Baseball America

2020 PROSPECT HANDBOOK

BASEBALL AMERICA INC. DU

Baseball America 2020 PROSPECT HANDBOOK

Editors
J.J. COOPER, MATT EDDY,
KYLE GLASER AND JOSH NORRIS

Assistant Editors
BEN BADLER, MICHAEL BROWN,
TEDDY CAHILL, JUSTIN COLEMAN,
JOE HEALY, CHRIS HILBURN-TRENKLE
AND CARLOS COLLAZO

Database and Application Development
BRENT LEWIS

Scouting Consultant
LEE MACPHAIL

Contributing Writers
MIKE DIGIOVANNA, TOM HAUDRICOURT,
KEGAN LOWE, LACY LUSK, JON MEOLI,
BILL MITCHELL, NICK PIECORO,
ALEX SPEIER, TRACY RINGOLSBY,
EMILY WALDON AND TIM WILLIAMS

Photo Editor
BRENDAN NOLAN

Design & Production
JAMES ALWORTH AND LEAH TYNER

Cover Photo
WANDER FRANCO BY TOM DIPACE

FOR ADDITIONAL COPIES
VISIT OUR WEBSITE AT **BASEBALLAMERICA.COM** OR
CALL **1-800-845-2726** TO ORDER.

US $34.95, PLUS SHIPPING AND HANDLING PER ORDER.
EXPEDITED SHIPPING AVAILABLE.

DISTRIBUTED BY SIMON & SCHUSTER
ISBN: 978-1-932391-93-0

STATISTICS PROVIDED BY MAJOR LEAGUE BASEBALL
ADVANCED MEDIA AND COMPILED BY
BASEBALL AMERICA.

Baseball America

ESTABLISHED 1981 • P.O. Box 12877, Durham, NC 27709 • Phone (919) 682-9635

EDITOR AND PUBLISHER B.J. Schecter *@bjschecter*
EXECUTIVE EDITORS J.J. Cooper *@jjcoop36*, Matt Eddy *@MattEddyBA*
CHIEF REVENUE OFFICER Don Hintze
DIRECTOR OF BUSINESS DEVELOPMENT Ben Leigh
DIRECTOR OF DIGITAL STRATEGY Mike Salerno

EDITORIAL
SENIOR EDITOR Josh Norris *@jnorris427*
SENIOR WRITER Ben Badler *@benbadler*
NATIONAL WRITERS Teddy Cahill *@tedcahill*
Carlos Collazo *@CarlosACollazo*
Kyle Glaser *@KyleAGlaser*
ASSOCIATE EDITORS Justin Coleman
Chris Hilburn-Trenkle *@ChrisTrenkle*
STAFF WRITER Joe Healy *@JoeHealyBA*
DIRECTOR OF EDITORIAL PRODUCTION/ AUDIENCE DEVELOPMENT Mark Chiarelli *@Mark_Chiarelli*
SPECIAL CONTRIBUTOR Tim Newcomb *@tdnewcomb*

PRODUCTION
CREATIVE DIRECTOR James Alworth
GRAPHIC DESIGNER Leah Tyner

BUSINESS
TECHNOLOGY MANAGER Brent Lewis
ACCOUNT EXECUTIVE Kellen Coleman
MARKETING/ OPERATIONS COORDINATOR Angela Lewis
CUSTOMER SERVICE Melissa Sunderman

STATISTICAL SERVICE
MAJOR LEAGUE BASEBALL ADVANCED MEDIA

BASEBALL AMERICA ENTERPRISES

Alliance BASEBALL
CHAIRMAN & CEO Gary Green
PRESIDENT Larry Botel
GENERAL COUNSEL Matthew Pace
DIRECTOR OF MARKETING Amy Heart
INVESTOR RELATIONS Michele Balfour
DIRECTOR OF OPERATIONS Joan Disalvo
PARTNERS Jon Ashley
Stephen Alepa
Martie Cordaro
Brian Rothschild
Andrew Fox
Maurice Haroche
Dan Waldman
Sonny Kalsi
Glenn Isaacson
Robert Hernreich
Craig Amazeen
Peter Ruprecht
Beryl Snyder
Tom Steiglehner

3STEP
MANAGING PARTNER David Geaslen
CHIEF CONTENT OFFICER Jonathan Segal
CHIEF FINANCIAL OFFICER Sue Murphy
DIRECTOR OF DIGITAL CONTENT Tom Johnson
DIRECTOR OF OPERATIONS, DATABASE/VIDEO Brendan Nolan

INTRODUCTION

As we usher in the 2020s, we are proud to be celebrating our fifth decade of publishing Baseball America magazine. We are equally proud of the fact that you hold in your hands the 20th edition of the Baseball America Prospect Handbook. The Handbook itself is old enough to be a prospect if it could swing a bat and post a 4.0-second run time from home to first.

If you compare this year's Prospect Handbook to the first edition, you would be able to see the similarities. The general idea—we rank the top 30 prospects in each major league organization—remains the same. But like most everything, the expectations for the Prospect Handbook have risen over the past 20 years.

In 2001, it took a lot of effort to gather radar gun readings for all pitching prospects in the book. Now we work hard to include exit velocities, spin rates and other objective data that simply didn't exist when the first Handbook was published.

The Prospect Handbook is the biggest project the Baseball America staff undertakes each year. We're proud of that, and we want to make sure that it's well worth your purchase. We hope you enjoy it as much as we enjoyed spending the past year watching players, talking to scouts and writing these 900 scouting reports.

J.J. COOPER AND MATT EDDY
EXECUTIVE EDITORS, BASEBALL AMERICA

A NOTE ABOUT THIS EDITION

Baseball America introduced BA Grades in the 2012 edition of the Prospect Handbook. We also grade all tools for the 300 players who rank as Top 10 Prospects, providing an quick overview of each player's strengths and weaknesses. All grades are projected future grades.

We grade players' tools on the 20-80 scouting scale, where 50 is average. A key to the abbreviations:

Players		Pitchers*	
Hit	Ability to hit for average	**FB**	Fastball
Power	Power	**CB**	Curveball
Run	Speed	**SL**	Slider
Field	Fielding ability	**CHG**	Changeup
Arm	Throwing arm	**CTL**	Control

ALSO NEW IN THE 2020 EDITION:

- **PROJECTED 2023 LINEUPS:** Our crystal ball now includes Top 30 Prospects rankings in parentheses, where applicable, in addition to all players' baseball ages in 2023.
- **BASEBALL AGE:** For the first time, all players' baseball ages are included in their statistical registers. Baseball age is a player's age on June 30 of the year in question, which is the standard used by Baseball-Reference.com and other outlets. This allows the reader to better put prospects' age relative to level in context.
- **BATTER STATISTICS:** We removed caught stealing (CS) totals to accommodate baseball age.
- **PITCHER STATISTICS:** We removed complete games (CG) to accommodate baseball age.

EDITOR'S NOTE: The transactions deadline for this book was Dec. 15, 2019. You can find players who changed organizations by using the handy index in the back.

>> For the purposes of this book, a prospect is any player who is signed with a major league organization and who has not exceeded 130 at-bats, 50 innings or 30 pitching appearances or in the major leagues, regardless of major league service time.

>> The grades attached to each team's draft class, as evaluated by Teddy Cahill, are based solely on the quality of the players signed, with no consideration given to any players acquired by trading those draft picks or for how many draft picks a team might have lost.

L = Low. M = Medium. H = High. V = Very High. X= Extreme.

TABLE OF CONTENTS

ARIZONA DIAMONDBACKS

STARTS ON PAGE 18

No.	Player, Pos.	Grade/Risk
1.	Daulton Varsho, C	55/M
2.	Geraldo Perdomo, SS	55/H
3.	Kristian Robinson, OF	60/V
4.	Alek Thomas, OF	55/H
5.	Corbin Carroll, OF	55/V
6.	Blake Walston, LHP	55/X
7.	Liover Peguero, SS	55/X
8.	Corbin Martin, RHP	50/H
9.	Brennan Malone, RHP	55/X
10.	Luis Frias, RHP	55/X
11.	Levi Kelly, RHP	50/H
12.	J.B. Bukauskas, RHP	50/H
13.	Jon Duplantier, RHP	50/H
14.	Seth Beer, 1B	50/H
15.	Josh Green, RHP	50/H
16.	Wilderd Patino, OF	55/X
17.	Drey Jameson, RHP	50/H
18.	Pavin Smith, 1B	45/H
19.	Blaze Alexander, SS/2B	45/H
20.	Andy Young, 2B	40/M
21.	Matt Tabor, RHP	45/H
22.	Dominic Fletcher, OF	45/H
23.	Tommy Henry, LHP	45/H
24.	Eduardo Diaz, OF	45/H
25.	Kevin Ginkel, RHP	40/M
26.	Tristin English, 3B	50/X
27.	Ryne Nelson, RHP	50/X
28.	Taylor Widener, RHP	45/H
29.	Conor Grammes, RHP	50/X
30.	Justin Martinez, RHP	50/X

ATLANTA BRAVES

STARTS ON PAGE 34

No.	Player, Pos.	Grade/Risk
1.	Cristian Pache, OF	65/M
2.	Drew Waters, OF	60/M
3.	Ian Anderson, RHP	55/M
4.	Kyle Wright, RHP	55/M
5.	Kyle Muller, LHP	50/M
6.	Bryse Wilson, RHP	50/M
7.	Shea Langeliers, C	55/H
8.	William Contreras, C	55/H
9.	Braden Shewmake, SS	55/H
10.	Tucker Davidson, LHP	50/M
11.	Jasseel De La Cruz, RHP	50/H
12.	Patrick Weigel, RHP	55/V
13.	Michael Harris, OF	55/X
14.	Victor Vodnik, RHP	50/H
15.	Freddy Tarnok, RHP	50/H
16.	Huascar Ynoa, RHP	50/H
17.	Alex Jackson, C	45/M
18.	Bryce Ball, 1B	50/H
19.	Greyson Jenista, OF	45/H
20.	Kasey Kalich, RHP	45/H
21.	Trey Harris, OF	45/H
22.	Jeremy Walker, RHP	40/M
23.	Daysbel Hernandez, RHP	50/X
24.	Logan Brown, C	45/V
25.	Beau Philip, SS	45/V
26.	Justin Dean, OF	45/V
27.	AJ Graffanino, SS	45/V
28.	Stephen Paolini, OF	45/X
29.	Trey Riley, RHP	45/X
30.	Jefrey Ramos, OF	45/X

BALTIMORE ORIOLES

STARTS ON PAGE 50

No.	Player, Pos.	Grade/Risk
1.	Adley Rutschman, C	70/H
2.	Grayson Rodriguez, RHP	60/H
3.	DL Hall, LHP	60/H
4.	Austin Hays, OF	50/M
5.	Ryan Mountcastle, 1B	50/M
6.	Yusniel Diaz, OF	55/V
7.	Gunnar Henderson, SS	55/X
8.	Hunter Harvey, RHP	50/H
9.	Keegan Akin, LHP	45/M
10.	Mike Baumann, RHP	50/H
11.	Dean Kremer, RHP	50/H
12.	Zac Lowther, LHP	50/H
13.	Adam Hall, SS/2B	50/H
14.	Alex Wells, LHP	45/M
15.	Drew Rom, LHP	50/H
16.	Bruce Zimmermann, LHP	45/M
17.	Ryan McKenna, OF	45/M
18.	Kyle Stowers, OF	50/H
19.	Zach Watson, OF	45/H
20.	Cody Sedlock, RHP	45/H
21.	Gray Fenter, RHP	45/H
22.	Blaine Knight, RHP	45/H
23.	Brenan Hanifee, RHP	45/H
24.	Cadyn Grenier , SS	45/H
25.	Darell Hernaiz, SS	50/X
26.	Zach Pop, RHP	50/X
27.	Dillon Tate, RHP	40/M
28.	Mason McCoy, SS/2B	45/H
29.	Rylan Bannon, 3B	40/M
30.	Brandon Bailey, RHP	45/H

BOSTON RED SOX

STARTS ON PAGE 66

No.	Player, Pos.	Grade/Risk
1.	Triston Casas, 1B	60/H
2.	Bobby Dalbec, 3B	55/M
3.	Bryan Mata, RHP	55/H
4.	Jarren Duran, OF	50/H
5.	Darwinzon Hernandez, LHP	45/M
6.	Thad Ward, RHP	50/H
7.	Jay Groome, LHP	55/X
8.	Gilberto Jimenez, OF	55/X
9.	Noah Song, RHP	55/X
10.	Tanner Houck, RHP	45/M
11.	C.J. Chatham, SS/2B	45/M
12.	Matthew Lugo, SS	55/X
13.	Chris Murphy, LHP	50/H
14.	Brayan Bello, RHP	50/V
15.	Marcus Wilson, OF	45/H
16.	Brainer Bonaci, SS	50/X
17.	Ryan Zeferjahn, RHP	45/H
18.	Brandon Howlett, 3B	45/H
19.	Nick Decker, OF	50/X
20.	Cameron Cannon, 2B/SS	45/H
21.	Andrew Politi, RHP	45/H
22.	Ceddanne Rafaela, SS/2B	45/V
23.	Yoan Aybar, LHP	45/V
24.	Chih-Jung Liu, RHP	45/X
25.	Aldo Ramirez, RHP	45/X
26.	Tyler Esplin, OF	40/H
27.	Kyle Hart, LHP	40/H
28.	Chase Shugart, RHP	40/H
29.	Antoni Flores, SS	45/X
30.	Durbin Feltman, RHP	40/H

CHICAGO CUBS

STARTS ON PAGE 82

No.	Player, Pos.	Grade/Risk
1.	Brailyn Marquez, LHP	60/H
2.	Nico Hoerner, SS/2B	55/M
3.	Brennen Davis, OF	55/H
4.	Miguel Amaya, C	55/H
5.	Chase Strumpf, 2B	50/H
6.	Cole Roederer, OF	50/H
7.	Ryan Jensen, RHP	50/H
8.	Ethan Hearn, C	50/H
9.	Riley Thompson, RHP	50/H
10.	Cory Abbott, RHP	50/H
11.	Adbert Alzolay, RHP	45/M
12.	Tyson Miller, RHP	50/H
13.	Kohl Franklin, RHP	50/V
14.	Chris Clarke, RHP	50/V
15.	Michael McAvene, RHP	50/V
16.	Pedro Martinez, 2B/SS	50/V
17.	Edmond Americaan, OF	50/V
18.	Richard Gallardo, RHP	50/V
19.	Kevin Made, SS	50/X
20.	Ronnier Quintero, C	50/X
21.	Rafael Morel, SS	50/X
22.	Yohendrick Pinango, OF	50/X
23.	Fabian Pertuz, SS	50/X
24.	Brayan Altuve, C	50/X
25.	Justin Steele, LHP	45/H
26.	Aramis Ademan, SS	45/H
27.	Christopher Morel, 3B	45/H
28.	Zack Short, SS	40/M
29.	Manuel Rodriguez, RHP	40/H
30.	Jack Patterson, LHP	40/H

CHICAGO WHITE SOX

STARTS ON PAGE 98

No.	Player, Pos.	Grade/Risk
1.	Luis Robert, OF	70/M
2.	Andrew Vaughn, 1B	60/H
3.	Michael Kopech, RHP	60/H
4.	Nick Madrigal, 2B	55/M
5.	Matthew Thompson, RHP	55/X
6.	Jonathan Stiever, RHP	50/H
7.	Andrew Dalquist, RHP	55/X
8.	Dane Dunning, RHP	50/H
9.	Blake Rutherford, OF	50/H
10.	Luis Gonzalez, OF	50/H
11.	Micker Adolfo, OF	50/H
12.	Jimmy Lambert, RHP	50/V
13.	Bryce Bush, OF	50/V
14.	Gavin Sheets, 1B	45/H
15.	Zack Collins, C	40/M
16.	Luis Alexander Basabe, Of	45/H
17.	Konnor Pilkington, LHP	45/H
18.	Yolbert Sanchez, SS	50/X
19.	James Beard, OF	50/X
20.	Luis Mieses, OF	50/X
21.	Bryan Ramos, 3B	50/X
22.	Benyamin Bailey, OF	50/X
23.	Alexander Comas, OF	50/X
24.	Damon Gladney, 3B	50/X
25.	Victor Torres, C	50/X
26.	Codi Heuer, RHP	40/M
27.	Danny Mendick, 2B	40/M
28.	Jose Rodriguez, SS	45/V
29.	Ian Hamilton, RHP	40/M
30.	Jefferson Mendoza, C	45/H

CINCINNATI REDS

STARTS ON PAGE 114

No.	Player, Pos.	Grade/Risk
1.	Hunter Greene, RHP	60/X
2.	Jonathan India, 3B	55/H
3.	Nick Lodolo, LHP	55/H
4.	Tyler Stephenson, C	50/M
5.	Tony Santillan, RHP	50/H
6.	Jose Garcia, SS	50/H
7.	Lyon Richardson, RHP	50/V
8.	Stuart Fairchild, OF	45/H
9.	Mike Siani, OF	50/X
10.	Jameson Hannah, OF	45/H
11.	Rece Hinds, SS	50/X
12.	Vladimir Gutierrez, RHP	45/H
13.	Tyler Callihan, 3B/2B	50/X
14.	Michel Triana, 1B	50/X
15.	Noah Davis, RHP	50/X
16.	Packy Naughton, LHP	45/H
17.	Jose Siri, OF	40/M
18.	TJ Friedl, OF	40/M
19.	Joel Kuhnel, RHP	40/M
20.	Yan Contreras, SS	45/X
21.	Jared Solomon, RHP	40/H
22.	Tejay Antone, RHP	40/H
23.	Ivan Johnson, SS/2B	45/X
24.	Hendrik Clementina, C	40/H
25.	Mariel Bautista, OF	45/X
26.	James Marinan, RHP	45/X
27.	Debby Santana, RHP	45/X
28.	Ibandel Isabel, 1B	40/H
29.	Jacob Heatherly, LHP	45/X
30.	Ryan Hendrix, RHP	40/H

CLEVELAND INDIANS

STARTS ON PAGE 130

No.	Player, Pos.	Grade/Risk
1.	Nolan Jones, 3B	60/H
2.	Tyler Freeman, SS	55/H
3.	Bo Naylor, C	55/V
4.	George Valera, OF	55/V
5.	Brayan Rocchio, SS	55/V
6.	Daniel Espino, RHP	55/X
7.	Triston McKenzie, RHP	55/X
8.	Ethan Hankins, RHP	55/X
9.	Aaron Bracho, 2B	55/X
10.	Gabriel Rodriguez, SS	55/X
11.	Logan Allen, LHP	45/M
12.	Bobby Bradley, 1B	45/M
13.	Scott Moss, LHP	45/M
14.	Carlos Vargas, RHP	50/V
15.	Emmanuel Clase, RHP	50/H
16.	James Karinchak, RHP	45/M
17.	Sam Hentges, LHP	50/V
18.	Luis Oviedo, RHP	50/V
19.	Yordys Valdes, SS	50/X
20.	Angel Martinez, SS	50/X
21.	Ernie Clement, SS	40/M
22.	Yu Chang, 3B/SS	40/M
23.	Daniel Johnson, OF	40/M
24.	Lenny Torres, RHP	50/X
25.	Will Benson, OF	50/X
26.	Oscar Gonzalez, OF	45/H
27.	Jose Pastrano, SS	50/X
28.	Jose Tena, SS/2B	50/X
29.	Nick Sandlin, RHP	45/H
30.	Jean Carlos Mejia, RHP	45/V

COLORADO ROCKIES

STARTS ON PAGE 146

No.	Player, Pos.	Grade/Risk
1.	Brendan Rodgers, SS/2B	60/M
2.	Ryan Rolison, LHP	55/H
3.	Michael Toglia, 1B	55/H
4.	Grant Lavigne, 1B	55/V
5.	Colton Welker, 3B	50/H
6.	Sam Hilliard, OF	45/M
7.	Ryan Castellani, RHP	50/H
8.	Ryan Vilade, SS	50/H
9.	Aaron Schunk, 3B	50/H
10.	Tyler Nevin, 1B/3B	50/H
11.	Adael Amador, SS	55/X
12.	Ben Bowden, LHP	45/M
13.	Karl Kauffmann, RHP	50/H
14.	Terrin Vavra, SS	45/H
15.	Jacob Wallace, RHP	45/H
16.	Helcris Olivarez, LHP	50/X
17.	Brenton Doyle, OF	45/H
18.	Eddy Diaz, SS	50/X
19.	Tommy Doyle, RHP	45/H
20.	Julio Carreras, 3B	50/X
21.	Ezequiel Tovar, SS	50/X
22.	Yanquiel Fernandez, OF	50/X
23.	Ashton Goudeau, RHP	40/M
24.	Yonathan Daza, OF	40/M
25.	Christian Koss, INF	45/V
26.	Bladimir Restituyo, SS	50/X
27.	Josh Fuentes, 3B	40/H
28.	PJ Poulin, LHP	40/H
29.	Will Ethridge, RHP	40/H
30.	Riley Pint, RHP	45/X

DETROIT TIGERS

STARTS ON PAGE 162

No.	Player, Pos.	Grade/Risk
1.	Casey Mize, RHP	65/H
2.	Matt Manning, RHP	60/M
3.	Tarik Skubal, LHP	60/H
4.	Riley Greene, OF	60/V
5.	Isaac Paredes, SS/3B	55/H
6.	Alex Faedo, RHP	50/H
7.	Daz Cameron, OF	45/M
8.	Franklin Perez, RHP	55/X
9.	Willi Castro, SS	45/M
10.	Jake Rogers, C	45/M
11.	Joey Wentz, LHP	50/H
12.	Parker Meadows, OF	50/V
13.	Roberto Campos, OF	50/X
14.	Wenceel Perez, SS	45/H
15.	Beau Burrows, RHP	45/H
16.	Kody Clemens, 2B	45/H
17.	Bryan Garcia, RHP	45/H
18.	Elvin Rodriguez, RHP	45/H
19.	Anthony Castro, RHP	45/H
20.	Nick Quintana, 3B	45/H
21.	Sergio Alcantara, SS	40/M
22.	Derek Hill, OF	40/M
23.	Paul Richan, RHP	45/H
24.	Adinso Reyes, SS	50/X
25.	Jose De La Cruz, OF	50/X
26.	Wladimir Pinto, RHP	40/H
27.	Jose Azocar, OF	40/H
28.	Kyle Funkhouser, RHP	40/H
29.	Alex Lange, RHP	40/H
30.	Wilkel Hernandez, RHP	40/H

L = Low. M = Medium. H = High. V = Very High. X = Extreme.

TABLE OF CONTENTS

HOUSTON ASTROS

STARTS ON PAGE 178

No.Player, Pos.	Grade/Risk
1. Forrest Whitley, RHP	65/V
2. Jose Urquidy, RHP	45/M
3. Jeremy Pena, SS	50/H
4. Freudis Nova, SS	55/X
5. Bryan Abreu, RHP	50/H
6. Abraham Toro, 3B	45/M
7. Korey Lee, C	50/H
8. Cristian Javier, RHP	45/M
9. Hunter Brown, RHP	55/X
10. Grae Kessinger, SS	50/H
11. Tyler Ivey, RHP	50/H
12. Jordan Brewer, OF	50/H
13. Luis Garcia, RHP	50/H
14. Jairo Solis, RHP	55/X
15. Brandon Bielak, RHP	45/M
16. Colin Barber, OF	50/X
17. Jojanse Torres, RHP	45/H
18. Jose Alberto Rivera, RHP	50/X
19. Shawn Dubin, RHP	45/H
20. Jairo Lopez, RHP	45/H
21. Brett Conine, RHP	45/H
22. Blair Henley, RHP	45/H
23. Nivaldo Rodriguez, RHP	45/H
24. Garrett Stubbs, C	40/M
25. Peter Solomon, RHP	50/X
26. Rogelio Armenteros, RHP	40/M
27. Austin Hansen, RHP	45/H
28. Enoli Paredes, RHP	45/H
29. Dauri Lorenzo, SS	50/X
30. Chandler Taylor, OF	45/V

KANSAS CITY ROYALS

STARTS ON PAGE 194

No.Player, Pos.	Grade/Risk
1. Bobby Witt Jr., SS	65/V
2. Daniel Lynch, LHP	60/H
3. Jackson Kowar, RHP	55/H
4. Brady Singer, RHP	55/H
5. Kyle Isbel, OF	50/H
6. Erick Pena, OF	55/X
7. Khalil Lee, OF	45/M
8. Kris Bubic, LHP	50/H
9. Austin Cox, LHP	50/H
10. Nick Pratto, 1B	50/V
11. Jonathan Bowlan, RHP	50/V
12. MJ Melendez, C	50/V
13. Jeison Guzman, SS	45/H
14. Carlos Hernandez, RHP	45/H
15. Zach Haake, RHP	45/H
16. Seuly Matias, OF	50/X
17. Brady McConnell, SS	50/X
18. Kelvin Gutierrez, 3B	40/M
19. Brewer Hicklen, OF	45/H
20. Yefri Del Rosario, RHP	50/X
21. Daniel Tillo, LHP	45/H
22. Jon Heasley, RHP	45/H
23. Alec Marsh, RHP	45/H
24. Richard Lovelady, LHP	40/M
25. Josh Staumont, RHP	40/M
26. Nick Heath, OF	40/H
27. Michael Gigliotti, OF	45/X
28. Evan Steele, LHP	45/X
29. Foster Griffin, LHP	40/H
30. Yohanse Morel, RHP	45/X

LOS ANGELES ANGELS

STARTS ON PAGE 210

No.Player, Pos.	Grade/Risk
1. Jo Adell, OF	70/M
2. Brandon Marsh, OF	60/H
3. Jordyn Adams, OF	55/V
4. Jeremiah Jackson, SS	55/X
5. Chris Rodriguez, RHP	55/X
6. Patrick Sandoval, LHP	45/M
7. Jose Soriano, RHP	50/H
8. Arol Vera, SS	55/X
9. Hector Yan, LHP	50/H
10. Kyren Paris, SS	50/X
11. Jahmai Jones, 2B/OF	45/H
12. Jack Kochanowicz, RHP	50/X
13. D'Shawn Knowles, OF	50/X
14. Stiward Aquino, RHP	50/X
15. Alexander Ramirez, OF	50/X
16. Oliver Ortega, RHP	45/H
17. Sadrac Franco, RHP	50/X
18. Orlando Martinez, OF	45/H
19. Robinson Pina, RHP	45/H
20. William Holmes, RHP/OF	50/X
21. Jared Walsh, 1B/LHP	40/M
22. Jose D. Rodriguez, RHP	40/M
23. Livan Soto, SS	45/V
24. Adrian Placencia, SS/2B	45/X
25. Jose Bonilla, SS/3B	45/X
26. Erik Rivera, LHP/OF	45/X
27. Garrett Stallings, RHP	40/H
28. Jeremy Beasley, RHP	40/H
29. Matt Ball, RHP	40/H
30. Aaron Hernandez, RHP	40/H

LOS ANGELES DODGERS

STARTS ON PAGE 226

No.Player, Pos.	Grade/Risk
1. Gavin Lux, SS	60/M
2. Dustin May, RHP	60/M
3. Keibert Ruiz, C	55/H
4. Tony Gonsolin, RHP	50/M
5. Josiah Gray, RHP	55/H
6. Jeter Downs, SS	55/H
7. Diego Cartaya, C	60/X
8. Kody Hoese, 3B	55/H
9. Michael Busch, 2B/1B	55/H
10. Luis Rodriguez, OF	60/X
11. Dennis Santana, RHP	50/M
12. Mitchell White, RHP	50/H
13. Edwin Rios, 3B/1B	45/M
14. DJ Peters, OF	45/H
15. Connor Wong, C	45/H
16. Cristian Santana, 3B	45/H
17. Omar Estevez, 2B	40/M
18. Edwin Uceta, RHP	45/H
19. Devin Mann, 2B	45/H
20. Jacob Amaya, SS	45/H
21. Zach McKinstry, SS	40/M
22. Miguel Vargas, 3B	45/H
23. Andy Pages, OF	50/X
24. Jimmy Lewis, RHP	50/X
25. Andre Jackson, RHP	50/X
26. Alex De Jesus, SS	50/X
27. Gerardo Carrillo, RHP	45/H
28. Ryan Pepiot, RHP	45/H
29. Robinson Ortiz, LHP	45/H
30. Victor Gonzalez, LHP	40/M

MIAMI MARLINS

STARTS ON PAGE 242

No.Player, Pos.	Grade/Risk
1. Sixto Sanchez, RHP	65/H
2. JJ Bleday, OF	60/H
3. Jesus Sanchez, OF	55/M
4. Edward Cabrera, RHP	55/H
5. Jazz Chisholm, SS	55/H
6. Monte Harrison, OF	55/V
7. Lewin Diaz, 1B	50/H
8. Braxton Garrett, LHP	50/H
9. Trevor Rogers, LHP	50/H
10. Connor Scott, OF	50/H
11. Kameron Misner, OF	50/H
12. Nick Neidert, RHP	45/M
13. Jose Devers, SS	50/H
14. Jorge Guzman, RHP	50/H
15. Victor Victor Mesa, OF	50/H
16. Jerar Encarnacion, OF	50/H
17. Peyton Burdick, OF	50/H
18. Nasim Nuñez, SS	50/X
19. Will Banfield, C	45/H
20. Sterling Sharp, RHP	40/M
21. Jordan Holloway, RHP	50/V
22. Victor Mesa, Jr., OF	50/V
23. Jose Salas, SS	50/X
24. Evan Fitterer, RHP	50/X
25. Osiris Johnson, SS	50/X
26. Humberto Mejia, RHP	45/H
27. Brian Miller, OF	45/H
28. Robert Dugger, RHP	40/M
29. Chris Mokma, RHP	50/X
30. Will Stewart, LHP	45/H

L = Low. M = Medium. H = High. V = Very High. X= Extreme.

MILWAUKEE BREWERS

STARTS ON PAGE 258

No.	Player, Pos.	Grade/Risk
1.	Brice Turang, SS	55/H
2.	Tristen Lutz, OF	50/H
3.	Corey Ray, OF	45/M
4.	Ethan Small, LHP	50/H
5.	Aaron Ashby, LHP	50/H
6.	Mario Feliciano, C	50/H
7.	Antoine Kelly, LHP	50/H
8.	Eduardo Garcia, SS	55/X
9.	Drew Rasmussen, RHP	55/X
10.	Zack Brown, RHP	45/M
11.	Hedbert Perez, OF	55/X
12.	Carlos Rodriguez, OF	50/V
13.	Trey Supak, RHP	45/H
14.	Luis Medina, OF	50/X
15.	Devin Williams, RHP	40/M
16.	Payton Henry, C	45/H
17.	Nick Kahle, C	45/H
18.	Jesus Parra, 3B	50/X
19.	Jeferson Quero, C	50/X
20.	Alec Bettinger, RHP	45/H
21.	Dylan File, RHP	45/H
22.	Tyrone Taylor, OF	40/M
23.	Joe Gray, OF	50/X
24.	Thomas Dillard, 1B/OF	45/V
25.	Max Lazar, RHP	45/V
26.	Jheremy Vargas, SS	45/X
27.	Clayton Andrews, LHP/OF	40/H
28.	Micah Bello, OF	45/X
29.	Gabe Holt, SS	45/X
30.	Eduarqui Fernandez, OF	45/X

MINNESOTA TWINS

STARTS ON PAGE 274

No.	Player, Pos.	Grade/Risk
1.	Royce Lewis, SS/3B	65/V
2.	Alex Kirilloff, OF/1B	60/H
3.	Trevor Larnach, OF	55/M
4.	Brusdar Graterol, RHP	55/M
5.	Jordan Balazovic, RHP	55/H
6.	Jhoan Duran, RHP	55/H
7.	Ryan Jeffers, C	50/H
8.	Matt Canterino, RHP	50/H
9.	Blayne Enlow, RHP	50/H
10.	Misael Urbina, OF	55/X
11.	Keoni Cavaco, SS	55/X
12.	Devin Smeltzer, LHP	45/M
13.	Gilberto Celestino, OF	50/H
14.	Brent Rooker, OF	45/M
15.	Randy Dobnak, RHP	45/M
16.	Nick Gordon, SS	45/M
17.	Lewis Thorpe, LHP	45/M
18.	Jorge Alcala, RHP	50/H
19.	Lamonte Wade, OF	40/L
20.	Matt Wallner, OF	50/H
21.	Akil Baddoo, OF	50/H
22.	Cole Sands, RHP	50/H
23.	Travis Blankenhorn, 3B	45/H
24.	Luke Raley, OF	45/H
25.	Ben Rortvedt, C	45/H
26.	Emmanuel Rodriguez, OF	50/X
27.	Josh Winder, RHP	45/H
28.	Edwar Colina, RHP	45/H
29.	Cody Stashak, RHP	40/M
30.	Wander Javier, SS	50/X

NEW YORK METS

STARTS ON PAGE 290

No.	Player, Pos.	Grade/Risk
1.	Ronny Mauricio, SS	60/H
2.	Francisco Alvarez, C	60/V
3.	Brett Baty, 3B	55/X
4.	Matt Allan, RHP	55/X
5.	Andres Gimenez, SS	50/H
6.	Mark Vientos, 3B	50/H
7.	Thomas Szapucki, LHP	50/H
8.	Josh Wolf, RHP	55/X
9.	Kevin Smith, LHP	50/H
10.	David Peterson, LHP	45/M
11.	Jordan Humphreys, RHP	50/H
12.	Junior Santos, RHP	55/X
13.	Franklyn Kilome, RHP	50/H
14.	Michel Otanez, RHP	50/H
15.	Robert Dominguez, RHP	55/X
16.	Alexander Ramirez, OF	55/X
17.	Shervyen Newton, 2B/SS	50/V
18.	Freddy Valdez, OF	50/V
19.	Jose Butto, RHP	45/H
20.	Jaylen Palmer, 3B	50/X
21.	Dedniel Nunez, RHP	45/H
22.	Walker Lockett, RHP	40/M
23.	Sam Haggerty, OF/2B	40/M
24.	Tony Dibrell, RHP	45/H
25.	Daison Acosta, RHP	45/H
26.	Carlos Cortes, 2B	45/H
27.	Ryley Gilliam, RHP	40/H
28.	Ali Sanchez, C	40/H
29.	Quinn Brodey, OF	40/H
30.	Scott Ota, OF	40/H

NEW YORK YANKEES

STARTS ON PAGE 306

No.	Player, Pos.	Grade/Risk
1.	Jasson Dominguez, OF	65/X
2.	Clarke Schmidt, RHP	60/H
3.	Deivi Garcia, RHP	55/M
4.	Luis Gil, RHP	55/V
5.	Oswald Peraza, SS	55/V
6.	Anthony Volpe, SS	55/X
7.	Luis Medina, RHP	55/X
8.	Roansy Contreras, RHP	50/H
9.	Alexander Vizcaino, RHP	50/H
10.	Albert Abreu, RHP	50/H
11.	Miguel Yajure, RHP	50/H
12.	Yoendrys Gomez, RHP	50/H
13.	Michael King, RHP	45/M
14.	Estevan Florial , OF	50/H
15.	T.J. Sikkema, LHP	50/H
16.	Canaan Smith, OF	50/H
17.	Matt Sauer, RHP	50/V
18.	Everson Pereira, OF	50/X
19.	Antonio Cabello, OF	50/X
20.	Kevin Alcantara, OF	50/X
21.	Antonio Gomez, C	50/X
22.	Alexander Vargas, SS	50/X
23.	Anthony Seigler, C	50/X
24.	Ezequiel Duran, 2B	45/H
25.	Josh Smith, 2B	45/H
26.	Raimfer Salinas, OF	50/X
27.	Maikol Escotto, SS	50/X
28.	Nick Nelson, RHP	45/H
29.	Ryder Green, OF	45/H
30.	Josh Stowers, OF	45/H

OAKLAND ATHLETICS

STARTS ON PAGE 322

No.	Player, Pos.	Grade/Risk
1.	Jesus Luzardo, LHP	70/H
2.	A.J. Puk, LHP	65/H
3.	Sean Murphy, C	55/M
4.	Daulton Jefferies, RHP	55/V
5.	Austin Beck, OF	55/V
6.	Robert Puason, SS	55/X
7.	Sheldon Neuse, 3B	45/M
8.	Jorge Mateo, SS	50/H
9.	Logan Davidson, SS	50/H
10.	Nick Allen, SS	45/H
11.	Austin Allen, C/DH	40/M
12.	Lazaro Armenteros, OF	50/X
13.	Skye Bolt, OF	45/H
14.	James Kaprielian, RHP	50/X
15.	Tyler Baum, RHP	45/H
16.	Greg Deichmann, OF	50/X
17.	Grant Holmes, RHP	45/H
18.	Jordan Diaz, 3B	50/X
19.	Brayan Buelvas, OF	50/X
20.	Marcus Smith, OF	50/X
21.	Alfonso Rivas, 1B	40/M
22.	Parker Dunshee, RHP	40/M
23.	Luis Barrera, OF	40/M
24.	Jonah Heim, C	45/H
25.	Seth Brown, 1B/OF	40/M
26.	Jeremy Eierman, SS/2B	40/H
27.	Hogan Harris, LHP	40/H
28.	Miguel Romero, RHP	40/H
29.	Gus Varland, RHP	40/H
30.	Kyle McCann, C	40/H

L = Low. M = Medium. H = High. V = Very High. X= Extreme.

TABLE OF CONTENTS

PHILADELPHIA PHILLIES

STARTS ON PAGE 338

No.	Player, Pos.	Grade/Risk
1.	Spencer Howard, RHP	60/H
2.	Alec Bohm, 3B	55/M
3.	Bryson Stott, SS	55/H
4.	Francisco Morales, RHP	55/V
5.	Adonis Medina, RHP	50/H
6.	Rafael Marchan, C	50/H
7.	Luis Garcia, SS	50/H
8.	Enyel de los Santos, RHP	45/M
9.	Mickey Moniak, OF	45/H
10.	Nick Maton, SS	45/H
11.	Johan Rojas, OF	50/X
12.	Simon Muzziotti, OF	45/H
13.	Erik Miller, LHP	45/H
14.	Andrick Nava, C	50/X
15.	JoJo Romero, LHP	45/H
16.	Deivi Gruillon, C	40/M
17.	Cristopher Sanchez, LHP	50/X
18.	Damon Jones, LHP	45/H
19.	Jamari Baylor, SS	50/X
20.	Addison Russ, RHP	45/M
21.	Kendall Logan Simmons, 2B/3B	50/X
22.	Logan O'Hoppe, C	45/H
23.	Ethan Lindow, LHP	45/H
24.	Connor Brodgon, RHP	40/M
25.	Mauricio Llovera, LHP	45/X
26.	Abrahan Gutierrez, C	45/X
27.	Cole Irvin, LHP	40/M
28.	Jhailyn Ortiz, OF	45/X
29.	Jonathan Guzman, 2B/SS	40/H
30.	Connor Seabold, RHP	40/H

PITTSBURGH PIRATES

STARTS ON PAGE 354

No.	Player, Pos.	Grade/Risk
1.	Mitch Keller, RHP	55/M
2.	Ke'Bryan Hayes, 3B	55/M
3.	Oneil Cruz, SS	60/H
4.	Cody Bolton, RHP	50/H
5.	Tahnaj Thomas, RHP	55/X
6.	Quinn Priester, RHP	55/X
7.	Ji-Hwan Bae, SS/2B	50/H
8.	Sammy Siani, OF	55/X
9.	Travis Swaggerty, OF	50/H
10.	Braxton Ashcraft, RHP	50/V
11.	Michael Burrows, RHP	50/V
12.	Calvin Mitchell , OF	50/V
13.	Mason Martin, 1B	50/V
14.	Alexander Mojica, OF	50/X
15.	Travis MacGregor, RHP	50/X
16.	JT Brubaker, RHP	45/H
17.	Nick Mears, RHP	45/H
18.	Jared Oliva, OF	45/H
19.	Kevin Kramer, 2B	40/M
20.	Santiago Florez, RHP	50/X
21.	Max Kranick, RHP	45/H
22.	Will Craig, 1B	45/H
23.	Nick Burdi, RHP	50/X
24.	Osvaldo Bido, RHP	45/H
25.	Blake Cederlind, RHP	40/M
26.	Lolo Sanchez, OF	40/H
27.	Jack Herman, OF	40/H
28.	Jasiah Dixon, OF	45/X
29.	J.C. Flowers, RHP	45/X
30.	Matt Gorski, OF	45/X

ST. LOUIS CARDINALS

STARTS ON PAGE 370

No.	Player, Pos.	Grade/Risk
1.	Dylan Carlson, OF	60/M
2.	Nolan Gorman, 3B	60/H
3.	Genesis Cabrera, LHP	50/M
4.	Ryan Helsley, RHP	50/M
5.	Ivan Herrera, C	55/H
6.	Zack Thompson, LHP	55/H
7.	Andrew Knizner, C	45/M
8.	Lane Thomas, OF	45/M
9.	Elehuris Montero, 3B	55/X
10.	Randy Arozarena, OF	45/M
11.	Johan Oviedo, RHP	50/H
12.	Junior Fernandez, RHP	45/M
13.	Jake Woodford, RHP	45/M
14.	Jhon Torres, OF	55/X
15.	Julio Rodriguez, C	50/H
16.	Angel Rondon, RHP	50/H
17.	Malcom Nunez, 3B	55/X
18.	Kodi Whitley, RHP	45/M
19.	Justin Williams, OF	45/M
20.	Mateo Gil, SS	50/X
21.	Edmundo Sosa, SS	40/M
22.	Trejyn Fletcher, OF	50/X
23.	Tony Locey, RHP	45/H
24.	Seth Elledge, RHP	40/M
25.	Alvaro Seijas, RHP	45/H
26.	Ramon Urias, 2B/3B	40/M
27.	Griffin Roberts, RHP	50/X
28.	Luken Baker, 1B	45/H
29.	Justin Toerner, OF	40/H
30.	Connor Jones, RHP	40/H

SAN DIEGO PADRES

STARTS ON PAGE 386

No.	Player, Pos.	Grade/Risk
1.	MacKenzie Gore, LHP	70/H
2.	Luis Patino, RHP	65/H
3.	CJ Abrams, SS	65/V
4.	Taylor Trammell, OF	55/H
5.	Luis Campusano, C	55/H
6.	Adrian Morejon, LHP	55/H
7.	Andres Muñoz, RHP	55/H
8.	Michel Baez, RHP	50/M
9.	Gabriel Arias, SS	55/V
10.	Ryan Weathers, LHP	55/V
11.	Joey Cantillo, LHP	50/H
12.	Owen Miller, 2B	45/M
13.	Ronald Bolaños, RHP	45/M
14.	Reggie Lawson, RHP	50/H
15.	Jake Cronenworth, SS/RHP	45/M
16.	Hudson Potts, 3B	50/H
17.	Edward Olivares, OF	45/M
18.	Tucupita Marcano, 3B/SS	50/V
19.	Blake Hunt, C	50/V
20.	Hudson Head, OF	50/X
21.	Reggie Preciado, SS	50/X
22.	Joshua Mears, OF	50/X
23.	Javy Guerra, RHP	50/X
24.	Jeisson Rosario, OF	45/H
25.	Tirso Ornelas, OF	45/H
26.	Logan Driscoll, C	45/H
27.	Jorge Ona, OF	50/X
28.	Ismael Mena, OF	50/X
29.	Eguy Rosario, 3B/2B	40/H
30.	Lake Bachar, RHP	40/H

SAN FRANCISCO GIANTS

STARTS ON PAGE 402

No.	Player, Pos.	Grade/Risk
1.	Marco Luciano, SS	65/V
2.	Joey Bart, C	60/H
3.	Heliot Ramos, OF	60/H
4.	Hunter Bishop, OF	55/H
5.	Alexander Canario, OF	55/V
6.	Luis Toribio, 3B	55/V
7.	Seth Corry, LHP	55/V
8.	Luis Matos, OF	55/X
9.	Sean Hjelle, RHP	50/H
10.	Mauricio Dubon, 2B/SS	45/M
11.	Logan Webb, RHP	45/M
12.	Will Wilson, SS	50/H
13.	Logan Wyatt, 1B	50/H
14.	Tristan Beck, RHP	50/H
15.	Jairo Pomares, OF	50/V
16.	Jaylin Davis, OF	40/M
17.	Conner Menez, LHP	40/M
18.	Blake Rivera, RHP	45/H
19.	Kai-Wei Teng, RHP	45/H
20.	Jake Wong, RHP	45/H
21.	Gregory Santos, RHP	45/H
22.	Jose Marte, RHP	45/H
23.	Rayner Santana, C	50/X
24.	Victor Bericoto, OF	50/X
25.	Trevor McDonald, RHP	50/X
26.	Aeverson Arteaga, SS	50/X
27.	Esmerlin Vinicio, LHP	50/X
28.	Tyler Fitzgerald, SS	45/H
29.	Sandro Fabian, OF	45/H
30.	Dany Jimenez, RHP	45/H

SEATTLE MARINERS

STARTS ON PAGE 418

No. Player, Pos.	Grade/Risk
1. Julio Rodriguez, OF	70/H
2. Jarred Kelenic, OF	65/H
3. Evan White, 1B	55/M
4. Logan Gilbert, RHP	55/M
5. George Kirby, RHP	55/H
6. Noelvi Marte, SS	60/X
7. Justus Sheffield, LHP	50/M
8. Justin Dunn, RHP	50/M
9. Brandon Williamson, LHP	55/H
10. Kyle Lewis, OF	50/M
11. Jake Fraley, OF	45/M
12. Cal Raleigh, C	50/H
13. Isaiah Campbell, RHP	50/H
14. Juan Then, RHP	50/H
15. Austin Shenton, RHP	50/V
16. Milkar Perez, 3B	50/X
17. Dom Thompson-Williams, OF	45/H
18. Sam Delaplane, RHP	45/H
19. Braden Bishop, OF	40/M
20. Jose Corniel, RHP	50/X
21. Sam Carlson, RHP	50/X
22. Aaron Fletcher, LHP	45/H
23. Joey Gerber, RHP	45/H
24. Wyatt Mills, RHP	40/M
25. Jonatan Clase, OF	50/X
26. Juan Querecuto, SS	50/X
27. Donnie Walton, 2B	40/M
28. Anthony Misiewicz, LHP	40/M
29. Penn Murfee, RHP	40/H
30. Yeury Tatis, RHP	45/X

TAMPA BAY RAYS

STARTS ON PAGE 434

No. Player, Pos.	Grade/Risk
1. Wander Franco, SS	75/H
2. Brendan McKay, LHP/DH	60/M
3. Matthew Liberatore, LHP	60/H
4. Vidal Brujan, 2B/SS	55/M
5. Shane Baz, RHP	60/V
6. Brent Honeywell, RHP	60/V
7. Shane McClanahan, LHP	60/V
8. Xavier Edwards, 2B	55/H
9. Ronaldo Hernandez, C	55/H
10. Joe Ryan, RHP	55/H
11. Josh Lowe, OF	50/H
12. Greg Jones, SS	50/H
13. JJ Goss, RHP	55/X
14. Moises Gomez, OF	55/X
15. Taj Bradley, RHP	50/H
16. Nick Schnell, OF	50/H
17. Kevin Padlo, 3B	45/M
18. Seth Johnson, RHP	50/H
19. Taylor Walls, SS	45/M
20. Riley O'Brien, RHP	50/H
21. John Doxakis, LHP	50/H
22. Peter Fairbanks, RHP	45/M
23. Lucius Fox, SS	45/H
24. Caleb Sampen, RHP	45/H
25. Drew Strotman, RHP	50/X
26. Jhon Diaz, OF	50/X
27. Niko Hulsizer, OF	50/X
28. Michael Plassmeyer, LHP	40/M
29. Josh Fleming, LHP	40/M
30. Anthony Banda, LHP	45/H

TEXAS RANGERS

STARTS ON PAGE 450

No. Player, Pos.	Grade/Risk
1. Josh Jung, 3B	55/H
2. Sam Huff, C	55/H
3. Leody Taveras, OF	55/V
4. Nick Solak, 2B/OF	50/M
5. Maximo Acosta, SS	60/X
6. Hans Crouse, RHP	55/V
7. Joe Palumbo, LHP	45/M
8. Luisangel Acuna, SS	55/X
9. Bayron Lora, OF	55/X
10. Ronny Henriquez, RHP	50/H
11. Sherten Apostel, 3B	50/H
12. Ricky Vanasco, RHP	50/V
13. Osleivis Basabe, SS	50/V
14. Cole Winn, RHP	50/V
15. Davis Wendzel, 3B	50/V
16. DeMarcus Evans, RHP	45/M
17. Jonathan Hernandez, RHP	45/M
18. Anderson Tejeda, SS	50/V
19. Ryan Garcia, RHP	50/V
20. Heriberto Hernandez, OF/1B	50/V
21. Brock Burke, LHP	40/M
22. Steele Walker, OF	45/H
23. Bubba Thompson, OF	50/X
24. David Garcia, C	50/X
25. Keithron Moss, 2B/3B	50/X
26. Randy Florentino, C	50/X
27. Julio Pablo Martinez, OF	45/H
28. Taylor Hearn, LHP	40/M
29. Zion Bannister, OF	50/X
30. Tyler Phillips, RHP	45/H

TORONTO BLUE JAYS

STARTS ON PAGE 466

No. Player, Pos.	Grade/Risk
1. Nate Pearson, RHP	70/M
2. Jordan Groshans, SS	65/V
3. Simeon Woods Richardson, RHP	60/H
4. Alejandro Kirk, C	55/H
5. Alek Manoah, RHP	55/H
6. Orelvis Martinez, SS	60/V
7. Gabriel Moreno, C	55/H
8. Miguel Hiraldo, 3B	55/V
9. Anthony Kay, LHP	45/M
10. Adam Kloffenstein, RHP	55/V
11. Eric Pardinho, RHP	55/X
12. Otto Lopez, SS/2B	50/H
13. Estiven Machado, SS	55/X
14. Kendall Williams, RHP	55/X
15. Griffin Conine, OF	50/V
16. Leonardo Jimenez, SS	50/V
17. Rikelvin de Castro, SS	50/X
18. Patrick Murphy, RHP	45/H
19. Victor Mesia, C	50/X
20. Santiago Espinal, SS/2B	40/M
21. Alberto Rodriguez, OF	45/V
22. Dasan Brown, OF	50/X
23. Reese McGuire, C	40/M
24. Anthony Alford, OF	45/H
25. Kevin Smith, SS	45/V
26. Joey Murray, RHP	40/H
27. Yennsy Diaz, RHP	40/H
28. Tanner Morris, SS	40/H
29. Will Robertson, OF	40/H
30. Sem Robberse, RHP	45/X

WASHINGTON NATIONALS

STARTS ON PAGE 482

No. Player, Pos.	Grade/Risk
1. Carter Kieboom, SS	60/M
2. Luis Garcia, SS	55/H
3. Jackson Rutledge, RHP	60/X
4. Wil Crowe, RHP	50/M
5. Tim Cate, LHP	50/H
6. Drew Mendoza, 1B	50/H
7. Andry Lara, RHP	55/X
8. Mason Denaburg, RHP	55/X
9. Yasel Antuna, SS	55/X
10. Seth Romero, LHP	55/X
11. Tres Barrera, C	45/H
12. Eddy Yean, RHP	50/X
13. Jeremy De La Rosa, OF	50/X
14. Matt Cronin, LHP	45/H
15. Jake Irvin, RHP	45/H
16. Jackson Cluff, SS	45/H
17. Tyler Dyson, RHP	45/H
18. Reid Schaller, RHP	45/H
19. Israel Pineda, C	50/H
20. Ben Braymer, LHP	40/M
21. Cole Freeman, 2B/OF	45/H
22. James Bourque, RHP	40/H
23. Joan Adon, RHP	40/H
24. Jackson Tetreault, RHP	40/H
25. Malvin Pena, RHP	40/H
26. Nick Banks, OF	40/H
27. Steven Fuentes, RHP	40/V
28. Jakson Reetz, C	40/V
29. Nick Raquet, LHP	40/V
30. Jhonatan German, RHP	40/X

BA GRADES

For the ninth year, Baseball America has assigned Grades and Risk Factors for each of the 900 prospects in the Prospect Handbook. For the BA Grade, we used a 20-to-80 scale, similar to the scale scouts use, to keep it familiar. However, most major league clubs put an overall numerical grade on players, called the Overall Future Potential or OFP. Often the OFP is merely an average of the player's tools.

The BA Grade is not an OFP. It's a measure of a prospect's value, and it attempts to gauge the player's realistic ceiling. We've continued to adjust our grades to try to be more realistic, and less optimistic, and keep refining the grade vetting process. The majority of the players in this book rest in the 50 High/45 Medium range, because the vast majority of worthwhile prospects in the minors are players who either have a chance to be everyday regulars but are far from that possibility, or players who are closer to the majors but who are likely to be role players and useful contributors. Few future franchise players or perennial all-stars graduate from the minors in any given year. The goal of the Grade/Risk system is to allow readers to take a quick look at how strong their team's farm system is, and how much immediate help the big league club can expect from its prospect. Got a minor leaguer who was traded from one organization to the other after the book went to press? Use the player's Grade/Risk and see where he would rank in his new system.

It also helps with our Organization Rankings, but those will not simply flow, in formulaic fashion, from the Grade/Risk results as we incorporate a lot of factors into our talent rankings including the differences in risk between pitchers and hitters. Hitters have a lower injury risk and therefore are safer bets.

BA Grade Scale

GRADE	HITTER ROLE	PITCHER ROLE	EXAMPLES
75-80	Franchise Player	No. 1 starter	Mike Trout, Justin Verlander, Christian Yelich
65-70	Perennial All-Star	No. 2 starter	Freddie Freeman, Nolan Arenado, Patrick Corbin
60	Occasional All-Star	No. 3 starter, Game's best reliever	Michael Conforto, Jose Abreu, Josh Hader
55	First-Division Regular	No. 3/No. 4 starter, Elite closer	Nicholas Castellanos, Anibal Sanchez, Brad Hand
50	Solid-Average Regular	No. 4 starter, Elite set-up reliever	Cesar Hernandez, Tanner Roark, Adam Ottavino
45	Second-Division Regular/Platoon	No. 5 starter, Lower-leverage reliever	Jarrod Dyson, Kyle Gibson, Juan Nicasio
40	Reserve	Fill-in starter, relief specialist	Greg Allen, Aaron Brooks, Adam Kolarek

RISK FACTORS

LOW: Likely to reach realistic ceiling, certain big league career barring injury.

MEDIUM: Some work left to refine their tools, but a polished player.

HIGH: Most top draft picks in their first seasons, players with plenty of projection left, players with a significant flaw left to correct or players whose injury history is worrisome.

VERY HIGH: Recent draft picks with a limited track record of success or injury issues.

EXTREME: Teenagers in Rookie ball, players with significant injury histories or players whose struggle with a key skill (especially control for pitchers or strikeout rate for hitters).

Explaining The 20-80 Scouting Scale

None of the authors of this book is a scout, but we all have spoken to plenty of scouts to report on the prospects and scouting reports enclosed in the Prospect Handbook. So we use their lingo, and the 20-80 scouting scale is part of that. Many of these grades are measurable data, such as fastball velocity and speed (usually timed from home to first or in workouts over 60 yards). A fastball grade doesn't stem solely from its velocity—command and life are crucial elements as well—but throwing 100 mph will earn a player an 80 grade. Secondary pitches are graded in a similar fashion. The more swings-and-misses a pitch induces from hitters and the sharper the bite of the movement, the better the grade.

Velocity steadily has increased over the past decade. Not all that long ago an 88-91 mph fastball was considered major league average, but current data shows it is now below-average. Big league starting pitchers now sit 92-93 mph on average. You can reduce the scale by 1 mph for lefthanders as they on average throw with slightly reduced velocity. Fastballs earn their grades based on the average range of the pitch over the course of a typical outing, not touching or bumping the peak velocity on occasion.

A move to the bullpen complicates in another direction. Pitchers airing it out for one inning should throw harder than someone trying to last six or seven innings, so add 1-2 mph for relievers. Yes, nowadays an 80 fastball for a reliever needs to sit at 98-99 mph with some movement and command.

Hitting ability is as much a skill as it is a tool, but the physical elements—hand-eye coordination, swing mechanics, bat speed—are key factors in the hit tool grade. Raw power generally is measured by how far a player can hit the ball, but game power is graded by how many home runs the hitter projects to hit in the majors, preferably an average over the course of a career. We have tweaked our power grades based on the recent rise in home run rates.

Arm strength can be evaluated by observing the velocity and carry of throws, measured in workouts with radar guns or measured in games for catchers with pop times—the time it takes from the pop of the ball in the catcher's mitt to the pop of the ball in the fielder's glove at second base. Defense takes different factors into account by position but starts with proper footwork and technique, incorporates physical attributes such as hands, short-area quickness and fluid actions, then adds subtle skills such as instincts and anticipation as a last layer.

Not every team uses the wording below. Some use a 2-to-8 scale without half-grades, and others use above-average and plus synonymously. But for the Handbook, consider this BA's 20-80 scale.

20: As bad as it gets for a big leaguer. Think Billy Hamilton's power.
30: Poor, but not unplayable, such as Edwin Encarnacion's speed.
40: Below-average, such as Eloy Jimenez's defense, or Trevor Bauer's control.
45: Fringe-average. Reynaldo Lopez's control and Kurt Suzuki's arm qualify.
50: Major league average. Juan Soto's speed.
55: Above-average. Nick Castellanos' power.
60: Plus. Alex Bregman's speed or Stephen Strasburg's control.
70: Plus-Plus. Among the best tools in the game, such as Corey Seager's arm, Patrick Corbin's slider or Francisco Lindor's defense.
80: Top of the scale. Some scouts consider only one player's tool in all of the major leagues to be 80. Think of Aaron Judge's power tool, Byron Buxton's speed or Aroldis Chapman's fastball.

20-80 Measurables

SPEED 60-Yard Dash Times (In Seconds)

Grade	Time
80	< 6.44
70	6.45-6.64
60	6.65-6.84
50	6.85-6.99
40	7.00-7.24
30	7.25-7.44
20	> 7.45

SPEED Home-First (In Secs.)

Grade	RHH—LHH
80	4.00—3.90
70	4.10—4.00
65	4.15—4.05
60	4.20—4.10
55	4.25—4.15
50	4.30—4.20
45	4.35—4.25
40	4.40—4.30
30	4.50—4.40
20	4.60—4.50

POWER

Grade	Home Runs
80	45+
70	35-44
65	30-34
60	25-29
55	21-24
50	18-20
45	15-17
40	10-14
30	5-9
20	0-4

FASTBALL Velocity (Starters)

Grade	Velocity
80	97+ mph
70	96
65	95
60	94
55	93
50	91-92
45	90
40	88-89
30	86-87
20	85 or less

ARM STRENGTH Catcher: Pop Times To Second Base (In Seconds)

Grade	Time
80	< 1.74
70	1.75-1.84
60	1.85-1.94
50	1.95-2.04
40	2.05-2.14
30	2.15-2.24
20	> 2.25

MINOR LEAGUE DEPTH CHART

AN OVERVIEW

Another feature of the Prospect Handbook is a depth chart of every organization's minor league talent. This shows you at a glance what kind of talent a system has and provides even more prospects beyond the Top 30.

Players are usually listed on the depth charts where we think they'll ultimately end up. To help you better understand why players are slotted at particular positions, we show you here what scouts look for in the ideal candidate at each spot, with individual tools ranked in descending order.

LF
Power
Hitting
Fielding
Arm Strength
Speed

CF
Fielding
Hitting
Speed
Power
Arm Strength

RF
Power
Hitting
Arm Strength
Fielding
Speed

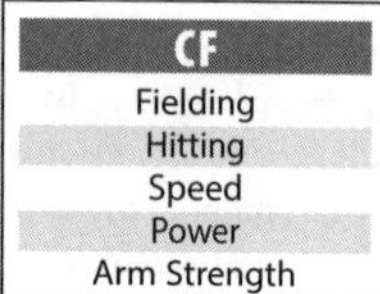

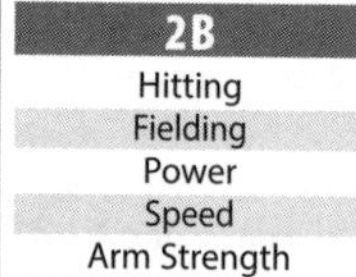

3B
Power
Hitting
Fielding
Arm Strength
Speed

SS
Fielding
Arm Strength
Hitting
Power
Speed

2B
Hitting
Fielding
Power
Speed
Arm Strength

1B
Power
Hitting
Fielding
Arm Strength
Speed

C
Fielding
Hitting
Arm Strength
Power
Speed

STARTING PITCHERS

No. 1 starter
- Two plus pitches
- Average third pitch
- Plus-plus command
- Plus makeup

No. 2 starter
- Two plus pitches
- Average third pitch
- Average command
- Average makeup

No. 3 starter
- One plus pitch
- Two average pitches
- Average command
- Average makeup

No. 4-5 starters
- Command of two major league pitches
- Average velocity
- Consistent breaking ball
- Decent changeup

CLOSER
- One dominant pitch
- Second plus pitch
- Plus command
- Plus-plus makeup

SETUP MAN
- Plus fastball
- Second above-average pitch
- Average command

POSITION RANKINGS

Context is crucial to prospect evaluations. So to provide yet another layer of context, we rank prospects at all all eight field positions plus righthanded and lefthanded starting pitchers. The rankings go deeper at the glamour positions, i.e. shortstop, center field and righthanded starter.

We grade players' tools on the 20-80 scouting scale, where 50 is average. The tools listed for position players are ability to hit for average (HIT), hit for power (POW), speed (SPD), fielding ability (FLD) and throwing arm (ARM). The tools listed for pitchers are fastball (FB), curveball (CB), slider (SL), changeup (CHG), other (OTH) and control (CTL). The "other" category can be a splitter, cutter or screwball.

Included as the final categories are BA Grades and Risk levels on a scale ranging from low to extreme.

CATCHER

No	Player	Org	HIT	POW	SPD	FLD	ARM	BA Grade	Risk
1	Adley Rutschman	Orioles	70	60	40	60	70	70	High
2	Joey Bart	Giants	50	60	40	50	60	60	High
3	Sean Murphy	Athletics	45	55	30	60	70	55	Medium
4	Francisco Alvarez	Mets	60	50	40	60	60	60	Very High
5	Daulton Varsho	D-backs	55	50	55	50	45	55	Medium
6	Keibert Ruiz	Dodgers	60	45	40	55	50	55	High
7	Luis Campusano	Padres	55	55	30	50	55	55	High
8	Sam Huff	Rangers	40	70	40	45	60	55	High
9	Shea Langeliers	Braves	50	55	40	70	60	55	High
10	Alejandro Kirk	Blue Jays	70	45	20	45	50	55	High

FIRST BASE

No	Player	Org	HIT	POW	SPD	FLD	ARM	BA Grade	Risk
1	Andrew Vaughn	White Sox	60	60	30	40	50	60	High
2	Evan White	Mariners	55	50	60	70	55	55	Medium
3	Triston Casas	Red Sox	55	60	40	60	50	60	High
4	Ryan Mountcastle	Orioles	60	55	45	40	30	50	Medium
5	Michael Toglia	Rockies	50	60	45	60	50	55	High
6	Lewin Diaz	Marlins	50	60	40	60	50	50	High
7	Seth Beer	D-backs	50	55	20	40	45	50	High
8	Grant Lavigne	Rockies	50	55	40	50	45	55	Very High
9	Bobby Bradley	Indians	40	60	20	50	45	45	Medium
10	Mason Martin	Pirates	40	60	30	40	45	50	Very High

SECOND BASE

No	Player	Org	HIT	POW	SPD	FLD	ARM	BA Grade	Risk
1	Brendan Rodgers	Rockies	60	55	50	55	60	60	Medium
2	Nick Madrigal	White Sox	60	30	60	60	40	55	Medium
3	Vidal Brujan	Rays	60	40	80	55	50	55	Medium
4	Xavier Edwards	Rays	60	30	70	55	45	55	High
5	Nick Solak	Rangers	55	50	60	40	50	50	Medium
6	Michael Busch	Dodgers	60	50	40	50	45	55	High
7	Aaron Bracho	Indians	55	50	55	50	45	55	Extreme
8	Chase Strumpf	Cubs	55	50	40	45	45	50	High
9	Mauricio Dubon	Giants	50	40	55	55	55	45	Medium
10	Owen Miller	Padres	55	40	55	50	45	45	Medium

THIRD BASE

No	Player	Org	HIT	POW	SPD	FLD	ARM	BA Grade	Risk
1	Alec Bohm	Phillies	55	55	40	45	50	55	Medium
2	Nolan Gorman	Cardinals	50	70	40	50	55	60	High
3	Nolan Jones	Indians	60	60	50	50	60	60	High
4	Ke'Bryan Hayes	Pirates	55	50	50	70	60	55	Medium
5	Bobby Dalbec	Red Sox	45	70	40	60	70	55	Medium
6	Jonathan India	Reds	55	50	50	60	55	55	High
7	Josh Jung	Rangers	60	50	40	50	60	55	High
8	Isaac Paredes	Tigers	55	50	40	45	50	55	High
9	Kody Hoese	Dodgers	55	55	50	50	55	55	High
10	Luis Toribio	Giants	55	50	40	40	55	55	Very High

POSITION RANKINGS

SHORTSTOP

No	Player	Org	HIT	POW	SPD	FLD	ARM	BA Grade	Risk
1	Wander Franco	Rays	80	60	50	55	50	75	High
2	Gavin Lux	Dodgers	60	55	60	50	55	60	Medium
3	Carter Kieboom	Nationals	60	50	45	50	55	60	Medium
4	Royce Lewis	Twins	45	60	60	55	55	65	Very High
5	Bobby Witt Jr.	Royals	55	60	60	70	60	65	Very High
6	CJ Abrams	Padres	70	55	70	60	55	65	Very High
7	Marco Luciano	Giants	60	70	40	50	60	65	Very High
8	Jordan Groshans	Blue Jays	60	60	50	50	60	65	Very High
9	Nico Hoerner	Cubs	60	50	55	50	50	55	Medium
10	Oneil Cruz	Pirates	50	70	60	50	60	60	High
11	Ronny Mauricio	Mets	50	60	40	50	60	60	High
12	Tyler Freeman	Indians	60	40	50	50	55	55	High
13	Jeter Downs	Dodgers	50	55	50	50	55	55	High
14	Geraldo Perdomo	D-backs	55	45	55	60	60	55	High
15	Orelvis Martinez	Blue Jays	60	60	45	40	60	60	Very High
16	Jazz Chisholm	Marlins	50	60	55	55	55	55	High
17	Brice Turang	Brewers	55	40	60	55	50	55	High
18	Bryson Stott	Phillies	50	50	55	55	55	55	High
19	Luis Garcia	Nationals	55	45	50	60	60	55	High
20	Gabriel Arias	Padres	50	55	40	70	70	55	Very High

CENTER FIELD

No	Player	Org	HIT	POW	SPD	FLD	ARM	BA Grade	Risk
1	Luis Robert	White Sox	55	70	70	60	70	70	Medium
2	Cristian Pache	Braves	45	60	70	70	70	65	Medium
3	Jarred Kelenic	Mariners	70	60	55	50	60	65	High
4	Jasson Dominguez	Yankees	60	70	70	60	60	65	Extreme
5	Heliot Ramos	Giants	50	55	50	55	55	60	High
6	Brandon Marsh	Angels	55	50	60	60	70	60	High
7	Taylor Trammell	Padres	55	50	60	50	40	55	High
8	Alek Thomas	D-backs	60	45	60	60	45	55	High
9	Corbin Carroll	D-backs	55	45	70	60	45	55	Very High
10	Austin Hays	Orioles	50	55	50	55	60	50	Medium
11	Luis Rodriguez	Dodgers	60	50	55	50	55	60	Extreme
12	Leody Taveras	Rangers	50	40	60	60	60	55	Very High
13	Monte Harrison	Marlins	40	60	60	60	60	55	Very High
14	Austin Beck	Athletics	45	55	60	60	60	55	Very High
15	Jordyn Adams	Angels	50	50	80	55	45	55	Very High
16	Jarren Duran	Red Sox	55	40	70	55	50	50	High
17	Josh Lowe	Rays	40	50	60	60	60	50	High
18	Kyle Isbel	Royals	55	45	60	60	50	50	High
19	Lane Thomas	Cardinals	45	50	60	60	55	45	Medium
20	Misael Urbina	Twins	60	40	60	60	45	55	Extreme

CORNER OUTFIELD

No	Player	Org	HIT	POW	SPD	FLD	ARM	BA Grade	Risk
1	Jo Adell	Angels	60	70	60	55	60	70	Medium
2	Julio Rodriguez	Mariners	70	70	45	50	70	70	High
3	Dylan Carlson	Cardinals	55	60	55	55	50	60	Medium
4	Drew Waters	Braves	55	55	60	60	55	60	Medium
5	Alex Kirilloff	Twins	60	55	45	50	50	60	High
6	JJ Bleday	Marlins	60	60	50	55	55	60	High
7	Riley Greene	Tigers	60	55	50	50	50	60	Very High
8	Trevor Larnach	Twins	50	60	50	45	45	55	Medium
9	Kristian Robinson	D-backs	50	70	60	55	50	60	Very High
10	Jesus Sanchez	Marlins	50	60	50	55	55	55	Medium

RIGHTHANDER

No	Pitcher	Team	FB	CB	SL	CHG	OTH	CTL	BA Grade	Risk
1	Nate Pearson	Blue Jays	80	45	60	55		55	70	Medium
2	Casey Mize	Tigers	60		60	70	55†	55	65	High
3	Dustin May	Dodgers	70	50		45	60†	70	60	Medium
4	Luis Patiño	Padres	70	50	60	55		55	65	High
5	Sixto Sanchez	Marlins	70		55	60		60	65	High
6	Forrest Whitley	Astros	60	60	60	60	60†	40	65	Very High
7	Matt Manning	Tigers	60	60		60		55	60	Medium
8	Michael Kopech	White Sox	80	50	60	50		50	60	High
9	Spencer Howard	Phillies	70	55	55	55		55	60	High
10	Grayson Rodriguez	Orioles	70	60	55	55		60	60	High
11	Ian Anderson	Braves	60	55		55		50	55	Medium
12	Mitch Keller	Pirates	70	60	60	45		55	55	Medium
13	Kyle Wright	Braves	60	55	55	55		45	55	Medium
14	S. Woods Richardson	Blue Jays	60	50	55	50		70	60	High
15	Brusdar Graterol	Twins	80		60	45		50	55	Medium
16	Logan Gilbert	Mariners	60	55	50	50		55	55	Medium
17	Clarke Schmidt	Yankees	60	55		60		50	60	High
18	Shane Baz	Rays	70	50	70	50		40	60	Very High
19	Brent Honeywell	Rays	60	55	55	60	70^	55	60	Very High
20	Hunter Greene	Reds	80		60	50		50	60	Extreme
21	Deivi Garcia	Yankees	60	55	60	50		55	55	Medium
22	Edward Cabrera	Marlins	70		60	50		50	55	High
23	Tony Gonsolin	Dodgers	60	55	50	70		50	50	Medium
24	Bryse Wilson	Braves	60		45	55		50	50	Medium
25	Jackson Kowar	Royals	55		50	70		55	55	High
26	Josiah Gray	Dodgers	60	55		50		55	55	High
27	Bryan Mata	Red Sox	70	40	60	55		45	55	High
28	Brady Singer	Royals	55		60	45		50	55	High
29	Jackson Rutledge	Nationals	80	55	60	50		45	60	Extreme
30	Jordan Balazovic	Twins	60		55	50		50	55	High
31	Alek Manoah	Blue Jays	60		55	50		50	55	High
32	Ryan Helsley	Cardinals	70	50		45		45	50	Medium
33	Joe Ryan	Rays	70	55	40	30		55	55	High
34	Jhoan Duran	Twins	70	45			70*	50	55	High
35	Andres Muñoz	Padres	80		50			45	55	High
36	George Kirby	Mariners	60	50	55	55		70	55	High
37	Hans Crouse	Rangers	60		60	50		50	55	Very High
38	Daulton Jefferies	Athletics	55		50	60		70	55	Very High
39	Justin Dunn	Mariners	55	40	60	45		50	50	Medium
40	Adam Kloffenstein	Blue Jays	55	55	55	50		50	55	Very High

LEFTHANDER

No	Pitcher	Team	FB	CB	SL	CHG	OTH	CTL	BA Grade	Risk
1	Mackenzie Gore	Padres	60	55	60	60		60	70	High
2	Jesus Luzardo	Athletics	60	55		70		60	70	High
3	A.J. Puk	Athletics	70		70	50		50	65	High
4	Brendan McKay	Rays	60	50		50		60	60	Medium
5	Tarik Skubal	Tigers	60	55	60	55		50	60	High
6	Daniel Lynch	Royals	60	50	60	60		55	60	High
7	Matthew Liberatore	Rays	60	60	45	55		55	60	High
8	Brailyn Marquez	Cubs	80		60	50		50	60	High
9	DL Hall	Orioles	70	60	50	60		50	60	High
10	Shane McClanahan	Rays	70	60	50	50		45	60	Very High
11	Adrian Morejon	Padres	60	60		55		45	55	High
12	Nick Lodolo	Reds	55	60		50		55	55	High
13	Kyle Muller	Braves	60	50		50		45	50	Medium
14	Ryan Rolison	Rockies	50	60	45	50		50	55	High
15	Justus Sheffield	Mariners	60		55	50		45	50	Medium

* Splitter. ^ Screwball. † Cutter.

TALENT RANKINGS

Team	2019	2018	2017	2016	2015
1. Tampa Bay Rays	2	5	11	13	17

The Rays have produced a steady stream of productive big leaguers thanks to solid drafting, player development and excellent pro scouting for trades. As impressive as their farm system has been, they haven't had a prospect like Wander Franco in quite a while.

Team	2019	2018	2017	2016	2015
2. San Diego Padres	1	3	9	25	14

Even after graduating Fernando Tatis Jr., Chris Paddack and others, the Padres' system still boasts both star power and depth. MacKenzie Gore and Luis Patiño lead a deep well of pitchers, while 2019 draftee CJ Abrams gives them a new potential frontline position player.

Team	2019	2018	2017	2016	2015
3 Los Angeles Dodgers	10	9	2	1	3

Gavin Lux and Dustin May give the Dodgers a pair of potential stars who have already seen the big leagues. With a deep group of prospects at all levels behind them, the Dodgers' player development machine shows no signs of slowing down. Very few teams maintain top farm systems this long while contending for World Series titles.

Team	2019	2018	2017	2016	2015
4. Atlanta Braves	4	1	1	3	29

The fall is coming. Two years from now, the Braves will likely rank among the bottom third in terms of farm system talent. By then, Atlanta will have graduated a steady stream of productive big leaguers, however, stretching back to Ozzie Albies' 2017 arrival.

Team	2019	2018	2017	2016	2015
5. Seattle Mariners	17	30	21	28	24

The Mariners' rebuild has picked up significant momentum thanks to the outfield duo of Julio Rodriguez and Jarred Kelenic. There's still plenty of work to do in Seattle, but having a pair of potential impact middle-of-the-order bats is a great start.

Team	2019	2018	2017	2016	2015
6. Toronto Blue Jays	3	8	20	24	9

Graduating two top 10 overall prospects like Vladimir Guerrero Jr. and Bo Bichette would usually sink a team in these rankings, but the Blue Jays still have one of the game's top farm systems. It's a balanced group with star potential at the top in Nate Pearson and Jordan Groshans and prospect depth throughout each level.

Team	2019	2018	2017	2016	2015
7. Minnesota Twins	8	12	22	10	2

The Twins led the American League Central last year with 102 wins. They also have the division's best farm system—just ahead of the nearly rebuilt White Sox. Minnesota has a nice mix of high-impact prospects followed by a large number of lower-impact, close-to-the-majors depth.

Team	2019	2018	2017	2016	2015
8. Chicago White Sox	6	4	5	23	20

Chicago's top four of Luis Robert, Andrew Vaughn, Michael Kopech and Nick Madrigal is hazardous enough to other teams that it should come with a warning from the surgeon general. The system's depth falls off quickly afterward.

Team	2019	2018	2017	2016	2015
9. Miami Marlins	25	24	29	29	25

The Marlins' steady stream of trades, plus some improved returns from the draft have paid off in a farm system that is significantly better than it has been in years. The system is still a little thinner than would be ideal, but the Top 10 Prospects have taken a big step forward.

Team	2019	2018	2017	2016	2015
10. Arizona Diamondbacks	21	26	28	22	6

If you want to pick a team that could climb into the top three next year, the D-backs are a good choice. The majority of their talent is at the lower levels. While there is plenty of risk, there's enough prospect depth here that several players could quickly climb into Top 100 Prospects consideration in 2020.

Team	2019	2018	2017	2016	2015
11. Detroit Tigers	14	20	25	26	30

Under general manager Al Avila, Detroit has amassed elite pitching at the top of the system. Casey Mize, the No. 1 pick of the 2018 draft, leads a crop of talented young arms that received a boost from breakout lefthander Tarik Skubal, who managed to dominate across two levels of the minors.

Team	2019	2018	2017	2016	2015
12. Baltimore Orioles	22	17	27	27	28

This system is on the rise and it's only going to get better. By next year's Prospect Handbook, the Orioles will have added yet another massive draft class to a system that is unlikely to graduate any of its top three prospects in 2020.

Team	2019	2018	2017	2016	2015
13. San Francisco Giants	28	25	24	19	26

If Marco Luciano is as good as scouts believe he can be, this will be the lowest the Giants will rank over the next few years. Some very astute signings on the international amateur side have helped pushed this farm system up the rankings.

Team	2019	2018	2017	2016	2015
14. St. Louis Cardinals	11	13	12	14	15

Dylan Carlson and Nolan Gorman give the Cardinals two potential standouts to work with, followed by a solid group of players ready to help in the majors soon. The system drops off considerably, however, particularly at the lower levels.

Team	2019	2018	2017	2016	2015
15. Oakland Athletics	9	18	17	18	19

It's always better to have stars than depth. Stars win titles, while depth can often be found on the free agent market at an inexpensive price. The A's have potential stars in Jesus Luzardo, A.J. Puk and even Sean Murphy. The depth? The front office will have to keep being creative to fill holes.

Team	2019	2018	2017	2016	2015
16. Los Angeles Angels	13	14	30	30	27

Jo Adell and Brandon Marsh are arguably the best pair of outfield prospects in any system. The system quickly drops off after that, but for an organization that has been making every move to try to not waste Mike Trout's prime years, having Adell ready to contribute is a big asset.

Team	2019	2018	2017	2016	2015
17. New York Yankees	20	2	3	16	19

After the threesome of multitalented newcomer Jasson Dominguez and upper-level righthanders Deivi Garcia and Clarke Schmidt, the Yankees system's strength is its upside. The group is filled with players with high-ceiling, high-variance futures who have years to go before they make an impact in the big leagues. Or not.

Team	2019	2018	2017	2016	2015
18. Kansas City Royals	27	29	26	21	13

In 2018, the Royals received excellent performances from the hitters they drafted in 2017. While Nick Pratto and MJ Melendez hit a wall when they moved to high Class A Wilmington in 2019, that was balanced out by the strong season by many of the pitchers the Royals drafted in 2018.

Team	2019	2018	2017	2016	2015
19. Cleveland Indians	15	21	18	17	23

The Indians have an extremely young farm system, which carries risks and possible rewards. The system is stacked with high-upside prospects who also have a wide range of potential outcomes. This system could climb or dive significantly in the next year.

Team	2019	2018	2017	2016	2015
20. Texas Rangers	24	22	23	7	11

The Rangers don't have an elite prospect, which is concerning for a team coming off three straight losing seasons. They do have a deep system, though, mostly at the lower levels and especially from their young Latin American signings. This system could climb significantly in 2020 as those young players mature.

Team	2019	2018	2017	2016	2015
21. Chicago Cubs	29	28	16	20	1

Towering lefty Brailyn Marquez took as big of a jump as any pitcher in the minors and has drawn comparisons with both Aroldis Chapman and David Price. Nico Hoerner got a taste of the big leagues, too. The system still has a ways to go to return to prominence, however.

Team	2019	2018	2017	2016	2015
22. Boston Red Sox	30	23	14	4	5

Not having a first-round pick in 2019 did not help the Red Sox climb out of the farm system cellar they occupied coming into 2019, but strong seasons by Bobby Dalbec, Bryan Mata and Jarren Duran gave the system a boost. The return of Jay Groome will be the fulcrum point for determining how this system looks in 2020.

Team	2019	2018	2017	2016	2015
23. Washington Nationals	16	15	19	5	12

Basking in the glow of the franchise's first World Series title, it's worth honoring the fact that Washington has produced three homegrown franchise talents in the past 10 years—Stephen Strasburg, Bryce Harper and Juan Soto. There's no Soto in the system right now, but the top handful of prospects are talented.

Team	2019	2018	2017	2016	2015
24. Pittsburgh Pirates	18	16	7	11	7

The Pirates have a new general manager and a revamped approach. It will be a while before everyone sees what that means for a system that has done a decent job at producing hitters but has struggled mightily to get its top pitchers to go from being prospects to successful big leaguers.

Team	2019	2018	2017	2016	2015
25. New York Mets	19	27	15	15	4

The Mets' system is long on upside but short on proximity or depth. A robust international scouting effort yielded shortstop Ronny Mauricio and catcher Francisco Alvarez, the system's top two prospects, while a high-upside 2019 draft class could pay off big if Brett Baty, Josh Wolf and Matt Allan click.

Team	2019	2018	2017	2016	2015
26. Philadelphia Phillies	12	7	6	8	22

Spencer Howard and Alec Bohm could help the big league club in the near future, but Philadelphia's impact talent drops off pretty quickly after that pair. There are a lot of potential role players and potential bullpen arms, but few regulars or starting pitchers.

Team	2019	2018	2017	2016	2015
27. Houston Astros	5	11	4	2	10

This is the normal life cycle of a team that continually contends. Trades and graduations have gutted much of the team's high-end prospect depth. Houston still has a large number of hard-throwing pitchers who could be big leaguers, but the team's position depth is thin.

Team	2019	2018	2017	2016	2015
28. Colorado Rockies	23	19	10	6	8

The Rockies have a number of bat-first prospects who all reside on the low end of the defensive spectrum. It's likely that this group will produce a first baseman or two who are useful big leaguers in the next few years, but the system is thinner at up-the-middle defensive positions.

Team	2019	2018	2017	2016	2015
29. Cincinnati Reds	7	10	13	12	16

The graduation of top prospect Nick Senzel and various trades have worn the system down. Hunter Greene is rehabbing from Tommy John surgery, but the team does have interesting positional talent, albeit far away from the big leagues.

Team	2019	2018	2017	2016	2015
30. Milwaukee Brewers	26	6	8	9	21

Yes, the Brewers rank 30th. They have graduated their best prospects—Keston Hiura had an impressive big league debut in 2019—and they now draft at the back of the first round. This system likely won't improve for a while, but that's a tradeoff for the Brewers' first back-to-back playoff appearances since 1981 and '82.

Arizona Diamondbacks

BY NICK PIECORO

The retooling of the Diamondbacks' organization went into full gear following the 2018 season—or, that is, the highest speed general manager Mike Hazen was willing to take it. In a nine-month span, Hazen traded away Paul Goldschmidt and Zack Greinke and watched Patrick Corbin and A.J. Pollock walk as free agents, but at the same time managed to keep his club in the playoff race into September.

Not interested in a full teardown, Hazen seems to be doing an admirable job following an alternative reconstruction model. For years, the sense around the game has been that teams who try to win and rebuild simultaneously often do a poor job of both. Hazen is trying to follow the same path the Brewers have to disprove that adage.

In terms of winning, his results have been mixed. The D-backs claimed a wild card in 2017 but fell short of the playoffs each of the next two seasons. The work on the farm is less debatable, though it too is open to interpretation.

When Hazen took over, the D-backs had one of the worst farm systems in the game. They'll open this year with one that ranks in the top 10 of baseball. The industry seems to have little dispute about the depth of talent the D-backs have assembled, with a large and growing collection of up-the-middle athletes with plate discipline and hard throwers with unrealized potential.

There is, however, one shortcoming: prospects who project as superstars. Three years ago, the White Sox signed outfielder Luis Robert and traded for Eloy Jimenez, adding them to a prospect stable that already included Yoan Moncada, Lucas Giolito and Michael Kopech.

Rival scouts see a lot to like about the D-backs' current collection, but it pales in comparison to what teams like the White Sox—that is, teams willing to tear down—are able to amass.

"I think it's a better system," a scout with an American League club said of the D-backs. "It's good but still not great. There are still quite a few talented guys at the lower levels. I like Daulton Varsho and Alek Thomas, but if those are your one and two guys, I don't know. They're everyday guys, but I don't know if they're the kind that anchor a championship ballclub."

Of course, players are bound to surprise. Perhaps Varsho, Thomas, Geraldo Perdomo or Corbin Carroll become even more impactful than initial impressions might suggest. Perhaps Kristian Robinson realizes his potential as a middle-of-the-order masher. Perhaps any of their half-dozen unrefined, lightning-armed prospects click and become frontline starters.

DUSTIN BRADFORD/GETTY IMAGES

The D-backs traded acquired righthander Zac Gallen from the Marlins at the trade deadline.

PROJECTED 2023 LINEUP

Position	Player	Age
Catcher	Carson Kelly	28
First Base	Seth Beer	26
Second Base	Daulton Varsho (1)	26
Third Base	Ketel Marte	29
Shortstop	Geraldo Perdomo (2)	23
Left Field	Alek Thomas (4)	23
Center Field	Corbin Carroll (5)	22
Right Field	Kristian Robinson (3)	22
No. 1 Starter	Madison Bumgarner	33
No. 2 Starter	Luke Weaver	29
No. 3 Starter	Zac Gallen	27
No. 4 Starter	Blake Walston (6)	22
No. 5 Starter	Corbin Martin (8)	27
Closer	Luis Frias (10)	25

Or, better yet, maybe the D-backs' current crop of big leaguers—headed by a collection of players acquired and groomed by Hazen like second baseman Ketel Marte, catcher Carson Kelly and righthanders Zac Gallen and Luke Weaver—make a deep postseason run in the near future.

With Hazen agreeing to a new contract extension in September, it seems clear that, for the first time in awhile, a D-backs GM will be around to see how his long-term plans play out. If everything goes as hoped, and if the club wins while rebuilding, Hazen will have turned an adage on its head.

DEPTH CHART

ARIZONA DIAMONDBACKS

TOP 2020 ROOKIE: Daulton Varsho, C/OF. The lefthanded hitter can do a bit of everything and that offensive and defensive versatility should help him find avenues to playing time.

BREAKOUT PROSPECT: Conor Grammes, RHP. He has electric stuff, and he showed good aptitude to make adjustments during his pro debut.

SLEEPER: Diomede Sierra, LHP. Armed with a fastball up to 96 mph, Sierra has a chance to burst onto the scene when he comes stateside in 2020.

SOURCE OF TOP 30 TALENT

Homegrown	**25**	**Acquired**	**5**
College	11	Trade	5
Junior college	0	Rule 5 draft	0
High school	7	Independent league	0
Nondrafted free agent	0	Free agent/waivers	0
International	7		

LF
- Buddy Kennedy
- Alvin Guzman
- Jorge Barrosa
- Jake McCarthy

CF
- Kristian Robinson (3)
- Alek Thomas (4)
- Corbin Carroll (5)
- Dominic Fletcher (22)
- Jeferson Espinal

RF
- Wilderd Patiño (16)
- Eduardo Diaz (24)
- Franyel Baez

3B
- Tristin English (26)
- Wyatt Mathisen
- Drew Ellis
- Ronny Polanco

SS
- Geraldo Perdomo (2)
- Liover Peguero (7)
- Blaze Alexander (19)
- Juan Corniel

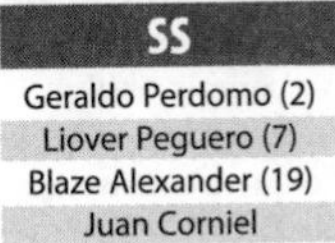

2B
- Andy Young (20)
- Domingo Leyba
- Lewin De La Cruz
- Glenallen Hill Jr.

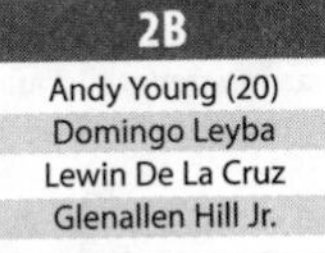

1B
- Seth Beer (14)
- Pavin Smith (18)
- Kevin Cron

C
- Daulton Varsho (1)
- Jose Herrera
- Dominic Miroglio

LHP

LHSP	LHRP
Blake Walston (6)	Mack Lemieux
Tommy Henry (23)	Andrew Saalfrank
Diomede Sierra	Cody Reed

RHP

RHSP	RHRP
Corbin Martin (8)	Kevin Ginkel (25)
Brennan Malone (9)	Taylor Widener (28)
Luis Frias (10)	Riley Smith
Levi Kelly (11)	Emilio Vargas
J.B. Bukauskas (12)	Matt Peacock
Jon Duplantier (13)	Cole Stapler
Josh Green (15)	Matt Brill
Drey Jameson (17)	Justin Lewis
Matt Tabor (21)	Bobby Ay
Ryne Nelson (27)	Junior Mieses
Conor Grammes (29)	Matt Mercer
Justin Martinez (30)	
Jhosmer Alvarez	

DRAFT ANALYSIS

2019

BEST PURE HITTER: OF Corbin Carroll (1) was one of the top-performing prep hitters throughout the summer showcase season prior to the draft and possesses excellent bat-to-ball skills. He also has surprising pop for his size and arguably the best strike zone understanding and approach of the 2019 prep class.

BEST POWER HITTER: 1B Tristin English (3) homered 18 times during his junior season with Georgia Tech before homering seven times during his pro debut in the short-season Northwest League. English has 60-grade raw power and above-average power in games.

FASTEST RUNNER: Carroll has an advanced toolset, but his loudest tool is perhaps his running ability. He's a 70-grade runner who uses that speed in the outfield and on the bases, where he is an aggressive and instinctual runner. He stole 18 bases and was caught just once in his pro debut in the Arizona and Northwest leagues.

BEST DEFENSIVE PLAYER: Carroll has all the tools to be a plus defender in center field. OF Dominic Fletcher (2s) runs terrific routes and makes excellent jumps, but lacks the elite foot speed that Carroll has. Fletcher's plus arm strength could make him a defensive asset in right field if he is ever forced away from center field.

BEST FASTBALL: The D-backs invested in several high-octane arms with their plethora of draft picks this year. RHPs Brennan Malone (1), Drey Jameson (1), Ryne Nelson (2) and Conor Grammes (5) all have fastballs that have been up to 97 mph or better.

BEST SECONDARY PITCH: It's a testament to the strength of LHP Andrew Saalfrank's (6) curveball that he's mentioned here despite the impressive collection of pitching talent drafted in front of him. It has big shape and depth and could be a legitimate 70-grade breaking ball.

BEST PRO DEBUT: Fletcher hit .318/.389/.463 with five home runs and 14 doubles in the Midwest League while playing all three outfield positions, while LHP Nick Snyder (11) posted a 0.53 ERA with 30 strikeouts and nine walks in 17 innings in the Arizona and Northwest leagues.

BEST ATHLETE: LHP Blake Walston (1), has impressive athleticism as well. He was a talented high school quarterback and his athleticism translates well to the mound, where he has a clean arm action and some of the best strike-throwing ability of the 2019 prep class.

MOST INTRIGUING BACKGROUND: SS Glenallen Hill Jr. (4) is the son of former 13-year major leaguer Glenallen Hill.

CLOSEST TO THE MAJORS: Fletcher can play all three outfield spots effectively and has impressive contact ability that could allow him to move quickly. He's extremely polished defensively and had an extensive track record of performing in college before his hot start to pro ball. Scouts laud his makeup as well.

BEST LATE-ROUND PICK: Snyder's terrific debut makes him a strong candidate for best late-round pick, though LHP Avery Short (12) is a good strike-thrower with a four-pitch mix. SS Ricky Martinez (18) had a solid debut with the bat and can play shortstop, second base and third.

THE ONE WHO GOT AWAY: OF Jerrion Ealy (31) was among the most athletic players in the 2019 class—high school or college—but was always going to be a tough sign as a two-sport commit to Mississippi. He has the toolset to become a star with improved all-around refinement to his game.

—CARLOS COLLAZO

TOP DRAFT PICKS OF THE DECADE

Year	Player, Pos.	2019 Org
2010	*Barret Loux, RHP	Did not play
2011	Trevor Bauer, RHP	Reds
2012	Stryker Trahan, C	Did not play
2013	Braden Shipley, RHP	D-backs
2014	Touki Toussaint, RHP	Braves
2015	Dansby Swanson, SS	Braves
2016	Anfernee Grier, OF (1st round supp)	D-backs
2017	Pavin Smith, 1B	D-backs
2018	*Matt McLain, SS	UCLA
2019	Corbin Carroll, OF	D-backs

* Did not sign

2018

The D-backs didn't get a deal done with SS Matt McLain (1), and OF Jake McCarthy (1s) missed most of 2019 due to injury. OF Alek Thomas (2) has impressed early, but he's having to do some heavy lifting here.

GRADE: C

2017

C Daulton Varsho (2s) has developed into the system's top prospect and is coming off a strong season at Double-A. The rest of the class, however, has scuffled, starting at the top with 1B Pavin Smith (1).

GRADE: C

2016

The D-backs have gotten three big leaguers from the group—RHP Jon Duplantier (3), LHP Colin Poche (14) and RHP Kevin Ginkel (22). But no one in that trio looks to be high impact.

GRADE: C

1 DAULTON VARSHO, C/OF

Born: July 2, 1996. **B-T:** L-R. **HT:** 5-10. **WT:** 190.
Drafted: Wisconsin-Milwaukee, 2017 (2nd round supp).
Signed by: Rick Short.

MIKE JANES/FOUR SEAM IMAGES

BA GRADE 55 **Risk:** Medium

SCOUTING GRADES **Hit:** 55. **Power:** 50. **Run:** 55. **Field:** 50. **Arm:** 45.

Projected future grades on 20-80 scouting scale.

TRACK RECORD: Varsho, the son of ex-big leaguer Gary Varsho, cemented his status as one of the Diamondbacks' most dynamic prospects last year when he put together one of the better seasons of any hitter at Double-A. In leading the Southern League in OPS, Varsho showed an ability to hit for average and get on base, displayed both power and speed and played well at two positions high on the defensive spectrum. Though he finally began to gain industry-wide recognition in 2019, his production generally fell in line with what he had done throughout his career since being selected 68th overall in the 2017 draft out of University of Wisconsin-Milwaukee.

SCOUTING REPORT: With short arms and a compact swing, Varsho finds the barrel often. He has a mature approach and will take his walks, and he also has good hand-eye skills that allow him to spray the ball to all fields. Even though he hit 18 home runs in 108 games at Double-A Jackson, his power potential generates mixed feelings, with some scouts anticipating 20-plus home runs while others see him merely reaching double digits.He has above-average speed (and not just for a catcher) and is a good baserunner; he became the first backstop at Double-A or Triple-A to steal 20-plus bases since at least 2006. He even runs well enough to hold his own in center field, which he did during a cameo there over the final two weeks of the season. Scouts and executives both inside and outside the organization believe he can be at least an average defensive major league catcher. He is athletic, is a decent receiver, blocks well and compensates for below-average arm strength with a quick transfer that leads to at least average times on throws to second base. D-backs officials were encouraged by Varsho's brief exposure to center field, which came as no surprise given the high marks he receives for his baseball instincts.

THE FUTURE: With Carson Kelly's emergence as a potential frontline catcher, the D-backs started to experiment with other paths toward big league at-bats for Varsho in August. His outfield experience was limited to center field, but club officials say he also could be exposed to left field and did not rule out the possibility of second base. Varsho is likely to open the year in Triple-A Reno and should give the D-backs the kind of flexibility their front office values.

TOP PROSPECTS OF THE DECADE

Year	Player, Pos.	2019 Org
2010	Jarrod Parker, RHP	Did not play
2011	Jarrod Parker, RHP	Did not play
2012	Trevor Bauer, RHP	Reds
2013	Tyler Skaggs, LHP	Angels
2014	Archie Bradley, RHP	D-backs
2015	Archie Bradley, RHP	D-backs
2016	Dansby Swanson, SS	Braves
2017	Anthony Banda, LHP	Rays
2018	Jon Duplantier, RHP	D-backs
2019	Jazz Chisholm, SS	Marlins

BEST TOOLS

Best Hitter for Average	Daulton Varsho
Best Power Hitter	Kevin Cron
Best Strike-Zone Discipline	Geraldo Perdomo
Fastest Baserunner	Leodany Perez
Best Athlete	Kristian Robinson
Best Fastball	Luis Frias
Best Curveball	Mack Lemieux
Best Slider	J.B. Bukauskas
Best Changeup	Shumpei Yoshikawa
Best Control	Matt Tabor
Best Defensive Catcher	Jose Herrera
Best Defensive Infielder	Geraldo Perdomo
Best Infield Arm	Blaze Alexander
Best Defensive Outfielder	Alek Thomas
Best Outfield Arm	Eduardo Diaz

Year	Age	Club (League)	Class	AVG	G	AB	R	H	2B	3B	HR	RBI	BB	SO	SB	OBP	SLG
2017	20	Hillsboro (NWL)	SS	.311	50	193	36	60	16	3	7	39	17	30	7	.368	.534
2018	21	Diamondbacks (AZL)	R	.500	3	12	4	6	2	1	1	1	0	1	0	.500	1.083
	21	Visalia (CAL)	HiA	.286	80	304	44	87	11	3	11	44	30	71	19	.363	.451
2019	22	Jackson (SL)	AA	.301	108	396	85	119	25	4	18	58	42	63	21	.378	.520
Minor League Totals				.301	241	905	169	272	54	11	37	142	89	165	47	.372	.507

2 GERALDO PERDOMO, SS

Born: Oct. 22, 1999. **B-T:** B-R. **HT:** 6-3. **WT:** 184. **Signed:** Dominican Republic, 2016. **Signed by:** Junior Noboa/Elvis Cruz.

RAWHIDE/JILL GEARIN

BA GRADE
55 Risk: High

TRACK RECORD: Following the trade deadline deal that sent Jazz Chisholm to the Marlins, Perdomo took the reins as the D-backs' shortstop of the future. His play earned him such a designation in 2019, a year in which he reached high Class A and put together a solid six weeks in the Arizona Fall League.

SCOUTING REPORT: The switch-hitting Perdomo is best known for his mature approach and on-base ability and stayed true to form by finishing last year with more walks than strikeouts. He has good bat speed and bat-to-ball ability, and scouts who watched him in the AFL saw him unload on a handful of balls, giving them reason to dream on potentially average power. Perdomo is an above-average runner whose speed plays up thanks to his instincts. He is a graceful defender with good range, a plus arm and an accurate internal clock. He is a consistent and dependable defender whom scouts have little doubt will stick at short.

THE FUTURE: Given his defense, speed and approach, Perdomo is on his way toward being an above-average everyday player. He grew an inch taller from 2018 to 2019 and still has plenty of maturing to do physically. If that leads to more pop, the D-backs could have an all-star.

SCOUTING GRADES: **Hitting:** 55 **Power:** 45 **Running:** 55 **Fielding:** 60 **Arm:** 60

Year	Age	Club (League)	Class	AVG	G	AB	R	H	2B	3B	HR	RBI	BB	SO	SB	OBP	SLG
2017	17	D-backs (DSL)	R	.238	63	214	42	51	3	2	1	11	60	37	16	.410	.285
2018	18	Diamondbacks (AZL)	R	.314	21	86	20	27	4	2	1	8	14	17	14	.416	.442
	18	Missoula (PIO)	R	.455	6	22	3	10	0	1	0	2	7	4	1	.586	.545
	18	Hillsboro (NWL)	SS	.301	30	103	20	31	3	2	3	14	18	23	9	.421	.456
2019	19	Kane County (MWL)	LoA	.268	90	314	48	84	16	3	2	36	56	56	20	.394	.357
	19	Visalia (CAL)	HiA	.301	26	93	15	28	5	0	1	11	14	11	6	.407	.387
Minor League Totals				.278	236	832	148	231	31	10	8	82	169	148	66	.411	.368

3 KRISTIAN ROBINSON, OF

Born: Dec. 11, 2000. **B-T:** R-R. **HT:** 6-3. **WT:** 190. **Signed:** Bahamas, 2017. **Signed by:** Cesar Geronimo/Craig Shipley.

CRAIG MITCHELDYER

TRACK RECORD: Robinson received a $2.5 million bonus in 2017 and put his massive skill-set on display in the short-season Northwest League in 2019, dominating against much older competition. Playing the entire season at age 18, he reached low Class A for the final month of the season.

SCOUTING REPORT: A physical specimen despite his age, Robinson has a chance for four plus tools, the exception being his arm. At the plate, he uses a simple stride with little movement in his setup followed by a compact swing. The raw power he generates is enormous, and he got to it often in games last season. Scouts are concerned by his strikeout total, but his chase rate is solid and his in-zone whiff rate isn't bad, either. He makes enough hard contact to offset the swing-and-miss in his game. Robinson gets good reads in center field, but scouts expect he will move to a corner once he fills out. He is mature for his age, a hard worker and routine-oriented. He has plus speed and stole bases at an 82 percent clip in Hillsboro.

THE FUTURE: Given his loud tools, Robinson arguably has more potential than any player in the D-backs system. If he continues his upward trajectory, he could find himself among baseball's top prospects in short order.

SCOUTING GRADES: **Hitting:** 50 **Power:** 70 **Running:** 60 **Fielding:** 55 **Arm:** 50

Year	Age	Club (League)	Class	AVG	G	AB	R	H	2B	3B	HR	RBI	BB	SO	SB	OBP	SLG
2018	17	Diamondbacks (AZL)	R	.272	40	162	35	44	11	0	4	31	16	46	7	.341	.414
	17	Missoula (PIO)	R	.300	17	60	13	18	1	0	3	10	11	21	5	.419	.467
2019	18	Hillsboro (NWL)	SS	.319	44	163	29	52	10	1	9	35	23	47	14	.407	.558
	18	Kane County (MWL)	LoA	.217	25	92	14	20	3	1	5	16	8	30	3	.294	.435
Minor League Totals				.281	126	477	91	134	25	2	21	92	58	144	29	.366	.474

4 ALEK THOMAS, OF

RAWHIDE/JILL GEARIN

BA GRADE
55 **Risk: High**

Born: April 28, 2000. **B-T:** L-L. **HT:** 5-11. **WT:** 175. **Drafted:** HS—Chicago, 2018 (2nd round). **Signed by:** Nate Birtwell.

TRACK RECORD: Thomas, the son of White Sox strength coach Allen Thomas, performed well in the low Class A Midwest League in his first full season as a pro and mostly held his own at high Class A Visalia after an August promotion. Fast, instinctual and with a nose for hitting, Thomas capped his season with a walk-off RBI double to give Visalia the California League championship.

SCOUTING REPORT: Thomas has a lot of moving parts with his swing, including a big leg kick and active hands before he loads. But he consistently manages to be in the right position and on time when he swings, and he is able to generate hard line drives on all types of pitches. He has an aggressive approach that will lead to strikeouts, but he will also take a walk. Thomas surprises with the power he generates from his undersized frame, but how that will translate in the majors remains a question among scouts, most of whom project 12-15 home run totals. He is a plus runner who could steal 20-plus bases. Thomas gets good reads and will have no trouble sticking in center field. His arm is improving but remains below-average.

THE FUTURE: Scouts love the way Thomas plays and compare him with Adam Eaton and Jon Jay. He will likely open 2020 back in Visalia.

SCOUTING GRADES: **Hitting:** 60 **Power:** 45 **Running:** 60 **Fielding:** 60 **Arm:** 45

Year	Age	Club (League)	Class	AVG	G	AB	R	H	2B	3B	HR	RBI	BB	SO	SB	OBP	SLG
2018	18	Diamondbacks (AZL)	R	.325	28	123	24	40	3	5	0	10	13	18	8	.394	.431
	18	Missoula (PIO)	R	.341	28	123	26	42	11	1	2	17	11	19	4	.396	.496
2019	19	Kane County (MWL)	LoA	.312	91	353	63	110	21	7	8	48	43	72	11	.393	.479
	19	Visalia (CAL)	HiA	.255	23	94	13	24	2	0	2	7	9	33	4	.327	.340
Minor League Totals				.312	170	693	126	216	37	13	12	82	76	142	27	.385	.455

5 CORBIN CARROLL, OF

BILL JACOBS

Born: Aug. 21, 2000. **B-T:** L-L. **HT:** 5-10. **WT:** 165. **Drafted:** HS—Seattle, 2019 (1st round). **Signed by:** Dan Ramsay.

TRACK RECORD: The D-backs' front office hasn't shied away from taking undersized position players high in the draft the past few years, and the 5-foot-10 Carroll became the latest such selection. The club was thrilled a player it had rated in the top 10 of the draft made it to No. 16 overall. Carroll signed for $3.75 million, forgoing his commitment to UCLA.

SCOUTING REPORT: Carroll, whose game is similar to fellow D-backs prospect Alek Thomas, described his play as "tools meets gamer." Scouts and coaches paint a similar picture. Carroll has a fluid swing with which he sprays line drives to all fields. He has surprising average raw power, which he put on display during an impressive batting practice session at Chase Field after he signed. In his pro debut in the Rookie-level Arizona League and short-season Northwest League, he showed some swing-and-miss tendencies but also carried an impressive 15.5 percent walk rate. Carroll is a burner whose plus-plus speed plays on the bases and in center field, where he projects to be a plus defender. He has an accurate but below-average arm. An advanced player for his age, he has good instincts and good baseball acumen.

THE FUTURE: Carroll will look to build on his strong pro debut in 2020, beginning at low Class A Kane County.

SCOUTING GRADES: **Hitting:** 55 **Power:** 45 **Running:** 70 **Fielding:** 60 **Arm:** 45

Year	Age	Club (League)	Class	AVG	G	AB	R	H	2B	3B	HR	RBI	BB	SO	SB	OBP	SLG
2019	18	Diamondbacks (AZL)	R	.288	31	111	23	32	6	3	2	14	24	29	16	.409	.450
	18	Hillsboro (NWL)	SS	.326	11	43	13	14	3	4	0	6	5	12	2	.408	.581
Minor League Totals				.299	42	154	36	46	9	7	2	20	29	41	18	.409	.487

6 BLAKE WALSTON, LHP

COURTESY OF HILLSBORO HOPS

BA GRADE
55 **Risk: Extreme**

Born: June 28, 2001. **B-T:** L-L. **HT:** 6-5. **WT:** 195. **Drafted:** HS—Wilmington, N.C., 2019 (1st round). **Signed by:** George Swain.

TRACK RECORD: The D-backs saw a projectable lefthander with plenty of stuff to dream on in Walston and surprised many, including Walston himself, when they selected him 26th overall in the 2019 draft. He signed for $2.45 million to forgo a North Carolina State commitment. Walston made huge strides in his first summer as a pro, adding both strength and velocity.

SCOUTING REPORT: In the world of high school pitchers, Walston checks all the boxes when it comes to projectability. He's tall and lanky with room to add strength; he has a clean arm action and delivery; he showed velocity and the ability to spin a breaking ball; and he is an excellent athlete, evidenced by his success as a high school quarterback. While his velocity fluctuated during the spring, he was more consistent after signing, regularly touching 96-97 mph. His plus curveball and average slider tended to bleed together, and some feel he could benefit from settling on one or the other. His changeup is lightly used but showed flashes of being an average pitch.

THE FUTURE: Walston excited the Diamondbacks with glimpses of his potential last summer, drawing comparisons to a young Barry Zito. He likely will open the season in extended spring training with a chance to push his way to low Class A Kane County.

SCOUTING GRADES: **Fastball:** 60 **Slider:** 50 **Curveball:** 60 **Changeup:** 50 **Control:** 55

Year	Age	Club (League)	Class	W	L	ERA	G	GS	SV	IP	H	HR	BB	SO	K/9	WHIP	AVG
2019	18	Diamondbacks (AZL)	R	0	0	1.80	3	2	0	5	2	0	0	11	19.8	0.40	.118
	18	Hillsboro (NWL)	SS	0	0	3.00	3	3	0	6	6	0	2	6	9.0	1.33	.261
Minor League Totals				0	0	2.45	6	5	0	11	8	0	2	17	13.9	0.91	.200

7 LIOVER PEGUERO, SS

COURTESY OF HILLSBORO HOPS

BA GRADE
55 **Risk: Extreme**

Born: Dec. 31, 2000. **B-T:** R-R. **HT:** 6-2. **WT:** 175. **Signed:** Dominican Republic, 2017. **Signed by:** Cesar Geronimo.

TRACK RECORD: When Latin American scouting director Cesar Geronimo first saw Peguero, he was a skinny, 5-foot-10 teenager who managed to hit the ball as hard as any of the bigger players around him. Peguero is still lean, but he's grown at least four inches and added at least 30 pounds since the club invested $475,000 in him. He starred at Rookie-level Missoula in his U.S. debut and finished at short-season Hillsboro.

SCOUTING REPORT: Regarded as a premium athlete, Peguero has a strong, wiry build and above-average speed. He has a feel for finding the barrel and regularly generates loud contact. With a body that still has room to fill out, his average power projection could continue to grow. Peguero's approach is aggressive, but he showed signs last year of being more selective. He won over skeptical coaches and evaluators with his improved defense last season, leading many to change their minds about his ability to stick at shortstop. If he does have to move, he could easily fit elsewhere on the infield or even in center field, where his long strides would cover a lot of ground.

THE FUTURE: Peguero has a ways to go, but his offensive-minded profile brings to mind a longer and leaner Jean Segura. He should make the jump to full-season ball in 2020.

SCOUTING GRADES: **Hitting:** 55 **Power:** 50 **Running:** 55 **Fielding:** 55 **Arm:** 55

Year	Age	Club (League)	Class	AVG	G	AB	R	H	2B	3B	HR	RBI	BB	SO	SB	OBP	SLG
2018	17	D-backs (DSL)	R	.309	22	81	14	25	3	3	1	16	6	12	4	.356	.457
	17	Diamondbacks (AZL)	R	.197	19	66	8	13	0	0	0	5	5	17	3	.254	.197
2019	18	Missoula (PIO)	R	.364	38	143	34	52	7	3	5	27	12	34	8	.410	.559
	18	Hillsboro (NWL)	SS	.262	22	84	13	22	4	2	0	11	8	17	3	.333	.357
Minor League Totals				.299	101	374	69	112	14	8	6	59	31	80	18	.354	.428

8 CORBIN MARTIN, RHP

BA GRADE
50 Risk: High

Born: Dec. 28, 1995. **B-T:** R-R. **HT:** 6-2. **WT:** 200. **Drafted:** Texas A&M, 2017 (2nd round). **Signed by:** Noel Gonzales-Luna (Astros).

TRACK RECORD: Martin reached the majors last season and made five starts for the Astros before being sent back to Triple-A Round Rock in June. Three starts later, he went down with elbow problems that ultimately required Tommy John surgery. The injury will sideline him for most, if not all, of the 2020 season, but it didn't deter the D-backs from acquiring him as part of the four-player package for righthander Zack Greinke at the 2019 trade deadline.

SCOUTING REPORT: The surgery will act as a bumper on what had been a fast-track career for Martin, who reached the big leagues less than two years after being drafted. He is a good athlete with clean arm action and a simple, repeatable delivery. Assuming he can get back to what he was, Martin will give the D-backs a polished starter with a four-pitch mix. His fastball sits in the 94-95 mph range, touching 98, and he commands it well to both sides of the plate. His slider and curveball both can be above-average pitches. His slider is more consistent, but when it's on his curveball can be better. His changeup comes in firm but with good armside run.

THE FUTURE: Martin's immediate future includes a lot of days rehabbing at Salt River Fields. If all goes well, he will return to game action after the all-star break.

SCOUTING GRADES: **Fastball:** 60 **Slider:** 50 **Curveball:** 55 **Changeup:** 50 **Control:** 55

Year	Age	Club (League)	Class	W	L	ERA	G	GS	SV	IP	H	HR	BB	SO	K/9	WHIP	AVG
2017	21	Astros (GCL)	R	0	0	0.00	2	1	0	5	0	0	1	5	9.0	0.20	.000
	21	Tri-City (NYP)	SS	0	1	2.60	8	3	1	28	20	1	8	38	12.4	1.01	.202
2018	22	Buies Creek (CAR)	HiA	2	0	0.00	4	3	1	19	4	0	7	26	12.3	0.58	.065
	22	Corpus Christi (TL)	AA	7	2	2.97	21	18	0	103	84	7	28	96	8.4	1.09	.221
2019	23	Houston (AL)	MAJ	1	1	5.59	5	5	0	19	23	8	12	19	8.8	1.81	.288
	23	Round Rock (PCL)	AAA	2	1	3.13	9	8	0	37	33	2	18	45	10.8	1.37	.243
Major League Totals				1	1	5.59	5	5	0	19	23	8	12	19	8.8	1.81	.288
Minor League Totals				11	4	2.58	44	33	2	192	141	10	62	210	9.8	1.06	.203

9 BRENNAN MALONE, RHP

ZACHARY LUCY/FOUR SEAM IMAGES

BA GRADE
55 Risk: Extreme

Born: Sept. 8, 2000. **B-T:** R-R. **HT:** 6-4. **WT:** 205. **Drafted:** HS—Bradenton, Fla., 2019 (1st round). **Signed by:** Matt Mercurio.

TRACK RECORD: Long regarded as one of the top prep arms in the 2019 class, Malone solidified his stock with a strong spring at IMG Academy, where the North Carolina native transferred for his senior year. The D-backs used the third of their seven first-day draft picks on Malone, taking him 33rd overall and signing him for $2.2 million to forgo a North Carolina commitment.

SCOUTING REPORT: Malone featured perhaps the best combination of present stuff and future projection of any high school pitcher in his class. He has a strong, durable frame and an athletic delivery with a loose, easy arm action. He showed plus fastball velocity consistently throughout the spring, sitting 93 mph while touching the upper 90s. His slider is his best secondary offering, a potential plus pitch with sharp, late break that he throws at the back foot of lefthanded hitters. His curveball and changeup are less consistent, but both project average. Malone has a mature, stoic demeanor on the mound. At times, his command deserts him and he can look more like a thrower than a pitcher.

THE FUTURE: Malone has the ingredients to become a power starter, with his upside to be determined by how his command and stuff progress.

SCOUTING GRADES: **Fastball:** 60 **Slider:** 60 **Curveball:** 50 **Changeup:** 50 **Control:** 50

Year	Age	Club (League)	Class	W	L	ERA	G	GS	SV	IP	H	HR	BB	SO	K/9	WHIP	AVG
2019	18	Diamondbacks (AZL)	R	1	2	5.14	6	3	0	7	4	0	5	7	9.0	1.29	.167
	18	Hillsboro (NWL)	SS	0	0	0.00	1	0	0	1	0	0	0	1	9.0	0.00	.000
Minor League Totals				1	2	4.50	7	3	0	8	4	0	5	8	9.0	1.13	.148

10 LUIS FRIAS, RHP

BA GRADE
55 Risk: Extreme

Born: May 23, 1998. **B-T:** R-R. **HT:** 6-3. **WT:** 235. **Signed:** Dominican Republic, 2015. **Signed by:** Jose Ortiz/Junior Noboa.

TRACK RECORD: Since signing for $50,000 in 2015, Frias has added size, strength and stuff to develop into one of the more intriguing pitching prospects in the organization. He took steps forward in 2019 by smoothing out his delivery and both refining and adding to his pitch mix, and as a result he reached full-season ball for the first time with low Class A Kane County.

SCOUTING REPORT: Frias comes with some reliever risk, but he has the ingredients of a frontline starter. He has a big, physical build, a fastball that reaches the upper 90s and a swing-and-miss breaking ball. He implemented a spike curveball grip in 2019 that made the pitch a plus offering and turned his changeup into more of a splitter, giving him a usable, average third pitch. Frias ironed out his delivery and began to shed his reputation for being erratic. He also kept his weight in check around the mid-230s after ballooning to more than 250 pounds a year ago.

THE FUTURE: Frias showed progress in 2019, but he will need to continue to refine his arsenal and show his command and control will play against more advanced hitters. He could be a force in the rotation if it all clicks. Otherwise, his path might lead him to a high-leverage relief role.

SCOUTING GRADES: **Fastball:** 70 **Curveball:** 60 **Splitter:** 50 **Control:** 50

Year	Age	Club (League)	Class	W	L	ERA	G	GS	SV	IP	H	HR	BB	SO	K/9	WHIP	AVG
2017	19	Did not play—Injured															
2018	20	Diamondbacks (AZL)	R	1	1	2.48	7	6	0	29	17	1	11	31	9.6	0.97	.167
	20	Hillsboro (NWL)	SS	0	4	3.16	7	7	0	26	21	0	15	27	9.5	1.40	.221
2019	21	Hillsboro (NWL)	SS	3	3	1.99	10	10	0	50	36	0	17	72	13.0	1.07	.205
	21	Kane County (MWL)	LoA	3	1	4.39	6	6	0	27	22	1	12	29	9.8	1.28	.225
Minor League Totals				10	11	3.10	43	40	0	182	141	2	83	206	10.2	1.23	.212

11 LEVI KELLY, RHP

BA GRADE
50 Risk: High

Born: May 14, 1999. **B-T:** R-R. **HT:** 6-4. **WT:** 205. **Drafted:** HS—Bradenton, Fla., 2018 (8th round). **Signed by:** Luke Wrenn.

TRACK RECORD: The Diamondbacks lean toward conservative when handling high school arms, keeping most at extended spring training their first full season. Kelly was so dominant in spring training he forced his way to low Class A Kane County, where he turned in an overpowering season in the Midwest League.

SCOUTING REPORT: Tall and lean, Kelly features a fastball that sits in the mid-90s along with a slider that some believe already is at least an above-average major league pitch. He switched his changeup grip to a splitter, a pitch that better fits his aggressive mindset, but it remains a distant third offering. Kelly has a max-effort delivery—some coaches think he might benefit from not going all-out on every pitch—and only fair command. Those attributes, combined with his still-developing splitter, lead to projections of a possible future in relief. He earns high marks for his makeup and maturity.

THE FUTURE: If everything comes together, Kelly could settle into a role as a back-end starter. If not, his slider gives him a go-to weapon that would shine in a late-inning relief role.

Year	Age	Club (League)	Class	W	L	ERA	G	GS	SV	IP	H	HR	BB	SO	K/9	WHIP	AVG
2018	19	Diamondbacks (AZL)	R	0	0	0.00	4	4	0	6	3	0	2	6	9.0	0.83	.143
2019	20	Kane County (MWL)	LoA	5	1	2.15	22	22	0	100	72	4	39	126	11.3	1.11	.199
Minor League Totals				5	1	2.03	26	26	0	106	75	4	41	132	11.2	1.09	.196

12 J.B. BUKAUSKAS, RHP

BA GRADE
50 Risk: High

Born: Oct. 11, 1996. **B-T:** R-R. **HT:** 6-0. **WT:** 201. **Drafted:** North Carolina, 2017 (1st round). **Signed by:** Tim Bittner (Astros).

TRACK RECORD: Pro ball has not been the smoothest ride for Bukauskas since the Astros selected him 15th overall in 2017. He missed two months with a bulging disk in his back following a car accident in 2018, then struggled to command his pitches in 2019, a year in which he was both traded to the Diamondbacks in the Zack Greinke trade and shut down in August with elbow discomfort.

SCOUTING REPORT: There are few questions about Bukauskas' stuff. He has a short arm stroke that produces deception and power and two plus pitches in his his fastball and slider. His fastball, though straight at times, touches the mid-to-upper 90s, and his slider is a true wipeout pitch in the upper 80s with sharp, late tilt. His changeup projects average. Bukauskas was his own worst enemy in 2019, falling behind in

counts and putting runners on as his command took a step back from the previous year. He has trouble repeating his delivery and remaining consistent with his release point.
THE FUTURE: Bukauskas has the weapons to start if he can clean things up, but most evaluators now view him as a reliever. Still, he could be a difference-maker in a late-inning role.

Year	Age	Club (League)	Class	W	L	ERA	G	GS	SV	IP	H	HR	BB	SO	K/9	WHIP	AVG
2017	20	Astros (GCL)	R	0	0	0.00	1	1	0	4	3	0	1	3	6.8	1.00	.231
	20	Tri-City (NYP)	SS	0	0	4.50	2	2	0	6	4	0	4	6	9.0	1.33	.191
2018	21	Astros (GCL)	R	0	0	10.80	1	1	0	2	5	0	0	2	10.8	3.00	.500
	21	Tri-City (NYP)	SS	0	0	0.00	3	3	0	8	8	0	2	9	9.7	1.20	.258
	21	Quad Cities (MWL)	LoA	1	2	4.20	4	4	0	15	15	0	7	21	12.6	1.47	.259
	21	Buies Creek (CAR)	HiA	3	0	1.61	5	5	0	28	13	1	13	31	10.0	0.93	.138
	21	Corpus Christi (TL)	AA	0	0	0.00	1	1	0	6	1	0	2	8	12.0	0.50	.056
2019	22	Corpus Christi (TL)	AA	2	4	5.25	20	14	1	86	81	8	54	98	10.3	1.58	.252
	22	Jackson (SL)	AA	0	1	7.71	2	2	0	7	10	0	5	11	14.1	2.14	.345
Minor League Totals				6	7	4.06	39	33	1	161	140	9	88	189	10.5	1.41	.235

13 JON DUPLANTIER, RHP

BA GRADE
45 Risk: Medium

Born: July 11, 1994. **B-T:** L-R. **HT:** 6-4. **WT:** 225. **Drafted:** Rice, 2016 (3rd round). **Signed by:** Rusty Pendergrass.
TRACK RECORD: Duplantier reached the majors in 2019, but he spent the year bouncing not only from Triple-A Reno to Arizona but also from the rotation to the bullpen, where the Diamondbacks primarily used him in the big leagues. He mostly struggled no matter the role or level as his season became a manifestation of the reservations scouts have harbored about him for years.
SCOUTING REPORT: Duplantier again battled injuries—this time, shoulder inflammation—and also struggled to maintain his velocity while showing below-average command. For some scouts, both Duplantier's injury and command issues stem from his high-maintenance delivery and long arm action. He spent the final months of the season working to correct those issues with then-Diamondbacks pitching coach Mike Butcher. At his best, Duplantier features a fastball that can touch the mid-90s along with a slider, curveball and changeup that all flash at least average, but consistency eludes him.
THE FUTURE: The Diamondbacks hope a more consistent role as a starter in 2020 will allow Duplantier to regain his previous form. His struggles last season led to more questions about whether he is best suited for relief.

Year	Age	Club (League)	Class	W	L	ERA	G	GS	SV	IP	H	HR	BB	SO	K/9	WHIP	AVG
2017	22	Kane County (MWL)	LoA	6	1	1.24	13	12	0	73	45	4	15	78	9.7	0.83	.180
	22	Visalia (CAL)	HiA	6	2	1.56	12	12	0	63	46	2	27	87	12.4	1.15	.204
2018	23	Diamondbacks (AZL)	R	0	0	1.29	2	2	0	7	5	0	2	9	11.6	1.00	.200
	23	Jackson (SL)	AA	5	1	2.69	14	14	0	67	52	4	28	68	9.1	1.19	.217
2019	24	Diamondbacks (AZL)	R	0	0	18.00	2	2	0	2	5	1	3	3	13.5	4.00	.455
	24	Visalia (CAL)	HiA	0	0	0.00	1	1	0	3	2	0	0	3	9.0	0.67	.222
	24	Reno (PCL)	AAA	1	2	5.21	13	11	0	38	31	1	28	44	10.4	1.55	.233
	24	Arizona (NL)	MAJ	1	1	4.42	15	3	1	37	39	2	18	34	8.3	1.55	.283
Major League Totals				1	1	4.42	15	3	1	36	39	2	18	34	8.4	1.55	.283
Minor League Totals				18	6	2.41	58	54	0	254	186	12	105	295	10.5	1.15	.208

14 SETH BEER, 1B

BA GRADE
50 Risk: High

Born: Sept. 18, 1996. **B-T:** L-R. **HT:** 6-3. **WT:** 205. **Drafted:** Clemson, 2018 (1st round). **Signed by:** Gavin Dickey (Astros).
TRACK RECORD: Beer is a former elite-level swimmer who chose to focus on baseball at age 13, a decision that has worked out nicely. After mashing his way through the Atlantic Coast Conference at Clemson, he was drafted 28th overall by the Astros in 2018 and hit his way to Double-A in his first full season. The Diamondbacks acquired him midway through the year as part of the Zack Greinke trade.
SCOUTING REPORT: Beer's calling card is his bat, but there's far from a consensus on what kind of player he is likely to become. His game includes a blend of hittability, power and a mature approach, but scouts wonder if he does well enough at any of them to be a first-division bat. Since he doesn't run well and is a poor defender—he's a first base-only type with below-average footwork and hands—he's going to have to really mash in order to profile at the position.
THE FUTURE: Despite the gaudy numbers, Beer is a divisive player in the industry. Analytically-inclined officials support him, while most traditional scouts remain uncertain, offering comps of modestly productive sluggers like Matt Adams and Allen Craig. Beer is likely to open 2020 back at Double-A Jackson.

Year	Age	Club (League)	Class	AVG	G	AB	R	H	2B	3B	HR	RBI	BB	SO	SB	OBP	SLG
2018	21	Tri-City (NYP)	SS	.293	11	41	9	12	3	0	4	7	6	10	0	.431	.659
	21	Quad Cities (MWL)	LoA	.348	29	112	15	39	7	0	3	16	15	17	1	.443	.491
	21	Buies Creek (CAR)	HiA	.262	27	107	15	28	4	0	5	19	4	22	0	.307	.439
2019	22	Fayetteville (CAR)	HiA	.328	35	128	24	42	8	0	9	34	14	30	0	.414	.602
	22	Corpus Christi (TL)	AA	.299	63	234	40	70	9	0	16	52	24	58	0	.407	.543
	22	Jackson (SL)	AA	.205	24	88	8	18	7	0	1	17	8	25	0	.297	.318
Minor League Totals				.294	189	710	111	209	38	0	38	145	71	162	1	.388	.508

15 JOSH GREEN, RHP

BA GRADE 50 Risk: High

Born: Aug. 31, 1995. **B-T:** R-R. **HT:** 6-3. **WT:** 210. **Drafted:** Southeastern Louisiana, 2018 (14th round). **Signed by:** Rusty Pendergrass.

TRACK RECORD: A 14th-round senior sign out of Southeastern Louisiana, Green opened eyes during his pro debut in 2018 before breaking out as a prospect in 2019. He led the organization in wins (11) and finished second in ERA (2.71) while advancing to Double-A and was named the Diamondbacks' minor league pitcher of the year.

SCOUTING REPORT: Riding a heavy, sinking fastball that harkens back to a different era, Green recorded one of the highest ground-ball rates in the minors. His sinker sits in the low-to-mid 90s, touching 96 at its best. His curveball improved to the point that it might be his best secondary offering ahead of his change-up, as an average pitch. He also has a cutter/slider. Green's secondaries are truly secondary, but he limits walks and homers and is something of a workhorse. He went at least five innings in all 22 of his starts.

THE FUTURE: Rival scouts believe Green's stuff is too light to compare to a turbo-sinkerballer like Dakota Hudson, but the Diamondbacks view him differently. They see enough stuff to go along with a durable frame and aptitude and believe he can become a back-end starter.

Year	Age	Club (League)	Class	W	L	ERA	G	GS	SV	IP	H	HR	BB	SO	K/9	WHIP	AVG
2018	22	Hillsboro (NWL)	SS	3	1	1.09	25	0	11	33	31	0	9	25	6.8	1.21	.250
2019	23	Visalia (CAL)	HiA	9	1	1.73	14	14	0	78	69	1	13	69	8.0	1.05	.247
	23	Jackson (SL)	AA	2	4	4.28	8	8	0	48	61	2	8	32	6.0	1.43	.318
Minor League Totals				14	6	2.37	47	22	11	159	161	3	30	126	7.1	1.20	.271

16 WILDERD PATIÑO, OF

BA GRADE 55 Risk: Extreme

Born: July 18, 2001. **B-T:** R-R. **HT:** 6-1. **WT:** 175. **Signed:** Venezuela, 2017. **Signed by:** Cesar Geronimo/Kristians Pereira.

TRACK RECORD: Patiño reportedly agreed to a $1.3 million deal with the Rangers before hurting his elbow prior to the start of the 2017 international signing period. The Rangers nixed the deal, allowing the Diamondbacks to swoop in and sign him for $985,000. Patiño underwent a second elbow surgery that sidelined him until the following June, but he played his first uninterrupted season in 2019.

SCOUTING REPORT: Once healthy, Patiño quickly showcased his ultra-athletic skill set. Built like a defensive back, he has a chance to develop into a five-tool talent. He has at least plus speed, above-average if not plus raw power, a chance to stick in center field and an above-average arm to go with his promising pure hitting ability. Patiño still has plenty of facets to fine tune. His approach can come and go, he chases too much and doesn't recognize spin particularly well. He also hits too many balls on the ground, which limits his capacity for extra-base hits.

THE FUTURE: Patiño's rough edges are standard for an 18-year-old with fewer than 300 professional at-bats.

Year	Age	Club (League)	Class	AVG	G	AB	R	H	2B	3B	HR	RBI	BB	SO	SB	OBP	SLG
2018	16	D-backs2 (DSL)	R	.225	28	89	10	20	5	0	0	7	14	19	2	.360	.281
	16	D-backs (DSL)	R	.409	6	22	4	9	1	0	0	2	2	5	4	.519	.455
2019	17	Diamondbacks (AZL)	R	.349	30	106	18	37	4	3	1	21	11	32	13	.403	.472
	17	Missoula (PIO)	R	.229	10	35	6	8	1	2	0	4	2	14	1	.300	.371
Minor League Totals				.294	74	252	38	74	11	5	1	34	29	70	20	.384	.389

17 DREY JAMESON, RHP

BA GRADE 50 Risk: High

Born: Aug. 17, 1997. **B-T:** R-R. **HT:** 6-0. **WT:** 165. **Drafted:** Ball State, 2019 (1st round). **Signed by:** Jeremy Kehrt.

TRACK RECORD: Jameson arrived at Ball State a two-way player but quickly turned himself into the Cardinals' best pitching prospect since Bryan Bullington went No. 1 overall in 2002. As a draft-eligible sophomore, he earned Mid-American Conference Pitcher of the Year honors in 2019 and was drafted 34th overall by the Diamondbacks.

SCOUTING REPORT: Jameson stands out for his pure stuff. Despite an undersized frame, his quick arm produces rising fastballs that regularly gets into the 93-97 mph range. He compliments his fastball with a swing-and-miss curveball, a potential above-average slider that elicits soft contact and a changeup that flashes plus with split action. All have intriguing potential but are inconsistent. Jameson's size and uptempo delivery create questions about whether he'll be able to maintain his stuff as a starter. He also did not throw enough strikes his freshman year, and while he improved as a sophomore, his control wasn't sharp in his abbreviated pro debut and will be worth watching moving forward.
THE FUTURE: Jameson is regarded as a tremendous athlete, giving the Diamondbacks hope he'll find a way to stick in the rotation. If he can't, his explosive stuff should play well in relief.

Year	Age	Club (League)	Class	W	L	ERA	G	GS	SV	IP	H	HR	BB	SO	K/9	WHIP	AVG
2019	21	Hillsboro (NWL)	SS	0	0	6.17	8	8	0	12	14	1	9	12	9.3	1.97	.292
Minor League Totals				0	0	6.17	8	8	0	11	14	1	9	12	9.3	1.97	.292

18 PAVIN SMITH, 1B/OF

BA GRADE
45 **Risk: High**

Born: Feb. 6, 1996. **B-T:** L-L. **HT:** 6-2. **WT:** 210. **Drafted:** Virginia, 2017 (1st round). **Signed by:** Rick Matsko.

TRACK RECORD: Smith long struggled to generate the kind of offensive production expected from him as the seventh overall pick of the 2017 draft, but he caught fire in the second half of last season to rekindle hopes of a major league future. Smith hit .329 with a .936 OPS at Double-A Jackson after the all-star break, finding a way to balance his top-notch plate discipline and contact skills with the ability to do damage.
SCOUTING REPORT: Smith had been trying to tinker with his swing and approach, but his hot finish seemed more like him getting back to his old self. A natural hitter who can find the barrel and rarely expands the zone, he went back to spraying balls to left and center and trying to pull the ball with power only occasionally. While he's always been a good defender at first, he also played a more passable corner outfield in 2019, showing a sneaky good arm.
THE FUTURE: Smith started to make his path toward a positive big league role more palatable. Whether he fully lives up to his draft slot remains to be seen, but he'll open 2020 in Triple-A Reno on the cusp of the majors.

Year	Age	Club (League)	Class	AVG	G	AB	R	H	2B	3B	HR	RBI	BB	SO	SB	OBP	SLG
2017	21	Hillsboro (NWL)	SS	.318	51	195	34	62	15	2	0	27	27	24	2	.401	.415
2018	22	Visalia (CAL)	HiA	.255	120	439	63	112	25	1	11	54	57	65	3	.343	.392
2019	23	Jackson (SL)	AA	.291	123	440	62	128	29	6	12	67	59	61	2	.370	.466
Minor League Totals				.281	294	1074	159	302	69	9	23	148	143	150	7	.364	.426

19 BLAZE ALEXANDER, SS/2B

BA GRADE
45 **Risk: High**

Born: June 11, 1999. **B-T:** R-R. **HT:** 6-0. **WT:** 160. **Drafted:** HS—Bradenton, Fla., 2018 (11th round). **Signed by:** Luke Wrenn.

TRACK RECORD: Alexander's father, Charles, pitched in the Indians organization and his older brother, C.J., is in the Braves' system. The Diamondbacks snapped up the youngest Alexander in the 11th round of the 2018 draft and signed him for an overslot $500,000 bonus. He produced right away with impressive numbers at two short-season levels, then put together a solid, if unspectacular, season in the low Class A Midwest League in 2019.
SCOUTING REPORT: Lean and athletic, Alexander's loudest tool is his arm, which scouts rate near the top of the scouting scale. He has good hands and actions, as well, convincing evaluators he could be at least a serviceable shortstop in the majors. He also saw time at second base and third base. Though his numbers (.262, 7 HR) weren't great, he made strides at the plate and showed better pitch selection. Even so, Alexander gave away too many at-bats without a consistent plan, something the Diamondbacks hope will come with maturity. Scouts give him a chance to hit for a decent average and close to average power.
THE FUTURE: With a crowded middle infield picture in the system, Alexander's versatility could help him carve out a role in the Chris Taylor/Chris Owings mold. He'll see high Class A Visalia in 2020.

Year	Age	Club (League)	Class	AVG	G	AB	R	H	2B	3B	HR	RBI	BB	SO	SB	OBP	SLG
2018	19	Diamondbacks (AZL)	R	.362	27	94	25	34	10	2	2	25	19	21	7	.475	.574
	19	Missoula (PIO)	R	.302	28	116	27	35	9	3	3	17	12	31	3	.364	.509
2019	20	Kane County (MWL)	LoA	.262	97	343	56	90	12	4	7	47	42	89	14	.355	.382
Minor League Totals				.288	152	553	108	159	31	9	12	89	73	141	24	.378	.441

20 ANDY YOUNG, 2B

BA GRADE **40** Risk: Medium

Born: May 10, 1994. **B-T:** R-R. **HT:** 6-0. **WT:** 195. **Drafted:** Indiana State, 2016 (37th round). **Signed by:** Jason Bryans (Cardinals).

TRACK RECORD: Though he wasn't as accomplished as Carson Kelly or Luke Weaver, Young was no throw-in to the Paul Goldschmidt trade but rather a player whose offensive upside the Diamondbacks found intriguing when they acquired him from the Cardinals. A 37th-round pick who signed for $3,000, Young continued to swing the bat with his new organization and hit 29 homers between Double-A Jackson and Triple-A Reno, tied for second-most in the D-backs' system.

SCOUTING REPORT: Young has a strong frame and a compact swing with little wasted movement, allowing him to generate real power. Most scouts envision a player who will provide quality at-bats and occasional power at the major league level. They are less convinced on what Young will bring defensively. He is at best a fringe-average defender at second base, while others don't see a position for him on the field at all. The Diamondbacks plan to expose him to the outfield in 2020, where he has played only sparingly.

THE FUTURE: The D-backs added Young to the 40-man roster in November. Comparisons put him somewhere between a Phil Gosselin and Jedd Gyorko type of contributor.

Year	Age	Club (League)	Class	AVG	G	AB	R	H	2B	3B	HR	RBI	BB	SO	SB	OBP	SLG
2017	23	Peoria (MWL)	LoA	.284	58	211	31	60	11	4	12	38	22	54	5	.379	.545
	23	Palm Beach (FSL)	HiA	.265	57	196	24	52	9	0	5	20	10	49	3	.327	.388
	23	Springfield, MO (TL)	AA	.667	2	3	2	2	0	0	0	1	1	1	0	.800	.667
2018	24	Palm Beach (FSL)	HiA	.276	84	297	43	82	10	2	12	34	31	59	4	.372	.444
	24	Springfield, MO (TL)	AA	.319	35	135	18	43	3	1	9	24	7	26	0	.395	.556
2019	25	Jackson (SL)	AA	.260	65	223	36	58	15	2	8	28	18	53	1	.363	.453
	25	Reno (PCL)	AAA	.280	68	239	53	67	10	3	21	53	24	68	2	.373	.611
Minor League Totals				.278	422	1496	240	416	63	18	70	222	130	357	18	.367	.485

21 MATT TABOR, RHP

BA GRADE **45** Risk: High

Born: July 14, 1998. **B-T:** R-R. **HT:** 6-2. **WT:** 180. **Drafted:** HS—Milton, Mass., 2017 (3rd round). **Signed by:** Dennis Sheehan.

TRACK RECORD: Drafted in the third round in 2017 as a projection play, Tabor hasn't taken any massive leaps forward with his stuff but continues to make gradual progress. That included refining a third pitch and his ability to miss bats consistently, and the result was a 2.93 ERA at low Class A Kane County.

SCOUTING REPORT: Tabor has a lean frame and a clean, athletic delivery. His fastball sits mostly in the low-90s, touching 93 mph, and since he's still maturing physically there remains potential for him to add another tick or two. He focused on his slider in the offseason and turned it into a useable weapon, a pitch that ranged from average to plus. The emphasis on his breaking ball came at the cost of his changeup, though he rediscovered the pitch late in the year to give him a solid three-pitch mix. Most impressive was his control—he walked only 16 batters in 95.1 innings.

THE FUTURE: Most evaluators see Tabor as a potential back-end starter, and he still has work to do to get there. He is likely to open 2020 with high Class A Visalia.

Year	Age	Club (League)	Class	W	L	ERA	G	GS	SV	IP	H	HR	BB	SO	K/9	WHIP	AVG
2017	18	Diamondbacks (AZL)	R	0	1	1.93	4	4	0	5	8	0	0	9	17.4	1.71	.348
2018	19	Hillsboro (NWL)	SS	2	1	3.26	14	14	0	61	59	4	13	46	6.8	1.19	.251
2019	20	Kane County (MWL)	LoA	5	4	2.93	21	21	0	95	79	6	16	101	9.5	1.00	.225
Minor League Totals				7	6	3.02	39	39	0	160	146	10	29	156	8.7	1.09	.240

22 DOMINIC FLETCHER, OF

BA GRADE **45** Risk: High

Born: Sept. 2, 1997. **B-T:** L-L. **HT:** 5-9. **WT:** 185. **Drafted:** Arkansas, 2019 (2nd round supplemental). **Signed by:** Nate Birtwell.

TRACK RECORD: The younger brother of Angels infielder David Fletcher, Dominic spent three years at Arkansas, where he developed a reputation as a terrific defensive center fielder and a solid hitter with surprising pop. The D-backs selected him 75th overall in 2019, making him the highest-drafted Razorback since Andrew Benintendi was drafted seventh overall by the Red Sox in 2015.

SCOUTING REPORT: Fletcher has a smooth, line-drive swing that generates impressive above-average raw power, which he can occasionally tap into during games. His amount of swings and misses was a concern for some clubs. He is only an average runner, but he gets good enough jumps that most project him as an above-average center fielder. Some are less certain about his position and paint him as an outfield tweener without the chops to play center or the offensive thump to profile in a corner.

THE FUTURE: Whether as an everyday center fielder or a fourth outfielder, Fletcher is viewed as a likely future big league contributor. He is likely to start 2020 at high Class A Visalia.

Year	Age	Club (League)	Class	AVG	G	AB	R	H	2B	3B	HR	RBI	BB	SO	SB	OBP	SLG
2019	21	Kane County (MWL)	LoA	.318	55	214	33	68	14	1	5	28	22	50	1	.389	.463
Minor League Totals				.318	55	214	33	68	14	1	5	28	22	50	1	.389	.463

23 TOMMY HENRY, LHP

BA GRADE 45 Risk: High

Born: July 29, 1997. **B-T:** L-L. **HT:** 6-3. **WT:** 205. **Drafted:** Michigan, 2019 (2nd round supplemental). **Signed by:** Jeremy Kehrt.

TRACK RECORD: Henry made his way through an up-and-down junior year at Michigan and was viewed as a volatile prospect when the Diamondbacks took him 74th overall, but his arrow began pointing up after a string of dominant outings led the Wolverines to the brink of a College World Series title. He finished the year owning the school's single-season strikeout record and was the highest drafted Michigan pitcher in 25 years.

SCOUTING REPORT: Henry doesn't have a dominant repertoire, but he is a strike-thrower who repeats his delivery and commands each of his three offerings: a fastball that sits in the low-90s along with a slider and changeup that operate in the 78-82 mph range. He is an excellent athlete so the Diamondbacks are hoping that athletic aptitude helps his stuff to tick up.

THE FUTURE: Henry is viewed as having a back-end rotation ceiling, but the Diamondbacks see him as a safer bet than most to pitch in the big leagues. He'll open 2020 at one of the Class A levels.

Year	Age	Club (League)	Class	W	L	ERA	G	GS	SV	IP	H	HR	BB	SO	K/9	WHIP	AVG
2019	21	Hillsboro (NWL)	SS	0	0	6.00	3	3	0	3	4	0	0	4	12.0	1.33	.286
Minor League Totals				0	0	6.00	3	3	0	3	4	0	0	4	12.0	1.33	.286

24 EDUARDO DIAZ, OF

BA GRADE 45 Risk: High

Born: July 19, 1997. **B-T:** R-R. **HT:** 6-2. **WT:** 175. **Signed:** Venezuela, 2015. **Signed by:** Gregorio Ramirez/Junior Noboa.

TRACK RECORD: Diaz has been viewed as a toolsy, high-risk prospect in the Diamondbacks system for years, and there were concerns he could be stalling out after an injury-plagued 2018 season. But he came back in 2019 and performed well across both Class A levels, rekindling hope that the club still has an intriguing prospect on its hands.

SCOUTING REPORT: Diaz's tools have never been in question. He is an above-average runner, thrower and defender who also shows the ability to hit and put a charge into balls. Diaz has a strong, athletic build and has always been an extremely aggressive player, but he continued to take steps toward refining his game. His approach has come a long way as he started looking to do damage but not longer at all costs, although he's still learning how to consistently tap into his above-average raw power.

THE FUTURE: Diaz can stick in center field, so his bat will determine whether he's an everyday player or a fourth outfielder. He'll face his toughest test yet at Double-A in 2020.

Year	Age	Club (League)	Class	AVG	G	AB	R	H	2B	3B	HR	RBI	BB	SO	SB	OBP	SLG
2017	19	Missoula (PIO)	R	.312	57	247	58	77	18	5	7	44	11	47	11	.357	.510
2018	20	Kane County (MWL)	LoA	.225	33	120	12	27	5	2	2	11	3	40	3	.262	.350
2019	21	Kane County (MWL)	LoA	.283	72	286	48	81	15	3	7	31	26	57	13	.355	.430
	21	Visalia (CAL)	HiA	.283	44	187	30	53	11	3	3	27	8	43	5	.318	.422
Minor League Totals				.287	268	1061	191	304	57	15	22	136	77	231	55	.346	.431

25 KEVIN GINKEL, RHP

BA GRADE 40 Risk: Medium

Born: March 24, 1994. **B-T:** L-R. **HT:** 6-4. **WT:** 210. **Drafted:** Arizona, 2016 (22nd round). **Signed by:** Doyle Wilson.

TRACK RECORD: After a difficult 2017 season in which his stuff regressed and he struggled to bounce back physically from outings, Ginkel feared he would be released. He reworked his delivery that offseason in a bid to save his career, and everything about his trajectory has changed. Ginkel posted a 1.41 ERA in 2018 and soared from Double-A to the majors in 2019, where he pitched well and now looks like a bullpen mainstay.

SCOUTING REPORT: Ginkel went to Arizona, but his revamped delivery is reminiscent of a Virginia product: He is bent at the knees as he comes set, a posture which helps him activate his lower half before driving toward home plate. The delivery allows him to generate elite extension, helping his mid-90s fastball play up. He pairs his fastball with a slider that proved to be nearly unhittable in his 25 appearances in the majors. The Diamondbacks did not hesitate to move Ginkel up the bullpen hierarchy, even giving

him a pair of save chances in the season's final two weeks.
THE FUTURE: Barring a disastrous spring, Ginkel seems assured of a role in the Diamondbacks' bullpen to open 2020, and potentially even a prominent one.

Year	Age	Club (League)	Class	W	L	ERA	G	GS	SV	IP	H	HR	BB	SO	K/9	WHIP	AVG
2017	23	Kane County (MWL)	LoA	1	1	14.85	6	0	0	7	8	1	9	5	6.8	2.55	.308
	23	Hillsboro (NWL)	SS	0	1	3.48	20	0	0	34	26	1	11	49	13.1	1.10	.213
2018	24	Visalia (CAL)	HiA	1	1	0.99	20	0	4	27	20	2	3	40	13.2	0.84	.200
	24	Jackson (SL)	AA	5	0	1.69	34	0	5	43	26	3	9	60	12.7	0.82	.176
2019	25	Diamondbacks (AZL)	R	0	0	0.00	2	0	0	2	0	0	1	1	4.5	0.50	.000
	25	Jackson (SL)	AA	1	2	2.16	14	0	5	17	9	2	5	26	14.0	0.84	.158
	25	Reno (PCL)	AAA	1	0	1.62	15	0	6	17	10	2	8	36	19.4	1.08	.170
	25	Arizona (NL)	MAJ	3	0	1.48	25	0	2	24	15	2	9	28	10.4	0.99	.174
Major League Totals				3	0	1.48	25	0	2	24	15	2	9	28	10.4	0.99	.174
Minor League Totals				10	5	2.60	129	0	22	166	116	11	52	239	12.9	1.01	.196

26 TRISTIN ENGLISH, 3B

BA GRADE **50** Risk: Extreme

Born: May 14, 1997. **B-T:** R-R. **HT:** 6-3. **WT:** 208. **Drafted:** Georgia Tech, 2019 (3rd round). **Signed by:** Hudson Belinsky.

TRACK RECORD: English was a two-way player viewed by most organizations as a pitcher in the long run throughout most of his playing career. It wasn't until he performed well in the Cape Cod League in 2018 and carried that success into his junior season at Georgia Tech that scouts began to see him as a hitter. The Diamondbacks drafted him in the third round in 2019, believing he could develop into an everyday big leaguer with a sole focus on hitting.

SCOUTING REPORT: English is a tall, lanky athlete with smooth, graceful actions. He has good hand-eye coordination and rarely swings and misses. He began to tap into above-average power last year. He can be overly aggressive in his approach but is working on being more selective. English bounced between first base, right field and third base and appeared to find a home at third, where his plus arm can thrive.

THE FUTURE: With pitching in his past, English will put his attention squarely on being a position player. He'll likely open 2020 at low Class A Kane County.

Year	Age	Club (League)	Class	AVG	G	AB	R	H	2B	3B	HR	RBI	BB	SO	SB	OBP	SLG
2019	22	Hillsboro (NWL)	SS	.290	50	193	32	56	12	2	7	30	13	24	1	.356	.482
Minor League Totals				.290	50	193	32	56	12	2	7	30	13	24	1	.356	.482

27 RYNE NELSON, RHP

Born: Feb. 1, 1998. **B-T:** R-R. **HT:** 6-3. **WT:** 184. **Drafted:** Oregon, 2019 (2nd round). **Signed by:** Dan Ramsay.

TRACK RECORD: A two-way player who stood out as a shortstop his first two years at Oregon, Nelson moved to pitching full-time in 2019. He featured some of the most electric stuff in his draft class, but while he missed bats at a high clip, he was also more hittable than the stuff would suggest. The Diamondbacks took a chance on the arm and athleticism, drafting him in the second round.

SCOUTING REPORT: Nelson has an athletic delivery and a long but lightning-quick arm action. His fastball touches 99-100 mph and his curveball was his best secondary pitch during his pro debut. He also throws a slider, split changeup and cutter, the latter of which might be shelved for the time being. Nelson began ironing out some mechanical issues after signing. The club is hopeful his above-average body control and athleticism will allow him to become consistent mechanically and develop the command to start.

THE FUTURE: An excellent athlete with a low-mileage arm, the Diamondbacks will work to develop Nelson as a starter, knowing he has a fallback as a power-armed reliever.

Year	Age	Club (League)	Class	W	L	ERA	G	GS	SV	IP	H	HR	BB	SO	K/9	WHIP	AVG
2019	21	Hillsboro (NWL)	SS	0	1	2.89	10	7	0	19	15	1	10	26	12.5	1.34	.227
Minor League Totals				0	1	2.89	10	7	0	18	15	1	10	26	12.5	1.34	.227

28 TAYLOR WIDENER, RHP

BA GRADE **45** Risk: High

Born: Oct. 24, 1994. **B-T:** L-R. **HT:** 6-0. **WT:** 195. **Drafted:** South Carolina, 2016 (12th round). **Signed by:** Billy Godwin (Yankees).

TRACK RECORD: Widener won Diamondbacks minor league pitcher of the year in his first season with the club after they acquired him from the Yankees in a three-team deal in Feb. 2018. The wheels came off in year two, however, as Widener was unable to survive the harsh conditions of Triple-A Reno, particularly

with livelier baseballs. He finished the year with an 8.10 ERA and missed a month with elbow soreness.
SCOUTING REPORT: Widener has always thrived by relying on his fastball, a pitch that has good ride through the zone and plays above its 92-95 mph velocity. His changeup and slider never have been dominant or consistent, but he struggled with both in 2019, leaving him overly reliant on his fastball. Making matters worse, his velocity was down at times, and scouts thought he was working so hard to add velocity that his command suffered. The end result was a fastball he couldn't control that hitters sat on, and summarily punished.
THE FUTURE: Widener's year created doubt about his future as a starter. He will need to rediscover his fastball velocity and command and find a consistent secondary pitch to succeed in any role.

Year	Age	Club (League)	Class	W	L	ERA	G	GS	SV	IP	H	HR	BB	SO	K/9	WHIP	AVG
2017	22	Tampa (FSL)	HiA	7	8	3.39	27	27	0	119	87	5	50	129	9.7	1.15	.206
2018	23	Jackson (SL)	AA	5	8	2.75	26	25	0	137	99	12	43	176	11.5	1.03	.197
2019	24	Reno (PCL)	AAA	6	7	8.10	23	23	0	100	133	23	41	109	9.8	1.74	.324
Minor League Totals				21	23	4.08	89	77	4	395	336	42	141	473	10.8	1.21	.230

29 CONOR GRAMMES, RHP

BA GRADE
50 Risk: Extreme

Born: July 13, 1997. **B-T:** R-R. **HT:** 6-1. **WT:** 200. **Drafted:** Xavier, 2019 (5th round). **Signed by:** Jeremy Kehrt.
TRACK RECORD: Grammes was a position player and a wrestler in high school, barely stepping foot on the mound. He became a two-way player at Xavier, but as his velocity climbed and ultimately touched triple digits, it became clear where his future would lie. The Diamondbacks selected him in the fifth round and signed him for $300,000, and already think he has a chance to be a steal.
SCOUTING REPORT: Grammes has an explosive arm that generates fastballs in the mid-to-upper 90s. He has two breaking balls, a curveball he can throw for strikes or bounce and a slider he buries in on left-handed hitters. He began to get a better feel for his little-used changeup late in his pro debut at short-season Hillsboro. His high-effort delivery occasionally broke down across multiple innings in college and led to a walk rate of more than six batters-per-nine innings, and after signing he had issues with maintaining his arm slot and keeping his backside from collapsing. Given Grammes' athleticism and limited pitching experience, the organization is hopeful his delivery and strike-throwing will become more consistent with time.
THE FUTURE: The Diamondbacks believe the upside with Grammes is significant. He has obvious reliever risk, but the organization will develop him as a starter.

Year	Age	Club (League)	Class	W	L	ERA	G	GS	SV	IP	H	HR	BB	SO	K/9	WHIP	AVG
2019	21	Hillsboro (NWL)	SS	0	1	4.11	9	6	0	15	11	0	8	20	11.7	1.24	.200
Minor League Totals				0	1	4.11	9	6	0	15	11	0	8	20	11.7	1.24	.200

30 JUSTIN MARTINEZ, RHP

BA GRADE
50 Risk: Extreme

Born: July 30, 2001. **B-T:** R-R. **HT:** 6-3. **WT:** 195. **Signed:** Dominican Republic, 2018. **Signed by:** Cesar Geronimo/Jose Ortiz.
TRACK RECORD: Martinez converted from outfield to the mound less than six months before the Diamondbacks took a $50,000 flyer on him in March, 2018. He debuted in the Dominican Summer League a few months later, topping out at 95 mph, and added a few more ticks to his fastball last year to suddenly look like an intriguing, under-the-radar arm.
SCOUTING REPORT: Martinez flashes electric stuff with his arm strength and athleticism. He sits 95-96 mph on his fastball, touching 98, and can show a powerful, swing-and-miss slider, albeit inconsistently. He also shows feel for a changeup. Despite a clean arm action and an uncomplicated, low-effort delivery, he has difficulty repeating and syncing up his levers. Even so, his strike-throwing improved year-to-year, and given his athleticism and how far he has come so quickly for a converted player, the Diamondbacks see reason to believe he'll continue to get better in time
THE FUTURE: Martinez has the ingredients to become a tantalizing pitching prospect, but he still has a long way to turn that potential into reality. He'll open 2020 in extended spring training.

Year	Age	Club (League)	Class	W	L	ERA	G	GS	SV	IP	H	HR	BB	SO	K/9	WHIP	AVG
2018	16	D-backs (DSL)	R	0	2	7.33	7	7	0	23	26	2	20	15	5.8	1.97	.277
	16	D-backs2 (DSL)	R	0	3	7.84	8	5	0	21	25	1	18	15	6.5	2.08	.298
2019	17	D-backs2 (DSL)	R	1	2	3.06	9	8	0	35	29	0	22	48	12.2	1.44	.220
	17	Diamondbacks (AZL)	R	0	1	3.24	6	2	1	17	12	0	11	23	12.4	1.38	.191
	17	Missoula (PIO)	R	0	0	0.00	3	0	0	4	1	0	4	7	15.8	1.25	.067
Minor League Totals				1	8	4.95	33	22	1	100	93	3	75	108	9.7	1.68	.240

Atlanta Braves

BY CARLOS COLLAZO

After something of a surprise National League East title in 2018, the Braves topped the division again in 2019 despite win-now offseasons from the Mets and Phillies and another strong year from the Nationals.

Atlanta went 97-65 and was the fifth-best team in baseball by record. Yet again they hit a wall in the playoffs, losing their eighth consecutive postseason series by dropping the Division Series to the Cardinals.

Led by center fieler Ronald Acuña Jr., second baseman Ozzie Albies, third baseman Josh Donaldson and first baseman Freddie Freeman, the Braves had one of the best offensive cores in the game. The team ranked third in the National League in runs scored, and while Donaldson was signed to a one-year deal, the team signed both Acuña and Albies to team-friendly extensions that will keep them in Atlanta together through 2028.

The core of Acuña, Albies and Freeman should keep the Braves competitive well into the 2020s.

While Atlanta hasn't gotten the expected results from its bevy of pitching prospects, righthander Mike Soroka established himself as one of the best young pitchers in the game in 2019. He finished second in the NL Rookie of the Year award voting by going 13-4, 2.68 with the fourth-best park-adjusted ERA+ of 169 in baseball.

Having so much quality young talent should allow general manager Alex Anthopoulos to add established veteran pieces to the roster to take the next step. While it would be surprising to see the Liberty Media-owned Braves dive into the premier free agent market, Anthopoulos did act aggressively early in the offseason to solidify what was previously a shaky bullpen, signing closer Will Smith to a three-year, $40 million deal. He later bolstered the rotation by signing 36-year-old lefthander Cole Hamels for one year and $18 million.

The Braves enter 2020 with more upper-level pitching prospects and young major league arms than roster spots available. That could benefit the team by creating a deep crop of arms to use as a safety net for injuries during the season, or more likely, pieces to add in a trade for additional major league assets that will help improve the team.

While pitching was at the heart of Atlanta's rebuild, their top two prospects are outfielders, and both Cristian Pache and Drew Waters made it to Triple-A in 2019 and look to impact the club at some point in 2020.

The Braves also seemed to shift their draft philosophy after letting longtime scouting director Brian Bridges go just before the season. They targeted safer college players like Baylor catcher Shea Langeliers at No. 9 overall and Texas A&M shortstop Braden Shewmake 21st overall. Both could move quickly through the system and more easily fit into the team's current competitive window.

Still, graduations of top prospects like Acuña, Soroka and third baseman Austin Riley, as well as international signing sanctions, have thinned Atlanta's previously dynamic farm system and instead given them a solid one, with immediate help in the upper minors, but little to speak of at the lower levels.

Fortunately for the Braves, they probably won't need to worry about that for some time.

JAMIE SQUIRE/GETTY IMAGES

Mike Soroka logged a 2.68 ERA in 29 starts and finished second in NL Rookie of the Year voting.

PROJECTED 2023 LINEUP

Position	Player	Age
Catcher	Shea Langeliers (7)	25
First Base	Freddie Freeman	33
Second Base	Ozzie Albies	26
Third Base	Austin Riley	26
Shortstop	Dansby Swanson	29
Left Field	Drew Waters (2)	24
Center Field	Cristian Pache (1)	24
Right Field	Ronald Acuña Jr.	25
No. 1 Starter	Mike Soroka	25
No. 2 Starter	Mike Foltynewicz	31
No. 3 Starter	Ian Anderson (3)	25
No. 4 Starter	Max Fried	30
No. 5 Starter	Kyle Wright (4)	27
Closer	Touki Toussaint	27

DEPTH CHART

ATLANTA BRAVES

TOP 2020 ROOKIE: Cristian Pache, OF. He will immediately become one of the best defensive center fielders in the majors when he is called up.
BREAKOUT PROSPECT: Michael Harris, OF. There's some work needed to be done in refining his swing, but Harris has the toolset to become an impact player on both sides of the ball.
SLEEPER: Jared Johnson, RHP. Johnson is incredibly raw, but the 2019 draftee has a fastball that gets up to 97 mph with little effort. Atlanta's player development should have fun with his natural talent.

SOURCE OF TOP 30 TALENT			
Homegrown	**29**	**Acquired**	**1**
College	13	Trade	1
Junior college	2	Rule 5 draft	0
High school	8	Independent league	0
Nondrafted free agent	0	Free agent/waivers	0
International	6		

LF
Greyson Jenista (19)
Trey Harris (21)
Jefrey Ramos (30)

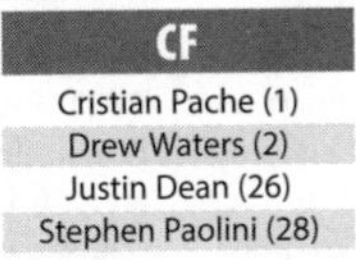

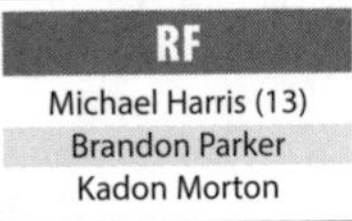

3B
CJ Alexander

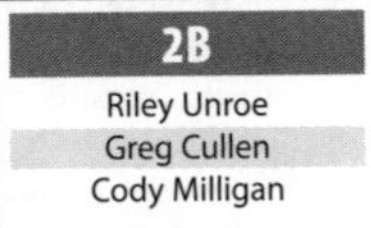

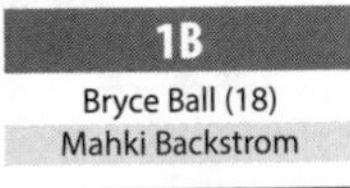

C
Shea Langeliers (7)
William Contreras (8)
Alex Jackson (17)
Logan Brown (24)

LHP

LHSP	LHRP
Kyle Muller (5)	Thomas Burrows
Tucker Davidson (10)	Dilmer Mejia
Mitch Stallings	Phil Pfeifer
Hayden Deal	Jake Higginbotham
	Corbin Clouse
	Tanner Lawson

RHP

RHSP	RHRP
Ian Anderson (3)	Patrick Weigel (12)
Kyle Wright (4)	Victor Vodnik (14)
Bryse Wilson (6)	Freddy Tarnok (15)
Jasseel de la Cruz (11)	Huascar Ynoa (16)
Tanner Gordon	Kasey Kalich (20)
	Jeremy Walker (22)
	Daysbell Hernandez (23)
	Trey Riley (29)
	Tyler Owens
	Luis Mora
	Josh Graham
	Kurt Hoekstra
	Ricky DeVito
	Darius Vines
	Jared Johnson

DRAFT ANALYSIS

2019

BEST PURE HITTER: SS Braden Shewmake (1) was one of the most consistent hitters in the SEC over his collegiate career—he hit .323/.381/.487 at Texas A&M—and did well during his pro debut at low Class A Rome, where he hit .318/.389/.473 before a late-season promotion to Double-A Mississippi.

BEST POWER: 1B Bryce Ball (24) has a 6-foot-6, 235-pound frame and plus raw power that should be his carrying tool. He tapped into that power well during his pro debut, hitting .329/.395/.628 with 17 home runs and 18 doubles between Rookie-level Danville and low Class A Rome.

FASTEST RUNNER: OF Drew Campbell (23) is an above-average runner, though he stole a modest 14 bags over two seasons with Louisville and just one during a 28-game stint with low Class A Rome, where he played left and right field. OF Stephen Paolini (5) is also an impressive runner.

BEST DEFENSIVE PLAYER: C Shea Langeliers (1) has plus arm strength, great blocking and receiving ability, and he threw out 41 percent of basestealers in the South Atlantic League during his debut. Shewmake is a solid defender with the versatility to play any position outside of catcher.

BEST ATHLETE: Paolini was something of an under-the-radar prospect. Many teams were unaware of him, but the Braves liked his plus running ability and standout athleticism that offers him significant upside. So much so that they signed him for $597,500.

BEST FASTBALL: RHP Ricky DeVito (8) has a fastball that gets into the mid-90s, while RHP Kasey Kalich (4) has a heater that can get up to 98 mph. Kalich has a more clear role as a reliever at this point in his career, while DeVito has a three-pitch mix that could allow him to start.

BEST SECONDARY PITCH: RHP Darius Vines (7) has a solid four-pitch mix, but his best offering is a power curveball that amateur scouts believed was already a big league-quality pitch—a downer breaking ball in the 78-80 mph range that has late biting action and tunnels with his fastball well.

BEST PRO DEBUT: Ball was named the 2019 Appalachian League player of the year after posting a 1.086 OPS with 13 home runs for Danville. Ball also showed solid plate discipline.

MOST INTRIGUING BACKGROUND: RHP Jared Johnson (14) didn't pitch in any summer showcases, but he blew up during the spring after reaching back and touching 97 mph with his fastball in small-town Smithville, Miss.

CLOSEST TO THE MAJORS: Shewmake doesn't have the largest toolset, but he has a polished all-around game—led by his hit tool—and could fill a number of holes at the big league level, including a super-utility bench role if needed.

BEST-LATE ROUND PICK: The Braves have done a nice job getting late-round gems in the draft, and it seems like Ball is the next in line. He gives the organization some much-needed prospect excitement in the lower levels.

THE ONE WHO GOT AWAY: 3B Riley King (26) opted to return to Georgia for his redshirt junior season after hitting .295/.403/.440 with eight home runs in 2019. King then posted a .323/.373/.427 line in the Cape Cod League.

—CARLOS COLLAZO

TOP DRAFT PICKS OF THE DECADE

Year	Player, Pos.	2019 Org
2010	Matt Lipka, SS (1st round supplemental)	Yankees
2011	Sean Gilmartin, LHP	Orioles
2012	Lucas Sims, RHP	Reds
2013	Jason Hursh, RHP	Braves
2014	Braxton Davidson, OF	Braves
2015	Kolby Allard, LHP	Rangers
2016	Ian Anderson, RHP	Braves
2017	Kyle Wright, RHP	Braves
2018	*Carter Stewart, RHP	SoftBank (Japan)
2019	Shea Langeliers, C	Braves

* Did not sign

2018

The Braves failed to come to terms with RHP Carter Stewart (1) and they didn't have a third-round pick, leading to a light class. Trading RHP Tristan Beck (4) helped them land Mark Melancon in July.

GRADE: C

2017

RHP Kyle Wright (1) raced to the big leagues in his first full professional season. OF Drew Waters (2), now the No. 2 prospect in the system, is hot on his tail and reached Triple-A in 2019 as a 20-year-old.

GRADE: A

2016

RHPs Ian Anderson (1) and Kyle Muller (2) rank as two of the system's best prospects and are knocking on the door of the big leagues. RHPs Bryse Wilson (4) and Jeremy Walker (5) have already reached Atlanta.

GRADE: B

1 CRISTIAN PACHE, OF

Born: Nov. 19, 1998. **B-T:** R-R. **HT:** 6-2. **WT:** 185.
Signed: Dominican Republic, 2015.
Signed by: Matias Laureano.

TRACK RECORD: After failing to hit a home run over his first two pro seasons, Pache has completely shed his reputation as a glove-first, light-hitting center fielder by getting bigger and stronger and learning which pitches he can drive. After hitting a career high nine home runs in 2018, Pache topped that by hitting 12 in 2019, in a season spent primarily in the pitcher-friendly Double-A Southern League.

SCOUTING REPORT: Pache continues to stand out for his elite defensive ability. As a 70-grade runner with a tremendous first step and a 70-grade arm, it's easy to project Pache as a Gold Glove center fielder. He aggressively tracks down balls in the gaps and has well above-average range and impressive route-running ability. What has raised Pache's ceiling, though, is his increased power production. Previously expected to hit between 10-15 homers a season, Pache is now projected by scouts to hit 20-25 home runs. Some have even gone as far as saying 30 home runs are a possibility because of the increased strength and better leverage in his swing. Yet Pache does need to continue refining his approach to get to an average hit tool. He has the physical skills—with electric bat speed, as well as solid pitch selection and strike zone recognition—but he continues to be an extreme pull-oriented hitter who sent more than 55 percent of his batted balls to the left side in 2019. Learning to use the middle and opposite field will help him get on base more frequently and help him avoid being shifted upon. His pure speed will help him leg out infield hits. While Pache is a double-plus runner who clocks times of 4.15 seconds from home to first base from the right side, his speed continues to play better in the outfield. Pache has never been an efficient basestealer, and he showed little progress in that regard in 2019, going a dreadful 8-for-19 (42 percent) in stolen base attempts at Double-A Mississippi, before simply not attempting a stolen base in 26 games at Triple-A Gwinnett.

THE FUTURE: Pache made it to Triple-A as a 20-year-old in 2019, and could likely use some more time there in 2020. But he was ready to fill in if necessary with Atlanta in 2019 and should have a chance to break in as a regular in 2020, adding even more excitement to an outfield built around Ronald Acuña Jr.

MIKE JANES/FOUR SEAM

BA GRADE
65 **Risk: Medium**

SCOUTING GRADES
Hit: 45. **Power:** 60. **Run:** 70. **Field:** 70. **Arm:** 70.

Projected future grades on 20-80 scouting scale.

TOP PROSPECTS OF THE DECADE

Year	Player, Pos.	2019 Org
2010	Jason Heyward, OF	Cubs
2011	Julio Teheran, RHP	Braves
2012	Julio Teheran, RHP	Braves
2013	Julio Teheran, RHP	Braves
2014	Lucas Sims, RHP	Reds
2015	Jose Peraza, 2B	Reds
2016	Sean Newcomb, LHP	Braves
2017	Dansby Swanson, SS	Braves
2018	Ronald Acuña Jr., OF	Braves
2019	Austin Riley, 3B	Braves

BEST TOOLS

Best Hitter for Average	Drew Waters
Best Power Hitter	Bryce Ball
Best Strike-Zone Discipline	Riley Delgado
Fastest Baserunner	Cristian Pache
Best Athlete	Cristian Pache
Best Fastball	Kyle Muller
Best Curveball	Tucker Davidson
Best Slider	Kyle Wright
Best Changeup	Ian Anderson
Best Control	Ian Anderson
Best Defensive Catcher	Shea Langeliers
Best Defensive Infielder	Braden Shewmake
Best Infield Arm	Beau Philip
Best Defensive Outfielder	Cristian Pache
Best Outfield Arm	Cristian Pache

Year	Age	Club (League)	Class	AVG	G	AB	R	H	2B	3B	HR	RBI	BB	SO	SB	OBP	SLG
2017	18	Rome (SAL)	LoA	.281	119	469	60	132	13	8	0	42	39	104	32	.335	.343
2018	19	Florida (FSL)	HiA	.285	93	369	46	105	20	5	8	40	15	69	7	.311	.431
	19	Mississippi (SL)	AA	.260	29	104	10	27	3	1	1	7	5	28	0	.294	.337
2019	20	Mississippi (SL)	AA	.278	104	392	50	109	28	8	11	53	34	104	8	.340	.474
	20	Gwinnett (IL)	AAA	.274	26	95	13	26	8	1	1	8	9	18	0	.337	.411
Minor League Totals				.283	428	1649	207	467	76	30	21	171	115	347	58	.331	.404

2 DREW WATERS, OF

Born: Dec. 30, 1998. **B-T:** B-R. **HT:** 6-2. **WT:** 183. **Drafted:** HS—Woodstock, Ga., 2017 (2nd round). **Signed by:** Dustin Evans.

TRACK RECORD: A local high school product, Waters has steadily climbed the minor league ladder alongside Cristian Pache, and reached Triple-A Gwinnett for the first time in 2019. At Double-A, the athletic, switch-hitting outfielder won the Southern League batting title and MVP award.

SCOUTING REPORT: Waters has long been thought to be an above-average hitter thanks to a loose, handsy swing and a proclivity to use the entire field. However, scouts were concerned with the amount of swing-and-miss seen in his game this season—particularly from the righthanded side of the plate, where he also tends to get more pull-heavy. He still has a chance to be a solid-average hitter and has shown the ability to make adjustments within at-bats, but at the moment he gets beat inside too frequently and his swing can get long from the left side—where he shows plus raw power. Waters could stick in center field as a plus runner with above-average arm strength, and he's also an efficient and smart baserunner.

THE FUTURE: Waters should start 2020 in Triple-A, where he'll need to cut down his strikeout rate and improve his approach from the right side. If he does that, he could become a fixture in Atlanta during the season.

SCOUTING GRADES: **Hitting:** 55 **Power:** 55 **Running:** 60 **Fielding:** 60 **Arm:** 55

Year	Age	Club (League)	Class	AVG	G	AB	R	H	2B	3B	HR	RBI	BB	SO	SB	OBP	SLG
2017	18	Braves (GCL)	R	.347	14	49	13	17	3	1	2	10	7	11	2	.448	.571
	18	Danville (APP)	R	.255	36	149	20	38	11	1	2	14	16	59	4	.331	.383
2018	19	Rome (SAL)	LoA	.303	84	337	58	102	32	6	9	36	21	72	20	.353	.513
	19	Florida (FSL)	HiA	.268	30	123	14	33	7	3	0	3	8	33	3	.316	.374
2019	20	Mississippi (SL)	AA	.319	108	420	63	134	35	9	5	41	28	121	13	.366	.481
	20	Gwinnett (IL)	AAA	.271	26	107	17	29	5	0	2	11	11	43	3	.336	.374
Minor League Totals				.298	298	1185	185	353	93	20	20	115	91	339	45	.354	.461

3 IAN ANDERSON, RHP

BA GRADE
55 Risk: Medium

Born: May 2, 1998. **B-T:** R-R. **HT:** 6-3. **WT:** 170. **Drafted:** HS—Clifton Park, N.Y., 2016 (1st round). **Signed by:** Greg Morhardt.

TRACK RECORD: Anderson continued to dominate Double-A batters over 21 starts and ranked third in the Southern League with 147 strikeouts before earning a promotion to Triple-A Gwinnett.

SCOUTING REPORT: Anderson's stuff wasn't quite as electric in 2019 as he's shown in the past. While he's previously thrown a fastball in the 92-97 mph range, the pitch didn't have that sort of top-end velocity this season, sitting mostly in the 92-94 range. It's still a plus offering thanks to the angle that Anderson creates out of an overhand arm slot, and he's been effective with it pitching both up and down in the zone. Similarly, Anderson's 12-to-6 curveball hasn't shown the bite he's had in the past. It's more of a 55-grade offering he has learned to spot more consistently, but he struggles at times to get hitters to chase it out of the zone. Anderson also has a firm, mid-to-upper 80s changeup that he's shown feel for and it projects as an above-average pitch. Outside of his five-game stint in Triple-A, Anderson showed improved feel for throwing strikes and projects for above-average control despite stiffness in his delivery.

THE FUTURE: Anderson should start 2020 in Gwinnett and projects as more of a middle-of-the-rotation arm.

SCOUTING GRADES: **Fastball:** 60 **Curveball:** 55 **Changeup:** 55 **Control:** 50

Year	Age	Club (League)	Class	W	L	ERA	G	GS	SV	IP	H	HR	BB	SO	K/9	WHIP	AVG
2017	19	Rome (SAL)	LoA	4	5	3.14	20	20	0	83	69	0	43	101	11.0	1.35	.232
2018	20	Florida (FSL)	HiA	2	6	2.52	20	20	0	100	73	2	40	118	10.6	1.13	.198
	20	Mississippi (SL)	AA	2	1	2.33	4	4	0	19	14	0	9	24	11.2	1.19	.203
2019	21	Mississippi (SL)	AA	7	5	2.68	21	21	0	111	82	8	47	147	11.9	1.16	.202
	21	Gwinnett (IL)	AAA	1	2	6.57	5	5	0	25	23	5	18	25	9.1	1.66	.242
Minor League Totals				17	21	2.91	80	80	0	377	294	16	169	451	10.8	1.23	.214

4 KYLE WRIGHT, RHP

Born: Oct. 2, 1995. **B-T:** R-R. **HT:** 6-4. **WT:** 200. **Drafted:** Vanderbilt, 2017 (1st round). **Signed by:** Dustin Evans.

BA GRADE
55 Risk: Medium

TRACK RECORD: The top college pitcher in the 2017 draft, Wright sprinted to the big leagues and made his major league debut in September 2018. Since then, he has shuffled between Triple-A and Atlanta, primarily as a starter, but with a few big league relief outings.

SCOUTING REPORT: Wright still has some of the best pure stuff in the system, headlined by a plus fastball that sits around 94-95 mph and gets up to 99 at its best. The Vanderbilt product's slider and curveball each flash plus, but the pitches can blend together and are more consistently above-average offerings. Wright used his slider more frequently than his curve this season—a departure from previous pitch usage—and also showed much better feel for a mid-80s changeup that has solid depth and gives him a more effective secondary against lefties. The gap between his walk rate in the minors and majors continues to be drastic, though coaches believe that's more an issue of settling into a consistent schedule and role.

THE FUTURE: Wright should graduate from prospect status in 2020 and become a fixture in Atlanta's rotation, where he has the stuff to become a steady, mid-rotation arm.

SCOUTING GRADES: **Fastball:** 60 **Curveball:** 55 **Slider:** 55 **Changeup:** 55 **Control:** 45

Year	Age	Club (League)	Class	W	L	ERA	G	GS	SV	IP	H	HR	BB	SO	K/9	WHIP	AVG
2017	21	Braves (GCL)	R	0	0	1.59	3	3	0	6	3	0	2	8	12.7	0.88	.150
	21	Florida (FSL)	HiA	0	1	3.18	6	6	0	11	8	0	4	10	7.9	1.06	.205
2018	22	Mississippi (SL)	AA	6	8	3.70	20	20	0	109	103	6	43	105	8.6	1.34	.249
	22	Gwinnett (IL)	AAA	2	1	2.51	7	4	0	29	15	2	8	28	8.8	0.80	.152
	22	Atlanta (NL)	MAJ	0	0	4.50	4	0	0	6	4	2	6	5	7.5	1.67	.182
2019	23	Gwinnett (IL)	AAA	11	4	4.17	21	21	0	112	107	13	35	116	9.3	1.26	.252
	23	Atlanta (NL)	MAJ	0	3	8.69	7	4	0	20	24	4	13	18	8.2	1.88	.304
Major League Totals				0	3	7.71	11	4	0	25	28	6	19	23	8.1	1.83	.277
Minor League Totals				19	14	3.70	57	54	0	267	236	21	92	267	9.0	1.23	.237

5 KYLE MULLER, LHP

Born: Oct. 7, 1997. **B-T:** R-L. **HT:** 6-6. **WT:** 225. **Drafted:** HS—Dallas, 2016 (2nd round). **Signed by:** Nate Dion.

TRACK RECORD: No player has come as far in the Braves system as Muller. After failing to reach low Class A in his first full season and seeing his fastball sit in the upper 80s, Muller started training with Driveline Baseball. The results of that work have revitalized his prospect status.

SCOUTING REPORT: After trending in the right direction a season ago, Muller now has one of the best fastballs in the system. In 2019, he topped out at 98 mph and sat in the 90-97 mph range at Double-A, with solid downhill angle that makes it an easy plus pitch. He made some progress with both his curveball and changeup, which project as average with increased consistency. Muller's curveball flashes depth and bite and his changeup looks solid with slight fade, though he needs to learn to throw it with more conviction. Muller's control is below-average. He walked the second-most batters (68) in the Southern League and will need to improve his strike-throwing to take advantage of a solid three-pitch mix that overwhelms hitters when he's not overwhelming himself.

THE FUTURE: After dominating Double-A batters over a full season, Muller should start 2020 in Triple-A and could spend some time there learning how to sequence pitches more effectively as a starter, though he could help the big league club in a bullpen role right away.

SCOUTING GRADES: **Fastball:** 60 **Curveball:** 50 **Changeup:** 50 **Control:** 45

Year	Age	Club (League)	Class	W	L	ERA	G	GS	SV	IP	H	HR	BB	SO	K/9	WHIP	AVG
2017	19	Danville (APP)	R	1	1	4.15	11	11	0	48	43	5	18	49	9.3	1.28	.232
2018	20	Rome (SAL)	LoA	3	0	2.40	6	6	0	30	24	3	8	23	6.9	1.07	.222
	20	Florida (FSL)	HiA	4	2	3.24	14	14	0	81	80	2	32	79	8.8	1.39	.268
	20	Mississippi (SL)	AA	4	1	3.10	5	5	0	29	22	3	6	27	8.4	0.97	.206
2019	21	Mississippi (SL)	AA	7	6	3.14	22	22	0	112	81	5	68	120	9.7	1.33	.208
Minor League Totals				20	10	3.03	68	67	0	326	264	18	144	336	9.3	1.25	.223

6 BRYSE WILSON, RHP

Born: Dec. 20, 1997. **B-T:** R-R. **HT:** 6-1. **WT:** 225. **Drafted:** HS—Hillsborough, N.C., 2016 (4th round). **Signed by:** Billy Best.

BA GRADE
50 Risk: Medium

TRACK RECORD: A 2016 fourth-round pick out of high school, Wilson flew through the minors and dominated three levels before making his major league debut in 2018 as a 20-year-old. He spent the bulk of 2019 adding polish at Triple-A and as a big league spot starter.

SCOUTING REPORT: A strong, physical righthander, Wilson's fastball has long been his best pitch. It gets into the upper 90s at its best but sits in the 94-95 mph range. His pure velocity, natural sinking life and precision was more than enough to overwhelm minor league batters, but he was susceptible to the long ball in the major leagues. That might be due to the fact that Wilson currently lacks a swing-and-miss breaking ball. His firm, mid-80s slider has progressed, but he rarely generates whiffs with the pitch and relies more on an 84-87 mph changeup with fade and sink to get batters to swing and miss. There are few successful fastball/changeup righthanded starters in the big leagues, so Wilson will need to sharpen his breaking ball, but he has the strike-throwing ability and physicality to be a durable, innings-eating back-of-the-rotation type.

THE FUTURE: Wilson has done all he can do in the minors and will look to establish himself in the big leagues in 2020.

SCOUTING GRADES: **Fastball:** 60 **Slider:** 45 **Changeup:** 55 **Control:** 55

Year	Age	Club (League)	Class	W	L	ERA	G	GS	SV	IP	H	HR	BB	SO	K/9	WHIP	AVG
2017	19	Rome (SAL)	LoA	10	7	2.50	26	26	0	137	105	8	37	139	9.1	1.04	.211
2018	20	Florida (FSL)	HiA	2	0	0.34	5	5	0	27	16	0	7	26	8.8	0.86	.167
	20	Mississippi (SL)	AA	3	5	3.97	15	15	0	77	77	3	26	89	10.4	1.34	.258
	20	Gwinnett (IL)	AAA	3	0	5.32	5	3	0	22	20	6	3	28	11.5	1.05	.238
	20	Atlanta (NL)	MAJ	1	0	6.43	3	1	0	7	8	0	6	6	7.7	2.00	.308
2019	21	Gwinnett (IL)	AAA	10	7	3.42	21	21	0	121	120	12	26	118	8.8	1.21	.256
	21	Atlanta (NL)	MAJ	1	1	7.20	6	4	0	20	26	5	10	16	7.2	1.80	.321
Major League Totals				2	1	7.00	9	5	0	27	34	5	16	22	7.3	1.85	.318
Minor League Totals				29	20	2.94	81	76	0	410	354	29	107	429	9.4	1.12	.230

7 SHEA LANGELIERS, C

Born: Nov. 18, 1997**. B-T:** R-R. **HT:** 6-0. **WT:** 190. **Drafted:** Baylor, 2019 (1st round). **Signed by:** Darin Vaughan.

TRACK RECORD: Langeliers would have rated as the top catching prospect in a typical draft class, but had to settle for No. 2 thanks to first overall pick Adley Rutschman. The best defensive catcher in the 2019 draft, Langeliers missed parts of his junior season at Baylor with a broken hamate bone. He hit well when he returned, giving the Braves enough confidence to make him their first pick

SCOUTING REPORT: Langeliers shines on defense. He has an easy plus throwing arm and used that to throw out 41 percent of basestealers in his pro debut at low Class A Rome. Langeliers is also a polished pitch-framer who's handled plenty of premium stuff with USA Baseball's Collegiate National Team. He moves well behind the plate and consistently keeps balls in the dirt in front of him. Those defensive skills led to Austin Hedges comparisons, but Langeliers has a stronger offensive foundation than Hedges, with a chance to become an average hitter thanks to a balanced, fluid swing from the right side with gap power now that could get to above-average.

THE FUTURE: Langeliers' defense alone gives him a high floor as a major league backup, and if he reaches his offensive ceiling he could become a first-division regular. Langeliers could move quickly, but the Braves will look to maximize both his and William Contreras' at-bats.

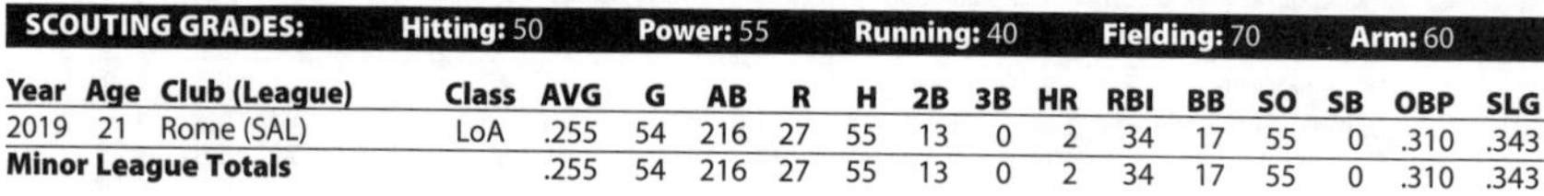

SCOUTING GRADES: **Hitting:** 50 **Power:** 55 **Running:** 40 **Fielding:** 70 **Arm:** 60

Year	Age	Club (League)	Class	AVG	G	AB	R	H	2B	3B	HR	RBI	BB	SO	SB	OBP	SLG
2019	21	Rome (SAL)	LoA	.255	54	216	27	55	13	0	2	34	17	55	0	.310	.343
Minor League Totals				.255	54	216	27	55	13	0	2	34	17	55	0	.310	.343

8 WILLIAM CONTRERAS, C

Born: Dec. 24, 1997. **B-T:** R-R. **HT:** 6-0. **WT:** 180. **Drafted:** Venezuela, 2015. **Signed by:** Rolando Petit.

TRACK RECORD: The younger brother of Cubs catcher Willson Contreras, William was one of the better catchers in the South Atlantic League a season ago before pushing to Double-A Mississippi in his age-21 season.

SCOUTING REPORT: Contreras has exciting tools on both sides of the ball, but is still maturing as a player. He wasn't as consistent as the team expected with high Class A Florida, but seemed to get energized and refocused after a promotion to Double-A. Contreras has plus raw power with the ability to use all fields with impact, and generally takes good at-bats as well, with a solid two-strike approach. He'll chase a bit at times which will be worth monitoring as he faces upper-level pitching, but he has all the skills to become an average hitter. Contreras stands out for his athleticism behind the dish. He has good hands and moves well for a catcher, with plus raw arm strength that plays a tick down from that thanks to a slightly long arm action. He needs to improve his game as a receiver, but at the moment it's a mental issue more than a physical one.

THE FUTURE: Contreras is less polished than Langeliers and is no longer the top catcher in the system but likely has more offensive upside.

SCOUTING GRADES: **Hitting:** 50 **Power:** 55 **Running:** 40 **Fielding:** 50 **Arm:** 55

Year	Age	Club (League)	Class	AVG	G	AB	R	H	2B	3B	HR	RBI	BB	SO	SB	OBP	SLG
2017	19	Danville (APP)	R	.290	45	169	29	49	10	1	4	25	24	30	1	.379	.432
2018	20	Rome (SAL)	LoA	.293	82	307	54	90	17	1	11	39	29	73	1	.360	.463
	20	Florida (FSL)	HiA	.253	23	83	3	21	7	0	0	10	6	16	0	.300	.337
2019	21	Florida (FSL)	HiA	.263	50	190	26	50	11	0	3	22	14	44	0	.324	.368
	21	Mississippi (SL)	AA	.246	60	191	24	47	9	0	3	17	15	40	0	.306	.340
Minor League Totals				.279	339	1184	165	330	68	6	22	153	110	239	4	.345	.402

9 BRADEN SHEWMAKE, SS

Born: Nov. 19, 1997. **B-T:** L-R. **HT:** 6-4. **WT:** 190. **Drafted:** Texas A&M, 2019 (1st round). **Signed by:** Darin Vaughan.

TRACK RECORD: A high-level performer at Texas A&M, Shewmake was a two-time All-Southeastern Conference performer who finished his career with a .323/.381/.487 batting line. In his pro debut, he more than held his own at low Class A before moving to Double-A.

SCOUTING REPORT: An athletic and lanky, 6-foot-4 infielder, Shewmake has a solid all-around game with impressive instincts and defensive versatility, but what he lacks is a carrying tool. His loudest tool is likely his plus speed, but his most valuable trait might be a polished lefthanded bat. Shewmake has an unorthodox setup, but has above-average bat speed and twitchy hands. While he has a projectable frame one would typically project for increased power, Shewmake was lanky throughout his college career and struggled to put on weight. If he fills out as a pro, scouts could project above-average power. Shewmake has a chance to stick at shortstop, with solid athleticism, hands and leadership traits that fit the position, but many scouts believed that he would be a more natural fit at second or third base.

THE FUTURE: Shewmake should start 2020 back at Double-A, where he'll look to continue his progress.

SCOUTING GRADES: **Hitting:** 55 **Power:** 50 **Running:** 60 **Fielding:** 50 **Arm:** 50

Year	Age	Club (League)	Class	AVG	G	AB	R	H	2B	3B	HR	RBI	BB	SO	SB	OBP	SLG
2019	21	Rome (SAL)	LoA	.318	51	201	37	64	18	2	3	39	21	29	11	.389	.473
	21	Mississippi (SL)	AA	.217	14	46	7	10	0	0	0	1	4	11	2	.288	.217
Minor League Totals				.300	65	247	44	74	18	2	3	40	25	40	13	.371	.425

10 TUCKER DAVIDSON, LHP

Born: March 25, 1996. **B-T:** L-L. **HT:** 6-2. **WT:** 215. **Drafted:** Midland (Texas) JC, 2016 (19th round). **Signed by:** Nate Dion.

TRACK RECORD: After taking a step back in 2018, Davidson had something of a breakout year in 2019. A 19th-round junior college pick, he took major strides forward with his pitching ability in 2019 and finished the season at Triple-A.

SCOUTING REPORT: Davidson's arsenal is led by two plus offerings—a fastball up to 97 mph and a 12-to-6 curveball. After struggling with his fastball control a season ago, Davidson impressed scouts with the pitchability that he showed in 2019. He tended to get into two-strike counts and then nibble around the zone rather than going after hitters, and he's a control-over-command arm. Davidson has an average changeup that should give him every opportunity to start, though there's some effort in his delivery and he pitches exclusively out of the stretch, which leads some scouts to believe he's a reliever.

THE FUTURE: Davidson was added to the 40-man roster in November to protect him from the Rule 5 draft. He will likely begin the season at Triple-A Gwinnett, but could make his big league debut later in 2020.

SCOUTING GRADES: **Fastball:** 60 **Curveball:** 55 **Changeup:** 50 **Control:** 50

Year	Age	Club (League)	Class	W	L	ERA	G	GS	SV	IP	H	HR	BB	SO	K/9	WHIP	AVG
2017	21	Rome (SAL)	LoA	5	4	2.60	31	12	2	104	96	4	30	101	8.8	1.22	.248
2018	22	Florida (FSL)	HiA	7	10	4.18	24	24	0	118	120	5	58	99	7.5	1.50	.270
2019	23	Mississippi (SL)	AA	7	6	2.03	21	21	0	111	88	5	45	122	9.9	1.20	.225
	23	Gwinnett (IL)	AAA	1	1	2.84	4	4	0	19	20	0	9	12	5.7	1.53	.286
Minor League Totals				20	24	2.86	91	62	2	381	356	15	146	366	8.6	1.32	.252

11 JASSEEL DE LA CRUZ, RHP

Born: June 26, 1997. **B-T:** R-R. **HT:** 6-1. **WT:** 215. **Signed:** Dominican Republic, 2015. **Signed by:** Matias Laureano.

TRACK RECORD: A late-blooming, hard-throwing prospect who signed as an 18-year-old in 2015, de la Cruz developed into an intriguing prospect in Atlanta's low minors thanks to pure stuff and a fast arm but took a step forward with his pitching ability and reached Double-A in 2019. Atlanta started de la Cruz in Rome which gave him a bit of a chip on his shoulder. He quickly advanced to Double-A Mississippi, where he spent the bulk of his time and posted the best walk rate of his domestic career.

SCOUTING REPORT: His fastball has touched 100 mph but he typically sits in the mid-90s with a plus fastball that he has learned to throw to both sides of the plate more consistently. De la Cruz has also improved the control of his offspeed offerings, which include a slider that flashes above-average and a previously below-average changeup that could now be projected as average. His arm action is long in the back, but he's shown enough improvement hitting his spots to give himself a shot at starting.

THE FUTURE: Some scouts believe de la Cruz is destined for the bullpen due to his demeanor and attacking mentality, but his improvement this year increases his likelihood to become a back-of-the-rotation arm.

Year	Age	Club (League)	Class	W	L	ERA	G	GS	SV	IP	H	HR	BB	SO	K/9	WHIP	AVG
2017	20	Braves (GCL)	R	2	1	1.89	4	4	0	19	13	1	7	17	8.1	1.05	.188
	20	Danville (APP)	R	0	2	5.32	7	6	0	24	25	1	11	19	7.2	1.52	.260
2018	21	Rome (SAL)	LoA	3	4	4.83	15	13	0	69	65	6	34	65	8.5	1.43	.250
2019	22	Rome (SAL)	LoA	0	1	2.50	4	4	0	18	19	1	5	22	11.0	1.33	.275
	22	Florida (FSL)	HiA	3	1	1.93	4	4	0	28	12	0	7	26	8.4	0.68	.128
	22	Mississippi (SL)	AA	4	7	3.83	17	16	0	87	71	7	37	73	7.6	1.24	.223
Minor League Totals				16	17	3.63	76	50	0	292	238	17	124	260	8.0	1.24	.223

12 PATRICK WEIGEL, RHP

BA GRADE
55 Risk: Very High

Born: July 8, 1994. **B-T:** R-R. **HT:** 6-6. **WT:** 240. **Drafted:** Houston, 2015 (7th round). **Signed by:** Darin Vaughan.

TRACK RECORD: The organization's minor league pitcher of the year in 2016, Weigel put himself on a fast track through the minors and pushed to Triple-A in 2017 before blowing out his elbow and having Tommy John surgery that wiped out his 2018 season. Weigel returned to the mound in 2019 and had a successful year while the Braves eased him back into his workload with limited innings and pitch counts.

SCOUTING REPORT: His pure stuff got back to the level of his pre-injury self at its best, but the consistency came and went. Weigel's fastball touched 97-98 mph at his best in shorter outings, but he pitched in the low-90s over longer outings. He paired that with a sharp slider that has the chance to be a plus offering and will occasionally mix in an average changeup, but that pitch needs more consistency as well. Weigel's control took a step back in his return and he will need to correct that to profile in a starting role.

THE FUTURE: Weigel has a chance to start, but could be a better fit in the bullpen, as his stuff plays up in shorter outings. The team used him in a reliever role in July and August to end the season.

Year	Age	Club (League)	Class	W	L	ERA	G	GS	SV	IP	H	HR	BB	SO	K/9	WHIP	AVG
2017	22	Mississippi (SL)	AA	3	0	2.89	7	7	0	37	32	2	11	38	9.2	1.15	.234
	22	Gwinnett (IL)	AAA	3	2	5.27	8	8	0	41	42	5	17	30	6.6	1.44	.269
2018	23	Braves (GCL)	R	0	0	0.00	4	3	0	4	2	0	0	6	13.5	0.50	.167
2019	24	Mississippi (SL)	AA	0	1	1.72	7	7	0	16	8	0	9	16	9.2	1.09	.146
	24	Gwinnett (IL)	AAA	6	1	2.98	21	11	0	63	42	9	32	55	7.8	1.17	.194
Minor League Totals				23	13	3.15	86	74	0	362	280	27	150	346	8.6	1.19	.215

13 MICHAEL HARRIS, OF

BA GRADE **55** Risk: Extreme

Born: March 7, 2001. **B-T:** B-L. **HT:** 6-0. **WT:** 195. **Drafted:** HS—Stockbridge, Ga., 2019 (3rd round). **Signed by:** Kirk Fredriksson.

TRACK RECORD: Scouts liked the athletic Harris as a lefthanded pitcher and as a hitter prior to the 2019 draft. Harris preferred hitting and the Braves drafted him in the third round and let him do that exclusively in his debut, where he impressed with a toolsy, high-upside profile.

SCOUTING REPORT: Harris might have the most exciting collection of tools in Atlanta's system outside of their top 10 prospects. A switch-hitter, Harris has above-average raw power with impressive bat speed, above-average running ability underway and easy plus arm strength that gives him a chance to be a plus defender in right field. He will need to shorten a swing that gets lengthy at times, with significant wrap, and clean up some of the holes in his swing. Moving forward, Harris will need to refine his approach and learn to trust his natural strength and bat speed to get the most out of his natural tools at the plate.

THE FUTURE: The Braves will look for Harris to add strength and return to the South Atlantic League in 2020. His focus will be on developing a professional approach at the plate.

Year	Age	Club (League)	Class	AVG	G	AB	R	H	2B	3B	HR	RBI	BB	SO	SB	OBP	SLG
2019	18	Braves (GCL)	R	.349	31	109	15	38	6	3	2	16	9	20	5	.403	.514
	18	Rome (SAL)	LoA	.183	22	82	11	15	2	1	0	11	9	22	3	.269	.232
Minor League Totals				.277	53	191	26	53	8	4	2	27	18	42	8	.344	.393

14 VICTOR VODNIK, RHP

BA GRADE **50** Risk: High

Born: Oct. 9, 1999. **B-T:** R-R. **HT:** 6-0. **WT:** 200. **Drafted:** HS—Rialto, Calif., 2018 (14th round). **Signed by:** Kevin Martin.

TRACK RECORD: Vodnik impressed as a high schooler thanks to his natural arm strength. The Braves took a shot on him in the 14th round of the 2018 draft and signed him for an above-slot $200,000 bonus despite the crude nature of his game. After a rough pro debut, Vodnik dominated in 2019 at low Class A Rome.

SCOUTING REPORT: An undersized but strong righthander, Vodnik had a strong season with low Class A Rome where he went right after hitters with a plus fastball that touches 96-98 mph, but sits in the 94-95 range. The pitch has some cutting action at times and he pairs it with a slider and changeup that both flash plus, but lack consistency. Vodnik's slider varies in shape and sits in the 83-85 mph range, while he showed a better changeup—an 87-89 mph offering with tumble—than he has in the past. Vodnik's delivery is still raw and presently below-average, which could impact his control and consistency moving forward.

THE FUTURE: Most scouts see Vodnik as a reliever with late-inning upside. He performed well enough that some think he should get a chance to start, especially with a three-pitch mix that's becoming more viable.

Year	Age	Club (League)	Class	W	L	ERA	G	GS	SV	IP	H	HR	BB	SO	K/9	WHIP	AVG
2018	18	Braves (GCL)	R	1	1	9.64	4	0	0	5	8	1	1	9	17.4	1.93	.364
2019	19	Rome (SAL)	LoA	1	3	2.94	23	3	3	67	55	1	24	69	9.2	1.17	.223
Minor League Totals				2	4	3.38	27	3	3	72	63	2	25	78	9.8	1.22	.234

15 FREDDY TARNOK, RHP

BA GRADE **50** Risk: High

Born: Nov. 24, 1998. **B-T:** R-R. **HT:** 6-3. **WT:** 185. **Drafted:** HS—Riverview, Fla., 2017 (3rd round). **Signed by:** Justin Clark.

TRACK RECORD: A converted shortstop, the Braves liked Tarnok's raw talent on the mound out of high school and have watched him slowly figure out the nuances of pitching during his first three years with the organization.

SCOUTING REPORT: After splitting time as a reliever and starter in 2018, Tarnok started the entire season

this year, and progressed to high Class A Florida, where he's focused on simplifying his delivery to improve his control and command. That improvement was borne out in the numbers, as Tarnok's walk rate improved by almost two batters per nine from 2018 to 2019. Tarnok has an average fastball in the 92-94 mph range that touches 95, but he's improved his secondaries this season. His changeup is among the better offerings in the system, and he throws that pitch with confidence to lefties and righties. He's also worked to get more aggressive with a curveball this season after previously throwing a slider, though his breaking ball is still his third-best offering. Tarnok missed a month of the season with a lat injury, but his improvement while on the mound during his second full season was obvious in many respects.
THE FUTURE: Tarnok should push to Double-A Mississippi at some point in 2020, where he'll work to improve his breaking ball and increase his chances of starting in the future, though a high-leverage reliever role is still a possibility.

Year	Age	Club (League)	Class	W	L	ERA	G	GS	SV	IP	H	HR	BB	SO	K/9	WHIP	AVG
2017	18	Braves (GCL)	R	0	3	2.57	9	9	0	14	11	0	3	10	6.4	1.00	.208
2018	19	Rome (SAL)	LoA	5	5	3.96	27	11	0	77	70	5	41	83	9.7	1.44	.235
2019	20	Braves (GCL)	R	0	1	3.38	3	3	0	8	3	1	1	9	10.1	0.50	.111
	20	Florida (FSL)	HiA	3	7	4.87	19	19	0	98	105	6	36	82	7.5	1.44	.276
Minor League Totals				8	16	4.29	57	41	0	197	189	12	81	184	8.4	1.37	.249

16 HUASCAR YNOA, RHP

Born: May 28, 1998. **B-T:** R-R. **HT:** 6-3. **WT:** 175. **Signed:** Dominican Republic, 2014. **Signed by:** Fred Guerrero (Twins).

TRACK RECORD: Prior to the 2019 season, Ynoa hadn't pitched above the high Class A Florida State League, but his pure stuff and the improvement of his slider pushed him all the way up the minor league ladder, and he was twice brought up to pitch in relief for the big league club.
SCOUTING REPORT: Ynoa's fastball is one of the best in the Braves system, sitting in the 92-97 mph range and touching 99-100 at its best. While the pure velocity is impressive, pitch metrics don't favor the offering, and he doesn't generate as many whiffs on the pitch as you might expect, with little movement or late life. However, that could be helped by a plus secondary offering, which is what scouts are now saying about Ynoa's power slurve in the mid-80s. The consistency of the offering got much better this season, and it features hard vertical movement. Ynoa also has a changeup in his arsenal, though he rarely used it as a reliever, and it is an average offering.
THE FUTURE: Ynoa has the pure stuff to project as a middle-of-the-rotation arm or high-leverage reliever, but he's currently a control-over-command type who will need to either miss bats more frequently or spot his fastball and slider more effectively to find success. He should return to Triple-A Gwinnett next year in his age-22 season for further refinement, but Atlanta clearly thinks he can help the big league club now.

Year	Age	Club (League)	Class	W	L	ERA	G	GS	SV	IP	H	HR	BB	SO	K/9	WHIP	AVG
2017	19	Elizabethton (APP)	R	0	1	5.26	6	6	0	26	28	1	14	23	8.1	1.64	.277
	19	Danville (APP)	R	0	3	5.26	7	7	0	26	24	1	15	27	9.5	1.52	.238
2018	20	Rome (SAL)	LoA	7	8	3.63	18	18	0	92	69	7	42	100	9.8	1.21	.205
	20	Florida (FSL)	HiA	1	4	8.03	6	6	0	25	33	1	12	31	11.3	1.82	.317
2019	21	Florida (FSL)	HiA	0	1	3.27	3	3	0	11	10	0	6	16	13.1	1.45	.233
	21	Mississippi (SL)	AA	1	2	5.27	6	0	1	14	17	2	5	15	9.9	1.61	.298
	21	Atlanta (NL)	MAJ	0	0	18.00	2	0	0	3	6	1	1	3	9.0	2.33	.400
	21	Gwinnett (IL)	AAA	3	5	5.33	17	14	0	73	80	14	34	79	9.8	1.57	.275
Major League Totals				0	0	18.00	2	0	0	3	6	1	1	3	9.0	2.33	.400
Minor League Totals				17	34	4.32	88	79	1	372	348	28	170	389	9.4	1.39	.243

17 ALEX JACKSON, C

BA GRADE
45 Risk: Medium

Born: Dec. 25, 1995. **B-T:** R-R. **HT:** 6-2. **WT:** 215. **Drafted:** HS—San Diego, 2014 (1st round). **Signed by:** Gary Patchett (Mariners).

TRACK RECORD: Jackson's prospect status dwindled after the Mariners moved him to the outfield and he struggled to hit, but the former BA High School Player of the Year has shown promising signs on both sides of the ball in his third year with Atlanta as a catcher.
SCOUTING REPORT: Jackson has steadily improved as a defender over the past couple years, and this season scouts lauded his receiving ability. Framing metrics reportedly reinforce that evaluation. Jackson has always had plus arm strength and this season that translated to throwing out a career-best 50 percent of runners. After his in-game power disappeared a season ago, Jackson had a career offensive year, with 28 home runs and showed over-the-fence power to all fields after being extremely pull-happy previously. While Jackson has double-plus raw power, there are still reasons to be skeptical of him getting to that in-game at the next level. He struggles to identify spin, and scouts believe he is still too pull-oriented. The Triple-A ball inflated

plenty of hitters' home run numbers this season, likely including Jackson as well.

THE FUTURE: Jackson made his major league debut and played in four games for the Braves, but he was put on the 60-day IL with a left knee sprain at the end of the season. Jackson's defensive improvement should allow him to be a serviceable backup option, but it's hard to project him as a first-division regular with well below-average pure hitting ability, though that bar for catchers is low.

Year	Age	Club (League)	Class	AVG	G	AB	R	H	2B	3B	HR	RBI	BB	SO	SB	OBP	SLG
2017	21	Florida (FSL)	HiA	.272	66	257	44	70	17	0	14	45	13	74	0	.333	.502
	21	Mississippi (SL)	AA	.255	30	110	12	28	4	0	5	20	10	32	0	.317	.427
2018	22	Mississippi (SL)	AA	.200	64	225	27	45	12	1	5	24	20	78	0	.282	.329
	22	Gwinnett (IL)	AAA	.204	35	108	15	22	11	2	3	17	12	42	0	.296	.426
2019	23	Atlanta (NL)	MAJ	.000	4	13	0	0	0	0	0	0	1	5	0	.133	.000
	23	Gwinnett (IL)	AAA	.229	85	306	52	70	9	0	28	65	20	118	1	.313	.533
Major League Totals				.000	4	13	0	0	0	0	0	0	1	5	0	.133	.000
Minor League Totals				.233	471	1692	245	395	96	7	76	280	145	567	6	.317	.433

18 BRYCE BALL, 1B

BA GRADE
50 Risk: High

Born: July 8, 1998. **B-T:** L-R. **HT:** 6-6. **WT:** 235. **Drafted:** Dallas Baptist, 2019 (24th round). **Signed by:** Ray Corbett.

TRACK RECORD: A 24th-round pick out of Dallas Baptist who signed for $197,500, Ball had one of the best debuts of any 2019 draftee, hitting .329/.395/.628 in the Appalachian and South Atlantic leagues, ranking as the No. 15 prospect in the Appy League.

SCOUTING REPORT: Ball is the best power hitter in the system, with 70-grade raw power, and has a solid understanding of the strike zone and a clean swing to go along with it. Ball stood out to Appy League managers for his ability to square up both fastballs and breaking balls, and he posted the best isolated slugging (.352) in the league among batters with at least 50 plate appearances. Ball doesn't chase much out of the zone now, but that will be worth monitoring as he progresses to higher levels. For now he has solid control of his long limbs, both at the plate and in the field. Defensively, Ball will be limited to first base where he's got a chance to be average with continued improvements. He's still figuring out the nuances and the footwork of the position but has the frame and power you'd like to see there.

THE FUTURE: There will be plenty of pressure on his bat as he progresses, but Ball's pro debut showed he could be a special hitter—and a late-round steal.

Year	Age	Club (League)	Class	AVG	G	AB	R	H	2B	3B	HR	RBI	BB	SO	SB	OBP	SLG
2019	20	Danville (APP)	R	.324	41	145	37	47	12	0	13	38	22	30	0	.410	.676
	20	Rome (SAL)	LoA	.337	21	86	14	29	6	0	4	14	4	20	0	.367	.547
Minor League Totals				.329	62	231	51	76	18	0	17	52	26	50	0	.395	.628

19 GREYSON JENISTA, OF

BA GRADE
45 Risk: High

Born: Dec. 7, 1996. **B-T:** L-R. **HT:** 6-3. **WT:** 210. **Drafted:** Wichita State, 2018 (2nd round). **Signed by:** Nate Dion.

TRACK RECORD: A career .318/.430/.487 hitter over three years with Wichita State, Jenista was seen as a polished college bat who would hit in pro ball, with raw power that might be further tapped into with a swing change.

SCOUTING REPORT: While Jenista did switch things up at the plate in his first full season and made his way to Double-A Mississippi, he struggled with consistency and most scouts attributed that to too much tinkering with his swing. His defensive profile means more will be expected out of his bat moving forward, as Jenista will be limited to a corner outfield spot, where he's an average defender, runner and thrower. Jenista played first base in the Arizona Fall League, though that's more for versatility's sake than an indictment of his outfield play—which is serviceable. Scouts still believe Jenista has above-average raw power, which is his best tool, but he's yet to show an ability to tap into that consistently in pro ball.

THE FUTURE: Jenista should repeat Double-A next year, where he's a bounce-back candidate in the mind of Braves evaluators and will look to find a consistent rhythm at the plate.

Year	Age	Club (League)	Class	AVG	G	AB	R	H	2B	3B	HR	RBI	BB	SO	SB	OBP	SLG
2018	21	Danville (APP)	R	.250	10	40	10	10	1	0	3	7	6	9	0	.348	.500
	21	Rome (SAL)	LoA	.333	32	117	20	39	5	3	1	23	10	17	4	.377	.453
	21	Florida (FSL)	HiA	.152	19	66	3	10	3	1	0	4	7	15	0	.230	.227
2019	22	Florida (FSL)	HiA	.223	56	202	24	45	14	1	4	29	27	70	1	.312	.361
	22	Mississippi (SL)	AA	.243	74	222	18	54	4	1	5	26	27	75	2	.324	.338
Minor League Totals				.244	191	647	75	158	27	6	13	89	77	186	7	.322	.365

20 KASEY KALICH, RHP

Born: April 25, 1998. **B-T:** R-R. **HT:** 6-3. **WT:** 220. **Drafted:** Texas A&M, 2019 (4th round). **Signed by:** Darin Vaughan.

TRACK RECORD: Kalich was the first pitcher the Braves selected in the 2019 draft, making him their fourth-round selection after striking out 51 batters in 34 innings in Texas A&M's bullpen. A pure reliever, Kalich is a candidate to be the first 2019 Atlanta draftee to make the majors.

SCOUTING REPORT: The Braves liked Kalich's fastball-slider combination enough to give him a $347,500 signing bonus as a draft-eligible sophomore, and he did well in his pro debut. He ran his fastball up to 97-98 mph at its best in college but topped out around 96 mph this summer, sitting in the 92-94 mph range with some tailing life. Kalich's out-pitch is a firm, upper-80s slider that some evaluators call a cutter, though that pitch clocked in the mid-80s during his pro debut. Both pitches are likely above-average now with plus potential and he is working on a changeup and curveball as well—though both pitches are below-average and in a reliever role he shouldn't have to use them much. Kalich showed average control as an amateur but that backed up in his brief pro debut.

THE FUTURE: Kalich should move quickly through the system as a straight reliever with arm strength.

Year	Age	Club (League)	Class	W	L	ERA	G	GS	SV	IP	H	HR	BB	SO	K/9	WHIP	AVG
2019	21	Braves (GCL)	R	0	0	0.00	1	0	0	1	1	0	1	2	18.0	2.00	.250
	21	Rome (SAL)	LoA	1	1	1.31	13	0	1	21	9	0	10	22	9.6	0.92	.136
Minor League Totals				1	1	1.25	14	0	1	21	10	0	11	24	10.0	0.97	.143

21 TREY HARRIS, OF

BA GRADE
45 Risk: High

Born: Jan. 15, 1996. **B-T:** R-R. **HT:** 5-8. **WT:** 215. **Drafted:** Missouri, 2018 (32nd round). **Signed by:** JD French.

TRACK RECORD: Harris didn't hit over .300 in college until his fourth year with Missouri, but after signing for just $10,000 in the 32nd round with the Braves, he's now hit above the .300 mark in each of his first two professional seasons.

SCOUTING REPORT: Harris' professional debut was strong, but brief, in 2018. A year later, the Braves aggressively pushed Harris to more age-appropriate leagues, and he continued to hit every step of the way. Harris has a fringe-average hit tool, but he can square up the fastball well and has a good understanding of the strike zone. He brings average power to the table and while most of that is pull-oriented, he can drive the ball out to the opposite field at times as well. An above-average runner now, that grade could go down in the future, as scouts noted increased weight on Harris towards the end of the season. He'll need to monitor that moving forward, but can capably handle either corner outfield spot, with average arm strength that likely makes him a better fit for left.

THE FUTURE: Harris should begin the 2020 season in Double-A where he will look to continue proving his hitting ability is strong enough to profile in a corner.

Year	Age	Club (League)	Class	AVG	G	AB	R	H	2B	3B	HR	RBI	BB	SO	SB	OBP	SLG
2018	22	Braves (GCL)	R	.314	31	105	24	33	9	2	1	18	21	13	4	.450	.467
	22	Rome (SAL)	LoA	.286	22	84	10	24	9	0	0	11	7	13	3	.351	.393
2019	23	Rome (SAL)	LoA	.366	56	202	38	74	14	4	8	44	20	32	4	.437	.594
	23	Florida (FSL)	HiA	.303	34	122	20	37	5	0	4	17	12	26	3	.388	.443
	23	Mississippi (SL)	AA	.281	41	146	15	41	7	3	2	12	4	33	1	.318	.411
Minor League Totals				.317	184	659	107	209	44	9	15	102	64	117	15	.395	.480

22 JEREMY WALKER, RHP

BA GRADE
40 Risk: Medium

Born: June 12, 1995. **B-T:** R-R. **HT:** 6-5. **WT:** 205. **Drafted:** Gardner-Webb, 2016 (5th round). **Signed by:** Billy Best.

TRACK RECORD: Undrafted out of high school, Walker developed into a prospect over three years at Gardner-Webb, culminating in something of a breakout campaign as a junior. With the Braves, Walker progressed to high Class A Florida before transitioning to a reliever full-time in 2019.

SCOUTING REPORT: The transition to the bullpen catapulted Walker to his big league debut this season. Primarily a two-pitch arm with a sinking fastball that sits in the low-90s and a hard, sweeping curveball in the low-80s, Walker debuted with the Braves in July and posted a 1.93 ERA over 9.1 innings and six appearances. An adjustment in his arm slot in 2019 allowed him to improve his control and while he doesn't have the overpowering pure stuff typical of most relievers in this era, his ability to keep the ball on the ground and prevent home runs could be an asset in the bullpen.

THE FUTURE: Walker doesn't have the upside of many players on this list, but he's a pretty safe bet to provide major league value out of the bullpen right away.

Year	Age	Club (League)	Class	W	L	ERA	G	GS	SV	IP	H	HR	BB	SO	K/9	WHIP	AVG
2017	22	Rome (SAL)	LoA	7	11	3.97	27	27	0	138	159	7	30	100	6.5	1.37	.288
2018	23	Florida (FSL)	HiA	5	11	4.07	25	25	0	135	148	10	46	95	6.3	1.44	.282
	23	Gwinnett (IL)	AAA	1	0	0.00	1	1	0	8	3	0	1	6	6.8	0.50	.115
2019	24	Mississippi (SL)	AA	1	6	2.45	21	1	6	59	56	2	5	57	8.7	1.04	.245
	24	Gwinnett (IL)	AAA	2	1	3.97	11	0	1	23	20	1	6	25	9.9	1.15	.233
	24	Atlanta (NL)	MAJ	0	0	1.93	6	0	0	9	9	0	4	6	5.8	1.39	.265
Major League Totals				0	0	1.93	6	0	0	9	9	0	4	6	5.8	1.39	.265
Minor League Totals				19	32	3.62	98	59	7	402	426	22	96	320	7.2	1.30	.270

23 DAYSBEL HERNANDEZ, RHP

BA GRADE 50 Risk: Extreme

Born: Sept. 15, 1996**. B-T:** R-R. **HT:** 5-10. **WT:** 220. **Signed:** Cuba, 2017. **Signed by:** Rolando Petit.

TRACK RECORD: Hernandez signed with the Braves in September of 2017 after pitching in the Cuban National Series during the 2014-15 and 2015-16 seasons.The Braves started Hernandez in the South Atlantic League in 2018 before watching him take a step forward this season with high Class A Florida.

SCOUTING REPORT: Hernandez has big league caliber pure stuff, but he previously struggled enough with his strike-throwing to limit his effectiveness. While he still lacks great command, his control took a big step forward in 2019. Hernandez has a plus-plus fastball that sits in the 96-99 mph range and pairs that with a firm slider in the upper-80s that has above-average potential as well. He'll need to improve the consistency of his slider moving forward, but a short arm action and above-average deception that comes from hiding the ball well in his delivery could create uncomfortable at-bats from hitters on both sides of the plate.

THE FUTURE: Scouts praise Hernandez's presence and mentality on the mound and think he has the stuff and demeanor to be a high-leverage reliever if he can keep his walk rate in check.

Year	Age	Club (League)	Class	W	L	ERA	G	GS	SV	IP	H	HR	BB	SO	K/9	WHIP	AVG
2017	20	Did not play															
2018	21	Rome (SAL)	LoA	1	0	3.33	13	0	1	24	15	0	15	26	9.6	1.23	.174
	21	Florida (FSL)	HiA	1	2	6.59	8	0	0	14	13	2	8	10	6.6	1.54	.260
2019	22	Florida (FSL)	HiA	5	2	1.71	35	0	7	53	34	2	23	70	12.0	1.08	.184
Minor League Totals				7	4	2.88	56	0	8	90	62	4	46	106	10.5	1.19	.193

24 LOGAN BROWN, C

BA GRADE 45 Risk: Very High

Born: Sept. 14, 1996**. B-T:** L-R. **HT:** 6-0. **WT:** 195. **Drafted:** Southern Indiana, 2018 (35th round). **Signed by:** Kevin Barry.

TRACK RECORD: A 35th round pick who signed for $125,000, Brown is the son of Kevin, who was a backup catcher in the majors for seven years and also attended Southern Indiana. The Braves were one of only a few teams interested in Brown during his junior year and loved his defensive skills.

SCOUTING REPORT: Brown has easy plus arm strength that will draw 70-grade evaluations on his best days and threw out 38 percent of runners in the Florida State League and 42 percent of runners in the South Atlantic League. Brown also has good hands and does a nice job receiving, blocking and handling a staff. He has all the tools and ability to become an above-average defender, but his bat needs plenty of work. His swing is stiff from the left side and he lacks present strength to impact the ball with much authority, with well below-average power currently. That said, the Braves were impressed with his contact ability and his improvements, and have hope that he will fill out and add strength in the future.

THE FUTURE: Brown has a solid backup catching profile, with some upside as a second-division regular who might do enough offensively to survive in the back of a lineup.

Year	Age	Club (League)	Class	AVG	G	AB	R	H	2B	3B	HR	RBI	BB	SO	SB	OBP	SLG
2018	21	Braves (GCL)	R	.272	37	114	13	31	5	0	3	16	11	16	0	.346	.395
2019	22	Rome (SAL)	LoA	.301	51	193	25	58	11	1	1	26	11	39	0	.351	.383
	22	Florida (FSL)	HiA	.240	48	175	12	42	7	0	0	20	6	44	0	.269	.280
Minor League Totals				.272	136	482	50	131	23	1	4	62	28	99	0	.321	.349

25 BEAU PHILIP, SS

BA GRADE 45 Risk: Very High

Born: Oct. 23, 1998**. B-T:** R-R. **HT:** 6-0. **WT:** 190. **Drafted:** Oregon State, 2019 (2nd round). **Signed by:** Cody Martin.

TRACK RECORD: Philip played two seasons at San Joaquin Delta (Calif.) JC before transferring to Oregon State for his junior season, where he hit .312 and capably replaced 2018 supplemental first-round pick Cadyn Grenier at shortstop. The Braves signed him to an underslot deal in the second round for $697,500.

SCOUTING REPORT: Philip is a defensive-oriented prospect who has advanced abilities and plus tools centered around shortstop. He has reliable hands and glove work, ranges well to both sides and particularly up the middle to his glove side and has plus arm strength. At San Joaquin Delta he threw 95 mph off the mound and could have a real fallback as a pitcher. Philip is also an above-average runner. There's a lot of work he needs to do offensively, however. Philip has always struggled to hit breaking pitches—dating back to his time in junior college and in the Pac-12 — and has below-average raw power. He doesn't project to have much in the future, meaning he'll need to make big strides with his hit tool to provide much value offensively.
THE FUTURE: Philip could have some value as a utility infielder or defensive specialist, but it's difficult to project more than that until he shows more promise with the bat.

Year	Age	Club (League)	Class	AVG	G	AB	R	H	2B	3B	HR	RBI	BB	SO	SB	OBP	SLG
2019	20	Danville (APP)	R	.193	55	207	27	40	6	0	4	20	26	51	5	.297	.280
Minor League Totals				.193	55	207	27	40	6	0	4	20	26	51	5	.297	.280

26 JUSTIN DEAN, OF

BA GRADE
45 **Risk: Very High**

Born: Dec. 6, 1996**. B-T:** R-R. **HT:** 5-6. **WT:** 185. **Drafted:** Lenoir-Rhyne (N.C.), 2018 (17th round**). Signed by:** Billy Best.

TRACK RECORD: A speedy center fielder out of Lenoir-Rhyne, the Braves signed Dean for $125,000 in the 17th round of the 2018 draft after a college career that saw him hit .367/.467/.532 over three years.
SCOUTING REPORT: Voted the best defensive outfielder in the South Atlantic League this season, Dean's prowess in center field is likely his biggest asset at the moment. He can run it down in the gaps well as a 70-grade runner who also posts 60-grade run times from home to first, and he plays with a lively, infectious energy. Dean uses his speed on the base paths as well, giving him an old school leadoff hitter profile on the surface. Dean could have average raw power in the tank down the line, though it's mostly pull-oriented at the moment—he hit just one opposite field home run in 2019. He's undersized, but pound-for-pound is well put together. Dean's hit tool is still raw, and scouts believe he's more likely to be a solid fourth outfielder type than a regular because of that.
THE FUTURE: If Dean continues to hit at more age-appropriate levels—he was old for the Sally League this season—he'll climb in the organization thanks to impressive supplemental tools and the ability to handle a premium position. For now, he profiles as a fourth outfielder.

Year	Age	Club (League)	Class	AVG	G	AB	R	H	2B	3B	HR	RBI	BB	SO	SB	OBP	SLG
2018	21	Danville (APP)	R	.308	32	130	28	40	8	4	1	15	22	32	7	.419	.454
	21	Rome (SAL)	LoA	.257	28	113	20	29	2	5	0	8	11	27	9	.333	.363
2019	22	Rome (SAL)	LoA	.284	109	429	85	122	18	9	9	46	62	115	47	.386	.431
Minor League Totals				.284	169	672	133	191	28	18	10	69	95	174	63	.384	.424

27 AJ GRAFFANINO, SS

BA GRADE
45 **Risk: Very High**

Born: July 16, 1997. **B-T:** L-R. **HT:** 6-2. **WT:** 170. **Drafted:** Washington, 2018 (8th round). **Signed by:** Brett Evert.

TRACK RECORD: A polished defender with major league bloodlines—his father Tony had a 13-year career—Graffanino was a needed addition to a system that lacked shortstop depth a year ago. Graffanino played in just one game this season after undiagnosed gastrointestinal issues sidelined him for the entirety of the season. The ailment lingered for Graffanino throughout the year before he started to recover in September, but at that point the season was lost. The injury left Graffanino behind in at-bats, which are sorely needed for the glove-first infielder.
SCOUTING REPORT: Graffanino has above-average range at shortstop with twitchy athleticism and above-average running ability, to go along with solid hands and above-average arm strength that will allow him to stick at the position long-term. His bat is the bigger question, as Graffanino has well below-average power and lacked much history hitting at a high level. He's leaned into being a slap-and-dash hitter too frequently in the past and will need to improve on that in the future.
THE FUTURE: He'll have to make up for lost time in 2020 and he should have his first full minor league season.

Year	Age	Club (League)	Class	AVG	G	AB	R	H	2B	3B	HR	RBI	BB	SO	SB	OBP	SLG
2018	20	Danville (APP)	R	.407	6	27	2	11	0	0	0	6	1	3	1	.400	.407
	20	Rome (SAL)	LoA	.301	37	143	19	43	8	0	1	11	8	24	4	.333	.378
2019	21	Florida (FSL)	HiA	.000	1	1	0	0	0	0	0	0	0	0	0	.000	.000
Minor League Totals				.316	44	171	21	54	8	0	1	17	9	27	5	.342	.380

28 STEPHEN PAOLINI, OF

Born: Nov. 23, 2000. **B-T:** L-L. **HT:** 6-2. **WT:** 195. **Drafted:** HS—Trumbull, Conn., 2019 (5th round). **Signed by:** Ted Lekas.

TRACK RECORD: The Braves were one of only a few teams interested in Paolini out of high school in the 2019 draft, but they believed in his swing, future power potential and center field profile enough to buy him out of an Elon commitment for $597,500 in the fifth round.

SCOUTING REPORT: Paolini was an under-the-radar prospect out of the Northeast who wasn't seen on the travel ball circuit during high school, but he checks a lot of boxes that look good on paper. He is a left-left centerfielder with plus speed and a projectable and athletic, 6-foot-2, 195-pound frame. The true ability of Paolini's hit tool will decide whether or not Atlanta's gamble will pay off, but he looked overmatched in a brief pro debut in the Rookie-level Gulf Coast League despite some solid on-base skills. Paolini has a chance to get to average raw power as he fills out physically, with solid bat speed, but he will need to quiet a swing that is aggressive and built from a big leg kick in his load that could lead to timing issues.

THE FUTURE: Paolini played all three outfield positions in his debut but should have the speed and athleticism to stick in center field. There's plenty of risk here, but if Paolini does improve his hitting ability there are a lot of supplemental tools and skills to get excited about. He should move slowly through the system.

Year	Age	Club (League)	Class	AVG	G	AB	R	H	2B	3B	HR	RBI	BB	SO	SB	OBP	SLG
2019	18	Braves (GCL)	R	.192	35	120	15	23	6	0	0	8	22	37	2	.315	.242
Minor League Totals				.192	35	120	15	23	6	0	0	8	22	37	2	.315	.242

29 TREY RILEY, RHP

BA GRADE
45 Risk: Extreme

Born: April 21, 1998. **B-T:** L-R. **HT:** 6-3. **WT:** 205. **Drafted:** John A. Logan (Ill.) JC, 2018 (5th round). **Signed by:** Kevin Barry.

TRACK RECORD: A popup arm in the 2018 draft who excelled at John A. Logan (Ill.) JC and showcased premium pure stuff, Riley signed for $450,000 in the fifth round before showing his control had a long way to go in his professional debut.

SCOUTING REPORT: After starting for most of the 2019 season, Riley moved to the bullpen during his last five games, where he struggled to find the strike zone, throwing just 47 percent of his pitches for strikes out of the bullpen compared to around 59 percent in a starting role. His pure stuff suits a reliever role, with a fastball that's been up to 96-97 mph at its best but this season was down into the low 90s more frequently. The slider is his best secondary, and it has a chance to be above-average, while Riley's curve and changeup lag behind.

THE FUTURE: Mechanically, Riley has a clean delivery and arm action, but his control is still limiting him from making the most of his pure stuff.

Year	Age	Club (League)	Class	W	L	ERA	G	GS	SV	IP	H	HR	BB	SO	K/9	WHIP	AVG
2018	20	Danville (APP)	R	0	0	8.00	6	2	0	9	10	1	10	13	13.0	2.22	.278
2019	21	Rome (SAL)	LoA	2	7	7.67	17	12	0	59	71	4	46	41	6.3	1.99	.317
Minor League Totals				2	7	7.71	23	14	0	67	81	5	56	54	7.2	2.02	.312

30 JEFREY RAMOS, OF

BA GRADE
45 Risk: Extreme

Born: Feb. 10, 1999. **B-T:** R-R. **HT:** 6-1. **WT:** 185. **Signed:** Dominican Republic, 2016. **Signed by:** Jonathan Cruz.

TRACK RECORD: After sanctions, Ramos is now the highest-ranked prospect in Atlanta's 2016 international class, which originally included players like Kevin Maitan (Angels) and Yunior Severino (Twins).

SCOUTING REPORT: Ramos faces a difficult path to the majors as a free-swinging right-right left fielder whose entire profile is dependent on his hit tool and power production. His raw power stacks up among the best in Atlanta's system, with scouts giving him plus grades or better in that department, but he has struggled to translate that into games consistently in two years of full-season ball. Ramos will need to make adjustments at the plate and get to at least fringe-average hitting ability to make up for below-average defensive ability that includes below-average speed and arm strength.

THE FUTURE: Ramos should start 2020 back in the Florida State League, where he'll hope to get the bat on the ball more and take advantage of his sole carrying tool.

Year	Age	Club (League)	Class	AVG	G	AB	R	H	2B	3B	HR	RBI	BB	SO	SB	OBP	SLG
2017	18	Braves (GCL)	R	.325	30	117	22	38	7	1	6	30	8	27	1	.374	.556
	18	Danville (APP)	R	.278	20	72	7	20	6	0	1	8	3	15	0	.308	.403
2018	19	Rome (SAL)	LoA	.245	122	469	57	115	24	6	16	69	27	89	2	.290	.424
2019	20	Florida (FSL)	HiA	.241	128	460	49	111	16	4	9	56	30	99	1	.291	.352
Minor League Totals				.252	333	1244	154	313	61	12	33	175	77	257	7	.299	.400

Baltimore Orioles

BY JON MEOLI

With their mid-decade run of relevance cratering in 2018, the Orioles embraced the need for change and began a "to-the-studs" rebuild that saw longtime executive vice president Dan Duquette and manager Buck Showalter replaced by former Astros scouting director Mike Elias and Cubs bench coach Brandon Hyde.

The ensuing season in 2019 saw them lose 108 games while cycling through waiver claims and bit parts all over their roster, although a few bright spots emerged like all-star rookie lefthander John Means and the continued progress of Trey Mancini.

But most of the focus from the new front office, including assistant general manager for analytics Sig Mejdal, was on beginning to revamp the scouting and player development infrastructures. Elias brought minor league pitching coordinator Chris Holt over from Houston to install a data-driven pitching program that emphasizes pitch mix over fastball command. Four affiliates—Double-A Bowie, low Class A Delmarva, short-season Aberdeen, and the Rookie-level Gulf Coast League Orioles—led their leagues in several pitching categories in the first year under Holt's instruction.

That pitching progress not only did wonders for recent high draft picks like Grayson Rodriguez and Mike Baumann but also helped get the careers of 2016 first-round pick Cody Sedlock and 2015 over-slot signee Gray Fenter back on track. Many pitchers embraced the new forms of instruction and the clear communication of goals that came with it.

No one, however, will be accelerated to the majors under a years-long plan of reloading before the Orioles are competitive again. Austin Hays, DJ Stewart, Chance Sisco and Anthony Santander were all well regarded young position players who had major league time coming into the year, but all started 2019 in the minors for further seasoning before coming up later in the season. Ryan Mountcastle hit 25 home runs in Triple-A and was named International League Most Valuable Player, but didn't get a September callup.

All that serves to delay the major league arrivals and create a bubble of talent that, combined with the impressive pitching from the last few drafts of the Duquette era under former scouting director Gary Rajsich, could make for an impressive system in the coming years.

The Orioles went heavy on position players early in the 2019 draft, with consensus No. 1 pick Adley Rutschman highlighting a polished group of hitters on the first two days before they turned their attention to pitching. And when it comes to pitching, they clearly had an idea of what would work. The 18 college pitchers signed in 2019 pitched 379.2 innings in their pro debuts to a combined 1.85 ERA, 1.07 WHIP and strikeout rate of 10.2 per nine innings.

Combined with a 2018 international signing class that included over $1 million in signings under the leadership of international scouting director Koby Perez and the largest July 2 class in club history, the Orioles made good on Elias' vow to improve the overall talent base in the organization, even if the major league team didn't see much benefit from that—and may not for years.

MARK CUNNINGHAM/MLB PHOTOS VIA GETTY IMAGES

Rookie lefthander John Means rode an improved changeup to the 2019 All-Star Game.

PROJECTED 2023 LINEUP

Position	Player	Age
Catcher	Adley Rutschman (1)	25
First Base	Ryan Mountcastle (5)	26
Second Base	Hanser Alberto	30
Third Base	Rio Ruiz	29
Shortstop	Gunnar Henderson (7)	22
Left Field	Cedric Mullins	28
Center Field	Austin Hays (4)	27
Right Field	Yusniel Diaz (6)	26
Designated Hitter	Trey Mancini	31
No. 1 Starter	Grayson Rodriguez (2)	23
No. 2 Starter	D.L. Hall (3)	24
No. 3 Starter	John Means	30
No. 4 Starter	Keegan Akin (9)	28
No. 5 Starter	Mike Baumann (10)	28
Closer	Hunter Harvey (8)	28

DEPTH CHART

BALTIMORE ORIOLES

TOP 2020 ROOKIE: Ryan Mountcastle, 1B. His feel for hitting, improved approach, and power potential will make him a plug-and-play standout in the middle of the lineup.

BREAKOUT PROSPECT: Adam Hall, SS. His first full season could have Hall primed for another contact-and-speed driven breakout and jump him into the organization's top 10.

SLEEPER: Dan Hammer, RHP. Hammer, with a 90-94 mph fastball and two present-average secondary pitches, could impress in his full-season debut.

SOURCE OF TOP 30 TALENT			
Homegrown	**23**	**Acquired**	**6**
College	11	Trade	6
Junior college	0	Rule 5 draft	1
High school	11	Independent league	0
Nondrafted free agent	0	Free agent/waivers	0
International	1		

LF
Ademar Rifaela
T.J. Nichting
Jaylen Ferguson

CF
Austin Hays (4)
Ryan McKenna (17)
Zach Watson (19)
Mason Janvrin

RF
Yusniel Diaz (6)
Kyle Stowers (18)
Zach Jarrett
Robbie Neustrom
Johnny Rizer

3B
Rylan Bannon (29)
JC Encarnacion
Willy Yahn
Toby Welk

SS
Gunnar Henderson (7)
Adam Hall (13)
Cadyn Grenier (24)
Darell Hernaiz (25)
Mason McCoy (28)
Joey Ortiz

2B
Chris Clare

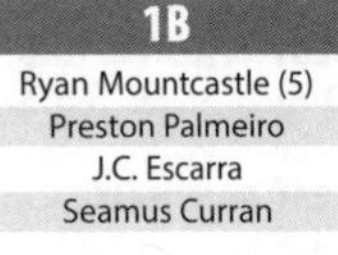

1B
Ryan Mountcastle (5)
Preston Palmeiro
J.C. Escarra
Seamus Curran

C
Adley Rutschman (1)
Cody Roberts

LHP

LHSP	LHRP
DL Hall (3)	Zack Muckenhirn
Keegan Akin (9)	Luis Gonzalez
Zac Lowther (12)	Tyler Erwin
Alex Wells (14)	Zach Matson
Drew Rom (15)	
Bruce Zimmermann (16)	

RHP

RHSP	RHRP
Grayson Rodriguez (2)	Hunter Harvey (8)
Mike Baumann (10)	Zach Pop (26)
Dean Kremer (11)	Dillon Tate (27)
Cody Sedlock (20)	Brandon Bailey (30)
Gray Fenter (21)	Francisco Jimenez
Blaine Knight (22)	Christian Alvarado
Brenan Hanifee (23)	Diogenes Almengo
Ofelky Peralta	Kyle Bradish
David Lebron	Isaac Mattson
Dan Hammer	
Leonardo Rodriguez	
Zach Peek	
Kyle Brnovich	

DRAFT ANALYSIS

2019

BEST PURE HITTER: C Adley Rutschman (1) projects as a 70-grade hitter with excellent feel for the zone and an advanced ability to make adjustments. He hit .325/.413/.481 in the New York-Penn League, but he struggled in shorter stints in the Gulf Coast and South Atlantic leagues.

BEST POWER HITTER: Rutschman has 60-grade in-game power from both sides of the plate. Some scouts will go so far as to give Rutschman 70-grade raw power, but it's at least plus.

FASTEST RUNNER: OF Mason Janvrin (14) was a menace on the basepaths in college, stealing 34 and 52 bases during his sophomore and junior seasons, respectively. Throughout his time at Central Missouri, Janvrin went 76-for-94 (80.1 percent) in stolen base attempts, and in his pro debut in the Gulf Coast and New York-Penn leagues, he went 17-for-21 (81 percent). He is an 80-grade runner.

BEST DEFENSIVE PLAYER: Rutschman is a polished receiver and game manager in addition to having a big arm. SS Joey Ortiz (4) is a plus defender at shortstop, and his arm plays up thanks to terrific exchange and footwork.

BEST ATHLETE: Rutschman was also a member of Oregon State's football team as a freshman place kicker.

BEST FASTBALL: Griffin McLarty (8) takes the prize for best fastball, despite a heater that tops out in the low 90s. However, McLarty seems to be one of those arms who can have success without massive velocity due to his precise strike-throwing ability and plus command.

BEST SECONDARY PITCH: RHP Shelton Perkins (16) has a slider that will flash double-plus potential, and he used that pitch to strike out each of the first six hitters he faced during his pro debut with low Class A Aberdeen.

BEST PRO DEBUT: Kade Strowd (12) didn't allow an earned run in 17 innings in the New York-Penn League. He mostly pitched in relief—making just one start—and struck out 19 batters (10.1 strikeouts per nine innings) while walking seven (3.7 walks per nine).

MOST INTRIGUING BACKGROUND: SS Gunnar Henderson (2) has athletic bloodlines, as his older brother, Jackson, is an infielder and outfielder at Auburn. It also seems like he was destined to be drafted by Baltimore. His younger brother, Cade, is a big Orioles fan and spent draft night watching in his Orioles pajamas, predicting the team would draft Gunnar.

CLOSEST TO THE MAJORS: Rutschman could hold his own in the majors as soon as late 2020, though it would be shocking for the team to move him that rapidly.

BEST LATE-ROUND PICK: The Orioles signed 3B Toby Welk (21) for just $1,000 on Day 3, and he dominated the New York-Penn League, hitting .344/.397/.500 with four home runs and 12 doubles.

THE ONE WHO GOT AWAY: Baltimore signed every one of their picks through the first 33 rounds before getting to SS Zach Arnold (34), who is an above-average runner with above-average arm strength and a chance to get to above-average power as well. Arnold was originally committed to Oregon, but he later flipped to Louisiana State.

—CARLOS COLLAZO

TOP DRAFT PICKS OF THE DECADE

Year	Player, Pos.	2019 Org
2010	Manny Machado, SS	Padres
2011	Dylan Bundy, RHP	Orioles
2012	Kevin Gausman, RHP	Reds
2013	Hunter Harvey, RHP	Orioles
2014	Brian Gonzalez, LHP (3rd round)	Orioles
2015	D.J. Stewart, OF	Orioles
2016	Cody Sedlock, RHP	Orioles
2017	D.L. Hall, LHP	Orioles
2018	Grayson Rodriguez, RHP	Orioles
2019	Adley Rutschman, C	Orioles

2018

RHP Grayson Rodriguez (1) gives the class a potential star. College All-Americans SS Cadyn Grenier (1s) and RHP Blaine Knight (2) have also provide solid value so far.

GRADE: B

2017

LHP DL Hall (1) is the class' frontman with fellow top 100 picks SS Adam Hall (2), LHP Zac Lowther (2s) and RHP Mike Baumann (3) off to strong starts as well.

GRADE: B

2016

OF Austin Hays (3) raced to Baltimore in 2017 but has struggled to repeat that success. Collegians RHP Cody Sedlock (1) and LHP Keegan Akin (2) could soon join him.

GRADE: C

1 ADLEY RUTSCHMAN, C

Born: Feb. 6, 1998. **B-T:** B-R. **HT:** 6-2. **WT:** 216.
Drafted: Oregon State, 2019 (1st round).
Signed by: Brandon Verley.

TRACK RECORD: A celebrated recruit who won Oregon high school state player of the year in 2016, Rutschman accomplished everything there was to do in college at Oregon State. He led the Beavers to the College World Series title and won CWS Most Outstanding Player in 2018, led USA Baseball's Collegiate National Team in nearly every offensive category the following summer and entered 2019 as the consensus top draft prospect in the class. He lived up to it by hitting .411 with a nation-leading .575 on-base percentage and won the BA College Player of the Year Award. The Orioles drafted him No. 1 overall and signed him for a draft-record $8.1 million. A case of mononucleosis after he signed delayed Rutschman's pro debut nearly a month, but he still climbed three levels after signing and wowed teammates and coaches at each stop, finishing with low Class A Delmarva for its playoff run.

SCOUTING REPORT: Despite Rutschman's reputation as a tireless worker, there are no apparent holes in his game. Defensively, he's a pitcher's dream in terms of his advanced framing and above-average pop times on throws to second base. He called some of his own games as an amateur and took well to game-calling once he signed. At the plate, the switch-hitting Rutschman shows a swing tooled for both average and power, with a consistent path from both sides geared towards line drives and hard contact. His future outlook as a plus hitter with plus in-game power will be aided by his standout approach, one honed as opposing teams pitched around him his last year in college. Rutschman showed a similarly sharp eye in his pro debut, to the point his coaches began using his at-bats as an example to his new teammates. That's not to say Rutschman often singles himself out. Instead, he's touted as a tremendous teammate who will put his own goals behind the team's, and he has spoken about how the turnaround in the Orioles' minors suits him in terms of his pursuit of winning.

THE FUTURE: A potential perennial all-star catcher with a middle-of-the-order bat landed on the Orioles' doorstep thanks to their dreadful 115-loss season in 2018. Already, Rutschman has become the face of the club's rebuild. The Orioles figure to start him at high Class A Frederick with an eye toward Double-A Bowie at midseason, which could put him on track for a 2021 debut in Baltimore.

TRACY PROFFITT/FOUR SEAM IMAGES

BA GRADE
70 Risk: High

SCOUTING GRADES
Hit: 70. **Power:** 60. **Run:** 40. **Field:** 60. **Arm:** 70.

Projected future grades on 20-80 scouting scale.

TOP PROSPECTS OF THE DECADE

Year	Player, Pos.	2019 Org
2010	Brian Matusz, LHP	Atlantic League
2011	Manny Machado, SS	Padres
2012	Dylan Bundy, RHP	Orioles
2013	Dylan Bundy, RHP	Orioles
2014	Dylan Bundy, RHP	Orioles
2015	Dylan Bundy, RHP	Orioles
2016	Dylan Bundy, RHP	Orioles
2017	Chance Sisco, C	Orioles
2018	Austin Hays, OF	Orioles
2019	Yusniel Diaz, OF	Orioles

BEST TOOLS

Best Hitter for Average	Adley Rutschman
Best Power Hitter	Ryan Mountcastle
Best Strike-Zone Discipline	Adley Rutschman
Fastest Baserunner	Mason Janvrin
Best Athlete	Austin Hays
Best Fastball	Hunter Harvey
Best Curveball	DL Hall
Best Slider	Mike Baumann
Best Changeup	Grayson Rodriguez
Best Control	Alex Wells
Best Defensive Catcher	Adley Rutschman
Best Defensive Infielder	Adam Hall
Best Infield Arm	JC Encarnacion
Best Defensive Outfielder	Austin Hays
Best Outfield Arm	Austin Hays

Year	Age	Club (League)	Class	AVG	G	AB	R	H	2B	3B	HR	RBI	BB	SO	SB	OBP	SLG
2019	21	Orioles (GCL)	R	.143	5	14	3	2	0	0	1	3	2	2	1	.250	.357
	21	Aberdeen (NYP)	SS	.325	20	77	11	25	7	1	1	15	12	16	0	.413	.481
	21	Delmarva (SAL)	LoA	.154	12	39	5	6	1	0	2	8	6	9	0	.261	.333
Minor League Totals				.254	37	130	19	33	8	1	4	26	20	27	1	.351	.423

2 GRAYSON RODRIGUEZ, RHP

Born: Nov. 16, 1999. **B-T:** L-R. **HT:** 6-5. **WT:** 220. **Drafted:** HS—Nacogdoches, Texas, 2018 (1st round). **Signed by:** Thom Dreier.

TRACK RECORD: A pop-up prospect who signed for $4.3 million after remaking his body and delivery before his senior spring, Rodriguez became the latest Orioles pitching prospect to dominate his full-season debut at low Class A Delmarva. Just nine minor league pitchers with at least 90 innings struck out more batters per nine innings than Rodriguez's 12.4, and people took notice. Rodriguez was a South Atlantic League all-star, pitched in the Futures Game and shared Orioles minor league pitcher of the year honors.

SCOUTING REPORT: The specialized training of his high school days allowed Rodriguez to grow significantly in 2019. His fastball sat 93-96 mph and got up to 98 late in the season. It projects as a potential plus-plus pitch with downhill plane and armside life. His curveball and slider alternate as his better breaking pitch depending on the day, but at their best his mid-70s curveball flashes plus and his low-to-mid-80s slider shows above-average. His changeup made great progress throughout the year and began flashing plus, giving him four pitches that miss bats to go with plus command.

THE FUTURE: Rodriguez's first full season made him the clear top pitching prospect in the organization and one of the best in baseball. He will begin 2019 at high Class A Frederick.

SCOUTING GRADES: **Fastball:** 70 **Slider:** 55 **Curveball:** 60 **Changeup:** 55 **Control:** 60

Year	Age	Club (League)	Class	W	L	ERA	G	GS	SV	IP	H	HR	BB	SO	K/9	WHIP	AVG
2018	18	Orioles (GCL)	R	0	2	1.40	9	8	0	19	17	0	7	20	9.3	1.24	.236
2019	19	Delmarva (SAL)	LoA	10	4	2.68	20	20	0	94	57	4	36	129	12.4	0.99	.171
Minor League Totals				10	6	2.46	29	28	0	113	74	4	43	149	11.8	1.03	.183

3 DL HALL, LHP

Born: Sept. 19, 1998. **B-T:** L-L. **HT:** 6-0. **WT:** 180. **Drafted:** HS—Valdosta, Ga., 2017 (1st round). **Signed by:** Arthur McConnehead.

TRACK RECORD: Hall's brief slide in the 2017 draft ended when the Orioles selected him 21st overall and signed him to a $3 million bonus. A dominant first full season in 2018 backed up the assessment that he was the top prep lefthander in his class. Hall spent too much time out of the strike zone in the first half of 2019 before a trip to the Futures Game set him straight. He logged a 2.67 ERA over his final five starts at high Class A Frederick before an oblique injury ended his season three weeks early.

SCOUTING REPORT: Hall's electric arsenal is highlighted by a fastball that comfortably sits 93-96 mph deep into outings and touches 97. The easy life on his fastball gives it plus-plus potential. Hall's upper-70s curveball has lived up to its pre-draft reputation as a future plus pitch he can drop in for strikes, and he's had additional success with an average short slider he's developed as a pro. His low-80s changeup has also flashed plus potential with late fade. Hall struggled to throw strikes in 2019, but his athletic delivery is repeatable. He should develop average control as he more consistently attacks hitters.

THE FUTURE: Hall has the raw stuff and pitch mix to be a mid-rotation starter or better. He'll open 2020 at Double-A.

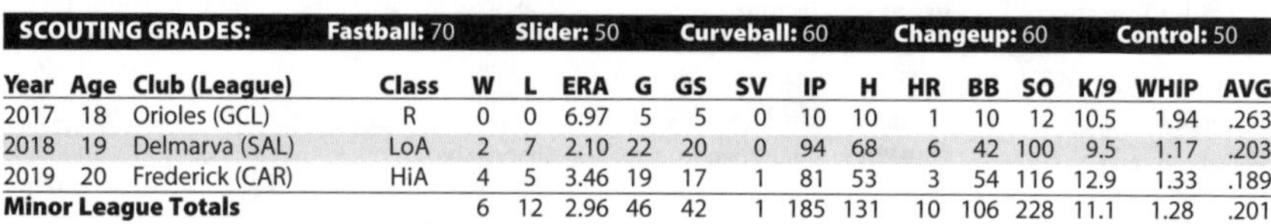

SCOUTING GRADES: **Fastball:** 70 **Slider:** 50 **Curveball:** 60 **Changeup:** 60 **Control:** 50

Year	Age	Club (League)	Class	W	L	ERA	G	GS	SV	IP	H	HR	BB	SO	K/9	WHIP	AVG
2017	18	Orioles (GCL)	R	0	0	6.97	5	5	0	10	10	1	10	12	10.5	1.94	.263
2018	19	Delmarva (SAL)	LoA	2	7	2.10	22	20	0	94	68	6	42	100	9.5	1.17	.203
2019	20	Frederick (CAR)	HiA	4	5	3.46	19	17	1	81	53	3	54	116	12.9	1.33	.189
Minor League Totals				6	12	2.96	46	42	1	185	131	10	106	228	11.1	1.28	.201

4 AUSTIN HAYS, OF

BA GRADE
50 Risk: Medium

Born: July 5, 1995. **B-T:** R-R. **HT:** 6-1. **WT:** 195. **Drafted:** Jacksonville, 2016 (3rd round). **Signed by:** Arthur McConnehead.

TRACK RECORD: Hays put together one of the more impressive full-season debuts of any player in 2017. He hit .332 with 32 home runs between high Class A Frederick and Double-A Bowie and made his big league debut in September, becoming the first player from the 2016 draft to reach the majors. But Hays struggled through an ankle injury in 2018, missed the beginning of 2019 with a thumb injury and also dealt with a midseason hamstring injury before finally making his way back to the majors in September.

SCOUTING REPORT: A highly aggressive hitter, Hays regained some of his opposite-field approach in 2019 after becoming too pull-heavy. His bat speed allows him to stay back on spin without sacrificing the ability to catch up to fastballs. He has above-average power and the raw tools to be an average hitter, though plate discipline has been a problem in the past. The Orioles looked at Hays' strikeout-to-walk ratio in September in the majors and deemed his year a success. He continues to show a plus arm with average range with good instincts in the outfield, earning him his first significant look in center field.

THE FUTURE: Hays will compete for an Opening Day roster spot for the third straight year in 2020. He showed enough in September to be considered an immediate center field solution.

SCOUTING GRADES: **Hitting:** 50 **Power:** 55 **Running:** 50 **Fielding:** 55 **Arm:** 60

Year	Age	Club (League)	Class	AVG	G	AB	R	H	2B	3B	HR	RBI	BB	SO	SB	OBP	SLG
2017	21	Frederick (CAR)	HiA	.324	64	262	42	85	15	3	16	41	12	40	4	.361	.588
	21	Bowie (EL)	AA	.330	64	261	39	86	17	2	16	54	13	45	1	.367	.594
	21	Baltimore (AL)	MAJ	.217	20	60	4	13	3	0	1	8	2	16	0	.238	.317
2018	22	Aberdeen (NYP)	SS	.189	9	37	6	7	2	0	0	3	2	7	0	.231	.243
	22	Bowie (EL)	AA	.242	66	273	34	66	12	2	12	43	12	59	6	.271	.432
2019	23	Frederick (CAR)	HiA	.162	9	37	3	6	0	0	2	6	1	11	0	.200	.324
	23	Bowie (EL)	AA	.268	14	56	9	15	5	0	3	11	5	11	3	.328	.518
	23	Aberdeen (NYP)	SS	.278	5	18	5	5	2	0	2	4	1	0	0	.350	.722
	23	Norfolk (IL)	AAA	.254	59	240	43	61	16	1	10	27	11	61	6	.304	.454
	23	Baltimore (AL)	MAJ	.309	21	68	12	21	6	0	4	13	7	13	2	.373	.574
Major League Totals				.266	41	128	16	34	9	0	5	21	9	29	2	.312	.453
Minor League Totals				.286	328	1324	195	379	78	10	65	210	68	266	24	.327	.508

5 RYAN MOUNTCASTLE, 1B

BA GRADE
50 Risk: Medium

Born: Feb. 18, 1997. **B-T:** R-R. **HT:** 6-3. **WT:** 195. **Drafted:** HS—Oviedo, Fla., 2015 (1st round)**. Signed by:** Kelvin Colon.

TRACK RECORD: A pure hitter who grew into power with a career-high 25 home runs in 2019, Mountcastle's bat has played at every level. He's been an all-star in each of the last three seasons, and his standout 2019 earned him the Triple-A International League's MVP award. But seemingly every promotion has come with a position change. Originally a shortstop and then moved to third base, Mountcastle played first base and left field in 2019.

SCOUTING REPORT: Mountcastle's swing has always been his premier asset. His loose but quick hands allow him to adjust to whatever he's seeing and make him a potentially plus hitter. Offseason work to improve his swing path and add strength only boosted that outlook. While he's more of an above-average power threat than an on-base threat, Mountcastle showed an improved situational approach in 2019 to show he's not just a masher. The Orioles believe Mountcastle's well-below average arm will play better with the different arm swing required from left field, but the farther he moves down the defensive spectrum—being average anywhere is a stretch—the more pressure is put on his bat.

THE FUTURE: Mountcastle is on the cusp of his major league debut in 2020. His bat is that of a first-division regular, but he has to find somewhere to play.

SCOUTING GRADES: **Hitting:** 60 **Power:** 55 **Running:** 45 **Fielding:** 40 **Arm:** 30

Year	Age	Club (League)	Class	AVG	G	AB	R	H	2B	3B	HR	RBI	BB	SO	SB	OBP	SLG
2017	20	Frederick (CAR)	HiA	.314	88	360	63	113	35	1	15	47	14	61	8	.343	.542
	20	Bowie (EL)	AA	.222	39	153	18	34	13	0	3	15	3	35	0	.239	.366
2018	21	Bowie (EL)	AA	.297	102	394	63	117	19	4	13	59	26	79	2	.341	.464
2019	22	Norfolk (IL)	AAA	.312	127	520	81	162	35	1	25	83	24	130	2	.344	.527
Minor League Totals				.295	524	2078	301	612	137	10	70	274	101	446	27	.328	.471

6 YUSNIEL DIAZ, OF

Born: Oct. 7, 1996. **B-T:** R-R. **HT:** 6-1. **WT:** 195. **Signed:** Cuba, 2015. **Signed by:** Ismael Cruz/Miguel Tosar/Roman Barinas (Dodgers).

BA GRADE
55 **Risk: Very High**

TRACK RECORD: Signed out of Cuba by the Dodgers for $15.5 million after the 2015 season, Diaz has spent three seasons in the U.S. trying to translate his considerable tools into consistent production. After being acquired in the Manny Machado trade in July 2018, Diaz impressed in his first big league camp with the Orioles, but a hamstring injury early and a quadriceps injury late limited him to 76 games in a stop-and-start year at Double-A Bowie.

SCOUTING REPORT: Diaz has been trying to find a swing path that best utilizes his plus bat speed since turning pro. He's found success closing his stance and standing closer to home plate to cover more of the plate, but he's still prone to selling out for pull power. He produces with runners in scoring position and will take a walk. Overall, he projects as an above-average hitter with 20-home run power. Diaz is capable of filling in at center field but is best in right field, where his average speed and plus arm profile. His in-game habits and overall instincts are inconsistent, but his pregame work draws praise from coaches.

THE FUTURE: Diaz has the tools to be an above-average everyday player, but hasn't consistently shown the production for it. He'll start 2020 at Triple-A Norfolk and will be in position to make his big league debut.

SCOUTING GRADES: **Hitting:** 55 **Power:** 50 **Running:** 50 **Fielding:** 50 **Arm:** 60

Year	Age	Club (League)	Class	AVG	G	AB	R	H	2B	3B	HR	RBI	BB	SO	SB	OBP	SLG
2017	20	R. Cucamonga (CAL)	HiA	.278	83	331	42	92	15	3	8	39	35	73	7	.343	.414
	20	Tulsa (TL)	AA	.333	31	108	15	36	8	0	3	13	10	29	2	.390	.491
2018	21	Tulsa (TL)	AA	.314	59	220	36	69	10	4	6	30	41	39	8	.428	.477
	21	Bowie (EL)	AA	.239	38	134	23	32	5	1	5	15	18	28	4	.329	.403
2019	22	Frederick (CAR)	HiA	.273	6	22	0	6	0	0	0	2	3	7	0	.360	.273
	22	Aberdeen (NYP)	SS	.333	3	9	0	3	3	0	0	0	1	1	0	.455	.667
	22	Bowie (EL)	AA	.262	76	286	45	75	19	4	11	53	32	67	0	.335	.472
Minor League Totals				.278	381	1440	210	401	68	19	42	209	169	318	28	.355	.440

7 GUNNAR HENDERSON, SS

Born: June 29, 2001. **B-T:** L-R. **HT:** 6-3. **WT:** 195. **Drafted:** HS—Selma, Ala., 2019 (2nd round)**. Signed by:** David Jennings.

BA GRADE
55 **Risk: Extreme**

TRACK RECORD: Alabama's reigning Mr. Baseball also averaged a double-double on the basketball court as a senior. The Orioles made him the first pick of the second round and signed him away from an Auburn commitment for $2.3 million. Henderson debuted slowly in the Rookie-level Gulf Coast League while adjusting to professional velocity on a daily basis, but he settled in to the Orioles' liking in August.

SCOUTING REPORT: The Orioles have taken three prep shortstops on the first day of the draft in the last five years—Ryan Mountcastle, Adam Hall and Henderson—and it's the prolific offensive profile of Mountcastle that Henderson most closely resembles, albeit from the left side of the plate. Henderson has the bat speed and swing control to be an above-average hitter, and the Orioles saw plus raw power during his senior spring they believe he can eventually tap into. Henderson has a plus arm and the defensive actions to stay on the left side of the infield. If he outgrows shortstop with his projectable frame, he has the range, quickness and hands for third base.

THE FUTURE: Henderson's offensive abilities alone give him a chance to become an above-average everyday player. He is set to begin 2020 at low Class A Delmarva.

SCOUTING GRADES: **Hitting:** 55 **Power:** 55 **Running:** 50 **Fielding:** 50 **Arm:** 60

Year	Age	Club (League)	Class	AVG	G	AB	R	H	2B	3B	HR	RBI	BB	SO	SB	OBP	SLG
2019	18	Orioles (GCL)	R	.259	29	108	21	28	5	2	1	11	11	28	2	.331	.370
Minor League Totals				.259	29	108	21	28	5	2	1	11	11	28	2	.331	.370

8 HUNTER HARVEY, RHP

Born: Dec. 9, 1994. **B-T:** R-R. **HT:** 6-3 WT: 175. **Drafted:** HS—Catawba, N.C., 2013 (1st round). **Signed by:** Chris Gale.

BA GRADE

50 Risk: High

TRACK RECORD: When the Orioles drafted Dylan Bundy, Kevin Gausman, and Hunter Harvey in the first round in three consecutive years, the trio was meant to be the foundation of their rotation. Harvey was spectacular in 2014, but he had Tommy John surgery in 2016 after two years of elbow soreness and made just nine starts in 2018 due to a shoulder injury. Fully healthy in 2019, he started in the Double-A rotation before moving to the pen and shooting to Baltimore.

SCOUTING REPORT: Armed with a fastball that sat 97-99 mph and bumped 100 in his new relief role, Harvey increasingly looks the part of a closer, like his all-star father Bryan. Harvey backs up his four-seamer with an above-average splitter like his father used, and he also has an above-average power curveball at 84-85 mph with good shape. Harvey's cross-body delivery still gives some observers pause and limits his control to average, at best. He has significantly filled out his frame, but his injury history affects his durability and likelihood of him ever starting. He has yet to show he can work back-to-back days regularly (he only did it once last year).

THE FUTURE: Harvey's major league cameo made it clear he can be a late-inning reliever and possible closer for the Orioles. He'll be back in 2021 pitching in late relief as long as his health allows.

SCOUTING GRADES:	Fastball: 70	Splitter: 60	Curveball: 55	Control: 50

Year	Age	Club (League)	Class	W	L	ERA	G	GS	SV	IP	H	HR	BB	SO	K/9	WHIP	AVG
2017	22	Orioles (GCL)	R	0	0	0.00	3	3	0	5	6	0	0	6	10.8	1.20	.300
	22	Aberdeen (NYP)	SS	0	0	0.00	2	2	0	5	1	0	3	10	18.0	0.80	.063
	22	Delmarva (SAL)	LoA	0	1	2.08	3	3	0	9	4	0	3	14	14.5	0.81	.133
2018	23	Bowie (EL)	AA	1	2	5.57	9	9	0	32	36	3	9	30	8.4	1.39	.290
2019	24	Bowie (EL)	AA	2	5	5.19	14	11	1	59	63	14	21	61	9.3	1.42	.274
	24	Norfolk (IL)	AAA	1	1	4.32	12	0	0	17	13	2	5	22	11.9	1.08	.206
	24	Baltimore (AL)	MAJ	1	0	1.42	7	0	0	6	3	1	4	11	15.6	1.11	.136
Major League Totals				1	0	1.42	7	0	0	6	3	1	4	11	15.6	1.11	.136
Minor League Totals				11	16	3.67	73	58	1	252	222	24	86	300	10.7	1.22	.236

9 KEEGAN AKIN, LHP

Born: April 1, 1995. **B-T:** L-L. **HT:** 6-0. **WT:** 225. **Drafted:** Western Michigan, 2016 (2nd round). **Signed by:** Dan Durst.

TRACK RECORD: Rare are the instances when one shares his organization's minor league pitcher of the year award, as Akin did in 2018, and follows it up with a purely developmental year in Triple-A. But that's what Akin did in 2019, when he was named an International League all-star and worked on the Orioles' mandate to get away from his fastball and feature his slider and changeup more heavily. He ended up with a career high strikeout rate (10.5), but also set a career high with 4.9 walks per nine innings.

SCOUTING REPORT: The owner of an "invisi-ball" 90-94 mph fastball that jumps on hitters to draw late swings, Akin spent most of the season working on his low-80s slider and changeup. Both have the potential to be average to slightly above-average pitches that will play off his deceptive fastball. Akin works quickly with a simple, low-effort delivery, giving the impression his pitches may play up in the bullpen. His control regressed in 2019 as he worked on his secondaries, but he has shown average control in the past. Of greater concern is Akin's husky body, which he will have to watch carefully to maintain balance and durability.

THE FUTURE: Akin will be in major league camp for the first time in 2020. He figures to be a rotation piece for the Orioles through their rebuild as a back-of-the-rotation starter.

SCOUTING GRADES:	Fastball: 55	Slider: 55	Changeup: 50	Control: 50

Year	Age	Club (League)	Class	W	L	ERA	G	GS	SV	IP	H	HR	BB	SO	K/9	WHIP	AVG
2017	22	Frederick (CAR)	HiA	7	8	4.14	21	21	0	100	89	12	46	111	10.0	1.35	.240
2018	23	Bowie (EL)	AA	14	7	3.27	25	25	0	138	114	16	58	142	9.3	1.25	.225
2019	24	Norfolk (IL)	AAA	6	7	4.73	25	24	0	112	109	10	61	131	10.5	1.51	.252
Minor League Totals				27	23	3.78	80	79	0	376	327	38	172	413	9.9	1.33	.233

10 MIKE BAUMANN, RHP

Born: Sept. 10, 1995. **B-T:** R-R. **HT:** 6-4. **WT:** 225. **Drafted:** Jacksonville, 2017 (3rd round). **Signed by:** Arthur McConnehead.

BA GRADE **50** Risk: High

TRACK RECORD: Each of Baumann's first two full seasons have included swift promotions, but the difference in 2019 was how things improved for him at his new level. Baumann pitched well at high Class A Frederick upon his promotion in 2018 and to start 2019, but he found another gear at Double-A Bowie in the second half. He threw a no-hitter on July 16 and anchored Bowie's playoff rotation on its playoff run, sharing the Orioles' minor league pitcher of the year award with Grayson Rodriguez.

SCOUTING REPORT: While consistency has at times eluded Baumann, he is a good strike-thrower who was one of the primary beneficiaries of the team's new pitching development program and saw strides with all four pitches. His four-seam fastball has good spin and explodes on hitters, sitting 93-96 mph and reaching 99. His above-average slider at 88-89 mph has cutter action and sharp bite, while his high-spin curveball and split-changeup each flash average potential. Baumann goes deep in his delivery, which impacts the consistent shape of his pitches and limits his control to average.

THE FUTURE: Baumann might have the biggest arm of any potential starter in the organization, but has to improve his control and find a consistent third pitch to reach his mid-rotation ceiling. He should see Triple-A Norfolk at some point in 2020.

SCOUTING GRADES: **Fastball:** 60 **Curveball:** 55 **Slider:** 50 **Changeup:** 50 **Control:** 50

Year	Age	Club (League)	Class	W	L	ERA	G	GS	SV	IP	H	HR	BB	SO	K/9	WHIP	AVG
2017	21	Orioles (GCL)	R	0	0	0.00	1	1	0	1	2	0	0	2	18.0	2.00	.400
	21	Aberdeen (NYP)	SS	4	2	1.31	10	9	0	41	25	2	19	41	8.9	1.06	.168
2018	22	Delmarva (SAL)	LoA	5	0	1.42	7	7	0	38	23	0	13	47	11.1	0.95	.180
	22	Frederick (CAR)	HiA	8	5	3.88	17	17	0	93	82	9	40	59	5.7	1.32	.238
2019	23	Frederick (CAR)	HiA	1	4	3.83	11	11	0	54	40	2	24	77	12.8	1.19	.203
	23	Bowie (EL)	AA	6	2	2.31	13	11	1	70	45	2	21	65	8.4	0.94	.186
Minor League Totals				24	13	2.82	59	56	1	297	217	15	117	291	8.8	1.12	.204

11 DEAN KREMER, RHP

Born: Jan. 7, 1996. **B-T:** R-R. **HT:** 6-3. **WT:** 180. **Drafted:** Nevada-Las Vegas, 2016 (14th round). **Signed by:** Brian Compton (Dodgers).

BA GRADE **50** Risk: High

TRACK RECORD: Kremer wasn't highly touted out of either high school or college, but work with the Dodgers' analytics staff made him a breakout player in 2018 and helped him lead the minors in strikeouts that year. Los Angeles traded him to the Orioles at the 2018 trade deadline as part of the return for Manny Machado. An oblique strain made his spring training invite moot, and forced him to miss the start of the season, but wasn't ultimately a hindrance.

SCOUTING REPORT: Kremer is a fearless pitcher who uses all four pitches and has an idea of when to use them to his advantage, He misses bats with a high-spin four-seam fastball that sits 91-95 mph and a plus curveball in the mid-70s. His slider and changeup lag behind that, but he saw progress on the former as the season progressed. Both could be average pitches that play up based on his intelligent usage. Kremer uses solid-average command to attack all parts of the plate, especially inside.

THE FUTURE: Kremer will return to Triple-A Norfolk to continue his fine-tuning for a possible future as a mid-rotation starter for the Orioles. He could be one of the first starters in their first wave of young pitching to join the rotation in 2019.

Year	Age	Club (League)	Class	W	L	ERA	G	GS	SV	IP	H	HR	BB	SO	K/9	WHIP	AVG
2017	21	R. Cucamonga (CAL)	HiA	1	4	5.18	33	6	3	80	86	6	34	96	10.8	1.50	.274
2018	22	R. Cucamonga (CAL)	HiA	5	3	3.30	16	16	0	79	67	7	26	114	13.0	1.18	.230
	22	Tulsa (TL)	AA	1	0	0.00	1	1	0	7	3	0	3	11	14.1	0.86	.130
	22	Bowie (EL)	AA	4	2	2.58	8	8	0	45	38	3	17	53	10.5	1.21	.228
2019	23	Frederick (CAR)	HiA	0	0	0.00	2	2	0	10	6	0	4	14	13.0	1.03	.177
	23	Bowie (EL)	AA	9	4	2.98	15	15	0	85	75	9	29	87	9.2	1.23	.239
	23	Norfolk (IL)	AAA	0	2	8.84	4	4	0	19	30	2	4	21	9.8	1.76	.366
Minor League Totals				22	16	3.61	91	58	3	356	324	27	124	431	10.9	1.26	.243

12 ZAC LOWTHER, LHP

BA GRADE **50** Risk: High

Born: April 30, 1996. **B-T:** L-L. **HT:** 6-2. **WT:** 235. **Drafted:** Xavier, 2017 (2nd round supplemental). **Signed by:** Adrian Dorsey.

TRACK RECORD: All Lowther did to follow up the Orioles' minor league pitcher of the year award he earned in his first full season in 2018 was nearly repeat in 2019, leading the organization and Eastern League with 13 wins and 154 strikeouts while earning an all-star nod.

SCOUTING REPORT: With elite extension out of a simple delivery, Lowther's fastball plays up from its 88-91 mph velocity and is difficult for hitters to square up in the zone. Without a plus secondary pitch—though his changeup flashes that more than his future-average, high-spin curveball—a pitcher like Lowther requires pitchability, deception and an ability to pitch to all quadrants with his fastball. Lowther has that, though he's liable to lose his command for spells.

THE FUTURE: Whether Lowther can remain in the rotation in the major leagues will depend on his ability to develop consistency with his command and secondary pitches. But even for this style of pitcher who needs to prove it all the way, Lowther has. He'll get his first crack at Triple-A Norfolk in 2020 to further prove that.

Year	Age	Club (League)	Class	W	L	ERA	G	GS	SV	IP	H	HR	BB	SO	K/9	WHIP	AVG
2017	21	Aberdeen (NYP)	SS	2	2	1.66	12	11	0	54	35	1	11	75	12.4	0.85	.182
2018	22	Delmarva (SAL)	LoA	3	1	1.16	6	6	0	31	12	2	9	51	14.8	0.68	.115
	22	Frederick (CAR)	HiA	5	3	2.53	17	16	0	93	74	6	26	100	9.7	1.08	.220
2019	23	Bowie (EL)	AA	13	7	2.55	26	26	0	148	102	8	63	154	9.4	1.11	.197
Minor League Totals				23	13	2.26	61	59	0	326	223	17	109	380	10.5	1.02	.194

13 ADAM HALL, SS/2B

BA GRADE **50** Risk: High

Born: May 22, 1999. **B-T:** R-R. **HT:** 6-0. **WT:** 170. **Drafted:** HS—London, Ont., 2017 (2nd round). **Signed by:** Chris Reitsma.

TRACK RECORD: It wasn't even a given that Hall, signed for an above-slot $1.3 million after impressing in the Canadian National Team program, would break extended spring training with an affiliate in 2018. But he really came on at short-season Aberdeen, and was the most consistent hitter on a 90-win low Class A Delmarva club in 2019, when he was a South Atlantic League all-star.

SCOUTING REPORT: While the only true plus tool Hall features is his speed, he spent 2019 showing he can do almost everything well for his age. He has a line-drive swing with gap power and the ability to create extra bases with his legs, with average hit potential and fringy power if he fills out. While his defensive actions at shortstop were considered a little raw, Hall can handle the position, and has a chance to be at least an average defender up the middle. Some even see some outfield potential in his future.

THE FUTURE: Players with Hall's skill set and makeup always have a place on a major league roster, and there's nothing stopping him in the Orioles' system from being an average everyday infielder. A trip to high Class A Frederick in 2020 awaits.

Year	Age	Club (League)	Class	AVG	G	AB	R	H	2B	3B	HR	RBI	BB	SO	SB	OBP	SLG
2017	18	Orioles (GCL)	R	.667	2	9	4	6	1	1	0	2	0	2	1	.667	1.000
2018	19	Aberdeen (NYP)	SS	.293	62	222	35	65	9	3	1	24	17	58	22	.368	.374
2019	20	Delmarva (SAL)	LoA	.298	122	463	78	138	22	4	5	45	45	117	33	.385	.395
Minor League Totals				.301	186	694	117	209	32	8	6	71	62	177	56	.382	.396

14 ALEX WELLS, LHP

BA GRADE **45** Risk: Medium

Born: Feb. 27, 1997. **B-T:** L-L. **HT:** 6-1. **WT:** 190. **Signed:** Australia, 2015. **Signed by:** Brett Ward/Mike Snyder.

TRACK RECORD: For the fourth season of his four professional seasons, Wells made his league's all-star game in 2019, this time in the Double-A Eastern League. He did so by posting a walk rate of 1.6 per nine innings and limiting hard contact.

SCOUTING REPORT: Wells' velocity has remained consistent, living in the 88-91 mph range. He has an aptitude for pitching in on the hands to both lefthanded and righthanded batters. He also was back to showing the plus command that evaded him a season ago. Hitters have no choice but to swing when Wells lives in the strike zone, and often look bad doing it. Still, there's not much projection left, and while he's flashed an above-average changeup and curveball, neither pitch has taken a major step forward. Wells is looking to further diversify with a slider. His flyball rate could portend issues should the lively ball live on, but he's avoided home runs at an astonishing rate in his career.

THE FUTURE: Wells has always had to prove it at every stop, and his likely assignment to Triple-A Norfolk in 2020 will be all that's left before he gets a shot to be a back-end starter or swingman in the majors.

Year	Age	Club (League)	Class	W	L	ERA	G	GS	SV	IP	H	HR	BB	SO	K/9	WHIP	AVG
2017	20	Delmarva (SAL)	LoA	11	5	2.38	25	25	0	140	118	16	10	113	7.3	0.91	.222
2018	21	Frederick (CAR)	HiA	7	8	3.47	24	24	0	135	142	19	33	101	6.7	1.30	.270
2019	22	Bowie (EL)	AA	8	6	2.95	24	24	0	137	123	10	24	105	6.9	1.07	.236
Minor League Totals				30	24	2.82	86	86	0	475	431	46	76	369	7.0	1.07	.239

15 DREW ROM, LHP

BA GRADE 50 Risk: High

Born: Dec. 15, 1999. **B-T:** L-L. **HT:** 6-2. **WT:** 170. **Drafted:** HS—Fort Thomas, Ky., 2018 (4th round). **Signed by:** Adrian Dorsey.

TRACK RECORD: Kentucky's Mr. Baseball in 2018 signed for an above-slot bonus of $650,000 and made a sparkling debut at age 19 in the low Class A South Atlantic League. He was a midseason all-star and one of five teenage pitchers in full-season ball to strike out more than 11 batters per nine innings with 11.5.

SCOUTING REPORT: The projectable but slight lefthander pitches with a fastball that ranges 88-92 mph, depending on the day. His changeup, curveball and slider aren't putaway pitches, but along with future-average command of his entire arsenal, there's hope within the Orioles' pitching system that one can emerge as a plus pitch in a group of offerings that currently has average potential. His ability to minimize hard contact and manipulate the ball, plus the fact he has a low-effort delivery with room to grow, allows plenty of room to dream.

THE FUTURE: Rom's growth into a back-end starter will hinge on the continued development of his secondary pitches and consistent command. That process will continue at high Class A Frederick in 2020.

Year	Age	Club (League)	Class	W	L	ERA	G	GS	SV	IP	H	HR	BB	SO	K/9	WHIP	AVG
2018	18	Orioles (GCL)	R	0	2	1.76	10	9	0	31	20	1	6	28	8.2	0.85	.183
2019	19	Delmarva (SAL)	LoA	6	3	2.93	21	15	1	95	83	5	33	122	11.5	1.22	.228
Minor League Totals				6	5	2.64	31	24	1	126	103	6	39	150	10.7	1.13	.218

16 BRUCE ZIMMERMANN, LHP

BA GRADE 45 Risk: Medium

Born: Feb. 9, 1995. **B-T:** L-L. **HT:** 6-2. **WT:** 215. **Drafted:** Mount Olive (N.C.), 2017 (5th round). **Signed by:** Billy Best (Braves).

TRACK RECORD: Zimmermann left his deep local roots as a Baltimore native who went to Towson University when that school threatened to cut baseball, but he signed as a senior for $10,000 with the Braves. He was already in Double-A in his first full season when he ended up back home as part of the July 2018 trade that sent Kevin Gausman and Darren O'Day to Atlanta.

SCOUTING REPORT: In a loaded Double-A Bowie rotation in 2019, Zimmermann was regarded by teammates as the toughest of the bunch. With a fastball that sits 90-93 mph but still misses bats, he is able to get hitters off balance with a solid-average changeup in the mid-80s and a curveball in the mid-70s. He has a slider that he'll throw to either side and get swinging strikes at 84-86 mph from a clean, repeatable delivery.

THE FUTURE: Zimmermann will be 25 when he begins 2020 at Triple-A Norfolk, but will get another chance to prove he has a No. 5 starter ceiling, even if there's some thought his stuff could tick up in a relief role.

Year	Age	Club (League)	Class	W	L	ERA	G	GS	SV	IP	H	HR	BB	SO	K/9	WHIP	AVG
2017	22	Danville (APP)	R	0	1	3.09	11	11	0	23	21	0	9	28	10.8	1.29	.244
2018	23	Rome (SAL)	LoA	7	3	2.76	14	14	0	85	74	5	18	99	10.5	1.09	.233
	23	Mississippi (SL)	AA	2	1	3.14	6	6	0	29	25	3	19	26	8.2	1.53	.243
	23	Bowie (EL)	AA	2	3	5.06	5	5	0	21	25	2	7	16	6.8	1.50	.287
2019	24	Bowie (EL)	AA	5	3	2.58	18	17	0	101	88	9	34	101	9.0	1.20	.227
	24	Norfolk (IL)	AAA	2	3	4.89	7	7	0	39	44	3	18	33	7.7	1.60	.291
Minor League Totals				18	14	3.20	61	60	0	298	277	22	105	303	9.2	1.28	.245

17 RYAN McKENNA, OF

BA GRADE 45 Risk: Medium

Born: Feb. 14, 1997. **B-T:** R-R. **HT:** 5-11. **WT:** 185. **Drafted:** HS—Dover, N.H., 2015 (4th round). **Signed by:** Kirk Fredriksson.

TRACK RECORD: What was always meant to be a slow and steady development for the New Hampshire native, as he competed with players who got in far more baseball than he could in New England, was jolted forward when he broke out in an all-star campaign at high Class A Frederick in 2018. A season at Double-A Bowie, however, has knocked some of that shine off.

SCOUTING REPORT: As far as carrying tools, the book on McKenna remains the same: he's a plus runner with at least an above-average arm who can steal a base and play center field. He also has an eye, but he got away from the all-fields, line-drive approach that best suits him in favor of a fly ball happy swing in 2019. This left a larger gap than previously existed between his average-hit ceiling with fringe power and the current reality.

THE FUTURE: McKenna's floor, given his defense and speed, was always as a bench outfielder. His 2019 season brought questions as to whether his ceiling would be as a part-time player as well. He might be asked to start the season at Double-A Bowie again before moving to Triple-A Norfolk in 2020.

Year	Age	Club (League)	Class	AVG	G	AB	R	H	2B	3B	HR	RBI	BB	SO	SB	OBP	SLG
2017	20	Delmarva (SAL)	LoA	.256	126	468	62	120	33	2	7	42	43	128	20	.331	.380
2018	21	Frederick (CAR)	HiA	.377	67	257	60	97	18	2	8	37	37	45	5	.467	.556
	21	Bowie (EL)	AA	.239	60	213	35	51	8	2	3	16	29	56	4	.341	.338
2019	22	Bowie (EL)	AA	.232	135	488	78	113	26	6	9	54	59	121	25	.321	.365
Minor League Totals				.264	460	1680	269	443	95	14	28	178	196	415	72	.350	.387

18 KYLE STOWERS, OF

BA GRADE
50 **Risk: High**

Born: Jan. 2, 1998 **B-T:** L-L. **HT:** 6-3. **WT:** 200. **Drafted:** Stanford, 2019 (2nd round supplemental). **Signed by:** Scott Walter.

TRACK RECORD: Stowers signed for $884,200 on the strength of a few powerful seasons at Stanford. His professional debut at short-season Aberdeen earned him an all-star nod.

SCOUTING REPORT: Premium lefthanded power potential drew the Orioles to Stowers, though it's accompanied by the inevitable swing-and-miss concerns and questions about the hit tool that often come with such raw power. The way he slashed his strikeout rate as a junior gives the team hope there's more of that to come. When he puts the ball in play, it's consistent hard contact that rated in the top 5 percent of college hitters in terms of exit velocity. Even an average hit tool, with that kind of power, will make for a premium corner bat, with the ability to fill in with average center field defense.

THE FUTURE: Stowers has the type of bat and draft pedigree to grow into one of the top-flight bats in the organization and push for an everyday spot as an average regular, should the strikeouts stay down. A full-season assignment to low Class A Delmarva should begin his journey in 2020.

Year	Age	Club (League)	Class	AVG	G	AB	R	H	2B	3B	HR	RBI	BB	SO	SB	OBP	SLG
2019	21	Aberdeen (NYP)	SS	.216	55	204	19	44	13	1	6	23	20	53	5	.289	.377
Minor League Totals				.216	55	204	19	44	13	1	6	23	20	53	5	.289	.377

19 ZACH WATSON, OF

BA GRADE
45 **Risk: High**

Born: June 25, 1997. **B-T:** R-R. **HT:** 6-0. **WT:** 160. **Drafted:** Louisiana State, 2019 (3rd round). **Signed by:** David Jennings.

TRACK RECORD: A Freshman All-American and three-year starter at Louisiana State, Watson was a popular draft-eligible sophomore in 2018, but he stayed an extra year and signed for slot at $780,400 as the first pick of the 2019 draft's second day. He jumped from short-season Aberdeen to low Class A Delmarva after a few weeks, but a mid-August wrist injury ended his season early.

SCOUTING REPORT: The game's current emphasis on power hasn't left much room for players like Watson, who despite some pop this summer projects to be a contact hitter who can run his way to extra bases. The Orioles were sold on an ability to play at least above-average defense in center field thanks to a quick first step and his reads off the bat. As a high-effort player who can cause havoc atop the lineup with at least plus speed, the production will be a result of his motor as much as his tools.

THE FUTURE: Watson's defense and speed give him an easy bench outfielder floor, but if his bat comes around, he will provide a fringe everyday package. A return to Delmarva will allow for a chance to begin that process in 2020.

Year	Age	Club (League)	Class	AVG	G	AB	R	H	2B	3B	HR	RBI	BB	SO	SB	OBP	SLG
2019	22	Aberdeen (NYP)	SS	.232	20	56	17	13	4	0	2	9	4	17	5	.295	.411
	22	Delmarva (SAL)	LoA	.217	16	60	9	13	5	0	3	8	6	13	0	.294	.450
Minor League Totals				.224	36	116	26	26	9	0	5	17	10	30	5	.295	.431

20 CODY SEDLOCK, RHP

BA GRADE
45 **Risk: High**

Born: June 19,1994. **B-T:** R-R. **HT:** 6-3. **WT:** 190. **Drafted:** Illinois, 2016 (1st round). **Signed by:** Dan Durst.

TRACK RECORD: Plenty has changed since the Orioles made Sedlock their top pick in 2016 and touted him as a future four-pitch horse in the rotation, but at least he's back on the mound. Sedlock struggled with a forearm issue in 2017 and a shoulder issue related to thoracic outlet syndrome in 2018 before a

return to health meant a return to form and a high Class A Carolina League all-star appearance in 2019.
SCOUTING REPORT: A change in approach from a two-seam heavy plan to using a four-seam fastball and mixing his pitches more helped Sedlock get back on track. He missed bats in the zone with his 90-93 mph fastball. His 81-83 mph changeup showed consistent fade and flashed plus, and his slider ticked up as well. Sedlock's delivery has never been smooth, but the Orioles are letting him work with what feels best for him and have overall unlocked a pitcher much closer to his draft pedigree.
THE FUTURE: A healthy 2019 got Sedlock to Double-A Bowie, where he'll likely continue to build his innings en route to a No. 5 starter or middle relief role in 2020.

Year	Age	Club (League)	Class	W	L	ERA	G	GS	SV	IP	H	HR	BB	SO	K/9	WHIP	AVG
2017	22	Frederick (CAR)	HiA	4	5	5.90	20	20	0	90	119	11	36	69	6.9	1.72	.313
2018	23	Orioles (GCL)	R	0	0	0.93	5	1	0	10	5	0	4	10	9.3	0.93	.161
	23	Aberdeen (NYP)	SS	0	1	2.57	2	2	0	7	6	0	2	5	6.4	1.14	.250
	23	Frederick (CAR)	HiA	0	2	7.97	6	6	0	20	27	3	12	13	5.8	1.92	.325
2019	24	Frederick (CAR)	HiA	4	1	2.36	13	10	0	61	38	4	26	66	9.7	1.05	.181
	24	Bowie (EL)	AA	1	2	3.71	9	6	1	34	30	3	20	34	9.0	1.47	.238
Minor League Totals				9	12	4.30	64	54	1	249	241	22	113	222	8.0	1.42	.252

21 GRAY FENTER, RHP

BA GRADE
45 **Risk: High**

Born: Jan. 25, 1996. **B-T:** R-R. **HT:** 6-0. **WT:** 200. **Drafted:** HS—West Memphis, Ark., 2015 (7th round). **Signed by:** Mike Boulanger/Nathan Showalter.
TRACK RECORD: A $1 million signee whose progress was stunted in 2016 when he had Tommy John surgery, Fenter's return to low Class A Delmarva in 2019 went far better than the previous year. He saw his strikeout rate climb to 11.7 per nine innings during the successful campaign.
SCOUTING REPORT: Fenter attracted attention in high school for his 96-97 mph fastball, but two years back from surgery, he was sitting 90-94 mph with significant rising action up in the zone. His primary pitch was always a 77-80 mph curveball that had above-average traits, but he added a slider in 2019 that flashed plus. Fenter has a maxed-out frame that doesn't lend itself to much projection, but he repeated his delivery well during the season.
THE FUTURE: The Orioles wanted Fenter to get a full season finished before moving him up. He'll be old (24) for the level at high Class A Frederick in 2020, where he'll begin in the rotation. But if the Orioles take him off the back-end starter track, he could quickly work into a major league middle relief role.

Year	Age	Club (League)	Class	W	L	ERA	G	GS	SV	IP	H	HR	BB	SO	K/9	WHIP	AVG
2017	21	Orioles (GCL)	R	0	1	3.45	11	11	0	29	17	0	10	33	10.4	0.94	.172
	21	Aberdeen (NYP)	SS	0	0	16.20	1	0	0	2	3	1	0	1	5.4	1.80	.375
2018	22	Delmarva (SAL)	LoA	3	3	6.75	14	2	0	27	31	2	13	31	10.5	1.65	.292
	22	Aberdeen (NYP)	SS	5	3	3.95	13	11	0	57	41	5	25	60	9.5	1.16	.200
2019	23	Delmarva (SAL)	LoA	8	2	1.81	22	17	0	94	61	4	43	123	11.7	1.10	.185
Minor League Totals				16	9	3.21	70	49	0	230	168	12	97	266	10.4	1.15	.204

22 BLAINE KNIGHT, RHP

BA GRADE
45 **Risk: High**

Born: June 28, 1996. **B-T:** R-R. **HT:** 6-3. **WT:** 165. **Drafted:** Arkansas, 2018 (3rd round). **Signed by:** Ken Guthrie.
TRACK RECORD: Knight was an All-American atop the Arkansas rotation who outdueled every top pitcher in the country as a junior and helped the Razorbacks to the College World Series before signing for an above-slot $1.1 million. He pitched like the experienced college arm he was at low Class A Delmarva to start the year before he lost his command and struggled to put hitters away later in the season.
SCOUTING REPORT: Knight came to the Orioles with elite spin rate on his slider and curveball, but the utility of those pitches came into question in 2019. Below-average command of those pitches undercut what could be above-average shape and movement on them, and while there's some life on his 91-94 mph fastball, he got into fastball counts and couldn't get it past hitters. Knight had no such problems in college and showed he was durable despite his slight frame. He came through a difficult year with quiet confidence.
THE FUTURE: Despite his struggles, Knight's potential for three above-average pitches if he irons out his command makes him a candidate to be at least a No. 5 starter and potentially better, though he may return to high Class A Frederick in 2020 to check that level off.

Year	Age	Club (League)	Class	W	L	ERA	G	GS	SV	IP	H	HR	BB	SO	K/9	WHIP	AVG
2018	22	Aberdeen (NYP)	SS	0	1	2.61	4	4	0	10	13	1	3	8	7.0	1.55	.302
2019	23	Delmarva (SAL)	LoA	3	0	0.68	5	5	0	27	11	1	4	33	11.1	0.56	.125
	23	Frederick (CAR)	HiA	1	12	6.13	18	17	0	84	89	10	39	56	6.0	1.53	.273
Minor League Totals				4	13	4.62	27	26	0	120	113	12	46	97	7.2	1.32	.247

23 BRENAN HANIFEE, RHP

BA GRADE 45 Risk: High

Born: May 29, 1998. **B-T:** R-R. **HT:** 6-5. **WT:** 180. **Drafted:** HS—Bridgewater, Va., 2016 (4th round). **Signed by:** Rich Morales.

TRACK RECORD: If Hanifee's first full season at low Class A Delmarva in 2018 was evocative of a past generation's mantra of sinkers at the knees and efficiency over all else, his follow-up at high Class A Frederick showed how the new Orioles' regime doesn't think that's enough.

SCOUTING REPORT: Routinely 90-93 mph at the knees with sinking action, Hanifee's fastball is still his best pitch. He relied on it too much in 2018, so the Orioles' new pitching model emphasized his offspeed pitches more. He still got weak contact and ground balls, but the new mandates easily explain the jump in walk rate from 1.5 per nine innings to nearly four. He threw his 80-82 mph slider and 85-86 mph changeup more often, with his slider showing above-average potential, though it wasn't consistent. His changeup is coming along.

THE FUTURE: Hanifee's overall profile isn't one that fits well with the Orioles' spin-centric pitching philosophy, but he has plenty of fans around the game. His sinker and relative youth will keep him on a starter's path toward the back-end of a major league rotation. A Double-A Bowie assignment in 2020 would show they like the progress he's made.

Year	Age	Club (League)	Class	W	L	ERA	G	GS	SV	IP	H	HR	BB	SO	K/9	WHIP	AVG
2017	19	Aberdeen (NYP)	SS	7	3	2.75	12	12	0	69	65	2	12	44	5.8	1.12	.249
2018	20	Delmarva (SAL)	LoA	8	6	2.86	23	23	0	132	120	8	22	85	5.8	1.08	.244
2019	21	Frederick (CAR)	HiA	9	10	4.60	24	22	0	129	126	12	57	78	5.4	1.42	.259
Minor League Totals				24	19	3.52	59	57	0	329	311	22	91	207	5.7	1.22	.251

24 CADYN GRENIER, SS

BA GRADE 45 Risk: High

Born: Oct. 31, 1996. **B-T:** R-R. **HT:** 5-11. **WT:** 188. **Drafted:** Oregon State, 2018 (2nd round). **Signed by:** Brandon Verley.

TRACK RECORD: A fixture up the middle on Oregon State's College World Series winner with fellow Orioles draftee Adley Rutschman and a host of other stars, Grenier was the Brooks Wallace Award winner as the best shortstop in the country in 2018 before signing with the Orioles and going right to low Class A Delmarva. He spent most of 2019 back there before an August promotion, but he struck out an alarming 30.3 percent of the time over the two levels.

SCOUTING REPORT: No one questions Grenier's defensive abilities. He has the hands, range and arm to be an average shortstop and an even better second baseman. Even with that defensive aptitude as a backdrop and a lower offensive profile required for that, Grenier may struggle to hit enough for it to play in the majors. His swing can be long and susceptible to spin, though he has a good understanding of the strike zone and shows the ability to work a walk.

THE FUTURE: Grenier's capabilities to impact a baseball will be what dictates whether he gets the chance to play defense off a major league bench, and his quest to improve that will continue at high Class A Frederick.

Year	Age	Club (League)	Class	AVG	G	AB	R	H	2B	3B	HR	RBI	BB	SO	SB	OBP	SLG
2018	21	Delmarva (SAL)	LoA	.216	43	162	23	35	12	2	1	13	17	53	3	.297	.333
2019	22	Delmarva (SAL)	LoA	.253	82	308	49	78	18	3	7	39	48	107	5	.360	.399
	22	Frederick (CAR)	HiA	.208	24	77	11	16	4	1	1	4	11	31	2	.337	.325
Minor League Totals				.236	149	547	83	129	34	6	9	56	76	191	10	.339	.369

25 DARELL HERNAIZ, SS

BA GRADE 50 Risk: Extreme

Born: Aug. 3, 2001. **B-T:** R-R. **HT:** 6-1. **WT:** 170. **Drafted:** HS—El Paso, 2019 (5th round). **Signed by:** John Gillette.

TRACK RECORD: Hernaiz was still 17 years old when the Orioles drafted and signed him for $400,000 to make him the highest drafted player from El Paso's Americas High and keep him from a longstanding Texas Tech commitment.

SCOUTING REPORT: Plenty of refinement is required for the slight Hernaiz, but there could be an interesting player to grow from his current package. Hernaiz is a great athlete in the middle of the field with the arm for third base if he outgrows shortstop. He displays great energy and zeal for the game. Hernaiz possesses plus bat speed with average raw power, though a flyball rate above 50 percent in his pro debut creates an interesting profile, especially if he grows into game power and those turn into extra-base hits.

THE FUTURE: A young, up-the-middle prep talent at this stage in the draft is irresistible, though it hasn't exactly panned out for the Orioles before. They see at least average, everyday potential in Hernaiz, and more if his power develops. A full-season assignment would be a challenge in 2020 but a worthwhile one.

Year	Age	Club (League)	Class	AVG	G	AB	R	H	2B	3B	HR	RBI	BB	SO	SB	OBP	SLG
2019	17	Orioles (GCL)	R	.263	29	99	19	26	2	1	2	8	17	26	5	.371	.364
Minor League Totals				.263	29	99	19	26	2	1	2	8	17	26	5	.371	.364

26 ZACH POP, RHP

BA GRADE
50 Risk: Extreme

Born: Sept. 20, 1996**. B-T:** R-R. **HT:** 6-4. **WT:** 220. **Drafted:** Kentucky, 2017 (7th round). **Signed by:** Marty Lamb (Dodgers).

TRACK RECORD: Pop was a fast riser after the Dodgers drafted the Canadian righthander in 2017. He climbed three levels in a 2018 season defined by his inclusion in the Manny Machado trade. The Orioles invited him to big league camp in 2019, but he dealt with forearm soreness that limited him to eight appearances and led to Tommy John surgery in May.

SCOUTING REPORT: When healthy, the tall, lanky Pop featured one of the most electric fastballs in the organization at 96-98 mph while topping out at 100 with sinking life from a low arm slot. That, combined with a mid-80s slider, has opponents batting just .173 off him in his career, with two-thirds of pro hitters he's faced either hitting the ball on the ground or striking out.

THE FUTURE: Pop likely won't be back on a mound in game action until midseason 2020 due to the timing of his surgery, but if he finds his form quickly, he could quickly find his way to Baltimore as a medium-leverage reliever.

Year	Age	Club (League)	Class	W	L	ERA	G	GS	SV	IP	H	HR	BB	SO	K/9	WHIP	AVG
2017	20	Dodgers (AZL)	R	0	0	0.00	5	0	0	5	2	0	2	5	9.0	0.80	.125
2018	21	Great Lakes (MWL)	LoA	0	2	2.20	11	0	0	16	12	1	7	24	13.2	1.16	.194
	21	R. Cucamonga (CAL)	HiA	1	0	0.33	19	0	7	27	13	0	6	23	7.7	0.70	.149
	21	Bowie (EL)	AA	1	1	2.53	14	0	1	21	14	0	6	17	7.2	0.94	.189
2019	22	Bowie (EL)	AA	1	0	0.84	8	0	0	11	7	0	4	11	9.3	1.03	.184
Minor League Totals				3	3	1.34	57	0	8	80	48	1	25	80	9.0	0.91	.173

27 DILLON TATE, RHP

BA GRADE
40 Risk: Medium

Born: May 1, 1994. **B-T:** R-R. **HT:** 6-2. **WT:** 195. **Drafted:** UC Santa Barbara, 2015 (1st round). **Signed by:** Todd Guggiana (Rangers).

TRACK RECORD: Two trades and four years after he was selected fourth overall in 2015, Tate made his major league debut with the Orioles in a bullpen role that he had expressed interest in returning to in spring training. As a starter since he signed, Tate struggled to stay healthy and limit big innings. In the bullpen, he found the role less cluttered and was able to just go out and pitch.

SCOUTING REPORT: It helps that those pitches played up significantly when he was able to crank them out of the bullpen. His fastball sat 94-97 mph with sink. His slider got up to 88 mph and his changeup registered in the mid-80s. While the action on all the pitches means they can be above-average, he has struggled to command them consistently.

THE FUTURE: Considering he asked and the Orioles acquiesced to a role change, it's safe to say that's where his future lies. He might not have the putaway pitch to close, but consistency could see him rise to a set-up role with a middle relief floor.

Year	Age	Club (League)	Class	W	L	ERA	G	GS	SV	IP	H	HR	BB	SO	K/9	WHIP	AVG
2017	23	Tampa (FSL)	HiA	6	0	2.62	9	9	0	58	48	4	15	46	7.1	1.08	.221
	23	Trenton (EL)	AA	1	2	3.24	4	4	0	25	23	3	9	17	6.1	1.28	.253
2018	24	Trenton (EL)	AA	5	2	3.38	15	15	0	83	67	7	25	75	8.2	1.11	.218
	24	Bowie (EL)	AA	2	3	5.75	7	7	0	41	48	3	9	21	4.6	1.40	.302
2019	25	Frederick (CAR)	HiA	0	0	5.40	1	1	0	2	3	1	0	3	16.2	1.80	.375
	25	Bowie (EL)	AA	2	3	3.48	17	2	5	34	28	4	9	30	8.0	1.10	.224
	25	Norfolk (IL)	AAA	2	0	2.00	4	0	2	9	7	1	1	7	7.0	0.89	.212
	25	Baltimore (AL)	MAJ	0	2	6.43	16	0	0	21	18	3	9	20	8.6	1.29	.231
Major League Totals				0	2	6.43	16	0	0	21	18	3	9	20	8.6	1.29	.231
Minor League Totals				22	13	3.76	87	60	7	342	326	30	104	277	7.3	1.26	.253

28 MASON MCCOY, SS/2B

BA GRADE
45 Risk: High

Born: June 19,1994. **B-T:** R-R. **HT:** 6-3. **WT:** 190. **Drafted:** Iowa, 2017 (6th round). **Signed by:** Scott Thomas.

TRACK RECORD: A senior signing in 2017 after winning MVP honors of the summer wood bat Northwoods League the previous summer, McCoy earned Eastern League all-star honors with 118 hits by the break —the most in all of minor league ball.

SCOUTING REPORT: Most of McCoy's success was attributable to an opposite-field approach in which he shortened up and hit the ball through the right side against the shift with great success. That mindset, with a low swinging-strike rate, could help him maximize his swing to be a fringe-average hitter with gap power, though there's not much by way of power projection in his future. He's a heady player both at the plate and at shortstop, where he maximizes his range and arm to play average defense. Because he is an average runner, it will be his glove that will carry him closer to the major leagues.

THE FUTURE: McCoy represents the Orioles' closest-to-the-majors shortstop option, even if he would be more of a bench option on a first-division club. Offseason activity may push him back to Double-A Bowie in 2020.

Year	Age	Club (League)	Class	AVG	G	AB	R	H	2B	3B	HR	RBI	BB	SO	SB	OBP	SLG
2017	22	Aberdeen (NYP)	SS	.301	53	186	34	56	11	3	1	29	26	28	4	.382	.409
2018	23	Delmarva (SAL)	LoA	.266	124	482	66	128	18	10	4	47	45	95	13	.331	.369
2019	24	Frederick (CAR)	HiA	.379	27	116	21	44	9	0	2	17	8	16	3	.416	.509
	24	Bowie (EL)	AA	.266	105	429	60	114	13	7	2	31	36	84	10	.326	.343
Minor League Totals				.282	309	1213	181	342	51	20	9	124	115	223	30	.346	.379

29 RYLAN BANNON, 3B

BA GRADE 40 Risk: Medium

Born: April 22, 1996. **B-T:** R-R. **HT:** 5-10. **WT:** 180. **Drafted:** Xavier, 2017 (8th round). **Signed by:** Marty Lamb (Dodgers).

TRACK RECORD: Bannon's full-season debut in 2018 was so impressive that he was named California League MVP for his time at high Class A Rancho Cucamonga despite being traded for Manny Machado in mid-July. He spent most of 2019 at Double-A Bowie, where he was an Eastern League all-star and took advantage of his August promotion to Triple-A Norfolk with 13 extra-base hits in 20 games.

SCOUTING REPORT: After coming to the Orioles with a wide-open stance, Bannon closed it off some but didn't sacrifice much of his power thanks to his strong hands, sturdy lower half and aggressive swing. His 47 extra-base hits were second most in the organization, and he cut down his strikeouts significantly in 2019. Bannon is an above-average runner, and he has the range to play second base and third base, with enough arm for the latter.

THE FUTURE: The lack of shortstop in his profile leaves a gap in Bannon's utility profile, but the possibility of some pop off the bench and defense all over the rest of the field gives him a solid chance at a major league bench role. He'll work toward that at Triple-A Norfolk in 2020.

Year	Age	Club (League)	Class	AVG	G	AB	R	H	2B	3B	HR	RBI	BB	SO	SB	OBP	SLG
2017	21	Ogden (PIO)	R	.336	40	149	39	50	8	0	10	30	19	29	5	.425	.591
2018	22	R. Cucamonga (CAL)	HiA	.296	89	338	58	100	17	6	20	61	59	103	4	.402	.559
	22	Bowie (EL)	AA	.204	32	98	16	20	6	0	2	11	22	24	0	.344	.327
2019	23	Bowie (EL)	AA	.255	110	388	45	99	22	4	8	42	47	72	8	.345	.394
	23	Norfolk (IL)	AAA	.317	20	82	18	26	10	0	3	17	3	14	0	.344	.549
Minor League Totals				.280	291	1055	176	295	63	10	43	161	150	242	17	.375	.481

30 BRANDON BAILEY, RHP

BA GRADE 45 Risk: Very High

Born: Oct. 19, 1994. **B-T:** R-R. **HT:** 5-10. **WT:** 175. **Drafted:** Gonzaga, 2016 (6). **Signed by:** Jim Coffman (Athletics).

TRACK RECORD: Coming into the 2019 season, Bailey Tweeted that only five percent of MLB pitchers are under six-feet tall. He also made it clear that he intended to be part of that five percent. A year later, that goal seems very obtainable. Already traded once (from the A's to the Astros for Ramon Laureano), he was the second pick in the 2019 Rule 5 draft. The Orioles front office, which knew Bailey from their time in Houston, were happy to bring him to Baltimore.

SCOUTING REPORT: Bailey survives and succeeds with solid, but unspectacular stuff. His average 91-94 mph fastball can get some swings and misses when he elevates, and he's consistently shown he can locate it to all four quadrants of the strike zone. That fastball sets up his plus changeup. His competitiveness, clean repeatable delivery and his average control could help him stick with the Orioles.

THE FUTURE: Bailey has a shot to fill a swingman, multi-inning reliever who can spot start for the Orioles. He has a decent shot to stick as a Rule 5 pick.

Year	Age	Club (League)	Class	W	L	ERA	G	GS	SV	IP	H	HR	BB	SO	K/9	WHIP	AVG
2017	22	Beloit (MWL)	LoA	1	1	2.68	15	11	0	57	40	4	21	73	11.5	1.07	.199
	22	Stockton (CAL)	HiA	2	1	4.24	9	6	1	34	28	4	10	47	12.4	1.12	.217
2018	23	Buies Creek (CAR)	HiA	5	8	2.49	20	16	0	98	69	6	43	113	10.4	1.15	.199
	23	Corpus Christi (TL)	AA	1	0	4.01	5	1	1	25	21	5	9	23	8.4	1.22	.221
2019	24	Corpus Christi (TL)	AA	4	5	3.30	22	17	0	93	72	12	41	103	10.0	1.22	.212
Minor League Totals				16	16	3.07	83	58	2	349	263	32	134	405	10.4	1.14	.208

Boston Red Sox

BY ALEX SPEIER

In August 2015, Dave Dombrowski inherited a talent goldmine. The Red Sox organization featured a core of emerging young big league stars and a cresting wave of prospects in the offing. Over the next four seasons, as president of baseball operations, he did with that group exactly what he was tasked with doing. He graduated several players to the big leagues while trading several others to scaffold that young group with veterans who contributed to three straight American League East titles and a 2018 World Series championship.

But in 2019, when the Red Sox slipped while going 84-78 and missing the playoffs for the first time since 2015, the bill for the prospect graduations and trades came due.

Though the upper levels were not barren—the team graduated second baseman Michael Chavis and relievers Josh Taylor and Darwinzon Hernandez—the next cornerstone players had not emerged, at a time when the big league roster was nearing significant change given the nearing free agency and growing cost of key position players.

The decision by Boston to fire Dombrowski in September, and eventually to replace him with Chaim Bloom, previously the senior vice president of baseball operations with the Rays, reflected the changing challenge confronting the organization and the need to re-establish a sustainable pipeline. Dombrowski had been brought in to work with and build upon a pre-existing infrastructure. Bloom is tasked with reshaping the organization's talent pool in the majors and minors while bringing fresh perspective to the team's scouting and player development infrastructure.

Still, Bloom is joining the Red Sox at a time when their farm system has started to improve. Triston Casas, the 2018 first-round pick, delivered an impressive first full pro season that allowed him to emerge as the organization's top prospect. Bobby Dalbec carried his breakout 2018 performance forward into the upper levels, and right-hander Bryan Mata, in his age-20 season, looked the part of a potential mid-rotation starter, one of several Red Sox pitching prospects who made considerable progress in either their performances, their pitch mixes, or both.

The organization still lacks players in the minor leagues who combine both high ceilings and floors. But the farm system moved closer in 2019 to providing the sort of depth that can sustain a big league club over the course of a season, and given a big league roster that still features cornerstone young to prime-age talents such as Xander Bogaerts and Rafael Devers, the charge of the minor league system is a supplementary rather than foundational one.

Against that backdrop, Bloom—whose imprint was felt everywhere in a Rays organization where he worked extensively in player development, amateur and international scouting, as well as on the big league roster—represented a natural fit. The Red Sox were undone in 2019 by the absence of depth, while Tampa Bay surged to a wild card berth because that same aspect represented a strength. His hiring represents a desire on the part of the organization to find balance between the present and future, to recalibrate in a fashion that yields not just improvement in 2020 but sustainability beyond it.

PAUL BERESWILL/GETTY IMAGES

Rookie Michael Chavis popped 18 home runs while splitting time at first base and second base.

PROJECTED 2023 LINEUP

Position	Player	Age
Catcher	Christian Vazquez	32
First Base	Triston Casas (1)	23
Second Base	Michael Chavis	27
Third Base	Rafael Devers	26
Shortstop	Xander Bogaerts	30
Left Field	Andrew Benintendi	28
Center Field	Jarren Duran (4)	26
Right Field	Mookie Betts	30
Designated Hitter	Bobby Dalbec (2)	28
No. 1 Starter	Chris Sale	34
No. 2 Starter	Eduardo Rodriguez	30
No. 3 Starter	Bryan Mata (3)	24
No. 4 Starter	Thad Ward (6)	26
No. 5 Starter	Jay Groome (7)	24
Closer	Darwinzon Hernandez (5)	26

DEPTH CHART

BOSTON RED SOX

TOP 2020 ROOKIE: Bobby Dalbec, 3B/1B. His righthanded power should show up at some point in the big leagues this year.

BREAKOUT PROSPECT: Andrew Politi, RHP. Though unnoticed due to his late move from the bullpen to the rotation, he was throwing as well as anyone in the Red Sox system at the end of 2019.

SLEEPER: Eduardo Vaughan, OF. Signed out of Panama for $500,000 in 2018, he combines athleticism and a strong arm with flashes of power that suggest a potentially impactful skill set.

SOURCE OF TOP 30 TALENT

Homegrown	**29**	**Acquired**	**1**
College	13	Trade	1
Junior college	0	Rule 5 draft	0
High school	6	Independent league	0
Nondrafted free agent	0	Free agent/waivers	0
International	10		

LF
Tyler Esplin (26)
Albert Feliz

CF
Jarren Duran (4)

RF
Gilberto Jimenez (8)
Marcus Wilson (15)
Nick Decker (19)
Eduardo Lopez
Bryan Gonzalez
Darel Belen
Eduardo Vaughan

3B
Bobby Dalbec (2)
Brandon Howlett (18)
Antoni Flores (29)
Danny Diaz
Nick Northcut

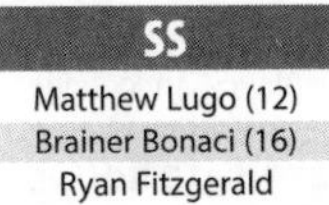

SS
Matthew Lugo (12)
Brainer Bonaci (16)
Ryan Fitzgerald

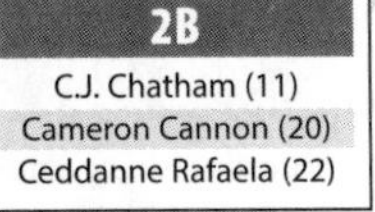

2B
C.J. Chatham (11)
Cameron Cannon (20)
Ceddanne Rafaela (22)

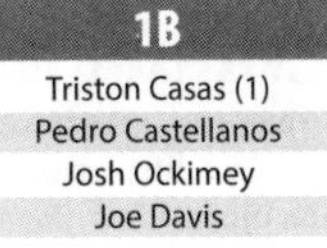

1B
Triston Casas (1)
Pedro Castellanos
Josh Ockimey
Joe Davis

C
Kole Cottam
Jhon Nunez

LHP

LHSP	LHRP
Jay Groome (7)	Darwinzon Hernandez (5)
Chris Murphy (13)	Yoan Aybar (23)
Kyle Hart (27)	Jhonathan Diaz
Jorge Rodriguez	Brendan Cellucci

RHP

RHSP	RHRP
Bryan Mata (3)	Tanner Houck (10)
Thad Ward (6)	Ryan Zeferjahn (17)
Noah Song (9)	Andrew Politi (21)
Brayan Bello (14)	Durbin Feltman (30)
Chih-Jung Liu (24)	Eduard Bazardo
Aldo Ramirez (25)	Travis Lakins
Chase Shugart (28)	Mike Shawaryn
Luis Perales	Dylan Spacke
Brock Bell	
Blake Loubier	
Denyi Reyes	
Kutter Crawford	

DRAFT ANALYSIS

2019

BEST PURE HITTER: SS Cameron Cannon (2) didn't have the best debut, hitting just .200/.284/.324 in the Gulf Coast and New York-Penn leagues, but he has an impressive track record in the Pacific-12 with standout plate discipline and solid feel for the barrel.

BEST POWER HITTER: 1B Dominic D'Alessandro (22) has 70-grade raw power and has no problem hitting with authority to the opposite field. The George Washington product hit 13 homers this spring before joining the Rookie-level Gulf Coast League, where he hit .292/.421/.415 with three home runs and five doubles.

FASTEST RUNNER: SS Matthew Lugo (2) has a chance for above-average tools across the board, but he's clocked 70-grade run times in the past. His speed plays closer to a 60-grade tool for the most part, however, and he's faster underway.

BEST DEFENSIVE PLAYER: Lugo always showed the tools to give himself a shot to play shortstop at a high level with impressive athleticism and gifted hands, but in his pro debut in the GCL and NYPL he impressed with defensive actions and instincts that were more polished than expected.

BEST FASTBALL: RHP Ryan Zeferjahn (3) has a fastball that gets into the upper 90s with tremendous late life, giving him impressive swing-and-miss qualities on the pitch.

BEST SECONDARY PITCH: RHP Noah Song (4) has made strides with his slider over the years, to the point where it's now considered a plus offering. The team was also impressed with the effectiveness of lefthander Chris Murphy's (6) changeup.

BEST PRO DEBUT: Song had an impressive debut in the NYPL, posting a 1.06 ERA in 17 innings with 19 strikeouts and five walks, but Murphy's was just as strong. In 10 starts and 33.1 innings of work in the NYPL, Murphy posted a 1.08 ERA with 34 strikeouts, seven walks and a 0.90 WHIP.

BEST ATHLETE: Lugo's standout athleticism gives him high upside in all phases of the game as a slick, up-the-middle defender.

MOST INTRIGUING BACKGROUND: Song's background has been detailed for some time now thanks to a Naval commitment that clouded his draft stock in 2018 and 2019, and it will continue to cloud his future.

CLOSEST TO THE MAJORS: Murphy has four solid weapons he can use now and showed much better strike-throwing ability in his pro debut than he displayed in college at San Diego. He should be a quick-mover.

BEST LATE-ROUND PICK: D'Alessandro had a strong debut and has a carrying tool in his power, though the Red Sox have a number of interesting candidates for this category. 2B Daniel Bakst (28) hit .306/.397/.469 with 15 walks and 19 strikeouts in 27 games in the GCL.

THE ONE WHO GOT AWAY: The Red Sox took a local product in RHP Sebastian Keane (11) with their first pick on Day 2, but they couldn't sign him out of a Northeastern commitment.

—**CARLOS COLLAZO**

TOP DRAFT PICKS OF THE DECADE

Year	Player, Pos.	2019 Org
2010	Kolbrin Vitek, 2B	Did not play
2011	Matt Barnes, RHP	Red Sox
2012	Deven Marrero, SS	Marlins
2013	Trey Ball, LHP	Red Sox
2014	Michael Chavis, SS	Red Sox
2015	Andrew Benintendi, OF	Red Sox
2016	Jay Groome, LHP	Red Sox
2017	Tanner Houck, RHP	Red Sox
2018	Triston Casas, 3B	Red Sox
2019	Cameron Cannon, SS (2nd round)	Red Sox

2018

1B Triston Casas (1) wasted no time becoming the system's top prospect with a solid first full pro season. OF Jarren Duran (7) has been the surprise of the group, using his hitting ability to race to the upper levels.

GRADE: B

2017

RHP Tanner Houck (1) and OF Tyler Esplin (7) are the only two members of this class to appear in the Handbook. Houck could reach Boston soon but how much impact he'll provide there remains to be seen.

GRADE: D

2016

After missing all of 2018 due to injury, LHP Jay Groome (1) got back in action in 2019 and still offers big upside. RHP Shaun Anderson (3), now in the Giants' rotation, is one of three big leaguers from the class.

GRADE: C

1 TRISTON CASAS, 1B

Born: Jan. 15, 2000. **B-T:** L-R. **HT:** 6-4. **WT:** 238.
Drafted: HS—Plantation, Fla., 2018 (1st round).
Signed by: Willie Romay.

TOM PRIDDY/FOUR SEAM

BA GRADE **60** **Risk: High**

SCOUTING GRADES **Hit:** 55. **Power:** 60. **Run:** 40. **Field:** 60. **Arm:** 50.

Projected future grades on 20-80 scouting scale.

TRACK RECORD: After reclassifying to enter the draft a year earlier than his peers, Casas emerged as one of the top high school position prospects in the 2018 draft by displaying standout all-fields power both with aluminum and, while playing in international competition for Team USA, wood bats. In 2019, he cemented his status as a standout player for his age and experience level, primarily at low Class A Greenville. He ranked in the top three of all 2018 high school draftees in OPS and homers while also joining Xander Bogaerts as the only Red Sox teenager in the last 50 years to hit at least 20 homers in one year at any level.

SCOUTING REPORT: Casas is gigantic, with size and strength in his lefthanded swing to generate easy power from left-center field to right. However, he sometimes fights his frame. In an effort to limit strikeouts, he opened the year employing a spread-out stance with a pronounced crouch, but the effort backfired and instead created extra movement in his swing that resulted in a high April strikeout rate. Casas showed aptitude and adaptability, employing a more natural, upright stance starting in May. The move showed not only standout power but also a versatile approach that suggested a solid overall hitting foundation that could help to control his strikeout rate. The lefthanded masher also chokes up with two strikes, and his willingness to use the whole field helps control his swings and misses. Casas played third base in high school (and a little bit in the minors), and his range at first base projects as above-average to plus, and his wingspan will be an asset. His arm is solid to above-average at first. He's a below-average runner, but his ceiling isn't predicated on speed. Team officials rave about his makeup, describing Casas as unusually mature in his routines, work ethic and preparation. He is a student of the game. Scouts see similarities to Freddie Freeman in his all-around game.

THE FUTURE: Casas is likely to open 2020 in high Class A Salem, and while it wouldn't be a shock to see him struggle at some point, it likewise wouldn't be surprising to see him remain on an aggressive development track. He projects as a player who could see the big leagues by early 2022 or even late 2021, with the potential to serve as a middle-of-the-order force and the organization's clear top prospect.

TOP PROSPECTS OF THE DECADE

Year	Player, Pos.	2019 Org
2010	Ryan Westmoreland, OF	Did not play
2011	Jose Iglesias, SS	Reds
2012	Will Middlebrooks, 3B	Did not play
2013	Xander Bogaerts, SS	Red Sox
2014	Xander Bogaerts, SS/3B	Red Sox
2015	Blake Swihart, C	D-backs
2016	Yoan Moncada, 3B	White Sox
2017	Andrew Benintendi, OF	Red Sox
2018	Jay Groome, LHP	Red Sox
2019	Bobby Dalbec, 3B	Red Sox

BEST TOOLS

Best Hitter for Average	Jarren Duran
Best Power Hitter	Bobby Dalbec
Best Strike-Zone Discipline	Triston Casas
Fastest Baserunner	Gilberto Jimenez
Best Athlete	Gilberto Jimenez
Best Fastball	Darwinzon Hernandez
Best Curveball	Jay Groome
Best Slider	Thad Ward
Best Changeup	Brayan Bello
Best Control	Noah Song
Best Defensive Catcher	Alan Marrero
Best Defensive Infielder	Triston Casas
Best Infield Arm	Bobby Dalbec
Best Defensive Outfielder	Tate Matheny
Best Outfield Arm	Gilberto Jimenez

Year	Age	Club (League)	Class	AVG	G	AB	R	H	2B	3B	HR	RBI	BB	SO	SB	OBP	SLG
2018	18	Red Sox (GCL)	R	.000	2	4	0	0	0	0	0	0	1	2	0	.200	.000
2019	19	Greenville (SAL)	LoA	.254	118	422	64	107	25	5	19	78	58	116	3	.349	.472
	19	Salem (CAR)	HiA	.429	2	7	2	3	1	0	1	3	0	2	0	.429	1.000
Minor League Totals				.254	122	433	66	110	26	5	20	81	59	120	3	.349	.476

2 BOBBY DALBEC, 3B

COURTESY OF PORTLAND SEA DOGS

BA GRADE
55 Risk: Medium

Born: June 29, 1995. **B-T:** R-R. **HT:** 6-4. **WT:** 225.
Drafted: Arizona, 2016 (4th round). **Signed by:** Vaughn Williams.

TRACK RECORD: Dalbec shows elite power, with his 59 homers over the last two seasons ranking as the sixth-most in the minors. Though high strikeout rates created caution about his floor, he has sustained the ability to slug and get on base while moving up the ladder, and he's also managed to cut his strikeout rate without compromising power.

SCOUTING REPORT: Dalbec is incredibly strong, allowing him to drive the ball out to all fields, sometimes even on mis-hits. His plate discipline is a strength that gives him solid on-base numbers regardless of his average. Still, his frame both creates holes in his swing and magnifies mechanical inefficiencies. Most of his struggles occur due to issues in the direction and timing of the weight transfer in his lower half, staying back for too long and then spinning off the ball while rushing forward. But when locked in, his homers come in bunches. Despite below-average speed on the bases and his size, Dalbec shows quickness, anticipation, and range in the field, with the hands and footwork to play solid defense at third. While he's still acclimating to first base and reads of the ball off the bat on the right side of the infield, he made considerable strides at the position with increased exposure to it in 2019.

THE FUTURE: With Rafael Devers anchoring third base for years to come, Dalbec—who is expected to open 2020 back in Triple-A—could find his way to the big leagues at first base or perhaps in left field if the Red Sox need righthanded thump.

SCOUTING GRADES: **Hitting:** 45 **Power:** 70 **Running:** 40 **Fielding:** 60 **Arm:** 70

Year	Age	Club (League)	Class	AVG	G	AB	R	H	2B	3B	HR	RBI	BB	SO	SB	OBP	SLG
2017	22	Red Sox (GCL)	R	.259	7	27	3	7	1	0	0	2	5	9	1	.375	.296
	22	Greenville (SAL)	LoA	.246	78	284	48	70	15	0	13	39	36	123	4	.345	.437
2018	23	Salem (CAR)	HiA	.256	100	344	59	88	27	2	26	85	60	130	3	.372	.573
	23	Portland (EL)	AA	.261	29	111	14	29	8	1	6	24	6	46	0	.323	.514
2019	24	Portland (EL)	AA	.234	105	359	57	84	15	2	20	57	68	110	6	.371	.454
	24	Pawtucket (IL)	AAA	.257	30	113	12	29	4	0	7	16	5	29	0	.301	.478
Minor League Totals				.261	383	1370	218	358	83	7	79	256	189	480	16	.362	.505

3 BRYAN MATA, RHP

BA GRADE
55 Risk: High

Born: May 3, 1999. **B-T:** R-R. **HT:** 6-3. **WT:** 220. **Signed:** Venezuela, 2016.
Signed by: Alex Requena/Eddie Romero.

TRACK RECORD: Signed for $25,000 in 2016, Mata quickly emerged as one of the organization's best starting pitching prospects. After he endured significant control struggles in 2018—attributed in no small part to continued physical growth and an effort to harness a two-seamer he started to incorporate—he nearly slashed his walk rate in half in 2019 while generating a high groundball rate. Though Mata struggled at times following a promotion as one of the youngest pitchers in Double-A, he took a major step forward in 2019.

SCOUTING REPORT: Mata has overhauled his arsenal considerably as a pro. He once relied on a four-seamer, curve and change, but the Red Sox determined that his arm slot was better suited to a two-seamer as a primary offering. He can also employ a four-seamer at the top of the zone while selectively mixing in his curve and change (a pitch with good action but inconsistent command). Mata's fastball sits in the mid-90s, topped out at 98 mph as a starter and hit triple-digits out of the bullpen in the Arizona Fall League. His slider typically comes in at 88-90 mph. While Mata's pitches don't generate tons of swings and misses, he throws hard enough to force early swing decisions.

THE FUTURE: Mata likely will open 2020 back in Double-A and is the team's most promising upper-level rotation prospect in recent years. He has No. 3 starter potential.

SCOUTING GRADES: **Fastball:** 70 **Slider:** 60 **Changeup:** 55 **Curveball:** 40 **Control:** 45

Year	Age	Club (League)	Class	W	L	ERA	G	GS	SV	IP	H	HR	BB	SO	K/9	WHIP	AVG
2017	18	Greenville (SAL)	LoA	5	6	3.74	17	17	0	77	75	3	26	74	8.6	1.31	.259
2018	19	Salem (CAR)	HiA	6	3	3.50	17	17	0	72	58	1	58	61	7.6	1.61	.229
2019	20	Salem (CAR)	HiA	3	1	1.75	10	10	0	51	38	1	18	52	9.1	1.09	.201
	20	Portland (EL)	AA	4	6	5.03	11	11	0	54	54	6	24	59	9.9	1.45	.271
Minor League Totals				22	20	3.40	69	69	0	315	279	13	145	307	8.8	1.35	.242

4 JARREN DURAN, OF

BA GRADE
50 Risk: High

Born: Sept. 5, 1996. **B-T:** L-R. **HT:** 6-2. **WT:** 200. **Drafted:** Long Beach State, 2018 (7th round). **Signed by:** Justin Horowitz.

TRACK RECORD: While Duran had a modest college statistical profile, then-area scout Justin Horowitz recognized a combination of impressive bat life with the ability to keep the barrel in the zone and game-changing speed that seemed wasted at second base. Now a full-time outfielder, Duran followed an outstanding 2018 pro debut with an even better performance in high Class A Salem in the first two months of 2019, flirting with .400 while showing excellent bat-to-ball skills, speed and occasional thump. While his numbers suffered after a promotion to Double-A, the quality of his at-bats improved.

SCOUTING REPORT: Duran has an extra gear when he senses opportunity, whether beating out routine grounders or taking an extra base. He takes advantage of that trait with a contact-heavy approach, albeit one in which he sometimes cuts off his swing. While he can make contact when expanding the strike zone, his tendency to do so results in weak contact. Still, his natural strength shows up at times with hard line drives to all fields and occasional long home runs. His bat-to-ball skills allow him to get to a variety of pitch types and locations from righties and lefties. Duran is still adjusting to center field, but his speed allows him to outrun route mistakes to represent at least an average future defender.

THE FUTURE: There's still some debate as to whether Duran's offensive profile is that of an everyday or fourth outfielder. Even with his speed, he must either hit for a high average or show more power to emerge as an everyday player. Still, he has the potential to be a catalyst.

SCOUTING GRADES: **Hitting:** 55 **Power:** 40 **Running:** 70 **Fielding:** 55 **Arm:** 50

Year	Age	Club (League)	Class	AVG	G	AB	R	H	2B	3B	HR	RBI	BB	SO	SB	OBP	SLG
2018	21	Lowell (NYP)	SS	.348	37	155	28	54	5	10	2	20	11	26	12	.393	.548
	21	Greenville (SAL)	LoA	.367	30	128	24	47	9	1	1	15	5	22	12	.396	.477
2019	22	Salem (CAR)	HiA	.387	50	199	49	77	13	3	4	19	23	44	18	.456	.543
	22	Portland (EL)	AA	.250	82	320	41	80	11	5	1	19	23	84	28	.309	.325
Minor League Totals				.322	199	802	142	258	38	19	8	73	62	176	70	.376	.446

5 DARWINZON HERNANDEZ, LHP

BA GRADE
45 Risk: Medium

Born: Dec. 17, 1996. **B-T:** L-L. **HT:** 6-2. **WT:** 245. **Signed:** Venezuela, 2013. **Signed by:** Rolando Pino/Ramon Mora.

TRACK RECORD: Signed for just $7,500 in 2013 after an injury sidelined him early in the 2013 international signing period, Hernandez emerged as a standout power pitcher. Significant control issues clouded his potential as a starter, but he showed dominant stuff once unleashed as a bullpen weapon in the big leagues in mid-July.

SCOUTING REPORT: Hernandez comes at hitters with an aggressive delivery, combining a low three-quarters slot with elite extension to create deception layered upon tremendous pure power. His 94-98 mph four-seam fastball features unpredictable movement based on fingers that sit on the side of the ball rather than behind it. Some compare his fastball to that of Josh Hader. Hernandez's low-80s slider has sharp, late, two-plane bite, generating ground balls and swings and misses. He employed a changeup and curve as a starter but left those pitches on the shelf in the bullpen. The lefthander will go through multi-batter stretches when he loses the strike zone, but out of the bullpen he limited the harm of his free passes by striking out bunches of batters.

THE FUTURE: The Red Sox have committed to Hernandez as a bullpen option. So long as he can throw enough strikes and stay healthy, he looks like a potential late-inning reliever.

SCOUTING GRADES: **Fastball:** 70 **Slider:** 55 **Curveball:** 45 **Control:** 40

Year	Age	Club (League)	Class	W	L	ERA	G	GS	SV	IP	H	HR	BB	SO	K/9	WHIP	AVG
2017	20	Greenville (SAL)	LoA	4	5	4.01	23	23	0	103	85	8	49	116	10.1	1.30	.221
2018	21	Salem (CAR)	HiA	9	5	3.56	23	23	0	101	80	1	60	124	11.0	1.39	.220
	21	Portland (EL)	AA	0	0	3.00	5	0	0	6	6	0	6	10	15.0	2.00	.250
2019	22	Portland (EL)	AA	1	4	5.13	10	9	0	40	33	2	32	59	13.2	1.61	.217
	22	Pawtucket (IL)	AAA	1	2	4.76	7	3	0	17	10	2	16	20	10.6	1.53	.175
	22	Boston (AL)	MAJ	0	1	4.45	29	1	0	30	27	1	26	57	16.9	1.75	.231
Major League Totals				0	1	4.45	29	1	0	30	27	1	26	57	16.9	1.75	.231
Minor League Totals				25	23	3.50	112	86	0	409	332	14	248	468	10.3	1.42	.220

6 THAD WARD, RHP

BA GRADE
50 Risk: High

Born: Jan. 16, 1997. **B-T:** R-R. **HT:** 6-3. **WT:** 182. **Drafted:** Central Florida, 2018 (5th round). **Signed by:** Stephen Hargett.

TRACK RECORD: Largely overlooked as a college swingman, Ward impressed the Red Sox with the movement and command of a low-90s sinker and a potential swing-and-miss slider. They committed to drafting him in the fifth round in 2018, figuring he had a solid reliever floor. But while working as a starter in his first full pro season, Ward rapidly surpassed the team's expectations with one of the best performances of any starter in the minors, posting the ninth-best ERA (2.13) and 20th-best strikeout rate (11.2 per nine innings) among those who threw at least 100 innings.

SCOUTING REPORT: Ward showed unexpected velocity in 2019, working at 93-96 mph with his sinker and topping out at 97. Yet it was the development of a cutter that tunneled off his two-seamer and mid-80s slider that allowed Ward to induce weak contact in the strike zone as well as chases outside of it. He also occasionally features a changeup and curveball. The rangy righty has an easy delivery without a ton of effort, creating the basis for command and hope for health, and he also shows an understanding of his mix that could keep him on an aggressive development track.

THE FUTURE: Ward is likely to begin 2020 in Double-A, where he'll hope to continue to build his case as a potential No. 4 starter.

SCOUTING GRADES:	Fastball: 50	Slider: 60	Cutter: 60	Control: 50

Year	Age	Club (League)	Class	W	L	ERA	G	GS	SV	IP	H	HR	BB	SO	K/9	WHIP	AVG
2018	21	Lowell (NYP)	SS	0	3	3.77	11	11	0	31	33	2	12	27	7.8	1.45	.275
2019	22	Greenville (SAL)	LoA	5	2	1.99	13	13	0	72	51	2	25	87	10.8	1.05	.194
	22	Salem (CAR)	HiA	3	3	2.33	12	12	0	54	38	4	32	70	11.7	1.30	.203
Minor League Totals				8	8	2.46	36	36	0	157	122	8	69	184	10.5	1.21	.214

7 JAY GROOME, LHP

BA GRADE
55 Risk: Extreme

Born: Aug. 23, 1998. **B-T:** L-L. **HT:** 6-6. **WT:** 220. **Drafted:** HS—Barnegat, N.J., 2016 (1st round). **Signed by:** Ray Fagnant.

TRACK RECORD: One of the best prep pitchers in the 2016 draft, Groome has thrown just 66 pro innings due to injuries, including a torn ulnar collateral ligament that required Tommy John surgery and cost him all of 2018 and most of 2019. Still, he returned to games by the end of 2019, showed flashes of swing-and-miss stuff, and continues to feature a ceiling that arguably surpasses that of any other pitcher in the Red Sox farm system.

SCOUTING REPORT: Groome received strong marks for the strength and conditioning work he did over his rehab from Tommy John. He has a prototypical starter's build, generating power stuff with an easy delivery. In his return, Groome sat at 92-94 mph and topped out at 96. His signature offering, however, is a hammer curveball—a pitch for which he was still looking to regain his feel in his return from Tommy John. Groome's changeup improved from fringy to average during his rehab, and his natural ability to manipulate the ball makes it easy to imagine the development of a cutter.

THE FUTURE: Groome likely will start 2020 in low Class A Greenville. If healthy, he could move quickly to high Class A Salem. At age 21, he's young enough to believe that his top-of-the-rotation upside remains intact, even if his poor health track record raises questions about whether he'll realize it.

SCOUTING GRADES:	Fastball: 60	Curveball: 60	Cutter: 55	Changeup: 50	Control: 50

Year	Age	Club (League)	Class	W	L	ERA	G	GS	SV	IP	H	HR	BB	SO	K/9	WHIP	AVG
2017	18	Lowell (NYP)	SS	0	2	1.64	3	3	0	11	5	0	5	14	11.5	0.91	.132
	18	Greenville (SAL)	LoA	3	7	6.70	11	11	0	44	44	6	25	58	11.8	1.56	.257
2018	19	Did not pitch—injured															
2019	20	Red Sox (GCL)	R	0	0	0.00	2	2	0	2	2	0	0	3	13.5	1.00	.250
	20	Lowell (NYP)	SS	0	0	4.50	1	1	0	2	3	0	1	3	13.5	2.00	.300
Minor League Totals				3	9	5.18	20	20	0	66	57	6	35	88	12.0	1.39	.227

8 GILBERTO JIMENEZ, OF

BA GRADE 55 Risk: Extreme

Born: July 8, 2000. **B-T:** B-R. **HT:** 5-11. **WT:** 160. **Signed:** Dominican Republic, 2017. **Signed by:** Eddie Romero/Manny Nanita.

TRACK RECORD: A raw athlete who fell through the scouting cracks in the 2017 signing period before joining the Red Sox for $10,000, Jimenez represents a moldable ball of clay whose athleticism, hand-eye coordination and incredible speed have allowed him to emerge as a standout performer while learning on the fly. After a strong Dominican Summer League debut in 2018, he excelled at short-season Lowell in 2019, leading the New York-Penn League in batting (.359) while finishing fourth in OPS (.863) and ninth in steals (14).

SCOUTING REPORT: Jimenez started switch-hitting after turning pro, and while his lefthanded swing remains inelegant and sometimes choppy, he has good enough feel for the barrel. Despite a very high groundball rate, his elite speed (sub-4.0 times from home to first) allowed him to garner loads of infield hits. It's possible that he'll be limited to a slap-and-run profile whose production decreases as defenses improve, but Jimenez also has flashed the bat speed to drive the ball, even if his current swing is geared for contact. Jimenez struggles with pitch recognition and plate discipline, but if experience yields refinement, he has the potential for average or better across-the-board tools. His speed and arm give him a big league outfielder's floor and his athleticism and strength making it easy to dream big.

THE FUTURE: Jimenez should open 2020 as a 19-year-old in at low Class A Greenville. He's raw and thus unlikely to fast track, but if everything clicks, he could sit near the top of Red Sox prospect lists in coming years.

SCOUTING GRADES: **Hitting:** 55 **Power:** 50 **Running:** 70 **Fielding:** 60 **Arm:** 60

Year	Age	Club (League)	Class	AVG	G	AB	R	H	2B	3B	HR	RBI	BB	SO	SB	OBP	SLG
2018	17	Red Sox1 (DSL)	R	.319	67	257	42	82	10	8	0	22	19	40	20	.384	.420
2019	18	Lowell (NYP)	SS	.359	59	234	35	84	11	3	3	19	13	38	14	.393	.470
Minor League Totals				.338	126	491	77	166	21	11	3	41	32	78	30	.388	.444

9 NOAH SONG, RHP

BA GRADE 55 Risk: Extreme

Born: May 28, 1997. **B-T:** R-R. **HT:** 6-4. **WT:** 200. **Drafted:** Navy, 2019 (4th round). **Signed by:** Reed Gragnani.

TRACK RECORD: When Song enrolled at Navy in possession of a mid-80s fastball and little else, he was convinced he'd pitch for four years in college and then never again. But his velocity soared and he went 11-1, 1.44 with 15.4 strikeouts per nine innings as a senior. Teams stayed away from Song in the draft due to questions about whether he'd be able to pursue a pro career given his two-year active military service commitment. The Red Sox decided Song's talent was worth the risk even if the start of his career was delayed and drafted him in the fourth round. He signed for $100,000 and dominated at short-season Lowell and for Team USA during the Olympic qualifying tournament.

SCOUTING REPORT: Song features a four-pitch mix from a powerful starter's build, anchored by a fastball that ranges from 94-98 mph. After working at the bottom of the zone in college, his fastball is likely to be more effective at the top of the zone in pro ball. While Song leaned chiefly on his slider as a secondary weapon at Navy, his changeup stood out as a potential plus offering in his pro debut. He still needs to define the velocities and shapes to his pitches that will generate the greatest effectiveness, but there's plenty with which to work. He is long, athletic and throws strikes

THE FUTURE: The Navy announced in December that Song, a commissioned Naval flight officer, will have to serve his military commitment immediately. He will spend the next two years as an active service member and can petition to serve his final three years in the reserves, which would allow him to resume his baseball career in 2022 at the earliest. He has the stuff, poise and mentality to project a mid-rotation starter, but it will be at least two years before he gets the chance to show he can rise to that level.

SCOUTING GRADES: **Fastball:** 60 **Slider:** 55 **Curveball:** 50 **Changeup:** 60 **Control:** 50

Year	Age	Club (League)	Class	W	L	ERA	G	GS	SV	IP	H	HR	BB	SO	K/9	WHIP	AVG
2019	22	Lowell (NYP)	SS	0	0	1.06	7	7	0	17	10	0	5	19	10.1	0.88	.167
Minor League Totals				0	0	1.06	7	7	0	17	10	0	5	19	10.1	0.88	.167

10 TANNER HOUCK, RHP

Born: June 29, 1996. **B-T:** R-R. **HT:** 6-5. **WT:** 220. **Drafted:** Missouri, 2017 (1st round). **Signed by:** Todd Gold.

BA GRADE
45 Risk: Medium

TRACK RECORD: Houck's development has traveled a crooked line since being taken in the first round in 2017. He tried to overhaul his pitch mix in early 2018 with initially disastrous results at high Class A Salem but found considerable success down the stretch with a balanced repertoire. In 2019, he alternated dominant performances—often against righty-heavy lineups—with struggles as a starter in Double-A and did the same out of the bullpen at Triple-A. He went back to starting in the Arizona Fall League.

SCOUTING REPORT: Houck's combination of a 92-97 mph two-seamer and four-seamer with a sweeping slider from a low three-quarters arm slot creates nightmares for righties, but he's struggled to show similar command against lefties, who have hit .283/.383/.363. On days where he flashes a solid changeup and locates his slider to both righties and lefties, Houck looks like a potential starter, but his difficulty in repeating a crossfire delivery with a lot of moving parts has convinced many that his future is in the bullpen.

THE FUTURE: Houck likely will open 2020 back in Triple-A, offering the Red Sox a spot-starting option or bullpen depth, with a potential future as a setup man. The Red Sox have resisted giving up on him as a starter, but his proximity to the big leagues suggests a decision about his role looms.

SCOUTING GRADES: **Fastball:** 55 **Slider:** 60 **Changeup:** 45 **Control:** 45

Year	Age	Club (League)	Class	W	L	ERA	G	GS	SV	IP	H	HR	BB	SO	K/9	WHIP	AVG
2017	21	Lowell (NYP)	SS	0	3	3.63	10	10	0	22	21	0	8	25	10.1	1.30	.239
2018	22	Salem (CAR)	HiA	7	11	4.24	23	23	0	119	110	11	60	111	8.4	1.43	.245
2019	23	Portland (EL)	AA	8	6	4.25	17	15	0	83	86	4	32	80	8.7	1.43	.270
	23	Pawtucket (IL)	AAA	0	0	3.24	16	2	1	25	19	3	14	27	9.7	1.32	.209
Minor League Totals				15	20	4.08	66	50	1	249	236	18	114	243	8.8	1.41	.249

11 C.J. CHATHAM, SS/2B

BA GRADE
45 Risk: Medium

Born: Dec. 22, 1994. **B-T:** R-R. **HT:** 6-4. **WT:** 185. **Drafted:** Florida Atlantic, 2016 (2nd round). **Signed by:** Willie Romay.

TRACK RECORD: Chatham's career has been plagued with a long list of injuries, dating back to a hip fracture in high school and recurring right shoulder and left hamstring injuries as a pro. He has been relatively injury-free since joining Salem in mid-May 2018 and has performed well across two levels in back-to-back years. He competed for a batting title into the final days of the season in the high Class A Carolina League in 2018 and then won the Eastern League's batting title in 2019.

SCOUTING REPORT: While Chatham gets the bat to the ball, he does so by spraying the ball to all fields rather than slugging. His aggressive approach caps his on-base abilities and limits his power, a notion reflected in his .105 isolated slugging percentage in 2019. His lack of strength and physicality also raises durability questions. Chatham does not wow with range and quickness but makes up for it with instincts, body control and solid hands. Consistent arm strength for the position has been an issue, tied to the nagging right shoulder injuries. Chatham moved around the dirt and saw time in left field during the AFL.

THE FUTURE: Chatham is likely at least a big league reserve. Some feel he could offer a credible everyday option, most likely at second base, if he adds offensive impact.

Year	Age	Club (League)	Class	AVG	G	AB	R	H	2B	3B	HR	RBI	BB	SO	SB	OBP	SLG
2017	22	Greenville (SAL)	LoA	.333	1	3	0	1	0	0	0	2	0	0	0	.333	.333
	22	Red Sox (GCL)	R	.313	6	16	5	5	0	0	1	3	2	1	0	.389	.500
2018	23	Greenville (SAL)	LoA	.307	19	75	13	23	6	1	0	9	3	14	1	.329	.413
	23	Salem (CAR)	HiA	.315	95	362	42	114	14	1	3	43	21	72	10	.355	.384
2019	24	Portland (EL)	AA	.297	90	350	39	104	26	1	3	36	18	66	7	.333	.403
	24	Pawtucket (IL)	AAA	.302	20	86	11	26	5	0	2	10	4	21	0	.330	.430
Minor League Totals				.298	266	1024	131	305	57	4	14	124	56	201	18	.337	.402

12 MATTHEW LUGO, SS

BA GRADE
55 Risk: Extreme

Born: May 9, 2001. **B-T:** R-R. **HT:** 6-1. **WT:** 185. **Drafted:** HS—Florida, P.R., 2019 (2nd round). **Signed by:** Edgar Perez.

TRACK RECORD: Lugo, the nephew of Carlos Beltran and a graduate of his star uncle's academy in Puerto Rico, distinguished himself prior to the 2019 draft with his size, athleticism, and lively bat. He got off to a tremendous start in the Rookie-level Gulf Coast League before wearing out down the stretch. Lugo made some spot appearances in the Puerto Rican Winter League as well.

SCOUTING REPORT: When scout Edgar Perez saw Lugo, he recognized the potential for plus power. Perhaps more intriguing, he also saw the ability to manipulate the barrel in a way that suggested Lugo could make the adjustments to advance through the minors. Lugo has advanced size and strength through his lower half, although he's still physically immature through his chest and shoulders. He has a solid base at the plate with a relatively simple swing with natural lift. Like most young hitters, Lugo is aggressive early in the count and will need to learn better selectivity. Lugo's physical lower half creates some questions defensively. The Sox hope to play Lugo at shortstop, although second base may be a more likely outcome. Lugo has enough arm for the left side but needs to improve his footwork and finish.

THE FUTURE: Lugo's power and middle-infield profile suggest a potential above-average regular.

Year	Age	Club (League)	Class	AVG	G	AB	R	H	2B	3B	HR	RBI	BB	SO	SB	OBP	SLG
2019	18	Red Sox (GCL)	R	.257	39	136	19	35	5	1	1	12	15	36	3	.342	.331
	18	Lowell (NYP)	SS	.250	2	8	0	2	0	0	0	1	0	2	0	.250	.250
Minor League Totals				.257	41	144	19	37	5	1	1	13	15	38	3	.337	.326

13 CHRIS MURPHY, LHP

BA GRADE 50 Risk: High

Born: June 5, 1998. **B-T:** L-L. **HT:** 6-1. **WT:** 175. **Drafted:** San Diego, 2019 (6th round). **Signed by:** J.J. Altobelli.

TRACK RECORD: Though he posted one of the top strikeout rates in Division I (12.2 per 9 innings) as a junior, Murphy's performance was obscured by unusually high walk rates (4.8) coming out of San Diego. The Sox took a chance on the former and were pleasantly surprised with a strong pro debut. In 10 starts spanning 33.1 innings with Lowell, Murphy forged a 1.08 ERA with 34 strikeouts, just seven walks, and allowed only one home run.

SCOUTING REPORT: While in Lowell, Murphy made some small tweaks to his delivery, including enhanced rhythm to his lower half, which in turn resulted in throwing from a slightly higher slot and generating better plane and more direct finish to the plate. The results were striking, allowing his 92-93 mph fastball to play much better than in college. Not only did Murphy elicit his share of swings and misses, he commanded his pitches in the zone more effectively and got ahead of hitters more frequently. Murphy also features a solid three-quarters slurve and changeup. He profiles as best as a starter during the development process.

THE FUTURE: While the 2019 debut was encouraging, Murphy will have to prove it was not a fluke, in contrast to his career log in college and the Cape. He should start the season at low Class A Greenville.

Year	Age	Club (League)	Class	W	L	ERA	G	GS	SV	IP	H	HR	BB	SO	K/9	WHIP	AVG
2019	21	Lowell (NYP)	SS	0	1	1.08	10	10	0	33	23	1	7	34	9.2	0.90	.197
Minor League Totals				0	1	1.08	10	10	0	33	23	1	7	34	9.2	0.90	.197

14 BRAYAN BELLO, RHP

BA GRADE 50 Risk: Very High

Born: May 17, 1999. **B-T:** R-R. **HT:** 6-1. **WT:** 170. **Signed:** Dominican Republic, 2017. **Signed by:** Manny Nanita/Todd Claus/Rollie Pino.

TRACK RECORD: Unlike most Latin players, Bello was already 18 years old when he signed. He has moved quickly due in part to his age, building on a dominant pro debut in the DSL in 2018 with a strong spring that convinced the Sox to push him to low Class A Greenville in his age-20 season.

SCOUTING REPORT: Bello has a medium build with a live, wiry body with room to fill. He also a loose, whippy arm. Lacking present core strength, Bello does not always repeat his direction and finish though he only needs minor adjustments. Bello's biggest challenge in 2019 came after a solid April, when he was getting hit hard making too many mistakes in the zone. After a rough two months, Bello adjusted his approach both in and out of the zone, resulting in better command of at-bats. Bello's fastball sits 94-95, mixed with a solid mid-80s slider and a mid-80s changeup with depth which each project as plus. The length of Bello's delivery will make creating deception an issue moving forward.

THE FUTURE: Bello will likely start next year at high Class A Salem, and if he cements his second-half improvements of 2019 he could reach the upper levels as a pitcher with a backend starter's ceiling.

Year	Age	Club (League)	Class	W	L	ERA	G	GS	SV	IP	H	HR	BB	SO	K/9	WHIP	AVG
2018	19	Red Sox2 (DSL)	R	6	2	1.68	13	13	0	64	37	0	10	68	9.5	0.73	.162
	19	Red Sox (GCL)	R	1	0	0.00	1	0	0	3	2	0	0	6	18.0	0.67	.182
2019	20	Greenville (SAL)	LoA	5	10	5.43	25	25	0	118	135	9	38	119	9.1	1.47	.286
Minor League Totals				12	12	4.04	39	38	0	185	174	9	48	193	9.4	1.20	.244

15 MARCUS WILSON, OF

Born: Aug. 15, 1996. **B-T:** R-R. **HT:** 6-2. **WT:** 175. **Drafted:** HS—Gardena, Calif., 2014 (2nd round supplemental). **Signed by:** Hal Kurtzman (D-backs).

TRACK RECORD: Wilson moved deliberately over five years in the Arizona system—finally reaching Double-A to open 2019—before being traded to the Red Sox in April for Blake Swihart and international pool money.

SCOUTING REPORT: Wilson has long been the athletic toolsy type, but he actually became more aggressive at the plate as his career progressed. That change enabled better control of counts and resulted in improved pitch selection and plate discipline. Wilson also adjusted his swing to add more life, which led to more fly balls and amplified power. Wilson split time both in center field and right field and profiles as an above-average defender with above-average range. Wilson's arm is fringy at best.

THE FUTURE: Wilson's righthanded power and defensive prowess are valuable. He will need to continue to refine his approach to make more consistent contact.

Year	Age	Club (League)	Class	AVG	G	AB	R	H	2B	3B	HR	RBI	BB	SO	SB	OBP	SLG
2017	20	Kane County (MWL)	LoA	.295	103	383	56	113	21	5	9	54	55	90	15	.383	.446
2018	21	Visalia (CAL)	HiA	.235	111	447	60	105	26	2	10	48	44	141	16	.309	.369
2019	22	Jackson (SL)	AA	.235	12	34	4	8	2	1	2	7	5	13	3	.350	.529
	22	Wilmington (CAR)	HiA	.667	1	3	0	2	0	0	0	1	0	0	0	.667	.667
	22	Salem (CAR)	HiA	.342	45	146	26	50	12	1	8	29	18	47	4	.413	.603
	22	Portland (EL)	AA	.223	62	206	35	46	14	0	8	22	28	82	6	.319	.408
Minor League Totals				.258	498	1794	273	463	102	15	40	224	250	546	80	.352	.399

16 BRAINER BONACI, SS

BA GRADE
50 Risk: Very High

Born: July 9, 2002. **B-T:** B-R. **HT:** 5-10. **WT:** 175. **Signed:** Venezuela, 2018. **Signed by:** Manny Padron/Junior Vizcaino/Eddie Romero.

TRACK RECORD: Signed as a small but physical 16-year-old with strong bat-to-ball skills and good baseball instincts, Bonaci had a strong pro debut in the Dominican Republic.

SCOUTING REPORT: In the DSL, Bonaci showed signs of plate discipline (8.8-percent walk rate), contact skills (15.3-percent strikeout rate), raw but impactful speed, and pop (.118 ISO). Defensively, he showed the standout arm strength to play on the left side of the infield, and the Red Sox will develop him primarily at short, though he did play some third this year. Some evaluators believe that his future is most likely as a versatile player who can move around the field while having a solid ability to play shortstop.

THE FUTURE: At an early stage of his pro career, Bonaci has shown the chance to have solid across-the-board tools with a chance at worst to be an offensive utility player.

Year	Age	Club (League)	Class	AVG	G	AB	R	H	2B	3B	HR	RBI	BB	SO	SB	OBP	SLG
2019	16	Red Sox1 (DSL)	R	.279	61	229	34	64	14	2	3	37	23	40	18	.356	.397
Minor League Totals				.279	61	229	34	64	14	2	3	37	23	40	18	.356	.397

17 RYAN ZEFERJAHN, RHP

BA GRADE
45 Risk: High

Born: Feb. 28, 1998. **B-T:** R-R. **HT:** 6-5. **WT:** 225. **Drafted:** Kansas, 2019 (3rd round). **Signed by:** Lane Decker.

TRACK RECORD: Zeferjahn has been a high-profile arm since his high school days, though he preferred to attend Kansas. Zeferjahn spent the last three years in the Jayhawks' rotation, punching out over 11 hitters per nine innings over his last two seasons. A blister on his nail limited his ability to throw his breaking ball once he arrived in short-season Lowell he still struck out 12.7 batters per nine innings.

SCOUTING REPORT: Despite quality stuff, Zeferjahn was still viewed as relatively raw for a college pitcher coming out of the draft due to command and consistency issues. His arm action created some concern due to depth in back, which impacted his timing. Primarily featuring a two-seamer, scouts believed Zeferjahn would be a better fit if he utilized his mid-to-high-90s four-seamer. Zeferjahn also has the makings of a potentially plus slider, but had a harder time getting to it due to erratic command and high pitch counts. Zeferjahn has had a harder time developing a usable changeup. His ability to spin the ball gives the Sox confidence that he'll have at least one solid secondary offering.

THE FUTURE: Zeferjahn will likely open 2020 in low Class A Greenville, with the need for pitch development resulting in a more deliberate development track than some college starters.

Year	Age	Club (League)	Class	W	L	ERA	G	GS	SV	IP	H	HR	BB	SO	K/9	WHIP	AVG
2019	21	Lowell (NYP)	SS	0	2	4.50	12	12	0	22	24	2	12	31	12.7	1.64	.279
Minor League Totals				0	2	4.50	12	12	0	22	24	2	12	31	12.7	1.64	.279

18 BRANDON HOWLETT, 3B

Born: September 12, 1999. **B-T:** R-R. **HT:** 6-1. **WT:** 205. **Drafted:** HS—Lakeland, Fla., 2018 (21st round). **Signed by:** Stephen Hargett.

TRACK RECORD: The Red Sox lured Howlett away as a later-round pick and a Florida State commitment, signing for $185,000 in 2018. Howlett dazzled in his pro debut in 2018, showing not only a surprisingly advanced offensive approach but also solid power in the Rookie-level Gulf Coast League. That performance, coupled with a strong spring, convinced the Sox to send Howlett to low Class A Greenville.

SCOUTING REPORT: Howlett has solid strength tools with a physically mature build for his age. Possessing plus raw power and an advanced approach, Howlett needs to be more efficient with contact. He is still quick to his front side with some effort that hinders consistent contact. While Howlett can generate hard contact now, staying on his backside will help him tap his raw power. A third baseman now, evaluators are still not sold on his ability to stay on the dirt. Athletic with solid effort, Howlett needs work on ground ball reads as well as footwork. He has the arm for the left side but raises his slot on throws, which gives doubt to his ability to vary angles and make throws needed for the position.

THE FUTURE: Howlett had a hard time self-correcting after a precipitous second-half slide during his first year in full season. A return to Greenville appears most likely in 2020.

Year	Age	Club (League)	Class	AVG	G	AB	R	H	2B	3B	HR	RBI	BB	SO	SB	OBP	SLG
2018	18	Red Sox (GCL)	R	.307	39	137	24	42	15	0	5	25	22	38	0	.405	.526
	18	Lowell (NYP)	SS	.133	5	15	5	2	1	0	1	2	6	3	1	.381	.400
2019	19	Greenville (SAL)	LoA	.231	113	390	48	90	23	1	8	35	56	144	1	.341	.356
Minor League Totals				.247	157	542	77	134	39	1	14	62	84	185	2	.359	.400

19 NICK DECKER, OF

BA GRADE
50 Risk: Extreme

Born: Oct. 2, 1999. **B-T:** L-L. **HT:** 6-0. **WT:** 200. **Drafted:** HS—Tabernacle, N.J., 2018 (2nd round). **Signed by:** Ray Fagnant.

TRACK RECORD: After selecting him in the second round in 2018, Decker's initial pro season was cut short after one game with a small fracture in his left wrist. Decker used the time away to understand nuances of the professional game, becoming the talk of the instructional league later that fall. After starting 2019 in extended spring training, Decker was pushed to short-season Lowell, Of the 31 teenagers who had at least 100 plate appearances in the New York-Penn League, Decker ranked second in isolated power (.224) and third in slugging (.471) while posting a .247/328/.471 line.

SCOUTING REPORT: Decker has offset the lack of high school game experience because of the typically colder northeast spring climates by adopting a physically and mentally mature approach. Decker has a compact stroke with strength through the zone that helps him generate hard contact while staying inside the ball. He has the ability to use all fields but also has natural lift in his swing built for power. Decker is solid runner underway though not a basestealer. Decker has played right field since signing and presents a solid defensive profile, including range, reactions and arm strength.

THE FUTURE: Decker showed enough flashes of offensive explosiveness—in tandem with a strong arm and solid defense in right field—to suggest a player with the upside of an everyday contributor. He should be in Greenville to start 2020.

Year	Age	Club (League)	Class	AVG	G	AB	R	H	2B	3B	HR	RBI	BB	SO	SB	OBP	SLG
2018	18	Red Sox (GCL)	R	.250	2	4	1	1	1	0	0	0	1	1	0	.400	.500
2019	19	Lowell (NYP)	SS	.247	53	170	23	42	10	5	6	25	21	59	4	.328	.471
Minor League Totals				.247	55	174	24	43	11	5	6	25	22	60	4	.330	.471

20 CAMERON CANNON, 2B/SS

BA GRADE
45 Risk: High

Born: Oct. 16, 1997. **B-T:** R-R. **HT:** 5-10. **WT:** 195. **Drafted:** Arizona, 2019 (2nd round). **Signed by:** Vaughn Williams.

TRACK RECORD: Vaughn Williams, the Red Sox area scout covering the Four Corners region, started following Cannon as a high school junior in Arizona. Over five seasons in high school and college, Williams watched Cannon evolve from someone with strong bat-to-ball skills to a player who began using his legs more as a junior to drive the ball en route to 40 extra-base hits, positioning himself as the top Red Sox draft pick in 2019. Cannon left Arizona with a career slash line of (.347/.443/.561).

SCOUTING REPORT: Cannon has an above-average to plus hit tool combined with the potential for average power. Though Cannon is viewed as capable at shortstop, he's a better fit at second due to arm strength concerns. Though his final line in Lowell was not overly impressive, the Red Sox were encouraged because he made approach adjustments in August allowing for better contact. The Red Sox trust that a

consistent amateur track record of hitting with a modest strikeout rate will show up in pro ball.
THE FUTURE: Cannon could open 2020 in high Class A Salem, although low Class A Greenville appears more likely.

Year	Age	Club (League)	Class	AVG	G	AB	R	H	2B	3B	HR	RBI	BB	SO	SB	OBP	SLG
2019	21	Red Sox (GCL)	R	.111	3	9	0	1	0	0	0	0	0	5	0	.200	.111
	21	Lowell (NYP)	SS	.205	42	161	17	33	12	0	3	21	12	37	1	.289	.335
Minor League Totals				.200	45	170	17	34	12	0	3	21	12	42	1	.284	.324

21 ANDREW POLITI, RHP

BA GRADE
45 Risk: High

Born: June 4, 1996. **B-T:** R-R. **HT:** 6-0. **WT:** 195. **Drafted:** Seton Hall, 2018 (15th round). **Signed by:** Ray Fagnant.
TRACK RECORD: The Red Sox plucked Politi on day three of the draft following a redshirt junior season in which the righthander posted a 5.44 ERA but struck out 12.6 batters per nine innings, punctuated by a dominant performance in the Big East Conference tournament.
SCOUTING REPORT: Politi's stuff has not been an issue. In addition to his four-seam fastball, which features elite spin and movement as well as a low-to-mid-80s curveball, the Red Sox worked with the righty to add a high-80s cutter-slider hybrid. Politi's approach has been mostly hard, with limited usage and conviction with his changeup. Command, durability and ideal usages remain in question. Politi features a max-effort delivery with lots of moving parts, which creates a lot of stress not only physically but also on repeating pitches. Although never pitch-efficient, Politi did a better job throwing strikes with a refined mix and approach, most notably vs. lefthanders in the second half, when he posted a 1.42 ERA with a 33.2-percent strikeout rate while holding hitters to a .146 average and .443 OPS over his final 50 innings of the year, including five late-season starts.
THE FUTURE: While Politi had success in the rotation late in the 2019, pitch efficiency and getting deep in games are still a challenge. Despite spot starts since college, Politi appears best suited as a bulk reliever if he can continue to refine his command. He should begin 2020 in Double-A Portland.

Year	Age	Club (League)	Class	W	L	ERA	G	GS	SV	IP	H	HR	BB	SO	K/9	WHIP	AVG
2018	22	Lowell (NYP)	SS	1	1	4.34	21	0	7	29	30	2	10	43	13.3	1.38	.270
2019	23	Wilmington (CAR)	HiA	0	0	0.00	1	1	0	4	2	0	0	6	13.5	0.50	—
	23	Salem (CAR)	HiA	5	2	3.55	33	5	1	79	56	4	37	96	11.0	1.18	.197
Minor League Totals				6	3	3.76	54	5	8	107	86	6	47	139	11.6	1.24	.217

22 CEDDANNE RAFAELA, SS/2B

Born: Sept. 18, 2000. **B-T:** R-R. **HT:** 5-8. **WT:** 145. **Signed:** Curacao, 2017. **Signed by:** Dennis Neuman/Rollie Pino/Todd Claus.
TRACK RECORD: Rafaela has been no stranger to the international scene, having played for Curacao in the 2012 Little World Series. Still, Rafaela was easy to overlook as a diminutive second baseman in Curacao. The Red Sox saw a player who had above-average speed, impressive bat speed and excellent makeup.
SCOUTING REPORT: Although listed at just 5-foot-8, Rafaela still intrigues, possessing longer limbs with a live, wiry build with room to fill. Over two years in pro ball, Rafaela has made strong impressions on evaluators who have been drawn to his high-energy style of play, hand-eye coordination and surprising pop. Rafaela shows good presence in the box with a loose, inside-out stroke and good balance. As an undersized aggressive hitter, he will need to be more selective to take advantage of contact potential with experience and maturity. He appears best suited as an athletic utility type.
THE FUTURE: After participating in the Red Sox's instructional league the past two years, Rafaela appears headed to Lowell in 2020.

Year	Age	Club (League)	Class	AVG	G	AB	R	H	2B	3B	HR	RBI	BB	SO	SB	OBP	SLG
2018	17	Red Sox1 (DSL)	R	.271	54	203	31	55	9	2	3	28	14	39	19	.326	.379
2019	18	Red Sox (GCL)	R	.248	41	153	30	38	1	4	6	17	14	28	9	.329	.425
	18	Lowell (NYP)	SS	.182	3	11	0	2	0	0	0	1	0	3	0	.167	.182
Minor League Totals				.259	98	367	61	95	10	6	9	46	28	70	28	.323	.392

23 YOAN AYBAR, LHP

BA GRADE
45 Risk: Very High

Born: July 3, 1997. **B-T:** L-L. **HT:** 6-2. **WT:** 165. **Signed:** Dominican Republic, 2013. **Signed by:** Jonathan Cruz/Eddie Romero.
TRACK RECORD: Aybar spent his four seasons in the Red Sox system as an outfielder, progressing as high

as Lowell in 2017. While Aybar possessed raw power, it never translated into games due in part to a 4 percent walk rate. Aybar has been pushed quickly over his two years on the mound, ending the season in the Arizona Fall League. Working out of the pen with a fastball-slider combination, Aybar has stood out early in his transition and has struck out 10.3 batters per nine innings over his career.

SCOUTING REPORT: Aybar works from the stretch only but has to fight to stay in sync. Aybar has a loose arm but the arm stroke is lengthy, which limits his deception. His fastball averaged 95 mph in 2019 and topped out at 99. Lack of deception, tendency to pitch armside only and a below-average strike percentage limits his impact now. He occasionally flashes a hard, high-80s cutter-slider hybrid. The pitch is still a work in progress but gets its share of swing and misses.

THE FUTURE: Aybar stands out simply by being a lefthander with top-end velocity. His delivery and pitch development are crucial. He likely will move level-to-level unless he can improve his command.

Year	Age	Club (League)	Class	W	L	ERA	G	GS	SV	IP	H	HR	BB	SO	K/9	WHIP	AVG
2018	20	Red Sox (GCL)	R	1	1	4.10	15	0	0	26	23	0	12	27	9.2	1.33	.232
	20	Lowell (NYP)	SS	1	0	4.50	2	0	0	2	2	0	2	0	0.0	2.00	.250
2019	21	Greenville (SAL)	LoA	1	3	4.88	40	0	0	52	34	1	40	67	11.7	1.43	.180
	21	Salem (CAR)	HiA	0	0	1.80	4	0	0	5	2	0	1	3	5.4	0.60	.125
Minor League Totals				3	4	4.45	61	0	0	85	61	1	55	97	10.3	1.36	.196

Year	Age	Club (League)	Class	AVG	G	AB	R	H	2B	3B	HR	RBI	BB	SO	SB	OBP	SLG
2017	19	Greenville (SAL)	LoA	.160	30	100	12	16	2	1	0	4	6	38	2	.206	.200
	19	Lowell (NYP)	SS	.267	50	187	25	50	7	5	2	28	6	67	5	.296	.390
Minor League Totals				.241	241	880	107	212	33	22	5	93	38	266	23	.279	.345

24 CHIH-JUNG LIU, RHP

BA GRADE
45 **Risk: Extreme**

Born: April 7, 1999. **B-T:** S-R. **HT:** 6-0. **WT:** 180. **Signed:** Taiwan, 2019.
Signed by: Louie Lin/Brett Ward/Chris Becerra/Eddie Romero.

TRACK RECORD: A two-way player in high school, Liu went to college as a shortstop before returning to the mound in 2019. He dominated and won MVP honors in the Asian Baseball Championship before signing with the Red Sox for $750,000 in October.

SCOUTING REPORT: Liu's delivery is already more westernized that most, lacking any noticeable pauses. He repeats it well though he tends to fall off at times, especially on his breaking stuff, which minimizes its velocity. His arm action has good finish. Working in short stints this year, Liu showed explosive stuff, including a 93-96 mph fastball that topped out at 98 during the Asian Games, an 82-83 mph slider, a curveball and a low-80s splitter. The split appears to be the most advanced of his secondary pitches with solid depth off his fastball. Size and durability could be an issue moving forward.

THE FUTURE: Liu has tremendous upside based on athleticism and stuff, but his role remains in doubt moving forward. Extended spring training and short-season Lowell appear in the offing next year.

Year	Age	Club (League)	Class	W	L	ERA	G	GS	SV	IP	H	HR	BB	SO	K/9	WHIP	AVG
2019	20	Did not play—Signed 2020 contract															

25 ALDO RAMIREZ, RHP

BA GRADE
45 **Risk: Extreme**

Born: May 6, 2001. **B-T:** R-R. **HT:** 6-0. **WT:** 180. **Signed:** Mexico, 2018.
Signed by: Sotero Torres/Eddie Romero/Todd Claus.

TRACK RECORD: When Ramirez was just 17, he showed impressive maturity and poise while pitching in the Mexican League against much older veterans. Those traits, in tandem with a good delivery, convinced the Sox to move aggressively to sign him. He was one of the younger pitchers in the short-season New York-Penn League in 2019, where he forged a 3.94 ERA with 9.2 strikeouts and just 2.3 walks per nine innings.

SCOUTING REPORT: Ramirez still is on the smallish side, raising questions about whether he has the size and physicality to handle a starter's workload. Despite makings of a solid delivery, Ramirez has a deep arm path which could create issues down the road. Ramirez features a fastball in the low 90s and topped out at 95-96 mph. He also has good feel for 12-to-6 curveball in the 75-80 mph range. The late fade of his changeup adds to a vertical mix, although command is still a work in progress.

THE FUTURE: Ramirez shows back-of-the-rotation potential but may slide into a long reliever's role should durability become an issue. He should open 2020 as a teenager at low Class A Greenville.

Year	Age	Club (League)	Class	W	L	ERA	G	GS	SV	IP	H	HR	BB	SO	K/9	WHIP	AVG
2018	17	Aguascalientes (MEX)	AAA	0	0	8.31	4	0	0	4	6	2	6	1	2.1	2.77	--
	17	Red Sox1 (DSL)	R	1	2	0.39	5	5	0	23	10	0	3	17	6.7	0.57	.127
2019	18	Lowell (NYP)	SS	2	3	3.94	14	13	0	62	59	5	16	63	9.2	1.22	.245
Minor League Totals				3	5	3.16	24	18	0	91	76	7	25	83	8.2	1.11	.221

26 TYLER ESPLIN, OF

BA GRADE **40** Risk: High

Born: July 6, 1999. **B-T:** L-R. **HT:** 6-4. **WT:** 220. **Drafted:** HS—Bradenton, Fla., 2017 (7th round). **Signed by:** Stephen Hargett.

TRACK RECORD: Esplin grew up in the midwest but went to IMG Academy (Fla.) to further his baseball development as a high school senior. At JetBlue Park, the lefthanded hitter commanded notice by clearing the 40-foot wall in left, part of an intriguing show of both power and balance.

SCOUTING REPORT: While Esplin's performances to date have been relatively modest, he signed as a 17-year-old and just completed his first year of full-season ball at age 19. His youth, impressive size, and increasing strength have convinced the Sox that there's considerable untapped potential in his game. Esplin had significantly better numbers against righties than lefties. Esplin's exit velocity has increased each season, topping out at 88.5 in 2019. While Esplin's launch angle has gotten better each year, he still hits more balls on the ground than in the air. Esplin has enough arm to stay in right field.

THE FUTURE: Team officials considered Esplin's 2019 season a huge developmental success and believe he has enough run production potential with the ability to offer average outfield defense, a formula that gives him a solid chance at a platoon future.

Year	Age	Club (League)	Class	AVG	G	AB	R	H	2B	3B	HR	RBI	BB	SO	SB	OBP	SLG
2017	17	Red Sox (GCL)	R	.271	22	85	16	23	4	0	2	11	7	26	1	.340	.388
2018	18	Lowell (NYP)	SS	.217	52	184	18	40	7	4	3	24	23	53	5	.303	.348
2019	19	Greenville (SAL)	LoA	.253	100	387	52	98	26	3	5	43	40	107	6	.326	.375
	19	Salem (CAR)	HiA	.200	2	5	0	1	0	0	0	0	1	2	0	.333	.200
Minor League Totals				.245	176	661	86	162	37	7	10	78	71	188	12	.322	.368

27 KYLE HART, LHP

BA GRADE **40** Risk: High

Born: Nov. 23, 1992. **B-T:** L-L. **HT:** 6-5. **WT:** 170. **Drafted:** Indiana, 2016 (19th round). **Signed by:** Blair Henry.

TRACK RECORD: A promising college career got derailed by Tommy John surgery in Hart's junior year, after which the lefty decided to stick around to finish his degree. Scout Blair Henry, who'd seen him shortly before the surgery, remained convinced that the lefthander's pitchability made him a solid gamble. Hart signed for $5,000 and an opportunity, and he's done nothing but take advantage.

SCOUTING REPORT: Hart's feel for pitching and command are his best traits, as his mix—a high-80s fastball that scrapes the low 90s, slider, curveball, and changeup helps keep hitters off-balance and generates soft contact. Hart, though, has a narrow margin for error and is prone to hard-hit mistakes in the zone.

THE FUTURE: Already 27 years old, the Sox thought enough of Hart's approach as well as performance in Pawtucket to add him to the 40-man roster in November, seeing him as a potential depth starter or potentially a bulk innings pitcher behind an opener in the near future.

Year	Age	Club (League)	Class	W	L	ERA	G	GS	SV	IP	H	HR	BB	SO	K/9	WHIP	AVG
2017	24	Greenville (SAL)	LoA	4	2	1.90	13	10	0	66	50	0	17	57	7.7	1.01	.211
	24	Salem (CAR)	HiA	2	3	2.49	9	9	0	51	45	5	23	52	9.2	1.34	.241
2018	25	Portland (EL)	AA	7	9	3.57	24	24	0	139	139	12	49	100	6.5	1.36	.258
2019	26	Portland (EL)	AA	3	6	2.91	9	9	0	56	39	3	17	60	9.7	1.01	.199
	26	Pawtucket (IL)	AAA	9	7	3.86	18	15	0	100	91	8	36	80	7.2	1.27	.251
Minor League Totals				25	29	3.13	77	71	0	423	376	28	144	368	7.8	1.23	.240

28 CHASE SHUGART, RHP

BA GRADE **40** Risk: High

Born: October 24, 1996. **B-T:** R-R. **HT:** 5-10. **WT:** 180. **Drafted:** Texas, 2018 (12th round). **Signed by:** Brandon Agamennone.

TRACK RECORD: After spending his first two years at Texas and on the Cape working as a part-time closer, Shugart's four-pitch mix convinced the Longhorns to convert him to the rotation. While the results were mixed, Shugart still showed an occasional big fastball, topping out at 97 mph. Shugart's season started late, after serving a 50-game suspension for a second positive test for a drug of abuse.

SCOUTING REPORT: Shugart has a simple, athletic, repeatable delivery with clean arm path. Listed at just 5-foot-10, deception is an issue, which is reflected in his 7.3 percent strikeout rate. Shugart's strengths are his command, ability to use both sides of the plate while working in the strike zone (2.3 walks per nine) and limiting hard contact (.101 ISO). While his fastball has topped out at 96 mph, Shugart works in the 91-93 range. Shugart's curveball is his most effective pitch now with good shape, spin and command. Shugart also has a solid changeup and a developing slider.

THE FUTURE: Shugart shows traits of a potential back-end starter or long reliever. He will need to continue to refine command and his pitchability as well as remaining comfortable with contact.

Year	Age	Club (League)	Class	W	L	ERA	G	GS	SV	IP	H	HR	BB	SO	K/9	WHIP	AVG
2018	21	Red Sox (GCL)	R	0	1	1.80	3	3	0	5	4	0	1	6	10.8	1.00	.211
	21	Lowell (NYP)	SS	0	0	0.00	1	1	0	3	0	0	0	3	9.0	0.00	.000
2019	22	Greenville (SAL)	LoA	6	4	2.81	16	16	0	90	89	4	23	73	7.3	1.25	.253
Minor League Totals				6	5	2.67	20	20	0	97	93	4	24	82	7.6	1.20	.244

29 ANTONI FLORES, SS

BA GRADE 45 Risk: Extreme

Born: October 14, 2000. **B-T:** R-R. **HT:** 6-1. **WT:** 190. **Signed:** Venezuela, 2017. **Signed by:** Angel Escobar/Eddie Romero.

TRACK RECORD: The Red Sox signed Flores for $1.4 million in 2017 based on his balanced overall game and the potential for an across-the-board tool set. In limited playing time in the DSL and GCL in 2018, he showed an advanced feel for the game that stood out among older peers, resulting in a 2019 assignment to short-season Lowell.

SCOUTING REPORT: As an amateur and in 2018, Flores showed plate discipline, an excellent feel to hit, flashes of power, and advanced defensive instincts. Flores started slowly in Lowell, hitting just .125 over his first seven games and was unable to right the ship for the remainder of the season. Basic skills such as swing and miss rate, hard contact and chase rates got worse each month as the spiral deepened. Flores continued to see a lot of pitches and started using the entire field more, lending hope that he will make better adjustments moving forward. The Sox believe his defensive fundamentals improved in a year when he spent most of his time at short, though some rival evaluators worried about his speed and range and thus his ability to stay in the middle infield.

THE FUTURE: The 2020 season will be significant in showing whether Flores has the ability to make the necessary adjustments to the game stateside to tap the promise he'd shown in the past or if he will relegated to the long list of toolsy prospects unable to adjust to the speed of the game.

Year	Age	Club (League)	Class	AVG	G	AB	R	H	2B	3B	HR	RBI	BB	SO	SB	OBP	SLG
2018	17	Red Sox2 (DSL)	R	.347	13	49	10	17	3	1	1	14	8	7	0	.439	.510
	17	Red Sox (GCL)	R	.250	2	4	0	1	0	1	0	0	1	1	0	.400	.750
2019	18	Lowell (NYP)	SS	.193	55	181	14	35	4	1	0	12	25	59	1	.293	.227
Minor League Totals				.226	70	234	24	53	7	3	1	26	34	67	1	.326	.295

30 DURBIN FELTMAN, RHP

BA GRADE 40 Risk: High

Born: April 18, 1997. **B-T:** R-R. **HT:** 6-0. **WT:** 205. **Drafted:** Texas Christian, 2018 (3rd round). **Signed by:** Brandon Agamennone.

TRACK RECORD: Drafted as a dominant college closer, the Red Sox plucked Feltman in the third round in 2018 anticipating he might be the first of his draft class to climb to the majors. The road has been less than smooth, however, and was filled with his share of growing pains in 2019, when he spent most of the season in Double-A Portland.

SCOUTING REPORT: In college, Feltman's fastball sat at 95-97 mph and topped out even higher while working mostly in high-leverage situations. In 2019, his fastball proved less effective against upper-level hitters, forcing the Sox to use Feltman earlier in games. While he still was able to hit 97 mph, Feltman's fastball needed to sit mostly between 93-94 to generate better quality in the zone. Moreover, after months of trying to elevate his fastball, Feltman returned to working the bottom half more frequently, which in turn resulted in a solid finish. Feltman's go to pitch has been his low 80s CB with solid spin and 12-6 break until the second half of last year when Feltman started using his slider more frequently, with mixed results.

THE FUTURE: As the Sox refine Feltman to develop his stuff to enhance his sustained value, they still remain optimistic in his ceiling: A reliever with the potential for two plus pitches and average command, a combination that would profile in the late innings.

Year	Age	Club (League)	Class	W	L	ERA	G	GS	SV	IP	H	HR	BB	SO	K/9	WHIP	AVG
2018	21	Lowell (NYP)	SS	0	0	0.00	4	0	0	4	0	0	0	7	15.8	0.00	.000
	21	Greenville (SAL)	LoA	0	1	2.57	7	0	3	7	6	0	1	14	18.0	1.00	.214
	21	Salem (CAR)	HiA	1	0	2.19	11	0	1	12	12	0	4	15	10.9	1.30	.261
2019	22	Portland (EL)	AA	2	3	5.26	43	0	5	51	42	8	31	54	9.5	1.42	.223
Minor League Totals				3	4	4.22	65	0	9	74	60	8	36	90	10.9	1.29	.218

Chicago Cubs

BY JOSH NORRIS

The era of good feelings in Chicago is over a mere three years removed from the team's first World Series championship since 1908. The 2019 season was the second consecutive in which the team squandered a division title in the season's final days, and this time it caused an organizational overhaul. The Cubs were done in by a late nine-game losing streak. Worse still, all nine games were against teams from the National League Central, including four in a row to the eventual division-champion Cardinals. The skid was a crushing blow for a team that had held a three and a half game lead as late as Aug. 8.

After the season, the Cubs fired manager Joe Maddon and replaced him with longtime catcher and World Series hero David Ross. It also promoted farm director Jaron Madison to assistant general manager and elevated one of his assistants, Bobby Basham, to farm director. There was also a series of moves made in the player development department designed to follow the industry trend of importing young, analytically minded talent and putting it in place up and down the organization.

The Cubs still have a young, talented core of hitters which includes Kris Bryant, Javier Baez, Kyle Schwarber, Willson Contreras and Anthony Rizzo, but the pitching staff is sorely lacking behind Kyle Hendricks and Yu Darvish. Because the organization hasn't been particularly good at developing pitchers outside of Hendricks in recent years, the team will likely have to turn to the free-agent market for help. The team's best pitching prospect, lefthander Brailyn Marquez, is still years away from Chicago, and the arms coming behind him aren't quite ready for prime time, either.

Marquez's breakthrough 2019 did perhaps represent a bit of an organizational turnaround. The fireballing lefty showed improved command and further development of his offspeed stuff en route to a stellar season, not to mention No. 1 prospect status in the organization.

Marquez was joined on the Top 100 Prospects by No. 2 prospect Nico Hoerner, a middle infielder and 2018 first-round pick who made his big league debut despite missing a chunk of the season with a broken hand. The Cubs showed faith in Hoerner early when they assigned him to Double-A Tennessee to begin his first full season as a pro. The move came after a scorching turn in the 2018 Arizona Fall League that saw him hit well against more experienced prospects.

The Cubs went off the board for their first pick in the 2019 draft when they selected Fresno State righthander Ryan Jensen, who showed intriguing fastball characteristics if not the best consistency or command. Jensen was part of a group of four college arms among their first five picks. The lone exception was UCLA's Chase Strumpf, a bat-first second baseman who put together a solid pro debut in the Northwest League.

The Cubs also added two of the better talents available on the 2019 international market in shortstop Kevin Made and catcher Ronnier Quintero on July 2. They added catcher Brayan Altuve to the mix later in the period and watched as several young Latin middle infielders put together strong seasons in the lowest levels of the minors.

The Cubs aren't far removed from the sport's highest peak, but they decided this offseason that sweeping changes were needed to help them reverse course and keep them from falling into another extended lull.

NUCCIO DINUZZO/GETTY IMAGES

Nico Hoerner continues the Cubs' tradition of graduating quality major league position players.

PROJECTED 2023 LINEUP

Position	Player	Age
Catcher	Willson Contreras	31
First Base	Anthony Rizzo	33
Second Base	Nico Hoerner (2)	26
Third Base	Kris Bryant	31
Shortstop	Javier Baez	30
Left Field	Kyle Schwarber	30
Center Field	Albert Almora	29
Right Field	Brennen Davis (3)	23
No. 1 Starter	Yu Darvish	36
No. 2 Starter	Brailyn Marquez (1)	24
No. 3 Starter	Kyle Hendricks	33
No. 4 Starter	Riley Thompson (9)	26
No. 5 Starter	Cory Abbott (10)	27
Closer	Ryan Jensen (7)	25

DEPTH CHART

CHICAGO CUBS

TOP 2020 ROOKIE: Nico Hoerner, SS/2B. After a solid big league cameo, Hoerner will carve out a role as a solid offensive piece in Chicago.
BREAKOUT PROSPECT: Kohl Franklin, RHP. He showed hints of a starter's ceiling in his first full pro year and could take big strides in 2020.
SLEEPER: Yovanny Cruz, RHP: Cruz has big velocity from an easy arm action and could make a big leap in 2020 with refined mechanics.

SOURCE OF TOP 30 TALENT

Homegrown	30	Acquired	0
College	10	Trade	0
Junior college	1	Rule 5 draft	0
High school	5	Independent league	0
Nondrafted free agent	0	Free agent/waivers	0
International	14		

LF
Cole Roederer (6)
D.J. Artis
Nelson Velazquez
Kevonte Mitchell

CF
Edmond Americaan (17)
Yohendrick Pinango (22)
Fernando Kelli
D.J. Wilson
Zac Taylor

RF
Brennen Davis (3)
Eddy Martinez

3B
Christopher Morel (27)
Grayson Byrd

SS
Nico Hoerner (2)
Pedro Martinez (16)
Kevin Made (19)
Rafael Morel (21)
Aramis Ademan (26)
Zack Short (28)

2B
Chase Strumpf (5)
Fabian Pertuz (23)
Reivaj Garcia
Luis Verdugo
Robel Garcia
Vimael Machin
Andy Weber

1B
Jared Young
Jake Slaughter

C
Miguel Amaya (4)
Ethan Hearn (8)
Ronnier Quintero (20)
Brayan Altuve (24)
P.J. Higgins
Jhonny Pereda

LHP

LHSP	LHRP
Brailyn Marquez (1)	Jack Patterson (30)
Justin Steele (25)	Brendon Little
D.J. Herz	Jordan Minch
	Wyatt Short

RHP

RHSP	RHRP
Ryan Jensen (7)	Michael McAvene (15)
Riley Thompson (9)	Manuel Rodriguez (29)
Cory Abbott (10)	Yovanny Cruz
Adbert Alzolay (11)	Scott Effross
Tyson Miller (12)	Brad Depperman
Kohl Franklin (13)	Hunter Bigge
Chris Clarke (14)	Jose Albertos
Richard Gallardo (18)	
Matt Swarmer	
Keegan Thompson	
Oscar De La Cruz	
Erich Uelmen	

DRAFT ANALYSIS

2019

BEST PURE HITTER: This category goes to UCLA product 2B Chase Strumpf (2). The Cubs were drawn to Strumpf for the maturity in his at-bats, his all-fields approach and the sneaky power he produces. He displayed all of those traits in his first pro season, spent predominantly at short-season Eugene.

BEST POWER: Alabama prep C Ethan Hearn (6) garnered the third-largest bonus in the Cubs' 2019 draft class on the strength of his bountiful raw juice. His muscular frame gives him the potential for plus power once he reaches the big leagues.

FASTEST RUNNER: Illinois OF Zac Taylor (25) is a 70-grade runner on the 20-to-80 scouting scale and swiped 12 bases in his pro debut, which took him from the Rookie-level Arizona League all the way to high Class A Myrtle Beach.

BEST DEFENSIVE PLAYER: This category goes to Hearn as well. In addition to his power, Hearn showed the Cubs athleticism, quick feet and small-space movement as an amateur and again in his pro debut. He also showed some pop times of less than 2.0 seconds.

BEST ATHLETE: Taylor has the speed and strength to show well in an NFL combine. He hits baseballs hard and is a near-elite runner. Those traits should benefit him at the plate and in the field.

BEST FASTBALL: Fresno State RHP Ryan Jensen (1) throws four- and two-seam fastballs that each averaged 96 mph in his pro debut, which was spent with short-season Eugene. The pitches also play well on TrackMan for their carry and rise or sink, depending on the version.

BEST SECONDARY PITCH: Southern California RHP Chris Clarke (4) throws a curveball that amateur scouts rated as a potential 70-grade pitch on the 20-to-80 scouting scale.

BEST PRO DEBUT: RHP Michael McAvene (3) was a reliever at Louisville but was used as a starter at short-season Eugene and struck out nearly 41 percent of the hitters he faced.

MOST INTRIGUING BACKGROUND: The Cubs drafted two players with big league bloodlines. Texas 3B Ryan Reynolds (14) is the son of former All-Star righthander Shane Reynolds, and Clemson INF Grayson Byrd (24) is the son of 14-year major leaguer Paul Byrd.

CLOSEST TO THE MAJORS: Jensen or McAvene could reach the majors quickly if moved to the bullpen, but both are starters at the moment and the Cubs see pitch mixes in both that will allow them to continue developing into potential rotation pieces.

BEST LATE-ROUND PICK: Taylor fits the bill here, with an intriguing mix of tools and athleticism that the Cubs were happy to select in the 25th round then watch as he zoomed through the low minors.

THE ONE WHO GOT AWAY: It's very rare for a team to draft a player in the top 10 rounds and then fail to sign him, but that's exactly what happened with C Wyatt Hendrie (10), an athletic backstop with good defensive ability and some contact skills. Hendrie was one of just two players in the 2019 draft to be selected among the top 10 rounds and not sign. RHP Brandon Sproat (Rangers, 7th round) was the other.

—JOSH NORRIS

TOP DRAFT PICKS OF THE DECADE

Year	Player, Pos	2019 Org
2010	Hayden Simpson, RHP	Did not play
2011	Javier Baez, SS	Cubs
2012	Albert Almora, OF	Cubs
2013	Kris Bryant, 3B	Cubs
2014	Kyle Schwarber, C	Cubs
2015	Ian Happ, OF	Cubs
2016	Thomas Hatch, RHP (3rd round)	Blue Jays
2017	Brendon Little, LHP	Cubs
2018	Nico Hoerner, SS	Cubs
2019	Ryan Jensen, RHP	Cubs

2018

SS Nico Hoerner (1) was the latest college hitter drafted by the Cubs to rocket to the big leagues. OF Brennan Davis (2) has also shown big potential, while RHP Paul Richan (2s) was a part of the deal for Nick Castellanos.

GRADE: A

2017

The Cubs went all-in on college pitching and, so far, have seen little return on that investment. RHP Cory Abbott (2) looks to be the best of the bunch, while RHP Alex Lange (1) helped land Nick Castellanos.

GRADE: D

2016

The Cubs didn't pick until the third round and then went heavy on college pitching. RHP Tyson Miller (4) is the best of that group, and they traded RHP Thomas Hatch (3) to Toronto in July for reliever David Phelps.

GRADE: F

1 BRAILYN MARQUEZ, LHP

Born: Jan. 30, 1999. **B-T:** L-L. **HT:** 6-4. **WT:** 185.
Signed: Dominican Republic, 2015. **Signed by:** Mario Encarnacion/Jose Serra/Alex Suarez/Louie Eljaua.

TRACK RECORD: When the Cubs gave Marquez $600,000 in 2015, they did so with the idea that his fastball, which sat in the low 90s, had the potential to give hitters nightmares. They were right. Marquez hinted at his potential in an excellent 2018 season that ended with him ranked as the No. 3 prospect in the Northwest League. He showed up even stronger in 2019, which ended in his first appearance on the Top 100 Prospects.

SCOUTING REPORT: Marquez's signature pitch is his fastball, which sits in the upper 90s and regularly reaches triple digits. He peaked at 102 mph, which he reached 24 times in 2019. Marquez pairs the fastball with a spike slider in the low 80s that, at its best, tunnels with his fastball and features short, late snap. He also throws a changeup in the 89-91 mph range that he can use to get swings and misses. The pitch needs more consistency to reach its projection as an average major league offering. The Cubs point to a two-year process Marquez went through to get his arms and legs to sync up during his delivery as one of the main drivers of his improved ability to throw quality strikes. They also worked to get his arm stroke back to the longer, smoother version he showed as an amateur instead of the shorter, choppier one it had morphed into. Once those elements were in place, he needed to learn how to sequence. Instead of using his velocity to blow fastballs by hitters, he needed to have the intuition and confidence to throw his offspeed pitches in appropriate counts. That process was part of the reason the Cubs kept Marquez at low Class A South Bend until Aug. 6. Even with his raised profile, there are still plenty of ways Marquez can continue to improve. Maintaining command will be a continual process, especially given his size and long levers. He needs to continue to refine his changeup, especially considering that it is thrown with similar velocity as his breaking ball.

THE FUTURE: For an organization that has struggled mightily to develop pitchers, Marquez represents hope. If he can maintain his delivery and bring his offspeed pitches forward, he could fit as a franchise starter at the front of a rotation. If not, his elite velocity from the left side could lead him into a closer's role. Either role would be an outcome befitting the organization's No. 1 prospect.

DAN ARNOLD

BA GRADE
60 Risk: High

SCOUTING GRADES
Fastball: 80. **Slider:** 60. **Changeup:** 50. **Control:** 50.

Projected future grades on 20-80 scouting scale.

TOP PROSPECTS OF THE DECADE

Year	Player, Pos	2019 Org
2010	Starlin Castro, SS	Marlins
2011	Chris Archer, RHP	Pirates
2012	Brett Jackson, OF	Did not play
2013	Javier Baez, SS	Cubs
2014	Javier Baez, SS	Cubs
2015	Kris Bryant, 3B	Cubs
2016	Gleyber Torres, SS	Yankees
2017	Eloy Jimenez, OF	White Sox
2018	Aramis Ademan, SS	Cubs
2019	Nico Hoerner, SS	Cubs

BEST TOOLS

Best Hitter for Average	Nico Hoerner
Best Power Hitter	Brennen Davis
Best Strike-Zone Discipline	Nico Hoerner
Fastest Baserunner	Edmond Americaan
Best Athlete	Brennen Davis
Best Fastball	Brailyn Marquez
Best Curveball	Jack Patterson
Best Slider	Cory Abbott
Best Changeup	Kohl Franklin
Best Control	Tyson Miller
Best Defensive Catcher	Miguel Amaya
Best Defensive Infielder	Nico Hoerner
Best Infield Arm	Luis Verdugo
Best Defensive Outfielder	Brennen Davis
Best Outfield Arm	Eddy Martinez

Year	Age	Club (League)	Class	W	L	ERA	G	GS	SV	IP	H	HR	BB	SO	K/9	WHIP	AVG
2017	18	Cubs (AZL)	R	2	1	5.52	11	9	0	44	50	3	12	52	10.6	1.41	.275
2018	19	Eugene (NWL)	SS	1	4	3.21	10	10	0	48	46	5	14	52	9.8	1.26	.257
	19	South Bend (MWL)	LoA	0	0	2.57	2	2	0	7	7	0	2	7	9.0	1.29	.259
2019	20	South Bend (MWL)	LoA	5	4	3.61	17	17	0	77	64	4	43	102	11.9	1.38	.228
	20	Myrtle Beach (CAR)	HiA	4	1	1.71	5	5	0	26	21	1	7	26	8.9	1.06	.214
Minor League Totals				16	12	3.19	57	55	0	257	232	14	101	287	10.1	1.30	.240

2 NICO HOERNER, SS/2B

Born: May 13, 1997. **B-T:** R-R. **HT:** 5-11. **WT:** 200. **Drafted:** Stanford, 2018 (1st round). **Signed by:** Gabe Zappin.

TRACK RECORD: During his career at Stanford and his summers in the Northwoods and Cape Cod leagues, Hoerner exhibited all the traits of a professional hitter. The Cubs were confident enough in Hoerner's hitting track record that they drafted him 24th overall in 2018, then watched as he made it to low Class A after just 10 games. An elbow strain ended his regular season, but Hoerner sidelined him until the Arizona Fall League, where he shined. Hoerner spent his first full year at Double-A. He missed the bulk of the regular season with a broken hand, but once again shined later in the season, this time as a September callup.

BA GRADE
55 Risk: Medium

SCOUTING REPORT: Hoerner entered pro ball as an accomplished hitter, but he still had polish to add. The Cubs focused early in the season on adjusting Hoerner's stance and approach to allow him to work the ball to the left-center field gap more often. The adjustments also allowed Hoerner to pull breaking balls in the air with more regularity. Those changes quickly took hold and made Hoerner into a more complete hitter and allowed him to put his best swing on more pitches. Defensively, he still has a chance to play shortstop, but he's more likely to slide over to second base as his career moves along—especially considering Javier Baez has shortstop well in hand. He's an average runner but his instincts amplify his pure speed.

THE FUTURE: Hoerner fared well in his big league debut and could compete for a return engagement out of spring training. Hoerner should settle in as an offensive-minded infielder.

SCOUTING GRADES: **Hitting:** 60 **Power:** 50 **Running:** 55 **Fielding:** 50 **Arm:** 50

Year	Age	Club (League)	Class	AVG	G	AB	R	H	2B	3B	HR	RBI	BB	SO	SB	OBP	SLG
2018	21	Cubs 1 (AZL)	R	.250	3	12	3	3	1	1	0	1	2	0	2	.400	.500
	21	Eugene (NWL)	SS	.318	7	22	6	7	0	1	1	2	5	3	4	.464	.545
	21	South Bend (MWL)	LoA	.400	4	15	1	6	1	0	1	3	2	1	0	.471	.667
2019	22	Cubs 2 (AZL)	R	.400	5	20	2	8	1	0	0	0	1	1	0	.429	.450
	22	Tennessee (SL)	AA	.284	70	268	37	76	16	3	3	22	21	31	8	.344	.399
	22	Chicago (NL)	MAJ	.282	20	78	13	22	1	1	3	17	3	11	0	.305	.436
Major League Totals				.282	20	78	13	22	1	1	3	17	3	11	0	.305	.436
Minor League Totals				.297	89	337	49	100	19	5	5	28	31	36	14	.365	.427

3 BRENNEN DAVIS, OF

Born: Nov. 2, 1999. **B-T:** R-R. **HT:** 6-4. **WT:** 175. **Drafted:** HS—Chandler, Ariz., 2018 (2nd round). **Signed by:** Steve McFarland.

TRACK RECORD: Davis came to the Cubs a bit raw in terms of his baseball skills after splitting his high school career between the diamond and the basketball court. The athleticism that allowed him to excel on the hardwood also provided Davis with considerable baseball upside. The Cubs spent a second-round pick on him and used a $1.1 million bonus to sign him.

BA GRADE
55 Risk: High

SCOUTING REPORT: Davis was originally slated to start in extended spring training before moving to short-season for the summer. He outplayed expectations, however, and forced the Cubs to push him to low Class A South Bend. Davis performed well in the Midwest League, but his season was disjointed because of a pair of pitches that hit him in nearly the same spot on his right index finger. The second pitch broke the finger and ended his season. Before the injury, the Cubs moved Davis off the plate a bit to allow his long levers a better chance to get extended and create torque against more pitches. He took to the changes quickly, and the result was an excellent first exposure to pitchers outside Rookie-level ball. The Cubs expect Davis to add considerably more strength to his lithe frame, which should add more power.

THE FUTURE: After a tantalizing glimpse of his tools becoming skills in 2019, Davis should get a chance to build on his success in 2020.

SCOUTING GRADES: **Hitting:** 50 **Power:** 60 **Running:** 60 **Fielding:** 50 **Arm:** 60

Year	Age	Club (League)	Class	AVG	G	AB	R	H	2B	3B	HR	RBI	BB	SO	SB	OBP	SLG
2018	18	Cubs 2 (AZL)	R	.298	18	57	9	17	2	0	0	3	10	12	6	.431	.333
2019	19	South Bend (MWL)	LoA	.305	50	177	33	54	9	3	8	30	18	38	4	.381	.525
Minor League Totals				.303	68	234	42	71	11	3	8	33	28	50	10	.394	.479

4 MIGUEL AMAYA, C

BA GRADE
55 Risk: High

Born: March 9, 1999. **B-T:** R-R. **HT:** 6-1. **WT:** 200. **Signed:** Panama, 2015.
Signed by: Marino Encarnacion/Jose Serra/Alex Suarez/Louie Eljaua.

TRACK RECORD: The Cubs thought enough of Amaya's combination of defensive and offensive skills to give him a $1 million signing bonus out of Panama. He's moved a level per year since signing, with full seasons at low Class A South Bend and high Class A Myrtle Beach in 2018 and 2019, respectively. Amaya has represented the Cubs at the Futures Game in each of the past two seasons as well.

SCOUTING REPORT: Slowly but surely, Amaya is developing into the player the Cubs envisioned. He spent 2019 adjusting his approach to hit the ball in the air more often. The concept is a tough sell at Myrtle Beach, where flyballs don't get rewarded as often as at other parks. Amaya's 11 home runs fell one short of the career high he set in 2018, but he did so in 73 fewer at-bats. Notably, Amaya opened the season as the youngest position player in the Carolina League. He can get overaggressive and get himself out early in counts, which is another area he'll work to improve. Amaya has work to do behind the plate, where he's still a bit of crude receiver. He has the arm strength to produce pop times of just more than 2.0 seconds and caught 35 percent of attempted basestealers.

THE FUTURE: After a full year at high Class A plus time in the Arizona Fall League, Amaya should move to Double-A Tennessee in 2020. He projects as a solid but not spectacular everyday catcher.

SCOUTING GRADES: **Hitting:** 50 **Power:** 55 **Running:** 20 **Fielding:** 50 **Arm:** 60

Year	Age	Club (League)	Class	AVG	G	AB	R	H	2B	3B	HR	RBI	BB	SO	SB	OBP	SLG
2017	18	Eugene (NWL)	SS	.228	58	228	21	52	14	1	3	26	11	49	1	.266	.338
2018	19	South Bend (MWL)	LoA	.256	116	414	54	106	21	2	12	52	50	91	1	.349	.403
2019	20	Myrtle Beach (CAR)	HiA	.235	99	341	50	80	24	0	11	57	54	69	2	.351	.402
Minor League Totals				.243	331	1191	154	289	71	3	27	157	136	236	13	.334	.375

5 CHASE STRUMPF, 2B

BA GRADE
50 Risk: High

Born: March 8, 1998. **B-T:** R-R. **HT:** 6-1. **WT:** 191. **Drafted:** UCLA, 2019 (2nd round). **Signed by:** Tom Myers.

TRACK RECORD: Strumpf put together a stellar career at California's prestigious JSerra HS, where he was teammates with 2017 No. 1 overall pick Royce Lewis. His five home runs led the 2013 15U National Team, which had a roster with 2016 No. 1 overall pick Mickey Moniak, 2019 No. 3 overall pick Andrew Vaughn and 2017 first-rounder Nick Pratto. After high school, Strumpf put together three excellent seasons at UCLA, including an outstanding sophomore season in which he hit .363/.475/.633 with 12 home runs. His numbers were down a bit in 2019, but the Cubs were convicted enough by his bat to draft him in the second round. He ranked No. 6 among the short-season Northwest League's Top 20 prospects.

SCOUTING REPORT: After scoring big in 2018 with Nico Hoerner, a bat-first middle infielder from the Pac-12 Conference, the Cubs went back to that well again in 2019. In Strumpf, Cubs scouts saw a polished hitter with a solid approach and a grinder's mentality both at the plate and in the field. He's shown mostly doubles power as a pro, but the Cubs believe a few tweaks can help him start putting more balls over the fence. Specifically, they want him to back off the plate a little bit more and use his long arms to generate the torque his frame and strength will allow. They'd also like to see him be a little more aggressive later in counts, especially on pitches he can impact. Strumpf is a serviceable second baseman with strong hands and feet who can make routine plays but is not likely to wow anyone his glove. He has fringe-average arm strength.

THE FUTURE: Given his pedigree, Strumpf should move to high Class A Myrtle Beach in 2020. He projects as a bat-first middle infielder.

SCOUTING GRADES: **Hitting:** 55 **Power:** 50 **Running:** 40 **Fielding:** 45 **Arm:** 45

Year	Age	Club (League)	Class	AVG	G	AB	R	H	2B	3B	HR	RBI	BB	SO	SB	OBP	SLG
2019	21	Cubs 2 (AZL)	R	.182	7	22	5	4	3	0	0	1	7	7	0	.406	.318
	21	Eugene (NWL)	SS	.292	26	89	17	26	8	0	2	14	15	28	2	.405	.449
	21	South Bend (MWL)	LoA	.125	6	24	3	3	1	0	1	2	1	7	0	.214	.292
Minor League Totals				.244	39	135	25	33	12	0	3	17	23	42	2	.374	.400

6 COLE ROEDERER, OF

Born: Sept. 24, 1999. **B-T:** L-L. **HT:** 6-0. **WT:** 175. **Drafted:** HS—Santa Clarita, Calif., 2018 (2nd round supplemental). **Signed by:** Tom Myers.

TRACK RECORD: Improved strength and power in his draft season led Roederer to make a quick move up draft boards. Even after he separated his shoulder and pulled his hamstring, the Cubs were sold enough to draft Roederer in the second supplemental round and sign him for $1.2 million. He put together a solid pro debut in the Rookie-level Arizona League, where he ranked as the league's No. 7 prospect.

SCOUTING REPORT: Roederer's value is tied mostly to his bat, which showed in 2019 that it will need a bit more polish. Specifically, Roederer tried too hard to pull the ball with power rather than shooting line drives to all fields. In turn, his numbers suffered. Still, evaluators both inside and outside the system see the potential for a solid hitter. He has a quick, direct swing and a still head which should allow him to make plenty of solid contact if he can adjust his approach. Pitchers in the MWL learned to set up Roederer with high fastballs followed by offspeed pitches low in the zone. Now it's on him to adjust. He's a solid defender whose above-average speed and fringe-average arm should fit well in left field.

THE FUTURE: Roederer projects as a solid regular in the outfield. He should see high Class A Myrtle Beach in 2020 but might start back in the Midwest League.

SCOUTING GRADES: **Hitting:** 55 **Power:** 50 **Running:** 55 **Fielding:** 50 **Arm:** 45

Year	Age	Club (League)	Class	AVG	G	AB	R	H	2B	3B	HR	RBI	BB	SO	SB	OBP	SLG
2018	18	Cubs 2 (AZL)	R	.275	36	142	30	39	4	4	5	24	18	37	13	.354	.465
2019	19	South Bend (MWL)	LoA	.224	108	384	45	86	19	4	9	60	52	112	16	.319	.365
Minor League Totals				.238	144	526	75	125	23	8	14	84	70	149	29	.328	.392

7 RYAN JENSEN, RHP

Born: Nov. 23, 1997. **B-T:** R-R. **HT:** 6-0. **WT:** 180. **Drafted:** Fresno State, 2019 (1st round). **Signed by:** Gabe Zappin.

TRACK RECORD: Jensen moved from the bullpen at Fresno State into the rotation in the middle of his sophomore year and saw mixed results. His stuff was plenty strong to thrive, but his scattershot command and control often counteracted his powerful pitch mix. Still, the Cubs were intrigued by Jensen's raw tools and what they could become when paired with pro coaching. They were so strongly convinced, in fact, that they used their first-round pick in 2019 on Jensen and signed him to a $2 million bonus. He made six starts in the short-season Northwest League before shutting it down after throwing a career-high 100 innings at Fresno State.

SCOUTING REPORT: The intrigue surrounding Jensen comes from his two-seam and four-seam fastballs. While plenty of pitchers have both of them in their repertoire, Jensen throws both pitches at the same velocity while keeping them as two distinct pitches. Both pitches average 96 mph, but the four-seamer features carrying life through the zone while the two-seamer shows power sink and armside run. He backs up the fastballs with a mid-80s slider with power break. His changeup is a distant fourth pitch and was seldom needed in college. The key will be honing Jensen's mechanics to make them more repeatable and helping him control the length of the movement on his pitches. He showed fatigue toward the end of the season, but area scout Gabe Zappin and West Coast crosschecker Shane Farrell noted that Jensen held his stuff throughout his outings despite a smaller than normal frame from a power pitcher.

THE FUTURE: After an offseason to recover, Jensen will likely move to one of the Cubs' Class A levels to begin 2020. His upside is as a high-end power arm in the rotation but he could be a power reliever as well and use his fastballs and slider to wipe out hitters.

SCOUTING GRADES: **Fastball:** 70 **Slider:** 55 **Changeup:** 40 **Control:** 40

Year	Age	Club (League)	Class	W	L	ERA	G	GS	SV	IP	H	HR	BB	SO	K/9	WHIP	AVG
2019	21	Eugene (NWL)	SS	0	0	2.25	6	6	0	12	7	0	14	19	14.3	1.75	.171
Minor League Totals				0	0	2.25	6	6	0	12	7	0	14	19	14.3	1.75	.171

8 ETHAN HEARN, C

BA GRADE
50 Risk: High

Born: Aug. 31, 2000. **B-T:** L-R. **HT:** 6-0. **WT:** 200. **Drafted:** HS—Mobile, Ala., 2019 (6th round). **Signed by:** Alex McClure.

TRACK RECORD: After plumbing the college ranks in the first five rounds, the Cubs made Hearn—a sturdily built catcher from Alabama—their first prep pick in 2019. He was a preseason first-team All-American entering the year, and then hit .482 with 11 doubles and 11 home runs in his draft year. He was the first high school catcher selected. The Cubs signed him for $950,000, the highest bonus for a sixth-rounder in the past two drafts, and assigned him to the Rookie-level Arizona League.

SCOUTING REPORT: Hearn looks like a player built to mash, and that's exactly what he does. He pairs a quick bat with strong hands, legs and forearms to generate above-average raw power from the left side. He has a power-over-hit profile and lived up to that rep by striking out at a 36.7-percent clip in his pro debut. The Cubs are working with Hearn to build more lift into his swing and prioritize hitting the ball deeper in the strike zone. Beyond his offensive skills, Hearn has the tools necessary to stay behind the plate. Baseball America ranked him as the second-best defensive catcher available in the high school ranks, and the Cubs see short-area quickness combined with plus arm strength that has allowed him to flash 1.9-second pop times.

THE FUTURE: Hearn projects as a catcher with a blend of offensive and defensive gifts. He should begin his first full season as a pro in extended spring training before moving to short-season Eugene.

SCOUTING GRADES: **Hitting:** 40 **Power:** 60 **Running:** 30 **Fielding:** 50 **Arm:** 60

Year	Age	Club (League)	Class	AVG	G	AB	R	H	2B	3B	HR	RBI	BB	SO	SB	OBP	SLG
2019	18	Cubs 1 (AZL)	R	.160	21	75	9	12	2	0	2	11	12	35	1	.283	.267
	18	Cubs 2 (AZL)	R	.200	2	5	1	1	1	0	0	3	1	1	0	.333	.400
Minor League Totals				.163	23	80	10	13	3	0	2	14	13	36	1	.286	.275

9 RILEY THOMPSON, RHP

BA GRADE
50 Risk: High

Born: July 9, 1996. **B-T:** L-R. **HT:** 6-3. **WT:** 205. **Drafted:** Louisville, 2018 (11th round). **Signed by:** Jacob Williams.

TRACK RECORD: Thompson transitioned into the starting rotation in the middle of his sophomore year at Louisville after being used exclusively as a reliever in 2017 both in college and in a five-game stint in the Cape Cod League. He was a draft-eligible sophomore, and the Cubs selected him in the 11th round. He had Tommy John surgery in 2016 and was a 37th-round pick of the Reds out of high school and a 27th-round pick of the Yankees as a redshirt freshman. He had a successful first half-season as a pro with short-season Eugene, which included a run to the Northwest League Championship Series.

SCOUTING REPORT: As a starter, Thompson has begun showing the makings of a true four-pitch mix. He starts with a fastball that averages 93 mph and touches around 96 mph while spinning at an above-average rate of 2,300 rpms. He pairs the fastball with a downer curveball that spins at better than 3,000 rpms and is thrown in the mid-80s. He's made great strides with his changeup, which the Cubs rebuilt during their instructional league in January 2019. After running through a variety of grips, Thompson and the Cubs settled on a split-fingered, "Vulcan" grip. The new version of the pitch tunnels well off of his fastball and is easiest for him to command. He's also shown the makings of a potentially average slider. Thompson finished his season in style with five perfect innings with 10 strikeouts in the decisive third game of South Bend's Midwest League Championship Series win over Clinton.

THE FUTURE: Thompson threw a career-high 94 innings in 2019 and will need to continue being built up to handle a starter's workload. The next step is high Class A Myrtle Beach.

SCOUTING GRADES: **Fastball:** 60 **Slider:** 50 **Curveball:** 50 **Changeup:** 50 **Control:** 50

Year	Age	Club (League)	Class	W	L	ERA	G	GS	SV	IP	H	HR	BB	SO	K/9	WHIP	AVG
2018	21	Eugene (NWL)	SS	0	2	2.84	9	8	0	25	24	1	9	25	8.9	1.30	.253
2019	22	South Bend (MWL)	LoA	8	6	3.06	21	21	0	94	85	9	31	87	8.3	1.23	.239
Minor League Totals				8	8	3.02	30	29	0	119	109	10	40	112	8.5	1.25	.242

10 CORY ABBOTT, RHP

Born: Sept. 20, 1995. **B-T:** R-R. **HT:** 6-2. **WT:** 210. **Drafted:** Loyola Marymount, 2017 (2nd round). **Signed by:** Tom Myers.

TRACK RECORD: Abbott's draft stock took off after he watched a video of Mets ace Noah Syndergaard throwing his slider and began replicating the pitch. He threw a perfect game in 2017 at Loyola Marymount, then was selected by the Cubs in the second round. He mastered both Class A levels in his first full season as a pro, then rung up 166 strikeouts at Double-A in 2019. That figure ranked 11th in the minor leagues and tops among Cubs farmhands.

SCOUTING REPORT: Abbott starts his arsenal with a fastball in the 89-93 mph range that can touch a few ticks higher when needed. The pitch is commanded well and has the characteristics to get swings and misses up in the zone. He backs it up with a hard curveball with 12-to-6 break that he uses to tunnel off of his fastball. He still uses the slider, which has the potential to be an above-average pitch with cutterish break, as a way to give hitters a look at something that breaks from east to west. His changeup is present but is a clear fourth pitch that needs further polish before it can project even as average. He's made considerable improvements to his body, especially his lower half, and the Cubs are fans of the cerebral, competitive mentality he brings to the mound.

THE FUTURE: After finding success in the Southern League, Abbott will move to the hitter's Hades of the Pacific Coast League in 2020. He has the upside of a back-end starter.

SCOUTING GRADES: **Fastball:** 50 **Slider:** 50 **Curveball:** 55 **Changeup:** 40 **Control:** 45

Year	Age	Club (League)	Class	W	L	ERA	G	GS	SV	IP	H	HR	BB	SO	K/9	WHIP	AVG
2017	21	Eugene (NWL)	SS	0	0	3.86	5	5	0	14	14	1	3	18	11.6	1.21	.269
2018	22	South Bend (MWL)	LoA	4	1	2.47	9	9	0	47	35	5	13	57	10.8	1.01	.207
	22	Myrtle Beach (CAR)	HiA	4	5	2.53	13	13	0	68	59	3	26	74	9.8	1.26	.234
2019	23	Tennessee (SL)	AA	8	8	3.01	26	26	0	147	112	15	52	166	10.2	1.12	.210
Minor League Totals				16	14	2.84	53	53	0	275	220	24	94	315	10.3	1.14	.218

11 ADBERT ALZOLAY, RHP

Born: May 1, 1995. **B-T:** R-R. **HT:** 6-0. **WT:** 179. **Signed:** Dominican Republic, 2012. **Signed by:** Julio Figueroa/Hector Ortega.

BACKGROUND: Alzolay was a low-profile signing as a 17-year-old out of the Dominican Republic in 2012 but took huge strides forward at high Class A Myrtle Beach and Double-A Tennessee in 2017. After injuries blunted his progress in 2018, Alzolay recovered and made his big league debut on June 20, 2019.

SCOUTING REPORT: Alzolay showed a three-pitch mix in 2019, fronted by a mid-90s fastball that can reach into the upper 90s as well. He backs it up with a high-70s curveball and a mid-80s changeup. He gets to his velocity from an effortful delivery, which sometimes leads to him overthrowing with command that will wander. He's got a strong makeup and the work ethic that will allow him to correct those issues and add polish as he continues to develop. The raw pieces are there—now it's a matter of learning how to best utilize what he has without trying to be something he's not. The Cubs have quickened Alzolay's delivery in the past to help him avoid overthinking on the mound.

THE FUTURE: Alzolay will have a shot at a spot in the big league rotation in 2020. If he doesn't make it there, he could go back to Triple-A Iowa for more seasoning or carve out a spot in the bullpen.

Year	Age	Club (League)	Class	W	L	ERA	G	GS	SV	IP	H	HR	BB	SO	K/9	WHIP	AVG
2017	22	Myrtle Beach (CAR)	HiA	7	1	2.98	15	15	0	82	65	8	22	78	8.6	1.07	.217
	22	Tennessee (SL)	AA	0	3	3.03	7	7	0	33	27	0	12	30	8.3	1.19	.229
2018	23	Iowa (PCL)	AAA	2	4	4.76	8	8	0	40	43	4	13	27	6.1	1.41	.281
2019	24	Myrtle Beach (CAR)	HiA	0	1	11.25	1	1	0	4	7	1	2	3	6.8	2.25	.389
	24	Iowa (PCL)	AAA	2	4	4.41	15	15	0	65	53	10	31	91	12.5	1.29	.215
	24	Chicago (NL)	MAJ	1	1	7.30	4	2	0	12	13	4	9	13	9.5	1.78	.260
Major League Totals				1	1	7.30	4	2	0	12	13	4	9	13	9.5	1.78	.260
Minor League Totals				33	27	3.63	105	84	0	491	425	41	145	448	8.2	1.16	.232

12 TYSON MILLER, RHP

Born: July 29, 1995. **B-T:** R-R. **HT:** 6-4. **WT:** 215. **Drafted:** Cal Baptist, 2016 (4th round). **Signed by:** Alex Lontayo.

BACKGROUND: When Miller was selected in the fourth round of the 2016 draft he became the highest-drafted player in California Baptist's history, topping the 2014 seventh-round selection of Trevor Oaks. He put together a solid first three seasons in pro ball, including a 2018 season when he struck out 126 hitters. That total ranked third-best among Cubs minor leaguers. He continued that progress in 2019, when he blitzed the competition at Double-A Tennessee before running into trouble after a promotion to Triple-A Iowa.

SCOUTING REPORT: Miller's pitch mix and approach have changed as he's moved through the system. In prior years he'd worked a sinker-slider combination, but he added or adjusted a changeup and curveball before the 2019 season and saw big results. The new repertoire allows him to work up in the zone with a low-90s fastball with riding action and follow it with a downer curveball to both sides of the plate. He still throws the slider, which functions as a short cutter and projects as a fringe-average pitch. The changeup, which he throws with a Vulcan-style grip that best fits his hands, also should be fringe-average with more development. He also needs to continue to work to keep his upper and lower halves in sync in his delivery.

THE FUTURE: Miller was hit hard at Triple-A and figures to return there in 2020. He projects as a back-end starter.

Year	Age	Club (League)	Class	W	L	ERA	G	GS	SV	IP	H	HR	BB	SO	K/9	WHIP	AVG
2017	21	South Bend (MWL)	LoA	6	7	4.48	28	20	0	121	122	10	38	99	7.4	1.33	.259
2018	22	Myrtle Beach (CAR)	HiA	9	9	3.54	23	23	0	127	104	12	35	126	8.9	1.09	.220
2019	23	Tennessee (SL)	AA	4	3	2.56	15	15	0	88	70	6	18	80	8.2	1.00	.219
	23	Iowa (PCL)	AAA	3	5	7.58	11	11	0	49	62	13	25	43	8.0	1.79	.304
Minor League Totals				24	25	4.05	85	74	0	413	386	45	123	365	8.0	1.23	.245

13 KOHL FRANKLIN, RHP

BA GRADE
50 **Risk: Very High**

Born: Sept. 9, 1999. **B-T:** R-R. **HT:** 6-4. **WT:** 190. **Drafted:** HS—Broken Arrow, Okla., 2018 (6th round). **Signed by:** Ty Nichols.

BACKGROUND: Franklin is the nephew of Ryan Franklin, who pitched for 12 seasons in the big leagues. Kohl missed much of his draft year at Owasso (Okla.) HS with a broken foot, but the Cubs believed enough in his projectability to draft him in the sixth round and sign him away from his commitment to Oklahoma for $540,000.

SCOUTING REPORT: The projectability the Cubs saw from Franklin started to take hold in 2019. After throwing his fastball 88-92 mph in high school, Franklin now sits in the low 90s and bumped as high as 97 in his first full season. Besides his natural growth, Franklin found the extra velocity by learning to use his legs more in his delivery. His 80-84 mph changeup projects as a solid-average offering because of its fade and the conviction with which Franklin throws the pitch. His mid-70s curveball is the key to his development. He wasn't allowed to throw the pitch until his senior year in high school, and the Cubs have toyed with the pitch to optimize it for his delivery. They settled on a spike grip and watched as the pitch gained four to five more inches of depth as a result.

THE FUTURE: Franklin finished the year at low Class A South Bend and is likely to return to the level in 2020. His next step is refining his command and throwing more quality strikes. Franklin has the ceiling of a No. 4 starter.

Year	Age	Club (League)	Class	W	L	ERA	G	GS	SV	IP	H	HR	BB	SO	K/9	WHIP	AVG
2018	18	Cubs 2 (AZL)	R	0	1	6.23	5	3	0	9	5	0	6	8	8.3	1.27	.161
2019	19	Eugene (NWL)	SS	1	3	2.31	10	10	0	39	31	2	14	49	11.3	1.15	.214
	19	South Bend (MWL)	LoA	0	0	3.00	1	1	0	3	0	0	5	3	9.0	1.67	.000
Minor League Totals				1	4	3.02	16	14	0	50	36	2	25	60	10.7	1.20	.194

14 CHRIS CLARKE, RHP

BA GRADE
50 **Risk: Very High**

Born: May 13, 1998. **B-T:** R-R. **HT:** 6-7. **WT:** 212. **Drafted:** Southern California, 2019 (4th round). **Signed by:** Tom Myers.

BACKGROUND: After beginning the year as Southern California's setup man, Clarke moved into the closer's role because of an injury to the team's regular ninth-inning option. He had Tommy John surgery in high school and scouts connected it to a drop-off in his stuff when he pitched back-to-back days. The Cubs saw starter traits in his pitch mix, took him in the fourth round and set him into the rotation at short-season Eugene for his first taste of pro ball.

SCOUTING REPORT: After being primarily a fastball-curveball reliever in the second half of his college career, Clarke began throwing a five-pitch mix as a starter in pro ball. He works with two fastballs—four-seam and sinker—in the low-to-mid 90s. He pairs them with a powerful spike curveball that was among the best collegiate curveballs available in the draft class and with a hard-darting slider with cutter-type break. He also has a changeup with deep fade action as well. Clarke throws all his pitches with a smooth, repeatable delivery that belies his massive, 6-foot-7 frame.

THE FUTURE: Clarke should move to low Class A South Bend in 2020 and has the makings of a back-end rotation piece with powerful stuff that could also fit well in the late innings if necessary.

Year	Age	Club (League)	Class	W	L	ERA	G	GS	SV	IP	H	HR	BB	SO	K/9	WHIP	AVG
2019	21	Eugene (NWL)	SS	0	1	1.96	9	8	0	23	20	2	4	26	10.2	1.04	.230
Minor League Totals				0	1	1.96	9	8	0	23	20	2	4	26	10.2	1.04	.230

15 MICHAEL MCAVENE, RHP

BA GRADE 50 Risk: Very High

Born: Aug. 24, 1997. **B-T:** R-R. **HT:** 6-3. **WT:** 210. **Drafted:** Louisville, 2019 (3rd round). **Signed by:** Jacob Williams.

BACKGROUND: McAvene made five starts as a freshman at Louisville before having Tommy John surgery. After a shortened sophomore season spent kicking off the rust, McAvene reemerged as a force out of the Cardinals' pen in 2019 and showed enough to convince the Cubs to spend $500,000 on him in the third round. He moved back into the rotation with short-season Eugene and struck out 20 in 12.2 innings.

SCOUTING REPORT: Unsurprisingly for someone with a reliever's history, McAvene has a high-effort delivery with a bit of a head whack at the end. The Cubs believe they can smooth it out, though, and that McAvene has enough athleticism to repeat his mechanics for multiple trips though a lineup. He starts his arsenal with an upper-90s fastball that draws a high percentage of in-zone swings and misses. He pairs it with a sharp, angry slider that he uses to wipe hitters out. He has a changeup as well but hasn't needed to use it much because of the success of his two best pitches.

THE FUTURE: Much as they did with fellow Louisville alum Riley Thompson in 2019, the Cubs will move McAvene to low Class A South Bend in 2020 and continue developing him as a starter. Like 2019 fourth-rounder Chris Clarke, the Cubs believe they can turn a college reliever into a big league rotation piece.

Year	Age	Club (League)	Class	W	L	ERA	G	GS	SV	IP	H	HR	BB	SO	K/9	WHIP	AVG
2019	21	Eugene (NWL)	SS	0	0	1.42	6	6	0	13	5	0	4	20	14.2	0.71	.119
Minor League Totals				0	0	1.42	6	6	0	12	5	0	4	20	14.2	0.71	.119

16 PEDRO MARTINEZ, 2B/SS

BA GRADE 50 Risk: Very High

Born: Jan. 28, 2001. **B-T:** S-R. **HT:** 5-11. **WT:** 165. **Signed:** Venezuela, 2018. **Signed by:** Hector Ortega/Louie Eljaua/Julio Figueroa.

BACKGROUND: The Cubs liked Martinez for his bat-to-ball skills as well as his strong baseball instincts. He put together strong performances in both complex leagues before moving to short-season Eugene in the middle of the summer. He ranked No. 18 and No. 19, respectively, among the Arizona League and Northwest League's Top 20 prospect lists.

SCOUTING REPORT: Martinez is one of the more advanced in a group of young, gifted middle infielders in the Cubs' system. Scouts inside and outside the organization saw strong hittability from both sides of the plate for Martinez, who more than held his own as a teenager in the short-season Northwest League. He's not the most powerful hitter at present, but with further strength gains and continued strike zone discipline he could reach double-digit home run totals once he makes the big leagues. Martinez alternated between shortstop and second base in his first full season as a pro and scouts see a plus defender at second base as he moves up the ladder. The Cubs still believe he can stick at shortstop, though, thanks to smooth hands, footwork and an above-average arm.

THE FUTURE: After ending the season in Eugene, Martinez could move up to full-season ball with low Class A South Bend to begin 2020. He has a future as a middle infielder with value on both sides of the ball.

Year	Age	Club (League)	Class	AVG	G	AB	R	H	2B	3B	HR	RBI	BB	SO	SB	OBP	SLG
2018	17	Cubs2 (DSL)	R	.310	54	197	37	61	3	5	2	25	26	26	31	.398	.406
2019	18	Cubs 1 (AZL)	R	.352	27	108	12	38	6	3	2	17	12	27	8	.417	.519
	18	Eugene (NWL)	SS	.265	27	98	15	26	2	3	0	7	12	36	11	.357	.347
Minor League Totals				.310	108	403	64	125	11	11	4	49	50	89	50	.393	.422

17 EDMOND AMERICAAN, OF

BA GRADE 50 Risk: Very High

Born: March 26, 1997. **B-T:** L-L. **HT:** 6-1. **WT:** 170. **Drafted:** Chipola (Fla.) JC, 2018 (35th round). **Signed by:** Tom Clark.

BACKGROUND: The Cubs bet big in 2018 that they could turn Americaan's intriguing set of tools into skills that would get him to the big leagues. Americaan spent two seasons at Chipola (Fla.) JC before the Cubs selected him in the 35th round of the 2018 draft and signed him for a round-high $208,950. He opened 2019 with low Class A South Bend and finished the year at short-season Eugene, where he showed well enough to rank No. 15 among the Northwest League's Top 20 prospects.

SCOUTING REPORT: Americaan's game is based on tools and projection. He's wiry strong with above-average bat speed that allows him to generate modest power to all fields. The Cubs backed him off the plate a touch before the season in an effort to get his barrel to more pitches more often while still letting his swing's natural arc put him in a position to pull breaking balls. He has a chance to stick in center field depending on the way his body develops. If he continues to be a wiry player, his plus speed and instincts will allow him to stay at the position. If not, his plus arm could help him play right field.

THE FUTURE: If Americaan shows hittability going forward, he could be an everyday player. If not, he fits into a fourth outfielder's role. He'll give low Class A another try in 2020.

Year	Age	Club (League)	Class	AVG	G	AB	R	H	2B	3B	HR	RBI	BB	SO	SB	OBP	SLG
2018	21	Cubs 1 (AZL)	R	.295	30	112	22	33	5	2	0	9	13	30	11	.373	.375
2019	22	South Bend (MWL)	LoA	.160	8	25	0	4	1	0	0	0	3	9	0	.276	.200
	22	Eugene (NWL)	SS	.282	66	255	38	72	17	5	4	32	19	65	16	.350	.435
Minor League Totals				.278	104	392	60	109	23	7	4	41	35	104	27	.352	.403

18 RICHARD GALLARDO, RHP

BA GRADE 50 Risk: Very High

Born: Sept. 6, 2001. **B-T:** R-R. **HT:** 6-1. **WT:** 180. **Signed:** Venezuela, 2018. **Signed by:** Hector Ortega/Louie Eljaua/Manuel Pestana/Carlos Figueroa.

BACKGROUND: After a strong showing at the 15U World Cup in Japan, Gallardo positioned himself as the second-best pitching prospect available on the 2018 international market, just behind Cuban righty Osiel Rodriguez. He put together a big showing at MLB's international showcase in 2018, then signed with the Cubs. He spent most of his first season as a pro at the Cubs' complex in Mesa, Ariz. in extended spring training and the Rookie-level Arizona League before making two starts at short-season Eugene.

SCOUTING REPORT: Evaluators inside and outside the organization have Gallardo pegged as a high-floor guy who shows a strong present feel to pitch. He starts his mix with a fastball that averaged 91 mph during the season and topped out at 94. Gallardo backed up the fastball with a downer curveball that he could spot to both sides of the plate as well as a changeup that is in the early stages of its development. To reach his ceiling, He needs to add strength. The Cubs believe he will do that because of a strong work ethic in the weight room. Beyond that, he needs to add power to his curveball and continue bringing his changeup forward.

THE FUTURE: Gallardo has the makings of a back-end type of starter with a chance for a little bit more depending on the way his body develops. He will pitch all season as an 18-year-old and is likely to start his second season in extended spring training.

Year	Age	Club (League)	Class	W	L	ERA	G	GS	SV	IP	H	HR	BB	SO	K/9	WHIP	AVG
2019	17	Cubs 1 (AZL)	R	0	2	4.15	11	9	0	30	32	1	12	23	6.8	1.45	.267
	17	Eugene (NWL)	SS	0	0	2.25	2	1	0	4	2	0	2	2	4.5	1.00	.154
Minor League Totals				0	2	3.93	13	10	0	34	34	1	14	25	6.6	1.40	.256

19 KEVIN MADE, SS

BA GRADE 50 Risk: Extreme

Born: Sept. 2, 2002. **B-T:** R-R. **HT:** 6-1. **WT:** 160. **Drafted:** Dominican Republic, 2019. **Signed by:** Louie Eljaua/Jose Serra/Gian Guzman.

BACKGROUND: Made was one of the Cubs' three big-time international signings during the 2019-20 period along with catchers Ronnier Quintero and Brayan Altuve. Like Quintero, Made trained in the Dominican Republic with Jaime Ramos. He signed for $1.5 million

SCOUTING REPORT: Made's ceiling is based on quite a bit of remaining projection on his athletic, high-waisted frame. He's put on roughly 15 pounds since the Cubs first laid eyes on him, and the club expects further strength gains as he matures. Despite the subpar strike-zone discipline one might expect from a 16-year-old, Made already makes plenty of contact. He's used his wiry frame and sneaky strength to generate surprising power for someone his size. Unlike some of the other middle infielders the Cubs have lurking in the lower minors, Made's build looks more like the classic shortstop. He's got smooth hands, sound footwork and a strong internal clock and arm strength that allow him to make plays in the hole and on the run. He maintains his accuracy while throwing from multiple angles.

THE FUTURE: The 2020 season will be Made's first official test as a pro. He'll begin the year in extended spring training before a likely move to the Rookie-level Arizona League.

Year	Age	Club (League)	Class	AVG	G	AB	R	H	2B	3B	HR	RBI	BB	SO	SB	OBP	SLG
2019	16	Did not play—signed 2020 contract															

20 RONNIER QUINTERO, C

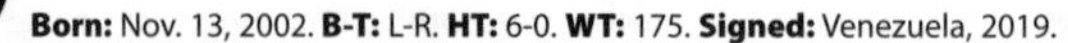

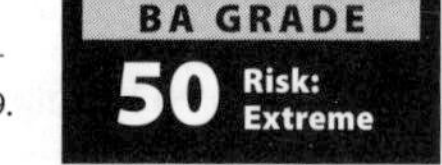

Born: Nov. 13, 2002. **B-T:** L-R. **HT:** 6-0. **WT:** 175. **Signed:** Venezuela, 2019. **Signed by:** Jose Serra/Gian Guzman/Louie Eljaua.

BACKGROUND: Quintero caught the Cubs' eye early because of his easy power from the left side. He was one of the team's three major signings during the 2019-20 period—along with shortstop Kevin Made and late-addition catcher Brayan Altuve.

SCOUTING REPORT: Despite not playing in an official game, Quintero has already opened eyes with his new organization. He was one of the stars of the team's Dominican instructional league program, posting exit velocities that ranked among the best of the entire camp. He gets to his power through a combination of strength and a swing with natural lift. Quintero has shown an ability to drive balls the opposite way as well. He turns on high-velocity fastballs and can recognize spin as well. Quintero's got a potential plus arm behind the plate and could become an average defender with further refinement, especially when it comes to receiving pitches.

THE FUTURE: Quintero's first official season as a pro will be in 2020, and he should begin in extended spring training. He projects as an offensive-minded catcher.

Year	Age	Club (League)	Class	AVG	G	AB	R	H	2B	3B	HR	RBI	BB	SO	SB	OBP	SLG
2019	16	Did not play—Signed 2020 contract															

21 RAFAEL MOREL, SS

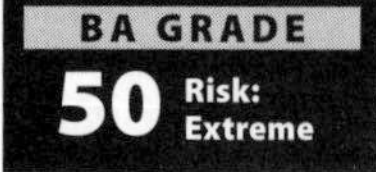

Born: Nov. 22, 2001. **B-T:** R-R. **HT:** 5-11. **WT:** 165. **Signed:** Dominican Republic, 2018. **Signed by:** Alejandro Peña/Gian Guzman/Jose Serra/Louie Eljaua.

BACKGROUND: The Cubs inked Morel—whose brother, Christopher, is also a Cubs farmhand—to an $850,000 deal in 2018 on the strength of a combination of athleticism and bat-to-ball skills. He showed off both traits in his stellar pro debut in the Dominican Summer League. His father was a basketball player in the Dominican Republic, which helps to explain some of Rafael's athleticism.

SCOUTING REPORT: At the plate, Morel showed the expected hittability during his first taste of pro ball. He put forth a strikeout rate of just 14.2 percent while walking at a 9.7 percent clip and showing enough power that 25 of his 65 hits went for extra bases. In the field, Morel's fast-twitch ability and plus speed will allow him to play shortstop, but he might be better suited for center field in the long run. He's got a plus arm and shows solid instincts for the game.

THE FUTURE: After spending all summer in the DSL, Morel's next step is the Rookie-level Arizona League, where he'll continue working toward his ceiling as a top-of-the-order hitter with more than a hint of impact power once he's done developing.

Year	Age	Club (League)	Class	AVG	G	AB	R	H	2B	3B	HR	RBI	BB	SO	SB	OBP	SLG
2019	17	Cubs1 (DSL)	R	.283	60	230	50	65	16	5	4	32	26	38	23	.373	.448
Minor League Totals				.283	60	230	50	65	16	5	4	32	26	38	23	.373	.448

22 YOHENDRICK PINANGO, OF

BA GRADE
50 Risk: Extreme

Born: May 7, 2002. **B-T:** L-L. **HT:** 5-11. **WT:** 170. **Signed:** Venezuela, 2018. **Signed by:** Julio Figueroa/Hector Ortega/Louie Eljaua.

BACKGROUND: The Cubs were drawn to Pinango because of his bat-to-ball skills and advanced knowledge of the strike zone for an amateur. Pinango trained with Jose Montero as an amateur and signed with the Cubs as part of their 2018-19 signing class. He tore up the Dominican Summer League in his professional debut and finished fourth in the league with a .358 average.

SCOUTING REPORT: Pinango still shows the same hitter's tool set that earned him a shot as a pro and had more walks (27) than strikeouts (20) in his first season. Now, the Cubs would like to see him add some power to his game. His contact-oriented swing doesn't have much lift, which means the raw power he shows in batting practice doesn't translate to games. Pinango also has more of an opposite-field approach, and the Cubs would like to see him pull more balls with authority. He's a plus runner and will stay in center field for now but is likely to move to a corner as he matures. To profile there, he'll need to add the power the Cubs already want to see.

THE FUTURE: After a strong turn in the DSL, Pinango should make his stateside debut in 2020 in the Rookie-level Arizona League. He has the ceiling of a corner outfielder with modest impact ability.

Year	Age	Club (League)	Class	AVG	G	AB	R	H	2B	3B	HR	RBI	BB	SO	SB	OBP	SLG
2019	17	Cubs1 (DSL)	R	.358	62	240	43	86	20	0	0	36	27	20	27	.427	.442
Minor League Totals				.358	62	240	43	86	20	0	0	36	27	20	27	.427	.442

23 FABIAN PERTUZ, SS

BA GRADE 50 Risk: Extreme

Born: Sept. 1, 2000. **B-T:** R-R. **HT:** 6-0. **WT:** 156. **Signed:** Colombia, 2017. **Signed by:** Manny Esquivia/Louie Eljaua/Hector Ortega.

BACKGROUND: With fellow middle infielders Reivaj Garcia and Luis Verdugo in the Rookie-level Arizona League, Pertuz stayed back and made his debut in 2018 in the Dominican Summer League. He showed hitting and on-base skills and tied for sixth in the league with 36 stolen bases.

SCOUTING REPORT: In the AZL, Pertuz's game changed a bit. He became more aggressive at the plate and started trying to tap into his raw power more often. The result was a dip in on-base percentage and a slight uptick in slugging percentage from his 2018 debut. He's got a simple, low-maintenance swing, impressive bat speed, strong hands to generate power and has shown the ability to turn on high-quality fastballs and do damage. Pertuz has average range and an above-average arm that could help him stick at shortstop, but the Cubs believe his offensive ability will allow him to move to either second or third base while still profiling at shortstop. He's a fringe-average runner.

THE FUTURE: After a strong turn in the AZL, Pertuz should be ready to move to low Class A South Bend. He has the skills to profile as an offensive, middle-diamond player.

Year	Age	Club (League)	Class	AVG	G	AB	R	H	2B	3B	HR	RBI	BB	SO	SB	OBP	SLG
2018	17	Cubs1 (DSL)	R	.298	62	218	49	65	10	6	2	39	38	32	36	.419	.427
2019	18	Cubs 1 (AZL)	R	.340	40	162	28	55	12	1	2	19	7	38	7	.371	.463
	18	Cubs 2 (AZL)	R	.257	9	35	5	9	2	0	0	6	2	8	2	.297	.314
Minor League Totals				.311	111	415	82	129	24	7	4	64	47	78	45	.392	.431

24 BRAYAN ALTUVE, C

BA GRADE 50 Risk: Extreme

Born: Jan. 22, 2003. **B-T:** R-R. **HT:** 5-11. **WT:** 160. **Signed:** Venezuela, 2019. **Signed by:** Hector Ortega/Manuel Pestana/Louie Eljaua.

BACKGROUND: Altuve was the third of the Cubs three premier international signings in the 2019 cycle, joining fellow catcher Ronnier Quintero and shortstop Kevin Made. Altuve, who trained in Venezuela with Carlos Azocar, was lauded for his mix of athleticism and tools.

SCOUTING REPORT: Altuve's athleticism jumps off the page, and not just for a catcher. He turned in plus run times in the 60-yard dash, although he's likely to see his speed wane as he gets older and catching takes its toll. Altuve has plus bat speed and can impact the ball thanks to a combination of strength and a swing with natural lift. Like most younger players, Altuve will overswing and has a bit of a pull-heavy approach. He has a solid-average arm behind the plate, and the athletic ability to become a solid blocker and receiver.

THE FUTURE: After signing late, Altuve should spend his first pro season in the Dominican Summer League. He has the ceiling of an everyday catcher.

Year	Age	Club (League)	Class	AVG	G	AB	R	H	2B	3B	HR	RBI	BB	SO	SB	OBP	SLG
2019	16	Did not play—Signed 2020 contract															

25 JUSTIN STEELE, LHP

BA GRADE 45 Risk: High

Born: July 11, 1995. **B-T:** L-L. **HT:** 6-2. **WT:** 195. **Drafted:** HS—Lucedale, Miss., 2014 (5th round). **Signed by:** J.P. Davis.

BACKGROUND: Steele showed steady production through his climb up the ladder until Tommy John surgery in 2017 kept him out until the middle of 2018. The injuries that plagued Steele in 2019 were less severe but limited him to just 38.2 innings at Double-A Tennessee.

SCOUTING REPORT: Despite the injuries, Steele brings an intriguing mix from the left side. He starts his repertoire with a low-to-mid 90s fastball that has touched as high as 97 mph. The pitch shows riding life up in the zone. His best offering is a potentially plus curveball in the 76-80 mph range as well as a seldom-used changeup. The Cubs are working to add a sinker to his arsenal, and he's shown a mid-80s slider.

THE FUTURE: Steele showed premium stuff in spurts, but 2019 was a lost year. The Cubs will try to get him back on track in 2020, when he'll work toward his ceiling as a back-end rotation option.

Year	Age	Club (League)	Class	W	L	ERA	G	GS	SV	IP	H	HR	BB	SO	K/9	WHIP	AVG
2017	21	Myrtle Beach (CAR)	HiA	6	7	2.92	20	20	0	99	100	6	36	82	7.5	1.38	.265
2018	22	Cubs 1 (AZL)	R	0	0	1.47	5	5	0	18	9	1	4	27	13.3	0.71	.143
	22	Myrtle Beach (CAR)	HiA	2	1	2.45	4	4	0	18	12	0	6	19	9.3	0.98	.185
	22	Tennessee (SL)	AA	0	1	3.60	2	2	0	10	8	1	3	7	6.3	1.10	.216
2019	23	Tennessee (SL)	AA	0	6	5.59	11	11	0	39	45	3	20	42	9.8	1.68	.308
Minor League Totals				16	23	3.62	80	75	0	320	320	14	131	316	8.9	1.41	.263

26 ARAMIS ADEMAN, SS

BA GRADE **45** Risk: High

Born: Sept. 13, 1998. **B-T:** L-R. **HT:** 5-11. **WT:** 160. **Signed:** Dominican Republic, 2015. **Signed by:** Jose Estevez/Gian Guzman/Jose Serra/Louie Eljaua.

BACKGROUND: After signing for $2 million and skipping over the Rookie-level Arizona League, Ademan has struggled. He followed a rough 2018 at high Class A Myrtle Beach with a similarly difficult 2019 season at the same level. The only saving grace was that, despite the repeat, Ademan was the ninth-youngest player in the Carolina League on Opening Day.

SCOUTING REPORT: Entering the year, Ademan needed to get stronger to withstand the grind of a full season. After the season, it's clear he still has a ways to go in that department. After a strong start to the season, he faded in the second half with a .172/.257/.289 line over 56 games. Scouts did see some bat-to-ball skills and a touch of pull power but for the most part were unimpressed. He's still a solid defender up the middle and is athletic. Ademan will have to work to maintain those skills, which appear at this point to be his carrying tools. He's an average runner.

THE FUTURE: After two seasons at high Class A, Ademan will likely move to Double-A Tennessee. He has the ceiling of a glove-first defensive utilityman in the big leagues.

Year	Age	Club (League)	Class	AVG	G	AB	R	H	2B	3B	HR	RBI	BB	SO	SB	OBP	SLG
2017	18	Eugene (NWL)	SS	.286	39	161	23	46	9	4	4	27	14	30	10	.365	.466
	18	South Bend (MWL)	LoA	.244	29	127	13	31	6	1	3	15	4	24	4	.269	.378
2018	19	Myrtle Beach (CAR)	HiA	.207	114	396	49	82	11	3	3	38	38	95	9	.291	.273
2019	20	Myrtle Beach (CAR)	HiA	.221	112	362	40	80	10	8	5	39	48	92	16	.318	.334
Minor League Totals				.233	353	1255	162	292	41	20	15	135	138	269	56	.319	.333

27 CHRISTOPHER MOREL, 3B

BA GRADE **45** Risk: High

Born: June 24, 1999. **B-T:** R-R. **HT:** 6-0. **WT:** 140. **Signed:** Dominican Republic, 2015. **Signed by:** Jose Estevez/Gian Guzman/Jose Serra.

BACKGROUND: The older brother of fellow Cubs farmhand Rafael Morel, Christopher was signed for $800,000 but had his pro debut delayed by injury. He's struggled to put together solid numbers until this past season at low Class A South Bend. Once again, though, his progress was cut off by injuries. In this case, he hurt his knee while going for a foul ball with low Class A South Bend. He compounded the injury by trying to play through the pain and was limited to 73 games before shutting it down for the year.

SCOUTING REPORT: Despite the lack of numbers, Morel's tools are still there. He's got a free-swinging approach at the plate that he'll need to temper if he's to reach his ceiling. When he does connect, however, the impact potential is obvious. He can get to plus velocity and scalds balls to all sectors with what the Cubs believe is potential double-plus power. They also believe he has a chance to be an average hitter, but there's a long way to go to get to that ceiling. Morel is a rangy, twitchy defender at third base who could play shortstop if needed. His power potential and strong arm play better at third base, though, and his range at the position would help him at shortstop as well. He's a smart, instinctive runner with above-average speed.

THE FUTURE: Morel has moved slowly so far. The Cubs could choose to accelerate his timetable by sending him to high Class A Myrtle Beach and hoping the warmer early-season weather helps him get off to a quick start.

Year	Age	Club (League)	Class	AVG	G	AB	R	H	2B	3B	HR	RBI	BB	SO	SB	OBP	SLG
2017	18	Cubs (DSL)	R	.220	61	223	44	49	6	2	7	40	35	37	23	.332	.359
2018	19	Eugene (NWL)	SS	.165	25	91	7	15	2	0	1	8	0	29	0	.172	.220
	19	Cubs 1 (AZL)	R	.257	29	113	20	29	6	0	2	12	11	28	1	.331	.363
2019	20	South Bend (MWL)	LoA	.284	73	257	36	73	15	7	6	31	11	60	9	.320	.467
Minor League Totals				.243	188	684	107	166	29	9	16	91	57	154	33	.308	.382

28 ZACK SHORT, SS

BA GRADE **40** Risk: Medium

Born: May 29, 1995. **B-T:** R-R. **HT:** 5-10. **WT:** 180. **Drafted:** Sacred Heart, 2016 (17th round). **Signed by:** Matt Sherman.

BACKGROUND: At Sacred Heart, Short was part of a talented team that also included fireballing reliever and current Tigers prospect Jason Foley. Since being drafted in 2016, Short has shown a consistent blend of strong defensive skills and sneaky impact at the plate. He missed roughly six weeks in the early portion of 2019 with a broken hand but recovered to make it to Triple-A Iowa, where he scuffled. He also made up for lost time in the Arizona Fall League, then was added to the Cubs' 40-man roster.

SCOUTING REPORT: Short's carrying skills are on defense. He's a rangy, instinctive defender with a plus arm who can make every play at shortstop. Those tools alone will likely get him to the big leagues. If he wants to stay there, he'll have to work to stay within himself and not get caught up with trying to hit for power. He has a short, quick stroke geared toward shooting line drives to all sectors with occasional home run power. Short has the strength to put the ball out of the park, but he gets in trouble when he tries to do it too often.

THE FUTURE: After being added to the 40-man roster, Short should make his big league debut sometime in 2020 after returning to Triple-A Iowa. He fits well as a defense-first backup with a sprinkling of offense.

Year	Age	Club (League)	Class	AVG	G	AB	R	H	2B	3B	HR	RBI	BB	SO	SB	OBP	SLG
2017	22	South Bend (MWL)	LoA	.237	66	236	50	56	17	3	7	26	54	54	15	.393	.424
	22	Myrtle Beach (CAR)	HiA	.263	65	232	34	61	11	3	6	21	40	50	3	.372	.414
2018	23	Tennessee (SL)	AA	.227	124	436	68	99	28	2	17	59	82	136	8	.356	.417
2019	24	Cubs 1 (AZL)	R	.375	6	16	5	6	2	0	0	3	8	4	0	.600	.500
	24	Tennessee (SL)	AA	.250	16	64	7	16	3	2	0	5	9	18	0	.338	.359
	24	Iowa (PCL)	AAA	.211	41	133	22	28	9	0	6	17	21	50	2	.338	.414
Minor League Totals				.241	371	1288	220	310	79	11	37	162	261	345	43	.377	.405

29 MANUEL RODRIGUEZ, RHP

BA GRADE
40 Risk: High

Born: Aug. 6, 1996. **B-T:** R-R. **HT:** 5-11. **WT:** 205. **Signed:** Mexico, 2016. **Signed by:** Sergio Hernandez/Louie Eljaua.

BACKGROUND: Rodriguez was the Cubs' top international signing in 2016, when they plunked down $400,000 to sign him away from the Leones de Yucatan in the Mexican League. Strictly a reliever, Rodriguez has moved slowly and steadily through the system. He completed his lower-level tour in 2019 with a full season at high Class A Myrtle Beach and was impressive enough to warrant a spot on the 40-man roster after the season.

SCOUTING REPORT: As was the case in the Mexican League, power is the key to Rodriguez's game. He brings a pair of mid-to-upper 90s fastballs from a short, stocky body and pounds the strike zone. His four-seamer is thrown at 95-98 mph, which is a touch higher than his 94-97 mph sinker. He backs up the fastballs with a powerful downer curveball that he likes to bury toward the bottom of the zone. He threw the pitch 29 percent of the time. Rodriguez has a seldom-used slider but primarily works with a mixture of fastballs and curveballs. A more consistent delivery helped Rodriguez slash his walks per nine innings from just over 8.0 in 2018 to 3.25 in 2019.

THE FUTURE: With further refined command, Rodriguez has the look of a big league setup man. He'll head to Double-A Tennessee in 2020.

Year	Age	Club (League)	Class	W	L	ERA	G	GS	SV	IP	H	HR	BB	SO	K/9	WHIP	AVG
2017	20	Eugene (NWL)	SS	1	0	3.52	12	0	0	23	20	1	6	33	12.9	1.13	.222
	20	South Bend (MWL)	LoA	0	0	5.40	4	0	2	7	8	2	5	5	6.8	1.95	.276
2018	21	South Bend (MWL)	LoA	3	5	7.59	32	0	3	40	52	2	36	64	14.3	2.18	.308
2019	22	Myrtle Beach (CAR)	HiA	1	3	3.45	35	0	2	47	43	1	17	65	12.4	1.28	.242
Minor League Totals				10	9	4.24	155	0	7	184	176	8	101	229	11.2	1.50	.249

30 JACK PATTERSON, LHP

BA GRADE
40 Risk: High

Born: Aug. 3, 1995. **B-T:** L-L. **HT:** 6-0. **WT:** 210. **Drafted:** Bryant, 2018 (32nd round). **Signed by:** Matt Sherman.

BACKGROUND: Patterson was the Northeastern Conference's pitcher of the year in his senior season in 2018 after going 6-3, 3.84 with 101 strikeouts in 82 innings. The Cubs took a flier on him in the 32nd round and then watched in 2019 as he had a breakout year.

SCOUTING REPORT: Patterson utilizes a smooth, easy delivery to bring an 88-91 mph fastball that he spots well to all quadrants of the strike zone. He's used better hip rotation to bring his fastball up that far, which represents a velocity spike from college. He backs up the pitch with a potentially average curveball with high spin and a slider that sometimes blends with the curveball but can be distinguished because of a touch more velocity. The Cubs would like to see Patterson's changeup come forth a little more, but scouts see a potentially average pitch there as well. Patterson uses strong hands and fingers to manipulate the baseball well both in and out of the zone.

THE FUTURE: Patterson has enough pitchability to give himself a chance as a situational reliever.

Year	Age	Club (League)	Class	W	L	ERA	G	GS	SV	IP	H	HR	BB	SO	K/9	WHIP	AVG
2018	22	Cubs 1 (AZL)	R	0	0	0.00	3	0	0	4	1	0	1	3	7.4	0.55	.091
	22	Cubs 2 (AZL)	R	2	1	3.08	7	5	0	26	28	3	7	24	8.2	1.33	.267
	22	Eugene (NWL)	SS	0	0	3.60	1	1	0	5	6	0	2	6	10.8	1.60	.286
2019	23	South Bend (MWL)	LoA	5	1	2.34	16	1	1	42	29	0	18	47	10.0	1.11	.195
	23	Myrtle Beach (CAR)	HiA	2	0	0.00	5	5	0	24	8	0	8	24	9.1	0.68	.104
	23	Tennessee (SL)	AA	1	0	2.63	3	3	0	14	11	1	6	9	5.9	1.24	.239
Minor League Totals				10	2	2.04	35	15	1	114	83	4	42	113	8.9	1.09	.203

Chicago White Sox

BY JOSH NORRIS

The light at the end of the tunnel is getting brighter for the White Sox. Though the 2019 season didn't bring much on-field success, their 72-89 record was a 10-win improvement from 2018. That jump was due in large part to development by, and debuts of, a host of young players and prospects. Chief among the players who experienced turnarounds were righthander Lucas Giolito and shortstop Tim Anderson.

Giolito went from the worst ERA among qualified pitchers in 2018 to third place in American League Cy Young Award voting in 2019. In all, Giolito—who headlined the 2017 deal that sent outfielder Adam Eaton to Washington—went 14-9, 3.41 with 228 strikeouts in 176.2 innings to pace the Chicago staff. Anderson, another former top prospect who had shown flashes of ability, went from hitting .240 in 2018 to a .335 mark in 2019 that earned him the AL batting title. Another trade headliner, Yoan Moncada, also took big steps forward. The former No. 1 overall prospect in baseball improved his OPS by 201 points as he switched positions from second base to third base. Moncada was the headliner in the 2017 deal that sent ace Chris Sale to Boston.

To those three pieces, the White Sox added outfielder Eloy Jimenez, another heralded trade acquisition—the premier piece in the 2017 deal that sent Jose Quintana to the Cubs. Jimenez was signed to an eight-figure extension before the season and hit 31 home runs while missing 40 games.

But that's not all. The White Sox have more help on the way. Outfielder Luis Robert rebounded from an injury-plagued first full season to blitz the minor leagues in 2019. Robert finished as just one of two players with 30 home runs and 30 stolen bases and appears poised to be a true five-tool impact player when he makes his big league debut sometime in 2020.

The White Sox are also likely to be aided by the early-season arrival of second baseman Nick Madrigal, the system's contact savant and first-round pick from 2018. Madrigal hit his way from high Class A Winston-Salem to Triple-A Charlotte over the course of the season and never showed a hint of trouble continuing to make line-drive contact against advanced pitching. Like Robert, he should be ready early in 2020.

The rotation should also get a big boost from the return of righthander Michael Kopech—another key piece of the Sale trade—who put forth an excellent big league debut in 2018 before having Tommy John surgery that cost him all of 2019.

RON VESELY/MLB PHOTOS VIA GETTY IMAGES

Rookie hitting prodigy Eloy Jimenez turned on the jets late with an .870 OPS in the second half.

PROJECTED 2023 LINEUP

Position	Player	Age
Catcher	Yasmani Grandal	34
First Base	Andrew Vaughn (2)	25
Second Base	Nick Madrigal (4)	26
Third Base	Yoan Moncada	28
Shortstop	Tim Anderson	30
Left Field	Eloy Jimenez	26
Center Field	Luis Robert (1)	25
Right Field	Nomar Mazara	28
Designated Hitter	Jose Abreu	36
No. 1 Starter	Lucas Giolito	28
No. 2 Starter	Michael Kopech (3)	27
No. 3 Starter	Dylan Cease	27
No. 4 Starter	Reynaldo Lopez	29
No. 5 Starter	Matt Thompson (5)	22
Closer	Jonathan Stiever (6)	26

Dane Dunning, a righthander who also came over in the Eaton deal, is returning from Tommy John surgery as well and could see his first big league time at some point during the year. Righthander Dylan Cease—yet another trade piece—graduated from prospectdom in 2019 and showed spurts of dominance in an otherwise inconsistent first test of the big leagues. The White Sox also believe big things are in store from their 2019 first-round pick Andrew Vaughn, a high-pedigree collegian who combines hard contact with a hitter's sensibility into what could become a classic masher's package.

The 2019 season wasn't great for the White Sox in the standings, but the tide is beginning to turn thanks to a farm system that continues to deliver.

DEPTH CHART

CHICAGO WHITE SOX

TOP 2020 ROOKIE: Luis Robert, OF. After he bides his time in the minors for a few more weeks, he should be ready to establish himself as a franchise cornerstone.

BREAKOUT PROSPECT: James Beard, OF. The speedster has the tools to be a force on the bases and at the top of the lineup.

SLEEPER: Jake Burger, 3B. Beset by injuries in his pro career, a return to health could finally put him on the path the White Sox expected.

SOURCE OF TOP 30 TALENT			
Homegrown	**26**	**Acquired**	**4**
College	11	Trade	4
Junior college	0	Rule 5 draft	0
High school	6	Independent league	0
Nondrafted free agent	0	Free agent/waivers	0
International	9		

LF
Blake Rutherford (9)
Joel Booker
Ian Dawkins

CF
Luis Robert (1)
Luis Basabe (16)
James Beard (19)
Luis Mieses (20)
Cabera Weaver

RF
Luis Gonzalez (10)
Micker Adolfo (11)
Bryce Bush (13)
Benyamin Bailey (22)
Anderson Comas (23)

3B
Bryan Ramos (21)
Damon Gladney (24)
Zach Remillard
Jake Burger
Ti'Quan Forbes

SS
Yolbert Sanchez (18)
Jose Rodriguez (28)
Lenyn Sosa
Luis Curbelo
Lency Delgado

2B
Nick Madrigal (4)
Danny Mendick (27)

1B
Andrew Vaughn (2)
Gavin Sheets (14)

C
Zack Collins (15)
Victor Torres (25)
Jefferson Mendoza (30)
Yermin Mercedes
Seby Zavala

LHP

LHSP	LHRP
Konnor Pilkington (17)	Kodi Medeiros
Bernardo Flores	Caleb Frare
Avery Weems	Bennett Sousa
Taylor Varnell	

RHP

RHSP	RHRP
Michael Kopech (3)	Codi Heuer (26)
Matthew Thompson (5)	Ian Hamilton (29)
Jonathan Stiever (6)	Zack Burdi
Andrew Dalquist (7)	Tyler Johnson
Dane Dunning (8)	McKinley Moore
Jimmy Lambert (12)	Hansen Butler
Lincoln Henzman	Alec Hansen
Kade McClure	Will Kincanon
Chase Solesky	Luis Ledo
Davis Martin	Zach Thompson
	Matt Foster

DRAFT ANALYSIS

2019

BEST PURE HITTER: This category easily goes to 1B Andrew Vaughn (1). The No. 3 overall pick in the draft, Vaughn projects as a plus hitter with plus power. The White Sox were drawn to him because of the way his swing allows the barrel of the bat to stay through the strike zone for a long time and with incredible impact.

BEST POWER HITTER: Vaughn's potential plus power makes him a fit here, too, but an under-the-radar candidate might be Illinois high school 3B Damon Gladney (16). Entering the spring, Gladney was known for more of a hit-over-power profile but showed better than expected pop during pre-draft workouts. He has the athleticism and makeup to continue tapping into that power as he moves up the ladder and could have above-average power in the big leagues.

FASTEST RUNNER: OF James Beard (4) wins this category easily. He's an 80-grade runner on the 20-to-80 scouting scale, was the fastest player available in the entire class, and swiped nine bases in his pro debut in the Rookie-level Arizona League.

BEST DEFENSIVE PLAYER: C Victor Torres (11) earns high marks for his receiving, throwing and ability to handle pitching staffs. He showed the aptitude to quickly learn how to call his own game and produced pop times in the 1.90- to 1.92-second range. He threw out 30 percent of runners in his pro debut.

BEST ATHLETE: Beard takes this category, too, but OF Cameron Simmons (20) was in consideration. Simmons, a Virginia product who missed time during his final season with a shoulder injury, socked five home runs and stole five bases between Rookie-level Great Falls and low Class A Kannapolis in his pro debut.

BEST FASTBALL: Arkansas-Little Rock RHP McKinley Moore (14) runs his fastball up to 98-99 mph and sits in the mid-90s, so he's the runaway winner here.

TOP DRAFT PICKS OF THE DECADE

Year	Player, Pos.	2019 Org
2010	Chris Sale, LHP	Red Sox
2011	Keenyn Walker, OF (1st round supp)	Did not play
2012	Courtney Hawkins, OF	Giants
2013	Tim Anderson, SS	White Sox
2014	Carlos Rodon, LHP	White Sox
2015	Carson Fulmer, RHP	White Sox
2016	Zack Collins, C	White Sox
2017	Jake Burger, 3B	White Sox
2018	Nick Madrigal, SS	White Sox
2019	Andrew Vaughn, 1B	White Sox

BEST SECONDARY PITCH: Houston high school RHP Matthew Thompson (2) has a four-pitch mix, but his best offspeed offering is his potentially plus curveball which shows excellent depth in the upper 70s.

BEST PRO DEBUT: Vaughn made it to high Class A Winston-Salem and showed the ability to make hard contact and control the strike zone.

MOST INTRIGUING BACKGROUND: RHP Nick Silva (40) is a nephew of former 14-time All-Star Alex Rodriguez.

CLOSEST TO THE MAJORS: Vaughn carries a strong college pedigree and posted a .760 OPS in the high Class A Carolina League. His hit tool and polish should allow him to move quickly.

BEST LATE-ROUND PICK: Gladney, who socked eight home runs in the Arizona League, fits the bill here. Other candidates include OF Logan Glass (22), who is a projectable athlete at 6-foot-4 and 215 pounds, and OF Chase Krogman (34) who is a little more polished than Glass.

THE ONE WHO GOT AWAY: The White Sox signed each of their players through the first 27 rounds before failing to sign Hillsboro (Texas) High OF Caeden Trenkle (28). The team also missed out on inking OF Logan Britt (35), who has a physical frame, plus power potential and a big arm.

—**JOSH NORRIS**

2018

2B Nick Madrigal (1) shot to Triple-A in his first full season and figures to soon reach Chicago. OF Steele Walker (2) was traded for Nomar Mazara and OF Bryce Bush (33) has been a quality late-round find.

GRADE: B

2017

3B Jake Burger (1) has missed the last two seasons due to a rotten run of injury luck that led to a pair of Achilles tears. 1B Gavin Sheets (2) and OF Luis Gonzalez (3) both reached Double-A and show promise.

GRADE: C

2016

C Zack Collins (1) and RHP Ian Hamilton (11) have reached the big leagues but Collins struggled, and Hamilton's year was lost to injury after getting hit by a line drive. RHP Jimmy Lambert (5) still has upside.

GRADE: D

1 LUIS ROBERT, OF

Born: Aug. 3, 1997. **B-T:** R-R. **HT:** 6-3. **WT:** 185.
Signed: Cuba, 2017.
Signed by: Kenny Williams/Marco Paddy.

TRACK RECORD: The White Sox signed Robert out of Cuba for $26 million, which went well past their previous franchise high for an amateur player. After spending his first pro season in the Dominican Summer League, Robert spent an inconsistent 2018 in the U.S. He opened eyes in spring training but a torn thumb ligament days before the season meant his debut didn't come until mid-June in the Rookie-level Arizona League. He re-injured the thumb with high Class A Winston-Salem later in the year, then dealt with nagging injuries in the Arizona Fall League as well. Robert then spent all of 2019 displaying strong signs of being a five-tool player once he reaches his peak.

SCOUTING REPORT: Robert is the most tooled-up player the White Sox have had in their system in years. Robert's pure hitting ability might be his weakest tool because of the swing-and-miss in his game. He will chase pitches out of the zone, and scouts have noticed that he has the tendency to commit a bit early on breaking balls. Internally, the White Sox believe that trait appears in part because pitchers have learned to stay away from the juicy parts of the strike zone, which leads Robert to get impatient and try to do damage on pitcher's pitches. If pitchers do bring the ball in the zone, Robert can use his strong hands, muscular frame and elite bat speed to pummel pitches out to all parts of the park. That power was best displayed in 2019 on a home run in Birmingham that cleared the batter's eye in center field. On defense, Robert uses near-elite speed to chase balls down in center field. His arm is double-plus as well—he had seven outfield assists in 2019—which gives him a weapon not present in the skill sets of most center fielders. While the Astros' Kyle Tucker joined him in the 30-30 club, Robert is the first player since 2009 to finish a season with 30 home runs and 10 or more triples.

THE FUTURE: Robert is likely to follow the typical path of the big league-ready super-prospect. On a team that in 2019 featured a pitcher who finished in the top three in the Cy Young voting and another who won the batting title, Robert has the tools and skills to become a true face of the franchise.

BRIAN WESTERHOLT/FOUR SEAM IMAGES

BA GRADE
70 **Risk: Medium**

SCOUTING GRADES
Hit: 55. **Power:** 70. **Run:** 70. **Field:** 60. **Arm:** 70.

Projected future grades on 20-80 scouting scale.

TOP PROSPECTS OF THE DECADE

Year	Player, Pos.	2019 Org
2010	Jared Mitchell, OF	Atlantic League
2011	Chris Sale, LHP	Red Sox
2012	Addison Reed, RHP	Twins
2013	Courtney Hawkins, OF	Giants
2014	Jose Abreu, 1B	White Sox
2015	Carlos Rodon, LHP	White Sox
2016	Tim Anderson, SS	White Sox
2017	Yoan Moncada, 2B/3B	White Sox
2018	Eloy Jimenez, OF	White Sox
2019	Eloy Jimenez, OF	White Sox

BEST TOOLS

Best Hitter for Average	Nick Madrigal
Best Power Hitter	Luis Robert
Best Strike-Zone Discipline	Zack Collins
Fastest Baserunner	Luis Robert
Best Athlete	Luis Robert
Best Fastball	Michael Kopech
Best Curveball	Jonathan Stiever
Best Slider	Michael Kopech
Best Changeup	Bernardo Flores
Best Control	Jonathan Stiever
Best Defensive Catcher	Seby Zavala
Best Defensive Infielder	Nick Madrigal
Best Infield Arm	Zach Remillard
Best Defensive Outfielder	Luis Robert
Best Outfield Arm	Micker Adolfo

Year	Age	Club (League)	Class	AVG	G	AB	R	H	2B	3B	HR	RBI	BB	SO	SB	OBP	SLG
2017	19	White Sox (DSL)	R	.310	28	84	17	26	8	1	3	14	22	23	12	.491	.536
2018	20	Kannapolis (SAL)	LoA	.289	13	45	5	13	3	1	0	4	4	12	4	.360	.400
	20	White Sox (AZL)	R	.389	5	18	5	7	2	1	0	2	0	3	3	.389	.611
	20	Winston-Salem (CAR)	HiA	.244	32	123	21	30	6	1	0	11	8	37	8	.317	.309
2019	21	Winston-Salem (CAR)	HiA	.453	19	75	21	34	5	3	8	24	4	20	8	.512	.920
	21	Birmingham (SL)	AA	.314	56	226	43	71	16	3	8	29	13	54	21	.362	.518
	21	Charlotte (IL)	AAA	.297	47	202	44	60	10	5	16	39	11	55	7	.341	.634
Minor League Totals				.312	200	773	156	241	50	15	35	123	62	204	63	.381	.551

2 ANDREW VAUGHN, 1B

BORN: April 3, 1998 B-T: R-R. **HT:** 6-0. **WT:** 214. **Drafted:** California, 2019 (1st round). **Signed by:** Adam Virchis

BA GRADE
60 Risk: High

TRACK RECORD: Vaughn started to open evaluators' eyes after his sophomore season, when he earned a spot on USA Baseball's Collegiate National Team and won the Golden Spikes Award. He carried that momentum into his draft year, when he hit .374/.539/.704 for California. The White Sox drafted him with the third overall pick, signed him for a bonus of $7,221,200 and then let him get his feet wet as a pro at both levels of Class A.

SCOUTING REPORT: The White Sox were drawn to Vaughn because of a simple, powerful swing that allowed his barrel to stay in the zone for a long time. Combined with excellent strength and bat speed, Vaughn projects as a classic masher who could produce average and power in the middle of an order. It's easy to envision him slotting into a lineup that includes Yoan Moncada, Tim Anderson, Luis Robert and Eloy Jimenez come 2021. If he succeeds, he'll have done his part to strip away the stigma associated with spending a high draft pick on a first baseman who both hits and throws righthanded. Vaughn is agile and has solid hands, so he should be a capable defender.

THE FUTURE: Because of his advanced pedigree, Vaughn should make his debut in the upper levels in 2020. Though a return to high Class A Winston-Salem to start the year, like Robert and Nick Madrigal did in 2019, isn't out of the question.

SCOUTING GRADES: Hitting: 60 Power: 60 Running: 30 Fielding: 40 Arm: 50

Year	Age	Club (League)	Class	AVG	G	AB	R	H	2B	3B	HR	RBI	BB	SO	SB	OBP	SLG
2019	21	White Sox (AZL)	R	.600	3	15	3	9	2	0	1	4	0	3	0	.625	.933
	21	Kannapolis (SAL)	LoA	.253	23	83	14	21	7	0	2	11	14	18	0	.388	.410
	21	Winston-Salem (CAR)	HiA	.252	29	107	16	27	8	0	3	21	16	17	0	.349	.411
Minor League Totals				.278	55	205	33	57	17	0	6	36	30	38	0	.384	.449

3 MICHAEL KOPECH, RHP

Born: April 30, 1996. **B-T:** R-R. **HT:** 6-3. **WT:** 205. **Drafted:** HS—Mount Pleasant, Texas, 2014 (1st round). **Signed by:** Tim Collinsworth (Red Sox).

TRACK RECORD: Kopech was a first-round pick of the Red Sox in 2014, then was dealt in the 2016 trade that sent Chris Sale to Boston. He impressed quickly over his first full season with his new organization, then made his big league debut on Aug. 21, 2018. His success in the majors gave the White Sox a peek at their bright future, but that optimism was scuttled when Kopech had Tommy John surgery. He spent all season recovering before returning in the fall instructional league.

SCOUTING REPORT: When healthy, Kopech showed the makings of a dynamic pitch mix. His fastball sat in the 95-98 mph range and touched 102. He added a two-seam fastball while with Triple-A Charlotte as well. The velocity was amplified by improved command achieved through a more repeatable delivery. His slider has earned plus grades since he was in high school and has been his best offspeed pitch throughout his pro career. The key for Kopech's development was the much-improved changeup he showed before his big league debut.

THE FUTURE: After rehabbing all season long, Kopech is likely to be ready to go for spring training and should quickly assume a place in Chicago's rapidly improving rotation.

SCOUTING GRADES: Fastball: 80 Slider: 60 Curveball: 50 Changeup: 50 Control: 50

Year	Age	Club (League)	Class	W	L	ERA	G	GS	SV	IP	H	HR	BB	SO	K/9	WHIP	AVG
2017	21	Birmingham (SL)	AA	8	7	2.87	22	22	0	119	77	6	60	155	11.7	1.15	.184
	21	Charlotte (IL)	AAA	1	1	3.00	3	3	0	15	15	0	5	17	10.2	1.33	.263
2018	22	Charlotte (IL)	AAA	7	7	3.70	24	24	0	126	101	9	60	170	12.1	1.27	.219
	22	Chicago (AL)	MAJ	1	1	5.02	4	4	0	14	20	4	2	15	9.4	1.53	.328
2019	23	Did Not Pitch—Injured															
Major League Totals				1	1	5.02	4	4	0	14	20	4	2	15	9.4	1.53	.328
Minor League Totals				24	22	3.05	85	84	0	395	286	18	194	514	11.7	1.21	.203

4 NICK MADRIGAL, 2B

Born: March 5, 1997. **B-T:** R-R. **HT:** 5-7. **WT:** 165. **Drafted:** Oregon State, 2018 (1st round). **Signed by:** Mike Gange.

LAURA WOLFF

BA GRADE
55 **Risk: Medium**

TRACK RECORD: All Madrigal does is hit. That has been true at Oregon State—where he was part of the Beavers' 2018 College World Series winning team—in summer collegiate leagues and as a pro. Madrigal has maintained a .309 average over his first season and a half in the minors and has walked more times (51) than he's struck out (21). He made it to Triple-A Charlotte by the end of 2019 and looks like another enviable piece in a White Sox lineup that is becoming younger and more talented.

SCOUTING REPORT: Madrigal's biggest strength is his ability to make contact, which he's done with aplomb. He has exceptional hand-eye coordination, which allows him to manipulate the barrel to any part of the strike zone with ease. After being an almost exclusively opposite-field hitter in his introduction to the minor leagues, Madrigal learned to pull the ball more in 2019 and produced an all-fields spray chart. He has shown almost no over-the-fence power as a pro or in college, with just 12 home runs over 1,240 combined at-bats. His last home run in 2019 stayed inside the park. After playing some shortstop in college, Madrigal has played exclusively second base as a pro and shows the hands, range and feet for the position, but there are scouts who question whether his arm is strong enough to turn double plays while a runner is bearing down on him. He is a plus runner.

THE FUTURE: Madrigal likely will return to Triple-A Charlotte to begin the year but should make his big league debut in 2020. He has all the skills to hit at the top or bottom of a lineup and provide defensive value up the middle.

SCOUTING GRADES: Hitting: 60 | Power: 30 | Running: 60 | Fielding: 60 | Arm: 40

Year	Age	Club (League)	Class	AVG	G	AB	R	H	2B	3B	HR	RBI	BB	SO	SB	OBP	SLG
2018	21	White Sox (AZL)	R	.154	5	13	2	2	0	0	0	1	1	0	0	.353	.154
	21	Kannapolis (SAL)	LoA	.341	12	44	9	15	3	0	0	6	1	0	2	.347	.409
	21	Winston-Salem (CAR)	HiA	.306	26	98	14	30	4	0	0	9	5	5	6	.355	.347
2019	22	Winston-Salem (CAR)	HiA	.272	49	191	20	52	10	2	2	27	17	6	17	.346	.377
	22	Birmingham (SL)	AA	.341	42	164	30	56	11	2	1	16	14	5	14	.400	.451
	22	Charlotte (IL)	AAA	.331	29	118	26	39	6	1	1	12	13	5	4	.398	.424
Minor League Totals				.309	163	628	101	194	34	5	4	71	51	21	43	.371	.398

5 MATTHEW THOMPSON, RHP

Born: Aug. 11, 2000. **B-T:** R-R. **HT:** 6-3. **WT:** 195. **Drafted:** HS—Cypress, Texas, 2019 (2nd round). **Signed by:** Chris Walker.

BILL MITCHELL

BA GRADE
55 **Risk: Extreme**

TRACK RECORD: Thompson had long been famous on the amateur circuit thanks to a 90-96 mph fastball, feel for spin and high-end athleticism. He showed all those characteristics during his senior season, but not as consistently as scouts would have wanted. Still, the White Sox were convinced that the pitcher they'd seen in previous seasons was the one they were going to get. He signed for $2.1 million instead of heading to Texas A&M.

SCOUTING REPORT: Though his stuff was up and down in his high school finale, the White Sox saw Thompson when he was throwing 93-96 with carry through the zone. That further reinforced his status in their minds as someone worthy of a high draft pick. He paired the four-seam fastball with a two-seamer in the low 90s that showed strong armside run and sink. Thompson's curveball is a deep breaker that the White Sox believe could get to plus as it develops. His slider—a two-plane breaker in the mid-80s—could get there as well. His breaking balls blend with one another at times, which is common for pitchers coming out of the prep ranks. His changeup is his clear fourth pitch, though it has a chance to get to average if he tweaks the way he delivers the pitch to let his shoulders and arm get all the way through. A wrist wrap left some scouts concerned about his future control.

THE FUTURE: Thompson's stuff, athleticism and projection give him the ceiling of a mid-rotation starter. He's likely to open 2020 in extended spring training before heading to Rookie-level Great Falls.

SCOUTING GRADES: Fastball: 60 | Curveball: 60 | Slider: 60 | Changeup: 50 | Control: 45

Year	Age	Club (League)	Class	W	L	ERA	G	GS	SV	IP	H	HR	BB	SO	K/9	WHIP	AVG
2019	18	White Sox (AZL)	R	0	0	0.00	2	2	0	2	2	0	0	2	9.0	1.00	.250
Minor League Totals				0	0	0.00	2	2	0	2	2	0	0	2	9.0	1.00	.250

6 JONATHAN STIEVER, RHP

Born: May 12, 1997. **B-T:** R-R. **HT:** 6-2. **WT:** 205. **Drafted:** Indiana, 2018 (5th round). **Signed by:** Justin Weschsler.

BA GRADE

50 Risk: High

TRACK RECORD: After a nondescript pro debut in his draft year, Stiever was the organization's biggest breakout story in 2019. He dominated both levels of Class A and finished with 154 strikeouts, which ranked second in the system. He turned it on in particular when he got to high Class A Winston-Salem, where he went 6-4, 2.15 with 77 strikeouts in 71 innings.

SCOUTING REPORT: Stiever's signature pitch is his fastball, which sears in at 92-97 mph with regularity. He backs it up with a pair of breaking balls that each have a chance to reach above-average with further consistency. His changeup is well behind his breaking balls but provides a bit of a wrinkle at times. The power associated with his arsenal also gives him a larger margin of error than is typically afforded to pitchers whose repertoire rely more on finesse. If he doesn't have his best command on a given day, he can rely on his fastball to simply blow hitters away. He controls his arsenal well despite a high-effort delivery that features a head-whack.

THE FUTURE: Evaluators see a forked path ahead for Stiever. If one of his breaking pitches steps forward, he's got a good chance to a be a high-value starter. If not, he could provide value as a setup man who dominates hitters with his fastball. He'll head to Double-A Birmingham in 2020.

SCOUTING GRADES: **Fastball:** 60 **Slider:** 55 **Curveball:** 55 **Changeup:** 40 **Control:** 45

Year	Age	Club (League)	Class	W	L	ERA	G	GS	SV	IP	H	HR	BB	SO	K/9	WHIP	AVG
2018	21	Great Falls (PIO)	R	0	1	4.18	13	13	0	28	23	3	9	39	12.5	1.14	.223
2019	22	Kannapolis (SAL)	LoA	4	6	4.74	14	14	0	74	88	10	14	77	9.4	1.38	.293
	22	Winston-Salem (CAR)	HiA	6	4	2.15	12	12	0	71	56	7	13	77	9.8	0.97	.216
Minor League Totals				10	11	3.59	39	39	0	173	167	20	36	193	10.0	1.17	.252

7 ANDREW DALQUIST, RHP

Born: Nov. 13, 2000. **B-T:** R-R. **HT:** 6-1. **WT:** 175. **Drafted:** HS—Redondo Beach, Calif., 2019 (3rd round). **Signed by:** Mike Baker.

BILL MITCHELL

BA GRADE

55 Risk: Extreme

TRACK RECORD: The second of two high school arms the White Sox took in the first three rounds of the 2019 draft, Dalquist showed an impressive three-pitch mix as an amateur at Redondo Union HS. He was considered to be a tough sign away from his commitment to Arizona, but the White Sox got their man by offering a signing bonus of $2 million. The figure was the third-highest in the third round. Dalquist made three one-inning starts in the Rookie-level Arizona League and a few more outings in the fall instructional league.

SCOUTING REPORT: Though his stuff isn't as explosive as Matthew Thompson, whom the White Sox took a round earlier, none of his pitches projects as worse than average, either. Dalquist starts his arsenal with a 90-94 mph fastball and combines it with a slider and a changeup that each could be average pitches. His changeup is farther along the developmental trail than the slider. Dalquist raised his profile in the eyes of the White Sox as the season progressed, and area scout Mike Baker stayed on him. He was impressed by the way he held his velocity through starts and the ease of operation in his delivery.

THE FUTURE: Dalquist is likely to stay back in extended spring training to begin his season before moving to Rookie-level Great Falls in the second half. He has the ceiling of a No. 4 starter in the big leagues

SCOUTING GRADES: **Fastball:** 55 **Slider:** 50 **Changeup:** 50 **Control:** 50

Year	Age	Club (League)	Class	W	L	ERA	G	GS	SV	IP	H	HR	BB	SO	K/9	WHIP	AVG
2019	18	White Sox (AZL)	R	0	0	0.00	3	3	0	3	2	0	2	2	6.0	1.33	.182
Minor League Totals				0	0	0.00	3	3	0	3	2	0	2	2	6.0	1.33	.182

8 DANE DUNNING, RHP

Born: Dec. 20, 1994. **B-T:** R-R. **HT:** 6-4. **WT:** 200. **Drafted:** Florida, 2016 (1st round). **Signed by:** Buddy Hernandez (Nationals).

TRACK RECORD: Just months after being drafted by the Nationals, Dunning was dealt to the White Sox with righties Lucas Giolito and Reynaldo Lopez as the price to bring outfielder Adam Eaton to Washington. He was impressive in his first two seasons with the White Sox but an elbow strain late in 2018 led to Tommy John surgery that cost him all of the 2019 season.

SCOUTING REPORT: Before the surgery, Dunning had the makings of a classic sinker/slider starter. He worked his low-to-mid-90s heater toward the bottom of the zone—he'd been making special effort to max out his extension to maximize the pitch's effectiveness—and couples that with a mid-80s slider with 10-to-4 break. He moved to a spike grip on his curveball, which has above-average potential. He also throws a mid-80s slider that could be above-average if it reaches its potential.

THE FUTURE: Dunning had Tommy John surgery in mid-March 2019, meaning he will likely miss the first part of the 2020 regular season. Dunning has returned to the mound, and was throwing at the team's complex in Glendale in November. If he returns to his pre-surgery form, he could nestle into the middle of a young, talented White Sox rotation.

SCOUTING GRADES: **Fastball:** 55 **Slider:** 60 **Curveball:** 60 **Changeup:** 55 **Control:** 55

Year	Age	Club (League)	Class	W	L	ERA	G	GS	SV	IP	H	HR	BB	SO	K/9	WHIP	AVG
2017	22	Kannapolis (SAL)	LoA	2	0	0.35	4	4	0	26	13	0	2	33	11.4	0.58	.143
	22	Winston-Salem (CAR)	HiA	6	8	3.51	22	22	0	118	114	15	36	135	10.3	1.27	.250
2018	23	Winston-Salem (CAR)	HiA	1	1	2.59	4	4	0	24	20	2	3	31	11.5	0.95	.215
	23	Birmingham (SL)	AA	5	2	2.76	11	11	0	62	57	0	23	69	10.0	1.29	.243
2019	24	Did not play—Injured															
Minor League Totals				17	13	2.74	49	49	0	266	230	18	71	300	10.2	1.13	.229

9 BLAKE RUTHERFORD, OF

HANNAH STONE/BARONS

Born: May 2, 1997. **B-T:** L-R. **HT:** 6-2. **WT:** 210. **Drafted:** HS—Canoga Park, Calif., 2016 (1st round). **Signed by:** Bobby Dejardin (Yankees).

TRACK RECORD: Rutherford was taken by the Yankees with the 18th overall pick in the first round of the 2016 draft, then dealt to the White Sox a year later in a trade that returned Todd Frazier, David Robertson and Tommy Kahnle to New York. He's spent the last two seasons trying to add enough strength to produce profile corner-outfield power from his sweet lefthanded swing.

SCOUTING REPORT: As an amateur and a professional, Rutherford has gained a reputation as a professional hitter from the left side. As a pro, he's matched a walk rate of 7.9 percent with a strikeout rate of 20.4 percent and has shown the ability every season to spray hits from line to line. The projected power, however, has not shown up. He's never topped seven home runs in a season and his over-the-fence power has shown up exclusively to the pull side. Evaluators within the organization believe Rutherford entered the year showing the type of power they'd been looking for, but a long season in the humid Southern League masked any gains Rutherford had made. His slightly below-average footspeed makes him an emergency option in center field, and his below-average throwing arm limits him to left field.

THE FUTURE: Rutherford will likely start 2020 back at Double-A Birmingham, but his power could spike once he gets to Triple-A Charlotte, where the cozy confines and the livelier MLB ball make for extremely hitter-friendly conditions. Until his power develops, Rutherford will continue to present a tricky profile problem.

SCOUTING GRADES: **Hitting:** 50 **Power:** 40 **Running:** 45 **Fielding:** 50 **Arm:** 40

Year	Age	Club (League)	Class	AVG	G	AB	R	H	2B	3B	HR	RBI	BB	SO	SB	OBP	SLG
2017	20	Charleston, SC (SAL)	LoA	.281	71	274	41	77	20	2	2	30	25	55	9	.342	.391
	20	Kannapolis (SAL)	LoA	.213	30	122	11	26	5	0	0	5	13	21	1	.289	.254
2018	21	Winston-Salem (CAR)	HiA	.293	115	447	67	131	25	9	7	78	34	90	15	.345	.436
2019	22	Birmingham (SL)	AA	.265	118	438	50	116	17	3	7	49	37	118	9	.319	.365
Minor League Totals				.280	367	1395	185	390	75	18	19	174	122	314	34	.337	.400

10 LUIS GONZALEZ, OF

HANNAH STONE

BA GRADE
50 Risk: High

Born: Sept. 10, 1995. **B-T:** L-L. **HT:** 6-1. **WT:** 190. **Drafted:** New Mexico, 2017 (3rd round). **Signed by:** John Kazanas.

TRACK RECORD: A two-way player at New Mexico, Gonzalez showed more potential as a hitter and the White Sox drafted him with their third-round pick in 2017. He put together a stellar first full season as a pro in 2018, when he cruised through both Class A levels while hitting for average and power.

SCOUTING REPORT: After a strong turn at Class A, things got more difficult for Gonzalez at Double-A. Scouts saw a player who'd abandoned his approach and had begun trying to pull everything for power. He didn't strike out at a particularly high clip (16.6 percent) but showed a willingness to expand the zone nonetheless. He got better in the second half of the season when he reverted to the shorter, more balanced swing that had helped him do damage the year prior. Gonzalez has the plus speed to play center field but is more suited for right field because of a plus throwing arm.

THE FUTURE: After a return to form in the second half, Gonzalez looks to be back on track. He'll return to Double-A in 2020 to keep working toward his ceiling as an everyday outfielder.

SCOUTING GRADES: **Hitting:** 50 **Power:** 45 **Running:** 50 **Fielding:** 50 **Arm:** 60

Year	Age	Club (League)	Class	AVG	G	AB	R	H	2B	3B	HR	RBI	BB	SO	SB	OBP	SLG
2017	21	Great Falls (PIO)	R	.118	4	17	3	2	1	0	0	3	4	3	0	.286	.176
	21	Kannapolis (SAL)	LoA	.245	63	233	26	57	13	4	2	12	38	50	2	.356	.361
2018	22	Kannapolis (SAL)	LoA	.300	55	230	35	69	16	2	8	26	21	57	7	.358	.491
	22	Winston-Salem (CAR)	HiA	.313	62	252	50	79	24	3	6	45	27	46	3	.376	.504
2019	23	Birmingham (SL)	AA	.247	126	473	63	117	18	4	9	59	47	89	17	.316	.359
Minor League Totals				.269	310	1205	177	324	72	13	25	145	137	245	29	.344	.412

11 MICKER ADOLFO, OF

BA GRADE
50 Risk: High

Born: Sept. 11, 1996. **B-T:** R-R. **HT:** 6-4. **WT:** 255. **Signed:** Dominican Republic, 2013. **Signed by:** Marco Paddy.

TRACK RECORD: The White Sox bet Adolfo would develop into massive power. After a slow track through the lower minors, he broke out in 2017. He socked 16 home runs that year and appeared to set expectations for what was to come. Adolfo mashed 11 more homers in 2018 at high Class A Winston-Salem, but his year was cut short by an elbow injury that eventually required Tommy John surgery. A setback in 2019 limited him to just 36 games before a stint in the Arizona Fall League.

SCOUTING REPORT: Adolfo's value continues to be centered around his massive raw power. Multiple scouts outside the organization noted that Adolfo is the only player they've seen hit balls onto the carousel in deep right-center field at high Class A Winston-Salem's ballpark. Adolfo produces that power in part because of a massive frame that is strapped with strength and swing mechanics with significant leverage. The question now is whether he'll have enough plate discipline to get to that power often enough to be productive. His timing and pitch recognition were understandably askew in 2019 after such a long time on the injured list, and he struck out 39 percent of the time between the regular season and the AFL. His arm before the surgery was among the best in the minors, a true 80 on the 20-80 scouting scale. He was exclusively a DH during the season but mixed in a bit of right field in the AFL. He's an average runner.

THE FUTURE: The 2020 season will be huge for Adolfo. If he can shake off the rust and get back on his track from 2018, he'll have a chance to regain some of his ceiling. If not, he might be destined for a role as a backup who can provide lightning in a bottle off the bench.

Year	Age	Club (League)	Class	AVG	G	AB	R	H	2B	3B	HR	RBI	BB	SO	SB	OBP	SLG
2017	20	Kannapolis (SAL)	LoA	.264	112	424	60	112	28	2	16	68	31	149	2	.331	.453
2018	21	Winston-Salem (CAR)	HiA	.282	79	291	48	82	18	1	11	50	34	92	2	.369	.464
2019	22	Birmingham (SL)	AA	.205	23	78	5	16	7	0	0	9	14	36	0	.337	.295
	22	White Sox (AZL)	R	.260	13	50	8	13	5	0	2	3	7	21	0	.362	.480
Minor League Totals				.249	364	1368	194	341	86	7	40	184	121	504	7	.323	.410

12 JIMMY LAMBERT, RHP

BA GRADE
50 Risk: Very High

Born: Nov. 18. 1994. **B-T:** R-R. **HT:** 6-2. **WT:** 190. **Drafted:** Fresno State, 2016 (5th round). **Signed by:** Adam Virchis.

TRACK RECORD: Lambert, the older brother of Rockies righthander Peter Lambert, showed enough in his junior season at Fresno State to earn a fifth-round selection and a $325,000 bonus from the White Sox in 2016. He moved slowly through the White Sox's two Class A levels before a strong five-game stint at Double-A Birmingham put him on the map in 2018. He continued to show swing-and-miss characteristics in 2019 (10.6 strikeouts per nine innings) in a return to Birmingham but had his season cut short by Tommy John surgery.

SCOUTING REPORT: Lambert's stuff doesn't jump off the page, but he gets hitters to swing through it nonetheless. His fastball typically works in the low 90s with flecks of 94 every now and then, but the riding action the pitch shows at the top part of the strike zone makes it play harder than its radar gun readings. He backs the fastball with a traditional complement of curveball, slider and changeup, and each of his three offspeed pitches projects as average if not a tick better. No one secondary pitch jumps out, but Lambert's ability to game plan and utilize opposition scouting reports helps him use each pitch in the optimal scenario.

THE FUTURE: Lambert is working out at the White Sox's spring training complex in Glendale, Ariz. and could possibly make an appearance late in 2020. He's on the White Sox's 40-man roster and projects as a back-end starter.

Year	Age	Club (League)	Class	W	L	ERA	G	GS	SV	IP	H	HR	BB	SO	K/9	WHIP	AVG
2017	22	Kannapolis (SAL)	LoA	7	2	2.19	12	12	0	74	77	1	11	43	5.2	1.19	.274
	22	Winston-Salem (CAR)	HiA	5	4	5.45	14	14	0	76	86	10	29	59	7.0	1.51	.290
2018	23	Winston-Salem (CAR)	HiA	5	7	3.95	13	13	0	71	57	5	21	80	10.2	1.10	.224
	23	Birmingham (SL)	AA	3	1	2.88	5	5	0	25	20	2	6	30	10.8	1.04	.217
2019	24	Birmingham (SL)	AA	3	4	4.55	11	11	0	59	62	11	27	70	10.6	1.50	.272
Minor League Totals				24	24	4.07	70	68	0	342	346	32	107	325	8.5	1.32	.265

13 BRYCE BUSH, OF

BA GRADE
50 **Risk: Very High**

Born: Dec. 14, 1999. **B-T:** R-R. **HT:** 6-0. **WT:** 200. **Drafted:** HS—Warren, Mich, 2018 (33rd round). **Signed by:** Justin Wechsler.

TRACK RECORD: A seemingly firm commitment to Mississippi State kept most teams off of Bush during the 2018 draft, but the White Sox took a flier in the 33rd round and signed him for $290,000. He opened his pro career by demolishing the Rookie-level Arizona League and ranked as the No. 19 prospect in the Rookie-level Pioneer League. Drafted as a third baseman, Bush moved to right field in 2019 at low Class A Kannapolis but had his season truncated by foot injuries and bronchitis.

SCOUTING REPORT: In his first full season as a pro, Bush showed tools without much production. He still has the top-end bat speed that earned him plaudits as an amateur and shows enough raw power to drive balls out to all sectors. He has exceptional bat control as well, which gives evaluators hope that he will eventually tap into his raw gifts. To do so, he needs to stay healthy and significantly improve his plate discipline and adopt a more level bat path to keep his barrel in the zone longer. He can murder fastballs but has a tendency to spin off of breaking pitches. Bush is understandably raw in right field, but the White Sox hope his athleticism and plus throwing arm will eventually translate into average defense.

THE FUTURE: After injuries blunted his 2019 season, Bush is likely to return to Kannapolis to see if he can make the necessary improvements. He's a bit of a lottery ticket but has the ceiling of a powerful regular in right field.

Year	Age	Club (League)	Class	AVG	G	AB	R	H	2B	3B	HR	RBI	BB	SO	SB	OBP	SLG
2018	18	White Sox (AZL)	R	.442	14	43	8	19	4	0	1	8	8	4	1	.538	.605
	18	Great Falls (PIO)	R	.250	24	96	16	24	5	1	2	10	10	21	3	.327	.385
2019	19	Kannapolis (SAL)	LoA	.201	67	254	29	51	12	5	5	33	27	92	4	.285	.346
	19	White Sox (AZL)	R	.000	4	9	0	0	0	0	0	0	0	2	0	.000	.000
Minor League Totals				.234	109	402	53	94	21	6	8	51	45	119	8	.318	.376

14 GAVIN SHEETS, 1B

BA GRADE
45 **Risk: High**

Born: April 23, 1996. **B-T:** L-L. **HT:** 6-4. **WT:** 230. **Drafted:** Wake Forest, 2017 (2nd round). **Signed by:** Abe Fernandez.

TRACK RECORD: A campaign with 21 home runs in his junior season at Wake Forest led the White Sox to draft Sheets with their second-round pick in 2017. Sheets—the son of former big leaguer Larry Sheets—struggled to replicate that power in his first two years as a pro. He hit just six home runs in a full season at high Class A Winston-Salem, which plays its home games just minutes from Sheets' alma mater. Despite the park's inviting short porch in right field, just two of Sheets' 2018 home runs came at home.

SCOUTING REPORT: Just as things were looking grim in his first season at Double-A, Sheets made an adjustment that unlocked the power he'll need to profile at first base. A suggestion from Birmingham hitting coach Charles Poe and White Sox hitting coordinator Mike Gellinger got Sheets to use his lower half more effectively in his swing, and the change produced stark results. His second-half OPS jumped 190 points, from .665 to .855, and helped him finish with more home runs (16) than he'd hit in the previous 641 at-bats over two seasons. Scouts are still somewhat skeptical because of an uppercut swing path and an all-or-nothing approach that might turn him into a one-trick pony, but the last two months of the season were just what Sheets needed to rebuild some of his prospect sheen.

THE FUTURE: Sheets has the profile of a second-division regular with power as his calling card.

Year	Age	Club (League)	Class	AVG	G	AB	R	H	2B	3B	HR	RBI	BB	SO	SB	OBP	SLG
2017	21	White Sox (AZL)	R	.500	4	12	3	6	2	0	1	3	3	0	0	.625	.917
	21	Kannapolis (SAL)	LoA	.266	52	192	16	51	10	0	3	25	20	34	0	.346	.365
2018	22	Winston-Salem (CAR)	HiA	.293	119	437	58	128	28	2	6	61	52	81	1	.368	.407
2019	23	Birmingham (SL)	AA	.267	126	464	56	124	18	1	16	83	54	99	3	.345	.414
Minor League Totals				.280	301	1105	133	309	58	3	26	172	129	214	4	.358	.408

15 ZACK COLLINS, C

Born: Feb. 6, 1995. **B-T:** L-R. **HT:** 6-3. **WT:** 220. **Drafted:** Miami, 2016 (1st round). **Signed by:** Jose Ortega.

TRACK RECORD: Collins stood out at Miami for three seasons before the White Sox selected him with the 10th overall pick in 2016 and signed him for $3,386,000. He jumped almost immediately to high Class A Winston-Salem in his debut season and then spent another 101 games there in his first full season as a pro. Collins made his big league debut on June 19 and hit his first MLB home run two days later.

SCOUTING REPORT: Collins has shown a classic three-true-outcomes skill set throughout his professional career—roughly half of his 1,533 minor league plate appearances have ended in either a strikeout, walk or home run. He has the best strike-zone discipline of any player in the system, but his willingness to work deep in counts leads to plenty of strikeouts as well. Collins has a timing mechanism in his swing that he counteracts with quick hands. He shows plus power to the opposite field. Collins is a well-below average defender behind the plate whose footwork and poor receiving get him in trouble. He has an above-average throwing arm, but his mechanics sometimes make it difficult to catch potential basestealers.

THE FUTURE: After a breakout season from James McCann, the White Sox doubled down by adding free agent Yasmani Grandal on a four-year deal and placing fellow catcher Yermin Mercedes on their 40-man roster. Collins might need to get better at first base if he wants a long-term role in the big leagues.

Year	Age	Club (League)	Class	AVG	G	AB	R	H	2B	3B	HR	RBI	BB	SO	SB	OBP	SLG
2017	22	Winston-Salem (CAR)	HiA	.223	101	341	63	76	18	3	17	48	76	118	0	.365	.443
	22	Birmingham (SL)	AA	.235	12	34	7	8	2	0	2	5	11	11	0	.422	.471
2018	23	Birmingham (SL)	AA	.234	122	418	58	98	24	1	15	68	101	158	5	.382	.404
2019	24	Charlotte (IL)	AAA	.282	88	294	56	83	19	1	19	74	62	98	0	.403	.548
	24	Chicago (AL)	MAJ	.186	27	86	10	16	3	1	3	12	14	39	0	.307	.349
Major League Totals				.186	27	86	10	16	3	1	3	12	14	39	0	.307	.349
Minor League Totals				.244	362	1218	209	297	70	5	59	213	283	431	5	.385	.455

16 LUIS ALEXANDER BASABE, OF

BA GRADE
45 **Risk: High**

Born: Aug. 26, 1996. **B-T:** B-R. **HT:** 6-0. **WT:** 160. **Signed:** Venezuela, 2012. **Signed by:** Eddie Romero/Luis Segovia (Red Sox).

TRACK RECORD: Basabe and his identical twin, Luis Alejandro, were each signed by the Red Sox in 2012. Luis Alexander came to Chicago as part of the Chris Sale trade in 2016 but has struggled to stay healthy since joining his new organization. He had knee surgery after the 2017 season to clean up a nagging injury, then performed respectably in a return to high Class A Winston-Salem the next season. Injuries to his hamstring, quadriceps and hamate bone limited Basabe in 2019, when he played just 74 games.

SCOUTING REPORT: Basabe still has an impressive set of tools but needs to stay out of the trainer's room to reach his full potential. Scouts who saw Basabe when he was healthy in 2019 saw a player with contact skills, bat control and athleticism but not enough of any one tool to be particularly high-impact. At his best, he showed a potential five-tool skill set but needed to refine his hittability. That was particularly true against breaking pitches and changeups. There is some power in there, which he showed on the big stage in the 2018 Futures Game when he crushed a 102 mph fastball for a long home run.

THE FUTURE: The tools are there for Basabe. Now he just needs to lock in the elusive sixth tool—health. He could begin 2020 back in Birmingham and has the ceiling of a quality backup outfielder.

Year	Age	Club (League)	Class	AVG	G	AB	R	H	2B	3B	HR	RBI	BB	SO	SB	OBP	SLG
2017	20	Winston-Salem (CAR)	HiA	.221	107	375	52	83	12	5	5	36	49	104	17	.320	.320
2018	21	Winston-Salem (CAR)	HiA	.266	58	207	36	55	12	5	9	30	34	64	7	.370	.502
	21	Birmingham (SL)	AA	.251	61	231	41	58	9	3	6	26	30	76	9	.340	.394
2019	22	Kannapolis (SAL)	LoA	.300	5	20	2	6	0	1	0	1	4	7	1	.417	.400
	22	Birmingham (SL)	AA	.246	69	256	31	63	12	1	3	30	29	85	9	.324	.336
Minor League Totals				.248	598	2198	366	546	104	40	44	257	311	639	116	.345	.392

17 KONNOR PILKINGTON, LHP

BA GRADE 45 Risk: High

Born: Sept. 12, 1997. **B-T:** L-L. **HT:** 6-3. **WT:** 225. **Drafted:** Mississippi State, 2018 (3rd round). **Signed by:** Warren Hughes.

TRACK RECORD: Pilkington put together three solid seasons at Mississippi State, an excellent 2016 season in the Cape Cod League and a 2.65 ERA for the 2017 Collegiate National Team. With the CNT, Pilkington played with a host of future White Sox system-mates, including Andrew Vaughn, Nick Madrigal and Steele Walker. The White Sox signed him for $650,000 as their 2018 third-round pick.

SCOUTING REPORT: Pilkington spent his first season kicking off the rust, then set to work in the fall instructional league tweaking his arsenal. He adopted an approach that centered more on his four-seam fastball and an improved version of his curveball. An analysis of his curveball with the help of high-speed cameras and other software helped him get on top of the pitch better and find a more consistent 10-4 shape that allowed for deeper break. He improved his changeup as well and got roughly eight mph of separation from his low-90s fastball. He's got a slider in his pitch package, but it's behind his three other pitches.

THE FUTURE: Even with the crisper stuff, Pilkington still doesn't have the knockout repertoire that evaluators would like to see in an impact starter. His body is somewhat maxed out, giving him less room for improvement. He'll move to Double-A in 2020 and has a ceiling as a No. 5 starter.

Year	Age	Club (League)	Class	W	L	ERA	G	GS	SV	IP	H	HR	BB	SO	K/9	WHIP	AVG
2018	20	White Sox (AZL)	R	0	0	18.00	2	1	0	2	7	0	1	2	9.0	4.00	.538
	20	Great Falls (PIO)	R	0	1	5.25	6	6	0	12	14	1	4	9	6.8	1.50	.292
2019	21	Kannapolis (SAL)	LoA	1	0	1.62	6	6	0	33	15	2	11	42	11.3	0.78	.132
	21	Winston-Salem (CAR)	HiA	4	9	4.99	19	19	0	96	99	7	39	96	9.0	1.44	.270
Minor League Totals				5	10	4.41	33	32	0	143	135	10	55	149	9.4	1.33	.249

18 YOLBERT SANCHEZ, SS

BA GRADE 50 Risk: Extreme

Born: March 3, 1997. **B-T:** R-R. **HT:** 5-11. **WT:** 184. **Signed:** Cuba, 2019. **Signed by:** Marco Paddy.

TRACK RECORD: The White Sox handed the top bonus of their 2019 international class to Sanchez, a 22-year-old shortstop from Cuba who was teammates with top White Sox prospect Luis Robert on their country's U18 World Cup squad. Also like Robert, Sanchez started his career in the Dominican Summer League despite being advanced for the level.

SCOUTING REPORT: Sanchez has strong bat-to-ball skills thanks to an uncomplicated approach geared toward line drives. He's a hit-over-power player who projects to have an average hit tool with the possibility of 8-12 home runs per season. He could fit nicely at the bottom of a lineup. Sanchez is a solid defender at shortstop with the potential to be above-average, though other clubs believed he might be better suited for second base. He's a solid-average runner with the hands, feet and above-average arm strength required to play on the left side.

THE FUTURE: Like Robert, Sanchez should start his first full season at low Class A Kannapolis and has a chance to move quickly through the system.

Year	Age	Club (League)	Class	AVG	G	AB	R	H	2B	3B	HR	RBI	BB	SO	SB	OBP	SLG
2019	22	White Sox (DSL)	R	.297	29	111	19	33	8	1	2	12	15	12	3	.386	.441
Minor League Totals				.297	29	111	19	33	8	1	2	12	15	12	3	.386	.441

19 JAMES BEARD, OF

BA GRADE 50 Risk: Extreme

Born: Sept. 24, 2000. **B-T:** R-R. **HT:** 6-1. **WT:** 175. **Drafted:** HS—Brookhaven, Miss., 2019 (4th round). **Signed by:** Warren Hughes.

TRACK RECORD: Beard was the fastest player in a draft class that also included Jerrion Ealy, who opted to play running back at Mississippi rather than turn pro on the diamond. Beard added strength between his junior and senior seasons in high school and enough thump to hit 11 home runs. The White Sox bet on his solid swing and burner tool set in the fourth round and gave him $350,000 to sign.

SCOUTING REPORT: Beard's carrying tool is his speed. He's a true 80 runner on the 20-to-80 scouting scale and has the best pure speed in the system. He swiped 25 bases in 26 tries in his draft year in high school and added nine more in 12 tries in the Rookie-level Arizona League upon turning pro. Scouts believe he has a sound enough swing with sufficient loft to project average hittability and perhaps 10-12 home runs. The elite speed, of course, will help him turn singles into doubles and doubles into triples. Beard's all-around game needs polish. His speed helps him overcome some circuitous routes in the outfield, and better instincts on the bases will turn him into a player who rarely gets caught trying to steal. He has the range and arm to stay in center field for the long term.

THE FUTURE: The White Sox knew Beard was going to be a project and are willing to wait for him to develop into what they believe could be an elite table-setter in the big leagues. He's likely to return to the AZL in 2020.

Year	Age	Club (League)	Class	AVG	G	AB	R	H	2B	3B	HR	RBI	BB	SO	SB	OBP	SLG
2019	18	White Sox (AZL)	R	.213	31	127	19	27	4	1	2	12	8	54	9	.270	.307
Minor League Totals				.213	31	127	19	27	4	1	2	12	8	54	9	.270	.307

20 LUIS MIESES, OF

Born: May 31, 2000. **B-T:** L-L. **HT:** 6-3. **WT:** 180. **Signed:** Dominican Republic, 2016. **Signed by:** Marino De Leon.

TRACK RECORD: Mieses was part of an impressive class of international outfielders the White Sox signed in 2016 that also included Anderson Comas and Josue Guerrero. Like his counterparts, Mieses was signed in part because of a projectable frame that offered offensive upside. He's yet to translate his tools into skills or production but still has plenty of time to grow and mature to unlock his potential.

SCOUTING REPORT: Mieses showed evaluators a short, compact swing from the left side with strong hands and wrists. The swing doesn't have much lift to it, though, which partially explains why he hasn't hit for the power evaluators expected that he'd grow into when he was an amateur. The power is going to have to start showing up because he doesn't fit in center field. He's not a graceful runner and doesn't have the range to make the plays required at the position.

THE FUTURE: Much like Comas, Mieses is going to need plenty of time to develop. If the White Sox want to be aggressive, they could push him to low Class A Kannapolis. If not, they could start him back at their Arizona complex before a return to Great Falls. He has the upside of a classic corner outfielder with lefty power.

Year	Age	Club (League)	Class	AVG	G	AB	R	H	2B	3B	HR	RBI	BB	SO	SB	OBP	SLG
2017	17	White Sox (DSL)	R	.263	59	247	24	65	8	3	0	25	10	42	3	.302	.320
2018	18	White Sox (AZL)	R	.226	48	195	19	44	10	2	2	26	4	35	3	.236	.328
2019	19	Great Falls (PIO)	R	.241	59	220	24	53	14	0	4	28	7	46	0	.264	.359
Minor League Totals				.245	166	662	67	162	32	5	6	79	21	123	6	.270	.335

21 BRYAN RAMOS, 3B

Born: March 12, 2002. **B-T:** R-R. **HT:** 6-2. **WT:** 190. **Signed:** Cuba, 2018. **Signed by:** Ruddy Moreta/Doug Laumann/Marco Paddy.

TRACK RECORD: Ramos was a standout on Cuba's youth circuits, where he consistently hit for average and power. He signed with the White Sox for $300,000 in 2018 and quickly impressed the club with his blend of righthanded thump and improved defense at third. The club jumped him over the Dominican Summer League in 2019 and watched as he put up a solid season in the Rookie-level Arizona League.

SCOUTING REPORT: Ramos already intrigues with his size and strength throughout his body and puts on impressive shows in batting practice. He stays inside the ball well, pulls the ball with authority and made a remarkable amount of contact for a player that young in his first taste of pro ball. Ramos has plus raw power and showed capability to hit for average and on-base skills in the AZL. He has some work to do defensively but shows good actions and an above-average arm at third base. Some evaluators believe he's best suited for a corner-outfield spot, but the White Sox have indicated they might try him at second base going forward to increase his defensive versatility. He's an average runner underway.

THE FUTURE: Ramos is likely to return to the team's Arizona complex to start 2020 before moving to Rookie-level Great Falls. He has the ceiling of a mashing third baseman.

Year	Age	Club (League)	Class	AVG	G	AB	R	H	2B	3B	HR	RBI	BB	SO	SB	OBP	SLG
2019	17	White Sox (AZL)	R	.277	51	188	36	52	10	2	4	26	19	44	3	.353	.415
Minor League Totals				.277	51	188	36	52	10	2	4	26	19	44	3	.353	.415

22 BENYAMIN BAILEY, OF

BA GRADE
50 Risk: Extreme

Born: Sept. 18, 2001. **B-T:** R-R. **HT:** 6-5. **WT:** 225. **Signed:** Panama, 2019. **Signed by:** Ricardo Ortiz.

TRACK RECORD: The White Sox came away with one of the more promising sleepers of the 2018-19 international class in Bailey, a Panamanian outfielder they gave $35,000 in April. Bailey went to the Dominican Summer League and immediately raked as a 17-year-old, hitting .324/.477/.454 with more walks (52) than strikeouts (40) in 55 games.

SCOUTING REPORT: Bailey, who turned 18 in September, is a physical 6-foot-5, 225 pounds and a power/speed threat, with both tools grading out above-average. Bailey has a short swing for a bigger guy and is a patient hitter with a good eye for the strike zone, which helped him hit immediately when he got to the DSL and faced better pitching than he was used to seeing in Panama. He's a corner outfielder who moves well for his size, though he might slow down as he gets older.

THE FUTURE: After a standout season in the DSL, Bailey should get his first stateside test in 2020 when he moves up to the Rookie-level AZL. He has a ceiling as an everyday corner outfielder with impact power.

Year	Age	Club (League)	Class	AVG	G	AB	R	H	2B	3B	HR	RBI	BB	SO	SB	OBP	SLG
2019	17	White Sox (DSL)	R	.324	55	185	41	60	12	3	2	19	52	40	10	.477	.454
Minor League Totals				.324	55	185	41	60	12	3	2	19	52	40	10	.477	.454

23 ALEXANDER COMAS, OF

BA GRADE
50 **Risk: Extreme**

Born: Feb. 10, 2000. **B-T:** L-L. **HT:** 6-3. **WT:** 185. **Drafted:** Dominican Republic, 2016. **Signed by:** Marino De Leon.

TRACK RECORD: The White Sox inked Comas for $425,000, on the strength of a lanky, projectable frame. His .306 batting average in the Rookie-level Arizona League in 2018 was fourth in the system, giving the organization hope that he might have gotten an early jump on translating his tools into skills.

SCOUTING REPORT: Comas still oozes with projection but didn't make the strength gains the White Sox had expected. He had a much tougher go at Rookie-level Great Falls in 2019 than he did in the complex league a season ago. Scouts from outside the organization saw a player who still has an enviable frame and above-average raw power in batting practice that doesn't translate well in games. When the lights come on, he tends to eschew the power profile he should have and instead plays like a scrappy player who should be hitting at the top of a lineup. Part of the issue, scouts said, was due to down angle in his swing that simply doesn't allow for power. He also showed a well below-average exit velocity of 81 mph. He has above-average speed and defensive skills.

THE FUTURE: Comas could move up to low Class A Kannapolis in 2020 but might be better served with more seasoning at the team's complex in Arizona. He has a corner outfielder's skills but needs to gain strength.

Year	Age	Club (League)	Class	AVG	G	AB	R	H	2B	3B	HR	RBI	BB	SO	SB	OBP	SLG
2017	17	White Sox (DSL)	R	.291	63	237	29	69	5	2	0	17	8	45	1	.316	.329
2018	18	White Sox (AZL)	R	.306	41	160	17	49	6	2	1	22	7	26	5	.339	.388
2019	19	Great Falls (PIO)	R	.222	54	194	19	43	7	6	2	33	7	58	0	.251	.351
Minor League Totals				.272	158	591	65	161	18	10	3	72	22	129	6	.301	.352

24 DAMON GLADNEY, 3B

BA GRADE
50 **Risk: Extreme**

Born: July 14, 2001. **B-T:** R-R. **HT:** 6-3. **WT:** 195. **Drafted:** HS—Dyer, Ind., 2019 (16th round). **Signed by:** J.J. Lally.

TRACK RECORD: Entering his 2019 season at Illiana Christian HS, Gladney had a reputation as more of a hitter than a masher. The White Sox had a previous relationship with Gladney, however, through their Amateur City Elite program, and believed Gladney's makeup would lead to further development. The power they expected showed up in their pre-draft workouts at U.S. Cellular Field, and the team decided to spend $225,000 in the 16th round to pull him away from a commitment to Eastern Kentucky. His eight home runs tied him for fifth in the Rookie-level Arizona League.

SCOUTING REPORT: Gladney's power started growing once he got a better understanding of his body. Earlier in his high school career his swing had been more rotational and focused around his upper body. Once he started utilizing his lower half, balls started flying and the door was opened to potential above-average power. He's going to have to shore up his plate discipline as well, as shown by 82 strikeouts in his first 220 plate appearances (37.2 percent). Gladney's defense at third base is a bit raw, and he's already begun dabbling at first base. He's got good enough hands to catch the ball at the hot corner, but there's work to be done on his transfers and the accuracy of his throws across the diamond.

THE FUTURE: Raw power is going to be Gladney's calling card as he moves up the ladder, but he'll need to eliminate some of the swing-and-miss from his game for it to play at the highest level. He'll likely start 2020 back in the AZL before moving to the Pioneer League during the summer.

Year	Age	Club (League)	Class	AVG	G	AB	R	H	2B	3B	HR	RBI	BB	SO	SB	OBP	SLG
2019	17	White Sox (AZL)	R	.264	50	201	27	53	5	2	8	25	10	82	1	.309	.428
Minor League Totals				.264	50	201	27	53	5	2	8	25	10	82	1	.309	.428

25 VICTOR TORRES, C

BA GRADE **50** Risk: Extreme

Born: July 29, 2000. **B-T:** R-R. **HT:** 6-0. **WT:** 180. **Drafted:** HS—Cieba, P.R., 2019 (11th round). **Signed by:** Jose Ortega.

TRACK RECORD: Torres was one of the best Puerto Rican prospects available, and the White Sox spent $175,000 on him in the 11th round. He had an inconsistent debut in the Rookie-level Arizona League.

SCOUTING REPORT: Torres was tabbed by the club as the best defensive player they selected in 2019. He earned that rep thanks to an advanced ability to handle a pitching staff and call his own games. He's quick behind the plate and has already shown a knack for controlling the running game. He caught 30.3 percent (10 of 33) of would-be basestealers in his pro debut but needs to work on handling balls in the lower part of the strike zone and blocking pitches in the dirt. That area for improvement showed up through 14 passed balls in 26 games, the worst mark in the AZL. The White Sox believe he has a chance to hit and will display solid bat-to-ball skills, but his body needs to fill out so he can handle the rigors of a full season.

THE FUTURE: Torres will likely start 2020 in extended spring training before either a return to the AZL or a move to Rookie-level Great Falls. He has the ceiling of a defense-first backup catcher.

Year	Age	Club (League)	Class	AVG	G	AB	R	H	2B	3B	HR	RBI	BB	SO	SB	OBP	SLG
2019	18	White Sox (AZL)	R	.219	26	96	5	21	2	0	0	9	3	28	2	.240	.240
Minor League Totals				.219	26	96	5	21	2	0	0	9	3	28	2	.240	.240

26 CODI HEUER, RHP

BA GRADE **40** Risk: Medium

Born: July 3, 1996. **B-T:** R-R. **HT:** 6-5. **WT:** 195. **Drafted:** Wichita State, 2018 (6th round). **Signed by:** Robbie Cummings.

TRACK RECORD: Heuer was a Friday starter at Wichita State in his junior year and showed enough potential for the White Sox to spend a sixth-round pick and $260,000 on him in 2018. He lasted just one season as a starter before moving to the bullpen full-time in 2019, when he finished the season in Double-A.

SCOUTING REPORT: Since moving to the bullpen, Heuer's fastball has jumped up the expected couple of ticks and now regularly bumps 96-97 mph. He comes at hitters from a low slot, which creates plenty of deception. His live arm also produces a slider that grades as potentially plus. That grade represents a marked improvement since his college days, when the slider was below-average. He has a changeup as well but is primarily a two-pitch reliever at this point. He finished the year with 8.6 strikeouts per nine innings.

THE FUTURE: Heuer will likely return to Double-A Birmingham in 2020 before a move to the pitching-adverse conditions of Triple-A Charlotte. He has a ceiling as a middle-relief arm.

Year	Age	Club (League)	Class	W	L	ERA	G	GS	SV	IP	H	HR	BB	SO	K/9	WHIP	AVG
2018	21	Great Falls (PIO)	R	0	1	4.74	14	14	0	38	49	4	14	35	8.3	1.66	.310
2019	22	Winston-Salem (CAR)	HiA	4	1	2.82	20	0	2	38	34	0	8	43	10.1	1.10	.233
	22	Birmingham (SL)	AA	2	3	1.84	22	0	9	29	25	0	7	22	6.8	1.09	.236
Minor League Totals				6	5	3.24	56	14	11	105	108	4	29	100	8.5	1.30	.263

27 DANNY MENDICK, 2B

BA GRADE **40** Risk: Medium

Born: Sept. 28, 1993. **B-T:** R-R. **HT:** 5-10. **WT:** 189. **Drafted:** Massachusetts-Lowell, 2015 (22nd round). **Signed by:** Joel Grampietro.

TRACK RECORD: Mendick found a bit of power in Double-A Birmingham in 2018 and then doubled down on that outburst in 2019 by socking 17 home runs before making his big league debut on Sept. 3.

SCOUTING REPORT: Throughout his career, Mendick has utilized a short, quick swing to spray line drives all over the diamond and uses above-average speed to create a little bit of havoc on the basepaths. Mendick's bat was always going to be the key to his game, but he has enough defensive chops to play virtually anywhere on the diamond without creating a hole. He has enough hittability and power to do a bit of damage every now and then, but he's at his best when he doesn't let himself get too power-conscious and instead focuses on staying within himself. He can play shortstop but is best suited as a utility player.

THE FUTURE: Mendick is the classic utility player who provides value on both sides of the ball.

Year	Age	Club (League)	Class	AVG	G	AB	R	H	2B	3B	HR	RBI	BB	SO	SB	OBP	SLG
2017	23	Winston-Salem (CAR)	HiA	.289	84	263	45	76	18	4	7	30	31	40	11	.373	.468
	23	Birmingham (SL)	AA	.197	41	147	14	29	5	0	3	21	17	27	1	.280	.293
2018	24	Birmingham (SL)	AA	.247	132	453	62	112	25	0	14	59	57	90	20	.340	.395
2019	25	Charlotte (IL)	AAA	.279	133	477	75	133	26	1	17	64	66	96	19	.368	.444
	25	Chicago (AL)	MAJ	.308	16	39	6	12	0	0	2	4	1	11	0	.325	.462
Major League Totals				.308	16	39	6	12	0	0	2	4	1	11	0	.325	.462
Minor League Totals				.259	554	1939	277	503	104	8	48	237	227	368	67	.344	.396

28 JOSE RODRIGUEZ, SS

Born: May 13, 2001. **B-T:** R-R. **HT:** 5-11. **WT:** 175. **Signed:** Dominican Republic, 2018. **Signed by:** Guillermo Peralta/Ruddy Moreta.

TRACK RECORD: Rodriguez signed out of the Dominican Republic in February 2018 and club officials watched as he put up a solid debut in the Dominican Summer League. He followed it up with a very strong campaign in the Rookie-level Arizona League in which he finished tied for fourth in the league with nine home runs.

SCOUTING REPORT: Rodriguez opened eyes with his play in the AZL. He showed evaluators a slightly over-aggressive approach, but his strong wrists and forearms translate into above-average raw power when he connects. He has average range and hands as well as solid footwork to go with a potentially plus arm. His fringe-average footspeed might fit better at second base in the long run if he has to move away from shortstop. He gets to average speed underway.

THE FUTURE: Rodriguez might have to move level by level as he develops and is someone who might profile as a bat-first second baseman or utilityman.

Year	Age	Club (League)	Class	AVG	G	AB	R	H	2B	3B	HR	RBI	BB	SO	SB	OBP	SLG
2018	17	White Sox (DSL)	R	.291	60	227	31	66	13	3	2	23	9	29	16	.318	.401
2019	18	White Sox (AZL)	R	.293	44	188	28	55	7	3	9	31	9	45	7	.328	.505
Minor League Totals				.292	104	415	59	121	20	6	11	54	18	74	23	.323	.448

29 IAN HAMILTON, RHP

BA GRADE
40 Risk: Medium

Born: June 16, 1995. **B-T:** R-R. **HT:** 6-0. **WT:** 200. **Drafted:** Washington State, 2016 (11th round). **Signed by:** Robbie Cummings.

TRACK RECORD: Hamilton racked up 10.8 strikeouts per nine innings in 2018 before earning his first big league callup. He went back to Triple-A for more seasoning in 2019 but found the new MLB ball didn't pair well with his game. Hamilton was struck in the face in the dugout by a line drive with enough force to cause multiple facial fractures and the loss of teeth. He had multiple surgeries to repair the injuries.

SCOUTING REPORT: At his best, Hamilton coupled an upper-90s fastball that touched triple-digits with a hard slider in the low 90s that projected as plus. Hamilton has a changeup as well, but it's a distant third pitch compared to his fastball and slider. He had worked in 2018 to stay behind the fastball to improve command of the pitch and in 2019 had shown the same ability to get swings and misses as before the injury. He ran into problems, however, when hitters got the ball in the air.

THE FUTURE: Once recovered, Hamilton will likely return to Triple-A Charlotte to try to rediscover the form that landed him in the big leagues. He has a future as a middle-innings reliever.

Year	Age	Club (League)	Class	W	L	ERA	G	GS	SV	IP	H	HR	BB	SO	K/9	WHIP	AVG
2017	22	Birmingham (SL)	AA	1	3	5.50	13	0	1	18	24	0	8	21	10.5	1.78	.317
	22	Winston-Salem (CAR)	HiA	3	3	1.71	30	0	6	53	32	1	8	52	8.9	0.76	.179
2018	23	Birmingham (SL)	AA	2	1	1.78	21	0	12	25	20	0	12	34	12.1	1.26	.211
	23	Charlotte (IL)	AAA	1	1	1.85	21	0	9	24	17	2	4	26	9.6	0.86	.198
	23	Chicago (AL)	MAJ	1	2	4.50	10	0	0	8	6	2	2	5	5.6	1.00	.207
2019	24	Charlotte (IL)	AAA	0	2	9.92	16	0	3	16	28	4	3	20	11.0	1.90	.378
Major League Totals				1	2	4.50	10	0	0	8	6	2	2	5	5.6	1.00	.207
Minor League Totals				8	11	3.24	125	0	40	172	147	10	50	185	9.7	1.14	.230

30 JEFFERSON MENDOZA, C

BA GRADE
45 Risk: High

Born: Jan. 16, 2001. **B-T:** R-R. **HT:** 6-0. **WT:** 180. **Signed:** Venezuela, 2017. **Signed by:** Amador Arias.

TRACK RECORD: Mendoza moved to the Dominican Summer League for his debut season but increased each of his three slash-line categories by better than 95 points in 2019.

SCOUTING REPORT: Despite his age, Mendoza had plenty of catching experience when he signed. The extra reps showed up in an advanced defensive skill set that included excellent blocking and receiving abilities and a plus throwing arm. Despite the arm strength, Mendoza caught just 16 percent of runners trying to steal in 2019. Mendoza has a middle-of-the-field approach and a sturdy frame, and should develop average power. He is buoyed by an ability to be selective when it comes to finding pitches he can drive.

THE FUTURE: Mendoza has the upside of a solid second-division catcher.

Year	Age	Club (League)	Class	AVG	G	AB	R	H	2B	3B	HR	RBI	BB	SO	SB	OBP	SLG
2018	17	White Sox (DSL)	R	.207	38	121	8	25	7	0	1	15	12	26	1	.289	.289
2019	18	White Sox (DSL)	R	.305	33	95	14	29	8	0	3	21	10	28	1	.391	.484
Minor League Totals				.250	71	216	22	54	15	0	4	36	22	54	2	.335	.375

Cincinnati Reds

BY JUSTIN COLEMAN

The Reds made significant changes in advance of the 2019 season, hiring David Bell as manager and bringing in a new coaching staff around him, headlined by famed pitching coach Derek Johnson. Matt Kemp, Yasiel Puig, Alex Wood and Kyle Farmer were acquired in a blockbuster trade with the Dodgers, while Sonny Gray was acquired from the Yankees and signed to a three-year extension.

The result was still the same. The Reds went 75-87, their sixth losing season in a row. After enduring a long rebuild with little to show for it, Reds owner Bob Castellini is getting impatient.

After trading top prospects Jeter Downs and Josiah Gray in the Kemp/Puig trade, Shed Long in the Gray trade and Tanner Rainey in a trade for Tanner Roark, the Reds made further win-now moves throughout 2019. They traded outfielder Taylor Trammell, the organization's No. 1 prospect, to the Padres at the trade deadline in a three-team deal that imported Trevor Bauer from the Indians. They opened December by signing all-star second baseman Mike Moustakas for four years and $64 million.

In less than 12 months, the Reds shipped out five of their top prospects in exchange for big league help, with mixed results. Kemp (released), Puig (traded) and Roark (traded) didn't make it through the season with the Reds, but Gray returned to all-star form to give them a front-of-the-rotation standout to pair with 26-year-old righthander Luis Castillo.

There were bright spots for the Reds to build on. Rookie outfielder Aristides Aquino came up and became the fastest player to reach 15 homers in major league history. Eugenio Suarez hit 49 home runs, the most in a single season for a Venezuelan-born player, a record previously held by Andres Galarraga in 1996.

After ranking 24th in ERA in 2018, the Reds ranked eighth in 2019. Castillo was the first Reds starting pitcher named to an All-Star Game since 2014, while Gray joined him as a late addition. Righthander Michael Lorenzen posted a 2.92 ERA in a team-high 73 games out of the bullpen and Amir Garrett appeared in at least 60 games for the second season in a row. Robert Stephenson settled into a bullpen role after years of shuttling back and forth to the rotation, finally delivering some value as a first-round pick.

Getting continued value from their first-round picks will be key for the Reds. Nick Senzel, the No. 2 overall pick in 2016, made his major league debut in May and took over as the Reds' everyday center fielder before going down with a torn labrum in September. Jonathan India, the No. 5 overall pick in 2018, rose to Double-A in his first full season while showing everyday skills on both sides of the ball. On the downside, 2017 first-round righthander Hunter Greene had Tommy John surgery and will likely miss the entire 2020 season in addition to 2019. The Reds added another top 10 pick in 2019, drafting Texas Christian lefthander Nick Lodolo No. 7 overall.

The continued growth of those young players will be key. While Aquino and Senzel figure to be impactful for the 2020 Reds, much of the club's remaining minor league talent is either coming back from injury, coming off an inconsistent season or is in the low minors.

JOE ROBBINS/GETTY IMAGES

Power righthander Luis Castillo morphed into a frontline starter in his third big league season.

PROJECTED 2023 LINEUP

Position	Player	Age
Catcher	Tyler Stephenson (4)	26
First Base	Joey Votto	39
Second Base	Mike Moustakas	34
Third Base	Eugenio Suarez	30
Shortstop	Jose Garcia (6)	24
Left Field	Jesse Winker	28
Center Field	Nick Senzel	28
Right Field	Jonathan India (2)	26
No. 1 Starter	Luis Castillo	28
No. 2 Starter	Hunter Greene (1)	23
No. 3 Starter	Sonny Gray	33
No. 4 Starter	Nick Lodolo (3)	25
No. 5 Starter	Tyler Mahle	28
Closer	Raisel Iglesias	33

DEPTH CHART

CINCINNATI REDS

TOP 2020 ROOKIE: Jose Siri, OF. He struggled to hit in the upper minors, but his speed, defense and occasional power can help in a complementary role.

BREAKOUT PROSPECT: Noah Davis, RHP. Davis showed well in his return from Tommy John surgery and has the stuff and feel to rise quickly if he stays healthy.

SLEEPER: Michael Beltre, OF. Beltre is athletic and has enough tools to reach the majors if he can get to his raw power.

SOURCE OF TOP 30 TALENT

Homegrown	26	Acquired	4
College	8	Trade	4
Junior college	1	Rule 5 draft	0
High school	10	Independent league	0
Nondrafted free agent	1	Free agent/waivers	0
International	6		

LF

Stuart Fairchild (8)
Jameson Hannah (10)
TJ Friedl (18)

CF

Mike Siani (9)
Jose Siri (17)
Mariel Bautista (25)
Andy Sugilio
Miles Gordon
Quin Coton

RF

Michael Beltre
Bren Spillane
Danny Lantigua

3B

Jonathan India (2)
Rece Hinds (11)
Debbie Santana (27)
Brantley Bell
Alejo Lopez
Juan Martinez

SS

Jose Israel Garcia (6)
Yan Contreras (20)
Alfredo Rodriguez
Blake Trahan
Braylin Minier

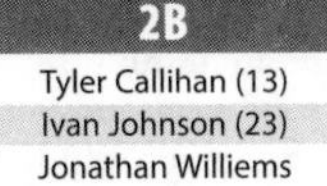

2B

Tyler Callihan (13)
Ivan Johnson (23)
Jonathan Williems

1B

Ibandel Isabel (28)
Gavin LaValley

C

Tyler Stephenson (4)
Hendrik Clementina (24)
Chris Okey
Mark Kolosczvary

LHP

LHSP	LHP
Nick Lodolo (3)	Reiver Sanmartin
Packy Naughton (16)	
Jacob Heatherly (29)	
Jose Salvador	

RHP

RHSP	RHP
Hunter Greene (1)	Ryan Hendrix (30)
Tony Santillan (5)	Connor Bennett
Lyon Richardson (7)	Jimmy Herget
Vladimir Gutierrez (12)	Ryan Dunne
Noah Davis (15)	Johnnie Schneider
Jared Solomon (21)	Jake Stevenson
Tejay Antone (22)	
James Marinan (26)	
Carlos Carreno	
Miguel Madrano	
Ricky Karcher	
Jose Lopez	

DRAFT ANALYSIS

2019

BEST PURE HITTER: 2B Tyler Callihan (3) showed plus bat speed from the left side, smashing 20 extra-base hits in 52 games in the Rookie-level Appalachian League before receiving a promotion to short-season Billings. He is an advanced prep bat who is mature enough to use the whole field and features developing power in his swing.

BEST POWER HITTER: Near top-of-the-scale raw power is what 3B Rece Hinds (2) brings to the table. His bat speed is plus and his swing has considerable loft, both of which could help him develop plus in-game power down the road.

FASTEST RUNNER: He isn't a double-plus runner, but OF Ashton Creal (21) has plus foot speed and wreaks havoc on the bases. Creal stole 50 bases in his junior college career, including 38 bags his final season with John A. Logan (Ill.) JC.

BEST DEFENSIVE PLAYER: 2B Ivan Johnson (4) shines at second base and has enough of a skill set to make shortstop work as well. He has a lively body with good footwork and a plus arm. His athleticism and glove should allow him to be a solid defender at second base.

BEST ATHLETE: Hinds played shortstop at IMG Academy despite his 6-foot-4, 215-pound frame. Even if his size pushes him to third base or the outfield, Hinds has a good arm and runs well underway. His athleticism should help him acclimate nicely to any positional changes in the future.

BEST FASTBALL: LHP Nick Lodolo (1) has a plus fastball and throws plenty of strikes with it. He works it comfortably in the low 90s and has natural angle on the pitch due to his 6-foot-6 frame.

BEST SECONDARY PITCH: Coming in with an advanced collegiate pedigree, Lodolo's slider is plus and he has good command of it. The key to his slider is that he can manipulate its break—Lodolo can spin it to have a large break or throw it with a shorter break.

TOP DRAFT PICKS OF THE DECADE

Year	Player, Pos	2019 Org
2010	Yasmani Grandal, C	Brewers
2011	Robert Stephenson, RHP	Reds
2012	Nick Travieso, RHP	Reds
2013	Phillip Ervin, OF	Reds
2014	Nick Howard, RHP	Royals
2015	Tyler Stephenson, C	Reds
2016	Nick Senzel, 3B	Reds
2017	Hunter Greene, RHP	Reds
2018	Jonathan India, 3B	Reds
2019	Nick Lodolo, LHP	Reds

BEST PRO DEBUT: Lodolo carved up hitters in the Rookie-level Pioneer League and then made two starts in the low Class A Midwest League. The lefthander consistently threw strikes, not walking a batter in his 18.1 innings. Callihan was one of the youngest hitters in the Rookie-level Appalachian League but showed promise at the plate.

MOST INTRIGUING BACKGROUND: C Luke Berryhill (13) not only had success as a catcher at South Carolina, but he is also a talented singer. He takes an interest in country music and could carve out a career in the field after baseball.

CLOSEST TO THE MAJORS: Lodolo's collegiate pedigree and advanced feel for how to pitch should allow him to climb to the big leagues quickly. His excellent control and three-pitch mix should push him along.

BEST LATE-ROUND PICK: Creal shows excellent athleticism in the outfield and has value as a late-round pick. RHP JC Keys (23) showed plus arm strength and a quality slider that could translate well in the bullpen.

THE ONE WHO GOT AWAY: Instead of signing, C Maxwell Romero (38) chose to play college baseball at Vanderbilt. He shows good power to all fields and has a solid arm, which should help him continue his development as a catcher.

—JUSTIN COLEMAN

2018

3B Jonathan India (1) reached Double-A in his first full pro season and figures to keep moving quickly. RHPs Lyon Richardson (2), Josiah Gray (2s) and Noah Davis (11) all are off to solid starts as well.

GRADE: B

2017

RHP Hunter Greene (1) missed 2019 with Tommy John surgery but still offers significant upside. SS Jeter Downs (1s) was traded to the Dodgers last offseason and has become a Top 100 prospect in baseball.

GRADE: B

2016

OF Nick Senzel (1) made his big league debut and is penciled in at center field. RHP Joel Kuhnel (11) has also made it, while OF Taylor Trammell (2) and LHP Scott Moss (4) helped land Trevor Bauer.

GRADE: A

1 HUNTER GREENE, RHP

Born: Aug. 6, 1999. **B-T:** R-R. **HT:** 6-4. **WT:** 215.
Drafted: HS—Sherman Oaks, Calif., 2017 (1st round).
Signed by: Rick Ingalls.

BRIAN WESTERHOLT/FOUR SEAM IMAGES

TRACK RECORD: The Reds drafted Greene second overall in 2017 and inked him to a $7.23 million bonus. Cincinnati opted to develop him as a pitcher rather than a shortstop or two-way player, which was at least a possibility given the power he showed in high school. His hitting ability raised some questions among evaluators, while his arm strength, pure stuff and athleticism on the mound were too enticing to put on the backburner. Greene saw 30 at-bats as a DH and tossed just 4.1 innings for Rookie-level Billings after signing in 2017. He didn't dominate in 2018 for low Class A Dayton, but he posted an impressive 11.72 strikeouts per nine innings thanks to his power stuff. He didn't throw a single fastball under 100 mph at the 2018 Futures Game. A sprained ulnar collateral ligament, however, cut his season short in late July. After attempting to rehab his elbow in the offseason, Greene suffered a setback in spring training and had Tommy John surgery, causing him to miss the entire 2019 season.

SCOUTING REPORT: Greene's easy delivery and top-of-the-scale fastball are his main calling cards. His delivery is clean and easy for him to repeat from his three-quarters arm slot. It allows him to be in and around the strike zone with sound command of his fastball. Greene's arm strength is premium. His fastball has touched 103 mph, most notably in the 2018 Futures Game, and sits comfortably in the 98-100 mph range. While his fastball is electric, evaluators have noted batters see the ball well out of his hand and are able to square it up more frequently than is optimal. In addition to his high-octane fastball, Greene has enough arm speed to snap off a slider with good angle and downward biting action. Greene's slider is his best secondary offering and projects as plus while showing the ability to miss bats. His changeup lags behind his other offerings but projects average with his ability to maintain consistent arm speed during his delivery.

THE FUTURE: Greene is slated to begin building up innings on the mound in 2020 barring any setbacks. Besides proving a clean bill of health, Greene needs to improve his changeup in order to have a true off-speed weapon and a stronger chance at staying in the rotation. The righthander's pure stuff and delivery should give him a chance to pitch at the front of a rotation, but the Reds will rightfully continue to exercise caution.

BA GRADE
60 **Risk: Extreme**

SCOUTING GRADES
Fastball: 80. **Slider:** 60
Changeup: 50. **Control:** 50.

Projected future grades on 20-80 scouting scale.

TOP PROSPECTS OF THE DECADE

Year	Player, Pos	2019 Org
2010	Todd Frazier, 3B	Mets
2011	Aroldis Chapman, LHP	Yankees
2012	Devin Mesoraco, C	Did not play
2013	Billy Hamilton, OF	Braves
2014	Robert Stephenson, RHP	Reds
2015	Robert Stephenson, RHP	Reds
2016	Robert Stephenson, RHP	Reds
2017	Nick Senzel, 3B/2B	Reds
2018	Nick Senzel, 3B/2B	Reds
2019	Nick Senzel, 3B/2B	Reds

BEST TOOLS

Best Hitter for Average	Tyler Stephenson
Best Power Hitter	Ibandel Isabel
Best Strike-Zone Discipline	Stuart Fairchild
Fastest Baserunner	Andy Sugilio
Best Athlete	Mike Siani
Best Fastball	Hunter Greene
Best Curveball	Vladimir Gutierrez
Best Slider	Ryan Hendrix
Best Changeup	Vladimir Gutierrez
Best Control	Packy Naughton
Best Defensive Catcher	Mark Kolozsvary
Best Defensive Infielder	Alfredo Rodriguez
Best Infield Arm	Jose Garcia
Best Defensive Outfielder	Mike Siani
Best Outfield Arm	Jose Siri

Year	Age	Club (League)	Class	W	L	ERA	G	GS	SV	IP	H	HR	BB	SO	K/9	WHIP	AVG
2017	17	Billings (PIO)	R	0	1	12.46	3	3	0	4	8	0	1	6	12.5	2.08	.400
2018	18	Dayton (MWL)	LoA	3	7	4.48	18	18	0	68	66	6	23	89	11.7	1.30	.251
2019	19	Did not play—Injured															
Minor League Totals				3	8	4.95	21	21	0	72	74	6	24	95	11.8	1.35	.261

2 JONATHAN INDIA, 3B

BA GRADE
55 **Risk: High**

Born: Dec. 15, 1996. **B-T:** R-R. **HT:** 6-0. **WT:** 200. **Drafted:** Florida, 2018 (1st round). **Signed by:** Sean Buckley.

TRACK RECORD: Drafted fifth overall in 2018, India blasted 21 home runs as a junior at Florida after hitting 10 home runs in his first two years combined. He hit eight home runs in the high Class A Florida State League during the first half of his first full season and received a promotion to Double-A Chattanooga in late July. He posted a .414 on-base percentage in his first taste of the upper minors.

SCOUTING REPORT: India brings a polished game on both offense and defense. He controls the strike zone and flashes an above-average hit tool, although he will go through spells where he swings and misses too much. India shows plus raw power, but evaluators are split on whether it will translate into games as he gets more experience. India has average range and plus arm strength at third base, and he has the hands and glove necessary for the position long-term. India is an average runner who will try to steal a bag on occasion.

THE FUTURE: India's athleticism, polish and well-rounded game give him a chance to grow into a solid everyday player. A shortstop in college, India has the tools to move to second base in deference to Eugenio Suarez if needed. Wherever he plays, his natural feel to hit should keep him in the lineup.

SCOUTING GRADES: **Hitting:** 55 **Power:** 50 **Running:** 50 **Fielding:** 60 **Arm:** 55

Year	Age	Club (League)	Class	AVG	G	AB	R	H	2B	3B	HR	RBI	BB	SO	SB	OBP	SLG
2018	21	Greeneville (APP)	R	.261	14	46	11	12	2	1	3	12	15	12	1	.452	.543
	21	Billings (PIO)	R	.250	3	8	1	2	0	0	0	0	0	4	0	.400	.250
	21	Dayton (MWL)	LoA	.229	27	96	17	22	7	0	3	11	13	28	5	.339	.396
2019	22	Daytona (FSL)	HiA	.256	87	317	50	81	15	5	8	30	37	84	7	.346	.410
	22	Chattanooga (SL)	AA	.270	34	111	24	30	3	0	3	14	22	26	4	.414	.378
Minor League Totals				.254	165	578	103	147	27	6	17	67	87	154	17	.369	.410

3 NICK LODOLO, LHP

BA GRADE
55 **Risk: High**

Born: Feb. 5, 1998. **B-T:** L-L. **HT:** 6-6. **WT:** 202. **Drafted:** Texas Christian, 2019 (1st round). **Signed by:** Paul Scott.

TRACK RECORD: Lodolo decided not to sign with the Pirates out of high school after they drafted him 41st overall in 2016. He made his way to Texas Christian and struck out 11.4 batters per nine innings as a junior to emerge as the consensus top pitcher in the 2019 draft. The Reds took him No. 7 overall and signed him for the full slot amount of $5,432,200. Lodolo struck out 30 batters and didn't issue a single walk in 18.1 innings after signing and reached low Class A Dayton.

SCOUTING REPORT: Highly competitive, Lodolo comes right after hitters with his three-pitch mix. He attacks with a fastball that sits 92-93 mph and tops out at 96 with life. He works off his fastball with a plus curveball that has good depth and late snap to it with occasional sweeping action, and he has especially good feel to command it. Lodolo's third offering is an upper-80s changeup that currently lacks separation from his fastball but could end up an average pitch over time. For a taller pitcher at 6-foot-6, Lodolo projects to have plus command and control with the ability to fill up the strike zone.

THE FUTURE: Lodolo has the stuff and aggressiveness to be a mid-rotation starter and has a chance to move quickly. He'll head to high Class A Daytona in 2020.

SCOUTING GRADES: **Fastball:** 55 **Curveball:** 60 **Changeup:** 50 **Control:** 60

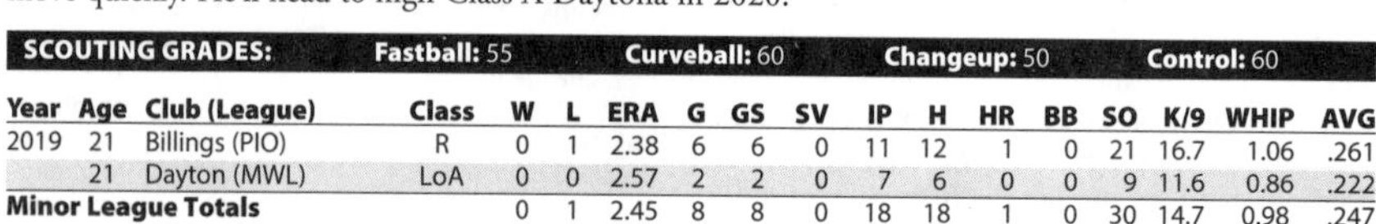

Year	Age	Club (League)	Class	W	L	ERA	G	GS	SV	IP	H	HR	BB	SO	K/9	WHIP	AVG
2019	21	Billings (PIO)	R	0	1	2.38	6	6	0	11	12	1	0	21	16.7	1.06	.261
	21	Dayton (MWL)	LoA	0	0	2.57	2	2	0	7	6	0	0	9	11.6	0.86	.222
Minor League Totals				0	1	2.45	8	8	0	18	18	1	0	30	14.7	0.98	.247

4 TYLER STEPHENSON, C

BA GRADE

50 Risk: Medium

Born: Aug. 16, 1996. **B-T:** R-R. **HT:** 6-4. **WT:** 225. **Drafted:** HS—Kennesaw, Ga., 2015 (1st round). **Signed by:** John Poloni.

TRACK RECORD: Stephenson was derailed by injuries for much of his first two seasons, including a concussion, wrist surgery and a sprained thumb. He stayed healthy in 2018 and showed defensive chops in the high Class A Florida State League, then took a step forward offensively in 2019. Stephenson's .372 on-base percentage ranked sixth among batters who had at least 300 plate appearances in the Double-A Eastern League.

SCOUTING REPORT: Stephenson has good feel for the strike zone with an average hit tool and an excellent approach. He starts his swing with a small leg kick and modest load before firing his hands through the zone to produce loud contact and average power. He rarely chases out of the strike zone and works his walks. The 6-foot-4, 225-pound Stephenson has a large frame behind the dish. He has solid hands but will have to continue to work on his receiving and framing skills. He has plus arm strength but doesn't always get a good release—he threw out just 26 percent of basestealers in 2019.

THE FUTURE: Stephenson's arm and offensive potential will be enticing if he can stick behind the plate. Some are concerned a lack of mobility may push him to first base or left field.

SCOUTING GRADES: **Hitting:** 55 **Power:** 50 **Running:** 30 **Fielding:** 50 **Arm:** 60

Year	Age	Club (League)	Class	AVG	G	AB	R	H	2B	3B	HR	RBI	BB	SO	SB	OBP	SLG
2017	20	Dayton (MWL)	LoA	.278	80	295	39	82	22	0	6	50	44	58	2	.374	.414
2018	21	Daytona (FSL)	HiA	.250	109	388	60	97	20	1	11	59	45	98	1	.338	.392
2019	22	Chattanooga (SL)	AA	.285	89	312	47	89	19	1	6	44	37	60	0	.372	.410
Minor League Totals				.263	376	1348	195	355	81	3	28	187	162	310	3	.350	.390

5 TONY SANTILLAN, RHP

BA GRADE

50 Risk: High

Born: Apr. 15, 1997. **B-T:** R-R. **HT:** 6-3. **WT:** 240. **Drafted:** HS—Arlington, Texas, 2015 (2nd round). **Signed by:** Byron Ewing.

TRACK RECORD: The 49th overall pick in 2015, Santillan experienced a breakthrough 2018 but fought shoulder issues and a strained triceps tendon throughout 2019, landing on the injured list three times. When he was healthy, Santillan walked nearly a batter every other inning in the first half of the season with Double-A Chattanooga and struggled to find the strike zone consistently even during an improved second half.

SCOUTING REPORT: Santillan works from a delivery that has some effort. He can run his fastball up to 96 mph, but he works more effectively in the low 90s. While his command has shown improvement at times, he lacks the ability to land his secondary offerings with any consistency, which has contributed to high walk totals throughout his career. Santillan's slider is a future plus pitch in terms of pure quality in the low-to-mid 80s with a good spin rate. His changeup is developing and grades as a potential average pitch, although it is a touch firm. He has also played around with a curveball, which helped him process and better develop the break on his slider.

THE FUTURE: Santillan's stuff is that of a mid-to-back-of-the-rotation starter, but his control may ultimately push him to the bullpen. He may need a third straight season at Double-A in 2020.

SCOUTING GRADES: **Fastball:** 55 **Slider:** 60 **Curveball:** 50 **Changeup:** 50 **Control:** 45

Year	Age	Club (League)	Class	W	L	ERA	G	GS	SV	IP	H	HR	BB	SO	K/9	WHIP	AVG
2017	20	Dayton (MWL)	LoA	9	8	3.38	25	24	0	128	104	9	56	128	9.0	1.25	.222
2018	21	Daytona (FSL)	HiA	6	4	2.70	15	15	0	87	81	5	22	73	7.6	1.19	.245
	21	Pensacola (SL)	AA	4	3	3.61	11	11	0	62	65	8	16	61	8.8	1.30	.264
2019	22	Chattanooga (SL)	AA	2	8	4.84	21	21	0	102	110	8	54	92	8.1	1.60	.280
Minor League Totals				24	28	3.94	95	93	0	468	434	38	199	457	8.8	1.35	.246

6 JOSE GARCIA, SS

Born: Apr. 5, 1998. **B-T:** R-R. **HT:** 6-2. **WT:** 175. **Signed:** Cuba, 2017. **Signed by:** Chris Buckley/Tony Arias/Miguel Machado/Jim Stoeckel/Bob Engle/Hector Otero.

BA GRADE **50** Risk: High

TRACK RECORD: The Reds tracked Garcia closely during his years on Cuba's junior national team and went over their international spending limit to sign him for $5 million in 2017. He struggled with an aggressive assignment to low Class A Dayton in his first season but, like many Cuban players, he made great strides in his second year in the U.S. in 2019. Garcia hit .278/.340/.432 in the pitcher-friendly Florida State League and led the circuit with 37 doubles.
SCOUTING REPORT: Primarily a second baseman in Cuba, Garcia has proven he can handle shortstop. His soft, quick hands give him a plus glove, and he has the footwork and quickness to cover the requisite ground. Garcia's arm strength is plus and has become better as his internal clock has improved. The game doesn't speed up on him anymore after previously being a problem. Garcia's swing is repeatable and he shows some ability to drive the ball, but he's a contact hitter who uses the whole field more than a home run threat. His footspeed is average and won't hurt his ability to stick up the middle.
THE FUTURE: Garcia's defense is an asset and should help him get to the big leagues. If he continues to progress as a hitter, he can be an everyday regular.

SCOUTING GRADES: **Hitting:** 55 **Power:** 45 **Running:** 50 **Fielding:** 60 **Arm:** 60

Year	Age	Club (League)	Class	AVG	G	AB	R	H	2B	3B	HR	RBI	BB	SO	SB	OBP	SLG
2018	20	Dayton (MWL)	LoA	.245	125	482	61	118	22	4	6	53	19	112	13	.290	.344
2019	21	Daytona (FSL)	HiA	.280	104	404	58	113	37	1	8	55	25	83	15	.343	.436
Minor League Totals				.261	229	886	119	231	59	5	14	108	44	195	28	.315	.386

7 LYON RICHARDSON, RHP

Born: Jan. 18, 2000. **B-T:** B-R. **HT:** 6-2. **WT:** 192. **Drafted:** HS—Jensen Beach, Fla., 2018 (2nd round). **Signed by:** Stephen Hunt.

BA GRADE **50** Risk: Very High

TRACK RECORD: Richardson quickly rose in the 2018 draft class after he showed premium velocity on the mound. He was ticketed to go to Florida as a pitcher/outfielder, but his upper-90s fastball and projectable frame helped him go in the second round and land a nearly $2 million signing bonus. After an inconsistent pro debut, Richardson took the ball every fifth day for low Class A Dayton and tied for the Midwest League lead with 26 starts.
SCOUTING REPORT: Richardson can run his fastball up to 95 mph but generally sits in the low 90s with the ability to throw it for strikes. He consistently attacks hitters and doesn't back down regardless of the situation. His low-to-mid-70s curveball has good spin with late depth, and he has shown the ability to land it in the lower part of the strike zone as an above-average pitch. As with many other prep draftees, Richardson's changeup is his third pitch, but it could develop into an average offering with improved arm speed. He is highly athletic and throws strikes with above-average control. Richardson has a frame built to log innings, although evaluators are split how much projection is left.
THE FUTURE: Richardson is set to open 2020 at high Class A Daytona. His arm strength, athleticism and control give him a shot at developing into a mid-to-back of the rotation starter.

SCOUTING GRADES: **Fastball:** 55 **Curveball:** 55 **Changeup:** 50 **Control:** 55

Year	Age	Club (League)	Class	W	L	ERA	G	GS	SV	IP	H	HR	BB	SO	K/9	WHIP	AVG
2018	18	Greeneville (APP)	R	0	5	7.14	11	11	0	29	37	3	16	24	7.4	1.83	.308
2019	19	Dayton (MWL)	LoA	3	9	4.15	26	26	0	113	126	10	33	106	8.5	1.41	.278
Minor League Totals				3	14	4.76	37	37	0	141	163	13	49	130	8.3	1.50	.284

8 STUART FAIRCHILD, OF

Born: Mar. 17, 1996. **B-T:** R-R. **HT:** 6-0. **WT:** 185. **Drafted:** Wake Forest, 2017 (2nd round). **Signed by:** Perry Smith.

BA GRADE
45 **Risk: High**

TRACK RECORD: Fairchild continued to adapt offensively in his third season of pro ball. While he hasn't shown the power he did at Wake Forest that made him a second-round pick in 2017, Fairchild managed to cut down on his strikeouts and hit .300 in May and June at high Class A Daytona to earn a promotion to Double-A Chattanooga in July.

SCOUTING REPORT: Fairchild isn't overly physical or toolsy, but he plays above his supposed limitations. He is known for being a grinder and a solid all-around contributor. Fairchild made the effort to simplify his swing and start it earlier, which has enabled him to put the barrel on the ball more consistently and show average or better hitting ability. With improvements to the timing of his lower and upper half, Fairchild has a chance to develop above-average power down the road. His plus instincts and plus speed give him the ability to play center field, and he has the average arm to man all three outfield positions as needed.

THE FUTURE: Fairchild should get plenty of at-bats in the upper minors in 2020. His continued offensive development will determine whether he becomes a solid everyday player or a useful fourth outfielder.

SCOUTING GRADES: **Hitting:** 50 **Power:** 55 **Running:** 60 **Fielding:** 50 **Arm:** 50

Year	Age	Club (League)	Class	AVG	G	AB	R	H	2B	3B	HR	RBI	BB	SO	SB	OBP	SLG
2017	21	Billings (PIO)	R	.304	56	204	36	62	5	4	3	23	19	35	12	.393	.412
2018	22	Dayton (MWL)	LoA	.277	67	235	40	65	12	5	7	37	31	65	17	.377	.460
	22	Daytona (FSL)	HiA	.250	63	220	25	55	14	1	2	20	17	63	6	.306	.350
2019	23	Daytona (FSL)	HiA	.258	67	248	32	64	17	2	8	37	25	60	3	.335	.440
	23	Chattanooga (SL)	AA	.275	42	153	25	42	12	1	4	17	19	23	3	.380	.444
Minor League Totals				.272	295	1060	158	288	60	13	24	134	111	246	41	.356	.421

9 MIKE SIANI, OF

Born: July 16, 1999. **B-T:** L-L. **HT:** 6-1. **WT:** 188. **Drafted:** HS—Philadelphia, 2018 (4th round). **Signed by:** Jeff Brookens.

BA GRADE
50 **Risk: Extreme**

TRACK RECORD: The Reds signed Siani for $2 million in 2018, a full $1 million more than any other fourth-round pick. After helping USA Baseball win the gold medal at the 18U World Cup, Siani showed a well-rounded game in the Rookie-level Appalachian League the following season. His first taste of full-season ball was a learning experience. The 19-year-old struck out 20 percent of the time but also led the Midwest League with 45 stolen bases.

SCOUTING REPORT: Siani is a pure center fielder with plus defensive ability. He is athletic with excellent body control and gets good jumps into both gaps. Siani's arm is plus with natural carry, and his footspeed is also plus. For a teenager, he shows the ability to take proper routes and closes well on fly balls. While Siani's bat path stays direct to the ball, he tends to overswing, which causes his contact ability to suffer. As he matures, his bat should develop to make more consistent contact and take advantage of his average raw power.

THE FUTURE: Siani will start the 2020 season with high Class A Daytona. While he has flaws to his game, he's young and is a solid all-around outfielder in a Reds system that lacks depth in center field.

SCOUTING GRADES: **Hitting:** 50 **Power:** 50 **Running:** 60 **Fielding:** 60 **Arm:** 60

Year	Age	Club (League)	Class	AVG	G	AB	R	H	2B	3B	HR	RBI	BB	SO	SB	OBP	SLG
2018	18	Greeneville (APP)	R	.288	46	184	24	53	6	3	2	13	16	35	6	.351	.386
2019	19	Dayton (MWL)	LoA	.253	121	466	75	118	10	6	6	39	46	109	45	.333	.339
Minor League Totals				.263	167	650	99	171	16	9	8	52	62	144	51	.338	.352

10 JAMESON HANNAH, OF

Born: Aug. 10, 1997. **B-T:** L-L. **HT:** 5-9. **WT:** 185. **Drafted:** Dallas Baptist, 2018 (2nd round). **Signed by:** Chris Reilly (Athletics).

BA GRADE **45** Risk: High

TRACK RECORD: The Athletics made Hannah the 50th overall pick in the 2018 draft, the second-highest player ever taken from Dallas Baptist. Hannah started his first full season strong at high Class A Stockton and made the California League All-Star Game, and the Reds acquired him at the trade deadline for Tanner Roark. Hannah hit just .224 in 18 games after the trade for high Class A Daytona before suffering a season-ending wrist sprain.

SCOUTING REPORT: Hannah is highly athletic and shows it on both sides of the ball. A plus athlete with good bat-to-ball skills and a nice lefthanded swing, Hannah grinds out at-bats and has a solid approach. He works counts and seldom chases out of the zone or swings and misses. He mostly hits grounders or low liners and racks up extra bases with his plus speed. His swing and size are not conducive to home runs, but he has the strength to drive the ball. Hannah's speed and plus range play in center field, but his fringy arm needs to improve.

THE FUTURE: Hannah's athleticism and on-base skills should help him get to the big leagues. Whether he becomes an everyday player or fourth outfielder will be determined by how much his bat continues to develop.

SCOUTING GRADES: Hitting: 50 Power: 40 Running: 60 Fielding: 50 Arm: 45

Year	Age	Club (League)	Class	AVG	G	AB	R	H	2B	3B	HR	RBI	BB	SO	SB	OBP	SLG
2018	20	Vermont (NYP)	SS	.279	23	86	14	24	4	1	1	10	9	24	6	.347	.384
2019	21	Stockton (CAL)	HiA	.283	92	375	48	106	25	3	2	31	29	88	6	.341	.381
	21	Daytona (FSL)	HiA	.224	18	67	6	15	3	1	0	6	9	16	2	.325	.299
Minor League Totals				.275	133	528	68	145	32	5	3	47	47	128	14	.340	.371

11 RECE HINDS, 3B

BA GRADE **50** Risk: Extreme

Born: Sept 5, 2000. **B-T:** R-R. **HT:** 6-4. **WT:** 215. **Drafted:** HS—Bradenton, Fla., 2019, (2nd round). **Signed by:** Sean Buckley.

TRACK RECORD: Hinds put his elite power on display at the 2018 Under Armor High School Home Run Derby, swatting 25 homers to end up as a finalist at Nationals Park. He impressed in the field as well, reaching 98 mph on the infield at Perfect Game's National Showcase that summer. Intrigued by his power and physicality, the Reds drafted him 49th overall and signed him for an overslot $1,797,500 bonus to keep him from a Louisiana State commitment.

SCOUTING REPORT: Hinds has top-of-the-scale raw power, showing the ability to crush baseballs to all fields due to his sheer strength. He combines those long home runs with gobs of swings and misses, however, projecting as a fringe-average hitter at best. While athletic, Hinds is raw and lacks the ability to track breaking pitches, often times getting into pitchers' counts. His frame will likely outgrow shortstop and fit best at third base or even right field, where his plus-plus should play, though he needs to improve the consistency of his glove work. He isn't a speedster but runs well under way.

THE FUTURE: Hinds has plenty of risk to his profile, but his extreme power fits as a masher in a corner if he can make enough contact.

Year	Age	Club (League)	Class	AVG	G	AB	R	H	2B	3B	HR	RBI	BB	SO	SB	OBP	SLG
2019	18	Greeneville (APP)	R	.000	3	8	1	0	0	0	0	1	2	3	0	.200	.000
Minor League Totals				.000	3	8	1	0	0	0	0	1	2	3	0	.200	.000

12 VLADIMIR GUTIERREZ, RHP

Born: Sept. 18, 1995. **B-T:** R-R. **HT:** 6-0. **WT:** 190. **Signed:** Cuba, 2016. **Signed by:** Tony Arias/Chris Buckley.

TRACK RECORD: The Reds signed Gutierrez for $4.7 million in Sept. 2016 after two successful seasons in Cuba's top baseball league, Serie Nacional. The 6-foot righthander rose quickly to the upper minors but hit a roadblock at Triple-A Louisville in 2019. His 6.04 ERA was third-highest in the International League, while his 26 homers allowed were tied for second-highest.

SCOUTING REPORT: Gutierrez's fastball sits in the low 90s and reaches 95 mph. It plays best when he pairs it with his plus changeup, but the consistency of his changeup was a problem in 2019. He often tried to manipulate it too much and, as a result, both his fastball and changeup played down. At his best, Gutierrez throws his changeup with similar arm speed to his fastball and has late fade with excellent deception. Gutierrez's spins an average curveball in the low-to-mid 80s that has sweeping action, but other times it is a true overhand, 12-to-6 offering. Usually in and around the strike zone, Gutierrez's control projects as average.

THE FUTURE: Gutierrez is best suited for the back of the rotation and could make his Reds debut in 2020. First, he has to prove his International League struggles are behind him.

Year	Age	Club (League)	Class	W	L	ERA	G	GS	SV	IP	H	HR	BB	SO	K/9	WHIP	AVG
2017	21	Daytona (FSL)	HiA	7	8	4.46	19	19	0	103	108	10	19	94	8.2	1.23	.267
2018	22	Pensacola (SL)	AA	9	10	4.35	27	27	0	147	139	18	38	145	8.9	1.20	--
2019	23	Louisville (IL)	AAA	6	11	6.04	27	27	0	137	144	26	48	117	7.7	1.40	.266
Minor League Totals				22	29	4.98	73	73	0	387	391	54	105	356	8.3	1.28	.259

13 TYLER CALLIHAN, 3B/2B

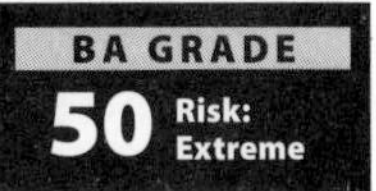

Born: June 22, 2000. **B-T:** L-R. **HT:** 6-1. **WT:** 205. **Drafted:** HS—Jacksonville, 2019, (3rd round). **Signed by:** Sean Buckley.

TRACK RECORD: Callihan emerged as one of the best hitters in his class on the showcase circuit, frequently barreling 90-plus mph velocity while showing in-game power. The catch, however, was he didn't have a defensive home. The Reds drafted Callihan in the third round anyway and signed him to an overslot $1,497,500 bonus to keep him from a South Carolina commitment. After playing shortstop and catcher in high school, Callihan played second base and third base in his pro debut at Rookie-level Greeneville and Billings.

SCOUTING REPORT: Callihan had no problems hitting high-velocity pitches as an amateur and showed the same prowess in pro ball thanks to plus bat speed. His hit tool projects to be above-average and his plus raw power will continue to translate as well. Like any prep hitter, he is prone to spells where he will swing and miss. Already moved off of shortstop, Callihan's future average glove and above-average arm fit at second or third base, with third his most likely destination.

THE FUTURE: Callihan's bat will drive his value moving forward. If all goes well, he should see low Class A Dayton in 2020.

Year	Age	Club (League)	Class	AVG	G	AB	R	H	2B	3B	HR	RBI	BB	SO	SB	OBP	SLG
2019	19	Greeneville (APP)	R	.250	52	204	27	51	10	5	5	26	9	46	9	.286	.422
	19	Billings (PIO)	R	.400	5	20	3	8	0	1	1	7	1	4	2	.429	.650
Minor League Totals				.263	57	224	30	59	10	6	6	33	10	50	11	.298	.442

14 MICHEL TRIANA, 1B

Born: Nov. 23, 1999. **B-T:** L-R. **HT:** 6-3. **WT:** 230. **Signed:** Cuba, 2019. **Signed by:** Reds international scouting department.

TRACK RECORD: Triana played first base for Cuba's 18U national team and worked out for teams at third base before signing with the Reds for $1.3 million on July 2. The organization held Triana back from the Dominican Summer League and instead opted to have him play in the unofficial Tricky League.

SCOUTING REPORT: Triana brings plus raw power to the plate with the ability to hit the ball out of any part of the park. He is strong and well built at 6-foot-3, 230 pounds. Even with his power potential, Triana's swing is more geared towards hard line drives. Thought he worked out at third base, Triana is a pure first baseman with the solid footwork and hands to project as an above-average defender down the road. He has a solid arm and runs well underway, which could allow him to play a corner outfield spot from time to time if necessary.

THE FUTURE: Triana has a chance to become an everyday first baseman if his power continues to develop. Already 20 years old, he should jump to the U.S. at some point in 2020.

Year	Age	Club (League)	Class	AVG	G	AB	R	H	2B	3B	HR	RBI	BB	SO	SB	OBP	SLG
2019	19	Did not play—Signed 2020 contract															

15 NOAH DAVIS, RHP

BA GRADE
50 Risk: Extreme

Born: April 22, 1997. **B-T:** R-R. **HT:** 6-2. **WT:** 195. **Drafted:** UC Santa Barbara, 2018 (11th round). **Signed by:** Rick Ingalls.

TRACK RECORD: Davis had Tommy John surgery that March after just two starts and fell out of top-10 rounds consideration. The Reds' were intrigued by his upside and signed him for $127,500 after taking him in the 11th round. Davis had a successful rehab process and got back on the mound in 2019. He stretched out to pitch two five-inning outings in the month of August, posting a 2.49 ERA that month

to close out the season.
SCOUTING REPORT: Davis is known for his competitive nature and attack-first mentality. His fastball topped out at 96 mph after his surgery, sitting more in the 90-93 mph range with good life. He already shows an advanced feel for his potentially plus changeup, which has good deception and movement off his fastball. Davis has two breaking pitches, a curveball and slider, but they tend to blend and he will need to focus on one for it to improve. He tends to walk batters and lose the strike zone at times, projecting for fringe-average control at best.
THE FUTURE: Davis' pure stuff and ability to attack hitters should help him move through the Reds' system as a starter. His health will determine his ultimate ceiling.

Year	Age	Club (League)	Class	W	L	ERA	G	GS	SV	IP	H	HR	BB	SO	K/9	WHIP	AVG
2018	21	Did not play—Injured															
2019	22	Reds (AZL)	R	0	2	7.88	5	5	0	8	13	4	0	5	5.6	1.63	.351
	22	Billings (PIO)	R	1	1	2.10	8	8	0	34	27	4	13	30	7.9	1.17	.218
Minor League Totals				1	3	3.19	13	13	0	42	40	8	13	35	7.4	1.25	.248

16 PACKY NAUGHTON, LHP

BA GRADE 45 Risk: High

Born: April 16, 1996. **B-T:** R-L. **HT:** 6-2. **WT:** 195. **Drafted:** Virginia Tech, 2017 (9th round). **Signed by:** Jeff Brookens.

TRACK RECORD: Naughton logged a 6.93 ERA in three years at Virginia Tech, but the Reds liked his stuff from the left side and drafted him in the ninth round in 2017. Naughton rewarded that faith as one of the system's most durable starters the last two years. He pitched more than 150 innings for the second straight season in 2019 and reached Double-A Chattanooga.
SCOUTING REPORT: Naughton works from a slightly funky, low-three-quarters arm slot that adds deception to his pitch mix. Naughton throws his fastball in the low-90s with average command despite his arm slot. His main weapon is his plus changeup, which has excellent deception, depth and armside run off of his heater. Naughton can spin a breaking ball with some shape, but it isn't nearly as effective as his other two offerings. He is able to repeat his arm slot despite his delivery and has developed above-average control as a professional.
THE FUTURE: Naughton's durability, pitch-mix and control give him a chance to stick as a back-of-the rotation starter. His stuff and arm slot give him a fallback as a lefty reliever.

Year	Age	Club (League)	Class	W	L	ERA	G	GS	SV	IP	H	HR	BB	SO	K/9	WHIP	AVG
2017	21	Billings (PIO)	R	3	3	3.15	14	12	0	60	58	5	20	63	9.5	1.30	.256
2018	22	Dayton (MWL)	LoA	5	10	4.03	28	28	0	154	168	12	34	137	8.0	1.31	.280
2019	23	Daytona (FSL)	HiA	5	2	2.63	9	9	0	51	49	2	9	50	8.8	1.13	.248
	23	Chattanooga (SL)	AA	6	10	3.66	19	19	0	106	109	8	26	81	6.9	1.28	.266
Minor League Totals				19	25	3.59	70	68	0	371	384	27	89	331	8.0	1.27	.267

17 JOSE SIRI, OF

BA GRADE 40 Risk: High

Born: July 22, 1995. **B-T:** R-R. **HT:** 6-2. **WT:** 175. **Signed:** Dominican Republic, 2012. **Signed by:** Richard Jimenez.

TRACK RECORD: Siri was hampered in 2018 by a sprained thumb he suffered when he crashed into a wall in spring training. He returned healthy in 2019 and advanced to Triple-A, although he hit just .186 in 30 games at the level after a pedestrian showing at Double-A Chattanooga.
SCOUTING REPORT: Siri doesn't have much discipline at the plate, and coupled with a penchant for swinging and missing, he projects to be a below-average hitter. His raw power is plus, but he doesn't make enough contact to get to it in games. When Siri does manage to get on base, his plus speed and good jumps make him a dangerous stolen base threat. Siri has an excellent glove and strong throwing arm to boot, allowing him to profile at any outfield position.
THE FUTURE: Siri is a high-energy player with plenty of tools, but his shortcomings at the plate may limit him to a reserve role. He will return to Triple-A Louisville in 2020.

Year	Age	Club (League)	Class	AVG	G	AB	R	H	2B	3B	HR	RBI	BB	SO	SB	OBP	SLG
2017	21	Dayton (MWL)	LoA	.293	126	498	92	146	24	11	24	76	33	130	46	.341	.530
2018	22	Daytona (FSL)	HiA	.261	30	119	15	31	9	2	1	9	4	32	9	.280	.395
	22	Pensacola (SL)	AA	.229	66	253	42	58	8	9	12	34	24	91	14	.300	.474
2019	23	Chattanooga (SL)	AA	.251	101	366	46	92	15	1	11	50	33	126	21	.313	.388
	23	Louisville (IL)	AAA	.186	30	102	10	19	4	1	0	3	9	39	5	.252	.245
Minor League Totals				.264	594	2233	368	589	98	54	68	270	147	675	155	.313	.447

18 TJ FRIEDL, OF

BA GRADE **40** Risk: Medium

Born: Aug 4, 1995. **B-T:** L-L. **HT:** 5-10. **WT:** 180. **Signed:** Nevada, 2016 (NDFA). **Signed by:** Rich Bordi/Sam Grossman

TRACK RECORD: Friedl put on a show with Team USA's Collegiate National team in 2016 after being overlooked as a draft-eligible sophomore earlier that summer. The Reds signed him for $735,000 afterhis Team USA performance, the largest bonus ever given to an undrafted player. After quickly climbing to Double-A, Friedl went on the injured list three times during the 2019 season and was limited to just 65 games. He suffered a shoulder injury in April after sliding head-first into a base and battled right ankle tendinitis that ultimately ended his season on July 4.

SCOUTING REPORT: Friedl is an undersized outfielder who knows his game. He uses a crouched, slightly closed stance at the plate with a swing built for contact, although he ran into trouble with strikeouts in the Southern League. He doesn't have much of strength and projects for below-average power. Friedl has plus speed and steals a fair amount of bases. He has above-average range in the outfield with a fringy arm that makes him best in either left or center field.

THE FUTURE: Health will be paramount for Friedl in 2020. His leadership skills and athletic ability give him a chance to carve out a role as a reserve outfielder.

Year	Age	Club (League)	Class	AVG	G	AB	R	H	2B	3B	HR	RBI	BB	SO	SB	OBP	SLG
2017	21	Dayton (MWL)	LoA	.284	66	250	47	71	20	6	5	25	29	46	14	.378	.472
	21	Daytona (FSL)	HiA	.257	48	179	15	46	6	2	2	13	10	39	2	.313	.346
2018	22	Daytona (FSL)	HiA	.294	64	228	40	67	10	4	3	35	38	44	11	.405	.412
	22	Pensacola (SL)	AA	.276	67	261	47	72	10	3	2	16	28	56	19	.359	.360
2019	23	Chattanooga (SL)	AA	.235	65	226	38	53	11	4	5	28	29	50	13	.347	.385
Minor League Totals				.277	339	1265	211	351	68	21	20	134	147	260	66	.369	.412

19 JOEL KUHNEL, RHP

BA GRADE **40** Risk: Medium

Born: Feb. 19, 1995. **B-T:** R-R. **HT:** 6-5. **WT:** 260. **Drafted:** Texas-Arlington, 2016 (11th round). **Signed by:** Byron Ewing.

TRACK RECORD: A starter at Texas-Arlington, Kuhnel promptly moved to the bullpen after the Reds drafted him in the 11th round and signed him for $125,000 in 2016. He steadily climbed the minors and made his major league debut in 2019, although his control became more erratic the higher he rose.

SCOUTING REPORT: Kuhnel's main weapon is a fastball that sits 96-97 mph and can touch 100. It's a premium fastball with a high spin rate and late life in the zone, although he struggled to throw it for strikes during his brief time in the majors. Kuhnel complements his heater with a hard mid-80s slider that can hit the low-90s. Like his fastball, however, his slider plays below its velocity due to his fringy control. It's an average pitch that still ranks ahead of his rarely-used changeup, which is firm in the upper 80s and flashes average.

THE FUTURE: Kuhnel should get more innings in the Reds' bullpen in 2020. His fastball will help him to stick as a seventh-inning option if he can throw it more often for strikes.

Year	Age	Club (League)	Class	W	L	ERA	G	GS	SV	IP	H	HR	BB	SO	K/9	WHIP	AVG
2017	22	Dayton (MWL)	LoA	2	4	4.36	48	0	11	64	78	6	10	54	7.6	1.38	.296
2018	23	Daytona (FSL)	HiA	1	4	3.04	44	0	17	53	54	2	11	56	9.5	1.22	.260
2019	24	Chattanooga (SL)	AA	3	2	2.27	25	0	10	36	26	5	8	30	7.6	0.95	.202
	24	Louisville (IL)	AAA	2	1	2.00	16	0	4	18	13	1	8	20	10.0	1.17	.200
	24	Cincinnati (NL)	MAJ	1	0	4.66	11	0	0	10	8	1	5	9	8.4	1.34	.216
Major League Totals				1	0	4.66	11	0	0	9	8	1	5	9	8.4	1.34	.216
Minor League Totals				8	12	3.28	151	0	46	192	199	15	38	174	8.2	1.23	.264

20 YAN CONTRERAS, SS

BA GRADE **45** Risk: Extreme

Born: Jan. 30. 2001. **B-T:** R-R. **HT:** 6-2. **WT:** 185. **Drafted:** HS—Gurabo, P.R., 2019 (12th round). **Signed by:** Hector Otero.

TRACK RECORD: Contreras signed for $249,000 as a 12th-round pick in 2019, turning down a commitment to San Jacinto (Texas) JC to turn pro. Known more for his defensive profile, Contreras showed enough with the bat to convince the Reds to draft him and pay him an overslot signing bonus, but he struggled to hit in the Rookie-level Arizona League before having his season cut short by a wrist injury.

SCOUTING REPORT: Despite his poor offensive performance in his pro debut, Contreras shows a balanced swing with the ability to use all fields. He will grow into some power, although he still figures to hit for average over power as he matures. Contreras' above-average speed is an asset on both offense and defense. His hands and arm are both plus for shortstop and he shows good range for the position. He has smooth actions in the field, which will help him to stick on the left side of the infield.

THE FUTURE: Contreras will hope for a clean bill of health in 2020. His actions up the middle and arm strength should help him stay at shortstop, though it's a very light bat profile.

Year	Age	Club (League)	Class	AVG	G	AB	R	H	2B	3B	HR	RBI	BB	SO	SB	OBP	SLG
2019	18	Reds (AZL)	R	.145	20	69	8	10	1	2	0	2	14	25	4	.298	.217
Minor League Totals				.145	20	69	8	10	1	2	0	2	14	25	4	.298	.217

21 JARED SOLOMON, RHP

BA GRADE
40 Risk: High

Born: June 10, 1997. **B-T:** R-R. **HT:** 6-2. **WT:** 192. **Drafted:** Lackawanna (Pa.) JC, 2017, (11th round). **Signed by:** Lee Seras.

TRACK RECORD: Solomon posted a lackluster season at Lackawanna (Pa.) JC in 2017, but his arm strength intrigued the Reds enough to draft him in the 11th round and give him an overslot $207,500 bonus. After pitching well at the Rookie levels, Solomon split 2019 between low Class A Dayton and high Class A Daytona and recorded nearly a strikeout an inning, but also struggled with walks.

SCOUTING REPORT: Solomon has a classic four-pitch mix, working primarily with a low-to-mid 90s fastball that has touched 97 mph. He throws it for strikes and mixes it with a hard slider that has lateral shape in the mid-80s and projects as average. Solomon can also spin a curveball in the upper-70s, but it lags behind the slider. At times his changeup is too firm to be effective, but it shows the movement necessary to project as average and is better than his breaking stuff. Solomon has had difficulty with walks throughout his career and projects to have fringe-average control. Besides arm strength and a four-pitch mix, Reds' executives applaud Solomon's makeup and work ethic.

THE FUTURE: Solomon has the ingredients to start, but he must improve his control in 2020.

Year	Age	Club (League)	Class	W	L	ERA	G	GS	SV	IP	H	HR	BB	SO	K/9	WHIP	AVG
2017	20	Reds (AZL)	R	2	2	4.26	11	6	0	38	39	2	16	43	10.2	1.45	.260
2018	21	Billings (PIO)	R	4	2	2.27	9	9	0	48	32	4	14	54	10.2	0.97	.187
	21	Dayton (MWL)	LoA	0	1	5.40	6	6	0	25	32	1	18	13	4.7	2.00	.305
2019	22	Dayton (MWL)	LoA	1	3	3.43	11	11	0	42	42	0	27	46	9.9	1.64	.258
	22	Daytona (FSL)	HiA	2	8	4.30	15	15	0	73	74	5	34	65	8.0	1.47	.265
Minor League Totals				9	16	3.82	52	47	0	226	219	12	109	221	8.8	1.45	.252

22 TEJAY ANTONE, RHP

BA GRADE
40 Risk: High

Born: Dec. 5, 1993. **B-T:** R-R. **HT:** 6-4. **WT:** 205. **Drafted:** Weatherford (Texas) JC, 2014 (5th round). **Signed by:** Byron Ewing.

TRACK RECORD: A 22nd-round pick of the Mets out of high school, Antone spent one year at Texas Christian before transferring to Weatherford (Texas) JC. The Reds picked him in the fifth round in 2014 and signed him for $308,400. Antone's ascent was interrupted by Tommy John surgery that cost him the entire 2017 season, but he steadily climbed the ladder after he returned and finished 2019 at Triple-A.

SCOUTING REPORT: Antone is known for his competitive nature and pitchability. His fastball sits in the low 90s and tops out at 93 mph, but he consistently pours it into the strike zone to keep batters on the defensive. His main secondary is a curveball that has good shape and projects to be an average pitch. Antone can also spin a fringe-average slider to give hitters a different look, and his average changeup helps him to get hitters off his fastball and induce soft contact on the ground. His above-average control helps him survive despite the lack of a plus pitch.

THE FUTURE: The Reds added Antone to their 40-man roster after the season. He is set to be starting rotation depth or a long man out of the bullpen.

Year	Age	Club (League)	Class	W	L	ERA	G	GS	SV	IP	H	HR	BB	SO	K/9	WHIP	AVG
2017	23	Did not play—Injured															
2018	24	Daytona (FSL)	HiA	6	3	4.03	17	17	0	96	95	6	29	82	7.7	1.29	.255
2019	25	Chattanooga (SL)	AA	7	4	3.38	13	13	0	75	63	4	22	63	7.6	1.14	.227
	25	Louisville (IL)	AAA	4	8	4.65	14	13	0	72	93	7	31	70	8.8	1.73	.322
Minor League Totals				39	35	3.74	111	109	0	611	679	39	164	460	6.8	1.38	.283

23 IVAN JOHNSON, SS/2B

BA GRADE
45 Risk: Extreme

Born: Oct. 11, 1998. **B-T:** B-R. **HT:** 6-0. **WT:** 190. **Drafted:** Chipola (Fla.) JC, 2019 (4th round). **Signed by:** John Poloni.

TRACK RECORD: After struggling his freshman year at Georgia, Johnson transferred to Chipola (Fla.) JC and led the team in every major offensive category in 2019. The Reds drafted him in the fourth round and signed him for $397,500. Johnson reported to Rookie-level Greenville after signing and showed the ability to play both shortstop and second base.

SCOUTING REPORT: Johnson has a long swing at times, but his quick hands handle velocity well from both sides of the plate. There are concerns regarding his swing-and-miss which places an average ceiling on his future hit tool. His frame has filled out some and has added strength to his swing which projects to have average power as he matures. Johnson is an above-average runner and handles both middle infield positions well, although executives think he is best suited for second base due to his average arm strength. His glove projects as average but is sturdy enough to move around the diamond and be effective.
THE FUTURE: There isn't a carrying tool present in Johnson's profile, but his all-around skillset has the ceiling of a second-division regular.

Year	Age	Club (League)	Class	AVG	G	AB	R	H	2B	3B	HR	RBI	BB	SO	SB	OBP	SLG
2019	20	Greeneville (APP)	R	.255	46	188	27	48	10	1	6	22	18	46	11	.327	.415
Minor League Totals				.255	46	188	27	48	10	1	6	22	18	46	11	.327	.415

24 HENDRIK CLEMENTINA, C

BA GRADE **40** Risk: High

Born: June 17, 1997. **B-T:** R-R. **HT:** 6-0. **WT:** 250. **Signed:** Curacao, 2013. **Signed by:** Rolando Chirino/Patrick Guerrero/Bob Engle (Dodgers).

TRACK RECORD: Clementina signed with the Dodgers for $50,000 in 2013 and spent four years in Rookie ball before the Reds acquired him for Tony Cingrani at the 2017 trade deadline. After showing power in his full-season debut in 2018, Clementina hit 14 home runs in the Florida State League.
SCOUTING REPORT: Clementina's calling card is his near top-of-the-scale power. He grinds out at-bats, but he has an inconsistent approach and doesn't make enough contact to be more than fringe-average as a hitter. His physically mature body limits his mobility as a catcher. Even though his arm is average, he threw out just 14 percent of would-be base stealers. His has strong hands but needs to improve his receiving skills.
THE FUTURE: Clementina's defense needs more reps, but his power may help him hit enough home runs to stick in a backup role in the majors. He'll move to Double-A in 2020.

Year	Age	Club (League)	Class	AVG	G	AB	R	H	2B	3B	HR	RBI	BB	SO	SB	OBP	SLG
2017	20	Ogden (PIO)	R	.370	24	92	17	34	5	0	4	25	10	16	0	.439	.554
	20	Billings (PIO)	R	.240	27	96	13	23	6	0	2	10	7	25	0	.302	.365
2018	21	Dayton (MWL)	LoA	.268	96	340	38	91	22	1	18	59	30	99	1	.327	.497
2019	22	Daytona (FSL)	HiA	.249	91	338	30	84	13	0	14	54	19	92	1	.296	.411
Minor League Totals				.264	357	1286	154	339	66	3	46	199	93	328	8	.320	.427

25 MARIEL BAUTISTA, OF

BA GRADE **45** Risk: Extreme

Born: Oct. 15, 1997. **B-T:** R-R. **HT:** 6-3. **WT:** 194. **Signed:** Dominican Republic, 2014. **Signed By:** Richard Jimenez.

TRACK RECORD: Bautista signed with the Reds for $60,000 and hit above .300 for three straight seasons at the Rookie levels, giving the Reds the belief they had a steal. But Bautista moved to the low Class A Midwest League in 2019 and was overmatched in full-season ball, posting a .635 OPS at Dayton and missing time with a shoulder issue.
SCOUTING REPORT: Bautista still has plenty of high-impact tools. Evaluators are enamored with his athleticism and projectable, wiry frame. He has plus bat speed and plus raw power, but he lacks feel for situations at the plate and had the swing-and-miss to his game exposed by better pitching. He is a plus runner with an average arm and plays a fine center field, though he may slow down as he fills out his frame.
THE FUTURE: Bautista's lack of feel for the game is concerning, but he has tools to work with and grow into. He will start 2020 back in the Midwest League.

Year	Age	Club (League)	Class	AVG	G	AB	R	H	2B	3B	HR	RBI	BB	SO	SB	OBP	SLG
2017	19	Reds (AZL)	R	.320	36	147	29	47	9	1	0	20	5	24	16	.353	.395
2018	20	Billings (PIO)	R	.330	56	209	43	69	12	4	8	37	16	29	16	.386	.541
2019	21	Reds (AZL)	R	.368	5	19	6	7	3	0	0	1	2	3	4	.429	.526
	21	Dayton (MWL)	LoA	.233	103	386	43	90	10	2	8	33	28	88	19	.303	.332
Minor League Totals				.288	313	1168	194	336	60	14	21	151	93	223	74	.355	.417

26 JAMES MARINAN, RHP

BA GRADE **45** Risk: Extreme

Born: Oct. 10, 1998. **B-T:** R-R. **HT:** 6-5. **WT:** 239. **Drafted:** HS—Lake Worth, Fla., 2017 (4th round). **Signed by:** Adrian Casanova (Dodgers).

TRACK RECORD: The Dodgers drafted Marinan in the fourth round and signed him for $822,500 in 2017 after he morphed from an interesting two-way prospect to a hard-throwing pitching prospect as a high school senior. The Reds acquired him one year later with reliever Aneurys Zabala in exchange for relievers Dylan Floro and Zach Neal. Marinan jumped to full-season ball in 2019 and struggled, posting a 5.56 ERA in 17 starts with low Class A Dayton.

SCOUTING REPORT: Marinan's fastball sits in the low 90s and touches 95 mph with sink. He is able to spin a curveball that has some depth, but it is inconsistent and needs refinement. Marinan's third offering is a changeup he shows nascent feel for and could become average in time. Control has been an issue for Marinan, whose large 6-foot-5 frame has caused him difficulty repeating his three-quarters arm slot.

THE FUTURE: Marinan's arm strength and feel for two secondary pitches give him potential, but only if he can rein in his control. He'll see high Class A Daytona in 2020.

Year	Age	Club (League)	Class	W	L	ERA	G	GS	SV	IP	H	HR	BB	SO	K/9	WHIP	AVG
2017	18	Dodgers (AZL)	R	2	0	1.59	9	6	0	17	14	0	14	14	7.4	1.65	.250
2018	19	Dodgers (AZL)	R	0	0	0.84	3	3	0	11	11	0	4	11	9.3	1.41	.289
	19	Billings (PIO)	R	3	2	3.98	11	11	0	43	49	1	19	39	8.2	1.58	.287
2019	20	Dayton (MWL)	LoA	2	9	5.56	17	17	0	79	96	10	30	48	5.4	1.59	.306
Minor League Totals				7	11	4.32	40	37	0	150	170	11	67	112	6.7	1.58	.294

27 DEBBY SANTANA, 3B

BA GRADE 45 Risk: Extreme

Born: Aug. 24, 2000. **B-T:** R-R. **HT:** 6-2. **WT:** 185. **Signed:** Dominican Republic, 2016. **Signed by:** Richard Jimenez.

TRACK RECORD: Santana got off to a hot start in pro ball after signing with the Reds for $70,000 during the 2016 international signing period. He excelled in the Dominican Summer League and was making strides in his second year in the Rookie-level Arizona League in 2019, but a nagging hip issue limited him to just 25 games.

SCOUTING REPORT: Santana is extremely raw but has shown he can hit. He has plus bat speed and a loose, whippy swing, but he does chase outside of the zone. His hit tool projects as above-average and shows growing power, which could be plus as he matures. Santana is gifted with a strong throwing arm that has natural carry, but his fringe-average glove may force him to move across the diamond from third base to first base.

THE FUTURE: While he is raw, Santana has considerable upside to his offensive game. He's a long way away, but has a chance to emerge as a bat-first regular.

Year	Age	Club (League)	Class	AVG	G	AB	R	H	2B	3B	HR	RBI	BB	SO	SB	OBP	SLG
2017	16	Reds (DSL)	R	.302	49	172	26	52	17	1	2	23	13	45	5	.356	.448
2018	17	Reds (AZL)	R	.250	50	188	23	47	7	4	6	25	10	44	0	.295	.426
2019	18	Reds (AZL)	R	.310	25	100	13	31	3	2	1	13	3	31	0	.327	.410
Minor League Totals				.283	124	460	62	130	27	7	9	61	26	120	5	.325	.430

28 IBANDEL ISABEL, 1B

BA GRADE 40 Risk: High

Born: June 20, 1995. **B-T:** R-R. **HT:** 6-4. **WT:** 225. **Signed:** Dominican Republic, 2013. **Signed by:** Bob Engle/Patrick Guerrero (Dodgers).

TRACK RECORD: Isabel signed with the Dodgers for $80,000 at 17 and grew into one of minor league baseball's most prolific home run hitters, as well as one of its easiest players to strike out. The Reds acquired him with reliever Zach Neal for Ariel Hernandez in April 2018. Isabel hit a Florida State League-record 35 home runs that year and led the Double-A Southern League with 26 home runs in 2019, but he also struck out a combined 314 times in those two seasons.

SCOUTING REPORT: Isabel has top-of-the-scale raw power and can hit the ball out of any ballpark. He has plus bat speed, but with a lot of moving parts to his swing, he frequently swings through pitches in the strike zone and has a penchant for chasing pitches out of the zone. When he connects he hits gargantuan home runs, but his max-effort swing and its resulting holes are problematic. Once a butcher in the field, Isabel has grown coordinated enough to handle first base and has an average arm. He committed just one error in 414.1 innings at the position in 2019.

THE FUTURE: Ibandel strikes out far too much to be a regular, but he might be an interesting power bat off the bench. He'll see Triple-A Louisville in 2019.

Year	Age	Club (League)	Class	AVG	G	AB	R	H	2B	3B	HR	RBI	BB	SO	SB	OBP	SLG
2017	22	R. Cucamonga (CAL)	HiA	.259	122	444	62	115	16	1	28	87	40	172	0	.327	.489
2018	23	R. Cucamonga (CAL)	HiA	.238	6	21	1	5	2	0	1	3	2	9	0	.304	.476
	23	Daytona (FSL)	HiA	.258	104	376	62	97	11	0	35	75	36	152	1	.333	.566
2019	24	Chattanooga (SL)	AA	.243	91	334	52	81	12	1	26	69	26	153	0	.307	.518
Minor League Totals				.271	521	1852	283	501	81	15	113	355	171	718	9	.340	.513

29 JACOB HEATHERLY, LHP

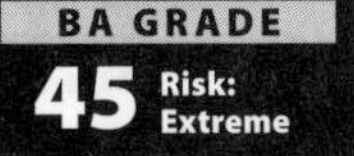

Born: May 20, 1998. **B-T:** L-L. **HT:** 6-1. **WT:** 215. **Drafted:** HS—Cullman, Ala., 2017 (3rd round). **Signed by:** Jim Moran.

TRACK RECORD: The Reds plucked Heatherly in the third round of the 2017 draft and signed him for an above-slot $1.047 million. He flashed high-quality stuff but also walked more than a batter per inning at Rookie-level Greeneville in 2018, then made only four starts for low Class A Dayton in 2019 before shoulder soreness ended his season.

SCOUTING REPORT: Heatherly uses a repeatable, compact delivery but doesn't have good control, some of which is due to his scarce time spent on the mound due to injury. He is armed with a fastball that ranges from 92-95 mph and tops out at 97 with life. Heatherly has the ability to spin the ball effectively, flashing a curveball that at times is near top-of-the-scale. His slider is behind his curveball but flashes average at times, while he shows feel for a changeup that is his decided fourth pitch.

THE FUTURE: With control issues hampering his success as a starter, Heatherly is destined for the bullpen. His fastball-curveball mix could play up as a late-inning power lefthander.

Year	Age	Club (League)	Class	W	L	ERA	G	GS	SV	IP	H	HR	BB	SO	K/9	WHIP	AVG
2017	19	Reds (AZL)	R	2	1	2.93	9	6	0	31	26	3	16	26	7.6	1.37	.224
	19	Billings (PIO)	R	0	1	12.00	3	3	0	9	17	0	4	5	5.0	2.33	.405
2018	20	Greeneville (APP)	R	1	5	5.82	11	11	0	39	34	3	40	49	11.4	1.91	.241
2019	21	Dayton (MWL)	LoA	1	2	8.31	4	4	0	9	12	0	6	10	10.4	2.08	.300
Minor League Totals				4	9	5.69	27	24	0	87	89	6	66	90	9.3	1.78	.263

30 RYAN HENDRIX, RHP

BA GRADE
40 Risk: High

Born: Dec. 16, 1994. **B-T:** R-R HT: 6-3. **WT:** 185. **Drafted:** Texas A&M, 2016 (5th round). **Signed by:** Byron Ewing.

TRACK RECORD: Control problems caused Hendrix to lose the closer's role at Texas A&M to his junior season. The Reds still selected the hard-throwing righthander in the fifth round because of his arm strength and ability to spin a breaking ball. Hendricks posted a 1.76 ERA at high Class A Daytona in 2018 and appeared primed to rocket up the system in 2019, but an elbow strain knocked him out for more than two months and limited him to 16 appearances at Double-A Chattanooga.

SCOUTING REPORT: Hendrix has premium arm strength with a fastball that can reach 97 mph. His main secondary weapon is a curveball that flashes plus-plus with late downward snap. It shows the ability to miss bats and put hitters away, although he lacks consistent command of it. Hendrix has a head whack in his delivery which can cause his control to waver from time to time. His third offering is a firm changeup that lags behind his other two offerings.

THE FUTURE: A clean bill of health would go a long way for Hendrix in 2020. If he can iron out his control issues, he has a chance to become a seventh-inning reliever.

Year	Age	Club (League)	Class	W	L	ERA	G	GS	SV	IP	H	HR	BB	SO	K/9	WHIP	AVG
2017	22	Dayton (MWL)	LoA	4	1	2.36	23	0	6	34	19	2	10	61	16.0	0.84	.161
	22	Daytona (FSL)	HiA	1	4	3.58	24	0	2	28	29	4	19	27	8.8	1.73	.266
2018	23	Daytona (FSL)	HiA	4	4	1.76	44	0	12	51	38	2	26	79	13.9	1.25	.205
2019	24	Reds (AZL)	R	1	0	0.00	4	2	0	5	1	0	0	8	14.4	0.20	.059
	24	Chattanooga (SL)	AA	3	0	2.33	16	0	2	19	14	0	8	23	10.7	1.14	.200
Minor League Totals				16	10	2.55	132	2	22	172	133	8	76	234	12.2	1.21	.211

Cleveland Indians

BY TEDDY CAHILL

The Indians won 93 games in 2019—two more than they did in 2018, when they won their third straight American League Central title—but for the first time since 2015 they missed the playoffs.

An October without baseball made for a bitter pill for the Indians and an uneasy early beginning to the offseason in Cleveland. In addition to missing the playoffs, the franchise must deal with a core that grows more expensive by the year—particularly Francisco Lindor, who is not signed to a long-term deal and has only two more seasons of team control, and Corey Kluber, who will turn 34 in April and is coming off a year in which he was limited by injury to 35.2 innings. Michael Brantley and Cody Allen both left Cleveland in free agency last year and Jason Kipnis this winter is expected to do the same, further marking the passage of time.

The Indians' payroll situation remains tight. The club ranked in the bottom half of the league in payroll in 2019 and figures to remain there, as it typically has in the 21st century. That reality helped precipitate the trade of Trevor Bauer, as the team walked a fine line of competing in 2019, while also managing an increasingly expensive player fast approaching free agency. That makes signing Lindor to an extension that would easily exceed the franchise record unlikely and has opposing teams eyeing him on the trade market.

Despite that bleak background, however, the franchise remains well positioned. Lindor and Jose Ramirez give the Indians one of the best left sides of the infield in the game. Roberto Perez took over full-time behind the plate in 2019 and won a Gold Glove. The Tribe's pitching development pipeline continues to flow, and Shane Bieber was named All-Star Game MVP and finished fourth in AL Cy Young voting as a 24-year-old. He was one of four pitchers under 30 to make at least 20 starts for the club in 2019 and produce an ERA+ above league average.

The Indians' next big wave of talent continues to matriculate in the lower levels of the minor leagues. The club had one of the best collections of talent in low Class A and below in all of baseball. While it'll take some time for players like Daniel Espino, Ethan Hankins, Bo Naylor, Brayan Rocchio and George Valera to get to the big leagues, they also could form the core of a top-five farm system a year from now.

Ahead of that group, Nolan Jones and Tyler Freeman will soon make an impact in Cleveland. And after the farm has graduated Bieber, Aaron Civale, Mike Clevinger and Zach Plesac in quick succession, it is fair to expect Logan Allen, James Karinchak or Scott Moss to soon deliver a breakout campaign.

With franchise stars like Kluber and Lindor approaching the end of their tenures in Cleveland, uneasiness is understandable. The window for this core is beginning to close. But the Indians' front office under Chris Antonetti and Mike Chernoff have worked hard to ensure that the next wave will be able to make an easy transition.

It's not time to hand the torch off yet in Cleveland, but the plan to do so is starting to both become more relevant and come into sharper focus as the new decade and a potential climb back to the top begins.

DAVID MAXWELL/GETTY IMAGES

Rookie Oscar Mercado filled two vital roles: top-of-the-order hitter and center fielder.

PROJECTED 2023 LINEUP

Position	Player	Age
Catcher	Bo Naylor (3)	23
First Base	Jake Bauers	27
Second Base	Tyler Freeman (2)	24
Third Base	Jose Ramirez	30
Shortstop	Francisco Lindor	29
Left Field	Nolan Jones (1)	25
Center Field	Oscar Mercado	28
Right Field	George Valera (4)	22
Designated Hitter	Franmil Reyes	27
No. 1 Starter	Shane Bieber	28
No. 2 Starter	Mike Clevinger	32
No. 3 Starter	Daniel Espino (6)	22
No. 4 Starter	Triston McKenzie (7)	24
No. 5 Starter	Aaron Civale	28
Closer	Brad Hand	33

DEPTH CHART

CLEVELAND INDIANS

TOP 2020 ROOKIE: Logan Allen, LHP. The Indians have done well at graduating pitchers in recent years and Allen could be the next up as a solid all-around and versatile lefthander.

BREAKOUT PROSPECT: Angel Martinez, SS. There's a bit of Brayan Rocchio in Martinez's profile and with a strong 2020 campaign, during which he'll make his U.S. debut.

SLEEPER: Joe Naranjo, 1B. In a system loaded with athletic infielders, Naranjo—nicknamed Joey Barrels—has the offensive potential to make noise in 2020.

SOURCE OF TOP 30 TALENT			
Homegrown	**26**	**Acquired**	**4**
College	3	Trade	4
Junior college	0	Rule 5 draft	0
High school	11	Independent league	0
Nondrafted free agent	0	Free agent/waivers	0
International	12		

LF
George Valera (4)
Oscar Gonzalez (26)
Ka'ai Tom

CF
Luis Durango Jr.
Steven Kwan
Quentin Holmes

RF
Daniel Johnson (23)
Will Benson (25)
Johnathan Rodriguez

3B
Nolan Jones (1)
Yu Chang (22)
Junior Sanquintin
Christian Cairo
Jhonkensy Noel

SS
Tyler Freeman (2)
Brayan Rocchio (5)
Gabriel Rodriguez (10)
Yordys Valdes (19)
Angel Martinez (20)
Ernie Clement (21)
Jose Pastrano (27)
Jose Devers

2B
Aaron Bracho (9)
Jose Tena (28)
Jose Fermin
Richie Palacios
Raynel Delgado
Andrew Velazquez
Jesus Lara

1B
Bobby Bradley (12)
Joe Naranjo

C
Bo Naylor (3)
Bryan Lavastida
Eric Haase

LHP

LHSP	LHRP
Logan Allen (11)	Kyle Nelson
Scott Moss (13)	Anthony Gose
Sam Hentges (17)	Ben Krauth
Adam Scott	
Kirk McCarty	
Raymond Burgos	
Juan Hillman	

RHP

RHSP	RHRP
Daniel Espino (6)	Emmanuel Clase (15)
Triston McKenzie (7)	James Karinchak (16)
Ethan Hankins (8)	Nick Sandlin (29)
Carlos Vargas (14)	Robert Broom
Luis Oviedo (18)	Nick Mikolajchak
Lenny Torres (24)	Dalbert Siri
Jean Carlos Mejia (30)	
Cody Morris	
Hunter Gaddis	
Eli Morgan	
Sergio Morillo	

DRAFT ANALYSIS

2019

BEST PURE HITTER: You don't earn the nickname Joey Barrels without having premium hitting ability. 1B Joseph Naranjo (3) stood out for just that during his prep career thanks to his simple approach, direct swing, control of the strike zone and ability to use the whole field to hit.

BEST POWER HITTER: The Indians didn't draft any big sluggers this year, instead focusing on hittability and defense among position players. But OF Will Brennan (8) has extra-base pop and C Will Bartlett (9) has above-average power. OF Micah Pries (13) could also match that and hit 18 home runs this spring.Fastest Runner: The Indians didn't draft any true burners, but Palacios, OF Steven Kwan (5), OF Korey Holland (14) and SS Gionti Turner (27) all show plus run times.

FASTEST RUNNER: SS Christian Cairo (4) has above-average speed and his instincts help that play up on the bases and in the infield.

BEST DEFENSIVE PLAYER: SS Yordys Valdes (2) was arguably the most advanced defender in the draft class. The Cuban native has excellent instincts and feel for the game to go with a plus arm and range. SS Joab Gonzalez (24) is also a high-end defender with a plus arm and good range.

BEST FASTBALL: RHP Daniel Espino (1) was one of the best prep arms in the draft class and has a big fastball that reaches 99 mph. RHP Hunter Gaddis (5) saw his velocity tick up after the draft, and he touched 97 mph this summer.

BEST SECONDARY PITCH: RHP Nick Mikolajchak (11) stands out for his fastball-slider combination, and that slider has helped him pile up strikeouts throughout his career. Espino also has the chance to have a plus slider.

BEST PRO DEBUT: The Indians often draft premium high school players but just as often are very cautious with them at the outset of their careers. Still, Espino pitched well enough in the Rookie-level Arizona League to force their hand, and he became the first prep player to advance to short-season Mahoning Valley during his pro debut since 2011.

BEST ATHLETE: Espino has excellent athleticism, especially in terms of his flexibility, coordination and body control. His combination of explosiveness and flexibility is rare. Gaddis and Valdes are both also high-end athletes.

MOST INTRIGUING BACKGROUND: RHP Jacob Forrester (37) is the son of Mike Forrester, one of the world's best competitive timber sportsmen who was once profiled on the Colbert Report. RHP Kevin Kelly (19) is one of the smartest players in baseball and taught himself to code, including how to write SQL.

CLOSEST TO THE MAJORS: Mikolajchak's pro debut puts him on an accelerated path to Cleveland and, as a reliever, he could be in the big leagues soon. For a prep player in the Indians' system, Espino is now also on an accelerated track.

BEST LATE-ROUND PICK: Mikolajchak stands out among the Indians' Day 3 picks. RHPs Eric Mock (25) and Matt Waldron (18) also impressed this summer during their pro debuts and offer promise.

THE ONE WHO GOT AWAY: The Indians signed their first 25 picks before SS Armani Sanchez (26) got away. He and C Jonathan French (30) were the two most high-profile prep players the Indians took who went unsigned. Sanchez will go back in the draft this spring after a year at San Jacinto (Texas) JC, while French upheld his commitment to Clemson.

—TEDDY CAHILL

TOP DRAFT PICKS OF THE DECADE

Year	Player, Pos.	2019 Org
2010	Drew Pomeranz, LHP	Brewers
2011	Francisco Lindor, SS	Indians
2012	Tyler Naquin, OF	Indians
2013	Clint Frazier, OF	Yankees
2014	Bradley Zimmer, OF	Indians
2015	Brady Aiken, LHP	Indians
2016	Will Benson, OF	Indians
2017	Quentin Holmes, OF (2nd round)	Indians
2018	Bo Naylor, C	Indians
2019	Daniel Espino, RHP	Indians

2018

The Indians used their two first-round picks on C Bo Naylor and RHP Ethan Hankins and both are off to strong starts. RHPs Lenny Torres (1s) and Nick Sandlin (2) have also impressed.

GRADE: B

2017

The club didn't have a first-round pick, but SS Tyler Freeman (2s) has exceeded expectations and become a Top 100 Prospect. RHP James Karinchak (9) rocketed to Cleveland, already giving this class a big leaguer.

GRADE: B

2016

The Indians aren't sorry they drafted RHP Shane Bieber (4). RHPs Aaron Civale (3) and Zach Plesac (12) joined him in the big leagues, and 3B Nolan Jones (2) became the system's top prospect.

GRADE: A

1 NOLAN JONES, 3B

Born: May 7, 1998. **B-T:** L-R. **HT:** 6-2. **WT:** 185.
Drafted: HS—Bensalem, Pa., 2016 (2nd round).
Signed by: Mike Kanen.

TRACK RECORD: Jones was one of the players the Indians targeted with their first-round pick in 2016. The team instead selected Will Benson 14th overall and didn't expect to see Jones on the board when they next picked at No. 55. They didn't pass on Jones, one of the top prep hitters in his class, a second time. In 2017, he led the New York-Penn League in OPS (.912) as a 19-year old and has followed that up in full-season ball. He had a busy 2019, beginning the year with high Class A Lynchburg, where he played well enough in 79 games to be selected to the Carolina League all-star team. He also was selected for the Futures Game and the Arizona Fall League's Fall Stars Game, and in July was promoted to Double-A Akron. His season came to an end in October when he re-aggravated an injury to his right thumb and had surgery to repair a ligament.

SCOUTING REPORT: Jones has an easy lefthanded swing and uses the whole field to hit. He is a patient hitter and has led all Indians' minor leaguers in walks in back-to-back seasons (89 in 2018, 96 in 2019), though his patience also means that he often works in deep counts and will always strike out fairly often as a result. He has plus raw power and has started to turn that into in-game production. Jones fits the third-base profile but throughout his career has dealt with questions about his ability to stay at the position. He has plus arm strength and has worked hard to improve his defense and infield actions, especially when ranging to the right. He's improved his footwork and agility, giving him a strong chance to stay at the hot corner. While the Indians generally work to add versatility to all their position players, Jones has played exclusively third base since he was in Rookie ball. Still, his athleticism and speed should play in the outfield if required.

THE FUTURE: After his impressive 2019 and stint in the AFL, Jones is nearing the big leagues and will likely open 2020 at Triple-A Columbus. He's a potential impact bat who also stands out for his work ethic. His impending big league debut and Jose Ramirez's versatility gives the Indians options over the next couple of years, but even if Ramirez stays in the hot corner, Jones' offensive ability is such that the team will find a way to get them both into the lineup.

BRIAN WESTERHOLT/FOUR SEAM IMAGES

BA GRADE 60 Risk: High

SCOUTING GRADES Hit: 60. Power: 60. Run: 50. Field: 50. Arm: 60.

Projected future grades on 20-80 scouting scale.

TOP PROSPECTS OF THE DECADE

Year	Player, Pos.	2019 Org
2009	Carlos Santana, C	Indians
2010	Carlos Santana, C	Indians
2011	Lonnie Chisenhall, 3B	Pirates
2012	Francisco Lindor, SS	Indians
2013	Francisco Lindor, SS	Indians
2014	Francisco Lindor, SS	Indians
2015	Francisco Lindor, SS	Indians
2016	Bradley Zimmer, OF	Indians
2017	Francisco Mejia, C	Padres
2018	Francisco Mejia, C	Padres
2019	Triston McKenzie, RHP	Indians

BEST TOOLS

Best Hitter for Average	Tyler Freeman
Best Power Hitter	Bobby Bradley
Best Strike-Zone Discipline	Ernie Clement
Fastest Baserunner	Quentin Holmes
Best Athlete	Will Benson
Best Fastball	Daniel Espino
Best Curveball	James Karinchak
Best Slider	Kyle Nelson
Best Changeup	Eli Morgan
Best Control	Eli Morgan
Best Defensive Catcher	Bo Naylor
Best Defensive Infielder	Brayan Rocchio
Best Infield Arm	Nolan Jones
Best Defensive Outfielder	Steven Kwan
Best Outfield Arm	Johnathan Rodriguez

Year	Age	Club (League)	Class	AVG	G	AB	R	H	2B	3B	HR	RBI	BB	SO	SB	OBP	SLG
2017	19	Mahoning Valley (NYP)	SS	.317	62	218	41	69	18	3	4	33	43	60	1	.430	.482
2018	20	Lake County (MWL)	LoA	.279	90	323	46	90	12	0	16	49	63	97	2	.393	.464
	20	Lynchburg (CAR)	HiA	.298	30	104	23	31	9	0	3	17	26	34	0	.438	.471
2019	21	Lynchburg (CAR)	HiA	.286	77	252	48	72	12	1	7	41	65	85	5	.435	.425
	21	Akron (EL)	AA	.253	49	178	33	45	10	2	8	22	31	63	2	.370	.466
Minor League Totals				.283	340	1184	201	335	66	8	38	171	251	388	13	.409	.448

2 TYLER FREEMAN, SS

Born: May 21, 1999. **B-T:** R-R. **HT:** 6-0. **WT:** 170. **Drafted:** HS—Rancho Cucamonga, Calif., 2017 (2nd round supplemental). **Signed by:** Mike Bradford.

COURTESY OF LCCAPTAINS

BA GRADE
55 **Risk: High**

TRACK RECORD: Freeman turned in a stellar first full pro season in 2018 that saw him lead the New York-Penn League in a host of offensive categories, including batting (.352) and slugging (.511), as a 19-year-old. He followed that with an impressive 2019, earning a promotion to high Class A Lynchburg in his first taste of full-season ball. Despite being one of the youngest players in the Carolina League, he more than held his own after his promotion to Lynchburg and is now a career .319/.379/.441 hitter.

SCOUTING REPORT: Freeman stands out most for his hitting ability and excellent feel for the barrel. He has a very aggressive approach at the plate and rarely walks, but when he swings, he makes contact. Thanks to his ability to consistently square balls up, he has doubles pop now and may be able to add more power as he physically matures. Freeman was drafted as a shortstop and the Indians are developing him at that position. He's shown improvement with his hands, infield actions and instincts. He's still an average runner with average arm strength, however, which limits his range and might ultimately push him to second base, especially in a system with as many high-end defensive shortstops. Regardless of where he ends up defensively, his bat will stand out.

THE FUTURE: Freeman is on the leading edge of the Indians' group of young middle infielders, meaning he can move quickly through the system. That probably means he's ready for Double-A Akron in 2020.

SCOUTING GRADES: **Hitting:** 60 **Power:** 40 **Running:** 50 **Fielding:** 50 **Arm:** 55

Year	Age	Club (League)	Class	AVG	G	AB	R	H	2B	3B	HR	RBI	BB	SO	SB	OBP	SLG
2019	21	Indians 2 (AZL)	R	.217	21	69	7	15	3	0	0	9	3	18	1	.280	.261
	21	Lake County (MWL)	LoA	.103	12	39	4	4	0	0	0	4	4	13	0	.200	.103
Minor League Totals				.176	33	108	11	19	3	0	0	13	7	31	1	.250	.204

3 BO NAYLOR, C

Born: Feb. 21, 2000. **B-T:** L-R. **HT:** 6-0. **WT:** 195. **Drafted:** HS—Mississauga, Ont., 2018 (1st round). **Signed by:** Mike Kanen.

COURTESY OF LCCAPTAINS

BA GRADE
55 **Risk: Very High**

TRACK RECORD: Naylor, the younger brother of Padres first baseman Josh Naylor, compiled a long track record of success as an amateur, especially facing premium competition with the Canadian Junior National Team. That helped ease his transition into his first year of pro ball, when he found success as a 19-year-old in the Midwest League.

SCOUTING REPORT: Naylor, like his older brother, has standout offensive tools, but he's a different kind of hitter. He's more hit-over-power, though he has solid pop as well. He has an advanced hit tool thanks to his smooth swing, pitch recognition and approach. His power showed up more in 2019 than it had previously, and he makes consistent hard contact and has the ability to drive the ball. Naylor is an above-average runner and his athleticism plays well behind the plate. He earns high grades for pitch-framing, and his strong arm helped him throw out 37 percent of basestealers, but teams were still very willing to test him, attempting 128 stolen bases in 85 games. Still, Naylor has proven himself enough defensively to largely quell any talk of him moving to third base, where he played a lot as an amateur.

THE FUTURE: Naylor will continue to work on refining his defensive skills in 2020 at high Class A Lynchburg, when he will be just 20 years old.

SCOUTING GRADES: **Hitting:** 60 **Power:** 50 **Running:** 50 **Fielding:** 55 **Arm:** 60

Year	Age	Club (League)	Class	AVG	G	AB	R	H	2B	3B	HR	RBI	BB	SO	SB	OBP	SLG
2018	18	Indians 2 (AZL)	R	.274	33	117	17	32	3	3	2	17	21	28	5	.381	.402
2019	19	Lake County (MWL)	LoA	.243	107	399	60	97	18	10	11	65	43	104	7	.313	.421
Minor League Totals				.250	140	516	77	129	21	13	13	82	64	132	12	.329	.417

4 GEORGE VALERA, OF

PAXTON REMBIS

BA GRADE
55 **Risk: Very High**

Born: Nov. 13, 2000. **B-T:** L-L. **HT:** 5-10. **WT:** 160. **Signed:** Dominican Republic, 2017. **Signed by:** Jhonathan Leyba/Domingo Toribio.

TRACK RECORD: The Indians made a splash on the international market in 2017 and signed Valera, the fifth-ranked player in the class to a $1.3 million deal. He was born in New York and lived there until his family moved to the Dominican Republic when he was 13. After a broken hamate limited him to six games in 2018, he spent most of 2019 with short-season Mahoning Valley, where he was the youngest position player in the league, before a late-season promotion to low Class A Lake County.

SCOUTING REPORT: Valera has a loose, compact swing and keeps his bat in the zone for a long time. His feel for the barrel, bat-to-ball skills, pitch recognition and discipline all help him to make consistent, hard contact and give him the kind of hittability the Indians covet. He has above-average raw power and gets to it in games well, hitting eight home runs in 46 games as an 18-year-old in the New York-Penn League. Valera profiles as a corner outfielder with average speed and arm strength.

THE FUTURE: As an amateur, Valera drew comparisons to Juan Soto. He's not going to match Soto's meteoric rise to stardom, but he's proven to be advanced enough to handle challenging assignments. He'll likely return to Lake County to begin 2020 and another mid-season promotion could be in the cards.

SCOUTING GRADES: **Hitting:** 60 **Power:** 55 **Running:** 50 **Fielding:** 50 **Arm:** 50

Year	Age	Club (League)	Class	AVG	G	AB	R	H	2B	3B	HR	RBI	BB	SO	SB	OBP	SLG
2018	17	Indians 2 (AZL)	R	.333	6	18	4	6	1	0	1	6	3	3	1	.409	.556
2019	18	Mahoning Valley (NYP)	SS	.236	46	157	22	37	7	1	8	29	29	52	6	.356	.446
	18	Lake County (MWL)	LoA	.087	6	23	1	2	0	1	0	3	2	9	0	.192	.174
Minor League Totals				.227	58	198	27	45	8	2	9	38	34	64	7	.343	.424

5 BRAYAN ROCCHIO, SS

PAXTON REMBIS

BA GRADE
55 **Risk: Very High**

Born: Jan. 13, 2001. **B-T:** B-R. **HT:** 5-10. **WT:** 150. **Signed:** Venezuela, 2017. **Signed by:** Jhonathan Leyba.

TRACK RECORD: While the Indians made a big splash on the 2017 international market with the heralded signings of Aaron Bracho and George Valera, their move to ink Rocchio flew more under the radar. The Venezuelan native has quickly made his own mark, however. After a strong 2018 in Rookie Ball, he advanced to short-season Mahoning Valley, where he held his own as the third-youngest position player.

SCOUTING REPORT: Rocchio doesn't stand out physically but was nicknamed "The Professor" because of his high baseball IQ and game awareness when he was in the Rookie-level Arizona League. A switch-hitter, he has a smooth, consistent swing from both sides of the plate and excellent pitch recognition. He's an aggressive hitter and consistently barrels up the ball. He's likely always going hit be hit over power but as he physically matures he'll start sending some of his line drives over the fence. Rocchio has largely answered any questions about his ability to stick at shortstop. He's a plus runner, and his hands and arm are good enough for the position, especially because his instincts and baseball IQ help his tools play up.

THE FUTURE: Rocchio is on an accelerated track and there's no reason to slow him down now. He'll head to low Class A Lake County for his first taste of full-season ball.

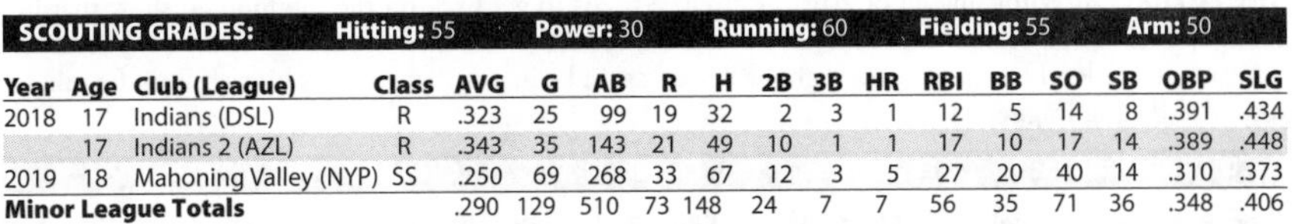

SCOUTING GRADES: **Hitting:** 55 **Power:** 30 **Running:** 60 **Fielding:** 55 **Arm:** 50

Year	Age	Club (League)	Class	AVG	G	AB	R	H	2B	3B	HR	RBI	BB	SO	SB	OBP	SLG
2018	17	Indians (DSL)	R	.323	25	99	19	32	2	3	1	12	5	14	8	.391	.434
	17	Indians 2 (AZL)	R	.343	35	143	21	49	10	1	1	17	10	17	14	.389	.448
2019	18	Mahoning Valley (NYP)	SS	.250	69	268	33	67	12	3	5	27	20	40	14	.310	.373
Minor League Totals				.290	129	510	73	148	24	7	7	56	35	71	36	.348	.406

6 DANIEL ESPINO, RHP

Born: Jan. 5, 2001. **B-T:** R-R. **HT:** 6-1. **WT:** 205. **Drafted:** HS—Statesboro, Ga., 2019 (1st round). **Signed by:** Ethan Purser.

BILL MITCHELL

BA GRADE
55 **Risk: Extreme**

TRACK RECORD: Espino was born in Panama before moving to the United States when he was 15. He enrolled at Georgia Premier Academy, where he was able to continue his education while also adopting a close to professional mindset. That approach was apparent when he arrived at the Indians' complex in Arizona after they drafted him 24th overall. His performance and mentality allowed him to become first prep player the Indians have promoted to short-season Mahoning Valley during his pro debut since Francisco Lindor in 2011.

SCOUTING REPORT: Espino was one of the best prep pitchers in the draft class and has big overall upside. He's on the shorter end of what teams look for in a righthander, but his excellent athleticism, explosiveness and flexibility help him access his lower half in a way most pitchers his size cannot. That helps him produce elite velocity and his fastball reach 99 mph and sit at 96. He throws both a curveball and slider, with the slider earning better grades as a potential plus pitch. He also throws a firm changeup that needs refinement but has a chance to give him a fourth at least average offering. He has a long arm action but typically pitches with average control. He'll need to refine his command as he faces more advanced hitters who are less susceptible to chasing his offspeed stuff.

THE FUTURE: Espino has put himself on an accelerated track already and he'll likely start his first full professional season with low Class A Lake County, where he and righthander Ethan Hankins will team up for a premium 1-2 punch the Indians hope will stick together all the way to Cleveland.

SCOUTING GRADES: **Fastball:** 70 **Slider:** 60 **Curveball:** 50 **Changeup:** 50 **Control:** 50

Year	Age	Club (League)	Class	W	L	ERA	G	GS	SV	IP	H	HR	BB	SO	K/9	WHIP	AVG
2019	18	Indians 1 (AZL)	R	0	1	1.98	6	6	0	14	7	1	5	16	10.5	0.88	.152
	18	Mahoning Valley (NYP)	SS	0	2	6.30	3	3	0	10	9	1	5	18	16.2	1.40	.225
Minor League Totals				0	3	3.80	9	9	0	23	16	2	10	34	12.9	1.10	.186

7 TRISTON MCKENZIE, RHP

Born: Aug. 2, 1997. **B-T:** R-R. **HT:** 6-5. **WT:** 165. **Drafted:** HS—Palm Beach, Fla., 2015 (1st round supplemental). **Signed by:** Juan Alvarez.

BA GRADE
55 **Risk: Extreme**

TRACK RECORD: McKenzie has ranked as the Indians' top prospect the last two years but that standing has slipped after an upper-back injury cost him all of 2019. The Indians have been very cautious with him throughout his career, partially due to his rail-thin frame. But he's always shown exceptional upside, and he pitched in the 2017 Futures Game and reached Double-A in 2018 as a 20-year-old.

SCOUTING REPORT: There have long been questions about McKenzie's durability. He suffered from some forearm soreness early in 2018, but his 2019 injury might speak even more to his durability because it may stem from a lack of strength in his shoulder. If he can avoid similar issues going forward, however, he should be able to get back to the high-end upside he's also long shown. His fastball sits at 92 mph and can touch 95. It plays up thanks to long extension and high spin rate. He also has a good feel for his curveball, which can be an out pitch, and his changeup has the potential to be an above-average offering. He commands the ball well and earns praise for his makeup and understanding of his craft.

THE FUTURE: After missing all of 2019, McKenzie needs to get back on the mound and show that he's ready to pitch a full season. He's still just 22 and hasn't been challenged much yet on the field. If he can get back to the level he was at a year ago, he'll soon again be in position to work himself into the mix for a spot in the big leagues.

SCOUTING GRADES: **Fastball:** 60 **Curveball:** 60 **Changeup:** 55 **Control:** 60

Year	Age	Club (League)	Class	W	L	ERA	G	GS	SV	IP	H	HR	BB	SO	K/9	WHIP	AVG
2017	19	Lynchburg (CAR)	HiA	12	6	3.46	25	25	0	143	105	14	45	186	11.7	1.05	.204
2018	20	Akron (EL)	AA	7	4	2.68	16	16	0	91	63	8	28	87	8.6	1.00	.191
2019	21	Did not play—Injured															
Minor League Totals				26	16	2.68	60	59	0	329	230	26	98	394	10.8	1.00	.194

8 ETHAN HANKINS, RHP

PAXTON REMBIS

BA GRADE
55 Risk: Extreme

Born: May 23, 2000. **B-T:** R-R. **HT:** 6-6. **WT:** 200. **Drafted:** HS—Gainesville, Ga., 2018 (1st round). **Signed by:** C.T. Bradford.

TRACK RECORD: The Indians were thrilled to draft Hankins with the final pick of the first round in 2018. Following his performance the previous summer and fall, he had been considered the best prep player in the draft class but a minor shoulder injury in the spring caused him to slide on draft day. After introducing him to pro ball, the Indians eased back on the leash during his first full pro season and in August sent him to low Class A Lake County.

SCOUTING REPORT: Hankins has a long, lean frame and uncommon athleticism for a pitcher of his size. At his best, he ran his fastball up to 97 mph and typically sits in the mid 90s with plus life. He has the makings of quality secondary pitches, but they'll need to become more consistent offerings.His slider and changeup both have the ability to be above-average offerings and he also throws a bigger curveball, though it lags behind his other pitches. Hankins controls his arsenal well, but it will be important for him to maintain his delivery as he grows into his large frame.

THE FUTURE: Hankins' impressive first full season was a reminder of just how big his upside can be. He's set to start back with Lake Countym where he and Daniel Espino will make for an impressive 1-2 punch that the Indians hope will stick together all the way to the big leagues.

SCOUTING GRADES: **Fastball:** 60 **Slider:** 55 **Changeup:** 50 **Control:** 50

Year	Age	Club (League)	Class	W	L	ERA	G	GS	SV	IP	H	HR	BB	SO	K/9	WHIP	AVG
2018	18	Indians 2 (AZL)	R	0	0	6.00	2	2	0	3	4	0	0	6	18.0	1.33	.308
2019	19	Mahoning Valley (NYP)	SS	0	0	1.40	9	8	0	39	23	1	18	43	10.0	1.06	.178
	19	Lake County (MWL)	LoA	0	3	4.64	5	5	0	21	20	3	12	28	11.8	1.50	.250
Minor League Totals				0	3	2.71	16	15	0	63	47	4	30	77	11.0	1.22	.212

9 AARON BRACHO, 2B

BILL MITCHELL

BA GRADE
55 Risk: Extreme

Born: Apr. 24, 2001. **B-T:** B-R. **HT:** 5-11. **WT:** 175. **Signed:** Venezuela, 2017. **Signed by:** Hernan Albornoz/Rafael Cariel.

TRACK RECORD: The Indians spent big on the 2017 international market. Bracho, who was ranked as a top-20 player in the class, as well as outfielder George Valera and shortstop Brayan Rocchio were a part of that class and now rank as top-10 prospects for the club. Bracho was banged up at the outset of his career and missed 2018 due to an arm injury. He was back to full health in 2019 and made his professional debut in the Rookie-level Arizona League and earned a late-season bump to short-season Mahoning Valley, where he joined Valera and Rocchio.

SCOUTING REPORT: A switch-hitter, Bracho has a smooth, compact swing from both sides of the plate and produces good bat speed. He has an advanced approach and walked more than he struck out in Arizona, a rarity for an 18-year-old with limited game experience. Listed at just 5-foot-11, he has more power than his frame suggests, and he could end up hitting for at least average power. Bracho was signed as a shortstop but he's already moved to second base. His hands and range are good enough to keep him there, but he's likely to be more of an offensive second baseman.

THE FUTURE: After an impressive debut, it's easy to see why Bracho had as much hype as he did as an amateur. He's probably advanced enough to start 2020 with low Class A Lake County as Rocchio's double-play partner, but the Indians middle-infield depth and his minimal game experience may lead to him coming back to Mahoning Valley to start the summer.

SCOUTING GRADES: **Hitting:** 55 **Power:** 50 **Running:** 55 **Fielding:** 50 **Arm:** 45

Year	Age	Club (League)	Class	AVG	G	AB	R	H	2B	3B	HR	RBI	BB	SO	SB	OBP	SLG
2018	17	Did not play—Injured															
2019	18	Indians 2 (AZL)	R	.296	30	108	25	32	10	2	6	29	23	21	4	.416	.593
	18	Mahoning Valley (NYP)	SS	.222	8	27	5	6	1	0	2	4	5	8	0	.344	.481
Minor League Totals				.281	38	135	30	38	11	2	8	33	28	29	4	.402	.570

10 GABRIEL RODRIGUEZ, SS

BILL MITCHELL

BA GRADE 55 **Risk: Extreme**

Born: Feb. 22, 2002 . **B-T:** R-R. **HT:** 6-2. **WT:** 174. **Signed:** Venezuela, 2018. **Signed by:** Hernan Albornoz.

TRACK RECORD: The Venezuelan native was the eighth-ranked player overall in the 2018 international class and lived up to the hype with an impressive pro debut in 2019, earning a midseason promotion to the Rookie-level Arizona League.

SCOUTING REPORT: Rodriguez stands out for his consistency and all-around tools. He has a short, simple swing and an advanced approach at the plate. As he physically matures, he figures to develop at least average power and he has already shown the ability to drive balls to all fields. He shows plenty of power potential during batting practice. The next step is to learn how to take it with him into games. His strong arm and instinctive actions will allow him to stay in the infield, likely at third base, if he does need to move.

THE FUTURE: Rodriguez is advanced enough to follow an aggressive developmental track, much like the premium players in the 2017 class. That would likely mean he starts 2020 back in Arizona and will have a chance to advance to short-season Mahoning Valley later in the summer.

SCOUTING GRADES: Hitting: 55 Power: 50 Running: 50 Fielding: 50 Arm: 55

Year	Age	Club (League)	Class	AVG	G	AB	R	H	2B	3B	HR	RBI	BB	SO	SB	OBP	SLG
2019	17	Indians (DSL)	R	.238	38	143	25	34	7	4	3	29	15	27	3	.335	.406
	17	Indians 1 (AZL)	R	.215	18	65	7	14	3	0	0	10	4	22	1	.288	.262
Minor League Totals				.231	56	208	32	48	10	4	3	39	19	49	4	.321	.361

11 LOGAN ALLEN, LHP

BA GRADE 45 **Risk: Medium**

Born: May 23, 1997. **B-T:** R-L. **HT:** 6-3. **WT:** 200. **Drafted:** HS—Bradenton, Fla., 2015 (8th round). **Signed by:** Stephen Hargett (Red Sox).

TRACK RECORD: Allen has been well traveled since the Red Sox drafted him in the eighth round in 2015 and signed him to an over-slot deal. He was traded that fall to the Padres as a part of the package for Craig Kimbrel and then climbed through the minor leagues to reach San Diego in June. He was traded a month later to Cleveland along with Franmil Reyes and Victor Nova a part of the three-team deal that sent Trevor Bauer to the Reds.

SCOUTING REPORT: Allen has a strong frame and a solid four-pitch mix, and his overall package makes for a potential No. 3 or 4 starter. His fastball sits in the low 90s and can get up to 96 mph in short stints. His changeup is his best secondary offering and it earns plus grades. His slider is an average offering and he'll occasionally mix in a curveball as well. He has average control and can throw his full arsenal for strikes, but he still needs to refine his command at the big league level.

THE FUTURE: He'll probably return to Columbus to start 2020 in the rotation and figures to be one of the first pitchers called up to Cleveland when a need arises.

Year	Age	Club (League)	Class	W	L	ERA	G	GS	SV	IP	H	HR	BB	SO	K/9	WHIP	AVG
2017	20	Fort Wayne (MWL)	LoA	5	4	2.11	13	13	0	68	49	1	26	85	11.2	1.10	.201
	20	Lake Elsinore (CAL)	HiA	2	5	3.97	11	10	0	57	60	2	18	57	9.1	1.38	.272
2018	21	San Antonio (TL)	AA	10	6	2.75	20	19	0	121	89	7	38	125	9.3	1.05	.205
	21	El Paso (PCL)	AAA	4	0	1.63	5	5	0	28	21	4	13	26	8.5	1.23	.206
2019	22	El Paso (PCL)	AAA	4	3	5.15	13	13	0	58	61	8	22	63	9.8	1.44	.269
	22	San Diego (NL)	MAJ	2	3	6.75	8	4	0	25	33	4	13	14	5.0	1.82	.330
	22	Cleveland (AL)	MAJ	0	0	0.00	1	0	0	2	3	0	0	3	11.6	1.29	.333
	22	Columbus (IL)	AAA	1	1	7.66	5	5	0	22	31	6	12	18	7.3	1.93	.341
Major League Totals				2	3	6.18	9	4	0	27	36	4	13	17	5.5	1.77	.330
Minor League Totals				29	24	3.31	94	88	0	440	386	30	154	459	9.4	1.23	.235

12 BOBBY BRADLEY, 1B

BA GRADE 45 **Risk: Medium**

Born: May 29, 1996. **B-T:** L-R. **HT:** 6-1. **WT:** 225. **Drafted:** HS—Gulfport, Miss., 2014 (3rd round). **Signed by:** Mike Bradford.

TRACK RECORD: Bradley has been one of the most productive players in the Indians' farm system since they drafted him in 2014 and in June he made his Major League debut.

SCOUTING REPORT: Bradley's raw power is the best in the system, and he has shown he is adept at getting to it in games. He has a strong, physical frame and creates excellent bat speed that allows him to drive the ball out to all fields. That power comes with a lot of swing and miss, and even in Triple-A he struck out in a third of his plate appearances. Bradley is a well-below average runner with an average arm, limiting him to first base.

THE FUTURE: Bradley will begin the 2020 season as a 23-year-old who has already gotten a taste of the big leagues. But breaking through to Cleveland's lineup won't be easy. Carlos Santana is signed through 2020 (with an option for 2021), while Franmil Reyes and Jake Bauers are still under long-term team control. Bradley will likely start back in Triple-A and again be in line for a callup if an opportunity arises in Cleveland.

Year	Age	Club (League)	Class	AVG	G	AB	R	H	2B	3B	HR	RBI	BB	SO	SB	OBP	SLG
2017	21	Akron (EL)	AA	.251	131	467	66	117	25	3	23	89	55	122	3	.331	.465
2018	22	Akron (EL)	AA	.214	97	369	49	79	19	3	24	64	45	105	1	.304	.477
	22	Columbus (IL)	AAA	.254	32	114	11	29	7	2	3	19	11	43	0	.323	.430
2019	23	Cleveland (AL)	MAJ	.178	15	45	4	8	5	0	1	4	4	20	0	.245	.356
	23	Columbus (IL)	AAA	.264	107	402	65	106	23	0	33	74	46	153	0	.344	.567
Major League Totals				.178	15	45	4	8	5	0	1	4	4	20	0	.245	.356
Minor League Totals				.254	647	2401	374	609	125	17	147	490	305	779	13	.342	.504

13 SCOTT MOSS, LHP

BA GRADE
45 **Risk: Medium**

Born: Oct. 6, 1994. **B-T:** L-L. **HT:** 6-6. **WT:** 225. **Drafted:** Florida, 2016 (4th round). **Signed by:** Greg Zunino (Reds).

TRACK RECORD: Tommy John surgery sidelined Moss for his first two seasons at Florida but he broke out with a dominant start in the 2016 Southeastern Conference Tournament, and the Reds liked the big lefthander enough to draft him in the fourth round. He rewarded their faith, and was pitching well in Double-A this summer when he was dealt to the Indians as part of the trade that sent Trevor Bauer to the Reds.

SCOUTING REPORT: Moss has a big, strong frame and since getting into pro ball has proved to be dependable. His fastball sits in the low 90s, getting up to 94 mph, and is capable of producing swings and misses. He combines it with a slider that can be a plus pitch and a changeup that makes for a quality third option thanks to its differentiation from his fastball. Moss pitched with average control early in his career but saw his walk rate balloon in 2019. The Indians helped him to throw more strikes down the stretch, but it's something he'll have continue to remain vigilant of and he'll likely never have better than average command.

THE FUTURE: The Indians were thrilled with what they saw from Moss after the trade and added him to the 40-man roster in the offseason. He'll start 2020 back with Columbus and figures to be in the mix for a spot in the big leagues at some point during the season.

Year	Age	Club (League)	Class	W	L	ERA	G	GS	SV	IP	H	HR	BB	SO	K/9	WHIP	AVG
2017	22	Dayton (MWL)	LoA	13	6	3.45	26	26	0	136	114	11	48	156	10.3	1.19	.224
2018	23	Daytona (FSL)	HiA	15	4	3.68	25	25	0	132	135	13	41	112	7.6	1.33	.262
2019	24	Chattanooga (SL)	AA	6	5	3.44	20	20	0	102	84	7	57	123	10.9	1.38	.227
	24	Akron (EL)	AA	2	0	0.00	2	2	0	10	3	0	5	13	11.7	0.80	.091
	24	Columbus (IL)	AAA	2	1	1.93	4	4	0	19	12	1	8	23	11.1	1.07	.179
Minor League Totals				41	17	3.28	87	87	0	436	383	34	173	456	9.4	1.27	.234

14 CARLOS VARGAS, RHP

BA GRADE
50 **Risk: Very High**

Born: Oct. 13, 1999. **B-T:** R-R. **HT:** 6-3. **WT:** 180. **Signed:** Dominican Republic, 2016. **Signed by:** Rafael Espinal.

TRACK RECORD: The Indians' international department went through a transition in 2016 and their biggest signing in that class was Vargas, who signed for just $275,000. Though he wasn't a particularly high-profile prospect at the time, the Indians landed a premium arm.

SCOUTING REPORT: When he signed as a 17-year-old in 2016, Vargas had an ultra-projectable frame and was already throwing 93 mph. His velocity has ticked up as expected and his fastball now reaches 100 mph and sits in the upper 90s. His slider sits around 90 mph and is a plus pitch at its best. He still needs to refine his command and learn how to get the most out of his electric stuff.

THE FUTURE: Vargas has considerable upside and has given plenty of reason for optimism at the outset of his career. He'll face another important test in 2020 as he advances to full-season ball with low Class A Lake County.

Year	Age	Club (League)	Class	W	L	ERA	G	GS	SV	IP	H	HR	BB	SO	K/9	WHIP	AVG
2018	18	Indians 2 (AZL)	R	1	2	3.93	10	9	0	34	33	2	24	41	10.7	1.66	.256
2019	19	Mahoning Valley (NYP)	SS	6	4	4.52	15	15	0	78	73	4	24	71	8.2	1.25	.250
Minor League Totals				7	6	4.34	25	24	0	112	106	6	48	112	9.0	1.38	.252

15 EMMANUEL CLASE, RHP

BA GRADE
50 Risk: High

Born: March 18, 1998. **B-T:** R-R. **HT:** 6-2. **WT:** 205. **Signed:** Dominican Republic, 2015. **Signed by:** Chris Kemp/Emengildo Diaz (Padres).

TRACK RECORD: Signed by the Padres for $125,000 out of the Dominican Republic in 2015 and traded to the Rangers in 2018 for catcher Brett Nicholas, Clase never pitched in a full-season league before 2019. That changed when he advanced to Double-A Frisco in late April. In August he reached Texas and was one of the team's top relievers. In December, the Rangers traded him as the headliner for Corey Kluber.

SCOUTING REPORT: Clase has an electric fastball that regularly registers in the upper 90s and hits 101 mph. He showed that same velocity in 2018, but his slider wasn't reliable. The pitch had good shape and depth, but it was inconsistent and he struggled to land it for strikes. That changed in 2019, as Clase made adjustments, throwing it with better arm speed to develop an average slider with improved ability to throw it for a strike or a chase pitch depending on the situation. Clase's fastball has natural cutting life.

THE FUTURE: Clase has the stuff to pitch as a high-leverage reliever in Cleveland right away.

Year	Age	Club (League)	Class	W	L	ERA	G	GS	SV	IP	H	HR	BB	SO	K/9	WHIP	AVG
2017	19	Tri-City (NWL)	SS	0	1	13.50	1	0	0	3	9	1	0	4	10.8	2.70	.474
	19	Padres (AZL)	R	2	4	5.30	9	6	0	36	40	4	22	42	10.6	1.74	.276
2018	20	Spokane (NWL)	SS	1	1	0.64	22	0	12	28	16	0	6	27	8.6	0.78	.163
2019	21	Down East (CAR)	HiA	2	0	0.00	6	0	1	7	4	0	1	11	14.1	0.71	.167
	21	Frisco (TL)	AA	1	2	3.35	33	1	11	38	34	1	8	39	9.3	1.12	.236
	21	Texas (AL)	MAJ	2	3	2.31	21	1	1	23	20	2	6	21	8.1	1.11	.230
Major League Totals				2	3	2.31	21	1	1	23	20	2	6	21	8.1	1.11	.230
Minor League Totals				10	9	3.06	92	19	24	191	178	7	70	195	9.2	1.30	.242

16 JAMES KARINCHAK, RHP

BA GRADE
45 Risk: Medium

Born: Sept. 22, 1995. **B-T:** R-R. **HT:** 6-3. **WT:** 230. **Drafted:** Bryant, 2017 (9th round). **Signed by:** Mike Kanen.

TRACK RECORD: Karinchak excelled during his first two seasons at Bryant before an injury slowed him as a junior in 2017 and he fell to the ninth round. He took off in pro ball, racing to Double-A Akron in his first full professional season. He pitched even better at the start of 2019, posting video game numbers to earn a promotion to Triple-A Columbus. A hamstring injury sidelined him for two months, but he came back strong and made his major league debut in September.

SCOUTING REPORT: Karinchak's fastball averages 97 mph and is good enough to produce swings and misses. His breaking ball can be a plus pitch and has the shape of a curveball but, at 85 mph, the velocity of a slider. His control is fringy and his somewhat funky delivery hinders his strike-throwing, though it does help his stuff play up.

THE FUTURE: Karinchak will head into 2020 competing for a spot in the Indians' bullpen. He has the stuff to pitch in high-leverage situations, though his control may need to improve to eventually become a closer or set-up man.

Year	Age	Club (League)	Class	W	L	ERA	G	GS	SV	IP	H	HR	BB	SO	K/9	WHIP	AVG
2017	21	Mahoning Valley (NYP)	SS	2	2	5.79	10	6	0	23	30	1	9	31	12.0	1.67	.319
2018	22	Lake County (MWL)	LoA	3	0	0.79	7	0	1	11	8	0	7	20	15.9	1.32	.200
	22	Lynchburg (CAR)	HiA	1	1	1.00	25	0	13	27	14	1	17	45	15.0	1.15	.161
	22	Akron (EL)	AA	0	1	2.61	10	0	0	10	7	1	12	16	13.9	1.84	.189
2019	23	Akron (EL)	AA	0	0	0.00	10	0	6	10	2	0	2	24	21.6	0.40	.061
	23	Indians 2 (AZL)	R	0	0	0.00	3	0	0	3	0	0	2	8	24.0	0.67	.000
	23	Columbus (IL)	AAA	1	1	4.67	17	0	2	17	14	2	13	42	21.8	1.56	.215
	23	Cleveland (AL)	MAJ	0	0	1.69	5	0	0	5	3	0	1	8	13.5	0.75	.150
Major League Totals				0	0	1.69	5	0	0	5	3	0	1	8	13.5	0.75	.150
Minor League Totals				7	5	2.73	82	6	22	102	75	5	62	186	16.4	1.34	.205

17 SAM HENTGES, LHP

BA GRADE
50 Risk: Very High

Born: July 18, 1996. **B-T:** L-L. **HT:** 6-8. **WT:** 245. **Drafted:** HS—Arden Hills, Minn., 2014 (4th round). **Signed by:** Les Pajari.

TRACK RECORD: Hentges didn't pitch much until he was a junior in high school and was one of the youngest players in the 2014 draft class. He started his professional career slowly, in part because he needed Tommy John surgery in 2016, but had a breakout 2018 with high Class A Lynchburg. He took a step back in 2019, though he improved as the season went on.

SCOUTING REPORT: His fastball averages about 93 mph and he can run it up to 97 mph. The pitch was good enough to overpower lower-level hitters, but against Eastern League hitters he needed to use his

secondary stuff more and the results weren't as good. His three offspeed offerings have potential – his curveball flashes plus, his changeup has promise and he added a cutter in 2018 that gives him another option. Like many big, young pitchers, Hentges needs to improve his control and take better advantage of his height to pitch down in the zone. His arm action can be long, hurting his ability to repeat pitches.
THE FUTURE: Hentges needs to refine some of the finer parts of his game, but the potential is still easy to see. He'll likely return to Akron to start the season with a chance to get back on track.

Year	Age	Club (League)	Class	W	L	ERA	G	GS	SV	IP	H	HR	BB	SO	K/9	WHIP	AVG
2017	20	Indians (AZL)	R	0	3	4.85	6	6	0	13	16	2	3	18	12.5	1.46	.296
	20	Mahoning Valley (NYP)	SS	0	1	2.04	5	5	0	18	5	1	12	23	11.7	0.96	.088
2018	21	Lynchburg (CAR)	HiA	6	6	3.27	23	23	0	118	114	4	53	122	9.3	1.41	.260
2019	22	Akron (EL)	AA	2	13	5.11	26	26	0	129	148	11	64	126	8.8	1.65	.289
Minor League Totals				14	32	4.34	95	85	0	406	420	30	193	433	9.6	1.51	.268

18 LUIS OVIEDO, RHP

BA GRADE 50 Risk: Very High

Born: May 15, 1999. **B-T:** R-R. **HT:** 6-4. **WT:** 250. **Signed:** Venezuela, 2015.
Signed by: Koby Perez/Luis Camacho.

TRACK RECORD: Oviedo was the top pitcher in the Indians' 2015 international class and has had some mixed results since signing but has stood out for his tools throughout his career. His performance didn't fully align with his tools in 2019 with low Class A Mahoning Valley and a lower back injury brought his season to an early end in mid-July.
SCOUTING REPORT: Oviedo since signing has filled out his big frame and refined his body, and his velocity has grown as a result. His fastball now reaches 98 mph with sinking action, up from the upper 80s when he signed. He's gotten back to throwing his big curveball, which along with his slider gives him two distinct breaking balls that can create swings and misses. He also has good feel for his changeup, which is advanced for his age. He's worked to refine his delivery to get it to be more controllable and allow him to throw strikes more consistently, but he will have to cut down on his walks after issuing 40 in 2019.
THE FUTURE: Oviedo has all the physical tools to develop into a workhorse starter but still has a lot of work to do. He'll head to high Class A Lynchburg for the next step of his development.

Year	Age	Club (League)	Class	W	L	ERA	G	GS	SV	IP	H	HR	BB	SO	K/9	WHIP	AVG
2017	18	Indians (AZL)	R	4	2	7.14	14	7	0	52	62	2	22	70	12.2	1.63	.286
2018	19	Mahoning Valley (NYP)	SS	4	2	1.88	9	9	0	48	34	3	10	61	11.4	0.92	.192
	19	Lake County (MWL)	LoA	1	0	3.00	2	2	0	9	5	0	7	6	6.0	1.33	.179
2019	20	Lake County (MWL)	LoA	6	6	5.38	19	19	0	87	80	6	40	72	7.4	1.38	.243
Minor League Totals				17	18	4.66	58	51	0	258	248	12	96	265	9.2	1.33	.249

19 YORDYS VALDES, SS

BA GRADE 50 Risk: Extreme

Born: Aug. 16, 2001. **B-T:** B-R. **HT:** 6-0. **WT:** 170. **Drafted:** HS—Hollywood, Fla., 2019 (2nd round). **Signed by:** Jhonathan Leyba.

TRACK RECORD: Valdes was born in Cuba, where his father played in the Serie Nacional, and moved with his family to Florida when he was 12. Though he was young for the 2019 draft class, he was one of the best defenders in the nation and the best prep prospect in South Florida.
SCOUTING REPORT: The natural righthanded hitter began switch-hitting when he got to America and almost all of his high school plate appearances came from the left side. He's made strides as a lefthanded hitter but he's still clearly better from the right side. He has a wiry frame and should be able to add more impact offensively as he physically matures. Defensively is where Valdes shines. He has a plus arm, can make all the throws from shortstop and gets rid of the ball quickly. He's an average runner, but that plays up on the bases and in the field thanks to his quickness and instincts.
THE FUTURE: The Indians have a bevy of exciting shortstops, especially in the lower levels of the system, and Valdes fits right in with the group. His age and need for further development offensively could make him a two-year rookie-ball player.

Year	Age	Club (League)	Class	AVG	G	AB	R	H	2B	3B	HR	RBI	BB	SO	SB	OBP	SLG
2019	17	Indians 1 (AZL)	R	.179	43	162	17	29	3	1	2	11	16	53	15	.251	.247
Minor League Totals				.179	43	162	17	29	3	1	2	11	16	53	15	.251	.247

20 ANGEL MARTINEZ, SS

BA GRADE 50 Risk: Extreme

Born: Jan. 27, 2002. **B-T:** B-R. **HT:** 6-0. **WT:** 165. **Signed:** Dominican Republic, 2018. **Signed by:** Jhonathan Leyba.

TRACK RECORD: Martinez is the son of former big league catcher Sandy Martinez, and his older brother

Sandy Martinez Jr. is a prospect in the D-backs system. As a result, Angel grew up around the diamond and has an advanced understanding of the game.

SCOUTING REPORT: Martinez isn't the most tooled out of the Indians' lower-level infielders, but his baseball IQ and maturity make all his tools play up. The switch-hitter has a simple swing from both sides and can drive the ball to all fields. He has advanced plate discipline and walked as much as he struck out in the DSL – a rarity – and has good physicality that plays as doubles power. Martinez is an average runner, but still covers a lot of ground thanks to his instincts and makes sound decisions defensively. That, as well as his plus arm, gives him a chance to stay at shortstop.

THE FUTURE: Gabriel Rodriguez is the most famous member of the Indians' 2018 international signing class and his impressive physical tools have him ranked higher on this list. But Martinez isn't far behind and has a chance to make a jump in 2020 as he makes his American debut in the Arizona League.

Year	Age	Club (League)	Class	AVG	G	AB	R	H	2B	3B	HR	RBI	BB	SO	SB	OBP	SLG
2019	17	Indians (DSL)	R	.306	56	222	37	68	10	7	1	27	29	29	11	.402	.428
Minor League Totals				.306	56	222	37	68	10	7	1	27	29	29	11	.402	.428

21 ERNIE CLEMENT, SS

BA GRADE
40 Risk: Medium

Born: March 22, 1996. **B-T:** R-R. **HT:** 6-0. **WT:** 170. **Drafted:** Virginia, 2017 (4th round). **Signed by:** Bob Mayer.

TRACK RECORD: During his three years at Virginia, Clement hit .306 and struck out just 31 times, earning him a reputation as a pure hitter. His college success translated well to the professional ranks and he raced to Double-A Akron in 2018, his first full professional season. A right abductor strain slowed him in 2019, but he still played well enough to finish the season with Triple-A Columbus and turned in a solid performance in the Arizona Fall League.

SCOUTING REPORT: Clement has an aggressive approach and an uncanny knack for putting the bat on the ball. He has minimal power and instead sprays the ball all over the field and takes advantage of his plus speed to get on base. Clement was a versatile defender in college but has almost exclusively played shortstop in pro ball. He has above-average instincts defensively and good hands. The biggest concern about his ability to stay at the position is his arm strength, which is fringy for a shortstop. His versatility allows him to play anywhere on the infield and he also has experience as a center fielder, giving him the ability to move around the diamond as needed.

THE FUTURE: Clement has proven to be capable of playing shortstop and—depending on how soon Francisco Lindor's tenure in Cleveland ends—he may get a chance to do so in Cleveland. He's fast approaching the major leagues and could put himself in position to debut as soon as 2020.

Year	Age	Club (League)	Class	AVG	G	AB	R	H	2B	3B	HR	RBI	BB	SO	SB	OBP	SLG
2017	21	Mahoning Valley (NYP)	SS	.280	45	175	32	49	9	1	0	13	6	12	6	.315	.343
2018	22	Lake County (MWL)	LoA	.267	54	221	34	59	14	1	1	15	23	21	11	.337	.353
	22	Lynchburg (CAR)	HiA	.346	33	133	29	46	7	0	1	13	15	7	5	.425	.421
	22	Akron (EL)	AA	.246	15	65	9	16	5	1	0	5	3	7	2	.279	.354
2019	23	Akron (EL)	AA	.261	98	394	46	103	15	3	1	24	26	33	16	.314	.322
	23	Columbus (IL)	AAA	.545	3	11	3	6	1	0	0	4	2	1	1	.615	.636
Minor League Totals				.279	248	999	153	279	51	6	3	74	75	81	41	.336	.351

22 YU CHANG, 3B/SS

BA GRADE
40 Risk: Medium

Born: Aug. 18, 1995. **B-T:** R-R. **HT:** 6-1. **WT:** 175. **Signed:** Taiwan, 2013. **Signed by:** Jason Lynn.

TRACK RECORD: Chang was a prominent prep player in Taiwan and was one of the top amateur free agents to sign out of Asia in 2013. His profile has risen in the last few years as his power has developed and he reached the upper levels. He made his major league debut in June 2019 and saw a healthy amount of action down the stretch in Cleveland.

SCOUTING REPORT: Chang has solid all-around offensive tools and he has produced well the last two years in Triple-A Columbus. He is a patient hitter, but his willingness to work deep in counts has led to strikeout rates in excess of 23 percent for three years in a row last two years. Though Chang may not pass the eye test at shortstop, he can play the position serviceably. He's an average runner with at least average arm strength. He's capable of playing anywhere on the infield—which he did in 2019—and he saw the majority of his big league action at third base.

THE FUTURE: Chang is unlikely to regularly play shortstop in Cleveland, but he's already shown he can help the Indians at a variety of positions. He'll enter spring training competing for a job somewhere on the infield.

Year	Age	Club (League)	Class	AVG	G	AB	R	H	2B	3B	HR	RBI	BB	SO	SB	OBP	SLG
2017	21	Akron (EL)	AA	.220	126	440	72	97	24	5	24	66	52	134	11	.312	.461
2018	22	Columbus (IL)	AAA	.256	127	457	56	117	28	2	13	62	44	144	4	.330	.411
2019	23	Columbus (IL)	AAA	.253	68	253	45	64	15	1	9	39	26	67	4	.322	.427
	23	Cleveland (AL)	MAJ	.178	28	73	8	13	2	1	1	6	11	22	0	.286	.274
Major League Totals				.178	28	73	8	13	2	1	1	6	11	22	0	.286	.274
Minor League Totals				.251	577	2119	342	532	122	24	74	314	212	586	41	.326	.436

23 DANIEL JOHNSON, OF

BA GRADE
40 **Risk: Medium**

Born: July 11, 1995. **B-T:** L-L. **HT:** 5-10. **WT:** 185. **Drafted:** New Mexico State, 2016 (5th round). **Signed by:** Mitch Sokol (Nationals).

TRACK RECORD: Johnson made steady progress in his first two professional seasons as a member of the Nationals' system. The Indians acquired him as a part of the package for Yan Gomes in November 2018 and Johnson produced a strong season with his new organization the following year. He led the system in doubles (34) and ranked third in hits (140).

SCOUTING REPORT: Johnson has quick hands at the plate and did a good job of barreling balls, especially against righthanded pitching. His strength and bat speed gives him above-average raw power, which he's done a good job of getting to in games. It does come with a fair amount of swing and miss, however. Johnson has plus speed and arm strength and can play all three outfield positions. He probably fits best in right field and that's where he has the most experience.

THE FUTURE: The Indians had a mostly open outfield picture as the offseason began. They added Johnson to their 40-man roster in November and he'll get a chance to compete for a job in spring training. Even if he starts 2020 in Triple-A Columbus he should find a way to Cleveland at some point during the season.

Year	Age	Club (League)	Class	AVG	G	AB	R	H	2B	3B	HR	RBI	BB	SO	SB	OBP	SLG
2017	21	Hagerstown (SAL)	LoA	.300	88	327	61	98	16	4	17	52	22	70	12	.361	.529
	21	Potomac (CAR)	HiA	.294	42	170	22	50	13	0	5	20	13	30	10	.346	.459
2018	22	Nationals (GCL)	R	.300	7	20	3	6	0	0	1	4	2	2	1	.417	.450
	22	Harrisburg (EL)	AA	.267	89	356	48	95	19	7	6	31	23	90	21	.321	.410
2019	23	Akron (EL)	AA	.253	39	146	25	37	7	2	10	33	16	39	6	.337	.534
	23	Columbus (IL)	AAA	.306	84	337	51	103	27	5	9	44	34	79	6	.371	.496
Minor League Totals				.284	411	1601	235	454	91	22	49	198	117	352	69	.344	.460

24 LENNY TORRES, RHP

BA GRADE
50 **Risk: Extreme**

Born: Oct. 15, 2000. **B-T:** R-R. **HT:** 6-1. **WT:** 190. **Drafted:** HS—Beacon, N.Y., 2018 (1st round supplemental). **Signed by:** Mike Kanen.

TRACK RECORD: Torres didn't pitch much growing up but quickly showed big upside on the mound after starting to focus on it late in his high school career. He made a smooth transition to pro ball and in 2018 excelled in the Arizona League. His progress was slowed in 2019, however, when he required Tommy John surgery in May and missed the whole season.

SCOUTING REPORT: Torres doesn't have a big frame, but he has a quick arm and, when healthy, can run his fastball up to 97 mph. He pairs the pitch with a slider that has plus potential. He is working to implement a changeup, which at its best has hard downer action, but is still a work in progress. His control is also an area of focus, though he surprised with his strike-throwing ability during his professional debut.

THE FUTURE: Before the draft, Torres faced lots of questions about whether he could be a starter in pro ball because of his size and lack of a third pitch. Those concerns are elevated by his injury, but he'll pitch all of the 2020 season as a 19-year-old and the Indians are optimistic he'll be able to take the necessary steps in his development. He should be ready to get back in action at short-season Mahoning Valley.

Year	Age	Club (League)	Class	W	L	ERA	G	GS	SV	IP	H	HR	BB	SO	K/9	WHIP	AVG
2018	17	Indians 2 (AZL)	R	0	0	1.76	6	5	0	15	14	0	4	22	12.9	1.17	.246
Minor League Totals				0	0	1.76	6	5	0	15	14	0	4	22	12.9	1.17	.246

25 WILL BENSON, OF

BA GRADE
50 **Risk: Extreme**

Born: June 16, 1998. **B-T:** L-L. **HT:** 6-5. **WT:** 215. **Drafted:** HS—Atlanta, 2016 (1st round). **Signed by:** C.T. Bradford.

TRACK RECORD: A heralded prep player coming out of the Atlanta prep ranks, Benson has long stood out for his athleticism and power. He started 2019 repeating low Class A Lake County as a 20-year-old and excelled. He was leading the Midwest League with 18 home runs in 61 games when he was promoted to high Class A Lynchburg, but his performance took a step back in the Carolina League.

SCOUTING REPORT: Benson produces exceptional bat speed thanks to his strength and quick hands and

turns that bat speed into tremendous lefthanded raw power, rivaling Bobby Bradley for the best in the system. Benson has a patient, bordering on passive, approach at the plate that helps him draw walks but also means he works deep in counts, contributing to his high strikeout rate. While he may just be on his way to becoming a three true outcomes player, Benson shows enough athleticism and tools to provide optimism that he can make necessary adjustments to become more consistent. He profiles well in right field thanks to his plus arm and solid speed, particularly once he is underway.
THE FUTURE: Benson's ceiling remains considerable, but he'll turn 22 in June and needs to show more hittability sooner than later to reach it. He'll return to Lynchburg to get back on track in 2020.

Year	Age	Club (League)	Class	AVG	G	AB	R	H	2B	3B	HR	RBI	BB	SO	SB	OBP	SLG
2017	19	Mahoning Valley (NYP)	SS	.238	56	202	29	48	8	5	10	36	31	80	7	.347	.475
2018	20	Lake County (MWL)	LoA	.180	123	416	54	75	11	1	22	58	82	152	12	.324	.370
2019	21	Lake County (MWL)	LoA	.272	62	217	44	59	12	3	18	55	37	78	18	.371	.604
	21	Lynchburg (CAR)	HiA	.189	61	217	29	41	9	2	4	23	31	73	9	.290	.304
Minor League Totals				.212	346	1210	187	256	50	14	60	199	203	443	56	.330	.425

26 OSCAR GONZALEZ, OF

BA GRADE
45 Risk: High

Born: Jan. 10, 1998. **B-T:** R-R. **HT:** 6-2. **WT:** 180. **Signed:** Dominican Republic, 2014. **Signed by:** Ramon Pena/Felix Nivar.

TRACK RECORD: Gonzalez, the Indians' top target in the 2014 international class, made a resounding U.S. debut in 2016, when he won MVP honors in the Arizona League. After a strong start to the 2019 season with high Class A Lynchburg, he earned a late-summer promotion to Double-A Akron.
SCOUTING REPORT: Gonzalez has good bat-to-ball skills and has ranked second in the system in hits in each of the last two years. But he's an ultra-aggressive hitter and has struggled with his plate discipline at times. He has above-average raw power and can get to it in games, but it more typically plays as doubles pop right now. Gonzalez is an average runner and has plus arm strength, giving him a chance to play right field, though he has mostly played left field since leaving the Dominican Summer League.
THE FUTURE: Whatever outfield corner Gonzalez ends up in, it will be up to his bat to push him through the minor leagues. Gonzalez will return to Double-A Akron to start 2020 and has the tools to eventually put himself in the big league picture.

Year	Age	Club (League)	Class	AVG	G	AB	R	H	2B	3B	HR	RBI	BB	SO	SB	OBP	SLG
2017	19	Mahoning Valley (NYP)	SS	.283	55	237	20	67	16	0	3	34	5	61	0	.301	.388
2018	20	Lake County (MWL)	LoA	.292	114	462	52	135	25	1	13	52	12	107	5	.310	.435
2019	21	Lynchburg (CAR)	HiA	.319	96	385	46	123	22	3	8	61	12	66	7	.342	.455
	21	Akron (EL)	AA	.188	29	96	7	18	5	0	1	9	3	17	0	.210	.271
Minor League Totals				.277	405	1584	180	439	95	7	37	220	60	374	17	.305	.416

27 JOSE PASTRANO, SS

Born: Sept. 12, 2002. **B-T:** B-R. **HT:** 5-11. **WT:** 145. **Signed:** Venezuela, 2019. **Signed by:** Gustavo Benzan.

TRACK RECORD: The Indians continued to be aggressive on the international market in 2019 and Pastrano, a Venezuelan native, was the club's biggest signing. His older brother, also named Jose Pastrano, plays in the Athletics' organization, but the younger Pastrano is viewed as the superior prospect.
SCOUTING REPORT: Pastrano stands out for his athleticism and understanding of the game. A switch-hitter, he has a short, direct swing and a good feel for the strike zone. He uses the whole field to hit and enough physical projection to see his doubles power increase in time, but he's likely to be hit-over-power in the long run. Pastrano has the defensive skills to stay at shortstop. He's a plus runner with quick hands, good infield actions and above-average arm strength.
THE FUTURE: Pastrano joins the burgeoning group of talented middle infielders at the lower levels of the Indians system. He'll make his debut in the Dominican Summer League in 2020.

Year	Age	Club (League)	Class	AVG	G	AB	R	H	2B	3B	HR	RBI	BB	SO	SB	OBP	SLG
2019	16	Did not play—Signed 2020 contract															

28 JOSE TENA, SS/2B

BA GRADE
50 Risk: Extreme

Born: March 20, 2001. **B-T:** L-R. **HT:** 5-9. **WT:** 159. **Signed:** Dominican Republic, 2017. **Signed by:** Anthony Roa/Jhonathan Leyba.

TRACK RECORD: The Indians' 2017 international signing class is fast turning into a blockbuster. It already features three players ranked among their top 10 prospects, and now Tena, a nephew of Juan Uribe, is making his own case. He stood out in the Arizona League for his offensive acumen and athleticism.

SCOUTING REPORT: Tena has a loose, easy swing and good feel for the bat, allowing him to consistently square up balls. He's an aggressive hitter who rarely walks and will need to learn to control the strike zone better as he advances. He's a plus runner who likely won't ever hit for much power. Tena has an above-average arm, good hands and solid range thanks to his speed and athleticism. He mostly played shortstop in Arizona and figures to be capable there, but he might end up as a plus defender at second base.
THE FUTURE: Tena is a step behind his more heralded classmates, but his early performance has been very encouraging. He'll look to continue that in 2020 with short-season Mahoning Valley.

Year	Age	Club (League)	Class	AVG	G	AB	R	H	2B	3B	HR	RBI	BB	SO	SB	OBP	SLG
2018	17	Indians (DSL)	R	.313	51	195	28	61	8	4	1	23	15	29	10	.367	.410
2019	18	Indians 2 (AZL)	R	.325	44	191	30	62	7	6	1	18	6	44	6	.352	.440
Minor League Totals				.319	95	386	58	123	15	10	2	41	21	73	16	.360	.425

29 NICK SANDLIN, RHP

BA GRADE **45** Risk: High

Born: Jan. 11, 1997. **B-T:** R-R. **HT:** 5-11. **WT:** 175. **Drafted:** Southern Mississippi, 2018 (2nd round). **Signed by:** Chuck Bartlett.

TRACK RECORD: As a junior at Southern Mississippi in 2018, Sandlin moved from closing to the front of the rotation and won the nation's ERA title (1.06). He shot up draft boards that spring and that momentum carried over into pro ball, as he finished the season in Double-A Akron. He started 2019 well and reached Triple-A Columbus in June, almost a year to the day after he was drafted, but he suffered a forearm strain that ended his season at the start of July.
SCOUTING REPORT: Sandlin is undersized and typically throws from a sidearm slot, though he'll also raise it to more of a three-quarters look. He's effective against both righthanders and lefthanders, though he's especially tough on righthanded hitters. His fastball sits in the low 90s with plenty of run and sink. He can manipulate his slider to make it a big, wipeout pitch or to land it for a strike. His changeup isn't as good as his sinker-slider combination, but it is a viable third offering. He has above-average command and stands out for his athleticism.
THE FUTURE: Sandlin has a tremendous feel for pitching and has already shown he can be effective against upper-level competition. He will likely be ready to help the Indians bullpen in 2020.

Year	Age	Club (League)	Class	W	L	ERA	G	GS	SV	IP	H	HR	BB	SO	K/9	WHIP	AVG
2018	21	Indians 1 (AZL)	R	0	0	0.00	3	0	0	3	2	0	0	4	12.0	0.67	.200
	21	Lake County (MWL)	LoA	0	0	1.74	10	0	1	10	9	0	0	15	13.1	0.87	.237
	21	Lynchburg (CAR)	HiA	1	0	1.42	7	0	4	6	2	0	2	10	14.2	0.63	.091
	21	Akron (EL)	AA	1	0	10.38	5	0	0	4	8	0	1	7	14.5	2.08	.400
2019	22	Akron (EL)	AA	0	0	1.56	15	0	2	17	13	2	8	27	14.0	1.21	.203
	22	Columbus (IL)	AAA	1	0	4.00	9	0	0	9	5	2	7	11	11.0	1.33	.172
Minor League Totals				3	0	2.68	49	0	7	50	39	4	18	74	13.2	1.13	.213

30 JEAN CARLOS MEJIA, RHP

BA GRADE **45** Risk: Very High

Born: Aug. 26, 1996. **B-T:** R-R. **HT:** 6-4. **WT:** 205. **Signed:** Dominican Republic, 2013. **Signed by:** Rafael Espinal/Ramon Pena.

TRACK RECORD: Mejia started his professional career slowly, spending three years in the Dominican Summer League. He made his U.S. debut in 2017 and started to build some buzz before breaking out in 2018—a performance that led him to be a popular name at the trade deadline and eventually added to the 40-man roster to protect him from the Rule 5 draft. He was unable to capitalize on that momentum in 2019, however, due to a hip injury that limited him to eight starts and ended his season in June.
SCOUTING REPORT: Mejia has a big, 6-foot-4 frame with a chance to develop into a solid starting pitcher. His fastball has been up to 96 mph and sits at 93. He has a good feel for spin and his curveball and slider both have plus potential. He also can generate swings-and-misses with his changeup. He pitches with above-average control. With a big frame and a solid four-pitch arsenal that he can throw for strikes, Mejia offers considerable upside but is also short on experience.
THE FUTURE: Mejia should be fully healthy for the start of the 2020 season and will look to make up for lost time. If he can get back to where he was before his injury, he should soon reach Double-A Akron.

Year	Age	Club (League)	Class	W	L	ERA	G	GS	SV	IP	H	HR	BB	SO	K/9	WHIP	AVG
2017	20	Indians (AZL)	R	1	0	3.14	10	0	6	14	13	0	5	19	11.9	1.26	.228
	20	Mahoning Valley (NYP)	SS	1	0	0.00	11	0	3	23	6	0	5	31	12.3	0.49	.083
2018	21	Lake County (MWL)	LoA	4	8	3.13	17	15	0	92	84	3	20	97	9.5	1.13	.241
	21	Lynchburg (CAR)	HiA	0	1	6.00	1	1	0	6	5	0	1	3	4.5	1.00	.227
2019	22	Lynchburg (CAR)	HiA	3	1	4.09	8	8	0	33	28	0	9	36	9.8	1.12	.226
Minor League Totals				18	17	2.79	99	25	16	274	221	4	72	262	8.6	1.07	.216

Colorado Rockies

BY TRACY RINGOLSBY

In an evaluation of minor league ballparks, it was determined five of the Rockies' farm teams play in the most offense-oriented ballparks in their leagues. The sixth team, Double-A Hartford, plays in a park that ranks No. 2 in the Eastern League.

Surprised? Don't be.

The Rockies call Coors Field home, which makes Triple-A Albuquerque, which like Denver has an altitude of 5,280, the perfect finishing school for Rockies pitchers.

What has become obvious over the years is importing high-priced free agents with a glossy résumé is not the answer to Coors Field. Ask Bill Swift, Bret Saberhagen, the late Darryl Kile, Mike Hampton and Denny Neagle, to name a few.

Success on the mound at Coors Field comes from journeymen who aren't worried about the neatness of the back of their baseball cards, like Jorge de la Rosa and Pedro Astacio, who preaches the key to success at Coors Field is simple: "Don't give up the next run."

The success on the mound at Coors Field comes from homegrown players, who wear a badge of honor when they have success at 5,280 feet.

In claiming the National League wild card in 2017 and 2018, the Rockies' rotation was heavy on homegrown arms.

There have been 11 pitchers in franchise history who won 35 or more games.

Three journeyman are on the list—de la Rosa (86 wins), Astacio (53) and Kevin Ritz (39)—and seven homegrown products—Aaron Cook (72), Jeff Francis (64), Jason Jennings (58), Ubaldo Jimenez (56), Jon Gray (43), Jhoulys Chacin (38) and Jamey Wright (35). The exception is German Marquez (38), who was in low Class A in the Rays' system when the Rockies acquired him.

To help along those lines, the Rockies purposely sought out ballparks that challenge pitchers, looking to develop the competitive mentality from day one among the prospects in the system. It also gives the Rockies insight as to the mental toughness of their pitchers.

In claiming the NL wild card in 2017, pitchers who arrived at Coors Field through the farm system started 137 of 162 games, the lone exception being Tyler Chatwood. And in claiming the wild card again in 2018, and advancing to the Division Series, all 163 regular season games were started by pitchers who made the jump from within the Rockies' farm system to the big leagues.

The Rockies reliance on homegrown players is not limited to its pitching staff. They had 18 players with 50 or more at-bats in 2019—13 of which were originally signed and developed by the organization, including six of the eight primary regulars in the lineup—second baseman Ryan McMahon, third baseman Nolan Arenado, shortstop Trevor Story, left fielder Raimel Tapia, center fielder David Dahl and right fielder Charlie Blackmon.

The Rockies' current farm system is lighter, in part because they've successfully graduated so many homegrown players to the big leagues. Next up are shortstop Brendan Rodgers, lefthander Ryan Rolison and a host of corner infielders. If they can continue the trend of homegrown Rockies finding success in the big leagues, the franchise could return to the playoffs.

JAMIE SABAU/GETTY IMAGES

Four-time top 100 prospect David Dahl stayed healthy and made his first all-star team.

PROJECTED 2023 LINEUP

Position	Player	Age
Catcher	Tony Wolters	31
First Base	Michael Toglia (3)	24
Second Base	Brendan Rodgers (1)	26
Third Base	Nolan Arenado	32
Shortstop	Trevor Story	30
Left Field	Raimel Tapia	29
Center Field	David Dahl	29
Right Field	Sam Hilliard (6)	29
No. 1 Starter	Jon Gray	31
No. 2 Starter	German Marquez	28
No. 3 Starter	Kyle Freeland	30
No. 4 Starter	Ryan Rolison (2)	25
No. 5 Starter	Peter Lambert	26
Closer	Jesus Tinoco	28

DEPTH CHART

COLORADO ROCKIES

TOP 2020 ROOKIE: Sam Hilliard, OF. He has the size and power to clear fences, but the speed and agility to cover center field, freeing David Dahl to settle into the vast expanse of left field.
BREAKOUT PROSPECT: Ben Bowden, LHP. The lefthander got his altitude indoctrination in the second half last year at Triple-A Albuquerque, and he can fill a bullpen void.
SLEEPER: Brian Mundell, 1B. Not a big power guy, Mundell has good strike-zone awareness and can drive the ball to the gaps. He has become a decent defensive first baseman.

SOURCE OF TOP 30 TALENT

Homegrown	**29**	**Acquired**	**1**
College	13	Trade	0
Junior college	1	Rule 5 draft	0
High school	7	Independent league	0
Nondrafted free agent	0	Free agent/waivers	1
International	8		

LF
Yanquiel Fernandez (22)
Vince Fernandez
Will Goslan
Walking Cabrera

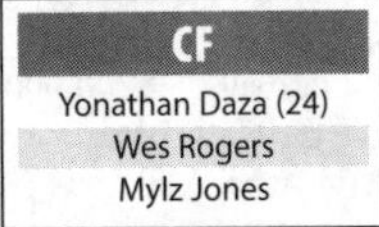

CF
Yonathan Daza (24)
Wes Rogers
Mylz Jones

RF
Sam Hilliard (6)
Brenton Doyle (17)
Niko Decolati

3B
Colton Welker (5)
Aaron Schunk (9)
Josh Fuentes (27)
Coco Montes

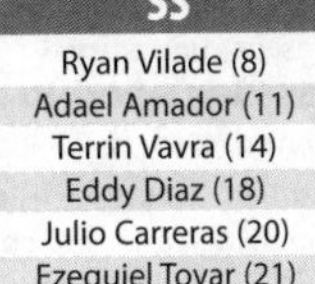

SS
Ryan Vilade (8)
Adael Amador (11)
Terrin Vavra (14)
Eddy Diaz (18)
Julio Carreras (20)
Ezequiel Tovar (21)

2B
Brendan Rodgers (1)
Christian Koss (25)
Bladimir Restituyo (26)

1B
Michale Toglia (3)
Grant Lavigne (4)
Tyler Nevin (10)
Roberto Ramos
Brian Mundell

C
Willie MacIver (29)
Dom Nunez
Max George
Brian Serven
Chris Rabago

LHP

LHSP
Ryan Rolison (2)
Helcris Olivarez (16)
Lucas Gilbreath

LHRP
Ben Bowden (12)
PJ Poulin (28)
Reagan Todd

RHP

RHSP
Ryan Castellani (7)
Karl Kauffmann (13)
Ashton Goudeau (23)
Robert Tyler (22)
Will Ethridge (29)
Ryan Feltner
Garrett Schilling
Will Gaddis

RHRP
Jacob Wallace (15)
Tommy Doyle (19)
Reid Humphreys (23)
Riley Pint (30)
Jesus Tinoco
Justin Lawrence
Alexander Martinez
Anderson Bido
Alexander Guillen
Rayan Gonzalez
Anderson Pilar

DRAFT ANALYSIS

2019

BEST PURE HITTER: 3B Aaron Schunk (2) led a strong Georgia team in average (.339) and slugging percentage (.556) this spring. After being drafted, Schunk—who gets 60 grades on his hit tool—hit .306/.370/.503 at short-season Boise.

BEST POWER: 1B Michael Toglia (1) easily takes this one with double-plus raw power. He'll need to keep his strikeouts in check to take full advantage of that power, but if he does he has enough in the tank to hit 30 home runs a season.

FASTEST RUNNER: 2B Isaac Collins (9) was limited a bit by a quad injury, but when he's healthy he's a plus runner with a tick more underway.

BEST DEFENSIVE PLAYER: Schunk has 70-grade arm strength from third base, and he ran a fastball up to 95 mph when on the mound in college. He also has good athleticism and defensive actions. SS Christian Koss (12) plays a more premium position with range, sure hands, above-average arm strength and good baseball IQ.

BEST ATHLETE: OF Brenton Doyle (4) has impressive, 60-grade speed and above-average arm strength that should help him in the outfield.

BEST FASTBALL: RHP Jacob Wallace (3) has a plus fastball that's been up to the 97-98 mph range at its best, though he doesn't currently pitch in that range. He was more 92-96 mph this summer after throwing 42 innings during the spring, but the Rockies won't be surprised if he comes out throwing harder next year.

BEST SECONDARY PITCH: RHP Karl Kauffmann (3) has a pair of secondaries that Colorado sees as plus in a changeup and a slider.

BEST PRO DEBUT: Doyle mashed at Rookie-level Grand Junction, hitting .383/.477/.611 with eight home runs and 11 doubles. C Colin Simpson (29) was named the MVP of the Pioneer League after hitting .309/.383/.667 with 18 home runs and 12 doubles.

TOP DRAFT PICKS OF THE DECADE

Year	Player, Pos.	2019 Org
2010	Kyle Parker, OF	Did not play
2011	Tyler Anderson, LHP	Rockies
2012	David Dahl, OF	Rockies
2013	Jon Gray, RHP	Rockies
2014	Kyle Freeland, LHP	Rockies
2015	Brendan Rodgers, SS	Rockies
2016	Riley Pint, RHP	Rockies
2017	Ryan Vilade, 3B (2nd round)	Rockies
2018	Ryan Rolison, LHP	Rockies
2019	Michael Toglia, 1B	Rockies

MOST INTRIGUING BACKGROUND: The Rockies drafted OF Yorvis Torrealba (20), the son of 13-year major leaguer Yorvit Torrealba, for $200,000 on Day 3 of the draft. What's crazier than Yorvis' major league bloodlines is the fact that he was kidnapped in Venezuela when he was just 11 years old for a $500,000 ransom.

CLOSEST TO THE MAJORS: Schunk and Toglia could both move quickly as fairly advanced college hitters in a system that has done well developing position players, while Wallace could move quickly as a late-inning reliever with power stuff and a closer's mentality.

BEST LATE-ROUND PICK: Koss played shortstop, second and third base in his pro debut in the Pioneer League, while hitting .332/.447/.605 with 11 home runs. He could wind up being a productive utility infielder with the athleticism and arm strength to capably handle each position.

THE ONE WHO GOT AWAY: The Rockies did an excellent job inking all of their top selections to deals. 3B Michael Curialle (31) is a toolsy infielder with a strong all-around skillset who could rapidly improve his draft stock if he hits at UCLA, while RHP Tyler Nesbitt (32) has shown flashes of impressive stuff, but will head to Florida.

—**CARLOS COLLAZO**

2018

No one from this class has taken off yet, but LHP Ryan Rolison (1) was solid in his first full pro season. 1B Grant Lavigne (1s) still offers upside, while C Willie MacIver (9) could be a nice late-round pick.

GRADE: C

2017

The Rockies had no first-round pick in 2017, leaving SS Ryan Vilade (2) and RHP Tommy Doyle (2s) as the top picks. Those two still have the most upside; the rest of the class hasn't provided much return.

GRADE: D

2016

RHPs Riley Pint (1) and Robert Tyler (1s) have stumbled so far, but 2B Garrett Hampson (3), RHP JD Hammer (24) and RHP Rico Garcia (30) have all made the big leagues, with Hampson leading the way.

GRADE: C

1 BRENDAN RODGERS, SS/2B

Born: Aug. 9, 1996. **B-T:** R-R. **HT:** 6-0. **WT.:** 185.
Drafted: HS—Lake Mary, Fla., 2015 (1st round).
Signed by: John Cedarburg.

TRACK RECORD: The Rockies selected Rodgers with the No. 3 overall pick in 2015, the third shortstop taken in the draft's first three picks. The other two are established in the big leagues—Dansby Swanson, who went No. 1 overall to the D-backs and was traded to the Braves; and Alex Bregman, taken second overall by the Astros and moved to third base. Swanson and Bregman were three years older than Rodgers, however, and debuted in the majors at the same age Rodgers was last May when he received his first big league callup. Rodgers played only 25 games for the Rockies before suffering an injury that eventually required season-ending surgery. Rodgers compiled a 1.035 OPS in 37 games at the high altitude of Triple-A Albuquerque to earn his callup, but he scuffled to hit .224 with two extra-base hits in 25 games with Colorado.

SCOUTING REPORT: Rodgers' bat gets most of the attention when he is the subject of conversation. He has high-level bat speed, consistently hits the ball off the barrel and makes frequent contact. He has legitimate, above-average power and can drive the ball hard the other way, an approach that works well with the large outfield at Coors Field. Rodgers rarely walks and needs to control his aggression, which he has worked on at higher levels, where experienced pitchers will exploit a free-swinger. A shortstop out of high school, the Rockies are confident Rodgers could play the position in the big leagues. With Trevor Story entrenched there, however, second base is likely to be Rodgers' long-term position. Rodgers played an increasing amount of second base in the minor leagues last year and his brief big league exposure. He is still working on going to his left and adjusting to a different angle for the throw to first base, and his hands have been a little stiff in his initial move to the right side of the infield, but he should become an above-average defender at the keystone in time.

THE FUTURE: A Rodgers-Story double play duo would give Colorado one of the most powerful middle infields in the game. Rodgers' initial struggles in Colorado fits his history. At each level he goes through a growth period before settling in. He will get a late start on the 2020 season as he recovers from shoulder surgery.

JOE SARGENT/GETTY IMAGES

BA GRADE
60 **Risk: Medium**

SCOUTING GRADES
Hit: 60. **Power:** 55. **Run:** 50. **Field:** 55. **Arm:** 60.

Projected future grades on 20-80 scouting scale.

TOP PROSPECTS OF THE DECADE

Year	Player, Pos.	2019 Org
2010	Tyler Matzek, LHP	Braves
2011	Tyler Matzek, LHP	Braves
2012	Drew Pomeranz, LHP	Brewers
2013	Nolan Arenado, 3B	Rockies
2014	Jon Gray, RHP	Rockies
2015	David Dahl, OF	Rockies
2016	Jon Gray, RHP	Rockies
2017	Brendan Rodgers, SS	Rockies
2018	Brendan Rodgers, SS	Rockies
2019	Brendan Rodgers, SS/2B	Rockies

BEST TOOLS

Best Hitter for Average	Brendan Rodgers
Best Power Hitter	Sam Hilliard
Best Strike-Zone Discipline	Grant Lavigne
Fastest Baserunner	Bladimir Restituyo
Best Athlete	Nico Decolati
Best Fastball	Jacob Wallace
Best Curveball	Ashton Goudeau
Best Slider	Tommy Doyle
Best Changeup	Ryan Rolison
Best Control	Antonio Santos
Best Defensive Catcher	Dom Nunez
Best Defensive Infielder	Ezequiel Tovar
Best Infield Arm	Julio Carreras
Best Defensive Outfielder	Yonathan Daza
Best Outfield Arm	Yonathan Daza

Year	Age	Club (League)	Class	AVG	G	AB	R	H	2B	3B	HR	RBI	BB	SO	SB	OBP	SLG
2017	20	Hartford (EL)	AA	.260	38	150	20	39	5	0	6	17	8	36	0	.323	.413
	20	Lancaster (CAL)	HiA	.387	51	222	44	86	21	3	12	46	6	35	2	.407	.671
2018	21	Hartford (EL)	AA	.275	95	357	49	98	23	2	17	62	30	76	12	.342	.493
	21	Albuquerque (PCL)	AAA	.232	19	69	5	16	4	0	0	5	1	16	0	.264	.290
2019	22	Albuquerque (PCL)	AAA	.350	37	143	34	50	10	1	9	21	14	27	0	.413	.622
	22	Colorado (NL)	MAJ	.224	25	76	8	17	2	0	0	7	4	27	0	.272	.250
Major League Totals				.224	25	76	8	17	2	0	0	7	4	27	0	.272	.250
Minor League Totals				.296	387	1526	247	452	102	8	66	245	109	325	24	.352	.503

2 RYAN ROLISON, LHP

Born: July 11, 1997. **B-T:** B-L. **HT:** 6-2. **WT:** 195. **Drafted:** Mississippi, 2018 (1st round). **Signed by:** Zack Zulli.

TONY FARLOW

BA GRADE
55 **Risk: High**

TRACK RECORD: Rolison was a potential top-five rounds pick out of high school in 2016, but his commitment to Mississippi was so strong he fell to the Padres in the 37th round. Two years later after a pair of excellent collegiate seasons, the Rockies drafted him 22nd overall as an eligible sophomore. Rolison opened his first full season at high Class A Lancaster and held his own in unforgiving conditions, making the California League all-star game and standing out as one of the league's best pitching prospects.

SCOUTING REPORT: Rolison has a good handle on his fastball, changeup and curveball and is experimenting with a slider. He varies the speed of his fastball from 89-94 mph depending on the situation and locates it to both sides of the plate. His plus power curveball is his swing-and-miss pitch in the upper 70s with varying break, and his changeup is an effective, average offering. Rolison throws everything for strikes, works quickly and pitches smart. He focuses on hitters' tendencies and adjusts to exploit their weaknesses.

THE FUTURE: Rolison is ready for Double-A in 2020, and if he adjusts quickly it won't be a surprise if he shows up in Triple-A Albuquerque by midseason. Given his maturity and ability to adjust, the Rockies won't hesitate to promote him.

SCOUTING GRADES: **Fastball:** 50 **Slider:** 45 **Curveball:** 60 **Changeup:** 50 **Control:** 50

Year	Age	Club (League)	Class	W	L	ERA	G	GS	SV	IP	H	HR	BB	SO	K/9	WHIP	AVG
2018	20	Grand Junction (PIO)	R	0	1	1.86	9	9	0	29	15	2	8	34	10.6	0.79	.149
2019	21	Asheville (SAL)	LoA	2	1	0.61	3	3	0	15	8	0	2	14	8.6	0.68	.157
	21	Lancaster (CAL)	HiA	6	7	4.87	22	22	0	116	129	22	38	118	9.1	1.44	.278
Minor League Totals				8	9	3.94	34	34	0	160	152	24	48	166	9.3	1.25	.247

3 MICHAEL TOGLIA, 1B

Born: Aug. 16, 1998. **B-T:** B-L. **HT:** 6-5. **WT:** 226. **Drafted:** UCLA, 2019 (1st round). **Signed by:** Matt Hattabaugh

COURTESY OF BOISE HAWKS

BA GRADE
55 **Risk: High**

TRACK RECORD: The Rockies have liked Toglia since his days at Gig Harbor (Wash.) High. They drafted him in the 37th round even though he was considered unsignable at the time. After Toglia spent three years at UCLA, the Rockies drafted him again with the 23rd overall pick in 2019 and signed him for $2.725 million. He went out to short-season Boise after signing and finished tied for second in the Northwest League with nine home runs.

SCOUTING REPORT: A switch-hitter with power from both sides of the plate, Toglia is a potential middle-of-the-lineup bat. He has an impressive understanding of the strike zone for a young player and is a tough out when his timing is right in the batter's box. His swing plane gets inconsistent and affects his ability to make contact, but when he's right he gets red hot and hits for both average and power. He controls the zone and figures to get better as he moves up because pitchers will have better control. Toglia has the soft hands and easy actions of a plus defender at first base. He is the type of first baseman who makes other infielders better.

THE FUTURE: Toglia will likely open his first full season at high Class A Lancaster. He is advanced enough to potentially move quickly to Double-A Hartford.

SCOUTING GRADES: **Hitting:** 50 **Power:** 60 **Running:** 45 **Fielding:** 60 **Arm:** 50

Year	Age	Club (League)	Class	AVG	G	AB	R	H	2B	3B	HR	RBI	BB	SO	SB	OBP	SLG
2019	20	Boise (NWL)	SS	.248	41	145	25	36	7	0	9	26	28	45	1	.369	.483
Minor League Totals				.248	41	145	25	36	7	0	9	26	28	45	1	.369	.483

4 GRANT LAVIGNE, 1B

Born: Aug. 27, 1999. **B-T:** L-R. **HT:** 6-4. **WT:** 220. **Drafted:** HS—Bedford, N.H., 2018 (1st round supplemental). **Signed by:** Mike Garlatti.

TRACK RECORD: Lavigne became the highest player ever drafted from New Hampshire when the Rockies took him 42nd overall in 2018. He signed for $2 million and delivered a promising pro debut, but he struggled with the grind of his first full season in 2019 at low Class A Asheville and slugged just .327 despite a favorable home park.

TONY FARLOW

BA GRADE

55 Risk: Very High

SCOUTING REPORT: Patience is key with Lavigne, who rarely faced good high school competition and is attempting to become the first New Hampshire high school draftee to ever reach the majors. Lavigne has potential as a hitter with an excellent feel for the strike zone and a strong lefthanded swing that produces plus raw power. He struggled to get to his power and posted below-average exit velocities in 2019, however, because he was often too passive, and evaluators noted he rarely drove the ball in games. Still, his approach, strength and youth earn him projections of at least an average hitter with at least average in-game power. Lavigne is a good athlete for his size who was a quarterback on his high school football team. He is comfortable in the field and moves well around the first base bag.

THE FUTURE: Lavigne showed signs of making adjustments late last year. He has the bat, strike-zone knowledge and mentality to be an everyday first baseman.

SCOUTING GRADES: **Hitting:** 50 **Power:** 55 **Running:** 40 **Fielding:** 50 **Arm:** 45

Year	Age	Club (League)	Class	AVG	G	AB	R	H	2B	3B	HR	RBI	BB	SO	SB	OBP	SLG
2018	18	Grand Junction (PIO)	R	.350	59	206	45	72	13	2	6	38	45	40	12	.477	.519
2019	19	Asheville (SAL)	LoA	.236	126	440	52	104	19	0	7	64	68	129	8	.347	.327
Minor League Totals				.272	185	646	97	176	32	2	13	102	113	169	20	.390	.389

5 COLTON WELKER, 3B/1B

Born: Oct. 9, 1997. **B-T:** R-R. **HT:** 6-2. **WT:** 235. **Drafted:** HS—Parkland, Fla., 2016 (4th round). **Signed by:** Rafael Reyes

TRACK RECORD: Welker hit .337 over his first three pro seasons and won the California League batting title in 2018. He moved up to Double-A Hartford in 2019 and met his stiffest challenge yet. He hit .308 through his first 50 games and was recognized by Eastern League managers as the circuit's best batting prospect. He hit just .190 the rest of the way in a season interrupted by a shoulder subluxation. He then hit .229 in the Arizona Fall League.

BA GRADE

50 Risk: High

SCOUTING REPORT: Welker's natural feel to hit has been his calling card throughout his career. Usually, his level swing path keeps his barrel in the zone for a long time, and he has the strike-zone discipline to be an on-base threat. Welker began chasing power and trying to loft the ball in 2019, and the result was an uppercut swing that went in and out of the zone quickly and dramatically reduced his ability to make contact. He has the natural skills to be an above-average hitter with 15-20 home runs, but only if he rediscovers his best swing. Welker has good hands and an above-average arm at third base, but his thickening body and lack of speed have some projecting him to first base.

THE FUTURE: The Rockies plan to keep developing Welker at both corners. He has the committed approach that should allow him to learn from the challenges of 2019.

SCOUTING GRADES: **Hitting:** 55 **Power:** 50 **Running:** 40 **Fielding:** 50 **Arm:** 55

Year	Age	Club (League)	Class	AVG	G	AB	R	H	2B	3B	HR	RBI	BB	SO	SB	OBP	SLG
2017	19	Asheville (SAL)	LoA	.350	67	254	32	89	18	1	6	33	18	42	5	.401	.500
2018	20	Lancaster (CAL)	HiA	.333	114	454	74	151	32	0	13	82	42	103	5	.383	.489
2019	21	Hartford (EL)	AA	.252	98	353	37	89	23	1	10	53	32	68	2	.313	.408
Minor League Totals				.313	330	1271	181	398	88	4	34	204	105	241	18	.364	.469

6 SAM HILLIARD, OF

Born: Feb. 21, 1994. **B-T:** L-L. **HT:** 6-5. **WT:** 238. **Drafted:** Wichita State 2015 (15th round). **Signed by:** Brett Baldwin

TRACK RECORD: Hilliard was a pitcher at Wichita State who only started to make the conversion to position player as a junior. The Rockies drafted Hilliard in the 15th round in 2015 and he methodically worked his way up the system. Hilliard reached the pinnacle in 2019, hitting 35 home runs and stealing 22 bases at Triple-A Albuquerque to receive his first big league callup.

SCOUTING REPORT: Hilliard's size is deceiving. Though he's 6-foot-5, 238 pounds, he showed well defensively in Coors Field's spacious center field and stole 24 bases in 29 attempts in 2019. He is a plus runner and has a strong arm that precludes runners from being overly brave. At the plate, Hilliard boasts plus-plus raw power he gets to in games. That power has long come with lots of strikeouts, but in the majors he refined his leg lift to give him a better swing path and make more contact without sacrificing any of his line-to-line home run power.

THE FUTURE: Hilliard's athleticism and power make him a legitimate lineup threat, and his ability to play all three outfield spots gives him a greater avenue to the majors. He has to trim his strikeout rate, which is the final step in his conversion from a pitcher.

SCOUTING GRADES: **Hitting:** 40 **Power:** 60 **Running:** 60 **Fielding:** 50 **Arm:** 60

Year	Age	Club (League)	Class	AVG	G	AB	R	H	2B	3B	HR	RBI	BB	SO	SB	OBP	SLG
2017	23	Lancaster (CAL)	HiA	.300	133	536	95	161	23	7	21	92	50	154	37	.360	.487
2018	24	Hartford (EL)	AA	.262	121	435	58	114	22	3	9	40	41	151	23	.327	.389
2019	25	Albuquerque (PCL)	AAA	.262	126	500	109	131	29	7	35	101	54	164	22	.335	.558
	25	Colorado (NL)	MAJ	.273	27	77	13	21	4	2	7	13	9	23	2	.356	.649
Major League Totals				.273	27	77	13	21	4	2	7	13	9	23	2	.356	.649
Minor League Totals				.277	567	2154	378	597	110	30	89	358	237	674	124	.349	.480

7 RYAN CASTELLANI, RHP

Born: April 1, 1996. **B-T:** R-R. **HT:** 6-1. **WT:** 190. **Drafted:** HS—Phoenix, 2014 (2nd round). **Signed by:** Chris Forbes

TRACK RECORD: Castellani overcame a failed effort to become a more traditional overhand pitcher in 2018 and returned to his usual three-quarters arm slot in 2019. He got off to an impressive start at Triple-A Albuquerque but he was slowed by bone chips in his right elbow and had season-ending surgery in June. He returned to pitch in the Arizona Fall League and posted a 2.16 ERA in five starts, reaffirmed his status as one of the Rockies' better pitching prospects.

SCOUTING REPORT: Castellani is an outlier who throws harder with from the three-quarters delivery than over the top. He has a three-pitch mix built around a fastball that can reach 97 mph, but he commands it best in the 91-94 mph range with heavy sink to induce ground balls. His best secondary pitch is an above-average hard slider and he also flashes a usable changeup. Castellani is a cerebral pitcher with thick, durable legs built to log innings, but his below-average command across the board makes him a likely reliever for many evaluators.

THE FUTURE: Castellani will get a shot to pitch in the Rockies' rotation at some point in 2020. How his elbow holds up and if his command improves will determine if he starts or relieves long term.

SCOUTING GRADES: **Fastball:** 55 **Slider:** 55 **Changeup:** 45 **Control:** 45

Year	Age	Club (League)	Class	W	L	ERA	G	GS	SV	IP	H	HR	BB	SO	K/9	WHIP	AVG
2017	21	Hartford (EL)	AA	9	12	4.81	27	27	0	157	163	16	47	132	7.6	1.33	.264
2018	22	Hartford (EL)	AA	7	9	5.49	26	26	0	134	135	15	70	91	6.1	1.53	.265
2019	23	Albuquerque (PCL)	AAA	2	5	8.31	10	10	0	43	54	14	30	47	9.8	1.94	.300
Minor League Totals				28	43	4.80	126	126	0	653	677	60	235	531	7.3	1.40	.267

8 RYAN VILADE, SS/3B

Born: Feb. 18, 1999. **B-T:** R-R. **HT:** 6-2. **WT:** 198. **Drafted:** HS—Stillwater, Okla., 2017 (2nd round). **Signed by:** Jesse Retzlaf

ZACHARY LUCY/FOUR SEAM IMAGES

BA GRADE
50 **Risk: High**

TRACK RECORD: The Rockies used their top pick in the 2017 draft on Vilade and signed him for just under $1.5 million. The son of a longtime coach, Vilade got off to a slow start before finishing strong at low Class A Asheville in 2018 and did the same at high Class A Lancaster in 2019. After hitting .250 the first two months, Vilade hit .330 from June through the end of the season and was one of just five minor leaguers to finish with double-digits in doubles (27), triples (10) and home runs (12).

SCOUTING: Vilade figures to develop more power but already has come to grips with basics of hitting—using the right side of the field, staying in the gaps and focusing on line drives to the middle of the field. He generally makes whatever adjustments he needs to and has the physicality and aptitude to drive the ball consistently and be at least an average hitter with average power. Vilade's challenge remains defense. His range, glove and arm are all below-average at shortstop and questionable even at third base.

THE FUTURE: Vilade was drafted because of his offensive potential and has shown that potential. He needs to find a defensive home, but the Rockies will find him one as long as he keeps hitting.

SCOUTING GRADES: **Hitting:** 50 **Power:** 50 **Running:** 50 **Fielding:** 40 **Arm:** 50

Year	Age	Club (League)	Class	AVG	G	AB	R	H	2B	3B	HR	RBI	BB	SO	SB	OBP	SLG
2017	18	Grand Junction (PIO)	R	.308	33	117	23	36	3	2	5	21	27	31	5	.438	.496
2018	19	Asheville (SAL)	LoA	.274	124	457	77	125	20	4	5	44	49	96	17	.353	.368
2019	20	Lancaster (CAL)	HiA	.303	128	509	92	154	27	10	12	71	56	95	24	.367	.466
Minor League Totals				.291	285	1083	192	315	50	16	22	136	132	222	46	.369	.428

9 AARON SCHUNK, 3B

Born: July 24, 1997. **B-T:** R-R. **HT:** 6-2. **WT:** 205. **Drafted:** Georgia, 2019 (2nd round). **Signed by:** Sean Gamble

BA GRADE
50 **Risk: High**

TRACK RECORD: A third baseman and reliever at Georgia, Schunk was drafted by the Rockies in the second round in 2019 to swing the bat. He signed for $1,102,700 and did just that in his pro debut, leading short-season Boise with a .306 average, .503 slugging percentage and .873 OPS.

SCOUTING: Schunk is a well-rounded player who plays a mature game. Offensively, he knows the strike zone, stays inside the ball and drives it from gap to gap. He has plenty of bat speed and makes contact out front, resulting in balls jumping off his bat when he gets it. He shows the overall foundation of a potential above-average hitter with average power, and most are confident he'll reach those benchmarks. Schunk still has growth ahead defensively third base, but he has the athleticism and arm strength to develop into at least an average defender. Just as important, he has the work ethic to get better. Schunk is a cerebral player always aware of the game situation and is a natural leader.

THE FUTURE: Schunk will open 2020 at high Class A Lancaster and could come quickly. He is mature beyond his years and consistently focused on getting better, which will only help him get the most out of his natural ability.

SCOUTING GRADES: **Hitting:** 55 **Power:** 50 **Running:** 45 **Fielding:** 50 **Arm:** 60

Year	Age	Club (League)	Class	AVG	G	AB	R	H	2B	3B	HR	RBI	BB	SO	SB	OBP	SLG
2019	21	Boise (NWL)	SS	.306	46	173	31	53	12	2	6	23	14	25	4	.370	.503
Minor League Totals				.306	46	173	31	53	12	2	6	23	14	25	4	.370	.503

10 TYLER NEVIN, 1B/3B

Born: May 29, 1997. **B-T:** R-R: **HT:** 6-4. **WT:** 214. **Drafted:** HS—Poway, Calif., 2015 (1st round supplemental). **Signed by:** Jon Lukens

TRACK RECORD: Nevin has performed when he's been on the field, but that hasn't been often since the Rockies drafted him 38th overall in 2015 and signed him for $2 million. He played more than 100 games for the first time at Double-A Hartford in 2019 and finished on a high note, winning Eastern League player of the month in August to cap an otherwise subpar season.

SCOUTING: The son of former all-star third baseman Phil Nevin, Tyler grew up around the ballpark. Like his dad, Tyler has a potent bat that drills hard line drives and a knack for hitting the ball the other way. Nevin is still learning to elevate for home runs, but he has enough natural strength and contact ability for evaluators to project a potential everyday corner infielder. Nevin is a well below-average third baseman who takes odd approaches and is destined for first base, where he is still gaining confidence and experience. Nevin is a resilient, tough individual who has rebounded from multiple injuries and responded well to his first extended struggles last year.

THE FUTURE: Nevin is really going to have to hit to profile at first base, but he may be up for it. He'll move to Triple-A Albuquerque in 2020 and has an outside chance to make his major league debut.

SCOUTING GRADES: **Hitting:** 50 **Power:** 45 **Running:** 40 **Fielding:** 40 **Arm:** 45

Year	Age	Club (League)	Class	AVG	G	AB	R	H	2B	3B	HR	RBI	BB	SO	SB	OBP	SLG
2017	20	Boise (NWL)	SS	.233	6	30	4	7	3	0	1	5	0	9	0	.233	.433
	20	Asheville (SAL)	LoA	.305	76	298	45	91	18	3	7	47	27	56	10	.364	.456
2018	21	Lancaster (CAL)	HiA	.328	100	378	59	124	25	1	13	62	34	77	4	.386	.503
2019	22	Hartford (EL)	AA	.251	130	466	60	117	26	2	13	61	65	90	6	.345	.399
Minor League Totals				.286	366	1362	198	390	88	7	36	193	155	274	23	.362	.441

11 ADAEL AMADOR, SS

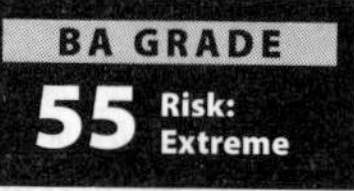

Born: April 11, 2003. **B-T:** R-R. **HT:** 5-11. **WT:** 180. **Signed:** Dominican Republic, 2019. **Signed by:** Rolando Fernandez/Martin Cabrera.

TRACK RECORD: Amador represented the Dominican Republic at multiple international tournaments as an amateur, including the COPABE 15U Pan American Championship, where he made the all-tournament team and won a gold medal. His combination of tools and ability to perform in games made him one of the best prospects in the 2019 international class when the Rockies signed him at 16 for $1.5 million.

SCOUTING REPORT: Amador is an advanced hitter for his age with a simple, compact swing from both sides of the plate. He stays balanced and recognizes pitches well, with the plate discipline and bat control to make frequent contact. Amador has a two-strike approach, but early in the count he looks to do damage, with his power ticking up to be able to drive the ball over the fence and the strength projection to get to at least average power. Amador has a chance to stay at shortstop, though some scouts think he might move off the position, and he's likely going to split time between shortstop and second base in 2020. An average runner, Amador has good defensive instincts, reading the ball off the bat well with a quick exchange to an average arm.

FUTURE: While Amador is far away, he's one of the most exciting young players in the system. He will make his pro debut in 2020.

Year	Age	Club (League)	Class	AVG	G	AB	R	H	2B	3B	HR	RBI	BB	SO	SB	OBP	SLG
2019	16	Did not play—Signed 2020 contract															

12 BEN BOWDEN, LHP

Born: Oct. 21, 1994. **B-T:** L-L. **HT:** 6-4. **WT:** 235. **Signed:** Vanderbilt, 2016 (2nd round). **Signed by:** Scott Corman.

TRACK RECORD: The closer for Vanderbilt's national championship team in 2016, Bowden has put together back-to-back impact seasons since missing his first potential full season, 2017, with hamstring and back injuries. He rose to Double-A Hartford in 2019 and set the Yard Goats record for saves (20) and ERA (1.05) in the first half alone before receiving a promotion to Triple-A Albuquerque, where he stayed strong pitching through difficult conditions. Bowden has struck out over 34 percent of hitters over the course of his pro career but has also battled control issues.

SCOUTING REPORT: Bowden's fastball, which he uses primarily up and away from hitters, sits 92-94 mph and reaches 97 from the left side. He backs up his heater with a plus, low 80s changeup which generates a high number of swings and misses from both lefties and righties. Bowden had lived largely on that two-pitch mix in the past but in 2019 significantly tightened his three-quarter breaking slurve and began generating a higher number of in-zone swings and misses with the pitch, particularly from lefthanders. Bowden struggles with his quality and intent in and out of the zone and needs to be more pitch-efficient, but the Rockies feel he took positive steps forward in 2019. Bowden is an excellent competitor with the stuff and mentality to be a late-inning reliever.

FUTURE: With a two-pitch mix and an ability to neutralize lefthanded hitters, Bowden is perfectly suited for relief role. There's still some seasoning to go, but he should make his big league debut in 2020

Year	Age	Club (League)	Class	W	L	ERA	G	GS	SV	IP	H	HR	BB	SO	K/9	WHIP	AVG
2017	22	Did not play—Injured															
2018	23	Asheville (SAL)	LoA	3	0	3.52	15	0	0	15	17	2	5	25	14.7	1.43	.274
	23	Lancaster (CAL)	HiA	4	2	4.17	34	0	0	37	35	6	15	53	13.0	1.36	.245
2019	24	Hartford (EL)	AA	0	0	1.05	26	0	20	26	8	1	7	42	14.7	0.58	.096
	24	Albuquerque (PCL)	AAA	1	3	5.88	22	0	1	26	29	4	17	37	12.8	1.77	.274
Minor League Totals				8	6	3.60	123	0	21	127	112	14	59	186	13.2	1.34	.232

13 KARL KAUFFMANN, RHP

BA GRADE **50** Risk: High

Born: Aug. 15, 1997. **B-T:** R-R. **HT:** 6-1. **WT:** 200. **Signed:** Michigan, 2019 (2nd round supplemental). **Signed by:** Ed Santa.

TRACK RECORD: Kauffmann enjoyed a successful three-year run at the Michigan, posting a 17-9, 2.74 mark while serving as a rotation stalwart in each of the last two seasons. Kauffmann signed with the Rockies for $805,600 soon after the Wolverines were bounced from the College World Series. After pitching a Michigan-record 130.2 innings, the Rockies used the rest of the summer as a chance for Kauffman to get acquainted with the organization.

SCOUTING REPORT: Kauffmann features an above-average, 91-95 mph sinking fastball that reminds the Rockies of the version used by former pitcher Aaron Cook. Kauffmann complements the sinker with a solid-average changeup. Scouts are mixed on the quality slider, which is still developing. Kauffmann is durable and has solid command of his pitches thanks to a smooth, athletic delivery. Kauffmann carries a reputation for mental toughness and gamesmanship from his amateur days.

FUTURE: Kauffmann projects as a potential back-end starter with the assortment of pitches designed for Coors Field, although some scouts the effort in his delivery may push him to the bullpen. With his savvy approach to pitching and strike-throwing ability, he could move quickly through the system.

Year	Age	Club (League)	Class	W	L	ERA	G	GS	SV	IP	H	HR	BB	SO	K/9	WHIP	AVG
2019	21	Did not play															

14 TERRIN VAVRA, SS

BA GRADE **45** Risk: High

Born: May 12, 1997. **B-T:** L-R. **HT:** 6-1. **WT:** 185. **Drafted:** Minnesota, 2018 (3rd round). **Signed by:** Brett Baldwin.

TRACK RECORD: Vavra's father, Joe, is the hitting coach for the Tigers, and both of his brothers played professionally. Vavra hit over .300 each of his three seasons with the Minnesota, including a .386 mark in his junior season with a 1.069 OPS. After being selected in the third round in 2018, Vavra had little trouble transitioning to pro ball. He posted a .302/.396/.467 slash line at short-season Boise in 2018, then won the South Atlantic League MVP with low Class A Asheville.

SCOUTING REPORT: There s little question about Vavra's offensive potential, highlighted by his production and his advanced knowledge of the strike zone. Vavra had a low swing-and-miss rate of just 18.2 percent and shows a line-drive, middle-of-the-field approach that should lead to more power in time because of a 14-degree launch angle. Scouts question his range and arm strength at shortstop and prefer him at second base. The Rockies plan to give Vavra playing time all around the infield to prepare him for a possible utility role, but his intangibles and feel for the game give him an extra edge.

FUTURE: Vavra will head to high Class A Lancaster in 2020. The Rockies envision him as a utilityman who finds his way into the lineup more often than not.

Year	Age	Club (League)	Class	AVG	G	AB	R	H	2B	3B	HR	RBI	BB	SO	SB	OBP	SLG
2018	21	Boise (NWL)	SS	.302	44	169	22	51	8	4	4	26	26	40	9	.396	.467
2019	22	Asheville (SAL)	LoA	.318	102	374	79	119	32	1	10	52	62	62	18	.409	.489
Minor League Totals				.313	146	543	101	170	40	5	14	78	88	102	27	.405	.483

15 JACOB WALLACE, RHP

Born: Aug. 13, 1998. **B-T:** R-R. **HT:** 6-1. **WT:** 190. **Signed:** Connecticut, 2019 (3rd round). **Signed by:** Mike Garlatti.

TRACK RECORD: Wallace is the third UConn reliever selected by the Rockies in the last eight drafts, joining PJ Poulin (11th round, 2018) and current big leaguer Scott Oberg (15th round, 2012). He got the attention of scouts when he struck out 12 of 15 batters in the 2019 college playoffs, including all seven batters he faced against Oklahoma State.

SCOUTING REPORT: Wallace is the prototypical power reliever with a mid-90s fastball and a plus slider. His fastball sits 93-95 mph and ramps up to 97, while his sharp 83-95 mph slider is a swing-and-miss offering more advanced than the typical college reliever. Northwest League hitters put Wallace's slider in play just 19 percent of the time while swing and missing on close to 60 percent of his offerings. Furthermore, Wallace's slider averaged 2,800 rpms during the summer, which is well above major league average. Wallace did not have a third pitch in college, but he has been working on a changeup since signing, though has yet to break it out in a regular-season game. Wallace is a quick twitch athlete with a very aggressive mound presence and delivery. His arm action is long and quick.

FUTURE: Wallace projects as a back-end bullpen arm. As he refines his command, he has a chance to rise through the system quickly

Year	Age	Club (League)	Class	W	L	ERA	G	GS	SV	IP	H	HR	BB	SO	K/9	WHIP	AVG
2019	20	Boise (NWL)	SS	0	0	1.29	22	0	12	21	9	1	9	29	12.4	0.86	.129
Minor League Totals				0	0	1.29	22	0	12	21	9	1	9	29	12.4	0.86	.129

16 HELCRIS OLIVAREZ, LHP

BA GRADE
50 Risk: Extreme

Born: Aug. 8, 2000. **B-T:** L/L. **HT:** 6-3. **WT:** 200. **Signed:** Dominican Republic, 2016. **Signed by:** Rolando Fernandez/Arnaldo Gomez/Orlando Medina/Frank Roa.

TRACK RECORD: Olivarez was little-known in the scouting community until he turned heads during extended spring training and became the buzz of the Arizona backfields. Olivarez pitched his first three seasons in the Dominican Summer League before coming stateside. He made three starts in the DSL in 2019 before moving to Rookie-level Grand Junction, where he struck out 28 percent of Pioneer League hitters.

SCOUTING REPORT: Olivarez already has an imposing frame at 6-foot-3, 200 pounds. He has a quick yet balanced delivery with a very quick arm from a low three-quarter slot with deeper plunge in back. His plus fastball sits 92-96 mph and has plenty of room to tick up as he gets stronger. His fastball plays up with life and good angle. Olivarez is still developing a breaking ball and changeup, both of which show potential but lack consistency due in part to inconsistent arm speed and finish. Olivarez has more confidence in his curveball, which has solid angle and spin when his delivery is on time, but he had more success in the Pioneer League commanding his changeup. Olivarez generates the majority of his strikeouts off his curveball, which demonstrates its potential ceiling. Olivarez's command is currently below-average, as shown by his 11.6 percent walk rate.

FUTURE: Olivarez is a long way off but has real rotation potential if he fills out and refines his pitches and command. The Rockies will monitor his innings, and extended Spring Training is a likely starting point before a move to either short-season Boise or low Class A Asheville.

Year	Age	Club (League)	Class	W	L	ERA	G	GS	SV	IP	H	HR	BB	SO	K/9	WHIP	AVG
2017	16	Rockies (DSL)	R	0	1	3.55	18	1	0	33	24	0	17	35	9.5	1.24	.200
2018	17	Rockies (DSL)	R	4	1	2.78	9	9	0	36	25	1	22	36	9.1	1.32	.205
	17	Colorado (DSL)	R	2	0	1.42	4	4	0	19	11	0	4	24	11.4	0.79	.164
2019	18	Rockies (DSL)	R	1	0	0.64	3	3	0	14	7	0	7	21	13.5	1.00	.149
	18	Grand Junction (PIO)	R	3	4	4.82	11	11	0	47	47	9	24	61	11.8	1.52	.260
Minor League Totals				10	6	3.22	45	28	0	148	114	10	74	177	10.7	1.27	.212

17 BRENTON DOYLE, OF

BA GRADE
45 Risk: High

Born: May 14, 1998. **B-T:** R-R. **HT:** 6-3. **WT:** 200. **Drafted:** Shepherd (W.Va.), 2019 (4th round). **Signed by:** Ed Santa.

TRACK RECORD: Doyle had originally committed to Virginia Military Institute, but as his skills improved he grew concerned about his ability to balance baseball along with the military obligations at VMI, so he opted instead to attend Division II Shepherd (W. Va) University. Doyle was two-time Mountain East Conference Player of the Year and finished his career with a .383/.438/.647 slash line. That performance earned him a fourth-round selection. Doyle opened his career by leading the Rookie-level Pioneer league in batting average (.383) and on-base percentage (.477) despite missing three weeks with a broken cheekbone suffered when he was hit by a fastball. His athleticism led scouts to speculate he might have been a first-round pick had he played at a more prominent school.

SCOUTING REPORT: Doyle is a plus runner with a plus arm and plus power and has shown the ability to adapt. He raised his stance at the Rockies' suggestion, and the move allowed him to create better leverage. It also gave him a longer look at pitches, which showed with a low strikeout rate and an average 4.08 pitches per plate appearance. One potential issue moving forward is a higher than average swing-and-miss rate of 30.4 percent and a particular vulnerability against sliders from righthanders. He has the potential to be a plus outfielder with a strong arm, and his speed makes him an option in center field.

FUTURE: Doyle could move quickly if he maintains the offensive adjustments he made at Grand Junction. He He should start 2020 at low Class A Asheville and has the makeup to continue to adapt to any roadblocks he may face.

Year	Age	Club (League)	Class	AVG	G	AB	R	H	2B	3B	HR	RBI	BB	SO	SB	OBP	SLG
2019	21	Grand Junction (PIO)	R	.383	51	180	42	69	11	3	8	33	31	47	17	.477	.611
Minor League Totals				.383	51	180	42	69	11	3	8	33	31	47	17	.477	.611

18 EDDY DIAZ, SS

BA GRADE
50 Risk: Extreme

Born: Feb. 14, 2000. **B-T:** R-R. **HT:** 5-11. **WT:** 171. **Signed:** Cuba, 2017. **Signed by:** Rolando Fernandez/Orlando Medina.

TRACK RECORD: Diaz became the Rockies' first-ever Cuban prospect when they signed him for $750,000 during the 2017 international signing period. His U.S. debut in 2019 was cut short by a knee injury that cost him the final month, but he was impressive when healthy.

SCOUTING REPORT: Diaz has proven particularly adept as a fastball hitter with a 9 percent swing-and-miss rate over his pro career. Diaz proved more vulnerable to pro breaking balls and will need to do a better job making contact. Diaz has yet to hit a professional home run in 555 plate appearances but can generate a decent slugging percentage by virtue of the doubles and triples his speed creates. A shortstop now, Diaz's arm is just average. He figures to settle in at second base and be a sparkplug.

FUTURE: It is tough to project power on Diaz, but he has bat speed, makes contact and delivers line drives. Add in his foot speed and first-step quickness, and he will fit nicely at the top of a lineup.

Year	Age	Club (League)	Class	AVG	G	AB	R	H	2B	3B	HR	RBI	BB	SO	SB	OBP	SLG
2017	17	Rockies (DSL)	R	.311	36	132	22	41	7	4	0	10	19	21	30	.403	.424
2018	18	Colorado (DSL)	R	.309	51	181	57	56	13	5	0	24	31	17	54	.417	.436
2019	19	Grand Junction (PIO)	R	.331	39	166	32	55	12	3	0	10	8	33	20	.366	.440
Minor League Totals				.317	126	479	111	152	32	12	0	44	58	71	104	.397	.434

19 TOMMY DOYLE, RHP

BA GRADE
45 Risk: High

Born: May 1, 1996. **B-T:** R-R. **HT:** 6-6. **Weight:** 235. **Signed:** Virginia, 2017 (2nd round supplemental). **Signed by:** Jordan Czarniecki.

TRACK RECORD: Doyle was drafted by the Nationals in 2014 but instead chose to head to Virginia, where he spent the next three seasons. After a transitional first season at Rookie-level Grand Junction, Doyle has strung together two quality seasons as a reliever at both levels of Class A, recording a combined 37 saves along with a 2.67 ERA and .548 OPS against.

SCOUTING REPORT: Doyle features a fastball that ranges from 95-98 mph with hard downer action that hitters usually beat into the ground. Doyle backs up the fastball with a power slurve in the 89-91 mph range that he now throws effectively to both sides of the plate. Doyle's changeup is still a work in progress due to deceleration issues in his delivery and timing. He often pulls the pitch to his gloveside, which gives it a cutterish look. While Doyle was able to use his slider in 2019 to neutralize lefthanded hitters, he may need to develop a pitch with more separation from his fastball in order to enhance his versatility and value in a major league pen. Doyle's delivery is solid with loose levers with leverage through his lower half and solid downhill plane. Doyle also added a higher front side to his delivery to enhance his plane to the plate.

FUTURE: Doyle should start 2020 at Double-A Hartford, where additional refinement changing speeds could put him on the fast track to a big league bullpen.

Year	Age	Club (League)	Class	W	L	ERA	G	GS	SV	IP	H	HR	BB	SO	K/9	WHIP	AVG
2017	21	Grand Junction (PIO)	R	3	3	5.14	20	0	3	21	29	2	10	18	7.7	1.86	.319
2018	22	Asheville (SAL)	LoA	7	6	2.31	52	0	18	58	52	2	12	66	10.2	1.10	.233
2019	23	Lancaster (CAL)	HiA	2	3	3.25	38	0	19	36	24	4	13	48	12.0	1.03	.185
Minor League Totals				12	12	3.12	110	0	40	115	105	8	35	132	10.3	1.21	.236

20 JULIO CARRERAS, 3B/SS

Born: Jan. 12, 2000. **B-T:** R-R. **HT:** 6-2. **WT:** 190. **Signed:** Dominican Republic, 2018. **Signed by:** Rolando Fernandez/Frank Roa.

TRACK RECORD: Carreras didn't garner much attention when the Rockies signed him for $15,000 before the 2018 season. But after a strong debut in the Dominican Summer League in 2018, Carreras followed it up by ranking as one of the top 20 prospects in the Rookie-level Pioneer League in 2019.

SCOUTING REPORT: Carreras has performed well at both stops since signing, with quick hands and a strong frame that give him a chance for 20-plus home run power. Carreras' swing gets long and it isn't the prettiest stroke, but despite some of his mechanical flaws, he has good hand-eye coordination, so he doesn't strike out excessively, though that might get challenged as he faces better competition. He moves surprisingly well for his size, with above-average speed underway. Carreras spent most of his time at third base, with exposure to shortstop and second base as well, but he profiles best at third. There's some stiffness to his actions that he will need to smooth out, but he has enough athleticism to stay at third base with a quick first step and an average arm.

THE FUTURE: Carreras should be advanced enough to advance to low Class A Asheville, where full-season pitching will give him a tougher test to show his swing will translate moving up.

Year	Age	Club (League)	Class	AVG	G	AB	R	H	2B	3B	HR	RBI	BB	SO	SB	OBP	SLG
2018	18	Rockies (DSL)	R	.252	41	135	32	34	5	3	3	14	23	28	8	.392	.400
	18	Colorado (DSL)	R	.344	27	93	26	32	6	4	3	17	8	18	8	.407	.591
2019	19	Grand Junction (PIO)	R	.294	67	262	51	77	14	8	5	38	25	63	14	.369	.466
Minor League Totals				.292	135	490	109	143	25	15	11	69	56	109	30	.383	.471

21 EZEQUIEL TOVAR, SS

BA GRADE
50 Risk: Extreme

Born: Aug. 1, 2001. **B-T:** S-R. **HT:** 6-0. **WT:** 162. **Signed:** Venezuela, 2017. **Signed by:** Rolando Fernandez/Orlando Medina.

TRACK RECORD: The Rockies signed Tovar the day he turned 16 then watched as he added the strength they expected. As an amateur he showed a projectable frame, the straight-line speed to run the 60-yard dash in 6.5 seconds and smooth, line-drive strokes from both sides of the plate. He's proved advanced enough that the Rockies split his time between the Rookie-level Pioneer League and the typically college-heavy Northwest League.

SCOUTING REPORT: Despite his youth (he was the youngest player with more than 50 plate appearances in the Pioneer League), Tovar showed impressive tools. He displayed enough bat speed to catch up with quality fastballs and a smooth enough swing that led rival evaluators to believe he'll have at least an average hit tool. The power isn't there quite yet, but Tovar still has to grow into his adult body. In the field, Tovar shows both quickness and speed as well as more than enough arm strength to make the throws required for a shortstop. He also impressed scouts with his high baseball IQ and ability to adjust quickly and learn from his mistakes.

THE FUTURE: Betting on Tovar is a long-term play, but he's already among the best defenders in the Rockies' system and has the potential to provide impact on both sides of the ball.

Year	Age	Club (League)	Class	AVG	G	AB	R	H	2B	3B	HR	RBI	BB	SO	SB	OBP	SLG
2018	16	Colorado (DSL)	R	.262	35	130	29	34	4	4	0	11	22	33	16	.369	.354
2019	17	Boise (NWL)	SS	.249	55	217	22	54	4	2	2	13	16	52	13	.304	.313
	17	Grand Junction (PIO)	R	.264	18	72	12	19	2	2	0	3	10	17	4	.357	.347
Minor League Totals				.255	108	419	63	107	10	8	2	28	48	102	33	.335	.332

22 YANQUIEL FERNANDEZ, OF

BA GRADE
50 Risk: Extreme

Born: Jan. 1, 2003. **B-T:** L-L. **HT:** 6-2 WT: 200. **Signed:** Cuba, 2019. **Signed by:** Rolando Fernandez/Marc Russo/Raul Gomez.

TRACK RECORD: Dominican shortstop Adael Amador was the prize signing of Colorado's 2019 international signing class, but Fernandez has made a loud impression as well. After Fernandez left Cuba, he signed with the Rockies at 16 for $295,0000.

SCOUTING REPORT: Fernandez is a strong, physical player with a chance to hit in the middle of a lineup. His strength and bat speed jump out, producing plus raw power with good leverage from a loose lefty stroke. He uses his hands well at the plate and does a good job of controlling the strike zone and recognizing pitches with advanced hitting instincts for his age. A smart player who is a student of the game, Fernandez uses the whole field and hangs in well against lefthanded pitching already. Fernandez has an arm that earns plus or better grades, but his value will come from what he does at the plate, as he's a below-average runner and athlete with limited range in an outfield corner.

THE FUTURE: Fernandez is far from the major leagues and has yet to make his pro debut, but he's one of the most exciting power bats in the organization.

Year	Age	Club (League)	Class	AVG	G	AB	R	H	2B	3B	HR	RBI	BB	SO	SB	OBP	SLG
2019	16	Did not play—Signed 2020 contract															

23 ASHTON GOUDEAU, RHP

BA GRADE **40** Risk: Medium

Born: July 23, 1992. **B-T:** R-R. **HT:** 6-6. **WT:** 205. **Drafted:** Maple Woods (Kan.) JC, 2012 (27th round). **Signed by:** Scott Melvin (Royals).

TRACK RECORD: Goudeau is an outlier—a 27-year-old who has gotten better every year and suddenly pushed himself into prospect status. A junior college draftee of the Royals in 2012, Goudeau chose pro ball over a scholarship to Louisiana-Lafayette. The Royals traded him to the Mariners during the waning stages of 2018 spring training. Change of scenery did little to advance Goudeau's performance, though he finally pitched in Triple-A for the first time. The Rockies signed him as a minor league free agent then watched as he posted a 2.07 ERA in 16 starts at Double-A and starred in the Arizona Fall League.

SCOUTING REPORT: Despite inflated ERAs and otherwise ordinary stat lines, Goudeau's peripheral numbers have gotten better each year. Goudeau has always had an excellent curveball, and throwing it more has led to favorable results. Goudeau complements the curveball with a 90-95 mph fastball and usable changeup. He keeps the changeup down in the zone and uses it against both against lefthanded and righthanded hitters. At 6-foot-6, he creates a strong downward angle on all of his pitches. Possessing a good pitcher's frame, Goudeau has continually improved his body, which has helped his athleticism and command.

FUTURE: Goudeau has pitched himself into position to be a major leaguer in 2020 but should begin 2020 at Triple-A Albuquerque.

Year	Age	Club (League)	Class	W	L	ERA	G	GS	SV	IP	H	HR	BB	SO	K/9	WHIP	AVG
2017	24	Royals (AZL)	R	0	0	0.00	2	1	0	3	2	0	1	3	9.0	1.00	.200
	24	NW Arkansas (TL)	AA	3	7	5.37	21	7	1	57	78	7	17	43	6.8	1.67	.322
2018	25	Tacoma (PCL)	AAA	1	5	8.20	20	2	0	37	59	6	19	31	7.5	2.09	.362
	25	Modesto (CAL)	HiA	1	1	4.50	3	3	0	14	14	2	6	12	7.7	1.43	.259
	25	Arkansas (TL)	AA	4	5	4.38	9	9	0	51	51	5	14	35	6.1	1.27	.264
2019	26	Hartford (EL)	AA	3	3	2.07	16	16	0	78	60	4	12	91	10.5	0.92	.215
Minor League Totals				29	48	4.81	171	70	4	563	638	55	153	499	8.0	1.40	.286

24 YONATHAN DAZA, OF

BA GRADE **40** Risk: Medium

Born: Feb. 28, 1994. **B-T:** R-R. **HT:** 6-2. **WT:** 210. **Signed:** Venezuela 2010. **Signed by:** Rolando Fernandez/Carlos Gonzalez/Orlando Medina.

TRACK RECORD: Daza has proven he can hit at the minor-league level, having put together batting averages of better than .300 in each of the last four years. That includes a .364 average at Triple-A Albuquerque in 2019 which earned him his first big league callup. That success didn't translate to the majors, where he hit .206 in 2019.

SCOUTING REPORT: Daza's strength has always been his ability to make contact, and he's produced a relatively low rate of swings and misses throughout his career. He's done the majority of his damage of fastballs in the minors, but those line drives turned into mishits in the big leagues. Selectively aggression coupled with a high contact rate has kept Daza from drawing many walks. Even with an increased launch angle over past few years, Daza has a relatively level swing and has produced more grounders than line drives or fly balls. Easily the best centerfielder in the organization, Daza covers plenty of ground with his plus speed and has a strong, accurate arm.

FUTURE: Daza should return to the majors in 2020 and has a ceiling of a backup outfielder who can handle all three positions while providing both speed and contact.

Year	Age	Club (League)	Class	AVG	G	AB	R	H	2B	3B	HR	RBI	BB	SO	SB	OBP	SLG
2017	23	Lancaster (CAL)	HiA	.341	125	519	93	177	34	11	3	87	30	88	31	.376	.466
2018	24	Hartford (EL)	AA	.306	54	219	27	67	18	2	4	29	7	24	4	.330	.461
2019	25	Albuquerque (PCL)	AAA	.364	89	387	67	141	30	4	11	48	25	52	12	.404	.548
	25	Colorado (NL)	MAJ	.206	44	97	7	20	1	1	0	3	7	21	1	.257	.237
Major League Totals				.206	44	97	7	20	1	1	0	3	7	21	1	.257	.237
Minor League Totals				.318	683	2624	401	834	170	28	30	365	133	378	96	.359	.438

25 CHRISTIAN KOSS, SS/2B/3B

BA GRADE
45 Risk: High

Born: Jan. 27, 1998. **B-T:** R-R. **HT:** 6-1. **WT:** 182. **Drafted:** UC Irvine, 2019 (12th round). **Signed by:** Jon Lukens.

TRACK RECORD: Koss entered the year as one of the top 2019 draft prospects on the West Coast. But he scuffled at the plate during his junior year at UC Irvine and fell to the 12th round, signing for $180,000. He rebounded well in the Rookie-level Pioneer League, where he ranked among the league's top prospects.

SCOUTING REPORT: In college, Koss stood out for his slick defense at shortstop. He's an athletic, high-energy player with good actions in the field and a quick transfer to a solid-average arm. Some scouts think he should stay at shortstop, though others think his range and inconsistency in the field might move him off the position. During his junior season, Koss changed his approach to try to hit for more power, and it ended up with him piling up strikeouts until he adjusted at the end, which carried over into his pro debut.

THE FUTURE: Koss could end up being a nice buy-low grab for the Rockies if he can replicate his early success higher up the ladder. Low Class A Asheville is up next.

Year	Age	Club (League)	Class	AVG	G	AB	R	H	2B	3B	HR	RBI	BB	SO	SB	OBP	SLG
2019	21	Grand Junction (PIO)	R	.332	53	190	45	63	11	4	11	51	35	43	10	.447	.605
Minor League Totals				.332	53	190	45	63	11	4	11	51	35	43	10	.447	.605

26 BLADIMIR RESTITUYO, 2B/OF

BA GRADE
50 Risk: Extreme

Born: July 2, 2001. **B-T:** R-R. **HT:** 5-10. **WT:** 151. **Signed:** Dominican Republic, 2001. **Signed by:** Rolando Fernandez/Frank Roa.

TRACK RECORD: For Restituyo, July 2, 2001 was doubly momentous. He celebrated his 16th birthday by signing a $200,000 contract to join the Rockies. Part of a class that also included Ezequiel Tovar and Eddy Diaz, Restituyo was lauded as an amateur for his quick-twitch athleticism and projectable body.

SCOUTING REPORT: The Rockies sent Restituyo to the college-heavy Northwest League for part of the season despite being just 17 years old on Opening Day. In the NWL, Restituyo showed evaluators the quick hands to turn around high-velocity fastballs and the footspeed to play center field. He's rough around the edges in the outfield but has plus speed to make up for some of the mistakes he makes running routes and chasing down balls in the gaps. He'll need to iron out his strike-zone discipline and learn to take a few more pitches to get to ones he can drive, but there's plenty of upside in a high-energy package.

THE FUTURE: Restituyo's future could be at second base or on the infield, but he has the profile of a player who could be pesky at the top or bottom of a lineup.

Year	Age	Club (League)	Class	AVG	G	AB	R	H	2B	3B	HR	RBI	BB	SO	SB	OBP	SLG
2018	16	Rockies (DSL)	R	.291	46	182	27	53	9	5	0	21	7	38	12	.337	.396
	16	Colorado (DSL)	R	.327	14	55	16	18	2	2	4	12	2	13	4	.339	.655
2019	17	Boise (NWL)	SS	.259	55	228	28	59	13	0	4	25	2	56	16	.266	.368
	17	Grand Junction (PIO)	R	.310	20	84	13	26	4	2	2	14	2	13	6	.326	.476
Minor League Totals				.284	135	549	84	156	28	9	10	72	13	120	38	.307	.423

27 JOSH FUENTES, 3B

Born: Feb. 19, 1993. **B-T:** R-R. **HT:** 6-2. **WT:** 215. **Signed:** Missouri Baptist (NDFA), 2014. **Signed by:** John Lukens.

TRACK RECORD: Signed as a non-drafted free agent out of NAIA Missouri Baptist in 2014 after his junior season for $10,000, Fuentes had a familiarity with the Rockies' organization thanks to his cousin Nolan Arenado. His continued success led to his big league debut on April 6.

SCOUTING REPORT: Fuentes features a strong inside-out swing, stays on the ball well, makes consistent contact and uses all fields. Fuentes tried to lift the ball for more power in 2019, which resulted in a career-high 17 home runs but career worsts in batting average and on-base percentage. His average exit velocity also dropped by 3.5 mph. Fuentes recorded a paltry .335 slugging percentage away from hitter-happy Albuquerque. Fuentes has the hands and reactions to play both third and first base adequately.

FUTURE: In 2020, Fuentes will be at a career crossroads. He'll need another strong season to prove himself as potential everyday player. If that doesn't happen, he could wind up as an up-and-down candidate.

Year	Age	Club (League)	Class	AVG	G	AB	R	H	2B	3B	HR	RBI	BB	SO	SB	OBP	SLG
2017	24	Hartford (EL)	AA	.307	122	414	48	127	28	7	15	72	24	92	8	.352	.517
2018	25	Albuquerque (PCL)	AAA	.327	135	551	93	180	39	12	14	95	21	103	3	.354	.517
2019	26	Albuquerque (PCL)	AAA	.254	101	402	66	102	23	2	17	64	25	118	1	.298	.448
	26	Colorado (NL)	MAJ	.218	24	55	8	12	1	0	3	7	1	20	1	.232	.400
Major League Totals				.218	24	55	8	12	1	0	3	7	1	20	1	.232	.400
Minor League Totals				.291	597	2238	334	651	150	26	66	353	132	492	28	.339	.470

28 PJ POULIN, LHP

BA GRADE **40** Risk: High

Born: July 25, 1996. **B-T:** R-L. **HT:** 6-1. **WT:** 185. **Drafted:** Connecticut, 2018 (11th round). **Signed by:** Mike Garlatti.

TRACK RECORD: After minimal work as a freshman at Connecticut, Poulin's workload increased over his final two years. He moved into the closer's role in 2018 and racked up 16 saves and 10.9 strikeouts per mine innings. He followed a strong pro debut with an even stronger turn in 2019, emerging as the closer yet again midway through the season at low Class A Asheville.

SCOUTING REPORT: Poulin works from a lower slot with command and no fear. His fastball sits between 88-91 mph and touches 93 with hard sink at the bottom of the zone. Poulin has a quick arm and aggressive approach in the strike zone and creates sneaky front-side deception. Poulin eliminated the spike on his curveball in the in 2018 offseason and started throwing a true slider.

FUTURE: Poulin has the tools to be a late-inning reliever. He'll jump to high Class A Lancaster in 2020.

Year	Age	Club (League)	Class	W	L	ERA	G	GS	SV	IP	H	HR	BB	SO	K/9	WHIP	AVG
2018	21	Boise (NWL)	SS	1	3	1.96	24	0	7	23	15	0	10	33	12.9	1.09	.176
2019	22	Asheville (SAL)	LoA	3	3	2.90	54	0	13	59	58	1	20	67	10.2	1.32	.256
Minor League Totals				4	6	2.63	78	0	20	82	73	1	30	100	11.0	1.26	.234

29 WILL ETHRIDGE, RHP

BA GRADE **40** Risk: High

Born: Dec. 20, 1997. **B-T:** R-R. **HT:** 6-5. **WT:** 240. **Drafted:** Mississippi, 2019 (5th round). **Signed by:** Zach Zulli.

TRACK RECORD: A 35th-round pick by the Mariners out of high school, Ethridge chose to attend Mississippi. Ethridge worked mostly in relief in his first two seasons with the Rebels before moving to the rotation as a junior. He quickly became the Rebels' Friday night starter and showed enough for the Rockies to draft him with their sixth-round pick and signed him for $327,500.

SCOUTING REPORT: Ethridge throws three average or better pitches for strikes while mostly pitching to contact. His fastball sits 90-93, topping out at 96 mph which sets up an above-average changeup he can throw to either side of the plate, serving as his chase pitch. He refined his hard slider in college to the point that it's now an average pitch. Ethridge threw the slider more in Boise, where it generated the highest swing-and-miss percentage of his mix. Ethridge's key is being comfortable throwing strikes and generating soft contact with all three pitches at the bottom of the zone.

FUTURE: Ethridge will get the chance to show he can remain a starter, and low Class A Asheville looks like a likely starting point in 2020. He has one of the higher floors in the Rockies' system.

Year	Age	Club (League)	Class	W	L	ERA	G	GS	SV	IP	H	HR	BB	SO	K/9	WHIP	AVG
2019	21	Boise (NWL)	SS	0	2	3.82	9	9	0	31	29	1	6	21	6.2	1.14	.250
Minor League Totals				0	2	3.82	9	9	0	30	29	1	6	21	6.2	1.14	.250

30 RILEY PINT, RHP

BA GRADE **45** Risk: Extreme

Born: Nov. 6, 1997. **B-T:** R-R. **HT:** 6-4. **WT:** 195. **Drafted:** HS—Overland Park, Kan., 2016 (1st round). **Signed by:** Bret Baldwin.

TRACK RECORD: The fourth overall pick in the 2016 draft, Pint has battled injuries and major control problems and has yet to advance past low Class A Asheville. Pint's control issues first surfaced at low Class A Asheville, where he uncorked 26 wild pitches and walked 59 hitters in 93 innings. Pint has thrown just 26 innings over the past two seasons, including a 2019 season in which he walked 31 batters in 17.2 innings, was demoted to the bullpen and didn't pitch after June 14 due to shoulder tendinitis.

SCOUTING REPORT: Pint still has a 97-100 mph fastball with dominant potential, a hard slurvy curveball and a true slider, but he has zero command of either. The move to the bullpen also allowed Pint him to focus solely on commanding his fastball before reintroducing offspeed pitches. Pint's stretch-only delivery appears sound through the start but also plenty of effort through his landing, finish and extension. That includes a head whack, which has contributed to the loss of a consistent release point.

FUTURE: Pint will try again to show he can take a step forward in 2020 and reestablish himself as someone who can at least provide bullpen value.

Year	Age	Club (League)	Class	W	L	ERA	G	GS	SV	IP	H	HR	BB	SO	K/9	WHIP	AVG
2017	19	Asheville (SAL)	LoA	2	11	5.42	22	22	0	93	96	3	59	79	7.6	1.67	.264
2018	20	Asheville (SAL)	LoA	0	1	81.00	1	1	0	0	2	0	2	0	0.0	12.00	.500
	20	Boise (NWL)	SS	0	2	1.13	3	3	0	8	4	0	9	8	9.0	1.63	.167
2019	21	Asheville (SAL)	LoA	0	1	8.66	21	3	0	18	12	0	31	23	11.7	2.43	.203
Minor League Totals				3	20	5.71	58	40	0	156	157	5	124	146	8.4	1.80	.266

Detroit Tigers

BY JUSTIN COLEMAN

The Tigers, in the midst of a full-blown rebuild, entered 2019 with few expectations and largely failed to meet even those. Their 47-114 record was not only the worst in the major leagues, but it was the second-worst record in the franchise's 119-year history behind only the atrocious 2003 Tigers. They lost 59 games at home, tying the 1939 St. Louis Browns for the most home losses during a season in the modern era.

It seems so long ago the Tigers made four straight postseason appearances, but it was only 2011-14. Detroit spent the earlier part of the decade infusing money into the big league club in an effort to win the World Series, with Justin Verlander, Max Scherzer, Prince Fielder and Miguel Cabrera the anchors of a star-studded, veteran team. They won the 2012 American League pennant but fell short in the Championship Series in 2011 and 2013. Their effort to win a World Series ultimately came up short, and when owner Mike Illitch died in February 2017, the Tigers decided to embrace a rebuild in order to create a more long-term competitive organization.

The list of players traded away since 2015 is a long and painful one: Yoenis Cespedes, David Price, Justin Upton, J.D. Martinez, Ian Kinsler and, of course, Verlander. Shane Greene and Nick Castellanos became the latest veterans moved when the Tigers shipped them to the Braves and Cubs, respectively, at the 2019 trade deadline for prospects. The only veteran holdovers, Cabrera and Jordan Zimmermann, remain with the club because they are largely unmovable due to their hefty contracts and track record of injuries.

The organization's focus has shifted from the majors to the minors. The scouting and player development staffs have been at the forefront of the Tigers' rebuild as the club aims to create a sustainable product through player development.

In that sense, the 2019 season saw positive steps, particularly with regard to the Tigers' pitching prospects. Casey Mize, the No. 1 overall pick in 2018, raced to Double-A in his first full season and showed why he was so highly touted with flashes of dominant stuff. His Double-A teammate Matt Manning was named the Eastern League Pitcher of the Year, while lefthander Tarik Skubal burst on the scene as perhaps the biggest breakout prospect in the minors.

While pitching is the strength of the Tigers system, Detroit also has a group of intriguing young outfielders. Daz Cameron, who they acquired as part of the return for Verlander, and Parker Meadows, drafted in the second round in 2018, are both athletic but far away. The Tigers added Cuban signee Roberto Campos for $2.85 million during the 2019 international signing period to give them another high-upside outfielder.

NUCCIO DINUZZO/GETTY IMAGES

Former Rule 5 pick Victor Reyes hit .304 and was a rare bright spot for the 114-loss Tigers.

PROJECTED 2023 LINEUP

Position	Player	Age
Catcher	Jake Rogers (10)	28
First Base	Jeimer Candelario	29
Second Base	Niko Goodrum	31
Third Base	Isaac Paredes (5)	24
Shortstop	Willi Castro (9)	26
Left Field	Daz Cameron (7)	26
Center Field	Victor Reyes	28
Right Field	Riley Greene (4)	22
Designated Hitter	Christin Stewart	29
No. 1 Starter	Casey Mize (1)	25
No. 2 Starter	Matt Manning (2)	25
No. 3 Starter	Tarik Skubal (3)	25
No. 4 Starter	Alex Faedo (6)	27
No. 5 Starter	Spencer Turnbull	30
Closer	Zack Hess	26

It would be easy to look past some athletic infielders that the organization has, such as third baseman Isaac Paredes and shortstops Willi Castro, Wenceel Perez and Sergio Alcantara. This group was assembled via trades and the international market, with Paredes having the best chance to be impactful with the bat.

The Tigers believe those players give them the foundation for future success in the major leagues, and they have a chance to fortify that prospect core with the No. 1 overall pick in the 2020 draft, their second top overall selection in three years.

DEPTH CHART

DETROIT TIGERS

TOP 2020 ROOKIE: Jake Rogers, C. Rogers brings elite defensive skills while also providing some pop from behind the plate

BREAKOUT PROSPECT: Parker Meadows, OF. The young outfielder struggled in his first full season, but his athleticism and raw tools still give him plenty of upside.

SLEEPER: Jason Foley, RHP. Foley is building innings as he comes back from Tommy John surgery. His near triple-digit fastball makes him enticing if he can regain his command.

SOURCE OF TOP 30 TALENT

Homegrown	**19**	**Acquired**	**11**
College	8	Trade	11
Junior college	0	Rule 5 draft	0
High school	5	Independent league	0
Nondrafted free agent	0	Free agent/waivers	0
International	6		

LF
Troy Stokes Jr.
Bryant Packard
Danny Woodrow

CF
Daz Cameron (7)
Parker Meadows (12)
Derek Hill (22)
Jose De La Cruz (25)
Jacob Robson
Kingston Liniak

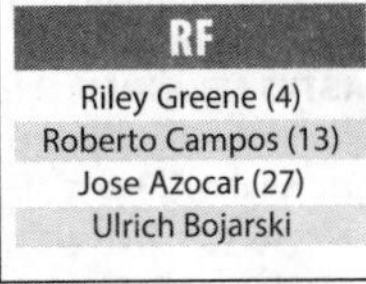

RF
Riley Greene (4)
Roberto Campos (13)
Jose Azocar (27)
Ulrich Bojarski

3B
Isaac Paredes (5)
Nick Quintana (20)
Adinso Reyes (24)
Chad Sedio
Andre Lipcius

SS
Willi Castro (9)
Wenceel Perez (14)
Sergio Alcantara (21)
Cole Peterson
Jose King
Ryan Kreidler

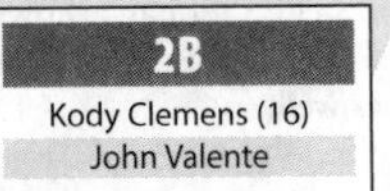

2B
Kody Clemens (16)
John Valente

1B
Reynaldo Rivera

C
Jake Rogers (10)
Joey Morgan
Cooper Johnson
Sam McMillan

LHP

LHSP
Tarik Skubal (3)
Joey Wentz (11)
Adam Wolf
Jack O'Loughlin

LHRP
Matt Hall
Trent Szkutnik

RHP

RHSP
Casey Mize (1)
Matt Manning (2)
Alex Faedo (6)
Franklin Perez (8)
Beau Burrows (15)
Elvin Rodriguez (18)
Paul Richan (23)
Kyle Funkhouser (28)
Wilkel Hernandez (30)
Logan Shore
Garrett Hill
Ethan DeCaster

RHRP
Bryan Garcia (17)
Anthony Castro (19)
Wladimir Pinto (26)
Alex Lange (29)
Jason Foley
Sandy Baez
Nolan Blackwood
Zack Hess
Xavier Javier

DRAFT ANALYSIS

2019

BEST PURE HITTER: The Tigers went position-heavy through the first six rounds of the draft, but OF Riley Greene (1) stands out. He has premium bat speed and barrels up pitches with consistency, showing the ability to use the whole field and work the count.

BEST POWER: Greene makes loud contact and shows enough power to project as plus thanks to his bat path and plus strength. 3B Nick Quintana (2) doesn't have the biggest frame at just 5-foot-10, but he has strong wrists and the ball jumps off his bat, projecting for power that should play down the road. Quintana hit 29 homers across his last two seasons at Arizona.

FASTEST RUNNER: He wasn't known as a basestealer during his three years at Arkansas, but SS Jack Kenley (8) is a plus runner who isn't twitchy but runs very well anyway. OF Connor Perry (28) is an above-average runner who shows feel to steal bags and should stick in center field thanks to his wheels.

BEST DEFENSIVE PLAYER: While his foot speed isn't plus, Greene has an above-average arm and shows natural feel in the outfield. Quintana shows a quick first step at the hot corner, coupled with a plus arm and good hands as well.

BEST ATHLETE: 3B Ryan Kreidler (4) has a large frame at 6-foot-4, 208 pounds but moves well around the diamond. He has good body control, moves well laterally and has excellent actions in the infield.

BEST FASTBALL: RHP Zack Hess (7) was converted into a starter at Louisiana State, but the Tigers quickly moved him back to the bullpen, where his fastball tops out at 98 mph with life.

BEST SECONDARY PITCH: Hess pairs his plus fastball with a wipeout slider that has hard, late bite. It gets swings and misses with good shape on it.

BEST PRO DEBUT: Greene was arguably the most advanced prep hitter of the 2019 draft class, and his feel for the game helped him to hold his own across three levels of the minors, including a stint at low Class A West Michigan. Greene hit .271/.347/.403 with 16 extra-base hits in his 57 pro games this season. OF Kerry Carpenter (19) showed an advanced approach out of Virginia Tech and went on to win the 2019 Gulf Coast League Most Valuable Player award. He led the league in homers (nine), total bases (100) and was fourth in hits (51).

MOST INTRIGUING BACKGROUND: 3B Andre Lipcius (3) comes from a family of educators and majored in nuclear engineering during his time at Tennessee.

CLOSEST TO THE MAJORS: Playing under the bright lights at LSU have helped Hess to mature on the mound, and his fastball-breaking ball combo should help him to climb to a major league bullpen in short order.

BEST LATE-ROUND PICK: Carpenter has the aptitude to continue learning and was one of the more advanced college bats in the draft.

THE ONE WHO GOT AWAY: SS Cade Doughty (39) declined to sign with the Tigers and opted to attend Louisiana State instead. The infielder receives praise for his hard-nosed play, sound swing and ability to run well.

—JUSTIN COLEMAN

TOP DRAFT PICKS OF THE DECADE

Year	Player, Pos.	2019 Org
2010	Nick Castellanos, 3B (1st round supp)	Cubs
2011	James McCann, C (2nd round)	White Sox
2012	Jake Thompson, RHP (2nd round)	Tigers
2013	Jonathon Crawford, RHP	Did not play
2014	Derek Hill, OF	Tigers
2015	Beau Burrows, RHP	Tigers
2016	Matt Manning, RHP	Tigers
2017	Alex Faedo, RHP	Tigers
2018	Casey Mize, RHP	Tigers
2019	Riley Greene, OF	Tigers

2018

No. 1 overall pick RHP Casey Mize has done his best to live up to that label early in his career and LHP Tarik Skubal (9) gives the class another potential star on the mound and great value as a ninth-round pick.

GRADE: A

2017

RHP Alex Faedo (1) pitched well in Double-A in 2019 and joins Detroit's burgeoning pitching ranks in the upper minors. But, right now, he's about it from this class—no other 2017 draftee made the Handbook.

GRADE: D

2016

The Tigers went pitching heavy in this draft and it has paid off. RHP Matt Manning (1) is their No. 2 prospect and is nearing Detroit. RHPs Bryan Garcia (6) and John Schreiber (15) have already made it.

GRADE: B

1 CASEY MIZE, RHP

Born: May 1, 1997. **B-T:** R-R. **HT:** 6-3. **WT:** 220.
Drafted: Auburn, 2018 (1st round).
Signed by: Justin Henry.

TRACK RECORD: Mize faced durability questions at Auburn after missing time with a flexor strain as a sophomore and pitching only sparingly that summer for USA Baseball's Collegiate National Team. As a junior, however, Mize cemented himself as the best player in the 2018 draft class and was picked No. 1 overall by the Tigers. He signed for $7.5 million, a then-record for the largest bonus under the current draft format implemented in 2012. Mize began his first full season at high Class A Lakeland and dominated Florida State League competition before receiving a promotion to Double-A Erie, where he spun a no-hitter in his first start. Mize pitched well initially for the SeaWolves but gave the Tigers a scare on June 13, when he left his start with right shoulder soreness. He returned to Erie a month later but was nowhere near as effective. He logged a 7.09 ERA in his final six starts before the Tigers shut him down.

SCOUTING REPORT: Mize's fastball touches 97 mph but sits comfortably in the 93-94 range. It plays up because he commands it with ease to both sides of the strike zone. Mize also uses a harder cutter in the upper 80s, which helps neutralize lefthanded hitters, as well as a slider in the low-to-mid-80s. The slider improved in 2019 with better shape and consistency. His main secondary offering is a double-plus splitter that has late, hard downward tumble. Mize disguises his splitter well and it tunnels off the plane of his fastball, generating plenty of swings and misses. All of his pitches are firm but work to different parts of the strike zone effectively. Mize projects to have future plus control despite a herky-jerky delivery. He throws all of his pitches for strikes with above-average command and shows maturity on the mound.

THE FUTURE: After dominating the Eastern League, Mize should continue his quick rise through the minors. He should continue to log innings in the upper minors as he prepares for the rigors of a major league season. If all goes well, Mize may get his first taste of big league competition at the end of the 2020 season. His pitch mix, advanced control and double-plus splitter paint the picture of a future front-of-the-rotation starter around whom the Tigers can build.

MIKE JANES/FOUR SEAM IMAGES

BA GRADE
65 **Risk: High**

SCOUTING GRADES
Fastball: 60. **Splitter:** 70. **SL:** 60. **Cutter:** 55. **Control:** 55.
Projected future grades on 20-80 scouting scale.

TOP PROSPECTS OF THE DECADE

Year	Player, Pos.	2019 Org
2010	Jacob Turner, RHP	Korea
2011	Jacob Turner, RHP	Korea
2012	Jacob Turner, RHP	Korea
2013	Nick Castellanos ,3B/OF	Cubs
2014	Nick Castellanos, 3B/OF	Cubs
2015	Steven Moya, OF	Japan
2016	Michael Fulmer, RHP	Tigers
2017	Matt Manning, RHP	Tigers
2018	Franklin Perez, RHP	Tigers
2019	Casey Mize, RHP	Tigers

BEST TOOLS

Best Hitter for Average	Riley Greene
Best Power Hitter	Riley Greene
Best Strike-Zone Discipline	Isaac Paredes
Fastest Baserunner	Parker Meadows
Best Athlete	Parker Meadows
Best Fastball	Jason Foley
Best Curveball	Matt Manning
Best Slider	Alex Faedo
Best Changeup	Casey Mize
Best Control	Paul Richan
Best Defensive Catcher	Jake Rogers
Best Defensive Infielder	Sergio Alcantara
Best Infield Arm	Sergio Alcantara
Best Defensive Outfielder	Derek Hill
Best Outfield Arm	Jose Azocar

Year	Age	Club (League)	Class	W	L	ERA	G	GS	SV	IP	H	HR	BB	SO	K/9	WHIP	AVG
2018	21	Tigers West (GCL)	R	0	0	0.00	1	1	0	2	0	0	1	4	18.0	0.50	.000
	21	Lakeland (FSL)	HiA	0	1	4.63	4	4	0	12	13	2	2	10	7.7	1.29	.295
2019	22	Lakeland (FSL)	HiA	2	0	0.88	6	6	0	31	11	0	5	30	8.8	0.52	.110
	22	Erie (EL)	AA	6	3	3.20	15	15	0	79	69	5	18	76	8.7	1.11	.234
Minor League Totals				8	4	2.71	26	26	0	123	93	7	26	120	8.8	0.97	.209

2 MATT MANNING, RHP

Born: Jan. 28, 1998. **B-T:** R-R. **HT:** 6-6. **WT:** 215. **Drafted:** HS—Sacramento, 2016 (1st round). **Signed by:** Scott Cerny.

BA GRADE
60 Risk: Medium

TRACK RECORD: Manning comes from athletic bloodlines as his father Rich played two seasons in the NBA. After climbing two levels and reaching Double-A to end his 2018 campaign, Manning took leaps forward in 2019. May was his best month, as the righthander allowed five earned runs across 31.1 innings pitched. The 21-year-old was named the Eastern League Pitcher of the Year thanks to his consistency and ability to throw all three of his pitches for strikes. His 148 strikeouts were second on the circuit.

SCOUTING REPORT: Manning's fastball plays up thanks to the extension he gets from his 6-foot-6 frame. He can ramp it up to 97 mph but sits more in the 92-95 range with life. Manning throws a high-spin curveball with sharp downer break that projects as plus. He will need to make sure it comes out of the same slot as his fastball as he matures. Manning's third offering is a changeup that flashes plus thanks to sinking action. His tempo, athleticism and ability to attack the strike zone help him project to have future above-average control.

THE FUTURE: Manning has to continue to hone his delivery while improving his ability to throw his changeup. His athleticism and competitive nature give him a mid-rotation ceiling.

SCOUTING GRADES: **Fastball:** 60 **Curveball:** 60 **Changeup:** 60 **Control:** 55

Year	Age	Club (League)	Class	W	L	ERA	G	GS	SV	IP	H	HR	BB	SO	K/9	WHIP	AVG
2017	19	Connecticut (NYP)	SS	2	2	1.89	9	9	0	33	27	0	14	36	9.7	1.23	.223
	19	West Michigan (MWL)	LoA	2	0	5.60	5	5	0	18	14	0	11	26	13.2	1.42	.209
2018	20	West Michigan (MWL)	LoA	3	3	3.40	11	11	0	56	47	3	28	76	12.3	1.35	.229
	20	Lakeland (FSL)	HiA	4	4	2.98	9	9	0	51	32	4	19	65	11.4	0.99	.176
	20	Erie (EL)	AA	0	1	4.22	2	2	0	11	11	0	4	13	11.0	1.41	.282
2019	21	Erie (EL)	AA	11	5	2.56	24	24	0	134	93	7	38	148	10.0	0.98	.192
Minor League Totals				22	17	3.04	70	70	0	331	251	16	121	410	11.1	1.12	.207

3 TARIK SKUBAL, LHP

Born: Nov. 20, 1996. **B-T:** L-L. **HT:** 6-3. **WT:** 215. **Drafted:** Seattle, 2018 (9th round). **Signed by:** Dave Dangler.

TRACK RECORD: Skubal was excellent as a freshman at Seattle, where he posted a 7-4, 3.24 record. He had Tommy John surgery and redshirted for the 2017 season in what would have been his junior year, but was still drafted by Arizona in the 29th round that June. A year later, the Tigers took a flier on him in the ninth round. His control numbers suffered but quickly returned once he moved into pro ball. The lefthander reached Double-A in 2019 and tallied 17.43 strikeouts per nine innings over 15 starts with Erie and finished with 179 strikeouts overall. That mark—as well as his 13.13 strikeouts per nine innings on the season—was good for third-best in the minors.

SCOUTING REPORT: Skubal's fastball sits at 94-95 mph and tops out at 97 mph. He hits both sides of the plate and works it inside on hitters. He throws two different breaking pitches and lands them both in the strike zone. His curveball is in the upper 70s and flashes above-average but tends to get on the same plane as his slider. Skubal uses his potentially plus slider to work down and in on righthanders. The lefthander's changeup has plus movement but needs more consistency.

THE FUTURE: Skubal's frontline stuff and pitchability should help him reach the ceiling of a No. 2 starter in the big leagues.

SCOUTING GRADES: **Fastball:** 60 **Slider:** 60 **Curveball:** 55 **Changeup:** 55 **Control:** 50

Year	Age	Club (League)	Class	W	L	ERA	G	GS	SV	IP	H	HR	BB	SO	K/9	WHIP	AVG
2018	21	Tigers West (GCL)	R	1	0	0.00	2	1	0	3	2	0	1	5	15.0	1.00	.167
	21	Connecticut (NYP)	SS	0	0	0.75	4	0	1	12	8	0	2	17	12.8	0.83	.195
	21	West Michigan (MWL)	LoA	2	0	0.00	3	0	1	7	5	0	1	11	13.5	0.82	.200
2019	22	Lakeland (FSL)	HiA	4	5	2.58	15	15	0	80	62	5	19	97	10.9	1.01	.210
	22	Erie (EL)	AA	2	3	2.13	9	9	0	42	25	2	18	82	17.4	1.02	.168
Minor League Totals				9	8	2.11	33	25	2	145	102	7	41	212	13.2	0.99	.195

4 RILEY GREENE, OF

Born: Sept. 28, 2000. **B-T:** L-L. **HT:** 6-3. **WT:** 200. **Drafted:** HS—Oviedo, Fla., 2019 (1st round). **Signed by:** R.J. Burgess.

MIKE JANES/FOUR SEAM IMAGES

BA GRADE
60 Risk: Very High

TRACK RECORD: Greene finished his senior season at Hagerty HS with a .420 average and was a BA first-team High School All-American. Greene was the best prep hitter in the draft class and was taken by Detroit with the fifth overall pick. He signed for $6,180,700 then quickly zoomed to low Class A West Michigan after just 33 games in the Rookie-level Gulf Coast League and short-season Connecticut. He earned a spot as the No. 2 prospect in the New York-Penn League, behind only No. 1 overall pick Adley Rutschman.

SCOUTING REPORT: Greene features a smooth, strong lefthanded swing that gets on plane quickly and stays there throughout his swing. He shows good barrel control for a prep draftee and has displayed the ability to stay within the strike zone. Greene shows plus raw power that should translate into above-average in-game power as he gets more at-bats and continues to gain strength. While he has played center field during his brief time in the minors, executives believe he profiles best in right field. His speed is average at best and he lacks the acceleration and closing ability to track down balls as a center fielder. His arm is average, as well.

THE FUTURE: Even though his hit tool is advanced, Greene is still raw and far away from the big leagues. His overall skill set profiles best as a first-division regular in right field.

SCOUTING GRADES: **Hitting:** 60 **Power:** 55 **Running:** 50 **Fielding:** 50 **Arm:** 50

Year	Age	Club (League)	Class	AVG	G	AB	R	H	2B	3B	HR	RBI	BB	SO	SB	OBP	SLG
2019	18	Tigers West (GCL)	R	.351	9	37	9	13	3	0	2	8	5	12	0	.442	.595
	18	Connecticut (NYP)	SS	.295	24	88	12	26	3	1	1	7	11	25	1	.380	.386
	18	West Michigan (MWL)	LoA	.219	24	96	13	21	2	2	2	13	6	26	4	.278	.344
Minor League Totals				.271	57	221	34	60	8	3	5	28	22	63	5	.347	.403

5 ISAAC PAREDES, 3B/SS

Born: Feb. 18, 1999. **B-T:** R-R. **HT:** 5-11. **WT:** 225. **Signed:** Mexico, 2015. **Signed by:** Sergio Hernandez/Louie Eljaua (Cubs).

BA GRADE
55 Risk: High

TRACK RECORD: Paredes' bat is what made him a valuable pickup for Detroit when they acquired him in July of 2017 from the Cubs in a deal for catcher Alex Avila and lefthander Justin Wilson. After reaching Double-A as a 19-year old during the 2018 season, Paredes returned in 2019 and posted a career-high in homers (13) and hits (135) as the second youngest player in the league. He didn't chase much at all out of the zone and drew nearly as many walks (57) as strikeouts (61).

SCOUTING REPORT: Natural bat-to-ball skills and elite plate discipline are the highlights of Paredes' profile. He hits for some power and projects to be above-average in that department. He will have to move from shortstop to third base, where his hands will play, although executives wonder if his maxed out frame means he will ultimately end up at first base. Paredes has arm strength but needs to work on throwing mechanics and consistency of his throws. At best, his range projects as fringe-average. While he won't clog up the bases, he is a below-average runner.

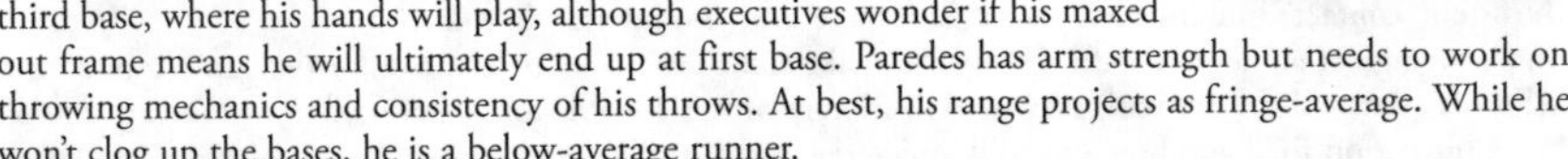

THE FUTURE: Paredes' ability to mash should get him to the big leagues. With developing power, it's conceivable that he will get the chance to be an everyday regular even with fringe-average defense.

SCOUTING GRADES: **Hitting:** 55 **Power:** 50 **Running:** 40 **Fielding:** 45 **Arm:** 50

Year	Age	Club (League)	Class	AVG	G	AB	R	H	2B	3B	HR	RBI	BB	SO	SB	OBP	SLG
2017	18	South Bend (MWL)	LoA	.264	92	337	49	89	25	0	7	49	29	54	2	.343	.401
	18	West Michigan (MWL)	LoA	.217	32	115	16	25	3	0	4	21	13	13	0	.323	.348
2018	19	Lakeland (FSL)	HiA	.259	84	301	50	78	19	2	12	48	32	54	1	.338	.455
	19	Erie (EL)	AA	.321	39	131	20	42	9	0	3	22	19	22	1	.406	.458
2019	20	Erie (EL)	AA	.282	127	478	63	135	23	1	13	66	57	61	5	.368	.416
Minor League Totals				.274	424	1541	221	422	93	6	40	232	163	226	13	.355	.420

6 ALEX FAEDO, RHP

BA GRADE
50 Risk: High

Born: Nov. 12, 1995. **B-T:** R-R. **HT:** 6-5. **WT:** 230. **Drafted:** Florida, 2017 (1st round). **Signed by:** R.J. Burgess.

TRACK RECORD: Faedo won the Most Outstanding Player honors during Florida's run to the 2017 College World Series win. The righthander endured surgeries on both knees before his junior season but bounced back and showed the stuff necessary to be selected 18th overall by Detroit. Questions arose when Faedo didn't show the fastball velocity he did as an amateur during his first full season as a pro. The velo returned in 2019, and his performance responded in kind. His strikeouts per nine innings jumped from 8.85 in 2018 with Double-A Erie to 10.46 in 2019 at the same level. Faedo ranked as the Eastern League's No. 12 prospect.

SCOUTING REPORT: Faedo's fastball tops out in the mid-90s but usually averages around 92 mph. Faedo's main secondary is his slider, which was one of the best in his draft class and generates swings and misses thanks to improved depth. His feel to throw it and miss bats lends it to project as an above-average pitch. Faedo's seldom-used changeup has plenty of natural run, but he needs to command the pitch better for it to project as better than fringe-average. Faedo also earns praise from Tigers executives for his aggressive nature on the mound.

THE FUTURE: His arsenal is effective but doesn't feature a wipeout pitch. His competitiveness and above-average control create a profile of a back-end starter.

SCOUTING GRADES: **Fastball:** 55 **Slider:** 55 **Changeup:** 45 **Control:** 55

Year	Age	Club (League)	Class	W	L	ERA	G	GS	SV	IP	H	HR	BB	SO	K/9	WHIP	AVG
2018	22	Lakeland (FSL)	HiA	2	4	3.10	12	12	0	61	49	3	13	51	7.5	1.02	.217
	22	Erie (EL)	AA	3	6	4.95	12	12	0	60	54	15	22	59	8.9	1.27	.239
2019	23	Erie (EL)	AA	6	7	3.90	22	22	0	115	104	17	25	134	10.5	1.12	.235
Minor League Totals				11	17	3.96	46	46	0	236	207	35	60	244	9.3	1.13	.232

7 DAZ CAMERON, OF

BA GRADE
45 Risk: Medium

Born: Jan. 15, 1997. **B-T:** B-R. **HT:** 6-2. **WT:** 195. **Drafted:** HS—McDonough, Ga., 2015 (1st round supplemental). **Signed by:** Gavin Dickey (Astros).

TRACK RECORD: The son of former all-star outfielder Mike Cameron was flipped at the 2017 deadline as part of the package sent to Houston to acquire ace Justin Verlander for their postseason run. Cameron hit a career-high 14 home runs in 2017 but saw his power nearly cut in half the following season when he hit eight homers between three levels. While his power returned in 2019 with 13 home runs, the outfielder posted a sub-.200 average in the months of April, July and August.

SCOUTING REPORT: Cameron receives high praise from Tigers' personnel for the way he handles himself both on and off the field. He is athletic and has bat speed, but his hit tool projects as future average at best. Cameron doesn't make consistent contact, but his raw power is average and should translate into fringe-average in-game power if he is able to make some adjustments. His feel for the game is plus, and helps his average defensive tools play up. His average arm is suitable for center field or a corner. Cameron isn't a burner on the bases but runs well underway in the outfield.

THE FUTURE: Cameron's contact woes are alarming and didn't get any better at Triple-A this season. His maturity and near-average tools across the board have the future of a second-division regular if his bat comes around at all.

SCOUTING GRADES: **Hitting:** 45 **Power:** 55 **Running:** 50 **Fielding:** 50 **Arm:** 50

Year	Age	Club (League)	Class	AVG	G	AB	R	H	2B	3B	HR	RBI	BB	SO	SB	OBP	SLG
2017	20	Quad Cities (MWL)	LoA	.271	120	446	79	121	29	8	14	73	45	108	32	.349	.466
	20	West Michigan (MWL)	LoA	.250	3	8	1	2	0	0	0	1	3	4	0	.455	.250
2018	21	Lakeland (FSL)	HiA	.259	58	216	35	56	9	3	3	20	25	69	10	.346	.370
	21	Erie (EL)	AA	.285	53	200	32	57	12	5	5	35	25	53	12	.367	.470
	21	Toledo (IL)	AAA	.211	15	57	8	12	4	1	0	6	2	15	2	.246	.316
2019	22	Toledo (IL)	AAA	.214	120	448	68	96	22	6	13	43	62	152	17	.330	.377
Minor League Totals				.247	460	1706	275	421	85	29	37	215	201	509	109	.338	.396

8 FRANKLIN PEREZ, RHP

BA GRADE 55 Risk: Extreme

Born: Dec. 6, 1997. **B-T:** R-R. **HT:** 6-3. **WT:** 197. **Signed:** Venezuela, 2014. **Signed by:** Oz Ocampo/Oscar Alvarado (Astros).

TRACK RECORD: Perez's arm strength helped facilitate a return to the mound after he trained temporarily as a third baseman at Carlos Guillen's academy in Venezuela as an amateur. The No. 14 international ranked prospect in 2014 inked for a $1 million bonus with the Astros before being flipped to Detroit as part of the package for righthander Justin Verlander in 2017. A cluster of injuries has slowed down Perez, who has made nine starts in his last two seasons combined. A knee injury in 2017 was followed by a lat strain and shoulder woes in 2018, and the shoulder woes returned in 2019 and derailed much of his season

SCOUTING REPORT: When healthy, Perez's stuff offers significant upside. His fastball has a high spin rate, tops out in the mid-90s and projects as plus. He shows particularly good feel for a low-to-mid 80s changeup with excellent armside run. The pitch misses plenty of bats with hard, late sinking action. Perez's curveball flashes above-average with good depth down in the strike zone. His slider has the potential to be a plus pitch as he's become more comfortable with it.

THE FUTURE: Perez needs a healthy 2020 to get back on track. His age, control and four-pitch mix point toward a future as a mid-rotation arm if he can stay healthy.

SCOUTING GRADES: **Fastball:** 55 **Slider:** 60 **Curveball:** 55 **Changeup:** 60 **Control:** 50

Year	Age	Club (League)	Class	W	L	ERA	G	GS	SV	IP	H	HR	BB	SO	K/9	WHIP	AVG
2017	19	Buies Creek (CAR)	HiA	4	2	2.98	12	10	2	54	38	4	16	53	8.8	0.99	.191
	19	Corpus Christi (TL)	AA	2	1	3.09	7	6	1	32	33	2	11	25	7.0	1.38	.266
2018	20	Tigers East (GCL)	R	0	1	4.50	3	3	0	8	3	0	0	5	5.6	0.38	.120
	20	Lakeland (FSL)	HiA	0	1	7.94	4	4	0	11	15	2	8	9	7.1	2.03	.341
2019	21	Lakeland (FSL)	HiA	0	0	2.35	2	2	0	8	7	1	5	6	7.0	1.57	.259
Minor League Totals				10	12	3.56	59	45	4	230	212	11	73	234	9.2	1.24	.243

9 WILLI CASTRO, SS

BA GRADE 45 Risk: Medium

Born: Apr. 24, 1997. **B-T:** B-R. **HT:** 6-1. **WT:** 205. **Signed:** Dominican Republic, 2013. **Signed by:** Ramon Pena/Felix Nivar (Indians).

TRACK RECORD: Castro was born in Puerto Rico but raised in the Dominican Republic and became the Indians' top non-Cuban international signee in 2013 when he signed for $825,000. Detroit acquired Castro in exchange for Leonys Martin and Kyle Dowdy at the 2018 trade deadline. He has been one of the youngest players at every level he's reached. Castro made it to the big leagues in August and started 28 games at shortstop for the Tigers.

SCOUTING REPORT: Castro features good bat-to-ball skills from both sides of the plate. His contact has helped him to maintain a similar OPS from both sides of the plate in the minors, but he has more natural power from the left side. His raw power is a tick above-average but won't translate to more than fringe-average power. He has the necessary range, speed and hands to stick at shortstop. Even with average tools, he showed inconsistency in his brief callup, botching routine plays yet making difficult ones look easy. He's an average runner.

THE FUTURE: His time in the big leagues wasn't pretty, but his ability to get on base and athletic actions could eventually help him reach his ceiling of a second-division regular or a utility option.

SCOUTING GRADES: **Hitting:** 50 **Power:** 45 **Running:** 50 **Fielding:** 50 **Arm:** 50

Year	Age	Club (League)	Class	AVG	G	AB	R	H	2B	3B	HR	RBI	BB	SO	SB	OBP	SLG
2017	20	Lynchburg (CAR)	HiA	.291	123	468	69	136	24	3	11	58	28	90	19	.337	.425
2018	21	Akron (EL)	AA	.245	97	371	55	91	20	2	5	39	28	84	13	.303	.350
	21	Erie (EL)	AA	.324	26	105	12	34	9	2	4	13	6	25	4	.366	.562
	21	Toledo (IL)	AAA	.286	5	21	0	6	0	0	0	2	0	5	1	.286	.286
2019	22	Toledo (IL)	AAA	.301	119	465	75	140	28	8	11	62	37	110	17	.366	.467
	22	Detroit (AL)	MAJ	.230	30	100	10	23	6	1	1	8	6	34	0	.284	.340
Major League Totals				.230	30	100	10	23	6	1	1	8	6	34	0	.284	.340
Minor League Totals				.273	606	2386	344	652	116	29	41	259	134	476	99	.320	.398

10 JAKE ROGERS, C

Born: Apr. 18, 1995. **B-T:** R-R. **HT:** 6-1. **WT:** 205. **Drafted:** Tulane, 2016 (3rd round). **Signed by:** Justin Cryer (Astros).

TRACK RECORD: Rogers was drafted by the Astros in 2016 and sent to Detroit as part of the package for Justin Verlander. While he has shown power, the defense-first backstop hasn't done much with the bat as a pro. His maturity behind home plate and ability to connect with his pitchers helped him earn his first big league callup on July 30.

SCOUTING REPORT: Rogers holds Tulane's record for caught-stealing percentage (56.8) and nabbed just under 50 percent of potential basestealers in the International League. His arm strength is plus but gets amplified by excellent footwork and transfer ability. Rogers receives praise for his work ethic and the way he studies the game. Utilizing a pronounced leg kick, Rogers' hit tool is considered well below-average. He tends to swing uphill and gets off plane too quickly to make consistent contact. His raw power is plus and should allow him to show average power in games. As with plenty of other catchers, Rogers has below-average speed but it doesn't hinder his athletic ability behind the dish.

THE FUTURE: If he can adjust to big league pitching, he could be a 20-homer backstop who brings elite defensive skills to the position. If not, his ceiling is that of a backup catcher.

SCOUTING GRADES: **Hitting:** 40 **Power:** 55 **Running:** 30 **Fielding:** 60 **Arm:** 70

Year	Age	Club (League)	Class	AVG	G	AB	R	H	2B	3B	HR	RBI	BB	SO	SB	OBP	SLG
2017	22	Quad Cities (MWL)	LoA	.255	27	102	17	26	7	1	6	15	9	28	1	.336	.520
	22	Buies Creek (CAR)	HiA	.265	83	313	43	83	18	3	12	55	44	72	13	.357	.457
	22	Lakeland (FSL)	HiA	.143	2	7	0	1	0	0	0	0	1	2	0	.250	.143
2018	23	Erie (EL)	AA	.219	99	352	57	77	15	1	17	56	41	112	7	.305	.412
2019	24	Erie (EL)	AA	.302	28	86	17	26	3	1	5	21	19	26	0	.429	.535
	24	Toledo (IL)	AAA	.223	48	166	29	37	10	1	9	31	18	53	0	.321	.458
	24	Detroit (AL)	MAJ	.125	35	112	11	14	3	0	4	8	13	51	0	.222	.259
Major League Totals				.125	35	112	11	14	3	0	4	8	13	51	0	.222	.259
Minor League Totals				.242	333	1185	181	287	63	9	52	194	153	336	22	.338	.442

11 JOEY WENTZ, LHP

BA GRADE
50 **Risk: High**

Born: Oct 6, 1997. **B-T:** L-L. **HT:** 6-5. **WT:** 210. **Drafted:** HS—Prairie Village, Kan., 2016 (1st round supplemental) **Signed by:** Nate Dion (Braves).

TRACK RECORD: Drafted 40th overall by the Braves in 2016, Wentz missed much of 2018 with an oblique injury but bounced back to pitch more than 125 innings for the second time in three seasons in 2019. The Tigers acquired him at the trade deadline as part of the package for closer Shane Greene. Wentz cut down on his walks after reporting to Double-A Erie and finished the year with a flourish.

SCOUTING REPORT: Wentz works comfortably in the low-90s with his fastball. While it doesn't have blazing velocity, his fastball plays up with plus vertical movement and works effectively at the top of the zone and above it. Wentz's breaking ball is a mid-to-upper 70s slider that has inconsistent shape and blends with the appearance of an overhand curveball. His best secondary offering is a changeup in the low-to-mid 80s that projects as a future above-average pitch. His control has improved but doesn't project as more than average.

THE FUTURE: Wentz has a frame built for innings and a three-pitch mix that allow him to project as a starter. He has a chance to pitch at the back of a rotation.

Year	Age	Club (League)	Class	W	L	ERA	G	GS	SV	IP	H	HR	BB	SO	K/9	WHIP	AVG
2017	19	Rome (SAL)	LoA	8	3	2.60	26	26	0	132	99	4	46	152	10.4	1.10	.209
2018	20	Florida (FSL)	HiA	3	4	2.28	16	16	0	67	49	3	24	53	7.1	1.09	.206
2019	21	Mississippi (SL)	AA	5	8	4.72	20	20	0	103	90	13	45	100	8.7	1.31	.239
	21	Erie (EL)	AA	2	0	2.10	5	5	0	26	20	3	4	37	13.0	0.94	.213
Minor League Totals				19	19	3.22	79	79	0	371	292	23	144	395	9.6	1.17	.219

12 PARKER MEADOWS, OF

Born: Nov. 2, 1999. **B-T:** L-R. **HT:** 6-5. **WT:** 205. **Drafted:** HS—Loganville, Ga., 2018 (2nd round) **Signed by:** Bryson Barber.

TRACK RECORD: The younger brother of Rays' outfielder Austin Meadows, Parker was a third-team All-American in 2018. The Tigers drafted him with the first pick of the second round, No. 44 overall, and gave him a $2.5 million signing bonus to forgo a Clemson commitment. Meadows spent his first

full season at low Class A West Michigan and struggled as one of the Midwest League's youngest players.
SCOUTING REPORT: Meadows features plus raw power but there is concern about his overall feel to hit. He has bat speed, but his long levers and lengthy swing cause him to miss hittable pitches. He has a power-over-hit offensive profile with a fringy ability to make contact. Defensively, he has near top-of-the-scale speed and good range in the outfield. Even with good foot speed, executives are split as to whether he has enough acceleration to stick in center field long term. Meadows has an average arm that should work in any spot in the outfield.
THE FUTURE: Meadows is one of the few Tigers prospects with extreme variance to his profile. If his hit tool significantly improves as he matures, he could reach his ceiling of an everyday, above-average center fielder. If he doesn't improve his routes and contact ability, he is ticketed for a fourth-outfielder role.

Year	Age	Club (League)	Class	AVG	G	AB	R	H	2B	3B	HR	RBI	BB	SO	SB	OBP	SLG
2018	18	Tigers West (GCL)	R	.284	22	74	16	21	2	1	4	8	8	25	3	.376	.500
	18	Connecticut (NYP)	SS	.316	6	19	4	6	1	0	0	2	2	6	0	.381	.368
2019	19	West Michigan (MWL)	LoA	.221	126	443	52	98	15	2	7	40	47	113	14	.296	.312
Minor League Totals				.233	154	536	72	125	18	3	11	50	57	144	17	.310	.340

13 ROBERTO CAMPOS, OF

BA GRADE
50 **Risk: Extreme**

Born: June 14, 2003. **B-T:** R-R. **HT:** 6-3. **WT:** 200. **Signed:** Cuba, 2019. **Signed by:** Aldo Perez/Oliver Arias.

TRACK RECORD: Campos received the largest bonus for any Cuban signee during the 2019 international period, signing with the Tigers for $2.85 million. He left Cuba to work out in the Dominican Republic with his brother Raul, a 2018 Marlins signee, and trained in San Pedro de Macoris. Considering his frame, Campos made the transition from the infield to the outfield before signing with Detroit.
SCOUTING REPORT: Campos has plus-plus raw power and can hit balls out to any part of the ballpark. He is athletic and strong, showing the ability to tap into his strength during his swing. For a 16-year old, he has an advanced ability to track pitches and stay within the strike zone. Campos does strike out some, but his approach should help him overcome that as he matures. He is learning to play the outfield and runs well under way, but doesn't have the type of range to profile in center field. His plus arm strength profiles best in right field long term.
THE FUTURE: While far away from the big leagues, Campos' strength and ability to hit for power make for a potential right field masher in the future.

Year	Age	Club (League)	Class	AVG	G	AB	R	H	2B	3B	HR	RBI	BB	SO	SB	OBP	SLG
2019	16	Did not play—Signed 2020 contract															

14 WENCEEL PEREZ, SS

BA GRADE
45 **Risk: High**

Born: Oct. 30, 1999. **B-T:** R-R. **HT:** 5-11. **WT:** 170. **Signed:** Dominican Republic, 2016. **Signed by:** Ramon Perez/Carlos Santana.

TRACK RECORD: Perez signed for $550,000 in July 2016 and made a strong first impression. He crushed the Dominican Summer League and advanced three levels all the way to low Class A West Michigan as an 18-year old, where he appeared in 16 games. He returned to the Midwest League in 2019 and made some adjustments, but still struggled overall.
SCOUTING REPORT: Perez projects as an average defender up the middle with some feel to play shortstop. He has good footwork with plus foot speed and range. His arm is average and profiles at the position. Perez's bat is much more in question. He has bat speed from both sides of the plate but projects to have well below-average power. He can barrel up pitches thanks to quick hands and shows glimpses of impact but lacks consistency with his hitting approach, resulting in low averages and on-base percentages. He is still working to get the most from his speed and was successful on just 21 of 34 stolen base attempts in 2019.
THE FUTURE: Perez's ceiling is a second-division regular, but his likelier role may be a sturdy utility infielder.

Year	Age	Club (League)	Class	AVG	G	AB	R	H	2B	3B	HR	RBI	BB	SO	SB	OBP	SLG
2017	17	Tigers (DSL)	R	.314	61	226	31	71	8	1	0	22	27	21	16	.387	.358
2018	18	Tigers West (GCL)	R	.383	20	81	20	31	7	0	2	14	12	14	2	.462	.543
	18	Connecticut (NYP)	SS	.244	21	82	8	20	2	0	1	8	5	12	7	.287	.305
	18	West Michigan (MWL)	LoA	.309	16	68	8	21	3	3	0	9	2	8	4	.324	.441
2019	19	West Michigan (MWL)	LoA	.233	124	459	59	107	16	6	3	30	45	87	21	.299	.314
Minor League Totals				.273	242	916	126	250	36	10	6	83	91	142	50	.337	.354

15 BEAU BURROWS, RHP

BA GRADE
45 Risk: High

Born: Sept. 18, 1996. **B-T:** R-R. **HT:** 6-2. **WT:** 215. **Drafted:** HS—Weatherford,Texas, 2015 (1st round). **Signed by:** Chris Wimmer.

TRACK RECORD: The 22nd overall pick in 2015, Burrows quickly made it to Double-A Erie but needed three years to advance to Triple-A. Burrows dealt with biceps tendonitis and shoulder inflammation in April that put him on the shelf for nearly two months, returned in June but went back on the injured list in August for a season-ending oblique injury.

SCOUTING REPORT: Burrows works with a four-pitch mix including a fastball that tops out at 96 mph. It can be straight at times, but it gets swings and misses at its best. Burrows doesn't have great control in part due to a high-front side in his delivery, which makes consistency tough to come by. He throws two breaking pitches, including a curveball in the low-70s that projects as above-average. His slider isn't particularly effective, but his changeup shows flashes of being above-average to give him a useful third pitch.

THE FUTURE: The Tigers added Burrows to the 40-man roster in the offseason. Without a true out pitch, Burrows is best suited as an occasional starter or bullpen arm, where his fastball should play up in short stints.

Year	Age	Club (League)	Class	W	L	ERA	G	GS	SV	IP	H	HR	BB	SO	K/9	WHIP	AVG
2017	20	Lakeland (FSL)	HiA	4	3	1.23	11	11	0	59	44	3	11	62	9.5	0.94	.221
	20	Erie (EL)	AA	6	4	4.72	15	15	0	76	79	5	33	75	8.8	1.47	.269
2018	21	Erie (EL)	AA	10	9	4.10	26	26	0	134	126	12	56	127	8.5	1.36	.251
2019	22	Lakeland (FSL)	HiA	0	0	0.00	1	1	0	4	1	0	2	5	11.3	0.75	.083
	22	Erie (EL)	AA	1	0	0.00	1	1	0	5	2	0	2	3	5.4	0.80	.125
	22	Toledo (IL)	AAA	2	6	5.51	15	15	0	65	68	12	32	61	8.4	1.53	.267
Minor League Totals				30	26	3.61	100	98	0	468	426	34	177	433	8.3	1.29	.245

16 KODY CLEMENS, 2B

BA GRADE
45 Risk: High

Born: May 15, 1996. **B-T:** L-R. **HT:** 6-1. **WT:** 170. **Drafted:** Texas, 2018 (3rd round). **Signed by:** Matt Lea.

TRACK RECORD: The youngest of Roger Clemens' sons, Clemens was drafted out of high school by the Astros but opted to head to college. He hit 24 homers as a junior at Texas, good for second in the NCAA, after a Tommy John surgery left him limited to designated hitter duties as a sophomore. After hitting 11 homers in the Florida State League in 2019, he was promoted to Double-A Erie in late August.

SCOUTING REPORT: Clemens is known for his competitive nature and feel for the game. He is trending as more of a power-over-hit type of player as some swing-and-miss issues have mounted, including striking out in nearly a quarter of his at-bats last season. Clemens has some developing power from the left side, although he struggles against lefthanded pitching. He runs the bases well and has average defensive tools at second base that are good enough for him to stick there.

THE FUTURE: Clemens will be ticketed for more at-bats against Eastern League pitching. His polish on the field should help him become a useful backup infielder or platoon bat if he doesn't handle lefties down the road.

Year	Age	Club (League)	Class	AVG	G	AB	R	H	2B	3B	HR	RBI	BB	SO	SB	OBP	SLG
2018	22	West Michigan (MWL)	LoA	.302	41	149	18	45	10	2	4	17	21	27	3	.387	.477
	22	Lakeland (FSL)	HiA	.238	11	42	6	10	2	0	1	3	2	12	1	.283	.357
2019	23	Dunedin (FSL)	HiA	.333	2	6	2	2	2	0	0	0	2	2	0	.500	.667
	23	Lakeland (FSL)	HiA	.238	115	411	43	98	24	7	11	59	45	101	11	.314	.411
	23	Erie (EL)	AA	.170	13	47	5	8	2	0	1	4	6	18	0	.278	.277
Minor League Totals				.248	180	649	72	161	38	9	17	83	74	158	15	.327	.413

17 BRYAN GARCIA, RHP

BA GRADE
45 Risk: High

Born: April 19, 1995. **B-T:** R-R. **HT:** 6-1. **WT:** 203. **Drafted:** Miami, 2016 (6th round). **Signed by:** Nick Avila.

TRACK RECORD: Garcia rocketed all the way to Triple-A in 2016 in his first full season, but Tommy John surgery derailed his ascent and wiped out his 2018 campaign. Garcia returned to the mound in 2019 and reached the majors after building up innings across three levels of the minors.

SCOUTING REPORT: Garcia receives high marks for his work ethic and mound presence. His fastball is a plus pitch that tops out in the upper-90s. With plus arm speed, Garcia throws an average slider that has good movement. He throws a changeup in the upper-80s that doesn't have much separation from his fastball, but he sells it well with similar arm speed. It grades as a future above-average offering.

THE FUTURE: Garcia should get plenty of outings in the majors for Detroit in 2020. His control is still suspect, but Garcia's aggressive mentality and two-pitch mix make for a quality late-inning reliever.

Year	Age	Club (League)	Class	W	L	ERA	G	GS	SV	IP	H	HR	BB	SO	K/9	WHIP	AVG
2017	22	West Michigan (MWL)	LoA	1	2	3.14	14	0	9	14	12	0	4	27	17.0	1.12	.218
	22	Lakeland (FSL)	HiA	2	0	0.00	7	0	0	9	7	0	2	15	15.6	1.04	.233
	22	Erie (EL)	AA	1	1	0.96	17	0	8	19	7	1	8	24	11.6	0.80	.115
	22	Toledo (IL)	AAA	1	0	4.05	14	0	0	13	10	1	8	12	8.1	1.35	.213
2018	23	Did not play—Injured															
2019	24	Lakeland (FSL)	HiA	0	0	4.50	4	0	1	4	3	1	2	6	13.5	1.25	.214
	24	Erie (EL)	AA	0	0	2.25	3	0	1	4	1	1	0	8	18.0	0.25	.077
	24	Toledo (IL)	AAA	3	0	2.97	31	0	0	33	26	4	14	33	8.9	1.20	.210
	24	Detroit (AL)	MAJ	0	0	12.15	7	0	0	7	9	1	5	7	9.5	2.10	.321
Major League Totals				0	0	12.15	7	0	0	6	9	1	5	7	9.5	2.10	.321
Minor League Totals				8	5	2.50	107	0	25	115	82	9	41	147	11.5	1.07	.197

18 ELVIN RODRIGUEZ, RHP

BA GRADE 45 Risk: High

Born: March 21, 1998. **B-T:** R-R. **HT:** 6-3. **WT:** 160. **Signed:** Dominican Republic, 2014. **Signed by:** Domingo Garcia/Alfredo Ulloa (Angels).

TRACK RECORD: Rodriguez signed with the Angels during the 2014 international signing period. His pitchability helped him to navigate his way to the low Class A Midwest League as a 19-year-old in 2017. That September, the Angels sent him to the Tigers as the player to be named later in the Justin Upton trade.

SCOUTING REPORT: Rodriguez tops out at 93 mph with his fastball, but there is room for growth with his projectable frame. His delivery is smooth and allows him to throw plenty of strikes. Rodriguez uses a changeup that flashes plus with horizontal movement and gets under the barrel consistently. He throws it in the low-80s and also features a mid-to-upper 70s curveball. His curveball is his decided third pitch. It has nice shape but tends to roll into the zone without much downward snap.

THE FUTURE: Rodriguez's delivery, projectable frame and three-pitch mix point towards a potential role as a back-of-the-rotation starter. He should see Double-A Erie in 2020.

Year	Age	Club (League)	Class	W	L	ERA	G	GS	SV	IP	H	HR	BB	SO	K/9	WHIP	AVG
2017	19	Orem (PIO)	R	5	1	2.50	11	11	0	54	45	5	11	49	8.2	1.04	.224
	19	Burlington (MWL)	LoA	0	2	4.50	3	3	0	14	20	2	3	12	7.7	1.64	.345
2018	20	West Michigan (MWL)	LoA	8	7	3.34	21	21	0	113	108	9	32	109	8.7	1.24	.255
2019	21	Lakeland (FSL)	HiA	11	9	3.77	24	23	0	134	113	12	44	112	7.5	1.17	.228
Minor League Totals				28	27	3.31	85	80	2	424	366	35	123	375	8.0	1.15	.233

19 ANTHONY CASTRO, RHP

BA GRADE 45 Risk: High

Born: April 13, 1995. **B-T:** R-R. **HT:** 6-2. **WT:** 180. **Signed:** Venezuela, 2011. **Signed by:** Oscar Garcia/Pedro Chavez.

TRACK RECORD: It's been a slow rise for Castro in the Tigers' system after signing as a 16-year-old in 2011. It took him four seasons to reach full-season ball and he missed 2015 after having Tommy John surgery. He finally got on track post-surgery and spent of all 2019 at Double-A Erie.

SCOUTING REPORT: Castro uses a 93-97 mph fastball that has excellent cutting action. The pitch flashes plus-plus and misses bats. His curveball has slurve-like shape with two-plane break. While it's a weapon for him, he doesn't land it in the strike zone with frequency. His third offering is a changeup that is often firm, registering in the low-80s. Castro's had difficulty with his control and command; making it questionable that he can stick in a rotation.

THE FUTURE: Castro's cut fastball and slurve fit best in the bullpen. His arm is intriguing and helps him profile as a seventh-inning type.

Year	Age	Club (League)	Class	W	L	ERA	G	GS	SV	IP	H	HR	BB	SO	K/9	WHIP	AVG
2017	22	West Michigan (MWL)	LoA	10	6	2.49	21	21	0	108	91	4	35	95	7.9	1.16	.226
2018	23	Erie (EL)	AA	0	0	8.10	3	3	0	10	8	1	12	4	3.6	2.00	.229
	23	Lakeland (FSL)	HiA	9	4	2.93	22	20	0	117	112	8	43	101	7.8	1.33	.253
2019	24	Erie (EL)	AA	5	3	4.40	27	18	1	102	75	9	65	116	10.2	1.37	.207
Minor League Totals				36	23	3.48	123	108	1	556	476	27	248	521	8.4	1.30	.233

20 NICK QUINTANA, 3B

BA GRADE 45 Risk: High

Born: Oct. 13, 1997. **B-T:** R-R. **HT:** 5-10. **WT:** 187. **Drafted:** Arizona, 2019 (2nd round). **Signed by:** Joey Lothrop.

TRACK RECORD: Quintana opted to attend Arizona after being selected in the 11th round by the Red Sox in the 2016 draft. He led the Wildcats in homers his sophomore season with 14 and led the Pac-12 Conference with 77 RBI his junior year before Detroit took him 47th overall. Quintana was challenged with his first assignment at low Class A West Michigan, where he hit .158/.228/.226. He wore down after a large workload in the summer and was sent down to short-season Connecticut in early August to finish the season.

SCOUTING REPORT: Quintana brings a power swing to the table with above-average raw power. He struggles to make consistent contact and is wholly dependent on home runs to provide offensive contributions. Quintana has plus bat speed but sometimes features a stiff swing, causing him difficulty making adjustments. Quintana has a quick first step at third base with good hands that profile at the position long term. He also has a plus arm with good natural carry.

THE FUTURE: After struggling his first season in pro ball, a return to low Class A West Michigan will be on the agenda for Quintana in 2020.

Year	Age	Club (League)	Class	AVG	G	AB	R	H	2B	3B	HR	RBI	BB	SO	SB	OBP	SLG
2019	21	West Michigan (MWL)	LoA	.158	41	146	14	23	5	1	1	13	13	51	3	.228	.226
	21	Connecticut (NYP)	SS	.256	25	86	12	22	7	0	1	4	12	31	1	.347	.372
Minor League Totals				.194	66	232	26	45	12	1	2	17	25	82	4	.273	.280

21 SERGIO ALCANTARA, SS

Born: July 10, 1996. **B-T:** B-R. **HT:** 5-9. **WT:** 170. **Signed:** Dominican Republic, 2012. **Signed by:** Junior Noboa (D-backs).

TRACK RECORD: Alcantara was part of the three-infielder package the Tigers acquired from the D-backs in exchange for J.D. Martinez at the 2017 trade deadline. Alcantara repeated Double-A in 2019 and walked more while striking out less, but he also made less quality contact and hit for less power.

SCOUTING REPORT: Alcantara is a plus defender at shortstop with easy actions in the field. He has soft hands and good footwork. A near top-of-the-scale arm allows him to project as an impact defender at the position. A thin, twitchy 5-foot-9, he has below-average power but has a chance to be an average hitter if he can start hitting the ball harder. Alcantara shows the ability to work the count and get on base via walk. He is an average runner and steals bases on occasion.

THE FUTURE: After struggling for two seasons at Double-A with the bat, it's hard to see a ceiling higher than that of a utility role for Alcantara. His athleticism and fielding would be impactful off the bench.

Year	Age	Club (League)	Class	AVG	G	AB	R	H	2B	3B	HR	RBI	BB	SO	SB	OBP	SLG
2017	20	Visalia (CAL)	HiA	.279	86	340	44	95	15	2	3	28	34	57	11	.344	.362
	20	Lakeland (FSL)	HiA	.230	35	126	18	29	4	1	0	7	14	23	4	.307	.278
2018	21	Erie (EL)	AA	.271	120	442	53	120	18	3	1	37	42	95	8	.335	.333
2019	22	Erie (EL)	AA	.247	102	324	46	80	10	0	2	27	48	71	7	.346	.296
Minor League Totals				.256	631	2266	317	580	86	14	9	187	289	447	57	.340	.318

22 DEREK HILL, OF

BA GRADE
40
Risk:
Medium

Born: Dec. 30, 1995. **B-T:** R-R. **HT:** 6-2. **WT:** 195. **Drafted:** HS—Elk Grove, Calif., 2014 (1st round). **Signed by:** Scott Cerny.

TRACK RECORD: The son of former player and now Dodgers scout Orsino Hill, Derek's pro career began with a myriad of injuries. The 2014 first rounder went through issues with his back and quadriceps his first two seasons before needing Tommy John surgery. The operation caused him to miss significant time in 2017. Hill reached Double-A for the first time in 2019 and managed to play a career-high 120 games, which allowed him to hit a career-high 14 home runs.

SCOUTING REPORT: Hill is extremely athletic and has started to show more thump with the bat with full health. He makes loud contact and shows growing power, but his hit tool projects to be fringe-average at best due to an inconsistent approach and strikeout issues. Defensively, Hill is one of the best outfielders in the minors. His plus-plus speed and a strong throwing arm help him grade as a future plus-plus defender in center field.

THE FUTURE: Hill's future role is that of a backup outfielder. His defensive ability can change a game, but his bat is most suitable off the bench.

Year	Age	Club (League)	Class	AVG	G	AB	R	H	2B	3B	HR	RBI	BB	SO	SB	OBP	SLG
2017	21	Tigers West (GCL)	R	.163	14	49	11	8	1	1	1	7	10	15	7	.300	.286
	21	West Michigan (MWL)	LoA	.285	35	144	28	41	8	6	1	21	16	38	12	.367	.444
	21	Lakeland (FSL)	HiA	.194	9	31	3	6	1	0	0	2	5	10	10	.324	.226
2018	22	Lakeland (FSL)	HiA	.239	106	343	45	82	9	3	4	33	33	109	35	.307	.318
2019	23	Erie (EL)	AA	.243	120	470	78	114	19	5	14	45	38	147	21	.311	.394
Minor League Totals				.243	477	1804	284	439	64	29	23	169	164	513	156	.313	.349

23 PAUL RICHAN, RHP

Born: March 26, 1997. **B-T:** R-R. **HT:** 6-2. **WT:** 200. **Drafted:** San Diego, 2018 (2nd round supplemental). **Signed by:** Alex Lontayo (Cubs).

TRACK RECORD: Richan pitched himself into the supplemental second round in 2018 with an excellent season at San Diego. The Cubs drafted him 78th overall and traded him one year later to the Tigers with righthander Alex Lange for Nicholas Castellanos. Richan made five starts with high Class A Lakeland after the trade and notched 29 strikeouts against just two walks in 30.2 innings.

SCOUTING REPORT: Richan's delivery is low-effort and repeatable despite a long arm action, allowing him to throw plenty of strikes. His fastball projects near average, topping out at 93 mph, and he commands it to both sides of the plate. Richan snaps off a slider in the low-80s that projects above-average with good tilt. It gets more swings and misses than his changeup, which projects average but currently lags behind his other pitches.

THE FUTURE: With future plus control, Richan profiles as a potential back-of-the-rotation starter. He should get his first taste of the upper minors in 2020.

Year	Age	Club (League)	Class	W	L	ERA	G	GS	SV	IP	H	HR	BB	SO	K/9	WHIP	AVG
2018	21	Eugene (NWL)	SS	0	2	2.12	10	9	0	30	19	2	5	31	9.4	0.81	.183
2019	22	Myrtle Beach (CAR)	HiA	10	5	3.97	17	17	0	93	96	10	18	86	8.3	1.23	.265
	22	Lakeland (FSL)	HiA	2	2	4.11	5	5	0	31	39	2	2	29	8.5	1.34	.317
Minor League Totals				12	9	3.64	32	31	0	153	154	14	25	146	8.6	1.17	.261

24 ADINSO REYES, SS

BA GRADE
50 Risk: Extreme

Born: Oct. 22, 2001. **B-T:** R-R. **HT:** 6-1. **WT:** 195. **Signed:** Dominican Republic, 2018. **Signed by:** Aldo Perez.

TRACK RECORD: The Tigers signed Reyes for $1.45 million during the 2018 international signing period because they were impressed with his bat and physical frame. He made his pro debut in the Dominican Summer League in 2019 and had instant success. Reyes' smacked seven home runs, all against righthanded pitchers, and hit .331.

SCOUTING REPORT: Reyes is strong and has loft in his swing that should develop into plus power as he matures. He shows the ability to use the whole field, although he is raw at tracking breaking pitches. His swing is long at times, which causes him to swing and miss, but he has the power potential to make up for it. He moves well in the field but his defense lags behind his bat. Reyes' arm should help him stick on the left side of the infield.

THE FUTURE: Reyes originally signed as a shortstop, but his physicality and strong arm would also be suitable at third base where his bat will play. He'll make the jump to the Rookie-level Gulf Coast League in 2020.

Year	Age	Club (League)	Class	AVG	G	AB	R	H	2B	3B	HR	RBI	BB	SO	SB	OBP	SLG
2019	17	Tigers1 (DSL)	R	.331	62	242	44	80	20	1	7	48	14	51	3	.379	.508
Minor League Totals				.331	62	242	44	80	20	1	7	48	14	51	3	.379	.508

25 JOSE DE LA CRUZ, OF

BA GRADE
50 Risk: Extreme

Born: Jan. 3, 2002. **B-T:** R-R. **HT:** 6-1. **WT:** 195. **Signed:** Dominican Republic, 2018. **Signed by:** Aldo Perez/Carlos Santana.

TRACK RECORD: The Tigers spent aggressively during the 2018 international signing period and gave their largest bonus to De La Cruz, who signed for $1.85 million. He hit the ground running in the Dominican Summer League in his first taste of pro ball. The outfielder showed off his power as well, ending up in a three-way tie for the DSL lead in home runs with 11.

SCOUTING REPORT: De La Cruz has a mature skill set for a 17-year-old outfielder and plays the game hard. He has plus bat speed and makes loud contact with a chance to grow into plus power. There are questions surrounding his hit tool, as he has shown swing-and-miss tendencies against both fastballs and breaking pitches. De La Cruz should be a true center fielder due to his plus speed and arm. Even if he fills out, De La Cruz's arm and defensive prowess will fit in right field.

THE FUTURE: If everything clicks, De La Cruz has the chance to be a power-hitting center fielder down the road. He'll move to the Rookie-level Gulf Coast League in 2020.

Year	Age	Club (League)	Class	AVG	G	AB	R	H	2B	3B	HR	RBI	BB	SO	SB	OBP	SLG
2019	17	Tigers2 (DSL)	R	.307	56	225	55	69	13	5	11	39	18	75	16	.375	.556
Minor League Totals				.307	56	225	55	69	13	5	11	39	18	75	16	.375	.556

26 WLADIMIR PINTO, RHP

BA GRADE
40 Risk: High

Born: Feb. 12, 1998. **B-T:** R-R. **HT:** 5-11. **WT:** 170. **Signed:** Venezuela, 2014. **Signed by:** Delvis Pacheco.

TRACK RECORD: After recovering from a lat strain that dismantled his 2017 season, Pinto reached the Florida State League the following season but struggled with his control. The flame-thrower started back in the FSL in 2019 and saw great success, working briefly as the closer for high Class A Lakeland before reaching the Eastern League, where he averaged 12.2 strikeouts per nine innings.

SCOUTING REPORT: Pinto's main weapon is a plus fastball that has good riding action up in the zone. It now tops out at 96 mph after reaching the upper 90s in the past. His main secondary is a curveball that tops out at 82 mph but doesn't project as plus. Pinto's command is inconsistent and leads to below-average control numbers, evidenced by his 5.1 walks per nine innings in 2019. He is purely a reliever who has never started as a pro.

THE FUTURE: Pinto's plus fastball gives him a chance to pitch in the sixth or seventh inning. He will try to harness his breaking ball in 2020 to reach that ceiling.

Year	Age	Club (League)	Class	W	L	ERA	G	GS	SV	IP	H	HR	BB	SO	K/9	WHIP	AVG
2017	19	Connecticut (NYP)	SS	1	0	0.00	8	0	4	10	2	0	0	18	16.8	0.21	.065
	19	West Michigan (MWL)	LoA	0	0	0.00	1	0	0	0	1	0	0	0	0.0	3.00	.500
2018	20	West Michigan (MWL)	LoA	1	0	0.00	11	0	7	17	4	0	12	30	16.2	0.96	.077
	20	Lakeland (FSL)	HiA	3	2	6.75	25	0	0	33	26	5	21	47	12.7	1.41	.213
2019	21	Lakeland (FSL)	HiA	3	3	2.14	23	0	6	34	16	2	20	49	13.1	1.07	.140
	21	Erie (EL)	AA	0	1	2.57	16	0	0	28	25	2	15	38	12.2	1.43	.238
Minor League Totals				11	8	3.12	116	0	19	173	101	9	106	238	12.4	1.20	.167

27 JOSE AZOCAR, OF

BA GRADE
40 Risk: High

Born: May 11, 1996. **B-T:** R-R. **HT:** 6-0. **WT:** 185. **Signed:** Venezuela, 2012. **Signed by:** Pedro Chavez.

TRACK RECORD: It's been a slow rise through the minors for Azocar, who reached the upper minors in 2019 for the first time after six seasons in the lower levels. The 2012 international signee hadn't shown much power up to this point, but went out and hit a career-high 10 homers at Double-A Erie after previously never hitting more than three in a season.

SCOUTING REPORT: Azocar's offensive ceiling isn't particularly high due to below-average power and a propensity to chase pitches. He hunts fastballs and does have some natural bat-to-ball ability. Azocar is a standout defensively in the outfield with a double-plus arm. It is strong and accurate, allowing him to throw behind runners at bases. He runs well under way and can play a plus right field and a playable center field.

THE FUTURE: With the ability to be an impact defender, Azocar may be limited to a backup outfielder who gets the occasional start. Without much power or on-base ability, it's tough to envision him progressing further than that.

Year	Age	Club (League)	Class	AVG	G	AB	R	H	2B	3B	HR	RBI	BB	SO	SB	OBP	SLG
2017	21	Lakeland (FSL)	HiA	.220	119	431	38	95	10	6	3	37	14	122	12	.246	.292
2018	22	West Michigan (MWL)	LoA	.317	27	104	19	33	3	6	1	16	5	21	6	.355	.490
	22	Lakeland (FSL)	HiA	.290	82	300	34	87	14	3	1	34	9	64	5	.308	.367
2019	23	Erie (EL)	AA	.286	129	504	65	144	21	3	10	58	21	132	10	.317	.399
Minor League Totals				.278	671	2512	301	698	88	39	16	277	96	587	71	.306	.363

28 KYLE FUNKHOUSER, RHP

Born: March 16, 1994. **B-T:** R-R. **HT:** 6-2. **WT:** 230. **Drafted:** Louisville, 2016 (4th round). **Signed by:** Harold Zonder.

TRACK RECORD: The Dodgers drafted Funkhouser with one of their two first round picks in 2015, but the righthander opted to return to Louisville for his senior season. The move backfired as he fell to the fourth round of the 2017 draft to the Tigers. After breaking his foot in 2018 and dealing with shoulder soreness in May, Funkhouser struggled badly at Triple-A Toledo in 2019. He logged an 8.53 ERA and walked 54 batters across 63.1 innings in the International League.

SCOUTING REPORT: Funkhouser relies on his excellent arm strength. He throws his fastball in the 92-96 mph range and can manipulate it to throw a sinker, which is a touch below the velocity of his four-seam fastball. Funkhouser can spin a slider in the low-to-mid 80s that grades as future average but doesn't generate many swings and misses. His third offering is a changeup in the upper-80s that doesn't present much variance off his heater. Funkhouser's control is well below average, with many unsure he'll throw enough strikes to even be a reliable option in relief.

THE FUTURE: Funkhouser's control may push him out of the rotation and into the bullpen soon enough. His pitch mix and arm strength still have upside for the rebuilding Tigers.

Year	Age	Club (League)	Class	W	L	ERA	G	GS	SV	IP	H	HR	BB	SO	K/9	WHIP	AVG
2017	23	West Michigan (MWL)	LoA	4	1	3.16	7	7	0	31	30	3	13	49	14.1	1.37	.254
	23	Lakeland (FSL)	HiA	1	1	1.72	5	5	0	31	23	1	6	34	9.8	0.93	.205
2018	24	Erie (EL)	AA	4	5	3.74	17	17	0	89	88	10	39	89	9.0	1.43	.266
	24	Toledo (IL)	AAA	0	2	6.23	2	2	0	9	8	0	10	7	7.3	2.08	.258
2019	25	Lakeland (FSL)	HiA	0	0	0.00	1	1	0	5	2	0	1	4	7.2	0.60	.118
	25	Erie (EL)	AA	3	1	1.90	4	4	0	24	16	2	3	29	11.0	0.80	.195
	25	Toledo (IL)	AAA	3	7	8.53	18	18	0	63	79	3	54	65	9.2	2.10	.310
Minor League Totals				15	19	4.23	67	67	0	289	280	19	134	311	9.7	1.43	.258

29 ALEX LANGE, RHP

BA GRADE 40 **Risk:** High

Born: Oct. 2, 1995. **B-T:** R-R. **HT:** 6-3. **WT:** 197. **Drafted:** Louisiana State, 2017 (1st round). **Signed by:** Kevin Ellis (Cubs).

TRACK RECORD: Lange compiled a 30-9, 2.91 record across three seasons at Louisiana State before being selected by the Cubs 30th overall in the 2017 draft. Lange pitched well in the Carolina League in 2018, but opened the season there once again this season and his ERA soared to 7.36 across 11 starts. He fared much better for Double-A Tennessee before being traded to the Tigers as part of the package for outfielder Nicholas Castellanos at the trade deadline. Lange was strictly used as a reliever after the trade for the first time in pro ball.

SCOUTING REPORT: Control has been an issue for Lange with his high-effort delivery and head whack. He tops out at 93 mph with his fastball, but sits 90-92 most outings. It doesn't have much life and projects as average at best. He throws a power curveball with hard downward drop and a slider with short break on it, both of which are effective but not plus. His changeup is firm but flashes above-average at times with sinking action.

THE FUTURE: Even with a four-pitch mix, Lange's delivery and fringe command make the bullpen his long-term spot. He'll see Triple-A in 2020.

Year	Age	Club (League)	Class	W	L	ERA	G	GS	SV	IP	H	HR	BB	SO	K/9	WHIP	AVG
2017	21	Eugene (NWL)	SS	0	1	4.82	4	4	0	9	9	0	3	13	12.5	1.29	.243
2018	22	Myrtle Beach (CAR)	HiA	6	8	3.74	23	23	0	120	104	6	38	101	7.6	1.18	.234
2019	23	Myrtle Beach (CAR)	HiA	1	9	7.36	11	11	0	48	58	4	26	51	9.6	1.76	.290
	23	Tennessee (SL)	AA	2	3	3.92	7	7	0	39	36	4	19	28	6.5	1.41	.252
	23	Erie (EL)	AA	2	1	3.45	9	0	0	16	13	0	8	15	8.6	1.34	.245
Minor League Totals				11	22	4.54	54	45	0	232	220	14	94	208	8.1	1.35	.251

30 WILKEL HERNANDEZ, RHP

BA GRADE 40 **Risk:** High

Born: April 13, 1999. **B-T:** R-R. **HT:** 6-3. **WT:** 180. **Signed:** Venezuela, 2015. **Signed by:** Marlo Zerpa/Marlon Urdaneta (Angels).

TRACK RECORD: The Angels signed Hernandez in 2015 on the promise of his projectable frame and mid-80s fastball. After spending 2017 in Rookie ball, the Angels dealt him to the Tigers for Ian Kinsler at the Winter Meetings. Hernandez made his full-season debut at low Class A West Michigan in 2019. He logged over 100 innings and posted a career-best 2.3 walks per nine innings.

SCOUTING REPORT: Hernandez attacks hitters with a fastball that now sits 92-93 mph and tops out at 95. He still has room to add strength and grow into more velocity, allowing it to project as a potential plus pitch as he fills out. His curveball needs refinement but shows signs of being an average pitch down the road. Hernandez also uses his changeup a fair amount, but like his breaking ball, it projects near average at best. While his control has been suspect in the past, it has started to trend positively and could end up being near above-average.

THE FUTURE: Executives are split as to whether Hernandez's stuff would hold up in the rotation. He will try to show it can at high Class A Lakeland in 2020.

Year	Age	Club (League)	Class	W	L	ERA	G	GS	SV	IP	H	HR	BB	SO	K/9	WHIP	AVG
2017	18	Angels (AZL)	R	3	1	2.61	11	7	0	41	23	1	20	42	9.1	1.04	.161
	18	Orem (PIO)	R	1	0	3.00	1	0	0	3	2	0	2	2	6.0	1.33	.222
2018	19	Connecticut (NYP)	SS	0	2	7.94	3	3	0	6	6	2	4	11	17.5	1.76	.250
	19	West Michigan (MWL)	LoA	2	5	4.71	10	10	0	42	40	4	16	34	7.3	1.33	.250
2019	20	West Michigan (MWL)	LoA	9	7	3.73	21	21	0	101	97	5	26	90	8.0	1.21	.246
Minor League Totals				17	15	3.63	50	45	0	208	180	12	74	193	8.3	1.22	.230

Houston Astros

BY J.J. COOPER

In the end, losing the World Series ended up being only the third-worst aspect of the Astros' 2019 season.

Losing a World Series is something heartbreaking for fans, but it's the culmination of a strong season.

But when the 2019 World Series is remembered, and when the story of the Astros of the late 2010s is recounted, what will assuredly be mentioned quickly is everything that happened around that Series loss to the Nationals.

During the World Series, the Astros fired assistant general manager Brandon Taubman, the culmination of a week-long public relations disaster where the team initially attacked reporting that had described Taubman's disparaging remarks to female sports writers. Eventually, the team had to acknowledge that the reporting was accurate and fired Taubman.

Taubman's actions led MLB to conduct an investigation, which quickly grew to also include a deep dive into the Astros' use of technology to steal signs during the 2017 season as well as efforts to determine if they did so in any other year as well. That investigation hovered over the club during the first half of the offseason.

In addition to the MLB investigation, the Astros faced several other challenges as the 2020s began. The farm system has thinned because of graduations and trades for major league assets. Houston continues to have a significant number of fast arms who can spin breaking balls in the minors, but the position player depth is limited, and many of the club's best pitching prospects carry reliever risk.

That same skepticism now follows the Astros when it comes to trades. Scouts for a significant number of other teams say they are hesitant to recommend acquiring Astros pitching prospects, because they believe the Astros' emphasis on velocity and high spin rates has not paid off in MLB success. They note that many of the Astros' pitching prospects dealt in trades have struggled to meet expectations with their new teams.

That skepticism didn't prevent the Astros from swinging a deal to acquire Zack Greinke, a move that helped get the team to the World Series. But the Astros are going to need to find some less-expensive arms to bolster a rotation that is now quite expensive and is getting old.

The Astros have also endured quite the brain drain in recent years. GM Jeff Luhnow has always emphasized a lean, cost-controlled front office, which has meant that the Astros have fewer directors and special assistants to the GM than other teams—most teams with the Astros' recent success would have a president, a GM and a large number of special assistants.

In recent years, Luhnow has lost David Stearns and Mike Elias to GM jobs elsewhere, but a number of other high-level officials like Sig Mejdal, Mike Fast, Eve Rosenbaum and Oz Ocampo have also left in recent years. In some cases, they left without having their next jobs lined up.

The Astros' approach has always been to grow their own executives, but the number of recent departures means some people will have to quickly grow to fill significant roles.

BOB LEVEY/GETTY IMAGES

AL Rookie of the Year Yordan Alvarez hit 27 home runs and drove in 78 runs in 87 games.

PROJECTED 2023 LINEUP

Position	Player	Age
Catcher	Korey Lee (7)	24
First Base	Abraham Toro (6)	26
Second Base	Jose Altuve	33
Third Base	Alex Bregman	29
Shortstop	Carlos Correa	28
Left Field	Kyle Tucker	26
Center Field	Myles Straw	28
Right Field	George Springer	33
Designated Hitter	Yordan Alvarez	26
No. 1 Starter	Lance McCullers Jr.	29
No. 2 Starter	Forrest Whitley (1)	25
No. 3 Starter	Jose Urquidy (2)	28
No. 4 Starter	Cristian Javier (8)	26
No. 5 Starter	Hunter Brown (9)	24
Closer	Bryan Abreu (5)	26

DEPTH CHART

HOUSTON ASTROS

TOP 2020 ROOKIE: Jose Urquidy, RHP. Forrest Whitley is more talented, but Urquidy is ready to help right now.

BREAKOUT PROSPECT: Blair Henley, RHP. Henley took to many of the Astros' pitching development program suggestions. With his ability to spin a breaking ball and improving velocity, he could be the next rising pitcher.

SLEEPER: Yohander Martinez, SS. Martinez was one of the more impressive bats in the Dominican Summer League in 2019. He's a smart, heady player with the tools to post high on-base percentages.

SOURCE OF TOP 30 TALENT			
Homegrown	**30**	**Acquired**	**0**
College	13	Trade	0
High School	2	Rule 5 draft	0
Junior College	2	Independent leagues	0
Nondrafted free agent	0	Free agents/waivers	0
International	13		

LF
Colin Barber (16)
Bryan de la Cruz
Chas McCormick
Marty Costes

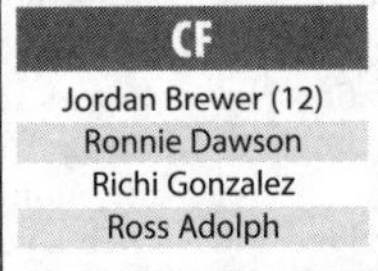

CF
Jordan Brewer (12)
Ronnie Dawson
Richi Gonzalez
Ross Adolph

RF
Chandler Taylor (30)

3B
Abraham Toro (6)
Grae Kessinger (10)
Joe Perez

SS
Jeremy Pena (3)
Freudis Nova (4)
Dauri Lorenzo (29)
Yohander Martinez
Miguelangel Sierra
Deury Carrasco

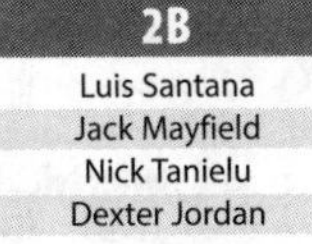

2B
Luis Santana
Jack Mayfield
Nick Tanielu
Dexter Jordan

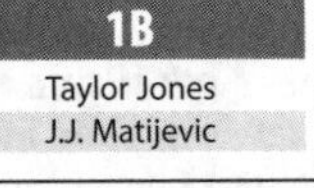

1B
Taylor Jones
J.J. Matijevic

C
Korey Lee (7)
Garrett Stubbs (24)
Chuckie Robinson
Juan Santander
Fernando Caldera
Colton Shaver

LHP

LHSP	LHRP
Kent Emmanuel	Parker Mushinski
Ryan Hartman	

RHP

RHSP	RHRP
Forrest Whitley (1)	Bryan Abreu (5)
Jose Urquidy (2)	Jojanse Torres (17)
Cristian Javier (8)	Jose A. Rivera (18)
Hunter Brown (9)	Shawn Dubin (19)
Tyler Ivey (11)	Austin Hansen (27)
Luis Garcia (13)	Enoli Paredes (28)
Jairo Solis (14)	Carlos Sanabria
Brandon Bielak (15)	Dean Deetz
Jairo Lopez (20)	Manny Ramirez
Brett Conine (21)	Andre Scrubb
Blair Henley (22)	Willy Collado
Nivaldo Rodriguez (25)	
Peter Solomon (25)	
Rogelio Armenteros (26)	
Elvis Garcia	
Jayson Schroeder	

DRAFT ANALYSIS

2019

BEST PURE HITTER: OF Colin Barber (4) was the Astros' fourth pick, but he received the second-largest signing bonus in the organization's draft class. He has an advanced approach for a high school draftee with solid bat-to-ball skills and developing strength and power. OF Jordan Brewer (3) was one of the best hitters in the Big Ten conference last year, learning how to better use his lower half in his swing while at Michigan.

BEST POWER HITTER: C Korey Lee (1) didn't have a massive pro debut, but he showed plenty of power last spring, hitting 15 home runs for California (matching the home runs hit by No. 3 overall pick and college teammate Andrew Vaughn). Lee posts excellent exit velocities, but the Astros are working to help him generate more loft with his swing.

FASTEST RUNNER: OF Matthew Barefoot (6) has above-average speed and stole 25 bases in 31 attempts as a junior at Campbell. OF James Nix (35) runs well and stole 24 bases for Central Florida JC.

BEST DEFENSIVE PLAYER: OF Preston Pavlica (24) didn't hit in his pro debut, but he continued to make highlight-reel catches in center field, showing range and an ability to make tough, diving catches.

BEST ATHLETE: Brewer was planning on walking on to play football at Michigan before he injured his shoulder on the football field during his senior year of high school. He decided instead to head to junior college to play baseball at Lincoln Trail (Ill.) JC. Brewer continues to have the strength and speed that helped him as a wide receiver.

BEST FASTBALL: RHP Hunter Brown (5) touched 99 mph and sat at 94-97 mph this summer. His fastball has plenty of backspin and can generate swings and misses up in the strike zone.

BEST SECONDARY PITCH: RHP Blair Henley (7) relied on his plus curveball heavily at Texas, and he'll continue to do so as a pro. It's a 3,200-3,300 rpm pitch, putting it in the upper echelons of curveball spin rates.

BEST PRO DEBUT: Henley went 1-1, 1.60 with a 46-to-8 strikeout-to-walk ratio, largely with short-season Tri-City. He was held to 50 or 60 pitches per outing after a busy spring at Texas, but he was often able to get through three or four innings in that pitch restriction.

MOST INTRIGUING BACKGROUND: SS Grae Kessinger's (2) grandfather, Don Kessinger, was a six-time All-Star and won two Gold Gloves. C C.J. Stubbs' (10) older brother, Garrett Stubbs, is a catcher who made his major league debut with the Astros this year.

CLOSEST TO THE MAJORS: Kessinger's ability to play multiple infield positions, solid bat-to-ball skills and knack for leadership should help him move quickly.

BEST LATE-ROUND PICK: RHP Cole McDonald (15) doesn't have a plus pitch and he has average velocity, but his feel for pitching and his ability to locate give it a chance to all work. And the Astros have had a knack of helping pitchers add velocity and sharpen their breaking balls.

THE ONE WHO GOT AWAY: The Astros made an attempt to sign RHP Oscar Carvajal (32), but the redshirt sophomore decided to return to Fresno State. His split-changeup is an impressive pitch.

—J.J. COOPER

TOP DRAFT PICKS OF THE DECADE

Year	Player, Pos.	2019 Org
2010	Mike Foltynewicz, RHP	Braves
2011	George Springer, OF	Astros
2012	Carlos Correa, SS	Astros
2013	Mark Appel, RHP	Did not play
2014	*Brady Aiken, LHP	Indians
2015	Alex Bregman, SS	Astros
2016	Forrest Whitley, RHP	Astros
2017	J.B. Bukauskas, RHP	D-backs
2018	Seth Beer, OF	D-backs
2019	Korey Lee, C	Astros

* Did not sign

2018

OF Seth Beer (1) and SS Jeremy Peña (3) got off to solid starts as pros and both were advanced enough to go to the Arizona Fall League. Beer was traded to the D-backs as a part of the deal for Zack Greinke.

GRADE: C

2017

Hard-throwing RHPs J.B. Bukauskas (1) and Corbin Martin (2) and 2B Josh Rojas (26) were traded to the D-backs as apart of the deal for Greinke. Martin and Rojas have both already reached the big leagues.

GRADE: B

2016

Limited by injury in 2019, RHP Forrest Whitely (1) still offers big upside and bounced back in the Arizona Fall League. C Jake Rogers (3), with Detroit, and 3B Abraham Toro (5) made their MLB debuts.

GRADE: A

1 FORREST WHITLEY, RHP

Born: Sept. 15, 1997. **B-T:** R-R. **HT:** 6-7. **WT:** 207.
Drafted: HS—San Antonio, 2016 (1st round).
Signed by: Noel Gonzales-Luna.

TRACK RECORD: Whitley was supposed to be a part of the Astros' rotation by now. He reached Double-A in 2017 and seemed poised to help Houston's playoff run in 2018. Instead, his season was derailed by a 50-game drug suspension. Whitley's 2019 season proved to be even rockier. He struggled with command in eight outings with Triple-A Round Rock and was eventually shut down with shoulder fatigue, though the break was a mental respite as much as anything. Sent to the Gulf Coast and Carolina leagues to rehab, he continued to struggle with big innings upon his assignment to Double-A Corpus Christi. He pitched well in the Arizona Fall League.

SCOUTING REPORT: Whitley's command backed up by a grade or even two in 2019. He missed badly high and low throughout the season. He would often struggle to finish his delivery, leaving his fastball up far out of the zone, and then he would bounce the next pitch trying to adjust. When Whitley was in the zone, he often caught too much of it. He allowed too many no-doubt home runs. After Whitley's early-season struggles, the Astros junked his windup and had him pitch exclusively from the stretch. He also moved from the third base side of the rubber to the first base side. The Astros had already worked to reduce Whitley's shoulder tilt in his delivery, which lowered his release point. If the alteration works, it will help Whitley stay behind the ball more and get more ride at the top of the zone—though in 2019 it did not work. When he is on, Whitley still shows five plus pitches. His 92-97 mph fastball touched 99. His low-90s cutter darts away from opponents' barrels. His 85-87 mph slider has power and depth and his 12-to-6 curveball does too, though it tends to get loopy and slow. His plus changeup wasn't as dominating in 2019 as it was in previous years, but it still had late drop at times. Whitley's fastball, changeup and slider all could get to plus-plus, but it will require he significantly improve his below-average control and command.

THE FUTURE: Whitley's 2019 season can only be described as disastrous. His stuff is still that of a front-of-the-rotation ace, but he will need to find at least fringe control to reach his upside.

JOSHUA SARNER/ICON SPORTSWIRE VIA GETTY IMAGES

BA GRADE 65 **Risk:** Very High

SCOUTING GRADES **Fastball:** 60. **CB:** 60. **SL:** 60. **CHG:** 60. **Cut:** 60. **Control:** 40.

Projected future grades on 20-80 scouting scale.

TOP PROSPECTS OF THE DECADE

Year	Player, Pos.	2019 Org
2010	Jason Castro, C	Twins
2011	Jordan Lyles, RHP	Brewers
2012	Jon Singleton, 1B/OF	Did not play
2013	Carlos Correa, SS	Astros
2014	Carlos Correa, SS	Astros
2015	Carlos Correa, SS	Astros
2016	A.J. Reed, 1B	White Sox
2017	Francis Martes, RHP	Astros
2018	Forrest Whitley, RHP	Astros
2019	Forrest Whitley, RHP	Astros

BEST TOOLS

Best Pure Hitter	Abraham Toro
Best Power	Chandler Taylor
Fastest Baserunner	Jordan Brewer
Best Strike-Zone Discipline	Jeremy Peña
Best Athlete	Jordan Brewer
Best Fastball	Jose Rivera
Best Curveball	Bryan Abreu
Best Slider	Enoli Paredes
Best Changeup	Forrest Whitely
Best Control	Jose Urquidy
Best Defensive Catcher	Chuckie Robinson
Best Defensive Infielder	Jeremy Peña
Best Infield Arm	Freudis Nova
Best Defensive Outfielder	Ronnie Dawson
Best Outfield Arm	Chandler Taylor.

Year	Age	Club (League)	Class	W	L	ERA	G	GS	SV	IP	H	HR	BB	SO	K/9	WHIP	AVG
2017	19	Quad Cities (MWL)	LoA	2	3	2.91	12	10	0	46	42	2	21	67	13.0	1.36	.247
	19	Buies Creek (CAR)	HiA	3	1	3.16	7	6	0	31	28	2	9	50	14.4	1.18	.237
	19	Corpus Christi (TL)	AA	0	0	1.84	4	2	0	15	8	1	4	26	16.0	0.82	.157
2018	20	Corpus Christi (TL)	AA	0	2	3.76	8	8	0	26	15	2	11	34	11.6	0.99	.160
2019	21	Round Rock (PCL)	AAA	0	3	12.21	8	5	0	24	35	9	15	29	10.7	2.05	.343
	21	Astros (GCL)	R	0	2	8.31	2	2	0	4	2	0	9	10	20.8	2.54	.125
	21	Fayetteville (CAR)	HiA	1	0	2.16	2	2	0	8	4	0	1	11	11.9	0.60	.138
	21	Corpus Christi (TL)	AA	2	2	5.56	6	6	0	23	18	2	19	36	14.3	1.63	.222
Minor League Totals				9	15	4.71	57	47	0	197	171	18	95	289	13.2	1.35	.232

2 JOSE URQUIDY, RHP

MARY DECICCO/MLB PHOTOS VIA GETTY IMAGES

BA GRADE
45 **Risk: Medium**

Born: May 1, 1995. **B-T:** R-R. **Ht.:** 6-0. **Wt.:** 212. **Signed:** Mexico, 2015. **Signed by:** Oz Ocampo/Carlos Alfonso/Raul Lopez.

TRACK RECORD: When other Astros' prospects proved unready to break into the rotation, Urquidy stepped in and even picked up a win in Game 4 of the World Series after throwing five scoreless innings. Urquidy, who was known as Jose Luis Hernandez until the 2019 season, had Tommy John surgery in 2017 and came into 2019 having not pitched above Class A.

SCOUTING REPORT: The Astros have a large number of pitching prospects who can throw harder than Urquidy and several who can spin a ball better. But his consistent ability to locate with plus control and command makes him quite effective. Urquidy has touched as high as 96-97 mph, but his average fastball generally sits 92-94. He throws his plus 82-84 mph changeup with excellent conviction. He's happy to double or triple-up with it as he believes in its deception and late-drop. He also has an average slider and a fringe-average curve. His slider plays up because it lives on the glove-side low-and-away corner.

THE FUTURE: Urquidy doesn't wow and his body is already mature, but he showed he can deceive and keep hitters uncomfortable. He's a solid back-end starter thanks to his control.

SCOUTING GRADES: **Fastball:** 50 **Slider:** 50 **Curveball:** 45 **Changeup:** 60 **Control:** 60

Year	Age	Club (League)	Class	W	L	ERA	G	GS	SV	IP	H	HR	BB	SO	K/9	WHIP	AVG
2017	22	Did not play—Injured															
2018	23	Tri-City (NYP)	SS	0	0	2.38	4	4	0	11	15	0	2	10	7.9	1.50	.313
	23	Buies Creek (CAR)	HiA	2	2	2.35	9	7	0	46	40	2	8	38	7.4	1.04	.234
2019	24	Corpus Christi (TL)	AA	2	2	4.09	7	6	0	33	28	2	5	40	10.9	1.00	.222
	24	Round Rock (PCL)	AAA	5	3	4.63	13	12	0	70	67	15	16	94	12.1	1.19	.245
	24	Houston (AL)	MAJ	2	1	3.95	9	7	0	41	38	6	7	40	8.8	1.10	.241
Major League Totals				2	1	3.95	9	7	0	41	38	6	7	40	8.8	1.10	.241
Minor League Totals				17	13	3.37	68	55	2	323	309	29	64	351	9.8	1.15	.248

3 JEREMY PEÑA, SS

BA GRADE
50 **Risk: High**

Born: Sept. 22, 1997. **B-T:** R-R. **HT:** 6-0. **WT:** 179. **Drafted:** Maine, 2018 (3rd round). **Signed by:** Bobby St. Pierre.

TRACK RECORD: The son of Geronimo Peña, Jeremy was a defensive whiz at Maine. Since signing with the Astros, Pena has remade his upper body and is now more physical, but he's done so without losing any of his athleticism.

SCOUTING REPORT: Peña has the range, hands, actions to make all the plays at shortstop. He has the reactions to slide to third if needed as well and his plus arm plays well at either spot. Multiple scouts gave him plus-plus defensive grades. He's also an above-average runner. Scouts have much more trouble getting excited about his below-average hit tool. Pena has added a significant amount of muscle and good weight and developed gap power with the ability to run into 10-12 home runs a year. But his swing is now geared almost exclusively to pulling balls. He does have a solid understanding of the strike zone, so he can work pitchers to get to situations in his zone and he'll add enough walks to post solid on-base percentages.

THE FUTURE: Pena's defense is good enough to allow him to be a productive player even if he hits .230, and he could be a long-time regular if he can hit .250-.260. He's ready for Double-A Corpus Christi.

SCOUTING GRADES: **Hitting:** 40 **Power:** 40 **Running:** 55 **Fielding:** 70 **Arm:** 60

Year	Age	Club (League)	Class	AVG	G	AB	R	H	2B	3B	HR	RBI	BB	SO	SB	OBP	SLG
2018	20	Tri-City (NYP)	SS	.250	36	136	22	34	5	0	1	10	18	19	3	.340	.309
2019	21	Quad Cities (MWL)	LoA	.293	66	242	44	71	8	4	5	41	35	57	17	.389	.421
	21	Fayetteville (CAR)	HiA	.317	43	167	28	53	13	3	2	13	12	33	3	.378	.467
Minor League Totals				.290	145	545	94	158	26	7	8	64	65	109	23	.374	.407

4 FREUDIS NOVA, SS

COURTESY OF QC RIVER BANDITS

Born: Jan. 12, 2000. **B-T:** R-R. **HT:** 6-1. **WT:** 180. **Signed:** Dominican Republic, 2016. **Signed by:** Oz Ocampo/Roman Ocumarez/Jose Lima.

TRACK RECORD: Nova was supposed to be the key player in the Marlins 2016 international class, but a positive drug test meant he instead signed with the Astros for $1.2 million, less than half of what he was supposed to receive. After a strong 2018, Nova had a more modest season in 2019, as he showed flashes of his talent but struggled with consistency.

SCOUTING REPORT: Nova has a projectable body with a plus-plus arm that plays well at any infield spot. He looked truly lost at third base in 2019 and didn't turn double plays well at second, but there are scouts who see his upright style of play defensively and project he will eventually fit best at third. At the plate, Nova has above-average bat speed and above-average power potential, but his aggressiveness gets him into big trouble. In 2019, his success depended on whether he got ahead of behind in the count. If he fell behind, pitchers knew he'd chase out of the strike zone and was an easy strikeout.

THE FUTURE: Of all Astros' minor league position players, Nova is the one with the biggest chance of being a star. Figuring out how to lay off pitches well off the plate will determine if he reaches his lofty ceiling.

SCOUTING GRADES: **Hitting:** 40 **Power:** 55 **Running:** 55 **Fielding:** 50 **Arm:** 70

Year	Age	Club (League)	Class	AVG	G	AB	R	H	2B	3B	HR	RBI	BB	SO	SB	OBP	SLG
2017	17	Astros Orange (DSL)	R	.247	47	166	30	41	6	0	4	16	15	33	8	.342	.355
2018	18	Astros (GCL)	R	.308	41	146	21	45	3	1	6	28	6	21	9	.331	.466
2019	19	Quad Cities (MWL)	LoA	.259	75	282	35	73	20	1	3	29	15	68	10	.301	.369
Minor League Totals				.268	163	594	86	159	29	2	13	73	36	122	27	.320	.389

5 BRYAN ABREU, RHP

MARY DECICCO/MLB PHOTOS VIA GETTY IMAGES

BA GRADE
50 Risk: High

Born: April 22, 1997. **B-T:** R-R. **HT:** 6-1. **WT:** 204. **Signed:** Dominican Republic, 2013. **Signed by:** Oz Ocampo/Marc Russo/Rafael Belen.

TRACK RECORD: The Astros added Abreu to the 40-man roster after the 2018 season even though he had just 38 innings above short-season ball. A year later, he left from high Class A to the big leagues, making eight relief appearances as a September callup.

SCOUTING REPORT: Abreu's high rpm breaking ball is a work of art. It morphs between a hard, mid-80s curve with a short 12-to-6 break and a similarly hard mid-80s slider that dives down and away from righthanded hitters. It's a plus-plus pitch that gets swings-and-misses. The arm speed and effort to spin such a dominating breaker has also ensured he's always had below-average control as he struggles to sync his arm and his lower half. His release point is inconsistent. His 93-97 mph plus fastball is relatively true, but has enough velocity to be effective when he spots it well. He has thrown a below-average change, but didn't use it once he moved to the bullpen.

THE FUTURE: Abreu has a chance to start if given time to try to fix his control issues, but the Astros have a bigger need right now for him to be a potential high-leverage reliever. He has the stuff to pitch in the eighth or the ninth, but his poor control could hold him back.

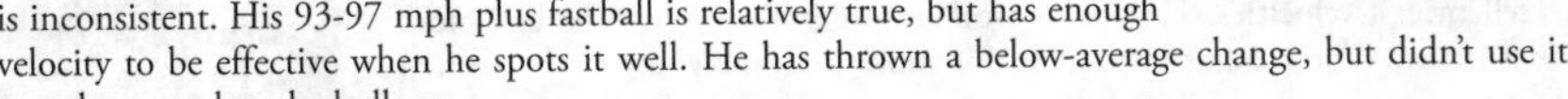
SCOUTING GRADES: **Fastball:** 60 **Slider:** 60 **Curveball:** 70 **Changeup:** 30 **Control:** 40

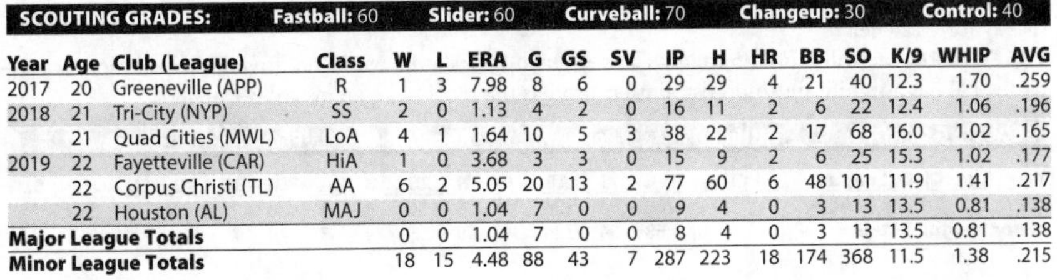

Year	Age	Club (League)	Class	W	L	ERA	G	GS	SV	IP	H	HR	BB	SO	K/9	WHIP	AVG
2017	20	Greeneville (APP)	R	1	3	7.98	8	6	0	29	29	4	21	40	12.3	1.70	.259
2018	21	Tri-City (NYP)	SS	2	0	1.13	4	2	0	16	11	2	6	22	12.4	1.06	.196
	21	Quad Cities (MWL)	LoA	4	1	1.64	10	5	3	38	22	2	17	68	16.0	1.02	.165
2019	22	Fayetteville (CAR)	HiA	1	0	3.68	3	3	0	15	9	2	6	25	15.3	1.02	.177
	22	Corpus Christi (TL)	AA	6	2	5.05	20	13	2	77	60	6	48	101	11.9	1.41	.217
	22	Houston (AL)	MAJ	0	0	1.04	7	0	0	9	4	0	3	13	13.5	0.81	.138
Major League Totals				0	0	1.04	7	0	0	8	4	0	3	13	13.5	0.81	.138
Minor League Totals				18	15	4.48	88	43	7	287	223	18	174	368	11.5	1.38	.215

6 ABRAHAM TORO, 3B

Born: Dec. 20, 1996. **B-T:** B-R. **HT:** 6-0. **WT:** 210. **Drafted:** Seminole State (Okla.) JC, 2016 (5th round). **Signed by:** Jim Stevenson.

MARY DECICCO/MLB PHOTOS VIA GETTY IMAGES

BA GRADE
45 **Risk: Medium**

TRACK RECORD: If not for Yordan Alvarez's incredible year, Toro would have had a case for having the best season by an Astros minor league hitter. He hit at Double-A Corpus Christi, was even better with Triple-A Round Rock and earned a callup to Houston a week before the September roster expansion.

SCOUTING REPORT: Nothing Toro does looks easy. He has short legs and a long torso that, combined with an unorthodox gait, makes everything look effortful. But Toro is more athletic than he looks. He is actually an average runner who will turn in the sporadic above-average time. Defensively, he has worked hard to get himself to being a below-average third baseman who can generally make the routine play He's fringe-average defensively at first. He has an above-average arm. Toro is a pure hitter and has a knack for hitting offspeed pitches, but he has also shown that he can catch up to good fastballs—his two MLB home runs came on 96 and 97 mph fastballs. He generally lines balls to the gaps but has the power to hit 15-18 home runs.

THE FUTURE: Toro's defensive limitations make it hard to find a good fit for him in Houston, but his bat and his ability to switch-hit makes him a useful pinch-hitter with modest defensive versatility.

SCOUTING GRADES: **Hitting:** 50 **Power:** 45 **Running:** 50 **Fielding:** 45 **Arm:** 55

Year	Age	Club (League)	Class	AVG	G	AB	R	H	2B	3B	HR	RBI	BB	SO	SB	OBP	SLG
2017	20	Tri-City (NYP)	SS	.292	32	106	21	31	8	0	6	16	19	21	1	.414	.538
	20	Quad Cities (MWL)	LoA	.209	37	134	25	28	3	2	9	17	21	30	2	.323	.463
2018	21	Buies Creek (CAR)	HiA	.257	83	296	54	76	20	1	14	56	45	62	5	.361	.473
	21	Corpus Christi (TL)	AA	.230	50	178	16	41	15	2	2	22	17	46	3	.317	.371
2019	22	Corpus Christi (TL)	AA	.306	98	376	65	115	22	4	16	70	48	77	4	.393	.513
	22	Round Rock (PCL)	AAA	.424	16	66	17	28	9	0	1	10	10	5	0	.506	.606
	22	Houston (AL)	MAJ	.218	25	78	13	17	3	2	2	9	9	19	1	.303	.385
Major League Totals				.218	25	78	13	17	3	2	2	9	9	19	1	.303	.385
Minor League Totals				.273	360	1333	218	364	83	12	48	210	170	272	17	.365	.461

7 KOREY LEE, C

Born: July 25, 1998. **B-T:** R-R. **HT:** 6-2. **WT:** 205. **Drafted:** California, 2019 (1st round). **Signed by:** Tim Costic.

BA GRADE
50 **Risk: High**

TRACK RECORD: Lee was the second best hitter for California in 2019, which was understandable when you consider he was teammates with the White Sox's Andrew Vaughn, the No. 3 pick in the draft. Lee was not seen as a first-round pick by most teams, but the Astros really believed in his bat, which gave the Bears two first-round picks in the same year for the first time in school history.

SCOUTING REPORT: Lee hit 15 home runs for California as a junior and posts excellent exit velocities. The Astros worked to get him to loft the ball more consistently. Those adjustments and his more pull-heavy approach resulted in a very modest pro debut. If the Astros are right about Lee's latent power potential, they could have found a late first-round steal, but area scouts and pro scouts for other teams are more skeptical, seeing modest power and a decent feel for hitting. Lee needs to work on his framing and receiving, but he has the athleticism to be at least an average receiver and he has a 70 arm on the 20-to-80 scale, although he needs to improve his accuracy. He is a 40 runner—pretty speedy for a catcher.

THE FUTURE: Lee will move up to low Class A Quad Cities as he works on driving the ball more consistently. He has a significant to-do list, but he also has the tools to be an everyday catcher.

SCOUTING GRADES: **Hitting:** 50 **Power:** 45 **Running:** 40 **Fielding:** 45 **Arm:** 70

Year	Age	Club (League)	Class	AVG	G	AB	R	H	2B	3B	HR	RBI	BB	SO	SB	OBP	SLG
2019	20	Tri-City (NYP)	SS	.268	64	224	31	60	6	4	3	28	28	49	8	.359	.371
Minor League Totals				.268	64	224	31	60	6	4	3	28	28	49	8	.359	.371

8 CRISTIAN JAVIER, RHP

BA GRADE
45 Risk: Medium

Born: March 26, 1997. **B-T:** R-R. **HT:** 6-1. **WT:** 204. **Drafted:** Dominican Republic, 2015. **Signed by:** Oz Ocampo/Roman Ocumarez/Leocadio Guevara.

TRACK RECORD: Javier is a pitcher who is more impressive when watched over longer stints than in a showcase setting. He began 2019 at high Class A Fayetteville, but pitched his way to Triple-A Round Rock by the end of the season and earned a spot on the Astros' 40-man roster in the offseason.

SCOUTING REPORT: Javier can touch 93-94 mph with his fastball, but he varies his fastball velocity by up to 5-6 mph to mess with hitter's timing. Javier's delivery hides the ball behind his back for a significant portion of his delivery. His average changeup has solid deception and some fade and his slow, average curveball is effective because of location and some depth. He uses an above-average slider against righthanders that sweeps across the plate. No pitch on its own is exceptional, but the fact is he was unhittable in 2019—righthanders hit .120 against him and lefties hit .144. If he falls behind, he's not going to throw a down-the-throat fastball.

THE FUTURE: Skeptical evaluators still see him as a No. 5 starter due to his lack of plus stuff, but Javier's ability to thrive after being promoted to Double-A is an indicator that his stuff will play in the majors. He could help Houston as a spot starter or reliever in 2020.

SCOUTING GRADES: **Fastball:** 55 **Slider:** 55 **Curveball:** 50 **Changeup:** 50 **Control:** 40

Year	Age	Club (League)	Class	W	L	ERA	G	GS	SV	IP	H	HR	BB	SO	K/9	WHIP	AVG
2017	20	Buies Creek (CAR)	HiA	1	0	0.00	2	0	0	6	2	0	3	9	14.3	0.88	.105
	20	Tri-City (NYP)	SS	0	0	2.70	4	2	0	17	11	0	9	24	13.0	1.20	.183
	20	Quad Cities (MWL)	LoA	2	0	2.39	8	7	1	38	25	3	15	47	11.2	1.06	.188
2018	21	Quad Cities (MWL)	LoA	2	2	1.82	11	7	1	49	28	3	23	80	14.6	1.03	.165
	21	Buies Creek (CAR)	HiA	5	4	3.41	14	11	0	61	44	6	27	66	9.8	1.17	.201
2019	22	Fayetteville (CAR)	HiA	2	0	0.94	7	5	1	29	15	1	16	40	12.6	1.08	.147
	22	Corpus Christi (TL)	AA	6	3	2.07	17	11	3	74	31	5	39	114	13.9	0.95	.124
	22	Round Rock (PCL)	AAA	0	0	1.64	2	2	0	11	5	1	4	16	13.1	0.82	.128
Minor League Totals				26	11	2.22	92	55	7	377	225	22	163	512	12.2	1.03	.170

9 HUNTER BROWN, RHP

BA GRADE
55 Risk: Extreme

Born: Aug. 29, 1998. **B-T:** R-R. **HT:** 6-2. **WT:** 203. **Drafted:** Wayne State, 2019 (5th round). **Signed by:** Scott Oberhelman.

TRACK RECORD: Coming into 2019, Brown was a pitcher who had struggled to earn a significant role in two seasons with Division II Wayne State (Mich.). But he improved his delivery, found some extra velocity and earned a spot in Wayne State's rotation. He had a dominating year and vaulted into the fifth round.

SCOUTING REPORT: Brown's rise from obscurity has been tied to a fastball that has turned into a fire-breathing monster. Brown will throw it anywhere from 92-100 mph in a normal outing, and he uses the extra gear to surprise hitters when he needs it. Brown gets good angle on his fastball, with that little hop at the top of the zone to miss bats. He has a durable frame with a thick midsection. The Astros will have to work hard to help him improve his well below-average control. He already has made some strides. He walked 16 in 14 innings over his first seven outings, but only four in 12 innings over his final six outings. Brown's 82-84 mph curveball is also a plus pitch. His changeup and slider both have average potential.

THE FUTURE: Brown is a high-risk, high-upside starter who has the stuff to be a middle-of-the-rotation starter. His fastball and curveball gives him several fallback options if his control doesn't improve as much as the Astros hope.

SCOUTING GRADES: **Fastball:** 70 **Slider:** 50 **Curveball:** 60 **Changeup:** 50 **Control:** 40

Year	Age	Club (League)	Class	W	L	ERA	G	GS	SV	IP	H	HR	BB	SO	K/9	WHIP	AVG
2019	20	Tri-City (NYP)	SS	2	2	4.56	12	6	0	24	13	0	18	33	12.5	1.31	.157
Minor League Totals				2	2	4.56	12	6	0	23	13	0	18	33	12.6	1.31	.157

10 GRAE KESSINGER, SS

Born: Aug. 25, 1997. **B-T:** R-R. **HT:** 6-2. **WT:** 200. **Drafted:** Mississippi, 2019 (2nd round). **Signed by:** Travis Coleman.

TRACK RECORD: Baseball is in Kessinger's blood. His grandfather Don was a six-time all-star shortstop for the Cubs before becoming Mississippi's baseball coach. His father was a minor leaguer for the Cubs and his uncle Keith played in the majors with the Reds. Grae was the undisputed team leader for Ole Miss for three seasons.

SCOUTING REPORT: Kessinger has above-average barrel control, showing a knack for making solid contact no matter what the count. He's a hitter more than a slugger, showing modest pull power that should produce below-average power. He is an average runner. Scouts do not see him having the quick reactions and smooth actions to remain at shortstop—everything he does is just a tick slower than ideal. But Kessinger is more playable at shortstop than most range-limited players because of his steady reliability. His average arm is not ideal at third base, but that spot could be a long-term fit. If not, he could be an offensive second baseman or a hit-first left fielder.

THE FUTURE: Kessinger is the kind of well-rounded college performer who usually figures out a way to get to the majors. His bat and reliability could make him a multi-position backup, but usually teams prefer a better shortstop for that role.

SCOUTING GRADES: **Hitting:** 55 **Power:** 40 **Running:** 50 **Fielding:** 45 **Arm:** 50

Year	Age	Club (League)	Class	AVG	G	AB	R	H	2B	3B	HR	RBI	BB	SO	SB	OBP	SLG
2019	21	Tri-City (NYP)	SS	.268	12	41	5	11	4	0	0	3	3	4	1	.333	.366
	21	Quad Cities (MWL)	LoA	.224	50	170	25	38	6	0	2	17	26	32	8	.333	.294
Minor League Totals				.232	62	211	30	49	10	0	2	20	29	36	9	.333	.308

11 TYLER IVEY, RHP

BA GRADE
50 Risk: High

Born: May 12, 1996. **B-T:** R-R. **HT:** 6-4. **WT:** 195. **Drafted:** Grayson (Texas) JC, 2017 (3rd round). **Signed by:** Jim Stevenson.

TRACK RECORD: Ivey has been effective in two seasons with the Astros, but he needs to stay on the mound more regularly. He missed half of May and all of June with elbow soreness and returned to the injured list for the final two weeks of the season. In addition to missing time with a sore elbow, Ivey was ejected from his second start of the season when umpires found a foreign substance on his glove.

SCOUTING REPORT: Ivey's funky delivery seems like something out of the 1940s. It's somewhat segmented, but he's steadily refined it, eliminating the head whack and some effort. His arm is generally on time and he has shown he can locate with above-average control and average command. In a system that has a lot of fireballing starters who haven't shown they have the control and feel to start, Ivey is an exception. He has three above-average pitches. His 90-95 mph fastball is effective up in the zone and he used both a big, slower curve and a hard cutter-ish slider.

THE FUTURE: Ivey is a potential No. 4 starter with a chance to be a No. 3, He's ready for Triple-A and could fill-in in Houston in the second half of the season.

Year	Age	Club (League)	Class	W	L	ERA	G	GS	SV	IP	H	HR	BB	SO	K/9	WHIP	AVG
2017	21	Astros (GCL)	R	0	0	0.00	1	1	0	2	1	0	2	3	13.5	1.50	.167
	21	Tri-City (NYP)	SS	0	3	5.94	11	7	0	36	41	2	12	41	10.2	1.46	.281
2018	22	Quad Cities (MWL)	LoA	1	3	3.46	9	6	2	42	36	2	8	53	11.4	1.06	.221
	22	Buies Creek (CAR)	HiA	3	3	2.69	15	12	1	70	50	3	21	82	10.5	1.01	.196
2019	23	Astros (GCL)	R	0	0	0.00	2	2	0	3	0	0	3	5	15.0	1.00	.000
	23	Fayetteville (CAR)	HiA	0	0	0.00	1	1	0	3	0	0	1	2	6.0	0.33	.000
	23	Corpus Christi (TL)	AA	4	0	1.57	11	8	0	46	28	5	16	61	11.9	0.96	.170
Minor League Totals				8	9	3.07	50	37	3	202	156	12	63	247	11.0	1.08	.207

12 JORDAN BREWER, OF

BA GRADE
50 Risk: High

Born: Aug. 1, 1997. **B-T:** R-L. **HT:** 6-1. **WT:** 195. **Drafted:** Michigan, 2019 (3rd round). **Signed by:** Scott Oberhelman.

TRACK RECORD: Brewer was a football/baseball star in high school who went to Lincoln Trail (Ill.) JC. After two years there, he transferred to Michigan, reworked his swing and blossomed as the Big 10 Player of the Year, helping lead the Wolverines to the College World Series finals. His pro debut was interrupted by a toe injury that cost him almost the entire Tri-City season.

SCOUTING REPORT: Astros draftees generally are picked for their bats and not their athleticism, so

Brewer's well-rounded toolset stands out. He has plus speed, plus power and a chance to stick in center field, even though he generally played in the corners with Michigan. He is even an adept first baseman—he throws lefty even though he hits righty. At the plate, Brewer's swing is a work in progress, but it's one that has come a long away already. He learned to use his lower half in his year at Michigan, but his swing is still a little grooved at times. The Astros are counting on his ability to continue to make adjustments.
THE FUTURE: There are some questions over how well Brewer can tweak his swing to be selective while still getting to his significant power potential, but the aptitude he displayed at Michigan is a positive sign.

Year	Age	Club (League)	Class	AVG	G	AB	R	H	2B	3B	HR	RBI	BB	SO	SB	OBP	SLG
2019	21	Tri-City (NYP)	SS	.130	16	54	5	7	0	0	1	3	2	6	2	.161	.185
Minor League Totals				.130	16	54	5	7	0	0	1	3	2	6	2	.161	.185

13 LUIS GARCIA, RHP

BA GRADE 50 Risk: High

Born: Dec. 13, 1996. **B-T:** R-R. **HT:** 6-1. **WT:** 238. **Signed:** Venezuela, 2016.
Signed by: Oz Ocampo/Tom Shafer/Roman Ocumarez/David Brito.

TRACK RECORD: Luis Garcia is a rather common name around baseball with six players with that moniker playing in the affiliated minors in 2019. Any evaluator who saw Luis H. Garcia pitch for the Astros in 2018 and 2019 may wonder if they were confusing him with another Lus Garcia. In 2018, he was just a run-of-the-mill righthander with an 89-92 mph fastball and a promising changeup. By the end of the 2019 season, he was showing flashes of three plus pitches with a dominating fastball.
SCOUTING REPORT: Garcia was the most well-rounded of Fayetteville's wave of hard-throwing starters. He figured out how to pitch with average stuff before he developed velocity. Garcia was sitting 92-97 mph in the second half of the season with a plus changeup and an average curve and slider. Garcia isn't just a thrower—there's some feel for setting up hitters. He has fringe-average control.
THE FUTURE: Garcia has more starter traits than most of the hard-throwing young Astros arms. Thanks to his fastball/changeup combo and his chance of developing average control, he has mid-rotation potential.

Year	Age	Club (League)	Class	W	L	ERA	G	GS	SV	IP	H	HR	BB	SO	K/9	WHIP	AVG
2017	20	Astros Blue (DSL)	R	1	1	1.64	6	1	0	11	13	1	4	18	14.7	1.55	.310
2018	21	Tri-City (NYP)	SS	0	0	0.00	5	3	0	16	7	0	8	28	15.4	0.92	.121
	21	Quad Cities (MWL)	LoA	7	2	2.48	19	10	0	69	58	4	33	70	9.1	1.32	.230
2019	22	Quad Cities (MWL)	LoA	4	0	2.93	9	6	1	43	23	4	16	60	12.6	0.91	.153
	22	Fayetteville (CAR)	HiA	6	4	3.02	15	12	0	66	43	5	34	108	14.8	1.17	.185
Minor League Totals				18	7	2.50	54	32	1	205	144	14	95	284	12.5	1.17	.196

14 JAIRO SOLIS, RHP

BA GRADE 55 Risk: Extreme

Born: Dec. 22, 1999. **B-T:** R-R. **HT:** 6-2. **WT:** 209. **Signed:** Venezuela, 2016.
Signed by: Oz Ocampo/Tom Shafer/Roman Ocumarez/Enrique Brito.

TRACK RECORD: Solis understandably has become a somewhat forgotten prospect for the Astros because he missed the end of 2018 and all of 2019 recovering from Tommy John surgery. Before his injury, he was seen as one of the Astros' most promising pitching prospects thanks to steadily improving velocity.
SCOUTING REPORT: Solis will begin 2020 having not pitched in an official game in 19 months. Before the injury, he was attacking hitters with a 93-95 mph plus fastball that can touch 98. He also was featuring an above-average 82-85 mph changeup. Solis' curveball and slider should reach average at least. Solis' control wavered between below-average and above-average pre-injury.
THE FUTURE: Solis should get a chance to pick up where he left off in 2018. If he can quickly shake off the rust he could quickly once again be one of the best pitching prospects in the Astros' system.

Year	Age	Club (League)	Class	W	L	ERA	G	GS	SV	IP	H	HR	BB	SO	K/9	WHIP	AVG
2017	17	Astros Orange (DSL)	R	1	1	2.73	6	4	0	26	20	2	8	28	9.6	1.06	.220
	17	Astros (GCL)	R	1	0	3.00	5	4	0	21	19	1	7	24	10.3	1.24	.229
	17	Greeneville (APP)	R	1	1	1.93	4	2	0	14	12	0	6	17	10.9	1.29	.226
2018	18	Quad Cities (MWL)	LoA	2	5	3.55	13	11	0	51	49	1	32	51	9.1	1.60	.259
2019	19	Did not play—Injured															
Minor League Totals				5	7	3.05	28	21	0	112	100	4	53	120	9.6	1.37	.240

15 BRANDON BIELAK, RHP

BA GRADE 45 Risk: Medium

Born: April 2, 1996. **B-T:** L-R. **HT:** 6-2. **WT:** 211. **Drafted:** Notre Dame, 2017 (11th round). **Signed by:** Nick Venuto.

TRACK RECORD: After a dominating sophomore season as a reliever at Notre Dame, Bielak's junior year was one struggle after another as a starter. The Astros were still intrigued and saw him post a 2.23 ERA that was best in the system in 2018. In 2019, he made it to Triple-A, but struggled with the livelier ball and pitched to a 8-4, 4.41 record.

SCOUTING REPORT: Bielak does everything he can to avoid being predictable. There's no plus pitch, but hitters never really know what they are going to get as Bielak throws six pitches (he added a screwball in 2019). Bielak's 91-94 mph fastball is average, as is his mid-80s changeup, curve and cutter. His slider is below-average and he added the screwball to give hitters something else to worry about. His command is above-average, but his control is fringe-average because he has to nibble around the edges of the zone.

THE FUTURE: Bielak is a back-of-the-rotation starter. Being regularly around the zone, he suffered adjusting to the Triple-A ball, as being in the zone often led to long home runs. The Astros will not be likely to count on Bielak in 2020, but he can fill in as needed. Mastering Triple-A in the meantime is a solid goal for Bielak.

Year	Age	Club (League)	Class	W	L	ERA	G	GS	SV	IP	H	HR	BB	SO	K/9	WHIP	AVG
2017	21	Astros (GCL)	R	1	0	0.00	2	0	0	4	3	0	1	5	10.4	0.92	.188
	21	Tri-City (NYP)	SS	1	1	0.92	8	4	1	29	18	0	4	37	11.4	0.75	.171
2018	22	Buies Creek (CAR)	HiA	5	3	2.10	14	7	2	56	44	2	17	74	12.0	1.10	.217
	22	Corpus Christi (TL)	AA	2	5	2.35	11	10	0	61	52	4	22	57	8.4	1.21	.235
2019	23	Corpus Christi (TL)	AA	3	0	3.75	8	6	0	36	29	3	14	33	8.3	1.19	.220
	23	Round Rock (PCL)	AAA	8	4	4.41	15	14	0	86	69	10	36	86	9.0	1.23	.220
Minor League Totals				20	13	2.94	58	41	3	272	215	19	94	292	9.7	1.13	.217

16 COLIN BARBER, OF

BA GRADE
50 Risk: Extreme

Born: Dec. 4, 2000. **B-T:** L-L. **HT:** 6-0. **WT:** 185. **Drafted:** HS—Chico, Calif., 2019 (4th round). **Signed by:** Tim Costic.

TRACK RECORD: Barber is the highest-drafted player ever picked out of Chico, Calif.'s Pleasant Valley High (and only the third player ever drafted from that high school). He had impressed at the Area Code Games, which was very useful for him as he didn't face much competition during the high school season. The Astros spent $1 million (far above slot for a fourth-round pick). After a slow start as a pro, Barber hit .306/.433/.429 in August.

SCOUTING REPORT: Barber has a chance to be a special hitter. He has excellent bat speed and advanced bat-to-ball skills. He has above-average raw power right now, largely to the pull side, but he right now focuses on putting together quality at-bats. He has enough of a batting eye to let a wild pitcher walk him, although he still has work to do on his two-strike approach. Defensively, Barber played all three outfield spots in his debut and is currently a plus runner. But there is some belief that he will eventually slow down and fit better in a corner outfield spot.

THE FUTURE: The Astros do not have many position players who project as MLB regulars, but Barber does and could quickly become one of the team's best prospects. He should be ready for low Class A Quad Cities in 2020.

Year	Age	Club (League)	Class	AVG	G	AB	R	H	2B	3B	HR	RBI	BB	SO	SB	OBP	SLG
2019	18	Astros (GCL)	R	.263	28	99	19	26	5	1	2	6	19	29	2	.387	.394
Minor League Totals				.263	28	99	19	26	5	1	2	6	19	29	2	.387	.394

17 JOJANSE TORRES, RHP

BA GRADE
45 Risk: High

Born: Aug. 4, 1995. **B-T:** R-R. **HT:** 6-1. **WT:** 175. **Signed:** Dominican Republic, 2018. **Signed by:** Roman Ocumarez.

TRACK RECORD: Even in an organization that has no problem signing international arms who are considered quite old by normal standards, Torres is remarkable. He was already 22 when he signed and turned 23 at the end of his first season in the Dominican Summer League. He's made up for lost time by making it to high Class A just 13 months after he signed.

SCOUTING REPORT: Torres simply rears back and fires. There's little sublety or nuance to his approach on the mound. He peppers the strike zone and a foot around the edge of the zone with 95-100 mph fastballs, using a simple, aggressive delivery. His changeup is effective because it has 10 mph separation off his fastball—which hitters have to respect. Every now and then Torres will sync up and spin a plus slider, but he'll also throw a cement mixer that is a slider in name only. The same can be said for his curveball.

THE FUTURE: Arm strength like Torres cannot be ignored. He seems eventually ticketed to be a low-leverage reliever unless his well-below-average control and inconsistent breaking balls improve. But it's worth remembering he has just 135 pro innings under his belt so far.

Year	Age	Club (League)	Class	W	L	ERA	G	GS	SV	IP	H	HR	BB	SO	K/9	WHIP	AVG
2018	22	Astros (DSL)	R	1	2	2.20	13	8	1	41	36	1	8	48	10.5	1.07	.232
2019	23	Quad Cities (MWL)	LoA	3	0	0.56	7	1	0	16	9	1	8	26	14.6	1.06	.161
	23	Fayetteville (CAR)	HiA	9	0	1.94	17	9	1	79	50	2	38	81	9.3	1.12	.178
Minor League Totals				13	2	1.86	37	18	2	135	95	4	54	155	10.3	1.10	.193

18 JOSE ALBERTO RIVERA, RHP

BA GRADE
50 Risk: Extreme

Born: Feb. 14, 1997. **B-T:** R-R. **HT:** 6-3. **WT:** 160. **Signed:** Dominican Republic, 2016. **Signed by:** Oz Ocampo/Roman Ocumarez/Leocadio Guevara.

TRACK RECORD: The Astros love to sign older (18/19-year-old) international amateurs with a chance to add velocity. Much like Jorge Guzman, Rivera was an old signee who quickly found a way to reach triple-digits with his fastball.

SCOUTING REPORT: In a system filled with fast arms, Rivera has the quickest. There's very little subtlety to Rivera—he just rears back and asks hitters to try to catch up to a 97-102 mph fastball that has plenty of arm-side run. Rivera throws a mid-80s split-change that got better and better, flashing plus as the season wore on. He also throws a mid-80s slider that is often a 58 footer. His secondaries need to improve, but the trends are in the right direction.

THE FUTURE: For a flamethrower, Rivera has a chance to throw strikes. His delivery is high-energy but he's around the zone. For now, there's every reason to keep letting him be a tandem starter, but long-term, he's likely a power reliever.

Year	Age	Club (League)	Class	W	L	ERA	G	GS	SV	IP	H	HR	BB	SO	K/9	WHIP	AVG
2017	20	Astros Orange (DSL)	R	2	3	3.44	12	5	0	37	20	3	24	37	9.1	1.20	.158
2018	21	Astros (GCL)	R	1	2	3.23	10	4	0	39	30	4	6	39	9.0	0.92	.205
	21	Tri-City (NYP)	SS	1	2	4.50	4	1	0	10	9	2	8	14	12.6	1.70	.237
2019	22	Quad Cities (MWL)	LoA	5	5	3.81	18	11	1	76	61	2	36	95	11.3	1.28	.222
Minor League Totals				9	12	3.63	44	21	1	161	120	11	74	185	10.3	1.20	.205

19 SHAWN DUBIN, RHP

BA GRADE
45 Risk: High

Born: Sept. 6, 1995. **B-T:** R-R. **HT:** 6-1. **WT:** 154. **Drafted:** Georgetown (Ky.), 2018 (13th round). **Signed by:** Travis Coleman.

TRACK RECORD: Dubin had to transfer from Buffalo to Georgetown (Ky.) for his senior season when Buffalo shut down its program. A $1,000 senior sign, when the Astros drafted him he pitched with a fringe-average straight fastball. In the second half of the 2019 season, he was throwing five-to-seven mph harder than he was just a year before.

SCOUTING REPORT: Dubin's newfound velocity has come even though he still has the frame of a telephone pole. Dubin barely weighs 160 pounds, but he has an extremely fast arm and he gets all of his momentum directed to the plate. Dubin's 93-98 mph plus-plus fastball now has solid carry up in the strike zone. It sets up an erratic slider. At its best, it's a plus pitch with depth and bite, but too often it's short and more cutter-ish than his best ones. He also needs to show he can land it, as too often it's a pure chase pitch that worked against Class A hitters, but won't be as effective against more advanced batters. His change is unremarkable with modest deception, but it plays average because hitters are gearing up for the fastball.

THE FUTURE: Dubin's slim frame, all-out delivery and hit-or-miss slider all seem to indicate he'll end up in the bullpen, but considering he's gone from being an org arm to a solid prospect in one year, there's no reason to limit his opportunities to improve. He could start for Double-A Corpus Christi in 2020.

Year	Age	Club (League)	Class	W	L	ERA	G	GS	SV	IP	H	HR	BB	SO	K/9	WHIP	AVG
2018	22	Tri-City (NYP)	SS	2	1	4.60	14	5	0	29	23	4	11	31	9.5	1.16	.215
2019	23	Quad Cities (MWL)	LoA	1	0	0.75	3	1	2	12	7	0	4	19	14.3	0.92	.167
	23	Fayetteville (CAR)	HiA	6	5	3.92	22	18	1	99	71	3	42	132	12.0	1.15	.196
Minor League Totals				9	6	3.79	39	24	3	140	101	7	57	182	11.7	1.13	.198

20 JAIRO LOPEZ, RHP

BA GRADE
45 Risk: High

Born: Nov. 21, 2000. **B-T:** R-R. **HT:** 5-11. **WT:** 150. **Signed:** Venezuela, 2017. **Signed by:** Oz Ocampo/Roman Ocumarez/David Brito.

TRACK RECORD: The Astros love fast arms, and they do not really matter what size or shape is attached to that arm. Lopez is yet another of the Astros' pack of short righthanders with big fastballs.

SCOUTING REPORT: Lopez has the foundations teams look for in a starting pitching prospect with three pitches and a delivery that allows him to get to above-average velocity with modest effort. He has an above-average 92-95 mph fastball and a plus curveball. His changeup shows signs of eventually being an average pitch as well.

THE FUTURE: Lopez's arm works well enough for fit as either a starter or reliever, and he shows enough feel that there's a solid chance to develop him as a starter. Low Class A Quad Cities shoud be a solid challenge, but the Astros don't have any hesitation to move pitchers quickly if they show they have handled a level, so he could reach Fayetteville in 2020 if he has a strong first half.

Year	Age	Club (League)	Class	W	L	ERA	G	GS	SV	IP	H	HR	BB	SO	K/9	WHIP	AVG
2018	17	Astros (DSL)	R	1	3	3.32	14	6	0	43	37	1	15	41	8.5	1.20	.222
2019	18	Astros (GCL)	R	2	1	1.09	6	2	0	25	15	1	7	25	9.1	0.89	.163
	18	Tri-City (NYP)	SS	2	2	1.71	7	2	0	26	10	0	16	36	12.3	0.99	.116
Minor League Totals				5	6	2.29	27	10	0	94	62	2	38	102	9.7	1.06	.180

21 BRETT CONINE, RHP

BA GRADE 45 Risk: High

Born: Oct. 16, 1996. **B-T:** R-R. **HT:** 6-3. **WT:** 210. **Drafted:** Cal State Fullerton, 2018 (11th round). **Signed by:** Ryan Leake.

TRACK RECORD: Cal State Fullerton's closer for two seasons, the Astros quickly moved Conine back into the rotation while working to get him more consistently to the upper ends of his velocity range. It's worked so far—he's been effective at four levels.

SCOUTING REPORT: In an organization where seemingly everyone has added three-to-six mph to pitch with a plus fastball, Conine is the crafty pitcher who succeeds based on plus control with average stuff. Conine sits 90-94 mph (which is actually a 2 mph bump from what he was as a reliever at Fullerton), setting up an average changeup and an above-average power curve—it's short and tight and sometimes gets described as a slider. His above-average command is key to his success.

THE FUTURE: There are evaluators who see Conine as an up-and-down arm who has feasted on less-advanced hitters, but he has the stuff to play his way to the majors. He'll return to Double-A Corpus Christi.

Year	Age	Club (League)	Class	W	L	ERA	G	GS	SV	IP	H	HR	BB	SO	K/9	WHIP	AVG
2018	21	Tri-City (NYP)	SS	1	1	1.99	11	3	0	32	23	0	11	37	10.5	1.07	.198
2019	22	Quad Cities (MWL)	LoA	3	2	1.91	6	5	0	33	19	3	6	40	10.9	0.76	.162
	22	Fayetteville (CAR)	HiA	4	2	2.42	15	8	0	63	52	3	17	80	11.4	1.09	.222
	22	Corpus Christi (TL)	AA	1	0	2.00	4	2	0	18	20	1	6	14	7.0	1.44	.282
Minor League Totals				9	5	2.16	36	18	0	146	114	7	40	171	10.5	1.05	.212

22 BLAIR HENLEY, RHP

Born: May 14, 1997. **B-T:** R-R. **HT:** 6-3. **WT:** 190. **Drafted:** Texas, 2019 (7th round). **Signed by:** Kris Gross.

TRACK RECORD: A 22nd-round pick of the Yankees out of high school, Henley was a reliable starter for three years for Texas. But scouts weren't all that thrilled with his pedestrian velocity. Already with the Astros, he's gained a tick of velocity and he was dominating in his pro debut.

SCOUTING REPORT: Keep an eye on Henley in 2020, as he seems like the perfect candidate to benefit from the Astros' program to increase velocity. He already spins a plus breaking ball with elite spin rates (3,200 rpm) and he's touching 93-94 mph. His below-average changeup needs to improve. His control needs to improve along with his stuff, but the pieces are there for him to be a mid-rotation starter.

THE FUTURE: Henley was able to work three to four innings on a strict 50-60 pitch limit. The pitch efficiency combined with his strikeout stuff gives him a path to being a back-of-the-rotation MLB starter.

Year	Age	Club (League)	Class	W	L	ERA	G	GS	SV	IP	H	HR	BB	SO	K/9	WHIP	AVG
2019	22	Astros (GCL)	R	0	0	0.00	1	1	0	3	1	0	1	4	12.0	0.67	.100
	22	Tri-City (NYP)	SS	1	1	1.60	11	2	1	34	29	1	8	46	12.3	1.10	.228
Minor League Totals				1	1	1.47	12	3	1	36	30	1	9	50	12.3	1.06	.219

23 NIVALDO RODRIGUEZ, RHP

BA GRADE 45 Risk: High

Born: April 16, 1997. **B-T:** R-R. **HT:** 6-1. **WT:** 170. **Signed:** Venezuela, 2016. **Signed by:** Oz Ocampo/Tom Shafer/Roman Ocumarez.

TRACK RECORD: A low-cost signing, Rodriguez is yet another Astros arm who has steadily gotten better. Signed as a 19-year-old, Rodriguez had to be moved quickly in 2019 to see if he was worthy of a 40-man roster spot. He responded by helping Fayetteville to the Carolina League championship series.

SCOUTING REPORT: Rodriguez has some of the best control in the Astros farm system, which helps him succeed without a real plus pitch. He has above-average pitchability, spotting his 91-95 mph fastball

and above-average slider. While his fastball and breaking ball are both effective, his changeup is standing between him and a future as a starter. Most of his changeups are well-below average. They are slow enough (78-80 mph) but he telegraphs them and leaves them up in the zone, making them quite hittable.
THE FUTURE: The Astros added Rodriguez to the 40-man roster ahead of several harder-throwing but less-refined relievers. He should reach Double-A Corpus Christi in 2020.

Year	Age	Club (League)	Class	W	L	ERA	G	GS	SV	IP	H	HR	BB	SO	K/9	WHIP	AVG
2017	20	Astros Blue (DSL)	R	3	0	0.35	6	4	1	26	17	0	6	29	10.0	0.88	.181
	20	Astros (GCL)	R	1	2	3.48	9	3	0	31	32	1	11	34	9.9	1.39	.267
2018	21	Tri-City (NYP)	SS	4	1	2.91	14	7	1	56	45	3	13	50	8.1	1.04	.218
2019	22	Quad Cities (MWL)	LoA	3	1	1.16	6	6	0	31	23	2	4	39	11.3	0.87	.200
	22	Fayetteville (CAR)	HiA	3	5	2.92	18	9	2	74	46	5	31	75	9.1	1.04	.175
Minor League Totals				15	9	2.40	58	29	4	225	169	11	69	235	9.4	1.06	.204

24 GARRETT STUBBS, C

BA GRADE
40 Risk: Medium

Born: May 26, 1993. **B-T:** L-R. **HT:** 5-10. **WT:** 175. **Drafted:** Southern California, 2015 (8th round). **Signed by:** Tim Costic.

TRACK RECORD: Stubbs has long been one of the most athletic catchers around—he also has played in the outfield and middle infield sporadically in college and as a pro. A star at Southern Cal, he's one of the smallest catchers in pro ball, and his workload has reflected that—he's never caught 100 games in a season.
SCOUTING REPORT: Most backup catchers are awful hitters, but have plus power for when they do run into a pitch. Stubbs has a chance to be an average hitter with a simple stroke that is low-maintenance—he can handle sitting on the bench for two or three days without getting rusty. It's a somewhat one-plane swing. He has very little power. Most catchers are bottom-of-the-scale runners. Stubbs is a plus runner. Defensively, he's athletic and moves well with an above-average and accurate arm (he's thrown out 43 percent of basestealers for his career). But his framing metrics are poor, which makes him much less appealing as a backup.
THE FUTURE: Stubbs will likely get a much better shot to be the backup with the Astros catching situation scrambled. If given at-bats, he has a chance to hit for average and provide some versatility as he can also play in the outfield.

Year	Age	Club (League)	Class	AVG	G	AB	R	H	2B	3B	HR	RBI	BB	SO	SB	OBP	SLG
2017	24	Corpus Christi (TL)	AA	.236	75	263	36	62	13	0	4	25	32	44	8	.324	.331
	24	Fresno (PCL)	AAA	.221	23	77	11	17	5	0	0	12	11	15	3	.341	.286
2018	25	Fresno (PCL)	AAA	.310	84	297	60	92	19	6	4	38	35	53	6	.382	.455
2019	26	Round Rock (PCL)	AAA	.240	63	204	33	49	11	0	7	23	24	38	12	.332	.397
	26	Houston (AL)	MAJ	.200	19	35	8	7	3	0	0	2	4	7	1	.282	.286
Major League Totals				.200	19	35	8	7	3	0	0	2	4	7	1	.282	.286
Minor League Totals				.272	367	1285	218	350	75	7	25	159	166	203	47	.361	.400

25 PETER SOLOMON, RHP

BA GRADE
50 Risk: Extreme

Born: Aug. 16, 1996. **B-T:** R-R. **HT:** 6-4. **WT:** 201. **Drafted:** Notre Dame, 2017 (4th round). **Signed by:** Nick Venuto.

TRACK RECORD: After a dominating stint in the Cape Cod League as a rising junior, Solomon was seen as a potential first-round pick. All that quickly dissolved as Notre Dame moved him back to the bullpen after just four starts. With the Astros, he has shown he can start, but his 2019 season ended after just two starts when he blew out his elbow.
SCOUTING REPORT: Solomon has made significant strides since his days as a Fighting Irish reliever. If he can recover from the surgery, there is nothing in his delivery or his wide array of pitches that should dissuade him starting—his delivery is fluid and clean. He now has a very varied approach. Everything starts with a low-to-mid-90s above-average fastball. His 12-to-6 curveball flashes above-average but he has a long way to go to find the command to make it more than a chase pitch. He also mixes in a fringier-slider and cutter. His below-average changeup needs further refinement.
THE FUTURE: Solomon will miss most of 2020 as he continues to recover from elbow surgery. Because of the timing of his surgery, the Astros could decide to hold him out of game action until 2021.

Year	Age	Club (League)	Class	W	L	ERA	G	GS	SV	IP	H	HR	BB	SO	K/9	WHIP	AVG
2017	20	Astros (GCL)	R	0	0	0.00	1	1	0	1	0	0	0	0	0.0	0.00	.000
2018	21	Quad Cities (MWL)	LoA	8	1	2.43	19	10	0	78	62	2	28	88	10.2	1.16	.218
	21	Buies Creek (CAR)	HiA	1	0	1.96	5	3	0	23	16	0	4	26	10.2	0.87	.195
2019	22	Fayetteville (CAR)	HiA	0	0	2.35	2	2	0	8	7	1	4	14	16.4	1.43	.241
Minor League Totals				9	1	2.30	27	16	0	109	85	3	36	128	10.5	1.11	.213

26 ROGELIO ARMENTEROS, RHP

BA GRADE
40 Risk: Medium

Born: June 30, 1994. **B-T:** R-R. **HT:** 6-1. **WT:** 215. **Signed:** Cuba, 2014. **Signed by:** Alex Jacobs.

TRACK RECORD: When Armenteros made his MLB debut on June 14, it was the capstone of an eight-year journey that began with him pitching as a 17-year-old for Industriales of Cuba's Serie Nacional. After leaving Cuba, then-Astros scout Alex Jacobs saw him pitching in a workout for Rusney Castillo and signed him for $40,000.

SCOUTING REPORT: Armenteros was added to the Astros 40-man roster before the 2019 season and seemed poised to be a fill-in starter. But Jose Urquidy ended up leap-frogging him into that role. Armenteros can work as either a spot starter or a multi-inning reliever, but other than a plus changeup, nothing in Armenteros' arsenal is particularly overwhelming. He can touch 95 mph with his average fastball, but more often he sits 90-92. He throws a below-average curve and will mix in a sporadic below-average slider almost entirely as a chase pitch for righthanded hitters. He has above-average control, but he's forced to stay around the edges of the zone and if he falls behind in the count, he'd rather walk the batter than give in.

THE FUTURE: Armenteros is unlikely to be the Astros first option for a spot in the rotation in 2020, but he should get a shot at contributing at some point during the season. He's more crafty than anything, but can be a useful swingman.

Year	Age	Club (League)	Class	W	L	ERA	G	GS	SV	IP	H	HR	BB	SO	K/9	WHIP	AVG
2017	23	Corpus Christi (TL)	AA	2	3	1.93	14	10	1	65	49	3	19	74	10.2	1.04	.207
	23	Fresno (PCL)	AAA	8	1	2.16	10	10	0	58	42	5	19	72	11.1	1.05	.203
2018	24	Fresno (PCL)	AAA	8	1	3.74	22	21	1	118	106	15	48	134	10.2	1.31	.237
2019	24	Houston (AL)	MAJ	1	1	4.00	5	2	1	18	17	1	5	18	9.0	1.22	.243
	24	Round Rock (PCL)	AAA	6	7	4.80	19	18	0	84	90	14	31	85	9.1	1.43	.276
Major League Totals				1	1	4.00	5	2	1	18	17	1	5	18	9.0	1.22	.243
Minor League Totals				35	20	3.45	106	93	3	514	456	55	185	566	9.9	1.25	.237

27 AUSTIN HANSEN, RHP

BA GRADE
45 Risk: High

Born: Aug. 25, 1996. **B-T:** R-R. **HT:** 6-0. **WT:** 195. **Drafted:** Oklahoma, 2018 (8th round). **Signed by:** Jim Stevenson.

TRACK RECORD: The Astros are quite happy to pick college relievers who they see as having some starter traits—the tandem starter approach they use helps them then ease into starting. Hansen was the Sooners closer. With Houston, he transitioned to a tandem starter role in 2019 and was effective at two levels.

SCOUTING REPORT: Hansen steadily gained velocity as the weather warmed up in 2019. He began the season sitting 90-94 mph, but by the end of the year he was sitting 93-96 and touching 98. That plus fastball and above-average, hard slider and 12-to-6 curveball gives him a chance for three above-average pitches. He hides the ball well in his delivery. Like many Astros prospects, he's coached to take walks rather than give in and give up hard contact and has below-average control. His command is also below average. His changeup has improved, but is still a below-average chase pitch largely just for lefties. Scouts laud his makeup and competitiveness.

THE FUTURE: Hansen very well could end up back in the relief role he thrived in at Oklahoma, but he has shown enough starter traits to stay in the rotation for now.

Year	Age	Club (League)	Class	W	L	ERA	G	GS	SV	IP	H	HR	BB	SO	K/9	WHIP	AVG
2018	21	Tri-City (NYP)	SS	2	3	1.76	14	2	2	31	14	2	13	45	13.2	0.88	.130
2019	22	Quad Cities (MWL)	LoA	4	1	0.86	9	7	1	42	20	1	19	52	11.2	0.94	.140
	22	Fayetteville (CAR)	HiA	3	2	3.10	14	7	1	52	32	4	32	76	13.1	1.22	.174
Minor League Totals				9	6	2.02	37	16	4	124	66	7	64	173	12.5	1.04	.152

28 ENOLI PAREDES, RHP

BA GRADE
45 Risk: High

Born: Sept. 28, 1995. **B-T:** R-R. **HT:** 5-11. **WT:** 168. **Signed:** Dominican Republic, 2015. **Signed by:** Oz Ocampo/Roman Ocumarez.

TRACK RECORD: Paredes was another bargain signing ($10,000) who has added 5-6 mph while being nearly unhittable in the lower minors. He wants to dominate hitters and sometimes focuses on embarrassing hitters more than just getting them out.

SCOUTING REPORT: Paredes has an extremely fast arm, which allows him to simply overwhelm many hitters with a 94-98 mph four-seam fastball (and a quality two-seamer too) and a plus slider. In a starter role, he throws a spike curve and below-average changeup as well. That fast arm also at times gets him into trouble, as he struggles with below-average control and even worse command—he's aiming for the strike zone more than he's trying to hit a spot. Paredes' delivery is high energy if you like it and effortful and hard to maintain if you don't.

THE FUTURE: Most pitchers with frames and deliveries like Paredes end up in the bullpen, but every now and then someone like Yordano Ventura makes it work. Paredes has been extremely hard to hit everywhere he's pitched. He will likely start back in Corpus Christi but with his stuff, he could be a viable option to pitch in Houston by the end of the year.

Year	Age	Club (League)	Class	W	L	ERA	G	GS	SV	IP	H	HR	BB	SO	K/9	WHIP	AVG
2017	21	Quad Cities (MWL)	LoA	1	3	2.11	8	6	0	38	21	3	13	33	7.7	0.89	.163
2018	22	Quad Cities (MWL)	LoA	2	3	1.46	16	5	2	56	28	0	26	71	11.5	0.97	.143
	22	Buies Creek (CAR)	HiA	4	1	1.35	8	0	0	13	6	1	3	19	12.8	0.68	.133
2019	23	Fayetteville (CAR)	HiA	3	1	1.64	10	6	0	44	21	3	21	59	12.1	0.95	.141
	23	Corpus Christi (TL)	AA	2	3	3.78	12	6	1	50	29	1	21	69	12.4	1.00	.167
Minor League Totals				13	14	2.41	66	26	6	235	130	8	103	297	11.4	0.99	.160

29 DAURI LORENZO, SS

Born: Oct. 29, 2002. **B-T:** B-R. **Ht:** 6-1. **Wt.:** 165. **Signed:** Dominican Republic, 2019. **Signed by:** Roman Ocumarez/Francisco Ulloa/Leocadio Guevara.

TRACK RECORD: The Astros spent $1.8 million to land Lorenzo, a switch-hitting shortstop who stands out more for his bat than his glove.

SCOUTING REPORT: Lorenzo has a chance to be an above-average or better hitter thanks to a smooth swing as a lefthanded and righthanded hitter. He has above-average barrel control, a level swing and the hand-eye to make plenty of contact and his hands work very well. Lorenzo projects as a high-average, high on-base hitter with modest gap/doubles power. Defensively, Lorenzo will have to work hard to stay at shortstop. He has shown steady improvement as an amateur but he still doesn't have the short-range quickness and actions teams often look for in a shortstop. If he does eventually have to move his athleticism, average speed and average arm should work at second or third base or even center field.

THE FUTURE: Lorenzo is expected to begin his pro career in the Dominican Summer League. His advanced bat should allow him to move quicker than the average teenager.

Year	Age	Club (League)	Class	AVG	G	AB	R	H	2B	3B	HR	RBI	BB	SO	SB	OBP	SLG
2019	16	Did not play—Signed 2020 contract															

30 CHANDLER TAYLOR, OF

Born: Feb. 7, 1996. **B-T:** L-L. **HT:** 6-1. **WT:** 210. **Drafted:** Alabama, 2018 (10th round). **Signed by:** Travis Coleman.

TRACK RECORD: A 27th-round pick of the Twins as a sophomore, Taylor hit 13 home runs for the Tide as a junior, moving into ninth on the school's career home run list (38). He also ranks sixth in career walks for Alabama (110). A hamate injury barely slowed Taylor, as he hit 14 home runs in his first full pro season.

SCOUTING REPORT: Taylor swings and misses baseballs at a frightening rate. In 2019, nearly 40 percent of Taylor's plate appearances ended in strikeouts. However, when he does make contact, he hits the ball in the air and he clears fences. He has the best raw power in the Astros farm system now that Yordan Alvarez has graduated. Taylor also has a plus arm and his average speed works in right field—he's a fringe-average defender. Taylor's plate demeanor doesn't help his swing-and-miss tendencies. Umpires aren't always thrilled with his demonstrative disagreements with called strikes. Very rarely do bottom-of-the-scale hitters with 70 power play in the majors—usually either the hit tool gets better or the player doesn't make it. So Taylor has to figure out how to make enough contact to be at least a .230-.240 hitter long-term.

THE FUTURE: The chances of Taylor fixing his contact problems enough to be a playable big leaguer are slim. Most players with his profile (Cody Johnson and Chris Carter are examples) end up flaming out somewhere short of a lengthy MLB career. Taylor's massive power gives him that slim shot of being a future home run champ, if he can make massive adjustments.

Year	Age	Club (League)	Class	AVG	G	AB	R	H	2B	3B	HR	RBI	BB	SO	SB	OBP	SLG
2018	22	Quad Cities (MWL)	LoA	.214	63	215	26	46	9	2	9	27	46	92	3	.351	.400
2019	23	Fayetteville (CAR)	HiA	.223	80	274	40	61	13	2	14	50	50	129	8	.345	.438
Minor League Totals				.219	143	489	66	107	22	4	23	77	96	221	11	.348	.421

Kansas City Royals

BY BILL MITCHELL

The 2019 season looked a lot like 2018 for the rebuilding Royals. The big league team finished with a 59-103 record, only one win better than the previous season.

The biggest loss was the yearlong injury suffered during spring training by stalwart catcher Salvador Perez. Unlike 2018, when the Royals saw an infusion of young talent from the farm system, the 2019 club relied on a steady influx of major league retreads to fill out the roster.

The only rookie to earn a significant amount of playing time was Nicky Lopez, who filled in at both middle infield positions for 103 games. The most positive news on the field in 2019 were the breakouts of DH Jorge Soler, who led the American League with 48 home runs, and third baseman Hunter Dozier, who finally justified his first-round selection in 2013 by putting up a .870 OPS with 26 long balls.

KC™

The most notable Royals transactions occurred off the field. David Glass sold the team to a group led by local businessman John Sherman for $1 billion, followed later by longtime manager Ned Yost announcing his retirement on Sept. 23. The Royals' manager since 2010, Yost finished his career with the most victories in franchise history, two AL pennants and the 2015 World Series title. He was replaced by former Cardinals manager and 13-year big league catcher Mike Matheny.

The Royals have used extra draft picks over the last two years to bolster what had been a weak farm system. In particular, they have focused on adding a significant number of advanced college pitchers. To the credit of the player development staff, many of these pitchers made a big jump forward in 2019. Righthanders Brady Singer and Kris Bubic, both products of the 2018 draft, represented the Royals in the Futures Game, and lefty Daniel Lynch was the starting pitcher in the Arizona Fall League's championship game. Singer and Jackson Kowar, former teammates at Florida, both advanced to Double-A in their first full seasons in the organization.

The Royals drafted Texas high school shortstop Bobby Witt Jr. with the second overall pick in 2019, adding another major talent to the system. Witt spent his pro debut in the Rookie-level Arizona League, but his advanced instincts and feel for the game should allow the Texas high school product to move quickly through the system.

Three of the top young hitters in the organization—first baseman Nick Pratto, catcher M.J. Melendez and outfielder Seuly Matias—all struggled with their move to high Class A Wilmington. They will all likely return there for the start of the 2020 season.

ED ZURGA/GETTY IMAGES

Jorge Soler broke out at age 27 by blasting an American League-leading 48 home runs.

PROJECTED 2023 LINEUP

Position	Player	Age
Catcher	Salvador Perez	33
First Base	Nick Pratto (10)	24
Second Base	Adalberto Mondesi	27
Third Base	Hunter Dozier	31
Shortstop	Bobby Witt Jr. (1)	23
Left Field	Whit Merrifield	34
Center Field	Kyle Isbel (5)	26
Right Field	Erick Peña (6)	20
Designated Hitter	Jorge Soler	31
No. 1 Starter	Daniel Lynch (2)	26
No. 2 Starter	Jackson Kowar (3)	26
No. 3 Starter	Brady Singer (4)	26
No. 4 Starter	Brad Keller	27
No. 5 Starter	Kris Bubic (8)	25
Closer	Josh Staumont	29

The Royals also added outfielder Erick Peña to their system when they signed him out of the Dominican Republic for a bonus just south of $4 million. Already ranked among their Top 10 Prospects, Peña has a chance to hit for a combination of average and power.

For an organization attempting to build a winning culture with its young players, the most significant accomplishment from the minor league system came during a three-day span in September. Three of the Royals' minor league affiliates—high Class A Wilmington, low Class A Lexington and Rookie-level Idaho Falls—each won their respective league championship.

DEPTH CHART

KANSAS CITY ROYALS

TOP 2020 ROOKIE: Josh Staumont, RHP. If Staumont can finally get command of his pitches, he'll be a useful piece in the bullpen.
BREAKOUT PROSPECT: Zach Haake, RHP. Haake continues to intrigue with his long, lean, projectable pitcher's frame and electric stuff.
SLEEPER: Omar Hernandez, C. A Cuban native who defected to Spain, Hernandez played in the Arizona League at 17 and showed plus defense behind the plate and plus arm strength.

SOURCE OF TOP 30 TALENT

Homegrown	**27**	**Acquired**	**2**
College	16	Trade	2
Junior college	2	Rule 5 draft	0
High school	4	Independent league	0
Nondrafted free agent	0	Free agent/waivers	0
International	5		

LF
Brewer Hicklen (19)
Darryl Collins

CF
Kyle Isbel (5)
Erick Pena (6)
Khalil Lee (7)
Nick Heath (26)
Michael Gigliotti (27)

RF
Seuly Matias (16)
Juan Carlos Negret
Kort Peterson

3B
Kelvin Gutierrez (18)
Emmanuel Rivera

SS
Bobby Witt Jr. (1)
Jeison Guzman (13)
Brady McConnell (17)
Maikel Garcia
Wilmin Candelario
Clay Dungan
Omar Florentino
Kevin Merrell

2B
Gabriel Cancel
Erick Mejia
Michael Massey

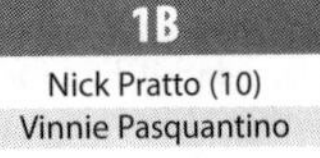

1B
Nick Pratto (10)
Vinnie Pasquantino

C
M.J. Melendez (12)
Omar Hernandez
Sebastian Rivero

LHP

LHSP
Daniel Lynch (2)
Kris Bubic (8)
Austin Cox (9)
Daniel Tillo (21)
Evan Steele (28)
Foster Griffin (29)
Angel Zerpa
Anthony Veneziano

LHRP
Richard Lovelady (24)
Josh Dye
Robert Garcia
Gabe Speier

RHP

RHSP
Jackson Kowar (3)
Brady Singer (4)
Jonathan Bowlan (11)
Carlos Hernandez (14)
Zach Haake (15)
Yefri Del Rosario (20)
Jon Heasley (22)
Alec Marsh (23)
Yohanse Morel (30)
Noah Murdock
Scott Blewett
Charlie Neuweiler
Grant Gambrell

RHRP
Josh Staumont (25)
Kyle Zimmer
Tyler Zuber
Brandon Marklund
Yunior Marte
Tad Ratliff

DRAFT ANALYSIS

2019

BEST PURE HITTER: SS Bobby Witt Jr. (1) has the ability to use the entire field with authority and has a solid approach at the plate, although there is still some swing-and-miss in his game.

BEST POWER HITTER: 1B Vinnie Pasquantino (11) has a big, physical frame and showed an ability to tap into his power while healthy at Old Dominion. In his pro debut, Pasquantino hit 14 home runs in 57 games at Rookie-level Burlington.

FASTEST RUNNER: SS Tyler Tolbert's (13) 70-grade speed played just fine during his pro debut in the Rookie-level Pioneer and Arizona leagues, where he combined for 28 steals in 50 games while being caught just once.

BEST DEFENSIVE PLAYER: Witt Jr. has the hands, range, arm strength, body control and footwork to become a more than reliable shortstop in the big leagues. He's consistent on the routine plays and has enough speed and athleticism to make plenty of highlight-reel plays as well.

BEST ATHLETE: SS Brady McConnell (2) has never lacked for tools and athleticism, dating back to his high school days with Merritt Island (Fla.), and if he's forced off shortstop in pro ball he should have the athleticism and speed—he's a 60-grade runner—to play center field.

BEST FASTBALL: RHP Noah Murdock (7) was touching 94-95 mph as a high schooler before he underwent Tommy John surgery, and he has since rediscovered that velocity.

BEST SECONDARY PITCH: Marsh has impressive control of a deep arsenal of pitches, which includes a pair of breaking balls that he can rely on. He has both a slider and a curveball that could become above-average offerings in the future.

BEST PRO DEBUT: Pasquantino was older than the average hitter in the Rookie-level Appalachian League this summer, but hitting .294/.371/.592 with 14 home runs and 17 doubles isn't anything to scoff at for a pro debut, regardless of age or level.

MOST INTRIGUING BACKGROUND: A converted outfielder who spent most of his time in college as a hitter, RHP Josh Broughton (25) was used on the mound exclusively in his pro debut with the Royals. He's got a big arm and touched 98 mph in the Arizona League, and he has athletic bloodlines with three family members in the NFL.

CLOSEST TO THE MAJORS: Marsh's variety of pitches and advanced feel for throwing strikes and sequencing on the mound should allow him to move quickly. He posted a 9.5-to-1 strikeout-to-walk ratio in his pro debut in the Pioneer League.

BEST LATE-ROUND PICK: The Royals signed 2B Jimmy Govern (30) for just $5,000 on Day 3 of the draft after a solid four-year career with Eastern Illinois. Govern isn't super toolsy, but he has an advanced hitting approach.

THE ONE WHO GOT AWAY: C Saul Garza (32) impressed both offensively and defensively during the spring for Louisiana State, but as a draft-eligible sophomore he proved too difficult to sign.

—CARLOS COLLAZO

TOP DRAFT PICKS OF THE DECADE

Year	Player, Pos.	2019 Org
2010	Christian Colon, SS	Reds
2011	Bubba Starling, OF	Royals
2012	Kyle Zimmer, RHP	Royals
2013	Hunter Dozier, SS	Royals
2014	Brandon Finnegan, LHP	Reds
2015	Ashe Russell, RHP	Royals
2016	A.J. Puckett, RHP (2nd round)	White Sox
2017	Nick Pratto, 1B	Royals
2018	Brady Singer, RHP	Royals
2019	Bobby Witt Jr., SS	Royals

2018

The Royals went heavy on college pitching and it has paid off. Top 100 draft picks RHP Jonathan Bowlan, LHP Kris Bubic, RHP Jackson Kowar, LHP Daniel Lynch and RHP Brady Singer all impressed early.

GRADE: A

2017

The class still shows upside, but 1B Nick Pratto (1) and C M.J. Melendez (2) are licking their wounds after a rough season in the Carolina League. How much impact the group provides is an open question.

GRADE: C

2016

This low-impact class has produced three big leaguers—SS Nicky Lopez (5), LHP Richard Lovelady (10) and RHP David McKay (14)—and RHP A.J. Puckett (2) helped land Melky Cabrera in a trade.

GRADE: D

1 BOBBY WITT JR., SS

Born: June 14, 2000. **B-T:** R-R. **HT:** 6-1. **WT:** 185.
Drafted: HS—Colleyville, Texas, 2019 (1st round).
Signed by: Chad Lee

TRACK RECORD: Witt Jr. topped his father by one draft slot when the Royals picked him second overall in 2019. Witt Jr. was a regular on the showcase circuit as an amateur. He won the high school home run derby at Nationals Park during 2018 all-star weekend and led USA Baseball's 18U National Team to a gold medal at the 2018 Pan-American Championships. He followed that up by winning the BA High School Player of the Year award his senior year and signed with the Royals for $7,789,000, the largest draft bonus in franchise history.

SCOUTING REPORT: Witt checks all the boxes for what is expected of a major league shortstop, with a super-athletic frame reminiscent of longtime Rockies star Troy Tulowitzki. Witt struggled with his timing in the Rookie-level Arizona League after a long layoff, however. Scouts noted Witt was too passive at the plate instead of driving pitches he could hit, but during instructional league he showed a much more aggressive approach with the ability to hit the ball to all fields. At his best, Witt shows good feel to hit, plus bat speed and a short, compact swing. He projects as an above-average hitter who should tap into his plus raw power. In addition to being a potential force as a hitter, Witt is a smart baserunner with above-average speed that ticks up to plus underway. His combination of power and speed gives him 20-home run, 20-stolen base potential, with a chance to possibly reach 30-30 in his best years. Defensively, Witt projects to be a top-tier shortstop with elite hands, a quick first step and good body control. He tends to get crossed up on balls in the hole and needs to improve his footwork, but that should come with time. Witt rounds out his supremely athletic package with a plus, accurate arm. While Witt's physical tools are considerable, his outstanding makeup and instincts stand out even more. Spending his first summer of pro ball in the AZL, he quickly bonded with teammates and demonstrated an enthusiasm and positivity readily evident to observers.

THE FUTURE: Witt is a five-tool talent with the potential to become a franchise player, though not everyone is convinced he will hit for a high average. After the Royals were conservative with him during his first pro season, the gloves will be off in 2020 with a likely assignment to low Class A Lexington and early success could result in a move to high Class A Wilmington by midsummer.

BILL MITCHELL

BA GRADE
65 **Risk: Very High**

SCOUTING GRADES
Hit: 55. **Power:** 60. **Run:** 60. **Field:** 70. **Arm:** 60.

Projected future grades on 20-80 scouting scale.

TOP PROSPECTS OF THE DECADE

Year	Player, Pos.	2019 Org
2010	Mike Montgomery, LHP	Royals
2011	Eric Hosmer, 1B	Padres
2012	Mike Montgomery, LHP	Royals
2013	Kyle Zimmer, RHP	Royals
2014	Kyle Zimmer, RHP	Royals
2015	Adalberto Mondesi, SS	Royals
2016	Adalberto Mondesi, SS	Royals
2017	Josh Staumont, RHP	Royals
2018	Nick Pratto, 1B	Royals
2019	Brady Singer, RHP	Royals

BEST TOOLS

Best Hitter for Average	Kyle Isbel
Best Power Hitter	Seuly Matias
Best Strike-Zone Discipline	Clay Dungan
Fastest Baserunner	Nick Heath
Best Athlete	Bobby Witt Jr.
Best Fastball	Daniel Lynch
Best Curveball	Austin Cox
Best Slider	Brady Singer
Best Changeup	Jackson Kowar
Best Control	Jonathan Bowlan
Best Defensive Catcher	MJ Melendez
Best Defensive Infielder	Bobby Witt Jr.
Best Infield Arm	Kelvin Gutierrez
Best Defensive Outfielder	Khalil Lee
Best Outfield Arm	Seuly Matias

Year	Age	Club (League)	Class	AVG	G	AB	R	H	2B	3B	HR	RBI	BB	SO	SB	OBP	SLG
2019	19	Royals (AZL)	R	.262	37	164	30	43	2	5	1	27	13	35	9	.317	.354
Minor League Totals				.262	37	164	30	43	2	5	1	27	13	35	9	.317	.354

2 DANIEL LYNCH, LHP

BA GRADE
60 Risk: High

Born: Nov. 17, 1996. **B-T:** L-L. **HT:** 6-6. **WT:** 190. **Drafted:** Virginia, 2018 (1st round). **Signed by:** Jim Farr.

TRACK RECORD: Lynch experienced a velocity bump in his draft year, and the Royals took him 34th overall in 2018 out of Virginia. He quickly emerged as a potential steal. Arm discomfort shut Lynch down for part of the 2019 season, but the lanky lefty still showed some of the best stuff in the high Class A Carolina League and touched 98 mph in the Arizona Fall League, where he started both the Fall Stars Game and the AFL championship game.

SCOUTING REPORT: Lynch comes at hitters with a pair of plus pitches. First is his 92-97 mph fastball with a high spin rate that gets hitters chasing up in the zone. He backs it up with a hard, mid-80s slider with late bite and depth at the bottom of the zone. Those two pitches alone make him an uncomfortable at-bat, but he also has an average curveball he can land on the back foot of righthanded hitters and a mid-80s changeup that has gradually improved and started flashing plus. Lynch's three-quarters delivery features a clean arm action and should yield above-average control, even with the long limbs of his skinny, 6-foot-6 frame.

THE FUTURE: Lynch's summer shutdown prevented him from reaching Double-A during the season, but he made up for lost time with his outstanding AFL. He is on track for Double-A in 2020.

SCOUTING GRADES: **Fastball:** 60 **Slider:** 60 **Changeup:** 60 **Curveball:** 50 **Control:** 55

Year	Age	Club (League)	Class	W	L	ERA	G	GS	SV	IP	H	HR	BB	SO	K/9	WHIP	AVG
2018	21	Burlington (APP)	R	0	0	1.59	3	3	0	11	9	0	2	14	11.1	0.97	.209
	21	Lexington (SAL)	LoA	5	1	1.58	9	9	0	40	35	1	6	47	10.6	1.03	.243
2019	22	Royals (AZL)	R	0	0	1.00	3	3	0	9	6	0	3	12	12.0	1.00	.200
	22	Burlington (APP)	R	1	0	4.00	2	2	0	9	13	1	3	7	7.0	1.78	.361
	22	Wilmington (CAR)	HiA	5	2	3.10	15	15	0	78	76	4	23	77	8.8	1.26	.253
Minor League Totals				11	3	2.50	32	32	0	147	139	6	37	157	9.6	1.19	.251

3 JACKSON KOWAR, RHP

Born: Oct. 4, 1996. **B-T:** R-R. **HT:** 6-5. **WT:** 180. **Drafted:** Florida, 2018 (1st round). **Signed by:** Jim Buckley.

TRACK RECORD: Kowar teamed with Brady Singer to lead Florida to a College World Series win in 2017. The Royals drafted Singer 18th overall a year later and selected Kowar shortly after with the 33rd overall pick. Both made the jump to Double-A in their first full seasons, with Kowar pulling ahead of Singer in the eyes of many evaluators.

SCOUTING REPORT: Kowar is defined by his changeup. It's a lethal, plus-plus offering that comes at hitters in the mid-80s before falling through a trap door, drawing foolish swings and leaving opponents confounded. He pairs his changeup with a 93-96 mph fastball that has two-seam life in on righthanded batters, and that fastball-changeup combination is often all he needs to dominate. Kowar's low-70s curveball with three-quarters break is still developing, but he has gained more confidence in it to take pressure off his changeup. It has average potential but could improve as his comfort level grows. Kowar is a fierce competitor on the mound who never backs down from a challenge. He is an effective strike-thrower and can expand the zone when needed.

THE FUTURE: Kowar will spend 2020 at the upper levels of the minors, with Triple-A Omaha on the horizon. Developing his breaking ball is his top priority.

SCOUTING GRADES: **Fastball:** 55 **Changeup:** 70 **Curveball:** 50 **Control:** 55

Year	Age	Club (League)	Class	W	L	ERA	G	GS	SV	IP	H	HR	BB	SO	K/9	WHIP	AVG
2018	21	Lexington (SAL)	LoA	0	1	3.42	9	9	0	26	19	2	12	22	7.5	1.18	.200
2019	22	Wilmington (CAR)	HiA	5	3	3.53	13	13	0	74	68	4	22	66	8.0	1.22	.246
	22	NW Arkansas (TL)	AA	2	7	3.51	13	13	0	74	73	8	21	78	9.4	1.26	.254
Minor League Totals				7	11	3.50	35	35	0	174	160	14	55	166	8.6	1.23	.243

4 BRADY SINGER, RHP

BA GRADE
55 Risk: High

Born: Aug. 4, 1996. **B-T:** R-R. **HT:** 6-5. **WT:** 210. **Drafted:** Florida, 2018 (1st round). **Signed by:** Jim Buckley.

TRACK RECORD: The Blue Jays drafted Singer in the second round out of high school but they failed to come to terms. Singer made his way to Florida and delivered one of the most decorated careers in school history, leading the Gators to a College World Series championship as a sophomore and winning BA College Player of the Year award as a junior. The Royals drafted him 18th overall in 2018 and signed him for just under $4.25 million. Singer cruised to Double-A in his first full season, earning a selection to the Futures Game.

SCOUTING REPORT: Singer thrives on a sinker-slider combination that induces a large number of ground balls. His fastball sits 91-94 mph with late life in on the hands of righthanded batters. His sharp, mid-80s slider is already a plus pitch he can use to draw swings and misses. Singer rarely uses his 85-87 mph changeup, which—along with his low arm slot—has hampered his effectiveness at times against lefthanded hitters. Evaluators saw no issues in 2019 and give him the benefit of the doubt. Singer's changeup is still a bit too firm, but he is gaining confidence in it and could make it an average pitch in time.

THE FUTURE: Singer will likely see Triple-A at some point in 2020 and could reach the majors if his changeup develops.

SCOUTING GRADES: **Fastball:** 55 **Slider:** 60 **Changeup:** 45 **Control:** 50

Year	Age	Club (League)	Class	W	L	ERA	G	GS	SV	IP	H	HR	BB	SO	K/9	WHIP	AVG
2019	22	Wilmington (CAR)	HiA	5	2	1.87	10	10	0	58	51	1	13	53	8.3	1.11	.248
	22	NW Arkansas (TL)	AA	7	3	3.47	16	16	0	91	86	8	26	85	8.4	1.24	.247
Minor League Totals				12	5	2.85	26	26	0	148	137	9	39	138	8.4	1.19	.247

5 KYLE ISBEL, OF

BA GRADE
50 Risk: High

Born: March 3, 1997. **B-T:** L-R. **HT:** 5-11. **WT:** 183. **Drafted:** Nevada-Las Vegas, 2018 (3rd round). **Signed by:** Kenny Munoz.

TRACK RECORD: Isbel got off to a hot start after the Royals made him their third-round pick in 2018, but injuries sidetracked him in 2019. A hamstring injury followed by a hamate injury largely kept him on the sidelines from mid-April until July 4 and led to a lost season. Isbel started hot at high Class A Wilmington, hitting .348 with power through 13 games, but he lost his timing at the plate with the layoff and hit .176 in his last 39 games. He rebounded to hit .315/.429/.438 in the Arizona Fall League.

SCOUTING REPORT: A fast-twitch athlete who puts together good at-bats, Isbel uses a short, line-drive stroke to all fields to project as an above-average hitter. While he doesn't look like a power hitter at 5-foot-11, 183 pounds, he has sneaky pop and could hit 10-15 home runs. Often described as a gamer, Isbel has solid tools across the board. He is a plus runner who has a chance to be a plus defender in center field with a quick first step and an average arm. He is still learning his routes and reads in the outfield after primarily playing second base in college.

THE FUTURE: Isbel looks to be the Royals' center fielder of the future. Even if he falls short of that outcome, he has the skills to be a valuable semi-regular who can play the outfield and second base. He will head to Double-A Northwest Arkansas in 2020.

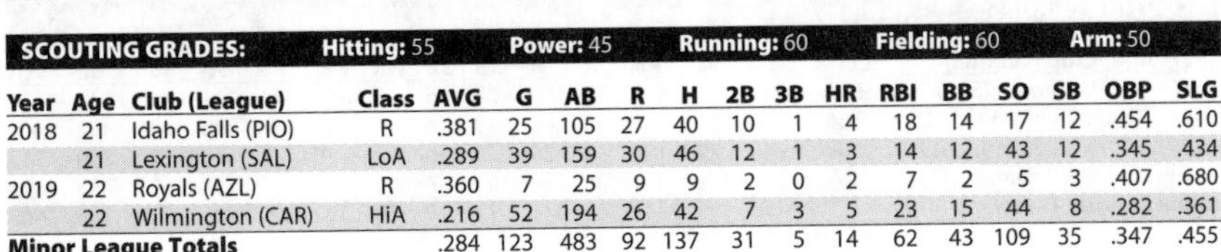

SCOUTING GRADES: **Hitting:** 55 **Power:** 45 **Running:** 60 **Fielding:** 60 **Arm:** 50

Year	Age	Club (League)	Class	AVG	G	AB	R	H	2B	3B	HR	RBI	BB	SO	SB	OBP	SLG
2018	21	Idaho Falls (PIO)	R	.381	25	105	27	40	10	1	4	18	14	17	12	.454	.610
	21	Lexington (SAL)	LoA	.289	39	159	30	46	12	1	3	14	12	43	12	.345	.434
2019	22	Royals (AZL)	R	.360	7	25	9	9	2	0	2	7	2	5	3	.407	.680
	22	Wilmington (CAR)	HiA	.216	52	194	26	42	7	3	5	23	15	44	8	.282	.361
Minor League Totals				.284	123	483	92	137	31	5	14	62	43	109	35	.347	.455

6 ERICK PEÑA, OF

Born: Feb. 20, 2003. **B-T:** L-R. **HT:** 6-3. **WT:** 180. **Signed:** Dominican Republic, 2019. **Signed by:** Edis Perez

BILL MITCHELL

BA GRADE
55 **Risk: Extreme**

TRACK RECORD: Peña was one of the top players in the 2019 international class, with the Royals signing the Dominican outfielder for a $3,897,500 bonus on July 2. He spent the latter half of the summer working out at the organization's complex in Arizona before getting into games during instructional league.

SCOUTING REPORT: Peña didn't look out of place in instructs with plus athleticism and advanced feel for the game, especially considering he was playing against older competition. He's got a good work ethic, goes about his business on the field, and is already a fluent English speaker. At the plate, Pena has good balance with strong hands and a level swing, projecting to be an average or better hitter with plus power, but he doesn't yet show the necessary plate coverage to limit the strikeouts. He's got good feel for fielding, taking solid breaks in the outfield and an average arm. Pena is an average runner now but his future speed grade will depend on how his tall, lean body develops with maturity.

THE FUTURE: Peña won't turn 17 until spring training. Since he's already spent the bulk of his time in Arizona since signing with the Royals, he'll most likely skip over the Dominican Summer League to make his official pro debut in the Rookie-level Arizona League in 2020.

SCOUTING GRADES: **Hitting:** 55 **Power:** 60 **Running:** 50 **Fielding:** 55 **Arm:** 50

Year	Age	Club (League)	Class	AVG	G	AB	R	H	2B	3B	HR	RBI	BB	SO	SB	OBP	SLG
2019	16	Did not play—Signed 2020 contract															

7 KHALIL LEE, OF

Born: June 26, 1998. **B-T:** L-L. **HT:** 5-10. **WT:** 192. **Drafted:** HS—Oakton, Va., 2016 (3rd round). **Signed by:** Jim Farr.

BA GRADE
45 **Risk: Medium**

TRACK RECORD: Lee has been young for his level every year since the Royals drafted him in the third round in 2016. He spent the entire 2019 season at Double-A Northwest Arkansas after first heading there partway through the 2018 season on his 20th birthday. Lee's numbers improved his second time through the Texas League, headlined by a league-leading 53 stolen bases.

SCOUTING REPORT: Lee presents an intriguing mix of power and speed, though how much he will get out of each is an open question. At the plate, Lee drives the ball into the gaps when he makes contact, but his swing gets stiff and at times he gets too passive at the plate. His strikeout rate remains alarmingly close to 30 percent and has improved only modestly over the years. These factors contribute to a below-average feel for hitting. Lee's above-average speed is sufficient and plays on the bases, but he doesn't always show the instincts or closing speed for center field. As such, most evaluators prefer him on an outfield corner, where his plus arm will play in either right or left.

THE FUTURE: Lee will still be only 21 on Opening Day and should get a crack at Triple-A Omaha. He will be tested by the advanced pitching at the level, but has a chance to make his major league debut during the season.

SCOUTING GRADES: **Hitting:** 45 **Power:** 50 **Running:** 55 **Fielding:** 55 **Arm:** 60

Year	Age	Club (League)	Class	AVG	G	AB	R	H	2B	3B	HR	RBI	BB	SO	SB	OBP	SLG
2017	19	Lexington (SAL)	LoA	.237	121	451	71	107	24	6	17	61	65	171	20	.344	.430
2018	20	Wilmington (CAR)	HiA	.270	71	244	42	66	13	4	4	41	48	75	14	.402	.406
	20	NW Arkansas (TL)	AA	.245	29	102	15	25	5	0	2	10	11	28	2	.330	.353
2019	21	NW Arkansas (TL)	AA	.264	129	470	74	124	21	3	8	51	65	154	53	.363	.372
Minor League Totals				.256	399	1449	245	371	72	19	37	192	222	485	97	.366	.409

8 KRIS BUBIC, LHP

Born: Aug. 19, 1997. **B-T:** L-L. **HT:** 6-3. **WT:** 220. **Drafted:** Stanford, 2018 (1st round supplemental). **Signed by:** Josh Hallgren.

BA GRADE
50 Risk: High

TRACK RECORD: Often thought of as the fourth pitcher in the Royals' 2018 draft quartet with Brady Singer, Daniel Lynch and Jackson Kowar, Bubic delivered a first full season that stacked up with any of them. The Stanford product led the minors with 185 strikeouts and posted a 2.24 ERA at a pair of Class A stops between low Class A Lexington and high Class A Wilmington, earning a selection to the Futures Game along the way.

SCOUTING REPORT: Considered a touch-and-feel lefty when he was drafted, Bubic as a pro has shown an above-average fastball that is tough to hit when he keeps it down in the zone. Bubic can run his heater up to 94 mph and it plays up with heavy sink and armside run, though his velocity fluctuates quite a bit. Bubic pairs his fastball with a plus changeup which stands as the gem of his arsenal. The pitch sinks and dives to generate swings and misses, though he doesn't always throw it as much as he should. Bubic's 1-to-7 curveball has solid bite and projects to average to give him a usable third offering. Bubic has a big, durable body that he keeps under control on the mound. A stab and pause in his delivery provide deception but do not hamper his above-average control.

THE FUTURE: Bubic has all the makings of a solid back-end starter. He will head to Double-A Northwest Arkansas in 2020.

SCOUTING GRADES: **Fastball:** 50 **Changeup:** 60 **Curveball:** 50 **Control:** 55

Year	Age	Club (League)	Class	W	L	ERA	G	GS	SV	IP	H	HR	BB	SO	K/9	WHIP	AVG
2018	20	Idaho Falls (PIO)	R	2	3	4.03	10	10	0	38	38	2	19	53	12.6	1.50	.253
2019	21	Lexington (SAL)	LoA	4	1	2.08	9	9	0	48	27	3	15	75	14.2	0.88	.164
	21	Wilmington (CAR)	HiA	7	4	2.30	17	17	0	102	76	3	27	110	9.7	1.01	.215
Minor League Totals				13	8	2.59	36	36	0	187	141	8	61	238	11.4	1.08	.211

9 AUSTIN COX, LHP

Born: Mar. 28, 1997. **B-T:** L-L. **HT:** 6-4. **WT:** 185. **Drafted:** Mercer, 2018 (5th round). **Signed by:** Jim Buckley.

BA GRADE
50 Risk: High

TRACK RECORD: The Royals drafted five pitchers before calling Cox's name in the fifth round in 2018, but the Mercer product quickly impressed after a strong 2019 season. An erratic pitcher in college, Cox impressed both Royals personnel and opposing scouts alike with a 2.76 ERA at two Class A levels, a lower figure than he ever posted in the hitter-friendly Southern Conference.

SCOUTING REPORT: Cox pitches aggressively with a plus fastball he gets to both sides of the plate. He sits 90-93 mph and touches 96. He stands out for his plus control and feel to pitch and complements his heater with a true 12-to-6 curveball the Royals consider the best in their organization. Cox is still developing an average mid-80s changeup he throws with the same arm speed as his other pitches. The key to Cox's improvement has been his control and command. A big lefty who took time to grow into his body, he now features a free and easy overhand delivery that is simple and repeatable. As such, his walk rate dropped dramatically from 4.4 per nine innings his final year in college to 2.6 per nine in his first full pro season.

THE FUTURE: Some observers believe Cox has more upside than many of the more touted pitchers in the Royals' system. He'll get a chance to prove it at Double-A Northwest Arkansas in 2020.

SCOUTING GRADES: **Fastball:** 55 **Curveball:** 60 **Changeup:** 50 **Control:** 55

Year	Age	Club (League)	Class	W	L	ERA	G	GS	SV	IP	H	HR	BB	SO	K/9	WHIP	AVG
2018	21	Burlington (APP)	R	1	1	3.78	9	9	0	33	29	1	15	51	13.8	1.32	.228
2019	22	Lexington (SAL)	LoA	5	3	2.75	13	13	0	75	59	5	22	77	9.2	1.08	.206
	22	Wilmington (CAR)	HiA	3	3	2.77	11	10	0	55	53	6	16	52	8.5	1.25	.260
Minor League Totals				9	7	2.96	33	32	0	164	141	12	53	180	9.9	1.18	.229

10 NICK PRATTO, 1B

BA GRADE 50 **Risk:** Very High

Born: Oct. 6, 1998. **B-T:** L-L. **HT:** 6-1. **WT:** 195. **Drafted:** HS—Huntington Beach, Calif., 2017 (1st round). **Signed by:** Rich Amaral.

TRACK RECORD: Pratto entered the 2017 draft with a decorated track record that included multiple gold medals playing for USA Baseball's junior national teams. The Royals drafted him 14th overall and signed him for $3.45 million. Pratto's amateur success has not translated to pro ball. He hit just .191 in a miserable season for high Class A Wilmington in 2019, though he hit seven of his nine home runs in the second half and got hot in time to help the Blue Rocks win the Carolina League championship.

SCOUTING REPORT: While the results were subpar, Pratto impressed observers by consistently putting together good at-bats and staying mentally tough through his struggles. He shows good instincts at the plate but needs to be more aggressive and avoid deep counts. He flashes average power and has the physical tools to hit .260 or better with an improved approach. Pratto's struggles at the plate didn't affect his work in the field, where he projects as a plus defender at first base with sound footwork, soft hands and an above-average arm. He is a fringe-average runner, but his advanced baserunning instincts have led to at least 10 stolen bases every year.

THE FUTURE: Pratto spent the fall working with new Royals hitting coordinators Drew Saylor and Keoni De Renne. His offseason progress will determine where he opens 2020.

SCOUTING GRADES: **Hitting:** 55 **Power:** 50 **Running:** 45 **Fielding:** 60 **Arm:** 55

Year	Age	Club (League)	Class	AVG	G	AB	R	H	2B	3B	HR	RBI	BB	SO	SB	OBP	SLG
2017	18	Royals (AZL)	R	.247	52	198	25	49	15	3	4	34	24	58	10	.330	.414
2018	19	Lexington (SAL)	LoA	.280	127	485	79	136	33	2	14	62	45	150	22	.343	.443
2019	20	Wilmington (CAR)	HiA	.191	124	419	48	80	21	1	9	46	49	164	17	.278	.310
Minor League Totals				.240	303	1102	152	265	69	6	27	142	118	372	49	.316	.387

11 JONATHAN BOWLAN, RHP

BA GRADE 50 **Risk:** Very High

Born: Dec. 1, 1996. **B-T:** R-R. **HT:** 6-6. **WT:** 262. **Drafted:** Memphis, 2018 (2nd round). **Signed by:** Travis Ezi

TRACK RECORD: A second-round pick in 2018, the burly Bowlan reported to spring training in better shape and rode his improved conditioning to a strong season at both Class A levels. The highlight of his season was a no-hitter in his fifth game after being promoted to high Class A Wilmington.

SCOUTING REPORT: Bowlan, who checks in at 262 pounds, stands out for how well he commands his pitches and is credited with having the best control in the Royals' system. He throws a heavy fastball from a full windup, sitting 90-95 mph and touching 97. Bowlan has two more potential plus pitches—a slider that got better tilt to it while working with Wilmington pitching coach Steve Luebber, and a changeup for which he has good feel. All pitches show above-average life and deception from a delivery that he repeats well. He's got good pitchability with a good idea of what he's doing on the mound.

THE FUTURE: Bowlan is the prototypical workhorse who projects in the middle or back of a rotation, but he has to watch his weight. He is set to see Double-A in 2020.

Year	Age	Club (League)	Class	W	L	ERA	G	GS	SV	IP	H	HR	BB	SO	K/9	WHIP	AVG
2018	21	Idaho Falls (PIO)	R	1	4	6.94	9	9	0	35	51	6	9	23	5.9	1.71	.329
2019	22	Lexington (SAL)	LoA	6	2	3.36	13	11	1	70	55	4	10	74	9.6	0.93	.216
	22	Wilmington (CAR)	HiA	5	3	2.95	13	12	0	76	66	5	13	76	9.0	1.03	.237
Minor League Totals				12	9	3.88	35	32	1	181	172	15	32	173	8.6	1.13	.250

12 M.J. MELENDEZ, C

BA GRADE 50 **Risk:** Very High

Born: Nov. 28, 1998. **B-T:** L-R. **HT:** 6-1. **WT:** 185. **Drafted:** HS—Palmetto Bay, Fla., 2017 (2nd round). **Signed by:** Alex Mesa.

TRACK RECORD: While many of the young hitters at Wilmington had difficulties adjusting to Carolina League pitching, none had as tough a time as Melendez. His .163 batting average and 24.2-percent swinging-strike rate were worst among all minor league hitters with at least 350 plate appearances.

SCOUTING REPORT: Melendez's problems stem from not having a real plan at the plate, using an all-or-nothing swing and having trouble hitting good velocity. He has good hands and makes hard contact with a level swing, but he needs to change his approach to use more of the field instead of pulling everything. Melendez's catch-and-throw skills keep him on the radar. He's athletic and moves well behind the plate,

although there is still improvement to be made in framing and blocking. A plus arm is his best tool, as seen in 2019 when he threw out 60 percent of basestealers, tops in the Carolina League by a wide margin.
THE FUTURE: Melendez will return to Wilmington in 2020 looking to restore his prospect stock. Some scouts now project a backup catcher's ceiling but he's still young enough to change their minds.

Year	Age	Club (League)	Class	AVG	G	AB	R	H	2B	3B	HR	RBI	BB	SO	SB	OBP	SLG
2017	18	Royals (AZL)	R	.262	47	168	25	44	8	3	4	30	26	60	4	.374	.417
2018	19	Lexington (SAL)	LoA	.251	111	419	52	105	26	9	19	73	43	143	4	.322	.492
2019	20	Salem (CAR)	HiA	.000	1	2	0	0	0	0	0	0	1	1	0	.333	.000
	20	Wilmington (CAR)	HiA	.163	110	363	34	59	23	2	9	54	44	165	7	.260	.311
Minor League Totals				.219	268	950	111	208	57	14	32	157	113	368	15	.308	.409

13 JEISON GUZMAN, SS

BA GRADE **45** **Risk: High**

Born: Oct. 8, 1998. **B-T:** L-R. **HT:** 6-2. **WT:** 180. **Signed:** Dominican Republic, 2015. **Signed by:** Edis Perez/Fabio Herrera.
TRACK RECORD: Originally signed by the Royals for $1.5 million during the 2015 international signing period, Guzman took four years to start tapping into his potential. He put himself back on the prospect radar in 2019 with a respectable season at low Class A Lexington, followed by time with the Dominican Republic national team at the Premier 12 tournament.
SCOUTING REPORT: Guzman's defense alone may get him to the big leagues. He's a plus defender with at shortstop solid footwork and a good arm, and the leadership he shows on the field stands out. Guzman showed growth at the plate in 2019. He is slowly generating more quality at-bats, staying in the zone better and staying on the ball through his swing. He hasn't moved completely away from his free-swinging ways and will need to cut down on strikeouts. While Guzman has gotten stronger, he is still a light hitter overall.
THE FUTURE: Guzman's ceiling may not get much above the role of a utility infielder, but if he continues making strides at the plate he could project as a regular shortstop batting at the bottom of the order. He will head to high Class A Wilmington in 2020.

Year	Age	Club (League)	Class	AVG	G	AB	R	H	2B	3B	HR	RBI	BB	SO	SB	OBP	SLG
2017	18	Burlington (APP)	R	.207	54	193	21	40	4	2	0	15	21	45	3	.286	.249
2018	19	Burlington (APP)	R	.283	25	106	17	30	1	1	2	8	12	16	14	.356	.368
	19	Lexington (SAL)	LoA	.239	60	209	27	50	11	3	2	21	18	58	12	.312	.349
2019	20	Lexington (SAL)	LoA	.253	121	450	51	114	23	5	7	48	25	98	15	.296	.373
Minor League Totals				.245	314	1181	155	289	50	16	12	111	97	267	51	.306	.345

14 CARLOS HERNANDEZ, RHP

BA GRADE **45** **Risk: High**

Born: March 11, 1997. **B-T:** R-R. **HT:** 6-4. **WT:** 241. **Signed:** Venezuela, 2016. **Signed by:** Richard Castro/Joelvis Gonzalez.
TRACK RECORD: Coming off a promising 2018 season at low Class A Lexington, Hernandez was ready to move up to the next level before breaking a rib during spring training. The hefty Venezuelan didn't get back on the mound for an official game until mid-June but finished with seven strong starts back at Lexington.
SCOUTING REPORT: Hernandez's fastball sits 93-97 mph and regularly touches the high 90s, with at least one report of him up to 101 during instructs. He has an easy delivery that helps the ball explode out of his hand. The pitch is fairly true but benefits from solid downhill angle. All of Hernandez's secondary pitches—slider, curveball, changeup—are below-average now, although his 80-83 mph curveball flashes plus. He needs to improve the command and the quality of those pitches to keep hitters off-balance.
THE FUTURE: Hernandez will get a second chance to make the high Class A Wilmington squad. If the command and secondaries come together with experience, Hernandez could be a force either in the rotation or in the back end of the bullpen. The latter role is more likely. The Royals added Hernandez to the 40-man roster after the season to protect him from the Rule 5 draft.

Year	Age	Club (League)	Class	W	L	ERA	G	GS	SV	IP	H	HR	BB	SO	K/9	WHIP	AVG
2017	20	Burlington (APP)	R	1	4	5.49	12	11	0	62	64	6	27	62	9.0	1.46	.266
2018	21	Lexington (SAL)	LoA	6	5	3.29	15	15	0	79	71	7	23	82	9.3	1.18	.236
2019	22	Royals (AZL)	R	0	2	7.36	5	5	0	11	14	1	3	12	9.8	1.55	.304
	22	Burlington (APP)	R	0	0	9.28	3	3	0	11	11	1	12	13	11.0	2.16	.262
	22	Lexington (SAL)	LoA	3	3	3.50	7	7	0	36	34	5	9	43	10.8	1.19	.250
Minor League Totals				10	14	4.56	42	41	0	199	194	20	74	212	9.6	1.34	.253

15 ZACH HAAKE, RHP

BA GRADE 45 **Risk:** High

Born: Oct. 8, 1996. **B-T:** R-R. **HT:** 6-4. **WT:** 186. **Drafted:** Kentucky, 2018 (6th round). **Signed by:** Mike Farrell.

TRACK RECORD: Haake is perhaps the poster child for both outstanding amateur scouting and player development. He posted an 8.47 ERA in his one year at Kentucky, but the Royals were astute enough to pick him in the sixth round in 2018 and sign him to a $297,500 bonus.

SCOUTING REPORT: Haake missed part of the 2019 season at low Class A Lexington with shoulder soreness but pitched well in his 18 starts at the level. He's two or three inches taller than his listed height, with a lanky frame that can add strength. With a big fastball in the mid-to-upper-90s, he's capable of beating hitters with it up in the zone but needs more consistency with the pitch. Haake's best secondary pitch is a potential plus changeup that looks like a slider because it moves so much before dropping quickly. He needs to develop consistency with the slider, a potential plus pitch with 11-to-5 break getting good depth and late movement.

THE FUTURE: There's still some rawness to Haake's game and questions persist as to how deep into games he'll be able to get, but he's got the tools and athleticism to take a big jump forward over the next year. He's slated for high Class A Wilmington.

Year	Age	Club (League)	Class	W	L	ERA	G	GS	SV	IP	H	HR	BB	SO	K/9	WHIP	AVG
2018	21	Royals (AZL)	R	0	0	1.86	5	4	0	10	7	1	2	10	9.3	0.93	.200
	21	Idaho Falls (PIO)	R	0	0	1.59	2	2	0	6	2	0	2	4	6.4	0.71	.111
2019	22	Idaho Falls (PIO)	R	0	0	0.00	1	1	0	4	2	0	3	4	8.3	1.15	.154
	22	Lexington (SAL)	LoA	4	6	2.85	18	18	0	76	60	2	36	90	10.7	1.27	.221
Minor League Totals				4	6	2.55	26	25	0	95	71	3	43	108	10.2	1.20	.210

16 SEULY MATIAS, OF

BA GRADE 50 **Risk:** Extreme

Born: Sept. 4, 1998. **B-T:** R-R. **HT:** 6-3. **WT:** 204. **Signed:** Dominican Republic, 2015. **Signed by:** Fausto Morel.

TRACK RECORD: Matias was showing little of his raw potential and sky-high ceiling during the early months of the Carolina League season, even after a good start in the first couple of weeks. It turns out that Matias was playing with a broken hand, with his season ending for good on June 11.

SCOUTING REPORT: When he's right, Matias has an impressive set of tools that come with plenty of risk. He might never be more than a below-average hitter but with the plus-plus power to compensate for any other shortcomings. Matias had made strides in pitch-recognition prior to the 2019 season but went backward due to the hand injury. Scouts still see an above-average defender with prototypical right field skills, with a plus or better arm.

THE FUTURE: Reports on his batting practice sessions in the fall instructional league were positive, so he should be ready to go in the spring with an almost certain return to Wilmington. Missing a year of development wasn't the optimal situation for Matias, but he'll play all of next year while still only 21.

Year	Age	Club (League)	Class	AVG	G	AB	R	H	2B	3B	HR	RBI	BB	SO	SB	OBP	SLG
2017	18	Burlington (APP)	R	.243	57	222	27	54	13	3	7	36	16	72	2	.297	.423
2018	19	Lexington (SAL)	LoA	.231	94	338	62	78	13	1	31	63	24	131	6	.303	.550
2019	20	Wilmington (CAR)	HiA	.148	57	189	23	28	10	4	4	22	25	98	2	.259	.307
Minor League Totals				.218	261	945	146	206	48	10	50	152	89	387	12	.299	.449

17 BRADY MCCONNELL, SS

BA GRADE 50 **Risk:** Extreme

Born: May 24, 1998. **B-T:** R-R. **HT:** 6-3. **WT:** 195. **Drafted:** Florida, 2019 (2nd round). **Signed by:** Jim Buckley.

TRACK RECORD: McConnell got off to a good start in his first pro season, but then went out for two weeks with a hip flexor injury less than a month into his time in the Pioneer League. He wasn't the same hitter when he came back. His season ended for good when an errant groundball caught him in the head, giving him a concussion that kept him out through the fall instructional league.

SCOUTING REPORT: McConnell has a well-rounded skill set, possessing an intriguing blend of plus raw power and plus speed. The ball makes a different sound when he barrels it up, thanks to strong, quick hands. There's plenty of swing-and-miss to his approach. While he's a shortstop now, it's more likely that McConnell moves around the field in the future, with the athleticism, arm strength and footwork to play multiple positions in a super utility role.

THE FUTURE: McConnell should head to low Class A Lexington after spring training. Expect him to get time around the field to see if that super utility projection still fits.

Year	Age	Club (League)	Class	AVG	G	AB	R	H	2B	3B	HR	RBI	BB	SO	SB	OBP	SLG
2019	21	Royals (AZL)	R	.250	2	8	3	2	1	0	1	1	1	2	0	.333	.750
	21	Idaho Falls (PIO)	R	.211	38	152	25	32	12	1	4	22	14	66	5	.286	.382
Minor League Totals				.213	40	160	28	34	13	1	5	23	15	68	5	.288	.400

18 KELVIN GUTIERREZ, 3B

Born: Aug. 28, 1994. **B-T:** R-R. **HT:** 6-3. **WT:** 215. **Signed:** Dominican Republic, 2013. **Signed by:** Modesto Ulloa (Nationals).

TRACK RECORD: Gutierrez made it to the big leagues in his age-25 season, getting into 20 games just over a year after being acquired from the Nationals as part of the deal for Kelvin Herrera. He spent the rest of the year at Triple-A Omaha for 75 games before a fractured toe ended his season early.

SCOUTING REPORT: If he could hit a little better, Gutierrez would be easy to pencil in as the Royals' third baseman of the future. He's often graded as a plus defender at the hot corner, with good hands and a plus-plus arm. At the plate he's a free swinger who struggles to cover the outer half of the plate and is susceptible to spin away. He has raw power but sells out for it.

THE FUTURE: Gutierrez will get a chance at regular playing time during spring training, with the hope that he'll start tapping into the power needed for a corner-infield position.

Year	Age	Club (League)	Class	AVG	G	AB	R	H	2B	3B	HR	RBI	BB	SO	SB	OBP	SLG
2017	22	Potomac (CAR)	HiA	.288	58	222	34	64	10	6	2	16	19	59	3	.347	.414
	22	Nationals (GCL)	R	.212	10	33	6	7	3	1	0	1	4	7	2	.297	.364
2018	23	Harrisburg (EL)	AA	.274	58	230	36	63	6	3	5	26	16	62	10	.321	.391
	23	NW Arkansas (TL)	AA	.277	65	242	29	67	8	3	6	40	20	46	10	.337	.409
2019	24	Kansas City (AL)	MAJ	.260	20	73	4	19	2	1	1	11	5	24	1	.304	.356
	24	Omaha (PCL)	AAA	.287	75	286	41	82	9	2	9	43	35	71	12	.367	.427
Major League Totals				.260	20	73	4	19	2	1	1	11	5	24	1	.304	.356
Minor League Totals				.284	556	2098	309	596	99	27	27	260	191	437	77	.347	.396

19 BREWER HICKLEN, OF

BA GRADE
45 Risk: High

Born: Feb. 9, 1996. **B-T:** R-R. **HT:** 6-2. **WT:** 208. **Drafted:** Alabama-Birmingham, 2017 (7th round). **Signed by:** Nick Hamilton.

TRACK RECORD: Hicklen will always carry the reputation of possessing a football mentality, having been a member of the Alabama-Birmingham team during the period when the program was being reinstated. That mindset has helped him in the pros and he's been labeled as a leader and credited with strong makeup. After a brief stint with high Class A Wilmington in 2018 when the Blue Rocks won the Carolina League championship, Hicklen returned there in 2019 to help the team earn its second straight crown.

SCOUTING REPORT: Standing out for his athleticism and plus speed, Hicklen is still a bit behind his counterparts in learning the nuances of baseball and catching up to the speed of the game. He has plus raw power but projects to be more hit over power because his swing lacks the necessary loft. He controls the zone and draws a fair share of walks and does damage when getting on base. An average defender, Hicklen can handle all three outfield positions, which fits with his likely projection as a solid fourth outfielder.

THE FUTURE: Hicklen will get to Double-A Northwest Arkansas in 2020.

Year	Age	Club (League)	Class	AVG	G	AB	R	H	2B	3B	HR	RBI	BB	SO	SB	OBP	SLG
2017	21	Royals (AZL)	R	.348	19	69	19	24	3	3	3	13	9	24	13	.439	.609
	21	Idaho Falls (PIO)	R	.299	20	87	19	26	8	2	1	10	9	22	3	.384	.471
2018	22	Wilmington (CAR)	HiA	.211	22	71	11	15	4	0	1	3	4	26	6	.263	.310
	22	Lexington (SAL)	LoA	.307	82	306	59	94	18	3	17	65	24	98	29	.378	.552
2019	23	Salem (CAR)	HiA	.333	1	3	0	1	0	0	0	0	0	0	0	.333	.333
	23	Wilmington (CAR)	HiA	.263	125	419	70	110	13	7	14	51	55	140	39	.363	.427
Minor League Totals				.283	268	952	178	269	46	15	36	142	101	310	90	.368	.476

20 YEFRI DEL ROSARIO, RHP

BA GRADE
50 Risk: Extreme

Born: Sept. 23, 1999. **B-T:** R-R. **HT:** 6-2. **WT:** 180. **Signed:** Dominican Republic, 2016. **Signed by:** Jonathan Cruz (Braves).

TRACK RECORD: Del Rosario started his career in the Braves organization before being declared a free agent as part of Atlanta's penalties for circumventing international signing rules. All looked rosy for the native Dominican during a strong spring training in 2019, but he missed the entire regular season with a nerve issue in his arm.

SCOUTING REPORT: Prior to the injury, Del Rosario showed good command of a mid-90s fastball with late life to both sides of the plate. The pitch topped at 96 in the spring. He complements the fastball with a potential plus curveball around 80 mph and a firm 88-89 mph changeup. His funky delivery has some deception when he doesn't throw across his body.

THE FUTURE: Del Rosario's likely landing spot will be high Class A Wilmington.

Year	Age	Club (League)	Class	W	L	ERA	G	GS	SV	IP	H	HR	BB	SO	K/9	WHIP	AVG
2017	17	Braves (DSL)	R	0	0	1.80	2	2	0	5	1	0	4	7	12.6	1.00	.067
	17	Braves (GCL)	R	1	1	3.90	11	6	0	32	37	1	10	29	8.1	1.45	.285
2018	18	Lexington (SAL)	LoA	6	5	3.19	15	15	0	79	69	10	29	72	8.2	1.24	.227
Minor League Totals				7	6	3.33	28	23	0	116	107	11	43	108	8.4	1.29	.238

21 DANIEL TILLO, LHP

BA GRADE 45 Risk: High

Born: June 13, 1996. **B-T:** L-L. **HT:** 6-5. **WT:** 215 Drafted: Iowa Western, 2017 (3rd round). **Signed by:** Scott Melvin.

TRACK RECORD: Tillo popped back on the prospect radar in 2019 with a strong season at high Class A Wilmington and Double-A Northwest Arkansas. He then had a busy fall, with an assignment to the Arizona Fall League before joining the USA Baseball's Premier12 team on trips to Mexico and Japan.

SCOUTING REPORT: An all-state basketball player in high school, Tillo is athletic with a tall, strong body. Using a low slot, he delivers a four-seam fastball that sits 91-96 mph and touches 97 with good life through the zone. Tillo's mid-80s slider and solid-average changeup lag behind the heater due to fringe command.

THE FUTURE: Still relatively inexperienced compared to other pitchers at the same level, Tillo has growth potential if he improves his command. Scouts see him as a potential piece out of the bullpen, where his stuff could get sharper and tick up. He'll head back to Double-A in 2020.

Year	Age	Club (League)	Class	W	L	ERA	G	GS	SV	IP	H	HR	BB	SO	K/9	WHIP	AVG
2017	21	Royals (AZL)	R	0	0	9.53	3	2	0	6	8	0	0	7	11.1	1.41	.333
	21	Burlington (APP)	R	3	2	3.48	7	7	0	31	35	1	6	25	7.3	1.32	.285
2018	22	Lexington (SAL)	LoA	1	1	4.35	7	7	0	41	37	3	14	31	6.8	1.23	.233
	22	Wilmington (CAR)	HiA	3	5	4.94	19	19	0	93	99	3	51	69	6.7	1.61	.279
2019	23	Wilmington (CAR)	HiA	7	8	3.77	20	20	0	107	95	5	43	64	5.4	1.29	.238
	23	NW Arkansas (TL)	AA	1	1	3.47	9	3	0	23	22	1	11	21	8.1	1.41	.256
Minor League Totals				15	17	4.27	65	58	0	301	296	13	125	217	6.5	1.40	.258

22 JON HEASLEY, RHP

BA GRADE 45 Risk: High

Born: Jan. 27, 1997. **B-T:** R-R. **HT:** 6-3. **WT:** 215. **Drafted:** Oklahoma State, 2018 (13th round). **Signed by:** Chad Lee.

TRACK RECORD: Heasley didn't live up to expectations in his two years at Oklahoma State before the Royals picked him in the 13th round in 2018, signing the draft-eligible sophomore for an over-slot $247,500 bonus. His first pro season did nothing to put him on prospect lists, but improved confidence in his arsenal in 2019 helped change his projection.

SCOUTING REPORT: Heasley uses a 90-95 mph higher-spin fastball that he commands well. A new, higher slot led to even more velocity, including a few brushes with 97 during the Carolina League playoffs. Heasley complements the heater with three secondary pitches, the best being a 12-to-6 curveball that flashes plus. That pitch is down and late when thrown to the outer portion of the strike zone. The changeup could be a plus pitch in time, as it's tough on righthanded batters when he stays on it longer and finishes it better. Heasley is very competitive on the mound and repeats his delivery.

THE FUTURE: Another year of continued improvement could make Heasley next year's pop-up prospect, although many scouts see him as a reliever. He'll head to high Class A Wilmington in 2020.

Year	Age	Club (League)	Class	W	L	ERA	G	GS	SV	IP	H	HR	BB	SO	K/9	WHIP	AVG
2018	21	Idaho Falls (PIO)	R	1	3	5.15	12	11	0	51	55	4	16	35	6.2	1.40	.264
2019	22	Lexington (SAL)	LoA	8	5	3.12	25	20	0	113	93	11	34	120	9.6	1.13	.222
Minor League Totals				9	8	3.75	37	31	0	163	148	15	50	155	8.5	1.21	.236

23 ALEC MARSH, RHP

BA GRADE 45 Risk: High

Born: May 14, 1998. **B-T:** R-R. **HT:** 6-2. **WT:** 220. **Drafted:** Arizona State, 2019 (2nd round supplemental). **Signed by:** Kenny Munoz.

TRACK RECORD: Marsh soared up draft boards during his junior year at Arizona State, where he excelled as the Sun Devils' Friday night ace. His first pro experience with Idaho Falls of the rookie-level Pioneer League was quite good, and he finished with a strikeout-to-walk ratio of 38-to-4.

SCOUTING REPORT: Marsh is aggressive on the mound and pitches to contact, with his best pitch being a 90-94 mph fastball that he throws as a two-seamer and a four-seamer. He has both a slider and a curveball that flash as plus pitches, but he needs to get more separation between the two breaking balls and gain more confidence. Marsh has feel for a solid-average changeup that he throws with good arm speed and natural sink. He delivers all of his pitches from the same arm slot with a clean, repeatable delivery.
THE FUTURE: Marsh is ready to form an orderly line with the multitude of Royals pitching prospects heading to full-season ball, with his likely destination being low Class A Lexington. He projects as a solid-bodied back-end starter.

Year	Age	Club (League)	Class	W	L	ERA	G	GS	SV	IP	H	HR	BB	SO	K/9	WHIP	AVG
2019	21	Idaho Falls (PIO)	R	0	1	4.05	13	13	0	33	30	5	4	38	10.3	1.02	.238
Minor League Totals				0	1	4.05	13	13	0	33	30	5	4	38	10.3	1.02	.238

24 RICHARD LOVELADY, LHP

BA GRADE
40 **Risk: Medium**

Born: July 7, 1995. **B-T:** L-L. **HT:** 6-0. **WT:** 175. **Drafted:** Kennesaw State, 2016 (10th round). **Signed by:** Sean Gibbs.
TRACK RECORD: After zooming through the Royals' system, Lovelady made it to the big leagues for two stints less than three years after being drafted in the 10th round from Kennesaw State. While just as effective with Triple-A Omaha in 2019 as in the previous year, Lovelady's major league time had mixed results. He especially struggled in August, giving up runs in each of his last seven appearances.
SCOUTING REPORT: The key to Lovelady's arsenal is an electric mid-90s four-seam fastball with plenty of sinking action. He throws the pitch from a funky, slingshot arm action. The heater has an extra gear to it because of his elite extension. He complements the pitch with a potentially plus slider in the upper 80s. He worked to incorporate a changeup in 2019 but seldom used it during his time in the big leagues.
THE FUTURE: Lovelady had offseason surgery on his right knee but should be all clear by spring training. He stands a good chance of breaking camp in the Royals bullpen because of his ability to get righthanded batters out, indicating that he can be more than just a lefty specialist.

Year	Age	Club (League)	Class	W	L	ERA	G	GS	SV	IP	H	HR	BB	SO	K/9	WHIP	AVG
2017	21	Wilmington (CAR)	HiA	1	0	1.08	21	0	7	33	18	0	4	41	11.1	0.66	.154
	21	NW Arkansas (TL)	AA	3	2	2.16	21	0	3	33	28	1	13	36	9.7	1.23	.228
2018	22	Omaha (PCL)	AAA	3	3	2.47	46	0	9	73	53	3	21	71	8.8	1.01	.204
2019	23	Kansas City (AL)	MAJ	0	3	7.65	25	0	0	20	30	2	8	17	7.7	1.90	.353
	23	Omaha (PCL)	AAA	1	2	3.08	24	0	4	26	26	1	7	29	9.9	1.25	.265
Major League Totals				0	3	7.65	25	0	0	20	30	2	8	17	7.7	1.90	.353
Minor League Totals				10	8	2.17	133	0	32	191	139	5	54	207	9.8	1.01	.203

25 JOSH STAUMONT, RHP

BA GRADE
40 **Risk: Medium**

Born: Dec. 21, 1993. **B-T:** R-R. **HT:** 6-3. **WT:** 200. **Drafted:** Azusa (Calif.) Pacific, 2015 (2nd round). **Signed by:** Colin Gonzalez.
TRACK RECORD: Ever since taking him in the second round in 2015, the Royals have waited for Staumont to harness his command to best utilize his triple-digit fastball. After returning to Triple-A Omaha for a third season, Staumont made it to Kansas City for his major league debut last year and delivered 16 fairly effective relief appearances.
SCOUTING REPORT: Staumont is hard to hit when he throws strikes, but therein lies the problem. He walked 6.49 batters per nine innings with Omaha, about the same as the previous year. Staumont's fastball explodes out of his hand from an easy delivery and arrives in the upper 90s with natural sinking action. When thrown for strikes, it's a devastating pitch. Staumont also gets swings and misses on a low-80s curveball that has 11-to-5 tilt. Because he doesn't get his fastball in the strike zone enough, however, opposing hitters don't often find themselves in unfavorable counts.
THE FUTURE: Staumont has settled into a relief role but has made a few starts at Omaha in an opener's role. The Royals need pitching, so he has a strong chance to break camp on their Opening Day roster.

Year	Age	Club (League)	Class	W	L	ERA	G	GS	SV	IP	H	HR	BB	SO	K/9	WHIP	AVG
2017	23	Omaha (PCL)	AAA	3	8	6.28	16	15	0	76	64	14	63	93	11.0	1.67	.227
	23	NW Arkansas (TL)	AA	3	4	4.44	10	10	0	49	42	2	34	45	8.3	1.56	.244
2018	24	Omaha (PCL)	AAA	2	5	3.51	41	5	1	74	59	4	52	103	12.5	1.49	.217
2019	25	Omaha (PCL)	AAA	1	5	3.16	32	12	2	51	31	4	37	74	13.0	1.32	.172
	25	Kansas City (AL)	MAJ	0	0	3.72	16	0	0	19	21	4	10	15	7.0	1.60	.273
Major League Totals				0	0	3.72	16	0	0	19	21	4	10	15	7.0	1.60	.273
Minor League Totals				16	34	4.20	146	72	4	413	321	29	322	540	11.8	1.55	.215

26 NICK HEATH, OF

BA GRADE
40 Risk: High

Born: Nov. 27, 1993. **B-T:** L-L. **HT:** 6-1. **WT:** 187. **Drafted:** Northwestern State, 2016 (16th round). **Signed by:** Travis Ezi.

TRACK RECORD: Heath has perennially intrigued with elite athleticism and plus-plus speed, with observers waiting for the baseball skills to catch up. He showed his potential with a strong Arizona Fall League season in 2018 and rose to Triple-A Omaha in 2019.

SCOUTING REPORT: Heath is a plus-plus athlete with plus-plus speed and the defensive skills to stick in center field. While he doesn't have good baseball instincts, he's coachable and has the makeup to continue learning the game. His tick below-average arm is enough to handle any outfield position in a utility role. At the plate, Heath uses a simple, handsy swing but doesn't efficiently use his lower half. He flashes sneaky power in batting practice, but Heath's game is to make contact and create hits with his speed. That doesn't jive well with his alarming propensity for swinging and missing in the strike zone.

THE FUTURE: Heath is the type of player the Royals like to carry as a speedy fourth or fifth outfielder and he's now been added to the 40-man roster. He will start the year back at Triple-A Omaha.

Year	Age	Club (League)	Class	AVG	G	AB	R	H	2B	3B	HR	RBI	BB	SO	SB	OBP	SLG
2017	23	Lexington (SAL)	LoA	.400	2	5	1	2	0	0	0	1	0	1	1	.400	.400
	23	Royals (AZL)	R	.250	4	16	3	4	1	0	0	3	3	2	3	.368	.313
	23	Wilmington (CAR)	HiA	.250	60	224	27	56	7	0	1	12	19	59	21	.310	.295
2018	24	Wilmington (CAR)	HiA	.284	54	194	37	55	8	1	2	20	35	65	29	.397	.366
	24	NW Arkansas (TL)	AA	.257	36	105	22	27	3	3	0	7	13	33	10	.336	.343
2019	25	NW Arkansas (TL)	AA	.255	84	330	55	84	10	7	6	27	39	116	50	.332	.382
	25	Omaha (PCL)	AAA	.256	21	78	17	20	4	1	2	9	17	27	10	.392	.410
Minor League Totals				.266	323	1182	201	315	41	16	13	107	147	364	160	.348	.361

27 MICHAEL GIGLIOTTI, OF

BA GRADE
45 Risk: Extreme

Born: Feb. 14, 1996. **B-T:** L-L. **HT:** 6-1. **WT:** 180. **Drafted:** Lipscomb, 2017 (4th round). **Signed by:** Nick Hamilton.

TRACK RECORD: At Lipscomb, Gigliotti fit the profile of a speedster who takes good at-bats, which led the Royals to draft him in the fourth round in 2017. His problem as a pro has been staying on the field. Gigliotti missed almost all of 2018 with a serious knee injury and played just 87 games in 2019.

SCOUTING REPORT: The best news is that Gigliotti's knee is as strong as ever, exceeding his pre-injury marks in speed tests and re-affirming his grade as a plus-plus runner. He has good instincts on the basepaths and stole 36 bags during his abbreviated 2019 season. Gigliotti is a patient gap-to-gap hitter with feel to hit and good hands, although he lacks home run power. A plus defender in center field, he takes good routes and gets jumps on balls. His average arm works in all three outfield spots, and he is an intelligent and instinctual ballplayer.

THE FUTURE: Gigliotti will turn 24 just before spring training and will likely start the year at Double-A Northwest Arkansas. Most see him as a future fourth outfielder or better, but only if he can stay healthy.

Year	Age	Club (League)	Class	AVG	G	AB	R	H	2B	3B	HR	RBI	BB	SO	SB	OBP	SLG
2017	21	Burlington (APP)	R	.329	42	155	30	51	8	3	3	30	32	21	15	.442	.477
	21	Lexington (SAL)	LoA	.302	22	86	14	26	5	1	1	8	8	20	7	.378	.419
2018	22	Lexington (SAL)	LoA	.235	6	17	3	4	1	0	1	2	6	5	1	.435	.471
2019	23	Lexington (SAL)	LoA	.309	59	236	42	73	19	1	1	23	27	49	29	.394	.411
	23	Salem (CAR)	HiA	.000	1	3	0	0	0	0	0	0	0	1	0	.000	.000
	23	Royals (AZL)	R	.429	4	14	3	6	1	0	0	2	3	3	2	.529	.500
	23	Wilmington (CAR)	HiA	.184	24	87	8	16	2	1	0	5	8	23	5	.268	.230
Minor League Totals				.296	157	595	100	176	36	6	6	70	84	121	59	.392	.407

28 EVAN STEELE, LHP

BA GRADE
45 Risk: Extreme

Born: Nov. 14, 1996. **B-T:** R-L. **HT:** 6-5. **WT:** 210. **Drafted:** Chipola (Fla.) JC, 2017 (2nd round supplemental). **Signed by:** Jim Buckley.

TRACK RECORD: After missing all of 2018 with a shoulder injury, Steele's season didn't start until mid-May and ended just two months later. He pitched effectively when he was on the mound, logging a 2.39 ERA over 11 starts at low Class A Lexington.

SCOUTING REPORT: Steele's fastball sits 91-92 mph, touches 94 and plays up with the extra movement and sink he gets on it. There were times that the fastball sat more in the high 80s because he was still getting his feet back under him after so much downtime. His arm action and delivery allow him to command all four of his pitches. The effectiveness of the curveball and slider vary depending on the day, but there's enough separation between the two. He uses a funky, lower slot delivery to give lefthanded hitters tough

at-bats. The changeup improved during the season and shows a bit more depth when he stays behind the pitch through his delivery.
THE FUTURE: Steele may again start his season in extended spring training before returning to Lexington or heading to high Class A Wilmington. Steele has starter potential, but his deceptive delivery from the left side means he could do well in a bullpen role.

Year	Age	Club (League)	Class	W	L	ERA	G	GS	SV	IP	H	HR	BB	SO	K/9	WHIP	AVG
2017	20	Royals (AZL)	R	0	2	5.63	5	5	0	8	11	2	2	16	18.0	1.63	.306
2019	22	Lexington (SAL)	LoA	4	3	2.39	11	11	0	49	40	2	15	56	10.3	1.12	.225
Minor League Totals				4	5	2.84	16	16	0	57	51	4	17	72	11.4	1.19	.238

29 FOSTER GRIFFIN, LHP

BA GRADE **40** Risk: High

Born: July 27, 1995. **B-T:** R-L. **HT:** 6-3. **WT:** 220. **Drafted:** HS—Orlando, 2014 (1st round). **Signed by:** Jim Buckley.

TRACK RECORD: Griffin was coming off a rough 2018 season in Double-A, where the southpaw struggled to command his fastball, but the Royals still challenged him with an assignment to the hitter-friendly Pacific Coast League. He fared better than the numbers would indicate. Griffin finished the calendar year in the Dominican Winter League pitching in a relief role with impressive results, striking out 31 in 23.1 innings while walking just six.
SCOUTING REPORT: Griffin was a better pitcher in the second half as the fastball ticked up to 92-94 mph with better command and more confidence throwing it. He adds cut to some of his fastballs resulting in more lateral movement than the regular heater, giving a different look to hitters. His go-to pitch is an 81-82 mph changeup that has good deception and break and is thrown with the same arm speed. Griffin commands his low-80s curveball, getting good spin and using it as a chase pitch below the zone.
THE FUTURE: The Royals showed their confidence in Griffin by adding him to the 40-man roster. The bullpen experience in winter ball makes him a little more intriguing heading into the 2020 season, with his fastball velocity ticking up a notch and his stuff being a bit crisper in shorter stints.

Year	Age	Club (League)	Class	W	L	ERA	G	GS	SV	IP	H	HR	BB	SO	K/9	WHIP	AVG
2017	21	Wilmington (CAR)	HiA	4	2	2.86	10	10	0	57	43	2	20	60	9.5	1.11	.210
	21	NW Arkansas (TL)	AA	11	5	3.61	18	18	0	105	108	11	34	81	7.0	1.36	.271
2018	22	NW Arkansas (TL)	AA	10	12	5.13	28	26	0	153	197	20	40	117	6.9	1.55	.315
2019	23	Omaha (PCL)	AAA	8	6	5.23	25	25	0	131	134	20	64	111	7.6	1.52	.259
Minor League Totals				43	47	4.77	141	139	0	708	789	75	257	564	7.2	1.48	.282

30 YOHANSE MOREL, RHP

BA GRADE **45** Risk: Extreme

Born: August 23, 2000. **B-T:** R-R. **HT:** 6-0. **WT:** 170. **Signed:** Dominican Republic, 2017. **Signed by:** Moises de la Mota/Johnny DiPuglia (Nationals).

TRACK RECORD: Morel was acquired by the Royals as one of three prospects in the deal for big league reliever Kelvin Herrera. He draws comparisons to Herrera for having a live arm with big velocity from a smaller frame. After starting the year in extended spring training at age 18, Morel went to low Class A Lexington for the remainder of the season.
SCOUTING REPORT: Morel has feel to pitch and a competitive nature on the mound. The fastball sits 91-95 mph and he uses both a four-seamer and a two-seamer, with the latter being his preference to get grounders. He needs to improve the command of his fastball, especially to the inside part of the plate. Morel complements his fastballs with a wipeout 81-84 mph slider that flashes plus, a swing-and-miss pitch held like a spike curveball that he tunnels well to the plate with late break. Rounding out Morel's bag of tricks is a hard changeup at 86-88 mph that drops into the zone from the same arm slot and arm speed as the fastball. Both the fastball and the changeup are plus pitches.
THE FUTURE: Morel will be only 19 for most of the 2020 season, so a return to Lexington is likely. He could thrive in a bullpen role pitching in shorter stints, but that decision is years away.

Year	Age	Club (League)	Class	W	L	ERA	G	GS	SV	IP	H	HR	BB	SO	K/9	WHIP	AVG
2018	17	Nationals (DSL)	R	0	0	8.10	1	1	0	3	6	0	1	5	13.5	2.10	.375
	17	Royals (AZL)	R	1	2	3.71	12	7	0	44	40	1	16	47	9.7	1.28	.240
2019	18	Lexington (SAL)	LoA	2	6	6.02	14	11	1	52	64	7	21	57	9.8	1.62	.295
Minor League Totals				3	8	5.07	27	19	1	99	110	8	38	109	9.9	1.49	.275

Los Angeles Angels

BY MIKE DIGIOVANNA

Three-time American League MVP Mike Trout was secured to what amounts to a lifetime contract—12 years, $426.5 million—last spring. Two-way star Shohei Ohtani, under club control through 2023, is poised to return from Tommy John surgery that relegated him solely to DH in 2019. A potential superstar in top outfield prospect Jo Adell is on the cusp of the big leagues.

The foundational pieces on which the Angels should be able to build entering a new decade are firmly in place, but that doesn't necessarily mean their house is in order.

Despite having the best player in baseball since 2012, the Angels have not won a playoff game in 10 years. They've endured four straight losing seasons and are coming off a 90-loss season that was marred by the death of lefthander Tyler Skaggs and the firing of first-year manager Brad Ausmus.

While the top of the farm system features potential impact players in Adell and outfielder Brandon Marsh and the Angels continue to infuse the organization with elite middle-of-the-field athletes, the overall talent—especially at the upper levels—appears thin.

There might not be an everyday big league catcher, first baseman or third baseman in the system, though the Angels signed Anthony Rendon in free agency to fill the latter hole. The Angels also entered the winter without a shortstop-in-waiting to replace Andrelton Simmons after 2020.

There are questions about the three top pitching prospects who graduated to the big leagues in 2019. Griffin Canning's rookie season was cut short by an elbow injury. Jose Suarez, a 20-year-old lefthander, was rushed to Anaheim because of injuries and looked overmatched while going 2-6, 7.11. Patrick Sandoval showed flashes in his big league debut but still finished with a 5.03 ERA.

The most intriguing arms in the system belong to teenagers such as Hector Yan, Jack Kochanowicz, Stiward Aquino, Sadrac Franco, William Holmes and Erik Rivera, who are three to five years from the big leagues. The addition of Julio Teheran in free agency gives the team a solid innings-eating starter.

There are reasons for optimism. Under general manager Billy Eppler and scouting director Matt Swanson, the Angels have drafted and signed more high-risk, high-reward prospects, giving coaches and instructors better raw material to work with—even after trading 2019 first-rounder Will Wilson to the Giants for salary relief by attaching the contract of Zack Cozart to the deal.

The Angels have reinvested so heavily in Latin America that 12 of their top 30 prospects—including top 2019 signings Arol Vera ($2 million) and Alexander Ramirez ($1 million)—hail from the Dominican Republic, Venezuela, Panama, Cuba or the Bahamas.

There are more pitchers with better pure stuff and more position players with dynamic tools—power, speed, arm strength, bat-to-ball skills—than the Angels have had in years.

The long-term future could be bright if the Angels hit on a number of their youngsters, but if the team is going compete for a playoff spot in 2020 and 2021, it will need considerable outside help. The good news is, owner Arte Moreno appears ready to spend to acquire it.

JOHN MCCOY/GETTY IMAGES

Drafted in 2017, Griffin Canning rocketed to Anaheim and showed swing-and-miss stuff.

PROJECTED 2023 LINEUP

Position	Player	Age
Catcher	Max Stassi	32
First Base	Matt Thaiss	28
Second Base	David Fletcher	29
Third Base	Anthony Rendon	33
Shortstop	Jeremiah Jackson (4)	23
Left Field	Brandon Marsh (2)	25
Center Field	Mike Trout	31
Right Field	Jo Adell (1)	24
Designated Hitter	Shohei Ohtani	28
No. 1 Starter	Shohei Ohtani	28
No. 2 Starter	Griffin Canning	27
No. 3 Starter	Chris Rodriguez (5)	24
No. 4 Starter	Patrick Sandoval (6)	26
No. 5 Starter	Jose Suarez	25
Closer	Ty Buttrey	30

DEPTH CHART

LOS ANGELES ANGELS

TOP 2020 ROOKIE: Jo Adell, OF. The five-tool prospect may not open season with the Angels, but he should be starting in right field by the all-star break.

BREAKOUT PROSPECT: Robinson Pina, RHP. Pina's growing mastery of a split-fingered fastball has turned him into a different pitcher who can miss bats with the best in the Angels' system.

SLEEPER: Nathan Bates, RHP. Bates' 98 mph fastball headlines a potent three-pitch mix he'll lean on as he tries to rebound from elbow surgery and a drug suspension.

SOURCE OF TOP 30 TALENT

Homegrown	**27**	**Acquired**	**3**
College	6	Trades	1
Junior college	0	Rule 5 draft	1
High school	10	Independent leagues	0
International	11	Free agents/waivers	1
Nondrafted free agents	0		

LF
Alexander Ramirez (15)
Michael Hermosillo
Darwin Moreno

CF
Brandon Marsh (2)
Jordyn Adams (3)
D'Shawn Knowles (13)
Trent Deveaux
Torii Hunter Jr.

RF
Jo Adell (1)
Orlando Martinez (18)
Brennon Lund
Gareth Morgan
Spencer Griffin

3B
Jose Bonilla (25)
Kevin Maitan
Jordan Zimmerman

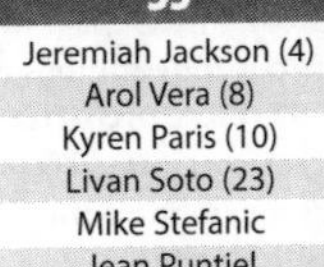

SS
Jeremiah Jackson (4)
Arol Vera (8)
Kyren Paris (10)
Livan Soto (23)
Mike Stefanic
Jean Puntiel

2B
Jahmai Jones (11)
Adrian Placencia (24)
Leonardo Rivas

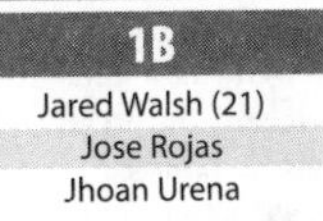

1B
Jared Walsh (21)
Jose Rojas
Jhoan Urena

C
Jack Kruger
Franklin Torres
Anthony Mulrine
Keinner Pina

LHP

LHSP	LHRP
Patrick Sandoval (6)	Erik Rivera (26)
Hector Yan (9)	Connor Higgins
Dakota Donovan	Jerryell Rivera
Jenrry Gonzalez	Adrian Almeda

RHP

RHSP:	RHRP
Chris Rodiguez (5)	Stiward Aquino (14)
Jose Soriano (7)	Oliver Ortega (16)
Jack Kochanowicz (12)	Robinson Pina (19)
Sadrac Franco (17)	Jose D. Rodriguez (22)
William Holmes (20)	Jeremy Beasley (28)
Garrett Stallings (27)	Aaron Hernandez (30)
Matt Ball (29)	Jake Jewell
Luis Madero	Brett Hanewich
Christopher Molina	Denny Brady

DRAFT ANALYSIS

2019

BEST PURE HITTER: SS Will Wilson (1), out of North Carolina State, has an extensive track record of high-level hitting over three years in the ACC and managed a .275/.328/.439 line in the Rookie-level Pioneer League in his pro debut. He has all the tools to become a plus hitter.

BEST POWER HITTER: While Wilson's hit tool is more advanced than his in-game power at the moment, scouts thought he had plus raw power as an amateur, and Angels evaluators believe he's the type of hitter who knows the barrel well enough to tap into at least average in-game power.

FASTEST BASERUNNER: The Angels took a shot on West Virginia OF Brandon White (17) on Day 3 of the draft after consistently receiving 60- and 70-grade run times on him throughout his college career. White went 61-for-85 (71.8 percent) in stolen base attempts in college, and he went 11-for-16 (68.8 percent) with Rookie-level Orem.

BEST DEFENSIVE PLAYER: White's speed could allow him to become a plus defensive center fielder at the next level, and he's athletic enough to make plenty of highlight-reel catches. SS Kyren Paris (2) has all the tools to become a standout defender as well, as a plus runner with quick-twitch athleticism, impressive hand-eye coordination and reliable hands.

BEST ATHLETE: Paris is a smooth runner and shows impressive ability at shortstop, where he'll use active footwork and standout body control.

BEST FASTBALL: Tennessee RHP Zach Linginfelter (9) has been up to 97 mph, and he's joined by a group of Day 3 college arms who have gotten into the mid-to-high 90s, including RHPs Zac Kristofak (14), Greg Veliz (15), Andrew Blake (21), and Shane Kelso (24) and LHP Ryan Smith (18).

BEST SECONDARY PITCH: The first pitcher the Angels selected was 6-foot-6 prep RHP Jack Kochanowicz (3), who showed a lot of potential with a mid-70s, 11-to-5 breaking ball that has impressive spin and depth. He also showed good feel for a changeup, as did Winthrop RHP Zach Peek (6).

BEST PRO DEBUT: After posting a 2.55 ERA over 42.1 innings with Miami, Veliz threw 29.1 innings in the Pioneer and Midwest leagues and didn't miss a beat. He posted a 3.68 ERA across both levels, with 36 strikeouts and nine walks in 29.1 innings.

CLOSEST TO THE MAJORS: RHP Garrett Stallings (5) didn't throw as a professional after handling 102.2 innings with Tennessee this spring, but scouts laud him for his makeup and competitive history in the SEC, where he walked just 1.3 batters per nine innings over his collegiate career.

BEST LATE-ROUND PICK: The Angels signed Kelso for just $10,000 in the 24th round, and he's been into the upper 90s as a professional while posting a 2.18 ERA across 20.2 innings in the Pioneer and Midwest leagues.

THE ONE WHO GOT AWAY: The Angels took a shot on RHP Kenyon Yovan (26) late in the draft, but he elected to return to school after an injury wiped out his junior season. Yovan was thought of as potentially a Day 1 talent prior to the 2019 season, and he'll look to get healthy and reclaim his draft stock next year.

—CARLOS COLLAZO

TOP DRAFT PICKS OF THE DECADE

Year	Player, Pos.	2019 Org
2010	Cam Bedrosian, RHP	Angels
2011	C.J. Cron, 1B	Rays
2012	R.J. Alvarez, RHP (3rd round)	Marlins
2013	Hunter Green, LHP (2nd round)	Did not play
2014	Sean Newcomb, LHP	Braves
2015	Taylor Ward, C	Angels
2016	Matt Thaiss, C	Angels
2017	Jo Adell, OF	Angels
2018	Jordyn Adams, OF	Angels
2019	Will Wilson, SS	Angels

2018

OF Jordyn Adams (1) and SS Jeremiah Jackson (2) were risky picks to lead off the draft, but so far it's paid off and they're both top five-prospects in the system. RHP Kyle Bradish (4) helped land Dylan Bundy.

GRADE: B

2017

OF Jo Adell (1) is close to saying hello to Angels fans and is one of the game's best and brightest prospects. RHP Griffin Canning (2) stepped into the rotation this year and pitched well in the role.

GRADE: A

2016

OF Brandon Marsh (2) ranks as the system's No. 2 prospect and is coming off a strong year in Double-A. 3B Matt Thaiss (1) in 2019 made his big league debut and RHP Chris Rodriguez (4) has impressed.

GRADE: C

1 JO ADELL, OF

Born: April 8, 1999. **B-T:** R-R. **HT:** 6-3. **WT:** 215.
Drafted: HS—Louisville, 2017 (1st round).
Signed by: John Burden.

TRAVIS BERG/FOUR SEAM IMAGES

TRACK RECORD: Adell missed most of April and May because of hamstring and ankle injuries he suffered on a baserunning mishap in spring training, but that did little to slow his ascent. The 10th overall pick in 2017, Adell slashed .289/.359/.475 in 76 games across three levels, though his strikeouts (94) were a bit high and his walks (30) were a little low. Adell did most of his damage at Double-A Mobile and starred in the Futures Game before cooling at Triple-A Salt Lake, where he struggled adjusting to a higher level of pitching. Adell rebounded with a standout showing in the Arizona Fall League and spent November playing for Team USA at the qualifying tournament for the 2020 Olympics. Facing almost exclusively older competition, Adell led the tournament in hits and tied for the lead in home runs.

SCOUTING REPORT: Adell's physical tools are plentiful. He is a broad-shouldered, dynamic athlete with high-end power, excellent bat speed and quick hands that allow him to drive the ball to all fields and get to high pitches. Adell has always destroyed fastballs and made an effort to avoid chasing breaking balls out of the zone last season. That hurt him when he first got to Salt Lake, where his passivity caused him to miss good pitches to hit, but he found the balance at the end of the season to round into form. There is maturity and a purpose in Adell's preparation and approach, and he is intelligent enough to make the adjustments necessary to hit the pitches he can handle and lay off the pitches he can't. The sum of his skills and approach should annually produce 30-plus home runs, with a plenty-high batting average to go with it. Adell's plus speed may not translate to double-digit stolen bases, but it benefits him going first to third and second to home. Adell made big strides defensively last season, improving his jumps and reads off the bat, and he must continue to hone those skills. His plus arm is good enough to play all three outfield spots.

THE FUTURE: Scouting director Matt Swanson described Adell as "a potential franchise player" the night the Angels drafted him. Adell has done little to dispel that notion and should take over as the Angels' right fielder in 2020.

BA GRADE

70 **Risk: Medium**

SCOUTING GRADES

Hit: 60. **Power:** 70. **Run:** 60.
Field: 55. **Arm:** 60.

Projected future grades on 20-80 scouting scale.

TOP PROSPECTS OF THE DECADE

Year	Player, Pos.	2019 Org
2010	Hank Conger, C	Did not play
2011	Mike Trout, OF	Angels
2012	Mike Trout, OF	Angels
2013	Kaleb Cowart, 3B	Angels
2014	Taylor Lindsey, 2B	Did not play
2015	Andrew Heaney, LHP	Angels
2016	Taylor Ward, C	Angels
2017	Jahmai Jones, OF	Angels
2018	Shohei Ohtani, RHP/DH	Angels
2019	Jo Adell, OF	Angels

BEST TOOLS

Best Hitter for Average	Brandon Marsh
Best Power Hitter	Jo Adell
Best Strike-Zone Discipline	Brandon Marsh
Fastest Baserunner	Jordyn Adams
Best Athlete	Jo Adell
Best Fastball	Jose Soriano
Best Curveball	Joey Gatto
Best Slider	Chris Rodriguez
Best Changeup	Patrick Sandoval
Best Control	Jose D. Rodriguez
Best Defensive Catcher	Keinner Pina
Best Defensive Infielder	Livan Soto
Best Infield Arm	Kevin Maitan
Best Defensive Outfielder	Brandon Marsh
Best Outfield Arm	Brandon Marsh

Year	Age	Club (League)	Class	AVG	G	AB	R	H	2B	3B	HR	RBI	BB	SO	SB	OBP	SLG
2017	18	Angels (AZL)	R	.288	31	118	18	34	6	6	4	21	10	32	5	.351	.542
	18	Orem (PIO)	R	.376	18	85	25	32	5	2	1	9	4	17	3	.411	.518
2018	19	Burlington (MWL)	LoA	.326	25	95	23	31	7	1	6	29	11	26	4	.398	.611
	19	Inland Empire (CAL)	HiA	.290	57	238	46	69	19	3	12	42	15	63	9	.345	.546
	19	Mobile (SL)	AA	.238	17	63	14	15	6	0	2	6	6	22	2	.324	.429
2019	20	Inland Empire (CAL)	HiA	.280	6	25	4	7	1	0	2	5	1	10	0	.333	.560
	20	Mobile (SL)	AA	.308	43	159	28	49	15	0	8	23	19	41	6	.390	.553
	20	Salt Lake (PCL)	AAA	.264	27	121	22	32	11	0	0	8	10	43	1	.321	.355
Minor League Totals				.298	224	904	180	269	70	12	35	143	76	254	30	.361	.518

2 BRANDON MARSH, OF

Born: Dec. 18, 1997. **B-T:** L-R. **HT:** 6-4. **WT:** 215. **Drafted:** HS—Buford, Ga., 2016 (2nd round). **Signed by:** Todd Hogan.

TRACK RECORD: Marsh did not impress scouts in the early part of last season. Batting from a crouched position, he slashed at pitches, his hands were not in position to get the barrel to the zone on time and he did not drive the ball with much authority. A midseason adjustment to stand more upright in the box helped free Marsh up, and he proceeded to hit .306 with a .829 OPS from July on at Double-A Mobile. He wrapped his year up by batting .328/.387/.522 in the Arizona Fall League.

SCOUTING REPORT: Once Marsh got comfortable with his new stance, his swing path improved and his bat stayed through the zone longer, allowing him to use his strength and generate more loft. His understanding of how opponents are pitching him continues to grow, and his improved pull-side power in the second half of last season fueled even more optimism about his offensive future. Marsh is an elite athlete with plus defensive instincts in center field, plus speed and route-running abilities and a strong, accurate arm. He also impressed coaches with his leadership and ability to battle through nagging injuries.

THE FUTURE: Marsh has the skills to be an everyday outfielder at the highest level. He'll move to Triple-A in 2020.

SCOUTING GRADES: Hitting: 55 | Power: 50 | Running: 60 | Fielding: 60 | Arm: 70

Year	Age	Club (League)	Class	AVG	G	AB	R	H	2B	3B	HR	RBI	BB	SO	SB	OBP	SLG
2017	19	Orem (PIO)	R	.350	39	177	47	62	13	5	4	44	9	35	10	.396	.548
2018	20	Burlington (MWL)	LoA	.295	34	132	26	39	12	1	3	24	21	40	4	.390	.470
	20	Inland Empire (CAL)	HiA	.256	93	371	59	95	15	6	7	46	52	118	10	.348	.385
2019	21	Angels (AZL)	R	.048	5	21	1	1	0	0	0	2	0	8	1	.048	.048
	21	Mobile (SL)	AA	.300	96	360	48	108	21	2	7	43	47	92	18	.383	.428
Minor League Totals				.287	267	1061	181	305	61	14	21	159	129	293	43	.368	.431

3 JORDYN ADAMS, OF

Born: Oct. 18, 1999. **B-T:** R-R. **HT:** 6-2. **WT:** 180. **Drafted:** HS—Cary, N.C., 2018 (1st round). **Signed by:** Chris McAlpin.

BA GRADE
55 Risk: Very High

TRACK RECORD: The 17th overall pick in 2018, Adams turned down a chance to play baseball and football at North Carolina and signed for an over-slot $4.1 million bonus. He showed elite athleticism but raw baseball skills in his first full season, though he held his own at low Class A Burlington and managed to touch high Class A Inland Empire as a 19-year-old.

SCOUTING REPORT: Adams is an elite runner with excellent bat speed and wiry strength. He makes contact and hit for more power after he reinstituted the modified leg kick he used in high school last July, though he is still working on his swing path to more consistently impact the ball. Adams has a mature feel for the strike zone and rarely chases offspeed pitches, leaving him more advanced than many other raw athletes of his ilk. Adams' 80-grade speed allows him to outrun some of his mistakes in center field. He is working on his pre-pitch routine and learning how to read balls off the bat, get better jumps and run cleaner routes.

THE FUTURE: Adams has the speed to lead off and wreak havoc on the basepaths. He also has room to add 20 pounds to his frame and grow into a middle-of-the-order bat. His hitting development will be key to watch at Inland Empire in 2020.

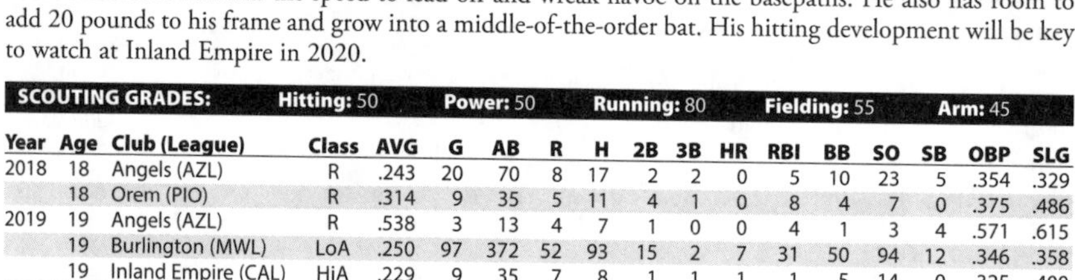

SCOUTING GRADES: Hitting: 50 | Power: 50 | Running: 80 | Fielding: 55 | Arm: 45

Year	Age	Club (League)	Class	AVG	G	AB	R	H	2B	3B	HR	RBI	BB	SO	SB	OBP	SLG
2018	18	Angels (AZL)	R	.243	20	70	8	17	2	2	0	5	10	23	5	.354	.329
	18	Orem (PIO)	R	.314	9	35	5	11	4	1	0	8	4	7	0	.375	.486
2019	19	Angels (AZL)	R	.538	3	13	4	7	1	0	0	4	1	3	4	.571	.615
	19	Burlington (MWL)	LoA	.250	97	372	52	93	15	2	7	31	50	94	12	.346	.358
	19	Inland Empire (CAL)	HiA	.229	9	35	7	8	1	1	1	1	5	14	0	.325	.400
Minor League Totals				.259	138	525	76	136	23	6	8	49	70	141	21	.353	.371

4 JEREMIAH JACKSON, SS/2B

ZACHARY LUCY/FOUR SEAM IMAGES

BA GRADE

55 Risk: Extreme

Born: March 26, 2000. **B-T:** R-R. **HT:** 6-0. **WT:** 165. **Drafted:** HS—Mobile, Ala., 2018 (2nd round). **Signed by:** J.T. Zink.

TRACK RECORD: Jackson emerged as the top prep prospect in Alabama in the 2018 draft and signed with the Angels for $1.194 million after they made him the 57th overall pick. After racing up to Rookie-level Orem in his pro debut, Jackson returned to the Owlz in 2019 and hit 23 home runs to tie the Pioneer League single-season record. That power, however, came with a concerning 33 percent strikeout rate.

SCOUTING REPORT: Jackson has eye-popping power for his skinny, 6-foot frame. He generates plus bat speed with an old-school flick of the wrist and should hit even more homers as he matures physically, though he's already driving balls out of the park to the opposite field. Jackson swings at strikes but often sells out for power and misses pitches in the zone, an issue he will have to correct in order to make enough contact against upper-level pitching. Jackson has the athletic actions for shortstop and improved his angles to the ball and throwing accuracy in 2019, two issues that previously hampered him. He also started 20 games at second base and made significant strides there as well.

THE FUTURE: Jackson is a high-risk prospect whose future depends on his ability to cut down on his strikeouts. If he can, he has huge upside as a power-hitting middle infielder.

SCOUTING GRADES: **Hitting:** 45 **Power:** 60 **Running:** 55 **Fielding:** 45 **Arm:** 55

Year	Age	Club (League)	Class	AVG	G	AB	R	H	2B	3B	HR	RBI	BB	SO	SB	OBP	SLG
2018	18	Angels (AZL)	R	.317	21	82	13	26	4	2	5	14	7	25	6	.374	.598
	18	Orem (PIO)	R	.198	22	91	13	18	6	3	2	9	8	34	4	.260	.396
2019	19	Orem (PIO)	R	.266	65	256	47	68	14	2	23	60	24	96	5	.333	.605
Minor League Totals				.261	108	429	73	112	24	7	30	83	39	155	15	.326	.559

5 CHRIS RODRIGUEZ, RHP

BILL MITCHELL

BA GRADE

55 Risk: Extreme

Born: July 20, 1998. **B-T:** R-R. **HT:** 6-2. **WT:** 185. **Drafted:** HS—Miami, 2016 (4th round). **Signed by:** Ralph Reyes.

TRACK RECORD: After sitting out the entire 2018 season with a stress reaction in his back, Rodriguez came out firing in 2019 with 13 strikeouts over 9.1 scoreless innings at high Class A Inland Empire. But his back flared up again in late April, and he had season-ending surgery to repair the stress fracture once and for all.

SCOUTING REPORT: Rodriguez flashed pure stuff in his brief return that rivaled anyone in the California League. He throws a four-seam fastball that averages 94 mph and touches 97 with late movement, and his two-seam fastball operates in the mid-90s with heavy sink and late life in on righthanded hitters. Rodriguez's best secondary pitches are a nasty, plus slider that averages 89 mph and an upper-80s changeup with screwball-like fading action. His big overhand curveball is more of a show-me pitch in the low 80s he flips in on occasion. He throws everything for strikes and earns high marks for his above-average command of such a vast repertoire. Angels officials rave about his competitive nature on the mound.

THE FUTURE: Two lost seasons have stunted Rodriguez's growth, but not his potential. Strength and conditioning will clearly be a focus in 2020, but if Rodriguez can stay healthy, he has the stuff, command and makeup to blossom into a front-of-the-rotation starter.

SCOUTING GRADES: **Fastball:** 70 **Slider:** 60 **Changeup:** 60 **Curveball:** 50 **Control:** 55

Year	Age	Club (League)	Class	W	L	ERA	G	GS	SV	IP	H	HR	BB	SO	K/9	WHIP	AVG
2017	18	Orem (PIO)	R	4	1	6.40	8	8	0	32	35	1	7	32	8.9	1.30	.271
	18	Burlington (MWL)	LoA	1	2	5.84	6	6	0	25	32	1	7	24	8.8	1.58	.314
2018	19	Did not play—Injured															
2019	20	Inland Empire (CAL)	HiA	0	0	0.00	3	3	0	9	6	0	4	13	12.5	1.07	.188
Minor League Totals				5	3	4.75	24	22	0	77	79	2	21	86	10.0	1.29	.262

6 PATRICK SANDOVAL, LHP

Born: Oct. 18, 1996. **B-T:** L-L. **HT:** 6-3. **WT:** 190. **Drafted:** HS—Mission Viejo, Calif., 2015 (11th round). **Signed by:** Brad Budzinksi (Astros).

BLAINE OHIGASHI

BA GRADE 45 **Risk:** Medium

TRACK RECORD: Sandoval grew up 20 minutes south of Anaheim in Mission Viejo and was committed to Southern California before the Astros picked him in the 11th round in 2015. The Angels acquired him from Houston for Martin Maldonado during a breakout 2018 season.

SCOUTING REPORT: Sandoval has grown into his body and now sits 93-96 mph on his fastball, compared to 88-94 only a year ago. He has good feel for an upper-70s curveball and upper-80s slider, but his best pitch is a plus mid-80s changeup he throws with great arm speed and deception in any count. The pitch, which he throws to lefties and righties, does not have exceptional vertical movement or much fading action, but it seems to pop a parachute as it approaches the plate. Big leaguers hit just .196 against it with a swinging strike rate of 25 percent. Sandoval's high-effort, up-tempo delivery makes him difficult for hitters to pick up, but also results in fringy control. He is a fierce competitor who had a few mound meltdowns when innings got away from him at Triple-A Salt Lake, but he did a better job controlling those emotions in the big leagues.

THE FUTURE:. Sandoval is ready to assume a rotation spot in 2020. He projects as a solid No. 4 starter.

SCOUTING GRADES: **Fastball:** 55 **Slider:** 50 **Curveball:** 50 **Changeup:** 60 **Control:** 45

Year	Age	Club (League)	Class	W	L	ERA	G	GS	SV	IP	H	HR	BB	SO	K/9	WHIP	AVG
2017	20	Buies Creek (CAR)	HiA	0	1	10.13	1	0	0	3	4	0	1	2	6.8	1.88	.333
	20	Tri-City (NYP)	SS	1	1	3.79	4	4	0	19	19	0	6	28	13.3	1.32	.257
	20	Quad Cities (MWL)	LoA	2	2	3.83	9	7	1	40	38	1	16	48	10.8	1.35	.244
2018	21	Quad Cities (MWL)	LoA	7	1	2.49	14	10	1	65	58	4	11	71	9.8	1.06	.231
	21	Buies Creek (CAR)	HiA	2	0	2.74	5	3	1	23	12	1	4	26	10.2	0.70	.156
	21	Inland Empire (CAL)	HiA	1	0	0.00	3	3	0	15	6	0	6	21	12.9	0.82	.118
	21	Mobile (SL)	AA	1	0	1.37	4	4	0	20	12	0	8	27	12.4	1.02	.174
2019	22	Mobile (SL)	AA	0	3	3.60	5	4	0	20	14	1	7	32	14.4	1.05	.187
	22	Salt Lake (PCL)	AAA	4	4	6.41	15	15	0	60	84	7	35	66	9.8	1.97	.319
	22	Los Angeles (AL)	MAJ	0	4	5.03	10	9	0	39	35	6	19	42	9.6	1.37	.240
Major League Totals				0	4	5.03	10	9	0	39	35	6	19	42	9.6	1.37	.240
Minor League Totals				20	18	4.01	79	64	3	330	322	19	123	383	10.4	1.35	.250

7 JOSE SORIANO, RHP

Born: Oct. 20, 1998. **B-T:** R-R. **HT:** 6-3. **WT:** 210. **Signed:** Dominican Republic, 2016. **Signed by:** Domingo Garcia/Alfredo Ulloa.

BA GRADE 50 **Risk:** High

TRACK RECORD: Soriano weighed about 170 pounds when he signed for $70,000 in 2016, but he gradually added weight and now looks more like an NFL wide receiver than a marathon runner. With added size and strength has come increased velocity and durability. After struggling at low Class A Burlington in 2018, Soriano repeated the level in 2019 and dominated.

SCOUTING REPORT: Soriano has the perfect pitcher's body: 6-foot-3, 210 pounds, athletic with long and loose limbs. He has an easy, rhythmic delivery that is repeatable and does not put much stress on his arm. After previously sitting in the low 90s, Soriano averaged 96 mph on his four-seam fastball and touched 100 in 2019. He backs up his heater with a plus, high-spin curveball with 11-to-5 shape and low-80s velocity. His firm changeup sits around 90 mph but still has enough separation to get swings and misses. Soriano currently struggles with walks, but evaluators believe he will have average control in time as he grows into his still-developing body.

THE FUTURE: Soriano will begin 2020 at high Class A Inland Empire. As he continues to mature physically and improve the timing and mechanics of his delivery, he has a chance to develop into a hard-throwing, mid-rotation starter.

SCOUTING GRADES: **Fastball:** 70 **Curveball:** 60 **Changeup:** 50 **Control:** 45

Year	Age	Club (League)	Class	W	L	ERA	G	GS	SV	IP	H	HR	BB	SO	K/9	WHIP	AVG
2017	18	Angels (AZL)	R	2	2	2.94	12	10	0	49	43	2	14	37	6.8	1.16	.234
	18	Orem (PIO)	R	0	0	2.70	1	1	0	3	4	0	4	2	5.4	2.40	.308
2018	19	Burlington (MWL)	LoA	1	6	4.47	14	14	0	46	34	1	35	42	8.2	1.49	.217
2019	20	Angels (AZL)	R	0	1	1.93	3	3	0	5	5	0	3	8	15.4	1.71	.263
	20	Burlington (MWL)	LoA	5	6	2.55	17	15	0	78	53	5	48	84	9.7	1.30	.197
Minor League Totals				11	20	2.76	61	57	0	238	176	10	134	218	8.2	1.30	.210

8 AROL VERA, SS

BILL MITCHELL

BA GRADE
55 **Risk: Extreme**

Born: Sept. 12, 2002. **B-T:** B-R. **HT:** 6-3. **WT:** 187. **Signed:** Venezuela, 2019. **Signed by:** Marion Urdaneta/Andres Garcia/Joel Chicarelli.

TRACK RECORD: Few players better illustrate the Angels' quest to accrue athletic middle infielders and their renewed commitment to Latin America than Vera, a switch-hitter who signed as a 16-year-old last July. He did not play for an affiliate after signing but participated in fall instructional league.

SCOUTING REPORT: Vera has an advanced understanding of the strike zone and good bat-to-ball skills from both sides of the plate. He works counts and rarely swings at pitches outside the zone. Vera has grown taller and gotten stronger over the past year, making him a more physical player. He's more of a line-drive hitter but should hit for more power as he matures physically, with some seeing plus power potential. Lean and athletic, Vera has quick hands, a strong arm and an ability to throw from all angles at shortstop. There is a polish to the way he moves around and fields his position. He is an average runner now and will likely slow down as he fills out, causing some evaluators to project him at third base. Vera has impressed scouts with his makeup and work ethic

THE FUTURE: Vera will likely spend his first pro season in the Dominican Summer League. He is talented enough to potentially push for an assignment to the Rookie-level Arizona League.

SCOUTING GRADES: **Hitting:** 55 **Power:** 60 **Running:** 45 **Fielding:** 50 **Arm:** 55

Year	Age	Club (League)	Class	AVG	G	AB	R	H	2B	3B	HR	RBI	BB	SO	SB	OBP	SLG
2019	16	Did not play—Signed 2020 contract															

9 HECTOR YAN, LHP

BA GRADE
50 **Risk: High**

Born: April 26, 1999. **Age:** 20. **B-T:** L-L. **HT:** 5-11. **WT:** 209. **Signed:** Dominican Republic, 2015. **Signed by:** Domingo Garcia/Alfredo Ulloa.

TRACK RECORD: After signing for $80,000 in 2015 and spending the next three years in Rookie ball, Yan made his full-season debut in 2019 at low Class A Burlington and did not disappoint. He finished second in the Midwest League with 148 strikeouts, the most in the Angels system, and limited opponents to a .190 average while flashing premium stuff from the left side.

SCOUTING REPORT: Yan weighed 180 pounds when he signed but has gradually added weight, strength and velocity. After previously sitting in the low 90s, his fastball averaged 94 mph and reached 98 in 2019. Yan's velocity is only part of the equation. He has a funky, low three-quarters arm slot, cross-body delivery that has perplexed pitching coaches and coordinators, who debate whether to straighten him up or leave him alone. Yan's above-average splitter plays like a slider with late depth to give him a second weapon, and he also has a low-80s breaking ball with excellent depth and an average mid-80s changeup with late fade. Yan's control is fringy because of his delivery, but he throws enough strikes to be effective.

THE FUTURE: Yan has the repertoire to pitch in the middle of a rotation if he improves his control. If not, he has the stuff to pitch high-leverage relief.

SCOUTING GRADES: **Fastball:** 60 **Splitter:** 55 **Changeup:** 50 **Curveball:**45 **Control:** 45

Year	Age	Club (League)	Class	W	L	ERA	G	GS	SV	IP	H	HR	BB	SO	K/9	WHIP	AVG
2017	18	Angels (AZL)	R	0	1	4.96	10	5	1	16	10	0	11	21	11.6	1.29	.179
2018	19	Orem (PIO)	R	0	4	4.55	10	10	0	30	29	3	20	29	8.8	1.65	.274
2019	20	Burlington (MWL)	LoA	4	5	3.39	26	20	1	109	74	5	52	148	12.2	1.16	.190
Minor League Totals				6	10	3.30	53	42	2	185	136	8	98	231	11.2	1.26	.207

10 KYREN PARIS, SS

BA GRADE
50 Risk: Extreme

Born: Nov. 11, 2001. **B-T:** R-R. **HT:** 6-0. **WT:** 175. **Drafted:** HS—Oakley, Calif., 2019 (2nd round). **Signed by:** Brian Tripp.

TRACK RECORD: Paris played his entire senior season at 17 and held his own to emerge as a top draft prospect. The Angels drafted him in the second round, No. 55 overall, and gave him an above-slot $1.4 million bonus to forgo a California commitment. Paris broke his hamate bone during batting practice just before the start of the Rookie-level Arizona League and was limited to three games in his pro debut.

SCOUTING REPORT: Paris has a sound righthanded swing and a line-drive approach that allows him to drive the ball with authority to the opposite field. He has quick hands and good timing and possesses a natural feel to hit. Paris hit just two homers in 91 high school games, but his burgeoning power seems to show up whenever he plays with a wood bat. With his bat speed and wiry strength, he could develop 15-home run power as he matures. Paris has nice actions in the infield and carries himself with a lot of confidence at shortstop. He should stick at the position with his above-average speed and arm.

THE FUTURE: Paris is a high-end athlete who could end up a starting middle infielder if he adds strength. He'll be 18 years old the entire 2020 season and has plenty of time to mature physically.

SCOUTING GRADES: **Hitting:** 50 **Power:** 40 **Running:** 60 **Fielding:** 55 **Arm:** 55

Year	Age	Club (League)	Class	AVG	G	AB	R	H	2B	3B	HR	RBI	BB	SO	SB	OBP	SLG
2019	17	Angels (AZL)	R	.300	3	10	4	3	1	0	0	2	3	4	0	.462	.400
Minor League Totals				.300	3	10	4	3	1	0	0	2	3	4	0	.462	.400

11 JAHMAI JONES, 2B

BA GRADE
45 Risk: High

Born: Aug. 4, 1997. **B-T:** R-R. **HT:** 6-0. **WT:** 215. **Drafted:** HS—Norcross, Ga., 2015 (2nd round). **Signed by:** Todd Hogan.

TRACK RECORD: A onetime top prospect, Jones was a mess his first two months at Double-A Mobile as he struggled to implement a swing change intended to incorporate a greater launch angle. The Angels finally let him revert to his old stance in the summer and he promptly began hitting. Jones hit .292 with a .370 on-base percentage from July through the end of the season, then hit .302 with an .886 OPS in the Arizona Fall League.

SCOUTING REPORT: Consistency has eluded Jones the last two seasons, and not always because it was his fault. The Angels converted him from center field to second base in 2018, then attempted to overhaul his swing in 2019. Jones battled through the challenges presented to him, and the Angels love his athleticism, plate discipline, attitude and work ethic. When right, Jones controls the strike zone, lines the ball to the gaps and amasses doubles with his above-average speed. He gets in trouble when he gets uphill in his swing path and tries to hit home runs. Jones is still learning the finer points of second base but is improving and has a chance to be a playable, if only fringe-average, defender there.

THE FUTURE: Jones salvaged his stock with a strong second half and was added to the 40-man roster in the offseason. He should open 2020 at Triple-A Salt Lake.

Year	Age	Club (League)	Class	AVG	G	AB	R	H	2B	3B	HR	RBI	BB	SO	SB	OBP	SLG
2017	19	Burlington (MWL)	LoA	.272	86	346	54	94	18	4	9	30	32	63	18	.338	.425
	19	Inland Empire (CAL)	HiA	.302	41	172	32	52	11	3	5	17	13	43	9	.368	.488
2018	20	Inland Empire (CAL)	HiA	.235	75	298	47	70	10	5	8	35	43	63	13	.338	.383
	20	Mobile (SL)	AA	.245	48	184	33	45	10	4	2	20	24	51	11	.335	.375
2019	21	Mobile (SL)	AA	.234	130	482	66	113	22	3	5	50	50	109	9	.308	.324
Minor League Totals				.258	484	1900	317	491	90	24	35	202	205	404	96	.338	.386

12 JACK KOCHANOWICZ, RHP

BA GRADE
50 Risk: Extreme

Born: Dec. 22, 2000. **B-T:** L-R. **HT:** 6-6 **WT**: 220. **Drafted:** HS—Philadelphia, 2019 (3rd round). **Signed by:** Kennard Jones.

TRACK RECORD: While the Angels have been aggressive picking high school position players in the early rounds, they have not pursued many prep pitchers high in the draft. They made an exception for Kochanowicz, drafting the burly but athletic righthander in the third round and giving him an overslot $1.25 million signing bonus to sway him from a Virginia commitment. Kochanowicz did not pitch for an affiliate after signing and spent most of the summer working on his strength and conditioning.

SCOUTING REPORT: Kochanowicz's above-average fastball sits 90-93 mph and touches 95 with late, riding life up in the zone. He generates good spin on his low-80s curveball, and it should become an above-average pitch as he gets stronger and adds velocity to it. He already has a good feel for an upper-80s changeup with depth. Kochanowicz generates plenty of downhill plane with his height and high-three-quarters arm slot. He is very fluid in the way he moves and appears comfortable in his delivery, allowing him average control.

THE FUTURE: Kochanowicz is far from a finished product but is very projectable with his size, athleticism and easy velocity. He will likely start 2020 in extended spring training before pitching in the Rookie-level Arizona League.

Year	Age	Club (League)	Class	W	L	ERA	G	GS	SV	IP	H	HR	BB	SO	K/9	WHIP	AVG
2019	18	Did not play															

13 D'SHAWN KNOWLES, OF

BA GRADE 50 Risk: Extreme

Born: Jan. 16, 2001. **B-T:** B-R. **HT:** 6-0. **WT:** 165. **Signed:** Bahamas, 2017. **Signed by:** Carlos Gomez.

TRACK RECORD: Signed out of the Bahamas for $850,000 in 2017, Knowles was so raw when he signed the Angels had to teach him how to take a professional batting practice. He proved a quick study and raced up to Rookie-level Orem to finish his first season. He returned to Pioneer League in 2019 and regressed, but he was still only 18 and one of the league's youngest players.

SCOUTING REPORT: Knowles is mainly a contact hitter with a clean, compact, quiet swing from both sides of the plate. He has average raw power potential, with more pop coming from the left side. A high-end athlete with plus speed, Knowles is still learning the nuances of baserunning. He is so athletic and versatile the Angels introduced him to second base in instructional league, and he will continue to explore the position moving forward. His arm is strong enough to play all three outfield spots, and it should play up in the infield.

THE FUTURE: Knowles turned 19 in January and still has plenty of time to mature physically and mentally. He might project more as a high on-base-percentage, speedy utility man than a regular. He is set to open 2020 at low Class A Burlington.

Year	Age	Club (League)	Class	AVG	G	AB	R	H	2B	3B	HR	RBI	BB	SO	SB	OBP	SLG
2018	17	Angels (AZL)	R	.301	30	113	19	34	4	1	1	14	15	27	7	.385	.381
	17	Orem (PIO)	R	.321	28	109	27	35	9	2	4	15	13	38	2	.398	.550
2019	18	Orem (PIO)	R	.241	64	253	38	61	11	4	6	28	26	76	5	.310	.387
Minor League Totals				.274	122	475	84	130	24	7	11	57	54	141	14	.348	.423

14 STIWARD AQUINO, RHP

BA GRADE 50 Risk: Extreme

Born: June 20, 1999. **B-T:** R-R. **HT:** 6-6. **WT:** 215. **Signed:** Dominican Republic, 2016. **Signed by:** Domingo Garcia/Frankie Thon.

TRACK RECORD: Aquino signed for $100,000 in 2017 and showed immense promise before Tommy John sidelined him for the entire 2018 season. He returned in 2019 and appeared fully recovered, touching 96 mph and striking out 49 batters in 36.2 innings at two Rookie levels.

SCOUTING REPORT: The gangly Aquino missed a year of development because of his elbow injury, but he benefitted from the strength and conditioning program that came with rehabilitation. He has plenty of room to grow physically, and as he adds muscle to his thin frame, he should add even more velocity to a fastball that currently sits 93-95 mph. Aquino complements his heater with a low-80's power curveball that has good downhill bite and an improving changeup. He is coordinated for his size and has a clean, simple, repeatable delivery. He has a tick of deception in his delivery that, combined with his velocity, makes for a very uncomfortable at-bat for righthanded hitters.

THE FUTURE: Aquino will likely open 2020 in the rotation at low Class A Burlington. With his power repertoire and competitive nature, he may project more as a reliever in the big leagues.

Year	Age	Club (League)	Class	W	L	ERA	G	GS	SV	IP	H	HR	BB	SO	K/9	WHIP	AVG
2017	18	Angels (DSL)	R	0	2	4.56	7	4	0	24	25	1	9	29	11.0	1.44	.272
	18	Angels (AZL)	R	1	0	1.59	2	0	0	6	5	0	4	2	3.2	1.59	.250
2018	19	Did not play—Injured															
2019	20	Angels (AZL)	R	0	4	7.71	8	8	0	21	27	1	10	26	11.1	1.76	.321
	20	Orem (PIO)	R	0	1	5.74	4	4	0	16	19	3	6	23	13.2	1.60	.307
Minor League Totals				1	7	5.59	21	16	0	66	76	5	29	80	10.9	1.59	.295

15 ALEXANDER RAMIREZ, OF

BA GRADE **50** Risk: Extreme

Born: Aug. 29, 2002. **B-T:** R-R. **HT:** 6-2. **WT:** 205. **Signed:** Dominican Republic, 2018. **Signed by:** Frank Tejeda.

TRACK RECORD: The Angels signed Ramirez for $1 million during the 2018 international signing period based on the belief that he has the power potential to grow into a middle-of-the-order slugger. The 17-year-old showed extra-base pop in his professional debut with eight doubles, five triples and four homers in 39 Dominican Summer League games, but he also struck out in one-third of his plate appearances.

SCOUTING REPORT: Ramirez is big, strong and muscular with an athletic frame that has very little baby fat. He has plus power and can hit a ball a long, long way. Ramirez has good bat speed and decent bat-to-ball skills but, like most youngsters, he is still learning to hit breaking balls. Despite Ramirez's youth and size, he has good coordination, flexibility and mobility, and his stride length and gait are improving. An average runner with solid defensive instincts and a strong throwing arm, Ramirez projects as a power-hitting corner outfielder, but the Angels will continue to challenge him by playing him in center field.

THE FUTURE: Ramirez is set to move stateside to the Rookie-level Arizona League in 2020. His growth as a hitter will be key to watch.

Year	Age	Club (League)	Class	AVG	G	AB	R	H	2B	3B	HR	RBI	BB	SO	SB	OBP	SLG
2019	16	Angels (DSL)	R	.234	39	154	37	36	8	5	4	19	16	59	6	.328	.429
Minor League Totals				.234	39	154	37	36	8	5	4	19	16	59	6	.328	.429

16 OLIVER ORTEGA, RHP

BA GRADE **45** Risk: High

Born: Oct. 2, 1996. **B-T:** R-R. **HT:** 6-0. **WT:** 200. **Signed:** Dominican Republic, 2014. **Signed by:** Domingo Garcia/Alfredo Ulloa.

TRACK RECORD: Ortega signed for just $10,000 during the 2014 international signing period. He missed all of 2017 with a stress reaction in his back and largely stayed off the radar until 2019, when he emerged as a hidden gem. The hard-throwing righthander took advantage of a velocity bump to rack up 135 strikeouts in 111 innings in a breakout season, which included a star turn in the California League all-star game and a late promotion to Double-A.

SCOUTING REPORT: Ortega's fastball is the bedrock of his success. His heater sits 93-96 mph as a starter and 95-98 mph in relief. He complements it with a 12-to-6 knuckle-curveball in the low 80s that induced a 48 percent swing-and-miss rate in 2019. His upper-80s changeup is his clear third pitch, but has improved it to the point it could potentially be an average offering. Strong and athletic, Ortega attacks hitters with an even-keeled tempo and rhythm. He walked 4.6 batters per nine innings over his last two seasons, so he will have to find the strike zone more consistently to remain a starter.

THE FUTURE: Most scouts believe Ortega's power fastball-breaking ball combination will play best in shorter stints out of the bullpen. He will start 2020 back at Double-A.

Year	Age	Club (League)	Class	W	L	ERA	G	GS	SV	IP	H	HR	BB	SO	K/9	WHIP	AVG
2017	20	Did not play—Injured															
2018	21	Burlington (MWL)	LoA	4	5	3.51	19	18	0	82	64	6	41	86	9.4	1.28	.215
2019	22	Inland Empire (CAL)	HiA	4	5	3.34	21	16	2	94	67	8	49	121	11.5	1.23	.198
	22	Mobile (SL)	AA	0	3	8.64	5	5	0	17	23	0	8	14	7.6	1.86	.319
Minor League Totals				11	19	3.83	72	46	2	265	212	15	126	285	9.7	1.27	.218

17 SADRAC FRANCO, RHP

BA GRADE **50** Risk: Extreme

Born: June 4, 2000. **B-T:** R-R. **HT:** 6-0 WT:190. **Signed:** Panama, 2017. **Signed by:** Carlos Ramirez/Lebi Ochoa.

TRACK RECORD: Franco, who signed for $50,000 in 2017, spent the first two and a half months of last year rehabilitating a forearm injury in extended spring training. He joined Rookie-level Orem in mid-June and set the tone for a breakout season with four innings of one-run ball with no walks and nine strikeouts in his first start.

SCOUTING REPORT: Franco soared up the depth chart because of his command of a fastball that has touched 98 mph with ride at the top of the zone, a considerable boost from his peak velocity of 94 mph in 2018. Franco has already added 25-30 pounds since he signed, and as he continues to fill out physically, gain strength and further distance himself from his arm injury, he should be able to maintain his velocity for longer stretches. Franco's secondary pitches need some work. He has flashed a swing-and-miss, mid-80s changeup with significant fade and depth, while his upper-70s curveball lags behind his changeup at this point. His delivery is smooth and repeatable.

THE FUTURE: Franco will head to low Class A Burlington in 2020. He may have another velocity jump in him.

Year	Age	Club (League)	Class	W	L	ERA	G	GS	SV	IP	H	HR	BB	SO	K/9	WHIP	AVG
2017	17	Angels (DSL)	R	1	3	3.45	7	1	0	16	15	0	3	14	8.0	1.15	.246
2018	18	Angels (AZL)	R	1	1	4.94	12	3	1	31	30	1	19	32	9.3	1.58	.250
	18	Orem (PIO)	R	1	1	14.54	2	0	0	4	7	0	2	4	8.3	2.08	.389
2019	19	Orem (PIO)	R	0	2	5.04	8	8	0	25	28	5	13	25	9.0	1.64	.272
Minor League Totals				3	7	5.21	29	12	1	76	80	6	37	75	8.9	1.54	.265

18 ORLANDO MARTINEZ, OF

BA GRADE 45 Risk: High

Born: Feb. 17, 1998. **B-T:** L-L. **HT:** 6-0. **WT:** 185. **Signed:** Cuba, 2017. **Signed by:** Frankie Thon Jr.

TRACK RECORD: Martinez participated in Cuba's 18U national league in 2016 and led the circuit in batting average while finishing second in slugging percentage behind only Luis Robert. The Angels signed him for $250,000 the following year. Martinez stood out early at high Class A Inland Empire last season before missing nearly two months with a broken finger, but he bounced back to post a .759 OPS in 88 games while playing all three outfield spots.

SCOUTING REPORT: Martinez's tools don't necessarily jump out at you, but he's a solid all-around athlete with good instincts and makeup. He has a solid swing and contact skills and an overall hit-over-power profile. When he gets the pitch he's looking for he can do damage, especially to the pull-side gap. He has a smooth lefthanded swing with the potential to add more power, and he knows how to manage an at-bat. Martinez is an above-average runner and defender with a strong throwing arm. He gets good reads off the bat and runs efficient routes in all three outfield spots.

THE FUTURE: Martinez will likely start 2020 at Double-A Rocket City. He doesn't project as a big-league starter, but has the potential to be a quality fourth outfielder.

Year	Age	Club (League)	Class	AVG	G	AB	R	H	2B	3B	HR	RBI	BB	SO	SB	OBP	SLG
2018	20	Orem (PIO)	R	.375	12	48	11	18	5	0	2	10	4	9	3	.415	.604
	20	Burlington (MWL)	LoA	.289	53	218	27	63	12	1	3	25	17	56	6	.340	.394
2019	21	Inland Empire (CAL)	HiA	.263	88	380	55	100	21	4	12	49	36	79	5	.325	.434
Minor League Totals				.280	153	646	93	181	38	5	17	84	57	144	14	.337	.433

19 ROBINSON PINA, RHP

BA GRADE 45 Risk: High

Born: Nov. 26, 1998. **B-T:** R-R. **HT:** 6-4. **WT:** 200. **Signed:** Dominican Republic, 2017. **Signed by:** Francisco Tejeda.

TRACK RECORD: Pina signed with the Angels for $50,000 in 2017 and did little to distinguish himself until the Angels taught him a split-fingered fastball in instructional league after the 2018 season. The big-bodied, broad-shouldered righthander took off with the new pitch and finished second in the organization with 146 strikeouts at low Class A Burlington.

SCOUTING REPORT: Pina's fastball averages 93 mph and tops out at 96 with late life up in the zone. His low-80s curveball was his best secondary pitch until he scrapped his changeup in favor of the split-fingered fastball, an upper-80s pitch the Angels thought suited Pina because of his over-the-top delivery and huge hands. Pina walked 5.1 batters per nine innings last season, but his below-average command and control should improve as he grows into his body and learns to repeat his delivery. The Angels love Pina's competitive nature—he hates coming out of games—and the way he attacks hitters.

THE FUTURE: Pina will remain in the rotation at high Class A Inland Empire in 2020. With his repertoire and mentality, he could eventually find himself in the back of a big-league bullpen.

Year	Age	Club (League)	Class	W	L	ERA	G	GS	SV	IP	H	HR	BB	SO	K/9	WHIP	AVG
2017	18	Angels (DSL)	R	1	2	3.68	15	10	0	51	35	0	24	47	8.2	1.15	.188
2018	19	Angels (DSL)	R	2	0	4.02	8	0	1	16	12	0	6	26	14.9	1.15	.214
	19	Angels (AZL)	R	1	1	3.14	6	1	0	14	12	0	5	17	10.7	1.19	.218
	19	Orem (PIO)	R	1	1	3.21	5	0	0	14	13	1	8	18	11.6	1.50	.245
2019	20	Burlington (MWL)	LoA	5	8	3.83	26	21	1	108	85	5	61	146	12.2	1.35	.213
Minor League Totals				10	12	3.72	60	33	2	203	157	6	104	254	11.2	1.28	.210

20 WILLIAM HOLMES, RHP/OF

BA GRADE 50 Risk: Extreme

Born: Dec. 22, 2000. **B-T:** R-R. **HT:** 6-3. **WT:** 220. **Drafted:** HS—Detroit, 2018 (5th round). **Signed by:** Drew Dominguez.

TRACK RECORD: The Angels drafted Holmes, formerly known as William English, as a two-way player in the fifth round in 2018 and signed him for an over-slot $700,000 bonus. Holmes showed why the Angels took the bold step of drafting him as a two-way player by batting .326 with a .920 OPS as a hitter and

striking out 38 batters in 24.1 innings as a pitcher between two Rookie-level stops in his first full season.
SCOUTING REPORT: Holmes is a physical specimen with a broad-shouldered, muscular, athletic frame and huge hands. He has shown good raw power and speed as a hitter, but he appears to have more upside as a pitcher. Holmes features a lively fastball that averages 94 mph and touches 97 with different action, either cutting, sinking or riding to the top of the zone. He complements the heater with a big-breaking upper-70s curveball and a low-80s changeup that replaced the split-fingered fastball he used to throw. He has a clean, athletic delivery but is still working to consistently throw strikes.
THE FUTURE: Holmes has a high ceiling, but he's still adjusting to life as a full-time baseball player and his tools are raw. He will need to improve his command as he rises through the system.

Year	Age	Club (League)	Class	W	L	ERA	G	GS	SV	IP	H	HR	BB	SO	K/9	WHIP	AVG
2019	18	Angels (AZL)	R	0	2	5.71	7	6	0	17	15	2	16	25	13.0	1.79	.238
	18	Orem (PIO)	R	0	0	3.86	2	2	0	7	4	2	4	13	16.7	1.14	.182
Minor League Totals				0	2	5.18	9	8	0	24	19	4	20	38	14.1	1.60	.224

21 JARED WALSH, 1B/LHP

Born: July 30, 1993. **B-T:** L-L. **HT:** 6-1 **WT:** 210. **Drafted**: Georgia, 2015 (39th round). **Signed by:** Todd Hogan.

TRACK RECORD: A senior sign from Georgia picked in the 39th round of the 2015 draft, Walsh defied odds by jumping from high Class A to Triple-A in 2018 and reaching the big leagues as a two-way player last season. He hit 36 home runs and led the minors with a 1.110 OPS at Triple-A Salt Lake last year, and he was more than functional as a pitcher with 14 strikeouts across 18 Triple-A and big-league innings.
SCOUTING REPORT: Walsh leveled out the uppercut in his swing in 2018 to produce a more consistent bat path through the zone. He began showing power to all fields with the change and delivering consistent hard contact. When Walsh connects he hits the ball hard, but he also has huge holes in his swing that were exploited in the majors. He's a smooth defender at first base with plus hands and a strong arm. On the mound, Walsh ranges from 90-94 mph with his fastball and can spin a decent curveball, but he hasn't focused enough on pitching to develop into a reliable major league reliever.
THE FUTURE: Walsh's lefthanded power and ability to eat innings in mop-up situations make him a unique option for the Angels. The addition of the 26th roster spot helps his chances of sticking in the big leagues in 2020.

Year	Age	Club (League)	Class	W	L	ERA	G	GS	SV	IP	H	HR	BB	SO	K/9	WHIP	AVG
2018	24	Inland Empire (CAL)	HiA	0	1	4.50	2	0	0	2	3	0	0	4	18.0	1.50	.333
	24	Mobile (SL)	AA	0	0	0.00	2	0	0	2	0	0	1	1	4.5	0.50	.000
	24	Salt Lake (PCL)	AAA	0	0	0.00	4	0	1	2	3	0	1	2	10.8	2.40	.375
2019	25	Salt Lake (PCL)	AAA	1	0	4.15	13	0	1	13	16	0	5	9	6.2	1.62	.291
	25	Los Angeles (AL)	MAJ	0	0	1.80	5	0	0	5	3	0	6	5	9.0	1.80	.177
Major League Totals				0	0	1.80	5	0	0	5	3	0	6	5	9.0	1.80	.176
Minor League Totals				2	2	3.32	23	0	2	21	25	0	9	20	8.3	1.57	.278

Year	Age	Club (League)	Class	AVG	G	AB	R	H	2B	3B	HR	RBI	BB	SO	SB	OBP	SLG
2017	23	Mobile (SL)	AA	.232	20	69	7	16	3	0	3	9	3	29	1	.274	.406
	23	Inland Empire (CAL)	HiA	.331	70	275	43	91	29	1	8	52	26	72	1	.395	.531
2018	24	Inland Empire (CAL)	HiA	.275	40	149	28	41	8	1	13	36	24	50	0	.365	.604
	24	Mobile (SL)	AA	.289	41	149	26	43	13	0	8	26	21	48	1	.382	.537
	24	Salt Lake (PCL)	AAA	.270	47	178	32	48	13	0	8	37	16	56	0	.333	.478
2019	25	Salt Lake (PCL)	AAA	.325	98	382	90	124	30	0	36	86	59	115	0	.423	.686
	25	Los Angeles (AL)	MAJ	.203	31	79	6	16	5	1	1	5	6	35	0	.276	.329
Major League Totals				.203	31	79	6	16	5	1	1	5	6	35	0	.276	.329
Minor League Totals				.301	458	1715	301	516	138	7	85	311	192	470	5	.375	.538

22 JOSE D. RODRIGUEZ, RHP

BA GRADE
40 Risk: Medium

Born: Aug. 29, 1995. **B-T:** R-R. **HT:** 6-2 **WT**: 205. **Signed:** Venezuela, 2012. **Signed by:** Lebi Ochoa/Mauro Zerpa.

TRACK RECORD: Rodriguez signed with the Angels for $40,000 in 2012 and spent most of his career as an unremarkable minor leaguer with an upper-80s fastball. Added strength, physical maturity and the adoption of a more rigorous throwing program led to a sharp velocity increase the last two seasons, and he jumped from Double-A to the majors in 2019.
SCOUTING REPORT: Rodriguez's fastball went from touching 92 mph in 2017 to 94 in 2018 and 96 in 2019. He now comfortably sits at 92-93 to give him an average major league fastball, although he has yet to completely harness his newfound velocity and has a long way to go with his fastball command. Rodriguez has an array of secondaries from his days as a pitchability righthander. He has a low-80s curve-

ball he locates more effectively than his fastball and two distinctly different changeups. One cuts toward his glove side at about 85 mph and is a swing-and-miss pitch, the other sinks and fades to his arm side at about 86 mph.

THE FUTURE: Rodriguez likely doesn't have the durability or command to win a spot in the Angels rotation, but he could compete for a middle- or long-relief role in 2020.

Year	Age	Club (League)	Class	W	L	ERA	G	GS	SV	IP	H	HR	BB	SO	K/9	WHIP	AVG
2017	21	Inland Empire (CAL)	HiA	8	12	5.18	27	27	0	149	178	11	44	134	8.1	1.49	.295
2018	22	Mobile (SL)	AA	7	10	6.12	23	23	0	115	144	10	41	105	8.2	1.61	.304
2019	23	Mobile (SL)	AA	0	2	7.27	5	5	0	17	24	2	6	24	12.5	1.73	.324
	23	Salt Lake (PCL)	AAA	3	3	6.29	18	2	2	44	48	7	22	45	9.1	1.58	.274
	23	Los Angeles (AL)	MAJ	0	1	2.75	9	1	0	20	17	5	11	13	5.9	1.42	.233
Major League Totals				0	1	2.75	9	1	0	19	17	5	11	13	6.0	1.42	.233
Minor League Totals				33	39	4.73	146	105	4	589	673	41	178	548	8.4	1.44	.286

23 LIVAN SOTO, SS/2B

BA GRADE
45 Risk: Very High

Born: June 22, 2000. **B-T:** L-R. **HT:** 6-2. **WT:** 175. **Signed:** Venezuela, 2017. **Signed by:** Rolando Petit (Braves).

TRACK RECORD: Soto, one of 12 former Braves prospects who were declared free agents by MLB as punishment for Atlanta's violation of international signing rules, gained 15 pounds between 2018 and 2019, but the added strength did not result in more power. He hit only one homer and had seven doubles in 273 at-bats in between the Rookie-level Arizona League and low Class A Burlington.

SCOUTING REPORT: Soto has an advanced approach at the plate—he has almost as many walks (84) as strikeouts (94) in three minor league seasons—and his bat-to-ball skills should allow him to hit for average. He'll never be a 25-homer hitter, but the Angels believe Soto can develop the gap-to-gap power to generate more extra-base hits. He's one of the better defenders in the system, with good instincts and fast-twitch actions, a good first step, quick hands and a strong arm. Soto's best position is shortstop, but he's also grown into a plus defender at second base. He's an average runner.

THE FUTURE: If Soto retains his agility as he gains weight, he could develop into a big-league utility infielder. He doesn't turn 20 until midway through the 2020 season and still has time.

Year	Age	Club (League)	Class	AVG	G	AB	R	H	2B	3B	HR	RBI	BB	SO	SB	OBP	SLG
2017	17	Braves (GCL)	R	.225	47	173	24	39	5	0	0	14	27	26	7	.332	.254
2018	18	Orem (PIO)	R	.291	44	172	31	50	10	0	0	11	24	24	9	.385	.349
2019	19	Angels (AZL)	R	.214	7	28	4	6	2	0	0	1	1	4	0	.241	.286
	19	Burlington (MWL)	LoA	.220	64	245	24	54	5	0	1	20	32	40	6	.311	.253
Minor League Totals				.241	162	618	83	149	22	0	1	46	84	94	22	.335	.282

24 ADRIAN PLACENCIA, SS

BA GRADE
45 Risk: Extreme

Born: June 2, 2003. **B-T:** B-R. **HT:** 5-11. **WT:** 170. **Signed:** Dominican Republic, 2019. **Signed by:** Jochy Cabrera.

TRACK RECORD: Placencia drew attention early in the 2019 international signing class as a baseball rat with a competitive edge. He progressively became more and more of a prospect as he grew into his 5-foot-11 frame, and the Angels gave him a $1.1 million bonus to sign on July 2.

SCOUTING REPORT: Placencia is presently scrawny at a generously-listed 170 pounds, but he drives the ball hard for his size. He has a sound swing, puts together quality at-bats and makes hard contact when he finds the barrel. Despite his size, the natural lift in his swing gives him a chance to develop average or better raw power as he matures. Placencia signed as a shortstop, but he is a below-average runner expected to eventually move to second base. He has soft hands and an average arm with a quick exchange.

THE FUTURE: Placencia will still be 16 on Opening Day and has a long road ahead. He is slated to spend most of 2020 in the Dominican Summer League.

Year	Age	Club (League)	Class	AVG	G	AB	R	H	2B	3B	HR	RBI	BB	SO	SB	OBP	SLG
2019	16	Did not play—Signed 2020 contract															

25 JOSE BONILLA, SS/3B

BA GRADE
45 Risk: Extreme

Born: April 2, 2002. **B-T:** R-R. **HT:** 6-0. **WT:** 185. **Signed:** Dominican Republic, 2019. **Signed by:** Domingo Garcia.

TRACK RECORD: Bonilla signed with the Angels for $600,000 on July 2 and immediately went out and hit in the Dominican Summer League. He batted .284 with an .808 OPS in 20 games, showing good pull-side power with occasional opposite-field pop.

SCOUTING REPORT: Bonilla has a clean bat path that allows him to barrel baseballs consistently and produce high-end exit velocities. He should add muscle as he grows, and with a natural launch angle that helps him hit the ball into the air, he has the chance to hit for average power. Bonilla has a stout frame and is not quite as athletic as some of the organization's other Latin American infielders, but he's a polished, smooth fielder with a plus-plus arm that allows him make throws from deep in the hole at shortstop. He is a fringe-average runner who is likely to slow down as he ages.
THE FUTURE: The Angels plan to groom Bonilla as both a shortstop and third baseman, with third base seen as his most likely long-term position. He is slated to make the jump to the Rookie-level Arizona League in 2020.

Year	Age	Club (League)	Class	AVG	G	AB	R	H	2B	3B	HR	RBI	BB	SO	SB	OBP	SLG
2019	17	Angels (DSL)	R	.284	20	74	13	21	5	2	0	6	14	19	0	.402	.405
Minor League Totals				.284	20	74	13	21	5	2	0	6	14	19	0	.402	.405

26 ERIK RIVERA, OF/LHP

BA GRADE **45** Risk: Extreme

Born: Feb. 4, 2001. **B-T:** L-L. **HT:** 6-2. **WT:** 200. **Drafted:** HS—Gurabo, P.R., 2019 (4th round). **Signed by:** Omar Rodriguez.
TRACK RECORD: Rivera wasn't sure he would be able to pursue his dreams of playing professional baseball after hurricanes battered his home island of Puerto Rico in Sept. 2017. He stuck with it and impressed enough scouts at the Puerto Rico Baseball Academy last spring to be selected in the fourth round and signed to a $597,500 bonus by the Angels, who announced him as a two-way player.
SCOUTING REPORT: Rivera, who passed on a commitment to Florida International, has plenty of raw power but has struggled at times to make consistent contact. His athleticism was apparent in the outfield, where his arm strength as a pitcher is an asset. On the mound, Rivera has a very fluid, athletic delivery. His fastball sits 88-92 mph and has touched 96 mph, and he backs it up with a promising hard curveball. Rivera's early emphasis will be on improving his overall control and developing a third pitch.
THE FUTURE: The Angels have been aggressive in their efforts to develop two-players such as Shohei Ohtani, Jared Walsh, Bo Way and William Holmes. They plan to give Rivera the opportunity to develop as both a pitcher and hitter, though most of his at-bats will likely come as a designated hitter.

Year	Age	Club (League)	Class	AVG	G	AB	R	H	2B	3B	HR	RBI	BB	SO	SB	OBP	SLG
2019	18	Angels (AZL)	R	.208	21	72	8	15	4	0	0	9	9	31	0	.313	.264
Minor League Totals				.208	21	72	8	15	4	0	0	9	9	31	0	.313	.264

27 GARRETT STALLINGS, RHP

Born: Aug. 8, 1997. **B-T:** R-R. **HT:** 6-1. **WT:** 210. **Drafted:** Tennessee, 2019 (5th round). **Signed by:** Joel Murrie.
TRACK RECORD: Stallings worked as Tennessee's Friday night starter last spring and held his own in the Southeastern Conference, going 8-5, 3.33 with 106 strikeouts and only 16 walks in 102.2 innings. The Angels drafted him in the fifth round and signed him for $312,500. Stallings threw several bullpen sessions in Arizona after signing but did not pitch for an affiliate.
SCOUTING REPORT: Stallings doesn't overpower hitters and lacks a true plus pitch. Where he succeeds is with a smooth, up-tempo and easy-to-repeat delivery that allows him to command and sequence his four-pitch repertoire effectively. His fastball sits between 88-91 mph with a peak of 93 mph and has some sinking action. He complements his heater with an average slider and changeup that are slightly ahead of his curveball at this point, although his curveball showed better than his changeup in college. Stallings' ability to throw four pitches from the same arm slot and release point adds to his deception.
THE FUTURE: Stallings has a chance to move fast because of his advanced feel for pitching, overall command and his business-like approach. He will likely start 2020 at high Class A Inland Empire and could reach Double-A Rocket City by the second half.

Year	Age	Club (League)	Class	W	L	ERA	G	GS	SV	IP	H	HR	BB	SO	K/9	WHIP	AVG
2019	21	Did not play															

28 JEREMY BEASLEY, RHP

BA GRADE **40** Risk: High

Born: Nov. 20, 1995. **B-T:** R-R. **HT:** 6-3. **WT:** 215. **Drafted:** Clemson, 2017 (30th round.) **Signed by:** Chris McAlpin.
TRACK RECORD: Beasley posted a 5.79 ERA in his one season at Clemson and couldn't crack the Tigers' starting rotation, but the Angels saw untapped potential and signed him for $3,000 as a 30th-round pick

in 2017. Beasley moved to the rotation in his first season and made good on that hunch by skyrocketing to Double-A. He continued to pitch well in 2019 and reached Triple-A for three starts at the end of the year.
SCOUTING REPORT: Beasley's fastball sits at 92 mph and touches 95-96 mph. His best secondary pitch is a sharp, 83-84-mph splitter with tumble that can miss bats or induce weak contact. He has a decent slider, but the splitter is clearly his out-pitch. Beasley's high-tempo delivery and his bulldog mentality on the mound—he grunts and snarls his way through many games—lead most to believe he's bound for the bullpen, but he holds his stuff and throws strikes enough to remain a starter for now.
THE FUTURE:. Beasley is on the cusp of his major league debut in 2020. His splitter gives him an out-pitch that will serve him well as either a starter or multi-inning reliever.

Year	Age	Club (League)	Class	W	L	ERA	G	GS	SV	IP	H	HR	BB	SO	K/9	WHIP	AVG
2017	21	Angels (AZL)	R	1	0	3.18	4	0	0	6	3	0	0	6	9.5	0.53	.150
	21	Orem (PIO)	R	2	1	3.12	13	0	1	26	21	3	12	31	10.7	1.27	.219
2018	22	Burlington (MWL)	LoA	0	2	2.35	6	5	0	23	16	0	7	19	7.4	1.00	.198
	22	Inland Empire (CAL)	HiA	3	2	3.05	9	6	1	44	48	4	11	48	9.7	1.33	.281
	22	Mobile (SL)	AA	3	3	2.44	10	7	0	44	32	3	14	37	7.5	1.04	.206
2019	23	Mobile (SL)	AA	6	7	4.06	23	22	0	109	110	13	42	102	8.4	1.40	.258
	23	Salt Lake (PCL)	AAA	1	0	7.90	3	3	0	14	19	1	6	13	8.6	1.83	.322
Minor League Totals				16	15	3.56	68	43	2	265	249	24	92	256	8.7	1.28	.247

29 MATT BALL, RHP

BA GRADE **40** Risk: High

Born: Jan. 23, 1995. **B-T:** R-R. **HT:** 6-5. **WT:** 200. **Drafted:** HS—Chula Vista, Calif. , 2013 (11th round). **Signed by:** George Kachigian (White Sox).

TRACK RECORD: Ball has bounced around quite a bit since the White Sox drafted him in the 11th round in 2013. The Rangers acquired him in a trade for Anthony Ranaudo in 2016, and the Angels selected him from Texas in the minor league portion of the 2017 Rule 5 draft. After not advancing past low Class A his first five seasons, Ball jumped to Double-A in is first season with the Angels and reached Triple-A Salt Lake last year.
SCOUTING REPORT: The big-bodied, broad-shouldered Ball combines a fastball that averages 93 mph and tops out at 96 with a slider, curveball and changeup. He induced a 50 percent swing-and-miss rate last season with his mid-80s slider, which has side-to-side and sinking action. He throws his overhand curve in the upper 70s and his sinking changeup in the mid-80s. Ball's control is below-average, but he's not excessively wild.
THE FUTURE: Ball will likely start 2020 in the rotation at Triple-A. He could be a fill-in option for the Angels when one of their starters or middle relievers goes on the injured list.

Year	Age	Club (League)	Class	W	L	ERA	G	GS	SV	IP	H	HR	BB	SO	K/9	WHIP	AVG
2017	22	Hickory (SAL)	LoA	0	1	5.67	11	5	3	33	39	4	10	38	10.3	1.47	.283
2018	23	Inland Empire (CAL)	HiA	4	1	3.81	14	13	0	54	44	5	12	55	9.1	1.03	.223
	23	Mobile (SL)	AA	1	3	5.79	4	4	0	19	22	0	7	13	6.3	1.55	.301
2019	24	Mobile (SL)	AA	1	3	3.57	8	8	0	35	33	2	13	45	11.5	1.30	.243
	24	Salt Lake (PCL)	AAA	0	2	5.82	14	7	0	43	48	9	28	43	8.9	1.75	.291
Minor League Totals				15	28	5.24	125	69	7	391	440	37	155	374	8.6	1.52	.283

30 AARON HERNANDEZ, RHP

BA GRADE **40** Risk: High

Born: Dec. 2, 1996. **B-T:** R-R. **HT:** 6-1. **WT:** 170. **Drafted:** Texas A&M-Corpus Christi, 2018. (3rd round). **Signed by:** Rudy Vasquez.

TRACK RECORD: The Angels made Hernandez their third-round pick in 2018 after a strong junior year, but his first pro season was a struggle at high Class A Inland Empire. He showed less velocity than expected, walked 5.7 batters per nine and allowed a .269 opponent average. He bounced back in the Arizona Fall League with a 3.38 ERA over six starts.
SCOUTING REPORT: Hernandez flashed 96 mph in college, but in his pro debut he sat 90-94 and struggled to hold his velocity for more than three or four innings. He heavily uses his 80-83 mph slurvy breaking ball, throwing it as often as his fastball at times, and flashes a tumbling mid-80s changeup that is his best pitch when he uses it. Hernandez's stuff is ahead of his command at this point, but the hope is both will tick up with a move to the bullpen.
THE FUTURE: Hernandez rebuilt his stock somewhat with his AFL showing and will continue starting for now. He'll head to Double-A Rocket City intent to show he can stay in the rotation long-term.

Year	Age	Club (League)	Class	W	L	ERA	G	GS	SV	IP	H	HR	BB	SO	K/9	WHIP	AVG
2018	21	Did not play															
2019	22	Inland Empire (CAL)	HiA	1	4	4.46	20	15	0	73	75	6	46	81	10.0	1.67	.269
Minor League Totals				1	4	4.46	20	15	0	72	75	6	46	81	10.0	1.67	.269

Los Angeles Dodgers

BY KYLE GLASER

The Dodgers enter 2020 the same way they've entered most of their recent offseasons—as one of the most talented teams in baseball, but without a World Series ring to show for it.

The Dodgers won a franchise-record 106 games in 2019 and entered the postseason as heavy favorites to reach the World Series for a third straight year. Instead, they were stunned by the Nationals in five games in the National League Division Series for their earliest postseason exit since 2015. While the Nationals were an excellent team and went on to win the World Series, the core reasons for the Dodgers' early playoff exit were self-inflicted, including a series of baffling pitching decisions made by manager Dave Roberts in Game 5 of the NLDS as the Dodgers watched a 3-1, eighth-inning lead slip away.

The Dodgers once again received a boost from a series of excellent rookies, this time outfielder Alex Verdugo, catcher Will Smith and utilityman Matt Beaty. The club's player development excellence was best exemplified by a magical three-game stretch in June when the they won three straight games on walkoff home runs by rookies. Righthanders Tony Gonsolin and Dustin May debuted later in the summer and ably fortified the pitching staff, while infielder Gavin Lux exploded in the upper minors to win BA Minor League Player of the Year and made his major league debut in September.

The Dodgers rookies of yesteryear continued to produce as well. Cody Bellinger rode one of the hottest starts in MLB history to the National League Most Valuable Player Award, while Walker Buehler delivered a stellar sophomore campaign and surpassed an aging Clayton Kershaw as the ace of the Dodgers' rotation.

Which is to say the Dodgers are once again loaded with a young talent base that is the envy of Major League Baseball, and yet they still can't get over the hump and win the World Series.

Patience is running thin among Dodgers fans, and the declining performance of onetime stars like Kershaw and Kenley Jansen only adds to the franchise's sense of urgency.

The Dodgers figure to have plenty more opportunities to win a World Series in the coming decade. In addition to their young major league core, the club continues to add talented prospects through savvy trades, such as acquiring Josiah Gray and Jeter Downs from the Reds prior to last season, and renewed international investment, exemplified by landing Venezuela's No. 1 prospect two years in a row in Diego Cartaya and Luis Rodriguez. Combined with an amateur scouting group that has a sterling record and a player development apparatus unmatched in MLB, the Dodgers have the talent and infrastructure in place to continue their run of eight straight National League West Division titles.

But for all their talent, the Dodgers have repeatedly shot themselves in the foot in the postseason with poor decisions like removing Rich Hill in Game 2 of the 2017 World Series and Roberts' bullpen management in Game 5 of the 2019 NLDS. Until that changes, and better decisions are made when the stakes are highest, all the talent in the world won't be enough to bring the Dodgers a long-awaited World Series title. The clock is ticking to show they've learned from their mistakes.

JOHN MCCOY/GETTY IMAGES

Rookie outfielder Alex Verdugo hit his way into regular at-bats but finished on the IL.

PROJECTED 2023 LINEUP

Position	Player	Age
Catcher	Will Smith	28
First Base	Max Muncy	32
Second Base	Gavin Lux (1)	25
Third Base	Corey Seager	29
Shortstop	Jeter Downs (6)	24
Left Field	Joc Pederson	31
Center Field	Cody Bellinger	27
Right Field	Alex Verdugo	27
No. 1 Starter	Walker Buehler	28
No. 2 Starter	Dustin May (2)	25
No. 3 Starter	Julio Urias	26
No. 4 Starter	Tony Gonsolin (4)	29
No. 5 Starter	Josiah Gray (5)	25
Closer	Dennis Santana (11)	27

DEPTH CHART

LOS ANGELES DODGERS

TOP 2020 ROOKIE: Gavin Lux, 2B. Lux is ready to take over as the Dodgers' everyday second baseman and keeps getting better every year.

BREAKOUT PROSPECT: Alex De Jesus, SS. De Jesus looks the part of an impact hitter and has the athletcism to stay on the infield.

SLEEPER: Brandon Lewis, 3B. Lewis' massive power changes games in an instant and gives him a carrying tool.

SOURCE OF TOP 30 TALENT

Homegrown	**28**	**Acquired**	**2**
College	10	Trade	2
Junior college	1	Rule 5 draft	0
High school	4	Independent league	0
Nondrafted free agent	0	Free agent/waivers	0
International	13		

LF
Kyle Garlick
Zach Reks
Drew Avans

CF
DJ Peters (14)
Jeren Kendall
James Outman

RF
Luis Rodriguez (10)
Andy Pages (23)
Donovan Casey
Cody Thomas

3B
Kody Hoese (8)
Cristian Santana (16)
Miguel Vargas (22)
Brandon Lewis
Sauryn Lao

SS
Gavin Lux (1)
Jeter Downs (6)
Jacob Amaya (20)
Alex De Jesus (26)

2B
Michael Busch (9)
Omar Estevez (17)
Devin Mann (19)
Zach McKinstry (21)

1B
Edwin Rios (13)
Connor Joe
Dillon Paulson

C
Keibert Ruiz (3)
Diego Cartaya (7)
Connor Wong (15)
Yeiner Fernandez

LHP

LHSP	LHRP
Robinson Ortiz (29)	Victor Gonzalez (30)
John Rooney	Logan Salow
Leo Crawford	

RHP

RHSP	RHRP
Dustin May (2)	Dennis Santana (11)
Tony Gonsolin (4)	Josh Sborz
Josiah Gray (5)	Jordan Sheffield
Mitchell White (12)	Yadier Alvarez
Edwin Uceta (18)	Brett de Geus
Jimmy Lewis (24)	Mashall Kasowski
Andre Jackson (25)	Willis Montgomerie
Gerardo Carrillo (27)	Max Gamboa
Ryan Pepiot (28)	Zach Willeman
Michael Grove	Melvin Jimenez
Hyun Il-Choi	
Jerming Rosario	
Braydon Fisher	
Jose Martinez	

DRAFT ANALYSIS

2019

BEST PURE HITTER: The Dodgers felt 2B Michael Busch (1) had the best pure swing in the draft and consider him a future plus hitter. Busch controls the strike zone, has excellent hand-eye coordination and frequently barrels balls with a pure, line-drive stroke.

BEST POWER HITTER: 3B Brandon Lewis (4) hit some of the nation's longest home runs in college last spring and showcased plus-plus power into his pro debut. He is a physical, strong hitter with the loose hands, bat speed and torque to project 30 or more home runs annually.

FASTEST RUNNER: OF Justin Washington (35) is a long, lean runner who covers a lot of ground quickly with his plus speed and stride length. His speed ticks up to double-plus underway in the outfield, but he is still learning to get the most from his speed on the basepaths.

BEST DEFENSIVE PLAYER: 3B Kody Hoese (1) drew middling reviews at third base at Tulane. The Dodgers, however, see Hoese as a potential plus defensive third baseman who has plus hands, reads hops well, picks the ball up off the bat and has an above-average arm.

BEST ATHLETE: OF Joe Vranesh (15) was a standout linebacker in high school at famed De La Salle (Concord, Calif.) High. He combines the speed and strength of football player as a powerful, plus runner at 6-foot-2, 200 pounds.

BEST FASTBALL: RHP Nick Robertson (7) sits 94-96 mph and his fastball gets on hitters quickly with his plus deception. Robertson hides the ball well behind his 6-foot-6, 265-pound frame, preventing hitters from picking the ball up until it's too late.

BEST SECONDARY PITCH: RHP Ryan Pepiot (3) had arguably the best changeup in the draft. The Dodgers consider it a double-plus pitch at 83-85 mph with hard, late movement in the strike zone down and in.

TOP DRAFT PICKS OF THE DECADE

Year	Player, Pos.	2019 Org
2010	Zach Lee, RHP	Mets
2011	Chris Reed, LHP	Atlantic League
2012	Corey Seager, 3B	Dodgers
2013	Chris Anderson, RHP	Did not play
2014	Grant Holmes, RHP	Athletics
2015	Walker Buehler, RHP	Dodgers
2016	Gavin Lux, SS	Dodgers
2017	Jeren Kendall, OF	Dodgers
2018	*J.T. Ginn, RHP	Mississippi State
2019	Kody Hoese, 3B	Dodgers

* Did not sign

BEST PRO DEBUT: RHP Mitchell Tyranski (12) struck out 40 of the 77 batters he faced in the Rookie-level Arizona and Pioneer leagues. His curveball was his swing-and-miss pitch in relief and is the best breaking ball in the Dodgers' draft class.

MOST INTRIGUING BACKGROUND: LHP Jeff Belge (18) is legally blind in his right eye. He was skipping stones with a cousin at age 9 when a stone slipped from his cousin's hand and shattered Belge's cornea. He needed two surgeries just to keep his right eye.

CLOSEST TO THE MAJORS: Hoese's feel for hitting, above-average power, average speed and solid defense makes him a well-rounded player with few weaknesses. The Dodgers believe that will allow him to conquer the minors quickly.

BEST LATE-ROUND PICK: Belge flashed a 93-95 mph fastball and a plus curveball in relief after signing. His 6-foot-5 frame, promising lefthanded stuff and ability to overcome adversity made him a quick favorite of the Dodgers.

THE ONE WHO GOT AWAY: The Dodgers were optimistic about signing RHP Andrew Baker (16) and OF/1B Trey LaFleur (21), but Baker landed at Auburn and LaFleur stuck to his Ole Miss commitment.

—KYLE GLASER

2018

The Dodgers didn't sign RHP JT Ginn (1), who earned Freshman All-America honors at Mississippi State, and RHP Michael Grove (2) struggled in his pro debut. 3B Devin Mann (5) has been the class' bright spot.

GRADE: C

2017

OF Jeren Kendall (1) has struggled mightily and RHP Morgan Cooper (2) still hasn't debuted due to injury. C Connor Wong (3) has shown promise, and the Dodgers have been able to use four players in trades.

GRADE: D

2016

This has become an elite class, already producing five big leaguers. SS Gavin Lux (1) won Minor League Player of the Year honors, C Will Smith (1) excelled during the playoff run and RHP Dustin May (3) has big upside.

GRADE: A

1 GAVIN LUX, SS/2B

Born: Nov. 23, 1997. **B-T:** L-R. **HT:** 6-2. **WT:** 190.
Drafted: HS—Kenosha, Wis., 2016 (1st round).
Signed by: Trey Magnuson.

JOHN WILLIAMSON

BA GRADE		SCOUTING GRADES
60	Risk: Medium	**Hit:** 60. **Power:** 55. **Run:** 60. **Field:** 50. **Arm:** 55.

Projected future grades on 20-80 scouting scale.

TRACK RECORD: Wisconsin high school players are historically one of the draft's least successful demographics, but Lux was a unique case. His uncle Augie Schmidt won the 1982 Golden Spikes Award and later became the coach at Division III Carthage (Wis.) College, where Lux began accompanying him to practices as a 6-year-old. After blossoming physically as a high school senior, Lux became the first Wisconsin prep drafted in the first round in 37 years when the Dodgers selected him 20th overall in 2016. He struggled in his first full season, but after adding 20 pounds to his skinny frame and adjusting his bat path, Lux took off. He raised his batting average 80 points and his slugging percentage 152 points from 2017 to 2018, and in 2019 he upped his game again. Lux hit .347 with a 1.028 OPS, both fourth in the minors, between Double-A Tulsa and Triple-Oklahoma City and won BA Minor League Player of the Year. He received his first major league callup Sept. 2 and took over as the Dodgers' primary second baseman down the stretch.

SCOUTING REPORT: Dodgers president of baseball operations Andrew Friedman called Lux's approach "the most mature I've ever been around in someone his age." When Lux gets a pitch to hit, he explodes on it with above-average bat speed and a leveraged swing that allows him to drive the ball from gap to gap. Once a doubles hitter, Lux's liners have increasingly carried over the fence to right and center field as he's added muscle. With an advanced approach and an increasingly impactful swing, Lux projects as a consensus plus hitter with a chance to hit .300 in his best years and 20 or more home runs per season. Lux has maintained his plus speed and athleticism even as he added muscle. He doesn't run often, but he picks his spots well. Lux is a leader in the infield at shortstop. He attacks the ball, reads hops well and gets the ball out quickly. Lux has the athleticism, lateral range and above-average arm strength to stick at shortstop, but longstanding throwing accuracy issues make him more reliable at second base.

THE FUTURE: Lux is ready to step in as the Dodgers' everyday second baseman. He has a chance to become their No. 2 hitter and an all-star.

TOP PROSPECTS OF THE DECADE

Year	Player, Pos.	2019 Org
2010	Dee Gordon, SS	Mariners
2011	Dee Gordon, SS	Mariners
2012	Zach Lee, RHP	Mets
2013	Hyun-Jin Ryu, LHP	Dodgers
2014	Joc Pederson, OF	Dodgers
2015	Corey Seager, SS	Dodgers
2016	Corey Seager, SS	Dodgers
2017	Cody Bellinger, 1B	Dodgers
2018	Walker Buehler, RHP	Dodgers
2019	Keibert Ruiz, C	Dodgers

BEST TOOLS

Best Hitter for Average	Gavin Lux
Best Power Hitter	DJ Peters
Best Strike-Zone Discipline	Jacob Amaya
Fastest Baserunner	Brayan Morales
Best Athlete	Jeren Kendall
Best Fastball	Dustin May
Best Curveball	Mitchell White
Best Slider	Dennis Santana
Best Changeup	Ryan Pepiot
Best Control	Dustin May
Best Defensive Catcher	Diego Cartaya
Best Defensive Infielder	Jacob Amaya
Best Infield Arm	Cristian Santana
Best Defensive Outfielder	Jeren Kendall
Best Outfield Arm	Andy Pages

Year	Age	Club (League)	Class	AVG	G	AB	R	H	2B	3B	HR	RBI	BB	SO	SB	OBP	SLG
2017	19	Great Lakes (MWL)	LoA	.244	111	434	68	106	14	8	7	39	56	88	27	.331	.362
2018	20	R. Cucamonga (CAL)	HiA	.324	88	358	64	116	23	7	11	48	43	68	11	.396	.520
	20	Tulsa (TL)	AA	.324	28	105	21	34	4	1	4	9	14	20	2	.408	.495
2019	21	Tulsa (TL)	AA	.313	64	259	45	81	7	4	13	37	28	60	7	.375	.521
	21	Oklahoma City (PCL)	AAA	.392	49	199	54	78	18	4	13	39	33	42	3	.478	.719
	21	Los Angeles (NL)	MAJ	.240	23	75	12	18	4	1	2	9	7	24	2	.305	.400
Major League Totals				.240	23	75	12	18	4	1	2	9	7	24	2	.305	.400
Minor League Totals				.305	396	1578	293	481	79	29	48	193	202	329	52	.383	.483

2 DUSTIN MAY, RHP

Born: Sept. 6, 1997. **B-T:** R-R. **HT:** 6-6. **WT:** 180. **Drafted:** HS—Justin, Texas, 2016 (3rd round). **Signed by:** Josh Herzenberg.

RON VESELY/MLB PHOTOS VIA GETTY IMAGES

BA GRADE
60 Risk: Medium

TRACK RECORD: May's fastball sat 88-92 mph in high school, but the Dodgers liked his projectable 6-foot-6 frame and bet he would add weight and velocity. He did just that after signing as a third-round pick, progressively adding a few ticks every year up to a breakthrough 2019. May broke camp sitting 95 mph and touching 99, and he vaulted from Double-A to the majors by early August.

SCOUTING REPORT: May's sinker is a plus-plus pitch that draws comparisons with Kevin Brown's. It comes in at 95-99 mph from his towering release point and stays off of barrels with late, hard bite. His sinker touched 100 mph during a postseason relief appearance, and batters often can't do anything except pound it into the dirt. May's 90-92 mph cutter is his primary swing-and-miss pitch. He can alter its shape and locate it both sides of the plate, back-dooring it to lefties and leaving righties waving through it on the outside corner. May primarily uses his sinker and cutter, but also flashes an average power curveball and fringe-average changeup that will play up with better command. His control is impeccable.

THE FUTURE: May is slated to open 2020 in the Dodgers' rotation. He is their potential future No. 2 starter behind Walker Buehler.

SCOUTING GRADES: **Fastball:** 70 **Cutter:** 60 **Curveball:** 50 **Changeup:** 45 **Control:** 70

Year	Age	Club (League)	Class	W	L	ERA	G	GS	SV	IP	H	HR	BB	SO	K/9	WHIP	AVG
2017	19	Great Lakes (MWL)	LoA	9	6	3.88	23	23	0	123	121	8	26	113	8.3	1.20	.250
	19	R. Cucamonga (CAL)	HiA	0	0	0.82	2	1	0	11	6	0	1	15	12.3	0.64	.150
2018	20	R. Cucamonga (CAL)	HiA	7	3	3.29	17	17	0	98	91	9	17	94	8.6	1.10	.241
	20	Tulsa (TL)	AA	2	2	3.67	6	6	0	34	27	0	12	28	7.3	1.14	.209
2019	21	Tulsa (TL)	AA	3	5	3.74	15	15	0	79	71	5	20	86	9.8	1.15	.237
	21	Oklahoma City (PCL)	AAA	3	0	2.30	5	5	0	27	21	0	9	24	7.9	1.10	.212
	21	Los Angeles (NL)	MAJ	2	3	3.63	14	4	0	35	33	2	5	32	8.3	1.10	.250
Major League Totals				2	3	3.63	14	4	0	34	33	2	5	32	8.3	1.10	.250
Minor League Totals				24	17	3.50	78	73	1	403	374	22	89	394	8.8	1.15	.240

3 KEIBERT RUIZ, C

Born: July 20, 1998. **B-T:** B-R. **HT:** 6-0. **WT:** 200. **Signed:** Venezuela, 2014. **Signed by:** Francisco Cartaya/Pedro Avila.

BA GRADE
55 Risk: High

TRACK RECORD: Ruiz signed with the Dodgers for $140,000 at 16 and skyrocketed through the system, playing a full season at Double-A at age 19. He repeated Double-A in 2019 due to the organization's catching logjam and struggled with motivation, leading to an underwhelming 76 games at Tulsa. He appeared rejuvenated after a July promotion Triple-A, but soon suffered a season-ending finger fracture.

SCOUTING REPORT: Ruiz's tools remained apparent even in a down year. His elite-hand eye coordination and ability to manipulate the barrel give him the foundation of a plus hitter, and he almost never swings and misses. Ruiz is often too passive early in counts and has to swing at pitches he can't drive after pitchers get ahead, so the Dodgers have implored him to be more aggressive. The switch-hitting Ruiz flashes average power from the left side but almost none from the right. He should reach 12-15 homers once he starts picking out better pitches to drive. Ruiz is an improving game-caller behind the plate who flashes above-average receiving and blocking skills when he's motivated. His average arm strength is hampered by below-average accuracy.

THE FUTURE: Ruiz will try to get back on track at Triple-A in 2020. He's still far ahead of most catchers his age and has a chance to make his major league debut by 22.

SCOUTING GRADES: **Hitting:** 60 **Power:** 45 **Running:** 40 **Fielding:** 55 **Arm:** 50

Year	Age	Club (League)	Class	AVG	G	AB	R	H	2B	3B	HR	RBI	BB	SO	SB	OBP	SLG
2017	18	Great Lakes (MWL)	LoA	.317	63	227	34	72	16	1	2	24	18	30	0	.372	.423
	18	R. Cucamonga (CAL)	HiA	.315	38	149	24	47	7	1	6	27	7	23	0	.344	.497
2018	19	Tulsa (TL)	AA	.268	101	377	44	101	14	0	12	47	26	33	0	.328	.401
2019	20	Tulsa (TL)	AA	.254	76	276	33	70	9	0	4	25	28	21	0	.329	.330
	20	Oklahoma City (PCL)	AAA	.316	9	38	6	12	0	0	2	9	2	1	0	.350	.474
Minor League Totals				.299	387	1439	188	430	76	6	29	199	104	150	4	.351	.420

4 TONY GONSOLIN, RHP

Born: May 14, 1994. **B-T:** R-R. **HT:** 6-2. **WT:** 180. **Drafted:** St. Mary's, 2016 (9th round). **Signed by:** Tom Kunis.

CODY ROPER

BA GRADE
50 **Risk: Medium**

TRACK RECORD: Gonsolin played both ways at St. Mary's and had more home runs (seven) than saves (six) his senior year. The Dodgers drafted him as a pitcher in the ninth round in 2016 and signed him for $2,500. Gonsolin rapidly added velocity once he focused on pitching and rocketed up the Dodgers system. After leading the organization in strikeouts in 2018 and winning Dodgers minor league pitcher of the year, he rose from Triple-A to the majors in 2019 and logged a 2.93 ERA in 40 innings in Los Angeles.

SCOUTING REPORT: After topping out at 95 mph in college, Gonsolin now holds his fastball at 93-96 mph late in games as a starter and touches 99 mph in relief. He pitches aggressively and is unafraid to throw his fastball to any part of the strike zone, beating hitters in all quadrants. Gonsolin gets ahead with his fastball and finishes batters with his devastating split-change, a plus-plus pitch in the mid-80s that dives below the zone and gets swings and misses. His above-average, low 80s curveball and average upper 80s slider show nice spin and shape and have a chance to play up with better command. Gonsolin is athletic and aggressive and stays around the strike zone, but his command is often scattered.

THE FUTURE: Gonsolin has a chance to open 2020 in the Dodgers' rotation. If he stumbles, his stuff and attacking mentality will play well in high-leverage relief.

SCOUTING GRADES: **Fastball:** 60 **Slider:** 50 **Curveball:** 55 **Changeup:** 70 **Control:** 50

Year	Age	Club (League)	Class	W	L	ERA	G	GS	SV	IP	H	HR	BB	SO	K/9	WHIP	AVG
2017	23	Great Lakes (MWL)	LoA	0	1	3.38	3	0	1	8	8	2	0	12	13.5	1.00	.242
	23	R. Cucamonga (CAL)	HiA	7	5	3.92	39	0	5	62	61	5	18	73	10.6	1.27	.254
2018	24	R. Cucamonga (CAL)	HiA	4	2	2.69	17	17	0	84	72	5	26	106	11.4	1.17	.227
	24	Tulsa (TL)	AA	6	0	2.44	9	9	0	44	32	3	16	49	9.9	1.08	.203
2019	25	Oklahoma City (PCL)	AAA	2	4	4.35	13	13	0	41	41	4	21	50	10.9	1.50	.249
	25	Los Angeles (NL)	MAJ	4	2	2.93	11	6	1	40	26	4	15	37	8.3	1.03	.178
Major League Totals				4	2	2.93	11	6	1	40	26	4	15	37	8.3	1.03	.178
Minor League Totals				20	14	3.33	100	39	10	270	243	20	89	315	10.5	1.23	.236

5 JOSIAH GRAY, RHP

Born: Dec. 21, 1997. **B-T:** R-R HT: 6-1. **WT:** 190. **Drafted:** Le Moyne (N.Y.), 2018 (2nd supp). **Signed by:** Lee Seras (Reds).

BA GRADE
55 **Risk: High**

TRACK RECORD: Gray entered Division II Le Moyne as a shortstop, began closing games as a sophomore and moved to pitching full-time his junior year. The Reds drafted him 72nd overall in 2018 and traded him to the Dodgers after the season in the deal that sent Matt Kemp and Yasiel Puig to Cincinnati. Gray jumped three levels to Double-A in his first season with the Dodgers. He led the system in ERA (2.28) and strikeouts (147) and was named the organization's minor league pitcher of the year.

SCOUTING REPORT: Gray is slightly undersized at 6-foot-1, but his strong, athletic physique allows him to pound the strike zone and hold his stuff deep into games. Gray's plus fastball sits 92-96 mph with running life away from lefties and into righties. Other pitchers throw harder, but Gray misses more bats because of the life on his fastball and his ability to maintain his top-end velocity and command late into games. Gray routinely lands his above-average 84-88 mph slider with late snap for strikes, and his firm upper 80s changeup flashes average with late sink. Gray's delivery is a bit crude, but he repeats it and flashes above-average control. He is highly intelligent and an elite competitor.

THE FUTURE: Gray cemented himself as part of the Dodgers future rotation plans with his breakthrough 2019. He'll head to Triple-A in 2020 and has a chance to reach Los Angeles by midsummer.

SCOUTING GRADES: **Fastball:** 60 **Slider:** 55 **Changeup:** 50 **Control:** 55

Year	Age	Club (League)	Class	W	L	ERA	G	GS	SV	IP	H	HR	BB	SO	K/9	WHIP	AVG
2018	20	Greeneville (APP)	R	2	2	2.58	12	12	0	52	29	1	17	59	10.1	0.88	.155
2019	21	Great Lakes (MWL)	LoA	1	0	1.93	5	5	0	23	13	0	7	26	10.0	0.86	.165
	21	R. Cucamonga (CAL)	HiA	7	0	2.14	12	12	0	67	52	3	13	80	10.7	0.97	.209
	21	Tulsa (TL)	AA	3	2	2.75	9	8	0	39	33	0	11	41	9.4	1.12	.228
Minor League Totals				13	4	2.37	38	37	0	182	127	4	48	206	10.2	0.96	.192

6 JETER DOWNS, SS/2B

Born: July 27, 1998. **B-T:** R-R. **HT:** 5-11. **WT:** 180. **Drafted:** HS—Miami Gardens, Fla., 2018 (1st round supplemental). **Signed by:** Hector Otero (Reds).

TRACK RECORD: Downs was one of the top high school players in the 2018 draft class and signed with the Reds for just over $1.8 million after they made him the 32nd overall pick. The Dodgers acquired him after the season in the trade that sent Matt Kemp and Yasiel Puig to Cincinnati. Downs started slow in his first season in the Dodgers' system, but he caught fire during the summer and finished as one of only 10 minor leaguers with 20 home runs (24) and 20 stolen bases (24).

BA GRADE
55 **Risk: High**

SCOUTING REPORT: Downs is a bat-first player with a pretty swing. His hands work, he stays on time and he turns around velocity with a quick, efficient path. Downs can be overly at passive and take at-bats off, limiting him to an average hitter, but he's a dynamic extra-base threat when he's focused. He drives the ball from gap-to-gap and projects for above-average power as he gets stronger. Downs is an intelligent baserunner whose average speed plays up on the bases. His reliable hands and above-average arm fit anywhere on the infield, but range is suboptimal for an everyday shortstop.

THE FUTURE: Evaluators see Downs as a multi-positional, everyday infielder in the mold of Josh Harrison. He finished last season at Double-A and will open back there in 2020.

SCOUTING GRADES: **Hitting:** 50 **Power:** 55 **Running:** 50 **Fielding:** 50 **Arm:** 55

Year	Age	Club (League)	Class	AVG	G	AB	R	H	2B	3B	HR	RBI	BB	SO	SB	OBP	SLG
2017	18	Billings (PIO)	R	.267	50	172	31	46	3	3	6	29	27	32	8	.370	.424
2018	19	Dayton (MWL)	LoA	.257	120	455	63	117	23	2	13	47	52	103	37	.351	.402
2019	20	R. Cucamonga (CAL)	HiA	.269	107	412	78	111	33	4	19	75	54	97	23	.354	.507
	20	Tulsa (TL)	AA	.333	12	48	14	16	2	0	5	11	6	10	1	.429	.688
Minor League Totals				.267	289	1087	186	290	61	9	43	162	139	242	69	.359	.458

7 DIEGO CARTAYA, C

Born: Sept. 7, 2001. **B-T:** R-R. **HT:** 6-2. **WT:** 199. **Signed:** Venezuela, 2018. **Signed by:** Luis Marquez/Roman Barinas/Cliff Nuiter/Jean Castro.

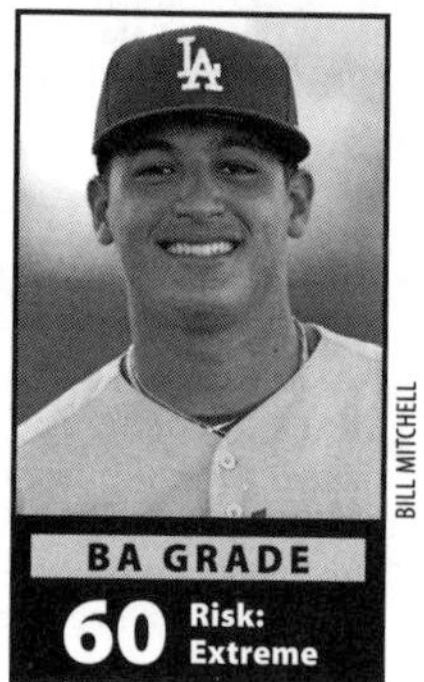

BILL MITCHELL

BA GRADE
60 **Risk: Extreme**

TRACK RECORD: Cartaya starred for Venezuela's junior national teams growing up and was regarded as the country's best prospect in the 2018 international signing class. The Dodgers established a relationship with him early and signed him for $2.5 million. Cartaya began 2019 in the Dominican Summer League but proved so advanced the Dodgers moved him stateside after just 13 games to the Rookie-level Arizona League, where he excelled as a 17-year-old.

SCOUTING REPORT: Cartaya is a highly advanced player on both sides of the ball. He has a short, quick swing with a sound bat path, drives the ball with an up-the-middle approach and makes adjustments to get to his power. He has strong hands and plenty of bat speed and should hit for both average and power as he matures. Cartaya presents a big target behind the plate and is flexible for his size. He's an above-average receiver with an above-average to plus arm, and some scouts think he's already a present major league-caliber defender. He has a strong, durable frame and a high baseball IQ, which he shows off with smart decisions on the basepaths.

THE FUTURE: Cartaya has the Dodgers dreaming of an above-average hitter and plus defender behind the plate. He'll be only 18 next season but has a chance to move quickly.

SCOUTING GRADES: **Hitting:** 55 **Power:** 55 **Running:** 40 **Fielding:** 60 **Arm:** 60

Year	Age	Club (League)	Class	AVG	G	AB	R	H	2B	3B	HR	RBI	BB	SO	SB	OBP	SLG
2019	17	Dodgers Bautista (DSL)	R	.240	13	50	11	12	2	2	1	9	5	11	0	.316	.420
	17	Dodgers Mota (AZL)	R	.296	36	135	25	40	10	0	3	13	11	31	1	.353	.437
Minor League Totals				.281	49	185	36	52	12	2	4	22	16	42	1	.343	.432

8 KODY HOESE, 3B

Born: July 13, 1997. **B-T:** R-R. **HT:** 6-4. **WT:** 200. **Drafted:** Tulane, 2019 (1st round). **Signed by:** Benny Latino.

TRACK RECORD: The Royals drafted Hoese in the 35th round in 2018 as a draft-eligible sophomore, but he returned to Tulane and became a first-rounder with a monster junior season. Hoese finished second in the nation with a .779 slugging percentage and tied for fifth with 23 home runs, leading the Dodgers to draft him 25th overall and sign him for $2,740,300. A tender right elbow limited Hoese after he signed, but he still posted an .863 OPS in 41 games and reached low Class A Great Lakes.

SCOUTING REPORT: Hoese is a mature hitter who has excellent pitch recognition and controls the strike zone. He rarely chases and forces pitchers to come to him. When they do, Hoese unloads on balls with his natural strength and leveraged swing to produce plus raw power. He can turn on balls for long home runs to left or drive them with authority the other way. With his approach, Hoese is a potential above-average hitter who should clear 20-25 home runs annually. Hoese is a fringe-average runner who ticks up to average underway. He reads balls of the bat well at third base and projects to be at least an average defender with plus hands and an above-average arm.

THE FUTURE: Hoese will rise as quickly as his bat takes him. He'll begin 2020 at high Class A Rancho Cucamonga as long as his elbow is healthy.

SCOUTING GRADES: **Hitting:** 55 **Power:** 55 **Running:** 50 **Fielding:** 50 **Arm:** 55

Year	Age	Club (League)	Class	AVG	G	AB	R	H	2B	3B	HR	RBI	BB	SO	SB	OBP	SLG
2019	21	Dodgers Mota (AZL)	R	.357	19	56	14	20	5	1	3	13	10	11	1	.456	.643
	21	Great Lakes (MWL)	LoA	.264	22	91	15	24	3	1	2	16	8	14	0	.330	.385
Minor League Totals				.299	41	147	29	44	8	2	5	29	18	25	1	.380	.483

9 MICHAEL BUSCH, 2B/1B

Born: Nov. 9, 1997. **B-T:** L-R. **HT:** 6-0. **WT:** 207. **Drafted:** North Carolina, 2019 (1st round). **Signed by:** Jonah Rosenthal

TRACK RECORD: One of eight children, Busch starred in baseball, football and hockey in high school in Minnesota before becoming one of college baseball's top hitters at North Carolina. The Dodgers drafted him 31st overall in 2019 and signed him for $2,312,000. Busch broke his right hand after getting hit by a pitch in just his fifth game, but he returned for the end of the Arizona Fall League and reached base in 12 of 22 plate appearances.

SCOUTING REPORT: Many teams thought Busch possessed the best pure swing of the 2019 draft. His swing mechanics are sound, he covers the whole plate and he can manipulate his hands to hit balls in all parts of the strike zone. Busch is more of a patient, line-drive hitter than a masher, but the Dodgers think they can make adjustments to his lower half and create more leverage in his swing to access average power. Though Busch played first base and left field in college, the Dodgers drafted him as a second baseman and believe his short-area quickness and elite work ethic will help him become playable, and possibly average, in time. He's a below-average runner with a fringe-average arm.

THE FUTURE: The Dodgers are confident they got a plus hitter in Busch. Now, it's about seeing how his power and defense develop.

SCOUTING GRADES: **Hitting:** 60 **Power:** 50 **Running:** 40 **Fielding:** 50 **Arm:** 45

Year	Age	Club (League)	Class	AVG	G	AB	R	H	2B	3B	HR	RBI	BB	SO	SB	OBP	SLG
2019	21	Great Lakes (MWL)	LoA	.182	5	11	4	2	0	0	0	2	6	3	0	.474	.182
Minor League Totals				.125	10	24	5	3	0	0	0	2	7	5	0	.371	.125

10 LUIS RODRIGUEZ, OF

BILL MITCHELL

Born: Sept. 16, 2002. **B-T:** R-R. **HT:** 6-2. **WT:** 175. **Signed:** Venezuela, 2019. **Signed by:** Roman Barinas/Laiky Uribe/Leon Canelon.

TRACK RECORD: Rodriguez starred in showcase events for years and ranked as Venezuela's top prospect in the 2019 international class. The Dodgers locked on to Rodriguez early in the process and signed him for $2,667,500 on July 2.

SCOUTING REPORT: Rodriguez was one of the most complete players in his class with an exciting combination of hitting ability, power and athleticism. He takes a patient, all-fields approach and has advanced plate discipline for his age. He turns around velocity with his smooth, righthanded swing and has a natural ability to lift the ball for power, especially to right-center field. Rodriguez has a long track record of performing against older competition, and his approach and swing hold the promise of a potentially plus hitter with 20-home run power. Rodriguez is an above-average runner with the instincts to stick in center field. He has plenty of room to grow into his 6-foot-2, 175-pound frame and could move to a corner as he fills out. His above-average arm strength profiles in right field, if needed.

THE FUTURE: Rodriguez has enormous potential, but he will be only 17 the entire 2020 season and is many years away. He is set to start his pro career in the Dominican Summer League.

SCOUTING GRADES: **Hitting:** 60 **Power:** 50 **Running:** 55 **Fielding:** 50 **Arm:** 55

Year	Age	Club (League)	Class	AVG	G	AB	R	H	2B	3B	HR	RBI	BB	SO	SB	OBP	SLG
2019	16	Did not play—signed 2020 contract															

11 DENNIS SANTANA, RHP

Born: April 12, 1996. **B-T:** R-R. **HT:** 6-2. **WT:** 190. **Signed:** Dominican Republic, 2012. **Signed by:** Bob Engle/Patrick Guerrero/Elvio Jimenez

TRACK RECORD: Santana signed with the Dodgers as a shortstop but converted to pitching after his first season. He earned All-Star honors in the low Class A Midwest League in 2016 and high Class A California League in 2017 before making his major league debut in 2018. Santana began 2019 in Triple-A expecting to be one of the Dodgers' first callups, but his fastball command disappeared and he spent the entire year at Oklahoma City.

SCOUTING REPORT: Santana is a long, lanky righthander with lively stuff. His fastball sits 93-94 mph and touches 97 mph with huge sink and run, and his mid-80s slider has developed into a plus pitch he can throw for strikes or expand the zone with. His upper 80s changeup has also flashes plus when he has a feel for it. Santana generates so much movement on his pitches he struggles to locate them, however, and he started nibbling as his struggles mounted in 2019. He regained his aggressiveness after a late move to the bullpen and posted a 1.72 ERA in relief, compared to 8.00 as a starter.

THE FUTURE: Santana's probability of starting has declined, but he has the stuff to be an impact, late-game reliever. He should return to the majors in 2020.

Year	Age	Club (League)	Class	W	L	ERA	G	GS	SV	IP	H	HR	BB	SO	K/9	WHIP	AVG
2017	21	R. Cucamonga (CAL)	HiA	5	6	3.57	17	14	0	86	87	5	22	92	9.7	1.27	.262
	21	Tulsa (TL)	AA	3	1	5.51	7	7	0	33	32	2	23	37	10.2	1.68	.256
2018	22	Tulsa (TL)	AA	0	2	2.56	8	8	0	39	26	3	14	51	11.9	1.03	.183
	22	Oklahoma City (PCL)	AAA	1	1	2.45	2	2	0	11	10	0	2	14	11.5	1.09	.238
	22	Los Angeles (NL)	MAJ	1	0	12.27	1	0	0	4	6	0	1	4	9.8	1.91	.375
2019	23	Los Angeles (NL)	MAJ	0	0	7.20	3	0	0	5	6	1	4	6	10.8	2.00	.300
	23	Oklahoma City (PCL)	AAA	5	9	6.94	27	17	0	93	111	16	53	105	10.1	1.76	.292
Major League Totals				1	0	9.35	4	0	0	8	12	1	5	10	10.4	1.96	.333
Minor League Totals				23	34	4.28	119	74	4	454	417	33	223	513	10.2	1.41	.241

12 MITCHELL WHITE, RHP

BA GRADE
50 Risk: High

Born: Dec. 28, 1994. **B-T:** R-R. **HT:** 6-4. **WT:** 207. **Drafted:** Santa Clara, 2016 (2nd round). **Signed by:** Tom Kunis.

TRACK RECORD: White had Tommy John surgery after high school but bounced back to become Santa Clara's ace as a redshirt sophomore. The Dodgers drafted him 65th overall in 2016 and signed him for $588,300. White looked like a potential No. 2 starter after rising to Double-A in a dominant first season, but injuries and inconsistency halted his rise and continued through 2019 at Triple-A Oklahoma City.

SCOUTING REPORT: At his best, White is "lights out" in the words of observers. His fastball sits 93-94

mph and gets up to 97, his plus curveball sets up hitters early in counts and his plus short slider finishes them for strikeouts. Too often, though, White sits in the low 90s and his curveball and slider are hit-or-miss, resulting in wildly inconsistent outings. Breakdowns in his mechanics affect his command and a long list of injuries, most recently two separate injured list stints for blisters, further affect his reliability. His changeup is below-average and resulted in lefties batting .271/.350/.571 against him in 2019.

THE FUTURE: White teases starter potential, but an increasing number of evaluators think his future is in the bullpen because of his health and consistency issues. He'll return to Triple-A in 2020.

Year	Age	Club (League)	Class	W	L	ERA	G	GS	SV	IP	H	HR	BB	SO	K/9	WHIP	AVG
2017	22	R. Cucamonga (CAL)	HiA	2	1	3.72	9	9	0	39	26	0	16	49	11.4	1.09	.187
	22	Dodgers (AZL)	R	0	0	0.00	3	3	0	7	2	0	2	8	10.3	0.57	.091
	22	Tulsa (TL)	AA	1	1	2.57	7	7	0	28	17	2	13	31	10.0	1.07	.168
2018	23	Tulsa (TL)	AA	6	7	4.53	22	22	0	105	114	12	34	88	7.5	1.41	.273
2019	24	Tulsa (TL)	AA	1	0	2.10	7	7	0	30	18	3	7	37	11.1	0.83	.165
	24	Oklahoma City (PCL)	AAA	3	6	6.50	16	13	0	64	73	13	24	68	9.6	1.52	.293
Minor League Totals				14	15	3.97	75	67	0	294	257	30	102	311	9.5	1.22	.231

13 EDWIN RIOS, 3B/1B

BA GRADE
45 **Risk: Medium**

Born: April 21, 1994. **B-T:** L-R. **HT:** 6-3. **WT:** 220. **Drafted:** Florida International, 2015 (6th round). **Signed by:** Adrian Casanova

TRACK RECORD: Rios finished second in the nation in home runs in 2015 at Florida International and signed with the Dodgers for $222,500 as a sixth-round pick. After hitting for power and average at every level, he overcame a slow start to make his major league debut in 2019 and finished with 35 home runs between Triple-A and the majors.

SCOUTING REPORT: Rios got into a rut early in 2019 when he began chasing balls out of the strike zone, but once he got back in the zone he returned to form as an average hitter with plus power. Rios' quick hands and natural timing allow him to hit all kinds of pitches and translate his massive power into games. He's a physical, lefthanded hitter capable of destroying baseballs, as he did with a 473-foot home run against the Padres on Sept. 26. He has a strong approach and keeps his strikeouts reasonable for a power hitter. Rios looks fine taking infield at third base but devolves to a fringe-average defender there in games. First base is the only position he inspires confidence.

THE FUTURE: Rios' bat is good enough to start. With the Dodgers set with Justin Turner, Cody Bellinger and Max Muncy on the corners, he likely needs a trade to get that opportunity.

Year	Age	Club (League)	Class	AVG	G	AB	R	H	2B	3B	HR	RBI	BB	SO	SB	OBP	SLG
2017	23	Tulsa (TL)	AA	.317	77	306	47	97	21	0	15	62	17	69	1	.358	.533
	23	Oklahoma City (PCL)	AAA	.296	51	169	23	50	13	0	9	29	18	42	0	.368	.533
2018	24	Oklahoma City (PCL)	AAA	.304	88	309	45	94	25	0	10	55	23	110	0	.355	.482
2019	25	Oklahoma City (PCL)	AAA	.270	104	393	72	106	23	2	31	91	37	153	2	.340	.575
	25	Los Angeles (NL)	MAJ	.277	28	47	10	13	2	1	4	8	9	21	0	.393	.617
Major League Totals				.277	28	47	10	13	2	1	4	8	9	21	0	.393	.617
Minor League Totals				.295	450	1670	264	492	115	4	95	326	126	514	6	.348	.539

14 DJ PETERS, OF

BA GRADE
45 **Risk: High**

Born: Dec. 12, 1995. **B-T:** R-R. **HT:** 6-6. **WT:** 225. **Drafted:** Western Nevada JC, 2016 (4th round). **Signed by:** Tom Kunis.

TRACK RECORD: Peters grew up rooting for the Dodgers in Los Angeles suburb Glendora and realized his childhood dream of playing for his favorite team when the Dodgers drafted him in the fourth round in 2016. He won MVP of the high Class A California League his first full season and led the Double-A Texas League in home runs in 2018 before reaching Triple-A in 2019.

SCOUTING REPORT: The 6-foot-6 Peters is a chiseled specimen whose strength and long limbs produce jaw-dropping raw power some scouts grade an "80." He demolishes anything left out over the plate with a leveraged swing that produces power to all fields, but his long arms leave him vulnerable to velocity inside and create huge holes in his swing. He has a career 36 percent career strikeout rate despite solid strike-zone discipline because he swings and misses in the zone so much. Peters is extremely athletic for his size and is a capable defender in center field with average speed and long strides. His above-average arm fits in right field, and he is also experienced playing left field.

THE FUTURE: Peters' power and ability to play all three outfield positions give him an avenue to the majors, but he won't be more than a reserve unless he gets his strikeouts under control. He'll open 2020 back at Triple-A Oklahoma City and has a chance to make his major league debut if he demonstrates the improvements needed.

Year	Age	Club (League)	Class	AVG	G	AB	R	H	2B	3B	HR	RBI	BB	SO	SB	OBP	SLG
2017	21	R. Cucamonga (CAL)	HiA	.276	132	504	91	139	29	5	27	82	64	189	3	.372	.514
2018	22	Tulsa (TL)	AA	.236	132	491	79	116	23	3	29	60	45	192	1	.320	.473
2019	23	Tulsa (TL)	AA	.241	68	249	31	60	10	1	11	42	28	93	1	.331	.422
	23	Oklahoma City (PCL)	AAA	.260	57	208	40	54	10	1	12	39	33	75	1	.388	.490
Minor League Totals				.269	455	1714	304	461	96	13	92	271	205	615	11	.363	.501

15 CONNOR WONG, C

BA GRADE 45 Risk: High

Born: May 9, 1996. **B-T:** R-R. **HT:** 6-1. **WT:** 181. **Drafted:** Houston, 2017 (3rd round). **Signed by:** Clint Bowers.

TRACK RECORD: Wong saw time at shortstop, third base and the outfield in college before becoming Houston's primary catcher as a sophomore. The Dodgers, with their affinity for infielders-turned-catchers, drafted Wong in the third round in 2017 and signed him for $547,500. Wong led high Class A Rancho Cucamonga to the California League championship in his first full season, but was sent back to the level due to the Dodgers organizational catching logjam. He struggled to stay motivated but exploded after a July promotion to Double-A Tulsa with a .997 OPS in 40 games.

SCOUTING REPORT: Wong's slight build is deceptive. He's twitchy in the box and can drive the ball, and when he stays in the middle of the field he's an advanced hitter with average power. Wong is an aggressive hitter who jumps on fastballs and drives them gap-to-gap, but he has career 31 percent strikeout rate and projects as a fringe-average hitter because he struggles against soft stuff. Wong is an athletic defender behind the plate who receives well and has an average arm, although his blocking needs work. He has played above-average defense in stints at second and third base, as well.

THE FUTURE: Wong could stick as a backup catcher, but he projects to be most valuable moving around the diamond and playing 2-3 positions a week. He'll see Triple-A in 2020.

Year	Age	Club (League)	Class	AVG	G	AB	R	H	2B	3B	HR	RBI	BB	SO	SB	OBP	SLG
2017	21	Dodgers (AZL)	R	.000	1	1	0	0	0	0	0	0	0	1	0	.000	.000
	21	Great Lakes (MWL)	LoA	.278	27	97	19	27	6	0	5	18	7	26	1	.336	.495
2018	22	R. Cucamonga (CAL)	HiA	.269	102	383	64	103	20	2	19	60	38	138	6	.350	.480
2019	23	R. Cucamonga (CAL)	HiA	.245	71	274	39	67	15	6	15	51	21	93	9	.306	.507
	23	Tulsa (TL)	AA	.349	40	149	17	52	9	1	9	31	11	50	2	.393	.604
Minor League Totals				.275	241	904	139	249	50	9	48	160	77	308	18	.342	.510

16 CRISTIAN SANTANA, 3B

BA GRADE 45 Risk: High

Born: Feb. 24, 1997. **B-T:** R-R. **HT:** 6-2. **WT:** 175. **Signed:** Dominican Republic, 2014. **Signed by:** Bob Engle/Patrick Guerrero/Franklin Taveras

TRACK RECORD: Santana spent three years in Rookie ball after signing with the Dodgers for $50,000, but he broke out in 2017 and finished tied for the high Class A California League lead in home runs (24) in 2018. He moved to Double-A Tulsa in 2019 and finished third in the Texas League in batting (.301).

SCOUTING REPORT: Santana is an aggressive hitter who hunts fastballs and punishes them. His broad physique and quick bat produce plus power when he connects, and he has as much opposite-field power as pull power. Santana struggles to recognize breaking balls and goes fishing for them below the zone. He swings early to avoid getting into breaking ball counts and walked only 10 times in 102 games in 2019. Santana isn't overly rangy at third base, but he makes highlight-reel reaction plays and has a plus-plus arm.

THE FUTURE: Santana's approach doesn't look great on paper, but it works for him and he keeps producing. He'll move to Triple-A in 2020.

Year	Age	Club (League)	Class	AVG	G	AB	R	H	2B	3B	HR	RBI	BB	SO	SB	OBP	SLG
2017	20	Ogden (PIO)	R	.537	10	41	18	22	2	1	5	16	6	6	0	.583	1.000
	20	Great Lakes (MWL)	LoA	.322	44	174	18	56	9	0	5	25	5	42	0	.339	.460
2018	21	R. Cucamonga (CAL)	HiA	.274	131	548	75	150	23	0	24	109	20	143	2	.302	.447
2019	22	Tulsa (TL)	AA	.301	102	399	45	120	22	1	10	57	10	88	0	.320	.436
Minor League Totals				.285	426	1669	219	476	82	5	55	260	68	389	7	.314	.439

17 OMAR ESTEVEZ, 2B/SS

BA GRADE 40 Risk: Medium

Born: Feb. 25, 1998. **B-T:** R-R. **HT:** 5-10. **WT:** 168. **Signed:** Cuba, 2015. **Signed by:** Roman Barinas/Mike Tosar.

TRACK RECORD: Signed out of Cuba for $6 million in 2015. Estevez struggled for two years before overhauling his swing during the second half of 2018. He advanced to Double-A in 2019 and performed despite missing nearly two months with a hamstring strain.

SCOUTING REPORT: Estevez began doing weighted ball drills in the second half of 2018 and turned into a different hitter. After previously pulling off the ball, he now makes frequent contact up the middle and drives the ball gap-to-gap for doubles. With increased success has come increased confidence, and Estevez now shows advanced feel and solid strike-zone discipline in the batter's box. Estevez lacks impact tools beyond his bat. He is a below-average runner with a thick lower half and limited twitch, making him a below-average shortstop and fringe-average second baseman. His arm strength is fringy and he's prone to sailing throws over the first baseman's head.

THE FUTURE: Estevez has to hit to rise, but he keeps doing exactly that. He'll move to Triple-A in 2020.

Year	Age	Club (League)	Class	AVG	G	AB	R	H	2B	3B	HR	RBI	BB	SO	SB	OBP	SLG
2017	19	R. Cucamonga (CAL)	HiA	.256	120	457	56	117	24	3	4	47	33	97	2	.309	.348
2018	20	R. Cucamonga (CAL)	HiA	.278	128	515	87	143	43	2	15	84	45	138	3	.336	.456
2019	21	Dodgers Mota (AZL)	R	.300	7	20	7	6	2	0	0	3	2	8	0	.364	.400
	21	Tulsa (TL)	AA	.291	83	299	34	87	24	0	6	36	31	70	0	.352	.431
Minor League Totals				.268	460	1762	230	473	125	7	34	231	137	434	8	.322	.405

18 EDWIN UCETA, RHP

BA GRADE **45** Risk: High

Born: Jan. 1, 1998. **B-T:** R-R. **HT:** 6-0. **WT:** 155. **Signed:** Dominican Republic, 2016. **Signed by:** Luis Marquez/Matt Doppelt.

TRACK RECORD: The Dodgers signed Uceta for just $10,000 as an 18-year-old out of the Dominican Republic, and he quickly emerged as a steal. He helped pitch Rookie-level Ogden to the Pioneer League championship in 2017 and high Class A Rancho Cucamonga to the California League championship in 2018. He split 2019 between high Class A and Double-A and finished second in the Dodgers' system in ERA (2.77) and strikeouts (141).

SCOUTING REPORT: Uceta is a slight-bodied righthander with an advanced feel to pitch and keeps adding velocity. His fastball ranges from 90-94 mph and plays up extension and riding life from his lower release height. He pairs his deceptive fastball with a plus mid-80s changeup that mirrors his fastball out of his hand before fading and dropping suddenly. His sweepy upper-70s breaking ball is highly effective against righties and gets nearly as many whiffs as his changeup. Uceta ties everything with average control and has improved at limiting his home runs allowed by staying out of the middle of the plate.

THE FUTURE: Uceta's plus-plus makeup and work ethic lead the Dodgers to believe he'll keep adding weight and velocity. If he does, he has a chance to became a back-of-the-rotation starter.

Year	Age	Club (League)	Class	W	L	ERA	G	GS	SV	IP	H	HR	BB	SO	K/9	WHIP	AVG
2017	19	Ogden (PIO)	R	2	3	6.59	14	14	0	56	63	8	14	62	10.0	1.38	.278
2018	20	Great Lakes (MWL)	LoA	5	6	3.25	20	20	0	100	91	9	27	103	9.3	1.18	.241
	20	R. Cucamonga (CAL)	HiA	0	0	6.97	5	5	0	21	17	7	12	28	12.2	1.40	.224
2019	21	R. Cucamonga (CAL)	HiA	4	0	2.15	10	10	0	50	47	6	16	65	11.6	1.25	.241
	21	Tulsa (TL)	AA	7	2	3.21	16	14	0	73	62	5	33	76	9.4	1.30	.238
Minor League Totals				20	12	3.73	76	66	0	331	300	36	105	362	9.8	1.22	.240

19 DEVIN MANN, 2B/3B

BA GRADE **45** Risk: High

Born: Feb. 11, 1997. **B-T:** R-R. **HT:** 6-3. **WT:** 180. **Drafted:** Louisville, 2018 (5th round). **Signed by:** Marty Lamb.

TRACK RECORD: Mann impressed with his natural hitting ability at Louisville, and the Dodgers drafted him in the fifth round in 2018 believing they could unlock untapped power with a few swing adjustments. Mann made the requested changes and emerged as one of the high Class A California League's top power threats in his first full season, finishing sixth in slugging percentage (.496) and tied for seventh in home runs (19) despite missing a month with a right MCL sprain.

SCOUTING REPORT: Mann looks the part of a major leaguer at 6-foot-3, 180 pounds with a strong core and long levers. Previously a contact hitter, he began using his legs more and added loft to his swing as part of the requested changes and now shows above-average power to all fields. Mann works counts, takes a short path to the ball and keeps his strikeouts reasonable for a power hitter, projecting as an average hitter overall. Mann has quickened his actions and improved his arm strength at second base, but he's still a touch stiff and is more natural at third base, where his range fits better.

THE FUTURE: The Dodgers internally compare Mann to David Freese and see the bat of a potential starter. He'll head to Double-A Tulsa in 2020.

Year	Age	Club (League)	Class	AVG	G	AB	R	H	2B	3B	HR	RBI	BB	SO	SB	OBP	SLG
2018	21	Dodgers (AZL)	R	.200	2	5	0	1	0	0	0	0	1	3	0	.333	.200
	21	Great Lakes (MWL)	LoA	.241	63	224	26	54	13	1	2	30	34	50	7	.348	.335
2019	22	Dodgers Mota (AZL)	R	.000	1	1	0	0	0	0	0	0	1	0	0	.500	.000
	22	R. Cucamonga (CAL)	HiA	.278	98	367	63	102	19	2	19	63	45	93	5	.358	.496
Minor League Totals				.269	168	610	91	164	34	3	21	94	82	147	12	.359	.438

20 JACOB AMAYA, SS

BA GRADE 45 Risk: High

Born: Sept. 3, 1998. **B-T:** R-R. **HT:** 6-0. **WT:** 180. **Drafted:** HS—West Covina, Calif., 2017 (11th round). **Signed by:** Bobby Darwin.

TRACK RECORD: Amaya grew up in suburban Los Angeles and signed with his hometown Dodgers for an above-slot $247,500 bonus as an 11th-round pick in 2017. He played his first full season in 2019 and tied for fifth in on-base percentage (.381) in the low Class A Midwest League before finishing at high Class A.

SCOUTING REPORT: Amaya possesses a promising foundation as a plus defensive shortstop who consistently gets on base. His chase rate is so low it's an outlier, and he rarely swings and misses. He has nearly as many walks (147) as strikeouts (180) in his pro career while being young for every level. Amaya's approach is the strength of his offensive game. He flashes pullside power but overall doesn't do much damage when he connects and projects mostly as a singles and doubles hitter. Amaya is a quick, polished athlete in the middle infield with range to both sides. He has a above-average arm strength and a good internal clock.

THE FUTURE: Amaya's continued offensive growth will determine his ceiling. He'll open 2020 back at Rancho Cucamonga.

Year	Age	Club (League)	Class	AVG	G	AB	R	H	2B	3B	HR	RBI	BB	SO	SB	OBP	SLG
2017	18	Dodgers (AZL)	R	.254	34	118	17	30	4	1	2	14	19	25	4	.364	.356
2018	19	Ogden (PIO)	R	.346	32	127	41	44	9	3	3	24	27	29	11	.465	.535
	19	Great Lakes (MWL)	LoA	.265	27	98	13	26	1	0	1	5	20	18	3	.390	.306
2019	20	Great Lakes (MWL)	LoA	.262	103	386	68	101	25	4	6	58	74	83	4	.381	.394
	20	R. Cucamonga (CAL)	HiA	.250	21	80	14	20	3	2	1	13	7	15	1	.307	.375
Minor League Totals				.273	217	809	153	221	42	10	13	114	147	170	23	.386	.398

21 ZACH McKINSTRY, 2B

BA GRADE 40 Risk: Medium

Born: April 29, 1995. **B-T:** L-R. **HT:** 6-0. **WT:** 180. **Drafted:** Central Michigan, 2016 (33rd round). **Signed by:** Trey Magnuson.

TRACK RECORD: McKinstry led Central Michigan with a .325 batting average as a draft-eligible sophomore in 2016. Most teams expected him to return to school, but the Dodgers grabbed him in the 33rd round and gave him $100,000 to sign. McKinstry hit just 11 home runs his first three seasons combined, but he overhauled his swing and hit 19 homers while advancing to Triple-A in 2019.

SCOUTING REPORT: McKinstry has long worked counts, recognized pitches and made consistent contact to project as an average hitter. What changed is McKinstry's power. He added muscle, tweaked his grip and altered his bat path to generate more loft last season. The result was newfound pop evaluators expect to translate to 10-15 home runs in the majors. McKinstry is a versatile athlete capable of playing second base, shortstop and third base at least average. He is an above-average runner with a plus, accurate arm.

THE FUTURE: The Dodgers added McKinstry to their 40-man roster after the season. He is set to debut as a utilityman in 2020.

Year	Age	Club (League)	Class	AVG	G	AB	R	H	2B	3B	HR	RBI	BB	SO	SB	OBP	SLG
2017	22	Great Lakes (MWL)	LoA	.308	17	52	10	16	7	0	1	3	17	10	2	.478	.500
	22	Tulsa (TL)	AA	.256	15	39	5	10	1	1	0	2	6	8	0	.356	.333
	22	R. Cucamonga (CAL)	HiA	.226	82	319	39	72	13	0	3	28	29	87	5	.299	.295
2018	23	Great Lakes (MWL)	LoA	.377	18	53	12	20	2	2	3	8	16	16	2	.542	.660
	23	R. Cucamonga (CAL)	HiA	.308	33	91	20	28	7	1	2	8	17	22	0	.447	.473
	23	Tulsa (TL)	AA	.193	25	83	7	16	2	1	2	8	4	21	0	.230	.313
2019	24	Tulsa (TL)	AA	.279	95	341	53	95	16	4	12	52	37	74	8	.352	.455
	24	Oklahoma City (PCL)	AAA	.382	26	89	17	34	8	2	7	26	6	18	0	.421	.753
Minor League Totals				.270	356	1226	182	331	61	14	30	149	147	288	23	.357	.416

22 MIGUEL VARGAS, 3B

BA GRADE 45 Risk: High

Born: Nov. 17, 1999. **B-T:** R-R. **HT:** 6-3. **WT:** 198. **Signed:** Cuba, 2017. **Signed by:** Roman Barinas/Mike Tosar.

TRACK RECORD: Vargas was one Cuba's top young hitters and left the island with his father, Cuban baseball legend Lazaro Vargas, in 2015. The Dodgers signed him for $300,000 nearly two years later. Vargas played his first full season in 2019 and ranked second in the low Class A Midwest League in batting (.325) before receiving a promotion to high Class A Rancho Cucamonga, where he excelled as a 19-year-old.

SCOUTING REPORT: Vargas takes an advanced approach and has supreme hand-eye coordination, allowing him to wait pitchers out and drive the ball he wants. He makes a conscious effort to drive the ball the other way with an inside-out swing. Vargas rarely pulls the ball in the air, but with his natural hitting gifts, he could become a plus hitter with 20 home run power once he starts turning on balls. Vargas is a slow mover at third base with limited lateral range and an average arm, so most believe his future is at first base.

THE FUTURE: Vargas will go as far as his bat takes him. He may see Double-A in 2020.

Year	Age	Club (League)	Class	AVG	G	AB	R	H	2B	3B	HR	RBI	BB	SO	SB	OBP	SLG
2017	17	Did not play															
2018	18	Dodgers (AZL)	R	.419	8	31	6	13	3	1	0	2	5	3	1	.514	.581
	18	Ogden (PIO)	R	.394	22	94	25	37	11	1	2	22	8	13	6	.447	.596
	18	Great Lakes (MWL)	LoA	.213	23	75	4	16	1	1	0	6	10	20	0	.307	.253
2019	19	Great Lakes (MWL)	LoA	.325	70	280	53	91	20	2	5	45	35	43	9	.399	.464
	19	R. Cucamonga (CAL)	HiA	.284	54	211	23	60	18	1	2	32	20	40	4	.353	.408
Minor League Totals				.314	177	691	111	217	53	6	9	107	78	119	20	.387	.447

23 ANDY PAGES, OF

BA GRADE
50 Risk: Extreme

Born: Dec. 8, 2000. **B-T:** R-R. **HT:** 6-1. **WT:** 180. **Signed:** Cuba, 2018. **Signed by:** Luis Marquez/Roman Barinas/Manelik Pimentel.

TRACK RECORD: Pages was one of top hitters in his age group in Cuba and signed with the Dodgers for $300,000 late in the 2017-18 international signing period. After struggling to hit in his debut season, Pages leaped forward in year two and finished second in the Rookie-level Pioneer League in home runs (19) and total bases (153).

SCOUTING REPORT: Pages is a strong, athletic hitter with a wild streak that calls to mind Yasiel Puig. He has the strength, bat speed and feel for the barrel to generate a swing path built for future plus power, and he has the hand-eye coordination to keep his strikeouts reasonable and be at least an average hitter. Pages moves well for his size with average speed and has played center field, but he projects best in right field where he can show off his plus-plus cannon for an arm. Pages plays with flair and at times tries to do too much, leading to overswinging at the plate. His effort is inconsistent on defense and the basepaths.

THE FUTURE: Pages' prodigious talent is widely apparent. His focus and maturity will be tested at low Class A Great Lakes in 2020.

Year	Age	Club (League)	Class	AVG	G	AB	R	H	2B	3B	HR	RBI	BB	SO	SB	OBP	SLG
2018	17	Dodgers Guerrero (DSL)	R	.236	42	140	34	33	8	0	9	33	23	31	9	.393	.486
	17	Dodgers (AZL)	R	.192	10	26	5	5	1	0	1	3	6	4	1	.382	.346
2019	18	Ogden (PIO)	R	.298	63	235	57	70	22	2	19	55	26	79	7	.398	.651
Minor League Totals				.269	115	401	96	108	31	2	29	91	55	114	17	.395	.574

24 JIMMY LEWIS, RHP

BA GRADE
50 Risk: Extreme

Born: Nov. 2, 2000. **B-T:** R-R. **HT:** 6-6. **WT:** 200. **Drafted:** HS—Austin, 2019 (2nd round supplemental). **Signed by:** Clint Bowers.

TRACK RECORD: Lewis teamed with third baseman Brett Baty to make Lake Travis (Austin, Texas) High a top destination for scouts in 2019. Baty became the 12th overall pick by the Mets while Lewis threw two one-hitters and a no-hitter in a dominant senior season. The Dodgers drafted him in the supplemental second round, No. 78 overall, and signed him for $1,097,500 to forgo Louisiana State commitment.

SCOUTING REPORT: Lewis is a prototypical big, Texas righthander. He stands an imposing 6-foot-6, 200 pounds and runs his two-seam fastball anywhere from 91-95 mph, with plenty of room to add velocity as he matures. Lewis' curveball is his signature offering. He shows advanced feel to manipulate the shape of the pitch and command it in the strike zone, earning consensus above-average to plus grades. Lewis' changeup is still developing but has flashed average, and he ties everything together with plus control. Lewis didn't pitch after signing because of shoulder issues, but his long-term prognosis is good.

THE FUTURE: The Dodgers plan to move Lewis slowly. If everything clicks, he has mid-rotation potential.

Year	Age	Club (League)	Class	W	L	ERA	G	GS	SV	IP	H	HR	BB	SO	K/9	WHIP	AVG
2019	18	Did not play — Injured															

25 ANDRE JACKSON, RHP

BA GRADE
50 Risk: Extreme

Born: May 1, 1996. **B-T:** R-R. **HT:** 6-3. **WT:** 210. **Drafted:** Utah, 2017 (12th round). **Signed by:** Brian Compton.

TRACK RECORD: Jackson primarily played the outfield at Utah, but his raw arm strength intrigued scouts during 11 relief appearances as a sophomore. He missed his junior season after having Tommy John surgery, but the Dodgers still drafted him as a pitcher in the 12th round and signed him for $247,500. Jackson returned to health in 2019 and emerged as one of the system's biggest breakouts. He tied for second in the organization in strikeouts (141) and ranked fourth in ERA (3.06) while jumping to high Class A Rancho Cucamonga.

SCOUTING REPORT: Jackson is extremely athletic with a quick arm and a natural feel for a delivery. He runs his fastball from 92-98 mph, sitting 94-96, and backs it up with an upper 80s cutter, mid-80s changeup and low 80s breaking ball. He is still learning what pitch to throw in which counts, and none of his secondaries show better than average. His control comes and goes and is below-average overall.
THE FUTURE: Jackson is still understandably raw given his lack of experience. His future outlook should become clearer in 2020.

Year	Age	Club (League)	Class	W	L	ERA	G	GS	SV	IP	H	HR	BB	SO	K/9	WHIP	AVG
2017	21	Did not play—Injured															
2018	22	Dodgers (AZL)	R	2	0	3.44	4	3	0	18	18	0	4	31	15.2	1.20	.254
	22	Great Lakes (MWL)	LoA	1	5	4.35	14	14	0	50	48	3	41	45	8.2	1.79	.257
2019	23	Great Lakes (MWL)	LoA	4	1	2.23	10	10	0	48	29	1	19	50	9.3	0.99	.172
	23	R. Cucamonga (CAL)	HiA	3	1	3.66	15	15	0	66	61	5	38	91	12.3	1.49	.248
Minor League Totals				10	7	3.45	43	42	0	182	156	9	102	217	10.7	1.41	.232

26 ALEX DE JESUS, SS

BA GRADE **50** Risk: Extreme

Born: March 22, 2002. **B-T:** R-R. **HT:** 6-2. **WT:** 170. **Signed:** Dominican Republic, 2018. **Signed by:** Luis Márquez/Laiky Uribe/Manelik Pimentel.

TRACK RECORD: De Jesus signed with the Dodgers for $500,000 in 2018 as a third baseman, but he became more athletic after he signed and moved to shortstop. The Dodgers pushed him from the Dominican Summer League to the Rookie-level Arizona League after only 13 games last year and he quickly became a favorite of rival scouts on Arizona's backfields.
SCOUTING REPORT: De Jesus is an advanced hitter who drives the baseball with a simple swing and growing bat speed. He has an athletic, projectable body and the natural loft to his swing to project 20-plus home runs at maturity, and possibly more. De Jesus shows natural, easy actions and a plus arm at shortstop. He has a quick first step and moves well for his size, but most evaluators think his fringy speed and range will eventually push him back to third base.
THE FUTURE: De Jesus is far away, but his bat and athleticism give him an everyday foundation.

Year	Age	Club (League)	Class	AVG	G	AB	R	H	2B	3B	HR	RBI	BB	SO	SB	OBP	SLG
2019	17	Dodgers Shoemaker (DSL)	R	.296	13	54	8	16	5	0	1	9	8	14		.381	.444
	17	Dodgers Mota (AZL)	R	.276	44	163	13	45	8	1	2	25	12	58	5	.326	.374
Minor League Totals				.281	57	217	21	61	13	1	3	34	20	72	5	.340	.392

27 GERARDO CARRILLO, RHP

Born: Sept. 3, 1998. **B-T:** R-R. **HT:** 6-1. **WT:** 180. **Signed:** Mexico, 2016. **Signed by:** Mike Brito/Roman Barinas/Juvenal Soto.

TRACK RECORD: The Dodgers purchased Carrillo for $75,000 from the Mexican League in 2016. He rapidly filled out to become one of the hardest-throwing pitchers in the Dodgers organization, but he struggled with his control and posted a 5.44 ERA at high Class A Rancho Cucamonga in 2019.
SCOUTING REPORT: Carrillo added 25 pounds since signing and saw his two-seam fastball jump from 90-94 mph to 94-98 mph last year. His two-seamer has special potential with its velocity and nearly 16 inches of run, but he has yet to harness his newfound power. He walked 51 batters and hit 17 more in 86 innings in 2019 and has well below-average control, especially to his armside. Carrillo complements his two-seamer with a swing-and-miss low 90s cutter and a potentially average changeup, as well as a below-average curveball. Carrillo shows some feel for pitching, and the Dodgers think he will grow into an average strikethrower in time even with his current wildness.
THE FUTURE: Carrillo is 21 and has time to harness his stuff. He will try to take a step forward in 2020.

Year	Age	Club (League)	Class	W	L	ERA	G	GS	SV	IP	H	HR	BB	SO	K/9	WHIP	AVG
2017	18	Dodgers2 (DSL)	R	5	2	2.79	14	10	0	48	44	1	14	32	6.0	1.20	.237
2018	19	Dodgers (AZL)	R	2	0	0.82	4	1	1	11	6	0	2	13	10.6	0.73	.154
	19	Great Lakes (MWL)	LoA	2	1	1.65	9	9	0	49	35	3	15	37	6.8	1.02	.200
2019	20	R. Cucamonga (CAL)	HiA	5	9	5.44	23	21	0	86	87	3	51	86	9.0	1.60	.263
Minor League Totals				14	12	3.57	50	41	1	194	172	7	82	168	7.8	1.31	.235

28 RYAN PEPIOT, RHP

BA GRADE **45** Risk: High

Born: Aug. 21, 1997. **B-T:** R-R. **HT:** 6-3. **WT:** 215. **Drafted:** Butler, 2019 (3rd round). **Signed by:** Stephen Head.

TRACK RECORD: Pepiot led the Big East Conference with 126 strikeouts as a junior, but he also had the conference's second-most hit batters (15) and third-most walks (44). The Dodgers bet on his stuff and made him the highest-drafted played in Butler history when they selected him in the third round, No. 102 overall, and signed him for $547,500.

SCOUTING REPORT: Pepiot is a big-bodied righthander with dominant stuff on his best days. His fastball sits 93-94 mph with plus life and his changeup was among the best in the 2019 draft class. It sits 83-85 mph with late action and movement in the strike zone, grading easily plus and sometimes plus-plus. He shows feel for spinning a low 80s slider and mid-70s curveball that flash average at their best. Pepiot's problem is inconsistent fastball command and execution. He goes through stretches of horrid wildness and often spirals and is unable to get out of them.

THE FUTURE: The Dodgers gave Pepiot a detailed plan to improve his fastball execution. How well he implements it will determine whether he reaches his starter ceiling.

Year	Age	Club (League)	Class	W	L	ERA	G	GS	SV	IP	H	HR	BB	SO	K/9	WHIP	AVG
2019	21	Dodgers Mota (AZL)	R	0	0	0.00	4	1	0	5	2	0	4	10	18.0	1.20	.118
	21	Great Lakes (MWL)	LoA	0	0	2.45	9	9	0	18	13	0	9	21	10.3	1.20	.197
Minor League Totals				0	0	1.93	13	10	0	23	15	0	13	31	12.0	1.20	.181

29 ROBINSON ORTIZ, LHP

BA GRADE **45** Risk: High

Born: Jan. 4, 2000. **B-T:** L-L. **HT:** 6-0. **WT:** 180. **Signed:** Dominican Republic, 2017. **Signed by:** Luis Marquez/Roman Barinas/Laiky Uribe.

TRACK RECORD: Ortiz was virtually unknown as an international amateur and didn't sign for nearly a year after becoming eligible. The Dodgers quietly signed him for $60,000. Ortiz impressed in two years in Rookie-ball and made his full season debut in 2019, where he overcame a slow start at low Class A Great Lakes to post a 3.26 ERA and .206 opponent average over his last 16 starts.

SCOUTING REPORT: Ortiz possesses a smooth, easy delivery and growing stuff from the left side. His 91-94 mph fastball plays up with armside life, giving it the potential to be a dynamic pitch if he adds velocity as he matures. Ortiz pairs his fastball with advanced feel for a changeup that creates swings and misses and weak contact against righthanders, and his slider misses barrels against lefthanders. Ortiz shows a feel for mixing his pitches, and his ease of operation allows him average control.

THE FUTURE: Ortiz has all the ingredients of a back-of-the-rotation starter. How well he matures and builds on his frame will determine if he gets there.

Year	Age	Club (League)	Class	W	L	ERA	G	GS	SV	IP	H	HR	BB	SO	K/9	WHIP	AVG
2017	17	Dodgers (DSL)	R	2	2	3.13	11	11	0	37	33	0	5	35	8.4	1.02	.229
2018	18	Dodgers (AZL)	R	2	2	4.18	11	9	0	32	27	2	12	42	11.7	1.21	.231
2019	19	Great Lakes (MWL)	LoA	4	5	4.59	19	18	0	86	73	10	40	74	7.7	1.31	.233
Minor League Totals				8	9	4.15	41	38	0	156	133	12	57	151	8.7	1.22	.232

30 VICTOR GONZALEZ, LHP

BA GRADE **40** Risk: Medium

Born: Nov. 16, 1995. **B-T:** L-L. **HT:** 6-0. **WT:** 180. **Signed:** Mexico, 2012. **Signed by:** Mike Brito

TRACK RECORD: Gonzalez failed to advance past low Class A in four seasons before Tommy John surgery wiped out his entire 2017 season and most of 2018. He returned a different pitcher post-surgery and vaulted three levels up to Triple-A in 2019.

SCOUTING REPORT: Gonzalez got considerably stronger during Tommy John rehab and returned throwing significantly harder. He now boasts a power fastball from the left side that sits 94-96 mph and reaches 98 in relief, and it plays up further with a hint of deception that allows the ball to get on hitters quicker than they expect. Gonzalez's fastball is dominant against lefthanded hitters and plenty effective against righties. His average changeup is his best secondary pitch, and he can land his curveball for an early-count strike. His currently fringy slider is an area of focus. Gonzalez throws everything for strikes with average control and goes after hitters with a fastball-dominant attack.

THE FUTURE: The Dodgers added Gonzalez to their 40-man roster after the season. His ability to get both lefties and righties out makes him a bullpen option in 2020.

Year	Age	Club (League)	Class	W	L	ERA	G	GS	SV	IP	H	HR	BB	SO	K/9	WHIP	AVG
2017	21	Did not play—Injured															
2018	22	Great Lakes (MWL)	LoA	0	3	5.61	6	6	0	26	33	3	5	18	6.3	1.48	.314
	22	Ogden (PIO)	R	1	2	13.50	4	2	0	8	18	1	4	7	7.9	2.75	.429
2019	23	R. Cucamonga (CAL)	HiA	2	1	1.65	8	5	0	27	17	0	14	36	11.9	1.13	.174
	23	Tulsa (TL)	AA	3	1	2.23	15	8	2	48	48	4	14	44	8.2	1.28	.260
	23	Oklahoma City (PCL)	AAA	0	0	3.86	15	0	0	14	16	3	4	13	8.4	1.43	.286
Minor League Totals				17	27	4.34	112	76	2	377	407	31	138	364	8.7	1.45	.275

Miami Marlins

BY KEGAN LOWE

The Marlins finished with the National League's worst record for the second consecutive season in 2019, losing 105 games for just the second time in franchise history and finishing 40 games out of first place in the NL East.

The organization has now suffered 10 straight losing seasons dating back to 2010, when the then-Florida Marlins finished 87-75. The 2019 season also marked the 16th consecutive season in which the Marlins failed to qualify for the playoffs, further extending the longest active postseason drought in the NL.

The sustained losing has had a direct impact on attendance numbers in Miami, with the Marlins finishing last in attendance among all 30 major league teams for the second straight season. Miami averaged just more than 10,000 fans per home game for a total of 811,302 in 2019, and it was the second straight year in which the Marlins were the only major league team that failed to draw at least one million fans for their 81 regular season home games.

Despite the noticeable lack of on-field success at the major league level, there is still reason for optimism surrounding the franchise—almost all of which has to do with an improving farm system.

Following the 2017 season, the Marlins had arguably the worst crop of minor league prospect talent in baseball. That offseason, a new ownership group led by venture capitalist Bruce Sherman and former Yankees shortstop Derek Jeter took over the club from former owner Jeffery Loria. Since then, the Marlins have gone from a farm system that was the worst in baseball to one that now resides in the top half of all major league clubs.

Of course, that improvement came as a direct result of trading away ultra-talented players like reigning MVP Giancarlo Stanton, future MVP Christian Yelich, all-star catcher J.T. Realmuto, slugger Marcell Ozuna and others, but the new-led Marlins have remained committed to building their next major league contender on the farm.

The minor league resurgence is led by the fact that five of the Marlins' top seven prospects have been acquired via trade since the new ownership group took over, and furthermore, 13 of Miami's best 15 prospects have been acquired since the summer of 2017. As a result, this offseason marked the first time since 2014 that the Marlins have had a farm system considered among the top 20 systems in baseball.

The Marlins added to their prospect core in 2019 by drafting Vanderbilt outfielder JJ Bleday with the fourth overall pick and by executing a series of trade deadline deals that fetched position prospects with both upside potential and Double-A experience. That group is headlined by outfielder Jesus Sanchez, shortstop Jazz Chisholm and first baseman Lewin Diaz.

Much of the Marlins' young minor league talent should be making its way to Miami in the next year or two, including top prospect Sixto Sanchez. Still, the current—and recent—state of affairs with the big league club is a stark reminder that the organization has a long way to go when it comes to contending at the major league level. But unlike the last several years, there is at least reason for optimism among the Marlins' faithful, headlined by an up-and-coming crop of talented prospects.

RICH SCHULTZ/GETTY IMAGES

Rookie Sandy Alcantara tossed 197 innings and pitched to a 2.73 ERA in his final 10 starts.

PROJECTED 2023 LINEUP

Position	Player	Age
Catcher	Jorge Alfaro	30
First Base	Lewin Diaz (7)	26
Second Base	Isan Diaz	27
Third Base	Brian Anderson	30
Shortstop	Jazz Chisholm (5)	25
Left Field	JJ Bleday (2)	25
Center Field	Monte Harrison (6)	27
Right Field	Jesus Sanchez (3)	25
No. 1 Starter	Sixto Sanchez (1)	24
No. 2 Starter	Sandy Alcantara	27
No. 3 Starter	Edward Cabrera (4)	25
No. 4 Starter	Braxton Garrett (8)	25
No. 5 Starter	Trevor Rogers (9)	25
Closer	Jorge Guzman	27

DEPTH CHART

MIAMI MARLINS

TOP 2020 ROOKIE: Jesus Sanchez, OF. After getting a taste of Triple-A in 2019, the 22-year-old should be ready for a role as the Marlins' everyday right fielder by mid-2020.

BREAKOUT PROSPECT: Peyton Burdick, OF. One of the minors' best hitters in the second half of 2019, Burdick has a chance to be the steal of the 2019 draft for the Marlins.

SLEEPER: Luis Palacios, LHP. The 19-year-old lefty is 13-0, 1.49 with 147 strikeouts and 21 walks in 150.2 career innings and should be ready for his first taste of full-season ball in 2020.

SOURCE OF TOP 30 TALENT

Homegrown	19	Acquired	11
College	4	Trade	10
Junior College	0	Rule 5 Draft	1
High School	9	Independent League	0
Nondrafted Free Agent	0	Free Agent/Waivers	0
International	6		

LF
JJ Bleday (2)
Peyton Burdick (17)
Victor Mesa Jr. (22)
Brian Miller (27)
Tristan Pompey
J.D. Orr

CF
Monte Harrison (6)
Connor Scott (10)
Victor Victor Mesa (15)

RF
Jesus Sanchez (3)
Kameron Misner (11)
Jerar Encarnacion (16)
Thomas Jones

3B
Joe Dunand
James Nelson
Nic Ready

SS
Jazz Chisholm (5)
Jose Devers (13)
Nasim Nunez (18)
Jose Salas (23)
Osiris Johnson (25)
Dalvy Rosario
Ian Lewis
Junior Sanchez

2B
Riley Mahan
Christopher Torres
Bryson Brigman

1B
Lewin Diaz (7)
Evan Edwards
Lazaro Alonso
Sean Reynolds

C
Will Banfield (19)
Nick Fortes
Cam Barstad

LHP

LHSP	LHRP
Braxton Garrett (8)	Alex Vesia
Trevor Rogers (9)	Dylan Lee
Will Stewart (30)	McKenzie Mills
Luis Palacios	Sean Guenther
	Zach Wolf

RHP

RHSP	RHRP
Sixto Sanchez (1)	Humberto Mejia (26)
Edward Cabrera (4)	Kyle Keller
Nick Neidert (12)	Tommy Eveld
Jorge Guzman (14)	Tyler Stevens
Sterling Sharp (20)	Vincenzo Aiello
Jordan Holloway (21)	Colton Hock
Evan Fitterer (24)	
Robert Dugger (28)	
Chris Mokma (29)	
Alberto Guerrero	
Josh Robertson	

DRAFT ANALYSIS

2019

BEST PURE HITTER: OF JJ Bleday (1) was a career .327/.448/.555 hitter at Vanderbilt before the Marlins selected the lefthanded hitter with the No. 4 overall pick. While in college, Bleday also drew more walks (119) than strikeouts (102), showing off a refined approach, smooth swing and solid bat speed. Bleday has the potential to be a future plus hitter.

BEST POWER HITTER: OF Peyton Burdick (3) saw his power translate more easily in his pro debut. A 6-foot, 210-pound righthander hitter, Burdick has 70-grade raw power and was able to regularly tap into that potential in games, hitting 11 home runs and 35 extra-base hits in 69 minor league games.

FASTEST RUNNER: OF J.D. Orr (10) has some scouts believing he is a legitimate 80-grade runner. His top-of-the-scale speed also helps him in the outfield, where he shows above-average range and is capable of playing all three spots.

BEST DEFENSIVE PLAYER: Undersized at just 5-foot-9, 160 pounds, SS Nasim Nunez (2) has a plus arm capable of making all of the throws, and his plus speed gives him with great range.

BEST ATHLETE: OF Kameron Misner (1s) has a chance to be a true, five-tool player. At 6-foot-4, 219 pounds, Misner is an above-average runner with an explosive first step, which helps him both on the bases and in the outfield.

BEST FASTBALL: RHP Evan Fitterer (5) regularly showcased a mid-90s fastball as an amateur, leading the Marlins to lure him away from his UCLA commitment with a $1.5 million signing bonus.

BEST SECONDARY PITCH: RHP M.D. Johnson (6) has a hard, tight slider that helped him rack up more than 10.4 strikeouts per nine innings in 15 relief appearances for short-season Batavia. Fitterer has a slider that can look more like a slurve at times, but the Marlins believe it has the potential to be a future plus pitch with more refinement.

BEST PRO DEBUT: Burdick's .950 OPS ranked third among all hitters who accumulated at least 250 plate appearances in the Midwest League.

MOST INTRIGUING BACKGROUND: 3B Nic Ready (23) is the son of former major league infielder Randy Ready, who played a combined 13 seasons for the Brewers, Padres, Phillies, Athletics and Montreal Expos from 1983-95.

CLOSEST TO THE MAJORS: After signing with the Marlins for north of $6.6 million, Bleday could be manning a corner outfield spot in the majors as soon as 2021.

BEST LATE-ROUND PICK: RHP Chris Mokma (12) signed with the Marlins for $557,000, which was a larger signing bonus than all but four of the organization's draft picks received in 2019. A 6-foot-4, 190-pound prep arm out of Michigan, Mokma impressed evaluators with his low-90s fastball, strike-throwing ability and a clean delivery.

THE ONE WHO GOT AWAY: 3B Parker Noland (31), a Vanderbilt commit, has an advanced lefthanded bat with above-average power potential and should be a productive hitter for the Commodores for years to come.

—KEGAN LOWE

TOP DRAFT PICKS OF THE DECADE

Year	Player, Pos	2019 Org
2010	Christian Yelich, OF	Brewers
2011	Jose Fernandez, RHP	Deceased
2012	Andrew Heaney, LHP	Angels
2013	Colin Moran, 3B	Pirates
2014	Tyler Kolek, RHP	Marlins
2015	Josh Naylor, 1B	Padres
2016	Braxton Garrett, LHP	Marlins
2017	Trevor Rogers, LHP	Marlins
2018	Connor Scott, OF	Marlins
2019	JJ Bleday, OF	Marlins

2018

Taking a trio of prep hitters at the top of the draft was a departure for the Marlins after a few pitching heavy years, but OF Connor Scott (1), SS Osiris Johnson (2) and C Will Banfield (2s) all offer upside.

GRADE: C

2017

After an injury-slowed start to his career, LHP Trevor Rogers (1) started in the right direction in 2019, reaching Double-A. OF Brian Miller (1s) is the only other player from the class to appear in the Handbook.

GRADE: D

2016

LHP Braxton Garrett (1) returned after missing 2018 due to injury and got to Double-A. RHP Mike King (12) dealt with his own injuries this season but made his major league debut with the Yankees.

GRADE: C

1 SIXTO SANCHEZ, RHP

Born: July 29, 1998. **B-T:** R-R. **HT:** 6-0. **WT:** 185.
Signed: Dominican Republic, 2015.
Signed by: Carlos Salas (Phillies).

TRACK RECORD: Originally signed by the Phillies for $35,000 in July 2015, Sanchez was traded to the Marlins in the Feb. 2019 trade for J.T. Realmuto. Prior to the trade, Sanchez established himself as one of the top pitching prospects in baseball on the strength of an explosive three-pitch arsenal. A 6-foot, 185-pound righthander, he struggled with right elbow inflammation in 2018, restricting him to just 46.2 innings in his final season with the Phillies. Sanchez enjoyed good health in 2019, pitched a career-high 114 innings and reached Double-A for the first time. Sanchez was the top-ranked pitching prospect in the Southern League, posting a 8-4, 2.53 record with 97 strikeouts and just 19 walks in 103 innings.

SCOUTING REPORT: Sanchez's three-pitch mix is headlined by a mid- to upper-90s fastball that can touch 101 mph. Complementing his double-plus fastball is a pair of above-average-to-plus secondary offerings in an upper-80s changeup with good sinking action and a hard, power slider that features two-plane tilt. Perhaps even more impressive than his stuff is Sanchez's ability to control all three offerings. He is an advanced strike-thrower with plus or better control, and he walked fewer than 1.7 batters per nine innings at both of his stops in 2019. A converted infielder, Sanchez is a good athlete whose control is aided by his relatively clean, smooth delivery. Previous concerns about Sanchez's elbow injury and his smaller stature limiting his effectiveness as a starter seemed to have quieted after an effective 2019. In all, he is one of the few pitching prospects still in the minors who can combine premium velocity, multiple swing-and-miss offspeed offerings, plus control and an easy, athletic delivery.

THE FUTURE: Sanchez will participate in big league spring training with the Marlins in 2020, but the likely scenario remains that he opens the regular season in Triple-A. A major league debut sometime next summer or in September is possible, but the Marlins seem content to let Sanchez continue to gain experience and build innings in the minors before finally breaking through with a regular rotation spot in 2021. Sanchez has the highest upside of any pitcher in the organization, and the Marlins hope he can be the frontline starter the franchise will need as it rises from its latest rebuilding effort.

TOM DIPACE

BA GRADE
65 Risk: High

SCOUTING GRADES
Fastball: 70. **Changeup:** 60.
Slider: 50. **Control:** 60.

Projected future grades on 20-80 scouting scale.

TOP PROSPECTS OF THE DECADE

Year	Player, Pos	2019 Org
2010	Giancarlo Stanton, OF	Yankees
2011	Matt Dominguez, 3B	Did not play
2012	Christian Yelich, OF	Brewers
2013	Jose Fernandez, RHP	Deceased
2014	Andrew Heaney, LHP	Angels
2015	Tyler Kolek, RHP	Marlins
2016	Tyler Kolek, RHP	Marlins
2017	Braxton Garrett, LHP	Marlins
2018	Sandy Alcantara, RHP	Marlins
2019	Victor Victor Mesa, OF	Marlins

BEST TOOLS

Best Hitter For Average	Jose Devers
Best Power Hitter	Jazz Chisholm
Best Strike-Zone Discipline	Victor Victor Mesa
Fastest Baserunner	Nasim Nuñez
Best Athlete	Monte Harrison
Best Fastball	Sixto Sanchez
Best Curveball	Braxton Garrett
Best Slider	Nick Neidert
Best Changeup	Edward Cabrera
Best Control	Sixto Sanchez
Best Defensive Catcher	Will Banfield
Best Defensive Infielder	Nasim Nuñez
Best Infield Arm	Christopher Torres
Best Defensive Outfielder	Monte Harrison
Best Outfield Arm	Jerar Encarnacion

Year	Age	Club (League)	Class	W	L	ERA	G	GS	SV	IP	H	HR	BB	SO	K/9	WHIP	AVG
2017	18	Lakewood (SAL)	LoA	5	3	2.41	13	13	0	67	46	1	9	64	8.6	0.82	.191
	18	Clearwater (FSL)	HiA	0	4	4.55	5	5	0	28	27	1	9	20	6.5	1.30	.252
2018	19	Clearwater (FSL)	HiA	4	3	2.51	8	8	0	47	39	1	11	45	8.7	1.07	.224
2019	20	Jupiter (FSL)	HiA	0	2	4.91	2	2	0	11	14	1	2	6	4.9	1.45	.318
	20	Jacksonville (SL)	AA	8	4	2.53	18	18	0	103	87	5	19	97	8.5	1.03	.225
Minor League Totals				23	18	2.58	68	59	0	335	278	9	64	294	7.9	1.02	.223

2 JJ BLEDAY, OF

Born: Nov. 10, 1997. **B-T:** L-L. **HT:** 6-3. **WT:** 205. **Drafted:** Vanderbilt, 2019 (1st round). **Signed by:** Christian Castorri.

BA GRADE
60 Risk: High

TRACK RECORD: Bleday enjoyed a breakout junior campaign at Vanderbilt before the Marlins signed him for a franchise-record $6.67 million as the No. 4 overall pick. A first-team All-American, Bleday led all Division I hitters with 27 home runs in 2019 and helped the Commodores win the program's second College World Series championship with a .347/.465/.701 slash line and more walks (61) than strikeouts (58). He made his pro debut for high Class A Jupiter on July 20 and posted a .747 OPS in August.

SCOUTING REPORT: Bleday is an advanced hitter with a smooth lefthanded swing and refined approach. As he showed in his final season at Vanderbilt, he can drive the ball with plus raw power when he connects, and he gets his barrel on the ball often. Bleday is an average runner with an above-average arm who profiles as an above-average defender in either outfield corner. Scouts routinely praise Bleday for his overall makeup, noting that his continued improvement over his three years at Vanderbilt was hardly a surprise when considering his work ethic and maturity.

THE FUTURE: Bleday has the pedigree, experience and talent to move quickly. After playing 38 games in the Florida State League in 2019, he should see plenty of time at Double-A in 2020. Bleday has the potential to be a high-average, middle-of-the-order hitter who should be able to hold down a corner outfield spot for years to come in Miami.

SCOUTING GRADES: **Hitting:** 60 **Power:** 60 **Running:** 50 **Fielding:** 55 **Arm:** 55

Year	Age	Club (League)	Class	AVG	G	AB	R	H	2B	3B	HR	RBI	BB	SO	SB	OBP	SLG
2019	21	Jupiter (FSL)	HiA	.257	38	140	13	36	8	0	3	19	11	29	0	.311	.379
Minor League Totals				.257	38	140	13	36	8	0	3	19	11	29	0	.311	.379

3 JESUS SANCHEZ, OF

Born: Oct. 7, 1997. **B-T:** L-R. **HT:** 6-3. **WT:** 230. **Signed:** Dominican Republic, 2014. **Signed by:** Danny Santana (Rays).

BA GRADE
55 Risk: High

TRACK RECORD: One of the top prospects traded at the 2019 deadline, Sanchez joined the Marlins' organization in the deal that sent righthanders Nick Anderson and Trevor Richards to the Rays. Sanchez originally signed with the Rays for $400,000 in 2014, and he received his first taste of Triple-A in 2019.

SCOUTING REPORT: Sanchez has elite bat speed and hand-eye coordination. Armed with plus raw power, the ball routinely jumps off his bat when he makes contact. Sanchez's swing can get too long at times, and he has occasionally struggled against high-end velocity, especially on the inside part of the plate as he's advanced through the upper minors. Defensively, Sanchez has an above-average arm and profiles best as an above-average right fielder. He'll likely settle in as an average runner as he continues to mature.

THE FUTURE: The combination of Sanchez and JJ Bleday gives the Marlins two potential high-end corner outfielders at the top of their system. Sanchez is better suited for a role in right field and is likely a year ahead of Bleday in terms of time line. Sanchez will start 2020 back in Triple-A, just one phone call or injury away from Miami.

SCOUTING GRADES: **Hitting:** 50 **Power:** 60 **Running:** 50 **Fielding:** 55 **Arm:** 55

Year	Age	Club (League)	Class	AVG	G	AB	R	H	2B	3B	HR	RBI	BB	SO	SB	OBP	SLG
2017	19	Bowling Green (MWL)	LoA	.305	117	475	81	145	29	4	15	82	32	91	7	.348	.478
2018	20	Charlotte, FL (FSL)	HiA	.301	90	359	56	108	24	2	10	64	15	71	6	.331	.462
	20	Montgomery (SL)	AA	.214	27	98	14	21	8	0	1	11	11	21	1	.300	.327
2019	21	Montgomery (SL)	AA	.275	78	287	32	79	11	1	8	49	24	65	5	.332	.404
	21	Durham (IL)	AAA	.206	18	63	6	13	2	1	1	5	6	20	0	.282	.317
	21	New Orleans (PCL)	AAA	.246	17	65	11	16	1	0	4	9	9	15	0	.338	.446
Minor League Totals				.296	464	1799	269	532	98	23	50	304	126	358	29	.342	.459

4 EDWARD CABRERA, RHP

BA GRADE
55 Risk: High

Born: April 13, 1998. **B-T:** R-R. **HT:** 6-4. **WT:** 175. **Signed:** Dominican Republic, 2015. **Signed by:** Albert Gonzalez/Sandy Nin/Domingo Ortega.

TRACK RECORD: A $100,000 signing out of the Dominican Republic in 2015, Cabrera had a breakout campaign in 2019. After showing an exciting arsenal with inconsistent results in his first three seasons, Cabrera ranked as best righthanded pitching prospect in the Florida State League. He reached Double-A Jacksonville in mid-June and struck out a career best 116 batters and allowed a .190 average in a combined 96.2 innings over the two stops.

SCOUTING REPORT: Cabrera has a heavy, mid-90s fastball with sink that has reached as high as 100 mph. While his fastball has seemingly always had the makings of a double-plus pitch and has only continued to improve, it was the development of Cabrera's breaking ball and changeup that has helped him become a more well-rounded pitcher. Though still firm at 88-90 mph, Cabrera's changeup brings enough separation from his fastball to keep hitters off-balance, while his low-80s breaking ball has both the tilt and depth necessary to be a swing-and-miss pitch. An athletic 6-foot-4, Cabrera's delivery can speed up at times, but he still managed to improve his control and walked fewer than three batters per nine innings in 2019.

THE FUTURE: Sixto Sanchez is the only pitching prospect in the Marlins' system with as high a ceiling as Cabrera, and even that gap might have closed slightly in 2019. Cabrera will likely begin the 2020 season back at Double-A Jacksonville, with a midseason move to Triple-A probable if he performs well.

SCOUTING GRADES: **Fastball:** 70 **Slider:** 60 **Changeup:** 50 **Control:** 50

Year	Age	Club (League)	Class	W	L	ERA	G	GS	SV	IP	H	HR	BB	SO	K/9	WHIP	AVG
2017	19	Batavia (NYP)	SS	1	3	5.30	13	6	0	36	42	1	8	32	8.1	1.40	.286
2018	20	Greensboro (SAL)	LoA	4	8	4.22	22	22	0	100	105	11	42	93	8.3	1.47	.270
2019	21	Jupiter (FSL)	HiA	5	3	2.02	11	11	0	58	37	1	18	73	11.3	0.95	.183
	21	Jacksonville (SL)	AA	4	1	2.56	8	8	0	39	28	6	13	43	10.0	1.06	.200
Minor League Totals				16	21	3.67	65	54	0	279	266	20	91	269	8.7	1.28	.250

5 JAZZ CHISHOLM, SS

Born: Feb. 1, 1998. **B-T:** L-R. **HT:** 5-11. **WT:** 165. **Signed:** Bahamas, 2015. **Signed by:** Craig Shipley (D-backs).

TRACK RECORD: Chisholm signed with the D-backs for $200,000 in July 2015 and worked his way up to becoming the organization's No. 1 prospect after an impressive 2018 season that he finished at high Class A Visalia. Chisholm was traded to the Marlins on July 31 in exchange for big league rookie righthander Zac Gallen.

SCOUTING REPORT: Chisholm is an athletic, 5-foot-11 shortstop with loud tools both offensively and defensively. A lefthanded hitter, Chisholm has a smooth, uppercut swing and strong wrists that leads to easy plus power but also significant swing-and-miss issues. He did manage to tone down his strike-out rate following the trade to the Marlins, however. He tends to be overly aggressive and hit just .220 in the Southern League this season. Still just 21 years old, Chisholm could be an all-around impact shortstop if he improves his approach, uses the entire field and puts the ball in play more often. Defensively, Chisholm is an above-average defender at shortstop who's capable of making all of the necessary plays. He's also an above-average runner capable of stealing 20-plus bases per season.

THE FUTURE: Chisholm is a high-risk, high-reward prospect. The Marlins could elect to start him back at Double-A to start 2020 with hopes of seeing an improved approach and a better hit tool. If Chisholm's tantalizing potential is realized, he could eventually be one of the majors' most exciting shortstops.

SCOUTING GRADES: **Hitting:** 50 **Power:** 60 **Running:** 55 **Fielding:** 55 **Arm:** 55

Year	Age	Club (League)	Class	AVG	G	AB	R	H	2B	3B	HR	RBI	BB	SO	SB	OBP	SLG
2017	19	Kane County (MWL)	LoA	.248	29	109	14	27	5	2	1	12	10	39	3	.325	.358
2018	20	Kane County (MWL)	LoA	.244	76	307	52	75	17	4	15	43	30	97	8	.311	.472
	20	Visalia (CAL)	HiA	.329	36	149	27	49	6	2	10	27	9	52	9	.369	.597
2019	21	Jackson (SL)	AA	.204	89	314	51	64	6	5	18	44	41	123	13	.305	.427
	21	Jacksonville (SL)	AA	.284	23	81	6	23	4	2	3	10	11	24	3	.383	.494
Minor League Totals				.255	315	1209	192	308	50	16	56	173	120	408	49	.327	.462

6 MONTE HARRISON, OF

Born: Aug. 10, 1995. **B-T:** R-R. **HT:** 6-3. **WT:** 220. **Drafted:** HS—Lee's Summit, Mo., 2014 (2nd round). **Signed by:** Drew Anderson (Brewers).

BA GRADE
55 **Risk:** **Very High**

TRACK RECORD: Drafted by the Brewers in the second round in 2014, Harrison joined outfielder Lewis Brinson, second baseman Isan Diaz and righthander Jordan Yamamoto as part of the return in the January 2018 trade that sent Christian Yelich to Milwaukee. Harrison struggled with swing-and-miss issues in his first year with the Marlins and then played in just 58 games in 2019 because of a right wrist injury he suffered while making a diving catch on June 26.

SCOUTING REPORT: Prior to his injury and subsequent surgery, Harrison was showing improvements at the plate. He toned down a high leg kick last offseason and turned it into a more subtle toe tap, helping him reduce his strikeout rate from 36.9 percent at Double-A in 2018 to 29.9 percent at Triple-A in 2019. It's a step in the right direction for a hitter who has excellent bat speed and plus raw power. Harrison is a plus runner with great instincts on the bases, and he stole 23 bases in 25 attempts in just 58 games this season. Capable of playing all three outfield spots, he has spent the majority of his time as an above-average center fielder. He could also be a plus defender with a plus arm in right field, if needed.

THE FUTURE: Harrison's injury torpedoed his chances of making his major league debut in 2019, but that should come sometime in 2020. Now healthy, Harrison was scheduled to play winter ball in Puerto Rico this offseason before potentially beginning the season with touch-up work at Triple-A.

SCOUTING GRADES: **Hitting:** 40 **Power:** 60 **Running:** 60 **Fielding:** 60 **Arm:** 60

Year	Age	Club (League)	Class	AVG	G	AB	R	H	2B	3B	HR	RBI	BB	SO	SB	OBP	SLG
2017	21	Wisconsin (MWL)	LoA	.265	63	223	32	59	12	1	11	32	29	70	10	.359	.475
	21	Carolina (CAR)	HiA	.278	59	230	41	64	16	1	10	35	14	69	16	.341	.487
2018	22	Jacksonville (SL)	AA	.240	136	521	85	125	20	3	19	48	44	215	28	.316	.399
2019	23	Jupiter (FSL)	HiA	.143	2	7	2	1	0	0	0	0	0	1	3	.143	.143
	23	New Orleans (PCL)	AAA	.274	56	215	41	59	7	2	9	24	25	73	20	.357	.451
Minor League Totals				.245	520	1921	314	471	84	15	61	221	195	677	138	.333	.400

7 LEWIN DIAZ, 1B

Born: Nov. 19, 1996. **B-T:** L-L. **HT:** 6-4. **WT:** 225. **Signed:** Dominican Republic, 2013. **Signed by:** Fred Guerrero (Twins).

BA GRADE
50 **Risk:** **High**

TRACK RECORD: Diaz signed with the Twins for $1.4 million out of the Dominican Republic in 2013 and found success at nearly every lower level until he reached high Class A Fort Myers and struggled mightily in 2018. This past offseason, the 6-foot-4 Diaz focused on dropping weight and getting into better shape, and his on-field production blossomed as a result. The rebuilding Marlins acquired Diaz on July 27 in a trade that sent righthanders Sergio Romo and Chris Vallimont to the Twins.

SCOUTING REPORT: A lefthander hitter capable of driving the ball to all fields, Diaz's leaner, stronger build and a thumb that healed from a late-season fracture in 2018 has helped him tap into his plus raw power more often. After never hitting more than 12 homers in a single season, Diaz launched a career-high 27 home runs in 2019. Though he doesn't draw a lot of walks, Diaz also doesn't strike out as much as a prototypical slugger, and he's at least an average hitter with strong bat-to-ball skills. Defensively, Diaz has the potential to be a plus defensive first baseman. He has below-average speed underway, but he showcases solid range, a strong arm and good footwork around the bag.

THE FUTURE: After proving capable of handling Double-A pitching in the second half of 2019, Diaz is expected to start 2020 season at Triple-A. Diaz is a potential middle-of-the-order hitter with plus defense at first base. He could find himself in the Marlins' lineup sometime in 2020.

SCOUTING GRADES: **Hitting:** 50 **Power:** 60 **Running:** 40 **Fielding:** 60 **Arm:** 50

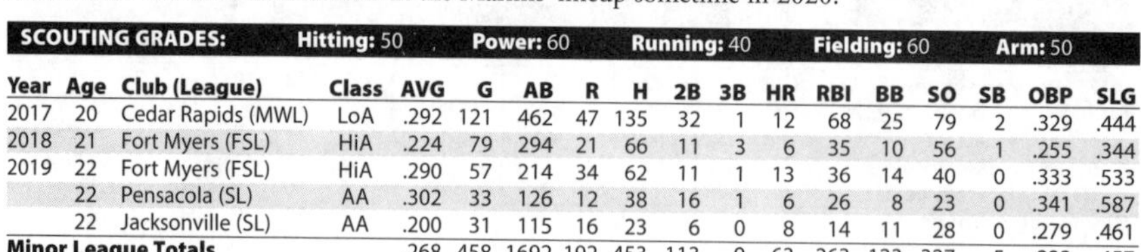

Year	Age	Club (League)	Class	AVG	G	AB	R	H	2B	3B	HR	RBI	BB	SO	SB	OBP	SLG
2017	20	Cedar Rapids (MWL)	LoA	.292	121	462	47	135	32	1	12	68	25	79	2	.329	.444
2018	21	Fort Myers (FSL)	HiA	.224	79	294	21	66	11	3	6	35	10	56	1	.255	.344
2019	22	Fort Myers (FSL)	HiA	.290	57	214	34	62	11	1	13	36	14	40	0	.333	.533
	22	Pensacola (SL)	AA	.302	33	126	12	38	16	1	6	26	8	23	0	.341	.587
	22	Jacksonville (SL)	AA	.200	31	115	16	23	6	0	8	14	11	28	0	.279	.461
Minor League Totals				.268	458	1692	192	453	113	9	63	263	123	327	5	.322	.457

8 BRAXTON GARRETT, LHP

BA GRADE
50 Risk: High

Born: Aug. 5, 1997. **B-T:** L-L. **HT:** 6-3. **WT:** 190. **Drafted:** HS—Florence, Ala., 2016 (1st round). **Signed by:** Mark Willoughby.

TRACK RECORD: The Marlins drafted Garrett with the No. 7 overall pick in 2016 and signed him for an above-slot deal north of $4.1 million. He made his pro debut in 2017 but made just four low Class A starts before having Tommy John surgery. After missing all of 2018, Garrett returned to the mound on April 9, striking out six batters and allowing only one run in four innings. In all, he threw 107 innings, struck out 119 batters and limited opponents to a .235 average in 2019.

SCOUTING REPORT: Armed with one the best offspeed offerings in the Marlins' system, Garrett's true, north-to-south curveball is a plus, swing-and-miss pitch. He pairs his big breaker with a 92-95 mph fastball and an average, third-pitch changeup that flashes above-average potential. Garrett still has room to add strength, and he could increase his fastball velocity as he continues to build innings. He has a smooth delivery, and he showed the makings of above-average command despite his long layoff in which he pitched just 15.1 innings over a span of nearly three years.

THE FUTURE: Garrett made a one-start cameo at Double-A Jacksonville at the end of 2019 and will return there in 2020. On a similar timeline to that of fellow first-round lefthander Trevor Rogers, Garrett could be a mid-rotation starter for the Marlins by late 2021 or early 2022.

SCOUTING GRADES: **Fastball:** 55 **Curveball:** 60 **Changeup:** 50 **Control:** 55

Year	Age	Club (League)	Class	W	L	ERA	G	GS	SV	IP	H	HR	BB	SO	K/9	WHIP	AVG
2017	19	Greensboro (SAL)	LoA	1	0	2.93	4	4	0	15	13	3	6	16	9.4	1.24	.220
2018	20	Did not play—Injured															
2019	21	Jupiter (FSL)	HiA	6	6	3.34	20	20	0	105	92	13	37	118	10.1	1.23	.230
	21	Jacksonville (SL)	AA	0	1	16.20	1	1	0	2	4	0	3	1	5.4	4.20	.444
Minor League Totals				7	7	3.47	25	25	0	122	109	16	46	135	10.0	1.27	.233

9 TREVOR ROGERS, LHP

BA GRADE
50 Risk: High

Born: Nov. 13, 1997. **B-T:** L-L. **HT:** 6-6. **WT:** 185. **Drafted:** HS—Carlsbad, N.M., 2017 (1st round). **Signed by:** Scott Stanley.

TRACK RECORD: The Marlins drafted Rogers with the 13th overall pick in 2017 and signed him for a below-slot $3.4 million. He did not make his pro debut until May 2018, however, with the Marlins citing general fatigue as the reason for his delayed start. After making 17 starts for low Class A Greensboro in 2018, Rogers pitched a career-high 136.1 innings in 2019, including a five-start cameo in Double-A Jacksonville.

SCOUTING REPORT: A lean, 6-foot-6, 185-pound lefthander, Rogers has worked to add strength and velocity to his low- to mid-90s fastball, which tops out at 96 mph. He has thrown both a changeup and slider in the past, with both grading out as average offerings but showing the potential for more. He's recently worked on adding a cutter to his arsenal, looking to find a go-to offspeed pitch in order to increase his strikeout rate. Rogers has a fluid delivery, and his control took a positive step forward in 2019 as he walked fewer than two batters per nine innings in 18 starts with high Class A Jupiter.

THE FUTURE: After getting a taste of Double-A, Rogers should return to the level to begin 2020. Possessing the likely ceiling of a mid- or back-end starter, Rogers could find himself in the Marlins' rotation as soon as 2021.

SCOUTING GRADES: **Fastball:** 55 **Slider:** 50 **Changeup:** 50 **Control:** 55

Year	Age	Club (League)	Class	W	L	ERA	G	GS	SV	IP	H	HR	BB	SO	K/9	WHIP	AVG
2018	20	Greensboro (SAL)	LoA	2	7	5.82	17	17	0	73	86	4	27	85	10.5	1.56	.295
2019	21	Jupiter (FSL)	HiA	5	8	2.53	18	18	0	110	97	7	24	122	10.0	1.10	.232
	21	Jacksonville (SL)	AA	1	2	4.50	5	5	0	26	25	3	9	28	9.7	1.31	.250
Minor League Totals				8	17	3.92	40	40	0	209	208	14	60	235	10.1	1.28	.256

10 CONNOR SCOTT, OF

BA GRADE
50 Risk: High

Born: Oct. 8, 1999. **B-T:** L-L. **HT:** 6-4. **WT:** 180. **Drafted:** HS—Tampa, 2018 (1st round). **Signed by:** Donavan O'Dowd.

TRACK RECORD: The 13th overall pick in 2018, Scott signed with the Marlins for just north of $4 million. He is a lanky, 6-foot-4, lefthanded hitter who draws comparisons with fellow Plant High alum and current Astros outfielder Kyle Tucker.

SCOUTING REPORT: Scott has plus speed that helps him both as a stolen base threat and at least an average center fielder. Some scouts believe he may eventually move to a corner outfield position, but his speed and plus arm strength would fit well in right field. Scott has above-average raw power, but he's yet to fully tap into that potential in games. Still young compared to his competition, Scott needs to refine his approach and learn how to turn and drive on hitter's pitches more often.

THE FUTURE: A potential five-tool outfielder with upside, the Marlins would like to see Scott drive the ball and make more of an offensive impact as he continues to mature, add strength and climb the ladder.

SCOUTING GRADES: **Hitting:** 50 **Power:** 50 **Running:** 60 **Fielding:** 55 **Arm:** 60

Year	Age	Club (League)	Class	AVG	G	AB	R	H	2B	3B	HR	RBI	BB	SO	SB	OBP	SLG
2018	18	Marlins (GCL)	R	.223	27	103	15	23	1	4	0	8	14	29	8	.319	.311
	18	Greensboro (SAL)	LoA	.211	23	76	4	16	2	0	1	5	10	27	1	.295	.276
2019	19	Clinton (MWL)	LoA	.251	95	378	56	95	24	4	4	36	31	91	21	.311	.368
	19	Jupiter (FSL)	HiA	.235	27	98	12	23	4	1	1	5	11	26	2	.306	.327
Minor League Totals				.240	172	655	87	157	31	9	6	54	66	173	32	.310	.342

11 KAMERON MISNER, OF

BA GRADE
50 Risk: High

Born: Jan. 8, 1998. **B-T:** L-L. **HT:** 6-4. **WT:** 219. **Drafted:** Missouri, 2019 (1st round supplemental). **Signed by:** Joe Dunigan.

TRACK RECORD: The Royals' 33rd-round pick in 2016, Misner instead went to Missouri, where he enjoyed a solid three-year career. A left foot fracture limited Misner to just 34 games in what was otherwise a breakout sophomore year in 2018, but he started his 2019 campaign strong before struggling with some swing-and-miss issues during conference play. After shaking off the rust post-signing in the Gulf Coast League, Misner finished the season in low Class A Clinton.

SCOUTING REPORT: While blessed with unrivaled tools within the Marlins system, Misner certainly looks the part of a major leaguer and has drawn comparisons to the Indians' Bradley Zimmer. Using a balanced yet spread-out stance, Misner has shown bat speed and an idea of the strike zone. Misner has been vulnerable to chasing stuff up in the zone, resulting in softer contact than expected. He still has an above-average power with good lift but will need to do a better managing counts and staying in control of at-bats. Misner is an above average runner with the tools to stay in center field though some scouts feel he may grow out of the position as he continues to fill out.

THE FUTURE: Misner should spend most of his time with high Class A Jupiter in 2020, when he will likely share an outfield with 2018 first-round pick Connor Scott.

Year	Age	Club (League)	Class	AVG	G	AB	R	H	2B	3B	HR	RBI	BB	SO	SB	OBP	SLG
2019	21	Marlins (GCL)	R	.241	8	29	2	7	2	0	0	4	9	7	3	.421	.310
	21	Clinton (MWL)	LoA	.276	34	134	25	37	7	0	2	20	21	35	8	.380	.373
Minor League Totals				.270	42	163	27	44	9	0	2	24	30	42	11	.388	.362

12 NICK NEIDERT, RHP

BA GRADE
45 Risk: Medium

Born: Nov. 20, 1996. **B-T:** R-R. **HT:** 6-1. **WT:** 202. **Drafted:** HS—Suwanee, Ga., 2015 (2nd round). **Signed by:** Dustin Evans (Mariners).

TRACK RECORD: Selected by the Mariners in the second round of the 2015 draft, Neidert quickly gained a reputation for both an advanced feel and command of his fastball-changeup mix. The Marlins netted Neidert as one of three Mariners prospects, along with Robert Dugger, in the Dec. 2017 deal that sent Dee Gordon to Seattle. Surgery to repair his meniscus cost Neidert a chunk of the season.

SCOUTING REPORT: Neidert's 90-94 mph fastball doesn't overpower hitters but the pitch plays up due to some deception through delivery, late movement as well as his ability to spot it to all parts of the plate. Neidert further expanded his fastball's value in 2019 by pitching up in the zone, which generated more soft contact to go along with an excellent swing-and-miss rate. Neidert's plus changeup keeps hitters off-balance. While Neidert still has a big 12-6 curveball, its early break and lack of true deception despite good spin relegates it to a fourth pitch. Neidert's success at the upper levels by the development of a cutter-slider hybrid with just enough angle and depth to both sides to keep hitters off-balance. Neidert generates a high front side with his glove and stays closed before generating tilt toward the plate. He maintains a consistent release point.

THE FUTURE: Neidert made up for the time lost due to his right knee injury by making five starts in the Arizona Fall League, where he went 2-0, 1.25 with 19 strikeouts and just two walks in 21.2 innings. With the ceiling of a mid-to-back of the rotation starter,

Year	Age	Club (League)	Class	W	L	ERA	G	GS	SV	IP	H	HR	BB	SO	K/9	WHIP	AVG
2017	20	Modesto (CAL)	HiA	10	3	2.76	19	19	0	104	95	7	17	109	9.4	1.07	.244
	20	Arkansas (TL)	AA	1	3	6.56	6	6	0	23	33	4	5	13	5.0	1.63	.324
2018	21	Jacksonville (SL)	AA	12	7	3.24	26	26	0	153	142	17	31	154	9.1	1.13	.250
2019	22	Marlins (GCL)	R	0	0	0.00	2	2	0	4	2	0	1	3	7.4	0.82	.154
	22	Jupiter (FSL)	HiA	0	1	4.82	2	2	0	9	10	1	4	6	5.8	1.50	.270
	22	New Orleans (PCL)	AAA	3	4	5.05	9	9	0	41	45	4	22	37	8.1	1.63	.280
Minor League Totals				33	23	3.20	94	94	0	460	427	41	102	414	8.1	1.15	.247

13 JOSE DEVERS, SS

BA GRADE 50 Risk: High

Born: Dec. 7, 1999. **B-T:** L-R. **HT:** 6-0. **WT:** 155. **Signed:** Dominican Republic, 2016. **Signed by:** Juan Rosario (Yankees).

TRACK RECORD: Originally signed by the Yankees for $250,000 out of the Dominican Republic, Devers was part of the Dec. 2017 deal that sent Giancarlo Stanton to the Yankees. Devers is also the cousin of current Red Sox third baseman Rafael Devers. Devers has struggled with a series of nagging injuries over the past two seasons, including shoulder and forearm issues, as well as a groin injury that limited him to just 47 games in 2019. Devers made up for lost time in the Arizona Fall League.

SCOUTING REPORT: Devers is a plus defensive shortstop with excellent instincts and solid footwork that help his average arm play up. Two years after being acquired, Devers is still a projection bat due in part to lack of strength as well as limited at-bats. Devers is a contact hitter with a selectively aggressive approach as evidenced by a 5.1-percent walk rate and a 14.7 percent strikeout rate. While Devers' power will never be average, he will need to do more to be competitive.

THE FUTURE: Having played in just 187 games over the past three seasons, the 20-year-old Devers simply needs to stay healthy. At full strength, Devers is a plus defensive shortstop with the potential to be a top-of-the-order hitter who should start back at high Class A Jupiter in 2020.

Year	Age	Club (League)	Class	AVG	G	AB	R	H	2B	3B	HR	RBI	BB	SO	SB	OBP	SLG
2017	17	Yankees1 (DSL)	R	.239	11	46	4	11	2	1	0	7	0	16	1	.255	.326
	17	Yankees1 (GCL)	R	.246	42	138	17	34	7	2	1	9	18	21	15	.359	.348
2018	18	Greensboro (SAL)	LoA	.273	85	337	46	92	12	4	0	24	15	49	13	.313	.332
	18	Jupiter (FSL)	HiA	.250	2	8	1	2	0	0	0	2	1	0	0	.333	.250
2019	19	Marlins (GCL)	R	.275	11	40	7	11	3	1	0	2	4	4	3	.370	.400
	19	Jupiter (FSL)	HiA	.325	33	126	13	41	3	1	0	3	8	20	5	.384	.365
	19	Clinton (MWL)	LoA	.455	3	11	5	5	2	0	0	2	2	2	0	.538	.636
Minor League Totals				.278	187	706	93	196	29	9	1	49	48	112	37	.339	.348

14 JORGE GUZMAN, RHP

BA GRADE 50 Risk: High

Born: Jan. 28, 1996. **B-T:** R-R. **HT:** 6-2. **WT:** 182. **Signed:** Dominican Republic, 2014. **Signed by:** Oz Ocampo/Ramon Ocumarez/Francis Mojica (Astros).

TRACK RECORD: Guzman was older than most Latin American signees, inking with the Astros for $22,500 at the age of 18 in 2014. Even more notable, Guzman hailed from Las Matas de Santa Cruz in the northwest Monte Cristi province, one of the more report parts of the Dominican. Guzman has been traded twice already—once to the Yankees as part of the Brian McCann deal, and then to the Marlins in the Giancarlo Stanton trade.

SCOUTING REPORT: Guzman is strong, physically mature and shows the makings of a solid delivery although his arm action is shorter and more rigid than most. While clean out front, Guzman is prone to rhythm and timing issues. To make up for it, Guzman possesses good downhill plane to the plate and a fastball in the mid-to-upper-90s that tops 100 frequently. Guzman's fastball quality took a step forward in 2019 because he utilized it up in the zone more often. Guzman also has an above-average slider that looks and feels more like a curveball family because of its hard, downer break. The pitch's quality in and out of the zone is still a work in progress despite good shape. Guzman's changeup may be key to his future role. It is often firm due to his arm action and delivery and is more of a timing pitch that needs to be thrown with more conviction.

THE FUTURE: If Guzman can learn to harness his stuff and lower his walk rate, he could have the ceiling of a hard-throwing, mid-rotation starter. However, some scouts believe he's best suited for a role as a high-leverage reliever working off his upper-90s fastball and above-average slider.

Year	Age	Club (League)	Class	W	L	ERA	G	GS	SV	IP	H	HR	BB	SO	K/9	WHIP	AVG
2017	21	Staten Island (NYP)	SS	5	3	2.30	13	13	0	67	51	4	18	88	11.9	1.04	.212
2018	22	Jupiter (FSL)	HiA	0	9	4.03	21	21	0	96	84	7	64	101	9.5	1.54	.239
2019	23	Jacksonville (SL)	AA	7	11	3.50	25	24	0	139	96	13	71	127	8.2	1.20	.201
Minor League Totals				18	31	3.70	89	78	0	396	323	27	200	399	9.1	1.32	.223

15 VICTOR VICTOR MESA, OF

BA GRADE
50 Risk: High

Born: July 20, 1996. **B-T:** R-R. **HT:** 5-10. **WT:** 165. **Signed:** Cuba, 2018. **Signed by:** Fernando Seguignol.

TRACK RECORD: Part of the second generation of impactful Mesas in Cuban baseball, Victor Victor's dad, Victor, was a standout player in Cuba, hitting .318. Victor Victor—not to be confused with his brother, Victor Jr., also a Marlins farmhand—made his debut at 15 in the Cuban major league and played six seasons before defecting. The Marlins signed Mesa out of Cuba in October 2018 for $5.25 million.

SCOUTING REPORT: While team officials expected a stark adjustment period for Mesa, who missed a lot of time in his final couple of years in Cuba due to injuries, he was behind even the most conservative of expectations when it came to his ability as a hitter. Too often, Mesa hit the ball either on the ground or with little impact to straightaway center and the opposite field. Some of this was due in part to Mesa's athletic, quick-twitch body, which too often caused him to open up too early and commit his lower half, robbing him of leverage. Despite the struggles, Mesa showed some encouraging signs, including a low swing-and-miss rate (18 percent) and a low strikeout rate (13.4 percent), displaying the ability to keep his hands back despite losing his base. Mesa is an above-average center fielder with plus arm strength and plus speed who uses a quick first step and good route-running ability to track down balls to either gap.

THE FUTURE: Mesa will likely begin 2020 back at Double-A Jacksonville, where the Marlins will hope to see a more experienced, well-adjusted hitter in his second season of pro ball.

Year	Age	Club (League)	Class	AVG	G	AB	R	H	2B	3B	HR	RBI	BB	SO	SB	OBP	SLG
2017	20	La Habana (CNS)	CNS	.237	21	76	19	18	5	0	0	9	12	9	6	.341	.303
2018	21	Did not play															
2019	22	Jupiter (FSL)	HiA	.252	89	357	37	90	5	3	0	26	19	48	15	.295	.283
	22	Jacksonville (SL)	AA	.178	27	107	8	19	2	0	0	3	3	16	3	.200	.196
Minor League Totals				.235	116	464	45	109	7	3	0	29	22	64	18	.274	.263

16 JERAR ENCARNACION, OF

BA GRADE
50 Risk: High

Born: Oct. 22, 1997. **B-T:** R-R. **HT:** 6-4. **WT:** 219. **Signed:** Dominican Republic, 2015. **Signed by:** Albert Gonzalez/Sandy Nin.

TRACK RECORD: Principally a basketball player growing up in the Dominican, baseball was never a true priority for Encarnacion. By the time that changed, Encarnacion was already 18, thereby making him older for free agents and leading to a bonus of just $78,000 in 2015. Encarnacion has shown glimpses of power but also contact issues as he's progressed through the Marlins system.

SCOUTING REPORT: Encarnacion struck out in more than 31 percent of his at-bats from 2017-18. He lowered that rate to a more palatable 25.3 percent in 2019, while also showing much-improved power numbers. Armed with a simple righthanded swing and a closed stance, Encarnacion has plus raw power to all fields. While he needs to continue to work on pitch recognition, Encarnacion did a much better job managing sliders, particularly from righthanded pitching. Encarnacion has plus arm strength and profiles best as an average to above-average defender with average speed.

THE FUTURE: The coming year will be key in determining Encarnacion's place in a suddenly crowded outfield picture.

Year	Age	Club (League)	Class	AVG	G	AB	R	H	2B	3B	HR	RBI	BB	SO	SB	OBP	SLG
2017	19	Marlins (GCL)	R	.266	42	154	25	41	7	3	5	26	10	51	3	.323	.448
2018	20	Batavia (NYP)	SS	.284	43	183	30	52	14	2	4	24	4	57	1	.305	.448
	20	Greensboro (SAL)	LoA	.074	16	54	3	4	0	0	0	2	5	23	0	.153	.074
2019	21	Clinton (MWL)	LoA	.298	68	255	34	76	16	0	10	43	23	69	3	.363	.478
	21	Jupiter (FSL)	HiA	.253	67	253	27	64	10	1	6	28	17	71	3	.298	.372
Minor League Totals				.261	250	954	125	249	49	7	26	130	60	282	10	.309	.409

17 PEYTON BURDICK, OF

BA GRADE **50** Risk: High

Born: Feb. 26, 1997. **B-T:** R-R. **HT:** 6-0. **WT:** 210. **Drafted:** Wright State, 2019 (3rd round). **Signed by:** Nate Adcock.

TRACK RECORD: A redshirt junior at Wright State due to a Tommy John surgery that forced him to miss the entire 2017 season, Burdick was named 2019 Horizon League player of the year. Ranked No. 183 on the BA 500, Burdick was drafted with the 82nd overall pick and signed him for just under $400,000.

SCOUTING REPORT: Armed with plus power and an above-average hit tool, Burdick was one of the minors' best hitters after making his pro debut in mid-June. More bat strength than looseness, Burdick showed an impressive ability to drive the ball to all fields while also showcasing a a walk rate above 11 percent at low Class A Clinton. Burdick's peripherals were particularly impressive during his first year in pro ball, including a 90.8 mph average exit velocity and 16.1-degree launch angle. Burdick should be an average defender in either corner-outfield spot with average speed and a slightly above-average arm.

THE FUTURE: Burdick will likely begin his age-23 season with an assignment to high Class A Jupiter. If he continues to impact the ball like he did in his pro debut, he could move quickly through the minors.

Year	Age	Club (League)	Class	AVG	G	AB	R	H	2B	3B	HR	RBI	BB	SO	SB	OBP	SLG
2019	22	Batavia (NYP)	SS	.318	6	22	3	7	0	1	1	5	2	5	1	.400	.545
	22	Clinton (MWL)	LoA	.307	63	238	57	73	20	3	10	59	32	67	6	.408	.542
Minor League Totals				.308	69	260	60	80	20	4	11	64	34	72	7	.407	.542

18 NASIM NUÑEZ, SS

BA GRADE **55** Risk: Extreme

Born: Aug. 18, 2000. **B-T:** B-R. **HT:** 5-9. **WT:** 160. **Drafted:** HS—Suwanee, Ga., 2019 (2nd round). **Signed by:** Christian Castorri.

TRACK RECORD: Considered one of the top defensive shortstops in the 2019 draft class, Nunez, was the Marlins' choice in the supplemental second round. After signing for an overslot $2.2 million, Nunez played in 48 games in the Rookie-level Gulf Coast League before a promotion to short-season Batavia.

SCOUTING REPORT: Nunez has long carried a defense-first reputation. He has all the makings of a plus defensive shortstop with excellent instincts, quick hands and smooth footwork to go alongside a very fast arm. Nunez showed off plus speed in his brief pro debut, stealing 28 bases in 30 attempts. Offensively, though, there are plenty of questions. While he has bat quickness from both sides with a swing geared for line drives, he fared far better lefthanders than righthanders.

THE FUTURE: A defense-first player now, Nunez's offensive development will be key to unlocking his potential as an impactful everyday shortstop. For now, he looks like an easy fit as defensive utilityman.

Year	Age	Club (League)	Class	AVG	G	AB	R	H	2B	3B	HR	RBI	BB	SO	SB	OBP	SLG
2019	18	Marlins (GCL)	R	.211	48	175	37	37	5	1	0	12	34	43	28	.340	.251
	18	Batavia (NYP)	SS	.000	3	10	1	0	0	0	0	0	1	5	0	.091	.000
Minor League Totals				.200	51	185	38	37	5	1	0	12	35	48	28	.327	.238

19 WILL BANFIELD, C

BA GRADE **45** Risk: High

Born: Nov. 18, 1999. **B-T:** R-R. **HT:** 6-0. **WT:** 200. **Drafted:** HS—Snellville, Ga., 2018 (2nd round). **Signed by:** Christian Castorri.

TRACK RECORD: Widely considered the draft's best defensive high school catcher in 2018, the Marlins drafted Banfield with the 69th overall pick in 2018 and signed him for an above-slot signing bonus of $1.8 million, nearly twice the slot value. Banfield has thrown out 46 percent of would-be basestealers.

SCOUTING REPORT: Behind the plate, Banfield has plus arm strength along with very quick feet to go with good lateral agility. While he is still an inexperienced receiver with some crudeness in his glove hand and framing, Banfield has shown the potential to be a plus defender. He's improved his shifting and blocking abilities notably since joining the organization. Banfield's strikeout rate has steadied between 28-30 percent, and his walk rate lowered to 5.8 percent in 2019. More alarming, he has well above-average swing-and-miss and chase rates. While Banfield has above-average raw power from the right side with plus launch angle, he has had a harder time with controlling at-bats and getting into advantage counts.

THE FUTURE: Banfield needs to improve his approach and shorten his swing, but if he can make strides offensively he has all of the defensive tools necessary to be a strong, defense-first catcher.

Year	Age	Club (League)	Class	AVG	G	AB	R	H	2B	3B	HR	RBI	BB	SO	SB	OBP	SLG
2018	18	Marlins (GCL)	R	.256	24	82	7	21	8	1	0	14	7	28	0	.330	.378
	18	Greensboro (SAL)	LoA	.208	15	48	5	10	0	0	3	4	4	15	0	.269	.396
2019	19	Clinton (MWL)	LoA	.199	101	397	44	79	13	2	9	55	25	121	0	.252	.310
Minor League Totals				.209	140	527	56	110	21	3	12	73	36	164	0	.266	.328

20 STERLING SHARP, RHP

BA GRADE **40** **Risk: Medium**

Born: May 30, 1995. **B-T:** R-R. **HT:** 6-3. **WT:** 170. **Drafted:** Drury (Mo.), 2016 (22nd round). **Signed by:** Brandon Larson (Nationals).

TRACK RECORD: Widely viewed as the best athlete in the Nationals' system, Sharp has a pinned tweet of himself dunking a basketball after moving the ball between his legs in mid-air. He was flying high again at the beginning of the 2019 season at Double-A Harrisburg, but an oblique injury kept him out of action for nearly three months. He made up for lost time in the Arizona Fall League, winning a pitcher of the week honor and achieving a 1.50 ERA, a 0.92 WHIP and 24 strikeouts in 24 innings. The Marlins picked him third overall in the Rule 5 major league draft in December.

SCOUTING REPORT: Sharp mostly throws sinkers in the 89-93 mph range and logged a 63 percent groundball rate in Double-A. He doesn't miss an overwhelming amount of bats, but he keeps the ball on the ground and limits damage. Sharp complements his sinker with an above-average changeup in the upper 80s and throws a low 80s breaking ball that grades out a tick below average. Sharp hides the ball well and repeats his delivery to give him average control. He has a lean build but has gained strength as he has risen through the minors.

THE FUTURE: Sharp has to stay on the major league roster all year with the Marlins. He has a chance to do so as a groundball-inducing reliever.

Year	Age	Club (League)	Class	W	L	ERA	G	GS	SV	IP	H	HR	BB	SO	K/9	WHIP	AVG
2017	22	Hagerstown (SAL)	LoA	4	9	3.69	18	17	0	93	100	8	14	69	6.7	1.23	.271
	22	Potomac (CAR)	HiA	2	2	4.78	6	5	0	32	39	4	13	26	7.3	1.63	.307
2018	23	Potomac (CAR)	HiA	5	3	3.16	14	14	0	80	82	4	21	58	6.6	1.29	.262
	23	Harrisburg (EL)	AA	6	3	4.33	13	13	0	69	72	6	26	47	6.2	1.43	.268
2019	24	Harrisburg (EL)	AA	5	3	3.99	9	9	0	50	56	1	14	45	8.2	1.41	.284
	24	Nationals (GCL)	R	0	0	0.00	1	1	0	2	1	0	0	2	9.0	0.50	.167
	24	Auburn (NYP)	SS	0	1	1.29	2	2	0	7	4	0	1	5	6.4	0.71	.191
Minor League Totals				25	21	3.71	75	69	2	378	407	25	95	290	6.9	1.33	.274

21 JORDAN HOLLOWAY, RHP

BA GRADE **50** **Risk: Very High**

Born: June 13, 1996. **B-T:** R-R. **HT:** 6-6. **WT:** 215. **Drafted:** HS—Arvada, Colo., 2014 (20th round). **Signed by:** Scott Stanley.

TRACK RECORD: After another slow start in 2017, Holloway had Tommy John surgery. Holloway returned for his first full season, post-surgery, in 2019, reaching high Class A Jupiter for the first time and completing a career-high 95 innings.

SCOUTING REPORT: Despite his early struggles, Holloway's fastball velocity has gotten better each season and averaged 97 mph during 2019. Holloway has very long limbs and has tried to limit excess movement, working stretch-only with a very short stride to simplify direction and repeat his delivery. Repeating, though, has been a challenge, along with maintaining direction to the plate, which has created erratic command and control in the zone. Holloway has the makings of a true plus curveball and an at least average changeup to round out his arsenal.

THE FUTURE: While few debate Holloway's stuff, his role remains in question. He has the body and the stuff to start but his delivery challenges may push him to the pen.

Year	Age	Club (League)	Class	W	L	ERA	G	GS	SV	IP	H	HR	BB	SO	K/9	WHIP	AVG
2017	21	Greensboro (SAL)	LoA	1	2	5.22	11	11	0	50	41	10	22	50	9.0	1.26	.220
2018	22	Marlins (GCL)	R	0	0	0.00	3	3	0	3	4	0	0	5	16.9	1.50	.286
	22	Batavia (NYP)	SS	0	0	0.00	2	2	0	5	0	0	0	4	7.2	0.00	.000
2019	23	Jupiter (FSL)	HiA	4	11	4.45	21	21	0	95	77	6	66	93	8.8	1.51	.220
Minor League Totals				13	30	4.64	76	72	0	304	280	24	166	245	7.3	1.47	.242

22 VICTOR MESA JR., OF

BA GRADE **50** **Risk: Very High**

Born: Sept. 8, 2001. **B-T:** L-L. **HT:** 5-11. **WT:** 175. **Signed:** Cuba, 2018. **Signed by:** Fernando Seguignol.

TRACK RECORD: The younger brother of fellow Marlins prospect Victor Victor Mesa and son of Cuban legend, Victor Mesa, Sr., Mesa Jr. signed with the Marlins for $1 million in Oct. 2018. He hit .284 while posting nearly as many walks (24) as strikeouts (27) in the Rookie-level Gulf Coast League in his debut.

SCOUTING REPORT: Mesa Jr. has impressed evaluators with a smooth, easy swing and advanced bat-to-ball skills. He opens his front side early, negatively impacting his base and present power, but has shown an uncanny ability to keep his hands back and made contact. Mesa Jr. projects as an average defender with above-average arm strength in right field. He's also an average runner.

THE FUTURE: The Marlins can afford to be patient with Mesa Jr., who will play in 2020 as an 18-year-old.

Year	Age	Club (League)	Class	AVG	G	AB	R	H	2B	3B	HR	RBI	BB	SO	SB	OBP	SLG
2019	17	Marlins (GCL)	R	.284	47	176	39	50	9	4	1	24	24	29	7	.366	.398
Minor League Totals				.284	47	176	39	50	9	4	1	24	24	29	7	.366	.398

23 JOSE SALAS, SS

BA GRADE 50 Risk: Extreme

Born: April 26, 2003. **B-T:** B-R. **HT:** 6-1. **WT:** 150. **Signed:** Venezuela, 2019. **Signed by:** Fernando Seguignol.

TRACK RECORD: The Marlins' top international signing in 2019, Salas' dad, uncle and grandfather all played pro ball in Venezuela. Salas was born in Florida and grew up in Orlando, but before high school he moved to Venezuela, worked out for clubs there, then went to the Dominican Republic before signing.

SCOUTING REPORT: Salas has a live, projectable body with lots of room to add strength. He's a quick-twitch athlete with plus speed. At his size, Salas might lose a step as he fills out, but he has significant physical upside to grow into more strength and power. The Marlins liked Salas' chance to hit for average and power, though other clubs were mixed on his hitting ability, with a tendency to get mechanical in his swing and inconsistent game performances. Salas' athleticism and strong arm play well at shortstop, where he gets quick reactions off the bat. He can get erratic in the field, however, so some scouts thought he might fit better in center field. There's also a chance he moves elsewhere in the infield.

THE FUTURE: Salas will make his pro debut in 2020, likely beginning the year in the Rookie-level Gulf Coast League.

Year	Age	Club (League)	Class	AVG	G	AB	R	H	2B	3B	HR	RBI	BB	SO	SB	OBP	SLG
2019	16	Did not Play—Signed 2020 contract															

24 EVAN FITTERER, RHP

BA GRADE 50 Risk: Extreme

Born: June 26, 2000. **B-T:** R-R. **HT:** 6-3. **WT:** 195. **Drafted:** HS—Aliso Viejo, Calif., 2019 (5th round). **Signed by:** Eric Brock.

TRACK RECORD: A strong commitment to UCLA and an apparent high price tag pushed Fitterer down teams' draft boards, but the Marlins, undeterred, drafted Fitterer in the fifth round and signed him for $1.5 million—the largest signing bonus given to any 2019 draftee outside of the top three rounds.

SCOUTING REPORT: Fitterer has an ideal, projectable pitcher's body, featuring broad shoulders and long limbs with lots of room to add strength. Fitterer starts his pitch mix with a fastball in the low-to-mid-90s that he can cut and sink effectively with late life through the zone. He throws three distinct offspeed pitches, including an upper-70s curveball that has the makings of a plus pitch, an above-average, low-80s slider and an average, fourth-pitch changeup. While Fitterer's delivery needs some refinement both in direction and base, due in part to limited core strength, he only needs to make minor adjustments. Fitterer is a good athlete on the mound, leading most scouts to project above-average control with refinement.

THE FUTURE: It is very easy to dream on Fitterer's ceiling as he matures. Due to limited innings, the team will continue to monitor his usage in the spring. While Fitterer will be given a chance to break with low Class A Clinton in 2020, he will most likely start in extended spring before moving to the New York-Penn League.

Year	Age	Club (League)	Class	W	L	ERA	G	GS	SV	IP	H	HR	BB	SO	K/9	WHIP	AVG
2019	19	Marlins (GCL)	R	0	1	2.38	9	8	0	23	20	1	12	19	7.5	1.41	.233
Minor League Totals				0	1	2.38	9	8	0	23	20	1	12	19	7.5	1.41	.233

25 OSIRIS JOHNSON, SS

BA GRADE 50 Risk: Extreme

Born: Oct. 18, 2000. **B-T:** R-R. **HT:** 6-0. **WT:** 181. **Drafted:** HS—Alameda, Calif., 2018 (2nd round). **Signed by:** John Hughes.

TRACK RECORD: The Marlins selected Johnson in the second round in 2018 and signed him for $1.35 million. He went to the same high school as former big leaguer Dontrelle Willis, and his second cousin is 2007 NL MVP Jimmy Rollins. His father, Marcel Johnson, played three seasons professionally. Johnson had surgery in March to repair a stress fracture in his right leg.

SCOUTING REPORT: Entering the 2018 draft, Johnson was highly regarded as a tooled-up, albeit raw, potential everyday shortstop. He has quick hands and at least average arm that should allow him to stick as an average to above-average defender at shortstop, but there are some scouts who question whether he may grow off the position and move to second base. Prior to his injury, Johnson was an above-average runner and the Marlins were intrigued by his potential as a power-speed threat. Johnson has plus raw power

but he showed a propensity to chase out of the zone too often during his pro debut in 2018. Improving quality contact and reducing his strike zone to make more contact will be key.
THE FUTURE: Johnson is expected to be fully healthy and ready for spring training in 2020. He will likely begin the season with low Class A Clinton in what will be his first full pro season in the minors.

Year	Age	Club (League)	Class	AVG	G	AB	R	H	2B	3B	HR	RBI	BB	SO	SB	OBP	SLG
2018	17	Marlins (GCL)	R	.301	25	103	12	31	8	2	1	13	4	19	7	.333	.447
	17	Greensboro (SAL)	LoA	.188	23	85	4	16	3	0	2	6	1	34	0	.205	.294
2019	18	Did not play—Injured															
Minor League Totals				.250	48	188	16	47	11	2	3	19	5	53	7	.276	.378

26 HUMBERTO MEJIA, RHP

BA GRADE 45 Risk: High

Born: March 3, 1997. **B-T:** R-R. **HT:** 6-3. **WT:** 175. **Signed:** Panama, 2013. **Signed by:** Luis Cordoba/Albert Gonzalez.
TRACK RECORD: Mejia signed for $50,000 in 2013 but didn't make his professional debut until 2015 and then missed all of 2017 due to shoulder injuries. He reached full-season ball for the first time in 2019 and logged a 2.09 ERA at the Class A levels before he was shut down at the end of June. The Marlins thought enough of Mejia to add him to their 40-man roster in November.
SCOUTING REPORT: Mejia has seen his fastball velocity gradually increase since signing, peaking as a low-to-mid-90s pitch that can touch 95 mph. Mejia throws strikes with his fastball, which features solid life through the zone. His curveball and slider both flash above-average. The slider, long-term, appears to have the better ceiling because it generates more chases and swings and misses. Mejia features a short stride with limited leverage through his lower half in his delivery, uncoiling with some effort due to stiffer hips.
THE FUTURE: Durability remains the biggest question mark for Mejia, who threw a career-high 90.1 innings in 2019. Many scouts believe his stuff will play up in the bullpen.

Year	Age	Club (League)	Class	W	L	ERA	G	GS	SV	IP	H	HR	BB	SO	K/9	WHIP	AVG
2017	20	Did not play—Injured															
2018	21	Batavia (NYP)	SS	1	6	3.30	15	12	0	63	55	8	14	59	8.5	1.10	.232
2019	22	Clinton (MWL)	LoA	5	1	2.03	13	10	1	67	42	4	19	68	9.2	0.92	.177
	22	Jupiter (FSL)	HiA	0	1	2.28	5	4	0	24	15	2	5	21	8.0	0.85	.177
Minor League Totals				13	16	2.40	59	43	1	277	218	17	62	268	8.7	1.01	.214

27 BRIAN MILLER, OF

Born: Aug. 20, 1995. **B-T:** L-R. **HT:** 6-1. **WT:** 186. **Drafted:** North Carolina, 2017 (1st round supplemental). **Signed by:** Blake Newsome.
TRACK RECORD: Miller hit .332 throughout his three years with North Carolina while posting a .872 OPS. Miller signed with the Marlins for $1.88 million as the 36th overall pick in 2017. He has continued to post high averages with low Class A Greensboro and high Class A Jupiter, hitting .324 over 534 plate appearances, but his numbers have dipped since reaching the upper levels.
SCOUTING REPORT: A lefthanded hitter with a smooth swing, Miller's ordinary numbers were the first struggles he'd experienced as a pro. Miller has continued to show above-average contact skills and low swing-and-miss rates, but scouts have noticed an effort to add lift to swing and pull the ball more, which has had a negative impact on quality contact. Always a good fastball hitter who has been able to handle velocity, Miller did not do so as effectively over the past years. Even with the changes in his swing path, power still has been minimal. He has plus speed but has a below-average stolen base percentage. Despite his speed, Miller has played most of his games in left, where he is an average defender with an average arm.
THE FUTURE: A potential .300 hitter with solid on-base skills and potential baserunning threat, Miller has the potential to be a useful top-of-the-order hitter and has a ceiling as an extra outfielder.

Year	Age	Club (League)	Class	AVG	G	AB	R	H	2B	3B	HR	RBI	BB	SO	SB	OBP	SLG
2017	21	Greensboro (SAL)	LoA	.322	57	233	42	75	17	1	1	28	23	35	21	.384	.416
2018	22	Jupiter (FSL)	HiA	.324	62	256	28	83	13	3	0	29	14	27	19	.358	.398
	22	Jacksonville (SL)	AA	.267	66	262	29	70	8	2	0	14	18	39	21	.319	.313
2019	23	Jacksonville (SL)	AA	.265	120	449	52	119	24	5	2	39	37	81	22	.326	.354
Minor League Totals				.289	305	1200	151	347	62	11	3	110	92	182	83	.343	.367

28 ROBERT DUGGER, RHP

BA GRADE 40 Risk: Medium

Born: July 3, 1995. **B-T:** R-R. **HT:** 6-2. **WT:** 180. **Drafted:** Texas Tech, 2016 (18th round). **Signed by:** Taylor Terrasas (Mariners).
TRACK RECORD: Dugger went undrafted out of high school, then pitched two seasons at Cisco (Texas)

JC. Dugger then moved to Texas Tech's bullpen for his draft year. The Mariners drafted Dugger with their 18th-round pick in 2016, then traded him to the Marlins as part of the Dee Gordon deal.

SCOUTING REPORT: Dugger makes the most of his average mix by throwing strikes, changing speeds and pitching to contact. He throws four- and two-seam fastballs, with his two-seamer acting more like an 88-92 mph sinker and his four-seamer coming in straighter at 90-93 mph. Dugger also throws a trio of average offspeed pitches, headlined by a low-80s slider that works as his go-to pitch against righthanders. Dugger uses his low-70s curveball effectively against lefthanders, and his changeup is used just enough to keep hitters off-balance.

THE FUTURE: Dugger was roughed up in his first taste of the majors in 2019, displaying the slim margin for error his stuff allows. He will likely continue to get chances in the Marlins' starting rotation in 2020.

Year	Age	Club (League)	Class	W	L	ERA	G	GS	SV	IP	H	HR	BB	SO	K/9	WHIP	AVG
2017	21	Clinton (MWL)	LoA	4	1	2.00	22	9	2	72	55	4	16	69	8.6	0.99	.206
	21	Modesto (CAL)	HiA	2	5	3.94	9	9	0	46	49	4	16	47	9.3	1.42	.272
2018	22	Jupiter (FSL)	HiA	3	1	2.40	7	7	0	41	40	2	7	34	7.4	1.14	.253
	22	Jacksonville (SL)	AA	7	6	3.79	18	18	0	109	100	13	36	107	8.8	1.24	.245
2019	23	Jacksonville (SL)	AA	6	6	3.31	13	13	0	71	57	6	21	73	9.3	1.10	.219
	23	New Orleans (PCL)	AAA	2	4	7.59	10	10	0	53	74	12	17	49	8.3	1.71	.332
	23	Miami (NL)	MAJ	0	4	5.77	7	7	0	34	33	6	17	25	6.6	1.46	.254
Major League Totals				0	4	5.77	7	7	0	34	33	6	17	25	6.6	1.46	.254
Minor League Totals				26	24	3.84	91	72	4	431	411	46	124	417	8.7	1.24	.250

29 CHRIS MOKMA, RHP

BA GRADE
50 Risk: Extreme

Born: Feb. 11, 2001. **B-T:** R-R. **HT:** 6-4. **WT:** 190. **Drafted:** HS—Holland, Mich., 2019 (12th round). **Signed by:** Nate Adcock.

TRACK RECORD: Mokma was committed to Michigan State, where he was originally planning to play alongside his older brother, Mike. Instead, the Marlins drafted Mokma with their 12th-round pick and signed him just before the deadline for $557,000.

SCOUTING REPORT: Mokma entered the draft cycle as a projectable, cold-weather high school arm with a very high ceiling. Mokma's fastball currently sits in the low 90s, but most evaluators feel there's plenty more velocity to tap as he adds core strength and fills out his athletic frame. Mokma showed feel to spin a potentially above-average curveball as an amateur while he used his third-pitch changeup much against lesser competition. Mokma's sound delivery leads scouts to project average or better control.

THE FUTURE: After an encouraging pro debut, Mokma most likely will start the season in extended spring training in 2020 as the team will manage his workload. He has the ceiling of a mid-rotation starter.

Year	Age	Club (League)	Class	W	L	ERA	G	GS	SV	IP	H	HR	BB	SO	K/9	WHIP	AVG
2019	18	Marlins (GCL)	R	0	1	2.19	5	5	0	12	12	0	2	12	8.8	1.14	.245
Minor League Totals				0	1	2.19	5	5	0	12	12	0	2	12	8.8	1.14	.245

30 WILL STEWART, LHP

BA GRADE
45 Risk: High

Born: July 14, 1997. **B-T:** L-L. **HT:** 6-2. **WT:** 175. **Drafted:** HS—Hazel Green, Ala., 2015 (20th round). **Signed by:** Mike Stauffer (Phillies).

TRACK RECORD: The Phillies' 20th-round pick in 2015, Stewart broke out in 2018 and impressed enough that the Marlins requested him as part of the J.T. Realmuto trade. Stewart's control took a step back in 2019, when he walked 2.9 batters per nine innings and found the middle of the plate more often.

SCOUTING REPORT: Stewart's fastball velocity dropped significantly in 2019, when the pitch spent most of the season sitting in the upper 80s. The velocity drop impacted the pitch's effectiveness in and out of the zone. Previously a strength, Stewart lost the ability to locate and generate soft contact or ground balls. Stewart shows the makings of an average slider with good angle and spin. While Stewart's slider lost its impact vs righthanded hitters, it remained effective against lefties as a swing-and-miss pitch in and out of the zone with good angle and depth. Previously a solid weapon vs righthanders, Stewart's changeup commanded less respect because hitters were able to adjust to the lack of separation from his fastball.

THE FUTURE: If Stewart can regain his velocity in 2020, his ceiling would rise in kind. He seems likely to return to Jupiter to start 2020 for a potential reboot.

Year	Age	Club (League)	Class	W	L	ERA	G	GS	SV	IP	H	HR	BB	SO	K/9	WHIP	AVG
2017	19	Williamsport (NYP)	SS	4	2	4.18	13	13	0	60	64	3	25	58	8.7	1.48	.267
2018	20	Lakewood (SAL)	LoA	8	1	2.06	20	20	0	114	90	5	21	90	7.1	0.98	.218
2019	21	Jupiter (FSL)	HiA	6	12	5.43	23	21	0	129	137	13	42	96	6.7	1.38	.275
Minor League Totals				21	18	3.98	79	61	0	368	343	25	122	299	7.3	1.26	.247

Milwaukee Brewers

BY TOM HAUDRICOURT

Since becoming Brewers general manager after the 2015 season and accelerating an organization-wide rebuild, David Stearns repeatedly emphasized the importance of building depth. In 2019, for the second consecutive September, that depth proved to be the difference in getting Milwaukee to the postseason.

After treading water for most of the first five months, the Brewers found their footing in September, winning 18 of 20 at one point and going 20-7 to claim the second National League wild card. It was reminiscent of the previous September, when the Brewers also went 20-7 to reel in the Cubs and set the stage for a Game No. 163 victory at Wrigley Field to claim the NL Central crown.

Simply put, the Brewers fared best with an expanded September roster. A lot of that had to do with manager Craig Counsell's expertise at using extra relievers to "bullpen" his way to victory.

That's what you do when you have no established ace, though hard-throwing righthander Brandon Woodruff was well on his way to filling that role before being sidelined for all of August and half of September with an oblique strain. And it's a lot easier to "bullpen" games when you have strikeout artist Josh Hader (37 saves, 138 strikeouts in 75.2 innings) to record the final outs.

The Brewers pulled off their September to remember despite losing reigning NL MVP Christian Yelich to a broken kneecap with two and a half weeks remaining. Yelich had put together another MVP-caliber season while continuing to show he has become one of the game's most dynamic offensive forces.

The free-agent additions of third baseman Mike Moustakas and catcher Yasmani Grandal proved huge in many ways, but the team's late push was aided by the contributions of two rookies who handled that pressure with aplomb. Second baseman Keston Hiura (.938 OPS in 84 games) showed he is a hitter to watch in the future, and outfielder Trent Grisham went from first-round disappointment to the organization's minor league player of the year. The Padres apparently took note because they traded 22-year-old second baseman Luis Urias to acquire Grisham in November.

In making the postseason in consecutive seasons for just the second time in franchise history, the Brewers fulfilled the promise to their fans of being relevant again. Team owner Mark Attanasio's commitment to Stearns and Counsell formed a 1-2 leadership punch that guided the club and put a winning culture in place, with the goal of being consistently competitive despite the budgetary restrictions of a small market.

QUINN HARRIS/GETTY IMAGES

Rookie second baseman Keston Hiura hit .303 with 19 home runs in just half a season.

PROJECTED 2023 LINEUP

Catcher	Mario Feliciano (6)	24
First Base	Keston Hiura	26
Second Base	Brice Turang (1)	23
Third Base	Luis Urias	26
Shortstop	Orlando Arcia	28
Left Field	Tristen Lutz (2)	24
Center Field	Corey Ray (3)	28
Right Field	Christian Yelich	31
No. 1 Starter	Brandon Woodruff	30
No. 2 Starter	Eric Lauer	28
No. 3 Starter	Adrian Houser	30
No. 4 Starter	Zack Brown (10)	28
No. 5 Starter	Ethan Small (4)	26
Closer	Josh Hader	29

Stearns' ability to improve the club from the outside, as he did with the acquisition of Yelich in January 2018, could continue to be tested with a farm system that thinned out after the promotions of Hiura and Grisham. Many of the other top prospects in the organization were plagued by inconsistent performances or injuries.

Developing pitchers from within will remain essential, particularly after the setbacks of Corbin Burnes and Freddy Peralta, who quickly pitched their way out of the 2019 rotation. But Woodruff has immense promise as a workhorse, and righthander Adrian Houser also showed improvement after joining the rotation late in the season.

DEPTH CHART

MILWAUKEE BREWERS

TOP 2020 ROOKIE: Devin Williams, RHP. He got his feet wet in the majors last year and showed he has the velocity to pitch in high-leverage situations.
BREAKOUT PROSPECT: Hedbert Perez, OF. He has a short, quick swing capable of producing above-average power and above-average speed.
SLEEPER: Victor Castaneda, RHP. He opened eyes with his overall stuff in the Arizona Fall League.

SOURCE OF TOP 30 TALENT

Homegrown	30	Acquired	0
College	10	Trade	0
Junior college	2	Rule 5 draft	0
High school	10	Independent league	0
Nondrafted free agent	0	Free agent/waivers	0
International	8		

LF
Tyrone Taylor (22)
Joantgel Segovia
Ryan Aguilar
Zach Clark
Cooper Hummel
Robert Henry
Arbert Cipion

CF
Corey Ray (3)
Hedbert Perez (11)
Carlos Rodriguez (12)
Joe Gray (23)
Eduarqui Fernandez (30)
Pablo Abreu

RF
Tristen Lutz (2)
Luis Medina (14)
Micah Bello (28)
Gabe Holt (29)
Je'Von Ward

3B
Jesus Parra (18)
Lucas Erceg
Weston Wilson

SS
Brice Turang (1)
Eduardo Garcia (8)
Jheremy Vargas (26)
Korry Howell
David Hamilton
Antonio Piñero

2B
Devin Hairston
Yeison Coca
Edwin Sano

1B
Luis Medina (14)
Thomas Dillard (24)
Jake Gatewood
Luis Castro

C
Mario Feliciano (6)
Payton Henry (16)
Nick Kahle (17)
Jeferson Quero (19)
Jacob Nottingham
David Fry

LHP

LHSP	LHRP
Ethan Small (4)	Clayton Andrews (27)
Aaron Ashby (5)	Angel Perdomo
Antoine Kelly (7)	Daniel Brown
Nick Bennett	Michael Mediavilla
Scott Sunitsch	
Brock Begue	

RHP

RHSP	RHRP
Drew Rasmussen (9)	Devin Williams (15)
Zack Brown (10)	Bobby Wahl
Trey Supak (13)	Victor Castaneda
Braden Webb (18)	Miguel Sanchez
Alec Bettinger (20)	Phil Bickford
Dylan File (21)	Matt Hardy
Max Lazar (25)	Luke Barker
Bubba Derby	J.T Hintzen
Noah Zavolas	Robbie Hitt
Justin Jarvis	
Thomas Jankins	
Bowden Francis	
Nelson Hernandez	

DRAFT ANALYSIS

2019

BEST PURE HITTER: The Brewers took OF/1B Thomas Dillard (5) in the middle of day two and signed him for $397,500 thanks to a potent, switch-hitting bat. The Mississippi product has impressive on-base skills and some power in the tank, though he hit .249/.391/.407 in his debut.

BEST POWER: The Brewers drafted a pair of physical hitters on Day 3. OF Andre Nnebe (28) is 6-foot-6, 230 pounds, while 1B Kevin Hardin (33) is 6-foot-5, 245 pounds. Both have plenty of raw power in the tank but will need to improve their ability to tap into that juice in games.

FASTEST RUNNER: SS David Hamilton (8) missed the entire season at Texas due to a ruptured Achilles tendon, but prior to the injury he was a plus runner, stealing 31 bases as a sophomore.

BEST DEFENSIVE PLAYER: Hamilton's speed and athleticism allowed him to play a strong shortstop in college, with a quick first step and hands that make scouts believe he can stay at the position.

BEST ATHLETE: Wilson's athleticism and speed should allow him to play all three outfield positions. Nnebe is athletic for his size, though he fills more of a corner profile.

BEST FASTBALL: LHP Antoine Kelly (2) had some of the best velocity from a southpaw in the 2019 draft class with a fastball that sits 93-95 mph and touches 97 mph. Kelly throws with an easy delivery and arm action, and most scouts figure he will touch 100 mph at some point in the future.

BEST SECONDARY PITCH: LHP Ethan Small (1) doesn't have huge pure stuff, but he has excellent command and is able to land a slurve-like breaking ball in any count. The pitch plays up thanks to his ability to mix and spot his entire arsenal, and the fact that he hides the ball well in his delivery.

BEST PRO DEBUT: Small has the exact skills you would assume translate quickly to the low minors, and that was the case in his pro debut. He threw 21 innings between the Arizona and Midwest leagues, posting a 0.86 ERA while striking out 36 batters and walking just four.

MOST INTRIGUING BACKGROUND: Kelly bet on himself after the Padres selected him in the 13th round of the 2018 draft thanks to his natural velocity. He opted for the junior college route at Wabash Valley (Ill.) JC, which turned into a $1,025,100 signing bonus a year later.

CLOSEST TO THE MAJORS: Small's polished command of a three-pitch arsenal should allow him to move quickly through the minors in a starting role.

BEST LATE-ROUND PICK: The Brewers were thrilled to get Nnebe in the 28th round, and he helped pay off a $190,000 signing bonus by hitting .302/.394/.496 with four home runs and nine doubles in 34 games in the Arizona League.

THE ONE WHO GOT AWAY: The Brewers drafted SS Jose Torres (24) on Day 3, but the slick-fielding shortstop opted to go to North Carolina State, where he has a chance to provide an immediate impact for the Wolfpack and will be a draft-eligible sophomore in 2021.

—CARLOS COLLAZO

TOP DRAFT PICKS OF THE DECADE

Year	Player, Pos	2019 Org
2010	*Dylan Covey, RHP	White Sox
2011	Taylor Jungmann, RHP	Japan
2012	Clint Coulter, C	Brewers
2013	Devin Williams, RHP (2nd round)	Brewers
2014	Kodi Medeiros, LHP	White Sox
2015	Trent Grisham, OF	Brewers
2016	Corey Ray, OF	Brewers
2017	Keston Hiura, 2B	Brewers
2018	Brice Turang, SS	Brewers
2019	Ethan Small, LHP	Brewers

*Did not sign

2018

Prep hitters SS Brice Turang (1) and OF Joe Gray (2) have shown off their upside. RHP Drew Rasmussen (6) has gotten healthy and impressed, while LHP Clayton Andrews (17) gives the class late-round value.

GRADE: B

2017

2B Keston Hiura (1) made his MLB debut and looked like a star once he took over an everyday role in the second half. He alone will make this a success, but OF Tristen Lutz (1s) gives the class another standout.

GRADE: A

2016

RHP Corbin Burnes (4) followed up his terrific 2018 MLB debut with a dreadful 2019, but he still has upside. OF Corey Ray (1) should soon join him in Milwaukee and C Mario Feliciano (2s) is progressing well.

GRADE: B

1 BRICE TURANG, SS

Born: Nov. 21, 1999. **B-T:** L-R. **HT:** 6-1. **WT:** 175.
Drafted: HS—Corona, Calif., 2018 (1st round).
Signed by: Wynn Pelzer.

TRACK RECORD: A star for USA Baseball in high school, Turang was viewed as one of the best prospects in the 2018 class for several years in the leadup to the draft. But instead of being in consideration for the first pick, Turang ended up sliding significantly. Turang became a victim of so-called "prospect fatigue." The Brewers went well over slot to sign him for $3,411,100 and keep him from a Louisiana State commitment. Turang immediately hit at two Rookie levels after signing and continued to perform in his first full season. He earned Midwest League all-star honors at low Class A Wisconsin and finished the year at high Class A Carolina as a 19-year-old.

SCOUTING REPORT: Turang's most obvious offensive skills are his plate discipline and ability to put the ball in play. He walked 83 times in 2019, compared to 101 strikeouts, and profiles as a leadoff hitter with his plus speed and on-base skills. Turang gets the most from his plus speed as a savvy baserunner. He stole 30 bases in 35 attempts at his two Class A stops and projects to keep his speed as he ages because of his thin frame and long legs. Turang has everything you would want at the top of the lineup as a lefthanded hitter who makes contact, puts the ball in play and creates pressure on the defense with his speed. He's gained about 10 pounds since being drafted and showed more pop at the plate, but most evaluators see him topping out at 10-15 home runs. Turang's speed helps him cover ground at shortstop, where his range and sure hands, combined with an average arm, should allow him to stay at that position. Opposing evaluators generally prefer Turang as a second baseman, where he played roughly one-third of his games in 2019, but the Brewers believe he can stick at shortstop and plan to develop him there. He plays the game hard and is something of a baseball gym rat. He has a solid pedigree as the son of former Mariners outfielder Brian Turang.

THE FUTURE: With Keston Hiura expected to be entrenched at second base in Milwaukee, the impetus is for Turang to develop as a shortstop. It's not easy to find shortstops with plus speed who profile as leadoff hitters, and the Brewers believe they have a good one in Turang. He will begin 2020 back at high Class A Carolina and could see Double-A Biloxi during the season if everything goes according to plan.

BRIAN WESTERHOLT/FOUR SEAM IMAGES

BA GRADE
55 Risk: High

SCOUTING GRADES
Hit: 55. **Power:** 40. **Run:** 60. **Field:** 55. **Arm:** 50.

Projected future grades on 20-80 scouting scale.

TOP PROSPECTS OF THE DECADE

Year	Player, Pos	2019 Org
2010	Alcides Escobar, SS	White Sox
2011	Jake Odorizzi, RHP	Twins
2012	Wily Peralta, RHP	Royals
2013	Wily Peralta, RHP	Royals
2014	Jimmy Nelson, RHP	Brewers
2015	Tyrone Taylor, OF	Brewers
2016	Orlando Arcia, SS	Brewers
2017	Lewis Brinson, OF	Marlins
2018	Lewis Brinson, OF	Marlins
2019	Keston Hiura, 2B	Brewers

BEST TOOLS

Best Hitter for Average	Brice Turang
Best Power Hitter	Mario Feliciano
Best Strike-Zone Discipline	Brice Turang
Fastest Baserunner	Reidy Mercado
Best Athlete	Corey Ray
Best Fastball	Drew Rasmussen
Best Curveball	Zack Brown
Best Slider	Aaron Ashby
Best Changeup	Devin Williams
Best Control	Dylan File
Best Defensive Catcher	Payton Henry
Best Defensive Infielder	Antonio Pinero
Best Infield Arm	Lucas Erceg
Best Defensive Outfielder	Carlos Rodriguez
Best Outfield Arm	Tristen Lutz

Year	Age	Club (League)	Class	AVG	G	AB	R	H	2B	3B	HR	RBI	BB	SO	SB	OBP	SLG
2018	18	Brewers (AZL)	R	.319	13	47	11	15	2	0	0	7	9	6	8	.421	.362
	18	Helena (PIO)	R	.268	29	112	26	30	4	1	1	11	22	28	6	.385	.348
2019	19	Wisconsin (MWL)	LoA	.287	82	303	57	87	13	4	2	31	49	54	21	.384	.376
	19	Carolina (CAR)	HiA	.200	47	170	25	34	6	2	1	6	34	47	9	.338	.276
Minor League Totals				.263	171	632	119	166	25	7	4	55	114	135	44	.374	.343

2 TRISTEN LUTZ, OF

TOM POLLARD

BA GRADE
50 **Risk: High**

Born: Aug. 22, 1998. **B-T:** R-R. **HT:** 6-3. **WT:** 210. **Drafted:** HS—Arlington, Texas, 2017 (1st round supplemental). **Signed by:** K.J. Hendricks.

TRACK RECORD: The Brewers have tested the mental toughness of Lutz, who grew up in the warmth of Texas but spent his first full season in 2018 at the cold climate at low Class A Wisconsin. The Brewers saw Lutz improve throughout that year and didn't hesitate to move him up to high Class A Carolina at age 20. He continued to have his ups and downs, particularly with swing-and-miss issues, but showed a promising skill set.

SCOUTING REPORT: Lutz's budding power remains his primary calling card. He displays bat speed and sheer strength, causing the ball to jump off his bat. High strikeout numbers have come with his above-average power, (139 in 2018 and 137 in 2019) but Lutz is more than an all-or-nothing slugger. He shows a willingness to hit to all fields and recognizes pitches well for a young player. Lutz is a good athlete who runs the bases well and has enough speed to play center field, though he has seen increasing action in right field, where his above-average arm plays well.

THE FUTURE: Lutz played most of 2019 at age 20 and should continue to develop as a hitter with more experience. His power potential, athleticism and work ethic have the Brewers believing he's their future everyday right fielder.

SCOUTING GRADES: **Hitting:** 50 **Power:** 55 **Running:** 50 **Fielding:** 50 **Arm:** 55

Year	Age	Club (League)	Class	AVG	G	AB	R	H	2B	3B	HR	RBI	BB	SO	SB	OBP	SLG
2017	18	Helena (PIO)	R	.333	24	93	23	31	1	1	6	16	12	21	2	.432	.559
	18	Brewers (AZL)	R	.279	16	68	12	19	4	3	3	11	4	21	1	.347	.559
2018	19	Wisconsin (MWL)	LoA	.245	119	444	63	109	33	3	13	63	46	139	9	.321	.421
2019	20	Carolina (CAR)	HiA	.255	112	420	62	107	24	3	13	54	46	137	3	.335	.419
Minor League Totals				.260	271	1025	160	266	62	10	35	144	108	318	15	.339	.442

3 COREY RAY, OF

DAVE MICHAEL/SA MISSIONS

BA GRADE
45 **Risk: Medium**

Born: Sept. 22, 1994. **B-T:** L-L. **HT:** 5-11. **WT:** 185. **Drafted:** Louisville, 2016 (1st round). **Signed by:** Jeff Simpson.

TRACK RECORD: Ray struggled after the Brewers took him fourth overall in 2016, but he appeared to break through when he won MVP of the Double-A Southern League in 2018. Instead of a strong follow-up season, Ray suffered a hand injury during spring training that hampered his swing the entire year. A wrist issue later in the year resulted in another stay on the injured list, and overall Ray hit just .218 over 69 games in what became a lost season.

SCOUTING REPORT: When healthy, Ray's combination of power and speed makes him a dynamic player. There is a lot of swing and miss to his game due to below-average pitch recognition, his aggressive nature and a long swing, but the trade-off is above-average power to all fields. When he does reach base, Ray is a difference-maker with plus speed and the willingness to run at any time. That speed also plays well in center field, where he chases down balls from gap to gap while displaying an average arm.

THE FUTURE: Ray never figures to hit for a high average but should compile enough extra-base hits to make up for it. He needs to show he can stay healthy in order to be a major league option in 2020.

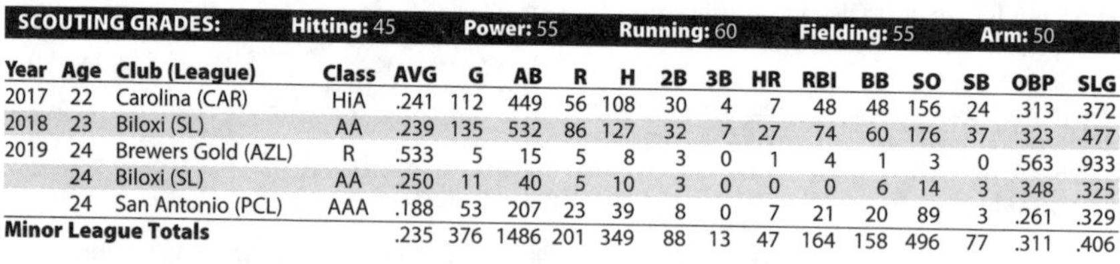

SCOUTING GRADES: **Hitting:** 45 **Power:** 55 **Running:** 60 **Fielding:** 55 **Arm:** 50

Year	Age	Club (League)	Class	AVG	G	AB	R	H	2B	3B	HR	RBI	BB	SO	SB	OBP	SLG
2017	22	Carolina (CAR)	HiA	.241	112	449	56	108	30	4	7	48	48	156	24	.313	.372
2018	23	Biloxi (SL)	AA	.239	135	532	86	127	32	7	27	74	60	176	37	.323	.477
2019	24	Brewers Gold (AZL)	R	.533	5	15	5	8	3	0	1	4	1	3	0	.563	.933
	24	Biloxi (SL)	AA	.250	11	40	5	10	3	0	0	0	6	14	3	.348	.325
	24	San Antonio (PCL)	AAA	.188	53	207	23	39	8	0	7	21	20	89	3	.261	.329
Minor League Totals				.235	376	1486	201	349	88	13	47	164	158	496	77	.311	.406

4 ETHAN SMALL, LHP

Born: Feb. 14, 1997. **B-T:** L-L. **HT:** 6-3. **WT:** 214. **Drafted:** Mississippi State, 2019 (1st round). **Signed by:** Scott Nichols.

BA GRADE
50 Risk: High

TRACK RECORD: Small improved his draft stock markedly with a huge junior season at Mississippi State. He led the Southeastern Conference in strikeouts (176), finished second in ERA (1.93) and ranked third in both innings (107) and opponent average (.164). Instead of going in the third to fifth rounds as expected, Small went 28th overall to the Brewers and signed for $1.8 million after leading the Bulldogs to the College World Series.

SCOUTING REPORT: Small compiles huge strikeout numbers by getting great extension with his long arms and using a deceptive delivery. He doesn't throw as hard as he did prior to Tommy John surgery in 2017 and sits mostly in the 89-92 mph range, but his advanced command, extension and deception make it appear much harder. He has also learned to vary the tempo of his delivery, adding some pauses with a bit of crossfire action. Small's above-average curveball is more of a "slurve" that generates swings and misses from lefthanded hitters, while his fringe-average changeup plays up with his deceiving arm action and late fade to neutralize righthanded hitters.

THE FUTURE: With no real plus pitch, Small profiles as more of a back-of-the-rotation starter, but he also has an advanced feel for pitching and has proven to be an overachiever. He will open 2020 at high Class A Carolina.

SCOUTING GRADES: **Fastball:** 50 **Curveball:** 55 **Changeup:** 45 **Control:** 60

Year	Age	Club (League)	Class	W	L	ERA	G	GS	SV	IP	H	HR	BB	SO	K/9	WHIP	AVG
2019	22	Brewers Gold (AZL)	R	0	0	0.00	2	2	0	3	0	0	0	5	15.0	0.00	.000
	22	Wisconsin (MWL)	LoA	0	2	1.00	5	5	0	18	11	0	4	31	15.5	0.83	.172
Minor League Totals				0	2	0.86	7	7	0	21	11	0	4	36	15.4	0.71	.151

5 AARON ASHBY, LHP

Born: May 24, 1998. **B-T:** R-L. **HT:** 6-1. **WT:** 175. **Drafted:** Crowder (Mo.) JC, 2018 (4th round). **Signed by:** Drew Anderson.

EVAN MOESTA

BA GRADE
50 Risk: High

TRACK RECORD: Ashby boosted his stock more than any player in the Brewers' system in 2019 and was named the organization's pitcher of the year. The reason was he gained better command of his pitches. He struck out 135 batters in 126 innings across both Class A levels, using a three-pitch mix that allowed him to control the action. It's what the Brewers had in mind when they drafted Ashby in the fourth round in 2018 after he averaged 18.8 strikeouts per nine innings at Crowder (Mo.) JC.

SCOUTING REPORT: Ashby doesn't throw overly hard, with a fastball that sits in the 92-95 mph range. What separates him is a devastating curveball. It's a true plus-pitch he sometimes throws tight and hard to give the appearance of a slider, and lefthanded hitters in particular are helpless against it. Same-side batters managed just .183 with six extra-base hits—all doubles. Ashby has made great strides with his changeup to give him a reliable third pitch. He has a deceptive, funky delivery that makes his pitches hard to pick up but also leads to occasional lapses of command and gives him fringe-average control overall.

THE FUTURE: Ashby has the stuff of a potential mid-rotation starter and just needs to keep making strides with his control. He is slated to start 2020 at Double-A Biloxi.

SCOUTING GRADES: **Fastball:** 55 **Curveball:** 70 **Changeup:** 50 **Control:** 45

Year	Age	Club (League)	Class	W	L	ERA	G	GS	SV	IP	H	HR	BB	SO	K/9	WHIP	AVG
2018	20	Helena (PIO)	R	1	2	6.20	6	3	1	20	18	3	8	19	8.4	1.28	.234
	20	Wisconsin (MWL)	LoA	1	1	2.17	7	7	0	37	40	1	9	47	11.3	1.31	.274
2019	21	Wisconsin (MWL)	LoA	3	4	3.54	11	10	0	61	47	4	28	80	11.8	1.23	.216
	21	Carolina (CAR)	HiA	2	6	3.46	13	13	0	65	54	1	32	55	7.6	1.32	.229
Minor League Totals				7	13	3.53	37	33	1	183	159	9	77	201	9.9	1.28	.235

6 MARIO FELICIANO, C

TOM POLLARD

BA GRADE
50 Risk: High

Born: Nov. 20, 1998. **B-T:** R-R. **HT:** 6-1. **WT:** 195. **Drafted:** HS—Florida, P.R., 2016 (2nd round supplemental). **Signed by:** Charlie Sullivan.

TRACK RECORD: After an injury-plagued 2018 limited Feliciano to just 42 games and resulted in offseason shoulder surgery, the Puerto Rican catcher needed to reestablish himself as a top prospect in the system. He did exactly that, leading the high Class A Carolina League with 19 homers, 81 RBIs, a .477 slugging percentage, 48 extra-base hits and 210 total bases at age 20 and winning the league's MVP award.

SCOUTING REPORT: A bat-first player, Feliciano finally made strides offensively but should also develop into a high-caliber defender with more games behind the plate. He has a compact swing and makes consistent hard contact to all fields and is learning to tap into his average power more and more in games. Feliciano is an aggressive hitter who rarely walks and is prone to striking out—his swinging-strike rate was one of the highest in the minors—but his plate discipline should improve with maturity and experience. Feliciano is a good athlete who runs well for a catcher and shows agility behind the plate. His plus arm strength and quick release discourages runners from taking liberties on the bases.

THE FUTURE: Feliciano has all the tools to develop into an everyday catcher, but he still needs to show he can repeat his breakout 2019. He will try to do that at Double-A Biloxi in 2020.

SCOUTING GRADES: **Hitting:** 55 **Power:** 50 **Running:** 45 **Fielding:** 55 **Arm:** 60

Year	Age	Club (League)	Class	AVG	G	AB	R	H	2B	3B	HR	RBI	BB	SO	SB	OBP	SLG
2017	18	Wisconsin (MWL)	LoA	.251	104	402	47	101	16	2	4	36	34	72	10	.320	.331
2018	19	Brewers (AZL)	R	.286	4	14	0	4	1	0	0	2	2	3	0	.375	.357
	19	Carolina (CAR)	HiA	.205	42	146	20	30	7	1	3	12	13	59	2	.282	.329
2019	20	Carolina (CAR)	HiA	.273	116	440	62	120	25	4	19	81	29	139	2	.324	.477
	20	Biloxi (SL)	AA	.167	3	12	2	2	0	1	0	0	0	4	0	.286	.333
Minor League Totals				.255	298	1131	147	288	54	11	26	147	85	296	16	.315	.391

7 ANTOINE KELLY, LHP

BA GRADE
50 Risk: High

Born: Dec. 5, 1999. **B-T:** L-L. **HT:** 6-6. **WT:** 205. **Drafted:** Wabash Valley (Ill.) JC, 2019 (2nd round). **Signed by:** Harvey Kuenn Jr.

TRACK RECORD: The Brewers went for upside when they drafted Kelly 65th overall in 2019 and signed him for just over $1 million. Kelly led all junior college pitchers with 19.1 strikeouts per nine innings with his overpowering fastball at Wabash Valley (Ill.) JC, then struck out 41 batters in 28.2 innings in the Rookie-level Arizona League after signing.

SCOUTING REPORT: Kelly's fastball sat in the low 90s in high school, but after adding weight and strength and working on his mechanics, he now sits 93-97 mph and has the projectable frame to one day touch 100. With a 6-foot-6 frame and loose arm action, he hasn't had to do much more than pump fastballs past hitters to succeed. Whether Kelly starts or relieves will depend on the development of his secondary pitches. He gets chases on his above-average slider, particularly from lefthanded hitters, but he must show more consistent command of it. His changeup is not much of a factor. Considering his long, lanky frame, Kelly has shown relatively good command, but it is still fringe-average overall.

THE FUTURE: Scouts already compare Kelly with Brewers closer Josh Hader, believing his future will be as a strikeout sensation out of the bullpen rather than in the rotation. He will open 2020 at a Class A level.

SCOUTING GRADES: **Fastball:** 60 **Slider:** 55 **Changeup:** 45 **Control:** 45

Year	Age	Club (League)	Class	W	L	ERA	G	GS	SV	IP	H	HR	BB	SO	K/9	WHIP	AVG
2019	19	Brewers (AZL)	R	0	0	1.26	9	9	0	29	21	0	5	41	12.9	0.91	.208
2019	19	Wisconsin (MWL)	LoA	0	1	18.00	1	1	0	3	5	2	4	4	12.0	3.00	.417
Minor League Totals				0	1	2.84	10	10	0	31	26	2	9	45	12.8	1.11	.230

8 EDUARDO GARCIA, SS

BILL MITCHELL

BA GRADE
55 Risk: Extreme

Born: July 10, 2002. **B-T:** R-R. **HT:** 6-2. **WT:** 160. **Signed:** Venezuela, 2018. **Signed by:** Reinaldo Hidalgo.

TRACK RECORD: Garcia was one of the youngest players in the 2018 international class and signed with the Brewers for $1.1 million on his 16th birthday. His glove immediately caught the attention of scouts during showcases in Colombia and the Dominican Republic. Assigned to the Dominican Summer League for his pro debut, Garcia got off to a hot start at the plate before suffering a season-ending broken ankle in mid-June while sliding into second base.

SCOUTING REPORT: It's not often that players as young as Garcia show such advanced defensive skills. He's a true plus defensive shortstop with a plus arm, and those tools could very well get even better as he matures physically and adds strength. At the plate, Garcia shows promise with a good approach and smooth swing that already yields gap power. He has quick hands and uses his lower half, and he might develop more pop over time. He is expected to be at least an average runner on the bases. It's Garcia's glove, above all else, that will fuel his rise.

THE FUTURE: Garcia is not expected to have any lingering effects from his ankle injury. He will likely be kept in extended spring training to start 2020.

SCOUTING GRADES: **Hitting:** 55 **Power:** 45 **Running:** 50 **Fielding:** 60 **Arm:** 60

Year	Age	Club (League)	Class	AVG	G	AB	R	H	2B	3B	HR	RBI	BB	SO	SB	OBP	SLG
2019	16	Brewers (DSL)	R	.313	10	32	6	10	2	0	1	3	6	9	1	.450	.469
Minor League Totals				.313	10	32	6	10	2	0	1	3	6	9	1	.450	.469

9 DREW RASMUSSEN, RHP

BA GRADE
55 Risk: Extreme

Born: July 27, 1995. **B-T:** R-R. **HT:** 6-1. **WT:** 211. **Drafted:** Oregon State, 2018 (6th round). **Signed by:** Shawn Whalen.

TRACK RECORD: The Rays drafted Rasmussen 31st overall in 2017 out of Oregon State but did not sign him over concerns about his elbow following the Tommy John surgery he had as a sophomore. He returned to OSU and needed a second TJ as a senior. Believing he would make a full recovery, the Brewers drafted him in the sixth round in 2018 and signed him for $135,000. After a year of rehab, Rasmussen re-emerged throwing in the upper 90s at 2019 spring training and rose three levels to Double-A.

SCOUTING REPORT: Rasmussen overpowers hitters with a mid-90s fastball that touches 99 mph. It has plus velocity and plays with life in the strike zone to make it a plus-plus pitch. Rasmussen backs up his fastball with an above-average power slider in the 88-91 mph range and an improving changeup which has a chance to be an average third pitch. Rasmussen quickly regained his feel for pitching post-surgery and fills up the strike zone with above-average control

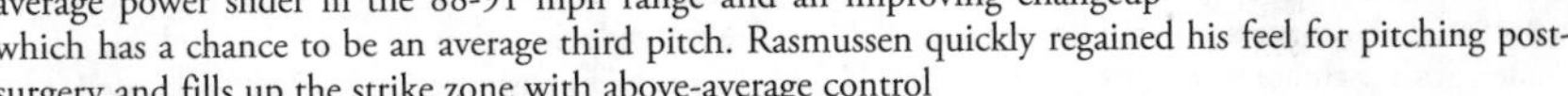

THE FUTURE: Rasmussen has starter stuff, but after two surgeries and a careful approach to pitch counts, his future could be in the bullpen. He will see Triple-A San Antonio in 2020 and has a shot at making his major league debut.

SCOUTING GRADES: **Fastball:** 70 **Slider:** 55 **Changeup:** 50 **Control:** 55

Year	Age	Club (League)	Class	W	L	ERA	G	GS	SV	IP	H	HR	BB	SO	K/9	WHIP	AVG
2018	22	Did not play—Injured															
2019	23	Wisconsin (MWL)	LoA	0	0	0.00	1	1	0	2	1	0	0	3	13.5	0.50	.167
	23	Carolina (CAR)	HiA	0	0	1.59	4	4	0	11	7	0	2	16	12.7	0.79	.184
	23	Biloxi (SL)	AA	1	3	3.54	22	18	0	61	49	4	29	77	11.4	1.28	.223
Minor League Totals				1	3	3.15	27	23	0	74	57	4	31	96	11.6	1.18	.216

10 ZACK BROWN, RHP

Born: Dec. 15, 1994. **B-T:** R-R. **HT:** 6-1. **WT:** 180. **Drafted:** Kentucky, 2016 (5th round). **Signed by:** Jeff Simpson.

DAVE MICHAEL/SA MISSIONS

BA GRADE
45 Risk: Medium

TRACK RECORD: The Brewers expected big things from Brown at Triple-A San Antonio after he won the organization's minor league pitcher of the year award in 2018, but he struggled with the introduction of the new ball to Triple-A and logged a 5.79 ERA with a rising walk rate and declining strikeout rate. Instead of getting his feet wet in the majors as expected, Brown lost confidence in his stuff and received a "time out" to regroup.

SCOUTING REPORT: At his best, Brown features a three-pitch mix and keeps his stuff deep into games. He uses both sides of the plate with a 92-95 mph fastball and goes to his two-seamer to induce weak ground balls. Brown mixes in a plus curveball when ahead in the count, keeping hitters off his hard stuff and inducing lots of swings and misses. He also has good feel for a promising changeup that also keeps opponents off his fastball. Brown struggled more with his command last season, but the Brewers like the way he competes on the mound and, when he's right, attacks the strike zone.

THE FUTURE: It remains to be seen if Brown can remain a starter or is better suited for a relief role with his fastball and breaking ball. After struggling at San Antonio, he'll be sent back there to get squared away.

SCOUTING GRADES: **Fastball:** 55 **Curveball:** 60 **Changeup:** 50 **Control:** 50

Year	Age	Club (League)	Class	W	L	ERA	G	GS	SV	IP	H	HR	BB	SO	K/9	WHIP	AVG
2017	22	Wisconsin (MWL)	LoA	4	5	3.39	18	13	0	85	78	7	34	84	8.9	1.32	.249
	22	Carolina (CAR)	HiA	3	0	2.16	4	4	0	25	24	1	2	23	8.3	1.04	.250
2018	23	Brewers (AZL)	R	0	0	0.00	1	1	0	2	3	0	1	3	13.5	2.00	.333
	23	Biloxi (SL)	AA	9	1	2.44	22	21	0	126	95	8	36	116	8.3	1.04	.207
2019	24	San Antonio (PCL)	AAA	3	7	5.79	25	23	0	117	138	16	64	98	7.6	1.73	.298
Minor League Totals				20	17	3.80	82	68	1	392	378	35	147	358	8.2	1.34	.253

11 HEDBERT PEREZ, OF

Born: April 4, 2003. **B-T:** L-L. **HT:** 5-11. **WT:** 180. **Signed:** Venezuela, 2019. **Signed by:** Reinaldo Hidalgo.

BA GRADE
55 Risk: Extreme

TRACK RECORD: As an amateur in Venezuela, Perez trained with his father, Robert Perez, an outfielder who played six seasons in the big leagues from 1994-2001, mostly with the Blue Jays. Perez was one of the elite players in the 2019 international class when the Brewers signed him, with an exciting combination of athleticism, tools and baseball skills on both sides of the ball for a 16-year-old.

SCOUTING REPORT: Perez is a high-contact hitter with an efficient, compact swing, barreling balls to all fields, with good performance in games. He's a disciplined hitter who has a chance to get on base at a high clip and has at least 55 raw power now that should be plus or better once he gets stronger. Along with his hitting ability and power, Perez is an excellent athlete with plus or better speed underway. He's a potential above-average defender in center field, where he reads the ball well off the bat and takes good routes, with accurate throws from a plus arm. He's also a fluent English speaker who draws praise for his confidence and leadership.

THE FUTURE: Perez will make his pro debut in 2020, and while he hasn't played yet, his impact potential offensively and defensively at a premium position makes him one of the most exciting players in the system.

Year	Age	Club (League)	Class	AVG	G	AB	R	H	2B	3B	HR	RBI	BB	SO	SB	OBP	SLG
2019	16	Did not play—signed 2020 contract															

12 CARLOS RODRIGUEZ, OF

Born: Dec. 7, 2000. **B-T:** L-L. **HT:** 5-10. **WT:** 150. **Signed:** Venezuela, 2017. **Signed by:** Jose Rodriguez.

BA GRADE
50 Risk: Very High

TRACK RECORD: Rodriguez was one of the more advanced hitting prospects to come out of Venezuela in 2017, and accordingly the Brewers gave the 16-year-old a signing bonus of $1.355 million.

SCOUTING REPORT: Not big in size, he stood out for his plus speed, which played well on the bases and in center field, but he also has advanced contact skills for his age. As might be expected for someone of his small stature, Rodriguez is more of a slasher than a slugger, making hard contact to all fields with a short, compact stroke. Once on the bases, he is a threat to steal but must work on reading pitchers and getting better jumps. His speed allows him to go gap-to-gap in center with little effort and he has all the makings of being the prototypical, contact leadoff hitter a la Juan Pierre, with the same below-average arm strength. He was considered one of the top prospects last season in the Rookie-level Pioneer League despite getting a late start while recovering from a broken hamate bone. That injury limited him to 43 games, but he made a healthy return in July with a brief stint in the AZL before moving to the new Rocky Mountain franchise and showing off his hitting prowess.

THE FUTURE: He has advanced skills on both sides of the ball and therefore could move quickly through the system. Rodriguez likely will move up to low Class A Wisconsin.

Year	Age	Club (League)	Class	AVG	G	AB	R	H	2B	3B	HR	RBI	BB	SO	SB	OBP	SLG
2018	17	Brewers (DSL)	R	.323	56	217	38	70	13	1	2	32	7	19	12	.358	.419
	17	Brewers (AZL)	R	.350	5	20	4	7	0	0	0	1	2	1	2	.409	.350
2019	18	Brewers Gold (AZL)	R	.318	7	22	5	7	1	0	0	1	0	2	1	.318	.364
	18	Rocky Mountain (PIO)	R	.331	36	151	20	50	3	1	3	12	4	20	4	.350	.424
Minor League Totals				.327	104	410	67	134	17	2	5	46	13	42	19	.356	.415

13 TREY SUPAK, RHP

BA GRADE
45 Risk: High

Born: May 31, 1996. **B-T:** R-R. **HT:** 6-5. **WT:** 235. **Drafted:** HS—La Grange, Texas, 2014 (2nd round supplemental). **Signed by:** Trevor Haley (Pirates).

TRACK RECORD: Supak pitched so well in 20 starts at Class AA Biloxi before being promoted to Triple-A San Antonio, he was named the pitcher of the year in the Southern League. He completely dominated opponents, logging 91 strikeouts in 122.2 innings, with only 23 walks, while limiting hitters to a .192 batting average. He did not fair nearly as well in the hitter-friendly PCL, compiling only 30 innings over seven starts, with opponents batting .325.

SCOUTING REPORT: Supak has a pitch-to-contact approach, making pinpoint command and mixing pitches well in his outings. He uses a four-pitch mix, with a fastball that sits in the low 90s. His slider and changeup have plus-pitch potential, and Supak uses them more than his curveball, with good command. He uses his height to pitch on a downhill plane but is a big-bodied player who must focus more on conditioning to succeed at the top level.

THE FUTURE: Pitching to contact can be risky at times, but Supak has the ingredients to be a successful starter in the majors because of his stuff and feel for pitching, and the Brewers like the way he competes on the mound. He is expected to start the 2020 season with San Antonio.

Year	Age	Club (League)	Class	W	L	ERA	G	GS	SV	IP	H	HR	BB	SO	K/9	WHIP	AVG
2017	21	Wisconsin (MWL)	LoA	2	2	1.76	8	7	0	41	21	1	10	53	11.6	0.76	.156
	21	Carolina (CAR)	HiA	3	4	4.60	15	11	1	72	65	12	28	57	7.1	1.29	.241
2018	22	Carolina (CAR)	HiA	2	1	1.76	9	9	0	51	37	2	16	48	8.5	1.04	.208
	22	Biloxi (SL)	AA	6	6	2.91	16	16	0	87	74	4	28	75	7.8	1.18	.232
2019	23	Biloxi (SL)	AA	11	4	2.20	20	20	0	123	84	6	23	91	6.7	0.87	.192
	23	San Antonio (PCL)	AAA	1	2	9.30	7	7	0	30	41	6	9	27	8.1	1.67	.325
Minor League Totals				30	28	3.48	106	92	2	514	442	40	148	446	7.8	1.15	.233

14 LUIS MEDINA, OF

Born: Feb. 24, 2003. **B-T:** L-L. **HT:** 6-2. **WT:** 170. **Signed:** Venezuela, 2019. **Signed by:** Jose Rodriguez.

TRACK RECORD: Nearly all of the Brewers' top bonuses in their 2019 international class went to Venezuelan players. That includes Medina, one of the top outfielders in the class.

SCOUTING REPORT: Medina stands out for his huge raw power from the left side. It grades out at least plus and shows flashes of becoming a 70 on the 20-80 scale. He's able to produce that power with a loose stroke, using his hands well and showing a solid sense for the strike zone. He gets in trouble when he gets pull-conscious, where his weight shifts out front too soon and he flies open early, which leads to empty swings. Even when he is caught out front, his hands are good enough for him to still be able to make contact sometimes, but better balance will help him handle pitches on the outer third. Medina will probably start out in center field, but he's more likely to end up in right field. He's an average runner and does have solid defensive instincts, but as he fills out he's likely to slow down. The tools are there for him to be a good defender in right field, with a 55 arm that could get stronger.

THE FUTURE: Medina is far away, but he immediately becomes one of the organization's most promising lower-level prospects. He should hit in the middle of the lineup for the Brewers in the Dominican Summer League in 2020.

Year	Age	Club (League)	Class	AVG	G	AB	R	H	2B	3B	HR	RBI	BB	SO	SB	OBP	SLG
2019	16	Did not play—signed 2020 contract															

15 DEVIN WILLIAMS RHP

BA GRADE
40 Risk: Medium

Born: Sept. 21, 1994. **B-T:** R-R. **HT:** 6-2. **WT:** 192. **Drafted:** HS—Hazelwood, Mo., 2013 (2nd round). **Signed by:** Harvey Kuenn Jr.

TRACK RECORD: Williams long has been considered to have one of the best arms in the organization but suffered a setback when Tommy John surgery forced him to miss the entire 2017 season. He got back on the mound in 2018 for 14 starts at high Class A Carolina, but it wasn't until last year at Double-A Biloxi that he used some added muscle to get his velocity back in a big way, throwing his fastball in the mid-to-high 90s, at times touching 100 mph. Accordingly, he became more aggressive with that pitch, attacking hitters up in the zone with late life, increasing his strikeout rate.

SCOUTING REPORT: He still flashes a sharp-breaking slider in the upper 80s but has gotten better feel for his changeup, which dips more than 10 mph below the velocity of his fastball and provides a new weapon that helped him dominate Double-A hitters (.181 batting average). Williams eventually was bumped up to Triple-A San Antonio, then to Milwaukee for his major league debut. Much of his newfound success came after being moved from a starting role to relief, with an appearance in the Futures Game signaling a return to prospect status. He made strides with his command but still has some work to do there.

THE FUTURE: Just like that, Williams' career is back on track. He will get a shot to make the Brewers' bullpen in the spring as a multi-inning reliever.

Year	Age	Club (League)	Class	W	L	ERA	G	GS	SV	IP	H	HR	BB	SO	K/9	WHIP	AVG
2017	22	Did not play—Injured															
2018	23	Carolina (CAR)	HiA	0	3	5.82	14	14	0	34	40	2	22	35	9.3	1.82	.301
2019	24	Biloxi (SL)	AA	7	2	2.36	31	0	4	53	34	3	29	76	12.8	1.18	.181
	24	San Antonio (PCL)	AAA	0	0	0.00	3	0	0	4	2	0	1	6	14.7	0.82	.167
	24	Milwaukee (NL)	MAJ	0	0	3.95	13	0	0	14	18	2	6	14	9.2	1.76	.310
Major League Totals				0	0	3.95	13	0	0	13	18	2	6	14	9.2	1.76	.310
Minor League Totals				22	29	3.73	120	53	7	378	344	19	176	405	9.6	1.37	.242

16 PAYTON HENRY, C

BA GRADE
45 Risk: High

Born: June 24, 1997. **B-T:** R-R. **HT:** 6-2. **WT:** 225. **Drafted:** HS—Pleasant Grove, Utah, 2016 (6th round). **Signed by:** Jeff Scholzen.

TRACK RECORD: The Brewers like both the tangibles and intangibles of Henry, which is why they invited him to their spring camp in 2019 after three seasons as a pro, without being on the 40-man roster. They wanted him to benefit from being around the big league catchers and continue to soak up knowledge while getting to watch how they go about their daily work. Henry then went out and put together a solid if not sensational season at high Class A Carolina while sharing time with another top catching prospect, Mario Feliciano.

SCOUTING REPORT: He has the physical strength to generate power at the plate as well as handle the rigorous duties of a catcher over a full season. As with many power hitters, Henry has some significant swing-and-miss to his offensive game and must work to improve a lopsided strikeout-to-walk ratio in 2019 (142 to 26). As he matures and learns not to chase so many pitches off the plate, his OBP should tick upward. Behind the plate, Henry has a strong arm that discourages opponents from taking liberties on the base paths. He has a quick release that helps with pop times and club officials love the way he works behind the plate, shows energy and takes charge of games.

THE FUTURE: No one will outwork him, and he certainly has the tools and work ethic to become an everyday, power-hitting catcher in the majors. He was scratched from an Arizona Fall League assignment because of an MCL sprain in his left knee but recovered fully from that injury.

Year	Age	Club (League)	Class	AVG	G	AB	R	H	2B	3B	HR	RBI	BB	SO	SB	OBP	SLG
2017	20	Helena (PIO)	R	.242	55	207	38	50	17	1	7	33	30	69	1	.344	.435
2018	21	Wisconsin (MWL)	LoA	.234	98	337	44	79	15	2	10	41	38	124	7	.327	.380
2019	22	Carolina (CAR)	HiA	.242	121	430	49	104	22	1	14	75	26	142	1	.315	.395
Minor League Totals				.241	298	1056	146	254	61	4	31	166	100	354	3	.326	.394

17 NICK KAHLE, C

BA GRADE
45 Risk: High

Born: Feb. 28, 1998. **B-T:** R-R. **HT:** 5-10. **WT:** 210. **Drafted:** Washington, 2019 (4th round). **Signed by:** Shawn Whalen.

TRACK RECORD: Kahle was a bit under-the-radar as a catcher in the Pac-12 during the same draft season as Oregon State backstop Adley Rutschman, but had a strong junior season, setting the single-season walk record (59) for the Huskies and leading the team in average (.339), on-base percentage (.506) and slugging (.532) before signing with the Brewers for $325,000 as a fourth-round pick in 2019.

SCOUTING REPORT: A compact, 5-foot-10 catcher, Kahle has some solid defensive tools and is a good receiver with soft hands who works well with pitchers thanks to his maturity and baseball IQ. Amateur scouts had mixed thoughts on his defensive ability though thanks to fringe-average arm strength and consistent tail on his throws, but his first stint in pro ball was strong in that area, as he threw out 53 percent of basestealers in the Rookie-level Pioneer League. Kahle's best tool is his natural hitting ability. He improved as a hitter each season with Washington and has a short, direct swing that's contact-oriented. He pairs that with a fairly polished approach, rarely chasing out of the strike zone and he also draws walks at a solid clip—12.4 percent of the time in the Pioneer and Carolina Leagues—as his college track record indicates. Kahle has below average power that will limit his offensive ceiling, with some scouts expecting around 10 homers over a full season.

THE FUTURE: Some scouts have questioned whether or not Kahle is physical enough to handle catching full time in pro ball, but if he can has a chance to profile nicely with a solid hit tool. Low Class A Wisconsin is up next.

Year	Age	Club (League)	Class	AVG	G	AB	R	H	2B	3B	HR	RBI	BB	SO	SB	OBP	SLG
2019	21	Carolina (CAR)	HiA	.000	2	5	0	0	0	0	0	0	1	2	0	.167	.000
	21	Rocky Mountain (PIO)	R	.255	40	141	25	36	11	1	6	25	20	36	2	.350	.475
Minor League Totals				.247	42	146	25	36	11	1	6	25	21	38	2	.343	.459

18 JESUS PARRA, 3B/2B

BA GRADE 50 Risk: Extreme

Born: Aug. 30, 2002. **B-T:** R-R. **HT:** 6-3. **WT:** 200. **Signed:** Venezuela, 2018.
Signed by: Jesus Rodriguez.

TRACK RECORD: Had Parra been born 48 hours later, he would have been a July 2 international signing for the 2019 class and would have made his pro debut in 2020. Instead, Parra narrowly made the cutoff to sign in the 2018 class, so the Brewers signed him for $210,000 when he turned 16 on Aug. 30, 2018. He played his first season in the DSL as a 16-year-old and hit .275/.398/.486 after the all-star break.

SCOUTING REPORT: Parra is a physical infielder with a promising mix of patience and power. He has above-average raw power now with the strength projection for that to potentially tick up as he gets into his prime. There is some swing-and-miss to his game—he struck out 26 percent of the time in the DSL—though that's somewhat mitigated by him being a 16-year-old in that league. His strike-zone judgment is sound, though, and he draws walks to go with his power. Parra split time between third base and second last year, with a traditional profile for third. He's a below-average runner but his hands and feet work well for his size and he can finish plays with a plus arm.

THE FUTURE: Parra will head to either the Rookie-level Arizona League or the Rookie-level Pioneer League in 2020, where he will again be one of the league's youngest players for his U.S. debut.

Year	Age	Club (League)	Class	AVG	G	AB	R	H	2B	3B	HR	RBI	BB	SO	SB	OBP	SLG
2019	16	Brewers (DSL)	R	.247	65	227	39	56	15	2	6	37	26	71	9	.361	.410
Minor League Totals				.247	65	227	39	56	15	2	6	37	26	71	9	.361	.410

19 JEFERSON QUERO, C

BA GRADE 50 Risk: Extreme

Born: Oct. 8, 2002. **B-T:** R-R. **HT:** 5-10. **WT:** 165. **Signed:** Venezuela, 2019.
Signed by: Reinaldo Hidalgo.

TRACK RECORD: Quero played for Venezuela in the 2015 Little League World Series, then four years later was one of the top catchers in the country when the Brewers signed him at 16 on July 2, 2019.

SCOUTING REPORT: Quero has a strong, durable frame and a chance to be a plus defender. His blocking and receiving technique are advanced for his age, with quick, athletic movements behind the plate. He also has a plus arm and a fast exchange, which produces pop times into the low 1.9s in games. Quero also draws praise for his leadership and intelligence that should help him as a catcher. Quero combines impressive defense with a promising bat that produced a low swing-and-miss rate as an amateur and hard contact when he connects. He has a good offensive approach for his age and drives the ball the other way well, with the ability to hit balls out from right-center over to his pull side already, so he could grow into plus power.

THE FUTURE: Before signing, Quero didn't have as high of a profile as some of the other catchers in his class, but he has trended up significantly. He has more breakout potential heading into his pro debut.

Year	Age	Club (League)	Class	AVG	G	AB	R	H	2B	3B	HR	RBI	BB	SO	SB	OBP	SLG
2019	16	Did not play—signed 2020 contract															

20 ALEC BETTINGER, RHP

Born: July 13, 1955. **B-T:** R-R. **HT:** 6-2. **WT:** 210. **Drafted:** Virginia, 2017 (10th round). **Signed by:** James Fisher.

TRACK RECORD: Expectations are usually modest for 10th-round draft picks who sign for $10,000, but Bettinger has become an overachiever in the Brewers' system. Selected after his senior season at Virginia, Bettinger had poor-to-modest results in his first two seasons as a pro before beginning to blossom last year at Double-A Biloxi.

SCOUTING REPORT: After getting past a poor start to the season (8.13 ERA through six outings), his strikeout rate improved (9.68 per nine innings), his walk rate declined (2.16) and he became the staff workhorse, leading the team with 146.1 innings. A major reason for that breakthrough was a bump up in velocity, with his fastball sitting in the low 90s and occasionally touching higher, allowing him to pitch up in the zone. Bettinger mixes in an above-average curveball and dependable cutter, giving him a mix that should allow him to remain a starting pitcher. His command has sharpened considerably, allowing him to miss more bats and he has some deception in a funky, crossfire delivery.

THE FUTURE: If Bettinger is unable to continue advancing as a starter, he at least projects as a multi-inning reliever in the major leagues. He likely will begin the 2020 season at Triple-A San Antonio, leaving him a phone call away from the top level.

Year	Age	Club (League)	Class	W	L	ERA	G	GS	SV	IP	H	HR	BB	SO	K/9	WHIP	AVG
2017	21	Helena (PIO)	R	3	3	4.97	15	9	0	51	52	1	23	39	6.9	1.48	.274
2018	22	Wisconsin (MWL)	LoA	5	4	3.73	12	11	0	63	59	6	17	50	7.2	1.21	.250
	22	Carolina (CAR)	HiA	1	6	6.91	13	12	0	55	70	10	17	56	9.2	1.59	.315
2019	23	Biloxi (SL)	AA	5	7	3.44	26	26	0	146	121	13	35	157	9.7	1.07	.223
Minor League Totals				14	20	4.35	66	58	0	314	302	30	92	302	8.7	1.25	.254

21 DYLAN FILE, RHP

BA GRADE
45 Risk: High

Born: June 4, 1996. **B-T:** R-R. **HT:** 6-1. **WT:** 205. **Drafted:** Dixie State (Utah), 2017 (21st round). **Signed by:** Jeff Scholzen.

TRACK RECORD: When the Brewers took File out of Division II Dixie State in the 21st round of the 2017 draft, the expectations were modest. But no pitcher in the system enjoyed more success last season than File, who split time between high Class A Carolina and Double-A Biloxi. Beyond the 15-6 record and 3.24 ERA, he had a tremendous strikeout-walk ratio (136 to 22) over 147 innings, no small sample size.

SCOUTING REPORT: File uses a four-pitch mix, with a fastball in the low 90s, a slider in the high 70s, a curveball in the mid 70s and a changeup in the low 80s. His slider is a true strikeout pitch, with a late, sharp break that is particularly effective against righthanded hitters. File throws his curveball more over the top, giving two distinct looks to his breaking pitches. He pitches ahead in the count, attacking hitters and forcing lots of weak contact. File dropped his arm slot a bit after being drafted, helping his pitches break more with a consistent delivery. He has confidence in his ability to throw strikes and it shows on the mound, with a real feel for setting up hitters.

THE FUTURE: File shows good athleticism on the mound and the Brewers believe he can remain a starting pitcher as he continues to advance through the system. After making 14 starts at Double-A to close 2019, he could be ready for Triple-A in 2020.

Year	Age	Club (League)	Class	W	L	ERA	G	GS	SV	IP	H	HR	BB	SO	K/9	WHIP	AVG
2017	21	Helena (PIO)	R	1	2	4.02	12	7	0	47	51	7	13	37	7.1	1.36	.273
2018	22	Wisconsin (MWL)	LoA	8	10	3.96	25	25	0	136	152	15	28	114	7.5	1.32	.284
2019	23	Carolina (CAR)	HiA	6	4	3.80	12	12	0	66	71	4	7	63	8.5	1.18	.277
	23	Biloxi (SL)	AA	9	2	2.79	14	14	0	81	74	5	15	73	8.1	1.10	.243
Minor League Totals				24	18	3.65	63	58	0	330	348	31	63	287	7.8	1.24	.271

22 TYRONE TAYLOR, OF

BA GRADE
40 Risk: Medium

Born: January 22, 1994. **B-T:** R-R. **HT:** 6-0. **WT:** 185. **Drafted:** HS—Torrance, Calif., 2012 (2nd round). **Signed by:** Dan Huston.

TRACK RECORD: Until 2019, Taylor seemed destined to be a top prospect who never made the majors. A high school football standout, Taylor ranked No. 1 on the Brewers Top 30 in 2015. He has struggled since then and missed much of 2017 due to a hamstring strain. He had a wrist issue in 2019, but he got hot late and received a September callup when Ryan Braun and Lorenzo Cain were injured.

SCOUTING REPORT: Taylor's value is tied to his athleticism and defensive ability. He fits in center field thanks to his instincts and ability to track down balls hit into the gaps. He is a plus runner whose speed plays better in the outfield than it does on the basepaths. Offensively, Taylor has solid bat-to-ball skills, and has seen his raw power translate better in games the past two seasons, but he remains a below-average hitter with below-average power. That's why he profiles more as an emergency callup rather than a fourth outfielder who sticks all season.

THE FUTURE: Taylor is on the Brewers' 40-man roster, so he will head to spring training competing for a backup outfield spot. Most likely he will return to Triple-A San Antonio.

Year	Age	Club (League)	Class	AVG	G	AB	R	H	2B	3B	HR	RBI	BB	SO	SB	OBP	SLG
2017	23	Brewers (AZL)	R	.435	7	23	6	10	1	0	4	7	3	3	2	.500	1.000
	23	Biloxi (SL)	AA	.247	25	85	15	21	6	1	1	6	8	18	2	.316	.376
2018	17	Brewers (AZL)	R	.240	39	154	25	37	4	3	1	15	18	41	10	.324	.325
2019	18	Rocky Mountain (PIO)	R	.232	50	177	30	41	9	3	6	20	18	47	5	.308	.418
Minor League Totals				.236	89	331	55	78	13	6	7	35	36	88	15	.315	.375

23 JOE GRAY, OF

BA GRADE **50** Risk: Extreme

Born: March 12, 2000. **B-T:** R-R. **HT:** 6-1. **WT:** 195. **Drafted:** HS—Hattiesburg, Miss., 2018 (2nd round). **Signed by:** Scott Nichols.

TRACK RECORD: After a bout of pneumonia during his rookie year and a hamstring strain in 2019, Gray has played in just 55 games, with mostly poor results (.171/.308/.310). He looked good in extended spring training last year before suffering the hamstring strain and never really caught up during a second season of rookie ball. As a result, he needs playing time more than any young, top prospect in the system.

SCOUTING REPORT: Power potential is Gray's calling card, though worries about his swing-and-miss tendencies caused him to drop out of the first round of the '18 draft. His other plus tool is arm strength, among the best in the prep ranks before being drafted. Gray also runs well and takes good routes in center, giving him a good chance to remain at that position. What remains to be seen is if he will make enough consistent contact to take full advantage of his power potential and speed on the bases.

THE FUTURE: He played the entire 2019 season so there is plenty of time for Gray to develop, but he has to stay out of the trainer's room. After missing so much time during his first two pro years, it remains to be seen if Gray will be deemed ready to go to low Class A in 2020 or have to play yet again in rookie ball.

Year	Age	Club (League)	Class	AVG	G	AB	R	H	2B	3B	HR	RBI	BB	SO	SB	OBP	SLG
2018	18	Brewers (AZL)	R	.182	24	77	14	14	5	0	2	9	18	25	6	.347	.325
2019	19	Rocky Mountain (PIO)	R	.164	31	110	19	18	4	1	3	9	13	36	3	.279	.300
Minor League Totals				.171	55	187	33	32	9	1	5	18	31	61	9	.308	.310

24 THOMAS DILLARD, OF/1B

BA GRADE **45** Risk: Very High

Born: Aug. 28, 1997. **B-T:** B-R. **HT:** 6-0. **WT:** 230. **Drafted:** Mississippi, 2019 (5th round). **Signed by:** Scott Nichols.

TRACK RECORD: Dillard was a hitter first at Ole Miss and a defender second, having moved from catcher to primarily an outfielder before the '19 draft. The Brewers envisioned him as a first baseman, however, and that was his primary position in his first season as a pro at low Class A Wisconsin.

SCOUTING REPORT: A switch-hitter, he saw far more action from the left side of the plate and therefore was more productive. He hit all of his home runs as a lefty and shows raw power with a short swing and natural loft in his swing. Dillard produces good at-bats, making consistent contact and showing mature plate discipline, giving him a chance to hit for average and power. He doesn't run particularly well but has good instincts and a feel for picking spots to steal. In the outfield, he has limited range and an average arm, explaining why the Brewers played him mostly at first base, where he showed surprising athleticism.

THE FUTURE: He will continue to see action as a catcher, and likely at third base as well because of the way the Brewers value versatility. Dillard probably will start the 2020 season at high Class A Carolina.

Year	Age	Club (League)	Class	AVG	G	AB	R	H	2B	3B	HR	RBI	BB	SO	SB	OBP	SLG
2019	21	Brewers (AZL)	R	.278	4	18	2	5	3	0	1	4	1	3	1	.316	.611
2019	21	Wisconsin (MWL)	LoA	.246	51	171	27	42	6	0	6	24	43	50	7	.398	.386
Minor League Totals				.249	55	189	29	47	9	0	7	28	44	53	8	.391	.407

25 MAX LAZAR, RHP

BA GRADE **45** Risk: Very High

Born: June 3, 1999. **B-T:** R-R. **HT:** 6-3. **WT:** 185. **Drafted:** HS—Coral Springs, Fla., 2017 (11th round). **Signed by:** Charlie Sullivan.

TRACK RECORD: Lazar pitched only 79 innings for low Class A Wisconsin in 2019, but was so impressive he received consideration for the organization's minor-league pitcher of the year. In those 79 innings, he had an impressive strikeout-to-walk ratio (109 to 15) with a 1.04 WHIP while limiting opponents to a

.226 batting average. Lazar was only 19 when the season began and his workload was carefully managed with a five-day, piggyback schedule in which he alternated starts and relief appearances. After growing up in southern Florida, he was pitching in the chilly Midwest League climate in the early weeks, so the Brewers took special care of his arm. He also was shut down for a period with a minor elbow issue that he moved past.

SCOUTING REPORT: Lazar's fastball tops out in the 88-90 mph range but has good life and rising action, and he learned to use it effectively up in the zone to record strikeouts. He mixed in an effective curveball and changeup with a good feel for pitching and was excellent while playing for his first full-season club.

THE FUTURE: With a good frame that can handle more weight, Lazar figures to get stronger as he matures, and the Brewers believe his velocity will tick upward. They like his work ethic and dedication to a solid routine between outings, and his conviction in what he is trying to accomplish on the mound is apparent.

Year	Age	Club (League)	Class	W	L	ERA	G	GS	SV	IP	H	HR	BB	SO	K/9	WHIP	AVG
2017	18	Brewers (AZL)	R	0	2	5.93	7	1	0	14	16	2	1	14	9.2	1.24	.291
2018	19	Helena (PIO)	R	3	3	4.37	14	14	0	68	74	7	15	55	7.3	1.31	.269
2019	20	Brewers Gold (AZL)	R	0	1	1.50	3	3	0	6	4	0	0	10	15.0	0.67	.191
	20	Wisconsin (MWL)	LoA	7	3	2.39	19	10	1	79	67	5	15	109	12.4	1.04	.226
Minor League Totals				10	9	3.46	43	28	1	166	161	14	31	188	10.2	1.15	.249

26 JHEREMY VARGAS, SS

BA GRADE
45 **Risk: Extreme**

Born: May 10, 2003. **B-T:** R-R. **HT:** 5-10. **WT:** 165. **Signed:** Venezuela, 2019. **Signed by:** Jose Rodriguez.

TRACK RECORD: Vargas grew up playing a lot of baseball in Venezuela, including when he represented his country at the COPABE 14U Pan American Championship in Chihuahua, Mexico in 2017. He joined a Venezuelan-heavy international signing class for the Brewers when he signed with them on July 2, 2019.

SCOUTING REPORT: In a workout, Vargas doesn't have tools that immediately jump out, but he looks better in games. He makes a lot of contact in games, with a line-drive stroke and gap power. Between his bat control and strike-zone discipline, Vargas has the potential to be a high on-base threat. Vargas isn't that big, but with his broad shoulders, there is strength projection for his power to tick up, but pure hitting ability will probably always be ahead of his power. He isn't as flashy in the field as other shortstops, but Vargas has a chance to stick at the position. He's an average runner with clean hands, good field awareness and a solid-average arm.

THE FUTURE: After hitting well in Tricky League and Dominican instructional league games since signing, Vargas will try to carry that early success to his pro debut in 2020 in the Dominican Summer League.

Year	Age	Club (League)	Class	AVG	G	AB	R	H	2B	3B	HR	RBI	BB	SO	SB	OBP	SLG
2017	17	Brewers (AZL)	R	.276	32	123	15	34	6	0	0	15	9	39	2	.326	.325
2018	18	Helena (PIO)	R	.307	64	238	40	73	13	2	2	21	32	57	13	.391	.403
2019	19	Wisconsin (MWL)	LoA	.225	109	373	35	84	16	7	2	46	47	107	7	.311	.322
Minor League Totals				.260	205	734	90	191	35	9	4	82	88	203	22	.340	.349

27 CLAYTON ANDREWS, LHP/OF

BA GRADE
40 **Risk: High**

Born: Jan. 4, 1997. **B-T:** L-L. **HT:** 5-6. **WT:** 165. **Drafted:** Long Beach State, 2018 (17th round). **Signed by:** Dan Houston.

TRACK RECORD: Brendan McKay isn't the only lefthanded two-way player in the minors. Andrews began hitting and playing center field as well on the days he wasn't pitching. He was a two-way player at Long Beach State as well before becoming the Brewers' 17th-round pick in 2018.

SCOUTING REPORT: On the mound, Andrews is a rarity who can offer four pitches out of the bullpen. None of his pitches is overwhelming, however, which limits his ceiling. He brings his fastball at 89-93 mph and complements with a sinking changeup that grades as fringe-average. He throws a sweepy slider as well and also has a more powerful but seldom-thrown curveball in the low 80s. He also offers deception from a crossfire delivery. He showed little power at the plate but a strong eye for the strike zone, albeit in a sample size of just 63 at-bats across two levels.

THE FUTURE: It remains to be seen where his future lies and if his two-way versatility will get him to the big leagues and overcome his size disadvantage. It seems his quickest path will be on the mound.

Year	Age	Club (League)	Class	W	L	ERA	G	GS	SV	IP	H	HR	BB	SO	K/9	WHIP	AVG
2018	21	Helena (PIO)	R	0	0	6.00	5	0	0	6	9	0	2	12	18.0	1.83	.346
	21	Wisconsin (MWL)	LoA	6	1	1.33	14	0	0	27	14	3	5	42	14.0	0.70	.156
2019	22	Carolina (CAR)	HiA	2	2	3.86	22	0	11	28	24	2	10	44	14.1	1.21	.240
	22	Biloxi (SL)	AA	3	0	2.59	17	0	0	31	19	3	15	33	9.5	1.09	.171
Minor League Totals				11	3	2.83	58	0	11	92	66	8	32	131	12.8	1.06	.202

28 MICAH BELLO, OF

BA GRADE 45 Risk: Extreme

Born: July 21, 2000. **B-T:** R-R. **HT:** 5-11. **WT:** 170. **Drafted:** HS—Hilo, Hawaii, 2018 (2nd round supplemental). **Signed by:** Shawn Whalen.

TRACK RECORD: Bello is part of a run of Hawaiians the Brewers have drafted in recent years, including since-traded pitchers Kodi Medeiros and Jordan Yamamoto. Bello was the best player available from Hawaii in his draft year, and the Brewers spent $550,000 to sign him from a commitment to St. Mary's.

SCOUTING REPORT: Evaluators who like Bello see a player with a combination of power and speed that will allow him to tally double-digits in home runs and stolen bases once he reaches the big leagues. Those who aren't as optimistic see a player without a standout tool. He can hit balls hard from time to time, but he has below-average bat speed and a below-average feel to hit. He has at least above-average speed that shows up underway and on defense more than it does from home to first base. Bello has a plus arm in the outfield that would serve him well in right field. He's not a particularly projectable player.

THE FUTURE: Bello's tool set gives him a future as a fourth outfielder.

Year	Age	Club (League)	Class	AVG	G	AB	R	H	2B	3B	HR	RBI	BB	SO	SB	OBP	SLG
2018	17	Brewers (AZL)	R	.240	39	154	25	37	4	3	1	15	18	41	10	.324	.325
2019	18	Rocky Mountain (PIO)	R	.232	50	177	30	41	9	3	6	20	18	47	5	.308	.418
Minor League Totals				.236	89	331	55	78	13	6	7	35	36	88	15	.315	.375

29 GABE HOLT, OF

BA GRADE 45 Risk: Extreme

Born: January 7, 1998. **B-T:** L-R. **HT:** 5-11. **WT:** 175. **Drafted:** Texas Tech, 2019 (7th round). **Signed by:** K.J. Hendricks.

TRACK RECORD: Holt was Texas Tech's leadoff hitter from the day he walked onto campus. Finding a defensive fit was a tougher task. He began his career at second base, then moved to right field late in his freshman season. He played in the outfield as a sophomore with the Red Raiders, but moved back to second base in pro ball. As a draft-eligible sophomore Holt signed for a well-above slot $400,000.

SCOUTING REPORT: Holt's best asset is his plus-plus speed. He forces infielders to stay on their toes–one bobble and he can turn a groundout into a single or an error. Holt sprays the ball around the field thanks to quick hands and a very simple swing with a very modest load. He is unlikely to ever hit for much power, but he can yank the ball enough to get to five-to-eight home runs with the livelier MLB ball. Holt's hands are hard and his actions need to speed up if he's going to stick at second base. He was also below-average in right field thanks to poor routes and reads. His speed might fit better one day in center because the reads are easier. His above-average arm will fit anywhere.

THE FUTURE: Holt's ability to be a table setter and to steal bases gives him a shot at being an MLB regular or useful reserve, but he has a lot of work to do to refine his glove.

Year	Age	Club (League)	Class	AVG	G	AB	R	H	2B	3B	HR	RBI	BB	SO	SB	OBP	SLG
2019	21	Brewers Gold (AZL)	R	.500	2	6	0	3	0	0	0	1	1	0	0	.571	.500
	21	Rocky Mountain (PIO)	R	.219	9	32	4	7	1	0	2	4	1	2	0	.265	.438
Minor League Totals				.263	11	38	4	10	1	0	2	5	2	2	0	.317	.447

30 EDUARQUI FERNANDEZ, OF

BA GRADE 45 Risk: Extreme

Born: Nov. 21, 2001. **B-T:** R-R. **HT:** 6-2. **WT:** 176. **Signed:** Dominican Republic, 2018. **Signed by:** Julio de la Cruz.

TRACK RECORD: The Brewers paid $1.1 million to sign Fernandez in 2018. At the time, he showed a chance to be a power-speed threat, albeit with a lot of risk in his hitting, which showed up in his pro debut in the Dominican Summer League. His 11 home runs were tied for the most in the DSL.

SCOUTING REPORT: Fernandez's tools are loud but his bat is raw. He's an athletic player with a well-proportioned build and plus raw power. He can hit balls out to straightaway center field and was able to tap into that power in games. He lacks natural feel for hitting, with a 33 percent strikeout rate that's a significant red flag in the DSL. Fernandez has power and speed as a plus runner with a good gait who could be a stolen base threat and projects to stay in center field. He's still improving his reads and routes in the outfield, but he has the speed and strong arm that should play in the middle of the field.

THE FUTURE: Fernandez's tools and athleticism are exciting, but he needs to make a lot of adjustments at the plate to make it work at higher levels. The Rookie-level Arizona League is up next in 2020.

Year	Age	Club (League)	Class	AVG	G	AB	R	H	2B	3B	HR	RBI	BB	SO	SB	OBP	SLG
2019	17	Brewers (DSL)	R	.214	72	266	48	57	9	0	11	31	29	98	15	.301	.372
Minor League Totals				.214	72	266	48	57	9	0	11	31	29	98	15	.301	.372

Minnesota Twins

BY J.J. COOPER AND JOSH NORRIS

A loss to the Royals on the final day of the season is all that kept the Twins from tying the 1965 club for the most wins in franchise history. Even with that mild disappointment, Minnesota's 101 wins was only the second time in team history that the club had reached triple digits in victories.

For a team that won 78 games in 2018 and 59 as recently as 2016, it was a reminder of how far this organization has come.

Yes, the Twins play in the American League Central, a division that had some of the worst teams in baseball. Minnesota went 41-16 (.719) against the White Sox, Royals and Tigers. Against everyone else they still went 60-45 (.571), good enough for a 92-win pace.

The Twins earned their division title and were clearly one of the better teams in baseball.

And then as soon as the AL Division Series began, the Twins were presented with clear evidence of how far they still have to go.

In the best-of-5 ALDS, the Twins started Jose Berrios in Game 1. He was clearly the team's best option, but against a deep Yankees lineup, he lasted just four innings in a loss. In Game 2, the Twins started Randy Dobnak. Dobnak was a great story—he went from the independent leagues to the playoffs in just a little over two years. But the fact that he was Minnesota's choice to start a nearly must-win playoff game showed how far this rotation needs to improve if it is going to be competitive against the Yankees and Astros in the AL playoffs.

The Twins had lost Michael Pineda to a suspension, and Martin Perez had crashed back to earth after an excellent start to the season. But even if everyone had been healthy and effective, the Twins would have found themselves in the playoffs battling aces with mid-rotation starters and trying to match mid-rotation starters with back-of-the-rotation starters.

Minnesota has an excellent lineup. The Bomba Squad gave the Twins a lineup with no clear weaknesses. The bullpen was excellent as well. But the Twins do not have the firepower in the rotation to match up with the best teams in baseball, and it will be hard for them to fix that without the Twins growing their own arms.

While pitchers like Gerrit Cole, Stephen Strasburg and Zack Wheeler all signed massive free agent contracts, the Twins' biggest move of the offseason as of mid-December was the re-signing of Pineda.

Minnesota does have a solid farm system that can fill needs as they arise. There's a nice blend of position players who should be MLB regulars as well as power pitchers who at the least should be solid relievers.

And beyond that, the club has done an excellent job of developing and acquiring players who should be useful MLB role players. That should allow the Twins to survive injuries that can often cause problems for a thinner team,

Players like Dobnak, Devin Smeltzer, Lewis Thorpe, Lamonte Wade, Luke Raley and Travis Blankenhorn give the club inexpensive depth. Few of those six will be counted on to be everyday regulars in Minnesota, but all should play in the big leagues in 2020, providing inexpensive homegrown depth.

MARK CUNNINGHAM/MLB PHOTOS VIA GETTY

Rookie second baseman Luis Arraez hit .334 with 36 walks and 29 strikeouts in 92 games.

PROJECTED 2023 LINEUP

Catcher	Mitch Garver	32
First Base	Alex Kirilloff (2)	25
Second Base	Luis Arraez	26
Third Base	Royce Lewis (1)	24
Shortstop	Jorge Polanco	29
Left Field	Trevor Larnach (3)	26
Center Field	Byron Buxton	29
Right Field	Max Kepler	30
Designated Hitter	Miguel Sano	30
No. 1 Starter	Jose Berrios	29
No. 2 Starter	Jake Odorizzi	33
No. 3 Starter	Michael Pineda	34
No. 4 Starter	Jordan Balazovic (5)	24
No. 5 Starter	Jhoan Duran (6)	25
Closer	Brusdar Graterol (4)	24

DEPTH CHART

MINNESOTA TWINS

TOP 2020 ROOKIE: Devin Smeltzer, LHP. Smeltzer has the inside track among the trio of young starters battling for a rotation spot.
BREAKOUT PROSPECT: Gilberto Celestino, OF. He has gotten bigger and stronger and already plays a great center field. If he keeps improving, he could crack the top 10 in 2021.
SLEEPER: Rhodery Diaz, OF. Diaz impressed in the Dominican Summer League. Diaz's bat is his best tool, but he's a center fielder as well and should move quicker than the average international signee.

SOURCE OF TOP 30 TALENT

Homegrown	**25**	**Acquired**	**5**
College	10	Trade	4
High School	9	Rule 5 draft	0
Junior College	0	Independent leagues	1
Nondrafted free agent	0	Free agents/waivers	0
International	6		

LF
Alex Kirilloff (2)
Lamonte Wade (19)
Malfrin Sosa

CF
Misael Urbina (10)
Gilberto Celestino (13)
Akil Baddoo (21)
Rhodery Diaz
Gabriel Maciel
Willie Jo Garry Jr.

RF
Trevor Larnach (3)
Matt Wallner (20)
Luke Raley (24)
Emmanuel Rodriguez (26)
Eduoard Julien

3B
Keoni Cavaco (11)
Travis Blankenhorn (23)
Jose Miranda
Seth Gray
Andrew Bechtold

SS
Royce Lewis (1)
Wander Javier (30)
Will Holland

2B
Nick Gordon (16)
Spencer Steer
Yunior Severino

1B
Brent Rooker (14)

C
Ryan Jeffers (7)
Ben Rortvedt (25)
David Banuelos

LHP

LHSP	LHRP
Devin Smeltzer (12)	Charlie Barnes
Lewis Thorpe (17)	

RHP

RHSP	RHRP
Brusdar Graterol (4)	Jhoan Duran (6)
Jordan Balazovic (5)	Jorge Alcala (18)
Matt Canterino (8)	Edwar Colina (28)
Blayne Enlow (9)	Cody Stashak (29)
Randy Dobnak (15)	Luis Rijo
Cole Sands (22)	Casey Legumina
Josh Winder (28)	Joseph Yabbour
Griffin Jax	Yennier Cano
Chris Vallimont	Moises Gomez
Landon Leach	
Bailey Ober	

DRAFT ANALYSIS

2019

BEST PURE HITTER: SS Spencer Steer (3) has proved his hitting ability at a high level from college to the Cape Cod League and now in pro ball. He has a balanced swing, manages the strike zone well and finds the barrel a lot.

BEST POWER: OF Matt Wallner (1s) began his college career as a two-way player with power both on the mound and at the plate. He's transitioned to a full-time outfielder, and his raw power helped him set Southern Mississippi's career home run record (54) and tie its single-season mark (23). 3Bs Seth Gray (4) and Edouard Julien (18) both have above-average raw power as well.

FASTEST RUNNER: SS Will Holland (5) is a plus runner, and that speed plays well both on the bases and in the infield. SS Keoni Cavaco (1) can also flash plus speed.

BEST DEFENSIVE PLAYER: Cavaco stands out most for his glove, and he has all the tools to be a plus defender on the left side of the infield. His arm is well above-average, he has smooth hands and excellent range. How he fills out as he physically matures will determine whether that happens at shortstop or third base.

BEST ATHLETE: Cavaco and Holland both offer high-end athleticism thanks to their fast-twitch ability, speed and body control.

BEST FASTBALL: RHP Matt Canterino (2) can run his fastball up to 96 mph with carrying life and the ability to locate it well. RHP Casey Legumina (8) got hurt this spring, but at his best also can get his fastball up to 95-96 mph.

BEST SECONDARY PITCH: Canterino throws both a curveball and slider that can be above-average offerings. His curveball is a hard downer and the better of the pair. Legumina has a power slider that he can throw up to 87 mph.

BEST PRO DEBUT: Canterino pitched well in his debut, reaching low Class A Cedar Rapids and going 1-1, 1.35 in 20 innings in the Midwest League. RHP Cody Laweryson (14) also reached Cedar Rapids after a stellar summer with Rookie-level Elizabethton that saw him post a 59-to-9 strikeout-to-walk ratio.

MOST INTRIGUING BACKGROUND: RHP Sawyer Gipson-Long (6) is studying chemistry at Mercer with the intention of attending medical school one day. He is serious enough about that goal to go back to campus this fall to take classes, even leaving before Elizabethton's season ended.

CLOSEST TO THE MAJORS: Canterino was already the most advanced member of the Twins' draft class even before his excellent pro debut. He's clearly ahead of the pack on the road to Minnesota.

BEST LATE-ROUND PICK: The Twins were able to sign Julien, a draft-eligible sophomore, for a well-above slot deal. The Canadian native has some loud raw tools, starting with his power, but was inconsistent this spring at Auburn, not altogether unlike Holland.

THE ONE WHO GOT AWAY: LHP Antoine Jean (17) was the only player the Twins drafted in the first 25 rounds who didn't sign. The projectable Canadian native came on strong late but is instead headed to Alabama. LHP Drew Gilbert (35) and RHP Will Frisch (36) were high school teammates and the best prep players in Minnesota this spring but chose to continue their careers in college—Gilbert at Tennessee and Frisch at Oregon State.

—TEDDY CAHILL

TOP DRAFT PICKS OF THE DECADE

Year	Player, Pos.	2019 Org
2010	Alex Wimmers, RHP	Did not play
2011	Levi Michael, SS	Giants
2012	Byron Buxton, OF	Twins
2013	Kohl Stewart, RHP	Twins
2014	Nick Gordon, SS	Twins
2015	Tyler Jay, LHP	Reds
2016	Alex Kirilloff, OF	Twins
2017	Royce Lewis, SS	Twins
2018	Trevor Larnach, OF	Twins
2019	Keoni Cavaco, SS	Twins

2018

OF Trevor Larnach (1) and C Ryan Jeffers (2) have proven to be the advanced hitters they were expected to be when the Twins took them out of college, advancing to Double-A in their first pro seasons.

GRADE: B

2017

SS Royce Lewis (1) had a tough 2019 season at the plate but has largely lived up to the hype as a No. 1 overall pick. OF Brent Rooker (1s) reached Triple-A and should soon be ready for the big leagues.

GRADE: C

2016

OF Alex Kiriloff (1) has become the best hitter in the Twins' system and has proven to be a quick mover. RHP Jordan Balazovic (5) impressed and has turned into one of the system's most promising pitchers.

GRADE: B

1 ROYCE LEWIS, SS/3B

Born: June 5, 1999. **B-T:** R-R. **HT:** 6-2. **WT:** 200.
Drafted: HS—San Juan Capistrano, Calif., 2017 (1st round).
Signed by: John Leavitt.

TRACK RECORD: After a decorated high school career at JSerra and multiple successful stints with Team USA, Lewis was the first overall pick in 2017 and signed for $6.725 million that was both a club record and a full $1 million under slot. He ranked as the No. 1 prospect in both the Midwest and Florida State leagues in 2018, his first full season, but holes started showing up in his game at high Class A. His day-to-day performance in 2019, when he returned to the FSL, was equal parts baffling and brilliant, but he showed the top tier of his talent at the Futures Game and again in the Arizona Fall League, where he was MVP.

SCOUTING REPORT: Lewis' future is going to come down to how well he can hit. Loud mechanics at the plate—a high leg kick, hand hitch and deep weight transfer—open plenty of holes for pitchers to exploit. As a result, he sputtered when he returned to the FSL, where he struck out 22 percent of the time. His hard contact is among the loudest in the game—it just doesn't come often enough. Lewis' hands work well, he has plenty of bat speed and he has some adaptability to his swing, but his timing is often off. That leads many to expect he'll eventually have to tone down his leg kick. His plus power has gotten more impressive. He now draws comparisons with a young George Springer as a plus athlete with power and hit-tool questions. Defensively, Lewis is an explosive athlete who can stick at shortstop because of lateral range, first-step quickness and a strong arm. He struggles with his throws at times when he has time to think and get mechanical. The Twins exposed Lewis to other positions—including second base, third base and center field—in the waning days of the season and in the AFL. He showed the speed and instincts to play center field in the AFL and fared well at the other spots around the infield. His eventual home will partly depend on the Twins' needs.

THE FUTURE: Lewis faces a likely return to Double-A to start 2020. There, he will work to continue smoothing his hitting mechanics in order to realize his upside. Minnesota didn't have a viable injury replacement for Byron Buxton in 2019. Lewis might be the club's best fill-in option in center field or at multiple infield spots by late 2020.

TOM DIPACE

BA GRADE
65 **Risk:** **Very High**

SCOUTING GRADES
Hit: 45. **Power:** 60. **Run:** 60. **Field:** 55. **Arm:** 55.

Projected future grades on 20-80 scouting scale.

TOP PROSPECTS OF THE DECADE

Year	Player, Pos.	2019 Org
2010	Aaron Hicks, OF	Yankees
2011	Kyle Gibson, RHP	Twins
2012	Miguel Sano ,3B/SS	Twins
2013	Miguel Sano, 3B	Twins
2014	Byron Buxton, OF	Twins
2015	Byron Buxton, OF	Twins
2016	Byron Buxton, OF	Twins
2017	Nick Gordon, SS	Twins
2018	Royce Lewis, SS	Twins
2019	Royce Lewis, SS	Twins

BEST TOOLS

Best Hitter for Average	Alex Kirilloff
Best Power Hitter	Royce Lewis
Best Strike-Zone Discipline	LaMonte Wade
Fastest Baserunner	Royce Lewis
Best Athlete	Royce Lewis
Best Fastball	Brusdar Graterol
Best Curveball	Josh Winder
Best Slider	Eduar Colina
Best Changeup	Jhoan Duran
Best Control	Griffin Jax
Best Defensive Catcher	Ben Rortvedt
Best Defensive Infielder	Wander Javier
Best Infield Arm	Keoni Cavaco
Best Defensive Outfielder	Gilberto Celestino
Best Outfield Arm	Gilberto Celestino

Year	Age	Club (League)	Class	AVG	G	AB	R	H	2B	3B	HR	RBI	BB	SO	SB	OBP	SLG
2017	18	Twins (GCL)	R	.271	36	133	38	36	6	2	3	17	19	17	15	.390	.414
	18	Cedar Rapids (MWL)	LoA	.296	18	71	16	21	2	1	1	10	6	16	3	.363	.394
2018	19	Cedar Rapids (MWL)	LoA	.315	75	295	50	93	23	0	9	53	24	49	22	.368	.485
	19	Fort Myers (FSL)	HiA	.255	46	188	33	48	6	3	5	21	19	35	6	.327	.399
2019	20	Fort Myers (FSL)	HiA	.238	94	383	55	91	17	3	10	35	27	90	16	.289	.376
	20	Pensacola (SL)	AA	.231	33	134	18	31	9	1	2	14	11	33	6	.291	.358
Minor League Totals				.266	302	1204	210	320	63	10	30	150	106	240	68	.331	.409

2 ALEX KIRILLOFF, OF/1B

BA GRADE

60 Risk: High

Born: Nov. 9, 1997. **B-T:** L-L. **HT:** 6-2. **WT:** 195. **Drafted:** HS—Pittsburgh, 2016 (1st round). **Signed by:** Jay Weitzel.

TRACK RECORD: Kirilloff won the MVP award in the Appalachian League in his pro debut but then sat out the 2017 season after having Tommy John surgery. When he returned in 2018, he hit .348 at two Class A stops and led the minors with 71 extra-base hits. His 2019 encore was limited to 94 games at Double-A Pensacola by a pair of wrist injuries. He was slated to go to the Arizona Fall League but Pensacola made a run through the Southern League playoffs and the Twins opted to have him sit out the AFL campaign as a result.

SCOUTING REPORT: Kirilloff is the definition of a pure hitter. He combines a balanced lefthanded swing with strong hands and quick wrists to produce line drives to all fields. Given those characteristics and his strong frame, he projects as a double-plus hitter with above-average power. His talent may have been obscured somewhat in 2019 because of his wrist injury, which obviously plays a key role in how much impact a hitter can make. Scouts saw a few nits to pick, specifically a hole on the outer half of the plate that pitchers exploited and some off-kilter mechanics that may have disrupted his rhythm. He's an average defender and runner with an average arm and should be serviceable in right field, but the bulk of his value will come at the plate. As he matures, he could begin to slow down and see most of his time at first base, where he made 35 starts in 2019.

THE FUTURE: Despite an inconsistent turn at Double-A, Kirilloff is likely to head to Triple-A Rochester in 2020. There, he will get the ultimate boost of the livelier baseballs that caused an offensive explosion at the level in 2019.

SCOUTING GRADES: **Hitting:** 60 **Power:** 55 **Running:** 45 **Fielding:** 50 **Arm:** 50

Year	Age	Club (League)	Class	AVG	G	AB	R	H	2B	3B	HR	RBI	BB	SO	SB	OBP	SLG
2017	19	Did not play—Injured															
2018	20	Cedar Rapids (MWL)	LoA	.333	65	252	36	84	20	5	13	56	24	47	1	.391	.607
	20	Fort Myers (FSL)	HiA	.362	65	260	39	94	24	2	7	45	14	39	3	.393	.550
2019	21	Pensacola (SL)	AA	.283	94	375	47	106	18	2	9	43	29	76	7	.343	.413
Minor League Totals				.317	279	1103	155	350	71	10	36	177	78	194	11	.365	.498

3 TREVOR LARNACH, OF

BA GRADE

55 Risk: Medium

Born: Feb. 26, 1997. **B-T:** L-R. **HT:** 6-4. **WT:** 223. **Drafted:** Oregon State, 2018 (1st round). **Signed by:** Kyle Blackwell.

TRACK RECORD: Larnach went to the Twins at No. 20 overall, but to get to that draft position he re-worked his swing to add more launch angle. That change amplified the strength supplied by his physical frame and unlocked his massive raw power, which he displayed in his pro debut.

SCOUTING REPORT: Larnach was one of the most eye-opening players in the minor leagues in 2019. Evaluators from April until September remarked about the unique opposite-field power Larnach showed off, but they were also a little confused about why he hit so few homers to his pull side. Unlocking his power to right field had been a point of emphasis since he entered the system, and his work with the player development staff began to take hold around the midpoint of 2019. Of the seven home runs he hit after his promotion to Double-A Pensacola, six went to center field and one went to right field. None went to the opposite field. Mission accomplished. He could stand to smooth out his route-running in right field, but a near-average arm and an excellent work ethic should allow him to become an average defender.

THE FUTURE: Larnach has all the markings of a classic corner outfield masher. He could enter the big league picture in late 2020 with a fringe-average hit tool whose power makes it well worth trading off some strikeouts. His first taste of Triple-A and the livelier baseballs should only amplify that profile.

SCOUTING GRADES: **Hitting:** 50 **Power:** 60 **Running:** 50 **Fielding:** 45 **Arm:** 45

Year	Age	Club (League)	Class	AVG	G	AB	R	H	2B	3B	HR	RBI	BB	SO	SB	OBP	SLG
2018	21	Elizabethton (APP)	R	.311	18	61	10	19	5	0	2	16	10	11	2	.413	.492
	21	Cedar Rapids (MWL)	LoA	.297	24	91	17	27	8	1	3	10	11	17	1	.373	.505
2019	22	Fort Myers (FSL)	HiA	.316	84	320	33	101	26	1	6	44	35	74	4	.382	.459
	22	Pensacola (SL)	AA	.295	43	156	26	46	4	0	7	22	22	50	0	.387	.455
Minor League Totals				.307	169	628	86	193	43	2	18	92	78	152	7	.385	.468

4 BRUSDAR GRATEROL, RHP

BRACE HEMMELGARN

BA GRADE
55 **Risk: Medium**

Born: Aug. 26, 1998. **B-T:** R-R. **HT:** 6-1. **WT:** 265. **Signed:** Venezuela, 2014. **Signed by:** Jose Leon.

TRACK RECORD: After a year off to recover from Tommy John surgery in 2016, Graterol started making waves at the end of 2017 and continued to progress throughout 2018 at a pair of Class A stops. Shoulder soreness shortened his season at Double-A Pensacola in 2019, but he recovered to make his big league debut as a reliever on Sept. 1. He was impressive enough that the Twins kept him on their roster in their Division Series loss to the Yankees.

SCOUTING REPORT: Graterol's selling point continues to be his electric fastball. The pitch averaged 99 mph in his limited time in the big leagues and showed hard, heavy movement when he located it in the bottom of the strike zone. It doesn't have the typical characteristics one likes to see in a fastball used up in the zone, but pure velocity should allow him to blow it by hitters regardless. He pairs the fastball with a hard slider at 87-90 mph that scouts project as plus if it achieves more consistency. His slider breaks somewhat like a cutter rather than a deep, downer version that can be used to back-foot hitters. He has feel for a low-90s changeup, but he's primarily a two-pitch guy at this point in his development. He's already a big-bodied pitcher who must watch his conditioning as he develops.

THE FUTURE: Graterol has the upside of a top-end starter and the floor of a power reliever. The development of his changeup and his conditioning will go a long way toward determining which path he takes.

SCOUTING GRADES: **Fastball:** 80 **Slider:** 60 **Changeup:** 45 **Control:** 50

Year	Age	Club (League)	Class	W	L	ERA	G	GS	SV	IP	H	HR	BB	SO	K/9	WHIP	AVG
2017	18	Twins (GCL)	R	2	0	1.40	5	2	0	19	10	1	4	21	9.8	0.72	.152
	18	Elizabethton (APP)	R	2	1	3.92	5	5	0	21	16	1	9	24	10.5	1.21	.213
2018	19	Cedar Rapids (MWL)	LoA	3	2	2.18	8	8	0	41	30	3	9	51	11.1	0.94	.195
	19	Fort Myers (FSL)	HiA	5	2	3.12	11	11	0	61	59	0	19	56	8.3	1.29	.261
2019	20	Twins (GCL)	R	0	0	0.00	2	2	0	3	1	0	0	4	12.0	0.33	.111
	20	Pensacola (SL)	AA	6	0	1.71	12	9	1	53	32	2	21	50	8.5	1.01	.179
	20	Rochester (IL)	AAA	1	0	5.06	4	0	0	5	4	1	2	7	11.8	1.13	.211
	20	Minnesota (AL)	MAJ	1	1	4.66	10	0	0	10	10	1	2	10	9.3	1.24	.278
Major League Totals				1	1	4.66	10	0	0	9	10	1	2	10	9.3	1.24	.278
Minor League Totals				19	6	2.48	51	41	1	214	164	8	65	230	9.7	1.07	.212

5 JORDAN BALAZOVIC, RHP

BA GRADE
55 **Risk: High**

Born: Sept. 17, 1998. **B-T:** R-R. **HT:** 6-5. **WT:** 215. **Drafted:** HS—Mississauga, Ont., 2016 (5th round). **Signed by:** Walt Burrows.

TRACK RECORD: After parts of two seasons in the Rookie-level Gulf Coast League, Balazovic started to hint at his potential in his 2018 tenure in the low Class A Midwest League. Still, he remained fairly anonymous until he returned to the level in 2019. His stellar start was rewarded with a trip to the Futures Game in Cleveland, and he also missed time to pitch for Team Canada in the Pan-American Games.

SCOUTING REPORT: Balazovic blew away MWL hitters with a fastball in the mid-to-upper 90s before he earned a promotion to high Class A Fort Myers. From there, he kept on dominating. He backed up the fastball with a slider and a changeup that each has a chance to be average or a tick better. The slider is a bit of a slurvier offering—so much so that evaluators occasionally mistake it for a curveball. The changeup has been a big point of emphasis in his development and ranks behind his slider in his arsenal's hierarchy and will be the key to whether he can remain in the rotation. Balazovic is also gifted with a strong, projectable frame befitting a power pitcher.

THE FUTURE: Balazovic will likely move to Double-A Pensacola, where he'll get to test his arsenal against more advanced hitters.

SCOUTING GRADES: **Fastball:** 60 **Slider:** 55 **Changeup:** 50 **Control:** 50

Year	Age	Club (League)	Class	W	L	ERA	G	GS	SV	IP	H	HR	BB	SO	K/9	WHIP	AVG
2017	18	Twins (GCL)	R	1	3	4.91	10	3	0	40	47	5	20	29	6.5	1.66	.298
2018	19	Cedar Rapids (MWL)	LoA	7	3	3.94	12	11	0	62	54	5	18	78	11.4	1.17	.233
2019	20	Cedar Rapids (MWL)	LoA	2	1	2.18	4	4	0	21	15	1	4	33	14.4	0.92	.195
	20	Fort Myers (FSL)	HiA	6	4	2.84	15	14	0	73	52	3	21	96	11.8	1.00	.193
Minor League Totals				18	12	3.32	49	38	1	227	194	14	68	252	10.0	1.15	.226

6 JHOAN DURAN, RHP

BA GRADE
55 Risk: High

Born: Jan. 8, 1998. **B-T:** R-R. **HT:** 6-5. **WT:** 230. **Signed:** Dominican Republic, 2014. **Signed by:** Jose Ortiz/Junior Noboa (D-backs).

TRACK RECORD: Duran was the centerpiece of the three-prospect package that Arizona used in 2018 to pry Eduardo Escobar from the Twins. The D-backs signed him in 2014 on the strength of a projectable body and fastball, which they watched move from the upper 80s to the mid 90s before he was dealt. He ranked as the No. 3 prospect in the short-season Northwest League in 2017 and No. 14 in the high Class A Florida State League in 2019.

SCOUTING REPORT: Duran still has the big four-seam fastball, which can touch triple digits. More interesting than his four-seamer is his split-fingered sinker, known colloquially as baseball's only "splinker." The pitch is thrown with the low-90s velocity of a sinker but the hard, sharp bottom of a split-fingered fastball. No matter how it was classified, the pitch baffled hitters in both the high Class A Florida State and Double-A Southern leagues. He also throws a hard, mid-80s curveball. Minnesota has altered Duran's approach to pitching, shifting him to work his arsenal north-south in the strike zone. The move will help him tunnel his four-seamer at the top of the strike zone with the downer break of his curveball at the bottom of the zone and make both pitches more effective in the process.

THE FUTURE: Duran will need to continue to refine his command in the strike zone and his overall control to stay in the rotation, where he projects as a powerful innings-eater. If he has to move, he could fit nicely in a late-innings role where his fastball can dominate hitters at the end of games.

SCOUTING GRADES: **Fastball:** 70 **Splitter:** 70 **Curveball:** 45 **Control:** 50

Year	Age	Club (League)	Class	W	L	ERA	G	GS	SV	IP	H	HR	BB	SO	K/9	WHIP	AVG
2017	19	Diamondbacks (AZL)	R	0	2	7.15	3	3	0	11	19	0	4	13	10.3	2.03	.352
	19	Hillsboro (NWL)	SS	6	3	4.24	11	11	0	51	44	5	17	36	6.4	1.20	.228
2018	20	Kane County (MWL)	LoA	5	4	4.73	15	15	0	65	69	6	28	71	9.9	1.50	.268
	20	Cedar Rapids (MWL)	LoA	2	1	2.00	6	6	0	36	19	2	10	44	11.0	0.81	.154
2019	21	Fort Myers (FSL)	HiA	2	9	3.23	16	15	0	78	63	5	31	95	11.0	1.21	.224
	21	Pensacola (SL)	AA	3	3	4.86	7	7	0	37	34	2	9	41	10.0	1.16	.243
Minor League Totals				23	26	3.94	77	76	0	374	348	23	131	366	8.8	1.28	.246

7 RYAN JEFFERS, C

BA GRADE
50 Risk: High

Born: June 3, 1997. **B-T:** R-R. **HT:** 6-4. **WT:** 230. **Drafted:** UNC Wilmington, 2018 (2nd round). **Signed by:** Matt Williams.

TRACK RECORD: The Twins plucked a bit of a wild card when they drafted Jeffers in the second round in 2018, who was not on many radars that high on the board. He put together a solid pro debut between the Appalachian and Midwest leagues, then reached Double-A at the end of 2019. He ranked as the No. 19 prospect in a loaded Florida State League.

SCOUTING REPORT: Jeffers was one of just 22 players in the pitcher-friendly Florida State League to hit double-digit homers and was the only non-first baseman to do so in 80 or fewer games. He added four more home runs after a promotion to Double-A. He'd shown burgeoning power in college, but scouts were skeptical about whether it would translate into pro ball. He produces the power thanks to the strength provided by his massive frame and a solid understanding of the strike zone that allows him to zero in on the pitches that give him the most potential for impact. Jeffers also adapted well to the new setups being taught to Twins catchers and used his strong hands to receive and frame pitches with aplomb. He allowed just six passed balls in 627.1 innings behind the plate while throwing out 26 percent of runners. As expected, Jeffers is a below-average runner.

THE FUTURE: Jeffers finished 2019 in Double-A Pensacola and is likely to return there in 2020. He has the upside of an offensive-minded catcher with value on both sides of the ball.

SCOUTING GRADES: **Hitting:** 50 **Power:** 55 **Running:** 40 **Fielding:** 55 **Arm:** 45

Year	Age	Club (League)	Class	AVG	G	AB	R	H	2B	3B	HR	RBI	BB	SO	SB	OBP	SLG
2018	21	Elizabethton (APP)	R	.422	28	102	29	43	7	0	3	16	20	16	0	.543	.578
	21	Cedar Rapids (MWL)	LoA	.288	36	139	19	40	10	0	4	17	14	30	0	.361	.446
2019	22	Fort Myers (FSL)	HiA	.256	79	281	35	72	11	0	10	40	28	64	0	.330	.402
	22	Pensacola (SL)	AA	.287	24	87	13	25	5	0	4	9	9	19	0	.374	.483
Minor League Totals				.296	167	609	96	180	33	0	21	82	71	129	0	.383	.453

8 MATT CANTERINO, RHP

BA GRADE
50 Risk: High

Born: Dec. 14, 1997. **B-T:** R-R. **HT:** 6-2. **WT:** 222. **Drafted:** Rice, 2019 (2nd round). **Signed by:** Greg Runser.

TRACK RECORD: A high school teammate of Padres' 2016 first-round pick Hudson Potts, Canterino was a part of the Rice weekend rotation for three years and he held opponents to a sub-.200 average while leading the team in strikeouts all three seasons.

SCOUTING REPORT: Canterino has an atypical delivery. Starting from a high hand set, he pumps his hands up over his head as he coils into his back leg. It leads to an unusual high hand break, but his arm is usually on time at foot strike. His delivery adds deception and he has above-average control. Canterino tweaked his fastball grip as a pro to help give his plus 92-95 mph fastball more carry up in the zone. He also rediscovered his average curveball that was his most effective offspeed pitch in 2018. Canterino was able to throw that 11-to-5 slow curve for strikes early in the count and the pitch sometimes lock up hitters late in counts, though it lacks the power to be a true bat-misser. It paired well with his elevated fastball allowing him to work up and down in the strike zone. His above-average 83-85 mph slider had moderate depth and tilt and he can bury it. He'll mix in a fringe-average changeup sporadically.

THE FUTURE: Canterino doesn't have overwhelming stuff, but he is coachable, durable and consistently effective. If either his curveball or slider can be tweaked to give him a second plus pitch, he could exceed his current back-end starter upside. After dominating in a short stint in the Midwest League, he should be ready for the Florida State League in 2020.

SCOUTING GRADES: **Fastball:** 60 **Slider:** 50 **Curveball:** 55 **Changeup:** 45 **Control:** 55

Year	Age	Club (League)	Class	W	L	ERA	G	GS	SV	IP	H	HR	BB	SO	K/9	WHIP	AVG
2019	21	Twins (GCL)	R	0	0	1.80	2	2	0	5	2	0	1	6	10.8	0.60	.118
	21	Cedar Rapids (MWL)	LoA	1	1	1.35	5	5	0	20	6	0	7	25	11.3	0.65	.091
Minor League Totals				1	1	1.44	7	7	0	25	8	0	8	31	11.2	0.64	.096

9 BLAYNE ENLOW, RHP

BA GRADE
50 Risk: High

Born: March 21, 1999. **B-T:** R-R. **HT:** 6-3. **WT:** 170. **Drafted:** HS—St. Amant, La., 2017 (3rd round). **Signed by:** Greg Runser.

TRACK RECORD: The Twins have succeeded drafting projectable young pitchers who grow into their velocity. Enlow was supposed to develop into a Friday starter at Louisiana State, but the Twins paid him a well above slot $2 million to turn pro. He has added a couple of miles per hour since signing, bumping his 90-94 mph fastball to 92-96.

SCOUTING REPORT: Enlow has gotten bigger and stronger, but despite above-average velocity, he's more crafty than dominating. His best asset is his plus control. He's almost always around the strike zone. He has a five-pitch mix, though there's not really a plus pitch among the quintet. Enlow was best known in high school for his curveball. He added a slider as a prep senior, but his once plus curve doesn't have the depth it had in high school. It's morphed into a slurvier average pitch. He has added an above-average cutter which is more promising than his slider thanks to solid depth and excellent life. His below-average changeup has not really developed and is still more of something he throws out of obligation than intent.

THE FUTURE: Enlow has a good frame. He's durable. He throws a lot of strikes. But he's going to have to develop an out pitch to be more than a back-end starter.

SCOUTING GRADES: **Fastball:** 50 **Slider:** 50 **Curveball:** 50 **Changeup:** 40 **Cutter:** 55 **Control:** 60

Year	Age	Club (League)	Class	W	L	ERA	G	GS	SV	IP	H	HR	BB	SO	K/9	WHIP	AVG
2017	18	Twins (GCL)	R	3	0	1.33	6	1	0	20	10	1	4	19	8.4	0.69	.141
2018	19	Cedar Rapids (MWL)	LoA	3	5	3.26	20	17	1	94	94	4	35	71	6.8	1.37	.263
2019	20	Cedar Rapids (MWL)	LoA	4	3	4.57	8	8	0	41	42	4	15	44	9.6	1.38	.250
	20	Fort Myers (FSL)	HiA	4	4	3.38	13	12	0	69	61	4	23	51	6.6	1.21	.237
Minor League Totals				14	12	3.36	47	38	1	225	207	13	77	185	7.4	1.26	.242

10 MISAEL URBINA, OF

BILL MITCHELL

Born: April 26, 2002. **B-T:** R-R. **Ht. 5-11. Wt.:** 170. **Signed:** Venezuela, 2018. **Signed by:** Fred Guerrero.

TRACK RECORD: The Twins targeted Urbina in 2018 after spending much of their international bonus pool to sign Yunior Severino. Urbina had an excellent debut in the Dominican Summer League in 2019.

SCOUTING REPORT: Urbina is an athletic center fielder with plus speed, future plus defense in center field thanks to good instincts and a quick first step and an advanced batting eye for a young hitter. In his debut he amassed a 12 percent swinging strike percentage and a 6.5 percent strikeout rate, which both ranked third best among all DSL qualified hitters. His swing is compact and is more geared to spraying the ball than lifting and lofting. He has average or better bat speed and should add more power as he matures and fills out. His fringe-average arm is playable in center.

THE FUTURE: Urbina has the tools to be an everyday regular center fielder who can be a top-of-the-lineup tablesetter. His advanced approach at the plate gives him a chance to skip over the Gulf Coast League and jump to Rookie-level Elizabethton.

SCOUTING GRADES: **Hitting:** 60 **Power:** 40 **Running:** 60 **Fielding:** 60 **Arm:** 45

Year	Age	Club (League)	Class	AVG	G	AB	R	H	2B	3B	HR	RBI	BB	SO	SB	OBP	SLG
2019	17	Twins (DSL)	R	.279	50	183	34	51	14	5	2	26	23	14	19	.382	.443
Minor League Totals				.279	50	183	34	51	14	5	2	26	23	14	19	.382	.443

11 KEONI CAVACO, SS/3B

BA GRADE
55 Risk: Extreme

Born: June 2, 2001. **B-T:** R-R. **HT:** 6-2. **WT:** 195. **Drafted:** HS—Chula Vista, Calif., 2019 (1st round). **Signed by:** John Leavitt.

TRACK RECORD: Cavaco was barely on teams' watch lists heading into his senior year, but he rocketed into first-round consideration by demonstrating massive tools. The Twins weren't the only team with first-round grades on him but there were other teams who were not on Cavaco at all because of his lack of track record and swing-and-miss tendencies. Those concerns were heightened by one of the worst pro debuts of any recent first-round pick. He struck out in every one of his 35 two-strike counts in his pro debut.

SCOUTING REPORT: While Cavaco played shortstop in his pro debut, he projects as a plus (or even plus-plus) defender at third base with the agility, range, hands and plus arm to make both routine and exceptional plays. He also posts excellent exit velocities, plus bat speed and 70 raw power. He's even an above-average runner. None of that will matter unless he can generate more consistent quality contact. Cavaco struggles to cover the outer half of the plate and is prone to stepping in the bucket.

THE FUTURE: Cavaco has a lot of work to do to reach his ceiling of an above-average regular. Unlike most prep first rounders, he's unlikely to be ready for low Class A to start 2020.

Year	Age	Club (League)	Class	AVG	G	AB	R	H	2B	3B	HR	RBI	BB	SO	SB	OBP	SLG
2019	18	Twins (GCL)	R	.172	25	87	9	15	4	0	1	6	4	35	1	.217	.253
Minor League Totals				.172	25	87	9	15	4	0	1	6	4	35	1	.217	.253

12 DEVIN SMELTZER, LHP

Born: Sept. 7, 1995. **B-T:** R-L. **HT:** 6-3. **WT:** 195. **Drafted:** San Jacinto (Texas) JC, 2015 (5th round). **Signed by:** Clint Bowers (Dodgers).

TRACK RECORD: A cancer survivor, Smeltzer helped San Jacinto (Texas) JC to a national title in 2016 by striking out 20 in a 140-pitch complete game semifinal victory. Smeltzer moved back to the rotation after the Twins acquired him at the 2018 trade deadline in a deal that sent Brian Dozier to Los Angeles.

SCOUTING REPORT: Smeltzer works up and down and in and out, but he is looking to get hitters to swing and miss at pitches outside of the strike zone. He has to do this because his 87-91 mph below-average fastball relies on deception and location. His 75-77 mph curveball is generally average and will flash above-average because of how well he can locate it. It is a slow, big breaker with good depth that he can backdoor to righthanded hitters or sweep inside to try to back them off the plate. It also sweeps away from lefties. His average, low-80s changeup can also flash above-average because it has solid deception and some late drop. Plus control and command are vital to Smeltzer's success.

THE FUTURE: Smeltzer's ability to locate and durability make him a valuable No. 5 starter or long reliever.

Year	Age	Club (League)	Class	W	L	ERA	G	GS	SV	IP	H	HR	BB	SO	K/9	WHIP	AVG
2017	21	Great Lakes (MWL)	LoA	2	3	3.78	10	10	0	52	40	6	12	57	9.8	0.99	.211
	21	R. Cucamonga (CAL)	HiA	5	4	4.40	16	15	0	90	107	10	18	102	10.2	1.39	.287
2018	22	Tulsa (TL)	AA	5	5	4.73	23	14	0	84	94	9	19	67	7.2	1.35	.281
	22	Chattanooga (SL)	AA	0	0	3.00	10	0	4	12	14	0	2	16	12.0	1.33	.280
2019	23	Pensacola (SL)	AA	3	1	0.60	5	5	0	30	19	0	3	33	9.9	0.73	.183
	23	Rochester (IL)	AAA	1	4	3.63	15	14	0	74	68	14	19	71	8.6	1.17	.241
	23	Minnesota (AL)	MAJ	2	2	3.86	11	6	1	49	50	8	12	38	7.0	1.27	.265
Major League Totals				2	2	3.86	11	6	1	49	50	8	12	38	7.0	1.27	.265
Minor League Totals				16	19	3.95	90	58	4	353	358	39	79	358	9.1	1.24	.260

13 GILBERTO CELESTINO, OF

BA GRADE 50 **Risk:** High

Born: Feb. 13, 1999. **B-T:** R-R. **HT:** 6-0. **WT:** 170. **Signed:** Dominican Republic, 2015. **Signed by:** Oz Ocampo/Roman Ocumarez (Astros).

TRACK RECORD: Celestino spent three seasons at rookie and short-season levels before making his full-season debut in 2019. The Twins acquired him from the Astros in July 2018 in the swap that sent right-hander Ryan Pressly to Houston. In 2019, he put forth his best season in pro ball to date.

SCOUTING REPORT: Celestino is a plus defender in center field thanks to excellent routes and reads. His speed is average, but he has excellent body control and goes back into gaps extremely well. He has a plus arm. Celestino adjusted his grip in 2018 and worked to better cover the outer half with an improved stance and a quicker trigger in 2019. His ability to make adjustments reflects well on his feel for hitting and is why it's possible to project him as a future above-average hitter. He also added some muscle and has shown the promise of future fringe-average power.

THE FUTURE: Even though he has just nine games above low Class A, the Twins added Celestino to the 40-man roster to keep him out of the Rule 5 draft. Celestino's center field defense gives him a solid shot to be a regular, but also makes him a viable fourth outfield candidate if his bat doesn't reach expectations.

Year	Age	Club (League)	Class	AVG	G	AB	R	H	2B	3B	HR	RBI	BB	SO	SB	OBP	SLG
2017	18	Greeneville (APP)	R	.268	59	235	38	63	10	2	4	24	22	59	10	.331	.379
2018	19	Corpus Christi (TL)	AA	.000	3	8	0	0	0	0	0	0	0	5	0	.000	.000
	19	Tri-City (NYP)	SS	.323	34	127	18	41	8	0	4	21	10	25	14	.387	.480
	19	Elizabethton (APP)	R	.266	27	109	13	29	4	1	1	13	6	16	8	.308	.349
2019	20	Cedar Rapids (MWL)	LoA	.276	117	450	52	124	24	3	10	51	48	81	14	.350	.409
	20	Fort Myers (FSL)	HiA	.300	8	30	6	9	4	0	0	3	2	4	0	.333	.433
Minor League Totals				.274	304	1150	156	315	62	10	21	131	121	229	61	.346	.400

14 BRENT ROOKER, OF/1B

BA GRADE 45 **Risk:** Medium

Born: Nov. 1, 1994. **B-T:** R-R. **HT:** 6-3. **WT:** 215. **Drafted:** Mississippi State, 2017 (1st round supplemental). **Signed by:** Derrick Dunbar.

TRACK RECORD: Rooker added loft to his swing for his senior season and led the nation in doubles and total bases at Mississippi State to gain notice from scouts. Rooker has averaged a home run every 20 plate appearances as a pro but saw his 2019 season hampered by a left wrist injury.

SCOUTING REPORT: Rooker has the power to hit 25 home runs or more while drawing enough walks to offset a below-average hit tool. Plenty of strikeouts are a price to be paid for his power. The Twins have tried Rooker in left field and at first base, but he's below-average at either spot. His hands and reactions are poor at first and his routes and below-average speed limit him in left. He runs the bases well.

THE FUTURE: Rooker has the power to be a productive regular, but without a clear defensive position it will be tough for him to earn that shot. He has a chance to fit in the Twins' DH/first base mix in 2020.

Year	Age	Club (League)	Class	AVG	G	AB	R	H	2B	3B	HR	RBI	BB	SO	SB	OBP	SLG
2017	22	Elizabethton (APP)	R	.282	22	85	19	24	5	0	7	17	11	21	2	.364	.588
	22	Fort Myers (FSL)	HiA	.280	40	143	23	40	6	0	11	35	16	47	0	.364	.552
2018	23	Chattanooga (SL)	AA	.254	130	503	72	128	32	4	22	79	56	150	6	.333	.465
2019	24	Rochester (IL)	AAA	.281	65	228	41	64	16	0	14	47	35	95	2	.398	.535
	24	Twins (GCL)	R	.333	2	6	2	2	0	0	0	0	1	0	0	.429	.333
Minor League Totals				.267	259	965	157	258	59	4	54	178	119	313	10	.357	.505

15 RANDY DOBNAK, RHP

BA GRADE 45 **Risk:** Medium

Born: Jan. 17, 1995. **B-T:** R-R. **HT:** 6-1. **WT:** 230. **Signed:** Utica (United Shore), 2017. **Signed by:** Billy Milos.

TRACK RECORD: Dobnak went undrafted and began his pro career with a successful stint with the independent United States Professional Baseball League. The Twins signed him, helped him make a few tweaks and watched him rocket through the minors in 2019. He started the year in high Class A and finished it by starting Game 2 of the Division Series at Yankee Stadium.

SCOUTING REPORT: Dobnak quickly took to the Twins' emphasis on one-seam fastballs, which added more sink to his heavy 90-95 mph fastball. He pairs the pitch with a 91-96 four-seamer used up in the zone. The fastballs are effective because he has plus control and command. He also spots his above-average mid-80s changeup well and his mid-80s average curveball is hard with modest downward break. Dobnak makes it all work by staying one step ahead of hitters, spotting all four pitches to the corners. None is a true swing-and-miss offering, but Dobnak throws all four with plus control.

THE FUTURE: The Twins have prospects with better stuff, but few have Dobnak's feel, control and guts. He can help the club as a swing starter/reliever.

Year	Age	Club (League)	Class	W	L	ERA	G	GS	SV	IP	H	HR	BB	SO	K/9	WHIP	AVG
2017	22	Utica (USL)	IND	3	0	2.31	6	6	0	35	22	2	6	29	7.5	0.80	--
	22	Elizabethton (APP)	R	2	0	2.39	5	3	1	26	19	3	6	22	7.5	0.95	.198
	22	Cedar Rapids (MWL)	LoA	0	0	2.57	1	1	0	7	6	0	1	1	1.3	1.00	.240
2018	23	Cedar Rapids (MWL)	LoA	10	5	3.14	24	20	0	129	138	6	25	84	5.9	1.26	.274
2019	24	Fort Myers (FSL)	HiA	3	0	0.40	4	4	0	22	18	0	4	14	5.6	0.99	.225
	24	Pensacola (SL)	AA	4	2	2.57	11	10	0	67	58	6	6	61	8.2	0.96	.231
	24	Rochester (IL)	AAA	5	2	2.15	9	7	0	46	28	0	18	34	6.7	1.00	.175
	24	Minnesota (AL)	MAJ	2	1	1.59	9	5	1	28	27	1	5	23	7.3	1.13	.246
Major League Totals				2	1	1.59	9	5	1	28	27	1	5	23	7.3	1.13	.245
Minor League Totals				24	9	2.57	54	45	1	297	267	15	60	216	6.5	1.10	.239

16 NICK GORDON, SS/2B

BA GRADE
45 **Risk: Medium**

Born: Oct. 24, 1995. **B-T:** L-R. **HT:** 6-0. **WT:** 160. **Drafted:** HS—Orlando, 2014 (1st round). **Signed by:** Brett Dowdy.

TRACK RECORD: After a setback in 2018 when he struggled in his first exposure to Triple-A, Gordon's 2019 season got off to a delayed start because of a stomach issue that led to lost weight and diminished strength. Gordon was still noticeably lighter at the end of the season, but he regained some of the strength later in the year. His season ended early thanks to a contusion on his left leg, but he was having a solid year for Triple-A Rochester before he went down.

SCOUTING REPORT: Gordon doesn't have a true plus tool, but he should have an MLB career thanks to his ability to play average defense at shortstop and above-average defense at second base. There's hope that he'll regain some pop in his bat as he regains weight, but he projects as a fringe-average hitter with below-average power. His arm got better as the season progressed and by the end of the season he was making plays from the hole that he was bouncing in spring training. He's an average runner.

THE FUTURE: With Jonathan Schoop departing, Gordon has a shot of playing in Minnesota in 2020 at second base or as a backup middle infielder.

Year	Age	Club (League)	Class	AVG	G	AB	R	H	2B	3B	HR	RBI	BB	SO	SB	OBP	SLG
2017	21	Chattanooga (SL)	AA	.270	122	519	80	140	29	8	9	66	53	134	13	.341	.408
2018	22	Chattanooga (SL)	AA	.333	42	162	22	54	10	3	5	20	11	27	7	.381	.525
	22	Rochester (IL)	AAA	.212	99	382	40	81	13	4	2	29	23	82	13	.262	.283
2019	23	Rochester (IL)	AAA	.298	70	292	49	87	29	3	4	40	18	65	14	.342	.459
Minor League Totals				.276	626	2532	372	698	133	35	25	293	178	528	102	.329	.385

17 LEWIS THORPE, LHP

BA GRADE
45 **Risk: Medium**

Born: Nov. 23, 1995. **B-T:** R-L. **Ht.:** 6-1. **Wt.:** 218. **Signed:** Australia, 2012. **Signed by:** Howard Norsetter.

TRACK RECORD: Considered one of the best amateur baseball prospects in Australian history, Thorpe's career was derailed when Tommy John surgery followed by mononucleosis cost him all of 2015 and 2016. When he returned in 2017, his velocity had diminished but not enough to keep him from making his big league debut in 2019.

SCOUTING REPORT: No longer a fireballer, Thorpe now relies on above-average command and some deception to make his average, 89-93 mph fastball effective. His best weapon is a plus slider that he can manipulate into behaving like a cutter. He can tighten it and make is a hard high-80s cutter and he can also throw a bigger, sweepier slider that he locates well to the bottom corner of the strike zone glove-side. His below-average mid-80s changeup and below-average mid-70s curveball are best used in small doses.

THE FUTURE: Thorpe has consistently picked up strikeouts in the minors thanks to his slider, but like Devin Smeltzer and Randy Dobnak, he's a back-of-the-rotation arm. There's likely room for one of them in the rotation, but it's hard to see all three fitting at the same time.

Year	Age	Club (League)	Class	W	L	ERA	G	GS	SV	IP	H	HR	BB	SO	K/9	WHIP	AVG
2017	21	Chattanooga (SL)	AA	1	0	6.00	1	1	0	6	5	2	2	7	10.5	1.17	.217
	21	Fort Myers (FSL)	HiA	3	4	2.69	16	15	0	77	62	3	31	84	9.8	1.21	.226
2018	22	Chattanooga (SL)	AA	8	4	3.58	22	21	0	108	105	13	30	131	10.9	1.25	.251
	22	Rochester (IL)	AAA	0	3	3.32	4	4	0	22	20	3	6	26	10.8	1.20	.244
2019	23	Rochester (IL)	AAA	5	4	4.58	20	19	0	96	91	13	25	119	11.1	1.20	.244
	23	Minnesota (AL)	MAJ	3	2	6.18	12	2	0	28	38	3	10	31	10.1	1.73	.336
Major League Totals				3	2	6.18	12	2	0	27	38	3	10	31	10.1	1.73	.336
Minor League Totals				24	18	3.50	91	84	0	424	377	43	136	511	10.8	1.21	.236

18 JORGE ALCALA, RHP

BA GRADE 50 Risk: High

Born: July 28, 1995. **B-T:** R-R. **HT:** 6-3. **WT:** 205. **Signed:** Dominican Republic, 2014. **Signed by:** Oz Ocampo/Roman Ocumarez/Leocadio Guevara (Astros).

BACKGROUND: The Astros have a propensity for signing projectable pitchers with fast arms who have been overlooked because they are a little older. Alcala fit that bill perfectly as the Astros signed him as an 18-year-old, helped him gain nearly 10 mph of velocity and then shipped him to the Twins in the Ryan Pressly swap in 2018. With the Twins, Alcala has struggled as a starter. He was moved to the bullpen to see if he could help the team during its playoff run, but he pitched very sparingly in Minnesota in September.

SCOUTING REPORT: Alcala has a big plus fastball, although it was more often in the mid-90s in 2019, down a tick from the high-90s he's shown in the past. It doesn't have elite spin or movement, but if he's throwing strikes, it still has enough hair on it to be effective. His 84-87 mph power slider has modest depth. Alcala has a problem with limiting damage in big innings. Once he gets in trouble, he struggles pitching from the stretch (opponents hit .306 against him with runners on). Alcala has shown flashes of having an average or even above-average changeup, but it's not a pitch he can regularly rely on.

THE FUTURE: Alcala continues to need to improve his below-average control to start or be an high-leverage reliever, but he should pitch in Minnesota in 2020.

Year	Age	Club (League)	Class	W	L	ERA	G	GS	SV	IP	H	HR	BB	SO	K/9	WHIP	AVG
2017	21	Quad Cities (MWL)	LoA	2	0	2.03	6	4	0	31	16	3	12	35	10.2	0.90	.155
	21	Buies Creek (CAR)	HiA	5	6	3.45	16	14	0	78	55	7	33	60	6.9	1.12	.200
2018	22	Buies Creek (CAR)	HiA	1	4	3.03	10	7	2	39	25	2	18	45	10.5	1.11	.182
	22	Corpus Christi (TL)	AA	2	3	3.54	9	5	1	41	36	1	17	37	8.2	1.30	.243
	22	Chattanooga (SL)	AA	0	4	5.85	5	4	0	20	23	4	14	22	9.9	1.85	.280
2019	23	Pensacola (SL)	AA	5	7	5.87	26	16	0	103	114	12	37	105	9.2	1.47	.284
	23	Rochester (IL)	AAA	1	0	0.00	5	0	0	8	4	0	2	11	12.9	0.78	.154
	23	Minnesota (AL)	MAJ	0	0	0.00	2	0	0	2	1	0	1	1	5.4	1.20	.167
Major League Totals				0	0	0.00	2	0	0	1	1	0	1	1	5.4	1.20	.167
Minor League Totals				21	27	3.80	104	62	5	407	346	30	170	405	9.0	1.27	.231

19 LAMONTE WADE, OF

BA GRADE 40 Risk: Low

Born: Jan. 1, 1994. **B-T:** L-L. **HT:** 6-1. **WT:** 205. **Drafted:** Maryland, 2015 (9th round). **Signed by:** John Wilson.

TRACK RECORD: Wade has had a knack for being a productive player wherever he plays. He missed some time in 2019 with a thumb injury, but returned to make his MLB debut. Wade's value is largely tied to a very discerning batting eye and his solid athleticism.

SCOUTING REPORT: Wade fits the profile of a useful backup outfielder. He is extremely patient at the plate. He has the barrel control to survive with two strikes, forcing pitchers to make an extra pitch or two. What keeps him from being a regular is his below-average power. He has some strength, but his swing is geared for line drives and ground balls. He is an above-average runner, but he's fringy defensively in center field and fits better in a left field because of a fringe-average arm.

THE FUTURE: Wade's ability to get on base makes him a useful fourth outfielder and he can play all three outfield spots, although he's not a viable long-term backup plan for oft-injured Byron Buxton in center field. He will compete for a big league roster spot in spring training.

Year	Age	Club (League)	Class	AVG	G	AB	R	H	2B	3B	HR	RBI	BB	SO	SB	OBP	SLG
2017	23	Chattanooga (SL)	AA	.292	117	424	74	124	22	3	7	67	76	71	9	.397	.408
2018	24	Chattanooga (SL)	AA	.298	46	171	30	51	2	1	7	27	26	20	5	.393	.444
	24	Rochester (IL)	AAA	.229	74	253	24	58	9	3	4	21	38	54	5	.337	.336
2019	25	Rochester (IL)	AAA	.246	77	264	47	65	12	1	5	24	56	48	7	.392	.356
	25	Cedar Rapids (MWL)	LoA	.133	4	15	1	2	0	0	0	0	3	5	0	.278	.133
	25	Pensacola (SL)	AA	.238	6	21	3	5	3	0	0	3	3	3	0	.333	.381
	25	Minnesota (AL)	MAJ	.196	26	56	10	11	2	1	2	5	11	9	0	.348	.375
Major League Totals				.196	26	56	10	11	2	1	2	5	11	9	0	.348	.375
Minor League Totals				.276	480	1710	265	472	70	17	40	238	303	281	44	.389	.407

20 MATT WALLNER, OF

Born: Dec. 12, 1997. **B-T:** L-R. **HT:** 6-5. **WT:** 220. **Drafted:** Southern Mississippi, 2019 (1st round supplemental). **Signed by:** Derrick Dunbar.

TRACK RECORD: Wallner arrived at Southern Miss as a potential two-way star but he preferred hitting to pitching and by his junior season he focused entirely on being an outfielder. He slugged over .600 in all three seasons at Southern Miss and ranked fifth in Division I with 23 home runs in 2019. He also holds Southern Miss' record for career home runs (58).

SCOUTING REPORT: Wallner fits the bill of a power-hitting right fielder with an excellent frame, power and a right fielder's arm. He has to produce 25-plus home run power to be a useful MLB regular because he's a below-average hitter who relies on pouncing on mistakes. He has the potential to do that, with plus-plus raw power and he's shown a consistent ability to get pitches to drive. He has a strong base and uses his legs well in his swing. He is a below-average outfielder, but his plus arm is quite useful in right.

THE FUTURE: The question Wallner has to answer moving forward is whether he has enough feel for hitting to survive against more advanced pitching. He likely will start with low Class A Cedar Rapids, but should spend plenty of time in Fort Myers if he starts strong.

Year	Age	Club (League)	Class	AVG	G	AB	R	H	2B	3B	HR	RBI	BB	SO	SB	OBP	SLG
2019	21	Elizabethton (APP)	R	.269	53	208	35	56	18	1	6	28	19	66	1	.361	.452
	21	Cedar Rapids (MWL)	LoA	.205	12	44	7	9	3	1	2	6	5	14	0	.340	.455
Minor League Totals				.258	65	252	42	65	21	2	8	34	24	80	1	.357	.452

21 AKIL BADDOO, OF

BA GRADE
50 Risk: High

Born: Aug. 16, 1998. **B-T:** L-L. **HT:** 6-1. **WT:** 210. **Drafted:** HS—Conyers, Ga., 2016 (2nd round supplemental). **Signed by:** Jack Powell.

TRACK RECORD: Baddoo was seen as a promising, athletic high school outfielder who may need a little extra development time as a supplemental second round pick. He spent two seasons in rookie ball, then produced a solid season at low Class A Cedar Rapids in 2018. Any chance to build on that in 2019 was wiped away by an elbow injury that required season-ending Tommy John surgery.

SCOUTING REPORT: Baddoo has gotten significantly bigger and more physical since signing with the Twins. He has plus speed with the potential to eventually have above-average power. He has a knack to avoid chasing pitches off the strike zone and projects as a fringe-average hitter with above-average power potential. Defensively, his plus speed gives him a shot to stay in center field, but he needs to continue to improve his routes and reads. His arm was below-average before surgery.

THE FUTURE: Baddoo's lost season turns 2020 into a pivotal year. If he has a strong return at high Class A Fort Myers he will likely play his way onto the 40-man roster before the 2021 season. He has the tools to be an MLB starting outfielder, although his bat has a ways to go to get to that upside.

Year	Age	Club (League)	Class	AVG	G	AB	R	H	2B	3B	HR	RBI	BB	SO	SB	OBP	SLG
2017	18	Twins (GCL)	R	.267	20	75	18	20	4	3	1	10	9	13	4	.360	.440
	18	Elizabethton (APP)	R	.357	33	126	39	45	15	2	3	19	27	19	5	.478	.579
2018	19	Cedar Rapids (MWL)	LoA	.243	113	437	83	106	22	11	11	40	74	124	24	.351	.419
2019	20	Fort Myers (FSL)	HiA	.214	29	117	15	25	3	3	4	9	12	39	6	.290	.393
Minor League Totals				.249	233	862	170	215	44	21	21	93	140	231	47	.357	.422

22 COLE SANDS, RHP

BA GRADE
50 Risk: High

Born: July 17, 1997. **B-T:** R-R. **HT:** 6-3. **WT:** 215. **Drafted:** Florida State, 2018 (5th round). **Signed by:** Brett Dowdy.

TRACK RECORD: The younger brother of Carson Sands, a lefthander who reached low Class A in four seasons with the Cubs, Cole went to Florida State and became the team's ace as a junior. The Twins didn't let him pitch in 2018, shutting him down to let him recover from bicep tendinitis he had that spring. In 2019, his bicep was fine. He did go on the injured list twice thanks to a calf injury and a blister.

SCOUTING REPORT: Sands is a strike-throwing righthander who succeeds thanks to plus control and a plus changeup. His 91-97 mph fastball sits at around 93 mph and is a solid average pitch. His changeup has some fade and sink, diving out of the zone. He needs to further develop his slider and curve, but both show promise. His slider has well-above-average 2,700 rpm spin rate. It has some depth to it, but is inconsistent. His curveball shows high spin rates but is slurvy. Both have promise to be potentially average pitches. His ability to locate and his command gives everything a chance to play up.

THE FUTURE: Sands has a clean delivery, a strong frame and an ability to find the strike zone. It gives him a solid path to being a back-end starter. The effectiveness of his changeup gives him a fallback option as a reliever if his breaking balls don't progress.

Year	Age	Club (League)	Class	W	L	ERA	G	GS	SV	IP	H	HR	BB	SO	K/9	WHIP	AVG
2018	20	Did not play—Injured															
2019	21	Cedar Rapids (MWL)	LoA	2	1	3.05	8	8	0	41	41	0	11	49	10.7	1.26	.258
	21	Fort Myers (FSL)	HiA	5	2	2.25	9	9	0	52	36	4	7	53	9.2	0.83	.199
	21	Pensacola (SL)	AA	0	0	4.50	1	1	0	4	4	0	1	6	13.5	1.25	.267
Minor League Totals				7	3	2.68	18	18	0	97	81	4	19	108	10.0	1.03	.228

23 TRAVIS BLANKENHORN, 2B/OF

BA GRADE
45 Risk: High

Born: August 3, 1996. **B-T:** L-R. **HT:** 6-2. **WT:** 228. **Drafted:** HS—Pottsville, Pa., 2015 (3rd round). **Signed by:** Jay Weitzel.

TRACK RECORD: A high school basketball star who also played cornerback and wide receiver, Blankenhorn has slowly climbed through the Twins minor league system, usually starting a season back where he finished the previous one. He's steadily improved and had his best year in 2019.

SCOUTING REPORT: Blankenhorn worked to better utilize his lower half in his swing in 2019. The results weren't immediately apparent and he struggled in the Arizona Fall League, but he has plus power potential, even if his aggressiveness and batting eye will likely limit him to a below-average hit tool. The biggest question is where he will play. He is a fringe-average defender at second base and below-average at third. His range is limited and his reactions and hands are stretched at third. His average speed also works in left field, which he began playing regularly in 2019. His average arm is adequate for either second or left.

THE FUTURE: The Twins added Blankenhorn to their 40-man roster, a sign of their belief that his power will help him find an MLB role. If he doesn't find a defensive home, he will likely be a role player.

Year	Age	Club (League)	Class	AVG	G	AB	R	H	2B	3B	HR	RBI	BB	SO	SB	OBP	SLG
2017	20	Cedar Rapids (MWL)	LoA	.251	117	438	68	110	22	11	13	69	46	119	13	.342	.441
2018	21	Fort Myers (FSL)	HiA	.231	124	442	52	102	24	6	11	57	34	127	6	.299	.387
2019	22	Fort Myers (FSL)	HiA	.269	15	52	6	14	4	0	1	3	9	12	0	.377	.404
	22	Pensacola (SL)	AA	.278	93	388	50	108	18	2	18	51	18	93	11	.312	.474
Minor League Totals				.257	462	1742	237	448	87	24	56	244	142	455	38	.325	.431

24 LUKE RALEY, OF

BA GRADE
45 Risk: High

Born: Sept. 19, 1994. **B-T:** L-R. **HT:** 6-4. **WT:** 235. **Drafted:** Lake Erie (Ohio), 2016 (7th round). **Signed by:** Marty Lamb (Dodgers).

TRACK RECORD: The Twins were very excited to receive Raley in the 2018 trade that sent Brian Dozier to Los Angeles. A season and a half later, they are still excited, but they also are hopeful they will finally get to see what he can do over a full season. A shoulder injury limited him to four games in the Arizona Fall League in 2018 and an ankle injury cost him most of the 2019 season.

SCOUTING REPORT: Raley has plus-plus raw power that he is beginning to better tap into in games He hits from an open, upright stance with quiet hands. Raley is aggressive at the plate and needs to better control the strike zone, but he has solid bat-to-ball skills and a simple, repeatable swing that gives him a shot to be an average hitter. He has always put together good at-bats against lefties. He's a good athlete with average speed and plays above-average defense in the corner outfield spots and is playable in a pinch in center. He has an above-average arm.

THE FUTURE: The Twins added Raley to the 40-man roster during the offseason. As a lefthanded power hitter who can play first base and the corner outfield spots capably, he isn't far from an MLB role, although his bat will have to continue to improve for him to be an MLB regular.

Year	Age	Club (League)	Class	AVG	G	AB	R	H	2B	3B	HR	RBI	BB	SO	SB	OBP	SLG
2017	22	R. Cucamonga (CAL)	HiA	.295	123	478	102	141	21	11	14	62	43	124	9	.375	.473
2018	23	Tulsa (TL)	AA	.275	93	386	65	106	17	5	17	53	24	105	3	.345	.477
	23	Chattanooga (SL)	AA	.276	27	98	15	27	2	3	3	16	12	32	1	.371	.449
2019	24	Rochester (IL)	AAA	.302	33	126	28	38	6	0	7	21	7	42	4	.362	.516
	24	Twins (GCL)	R	.368	5	19	1	7	0	0	1	2	0	2	0	.350	.526
Minor League Totals				.288	347	1347	245	388	60	25	46	178	104	355	21	.361	.472

25 BEN RORTVEDT, C

BA GRADE
45 Risk: High

Born: Sept. 25, 1997. **B-T:** L-R. **HT:** 5-10. **WT:** 205. **Drafted:** HS—Verona, Wis., 2016 (2nd round). **Signed by:** Mark Wilson.

TRACK RECORD: Concerns about Rortvedt's bat have somewhat come true, but he's proven to be an even better defender than projected. Rortvedt's season ended in early August as he finished the year on the injured list with a knee injury. He should be fine to start the 2020 season.

SCOUTING REPORT: Rortvedt is one of the more athletic and flexible receivers in the minors. He is a plus

defender with a plus arm and plus accuracy, making him a significant asset behind the plate. There's not a lot of projection in his bat. He has modest pull power, but he doesn't generate consistent enough contact to get to it regularly. With a slow bat, he projects as a below-average hitter with below-average power.
THE FUTURE: In a league where pitch framing is valued, Rortvedt can truly help a big league club thanks to his ability to help pitchers get borderline pitches called as strikes. But if MLB switches to an automated system for ball and strikes, his biggest asset disappears and he would be much less valuable as a prospect.

Year	Age	Club (League)	Class	AVG	G	AB	R	H	2B	3B	HR	RBI	BB	SO	SB	OBP	SLG
2017	19	Cedar Rapids (MWL)	LoA	.224	88	304	33	68	16	0	4	30	22	60	1	.284	.316
2018	20	Cedar Rapids (MWL)	LoA	.276	39	145	14	40	9	2	1	16	10	35	1	.325	.386
	20	Fort Myers (FSL)	HiA	.250	51	172	20	43	7	1	4	27	21	29	0	.337	.372
2019	21	Fort Myers (FSL)	HiA	.238	24	80	13	19	8	1	2	10	12	16	0	.340	.438
	21	Pensacola (SL)	AA	.239	55	197	19	47	8	0	5	19	23	51	0	.332	.355
Minor League Totals				.240	291	1001	104	240	51	4	16	112	98	201	2	.315	.347

26 EMMANUEL RODRIGUEZ, OF

BA GRADE 50 Risk: Extreme

Born: Feb. 28, 2003. **B-T:** L-L. **Ht.:** 5-11. **Wt.:** 200. **Signed:** Dominican Republic, 2019. **Signed by:** Manuel Luciano.

TRACK RECORD: The Twins' biggest-ticket signing of the 2019 international class, Rodriguez signed for $2.5 million. The Twins were impressed with his ability to potentially develop as a hitter and a slugger.
SCOUTING REPORT: Rodriguez has a low-maintenance swing with a simple setup and a direct bat path. He has shown an improved ability to use the whole field and is starting to develop the ability to drive the ball to the left-center power alley. Rodriguez is quickly morphing from a speedy center fielder into a slugging corner outfielder. He's slowed down to be an average runner as he's added weight and strength. His above-average arm should work in right field and he's reasonably advanced in his routes and reads.
THE FUTURE: Rodriguez is expected to head to the Dominican Summer League for his pro debut in 2020. His bat is reasonably advanced and should help him move quickly for a teenager.

Year	Age	Club (League)	Class	AVG	G	AB	R	H	2B	3B	HR	RBI	BB	SO	SB	OBP	SLG
2019	16	Did not play—Signed 2020 contract															

27 JOSH WINDER, RHP

BA GRADE 45 Risk: High

Born: Oct. 11, 1996. **B-T:** R-R. **HT:** 6-5. **WT:** 210. **Drafted:** Virginia Military Institute, 2018 (7th round). **Signed by:** Matt Williams.

TRACK RECORD: After an excellent sophomore season, Winder struggled as a junior. He continued to throw plenty of strikes, but those strikes were hit harder and more often. The Twins stayed on him however and a year later, he led the Midwest League with a 2.65 ERA, a .205 average against and a 0.98 WHIP.
SCOUTING REPORT: Winder attacks hitters up and down in the zone with an over-the-top delivery. His 91-94 mph fastball is average at its core, but he locates it well. His 12-to-6 low 80s curveball and his short mid-80s cutterish slider are both average as well. The fastball and curve pair well together and with his above-average changeup that has deception and some depth. He has above-average control and his feel for pitching helps him stay one step ahead of hitters.
THE FUTURE: The Twins were conservative with Winder in 2019, as they let him build on success by staying at low Class A Cedar Rapids all season. If he can do the same in 2020, his rate of advancement should speed up. He is a back-end starter who will have to back up his modest stuff against more advanced hitters.

Year	Age	Club (League)	Class	W	L	ERA	G	GS	SV	IP	H	HR	BB	SO	K/9	WHIP	AVG
2018	21	Elizabethton (APP)	R	3	1	3.72	9	9	0	39	37	1	6	42	9.8	1.11	.248
2019	22	Cedar Rapids (MWL)	LoA	7	2	2.65	21	21	0	126	93	10	30	118	8.5	0.98	.205
Minor League Totals				10	3	2.90	30	30	0	164	130	11	36	160	8.8	1.01	.216

28 EDWAR COLINA, RHP

BA GRADE 45 Risk: High

Born: May 3, 1997. **B-T:** R-R. **HT:** 5-11. **WT:** 240. **Signed:** Venezuela, 2015. **Signed by:** Jose Leon.

TRACK RECORD: Colina is a short righthander, but he's not small. And ever since the Twins signed him as an older-than-usual international signee, Colina has been effective. He climbed from the Dominican Summer League to Triple-A in just four years.
SCOUTING REPORT: If Colina has his way, he would join Royals righthander Brad Keller as the only MLB starter to qualify for the ERA title throwing two pitches more than 95 percent of the time. Like Keller, he's a fastball-slider pitcher without a real third pitch and his fastball and slider can both be quite impressive.

He sits 94-96 mph over longer outings (and 97-98 in bursts) and his plus fastball has premium sink and run when he elevates. His mid-80s slider is also plus, generating a lot of whiffs with tilt. Colina works East-West, busting righthanders on their hands with his fastball and then running his slider away from them. He has been effective against lefties as well, although they feasted on him in two late-season starts at Triple-A. His control has steadily gotten better, but it is only fringe-average.
THE FUTURE: Most likely, Colina ends up as a reliever thanks to his lack of a third pitch and what will likely be struggles against more advanced lefthanded hitters. But Keller gives him a template to try to follow. He's ready for Triple-A Rochester.

Year	Age	Club (League)	Class	W	L	ERA	G	GS	SV	IP	H	HR	BB	SO	K/9	WHIP	AVG
2017	20	Elizabethton (APP)	R	3	5	3.34	12	11	0	59	48	6	29	56	8.5	1.30	.219
2018	21	Cedar Rapids (MWL)	LoA	7	4	2.48	19	18	0	98	71	4	50	95	8.7	1.23	.200
	21	Fort Myers (FSL)	HiA	0	1	3.97	2	2	0	11	13	1	3	11	8.7	1.41	.289
2019	22	Fort Myers (FSL)	HiA	4	2	2.34	10	10	0	62	53	3	15	61	8.9	1.10	.233
	22	Pensacola (SL)	AA	4	0	2.03	7	4	0	31	21	0	15	37	10.7	1.16	.194
	22	Rochester (IL)	AAA	0	0	17.36	2	0	0	5	8	1	2	4	7.7	2.14	.364
Minor League Totals				19	15	2.80	66	58	0	324	257	16	140	316	8.8	1.22	.216

29 CODY STASHAK, RHP

BA GRADE
40 Risk: Medium

Born: June 4, 1994. **B-T:** R-R. **HT:** 6-2. **WT:** 169. **Drafted:** St. John's, 2015 (13th round). **Signed by:** John Wilson.

TRACK RECORD: After starting his collegiate career at Cumberland County (N.J.) JC, Stashak transferred to St. John's as a junior and was picked by the Twins in the 13th round of the 2015 draft.Four years later, Stashak made his MLB debut on July 23 and ended up on the club's postseason roster.
SCOUTING REPORT: When the Twins drafted Stashak, he was a skinny 170-pounder. He's still skinny now, but he has added 2-3 mph working out of the bullpen. Even with that, his velocity is pedestrian. He sits 91-93 mph with an average fastball but he locates it well thanks to plus command and plus-plus control. His fastball is best setting up his plus 81-83 mph slider. It's a short pitch with modest vertical depth, but it generates plenty of swinging strikes. He also mixes in a fringe-average changeup, mainly to lefties.
THE FUTURE: As a reliever with options who can throw strikes, Stashak should be a useful low-leverage member of the Twins bullpen.

Year	Age	Club (League)	Class	W	L	ERA	G	GS	SV	IP	H	HR	BB	SO	K/9	WHIP	AVG
2017	23	Fort Myers (FSL)	HiA	3	4	3.89	16	16	0	83	72	7	20	72	7.8	1.10	.236
	23	Twins (GCL)	R	1	0	3.18	3	0	0	6	5	0	0	8	12.7	0.88	.238
	23	Chattanooga (SL)	AA	0	0	0.00	3	0	0	6	4	0	0	10	15.0	0.67	.191
2018	24	Fort Myers (FSL)	HiA	1	0	4.50	2	0	0	4	2	1	2	5	11.3	1.00	.143
	24	Chattanooga (SL)	AA	1	1	2.75	35	2	4	56	47	4	13	69	11.2	1.08	.230
2019	25	Pensacola (SL)	AA	2	3	4.76	19	0	4	28	28	4	5	40	12.7	1.16	.250
	25	Rochester (IL)	AAA	5	0	1.44	14	2	0	25	17	1	4	34	12.2	0.84	.185
	25	Minnesota (AL)	MAJ	0	1	3.24	18	1	0	25	29	3	1	25	9.0	1.20	.287
Major League Totals				0	1	3.24	18	1	0	25	29	3	1	25	9.0	1.20	.287
Minor League Totals				28	15	3.15	123	50	9	374	317	25	88	381	9.2	1.08	.229

30 WANDER JAVIER, SS

BA GRADE
50 Risk: Extreme

Born: Dec. 29, 1998. **B-T:** R-R. **HT:** 6-1. **WT:** 165. **Signed:** Dominican Republic, 2015. **Signed by:** Fred Guerrero.

TRACK RECORD: Javier was one of the top amateur prospects in the 2015-2016 international signing class, as Minnesota signed him to a team-record $4 million bonus. He seemed right on track through his first two pro years, but he missed all of 2018 with left shoulder surgery. Slowed by a quad injury in spring training, he returned to action in 2019, but looked little like the five-tool prospect he was pre-injury.
SCOUTING REPORT: Javier did show some power for Cedar Rapids and he still is one of the best gloves the Twins have, but other than that, almost all of his tools suffered during his year-long layoff. He didn't have the explosiveness he had pre-injury as he didn't run as well. He looked lost at the plate for much of the season. He generally was battling from behind in the count and failed to make adjustments at the plate.
THE FUTURE: If 2018 was a lost season, the 2019 season was a big step backwards. Javier needs to show significant improvement in 2020. He was left unprotected for the Rule 5 draft.

Year	Age	Club (League)	Class	AVG	G	AB	R	H	2B	3B	HR	RBI	BB	SO	SB	OBP	SLG
2017	18	Elizabethton (APP)	R	.299	41	157	34	47	13	1	4	22	19	49	4	.383	.471
2018	19	Did not play—Injured															
2019	20	Cedar Rapids (MWL)	LoA	.177	80	300	43	53	9	1	11	37	35	116	2	.278	.323
Minor League Totals				.224	130	483	84	108	25	2	17	65	58	170	6	.319	.389

New York Mets

BY MATT EDDY

Jacob deGrom won his second straight National League Cy Young Award. Pete Alonso established a rookie record with 53 home runs. The club's offense ranked second in the NL in park-adjusted OPS+ and its starting pitchers turned in the fourth lowest ERA in the league.

Yet for all that individual and departmental achievement, the Mets failed to reach the postseason for a third straight season in 2019, undone by a shaky bullpen and porous defense, the same flaws that were evident in 2017 and 2018.

New York finished last in the NL with minus-91 defensive runs saved, a total that tied the 108-loss Orioles for the worst in baseball. Mets relievers registered a 4.99 ERA that ranked third worst in the NL.

The Mets' bullpen foibles were heightened by the collapse of offseason acquisition Edwin Diaz, who allowed 2.3 home runs per nine innings, the worst rate ever for a pitcher with at least 20 saves. Diaz regressed badly after an all-star season with the Mariners, but contrasting his season with that of the player for whom he was traded made the situation worse.

The Mets dealt 20-year-old outfielder Jarred Kelenic, the sixth overall pick in the 2018 draft, to Seattle in December 2018 as the centerpiece of their deal for Diaz and 36-year-old second baseman Robinson Cano. The deal was the first major transaction executed by incoming general manager Brodie Van Wagenen.

In his first year in the Mariners' system, Kelenic zoomed to Double-A and finished the season ranked as the No. 23 prospect in baseball. If Kelenic pans out and sticks in center field, his loss will be acutely felt by the Mets, who lack impact or depth at the position.

Kelenic was one of four top-10 caliber prospects surrendered by Van Wagenen in win-now trades in his first year on the job. The most notable other prospect traded was 18-year-old righthander Simeon Woods Richardson, a 2018 second-rounder, who was the headliner sent to the Blue Jays for Marcus Stroman at the 2019 trade deadline.

The GM also traded righthander Justin Dunn and lefty Anthony Kay. They have more modest ceilings as No. 4 or 5 starters but had proximity value in an organization sorely lacking in rotation depth to support its core of deGrom, Stroman, Noah Syndergaard and Steven Matz.

The Mets don't have another prospect who will impact the majors in 2020 the way Alonso did in 2019. The organization's highest-upside prospects are stationed in the low minors, headlined by Dominican shortstop Ronny Mauricio and Venezuelan catcher Francisco Alvarez, the club's top international signees in 2017 and 2018.

ALEX TRAUTWIG/MLB PHOTOS VIA GETTY IMAGES

First baseman Pete Alonso mashed a rookie record 53 home runs in a banner first season.

PROJECTED 2023 LINEUP

Position	Player	Age
Catcher	Francisco Alvarez (2)	21
First Base	Pete Alonso	28
Second Base	Jeff McNeil	31
Third Base	Ronny Mauricio (1)	22
Shortstop	Amed Rosario	27
Left Field	Brett Baty (3)	23
Center Field	Brandon Nimmo	30
Right Field	Michael Conforto	30
No. 1 Starter	Jacob deGrom	35
No. 2 Starter	Noah Syndergaard	30
No. 3 Starter	Marcus Stroman	32
No. 4 Starter	Steven Matz	32
No. 5 Starter	Matt Allan (4)	22
Closer	Edwin Diaz	29

To that foundation New York added three of the most promising prospects in the 2019 draft. The Mets drafted Texas high school third baseman Brett Baty with the No. 12 overall pick, then went over-slot to sign prep righthanders Josh Wolf in the second round and Matt Allan in the third.

Allan ranked as the top high school pitcher in the draft. He fell because of perceived signability concerns, but Florida area scout Jon Updike correctly assessed his price tag, and the Mets got a deal done for $2.5 million. To make the bonus pool money work, scouting director Marc Tramuta and his team had to focus on low-cost college seniors in rounds four through 10.

DEPTH CHART

NEW YORK METS

TOP 2020 ROOKIE: Kevin Smith, LHP. The 6-foot-5 lefty is a leading contender in what appears to be a weak Mets rookie crop. Something about Smith's angle and deception has flummoxed pro hitters.

BREAKOUT PROSPECT: Michel Otañez, RHP. The 22-year-old late bloomer has high-end velocity and a killer slider.

SLEEPER: Jace Beck, RHP. The 6-foot-9 Oklahoma prep righthander sits in the low 90s and has feel for spin. He struck out 10 and walked one in six Gulf Coast League appearances in his pro debut.

SOURCE OF TOP 30 TALENT

Homegrown	27	Acquired	3
College	7	Trade	3
Junior college	0	Rule 5 draft	0
High school	7	Independent league	0
Nondrafted free agent	0	Free agent/waivers	0
International	13		

LF
Quinn Brodey (29)
Adrian Hernandez

CF
Alexander Ramirez (16)
Sam Haggerty (23)
Hansel Moreno
Jake Mangum
Randy Adon
Blaine McIntosh
Gerson Molina

RF
Freddy Valdez (18)
Scott Ota (30)
Luis Medina
Stanley Consuegra

3B
Bretty Baty (3)
Mark Vientos (6)
Jaylen Palmer (20)
Will Toffey
William Lugo

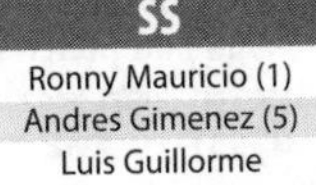

SS
Ronny Mauricio (1)
Andres Gimenez (5)
Luis Guillorme

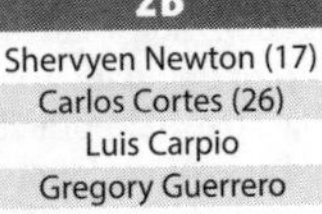

2B
Shervyen Newton (17)
Carlos Cortes (26)
Luis Carpio
Gregory Guerrero

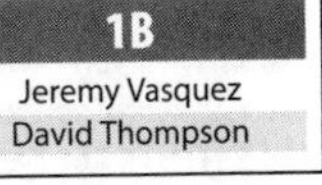

1B
Jeremy Vasquez
David Thompson

C
Francisco Alvarez (2)
Ali Sanchez (28)
Hayden Senger
Patrick Mazeika

LHP

LHSP
Thomas Szapucki (7)
Kevin Smith (9)
David Peterson (10)
Stephen Gonsalves

LHRP
Jake Simon

RHP

RHSP
Matt Allan (4)
Josh Wolf (8)
Jordan Humphreys (11)
Junior Santos (12)
Franklyn Kilome (13)
Michel Otañez (14)
Robert Dominguez (15)
Dedniel Nuñez (21)
Walker Lockett (22)
Tony Dibrell (24)
Nathan Jones
Jace Beck
Tylor Megill
Christian James
David Marcano

RHRP
Jose Butto (19)
Daison Acosta (25)
Ryley Gilliam (27)
Ryder Ryan
Drew Smith
Stephen Nogosek
Bryce Hutchinson
Corey Taylor
Matt Cleveland
Matt Blackham

DRAFT ANALYSIS

2019

BEST PURE HITTER: OF Jake Mangum (4) hit .357 in four years at Mississippi State and set the Southeastern Conference career record with 383 hits. The switch-hitter helped lead the Bulldogs to the College World Series in 2018 and 2019 but appeared gassed while making his pro debut at short-season Brooklyn this summer. Mangum hit .247 in 53 games with the third-lowest strikeout rate in the New York-Penn League.
BEST POWER: 3B Brett Baty (1) went deep seven times in 51 games in a pro debut focused at Rookie-level Kingsport and slugged .525 in his final 25 games in the Appalachian League. The lefthanded-hitting Baty had some of the best power in the high school draft class and proved it during a workout at Citi Field when he hit the ball into the upper deck during batting practice.
FASTEST RUNNER: The Mets threw a dart at OF Blaine McIntosh (13) based on his 70-grade speed and overall athleticism.
BEST DEFENSIVE PLAYER: OF Kennie Taylor (14) is a plus runner and outstanding defensive center fielder. Taylor stood out defensively at short-season Brooklyn, even when playing alongside Mangum and OF Antoine Duplantis (12) of Louisiana State.
BEST ATHLETE: Baty isn't a classic twitchy athlete, but he played three sports at Lake Travis High in Austin and can dunk a basketball. As a senior, he hit .624 with 19 homers in 93 at-bats; the year before he was the Gatorade high school player of the year in Texas.
BEST FASTBALL: The Mets regarded RHP Matt Allan (3) as the top pitcher available in the draft. He pitched at 93-96 mph in his 10-inning pro debut and touched 97 mph with a fastball that could play as double-plus one day. The Orlando area prep fell to the third round because of bonus demands, but the Mets were able to meet his $2.5 million asking price by saving money on picks in rounds four through 10.
BEST SECONDARY PITCH: Allan throws a hard curveball at 77-82 mph with an exceptional spin rate in excess of 2,500 rpm. The pitch projects as a 70-grade weapon and already draws comparisons with breaking pitches thrown by big leaguers. Allan shows advanced command of the pitch.
BEST PRO DEBUT: OF Scott Ota (10) from Illinois-Chicago, ranked fourth in the Rookie-level Appalachian League with a .519 slugging and fifth with an .874 OPS.
MOST INTRIGUING BACKGROUND: Samford SS Branden Fryman (21) is the son of five-time All-Star third baseman Travis Fryman. Branden hit .356 and played shortstop in the 13 games he started at short-season Brooklyn.
CLOSEST TO THE MAJORS: If Mangum doesn't rocket to Queens as an extra outfielder, then this race probably comes down to the top two prospects, Baty and Allan, who ranked 15th and 16th on the BA 500, respectively.
BEST LATE-ROUND PICK: Blanchard (Okla.) High RHP Jace Beck (22) is 6-foot-9, 200 pounds and already touches 92 mph. He offers the projection for more velocity and also could develop an above-average breaking ball.
THE ONE WHO GOT AWAY: The Mets drafted a pair of Florida high school pitchers, LHP Hunter Barco (24) and RHP Joseph Charles (25), as insurance in case they failed to sign Allan.

—MATT EDDY

TOP DRAFT PICKS OF THE DECADE

Year	Player, Pos	2019 Org
2010	Matt Harvey, RHP	Athletics
2011	Brandon Nimmo, OF	Mets
2012	Gavin Cecchini, SS	Mets
2013	Dominic Smith, 1B	Mets
2014	Michael Conforto, OF	Mets
2015	Desmond Lindsay, OF (2nd round)	Mets
2016	Justin Dunn, RHP	Mariners
2017	David Peterson, LHP	Mets
2018	Jarred Kelenic, OF	Mariners
2019	Brett Baty, 3B	Mets

2018

The Mets have mined this class heavily in trades, and OF Jarred Kelenic (1) and RHP Simeon Woods Richardson are thriving in their new organizations. LHP Kevin Smith (7) has emerged as a solid value pick.

GRADE: A

2017

In contrast to the 2018 class, the 2017 class is lacking impact. 3B Mark Vientos (2) is the best of the bunch and LHP David Peterson (1) is nearing Queens, but three years in it's an uninspiring group.

GRADE: D

2016

1B Pete Alonso (2) had a historic 2019 season and was named BA Rookie of the Year. RHP Justin Dunn (1) and LHP Anthony Kay (1) were both used in trades and reached the big leagues with their new teams.

GRADE: A

1 RONNY MAURICIO, SS

Born: April 4, 2001. **B-T:** B-R. **Ht.:** 6-3. **Wt.:** 166.
Signed: Dominican Republic, 2017.
Signed by: Marciano Alvarez/Gerardo Cabrera.

TRACK RECORD: Mauricio ranked as the No. 3 prospect in the 2017 international signing class—Rays shortstop Wander Franco was No. 1—and signed for $2.1 million. That set a franchise bonus record for a Latin American amateur that was surpassed by Venezuelan catcher Francisco Alvarez a year later. Mauricio shined in his pro debut in the Rookie-level Gulf Coast League in 2018. The Mets pushed him to the low Class A South Atlantic League in 2019, where he, Phillies shortstop Luis Garcia and Mariners outfielder Julio Rodriguez were the only 18-year-old regulars on Opening Day. Mauricio impressed scouts enough to rank as the league's No. 5 prospect.

SCOUTING REPORT: Mauricio has the potential to impact games with his bat and as a left-side-of-the-infield defender, though his rosiest outlook is predicated on projection. Mauricio is lanky and long-limbed, and it's an open question as to whether his narrow, 6-foot-3 frame will add significant mass. The good news is that he is an elite athlete who can stay on the dirt and already stands out for making loud contact with an easy swing from both sides of the plate. The bad news is that his long levers create unavoidable length to his swing that could impact his batting average down the line. Mauricio uses an all-fields hitting approach and adjusts well to breaking and offspeed stuff, but he tends to be overaggressive and puts too many pitchers' pitches in play. That contributed to him having one of the highest groundball rates in the SAL. He has no problem dropping the bat head on inside pitches for deep power to his pull side when he's locked in on a pitcher. Scouts came away pleasantly surprised by Mauricio's defensive play. He has the plus arm, body control and quick first step to make all the plays required at shortstop. He won't be a factor on the basepaths because he's a fringe runner who figures to slow down.

THE FUTURE: Scouts who like Mauricio see at least an average hitter with plus power who has the grace and hands of a major league shortstop or possibly a third baseman. The hot corner is probably the position for which he's destined with the Mets, who have pure shortstops Amed Rosario and Andres Gimenez ahead of him. Mauricio should spend the bulk of 2020 at high Class A St. Lucie and begin to enter the big league picture in 2022.

TOM PRIDDY/FOUR SEAM

BA GRADE
60 **Risk: High**

SCOUTING GRADES
Hit: 50. **Power:** 60. **Run:** 40.
Field: 50. **Arm:** 60.

Projected future grades on 20-80 scouting scale.

TOP PROSPECTS OF THE DECADE

Year	Player, Pos.	2019 Org
2010	Jenrry Mejia, RHP	Red Sox
2011	Jenrry Mejia, RHP	Red Sox
2012	Zack Wheeler, RHP	Mets
2013	Zack Wheeler, RHP	Mets
2014	Noah Syndergaard, RHP	Mets
2015	Noah Syndergaard, RHP	Mets
2016	Steven Matz, LHP	Mets
2017	Amed Rosario, SS	Mets
2018	Andres Gimenez, SS	Mets
2019	Andres Gimenez, SS	Mets

BEST TOOLS

Best Hitter for Average	Francisco Alvarez
Best Power Hitter	Brett Baty
Best Strike-Zone Discipline	Brett Baty
Fastest Baserunner	Ranfy Adon
Best Athlete	Ronny Mauricio
Best Fastball	Matt Allan
Best Curveball	Thomas Szapucki
Best Slider:	David Peterson
Best Changeup	Jose Butto
Best Control	Kevin Smith
Best Defensive Catcher	Ali Sanchez
Best Defensive Infielder	Andres Gimenez
Best Infield Arm	: Mark Vientos
Best Defensive Outfielder	Hansel Moreno
Best Outfield Arm	Hansel Moreno.

Year	Age	Club (League)	Class	AVG	G	AB	R	H	2B	3B	HR	RBI	BB	SO	SB	OBP	SLG
2018	17	Mets (GCL)	R	.279	49	197	26	55	13	3	3	31	10	31	1	.307	.421
	17	Kingsport (APP)	R	.233	8	30	6	7	3	0	0	4	3	9	1	.286	.333
2019	18	Columbia (SAL)	LoA	.268	116	470	62	126	20	5	4	37	23	99	6	.307	.357
Minor League Totals				.270	173	697	94	188	36	8	7	72	36	139	8	.306	.374

2 FRANCISCO ALVAREZ, C

TOM DIPACE

BA GRADE
60 Risk: Very High

Born: Nov. 19, 2001. **B-T:** R-R. **HT:** 5-11. **WT:** 220. **Signed:** Venezuela, 2018. **Signed by:** Andres Nunez/Ismael Perez.

TRACK RECORD: The Mets loved Alvarez's combination of tools when they signed him, but they were equally enamored of his work ethic and grinding mentality. Rival scouts mirrored the Mets' praise after getting a look at the 17-year-old catcher at a pair of Rookie-level stops in his 2019 pro debut. Alvarez hit .462 during a week in the Gulf Coast League before his manager implored the Mets to promote him. He continued to hit as the youngest player in the Appalachian League, ranking as the circuit's No. 1 prospect.

SCOUTING REPORT: Alvarez has the potential to be a franchise catcher. He handles velocity and stays on breaking balls, while showing elite bat-to-ball ability and power straightaway and to the opposite field. Alvarez has special potential with the bat and could be a plus overall hitter with power. He has all the ingredients behind the plate to start for a winning team, including a high energy level and the massive hands and forearms of a big league backstop. He receives well and keeps the running game in check with a plus arm. On his to-do list are fine-tuning his pitch-framing and game-calling.

THE FUTURE: Alvarez desires to be great and has put in the work to learn English and condition his body. Look for him to make a splash in full-season ball in 2020 and get on the big league radar in 2023.

SCOUTING GRADES: **Hitting:** 60 **Power:** 50 **Running:** 40 **Fielding:** 60 **Arm:** 60

Year	Age	Club (League)	Class	AVG	G	AB	R	H	2B	3B	HR	RBI	BB	SO	SB	OBP	SLG
2019	17	Mets (GCL)	R	.462	7	26	8	12	4	0	2	10	4	4	0	.548	.846
	17	Kingsport (APP)	R	.282	35	131	24	37	6	0	5	16	17	33	1	.377	.443
Minor League Totals				.312	42	157	32	49	10	0	7	26	21	37	1	.407	.510

3 BRETT BATY, 3B

BA GRADE
55 Risk: Extreme

Born: Nov. 13, 1999. **B-T:** L-R. **HT:** 6-3. **WT:** 210. **Drafted:** HS—Austin, 2019 (1st round). **Signed by:** Harry Shelton.

TRACK RECORD: Baty played basketball and football at Lake Travis High but shone brightest in baseball, where he was Gatorade player of the year as a junior and then even more prolific as a senior. He hit .624 with 19 homers in 93 at-bats in his draft year and was recognized by scouts as one of the top hitters, top power hitters and most disciplined hitters in the 2019 high school draft class. The complicating factor for Baty was his age—19 and a half on draft day—which dropped him to the Mets at No. 12. He signed for $3.9 million and showed power and patience in a 51-game pro debut focused at Rookie-level Kingsport.

SCOUTING REPORT: Baty's value is concentrated in his lefthanded bat, and he is a better athlete than his physical 6-foot-3 frame suggests. He might have fielded Division I offers as a quarterback had he not dropped football as a sophomore and he can dunk a basketball. His prodigious power plays to both his pull side and the opposite field and is supported by high-end exit velocities and a swing geared for loft. Baty can handle velocity, doesn't often chase out of the zone and takes his walks, so the Mets expect him to be a solid-average hitter or better. He is a notoriously hard worker who handled third base better than expected in his pro debut, showing average potential and a plus arm that once fired 92 mph heat off the mound in high school.

THE FUTURE: Baty turned 20 in November and because of his age doesn't have the typical grace period of a prep pick. He needs to hit the ground running at low Class A Columbia and move up at least one level during the season.

SCOUTING GRADES: **Hitting:** 55 **Power:** 60 **Running:** 40 **Fielding:** 50 **Arm:** 60

Year	Age	Club (League)	Class	AVG	G	AB	R	H	2B	3B	HR	RBI	BB	SO	SB	OBP	SLG
2019	19	Mets (GCL)	R	.350	5	20	5	7	3	0	1	8	5	6	0	.480	.650
	19	Kingsport (APP)	R	.222	42	158	30	35	12	2	6	22	24	56	0	.339	.437
	19	Brooklyn (NYP)	SS	.200	4	10	2	2	1	0	0	3	6	3	0	.529	.300
Minor League Totals				.234	51	188	37	44	16	2	7	33	35	65	0	.368	.452

4 MATT ALLAN, RHP

Born: April 17, 2001. **B-T:** R-R. **HT:** 6-3. **WT:** 225. **Drafted:** HS—Sanford, Fla., 2019 (3rd round). **Signed by:** Jon Updike.

TRACK RECORD: Allan ranked as the top high school pitching prospect in a 2019 draft class regarded by scouts as thin on prep arms. A mid-first round talent, Allan fell to the third round because he priced himself at $4 million in a draft in which only Quinn Priester, taken 18th overall by the Pirates, cleared $3 million. Allan signed for $2.5 million, the second-highest bonus for a high school pitcher in the draft and the most the Mets could offer after signing first-rounder Brett Baty and second-rounder Josh Wolf for a combined $6.05 million of their $8.225 million bonus pool. Allan signed in late June and made six brief appearances, mostly in the Rookie-level Gulf Coast League.

SCOUTING REPORT: The Mets viewed Allan as the best pitcher in the 2019 draft because of his combination of stuff, physicality, competitive makeup and a sound, repeatable, low-effort delivery. He already looks like a major league starter, and while that may preclude projection to the same degree as other teen pitchers, his present stuff is plenty good. He topped out at 97 mph in his pro debut and pitched at 93-96 with a plus fastball. His attention-getting 77-82 mph curveball has double-plus potential and a consistent spin rate in excess of 2,500 revolutions per minute. He locates his curve well but needs to fine-tune command of the pitch. Allan will receive a crash course in changeup usage in pro ball, but the pitch projects as solid-average.

THE FUTURE: Allan's stuff is firm and plays in the strike zone, giving him an absolute ceiling of a No. 2 starter and the chance to move quickly for a high school pitcher. He should have no trouble opening 2020 at low Class A Columbia.

SCOUTING GRADES: Fastball: 60 | Curveball: 70 | Changeup: 55 | Control: 55

Year	Age	Club (League)	Class	W	L	ERA	G	GS	SV	IP	H	HR	BB	SO	K/9	WHIP	AVG
2019	18	Mets (GCL)	R	1	0	1.08	5	4	0	8	5	0	4	11	11.9	1.08	.167
	18	Brooklyn (NYP)	SS	0	0	9.00	1	1	0	2	5	0	1	3	13.5	3.00	.500
Minor League Totals				1	0	2.61	6	5	0	10	10	0	5	14	12.2	1.45	.250

5 ANDRES GIMENEZ, SS

Born: Sept. 4, 1998. 21. **B-T:** L-R. **HT:** 6-0. **WT:** 161. **Signed:** Venezuela, 2015. **Signed by:** Robert Espejo/Hector Rincones.

TRACK RECORD: The No. 2 prospect in the 2015 international signing class, Gimenez shot to Double-A as a 19-year-old in 2018 but stalled offensively in a return to the Eastern League in 2019. He hit just .235 in the first half before showing signs of life in the second half, hitting .261/.306/.406 in 70 games with six of his nine home runs. He hit .358 with a .970 OPS in the Arizona Fall League, where he focused on keeping his upper and lower halves synced, trusting his hands and using all fields.

SCOUTING REPORT: Gimenez is a heady player who will flash all five tools but impacts games mostly with his glove, arm and plus speed. He is one of the best defensive shortstops in the minors and commands the infield at a tender age. He minimizes mistakes with reliable hands and a plus, accurate arm. Gimenez tinkered with his swing early in 2019 in an effort to generate more power, but it didn't take. At his best he is a disciplined, line drive-oriented hitter who should grow into double-digit power to go with an average overall bat. He has improved his speed to plus and tuned up his basestealing aggressiveness.

THE FUTURE: Gimenez is athletic, but a lack of physicality limits his offensive upside. His defensive acumen will afford him opportunities to develop his bat in the big leagues, where outlooks range from a starting middle infielder to a utility role.

SCOUTING GRADES: Hitting: 50 | Power: 40 | Running: 60 | Fielding: 60 | Arm: 60

Year	Age	Club (League)	Class	AVG	G	AB	R	H	2B	3B	HR	RBI	BB	SO	SB	OBP	SLG
2017	18	Columbia (SAL)	LoA	.265	92	347	50	92	9	4	4	31	28	61	14	.346	.349
2018	19	St. Lucie (FSL)	HiA	.282	85	308	43	87	20	4	6	30	22	70	28	.348	.432
	19	Binghamton (EL)	AA	.277	37	137	19	38	9	1	0	16	9	22	10	.344	.358
2019	20	Binghamton (EL)	AA	.250	117	432	54	108	22	5	9	37	24	102	28	.309	.387
Minor League Totals				.278	393	1438	218	400	80	18	22	152	129	277	93	.356	.405

6 MARK VIENTOS, 3B

BA GRADE
50 Risk: High

Born: Dec. 11, 1999. **B-T:** R-R. **HT:** 6-4. **WT:** 185. **Drafted:** HS—Plantation, Fla., 2017 (2nd round). **Signed by:** Cesar Aranguren.

TRACK RECORD: Following an encouraging 2018 season in Rookie ball that included 11 homers and nearly as many walks as strikeouts, Vientos didn't have much to show through his first month at low Class A Columbia in 2019. A struggle to pick up spin on breaking pitches from righthanders led him to a .233 average and .100 isolated slugging through 35 games. Vientos picked up the pace afterward and produced a .205 ISO over his next 65 games before tailing off in mid-August.

SCOUTING REPORT: Power is going to be Vientos' ticket to advancement, and making the best possible swing decisions will be the key to reaching that goal. He sees lefthanders well and can impact a pitch with plus bat speed, strong hand-eye coordination and loft power. He lacks the natural feel for barrel manipulation and fluidity to be anything more than an adequate hitter for average. Drafted as a shortstop, Vientos shifted to third base in 2018. He throws well and his hands work, but below-average speed, mobility and footwork limit his defensive upside.

THE FUTURE: Vientos is physically mature for his age and faces a possible move to first base down the line, but the thunder in his bat is real and could make him an attractive corner masher.

SCOUTING GRADES: **Hitting:** 45 **Power:** 60 **Running:** 30 **Fielding:** 40 **Arm:** 60

Year	Age	Club (League)	Class	AVG	G	AB	R	H	2B	3B	HR	RBI	BB	SO	SB	OBP	SLG
2017	17	Mets (GCL)	R	.259	47	174	22	45	12	0	4	24	14	42	0	.316	.397
	17	Kingsport (APP)	R	.294	4	17	1	5	2	0	0	2	1	4	0	.333	.412
2018	18	Kingsport (APP)	R	.287	60	223	32	64	12	0	11	52	37	43	1	.389	.489
2019	19	Columbia (SAL)	LoA	.255	111	416	48	106	27	1	12	62	22	110	1	.300	.411
Minor League Totals				.265	222	830	103	220	53	1	27	140	74	199	2	.329	.429

7 THOMAS SZAPUCKI, LHP

BA GRADE
50 Risk: High

Born: June 12, 1996. **B-T:** R-L. **HT:** 6-2. **WT:** 181. **Drafted:** HS—Palm Beach Gardens, Fla., 2015 (5th round). **Signed by:** Cesar Aranguren.

TRACK RECORD: Szapucki burst on the scene in 2016 when he struck out nearly 15 batters per nine innings at a pair of short-season stops. He failed to build on that success in 2017, when he had Tommy John surgery in July that knocked him out for all of 2018. Szapucki returned in 2019 and cruised through two Class A stops on tight pitch counts before making one Double-A start to close the season.

SCOUTING REPORT: Szapucki has experienced the highs and lows of professional baseball. Likewise, his pitches explore the highs and lows of the strike zone, and his high-spin rate arsenal makes him a prototype pitcher for baseball today. Szapucki's sneaky fastball sits 91-93 mph with carry up in the zone and he can reach 95 when needed. His curveball is the best in the system and features deep breaking action in the low 80s to change hitters' eye levels. He has good feel for a near-average changeup and began throwing it with more conviction as his comfort level grew in his return.

THE FUTURE: Szapucki has a major league arm, though it remains to be seen if it fits in the rotation or bullpen. His time table will be accelerated in 2020, his first year on the 40-man roster. His focus will remain building arm strength and gaining reps, most likely at Double-A.

SCOUTING GRADES: **Fastball:** 60 **Curveball:** 60 **Changeup:** 40 **Control:** 45

Year	Age	Club (League)	Class	W	L	ERA	G	GS	SV	IP	H	HR	BB	SO	K/9	WHIP	AVG
2017	21	Columbia (SAL)	LoA	1	2	2.79	6	6	0	29	24	0	10	27	8.4	1.17	.231
2018	22	Did not play—Injured															
2019	23	Columbia (SAL)	LoA	0	0	2.08	11	8	0	22	14	1	10	26	10.8	1.11	.182
	23	St. Lucie (FSL)	HiA	1	3	3.25	9	9	0	36	33	1	15	42	10.5	1.33	.241
	23	Binghamton (EL)	AA	0	0	0.00	1	1	0	4	2	0	1	4	9.0	0.75	.133
Minor League Totals				6	8	2.42	39	33	0	145	104	4	56	188	11.7	1.10	.199

8 JOSH WOLF, RHP

TOM DIPACE

Born: Sept. 1, 2000. **B-T:** R-R. **HT:** 6-3. **WT:** 170. **Drafted:** HS—Houston, 2019 (2nd round). **Signed by:** Harry Shelton.

TRACK RECORD: Wolf improved his velocity as a high school senior to sit in the mid-90s and occasionally reach 97 mph after he had ranged from 88-92 on the 2018 showcase circuit. Scouts took immediate notice of his velocity spike as well as his continued ability to throw strikes, making Wolf one of the more prominent pop-up prospects for the 2019 draft. The Mets selected him in the second round and went nearly $800,000 over slot to sign him. Wolf made five appearances in the Rookie-level Gulf Coast League, where he struck out 12 and walked only one in eight innings.

SCOUTING REPORT: Wolf throws two plus pitches, shows an aggressive mound demeanor that endears him to scouts and is a twitchy athlete with a quick arm and projectable frame. He pitched at 94 mph with life in his pro debut and ranged from 91-96 while continuing to throw strikes. Wolf shows aptitude for spinning a 79-83 mph curveball that projects as a plus pitch once he develops the command to shape it consistently. Like most high school righthanders, he doesn't have a lot of experience throwing a changeup but has the ingredients to develop an average one.

THE FUTURE: Wolf needs to add about 15 pounds to his frame, but his athleticism and presence give him a mid-rotation ceiling. He should be ready for low Class A in 2020.

SCOUTING GRADES: **Fastball:** 60 **Curveball:** 60 **Changeup:** 50 **Control:** 55

Year	Age	Club (League)	Class	W	L	ERA	G	GS	SV	IP	H	HR	BB	SO	K/9	WHIP	AVG
2019	18	Mets (GCL)	R	0	1	3.38	5	5	0	8	9	0	1	12	13.5	1.25	.281
Minor League Totals				0	1	3.38	5	5	0	8	9	0	1	12	13.5	1.25	.281

9 KEVIN SMITH, LHP

BA GRADE
50 Risk: High

Born: May 13, 1997. **B-T:** R-L. **HT:** 6-5. **WT:** 200. **Drafted:** Georgia, 2018 (7th round). **Signed by:** Tommy Jackson.

TRACK RECORD: The Mets had a good feeling about Smith in 2018, when they drafted him in the seventh round and watched him dominate New York-Penn League competition with a 0.76 ERA in 23.2 innings. He looked even better in 2019, when he reached Double-A in July of his full-season debut while striking out 10 and walking 3 per nine innings and allowing six home runs in 23 starts. He earned the Mets' minor league pitcher of the year award.

SCOUTING REPORT: The athletic, 6-foot-5 Smith has firm stuff but leans on deception and angle to succeed. He pitches at 90 mph from a slightly low three-quarters arm slot with plus arm speed and tailing life on his fastball. His low-80s slider features wide angle and high spin. The pitch is death on lefthanded hitters, who managed just .207 with three extra-base hits—all doubles—in 116 at-bats in 2019. Smith has developed a near-average changeup in pro ball.

THE FUTURE: Smith is one of the hardest workers and fiercest competitors in the system. He met the challenge of Double-A a year into his pro career and should be ready for Triple-A—and beyond—by the second half of 2020. He profiles as a No. 5-type starter or quality bullpen arm.

SCOUTING GRADES: **Fastball:** 50 **Curveball:** 60 **Changeup:** 45 **Control:** 50

Year	Age	Club (League)	Class	W	L	ERA	G	GS	SV	IP	H	HR	BB	SO	K/9	WHIP	AVG
2018	21	Brooklyn (NYP)	SS	4	1	0.76	12	3	0	24	12	1	6	28	10.6	0.76	.156
2019	22	St. Lucie (FSL)	HiA	5	5	3.05	17	17	0	86	83	5	24	102	10.7	1.25	.259
	22	Binghamton (EL)	AA	3	2	3.45	6	6	0	31	25	1	15	28	8.0	1.28	.227
Minor League Totals				12	8	2.75	35	26	0	140	120	7	45	158	10.1	1.17	.237

10 DAVID PETERSON, LHP

Born: Sept. 3, 1995. **B-T:** L-L. **HT:** 6-6. **WT:** 240. **Drafted:** Oregon, 2017 (1st round). **Signed by:** Jim Reeves.

BA GRADE
45 Risk: Medium

TRACK RECORD: Drafted 20th overall in 2017, Peterson spent the entirety of his third pro season in Double-A and made a career-high 24 starts. He ranked fifth in the Eastern League with 122 strikeouts while placing among the Double-A leaders in groundball rate (52.6 percent) and swinging-strike rate (13.7 percent) among pitchers with 100 innings.

SCOUTING REPORT: Peterson offers proof that looks can be deceiving. At 6-foot-6, 240 pounds, he looks like a power pitcher but instead relies on working ahead, location and sequencing. Peterson is a strike-thrower who generates late swings and mis-hits thanks to the extension in is delivery that makes his 87-92 mph fastball look faster. His swing-and-miss slider has been his primary weapon dating back to college. The pitch has slurvy shape, late break and plus depth. Peterson's below-average changeup is not a significant factor and is more of a show-me pitch.

THE FUTURE: Peterson's lack of fine command and sometimes questionable body language turn off some scouts, but he's lefthanded, throws strikes and has a plus slider. He could begin getting looks at the back of the rotation beginning in 2020.

SCOUTING GRADES: **Fastball:** 50 **Slider:** 60 **Changeup:** 40 **Control:** 60

Year	Age	Club (League)	Class	W	L	ERA	G	GS	SV	IP	H	HR	BB	SO	K/9	WHIP	AVG
2017	21	Brooklyn (NYP)	SS	0	0	2.45	3	3	0	4	4	0	1	6	14.7	1.36	.267
2018	22	Columbia (SAL)	LoA	1	4	1.82	9	9	0	59	46	1	11	57	8.6	0.96	.214
	22	St. Lucie (FSL)	HiA	6	6	4.33	13	13	0	69	74	1	19	58	7.6	1.35	.273
2019	23	Binghamton (EL)	AA	3	6	4.19	24	24	0	116	119	9	37	122	9.5	1.34	.263
Minor League Totals				10	16	3.63	49	49	0	247	243	11	68	243	8.8	1.26	.255

11 JORDAN HUMPHREYS, RHP

BA GRADE
50 Risk: High

Born: June 11, 1996. **B-T:** R-R. **HT:** 6-2. **WT:** 223. **Drafted:** HS—Crystal River, Fla., 2015 (18th round). **Signed by:** Jon Updike.

TRACK RECORD: The Mets love to throw darts at Florida high school pitchers in the later rounds of the draft. Humphreys is one of their more notable hits. He led the Rookie-level Appalachian League in strikeouts in 2016 and really began to pop at low Class A Columbia in the first half of 2017, when he went 10-1, 1.42 in 11 starts and earned a promotion to high Class A St. Lucie. After two Florida State League starts his season was over and he had Tommy John surgery that August.

SCOUTING REPORT: Those two FSL appearances were the last the Mets saw of Humphreys until a pair of 2019 rehab starts in the Rookie-level Gulf Coast League, followed by 12 innings in the Arizona Fall League. Humphreys succeeds more with command than pure stuff but has the ability to dot the corners and also pitch north-south effectively thanks to the spin and ride on his fastball. He pitches in the low 90s with a high near 94 mph and works both sides of the plate effectively. Humphreys' high-spin, high-70s curveball pairs well with his fastball and has average depth. His average changeup has action to his arm side. He began regaining feel for the pitch after the layoff in the AFL.

THE FUTURE: Despite missing nearly two and a half seasons, Humphreys showed enough in the AFL to convince the Mets to add him to the 40-man roster to shield him from the Rule 5 draft. He has the ceiling of a No. 4 starter and is probably two years away.

Year	Age	Club (League)	Class	W	L	ERA	G	GS	SV	IP	H	HR	BB	SO	K/9	WHIP	AVG
2017	21	Columbia (SAL)	LoA	10	1	1.42	11	11	0	70	41	2	9	80	10.3	0.72	.168
	21	St. Lucie (FSL)	HiA	0	0	4.09	2	2	0	11	17	1	3	3	2.5	1.82	.340
2018	22	Did not play—Injured															
2019	23	Mets (GCL)	R	0	0	4.50	2	2	0	2	2	0	1	2	9.0	1.50	.286
Minor League Totals				13	7	2.60	35	28	2	169	144	6	30	177	9.4	1.03	.227

12 JUNIOR SANTOS, RHP

BA GRADE
55 Risk: Extreme

Born: Aug. 16, 2001. **B-T:** R-R. **HT:** 6-8. **WT:** 218. **Signed:** Dominican Republic, 2017. **Signed by:** Anderson Taveras/Gerardo Cabrera.

TRACK RECORD: Mets international scouts don't typically recommend signing 16-year-old pitchers for large bonuses, but they made an exception for Santos, a 6-foot-8 righthander from Santiago in the mountainous northern region of the Dominican Republic. He signed for $275,000 in 2017 and two years later was impressing scouts and managers as an 18-year-old in the Rookie-level Appalachian League. The

teenager worked on tight pitch counts, never topping 73 pitches or 4.1 innings in a start for Kingsport.
SCOUTING REPORT: Santos embodies all the positive and negative attributes that come with a pitcher of his extreme height. He gets over his front side well and releases the ball closer to home plate than most pitchers thanks to the plus extension in his delivery. Syncing his long levers, repeating his arm action and holding baserunners are challenges for Santos, as they are for most extra tall pitchers. Santos is a strong, flexible athlete who easily generates 90-94 mph velocity and peaks at 95. His frame has room to add weight, giving him the potential to hold and possibly add velocity. Santos throws a slurvy breaking ball in the high 70s that has above-average spin and swing-and-miss potential, especially as he learns to stay on top of the ball more consistently. He needs to fine-tune his fastball command and develop his changeup.
THE FUTURE: Both the Mets and outside observers rave about Santos' work ethic and coachability, which coupled with his ease of operation gives him at least a chance to remain in the rotation. If control and command shortfalls force him to the bullpen, he has the potential to be a high-leverage reliever. Santos won't turn 19 until mid-August of 2020, so his Opening Day assignment is up in the air.

Year	Age	Club (League)	Class	W	L	ERA	G	GS	SV	IP	H	HR	BB	SO	K/9	WHIP	AVG
2018	16	Mets1 (DSL)	R	1	1	2.80	11	10	0	45	35	1	6	36	7.2	0.91	.219
	16	Mets (GCL)	R	0	0	0.00	3	0	0	5	4	0	0	3	5.4	0.80	.222
2019	17	Kingsport (APP)	R	0	5	5.09	14	14	0	41	46	4	25	36	8.0	1.75	.277
Minor League Totals				1	6	3.67	28	24	0	90	85	5	31	75	7.4	1.28	.247

13 FRANKLYN KILOME, RHP

BA GRADE
50 Risk: High

Born: June 25, 1995. **B-T:** R-R. **HT:** 6-6. **WT:** 175. **Signed:** Dominican Republic, 2013. **Signed by:** Koby Perez (Phillies).

TRACK RECORD: The Mets exchanged veteran second baseman Asdrubal Cabrera for Kilome at the 2018 trade deadline in a deal with the Phillies. He made seven starts for Double-A Binghamton after the trade but had Tommy John surgery in October and didn't appear in a game in 2019. Before his lost year, the tall, lean Kilome had recently turned a corner in his development and had spent a full season at Double-A.
SCOUTING REPORT: Keeping his long levers in sync has been a challenge for Kilome, but when he throws strikes his power arsenal is well suited to today's game. He fires high-spin, mid-90s fastballs that top out near 97 mph. The extension in Kilome's delivery helps the ball get on hitters quickly. His curveball is a strikeout weapon that combines velocity and top-to-bottom spin. He began to command the pitch with greater frequency in 2018 to lock up hitters with called strikes. Kilome also throws a distinct slider and has feel for a changeup but tends to rely on his top two pitches. He has tended to work with traffic on the bases because of higher than average walk rates and elevated hit rates.
THE FUTURE: Kilome lacks the type of command to be a front-of-the-rotation starter, but the quality of his top two pitches would make him at attractive relief option. He should be ready for Triple-A in short order in 2020 and could factor for the big league team if things go according to plan.

Year	Age	Club (League)	Class	W	L	ERA	G	GS	SV	IP	H	HR	BB	SO	K/9	WHIP	AVG
2017	22	Clearwater (FSL)	HiA	6	4	2.59	19	19	0	97	96	5	37	83	7.7	1.37	.265
	22	Reading (EL)	AA	1	3	3.64	5	5	0	30	25	2	15	20	6.1	1.35	.238
2018	23	Reading (EL)	AA	4	6	4.24	19	19	0	102	96	7	51	83	7.3	1.44	.257
	23	Binghamton (EL)	AA	0	3	4.03	7	7	0	38	31	3	10	42	9.9	1.08	.223
Minor League Totals				22	27	3.55	95	92	0	471	438	26	195	419	8.0	1.34	.251

14 MICHEL OTAÑEZ, RHP

BA GRADE
50 Risk: High

Born: July 3, 1997. **B-T:** R-R. **HT:** 6-3. **WT:** 215. **Signed:** Dominican Republic, 2016. **Signed by:** Marciano Alvarez.

TRACK RECORD: Otañez signed as an 18-year-old in 2016 and then missed the 2017 season while recovering from Tommy John surgery. He didn't begin to pop on scouts' radars until 2019, when he dominated the Rookie-level Appalachian League on his way to short-season Brooklyn in late July. In 14 starts total he recorded a 3.14 ERA in 63 innings with 70 strikeouts and a 1.27 WHIP.
SCOUTING REPORT: Otañez is tall, physical and long-limbed and appears to be a late bloomer after breaking out at age 21, in his fourth pro season. His 95-98 mph velocity stands out as does his three-pitch repertoire and durability. His fastball has good life to his arm side that he uses to work inside on righthanded hitters and set up a slider that projects as a plus pitch. Otañez also throws an above-average changeup that he locates away from lefthanded hitters. He can locate all his pitches for strikes but doesn't hide the ball well, which inhibits his deception.
THE FUTURE: Otañez has one of the more electric arms on the Mets' farm. Given his outstanding fastball/slider combination, it's easy to envision him as a future high-leverage reliever—but the quality of his changeup argues otherwise. Otañez has promise but a long climb ahead of him.

Year	Age	Club (League)	Class	W	L	ERA	G	GS	SV	IP	H	HR	BB	SO	K/9	WHIP	AVG
2017	19	Did not play															
2018	20	Mets (GCL)	R	1	6	7.64	11	7	0	35	42	2	24	33	8.4	1.87	.284
2019	21	Kingsport (APP)	R	2	2	3.31	7	7	0	33	26	1	11	44	12.1	1.13	.219
	21	Brooklyn (NYP)	SS	2	1	2.97	7	7	0	30	26	2	17	26	7.7	1.42	.232
Minor League Totals				6	10	4.74	30	26	0	119	117	5	58	124	9.3	1.46	.255

15 ROBERT DOMINGUEZ, RHP

Born: Nov. 30, 2001. **B-T:** R-R. **HT:** 6-4. **WT:** 200. **Signed:** Venezuela, 2019. **Signed by:** Ismael Perez/Andres Nuñez.

TRACK RECORD: A 16-year-old Dominguez didn't draw much attention in his native Venezuela in the 2018 international signing class. A move to the Dominican Republic to train completely reversed his fortune. Dominguez's velocity spiked to 97 mph during his two-month program in the Dominican after he made mechanical adjustments. The Mets signed him in November 2019, a few days before he turned 18.

SCOUTING REPORT: Dominguez topped out at 99 mph toward the end of Dominican instructional league and is one of the hardest-throwing 18-year-olds in the world. His sturdy 6-foot-4 frame, elite velocity and feel for a breaking ball him an exciting rotation prospect. Dominguez's curveball flashes average with late action and depth and could be developed as a plus pitch. He doesn't have much feel yet for a changeup.

THE FUTURE: Dominguez stands as one of the best pitching prospects in the 2019 international signing class, but like any teenage pitcher, he is a complete wild card. The Mets don't invest heavily in teen Latin pitchers, but the ones they have signed began their pro careers in the Dominican Summer League.

Year	Age	Club (League)	Class	W	L	ERA	G	GS	SV	IP	H	HR	BB	SO	K/9	WHIP	AVG
2019	17	Did not play—Signed 2020 contract															

16 ALEXANDER RAMIREZ, OF

BA GRADE
55 Risk: Extreme

Born: Jan. 13, 2003. **B-T:** R-R. **HT:** 6-3. **WT:** 170. **Signed:** Dominican Republic, 2019. **Signed by:** Gerardo Cabrera/Fernando Encarnacion.

TRACK RECORD: The Mets awarded their highest international bonus in 2019 to Ramirez, a 16-year-old Dominican outfielder who signed for $2.05 million. He signed a 2020 contract but made his first U.S. appearance at the Mets' instructional camp in the fall, where he showed off the physicality, athleticism and raw tools that excite scouts, particularly his chance to hit for impact power.

SCOUTING REPORT: Tall and athletic, Ramirez is a potential power-speed threat in center field. That projection hinges on his ability to remain light on his feet, but his frame has plenty of room to add strength without becoming bulky and sacrificing his plus speed. Ramirez shows present pull-side power and has the bat speed to impact velocity. Scouts are divided on his feel to hit. Ramirez has long arms, a lengthy swing and timing issues at the plate, which could inhibit his feel for hitting. The Mets like his barrel control and don't share those concerns. Ramirez tracks the ball well in the outfield and can be an above-average defender with an average arm.

THE FUTURE: Ramirez is a raw but exciting talent whose career could unfold in many different ways. His career will begin in Rookie ball in 2020.

Year	Age	Club (League)	Class	AVG	G	AB	R	H	2B	3B	HR	RBI	BB	SO	SB	OBP	SLG
2019	16	Did not play—Signed 2020 contract															

17 SHERVYEN NEWTON, 2B/SS

BA GRADE
50 Risk: Very High

Born: April 24, 1999. **B-T:** B-R. **HT:** 6-4. **WT:** 180. **Signed:** Curacao, 2015. **Signed by:** Sendly Reina/Hector Rincones/Harold Herrera/Chris Becerra.

TRACK RECORD: Newton spent two seasons in the Dominican Summer League before bursting on the prospect scene at Rookie-level Kingsport in 2018, when the shortstop led the Appalachian League with 16 doubles. He fell flat in his follow up at low Class A Columbia in 2019, hitting .209 with one of the highest strikeout rates (33 percent) in the South Atlantic League and a .613 OPS that ranked ninth worst.

SCOUTING REPORT: Newton missed time in spring training with a shoulder injury and never seemed to get into a groove. He made hard contact when he connected and had no trouble catching up with velocity, but breaking pitches gave him fits and led to a compromising swinging-strike rate. A 6-foot-4 switch-hitter, Newton shows easy plus power from the left side and has a chance to develop into a power-over-hit infielder. Newton spent most of his time at second base while playing on the same Columbia infield as shortstop Ronny Mauricio and third baseman Mark Vientos. Newton's height and physicality stand out at second base, where he has the requisite athleticism, sure hands and arm strength. Some scouts envision him settling in at third base or possibly an outfield corner.

THE FUTURE: The Mets left Newton unprotected in the Rule 5 draft, gambling that his rough edges would leave him without the skills needed to survive a season on the major league roster. They were right. He will need a big year with the bat to vault back into the Mets' plans.

Year	Age	Club (League)	Class	AVG	G	AB	R	H	2B	3B	HR	RBI	BB	SO	SB	OBP	SLG
2017	18	Mets2 (DSL)	R	.311	66	241	51	75	11	9	1	31	50	57	10	.433	.444
2018	19	Kingsport (APP)	R	.280	56	207	50	58	16	2	5	41	46	84	4	.408	.449
2019	20	Columbia (SAL)	LoA	.209	109	382	35	80	15	2	9	32	37	139	1	.283	.330
Minor League Totals				.246	266	948	154	233	47	14	15	109	155	312	15	.360	.372

18 FREDDY VALDEZ, OF

BA GRADE **50** Risk: Very High

Born: Dec. 6, 2001. **B-T:** R-R. **HT:** 6-3. **WT:** 210. **Signed:** Dominican Republic, 2018. **Signed by:** Fernando Encarnacion/Gerardo Cabrera.

TRACK RECORD: The Mets signed Valdez, a powerful righthanded-hitting corner outfielder, for $1.4 million in 2018. He embarked on his pro debut in the Dominican Summer League in 2019, where he clubbed 23 extra-base hits to rank in the 85th percentile for isolated slugging among DSL batters.

SCOUTING REPORT: The 6-foot-3 Valdez is physically mature for a 17-year-old, but his thin ankles and athletic bloodline are positive indicators that he won't become too thick. His present strength and quick swing translate to plus-plus raw power with a chance to reach plus game power. His flyball-oriented hitting approach will help him maximize power, as will his above-average plate discipline for a teen slugger. Valdez should hit for a respectable average but is definitely a power-over-hit profile. He is a solid defensive right fielder with a plus arm but below-average speed.

THE FUTURE: With a corner profile, Valdez will go as far as his bat takes him. His next step will be Rookie ball in the U.S. and he will require at least four seasons of development.

Year	Age	Club (League)	Class	AVG	G	AB	R	H	2B	3B	HR	RBI	BB	SO	SB	OBP	SLG
2019	17	Mets1 (DSL)	R	.268	57	220	36	59	15	3	5	36	28	46	6	.358	.432
	17	Mets (GCL)	R	.400	3	10	4	4	1	0	1	3	3	3	0	.538	.800
Minor League Totals				.274	60	230	40	63	16	3	6	39	31	49	6	.367	.448

19 JOSE BUTTO, RHP

BA GRADE **45** Risk: High

Born: March 19, 1998. **B-T:** R-R. **HT:** 6-1. **WT:** 160. **Signed:** Venezuela, 2017. **Signed by:** Hector Rincones.

TRACK RECORD: Butto signed as a 19-year-old out of Venezuela in 2017 and spent two seasons in short-season leagues before being assigned to low Class A Columbia in 2019. He rounded into shape after a rocky start and ranked inside the South Atlantic League top 10 with a 3.62 ERA and 1.17 WHIP.

SCOUTING REPORT: Butto throws the best changeup in the Mets' farm system. It elicits swings and misses from both lefthanded and righthanded batters with its diving action, coupled with Butto's convincing arm speed. That plus pitch allowed him to record the sixth highest swinging-strike rate in the SAL. Butto pitched in the low 90s early in the season but gained steam as the season progressed and he shifted to a two-inning role. He sat mid-90s and topped out at 98 mph late in the season, that extra velocity making his changeup even more devastating as batters geared up for heat. His below-average curveball shows slurve action and suffers from poor command.

THE FUTURE: Butto is primed to move quickly as a fastball/changeup reliever if the Mets want to pursue that route. He would need to make dramatic progress with his curve to profile in the rotation.

Year	Age	Club (League)	Class	W	L	ERA	G	GS	SV	IP	H	HR	BB	SO	K/9	WHIP	AVG
2017	19	Mets2 (DSL)	R	1	1	1.44	15	8	1	50	48	0	9	41	7.4	1.14	.258
2018	20	Kingsport (APP)	R	3	0	1.93	6	6	0	33	27	3	11	31	8.5	1.16	.227
	20	Brooklyn (NYP)	SS	1	2	6.11	6	5	0	28	31	6	11	24	7.7	1.50	.279
2019	21	Columbia (SAL)	LoA	4	10	3.62	27	25	0	112	100	8	31	109	8.8	1.17	.234
Minor League Totals				9	13	3.19	54	44	1	222	206	17	62	205	8.3	1.20	.244

20 JAYLEN PALMER, 3B/SS

BA GRADE **50** Risk: Extreme

Born: July 31, 2000. **B-T:** R-R. **HT:** 6-4. **WT:** 195. **Drafted:** HS—Flushing, N.Y., 2018 (22nd round). **Signed by:** John Kosciak.

TRACK RECORD: Palmer grew up in Flushing and played high school ball a few miles from Citi Field. The Mets liked what they saw and signed him for an over-slot $200,000 as a 22nd-round pick in 2018. Palmer hit .310 in his pro debut in the Rookie-level Gulf Coast League and continued to surpass expectations at Rookie-level Kingsport in 2019, when he ranked among the Appalachian League leaders with 63 hits, 31 walks and 100 total bases.

SCOUTING REPORT: Palmer is a twitchy athlete whose power potential is his most promising tool. He has grown to 6-foot-4 in the past few years, while his long limbs and broad shoulders suggest the potential for continued muscle gain. Palmer went deep seven times in the Appy League and hits the ball hard consistently when he connects. Making contact is an area for improvement after he registered a 39 percent strikeout rate and league-leading 108 whiffs. He tends to pull off the ball while trying to get to his power. Palmer split his time evenly between third base and shortstop and is projected by scouts to stay on the infield. He probably fits best at third because of his frame, average arm and fringe-average speed that figures to diminish.

THE FUTURE: Palmer shares some similarities with Shervyen Newton as a physical infielder with enticing power and high strikeout totals. He should get a crack at low Class A in 2020.

Year	Age	Club (League)	Class	AVG	G	AB	R	H	2B	3B	HR	RBI	BB	SO	SB	OBP	SLG
2018	17	Mets (GCL)	R	.310	25	87	13	27	4	1	1	11	8	27	5	.394	.414
2019	18	Kingsport (APP)	R	.260	62	242	41	63	12	2	7	28	31	108	1	.344	.413
Minor League Totals				.274	87	329	54	90	16	3	8	39	39	135	6	.357	.413

21 DEDNIEL NUÑEZ, RHP

BA GRADE
45 Risk: High

Born: June 5, 1996. **B-T:** R-R. **HT:** 6-2. **WT:** 180. **Signed:** Dominican Republic, 2016. **Signed by:** Fernando Encarnacion.

TRACK RECORD: Nuñez signed at age 20 in October 2016 and spent two seasons in Rookie ball before becoming more of a known commodity in 2019, when he pitched at two Class A levels. He didn't take the mound after July 11 because of a right shoulder injury, but when healthy he showed swing-and-miss stuff with 10.6 strikeouts per nine innings against just 2.6 walks per nine.

SCOUTING REPORT: Nuñez stands out most for his fastball, which he throws 92-96 mph with an elite spin rate in excess of 2,600 revolutions per minute. The pitch averages 93 mph and has natural cutting action that makes it difficult for opponents to square up. Nuñez's slurvy breaking ball averages about 80 mph and grades as an average pitch. He shows some feel for a changeup that grades near average. While Nuñez throws three pitches at or near average, he lacks a true out pitch, which puts his upside potential in doubt. His ability to execute pitches effectively is also hampered by a wrist wrap and wandering release point.

THE FUTURE: Nuñez turned 23 during the 2019 season and ended it on the injured list with a shoulder injury, so he is a wild card. His most likely big league outcome is medium- or low-leverage relief work.

Year	Age	Club (League)	Class	W	L	ERA	G	GS	SV	IP	H	HR	BB	SO	K/9	WHIP	AVG
2017	21	Mets (GCL)	R	1	3	5.24	10	8	0	45	51	3	16	46	9.3	1.50	.283
2018	22	Kingsport (APP)	R	4	1	3.79	11	7	1	40	38	2	16	36	8.0	1.34	.255
2019	23	Columbia (SAL)	LoA	3	1	4.03	4	3	0	22	14	2	3	33	13.3	0.76	.175
	23	St. Lucie (FSL)	HiA	2	3	4.53	12	12	0	58	59	3	20	61	9.5	1.37	.261
Minor League Totals				10	8	4.47	37	30	1	165	162	10	55	176	9.6	1.32	.255

22 WALKER LOCKETT, RHP

BA GRADE
40 Risk: Medium

Born: May 3, 1994. **B-T:** R-R. **HT:** 6-5. **WT:** 225. **Drafted:** HS—Jacksonville, 2012 (4th round). **Signed by:** Chris Kelly (Padres).

TRACK RECORD: Drafted by the Padres in 2012, Lockett missed most of his first three pro seasons with injuries. He then weathered two in-season demotions in 2015 before beginning his pro career in earnest in 2016. Two seasons later, Lockett had climbed to the big leagues, where he tossed 15 innings for San Diego. The Padres traded him to the Indians after the 2018 season, and Cleveland traded him to the Mets two months later as part of the return for Kevin Plawecki.

SCOUTING REPORT: Lockett reached the majors for a second straight season in 2019, only to be hit hard once again. He allowed 21 runs and 39 baserunners in 22.2 innings. Despite this, scouts regard Lockett as an intriguing young arm with a three-pitch mix who might find more success if he de-emphasized his fastball. He pitches at 92-93 mph and tops out at 96 with sinking, running action on his fastball and average extension. His low-80s slider has above-average spin and is his preferred second pitch, but his high-80s changeup actually produced more swinging strikes in the majors. Lockett throws strikes and keeps his pitches low in the strike zone, but he's not overpowering and requires weak contact to succeed.

THE FUTURE: Lockett, who turns 26 early in 2020, won't be the Mets' first choice as No. 5 starter or middle reliever, but he will be on hand if the club needs that role filled.

Year	Age	Club (League)	Class	W	L	ERA	G	GS	SV	IP	H	HR	BB	SO	K/9	WHIP	AVG
2017	23	El Paso (PCL)	AAA	5	2	4.39	10	10	0	55	67	9	13	33	5.4	1.45	.289
	23	Padres (AZL)	R	0	1	5.40	4	4	0	10	11	1	4	12	10.8	1.50	.262
2018	24	San Diego (NL)	MAJ	0	3	9.60	4	3	0	15	22	4	10	12	7.2	2.13	.333
	24	El Paso (PCL)	AAA	5	9	4.73	23	23	0	133	145	17	33	118	8.0	1.34	.279
2019	25	St. Lucie (FSL)	HiA	1	0	5.14	2	2	0	7	8	1	0	6	7.7	1.14	.276
	25	Syracuse (IL)	AAA	3	3	3.66	11	10	0	59	75	5	11	39	5.9	1.46	.305
	25	New York (NL)	MAJ	1	1	8.34	9	4	0	23	33	6	6	16	6.4	1.72	.347
Major League Totals				1	4	8.84	13	7	0	37	55	10	16	28	6.7	1.88	.342
Minor League Totals				28	31	4.11	114	97	0	547	591	49	124	418	6.9	1.31	.272

23 SAM HAGGERTY, 2B/OF

BA GRADE
40 Risk: Medium

Born: May 26, 1994. **B-T:** B-R. **HT:** 5-11. **WT:** 175. **Drafted:** New Mexico, 2015 (24th round). **Signed by:** Jon Heuerman (Indians).

TRACK RECORD: As a table-setting second baseman for New Mexico, Haggerty hit .311 with a high walk rate in the high altitude of Albuquerque. He spent four nondescript seasons in the Indians' farm system, reaching Double-A, before he was traded to the Mets in January 2019 as part of the return for catcher Kevin Plawecki. He went 0-for-4 as a September callup, serving primarily as a pinch-runner.

SCOUTING REPORT: Haggerty played every position but first base and catcher in the minors in 2019 and drew attention in the Eastern League for his play at second base and also as the league's best baserunner. Haggerty is an 70-grade runner and switch-hitter who draws walks but makes virtually no extra-base impact. He is a spray hitter with well below-average power. Scouts prefer Haggerty in the outfield or at second base. His arm and footwork don't play as well on the left side of the infield.

THE FUTURE: Haggerty has a modest ceiling afforded him by his speed, baserunning acumen and defensive versatility. His bat would need to find another gear to earn more than a utility role.

Year	Age	Club (League)	Class	AVG	G	AB	R	H	2B	3B	HR	RBI	BB	SO	SB	OBP	SLG
2017	23	Lynchburg (CAR)	HiA	.253	112	427	72	108	27	13	3	32	67	103	49	.355	.398
2018	24	Columbus (IL)	AAA	.176	7	17	3	3	0	0	0	2	2	6	2	.300	.176
	24	Akron (EL)	AA	.243	87	280	44	68	21	5	4	37	57	77	24	.373	.396
2019	25	Brooklyn (NYP)	SS	.333	6	21	5	7	3	0	0	4	4	8	0	.440	.476
	25	Binghamton (EL)	AA	.259	68	247	39	64	8	5	2	13	40	78	19	.370	.356
	25	Syracuse (IL)	AAA	.310	12	42	9	13	4	1	1	9	4	10	4	.383	.524
	25	New York (NL)	MAJ	.000	11	4	2	0	0	0	0	0	0	3	0	.000	.000
Major League Totals				.000	11	4	2	0	0	0	0	0	0	3	0	.000	.000
Minor League Totals				.249	408	1431	236	357	82	27	15	143	226	401	113	.355	.376

24 TONY DIBRELL, RHP

BA GRADE
45 Risk: High

Born: Nov. 8, 1995. **B-T:** R-R. **HT:** 6-3. **WT:** 190. **Drafted:** Kennesaw State, 2017 (4th round). **Signed by:** Tommy Jackson.

TRACK RECORD: A year after leading the South Atlantic League in strikeouts, Dibrell advanced to high Class A St. Lucie in 2019 and shined in the Florida State League until a mid-July promotion to Double-A. He found the going more difficult in the Eastern League, where he ran up a 9.31 ERA in 39 innings.

SCOUTING REPORT: Dibrell throws four pitches from a tall, lean frame and with a loose, easy arm stroke. He sits in the low 90s and dials up 95 mph occasionally. His standout tool is his plus changeup which generates swings and misses and plays up because of his command of the pitch. Dibrell throws an average slider and curveball, the latter of which is notable for its depth and spin, if not its power. He locates his fastball up in the zone and changes eye levels with his changeup and curveball.

THE FUTURE: Dibrell has the upside of a No. 4 starter, but first he must figure out how to tame Double-A. He will get another crack at them at the outset of 2020.

Year	Age	Club (League)	Class	W	L	ERA	G	GS	SV	IP	H	HR	BB	SO	K/9	WHIP	AVG
2017	21	Brooklyn (NYP)	SS	1	1	5.03	12	0	0	20	19	4	8	28	12.8	1.37	.253
2018	22	Columbia (SAL)	LoA	7	6	3.50	23	23	0	131	112	10	54	147	10.1	1.27	.228
2019	23	St. Lucie (FSL)	HiA	8	4	2.39	17	16	0	90	73	2	36	76	7.6	1.21	.225
	23	Binghamton (EL)	AA	0	8	9.31	9	8	0	39	51	10	21	37	8.6	1.86	.321
Minor League Totals				16	19	4.05	61	47	0	279	255	26	119	288	9.3	1.34	.243

25 DAISON ACOSTA, RHP

BA GRADE
45 Risk: High

Born: Aug. 24, 1998. **B-T:** R-R. **HT:** 6-2. **WT:** 160. **Signed:** Dominican Republic, 2016. **Signed by:** Daurys Nin.

TRACK RECORD: Acosta signed just shy of his 18th birthday in 2016 and spent three years in short-season

leagues. He breezed through the short-season New York-Penn League in 2019, recording an 0.98 ERA in 18 innings while striking out 25 and walking six to move to low Class A Columbia in early July.
SCOUTING REPORT: Acosta relies on a fastball and breaking ball that both have interesting characteristics. His fastball sits in the low 90s but plays up because of its spin and sinking life. Acosta's slider is his go-to strikeout pitch. It sweeps across the plate and has high spin, eliciting swings and misses. His changeup grades a distant third. Acosta's long arms help create unique angles but also inhibit his ability to time his delivery and repeat arm slot, which has contributed to chronically poor walk rates.
THE FUTURE: Acosta has swing-and-miss stuff and now a little success under his belt. He has the pitch profile of a future No. 5 starter or medium-leverage reliever.

Year	Age	Club (League)	Class	W	L	ERA	G	GS	SV	IP	H	HR	BB	SO	K/9	WHIP	AVG
2017	18	Mets (GCL)	R	0	2	3.27	6	4	0	22	18	0	7	19	7.8	1.14	.237
2018	19	Kingsport (APP)	R	2	5	4.46	10	9	0	42	38	8	18	46	9.8	1.32	.236
2019	20	Brooklyn (NYP)	SS	1	0	0.98	4	3	0	18	9	0	6	25	12.3	0.82	.150
	20	Columbia (SAL)	LoA	1	4	3.78	11	11	0	52	50	4	26	49	8.4	1.45	.244
Minor League Totals				4	12	3.56	34	30	0	146	129	12	63	147	9.0	1.31	.236

26 CARLOS CORTES, 2B

BA GRADE 45 **Risk:** High

Born: June 30, 1997. **B-T:** L-B. **HT:** 5-7. **WT:** 197. **Drafted:** South Carolina, 2018 (3rd round). **Signed by:** Daniel Coles.
TRACK RECORD: Cortes received one of just three seven-figure bonuses in the third round of the 2018 draft when he signed for $1 million. He advanced straight to high Class A St. Lucie in 2019 and put together a productive season in the Florida State League.
SCOUTING REPORT: The 5-foot-7, stocky Cortes bats lefthanded but is fully ambidextrous in the field, where he throws lefthanded in the outfield and righthanded at second base. He focused his time in the FSL at second base, where his fluidity has improved even though he lacks classic first-step quickness or arm strength. The batter's box is where Cortes shines. His picturesque swing and outstanding bat-to-ball skills give him average overall batting potential with the chance for a dozen home runs or more.
THE FUTURE: Cortes doesn't have a prototype body type or speed for the middle infield, but the Mets are convinced he will hit.

Year	Age	Club (League)	Class	AVG	G	AB	R	H	2B	3B	HR	RBI	BB	SO	SB	OBP	SLG
2018	20	Brooklyn (NYP)	SS	.264	47	178	26	47	5	2	4	24	17	34	1	.338	.382
2019	21	St. Lucie (FSL)	HiA	.255	127	458	64	117	26	3	11	68	52	77	6	.336	.397
Minor League Totals				.258	174	636	90	164	31	5	15	92	69	111	7	.337	.393

27 RYLEY GILLIAM, RHP

BA GRADE 40 **Risk:** High

Born: Aug. 11, 1996. **B-T:** R-R. **HT:** 5-10. **WT:** 170. **Drafted:** Clemson, 2018 (5th round). **Signed by:** Daniel Coles.
TRACK RECORD: The Mets were attracted to Gilliam in the fifth round of the 2018 draft because of his electric arm speed and high-spin breaking ball. He served as a closer at Clemson and continued in a bullpen role in pro ball, beginning his first full season at high Class A St. Lucie and reaching Triple-A Syracuse in June. His season concluded with seven appearances in the Arizona Fall League.
SCOUTING REPORT: Gilliam is a 5-foot-10 reliever with a chance for two plus pitches. His 93-96 mph fastball has good riding life up in the zone and gets on hitters quick because of how well he hides the ball in his delivery. His top-to-bottom curveball has 78-80 mph velocity and dramatic late break and spin. If Gilliam learns to command the pitch for called strikes he can be a high-leverage reliever.
THE FUTURE: Gilliam has advanced weaponry but a stuff-over-feel pitching profile. By finishing 2019 in the AFL, he has a chance to earn a major league look in 2020.

Year	Age	Club (League)	Class	W	L	ERA	G	GS	SV	IP	H	HR	BB	SO	K/9	WHIP	AVG
2018	21	Brooklyn (NYP)	SS	0	1	2.08	17	0	5	17	11	1	13	31	16.1	1.38	.180
2019	22	St. Lucie (FSL)	HiA	0	0	2.53	7	0	2	11	8	0	2	16	13.5	0.94	.200
	22	Binghamton (EL)	AA	3	0	4.34	12	0	1	19	15	1	7	28	13.5	1.18	.224
	22	Syracuse (IL)	AAA	2	0	13.50	10	0	0	9	19	3	9	12	11.6	3.00	.432
Minor League Totals				5	1	4.82	46	0	8	56	53	5	31	87	14.0	1.50	.250

28 ALI SANCHEZ, C

BA GRADE 40 **Risk:** High

Born: Jan. 20, 1997. **B-T:** R-R. **HT:** 6-1. **WT:** 196. **Signed:** Venezuela, 2013. **Signed by:** Robert Espejo/Hector Rincones.
TRACK RECORD: Sanchez is a gifted defensive catcher who signed in 2013 but didn't reach full-season ball

until 2017 because his bat was so light. His batting line ticked up near average at Double-A Binghamton in 2019 and he reached Triple-A for the first time late in the season.

SCOUTING REPORT: Sanchez impacts games while behind the plate, in both obvious and subtle ways. His plus arm plays up a grade because of his quick transfer and throwing accuracy. He threw out 44 percent of basestealers at the upper levels of the minors in 2019. Sanchez shines as a game-caller and pitch-framer, helping to win strikes for his pitchers. At the plate, Sanchez is a bottom-of-the-order hitter who uses all fields with an inside-out swing. He has 20-grade power but has shown greater skill at hitting for average and drawing walks in recent seasons.

THE FUTURE: If major league rosters expand to 26 players in 2020, as expected, it would create an extra 30 big league jobs, some of which could go to defensive-oriented backup catchers like Sanchez. That played a role in the Mets' decision to protect him from the Rule 5 draft.

Year	Age	Club (League)	Class	AVG	G	AB	R	H	2B	3B	HR	RBI	BB	SO	SB	OBP	SLG
2017	20	Columbia (SAL)	LoA	.231	56	182	20	42	3	0	1	15	13	26	2	.288	.264
2018	21	Columbia (SAL)	LoA	.259	50	193	26	50	11	1	4	22	10	23	1	.293	.389
	21	St. Lucie (FSL)	HiA	.274	38	135	11	37	9	0	2	16	5	15	1	.296	.385
2019	22	Binghamton (EL)	AA	.278	71	270	28	75	13	0	1	30	23	52	1	.337	.337
	22	Syracuse (IL)	AAA	.179	21	56	5	10	4	0	0	3	5	11	0	.277	.250
Minor League Totals				.259	381	1355	148	351	63	1	11	141	105	212	15	.317	.331

29 QUINN BRODEY, OF

BA GRADE
40 Risk: High

Born: Dec. 1, 1995. **B-T:** L-L. **HT:** 6-1. **WT:** 195. **Drafted:** Stanford, 2017 (3rd round). **Signed by:** Tyler Holmes.

TRACK RECORD: Drafted as a lefthanded pitcher out of high school, Brodey played both ways early in his college career before settling in as an outfielder. After two unremarkable seasons to begin his pro career, he had a brush with success at high Class A St. Lucie in the first half of 2019.

SCOUTING REPORT: Depending on one's viewpoint, Brodey is either a future fourth outfielder or a tweener who lacks a carrying tool. The lefthanded hitter makes hard line-drive contact and posts good exit velocity numbers with plus bat speed. His level stroke produces more doubles than home runs, but his balance and timing at the plate as well as a low chase rate mark him as at least an average hitter. He is a good baserunner and efficient basestealer. Brodey can play all three outfield positions because he gets good reads and jumps. His above-average arm plays up thanks to accuracy and a quick release.

THE FUTURE: Brodey has modest upside but a well-rounded set of skills that could carry him to the major leagues in a complementary role. He will spend another season in the upper minors before perhaps getting a big league look in 2021.

Year	Age	Club (League)	Class	AVG	G	AB	R	H	2B	3B	HR	RBI	BB	SO	SB	OBP	SLG
2017	21	Brooklyn (NYP)	SS	.257	54	210	20	54	9	2	2	30	14	49	10	.303	.348
	21	Columbia (SAL)	LoA	.229	9	35	4	8	1	1	1	7	4	14	0	.300	.400
2018	22	Columbia (SAL)	LoA	.217	84	314	36	68	14	5	10	46	26	93	7	.287	.389
	22	St. Lucie (FSL)	HiA	.245	31	102	11	25	3	1	3	17	10	31	4	.313	.382
2019	23	St. Lucie (FSL)	HiA	.285	53	200	30	57	13	1	5	38	18	46	8	.335	.435
	23	Binghamton (EL)	AA	.251	77	247	22	62	16	0	5	24	22	61	5	.314	.377
Minor League Totals				.247	308	1108	123	274	56	10	26	162	94	294	34	.308	.386

30 SCOTT OTA, OF

BA GRADE
40 Risk: High

Born: Aug. 16, 1997. **B-T:** L-L. **HT:** 5-11. **WT:** 195. **Drafted:** Illinois-Chicago, 2019 (10th round). **Signed by:** Chris Heidt.

TRACK RECORD: Ota ranked 15th in Division I by hitting 20 home runs as an Illinois-Chicago senior. He had the best pro debut of any Mets draft pick, ranking fourth in the Rookie-level Appalachian League with a .519 slugging percentage and fifth with an .874 OPS

SCOUTING REPORT: Ota takes a professional approach to hitting that helps him produce at a level above his average overall tool set. He has a disciplined approach and puts the ball in play with gap power to all fields. He uses a small leg lift and barred arm in his swing to emphasize contact over power. Ordinary power and speed make Ota's most likely career path that of an extra outfielder. He is a sound defender in right field who makes good decisions and has an average arm.

THE FUTURE: What Ota lacks in terms of a carrying tool he makes up for with his baseball IQ and all-around play. He will have to keep proving himself as he advances up the minor league ladder.

Year	Age	Club (League)	Class	AVG	G	AB	R	H	2B	3B	HR	RBI	BB	SO	SB	OBP	SLG
2019	21	Kingsport (APP)	R	.273	51	183	30	50	14	5	7	26	21	38	0	.355	.519
Minor League Totals				.273	51	183	30	50	14	5	7	26	21	38	0	.355	.519

New York Yankees

BY JOSH NORRIS

After coming up short in 2018, the Yankees seemed poised for a big run in 2019. Aaron Judge and Giancarlo Stanton were back to anchor the core of a powerful lineup. Standout rookies Gleyber Torres and Miguel Andujar were ready for encore performances. Luis Severino and Masahiro Tanaka would lead the way for a rotation that could feel confident handing the ball off to a stacked bullpen that included Aroldis Chapman, Dellin Betances, Zack Britton and new addition Adam Ottavino.

Then the season happened, and star after star was struck by injuries. Judge and Stanton played a combined 120 games (just 18 from Stanton), Andujar took just 47 at-bats and Severino and Betances combined for just 12.2 innings. Gary Sanchez, too, was limited to 106 games.

Despite all that, the Yankees fell two wins short of advancing to the World Series. The team was buoyed all season by smart pickups, including D.J. LeMahieu, who had a career year and finished fourth in the MVP balloting on a two-year deal. The team's other key pickup was third baseman Gio Urshela, who was signed toward the end of 2018, started 2019 in the minor leagues and then was forced into duty when Andujar went down with a season-ending shoulder injury.

Thought to be little more than minor league depth, Urshela finished the season with 21 home runs and an .881 OPS. His 3.4 wins above replacement—as measured by Baseball-Reference.com—put him in sixth on the team, just 0.2 points behind another stealth pickup in outfielder Mike Tauchman. The Yankees acquired Tauchman in a trade with the Rockies toward the end of spring training and watched as he became an outfield stalwart in Stanton's absence. Tauchman finished the year with 13 home runs and an .865 OPS.

The Yankees finished the year with the second-best record in the American League and coasted past Minnesota into a Championship Series matchup with the Astros, which they lost in six games on a walk-off home run from Jose Altuve.

The 2019 season also marked the end of lefthander CC Sabathia's career. He announced his planned retirement before the season, then went 5-8, 4.95 in the regular season before being used out of the bullpen in the playoffs.

The farm was led by righthander Deivi Garcia, who rocketed from high Class A Tampa to Triple-A Scranton/Wilkes-Barre with a stop at the Futures Game along the way. He racked up a system-best 165 strikeouts and appears to be on the cusp of the big leagues. Righthander Clarke Schmidt, with the reins removed in his second year back from Tommy John surgery, was also impressive, and took his place as the system's top starting pitching prospect.

The Yankees also made a huge splash on the international market when they signed Dominican outfielder Jasson Dominguez, whose extraordinary tool set commanded a $5.1 million bonus that stands as the largest outlay the franchise has given to an international amateur. On potential alone, he moved to the No. 1 ranking in the organization.

The Yankees hope that with returns to health from their key pieces, 2020 can finish just a few wins better than 2019.

ELSA/GETTY IMAGES

The emergence of journeyman third baseman Gio Urshela helped cover for myriad injuries.

PROJECTED 2023 LINEUP

Position	Player	Age
Catcher	Gary Sanchez	30
First Base	Luke Voit	32
Second Base	Oswald Peraza (5)	22
Third Base	Gio Urshela	31
Shortstop	Gleyber Torres	26
Left Field	Giancarlo Stanton	33
Center Field	Jasson Dominguez (1)	20
Right Field	Aaron Judge	31
Designated Hitter	Miguel Andujar	28
No. 1 Starter	Gerrit Cole	32
No. 1 Starter	Luis Severino	29
No. 2 Starter	James Paxton	34
No. 3 Starter	Domingo German	30
No. 4 Starter	Clarke Schmidt (2)	27
Closer	Luis Medina (7)	24

DEPTH CHART

NEW YORK YANKEES

TOP 2020 ROOKIE: Deivi Garcia, RHP. With a strong spring and a little more seasoning, Garcia could make an impact in New York in 2020.
BREAKOUT PROSPECT: Yoendrys Gomez, RHP. After another strong season, the projectable Gomez could fly through the system.
SLEEPER: Brandon Lockridge, OF. The Troy product posted a fine 2019 and could open even more eyes in 2020 with an encore performance.

SOURCE OF TOP 30 TALENT

Homegrown	**26**	**Acquired**	**4**
College	3	Trade	4
Junior college	1	Rule 5 draft	0
High school	5	Independent league	0
Nondrafted free agent	0	Free agent/waivers	0
International	17		

LF
Canaan Smith (16)
Jake Sanford
Trey Amburgey
Ben Ruta

CF
Jasson Dominguez (1)
Estevan Florial (14)
Kevin Alcantara (20)
Everson Pereira (18)
Antonio Cabello (19)
Raimfer Salinas (26)
Josh Stowers (30)
Brandon Lockridge

RF
Ryder Green (29)
Anthony Garcia
Madison Santos

3B
Oswaldo Cabrera
Enger Castellano
Andres Chaparro

SS
Oswald Peraza (5)
Anthony Volpe (6)
Alexander Vargas (22)
Thairo Estrada
Roberto Chirinos
Marcos Cabrera
Kyle Holder

2B
Ezequiel Duran (24)
Josh Smith (25)
Diego Castillo
Hoy Park

1B
Chris Gittens
Dermis Garcia
Brandon Wagner

C
Antonio Gomez (21)
Anthony Seigler (23)
Donny Sands

LHP

LHSP	LHRP
TJ Sikkema (15)	Trevor Lane
Jake Agnos	James Reeves
Ken Waldichuk	Anderson Severino
Josh Maciejewski	
Dalton Lehnen	
Alfredo Garcia	

RHP

RHSP	RHRP
Clarke Schmidt (2)	Brooks Kriske
Deivi Garcia (3)	Daniel Alvarez
Luis Gil (4)	Tanner Myatt
Luis Medina (7)	Glenn Otto
Roansy Contreras (8)	Aaron McGarity
Alexander Vizcaino (9)	Nelson Alvarez
Albert Abreu (10)	Frank German
Miguel Yajure (11)	Shawn Semple
Yoendrys Gomez (12)	Yoljeldriz Diaz
Michael King (13)	
Matt Sauer (17)	
Nick Nelson (28)	
Garrett Whitlock	
Hayden Wesneski	
Denny Larrondo	

DRAFT ANALYSIS

2019

BEST PURE HITTER: This is a virtual tie between SS Anthony Volpe (1) and SS Josh Smith (2), who each have swings geared for line drives now with power expected to develop as they move up the ladder in pro ball. Volpe's true ability was sapped by a bout of mononucleosis, while Smith posted a .927 OPS in the short-season New York-Penn League.

BEST POWER: Western Kentucky OF Jake Sanford (3) has an intriguing but unpolished set of tools, including raw power that ranks as a 70 on the 20-to-80 scouting scale.

FASTEST RUNNER: The Yankees' class lacked a true burner, but Volpe's plus run times give him the edge in this category.

BEST DEFENSIVE PLAYER: Volpe takes this category too, on the strength of the range and arm strength that will allow him a chance to stick at shortstop in the long term. Amateur scouts praised the consistency and sureness of his hands and thought of him as one of the better defenders at the position.

BEST ATHLETE: Sanford, who played hockey among a litany of other sports while growing up in Nova Scotia, Canada, is the winner here thanks to his diverse athletic background.

BEST FASTBALL: South Florida product RHP Nelson Alvarez (13) has touched 100 mph with his heater and can sit in the mid-90s. The pitch has the carrying life that typically gets swings and misses up in the zone.

BEST SECONDARY PITCH: Missouri LHP TJ Sikkema (1s) and St. Mary's LHP Ken Waldichuk (5) each showed sliders that project as plus pitches.

BEST PRO DEBUT: Smith's strong turn in the New York-Penn League, where he ranked as the league's No. 16 prospect, made him an easy choice for this category. Smith hit .324/.450/.477 with 25 walks to just 17 strikeouts in 33 games.

MOST INTRIGUING BACKGROUND: Sanford's long path to pro ball—a sparse high school career, two years at Mid-Plains (Neb.) JC, a year at Western Kentucky—plus a multi-sport background helps him stand out above the rest.

CLOSEST TO THE MAJORS: Smith's college pedigree and hot start as a pro could help him get there quickly. Alvarez's high-octane fastball and improved slider could put him on a fast track as well.

THE ONE WHO GOT AWAY: The Yankees selected RHP Jack Leiter (20)—the son of former big leaguer Al Leiter—in the 20th round knowing he was likely to head to Vanderbilt for two seasons before making himself available for pro ball. He is currently one of the top prospects in the 2021 draft class, when he will be a draft-eligible sophomore.

BEST LATE-ROUND PICK: Alvarez's powerful fastball-slider combination in the 13th round could prove to be a steal if he ascends through the system as the Yankees expect.

—**JOSH NORRIS**

TOP DRAFT PICKS OF THE DECADE

Year	Player, Pos.	2019 Org
2010	Cito Culver, SS	Can-Am League
2011	Dante Bichette Jr., 3B (1st round supp.)	Nationals
2012	Ty Hensley, RHP	Did not play
2013	Eric Jagielo, 3B	Did not play
2014	Jacob Lindgren, LHP (2nd round)	White Sox
2015	James Kaprielian, RHP	Athletics
2016	Blake Rutherford, OF	White Sox
2017	Clarke Schmidt, RHP	Yankees
2018	Anthony Seigler, C	Yankees
2019	Anthony Volpe, SS	Yankees

2018

It was not a good first full professional season for this class. C Anthony Siegler (1) has struggled mightily offensively and C Josh Breaux (2) was sidelined most of the year. OF Ryder Green (3) was a bright spot.

GRADE: D

2017

RHP Clarke Schmidt (1) has come back strong from Tommy John surgery and now ranks as the system's best pitcher. RHP Matt Sauer (2) and OF Canaan Smith (4) have also proven to be promising.

GRADE: B

2016

The Yankees have used this class heavily in trades, dealing four players, including OF Blake Rutherford (1) and 2B Nick Solak (2). Solak and LHP Phillip Diehl (27) give the class a pair of big leaguers already.

GRADE: C

1 JASSON DOMINGUEZ, OF

Born: Feb. 7, 2003. **B-T:** B-R. **HT:** 5-10. **WT:** 210.
Signed: Dominican Republic, 2019.
Signed by: Juan Rosario/Lorenzo Piron/Edgar Mateo.

TRACK RECORD: Dominguez had been on major league teams' radar screens since he was 13. He was training with Ivan Noboa in the Dominican Republic, as part of a group that also featured future Brewers prospect Larry Ernesto. He homered to center field on the first pitch he saw that day, and ran the 60-yard dash in somewhere between 6.3 and 6.4 seconds. He continued to impress over the next few years in showcases and simulated games while facing pitchers more advanced than are usually seen in that setting. The Yankees signed Dominguez in 2019 for $5.1 million, which tied Dominican shortstop Robert Puason, signed by the Athletics, for tops in the class and ranks as the largest international bonus the Yankees have ever handed an amateur.

SCOUTING REPORT: Yankees international scouting director Donny Rowland said Dominguez has "possibly the best combination of tools, athleticism and performance that (he's) run across." His body is built similarly to Yoan Moncada. Dominguez is shorter than Moncada, but both players have a combination of tightly packed muscle that produces strength and quick-burst athleticism. Dominguez is an advanced hitter from both sides of the plate with plate discipline, a low chase rate for someone his age and a swing path that allows his barrel to stay in the zone for a very long time. His sense of timing against all types of pitches mitigates the pre-pitch movement in his swing, and strong hands, wrists and forearms give him the potential for plenty of power from both sides of the plate. He has already shown exit velocities up to 108 mph from both sides of the plate in batting practice and has shown little problem turning around high-level velocity. The Yankees scouted Dominguez as a shortstop and catcher but decided that center field was the best fit. He has double-plus speed, which he combines with smooth, advanced route-running to help him track down balls in the far reaches of the outfield. His arm strength is plus or a tick better and is magnified by incredible accuracy. Internally, the Yankees describe Dominguez as a player who might be constructed by taking the best tools from other players throughout their system and molding them into a single player. His power, speed and athleticism rank among the best in the organization, which gives him the highest ceiling in the system.

THE FUTURE: Dominguez has yet to play his first official game and has a long way to go. But he has the blend of tools and baseball IQ to move as quickly as any of the current line of young stars from Latin America.

BA GRADE
65 **Risk: Extreme**

SCOUTING GRADES
Hit: 60. **Power:** 70. **Run:** 70. **Field:** 60. **Arm:** 60.

Projected future grades on 20-80 scouting scale.

TOP PROSPECTS OF THE DECADE

Year	Player, Pos.	2019 Org
2010	Jesus Montero, C	Did not play
2011	Jesus Montero, C	Did not play
2012	Jesus Montero, C	Did not play
2013	Mason Williams, OF	Orioles
2014	Gary Sanchez, C	Yankees
2015	Luis Severino, RHP	Yankees
2016	Jorge Mateo, SS	Athletics
2017	Gleyber Torres, SS	Yankees
2018	Gleyber Torres, SS	Yankees
2019	Estevan Florial, OF	Yankees

BEST TOOLS

Best Hitter for Average	Canaan Smith
Best Power Hitter	Dermis Garcia
Best Strike-Zone Discipline	Canaan Smith
Fastest Baserunner	Estevan Florial
Best Athlete	Jasson Dominguez
Best Fastball	Luis Medina
Best Curveball	Clarke Schmidt
Best Slider	Deivi Garcia
Best Changeup	Alexander Vizcaino
Best Control	Miguel Yajure
Best Defensive Catcher	Antonio Gomez
Best Defensive Infielder	Kyle Holder
Best Infield Arm	Oswald Peraza
Best Defensive Outfielder	Jasson Dominguez
Best Outfield Arm	Jasson Dominguez

Year	Age	Club (League)	Class	AVG	G	AB	R	H	2B	3B	HR	RBI	BB	SO	SB	OBP	SLG
2019	16	Did not play—Signed 2020 contract															

2 CLARKE SCHMIDT, RHP

Born: Feb. 20, 1996. **B-T:** R-R. **HT:** 6-1. **WT:** 200. **Drafted:** South Carolina, 2017 (1st round). **Signed by:** Billy Godwin.

BA GRADE
60 Risk: High

TRACK RECORD: The Yankees selected Schmidt in the first round in 2017 knowing he'd need Tommy John surgery. He missed all of 2017 recovering, then pitched just 23 innings in 2018 between the Rookie-level Gulf Coast League and short-season Staten Island. He skipped low Class A Charleston and then sped to Double-A Trenton, albeit with about six weeks on the injured list.

SCOUTING REPORT: Schmidt starts his repertoire with a 92-95 mph fastball that scouts saw up to 97 mph. The pitch shows boring, cutting action in on the hands of lefties. He backs it up with a potentially plus or better changeup with enough velocity and bottom that it can be mistaken for a split-fingered fastball. His curveball—which can behave like a slider—also earns above-average and plus grades. Schmidt also changes arm slots on his pitches, alternating between a high three-quarter and three-quarters, to give hitters different looks.

THE FUTURE: After a season that saw his pre-surgery stuff return in full, Schmidt has ceiling of a mid-rotation starter and looks like a wise gamble with the 16th overall pick.

SCOUTING GRADES: **Fastball:** 60 **Changeup:** 60 **Curveball:** 55 **Control:** 50

Year	Age	Club (League)	Class	W	L	ERA	G	GS	SV	IP	H	HR	BB	SO	K/9	WHIP	AVG
2017	21	Did not play—Injured															
2018	22	Yankees2 (GCL)	R	0	0	1.23	3	3	0	7	4	0	2	8	9.8	0.82	.167
	22	Yankees1 (GCL)	R	0	2	7.04	3	2	0	8	8	1	2	12	14.1	1.30	.267
	22	Staten Island (NYP)	SS	0	1	1.08	2	2	0	8	4	0	2	10	10.8	0.72	.143
2019	23	Yankees1 (GCL)	R	0	0	3.24	3	3	0	8	6	1	3	14	15.1	1.08	.200
	23	Tampa (FSL)	HiA	4	5	3.84	13	12	0	63	59	2	24	69	9.8	1.31	.247
	23	Trenton (EL)	AA	2	0	2.37	3	3	0	19	14	1	1	19	9.0	0.79	.200
Minor League Totals				6	8	3.39	27	25	0	114	95	5	34	132	10.4	1.13	.226

3 DEIVI GARCIA, RHP

Born: May 19, 1999. **B-T:** R-R. **HT:** 5-10. **WT:** 167. **Signed:** Dominican Republic, 2015. **Signed by:** Miguel Benitez.

TRACK RECORD: Garcia followed an impressive 2018 season with a strong 2019 campaign in which he rocketed from high Class A to Triple-A. He moved to the bullpen toward the end of his time with Triple-A as a means of managing his innings.

SCOUTING REPORT: Garcia entered 2019 with a big-breaking, high-spin curveball as his signature pitch. That pitch continued to be a weapon over the first half, but the Yankees made the decision to add a slider at the midway point of his season. The mid-80s slider gave him a breaking ball that showed hitters a pitch that moved from east to west instead of the rest of his repertoire, which was most effective at the top and bottom of the strike zone. His fastball, which sat in the 92-93 mph range and touched 96-97, showed excellent carry and elicited plenty of swings and misses when elevated. His fourth pitch is a mid-80s changeup.

THE FUTURE: There have long been questions about whether Garcia's slight frame will allow him to hold up as a starter over the course of a full season. Scouts are still split on whether his future is as a starter or a reliever, and he has earned comparisons with Octavio Dotel and Francisco Rodriguez.

SCOUTING GRADES: **Fastball:** 60 **Slider:** 60 **Curveball:** 55 **Changeup:** 50 **Control:** 55

Year	Age	Club (League)	Class	W	L	ERA	G	GS	SV	IP	H	HR	BB	SO	K/9	WHIP	AVG
2017	18	Yankees1 (DSL)	R	1	1	1.17	3	3	0	15	10	1	2	18	10.6	0.78	.196
	18	Yankees2 (GCL)	R	3	0	3.24	4	2	0	17	9	3	4	24	13.0	0.78	.155
	18	Pulaski (APP)	R	2	1	4.50	6	5	0	28	23	3	13	43	13.8	1.29	.232
2018	19	Charleston (SAL)	LoA	2	4	3.76	8	8	0	41	31	5	10	63	13.9	1.01	.205
	19	Tampa (FSL)	HiA	2	0	1.27	6	6	0	28	19	0	8	35	11.1	0.95	.192
	19	Trenton (EL)	AA	1	0	0.00	1	1	0	5	0	0	2	7	12.6	0.40	.000
2019	20	Tampa (FSL)	HiA	0	2	3.06	4	4	0	18	14	0	8	33	16.8	1.25	.215
	20	Trenton (EL)	AA	4	4	3.86	11	11	0	54	43	2	26	87	14.6	1.29	.213
	20	Scranton/W-B (IL)	AAA	1	3	5.40	11	6	0	40	39	8	20	45	10.1	1.48	.262
Minor League Totals				17	20	3.37	65	57	0	293	211	23	125	416	12.8	1.14	.202

4 LUIS GIL, RHP

BA GRADE
55 Risk: Very High

Born: June 3, 1998. **B-T:** R-R. **HT:** 6-3. **WT:** 200. **Signed:** Dominican Republic, 2014. **Signed by:** Luis Lajara (Twins).

TRACK RECORD: Gil was signed by the Twins in 2014 on the strength of a loose, live arm and a frame that projected to develop into that of a classic power pitcher. He was dealt to the Yankees in the winter of 2017 in a one-for-one deal for outfielder Jake Cave.

SCOUTING REPORT: Gil's calling card is his fastball, which sizzles into hitters in the upper 90s and touched as high as 101 mph in 2019. The pitch ranks as at least a 70 on the 20-to-80 scouting scale on velocity and movement, which has electric boring life in on the hands of lefthanders and extreme carry through the zone when he works to his gloveside. He backs up the fastball with a sweeping curveball in the low 80s and a changeup that averaged 91 mph. Scouts were uniformly impressed at the ease with which he produced that kind of velocity. Both offspeed pitches need considerable work in terms of command and consistency but each projects as a 50-to-55 grade pitch.

THE FUTURE: Gil's season ended a little early after he reported tightness in his right biceps after a side session but he might have been ready to go again were the Florida State League's last few games not canceled due to threat of hurricane. He will return to high Class A Tampa. If both of his offspeed pitches take steps forward he has a chance to be a mid-rotation starter. If only one does, he fits as a dynamic weapon toward the back of a bullpen.

SCOUTING GRADES: **Fastball:** 70 **Curveball:** 50 **Changeup:** 50 **Control:** 50

Year	Age	Club (League)	Class	W	L	ERA	G	GS	SV	IP	H	HR	BB	SO	K/9	WHIP	AVG
2017	19	Twins (DSL)	R	0	2	2.59	14	14	0	42	31	2	20	49	10.6	1.22	.205
2018	20	Pulaski (APP)	R	2	1	1.37	10	10	0	39	21	1	25	58	13.3	1.17	.154
	20	Staten Island (NYP)	SS	0	2	5.40	2	2	0	7	11	1	6	10	13.5	2.55	.344
2019	21	Charleston (SAL)	LoA	4	5	2.39	17	17	0	83	60	1	39	112	12.1	1.19	.200
	21	Tampa (FSL)	HiA	1	0	4.85	3	3	0	13	11	0	8	11	7.6	1.46	.234
Minor League Totals				8	12	2.74	62	46	2	207	149	7	124	264	11.5	1.32	.200

5 OSWALD PERAZA, SS

BA GRADE
55 Risk: Very High

Born: June 15, 2000. **B-T:** R-R. **HT:** 5-11. **WT:** 186. **Signed:** Venezuela, 2016. **Signed by:** Roney Calderon/Jose Gavidia.

TRACK RECORD: Peraza was part of an international class that also included righthander Roansy Contreras and the since-traded Jose Devers, and he has quickly proved to be one of the system's fastest risers. He made it to Rookie-level Pulaski as an 18-year-old, then moved to low Class A Charleston after just 15 games in short-season Staten Island as a 19-year-old. The Yankees laud Peraza for his all-around blend of tools and a solid makeup that allows him quickly turn them into skills.

SCOUTING REPORT: Evaluators both inside and outside the organization have been impressed with Peraza's tool set, which has shown up at each of his stops despite his accelerated development path. His polished baseball skills give him a high floor, and his high-end athleticism suggests a path to a high ceiling. His simple swing and sneaky strength have helped him show above-average or better raw power, though he hasn't shown much of it in games. He's also shown a smooth, simple swing that gives his barrel a direct path to the ball. The Yankees believe that, plus his advanced knowledge of the strike zone, will help him better select pitches on which he can do damage as he moves up the ladder. He shows smooth actions in the field and a strong arm that should keep him at shortstop. He also clocks in between 4.1 and 4.2 seconds to first base, which grades as plus speed.

THE FUTURE: Peraza is likely to return to Charleston to begin 2020 and should reach high Class A Tampa.

SCOUTING GRADES: **Hitting:** 50 **Power:** 40 **Running:** 60 **Fielding:** 60 **Arm:** 60

Year	Age	Club (League)	Class	AVG	G	AB	R	H	2B	3B	HR	RBI	BB	SO	SB	OBP	SLG
2017	17	Yankees1 (DSL)	R	.361	10	36	10	13	3	2	0	10	7	2	1	.467	.556
	17	Yankees2 (GCL)	R	.266	48	184	34	49	10	1	0	24	16	36	12	.363	.332
2018	18	Pulaski (APP)	R	.250	36	140	25	35	3	2	1	11	14	41	8	.333	.321
2019	19	Staten Island (NYP)	SS	.241	19	79	7	19	1	1	2	7	5	9	5	.294	.354
	19	Charleston (SAL)	LoA	.273	46	183	31	50	5	0	2	13	16	28	18	.348	.333
Minor League Totals				.267	159	622	107	166	22	6	5	65	58	116	44	.350	.346

6 ANTHONY VOLPE, SS

Born: April 28, 2001. **B-T:** R-R. **HT:** 5-11. **WT:** 180. **Drafted:** HS—Morristown, N.J, 2019 (1st round). **Signed by:** Matt Hyde.

TRACK RECORD: Volpe formed a dynamic duo at Delbarton High with right-hander and fellow Yankees draftee Jack Leiter. Volpe signed for $2,740,300 and headed directly to Rookie-level Pulaski. He contracted mononucleosis, however, which sapped his strength and cut his season short.

SCOUTING REPORT: Volpe doesn't have one standout tool, but the sum of his parts makes him an attractive player. He utilizes a short, quick swing to shoot line drives to all fields. The Yankees also like his ability and hand-eye coordination, which they believe will result in plenty of contact and a low strikeout rate. He's a gifted defender with smooth hands and feet that should allow him to stick up the middle. He's also got enough range and speed to stay at the position, even if his throwing arm is only average.

THE FUTURE: After an offseason to recover from the mono, Volpe is a strong candidate to head to low Class A Charleston to begin 2020.

SCOUTING GRADES: **Hitting:** 50 **Power:** 45 **Running:** 55 **Fielding:** 60 **Arm:** 50

Year	Age	Club (League)	Class	AVG	G	AB	R	H	2B	3B	HR	RBI	BB	SO	SB	OBP	SLG
2019	18	Pulaski (APP)	R	.215	34	121	19	26	7	2	2	11	23	38	6	.349	.355
Minor League Totals				.215	34	121	19	26	7	2	2	11	23	38	6	.349	.355

7 LUIS MEDINA, RHP

Born: May 3, 1999. **B-T:** R-R. **HT:** 6-3. **WT:** 195. **Signed:** Dominican Republic, 2015. **Signed by:** Juan Rosario.

TRACK RECORD: The Yankees signed Medina for $280,000 on the strength of a live arm that was already producing fastballs that touched triple-digits. He skipped straight to Rookie-level Pulaski for his pro debut in 2017, then proceeded to spend the better part of three seasons showing a strange combination of near-elite stuff with nearly nonexistent control or command.

SCOUTING REPORT: Medina's biggest strength is an elite fastball which averaged 98 mph in 2019 and peaked at 101 mph. Medina threw the fastball with enough life to induce a 32 percent swing-and-miss rate when the pitch was in the strike zone. For reference, the average is 15 percent. He backed up the fastball with a low-80s curveball—which sometimes broke like a true hammer and other times like a two-plane slider—that was swung at and missed 44 percent of the time. His third pitch is a high-80s changeup that flashes plus as well. A bit of inconsistency in his delivery—sometimes he landed a bit early and his arm slot wandered—plus a tendency to let mistakes compound led to a walk rate of just more than 6 hitters per nine innings. Something clicked on July 31 season, however, and Medina struck out 39 over the next 28 innings while allowing just five earned runs.

THE FUTURE: Medina will return to high Class A Tampa to see if he can continue building on his strong finish to 2019 and begin to scratch his sky-high potential.

SCOUTING GRADES: **Fastball:** 80 **Curveball:** 70 **Changeup:** 55 **Control:** 40

Year	Age	Club (League)	Class	W	L	ERA	G	GS	SV	IP	H	HR	BB	SO	K/9	WHIP	AVG
2017	18	Yankees1 (DSL)	R	1	1	5.74	4	3	0	16	17	0	10	17	9.8	1.72	.270
	18	Pulaski (APP)	R	1	1	5.09	6	6	0	23	14	1	14	22	8.6	1.22	.171
2018	19	Pulaski (APP)	R	1	3	6.25	12	12	0	36	32	3	46	47	11.8	2.17	.239
2019	20	Charleston (SAL)	LoA	1	8	6.00	20	20	0	93	86	9	67	115	11.1	1.65	.248
	20	Tampa (FSL)	HiA	0	0	0.84	2	2	0	11	7	0	3	12	10.1	0.94	.175
Minor League Totals				4	13	5.51	47	46	0	183	158	13	144	217	10.7	1.65	.232

8 ROANSY CONTRERAS, RHP

BA GRADE

50 Risk: High

Born: Nov. 7, 1999. **B-T:** R-R. **HT:** 6-0. **WT:** 197. **Signed:** Dominican Republic, 2016. **Signed by:** Juan Rosario.

TRACK RECORD: The Yankees were still in the international penalty box in 2016 but unearthed Contreras and signed him for $250,000. He experienced a bit of a breakout in 2018, when he ranked as the No. 5 prospect in the New York-Penn League after a strong performance in a typically college-heavy league before moving to low Class A Charleston and holding his own for seven starts. He is a product of the same Dominican program that produced Miguel Andujar and Gary Sanchez.

SCOUTING REPORT: Contreras was easily the most consistent piece of Charleston's extremely talented rotation and has as high an upside as anyone not named Luis Medina. He starts his arsenal with a low-90s fastball that can get to the mid-90s fairly consistently. The pitch is relatively straight but is thrown with considerable extension and downhill plane that somewhat mitigate the lack of movement. His best secondary offering is power changeup with sinking action thrown in the 85-89 mph range and sold well because it's thrown with the same conviction as his fastball. His curveball, a slurvy offering in the low 80s, is thrown with more consistent spin than the breaking balls of his rotation-mates in Charleston. Scouts noted more consistent hand position on the curveball led to a more consistent, higher quality offering. Contreras also impressed evaluators with his feel to pitch as situations dictated.

THE FUTURE: Contreras will move to high Class A Tampa in 2020. Scouts who like him see a solid back-end starter with a ceiling of a No. 3 if absolutely everything goes right.

SCOUTING GRADES: **Fastball:** 60 **Changeup:** 60 **Curveball:** 55 **Control:** 50

Year	Age	Club (League)	Class	W	L	ERA	G	GS	SV	IP	H	HR	BB	SO	K/9	WHIP	AVG
2017	17	Yankees1 (DSL)	R	0	3	3.68	6	6	0	22	25	2	5	17	7.0	1.36	.278
	17	Yankees1 (GCL)	R	4	1	4.26	8	5	0	32	35	2	12	17	4.8	1.48	.276
2018	18	Staten Island (NYP)	SS	0	0	1.26	5	5	0	29	15	1	9	32	10.0	0.84	.158
	18	Charleston (SAL)	LoA	0	2	3.38	7	7	0	35	29	4	12	28	7.3	1.18	.225
2019	19	Charleston (SAL)	LoA	12	5	3.33	24	24	0	132	105	10	36	113	7.7	1.07	.215
Minor League Totals				16	11	3.25	50	47	0	249	209	19	74	207	7.5	1.14	.225

9 ALEXANDER VIZCAINO, RHP

BA GRADE

50 Risk: High

Born: May 22, 1997. **B-T:** R-R. **HT:** 6-1. **WT:** 172. **Signed:** Dominican Republic, 2016. **Signed by:** Juan Rosario.

TRACK RECORD: Vizcaino was signed out of the Dominican Republic as a 19-year-old, then posted three underwhelming seasons—two of which were spent mostly at Rookie-level Pulaski— before a greatly improved changeup allowed him to jump into the Yankees' pack of intriguing pitching prospects.

SCOUTING REPORT: Vizcaino opened the year as one of the most nondescript members of a talented pitching staff at low Class A Charleston. Once scouts got a look, however, they saw a fastball that had jumped into the mid-90s and was touching as high as 98 mph. More than that, his changeup was a true weapon that was getting swings and misses by the bushel. The pitch, thrown in the low 90s, was effective not for its separation from his fastball, but because it showed sharp dive that mimicked a split-fingered fastball and was effective against hitters from both sides of the plate. The next step will be to sharpen his slider, which is thrown in the low 80s with a spin rate that averaged around 2,500 revolutions per minute and varied from potentially solid-average to below-average.

THE FUTURE: After a month-long stint in the Florida State League, Vizcaino will return there in 2020 to continue working on sharpening his breaking ball. Improvement in that area will greatly improve his chances of staying in the rotation.

SCOUTING GRADES: **Fastball:** 60 **Slider:** 45 **Changeup:** 60 **Control:** 50

Year	Age	Club (League)	Class	W	L	ERA	G	GS	SV	IP	H	HR	BB	SO	K/9	WHIP	AVG
2017	20	Pulaski (APP)	R	3	5	5.79	12	11	0	51	69	9	23	49	8.6	1.79	.321
2018	21	Pulaski (APP)	R	3	3	4.50	11	11	0	54	49	7	21	55	9.2	1.30	.239
	21	Charleston (SAL)	LoA	0	1	13.50	1	1	0	4	8	2	2	2	4.5	2.50	.421
2019	22	Charleston (SAL)	LoA	5	5	4.41	16	16	0	88	80	6	27	101	10.4	1.22	.242
	22	Tampa (FSL)	HiA	1	1	4.28	5	5	0	27	33	2	11	27	8.9	1.61	.320
Minor League Totals				12	20	4.89	56	50	0	259	279	30	97	261	9.1	1.45	.276

10 ALBERT ABREU, RHP

Born: Sept. 26, 1995. **B-T:** R-R. **HT:** 6-2. **WT:** 215. **Signed:** Dominican Republic, 2013. **Signed by:** Oz Ocampo/Rafael Belen/Francis Mojica (Astros).

BA GRADE
50 **Risk: High**

TRACK RECORD: Abreu was dealt from the Astros to the Yankees after the 2016 season as part of the package for catcher Brian McCann. He has teased evaluators with his blend of premium stuff that has been mitigated by injuries (an appendectomy and elbow inflammation in 2018) and inconsistency. He was added to the 40-man roster after the 2018 season, then put together a solid year at Double-A Trenton save for three weeks with right biceps inflammation.

SCOUTING REPORT: Abreu has an extra-large frame and a high-octane fastball that can reach the upper 90s with ease. He backs the pitch with a changeup and curveball, the former of which is his best offspeed weapon. The changeup, thrown in the 85-88 mph range shows excellent fading action away from lefties and is an effective option against same-side hitters as well. His curveball, a downer pitch in the mid-80s, flashes plus but not often enough to confidently project it will get there consistently. He doesn't get on top of the pitch often enough, which reduces the consistency of its break. Abreu's command is hampered by a short-stride delivery and inconsistency at foot strike that keeps his arm from producing his highest quality pitches.

THE FUTURE: After returning from the injured list on Aug. 13, Abreu made three starts of three or fewer innings before moving to the bullpen for the remainder of the season, including Trenton's run to the Eastern League championship. There's always been considerable reliever risk with Abreu, who is likely to return to the rotation in 2020 at Triple-A Scranton/Wilkes-Barre.

SCOUTING GRADES: **Fastball:** 70 **Curveball:** 55 **Changeup:** 55 **Control:** 40

Year	Age	Club (League)	Class	W	L	ERA	G	GS	SV	IP	H	HR	BB	SO	K/9	WHIP	AVG
2017	21	Charleston (SAL)	LoA	1	0	1.84	3	2	0	15	9	1	3	22	13.5	0.82	.180
	21	Yankees1 (GCL)	R	0	0	2.08	2	2	0	4	3	0	0	8	16.6	0.69	.177
	21	Tampa (FSL)	HiA	1	3	4.19	9	9	0	34	33	2	15	31	8.1	1.40	.252
2018	22	Yankees1 (GCL)	R	0	1	18.00	1	1	0	2	4	0	0	2	9.0	2.00	.400
	22	Yankees2 (GCL)	R	0	2	27.00	2	2	0	3	10	0	2	3	9.0	4.00	.476
	22	Tampa (FSL)	HiA	4	3	4.16	13	13	0	63	54	9	29	65	9.3	1.32	.229
	22	Trenton (EL)	AA	0	0	0.00	1	1	0	5	0	0	1	4	7.2	0.20	.000
2019	23	Trenton (EL)	AA	5	8	4.28	23	20	0	97	103	9	53	91	8.5	1.61	.276
Minor League Totals				19	30	3.77	105	87	5	439	373	31	211	446	9.1	1.33	.228

11 MIGUEL YAJURE, RHP

BA GRADE
50 **Risk: High**

Born: May 1, 1998. **B-T:** R-R. **HT:** 6-1. **WT:** 175. **Signed:** Venezuela, 2015. **Signed by:** Cesar Suarez/Ricardo Finol.

TRACK RECORD: The Yankees saw two impressive innings from Yajure in a tryout then signed him on the spot for $30,000. He had Tommy John surgery in 2017 and has slowly worked his way back onto the radar.

SCOUTING REPORT: Yajure started 2019 slowly at high Class A Tampa but turned it on after a rocky April. Evaluators saw a mostly mid-80s fastball in the early portion of the year but watched as the velocity began to tick up as the months passed. Even while shaking off the rust, Yajure kept his feel for a solid game plan with his four-pitch mix of a low-to-mid-90s fastball, cutter, downer curveball and changeup. As his velocity returned and his secondary pitches regained their sharpness, his feel to pitch remained. His changeup is a potential plus pitch and garners swings and misses from righthanders and lefthanders alike. His curveball projects as average, and his cutter blends nicely with his four-seamer.

THE FUTURE: Yajure earned a promotion to Double-A Trenton late in the year and should return to the level in 2020. He has the makings of a back-end starter if he continue making progress like he did during the 2019 season.

Year	Age	Club (League)	Class	W	L	ERA	G	GS	SV	IP	H	HR	BB	SO	K/9	WHIP	AVG
2017	19	Did not play—Injured															
2018	20	Charleston (SAL)	LoA	4	3	3.90	14	14	0	65	64	3	15	56	7.8	1.22	.258
2019	21	Tampa (FSL)	HiA	8	6	2.26	22	18	0	128	110	5	28	122	8.6	1.08	.233
	21	Trenton (EL)	AA	1	0	0.82	2	2	0	11	9	0	2	11	9.0	1.00	.214
Minor League Totals				14	13	2.47	61	54	0	291	261	10	70	246	7.6	1.13	.241

12 YOENDRYS GOMEZ, RHP

BA GRADE **50** Risk: High

Born: Oct. 5, 1999. **B-T:** R-R. **HT:** 6-3. **WT:** 181. **Signed:** Venezuela, 2016. **Signed by:** Alan Atacho.

TRACK RECORD: Gomez was a $50,000 signee because of a projectable body and a fastball that had already worked its way into the low 90s as a 16-year-old. He moved back and forth between the Dominican Summer League and Rookie-level Gulf Coast League over the first two seasons of his career and finished 2018 ranked No. 14 among the GCL's Top 20 prospects. Gomez made it all the way to low Class A Charleston in 2019 while continuing to show improved stuff.

SCOUTING REPORT: His fastball now sits in the low 90s and has touched as high as 97. His curveball, a downer breaker, is near average now and projects as plus, and his changeup could reach average as well. Combine the stuff with an advanced ability to throw strikes, an easy delivery and a frame that could take an extra 20-30 pounds, and it's easy to see why scouts are extremely high on his potential.

THE FUTURE: Gomez is likely to return to Charleston in 2020 and has the upside to fly through the system on his way to a spot in the big league rotation.

Year	Age	Club (League)	Class	W	L	ERA	G	GS	SV	IP	H	HR	BB	SO	K/9	WHIP	AVG
2017	17	Yankees1 (DSL)	R	0	3	4.78	10	8	0	32	36	2	12	32	9.0	1.50	.288
	17	Yankees2 (GCL)	R	0	0	12.00	1	1	0	3	5	0	6	1	3.0	3.67	.417
2018	18	Yankees (DSL)	R	1	0	1.00	2	2	0	9	2	0	7	7	7.0	1.00	.080
	18	Yankees1 (GCL)	R	3	1	2.33	10	9	0	39	27	1	15	43	10.0	1.09	.194
2019	19	Pulaski (APP)	R	4	2	2.12	6	6	0	30	26	1	10	28	8.5	1.21	.243
	19	Charleston (SAL)	LoA	0	3	6.08	6	6	0	27	28	2	9	25	8.4	1.39	.272
Minor League Totals				8	9	3.69	35	32	0	139	124	6	59	136	8.8	1.32	.243

13 MICHAEL KING, RHP

BA GRADE **45** Risk: Medium

Born: May 25, 1994. **B-T:** R-R. **HT:** 6-3. **WT:** 210. **Drafted:** Boston College, 2016 (12th round). **Signed by:** Steve Payne (Marlins).

TRACK RECORD: The Yankees acquired King during the 2017 offseason in a trade that sent Garrett Cooper and Caleb Smith to the Marlins. Smith and Cooper each emerged as productive pieces in Miami and King looked to be on the path to doing so as well. He raced from high Class A Tampa to Triple-A Scranton/Wilkes-Barre in 2018 on the way to earning the organization's pitcher of the year award. A stress fracture and then a setback during the rehab process kept King out until July 3. Despite that, the righthander made his big league debut on Sept. 27 with two scoreless innings against the Rangers.

SCOUTING REPORT: He uses a mix of two-seam, four-seam and cut fastballs to carve hitters up in all quadrants of the strike zone and produce plenty of weak contact. King complements the fastballs with a low-80s slider and a mid-80s changeup that each project as average pitches. All of his pitches play up because excellent command and control of his arsenal.

THE FUTURE: After a mostly lost season in 2019, King should compete for a spot at the back end of the rotation in 2020. If he doesn't make the big club, he'll head back to Triple-A Scranton/Wilkes-Barre for more seasoning.

Year	Age	Club (League)	Class	W	L	ERA	G	GS	SV	IP	H	HR	BB	SO	K/9	WHIP	AVG
2017	22	Greensboro (SAL)	LoA	11	9	3.14	26	25	0	149	141	14	21	106	6.4	1.09	.252
2018	23	Tampa (FSL)	HiA	1	3	1.79	7	7	0	40	33	1	10	45	10.0	1.07	.219
	23	Trenton (EL)	AA	6	2	2.09	12	11	0	82	65	4	13	76	8.3	0.95	.220
	23	Scranton/W-B (IL)	AAA	4	0	1.15	6	6	0	39	20	3	6	31	7.2	0.67	.147
2019	24	Yankees2 (GCL)	R	0	0	4.76	3	2	0	6	3	0	2	8	12.7	0.88	.150
	24	Staten Island (NYP)	SS	0	0	0.00	1	1	0	4	4	0	0	0	0.0	1.00	.308
	24	Trenton (EL)	AA	0	1	9.95	3	2	0	13	20	1	2	8	5.7	1.74	.351
	24	Scranton/W-B (IL)	AAA	3	1	4.18	4	3	0	24	20	3	6	28	10.6	1.10	.227
	24	New York (AL)	MAJ	0	0	0.00	1	0	0	2	2	0	0	1	4.5	1.00	.222
Major League Totals				0	0	0.00	1	0	0	2	2	0	0	1	4.5	1.00	.222
Minor League Totals				28	19	2.93	77	58	1	387	343	26	69	322	7.5	1.06	.238

14 ESTEVAN FLORIAL, OF

BA GRADE **50** Risk: High

Born: Nov. 25, 1997. **B-T:** L-L. **HT:** 6-1. **WT:** 199. **Signed:** Haiti, 2015. **Signed by:** Esteban Castillo.

TRACK RECORD: Florial's path to accessing his considerable talent has been littered with roadblocks. There was an identification snafu that led to a suspension and a lowered bonus, followed by two seasons lost to broken bones in his right wrist. The injuries have cost him half of the regular season each year, valuable developmental time for a player whose tools need a fair amount of polish.

SCOUTING REPORT: The development of Florial's hit tool has been the most impacted by his injuries.

He needed to control the strike zone better before the first injury, and all the time rehabbing has cost him chances to make improvements. The need was particularly glaring in 2019, when Florial whiffed at a 32.8 percent rate in the FSL. He's got above-average bat speed and enough leverage in his swing to hit for at least above-average power, but he's unlikely to reach that mark without better plate discipline and cutting down on swings and misses on pitches in the zone. Florial still has plus speed and enough instincts and athleticism to stick in center field, as well as a strong enough throwing arm to negate runners trying to take extra bases.

THE FUTURE: Despite another year lost to injury, the Yankees protected Florial on the 40-man roster to avoid certain selection in the Rule 5 Draft this winter. The raw tools are still there, and he'll try once again to access them, likely at Double-A Trenton.

Year	Age	Club (League)	Class	AVG	G	AB	R	H	2B	3B	HR	RBI	BB	SO	SB	OBP	SLG
2017	19	Charleston (SAL)	LoA	.297	91	344	64	102	21	5	11	43	41	124	17	.373	.483
	19	Tampa (FSL)	HiA	.303	19	76	13	23	2	2	2	14	9	24	6	.368	.461
2018	20	Yankees2 (GCL)	R	.429	4	14	5	6	0	0	1	3	2	3	2	.500	.643
	20	Yankees1 (GCL)	R	.647	5	17	5	11	3	1	2	5	2	2	3	.684	1.294
	20	Tampa (FSL)	HiA	.255	75	294	45	75	16	3	3	27	44	87	11	.354	.361
2019	21	Tampa (FSL)	HiA	.237	74	274	38	65	10	3	8	38	24	98	9	.297	.383
Minor League Totals				.273	392	1507	261	412	73	24	42	213	182	484	73	.353	.437

15 T.J. SIKKEMA, LHP

BA GRADE
50 Risk: High

Born: July 25, 1998. **B-T:** L-L. **HT:** 6-0. **WT:** 221. **Drafted:** Missouri, 2019 (1st round supplemental). **Signed by:** Steve Lemke.

TRACK RECORD: Sikkema started his college career as a high-end piece of Missouri's bullpen and immediately made an impact by tying Tanner Houck's school record for wins by a freshman. He moved into the rotation in the middle of his sophomore season and spent the next year and a half impressing scouts with his combination of aggressiveness and stuff.

SCOUTING REPORT: Sikkema starts his pitch mix with a low-90s fastball that he can run up to 95 mph and spot to both sides of the plate. He backs up the fastball with a full complement of secondaries, including a slurve that shows both power and depth. He also throws an average changeup. To mess with hitters' timing, Sikkema alternates between an overhand arm slot and a lower, three-quarters arm slot. His fastball ticks down in velo from the lower slot but gains significantly more armside run. Sikkema's body is maxed out already, so he likely has little projection remaining.

THE FUTURE: His ceiling is as a back-end starter or high-pressure reliever, and he's advanced enough to handle a jump directly to high Class A Tampa in his first full season as a pro.

Year	Age	Club (League)	Class	W	L	ERA	G	GS	SV	IP	H	HR	BB	SO	K/9	WHIP	AVG
2019	20	Staten Island (NYP)	SS	0	0	0.84	4	4	0	11	6	0	1	13	11.0	0.66	.158
Minor League Totals				0	0	0.84	4	4	0	10	6	0	1	13	11.0	0.66	.158

16 CANAAN SMITH, OF

Born: April 30, 1999. **B-T:** L-R. **HT:** 6-0. **WT:** 215. **Drafted:** HS—Rockwall, Texas, 2017 (4th round). **Signed by:** Mike Leuzinger.

TRACK RECORD: A two-sport star in high school, Smith was good enough on the diamond that scouts didn't get much chance to evaluate him—that's how often he was pitched around. Nonetheless, the Yankees got enough of a look to spend a fourth-round pick on Smith in 2017 and sign him away from an Arkansas commitment for $497,500. After a rough 2018 in the New York-Penn League, Smith broke out in 2019 with low Class A Charleston. He finished as one of just 15 players in the minors with 30 or more doubles, 10 or more home runs and 15 or more stolen bases.

SCOUTING REPORT: He doesn't have one standout tool but showed evaluators the potential for at least average hittability and above-average power. His power comes from extreme strength which produced some of the system's highest exit velocities despite an unorthodox swing that allows him to barrel pitches despite stepping in the bucket. He's an average runner with an average arm who fits best in left field.

THE FUTURE: After a strong showing in Charleston, he'll move to high Class A Tampa in 2020 and has the ceiling of an offensive-minded corner bat.

Year	Age	Club (League)	Class	AVG	G	AB	R	H	2B	3B	HR	RBI	BB	SO	SB	OBP	SLG
2017	18	Yankees1 (GCL)	R	.289	57	187	29	54	10	0	5	28	46	44	5	.430	.422
2018	19	Staten Island (NYP)	SS	.191	45	152	13	29	8	1	3	16	19	52	0	.281	.316
2019	20	Charleston (SAL)	LoA	.307	124	449	67	138	32	3	11	74	74	108	16	.405	.465
Minor League Totals				.280	226	788	109	221	50	4	19	118	139	204	21	.389	.426

17 MATT SAUER, RHP

BA GRADE
50 Risk: Very High

Born: Jan. 21, 1999. **B-T:** R-R. **HT:** 6-4. **WT:** 195. **Drafted:** HS—Santa Maria, Calif., 2017 (2nd round). **Signed by:** Bobby Dejardin.

TRACK RECORD: After a velocity jump during his senior season in high school led the Yankees to spend a second-round pick and just less than $2.5 million on him, Sauer has moved slowly but surely through the organization. He was impressive in the New York-Penn League in 2018 and started strong in his first test in full-season ball before tearing his ulnar collateral ligament and having Tommy John surgery.

SCOUTING REPORT: Before the injury, scouts inside and outside the organization were impressed by the progress Sauer had made year over year. His velocity had jumped to the 92-95 mph range and had touched a tick higher, and he was showing a slider and a changeup that each had the potential to be 55- or 60-grade pitches on the 20-to-80 scouting scale. The shape of his slider appeared to improve as well.

THE FUTURE: The surgery will likely cost him most of 2020 as well if he stays on the typical timetable of 12-18 months. Before the injury, he fit in well with the pack of high-upside pitching prospects at Charleston and he had the upside of a rotation piece.

Year	Age	Club (League)	Class	W	L	ERA	G	GS	SV	IP	H	HR	BB	SO	K/9	WHIP	AVG
2017	18	Yankees2 (GCL)	R	0	2	5.40	6	6	0	12	13	0	8	12	9.3	1.80	.271
2018	19	Staten Island (NYP)	SS	3	6	3.90	13	13	0	67	60	3	18	45	6.0	1.16	.236
2019	20	Charleston (SAL)	LoA	0	1	2.08	2	2	0	9	6	0	6	8	8.3	1.38	.188
Minor League Totals				3	9	3.92	21	21	0	87	79	3	32	65	6.7	1.27	.237

18 EVERSON PEREIRA, OF

BA GRADE
50 Risk: Extreme

Born: April 10, 2001. **B-T:** R-R. **HT:** 5-10. **WT:** 191. **Signed:** Venezuela, 2017. **Signed by:** Roney Calderon.

TRACK RECORD: Pereira was the jewel of the Yankees' 2017 international signing class and garnered a $1.5 million bonus as a result. The Yankees were impressed enough by Pereira that they jumped him over both the Dominican Summer League and Rookie-level Gulf Coast League in 2018 and instead sent him to Rookie-level Pulaski to begin his first official season. His numbers didn't jump off the board, but he played all season as a 17-year-old and was impressive enough to rank No. 7 among the league's Top 20 prospects.

SCOUTING REPORT: Pereira showed above-average bat speed and exit velocities in the New York-Penn League in 2019 but had issues with swinging and missing at pitches both in and out of the zone. Any chance at improvement was blunted on July 8, when an attempt at an acrobatic catch against the wall resulted in a sprained ankle that ended his season.

THE FUTURE: Scouts were still impressed by Pereira's tools, noting above-average speed and power and the potential to stick in center field. He has flaws to improve, but there's still plenty of ceiling remaining.

Year	Age	Club (League)	Class	AVG	G	AB	R	H	2B	3B	HR	RBI	BB	SO	SB	OBP	SLG
2018	17	Pulaski (APP)	R	.263	41	167	21	44	8	2	3	26	15	60	3	.322	.389
2019	18	Staten Island (NYP)	SS	.171	18	70	9	12	3	0	1	3	4	26	3	.216	.257
Minor League Totals				.236	59	237	30	56	11	2	4	29	19	86	6	.292	.350

19 ANTONIO CABELLO, OF

BA GRADE
50 Risk: Extreme

Born: Nov. 1, 2000. **B-T:** R-R. **HT:** 5-11. **WT:** 216. **Signed:** Venezuela, 2017. **Signed by:** Darwin Bracho.

TRACK RECORD: Cabello was signed with part of the money the Yankees had reserved to chase Shohei Ohtani when he was a free agent. When Ohtani eliminated the Yankees, the team pivoted and signed Cabello and Raimfer Salinas just before Christmas in 2017. Cabello was impressive enough in his first season as a pro to move to the Rookie-level Gulf Coast League after just six games in the DSL. He ranked as the GCL's No. 7 prospect after the season but a dislocated shoulder cost him more development time in the instructional league. Cabello recovered in time to open the second half of 2019 with Rookie-level Pulaski, where he struggled against more advanced pitching.

SCOUTING REPORT: Evaluators inside and outside the organization noted that his approach had gone backward and he'd become something of an all-or-nothing hitter. The Yankees spent the season working to improve Cabello's bat path to get it to stay in the zone longer. More concerning, though, was the direction his body seemed to be going. Scouts noted that he looked heavier than his listed weight, and was showing slower, stiffer actions than would be expected of a middle-of-the-diamond player. Part of Cabello's appeal in previous years included plus speed and defense to stick in center field, so he'll have to maintain his body to keep that part of his profile.

THE FUTURE: Cabello is likely to return to extended spring to begin 2020 before heading to short-season Staten Island.

Year	Age	Club (League)	Class	AVG	G	AB	R	H	2B	3B	HR	RBI	BB	SO	SB	OBP	SLG
2018	17	Yankees (DSL)	R	.227	6	22	5	5	0	1	0	1	6	6	5	.433	.318
	17	Yankees2 (GCL)	R	.321	40	137	21	44	9	4	5	20	21	34	5	.426	.555
2019	18	Pulaski (APP)	R	.211	56	227	31	48	10	4	3	19	19	77	5	.280	.330
Minor League Totals				.251	102	386	57	97	19	9	8	40	46	117	15	.344	.409

20 KEVIN ALCANTARA, OF

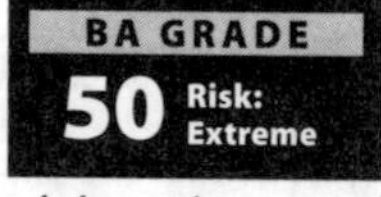

Born: July 12, 2002. **B-T:** R-R. **HT:** 6-6. **WT:** 188. **Signed:** Dominican Republic, 2018. **Signed by:** Edgar Mateo/Juan Piron.

TRACK RECORD: Alcantara was the No. 15-ranked player in the 2018 international class and was one of five from that group who wound up with the Yankees. Of that group, Alcantara might have the highest ceiling. He moved quickly from the Dominican Summer League to the Rookie-level Gulf Coast League in his pro debut and more than held his own as a 17-year-old.

SCOUTING REPORT: He caught the eye of managers and scouts around the GCL for his extremely projectable frame and easy actions in center field. He moves well in all directions and has the long strides and range to stick at the position long-term. Those same long levers, plus a sizable leg kick, will need to be controlled as he develops if he is to hit for average. Those long levers also should help him grow into plenty of power, which he already shows to the pull side, as his game matures and he gains strength.

THE FUTURE: There's a long way to go, but Alcantara's athleticism and natural gifts give him the potential for a very bright future.

Year	Age	Club (League)	Class	AVG	G	AB	R	H	2B	3B	HR	RBI	BB	SO	SB	OBP	SLG
2019	16	Yankees (DSL)	R	.237	9	38	7	9	3	1	0	6	5	9	2	.348	.368
	16	Yankees1 (GCL)	R	.260	32	123	19	32	5	2	1	13	3	27	3	.289	.358
Minor League Totals				.255	41	161	26	41	8	3	1	19	8	36	5	.305	.360

21 ANTONIO GOMEZ, C

BA GRADE
50 Risk: Extreme

Born: Nov. 13, 2001. **B-T:** R-R. **HT:** 6-2. **WT:** 216. **Signed:** Venezuela, 2018. **Signed by:** Edgar Mateo/Raul Gonzalez.

TRACK RECORD: After ranking as the No. 4 player available in the 2018 international class, Gomez signed with the Yankees and immediately cemented himself as one of the best defensive catchers in the system. His first test as a pro was delayed by triceps soreness that limited him to 14 games in the Rookie-level Gulf Coast League (plus one more in the DSL).

SCOUTING REPORT: The scouts who got the chance to see Gomez while he was healthy were impressed. He showed off plus arm strength behind the plate with a chance to reach a true 70-grade arm with further refinement. He also shows strong blocking and receiving abilities and works well with his pitching staffs. The Yankees praise Gomez for his ability to separate offense and defense as well and his fluent English speaking. At the plate he shows a patient, disciplined approach that has a chance to produce both average and power as he matures. He needs to gain strength so he can catch up to high-velocity fastballs.

THE FUTURE: Gomez had surgery on his non-throwing arm after the season but should be ready for 2020, which is likely to begin back in extended spring training. Gomez has little experience but one of the more exciting upsides in the system.

Year	Age	Club (League)	Class	AVG	G	AB	R	H	2B	3B	HR	RBI	BB	SO	SB	OBP	SLG
2019	17	Yankees (DSL)	R	.600	1	5	2	3	1	0	0	1	1	2	0	.667	.800
	17	Yankees1 (GCL)	R	.255	14	47	9	12	4	0	1	7	3	7	0	.314	.404
Minor League Totals				.288	15	52	11	15	5	0	1	8	4	9	0	.351	.442

22 ALEXANDER VARGAS, SS

Born: Oct. 29, 2001. **B-T:** B-R. **HT:** 5-11. **WT:** 154. **Signed:** Cuba, 2018. **Signed by:** Edgar Mateo/Esteban Castillo/Rudy Gomez.

TRACK RECORD: Another part of a pack of talented players the Yankees signed during the 2018 international signing period, Vargas was somewhat of a surprise signing. He was expected to ink with the Reds later in the period but agreed with the Yankees for $2.5 million. He made his pro debut mostly in the Rookie-level Gulf Coast League in 2019 and ranked No. 9 among the circuit's Top 20 prospects.

SCOUTING REPORT: Vargas' standout tool is his speed, which is at least double-plus. He produced home-to-first times of quicker than 4.15 seconds from both sides of the plate. Vargas is a spray-type hitter from both sides of the plate and showed no discernible platoon split in his first exposure to pro ball, although Yankees officials note that his launch angle was typically higher as a lefthanded hitter. At shortstop, Vargas shows tremendous hands and feet that somewhat make up for a fringe-average arm. He's got the upside of a table-setting shortstop who can cause havoc on the basepaths.

THE FUTURE: After starting in extended spring training, he should move to Rookie-level Pulaski in 2020.

Year	Age	Club (League)	Class	AVG	G	AB	R	H	2B	3B	HR	RBI	BB	SO	SB	OBP	SLG
2019	17	Yankees (DSL)	R	.289	8	38	6	11	5	2	0	2	4	6	2	.364	.526
	17	Yankees1 (GCL)	R	.219	40	155	23	34	5	5	1	16	14	22	13	.301	.335
Minor League Totals				.233	48	193	29	45	10	7	1	18	18	28	15	.313	.373

23 ANTHONY SEIGLER, C

BA GRADE
50 **Risk: Extreme**

Born: June 20, 1999. **B-T:** B-B. **HT:** 6-0. **WT:** 200. **Drafted:** HS—Cartersville, Ga., 2018 (1st round). **Signed by:** Darryl Monroe.

TRACK RECORD: Seigler entered the 2018 draft with one of the most intriguing profiles in the class. He starred in high school as both a switch-hitting catcher and a switch-pitcher who could sling fastballs in the upper 80s with both his right and left arms. The Yankees preferred him at catcher and gave him a bonus of $2,815,900 in the first round. He dealt with hamstring injuries and a concussion in his first taste of pro ball, which was limited to just 24 games. Seigler joined low Class A Charleston on June 10—eschewing either of the Yankees' half-season clubs—and struggled.

SCOUTING REPORT: Scouts liked Seigler's plate discipline and approach but couldn't project much impact because of below-average bat speed and a body with limited remaining projection. Behind the plate, Seigler showed athleticism, but his plus arm strength was counteracted by a slow release when trying to nab potential basestealers.

THE FUTURE: His season ended after five weeks in Charleston because of a broken left patella. He's likely to return in 2020 to low Class A, where he'll try to make a fresh start.

Year	Age	Club (League)	Class	AVG	G	AB	R	H	2B	3B	HR	RBI	BB	SO	SB	OBP	SLG
2018	19	Yankees2 (GCL)	R	.333	12	36	7	12	2	0	1	4	6	7	0	.429	.472
	19	Pulaski (APP)	R	.209	12	43	4	9	1	0	0	5	8	5	0	.340	.233
2019	20	Charleston (SAL)	LoA	.175	30	97	10	17	3	0	0	6	20	28	1	.328	.206
Minor League Totals				.216	54	176	21	38	6	0	1	15	34	40	1	.350	.267

24 EZEQUIEL DURAN, 2B

BA GRADE
45 **Risk: High**

Born: May 22, 1999. **B-T:** R-R. **HT:** 5-10. **WT:** 202. **Signed:** Dominican Republic, 2017. **Signed by:** Juan Rosario/Raymon Sanchez/Victor Mata.

TRACK RECORD: Duran could have signed earlier than he did but wasn't registered with Major League Baseball, so he had to wait until those issues were cleared up. He eventually inked with the Yankees for $10,000 and immediately raked in the Dominican Summer League. He stalled somewhat in 2018 at Rookie-level Pulaski but broke out in 2019 at short-season Staten Island. He was particularly explosive in July, when he hit .333/.392/.630 with seven doubles and seven homers in 26 games.

SCOUTING REPORT: Duran has quick hands, above-average bat speed and power to all fields. That last trait showed up in spades in 2019, when his 13 home runs were distributed fairly neatly to all fields. He's got the hands, feet and arm to play second base and could fill in at shortstop in a pinch as well.

THE FUTURE: Duran has the potential to be an offensive-minded middle infielder. He should get his first full-season test in 2020.

Year	Age	Club (League)	Class	AVG	G	AB	R	H	2B	3B	HR	RBI	BB	SO	SB	OBP	SLG
2017	18	Yankees1 (DSL)	R	.393	15	61	12	24	5	4	3	11	3	15	4	.415	.754
2018	19	Pulaski (APP)	R	.201	53	219	34	44	8	2	4	20	9	65	7	.251	.311
2019	20	Staten Island (NYP)	SS	.256	66	246	49	63	12	4	13	37	25	77	11	.329	.496
Minor League Totals				.249	134	526	95	131	25	10	20	68	37	157	22	.307	.449

25 JOSH SMITH, 2B

BA GRADE
45 **Risk: High**

Born: Aug. 7, 1997. **B-T:** L-R. **HT:** 5-9. **WT:** 175. **Drafted:** Louisiana State, 2019 (2nd round). **Signed by:** Mike Leuzinger.

TRACK RECORD: Buoyed by a set of solid tools across the board, Smith put together an excellent junior season at Louisiana State. He also proved himself with wood bats during a stellar season in the Cape Cod

League in 2017, when he hit .382/.478/.513 for Harwich. The Yankees, intrigued by his bat-to-ball skills and hard contact from the left side, used their 2019 second-round pick on Smith and signed him for $978,500. A strong college pedigree allowed Smith to make his pro debut at short-season Staten Island, where he showed the same blend of skills that should give him a relatively high floor.

SCOUTING REPORT: His blend of an above-average hit tool and average raw power gives him the profile of the classic professional hitter. He has average foot speed, strong instincts and smooth hands up the middle that will fit nicely at second base.

THE FUTURE: He has the potential to be an offensive-minded second-division regular and could skip over low Class A Charleston and begin his first full season in the Florida State League.

Year	Age	Club (League)	Class	AVG	G	AB	R	H	2B	3B	HR	RBI	BB	SO	SB	OBP	SLG
2019	21	Staten Island (NYP)	SS	.324	33	111	17	36	6	1	3	15	25	17	6	.450	.477
Minor League Totals				.324	33	111	17	36	6	1	3	15	25	17	6	.450	.477

26 RAIMFER SALINAS, OF

BA GRADE **50** Risk: Extreme

Born: Dec. 31, 2000. **B-T:** R-R. **HT:** 5-11. **WT:** 195. **Signed:** Venezuela, 2017. **Signed by:** Darwin Bracho.

TRACK RECORD: When Shohei Ohtani chose the Angels in 2017, the Yankees took the international slot money they'd accumulated and shifted it to Salinas and fellow outfielder Antonio Cabello. Salinas' 2018 season was truncated because of injuries to his knee and ring finger, so 2019 stood for all intents and purposes as his first extended test as a pro.

SCOUTING REPORT: Beyond what showed up on the field, Salinas' biggest strides in 2019 came behind the scenes. The Yankees worked with him to find a more consistent swing that kept the bat in the zone for a longer period of time. They also worked with him to sharpen his approach and keep him from chasing as many pitches out of the zone. Scouts outside the organization saw a player with plus bat speed, explosive footspeed and a chance to stick in center field. They also noted that his shorter arms could help him get the barrel to high-velocity fastballs sooner.

THE FUTURE: Salinas still has plenty of refinement to go, but his ceiling is still very high.

Year	Age	Club (League)	Class	AVG	G	AB	R	H	2B	3B	HR	RBI	BB	SO	SB	OBP	SLG
2018	17	Yankees (DSL)	R	.095	6	21	4	2	1	0	0	2	5	5	4	.321	.143
	17	Yankees2 (GCL)	R	.125	5	16	0	2	0	0	0	0	2	5	0	.300	.125
2019	18	Yankees2 (GCL)	R	.270	42	159	25	43	10	2	3	15	7	45	11	.329	.415
Minor League Totals				.240	53	196	29	47	11	2	3	17	14	55	15	.326	.362

27 MAIKOL ESCOTTO, SS

BA GRADE **50** Risk: Extreme

Born: June 4, 2002. **B-T:** R-R. **HT:** 5-11. **WT:** 180. **Signed:** Dominican Republic, 2018. **Signed by:** Juan Rosario/Esteban Castillo.

TRACK RECORD: The Yankees signed Escotto for $350,000 after seeing quick hands in the field and at the plate as well as above-average speed and gap power. In his pro debut, Escotto produced a .981 OPS that ranked eighth in the Dominican Summer League and a team-best eight home runs.

SCOUTING REPORT: More than the counting stats, Escotto continued showing off an interesting set of tools. He showed a compact swing that played well against both fastballs and offspeed pitches and produced top-end exit velocities of 106 miles per hour. He also showed solid plate discipline. In the field he has solid hands, strong footwork and arm strength that easily rates as plus. He's a plus runner with first-step quickness that shows up on offense and defense.

THE FUTURE: He continued his season in the instructional league at the team's complex in the D.R. and will likely come stateside for the first time in 2020.

Year	Age	Club (League)	Class	AVG	G	AB	R	H	2B	3B	HR	RBI	BB	SO	SB	OBP	SLG
2019	17	Yankees (DSL)	R	.315	45	181	47	57	11	4	8	26	32	57	13	.429	.552
Minor League Totals				.315	45	181	47	57	11	4	8	26	32	57	13	.429	.552

28 NICK NELSON, RHP

BA GRADE **45** Risk: High

Born: Dec. 5, 1995. **B-T:** R-R. **HT:** 6-0. **WT:** 216. **Drafted:** Gulf Coast State (Fla.) JC, 2016 (4th round). **Signed by:** Mike Wagner.

TRACK RECORD: Nelson was a two-way player at Gulf Coast State JC who led the team in both innings pitched and at-bats in his draft season. The Yankees liked Nelson better on the mound and spent a fourth-round pick and $350,000 to acquire him and see if they could unlock more by having him focus solely on pitching. His season was delayed by about a month in 2019 with a sore right shoulder but he still racked up an average of 11.4 strikeouts per nine innings over the rest of the season.

SCOUTING REPORT: Nelson combines a low-to-mid-90s fastball with a potentially above-average changeup he added as a pro and a pair of breaking balls fronted by a downer curveball. He added a slider last season and continued to develop the pitch in 2019.

THE FUTURE: Nelson struggled after a promotion to Triple-A Scranton/Wilkes-Barre and will need to see his offspeed pitches gain more polish in order to achieve his ceiling in the back of a rotation. If that doesn't happen, he could find himself in a middle-innings relief role. He'll return to Triple-A in 2020.

Year	Age	Club (League)	Class	W	L	ERA	G	GS	SV	IP	H	HR	BB	SO	K/9	WHIP	AVG
2017	21	Charleston(SAL)	LoA	3	12	4.56	22	22	0	101	103	5	50	110	9.8	1.52	.270
2018	22	Charleston (SAL)	LoA	1	1	3.65	5	5	0	25	18	1	7	35	12.8	1.01	.198
	22	Tampa (FSL)	HiA	7	5	3.36	18	17	0	88	69	1	47	99	10.1	1.31	.214
	22	Trenton (EL)	AA	0	0	5.19	3	3	0	9	10	1	9	10	10.4	2.19	.278
2019	23	Tampa (FSL)	HiA	0	0	0.00	1	1	0	4	4	0	1	7	17.2	1.36	.286
	23	Trenton (EL)	AA	7	2	2.35	13	12	0	65	48	4	35	83	11.5	1.28	.206
	23	Scranton/W-B (IL)	AAA	1	1	4.71	4	4	0	21	20	2	7	24	10.3	1.29	.247
Minor League Totals				19	24	3.65	76	74	0	333	286	14	178	387	10.5	1.39	.233

29 RYDER GREEN, OF

BA GRADE
45 Risk: High

Born: May 5, 2000. **B-T:** R-R. **HT:** 6-0. **WT:** 215. **Drafted:** HS—Knoxville, 2018 (3rd round). **Signed by:** Darryl Monroe.

TRACK RECORD: Green was one of the best prep prospects in Tennessee in the 2018 class, just behind lefthander Ryan Weathers. Green's calling card was big-time power, which he showed off with long home runs at showcases and in games during his high school season. He scuffled somewhat in his first pro season in the Rookie-level Gulf Coast League but rebounded in 2019 in the Appalachian League.

SCOUTING REPORT: Power is still Green's primary calling card, and scouts think he has a chance to produce plus power if he can refine his approach. He made strides in that area with Rookie-level Pulaski, where he cut his strikeout rate by 10 percent from the GCL. Green moves well in the outfield and played all three outfield positions but it is likely he fits in a corner rather than center field. He played some shortstop and third base in high school and should have enough arm to handle right field.

THE FUTURE: After a solid season that saw him rank No. 19 in the Appy League's Top 20 prospects, Green will likely head to low Class A Charleston in 2020. He has the upside of a second-division corner outfielder with power.

Year	Age	Club (League)	Class	AVG	G	AB	R	H	2B	3B	HR	RBI	BB	SO	SB	OBP	SLG
2018	18	Yankees1 (GCL)	R	.203	26	79	11	16	2	2	3	10	11	35	3	.316	.392
2019	19	Pulaski (APP)	R	.262	61	225	45	59	15	1	8	28	25	67	10	.343	.444
Minor League Totals				.247	87	304	56	75	17	3	11	38	36	102	13	.335	.431

30 JOSH STOWERS, OF

BA GRADE
45 Risk: High

Born: Feb. 25, 1997. **B-T:** R-R. **HT:** 6-1. **WT:** 200. **Drafted:** Louisville, 2018 (2nd round). **Signed by:** Jackson Laumann (Mariners).

TRACK RECORD: Stowers was the Mariners' second-round pick in 2018 after showing off a combination of speed and power for three seasons with the Cardinals. He finished his first season as a pro ranked No. 12 among the short-season Northwest League's Top 20 prospects. Stowers was shipped to the Yankees before the 2019 season in the three-way deal that sent righthander Sonny Gray to the Reds and then-Cincinnati prospect Shed Long to the Mariners. He made his Yankees debut with low Class A Charleston and showed scouts a tool package befitting a fourth outfielder.

SCOUTING REPORT: Stowers' hit tool and power are both fringe-average and he looks particularly vulnerable on quality offspeed pitches. He struggled mightily in the Arizona Fall League, where he struck out 27 times in 61 at-bats. He needs to improve his reads and routes in center field in order to help his plus speed become better utilized. He has a below-average throwing arm, which would likely limit him to left field if he had to move off of center field.

THE FUTURE: High Class A Tampa is the next step for Stowers, who will begin the season as a 23-year-old.

Year	Age	Club (League)	Class	AVG	G	AB	R	H	2B	3B	HR	RBI	BB	SO	SB	OBP	SLG
2018	21	Everett (NWL)	SS	.260	58	200	32	52	15	0	5	28	37	57	20	.380	.410
2019	22	Charleston (SAL)	LoA	.273	105	385	61	105	24	2	7	40	64	123	35	.386	.400
Minor League Totals				.268	163	585	93	157	39	2	12	68	101	180	55	.384	.403

Oakland Athletics

BY EMILY WALDON

After three consecutive last-place finishes in the American League West, the Athletics broke through with 97 wins in 2018 and made their first postseason appearance since 2014.

The 2019 season brought more of the same. Quite literally. Oakland once again won 97 games and secured an AL wild card, only to lose in the Wild Card Game.

In addition to the promising trend on the performance front, talks to secure a new ballpark for the A's were continuing in a positive direction as well. Set to be located at the Howard Terminal, north of Jack London Square, the new facility would be directly on the waterfront.

All of the positive improvements at the top tier of the organization have been gradually working their way down into the farm system, a system assistant general manager Billy Owens believes has been underrated for several years.

A new farm director will be overseeing the development of those prospects after Keith Lieppman stepped down after 28 seasons. Lieppman played in the Oakland system in the 1970s, then managed four of the organization's minor league affiliates in the '80s and ascended to farm director in 1992. He had an active role in developing core players for 10 Athletics playoff teams in his nearly three decades running the organization's player development.

Lieppman will occupy a front office advisory role as Ed Sprague Jr. ascends to farm director.

Sprague and the A's must contend with a bit of a gap in their farm system after gambling on Oklahoma outfielder Kyler Murray with the ninth overall pick in the 2018 draft. The two-sport star went on to win the Heisman Trophy as the Sooners' quarterback just months after being drafted. Murray ultimately chose to pursue football, spurning his commitment to the A's and going No. 1 overall in the NFL draft to the Arizona Cardinals. He never played a game in the Oakland system.

The A's focused on position players in the 2019 draft, led by Clemson shortstop Logan Davidson in the first round, prep outfielder Marcus Smith in the third, Georgia Tech catcher Kyle McCann in the fourth and prep shortstop Jalen Greer in the fifth.

The A's also made a big splash on their international market when they signed Dominican shortstop Robert Puason for an outlay of $5.1 million.

The A's caught a glimpse of their future when they called up their top three preseason prospects. Catcher Sean Murphy debuted in May, while lefthander A.J. Puk made his first appearance in August and lefty Jesus Luzardo made the jump in September. All three qualify as prospects again in 2020 and figure to lead the organization into the new decade.

JASON O. WATSON/GETTY IMAGES

Ramon Laureano has been a steady on-base source for Oakland the past two seasons.

PROJECTED 2023 LINEUP

Position	Player	Age
Catcher	Sean Murphy (3)	28
First Base	Matt Olson	29
Second Base	Robert Puason (6)	20
Third Base	Matt Chapman	30
Shortstop	Marcus Semien	32
Left Field	Austin Beck (5)	24
Center Field	Ramon Laureano	28
Right Field	Stephen Piscotty	32
Designated Hitter	Sheldon Neuse (7)	28
No. 1 Starter	Jesus Luzardo (1)	25
No. 2 Starter	A.J. Puk (2)	28
No. 3 Starter	Sean Manaea	31
No. 4 Starter	Frankie Montas	30
No. 5 Starter	Daulton Jefferies (4)	27
Closer	Liam Hendriks	34

Pitching coordinator Gil Patterson challenged each affiliate to lead its league in walk rate in 2019. Patterson and his staff once again are looking for ways to freshen and refocus their mantra.

All are moving parts behind the goal of strengthening every aspect of Oakland's system from the major league level all the way down to the Rookie-level Arizona League. These slow and steady improvements could be just enough to give the A's the push they need for an AL West title in the not-so-distant future.

DEPTH CHART

OAKLAND ATHLETICS

TOP 2020 ROOKIE: A.J. Puk, LHP. With his health finally intact and a taste of the big leagues, Puk's arsenal looks to only be more effective.

BREAKOUT PROSPECT: Bryan Buelvas, OF. The Colombian outfielder has loud tools and showed well in the Rookie-level Arizona League in his pro debut.

SLEEPER: Drew Millas, C. While there are questions about Millas' durability, his resume at Missouri State, including fighting for the role of best defensive catcher in his draft class, there is plenty to keep an eye on once he returns to full strength.

SOURCE OF TOP 30 TALENT

Homegrown	24	Acquired	6
College	16	Trade	6
Junior college	0	Rule 5 draft	0
High school	2	Independent league	0
Nondrafted free agent	0	Free agent/waivers	0
International	6		

LF
- Lazaro Armenteros (12)
- Tyler Ramirez
- Mark Payton
- Lawrence Butler

CF
- Austin Beck (5)
- Skye Bolt (13)
- Brayan Buelvas (19)
- Marcus Smith (20)
- Luis Barrera (23)
- Buddy Reed

RF
- Greg Deichmann (16)

3B
- Sheldon Neuse (7)
- Jordan Diaz (18)
- Mikey White
- Nate Mondou

SS
- Robert Puason (6)
- Jorge Mateo (8)
- Logan Davidson (9)
- Nick Allen (10)
- Jeremy Eierman (26)

2B
- Marcus Brito
- Trace Loehr

1B
- Alfonso Rivas (21)
- Seth Brown (25)
- Eric Campbell

C
- Sean Murphy (3)
- Austin Allen (11)
- Jonah Heim (24)
- Kyle McCann (30)
- Drew Millas
- Collin Theroux

LHP

LHSP	LHRP
Jesus Luzardo (1)	Zack Erwin
A.J. Puk (2)	Jhenderson Hurtado
Hogan Harris (27)	Cody Stull

RHP

RHSP	RHRP
Daulton Jefferies (4)	Miguel Romero (28)
James Kaprielian (14)	Wandisson Charles
Tyler Baum (15)	Ben Bracewell
Grant Holmes (17)	Jose Mora
Parker Dunshee (22)	Brian Howard
Gus Varland (29)	

DRAFT ANALYSIS

2019

BEST PURE HITTER: The quality of SS Logan Davidson's (1) hit tool was always the biggest question heading into the draft—he never hit .300 at Clemson—but he has the power and speed to become a solid offensive player even if he's never a plus hitter. OF Marcus Smith (3) has a chance to be an above-average hitter.

BEST POWER HITTER: The Athletics drafted C Kyle McCann (4) because of his powerful bat. He's got easy plus raw power from the left side and some scouts have put a 70 on it. He hit nine home runs in the Arizona and New York-Penn leagues in a 60-game pro debut.

FASTEST RUNNER: At his best, Smith is 70-grade runner who uses that speed in the outfield, where he's a plus defender. His wheels haven't yet translated to base stealing prowess, as he went just 1-for-2 in stolen base attempts through 29 games in the Rookie-level Arizona League.

BEST DEFENSIVE PLAYER: Smith would be a candidate for best defensive player thanks to his athleticism in the outfield, but Davidson has athleticism, above-average speed and a plus arm at shortstop.

BEST ATHLETE: Smith and Davidson both have cases for this category, though Smith gets the edge for his standout athleticism, which should translate to a number of impressive plays in the outfield.

BEST FASTBALL: RHP Tyler Baum (2) has a plus fastball that typically sits at 91-94 mph throughout starts, but he can ratchet the pitch into the upper 90s at any point if he needs the extra velocity.

BEST SECONDARY PITCH: Baum also has an impressive curveball, a sharp offering in the 79-81 mph range that has tight, 11-to-5 shape and could become a plus offering with more consistency.

BEST PRO DEBUT: Smith hit .361/.466/.443 with 20 walks, 29 strikeouts and six doubles in the Arizona League as an 18-year-old. 1B/3B Dustin Harris (11) played in the Arizona and New York Penn leagues and excelled in both. The St. Petersburg (Fla.) JC product hit .325/.403/.407 with 25 walks and 39 strikeouts.

MOST INTRIGUING BACKGROUND: Davidson's father, Mark Davidson, played in the majors for six years with the Twins and the Astros.

CLOSEST TO THE MAJORS: Baum will need to improve his consistency from outing to outing, but he has the stuff and enough strike-throwing ability to be a quick-mover. While he has a chance to start, the A's could speed up his timeline if they wanted to push him as a reliever, and he has the pure stuff for that role as well.

BEST LATE-ROUND PICK: Oakland has done a solid job developing position players and it'll be interesting to see what they do with Harris, who is a strong corner infielder with impressive feel to hit. His bat is his carrying tool, but he'll need to put in the work to give himself a chance to play third base full time. Most of his innings came as a first baseman in his debut season.

THE ONE WHO GOT AWAY: The Athletics only failed to sign three players in their 2019 draft class: C Ty Duvall (25), RHP Will Jensen (28) and OF Derek Lee (39).

—CARLOS COLLAZO

TOP DRAFT PICKS OF THE DECADE

Year	Player, Pos	2019 Org
2010	Michael Choice, OF	Mexican League
2011	Sonny Gray, RHP	Reds
2012	Addison Russell, SS	Cubs
2013	Billy McKinney, OF	Blue Jays
2014	Matt Chapman, 3B	Athletics
2015	Richie Martin, SS	Orioles
2016	A.J. Puk, LHP	Athletics
2017	Austin Beck, OF	Athletics
2018	Kyler Murray, OF	Arizona (NFL)
2019	Logan Davidson, SS	Athletics

2018

The A's gambled when they drafted OF Kyler Murray ninth overall. They got left with nothing when he chose football and went first overall in the NFL draft. OF Jameson Hannah (2) was traded for Tanner Roark.

GRADE: D

2017

This class is big on upside with OF Austin Beck (1), OF Greg Deichmann (2) and SS Nick Allen (3), but it also carries a lot of risk. Three players have been used in trades, chiefly SS Kevin Merrell (1s).

GRADE: C

2016

LHP A.J. Puk (1) and C Sean Murphy (3) both made their MLB debuts in 2019 and played well down the stretch to help Oakland win the wild card. Both have the potential to be core pieces for the A's.

GRADE: A

1 JESUS LUZARDO, LHP

Born: Sept. 30, 1997. **B-T:** L-L. **HT:** 6-0. **WT:** 209.
Drafted: HS—Parkland, Fla., 2016 (3rd round).
Signed by: Alex Morales (Nationals).

TRACK RECORD: Born in Peru, Luzardo was raised in Florida and attended Stoneman Douglas High in Parkland. He was on track to be a potential first-round pick in 2016 until he needed Tommy John surgery two months before the draft. He fell to the third round, where the Nationals picked him No. 94 overall and signed him for an above-slot $1.4 million. Luzardo made a full recovery and flashed big stuff when he returned, leading the Athletics to acquire him at the 2017 trade deadline with Blake Treinen and Sheldon Neuse in the trade that sent Ryan Madson and Sean Doolittle to the Nationals. With the A's, Luzardo bounded three levels up to Triple-A,started the Futures Game in a breakout 2018 and appeared on the precipice of the big leagues in 2019. Instead he suffered a rotator cuff strain in March and a lat strain in July, but he still managed to make his big debut in September and was so dominant that the A's carried him on their postseason roster.

SCOUTING REPORT: Luzardo tapped back into his fastball post-surgery, flirting with easy velocity up to 97 mph and impressive natural sink. Luzardo confidently works his heater to both sides of the plate, generating weak contact and plenty of swings and misses. His plus, mid-80s changeup features deceptive fade and is effective against both righties and lefties. His low-80s curveball is his third pitch, but it still projects as a future above-average offering. Luzardo is still gaining feel and confidence for his curve, but at its best he can land it for strikes with 1-to-7 action and alter its shape. Luzardo understands his body, which allows him to have a repeatable delivery and above-average control.

THE FUTURE: Luzardo's maturity, poise, confidence and steady development have him tracking to only become stronger with an already-dangerous arsenal. With nothing left to prove in the minors, Luzardo has the ingredients to become a front-of-the-rotation starter. As long as he shows he's healthy, he should open the year in Oakland.

JASON O. WATSON

BA GRADE
70 Risk: High

SCOUTING GRADES
Fastball: 60. **Changeup:** 70.
Curveball: 55. **Control:** 60.

Projected future grades on 20-80 scouting scale.

TOP PROSPECTS OF THE DECADE

Year	Player, Pos	2019 Org
2010	Chris Carter, OF	Mexican League
2011	Grant Green, SS	Did not play
2012	Jarrod Parker, RHP	Did not play
2013	Addison Russell, SS	Cubs
2014	Addison Russell, SS	Cubs
2015	Daniel Robertson, SS	Rays
2016	Franklin Barreto, SS	Athletics
2017	Franklin Barreto, SS	Athletics
2018	A.J. Puk, LHP	Athletics
2019	Jesus Luzardo, LHP	Athletics

BEST TOOLS

Best Hitter For Average	Sheldon Neuse
Best Power Hitter	Seth Brown
Best Strike-Zone Discipline	Alfonso Rivas
Fastest Baserunner	Jorge Mateo
Best Athlete	Jorge Mateo
Best Fastball	A.J. Puk
Best Curveball	Miguel Romero
Best Slider	Richard Gausch
Best Changeup	Jesus Luzardo
Best Control	Daulton Jefferies
Best Defensive Catcher	Sean Murphy
Best Defensive Infielder	Nick Allen
Best Infield Arm	Jeremy Eierman
Best Defensive Outfielder	Luis Barrera
Best Outfield Arm	Austin Beck

Year	Age	Club (League)	Class	W	L	ERA	G	GS	SV	IP	H	HR	BB	SO	K/9	WHIP	AVG
2017	19	Nationals (GCL)	R	1	0	1.32	3	3	0	14	14	1	0	15	9.9	1.02	.259
	19	Athletics (AZL)	R	0	1	1.54	4	3	0	12	9	0	1	13	10.0	0.86	.205
	19	Vermont (NYP)	SS	1	0	2.00	5	5	0	18	12	1	4	20	10.0	0.89	.188
2018	20	Stockton (CAL)	HiA	2	1	1.23	3	3	0	15	6	0	5	25	15.3	0.75	.120
	20	Midland (TL)	AA	7	3	2.29	16	16	0	79	58	5	18	86	9.8	0.97	.204
	20	Nashville (PCL)	AAA	1	1	7.31	4	4	0	16	25	2	7	18	10.1	2.00	.362
2019	21	Athletics Green (AZL)	R	0	0	0.00	1	1	0	2	1	0	0	5	22.5	0.50	.143
	21	Stockton (CAL)	HiA	1	0	0.90	3	1	0	10	6	1	0	18	16.2	0.60	.171
	21	Las Vegas (PCL)	AAA	1	1	3.19	7	7	0	31	29	3	8	34	9.9	1.19	.240
	21	Oakland (AL)	MAJ	0	0	1.50	6	0	2	12	5	1	3	16	12.0	0.67	.119
Major League Totals				0	0	1.50	6	0	2	12	5	1	3	16	12.0	0.67	.119
Minor League Totals				14	7	2.53	46	43	0	195	160	13	43	234	10.8	1.04	.219

2 A.J. PUK, LHP

Born: April 25, 1995. **B-T:** L-L. **HT:** 6-7. **WT:** 220. **Drafted:** Florida, 2016 (1st round). **Signed by:** Trevor Schaffer.

BA GRADE
65 Risk: High

TRACK RECORD: Puk missed the 2018 season after having Tommy John surgery, but he returned in 2019 and showed the same stuff that made him arguably the top player in the 2016 draft class. The Athletics called him up in August after he threw just 25 innings in the minors, and he earned a spot on the American League Wild Card Game roster.

SCOUTING REPORT: Puk returned from surgery with his premium stuff intact, headlined by a 70-grade fastball that tips the scales at 95-99 mph from the left side. Puk's upper-80s slider gives him another plus power offering he can bury in on righthanders and away from lefties, and his changeup continues to progress into a usable, if unspectacular, offering. Puk has never been known for pinpoint location, but makes up for it with an ability to elevate or drive in on both sides of the plate as needed. His sizzling velocity, combined with the natural downhill plane from his 6-foot-7 frame, makes for difficult, uncomfortable at-bats.

THE FUTURE: Puk still needs to build innings and may begin 2020 at Triple-A Las Vegas in order to do so. As long as he stays healthy, he should ascend to Oakland's rotation before long and could emerge as a front-of-the-rotation starter.

SCOUTING GRADES: **Fastball:** 70 **Slider:** 70 **Changeup:** 50 **Control:** 50

Year	Age	Club (League)	Class	W	L	ERA	G	GS	SV	IP	H	HR	BB	SO	K/9	WHIP	AVG
2017	22	Stockton (CAL)	HiA	4	5	3.69	14	11	0	61	44	1	23	98	14.5	1.10	.196
	22	Midland (TL)	AA	2	5	4.36	13	13	0	64	64	2	25	86	12.1	1.39	.256
2018	23	Did not play—Injured															
2019	24	Stockton (CAL)	HiA	0	0	6.00	3	3	0	6	5	2	4	9	13.5	1.50	.238
	24	Midland (TL)	AA	0	0	4.32	6	1	0	8	9	2	3	13	14.0	1.44	.281
	24	Las Vegas (PCL)	AAA	4	1	4.91	9	0	0	11	7	3	3	16	13.1	0.91	.175
	24	Oakland (AL)	MAJ	2	0	3.18	10	0	0	11	10	1	5	13	10.3	1.32	.238
Major League Totals				2	0	3.18	10	0	0	11	10	1	5	13	10.3	1.32	.238
Minor League Totals				10	15	3.98	55	38	0	183	152	10	70	262	12.9	1.21	.220

3 SEAN MURPHY, C

Born: Oct. 4, 1994. **B-T:** R-R. **HT:** 6-3. **WT:** 232. **Drafted:** Wright State, 2016 (3rd round). **Signed:** Rich Sparks.

DAVID DUROCHIK

BA GRADE
55 Risk: Medium

TRACK RECORD: Murphy began his career at Wright State as a walk-on and ended it as the program's highest-drafted player in 10 years. He battled a long list of injuries, including breaking both hamate bones and a torn left meniscus, but he still emerged as the club's primary catcher down the stretch.

SCOUTING REPORT: Murphy is an elite defensive catcher thanks to his athleticism and agility. His maturity as a game-caller, blocking and framing all receive plus grades, and his plus-plus arm was one of the strongest in the minors. At the plate, Murphy works the middle of the field with a compact swing and has the strength to produce 20-plus home run power. In addition to his work ethic, Murphy's leadership with his pitching staff draws rave reviews.

THE FUTURE: Murphy had a second surgery on his left knee in October. He is expected to be ready for spring training and is in prime position to be Oakland's Opening Day catcher.

SCOUTING GRADES: **Hitting:** 45 **Power:** 55 **Running:** 30 **Fielding:** 60. **Arm:** 70.

Year	Age	Club (League)	Class	AVG	G	AB	R	H	2B	3B	HR	RBI	BB	SO	SB	OBP	SLG
2017	22	Stockton (CAL)	HiA	.297	45	165	22	49	11	0	9	26	11	33	0	.343	.527
	22	Midland (TL)	AA	.209	53	191	25	40	7	0	4	22	21	34	0	.288	.309
2018	23	Athletics (AZL)	R	.200	2	5	1	1	1	0	0	0	0	1	0	.200	.400
	23	Midland (TL)	AA	.288	68	257	51	74	26	2	8	43	23	47	3	.358	.498
	23	Nashville (PCL)	AAA	.250	3	8	2	2	0	0	0	0	3	2	0	.500	.250
2019	24	Athletics Green (AZL)	R	.500	1	2	1	1	0	0	0	0	3	1	0	.800	.500
	24	Las Vegas (PCL)	AAA	.308	31	120	25	37	6	1	10	30	15	31	0	.386	.625
	24	Oakland (AL)	MAJ	.245	20	53	14	13	5	0	4	8	6	16	0	.333	.566
Major League Totals				.245	20	53	14	13	5	0	4	8	6	16	0	.333	.566
Minor League Totals				.267	235	855	146	228	54	3	34	129	89	165	4	.341	.456

4 DAULTON JEFFERIES, RHP

Born: Aug. 2, 1995. **B-T:** L-R. **HT:** 6-2. **WT:** 185. **Drafted:** California, 2016 (1st round supplemental). **Signed by:** Jermaine Clark

TRACK RECORD: The Athletics drafted Jefferies from the University of California with the 37th overall pick in 2016, but Tommy John surgery limited him to just three appearances combined in 2017 and 2018. Jefferies returned to full health in 2019 and showed the A's exactly what they hoped to see. He logged a 3.42 ERA while advancing to Double-A Midland, with an eye-popping 93 strikeouts against just nine walks in 79 innings.

SCOUTING REPORT: Jefferies has one of the most potent arsenals in the system and shows the ability to command all three of his pitches. His fastball sits 92-95 mph with cut life and plays up because of his command. He pairs his fastball with a potentially plus changeup in the upper 80s with two-seam dive and fade, and his tilting, upper-80s slider varies in length to take on cutter action and keep hitters unsure of how much it will break. Jefferies has a repeatable delivery and borderline elite control. His arm action, however, has rival evaluators concerned for his long-term health.

THE FUTURE: Jefferies will continue to log innings and build durability in 2020. He'll begin at Triple-A Las Vegas and has a chance to see Oakland if his workload allows.

BA GRADE
55 Risk: Very High

SCOUTING GRADES: Fastball: 55 | Slider: 50 | Changeup: 60 | Control: 70

Year	Age	Club (League)	Class	W	L	ERA	G	GS	SV	IP	H	HR	BB	SO	K/9	WHIP	AVG
2017	21	Stockton (CAL)	HiA	0	0	2.57	2	1	0	7	7	0	1	6	7.7	1.14	.241
2018	22	Athletics (AZL)	R	0	0	0.00	1	1	0	2	1	0	0	5	22.5	0.50	.143
2019	23	Stockton (CAL)	HiA	1	0	2.40	5	3	0	15	10	1	2	21	12.6	0.80	.182
	23	Midland (TL)	AA	1	2	3.66	21	12	0	64	63	7	7	72	10.1	1.09	.255
Minor League Totals				2	2	3.17	34	22	0	99	92	8	12	121	11.0	1.05	.242

5 AUSTIN BECK, OF

Born: Nov. 21, 1998. **B-T:** R-R. **HT:** 6-1. **WT:** 200. **Drafted:** HS—Lexington, N.C., 2017 (1st round). **Signed by:** Neil Avent.

TRACK RECORD: Beck suffered a torn anterior cruciate ligament prior to his senior season and had a limited track record against good competition at his small North Carolina high school, but the Athletics couldn't say no to his dripping athleticism and drafted him sixth overall in 2017. After a decent first full season, Beck battled a recurring quad strain that limited him to 85 games in 2019 and suffered through a difficult year at high Class A Stockton that included a 34-percent strikeout rate.

SCOUTING REPORT: Beck's athleticism stands out among the best of his peers. He is a plus runner, has plus arm strength and draws consistent reviews as an above-average to plus defender in center field. His bat, however, is a question mark. He flashes above-average raw power but is a below-average hitter who struggles to get to it. He frequently over-swings while chasing fastballs up and breaking stuff low and away, producing gobs of strikeouts and poor quality contact when he connects. Beck has plenty of bat speed, leaving some evaluators hopeful he'll hit once he refines his approach and improves his natural feel at the plate.

THE FUTURE: Beck will be 21 all of next year and still has time to figure out his swing. He may repeat high Class A Stockton before moving on to Double-A.

BA GRADE
55 Risk: Very High

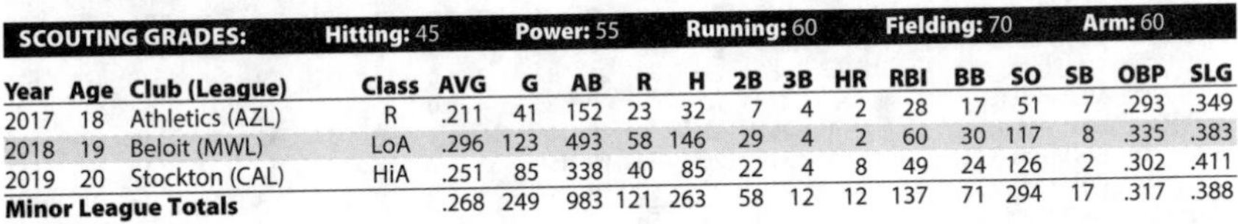

SCOUTING GRADES: Hitting: 45 | Power: 55 | Running: 60 | Fielding: 70 | Arm: 60

Year	Age	Club (League)	Class	AVG	G	AB	R	H	2B	3B	HR	RBI	BB	SO	SB	OBP	SLG
2017	18	Athletics (AZL)	R	.211	41	152	23	32	7	4	2	28	17	51	7	.293	.349
2018	19	Beloit (MWL)	LoA	.296	123	493	58	146	29	4	2	60	30	117	8	.335	.383
2019	20	Stockton (CAL)	HiA	.251	85	338	40	85	22	4	8	49	24	126	2	.302	.411
Minor League Totals				.268	249	983	121	263	58	12	12	137	71	294	17	.317	.388

6 ROBERT PUASON, SS

Born: Sept. 11, 2002. **Age:** 17. **B-T:** B-R. **HT:** 6-3. **WT:** 165. **Signed:** Dominican Republic, 2019. **Signed by:** Amauris Reyes

BA GRADE
55 Risk: Extreme

TRACK RECORD: Considered one of the top players in the Dominican Republic years before he was 16, Puason agreed to sign with the Braves when he was 14 but went back on the open market after Major League Baseball banned the Braves from signing international players for two years after finding numerous international signing violations. The Athletics jumped in and signed Puason for $5.1 million on July 2, tied for the largest signing bonus awarded to any player in the 2019-20 international class.

SCOUTING REPORT: Puason has a wiry, projectable frame and loads of tools on which to dream. A switch-hitter with plus speed, Puason produces hard contact from both sides of the plate and shows a mature feel for controlling the barrel. As he refines his swing mechanics and adds muscle, Puason could grow into above-average power and be at least an average hitter. His long swing and shoddy pitch recognition, however, give others pause about how much he'll hit. Puason is a sleek athlete with the athleticism and instincts to stick at shortstop. He has good footwork, clean hands and a plus arm that could still tick up as his body develops.

THE FUTURE: Puason played simulated games in Arizona after signing. He is set to open his pro career in the Rookie-level Arizona League in 2020.

SCOUTING GRADES: Hitting: 50 | Power: 50 | Running: 55 | Fielding: 60. | Arm: 70.

Year	Age	Club (League)	Class	AVG	G	AB	R	H	2B	3B	HR	RBI	BB	SO	SB	OBP	SLG
2019	16	Did not play—Signed 2020 Contract															

7 SHELDON NEUSE, 3B

Born: Dec. 10, 1994. **B-T:** R-R. **HT:** 6-0. **WT:** 218. **Drafted:** Oklahoma, 2016 (2nd round). **Signed by:** Ed Gustafson (Nationals).

DAVID DUROCHIK

BA GRADE
45 Risk: Medium

TRACK RECORD: The Athletics long liked Neuse's power and made sure to acquire him from the Nationals with Jesus Luzardo and Blake Treinen in exchange for Ryan Madson and Sean Doolittle at the 2017 trade deadline. Neuse scuffled in his first taste of Triple-A in 2018, but he cut his strikeout rate by 8 percent while repeating the Pacific Coast League in 2019 and earned his first big league callup in August.

SCOUTING REPORT: Neuse generates his power from the combination of a stocky frame and advanced barrel control. He drives the ball to the gaps and increased his loft in 2019 to hit career-high 27 home runs. Neuse is an aggressive hitter who often expands the strike zone early in seasons, especially chasing elevated fastballs, but tends to rein in his approach and cut down on his strikeouts as the year progresses. Neuse is bulky but sneakily athletic for his size with a quick first step, good instincts, and natural actions at both second and third base. He can also fill in at shortstop and left field, and his plus arm fits anywhere on the diamond.

THE FUTURE: Neuse primarily played second base during his callup. With Matt Chapman entrenched at third base, versatility will be Neuse's path to an everyday role in 2020.

SCOUTING GRADES: Hitting: 45 | Power: 50 | Running: 40 | Fielding: 55 | Arm: 60

Year	Age	Club (League)	Class	AVG	G	AB	R	H	2B	3B	HR	RBI	BB	SO	SB	OBP	SLG
2017	22	Hagerstown (SAL)	LoA	.291	77	292	40	85	19	3	9	51	25	66	12	.349	.469
	22	Stockton (CAL)	HiA	.386	22	83	21	32	3	0	7	22	9	25	2	.457	.675
	22	Midland (TL)	AA	.373	18	67	9	25	4	0	0	6	6	21	0	.427	.433
2018	23	Nashville (PCL)	AAA	.263	135	499	48	131	26	3	5	55	32	172	4	.304	.357
2019	24	Las Vegas (PCL)	AAA	.317	126	498	99	158	31	2	27	102	56	132	3	.389	.550
	24	Oakland (AL)	MAJ	.250	25	56	3	14	3	0	0	7	4	19	0	.295	.304
Major League Totals				.250	25	56	3	14	3	0	0	7	4	19	0	.295	.304
Minor League Totals				.294	414	1565	233	460	88	11	49	247	141	442	23	.354	.458

8 JORGE MATEO, SS

Born: June 23, 1995. **B-T:** R-R. **HT:** 6-0. **WT:** 192. **Signed:** Dominican Republic, 2012. **Signed by:** Juan Rosario (Yankees).

DAVID DUROCHIK

BA GRADE
50 Risk: High

TRACK RECORD: Viewed as one of the top prospects the A's received in the Sonny Gray trade with the Yankees, Mateo remains a head-scratcher who flashes big tools but struggles to produce consistently. He repeated the Triple-A Pacific Coast League in 2019 and took encouraging steps, cutting his strikeout rate while increasing his power output—but he also suffered a massive second half drop-off.

SCOUTING REPORT: Mateo's biggest tool is his 80-grade speed. He stole 82 bases in 2015 and 52 in 2017, though his stolen base totals have been more modest with Oakland. For Mateo to be at his sharpest, he needs to be on the basepaths, which has been a problem. Some days, he is on time in the box, stays within the strike zone and uses the whole field with a quick, direct swing. Other times he is tentative against velocity, swings from his heels and shows zero pitch-recognition. Evaluators don't know what to make of Mateo's offensive potential, but most see .250 with 15 home runs as the best possible outcome. Mateo is similarly inconsistent at shortstop, sometimes playing too aggressive and other times too passive. He has the athleticism and plus arm to play multiple positions.

THE FUTURE: Mateo needs to find some semblance of consistency. He'll return to Triple-A in 2020.

SCOUTING GRADES: **Hitting:** 45 **Power:** 40 **Running:** 80 **Fielding:** 50. **Arm:** 60.

Year	Age	Club (League)	Class	AVG	G	AB	R	H	2B	3B	HR	RBI	BB	SO	SB	OBP	SLG
2017	22	Tampa (FSL)	HiA	.240	69	275	39	66	16	8	4	11	16	79	28	.288	.400
	22	Trenton (EL)	AA	.300	30	120	26	36	9	3	4	26	15	32	11	.381	.525
	22	Midland (TL)	AA	.292	30	137	25	40	5	7	4	20	9	33	13	.333	.518
2018	23	Nashville (PCL)	AAA	.230	131	470	50	108	17	16	3	45	29	139	25	.280	.353
2019	24	Las Vegas (PCL)	AAA	.289	119	532	95	154	29	14	19	78	29	145	24	.330	.504
Minor League Totals				.267	702	2818	445	751	131	76	52	302	227	714	283	.325	.422

9 LOGAN DAVIDSON, SS

Born: Dec. 26, 1997. **B-T:** B-R. **HT:** 6-3. **WT:** 185. **Drafted:** Clemson, 2019 (1st round). **Signed by:** Neil Avent.

BA GRADE
50 Risk: High

TRACK RECORD: The Phillies drafted Davidson in the 30th round out of high school but he chose to follow his father Mark's footsteps and play baseball at Clemson. Davidson grew into a power hitter with 42 home runs and 142 RBIs over three collegiate seasons. The A's made him the 29th overall pick in 2019 and signed him for $2,424,600.

SCOUTING REPORT: Davidson never hit .300 in college and hit just .239 at short-season Vermont after signing, continuing longstanding concerns about his overall hitting ability. Opinions vary on Davidson's consistency at the plate. His supporters praise his natural feel for squaring up pitches, while detractors point to a long swing that results in too many swings and misses. He flashes above-average power when he connects. While the 6-foot-3 Davidson registers tall for a shortstop, he has the quick hands and natural athleticism to project to stick at the position. His plus arm strength allows him to profile at both shortstop or third base if he has to move. Davidson has bloodlines and a good role model in his corner. His father played six years in the majors with the Astros and Twins.

THE FUTURE: Davidson has work to do at the plate. His opening 2020 assignment will largely depend on how he looks in spring training.

SCOUTING GRADES: **Hitting:** 45 **Power:** 55 **Running:** 55 **Fielding:** 55 **Arm:** 60.

Year	Age	Club (League)	Class	AVG	G	AB	R	H	2B	3B	HR	RBI	BB	SO	SB	OBP	SLG
2019	21	Vermont (NYP)	SS	.239	54	205	42	49	7	0	4	12	31	55	5	.345	.332
Minor League Totals				.239	54	205	42	49	7	0	4	12	31	55	5	.345	.332

10 NICK ALLEN, SS

BA GRADE 45 **Risk:** High

Born: Oct. 8, 1998. **B-T:** R-R. **HT:** 5-9. **WT:** 166. **Drafted:** HS—San Diego, 2017 (3rd round). **Signed by:** Anthony Aliotti.

TRACK RECORD: The 5-foot-9 Allen has long held a reputation as a spectacular defender with a light bat, but he began changing that perception in 2019. Allen got stronger and adjusted his approach to use the whole field at high Class A Stockton, and he tied for the California League lead in doubles before suffering a season-ending ankle sprain on June 27.

SCOUTING REPORT: Allen is a twitchy, instinctive defender who moves well in every direction with plus speed. He makes highlight-reel plays and the routine ones, and he almost never makes a fielding error with his clean hands. Allen's arm ticked up to plus as he got stronger, burnishing his reputation as a potential Gold Glove shortstop. Scouts like Allen's swing and hand-eye coordination at the plate, but his compact frame limits his projection and caps most of his evaluations at an average hitter with well below-average power.

THE FUTURE: Allen's defense will earn him playing time, and he has started hitting just enough to profile as a potential starter rather than a pure backup. He'll try to keep it going at Double-A Midland in 2020.

SCOUTING GRADES: **Hitting:** 50 **Power:** 30 **Running:** 60 **Fielding:** 70 **Arm:** 60

Year	Age	Club (League)	Class	AVG	G	AB	R	H	2B	3B	HR	RBI	BB	SO	SB	OBP	SLG
2017	18	Athletics (AZL)	R	.254	35	138	26	35	3	2	1	14	13	28	7	.322	.326
2018	19	Beloit (MWL)	LoA	.239	121	460	51	110	17	6	0	34	34	85	24	.301	.302
2019	20	Stockton (CAL)	HiA	.292	72	288	45	84	22	5	3	25	28	52	13	.363	.434
Minor League Totals				.258	228	886	122	229	42	13	4	73	75	165	44	.324	.349

11 AUSTIN ALLEN, C

BA GRADE 40 **Risk:** Medium

Born: Jan. 16, 1994. **B-T:** L-R. **Ht.:** 6-2. **Wt.:** 220. **Drafted:** Florida Tech, 2015 (4th round). **Signed by:** Willie Bosque (Padres).

TRACK RECORD: The Padres made Allen the first Division II player drafted in 2015 when they selected him in the fourth round out of Florida Tech. He hit at least .280 with 20 home runs every season from 2017-19 and received his first major league callup last May. The A's acquired him in December for Jurickson Profar.

SCOUTING REPORT: Allen is a big-bodied catcher defined by his bat. He generates plus raw power with his supreme strength and leverage, frequently sending balls 400-plus feet to right-center. His bat speed isn't special, but he is consistently on time and has shown himself to be at least an average hitter with above-average power. Allen's catching has been a work-in-progress and still needs improvement. His hands are fine in the strike zone, but his thick body limits his mobility and ability to get out of the crouch. Opponents run freely on him and have stolen 436 bases in his 398 career games behind the plate. He also needs to improve his game-calling.

THE FUTURE: Allen's move to the American League opens up potential at-bats for him as a DH.

Year	Age	Club (League)	Class	AVG	G	AB	R	H	2B	3B	HR	RBI	BB	SO	SB	OBP	SLG
2017	23	Lake Elsinore (CAL)	HiA	.283	121	463	71	131	31	1	22	81	44	109	0	.353	.497
2018	24	San Antonio (TL)	AA	.290	119	451	59	131	31	0	22	56	37	97	0	.351	.506
2019	25	El Paso (PCL)	AAA	.330	67	270	52	89	27	0	21	67	22	56	0	.379	.663
	25	San Diego (NL)	MAJ	.215	34	65	4	14	4	0	0	3	6	21	0	.282	.277
Major League Totals				.215	34	65	4	14	4	0	0	3	6	21	0	.282	.277
Minor League Totals				.296	472	1800	258	532	121	2	75	300	153	369	1	.354	.490

12 LAZARO ARMENTEROS, OF

BA GRADE 50 **Risk:** Extreme

Born: May 22, 1999. **B-T:** R-R. **HT:** 6-0. **WT:** 182. **Drafted:** Cuba, 2016. **Signed by:** Raul Gomez.

TRACK RECORD: The A's made a big splash when they signed Armenteros for $3 million out of Cuba in 2016, but he has yet to deliver on his potential. Armenteros struggled to get to his power at low Class A Beloit in his full-season debut, then struggled to make contact at all at high Class A Stockton in 2019.

SCOUTING REPORT: Armenteros creates tremendous leverage in his swing and shows off at least plus raw power in batting practice. Armenteros rarely gets to that power in games, however, because he swings and misses at an alarming rate. His setup and swing path aren't conducive for contact, and his natural hitting instincts have a long way to go. Armenteros has plus speed and is improving his reads to become an average defender. His well below-average arm limits him to left field.

THE FUTURE: Armenteros' youth and raw tools are enticing, but he needs to make dramatic improvements as a hitter for them to matter. He'll still be 20 on Opening Day and has time on his side.

Year	Age	Club (League)	Class	AVG	G	AB	R	H	2B	3B	HR	RBI	BB	SO	SB	OBP	SLG
2017	18	Athletics (DSL)	R	.167	6	18	6	3	0	0	0	1	3	9	2	.385	.167
	18	Athletics (AZL)	R	.288	41	156	24	45	9	4	4	22	16	48	10	.376	.474
2018	19	Beloit (MWL)	LoA	.277	79	292	43	81	8	2	8	39	36	115	8	.374	.401
2019	20	Stockton (CAL)	HiA	.222	126	459	65	102	22	5	17	61	73	227	22	.336	.403
Minor League Totals				.250	252	925	138	231	39	11	29	123	128	399	42	.356	.410

13 SKYE BOLT, OF

BA GRADE 45 **Risk: High**

Born: Jan. 15, 1994. **B-T:** B-R. **HT:** 6-2. **WT:** 187. **Drafted:** North Carolina, 2015 (4th round). **Signed by:** Neil Avent.

TRACK RECORD: Since his selection as the Athletics' fourth-round pick in 2015, Bolt's has played mostly full seasons at each level before making his big league debut in May. Bolt was not initially recalled in September but was a late add following an injury to Mark Canha.

SCOUTING REPORT: Bolt possesses a solid combination of tools, skills and athleticism, though he lacks a true carrying tool. A switch-hitter, Bolt has made most of impact against righthanders and profiles as a platoon-type player. Bolt has solid-average speed that helps him on the bases and in the outfield. After playing mostly in center field, Bolt has divided time between right and center of late. His above-average arm gives him a chance at both positions.

THE FUTURE: After making his major league debut, Bolt will compete for a bench role in 2020.

Year	Age	Club (League)	Class	AVG	G	AB	R	H	2B	3B	HR	RBI	BB	SO	SB	OBP	SLG
2017	23	Stockton (CAL)	HiA	.243	114	432	76	105	24	7	15	66	53	134	9	.327	.435
2018	24	Stockton (CAL)	HiA	.266	46	169	28	45	8	4	9	32	31	47	9	.382	.521
	24	Midland (TL)	AA	.256	78	285	41	73	18	3	10	37	27	75	10	.325	.446
2019	25	Las Vegas (PCL)	AAA	.269	89	305	57	82	19	3	11	61	37	94	7	.350	.459
	25	Oakland (AL)	MAJ	.100	5	10	1	1	1	0	0	0	1	3	0	.182	.200
Major League Totals				.100	5	10	1	1	1	0	0	0	1	3	0	.182	.200
Minor League Totals				.249	480	1714	262	427	99	21	54	252	214	482	47	.335	.426

14 JAMES KAPRIELIAN, RHP

BA GRADE 50 **Risk: Extreme**

Born: March 2, 1994. **B-T:** R-R. **HT:** 6-3. **WT:** 210. **Drafted:** UCLA, 2015 (1st round). **Signed by:** Bobby DeJardin (Yankees).

TRACK RECORD: Kaprielian has been a premium prospect since his college days at UCLA. Unfortunately, injuries—including a forearm strain and Tommy John surgery—limited him to just 29.1 innings prior to 2019. Kaprielian threw no more than 73 pitches in any outing in 2019.

SCOUTING REPORT: While Kaprielian's velocity remained relatively consistent throughout the season, the quality of his stuff slowly returned. Prior to the injury, Kaprielian's fastball sat comfortably between 93-96 MPH, stretching as high as 99. In 2019, his fastball mostly sat between 90-93. Kaprielian's slider is above-average and flashes plus with good, tight shape. Kaprielian's curve and changeup are solid-average and play off each other nicely. His command proved more advanced than most pitchers in their first year back from Tommy John. His delivery is still effortful, which leaves him at risk for further injury

THE FUTURE: Triple-A Las Vegas seems a likely starting point in 2020, when he'll try to return to the track that could lead to a mid-rotation starter's role.

Year	Age	Club (League)	Class	W	L	ERA	G	GS	SV	IP	H	HR	BB	SO	K/9	WHIP	AVG
2017	23	Did not play—Injured															
2018	24	Did not play—Injured															
2019	25	Stockton (CAL)	HiA	2	2	4.46	11	10	0	36	35	6	8	43	10.7	1.18	.250
	25	Midland (TL)	AA	2	1	1.63	7	5	0	28	18	2	8	26	8.5	0.94	.186
	25	Las Vegas (PCL)	AAA	0	0	2.25	1	1	0	4	6	0	0	6	13.5	1.50	.333
Minor League Totals				6	5	2.96	27	22	0	97	77	9	23	111	10.3	1.03	.216

15 TYLER BAUM, RHP

BA GRADE 45 **Risk: High**

Born: Jan. 14, 1998. **B-T:** R-R. **HT:** 6-2. **WT:** 195. **Drafted:** North Carolina, 2019 (2nd round). **Signed by:** Neil Avent.

TRACK RECORD: Baum pulled his name from consideration in the 2016 draft to compete for the North Carolina, After three years in the Heels' rotation, Oakland selected Baum with its second-round pick in 2019. He pitched at short-season Vermont in his pro debut.

SCOUTING REPORT: Baum has a major league frame and arm to match. He features a 92-94 mph fastball that touches 97 with solid armside run. He backs it up with a a power slurve and has ability to change speeds and vary angles both to righties and lefties. Baum's changeup has been a work in progress and still lacks the touch and separation required for an average pitch. Baum's delivery and approach may be best suited for the pen due to a lengthy arm path that could affect his command.

THE FUTURE: Baum should be given every opportunity to start to refine his pitchability, feel and experience, but his stuff and approach could make for an easy fit in the bullpen.

Year	Age	Club (League)	Class	W	L	ERA	G	GS	SV	IP	H	HR	BB	SO	K/9	WHIP	AVG
2019	21	Vermont (NYP)	SS	0	3	4.70	11	11	0	31	29	4	7	34	10.0	1.17	.246
Minor League Totals				0	3	4.70	11	11	0	30	29	4	7	34	10.0	1.17	.246

16 GREG DEICHMANN, OF

BA GRADE
50 Risk: Extreme

Born: May 31, 1995. **B-T:** L-R. **HT:** 6-2. **WT:** 190. **Drafted:** Louisiana State, 2017 (2nd round). **Signed by:** Kelcey Mucker.

TRACK RECORD: Despite an impressive offensive track record coming out of Louisiana State, Deichmann has yet to stay healthy over a full season and injuries have impacted his performance. He finally appeared healthy in the Arizona Fall League, where his natural gifts began to show.

SCOUTING REPORT: After injuries limited Deichmmann to just 80 regular-season games, the LSU product showed what he can do by leading the Arizona Fall League with nine home runs. Deichmann profiles as a low-contact bat with high impact due to a lengthy stroke that produces plus power, an average exit velocity of 90 mph and a 17-degree launch angle. Deichmann does most of his damage against righthanders and will need to refine his approach versus lefties if he is to fill an everyday role. Right field has served as his primary home and his defensive profile should allow him to stay there long term.

THE FUTURE: Ticketed for Las Vegas in 2020, Deichmann's production befits the high-damage, low-contact hitter en vogue in today's game.

Year	Age	Club (League)	Class	AVG	G	AB	R	H	2B	3B	HR	RBI	BB	SO	SB	OBP	SLG
2017	22	Vermont (NYP)	SS	.274	46	164	31	45	10	4	8	30	28	40	4	.385	.530
2018	23	Athletics (AZL)	R	.289	11	38	9	11	2	2	1	7	5	8	0	.372	.526
	23	Stockton (CAL)	HiA	.199	47	166	18	33	14	0	6	21	17	63	0	.276	.392
2019	24	Midland (TL)	AA	.219	80	301	42	66	10	2	11	36	34	103	19	.300	.375
Minor League Totals				.232	184	669	100	155	36	8	26	94	84	214	23	.320	.426

17 GRANT HOLMES, RHP

BA GRADE
45 Risk: High

Born: March 22, 1996. **B-T:** L-R. **HT:** 6-0. **WT:** 224. **Drafted:** HS—Conway, SC., 2014 (1st round). **Signed by:** Lon Joyce (Dodgers).

TRACK RECORD: Holmes came to Oakland in 2016 in the trade that sent Rich Hill and Josh Reddick to the Dodgers. After missing the majority of 2018 with a right rotator cuff injury. Holmes returned to Midland in 2019 and got better every month, while cutting down his walks and increasing his strikeouts.

SCOUTING REPORT: Holmes is deceptively athletic despite a strong, athletic build. He's continued to develop as a starter though he may be best suited for the pen due to size and deception issues. Holmes has a solid, 92-96 mph fastball with life, but his go-to pitch continues to be a powerful mid-80s curveball with good depth in the zone. He has used a hard, 89-93 mph cutter over the past few years to open up the corners and also will also show a fringy changeup. While healthy in 2019, there are some lingering health concerns due to arm action and the stress his delivery puts on his shoulder.

THE FUTURE: Still just 24 despite entering his seventh season in pro ball, Holmes will likely make a return to Las Vegas after ending his season there in 2019.

Year	Age	Club (League)	Class	W	L	ERA	G	GS	SV	IP	H	HR	BB	SO	K/9	WHIP	AVG
2017	21	Midland (TL)	AA	11	12	4.49	29	24	0	148	149	15	61	150	9.1	1.42	.262
2018	22	Stockton (CAL)	HiA	0	0	4.50	2	2	0	6	4	1	2	8	12.0	1.00	.174
2019	23	Midland (TL)	AA	6	5	3.31	22	16	0	82	71	9	27	76	8.4	1.20	.235
	23	Las Vegas (PCL)	AAA	0	0	1.93	1	1	0	5	6	1	1	5	9.6	1.50	.353
Minor League Totals				36	31	3.98	115	100	1	526	502	45	211	538	9.2	1.35	.252

18 JORDAN DIAZ, 3B

BA GRADE
50 Risk: Extreme

Born: Aug. 13, 2000. **B-T:** R-R. **HT:** 5-10. **WT:** 175. **Signed:** Colombia, 2016. **Signed by:** Jose Quintero.

TRACK RECORD: Part of the burgeoning baseball scene in Colombia, Diaz made his debut as a 16-year-old in 2017 and advanced to short-season Vermont in 2019, ranking as the No. 8 prospect in the New York-Penn League.

SCOUTING REPORT: Diaz has impressed observers with his advanced approach on both sides of the ball. He has a good foundation at the plate with a low-maintenance swing, strong hands and the ability to generate hard contact. A leg kick sometimes leads Diaz tends to pull off the ball, which leaves him vulnerable against breaking balls from righthanders. Diaz has a sturdy frame with present strength with some power potential thanks to a solid base. Diaz appears to have skill set to stay at third base, displaying solid reactions and groundball reads with average range. While he has enough arm strength for the position, he needs work on his footwork and arm slots because he tends to sling the ball and not finish his throws.
THE FUTURE: Coming off a productive 2019, Diaz appears ticketed for low Class A Beloit in 2020.

Year	Age	Club (League)	Class	AVG	G	AB	R	H	2B	3B	HR	RBI	BB	SO	SB	OBP	SLG
2017	16	Athletics (AZL)	R	.185	8	27	2	5	0	0	0	2	0	4	1	.179	.185
	16	Athletics (DSL)	R	.255	42	137	14	35	7	0	0	18	6	22	2	.295	.307
2018	17	Athletics (AZL)	R	.277	48	159	23	44	11	2	1	25	19	22	0	.371	.390
2019	18	Vermont (NYP)	SS	.264	70	277	31	73	17	1	9	47	18	46	2	.307	.430
Minor League Totals				.262	168	600	70	157	35	3	10	92	43	94	5	.317	.380

19 BRAYAN BUELVAS, OF

BA GRADE
50 Risk: Extreme

Born: June 8, 2002. **B-T:** R-R. **HT:** 5-11. **WT:** 155. **Signed:** Colombia, 2019. **Signed by:** Tito Quintero.

TRACK RECORD: Buelvas is part of a growing influx of talent from Colombia. He moved quickly to the states in 2019, playing and performing during the season's second half in the Rookie-level Arizona League, where he ranked as the No. 19 prospect.
SCOUTING REPORT: Though not overly physical, Buelvas carries some deceptively loud tools, including an average exit velocity of 89 mph. He also shows solid bat speed and barrel control, but some evaluators believe the length of swing and overall balance at the plate could be problematic. While Buelvas still has projection remaining, any power uptick could be marginal. Buelvas' speed is an asset both on the bases and in the field. Scouts are confident Buelvas has the skill set and tools to stay in center field, and A's personnel have raved about his work ethic, energy and professional approach to the game.
THE FUTURE: Buelvas is likely to head back to Arizona in 2020, though his advanced approach and makeup could help him reach short-season Vermont by year's end.

Year	Age	Club (League)	Class	AVG	G	AB	R	H	2B	3B	HR	RBI	BB	SO	SB	OBP	SLG
2019	17	Athletics (DSL)	R	.244	23	78	4	19	5	1	0	14	8	14	4	.330	.333
	17	Athletics Green (AZL)	R	.300	44	160	26	48	10	7	3	27	22	46	12	.392	.506
Minor League Totals				.282	67	238	30	67	15	8	3	41	30	60	16	.372	.450

20 MARCUS SMITH, OF

BA GRADE
50 Risk: Extreme

Born: Sept. 11, 2000. **B-T:** L-L. **HT:** 5-11. **WT:** 190. **Drafted:** HS—Kansas City, Mo., 2019 (3rd round). **Signed by:** Steve Abney.

TRACK RECORD: Smith made the decision to forego a commitment Michigan to begin his professional career as the A's third-round pick in 2019 with a price tag of $400,000.
SCOUTING REPORT: Extremely athletic, Smith has advanced strength and physicality in his compact frame when compared to typical high school draftees. He has impressive tools at the plate, featuring quick, strong hands. He worked to widen his base, improve the use of his lower half as well as the balance and timing in his swing. He had a hard time centering the baseball in the Rookie-level Arizona League, where he generated over 60 percent ground balls. Smith's contact rate was encouraging despite the crudeness at the plate because of an average exit velocity of 88 mph. His speed and athleticism are assets on the basepaths and center field, though he will need to learn how to steal bases at the professional level.
THE FUTURE: An impressive athlete with a highly touted defensive resume, Smith will be given every chance to play in Vermont in 2020.

Year	Age	Club (League)	Class	AVG	G	AB	R	H	2B	3B	HR	RBI	BB	SO	SB	OBP	SLG
2019	18	Athletics (AZL)	R	.361	29	97	21	35	6	1	0	14	20	29	1	.466	.443
Minor League Totals				.361	29	97	21	35	6	1	0	14	20	29	1	.466	.443

21 ALFONSO RIVAS, 1B

BA GRADE
40 Risk: Medium

Born: Sept. 13, 1996. **B-T:** L-L. **HT:** 6-0. **WT:** 188. **Drafted:** Arizona, 2018 (4th round). **Signed by:** Scott Cousins

TRACK RECORD: Rivas has been one of faster movers from the 2018 draft. He ended the 2019 season at Triple-A Las Vegas and spent another five weeks playing in the Arizona Fall League.

SCOUTING REPORT: Rivas' has a balanced setup, a loose contact-oriented swing with limited extra movement in his swing. Rivas' approach has yielded limited dropoff when facing lefties. Profile questions for first base, though, will determine his ceiling. Although his swing has some natural lift, Rivas has generated mostly line-drive contact with gap power. Defensively, Rivas tighten up his hands and footwork to be average at first base. A former college hurler, Rivas has an above-average arm for each position.
THE FUTURE: Rivas had a solid fall in the AFL, which could propel him to bypass Double-A Midland and start 2020 in Las Vegas. He profiles as a bench player unless he increases his power or defensive versatility.

Year	Age	Club (League)	Class	AVG	G	AB	R	H	2B	3B	HR	RBI	BB	SO	SB	OBP	SLG
2018	21	Vermont (NYP)	SS	.285	61	214	33	61	16	1	1	28	36	44	7	.397	.383
2019	22	Stockton (CAL)	HiA	.283	114	431	60	122	24	3	8	55	66	113	2	.383	.408
	22	Las Vegas (PCL)	AAA	.406	8	32	2	13	2	1	1	5	2	7	0	.441	.625
Minor League Totals				.290	183	677	95	196	42	5	10	88	104	164	9	.390	.411

22 PARKER DUNSHEE, RHP

BA GRADE 40 **Risk: Medium**

Born: Feb. 12, 1995. **B-T:** R-R. **HT:** 6-0. **WT:** 215. **Drafted:** Wake Forest, 2017 (7th round). **Signed by:** Neil Avent.

TRACK RECORD: After returning for his senior year at Wake Forest, Dunshee made the most of his additional year of collegiate development and moved up seven rounds. That collegiate experience propelled him to the upper levels after just 100 innings. Dunshee thrived until a Triple-A promotion during the second half, when the hitter-friendly Pacific Coast League gave him his first taste of adversity.
SCOUTING REPORT: Dunshee generates good tilt while staying closed in his delivery and creating front-side deception. While his arm action is loose, it is funky in the back with a slight pause, effectively disrupting hitters timing and allowing his 88-92 mph fastball to play more effectively. Dunshee depends on changing speeds and looks with an 87-90 mph cutter-slider hybrid mix he uses to both sides of the plate to keep hitters off-balance. Dunshee mixes in a softer curveball to keep hitters honest early in counts but had issues effectively finishing off hitters in Triple-A. Dunshee's changeup is still a work in progress.
THE FUTURE: While he will be given every opportunity to start, Dunshee's performance markedly depreciates the second time through the lineup, which seemingly limits him to a bullpen role.

Year	Age	Club (League)	Class	W	L	ERA	G	GS	SV	IP	H	HR	BB	SO	K/9	WHIP	AVG
2017	22	Athletics (AZL)	R	0	0	13.50	1	0	0	2	5	1	0	3	13.5	2.50	.455
	22	Vermont (NYP)	SS	1	0	0.00	12	9	0	38	15	0	8	45	10.6	0.60	.119
2018	23	Stockton (CAL)	HiA	6	2	2.70	12	10	0	70	61	7	17	82	10.5	1.11	.238
	23	Midland (TL)	AA	7	4	2.01	12	12	0	81	59	5	14	81	9.0	0.90	.205
2019	24	Midland (TL)	AA	2	2	1.89	6	6	0	38	26	1	11	34	8.1	0.97	.196
	24	Las Vegas (PCL)	AAA	4	5	5.38	20	19	1	92	86	21	37	90	8.8	1.34	.245
Minor League Totals				20	13	2.94	63	56	1	321	252	35	87	335	9.4	1.06	.216

23 LUIS BARRERA, OF

BA GRADE 40 **Risk: Medium**

Born: Nov. 15, 1995. **B-T:** L-L. **HT:** 6-0. **WT:** 205. **Signed:** Dominican Republic, 2012. **Signed by:** Raymond Abreu.

TRACK RECORD: After playing two years in the Dominican Summer League, Barrera has steadily climbed through the A's system until repeating Double-A in 2019. Barrera's season was cut short in late June when he was shut down with a left shoulder strain.
SCOUTING REPORT: Possessing a lean build, Barrera has a solid start with a leg kick but tends to have balance and timing issues because he gets out on front side quickly and produces a high number of ground balls. Still just 24, Barrera has steadily increased his power numbers by learning how to drive the ball in favorable counts. Barrera's speed is more usable in center field but he's not a true basestealer. His easy play and strong arm in center field creates value, although his arm strength was sapped somewhat by his shoulder issues.
THE FUTURE: A start in Triple-A Las Vegas could be in the offing if the shoulder will allow. Defense will allow Barrera to play for a long time.

Year	Age	Club (League)	Class	AVG	G	AB	R	H	2B	3B	HR	RBI	BB	SO	SB	OBP	SLG
2017	21	Beloit (MWL)	LoA	.277	73	278	41	77	13	7	3	22	16	61	13	.320	.406
	21	Stockton (CAL)	HiA	.228	35	114	15	26	2	0	4	16	8	25	3	.276	.351
2018	22	Stockton (CAL)	HiA	.284	88	313	51	89	18	7	3	46	32	63	10	.354	.415
	22	Midland (TL)	AA	.328	36	131	24	43	8	4	0	18	9	18	13	.378	.450
2019	23	Midland (TL)	AA	.321	54	224	35	72	9	11	4	24	12	48	9	.357	.513
Minor League Totals				.280	438	1576	234	441	72	37	21	183	132	321	62	.337	.412

24 JONAH HEIM, C

BA GRADE 45 Risk: High

Born: June 27, 1995. **B-T:** B-R. **HT:** 6-4. **WT:** 220. **Drafted:** HS—Amherst, NY, 2013 (4th round). **Signed by:** Kirk Fredriksson (Orioles).

TRACK RECORD: Originally an Orioles fourth-round pick in 2013, Heim was traded to Tampa Bay for Steve Pearce in 2016, followed by another trade in 2017, this time to Oakland for Joey Wendle.

SCOUTING REPORT: A defense-first player, Heim has provided some surprising numbers since joining the Oakland organization. While still an aggressive hitter from both sides, Heim has done a better job of hitting strikes in favorable counts. Heim has a looser, more direct and rhythmic path from left side. With a more mature approach, Heim has also done a better job driving the ball to all fields. He has an above-average arm and advanced feel for his role behind the plate.

THE FUTURE: Heim will need to build on his offensive growth with a return ticket to Triple-A. His leadership and energy will be key areas of growth if he is to reach his ceiling as a big league backup.

Year	Age	Club (League)	Class	AVG	G	AB	R	H	2B	3B	HR	RBI	BB	SO	SB	OBP	SLG
2017	22	Bowling Green (MWL)	LoA	.268	77	291	45	78	17	1	9	53	27	57	0	.327	.426
	22	Charlotte, FL (FSL)	HiA	.218	16	55	3	12	3	0	0	8	3	17	1	.262	.273
2018	23	Stockton (CAL)	HiA	.292	80	312	41	91	21	1	7	49	29	60	3	.353	.433
	23	Midland (TL)	AA	.182	39	137	16	25	4	0	1	11	10	22	0	.238	.234
2019	24	Las Vegas (PCL)	AAA	.358	35	106	22	38	9	0	4	19	11	18	0	.412	.557
	24	Midland (TL)	AA	.282	50	181	20	51	12	0	5	34	24	27	0	.370	.431
Minor League Totals				.250	517	1802	214	451	106	4	36	236	164	326	10	.314	.373

25 SETH BROWN, 1B/OF

BA GRADE 40 Risk: Medium

Born: July 13, 1992. **B-T:** L-L. **HT:** 6-3. **WT:** 220. **Drafted:** Lewis-Clark State (Idaho), 2015 (19th round). **Signed by:** Jim Coffman.

TRACK RECORD: Brown hails from NAIA powerhouse Lewis-Clark State, which also produced Marvin Bernard and Brendan Ryan. Brown also fits the mold of player the Athletics appear to be able to accentuate through their player-development philosophy.

SCOUTING REPORT: After a nondescript 2016 at high Class A Stockton, Brown returned to California League at the age of 24, perhaps at a career crossroads. He responded adding more lift to his swing in 2019, which showed up in a 20-degree launch angle and 30 home runs. That was the start of a three-year run for Brown, which ended in the major leagues during the A's playoff chase. Brown has gotten better every year by narrowing the zone and maximizing impact in advantage counts. Brown has a classic platoon profile with most of his damage coming against righthanders.

THE FUTURE: Like Skye Bolt, Brown will have a chance to break with the big club due to the dearth of lefthanded options. Otherwise, a return ticket to Vegas seems likely.

Year	Age	Club (League)	Class	AVG	G	AB	R	H	2B	3B	HR	RBI	BB	SO	SB	OBP	SLG
2017	24	Stockton (CAL)	HiA	.270	135	518	80	140	18	7	30	109	56	146	7	.340	.506
2018	25	Midland (TL)	AA	.283	131	502	66	142	38	3	14	90	47	142	5	.342	.454
2019	26	Las Vegas (PCL)	AAA	.297	112	451	101	134	29	6	37	104	38	127	8	.352	.634
	26	Oakland (AL)	MAJ	.293	26	75	11	22	8	2	0	13	7	23	1	.361	.453
Major League Totals				.293	26	75	11	22	8	2	0	13	7	23	1	.361	.453
Minor League Totals				.274	573	2183	364	598	126	26	92	391	234	592	39	.344	.482

26 JEREMY EIERMAN, SS/2B

BA GRADE 40 Risk: High

Born: Sept. 10, 1996. **B-T:** R-R. **HT:** 6-0. **WT:** 205. **Drafted:** Missouri State, 2018 (second round supplemental). **Signed by:** Al Skorupa.

TRACK RECORD: Eierman become the third in his family to be drafted. Jeremy's Dad, John, and his brother Johnny both played pro ball. Jeremy had a productive offensive career at Missouri State but has had a tougher time translating to pro ball over two seasons.

SCOUTING REPORT: After a nondescript first season at short-season Vermont in 2018, Eierman struggled at high Class A Stockton. Possessing a balanced start, Eierman's contact issues stem from a late waggle in his swing that disrupts his timing. After playing shortstop most of 2018, Eierman teamed with Nick Allen in Stockton and moved to second base before Allen's season-ending injury. Possessing a strong, mature stocky build, Eierman seems better suited to second base based on range and quickness issues.

THE FUTURE: Eierman may repeat Stockton in 2020 to improve his contact rate.

Year	Age	Club (League)	Class	AVG	G	AB	R	H	2B	3B	HR	RBI	BB	SO	SB	OBP	SLG
2018	21	Vermont (NYP)	SS	.235	62	247	36	58	8	2	8	26	13	70	10	.283	.381
2019	22	Stockton (CAL)	HiA	.208	131	501	57	104	22	7	13	64	39	177	11	.270	.357
Minor League Totals				.217	193	748	93	162	30	9	21	90	52	247	21	.274	.365

27 HOGAN HARRIS, LHP

BA GRADE
40 Risk: High

Born: Dec. 26, 1996. **B-T:** R-L. **HT:** 6-3. **WT:** 230. **Drafted:** Louisiana-Lafayette, 2018 (3rd round). **Signed by:** Kelcey Mucker.

TRACK RECORD: Harris started his pro career later than most of his draft class after being slowed by an elbow strain. He finally made his pro debut in June at short-season Vermont before moving to high Class A Stockton, and logging 54 innings.

SCOUTING REPORT: Possessing a strong, durable build, Harris looks the part of a starter. In addition to health challenges, Harris' delivery has been in a work of progress and has undergone a series of transformations both in college and pro ball. The 2019 version was the cleanest yet, showing improved balance and tempo. Just a fair athlete, timing and connectivity issues have resulted in erratic command. Harris starts his mix with a 88-91 mph fastball that tops out at 95 with some movement. He backs it up with an effective changeup as well as a well-shaped curveball to combat righthanders. Scouts have noted that Harris' ability to manipulate the shape of his slider enhances his potential versatility at the upper levels although he needs to grow more comfortable attacking lefthanders with his current mix.

THE FUTURE: Just a fair athlete, Harris will need to refine both his command and sustain his health moving forward to profile as a low-ceiling starter. While he might have a chance to start in Midland, chances are he will return to Stockton.

Year	Age	Club (League)	Class	W	L	ERA	G	GS	SV	IP	H	HR	BB	SO	K/9	WHIP	AVG
2018	21	Did not play—Injured															
2019	22	Vermont (NYP)	SS	1	3	3.12	8	6	0	26	14	2	9	36	12.5	0.88	.154
	22	Stockton (CAL)	HiA	0	2	2.51	7	7	0	29	18	2	10	29	9.1	0.98	.184
Minor League Totals				1	5	2.80	15	13	0	54	32	4	19	65	10.7	0.93	.169

28 MIGUEL ROMERO, RHP

BA GRADE
40 Risk: High

Born: April 23, 1994. **B-T:** R-R. **HT:** 6-0. **WT:** 202. **Signed:** Cuba, 2017. **Signed by:** J.C. de la Cruz.

TRACK RECORD: Signed as an international free agent in Feb. 2017, Romero was already a veteran of the Cuban Industrial League. The experience helped him make a steady ascent through the minors. Romero has worked out of the bullpen for most of his career in Cuba and the United States.

SCOUTING REPORT: Romero's stuff has never been an issue. Featuring three major league-quality pitches, Romero has always looked the part of a big league reliever. The art of pitching, however, has always been a challenge. Romero's intangibles, deception, quality command and feel are lacking. He has been most effective against righthanders thanks to a fastball that sits in the mid-90s and tops out at 98. He backs it up with a hard-breaking, mid-80s slider. Lack of a change-of-pace pitch as well as erratic command and quality have limited his effectiveness. Romero's conviction and use of his knuckle-curveball to attack lefties has been slow, which has forced him into a platoon-type of role.

THE FUTURE: Romero, 25, enters 2020 with a chance to break with the A's as an extra arm due to his weapons versus righties, though his ceiling may be limited due to lack of true weapons against lefties.

Year	Age	Club (League)	Class	W	L	ERA	G	GS	SV	IP	H	HR	BB	SO	K/9	WHIP	AVG
2017	23	Athletics (DSL)	R	0	0	0.00	2	1	0	3	0	0	0	7	21.0	0.00	.000
	23	Athletics (AZL)	R	0	0	4.50	1	0	0	2	3	0	0	3	13.5	1.50	.333
	23	Beloit (MWL)	LoA	0	0	2.25	3	3	0	8	6	0	2	7	7.9	1.00	.200
	23	Stockton (CAL)	HiA	3	1	6.87	8	1	0	18	22	4	9	25	12.3	1.69	.301
2018	24	Stockton (CAL)	HiA	1	2	1.84	22	0	13	29	21	3	5	33	10.1	0.89	.202
	24	Midland (TL)	AA	1	1	6.00	22	0	1	30	35	4	12	33	9.9	1.57	.297
2019	25	Las Vegas (PCL)	AAA	4	1	3.96	45	1	3	73	65	11	36	81	10.0	1.39	.234
Minor League Totals				9	5	4.13	103	6	17	163	152	22	64	189	10.4	1.32	.245

29 GUS VARLAND, RHP

BA GRADE
40 Risk: High

Born: Nov. 6, 1996. **B-T:** L-R. **HT:** 6-1. **WT:** 205. **Drafted:** Concordia-St. Paul (Minn.), 2018 (14th round). **Signed by:** Derek Lee.

TRACK RECORD: Coming out of Division III Concordia College, Varland posted a 1.04 ERA and 11.7 strikeouts per nine innings over 60 innings. Despite pitching with elbow discomfort, Varland stuff translated well to pro ball, advancing quickly to Stockton in 2019 before being shut down with in July.

SCOUTING REPORT: Varland has made the most of deception and an advanced feel to pitch to maximize an average pitch mix. Raw boned with loose arm action, Varland has some extra length in the back, which enhances his deception and disrupts hitters' timing. The extra length has also increased the stress on his elbow and resulted in injury. When healthy, Varland works in the low 90s with a solid spin rate and an aggressive feel in the zone. He does an excellent job inducing soft contact up in the zone. Varland does well mixing his slider and generating weak contact, though the shape and sharpness of the pitch can vary due to his arm action. Varland needs further development with his changeup to increase his versatility.

THE FUTURE: Despite working as a starter, Varland projects as extra arm out of the bullpen.

Year	Age	Club (League)	Class	W	L	ERA	G	GS	SV	IP	H	HR	BB	SO	K/9	WHIP	AVG
2018	21	Athletics (AZL)	R	0	0	0.00	1	1	0	1	1	0	1	0	0.0	2.00	.333
	21	Vermont (NYP)	SS	0	1	1.02	7	5	0	18	14	0	4	22	11.2	1.02	.215
	21	Beloit (MWL)	LoA	0	0	0.93	5	5	0	19	8	1	3	28	13.0	0.57	.123
2019	22	Stockton (CAL)	HiA	2	1	2.39	5	4	0	26	23	3	8	27	9.2	1.18	.235
Minor League Totals				2	2	1.54	18	15	0	64	46	4	16	77	10.8	0.96	.199

30 KYLE McCANN, C

BA GRADE
40 Risk: High

Born: Dec. 2, 1997. **B-T:** L-R. **HT:** 6-2. **WT:** 217. **Drafted:** Georgia Tech, 2019 (4th round). **Signed by:** Jemel Spearman.

TRACK RECORD: After spending his first two seasons at first base at Georgia Tech, McCann moved behind the plate in 2019 after Joey Bart left for pro ball. McCann developed into a power lefthander for the Jackets while developing behind the plate.

SCOUTING REPORT: McCann has strength and a mature build and provides power over contact offensively. McCann has a quiet setup at the plate but has a small wrap through launch, which creates extra length and loop. He is a dead pull hitter with a lofted stroke geared for hard contact despite holes in the swing. Contact will be an issue moving forward based on his swing path, high swing-and-miss rate and challenges against lefthanders. Beyond pure strength, McCann's best asset is his advanced approach. He has a good feel for the strike zone and a selectively aggressive approach, though the walk rate in college did not translate during his pro debut. While he shows average arm strength, his receiving skills have been viewed as fringy based on lack of quickness and agility. First base remains a fallback option, though moving back would increase pressure on the bat.

THE FUTURE: With the questions surrounding McCann's defensive work, scouts have suggested a possible move back to first base. For now, he appears to be the level-to-level type who could start in Beloit in 2020.

Year	Age	Club (League)	Class	AVG	G	AB	R	H	2B	3B	HR	RBI	BB	SO	SB	OBP	SLG
2019	21	Vermont (NYP)	SS	.192	55	198	23	38	7	1	7	25	25	81	0	.289	.343
Minor League Totals				.211	60	218	33	46	9	3	9	32	30	87	0	.312	.404

Philadelphia Phillies

BY J.J. COOPER

A decade that started with the Phillies standing alone atop the National League East ended with them fighting with the Mets to try to be the third best team in one of baseball's most competitive divisions.

Philadelphia enters the 2020s looking up at both the Nationals and the Braves. The Nationals, long the kings of the division, won the World Series in 2019. The Braves, who began their rebuild around the same time as the Phillies, have won back-to-back NL East titles.

Philadelphia will enter 2020 looking for its first winning record since 2011. It's been a long climb to try to get back to contending.

The Phillies' 2019 season was ruined in part by injuries that devastated the bullpen. But the big league club also was left wanting by the organization's inability to draft and develop players in the way the Nationals and Braves have. The Braves have developed Ronald Acuña Jr. and Ozzie Albies while the Nationals have brought up Juan Soto and Victor Robles in recent years.

Philadelphia has wisely shifted into spend-now mode, because the club's rebuild has not produced cornerstone players to build around. Instead, the Phillies have to get creative with trades and free agency.

When Philadelphia traded Cole Hamels to the Rangers in 2015, it hoped the prospects it received in return would be part of the rebuild. As 2020 begins, the best return from that trade was Jorge Alfaro, who was part of a package (along with Phillies No. 1 prospect Sixto Sanchez) to acquire catcher J.T. Realmuto.

This offseason the Phillies have signed righthander Zack Wheeler and shortstop Didi Gregorius, adding significantly more free agent firepower to a team that signed Bryce Harper and Andrew McCutchen before the 2019 season.

They've done that because the club's farm system has not been as productive as some of their division rivals.

Righthander Aaron Nola, the club's first-round pick in 2014, is the team's undisputed ace. But three straight picks in the top 10 after Nola produced modest returns—at best. Outfielder Cornelius Randolph, the team's 2015 first-round pick, was left unprotected and unpicked in the Rule 5 draft. Mickey Moniak, the No. 1 pick in 2016, is projected by other teams as a second-division regular or backup outfielder. Adam Haseley, a 2017 first-round pick, made his major league debut in 2019, but like Randolph and Moniak, he's not projected to be an impact major leaguer.

There is some hope that Scott Kingery or Rhys Hoskins can give the club a homegrown star and Spencer Howard could join Nola in the Phillies' rotation before long. But if Philadelphia is going to catch the Nationals and Braves, it will require continued free agent spending, with the hope that the farm system can provide the depth around the stars acquired from elsewhere.

The Phillies' last two first-round picks, Alec Bohm and Bryson Stott, give them a pair of potentially fast-moving position players. There are prospects who could help the bullpen in 2020 and the system has a large number of catchers who project as potential major leaguers, though none of them are going to push Realmuto aside if the Phillies can extend his contract.

MADDIE MEYER/GETTY IMAGES

Scott Kingery played six positions in 2019 but focused his time at center field and third base.

PROJECTED 2023 LINEUP

Position	Player	Age
Catcher	J.T. Realmuto	32
First Base	Rhys Hoskins	30
Second Base	Bryson Stott (3)	25
Third Base	Alec Bohm (2)	26
Shortstop	Didi Gregorius	33
Left Field	Adam Haseley	27
Center Field	Scott Kingery	29
Right Field	Bryce Harper	30
No. 1 Starter	Aaron Nola	30
No. 2 Starter	Zack Wheeler	33
No. 3 Starter	Spencer Howard (1)	26
No. 4 Starter	Vince Velasquez	31
No. 5 Starter	Adonis Medina (5)	26
Closer	Francisco Morales (4)	23

DEPTH CHART

PHILADELPHIA PHILLIES

TOP 2002 ROOKIE: Spencer Howard, RHP. Howard has the potential to eventually join Zack Wheeler and Aaron Nola at the top of Philly's rotation.

BREAKOUT PROSPECT: Johan Rojas, OF. When the Phillies talk trade, teams regularly ask for Rojas because of his loud tools and potential.

SLEEPER: Juan Aparcio, C. On a crowded Phillies depth chart at catcher, Aparcio could leapfrog to near the top of the list in 2020.

SOURCE OF TOP 30 TALENT			
Homegrown	**28**	**Acquired**	**2**
College	9	Trades	2
Junior college	2	Rule 5 draft	0
High school	5	Independent leagues	0
Nondrafted free agents	0	Free agents/waivers	0
International	12		

LF
Mickey Moniak (9)
Cornelius Randolph
Josh Stephens

CF
Johan Rojas (11)
Simon Muzziotti (12)
Marcus Lee Sang
Hunter Markwardt

RF
Alec Bohm (2)
Matt Vierling

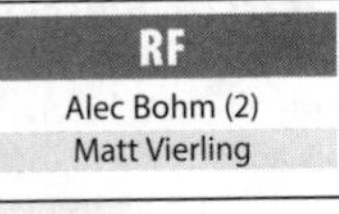

3B
Kendall Simmons (21)

SS
Bryson Stott (3)
Luis Garcia (7)
Nick Maton (10)
Jamari Baylor (19)
Jonathan Guzman (29)
Arquimedes Gamboa
Guarner Dipre

2B
Wilfredo Flores
Daniel Brito
Edgar Made

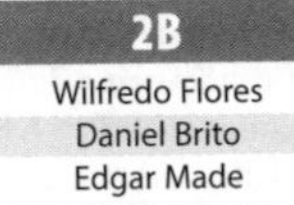

1B
Jhailyn Ortiz (27)
Darick Hall

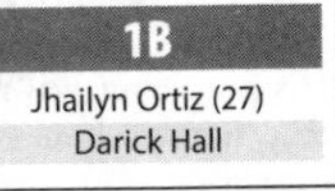

C
Rafael Marchan (6)
Andrick Nava (14)
Deivi Grullon (16)
Logan O'Hoppe (22)
Abrahan Gutierrez (26)
Juan Aparcio
Rodolfo Duran
Herbert Iser

LHP

LHSP	LHRP
Erik Miller (13)	JoJo Romero (15)
Ethan Lindow (23)	Damon Jones (18)
Cole Irvin (26)	Maurico Llovera (25)
Connor Seabold (30)	Zach Warren
David Parkinson	Kyle Dohy
Kyle Young	

RHP

RHSP	RHRP
Spencer Howard (1)	Adonis Medina (5)
Francisco Morales (4)	Cristopher Sanchez (17)
Enyel de los Santos (8)	Addison Russ (20)
Victor Santos	Connor Brogdon (24)
Colton Eastman	Andrew Schultz
Kevin Gowdy	Tyler McKay
Josh Gessner	Dominic Pipkin
Jean Hernandez	Brett Schulze
Connor Seabold	Ramon Rosso
Gunner Mayer	

DRAFT ANALYSIS

2019

BEST PURE HITTER: SS Bryson Stott (1) hit .356/.486/.599 for Nevada-Las Vegas after posting similar numbers as a sophomore. He followed that up by hitting .295/.391/.494 in his pro debut. Stott knows how to attack pitchers early in counts, but he also has a solid two-strike approach.

BEST POWER: C Herbert Iser (23) has plus-plus raw power. Iser never really hit in college, but the Phillies found that he has a vision issue that could be corrected with contact lenses which may help him at the plate. OF Marcus Lee Sang (11) has solid power potential as well, as does Stott.

FASTEST RUNNER: OF Hunter Markwardt (13) is a top-of-the-scale runner. His pro debut ended early because he crashed into the wall and broke his nose trying to catch a fly ball, which ultimately turned into an inside-the-park home run.

BEST DEFENSIVE PLAYER: The Phillies believe that Stott will be able to stay at shortstop. He's sure-handed and reliable with solid athleticism.

BEST ATHLETE: SS Jamari Baylor (2) has strength, athleticism, plus speed and an above-average arm. His pro debut was ruined by a hamstring injury that limited him to four games. RHP Dylan Castaneda (30) was an excellent wide receiver/defensive back for his high school football team.

BEST FASTBALL: RHP Andrew Schultz (6) works in short stints with an unconventional arm action, but he runs his fastball into the upper 90s and has touched 101 mph.

BEST SECONDARY PITCH: LHP Erik Miller (4) has a plus slider that he has an advanced feel for when considering his age. Schultz's slider is just as good when everything comes together, but the consistency of the pitch isn't there yet.

TOP DRAFT PICKS OF THE DECADE

Year	Player, Pos	2019 Org
2010	Jesse Biddle, LHP	Rangers
2011	Larry Greene, OF (1st round supp)	Did not play
2012	Shane Watson, RHP (1st round supp)	Did not play
2013	J.P. Crawford, SS	Mariners
2014	Aaron Nola, RHP	Phillies
2015	Cornelius Randolph, SS	Phillies
2016	Mickey Moniak, OF	Phillies
2017	Adam Haseley, OF	Phillies
2018	Alec Bohm, 3B	Phillies
2019	Bryson Stott, SS	Phillies

BEST PRO DEBUT: Stott hit in the New York-Penn League. Miller posted a 1.50 ERA with 52 strikeouts and 11 walks in 32 innings, reaching the South Atlantic League.

MOST INTRIGUING BACKGROUND: C Micah Yonamine (29) is the nephew of Wally Yonamine. Yonamine played in the NFL right after World War II before heading to Japan to play baseball. He became the first American-born player inducted into the Japanese Baseball Hall of Fame.

CLOSEST TO THE MAJORS: Stott and Miller are both polished college players who could move relatively quickly.

BEST LATE ROUND PICK: Castaneda has a 91-94 mph fastball and an intriguing breaking ball to go with solid athleticism. Sang has a chance to be a prototypical corner outfielder.

THE ONE WHO GOT AWAY: The Phillies signed every player they drafted in the top 30 rounds. LHP Michael Prosecky (35) is a promising pitcher with an 89-93 mph fastball, but his Louisville commitment was quite strong.

—BEN BADLER

2018

3B Alec Bohm (1) had an excellent first full season, reaching Double-A and establishing himself as the best hitter in the system. SS Kendall Simmons (6) and C Logan O'Hoppe (23) are providing solid value.

GRADE: B

2017

RHP Spencer Howard (2) was banged up in 2019 but returned from injury to pitch well in the second half and is the system's top prospect. OF Adam Haseley (1) is penciled in as the Phillies' starting center fielder.

GRADE: A

2016

It's been a tough go for the Phillies' top picks in this draft, starting with OF Mickey Moniak (1), who has disappointed as the first overall pick. LHP Cole Irvin (5) has given the class a big leaguer, however.

GRADE: D

1 SPENCER HOWARD, RHP

Born: July 28, 1996. **B-T:** R-R. **HT:** 6-2. **WT:** 205.
Drafted: Cal Poly, 2017 (2nd round).
Signed by: Shane Bowers.

BACKGROUND: When Howard arrived at Cal Poly he was an 83-85 mph walk-on who wasn't ready to be a college pitcher. He seemed destined for the club team, but he worked hard in the weight room during his redshirt freshman season and increased his velocity, which led to a solid summer as a reliever in the West Coast Collegiate League. He had an excellent redshirt freshman season as a reliever for Cal Poly, then moved into the rotation the next season. Howard's stuff has steadily gotten better as a pro. He battled through a dead arm period early in 2018 but by September he was touching 100 mph in a no-hitter in the playoffs with low Class A Lakewood. Howard missed two months in 2019 with shoulder soreness, but he showed no ill effects after he returned. Making up for lost innings, he was one of the most effective pitchers in the Arizona Fall League.

SCOUTING REPORT: Howard has a starter's build and the potential for three above-average or better offspeed pitches, although the consistency of his breaking balls varies dramatically. His 93-99 mph fastball is a reliable, plus-plus weapon. He's touched triple-digits and, unlike many fireballers, can stay on the edges of the strike zone. Howard's mid-80s changeup was below-average when he signed, started flashing average last year and by the end of 2019 it was regularly flashing plus thanks to solid deception and some late tumble. He can break off a swing-and-miss curveball as well, although it's not all that reliable. Sometimes his curve has a hump out of his hand, giving it the telltale signature that advanced hitters can recognize and lay off. He'll also throw his share of 58-footers. But when he syncs everything up, it's a 12-to-6 dive bomber that tunnels with his elevated fastball. His 85-88 mph plus slider is a little more consistent with late tilt but, like the curveball, there are nights when he doesn't have the feel for it. Howard's delivery is simple and repeatable and should lend him above-average control.

THE FUTURE: Howard's stint on the IL with shoulder stiffness was the only blemish in an outstanding season. He has taken strides in his two and a half pro seasons and now profiles as a potential No. 2 starter. He could be ready to pitch in Philadelphia by the second half of the 2020 season.

MIKE JANES/FOUR SEAM

BA GRADE
60 **Risk: High**

SCOUTING GRADES
Fastball: 70. **Slider:** 55. **CHG:** 55. **Curveball:** 55. **Control:** 55.

Projected future grades on 20-80 scouting scale.

TOP PROSPECTS OF THE DECADE

Year	Player, Pos	2019 Org
2010	Domonic Brown, OF	Mexican League
2011	Domonic Brown, OF	Mexican League
2012	Trevor May, RHP	Twins
2013	Jesse Biddle, LHP	Rangers
2014	Maikel Franco, 3B	Phillies
2015	J.P. Crawford, SS	Mariners
2016	J.P. Crawford, SS	Mariners
2017	J.P. Crawford, SS	Mariners
2018	J.P. Crawford, SS	Mariners
2019	Sixto Sanchez, RHP	Marlins

BEST TOOLS

Best Hitter	Alec Bohm
Best Power Hitter	Jhailyn Ortiz
Best Strike Zone Discipline	Alec Bohm
Fastest Baserunner	Corbin Williams
Best Athlete	Corbin Williams
Best Fastball	Spencer Howard
Best Slider	Francisco Morales
Best Curveball	Zach Warren
Best Changeup	Kyle Dohy
Best Control	Ethan Lindow
Best Defensive Catcher	Rafael Marchan
Best Defensive Infielder	Arquimedes Gamboa
Best Infield Arm	Jonathan Guzman
Best Defensive Outfielder	Simon Muzziotti
Best Outfield Arm	Jhailyn Ortiz

Year	Age	Club (League)	Class	W	L	ERA	G	GS	SV	IP	H	HR	BB	SO	K/9	WHIP	AVG
2017	20	Williamsport (NYP)	SS	1	1	4.45	9	9	0	28	22	0	18	40	12.7	1.41	.214
2018	21	Lakewood (SAL)	LoA	9	8	3.78	23	23	0	112	101	6	40	147	11.8	1.26	.240
2019	22	Phillies West (GCL)	R	0	0	0.00	1	1	0	3	1	0	1	5	15.0	0.67	.100
	22	Phillies East (GCL)	R	0	0	11.57	1	1	0	2	3	1	1	3	11.6	1.71	.300
	22	Clearwater (FSL)	HiA	2	1	1.29	7	7	0	35	19	1	5	48	12.3	0.69	.162
	22	Reading (EL)	AA	1	0	2.35	6	6	0	31	20	2	9	38	11.2	0.95	.180
Minor League Totals				13	10	3.28	47	47	0	211	166	10	74	281	12.0	1.14	.215

2 ALEC BOHM, 3B

Born: Aug. 3, 1996. **B-T:** R-R. **HT:** 6-5. **WT:** 225. **Drafted:** Wichita State (1st round), 2018. **Signed by:** Justin Munson.

BA GRADE
55 Risk: Medium

BACKGROUND: After hitting over .500 in his final two years of high school and over .300 in each of his three seasons at Wichita State, Bohm found pro ball much tougher after the Phillies drafted him third overall in 2018. He battled timing issues in his pro debut and hit a light .252. The Phillies sent him to low Class A Lakewood to start 2019, but he quickly put his problems behind him and hit his way to Double-A by June 21.

SCOUTING REPORT: The long-limbed Bohm has a straightforward swing that generates plenty of long fly balls. He has good plate coverage and uses the entire field, with the power to hit the ball out to center and right field. He has solid strike zone awareness and shows solid barrel control despite a long swing and long levers. He projects be an above-average hitter with above-average power. Kris Bryant and Troy Glaus are the only players 6-foot-5 or taller to play more than 200 games at third base in MLB history. Bohm is unlikely to become the third. His hands are adequate at best and his first-step reactions are a tick slow. His body type doesn't help him either. He's extremely long-legged and high-waisted. He most likely will end up as an average defender at first, although he could equal or top Rhys Hoskins' efforts in left field. His plus arm will play at any of those positions. He is expected to end up as a below-average runner.

THE FUTURE: After a solid six weeks in the Arizona Fall League, Bohm should be ready for Triple-A. His bat should clear his path to Philadelphia, but his defensive questions could slow his arrival.

SCOUTING GRADES: **Hitting:** 55 **Power:** 55 **Running:** 40 **Fielding:** 45 **Arm:** 50

Year	Age	Club (League)	Class	AVG	G	AB	R	H	2B	3B	HR	RBI	BB	SO	SB	OBP	SLG
2018	21	Phillies East (GCL)	R	.222	4	9	0	2	0	0	0	2	0	4	0	.200	.222
	21	Phillies West (GCL)	R	.391	7	23	8	9	1	1	0	3	2	0	2	.481	.522
	21	Williamsport (NYP)	SS	.224	29	107	9	24	5	1	0	12	10	19	1	.314	.290
2019	22	Lakewood (SAL)	LoA	.367	22	79	13	29	9	0	3	11	12	14	3	.441	.595
	22	Clearwater (FSL)	HiA	.329	40	158	25	52	10	3	4	27	17	21	1	.395	.506
	22	Reading (EL)	AA	.269	63	238	38	64	11	1	14	42	28	38	2	.344	.500
Minor League Totals				.293	165	614	93	180	36	6	21	97	69	96	9	.368	.474

3 BRYSON STOTT, SS

Born: Oct. 6, 1997. **B-T:** L-R. **HT:** 6-3. **WT:** 200. **Drafted:** Nevada-Las Vegas (1st round), 2019. **Signed by:** Mike Garcia.

BA GRADE
55 Risk: High

BACKGROUND: Stott led all Division I hitters with 30 doubles as a college sophomore, then was the shortstop for USA Baseball's Collegiate National Team. He followed up by showing improved power as a junior and was drafted 14th overall by the Phillies. He signed for $3.9 million and carried his power surge over to his pro debut.

SCOUTING REPORT: Stott has few clear weaknesses, but also few standout tools. He quickly showed that he can string together tough at-bats. He knows the strike zone and punishes mistakes. He can be beat by high heat but rarely chases pitches out of the zone. Stott's plate coverage needs to improve as he'll sometimes get pull-happy, even though he has the strength to drive the ball to the opposite field. He has average bat speed. Defensively, Stott has continued to improve. He has a shortstop's easy actions and above-average range to go with an above-average arm. Stott runs a tick above-average right now, but he'll need to watch his conditioning. Some scouts believe he could end up filling out to the point where he has to slide to third or second.

THE FUTURE: Stott should quickly leapfrog Luis Garcia as the Phillies' shortstop of the future. The two could end up sharing time early in 2020 at low Class A Lakewood, but Stott's polish should get him to high Class A Clearwater quickly, whether it's Opening Day or soon thereafter.

SCOUTING GRADES: **Hitting:** 50 **Power:** 50 **Running:** 55 **Fielding:** 55 **Arm:** 55

Year	Age	Club (League)	Class	AVG	G	AB	R	H	2B	3B	HR	RBI	BB	SO	SB	OBP	SLG
2019	21	Phillies East (GCL)	R	.667	4	9	3	6	1	1	1	3	2	0	0	.727	1.333
	21	Williamsport (NYP)	SS	.274	44	157	27	43	8	2	5	24	22	39	5	.370	.446
Minor League Totals				.295	48	166	30	49	9	3	6	27	24	39	5	.391	.494

4 FRANCISCO MORALES, RHP

MICHAEL DILL

BA GRADE
55 **Risk: Very High**

Born: Oct. 27, 1999. **B-T:** R-R. **HT:** 6-4. **WT:** 225. **Signed:** Venezuela, 2016. **Signed by:** Jesus Mendez.

BACKGROUND: The Phillies had the largest bonus allotment during the 2016-17 international signing period. They spent heavily in Venezuela and made Morales their top target. He had the best fastball in that year's international signing class, and it's only gotten better. He handled a piggy-back role well with low Class A Lakewood and got stronger as the season wore on.

SCOUTING REPORT: Morales has a simple delivery, which utilizes a modest hip turn to load to his balance point on the rubber before exploding to the plate. There's some effort to it and he has a moderate head whack. Refining the consistency of his release point was a point of emphasis in 2019. When he repeated his delivery and stayed on top of his release point he dominated hitters with his 93-97 mph fastball and plus 85-89 mph slider. When he's not consistent with his release point, his command suffers, his slider gets slurvier and his fastball loses some of its life. Morales' changeup remains more of an idea than a usable pitch—it's hard (86-88 mph) without much action or deception. Morales throws enough strikes but his command needs to improve.

THE FUTURE: Morales has some of the best pure stuff in the Phillies' organization, but he has a long way to go with his changeup and his consistency if he's going to remain a starter. Most likely he ends up as a two-pitch reliever, but there's no reason to not give him plenty of time to try to stay a starter. He's ready for high Class A Clearwater.

SCOUTING GRADES: **Fastball:** 70 **Slider:** 70 **Changeup:** 30 **Control:** 50

Year	Age	Club (League)	Class	W	L	ERA	G	GS	SV	IP	H	HR	BB	SO	K/9	WHIP	AVG
2017	17	Phillies (GCL)	R	3	2	3.05	10	9	0	41	34	1	20	44	9.6	1.31	.225
2018	18	Williamsport (NYP)	SS	4	5	5.27	13	13	0	56	54	6	33	68	10.9	1.54	.244
2019	19	Lakewood (SAL)	LoA	1	8	3.82	27	15	1	97	82	8	46	129	12.0	1.32	.226
Minor League Totals				8	15	4.08	50	37	1	194	170	15	99	241	11.2	1.38	.231

5 ADONIS MEDINA, RHP

BA GRADE
50 **Risk: High**

Born: Dec. 18, 1996. **B-T:** R-R. **HT:** 6-1. **WT:** 187. **Signed:** Dominican Republic, 2014. **Signed by:** Carlos Salas.

BACKGROUND: When Medina was 18 and carving up South Atlantic League hitters, it was easy to dream of just what the athletic, live-armed righthander would become. Since then Medina has shown flashes and made a Futures Game appearance but it's hard to say Medina is a much better pitcher heading into 2020 than he was in 2017. Medina struggled mightily in the second half at Double-A Reading, where he posted a 6.75 ERA after the all-star break.

SCOUTING REPORT: Medina still has the ingredients to end up as a solid No. 3 or No. 4 starter. He sits 91-96 mph with an above-average fastball that has average life. His slider will sporadically flash the two-plane tilt that can make it a true weapon, but too often he gets on the side of it and it becomes a slurvier pitch. His fringe-average changeup, which has long flashed plus potential, has not developed into a true weapon. Instead, more advanced hitters have found he struggles to throw it for strikes, so they can quickly recognize and eliminate the pitch from consideration. That helps explain why lefthanders hit .302/.385/.473 against him. The pieces are all still there for Medina to potentially turn into a three-pitch starter, but scouts want to see him take a step forward.

THE FUTURE: Medina was added to the 40-man roster before the 2019 season, so he has two options remaining. He still has time to add polish, but the clock is ticking–if he is going to end up as a reliever, teams generally want to take advantage of a player having options.

SCOUTING GRADES: **Fastball:** 55 **Slider:** 55 **Changeup:** 45 **Control:** 50

Year	Age	Club (League)	Class	W	L	ERA	G	GS	SV	IP	H	HR	BB	SO	K/9	WHIP	AVG
2017	20	Lakewood (SAL)	LoA	4	9	3.01	22	22	0	120	103	7	39	133	10.0	1.19	.227
2018	21	Clearwater (FSL)	HiA	10	4	4.12	22	21	0	111	103	11	36	123	9.9	1.25	.245
2019	22	Reading (EL)	AA	7	7	4.94	22	21	0	106	103	11	41	82	7.0	1.36	.254
Minor League Totals				31	28	3.60	100	87	1	473	420	35	156	429	8.2	1.22	.236

6 RAFAEL MARCHAN, C

MILES KENNEDY

BA GRADE
50 **Risk: High**

Born: Feb. 25, 1999. **B-T:** B-R. **HT:** 5-9. **WT:** 196. **Signed:** Venezuela, 2015. **Signed by:** Jesus Mendez.

BACKGROUND: As a kid, Marchan had dreams of emulating Omar Vizquel as defensive wizard at shortstop. But Marchan is both shorter and stockier than Vizquel, so at a 15U tournament he tried catching and quickly found it suited him. Marchan has impressed defensively wherever he has played. What he hasn't done is hit for any sort of power—his next home run will be his first.

SCOUTING REPORT: Marchan's an excellent defensive catcher with few weaknesses behind the plate. He is an agile backstop with soft, quiet hands that pluck strikes from the bottom and sides of the strike zone. He also embraces the challenge of working with pitchers on calling a good game, and he also has an accurate, plus arm that can produce 1.9-second pop times on throws to second base. Marchan's glove is going to need to be excellent because he doesn't provide much value as a hitter. The switch-hitter has a flat swing geared to produce line drives, and he has a solid understanding of what he wants to do, but he has below-average bat speed and well below-average power. He runs well for a catcher.

THE FUTURE: Marchan's excellent defense should give him a solid path to a big league job. Most players with his profile end up as backups, but Marchan's glove will give him plenty of at-bats over the next decade to develop offensively. Every now and then, someone with Marchan's profile ends up exceeding offensive expectations and becomes a regular.

SCOUTING GRADES: **Hitting:** 40 **Power:** 30 **Running:** 40 **Fielding:** 70 **Arm:** 60

Year	Age	Club (League)	Class	AVG	G	AB	R	H	2B	3B	HR	RBI	BB	SO	SB	OBP	SLG
2017	18	Phillies (GCL)	R	.238	30	84	10	20	5	0	0	10	4	8	1	.290	.298
2018	19	Williamsport (NYP)	SS	.301	51	196	28	59	8	2	0	12	11	18	9	.343	.362
2019	20	Lakewood (SAL)	LoA	.271	63	236	21	64	16	0	0	20	24	31	1	.347	.339
	20	Clearwater (FSL)	HiA	.231	22	78	6	18	4	0	0	3	6	8	1	.291	.282
Minor League Totals				.285	210	765	88	218	40	3	0	79	61	79	18	.342	.345

7 LUIS GARCIA, SS

BA GRADE
50 **Risk: High**

Born: Oct. 1, 2000. **B-T:** B-R. **HT:** 5-11. **WT:** 170. **Signed:** Dominican Republic, 2017. **Signed by:** Carlos Salas.

BACKGROUND: Garcia ranked as the 12th best prospect in the loaded 2017 international amateur class that also included Wander Franco, Ronny Mauricio, Julio Rodriguez and George Valera. Garcia had one of the loudest debuts, as he won the Gulf Coast League batting title in 2018. Garcia's second pro season was much rougher. His .186 batting average was 10th worst among all minor league hitters with 400 or more plate appearances and his .255 slugging percentage was fifth worst.

SCOUTING REPORT: Garcia's lack of physicality was apparent all season—he didn't get steadily better as he caught up to the league. Instead, he hit below .200 in all but one month of the season. He puts together solid at-bats, has excellent hand-eye coordination and has solid pitch recognition for his age. Because of a lack of snap in his wrists, Garcia simply doesn't hit the ball hard enough to make pitchers respect him. When pitchers challenge him, he makes a lot of soft contact. Outfielders played him shallow because they didn't need to worry about him hitting it over their heads. There is still hope for the future, though. Garcia is an above-average glove at shortstop with an above-average arm. While he's unlikely to ever have better than 30-grade power, improved strength will equate to harder line drives and make an average hit tool seem achievable. He's an average runner who might get a little faster if he gets stronger.

THE FUTURE: Garcia has the upside of an everyday shortstop, but many things have to come together to get him there. If he doesn't significantly develop, he's one of many good-glove, light-hitting shortstops that populate the minors.

SCOUTING GRADES: **Hitting:** 45 **Power:** 30 **Running:** 50 **Fielding:** 60 **Arm:** 55

Year	Age	Club (League)	Class	AVG	G	AB	R	H	2B	3B	HR	RBI	BB	SO	SB	OBP	SLG
2018	17	Phillies West (GCL)	R	.369	43	168	33	62	11	3	1	32	15	21	12	.433	.488
2019	18	Lakewood (SAL)	LoA	.186	127	467	36	87	14	3	4	36	44	132	9	.261	.255
Minor League Totals				.235	170	635	69	149	25	6	5	68	59	153	21	.306	.317

8 ENYEL DE LOS SANTOS, RHP

MIKE CARLSON

BA GRADE
45 Risk: Medium

Born: Dec. 25, 1995. **B-T:** R-R. **HT:** 6-3. **WT:** 170. **Signed:** Dominican Republic, 2014. **Signed by:** Eddy Toledo/Domingo Toribio (Mariners).

BACKGROUND: By the time he made his major league debut in July 2018, de los Santos was already pitching for his third different organization. A Mariners signee, he was swapped to San Diego in a trade that brought Joaquin Benoit to Seattle. San Diego then sent him to the Phillies for Freddy Galvis. De los Santos was second in the International League in ERA in 2018, but he struggled to match that success in Lehigh Valley in 2019.

SCOUTING REPORT: To be able to establish roots in Philadelphia, de los Santos is going to need to show he can locate his 92-98 mph above-average fastball to both sides of the plate. His control is fine, but his command is below-average. His fastball has exceptional armside run, but that run means when he tries to get to the outer corner against righthanded hitters the ball often leaks back over the middle of the plate. It's more effective when it runs in on righthanders. He was better in 2018 because his fringe-average changeup was more consistent—at its best it dives away from lefties. His average, 80-83 mph slider has modest depth and 12-to-6 curveball shape. Adding tilt would give hitters an east-west offspeed pitch to worry about and would greatly aid his overall pitchability.

THE FUTURE: De los Santos didn't appear in an MLB game after a rough start on June 23. He was not part of Philadelphia's September callups until the final two days of the season, when he was added as an emergency arm. His likely role is as a swingman, but improved command could help him get to a back-end starter.

SCOUTING GRADES: **Fastball:** 55 **Slider:** 50 **Changeup:** 45 **Control:** 50

Year	Age	Club (League)	Class	W	L	ERA	G	GS	SV	IP	H	HR	BB	SO	K/9	WHIP	AVG
2017	21	San Antonio (TL)	AA	10	6	3.78	26	24	0	150	131	12	48	138	8.3	1.19	.237
2018	22	Lehigh Valley (IL)	AAA	10	5	2.63	22	22	0	127	104	12	43	110	7.8	1.16	.226
	22	Philadelphia (NL)	MAJ	1	0	4.74	7	2	0	19	19	2	8	15	7.1	1.42	.271
2019	23	Philadelphia (NL)	MAJ	0	1	7.36	5	1	0	11	13	4	5	9	7.4	1.64	.317
	23	Lehigh Valley (IL)	AAA	5	7	4.40	19	19	0	94	81	16	35	83	7.9	1.23	.232
Major League Totals				1	1	5.70	12	3	0	30	32	6	13	24	7.2	1.50	.288
Minor League Totals				39	23	3.57	106	100	0	554	485	56	182	499	8.1	1.20	.237

9 MICKEY MONIAK, OF

BA GRADE
45 Risk: High

Born: May 13, 1998. **B-T:** L-R. **HT:** 6-2. **WT:** 188. **Drafted:** HS—Carlsbad, Calif., 2016 (1st round). **Signed:** Mike Garcia.

BACKGROUND: Moniak was the BA High School Player of the Year in 2016. In a class with no clear top prospect, the Phillies chose Moniak first overall. He has yet to live up to the lofty expectations that come with being the top pick, but 2019 was his best pro season. He led the Eastern League with 13 triples.

SCOUTING REPORT: Scouts regularly note that if you forget that Moniak went first overall, he's perfectly fine as a potential fourth outfielder. It's just that the expectations at No. 1 overall go far beyond being a useful role player. Moniak provides a reasonably well-rounded tool set, although there are no plus tools. He has gotten strong enough to project fringe-average power. He has some ability to put barrel on ball with a pull-heavy approach that suits his swing and his power, but he doesn't draw walks and it's hard to see him posting even league-average on-base percentages. Opinions on his defense differ widely, with some scouts saying he has no hope to play center and others saying he's perfectly fine there. He's an average runner.

THE FUTURE: Moniak should be a major leaguer, but he still has a long way to go to be a regular. He most likely ends up as a backup outfielder who can play all three spots. His improved power gives him a chance to be more than that, but he'll have to start being more selective as well.

SCOUTING GRADES: **Hitting:** 45 **Power:** 45 **Running:** 50 **Fielding:** 50 **Arm:** 50

Year	Age	Club (League)	Class	AVG	G	AB	R	H	2B	3B	HR	RBI	BB	SO	SB	OBP	SLG
2017	19	Lakewood (SAL)	LoA	.236	123	466	53	110	22	6	5	44	28	109	11	.284	.341
2018	20	Clearwater (FSL)	HiA	.270	114	433	50	117	28	3	5	55	22	100	6	.304	.383
2019	21	Reading (EL)	AA	.252	119	465	63	117	28	13	11	67	33	111	15	.303	.439
Minor League Totals				.256	402	1540	193	394	89	26	22	194	94	355	42	.302	.390

10 NICK MATON, SS

BA GRADE
45 Risk: High

Born: Feb. 18, 1997. **B-T:** L-R. **HT:** 6-2. **WT:** 183. **Drafted:** Lincoln Land (Ill) JC, 2017 (7th round). **Signed by:** Justin Morgenstern.

BACKGROUND: Maton's older brother Phil starred at Louisiana Tech and made it to the Padres' bullpen just two years after he was drafted. Younger brother Jacob is a pitcher at Coastal Carolina. Nick transferred to Lincoln Land (Ill.) JC after a solid freshman season at Eastern Illinois.

SCOUTING REPORT: Maton needs to continue to get stronger, but he's developed some wiry power, giving him a chance to hit 10-12 home runs down the road. Maton's bat speed is average, but he's consistently shown that he can catch up to premium velocity —in fact he seems to prefer when a pitcher tries to blow him away. Maton has gone from being a reliable defender with limited range to a reliable defender with average range at second or shortstop who can sometimes make a highlight-level play. His above-average arm plays up because of a quick release and a good internal clock.

THE FUTURE: Maton's excellent makeup, heady play and steady improvement give him a shot to be at least a solid and versatile backup, and you can find evaluators who believe he will top those expectations. He'll return to Double-A Reading.

SCOUTING GRADES: Hitting: 50 | Power: 40 | Running: 50 | Fielding: 55 | Arm: 55

Year	Age	Club (League)	Class	AVG	G	AB	R	H	2B	3B	HR	RBI	BB	SO	SB	OBP	SLG
2017	20	Williamsport (NYP)	SS	.252	58	210	34	53	9	1	2	13	30	47	10	.350	.333
2018	21	Lakewood (SAL)	LoA	.256	114	406	52	104	26	5	8	51	43	103	5	.330	.404
2019	22	Clearwater (FSL)	HiA	.276	93	337	35	93	14	3	5	45	41	71	11	.358	.380
	22	Reading (EL)	AA	.210	21	62	6	13	3	0	2	6	9	14	1	.306	.355
Minor League Totals				.259	286	1015	127	263	52	9	17	115	123	235	27	.342	.378

11 JOHAN ROJAS, OF

BA GRADE
50 Risk: Extreme

Born: Aug. 14, 2000. **B-T:** R-R. **HT:** 6-1. **WT:** 165. **Signed:** Dominican Republic, 2018. **Signed by:** Carlos Salas.

TRACK RECORD: The Phillies signed Rojas as part of its excellent 2017-2018 international class that also included shortstop Luis Garcia. Garcia made a much more impressive splash in 2018, but Rojas' wiry strength and speed gives him a chance to surpass Garcia eventually.

SCOUTING REPORT: Rojas is following in the footsteps of Simon Muzziotti and Carlos Tocci as an athletic center fielder who has the potential to be a plus runner and a plus defender with an average arm. And like Muzziotti and Tocci, the question is whether he'll hit enough for it to matter. Rojas has a solid swing, and he has the potential to hit for average power eventually–his two home runs were both opposite-field shots. Rojas is extremely aggressive at the plate right now–more than 50 percent of his plate appearances in 2019 were finished in one or two pitches. Scouts appreciate his high-energy approach, especially in the outfield.

THE FUTURE: In a system without many potential impact players, Rojas stands out because he has some strength potential to go with his speed and defense. He needs to improve his selectivity and get stronger, but few Phillies prospects can match his upside.

Year	Age	Club (League)	Class	AVG	G	AB	R	H	2B	3B	HR	RBI	BB	SO	SB	OBP	SLG
2018	17	Phillies Red (DSL)	R	.320	68	259	42	83	12	4	2	31	18	37	19	.376	.421
2019	18	Phillies West (GCL)	R	.311	18	74	13	23	6	5	0	4	9	12	3	.393	.527
	18	Williamsport (NYP)	SS	.244	42	164	17	40	5	6	2	11	5	29	11	.273	.384
Minor League Totals				.294	128	497	72	146	23	15	4	46	32	78	33	.346	.425

12 SIMON MUZZIOTTI, OF

BA GRADE
45 Risk: High

Born: Dec. 27, 1998. **B-T:** L-L. **HT:** 6-1. **WT:** 175. **Signed:** Venezuela, 2016. **Signed by:** Claudio Scerrato.

TRACK RECORD: Muzziotti was one of the best signees in the Red Sox's 2015 international class, but that contract was voided because MLB determined that Boston had used package deals to spread bonuses around to sign players for less than their value. He then signed with the Phillies for $750,000.

SCOUTING REPORT: Muzziotti is the best defensive center fielder the Phillies have, and his plus speed is very apparent on the basepaths. Muzziotti reads the ball off the bat well and takes direct routes. He had some arm soreness as an amateur but it hasn't been a problem as a pro. What he has yet to show is that

he can make enough offensive impact to project as more than a well-rounded backup outfielder. There's reasonable hope that Muzziotti will eventually be an above-average hitter. He doesn't swing and miss much and he has a solid feel for the strike zone, but he hits a lot of ground balls and has bottom-of-the-scale power. He will play all of 2020 as a 21-year-old, so he can still add some much-needed strength.
THE FUTURE: As a lefthanded hitter with a good glove, Muzziotti fits the profile of a fourth outfielder. So far nothing on his resume shows he can be a regular, but there are scouts who believe he will add the much-needed pop to play everyday.

Year	Age	Club (League)	Class	AVG	G	AB	R	H	2B	3B	HR	RBI	BB	SO	SB	OBP	SLG
2017	18	Clearwater (FSL)	HiA	.286	2	7	2	2	0	0	0	0	0	2	1	.286	.286
	18	Phillies (GCL)	R	.269	33	134	20	36	4	6	0	14	7	8	8	.305	.388
2018	19	Phillies East (GCL)	R	.091	6	22	2	2	0	0	0	2	2	1	1	.167	.091
	19	Lakewood (SAL)	LoA	.263	68	278	33	73	12	2	1	20	14	40	18	.299	.331
2019	20	Clearwater (FSL)	HiA	.287	110	425	52	122	21	3	3	28	32	60	21	.337	.372
Minor League Totals				.268	273	1069	130	287	43	13	4	86	70	127	57	.314	.344

13 ERIK MILLER, LHP

BA GRADE
45 **Risk: High**

Born: Feb. 13, 1998. **B-T:** L-L. **HT:** 6-5. **WT:** 240. **Drafted:** Stanford, 2019 (4th round). **Signed by:** Joey Davis.

TRACK RECORD: Miller has long carried lofty expectations as a big lefty who could be projected to one day have a big arm. Undrafted out of high school because of his strong Stanford commitment, Miller didn't fully find his groove until his junior year with the Cardinal. He went 8-3, 3.48 and pitched his way into the fourth round.

SCOUTING REPORT: Miller has touched 96-97 mph in shorter stints in the Cape Cod League and during fall ball at Stanford, but he generally sits 89-92 mph as a starter, which he did both at Stanford and for the Phillies in 2019. Miller's average fastball has solid life and is buoyed by a plus slider that he manipulates well. He also mixes in a changeup with average potential. It doesn't have exceptional movement but he maintains arm speed when throwing it. The Phillies have plenty of reasons to see if Miller can start, but a number of evaluators expect he'll eventually move to the bullpen thanks to his below-average control. Miller has long had a plunge in the back of his delivery and a long arm stroke. It's why he's consistently been a below-average strike thrower.

THE FUTURE: The Phillies don't have many starting pitching prospects, so there's plenty of reasons to see if Miller can improve his control and command. But a number of evaluators expect he'll end up as a fastball/slider lefty reliever with fringy control but above-average velocity in short stints.

Year	Age	Club (League)	Class	W	L	ERA	G	GS	SV	IP	H	HR	BB	SO	K/9	WHIP	AVG
2019	21	Phillies West (GCL)	R	0	0	3.00	2	1	0	3	2	0	2	6	18.0	1.33	.182
	21	Williamsport (NYP)	SS	0	0	0.90	6	4	0	20	13	0	7	29	13.1	1.00	.176
	21	Lakewood (SAL)	LoA	1	0	2.08	3	2	0	13	10	0	6	17	11.8	1.23	.208
Minor League Totals				1	0	1.50	11	7	0	36	25	0	15	52	13.0	1.11	.188

14 ANDRICK NAVA, C

BA GRADE
50 **Risk: Extreme**

Born: Oct. 6, 2001. **B-T:** B-R. **HT:** 5-11. **WT:** 175. **Signed:** Venezuela, 2018. **Signed by:** Rafael Alvarez/Romulo Oliveros.

TRACK RECORD: After signing for $400,000, Nava showed an advanced enough approach that the Phillies skipped him over the Dominican Summer League and sent him straight to the Gulf Coast League. He rewarded the Phillies by finishing sixth in the GCL batting race.

SCOUTING REPORT: In a system filled with catchers, Nava has the highest offensive upside. He has strong hands, above-average bat control and is comfortable from both sides of the plate. He recognizes spin well and shows an advanced approach. His power isn't really apparent yet–all seven of his extra-base hits in 2019 came as a lefthanded hitter–but he has strong hands and should eventually develop average power. Nava has a lot further to go as a receiver. He was raw defensively when he signed and even with significant improvement already as a pro, he needs to come a long way as a receiver and in blocking pitches in the dirt. His arm is average and he did throw out 32 percent of basestealers last season.

THE FUTURE: The Phillies' logjam of catchers could lead to sending him to the New York-Penn League in 2020, but Nava's advanced approach could handle a jump to low Class A Lakewood.

Year	Age	Club (League)	Class	AVG	G	AB	R	H	2B	3B	HR	RBI	BB	SO	SB	OBP	SLG
2019	17	Phillies West (GCL)	R	.314	44	156	25	49	6	0	1	20	8	20	1	.349	.372
Minor League Totals				.314	44	156	25	49	6	0	1	20	8	20	1	.349	.372

15 JOJO ROMERO, LHP

BA GRADE
45 Risk: High

Born: Sept. 9, 1996. **B-T:** L-L. **HT:** 5-11. **WT:** 190. **Drafted:** Yavapai (Ariz.) JC, 2016 (4th round). **Signed by:** Brad Holland.

TRACK RECORD: After a dominating 2017 season, it looked like Romero was a little over a year away from joining the Phillies rotation. Two years later, his timetable has slowed down and the optimism regarding his future major league role also has been significantly tempered.

SCOUTING REPORT: Romero's stuff ranged dramatically from intriguing to awful at different parts of 2019. In his worst outings, he struggled to top 90 with his fastball and had no above-average pitch. That led to a demotion back to Double-A Reading. He turned his season around there and he pitched better in a return to Triple-A, using a low-90s fastball and the above-average changeup that has been his calling card. In shorter stints of relief work in the Arizona Fall League, he was 94-96 mph in shorter stints while still showing a harder and tighter slider. Over the course of the season, it was an average slider at best getting more chases than swings and misses out of the strike zone. He does have average control.

THE FUTURE: Romero's inconsistency leads many to see a future in the bullpen, but he was just added to the 40-man roster.

Year	Age	Club (League)	Class	W	L	ERA	G	GS	SV	IP	H	HR	BB	SO	K/9	WHIP	AVG
2017	20	Lakewood (SAL)	LoA	5	1	2.11	13	13	0	77	61	2	21	79	9.3	1.07	.223
	20	Clearwater (FSL)	HiA	5	2	2.24	10	10	0	52	43	2	15	49	8.4	1.11	.223
2018	21	Reading (EL)	AA	7	6	3.80	18	18	0	107	97	13	41	100	8.4	1.29	.241
2019	22	Reading (EL)	AA	4	4	4.84	11	11	0	58	58	4	12	52	8.1	1.21	.261
	22	Lehigh Valley (IL)	AAA	3	5	6.88	13	13	0	54	68	8	35	40	6.7	1.92	.312
Minor League Totals				26	20	3.69	75	75	0	392	371	31	135	351	8.0	1.29	.250

16 DEIVY GRUILLON, C

BA GRADE
40 Risk: Medium

Born: Feb. 17, 1996. **B-T:** R-R. **HT:** 6-1. **WT:** 180. **Signed:** Dominican Republic, 2012. **Signed by:** Koby Perez.

TRACK RECORD: When the Phillies looked to reinvigorate their international program, Gruillon was one of their first major signings. He moved slowly early in his career, but back-to-back 20 home run seasons led to his MLB debut as a September callup in 2019.

SCOUTING REPORT: Gruillon has turned out to be a catcher with more offensive upside than most thanks to his above-average power. His swing isn't geared to hitting for average, as there is some length, but the power fits a backup catcher profile. He works well with pitchers and he has a plus arm. His thick trunk does limit his agility as a catcher. He sets up with one knee on the ground with no baserunners on to help him better present low pitches, but with runners on he struggles to get low in his setup. His hands are adequate, but he will get caught struggling to stab instead of block pitches that miss the strike zone badly.

THE FUTURE: As long as J.T. Realmuto is a Phillie, the club's backup catcher is a limited role. In 2019, Andrew Knapp started 30 games and got 160 plate appearances. Gruillon has a shot to fill that role while providing more value than Knapp as a pinch-hitter who can run into a home run every now and then.

Year	Age	Club (League)	Class	AVG	G	AB	R	H	2B	3B	HR	RBI	BB	SO	SB	OBP	SLG
2017	21	Clearwater (FSL)	HiA	.255	71	271	31	69	14	0	8	24	12	61	0	.287	.395
	21	Reading (EL)	AA	.229	23	83	10	19	3	0	4	13	5	19	0	.270	.410
2018	22	Reading (EL)	AA	.273	90	326	36	89	14	1	21	59	18	81	0	.310	.515
2019	23	Lehigh Valley (IL)	AAA	.283	108	407	55	115	24	0	21	77	45	133	1	.354	.496
	23	Philadelphia (NL)	MAJ	.111	4	9	0	1	1	0	0	1	0	2	0	.111	.222
Major League Totals				.111	4	9	0	1	1	0	0	1	0	2	0	.111	.222
Minor League Totals				.253	606	2195	235	556	116	3	70	308	155	553	4	.305	.405

17 CRISTOPHER SANCHEZ, LHP

Born: Dec. 12, 1996. **B-T:** L-L. **HT:** 6-5. **WT:** 165. **Signed:** Dominican Republic, 2013. **Signed by:** Daniel Santana (Rays).

TRACK RECORD: For the longest time, Sanchez's professional career was moving at the pace of a three-toed tree sloth. He spent three seasons in the Dominican Summer League and another two at Rookie-level Princeton. So he was left unprotected in the Rule 5 draft before he had ever thrown a pitch in full-season ball. In 2019, he started to speed up his development, dominating at low Class A Bowling Green and high Class A Charlotte. With the Rays facing a full 40-man roster, the Phillies acquired him for young Australian third baseman Curtis Mead and placed him on the 40-man.

SCOUTING REPORT: Sanchez has one of the best left arms in the Phillies system. He can attack hitters with a 94-98 mph fastball that comes out surprisingly easy. Sanchez throws from a cross-fire, low three-quarters delivery that makes it a little tougher for hitters to pick the ball up, but also makes it tougher

for him to command his fastball. His low-80s slider flashes plus and pairs well with his arm slot to sweep across the strike zone, getting down and in on righthanded hitters. He throws a low-80s straight change that he doesn't command as well as his fastball and slider.
THE FUTURE: Sanchez's clock has to speed up now that he's on the 40-man roster, but he should pitch in Double-A in 2020, so he still has time to develop at the upper levels. Sanchez's most likely landing spot is as a power lefty reliever.

Year	Age	Club (League)	Class	W	L	ERA	G	GS	SV	IP	H	HR	BB	SO	K/9	WHIP	AVG
2017	20	Princeton (APP)	R	1	6	10.01	13	7	0	39	61	8	16	30	7.0	1.99	.353
2018	21	Princeton (APP)	R	3	2	4.60	10	10	0	43	53	3	22	34	7.1	1.74	.308
	21	Hudson Valley (NYP)	SS	1	0	4.00	2	2	0	9	9	0	5	11	11.0	1.56	.273
2019	22	Bowling Green (MWL)	LoA	3	1	2.01	11	4	2	40	28	3	11	37	8.3	0.97	.191
	22	Charlotte, FL (FSL)	HiA	1	0	1.85	12	6	0	34	28	0	13	36	9.5	1.21	.231
	22	Durham (IL)	AAA	0	0	20.25	1	0	0	1	2	0	2	0	0.0	3.00	.400
Minor League Totals				17	16	4.53	90	40	5	270	287	14	113	219	7.3	1.48	.272

18 DAMON JONES, LHP

BA GRADE 45 Risk: High

Born: Sept. 30, 1994. **B-T:** L-L. **HT:** 6-5. **WT:** 225. **Drafted:** Washington State, 2017 (18th round). **Signed by:** Hilton Richardson.

TRACK RECORD: After two years at JC of Southern Idaho, Jones had two rather nondescript seasons at Washington State. As a redshirt junior, Jones never struck out more than four batters in any of his 13 starts but he allowed nine or more runs three different times. As a pro, he's been much more effective. He's added velocity after working with Driveline Baseball and he improved his control by junking his windup to throw exclusively from the stretch.
SCOUTING REPORT: Jones' improved above-average fastball now sits 92-94 mph and can touch 96 with good extension. He gets some swings and misses in the strike zone with it, but it is his plus 82-84 mph slider that finishes off hitters. Jones' slider has a high spin rate and sweeps across the strike zone with more horizontal movement than vertical depth. Jones can back-foot righthanded hitters, which is why he's just as effective against righties as he is lefties. His changeup is a below-average third pitch that is a little too hard (86-89 mph) and doesn't have enough movement to get swings and misses. Simplifying his delivery has helped, but he still has below-average control.
THE FUTURE: Jones is a steal of an 18th-round pick. He has a lot of work still to do with his control to be an major league starter, but his fastball and slider give him a fallback option as a power lefty reliever.

Year	Age	Club (League)	Class	W	L	ERA	G	GS	SV	IP	H	HR	BB	SO	K/9	WHIP	AVG
2017	22	Williamsport (NYP)	SS	2	3	4.85	13	0	3	26	23	0	20	38	13.2	1.65	.240
2018	23	Lakewood (SAL)	LoA	10	7	3.41	23	22	0	113	105	7	50	123	9.8	1.37	.247
2019	24	Clearwater (FSL)	HiA	4	3	1.54	11	11	0	58	38	3	24	88	13.6	1.06	.188
	24	Reading (EL)	AA	1	0	0.82	4	4	0	22	9	0	9	31	12.7	0.82	.129
	24	Lehigh Valley (IL)	AAA	0	1	6.62	8	8	0	34	27	4	26	33	8.7	1.56	.214
Minor League Totals				17	14	3.34	59	45	3	253	202	14	129	313	11.1	1.30	.220

19 JAMARI BAYLOR, SS

BA GRADE 50 Risk: Extreme

Born: Aug. 25, 2000. **B-T:** R-R. **HT:** 5-11. **WT:** 190. **Drafted:** HS—Richmond, 2019 (3rd round). **Signed by:** Kellum McKeon.

TRACK RECORD: Baylor impressed a number of scouts over the summer before the 2019 draft with his speed, athleticism, hitting ability and, most of all, his above-average makeup. The Phillies didn't get much of a chance to see what Baylor could do as a pro, as he badly pulled a hamstring just two games into the season. He didn't return to action until the final two games of the Gulf Coast League season.
SCOUTING REPORT: Baylor is a plus runner and has a shot to be an above-average hitter. He works counts well and seems allergic to strikeouts. He has a contact-oriented approach, but has enough strength to yank a home run if a pitcher gets sloppy, and he has the potential to add more muscle and strength. Baylor faces more skepticism about where he ends up defensively. He has a quick first step and an above-average arm, but his actions and his exchange are a little slow. If he can't stay at shortstop his arm and range could fit at second or third base or in the outfield, so he has plenty of options.
THE FUTURE: Baylor will be a little behind in 2020 because he missed so much time in his pro debut, so a jump to short-season Williamsport makes sense, especially with Luis Garcia needing to return to Lakewood.

Year	Age	Club (League)	Class	AVG	G	AB	R	H	2B	3B	HR	RBI	BB	SO	SB	OBP	SLG
2019	18	Phillies West (GCL)	R	.273	4	11	4	3	2	0	0	0	1	2	0	.333	.455
Minor League Totals				.273	4	11	4	3	2	0	0	0	1	2	0	.333	.455

20 ADDISON RUSS, RHP

BA GRADE
45 Risk: Medium

Born: Oct. 29, 1994. **B-T:** R-R. **HT:** 6-1. **WT:** 190. **Drafted:** Houston Baptist, 2017 (19th round). **Signed by:** Will Brunson.

TRACK RECORD: Russ is trying to become only the second player from Houston Baptist to make it to the major leagues. If he can throw 10 or more MLB innings, he will top Trever Enders for the longest major league career among Huskies. Russ was a starter at two different junior colleges and in his two years with Houston Baptist, but the senior sign has been a reliever for the entirety of his pro career. He has 52 saves in just 129 pro games.

SCOUTING REPORT: Opposing teams don't need to spend a long time trying to build a scouting report on Russ. He's going to attack hitters repeatedly with a 93-96 mph above-average fastball with some run and a plus 84-86 mph splitter that looks like the fastball out of his hand but dives toward the dirt with a little tail at the plate. The two tunnel well together. In addition, Russ does have a below-average slider, but when he's locating his fastball he can thrive with a two-pitch approach. Russ has average control as well, which is vital because he is much more effective when he can get ahead in counts to set up his splitter.

THE FUTURE: Russ has two pitches that should succeed in Philadelphia much like they have in the minors. He's ready to head to Triple-A Lehigh Valley and could make his MLB debut in 2020.

Year	Age	Club (League)	Class	W	L	ERA	G	GS	SV	IP	H	HR	BB	SO	K/9	WHIP	AVG
2017	22	Williamsport (NYP)	SS	0	0	8.10	2	0	0	3	5	0	1	4	10.8	1.80	.333
	22	Lakewood (SAL)	LoA	1	2	3.49	15	0	1	28	26	2	8	36	11.4	1.20	.241
2018	23	Lakewood (SAL)	LoA	5	2	1.67	25	0	13	32	19	3	4	37	10.3	0.71	.171
	23	Clearwater (FSL)	HiA	4	0	1.69	29	0	14	32	25	1	11	42	11.8	1.13	.205
2019	24	Reading (EL)	AA	5	6	2.54	55	0	22	57	47	5	20	81	12.9	1.18	.223
Minor League Totals				15	10	2.48	126	0	50	152	122	11	44	200	11.8	1.09	.215

21 KENDALL SIMMONS, 2B/3B

BA GRADE
50 Risk: Extreme

Born: April 11, 2000. **B-T:** R-R. **HT:** 6-2. **WT:** 180. **Drafted:** HS—Macon, Ga., 2018 (6th round). **Signed by:** Aaron Jersild.

TRACK RECORD: In high school, Simmons showed impressive power, but also struggled with strikeouts and his defense at shortstop. Two years later, he has impressive power and struggles with strikeouts and defense. He finished second in the New York-Penn League with 12 home runs while hitting .230.

SCOUTING REPORT: Simmons' defense requires plenty of work. The Phillies moved him from shortstop to primarily second and third base in 2019, but he's below-average at both spots now. His footwork isn't ideal, he struggles at turning double plays and his hands don't work all that well, especially to his backhand. He has an above-average arm. But Simmons is athletic enough that there is hope that with work, he can improve to fringe-average or even average at second and third. Offensively, he shows impressive power potential with plus-plus raw power, excellent exit velocities and the potential to hit 20-plus home runs one day. He currently chases a lot of pitches out of the zone.

THE FUTURE: Simmons has enough power and athleticism to develop to have potential to be an everyday regular, but he has a long ways to go. Low Class A Lakewood is the next step up the ladder.

Year	Age	Club (League)	Class	AVG	G	AB	R	H	2B	3B	HR	RBI	BB	SO	SB	OBP	SLG
2018	18	Phillies East (GCL)	R	.232	32	95	21	22	7	0	3	11	9	30	2	.345	.400
2019	19	Williamsport (NYP)	SS	.234	51	171	31	40	7	3	12	34	20	54	5	.333	.520
Minor League Totals				.233	83	266	52	62	14	3	15	45	29	84	7	.338	.477

22 LOGAN O'HOPPE, C

BA GRADE
45 Risk: High

Born: Feb. 9, 2000. **B-T:** R-R. **HT:** 6-2. **WT:** 185. **Drafted:** HS—West Islip, N.Y., 2018 (23rd round). **Signed by:** Alex Agostino.

TRACK RECORD: O'Hoppe announced himself as a worthwhile late-round sleeper by hitting .367 (thanks in part to an unsustainable .458 average on balls in play). O'Hoppe's slash line wasn't nearly as impressive in 2019, but he still showed some of the same underlying skills. O'Hoppe threw out 31 percent of basestealers while showing solid blocking skills behind the plate.

SCOUTING REPORT: O'Hoppe was seen as a glove-first catcher coming out of high school, but his bat has proven more advanced than expected. He has a fluid swing that is geared to hitting the ball in the air, and he should eventually have above-average power as he matures. He could eventually be a 45 hitter with 55 power. O'Hoppe has a solid understanding of the strike zone and a solid two-strike approach. He doesn't do anything spectacularly as a defender, but he moves reasonably well, has an above-average arm and the tools to eventually have average receiving ability. He doesn't run well now and will likely slow down.

THE FUTURE: Catcher is the deepest position among Phillies minor leaguers, but O'Hoppe has more offensive potential than most of Philadelphia's backstop prospects. He'll head to low Class A Lakewood.

Year	Age	Club (League)	Class	AVG	G	AB	R	H	2B	3B	HR	RBI	BB	SO	SB	OBP	SLG
2018	18	Phillies West (GCL)	R	.367	34	109	19	40	10	1	2	21	10	28	2	.411	.532
2019	19	Williamsport (NYP)	SS	.216	45	162	20	35	12	2	5	26	12	49	3	.266	.407
Minor League Totals				.277	79	271	39	75	22	3	7	47	22	77	5	.326	.458

23 ETHAN LINDOW, LHP

BA GRADE 45 **Risk: High**

Born: Oct. 15, 1998. **B-T:** R-L. **HT:** 6-3. **WT:** 180. **Drafted:** HS—Locust Grove, Ga., 2017 (5th round). **Signed by:** Aaron Jersild.

TRACK RECORD: Lindow was expected to be a two-way player for Alabama-Birmingham, but his mid-80s fastball steadily turned into a high-80s fastball that could touch 92 mph, which enticed the Phillies to draft him in the fifth round. Lindow played travel ball with Tom Glavine's son Peyton and he has learned some tricks of the trade from Glavine who, like Lindow, didn't light up a radar gun.

SCOUTING REPORT: If Lindow can find another 2-3 mph, he will be one of the better pitching prospects the Phillies have. As it stands right now, he has a lot of impressive attributes, but his fringe-average 87-92 mph fastball is a somewhat limiting factor. Lindow throws four pitches for strikes with plus control. His above-average changeup had fade and sink and solid deception, and his above-average mid-70s curveball had quality spin and depth and he can sometimes slow it down even further to lock up hitters looking for a fastball. His average 82-84 mph slider has modest depth, but is effective because he can spot it. He does a good job of hiding the ball from hitters in his delivery, adding to his effectiveness.

THE FUTURE: Lindow has made excellent progress in his two years as a pro. He's still young enough to add some more velocity. As far as feel, control and pitch selection, he's as impressive as any young Phillies pitcher. He'll head to high Class A Clearwater.

Year	Age	Club (League)	Class	W	L	ERA	G	GS	SV	IP	H	HR	BB	SO	K/9	WHIP	AVG
2017	18	Phillies (GCL)	R	2	2	4.55	8	8	0	28	26	2	12	34	11.1	1.37	.241
2018	19	Williamsport (NYP)	SS	3	2	2.19	13	13	0	70	58	2	19	63	8.1	1.10	.227
2019	20	Lakewood (SAL)	LoA	5	2	2.66	23	13	2	95	73	4	20	103	9.8	0.98	.208
	20	Clearwater (FSL)	HiA	0	2	1.69	3	3	0	16	17	0	2	16	9.0	1.19	.274
Minor League Totals				10	8	2.68	47	37	2	208	174	8	53	216	9.3	1.09	.224

24 CONNOR BRODGON, RHP

BA GRADE 40 **Risk: Medium**

Born: Jan. 29, 1995. **B-T:** R-R. **HT:** 6-6. **WT:** 192. **Drafted:** Lewis-Clark State (Idaho), 2017 (10th round). **Signed by:** Hilton Richardson.

TRACK RECORD: A 10th-round senior sign out of NAIA power Lewis-Clark State, Brogdon quickly moved to the bullpen as a pro. It's been a fortuitous move as he's turned himself into a viable prospect.

SCOUTING REPORT: Brogdon attacks hitters with a 92-96 mph above-average fastball that has solid riding life to go with excellent extension. He elevates it well and he has the plus spin rate to get swings and misses. His circle change is an 82-84 mph plus pitch with quality fade and sink. Brogdon relies mainly on those two pitches. He will sporadically throw a below-average slider that is a big breaker, but he doesn't have confidence to use it as more than a surprise pitch. He has average control.

THE FUTURE: The Phillies didn't opt to promote Brogdon to the majors in September but he can be expected to be part of the Phillies' 2020 bullpen plans. He projects as a solid middle-innings reliever.

Year	Age	Club (League)	Class	W	L	ERA	G	GS	SV	IP	H	HR	BB	SO	K/9	WHIP	AVG
2017	22	Williamsport (NYP)	SS	3	1	2.34	16	0	3	35	22	2	18	45	11.7	1.15	.177
2018	23	Lakewood (SAL)	LoA	5	3	2.47	31	7	5	69	59	3	16	79	10.3	1.08	.228
2019	24	Clearwater (FSL)	HiA	2	0	1.80	10	0	0	20	11	1	5	23	10.4	0.80	.164
	24	Reading (EL)	AA	1	1	2.66	15	0	2	24	12	4	7	39	14.8	0.80	.150
	24	Lehigh Valley (IL)	AAA	3	1	3.06	26	0	2	32	23	4	12	44	12.2	1.08	.193
Minor League Totals				14	6	2.50	98	7	12	180	127	14	58	230	11.5	1.03	.196

25 MAURICIO LLOVERA, RHP

BA GRADE 45 **Risk: Extreme**

Born: April 17, 1996. **B-T:** R-R. **HT:** 5-11. **WT:** 200. **Signed:** Venezuela, 2014. **Signed by:** Carlos Salas.

TRACK RECORD: Llovera was a revelation for the Phillies as he quickly went from low-cost $7,500 signing to one of the best arms in the system. Llovera sat in the mid-90s and touched 99 mph as a power reliever in 2017 then managed to retain that stuff as a starter in 2018. But his fastball backed up in 2019 and he ended up missing the second half of the season with forearm tightness.

SCOUTING REPORT: Llovera sat 92-94 mph after flirting with triple digits in the past. He doesn't get a

lot of extension or plane on his fastball and it's a low spin rate pitch that wasn't all that effective with less velocity. He relied more heavily on his plus changeup and average slider. He has fringe-average control.
THE FUTURE: Llovera's forearm soreness is concerning, but the Phillies' decision to add him to the 40-man roster was a strong vote of confidence. Most likely, he will move to the bullpen in the long-term.

Year	Age	Club (League)	Class	W	L	ERA	G	GS	SV	IP	H	HR	BB	SO	K/9	WHIP	AVG
2017	21	Lakewood (SAL)	LoA	2	4	3.35	30	10	0	86	81	2	33	94	9.8	1.33	.250
2018	22	Clearwater (FSL)	HiA	8	7	3.72	23	22	0	121	100	14	34	137	10.2	1.11	.221
2019	23	Reading (EL)	AA	3	4	4.55	14	12	0	65	60	7	28	72	9.9	1.35	.243
Minor League Totals				22	20	3.45	89	64	0	372	316	24	124	402	9.7	1.18	.228

26 ABRAHAN GUTIERREZ, C

BA GRADE
45 Risk: High

Born: Oct. 31, 1999. **B-T:** R-R. **HT:** 6-2. **WT:** 214. **Signed:** Venezuela, 2017. **Signed by:** Carlos Salas.

TRACK RECORD: A year after the Phillies signed Simon Muzziotti after Major League Baseball voided his contract, they inked Gutierrez after MLB voided his Braves contract. He made his full-season debut in 2019 at low Class A Lakewood.
SCOUTING REPORT: Gutierrez's quickly maturing body drew some concerns when he was an amateur, but he has managed to retain his flexibility despite thick hips and a heavy lower half. Gutierrez is able to get low in his crouch and sets a good, low target. He has an average arm and projects as a fringe-average or average defender. Gutierrez made zero offensive impact in 2019, as he didn't drive the ball despite his solid strength. He can shoot balls into the opposite field gap or yank them down the line, but generally, he hit a lot of ineffectual ground balls and shallow fly balls. He shows average power in batting practice, but his slow bat speed and long swing make it hard for him to get to his power in games.
THE FUTURE: Gutierrez has some building blocks of a backup catcher, but he has to speed up his bat.

Year	Age	Club (League)	Class	AVG	G	AB	R	H	2B	3B	HR	RBI	BB	SO	SB	OBP	SLG
2017	17	Braves (GCL)	R	.264	35	129	15	34	9	0	1	12	10	21	0	.319	.357
2018	18	Phillies West (GCL)	R	.315	41	162	24	51	10	1	1	30	10	16	2	.362	.407
2019	19	Lakewood (SAL)	LoA	.246	83	289	23	71	9	0	4	27	28	62	3	.314	.318
Minor League Totals				.269	159	580	62	156	28	1	6	69	48	99	5	.328	.352

27 COLE IRVIN, LHP

BA GRADE
40 Risk: Medium

Born: Jan. 31, 1994. **B-T:** L-L. **HT:** 6-4. **WT:** 180. **Drafted:** Oregon, 2016 (5th round). **Signed by:** Hilton Richardson.

TRACK RECORD: Irvin was a dominating 12-3, 2.48 as a freshman for Oregon. And then he blew out his elbow. When he returned from Tommy John surgery his stuff wasn't as sharp. Since the Phillies drafted him, he moved quickly to the majors thanks to guile and plus control.
SCOUTING REPORT: Irvin's below-average 87-91 mph fastball has arm-side run, but it doesn't have enough velocity or movement to frighten hitters. His above-average 82-84 mph slurvy slider dives away from lefties enough to be effective. His average 82-84 mph changeup relies on solid deception. It's aiming for weak contact and is effective against righties when he's dotting it to the edge of the plate.
THE FUTURE: Irvin should return to Triple-A Lehigh Valley to begin 2020. He's a useful depth piece for the Phillies who can fill in either in the bullpen or the rotation, but it would not be a good sign if he received a lot of innings in Philadelphia this year.

Year	Age	Club (League)	Class	W	L	ERA	G	GS	SV	IP	H	HR	BB	SO	K/9	WHIP	AVG
2017	23	Clearwater (FSL)	HiA	4	6	2.55	12	11	0	67	68	2	14	52	7.0	1.22	.265
	23	Reading (EL)	AA	5	3	4.06	13	13	0	84	72	12	24	66	7.0	1.14	.228
2018	24	Lehigh Valley (IL)	AAA	14	4	2.57	26	25	0	161	135	11	35	131	7.3	1.05	.227
2019	25	Lehigh Valley (IL)	AAA	6	1	3.94	17	16	0	94	113	13	14	65	6.2	1.36	.297
	25	Philadelphia (NL)	MAJ	2	1	5.83	16	3	1	42	45	7	13	31	6.7	1.39	.278
Major League Totals				2	1	5.83	16	3	1	41	45	7	13	31	6.7	1.39	.278
Minor League Total				34	15	3.07	78	72	0	452	424	40	95	351	7.0	1.15	.246

28 JHAILYN ORTIZ, OF

BA GRADE
45 Risk: Extreme

Born: Nov. 18, 1998. **B-T:** R-R. **HT:** 6-3. **WT:** 215. **Signed:** Dominican Republic, 2015. **Signed by:** Sal Agostinelli.

TRACK RECORD: The Phillies made a $4 million bet on Ortiz, believing he could make the adjustments to his swing and timing to unlock his best-in-class power. Instead, he has yet to advance past the Class A

levels in five years while strugging to make contact.
SCOUTING REPORT: When Ortiz connects, he not only clears fences but leaves balls bouncing out of stadiums. He takes big, massive swings with a big load to get to his plus-plus power. He is rarely on time with his big swings and is quite pitchable thanks to his inability to adjust to off-speed pitches. Ortiz has always moved well for his size and the Phillies have even let him play center field, but scouts see a below-average corner outfielder or first baseman He's a below-average runner, but he does have a plus arm.
THE FUTURE: Ortiz's top-of-the-scale raw power will earn him plenty of chances to improve his selectivity and swing. The Phillies left him unprotected and he went unpicked in the Rule 5 draft.

Year	Age	Club (League)	Class	AVG	G	AB	R	H	2B	3B	HR	RBI	BB	SO	SB	OBP	SLG
2017	18	Williamsport (NYP)	SS	.302	47	159	27	48	15	1	8	30	18	47	5	.401	.560
2018	19	Lakewood (SAL)	LoA	.225	110	405	51	91	18	2	13	47	35	148	2	.297	.375
2019	20	Clearwater (FSL)	HiA	.200	115	430	57	86	15	3	19	65	36	149	2	.272	.381
Minor League Totals				.227	319	1167	164	265	57	7	48	169	106	397	17	.307	.411

29 JONATHAN GUZMAN, 2B/SS

BA GRADE 40 **Risk: High**

Born: Aug. 17, 1999. **B-T:** R-R. **HT:** 6-0. **WT:** 156. **Signed:** Dominican Republic, 2015. **Signed by:** Carlos Salas.
TRACK RECORD: Guzman was a low-cost ($60,000) signing in 2015 who has proven to be a bargain. A switch-hitter as an amateur, Guzman has scrapped hitting lefty as a pro. He finished tied for fourth in the South Atlantic League in 2019 with 31 steals. He also made the Dominican Republic Premier 12 roster.
SCOUTING REPORT: Guzman is an excellent defender who has to prove he is anywhere near as capable with his bat. He is a plus defender with a plus arm who is equally comfortable at shortstop and second base. His hands are excellent and he has the smooth actions of a major league middle infielder. At the plate, Guzman strikes zero fear in the hearts of pitchers because even if they make a mistake, he's most likely to simply slap a single. Power can develop late, but if Guzman can get to 8-10 home runs a year, that would be a surprise.
THE FUTURE: The minors are filled with shortstops with great gloves who can't hit enough for it to matter. Guzman's arm is good enough that he might have a fallback option as a pitcher.

Year	Age	Club (League)	Class	AVG	G	AB	R	H	2B	3B	HR	RBI	BB	SO	SB	OBP	SLG
2017	17	Clearwater (FSL)	HiA	.000	1	3	0	0	0	0	0	0	0	3	0	.000	.000
	17	Williamsport (NYP)	SS	.263	6	19	2	5	0	0	1	2	4	3	0	.391	.421
	17	Phillies (GCL)	R	.248	38	153	17	38	4	2	1	13	11	24	5	.299	.320
2018	18	Williamsport (NYP)	SS	.210	62	243	28	51	7	1	2	14	10	61	3	.241	.272
2019	19	Lakewood (SAL)	LoA	.251	123	475	55	119	18	2	3	40	32	97	31	.298	.316
Minor League Totals				.252	294	1133	129	285	40	5	7	82	78	213	52	.303	.314

30 CONNOR SEABOLD, LHP

BA GRADE 40 **Risk: High**

Born: Jan. 24, 1996. **B-T:** R-R. **HT:** 6-2. **WT:** 190. **Drafted:** Cal State Fullerton, 2017 (3rd round). **Signed by:** Demerius Pittman.
TRACK RECORD: Cal State Fullerton produces crafty pitchers with impeccable control year after year. Seabold fits the same mold as Dylan Floro and teammate Thomas Eshelman as a pitcher who succeeds with control more than velocity. An oblique injury cost Seabold time early in the season, but he made up for it with a strong four outings in the Arizona Fall League.
SCOUTING REPORT: Seabold has added a little velocity since college, turning a fringy fastball into an 89-93 mph average pitch. His plus control helps it play up as he does a good job of avoiding hitter's happy zones. Seabold also has improved his above-average changeup–it has drop at the plate to generate poor swings and some whiffs. His fringe-average slider needs to improve as it lacks depth and bite.
THE FUTURE: Much like Cole Irvin, Seabold is a polished lefty whose control and guile make him a potentially useful MLB starter. But his lack of stuff keeps him from being more than a back-end starter. He heads to Triple-A ready to help if the Phillies need a fill-in start.

Year	Age	Club (League)	Class	W	L	ERA	G	GS	SV	IP	H	HR	BB	SO	K/9	WHIP	AVG
2017	21	Williamsport (NYP)	SS	2	0	0.90	5	0	0	10	5	0	2	13	11.7	0.70	.143
2018	22	Clearwater (FSL)	HiA	4	4	3.77	12	12	0	72	57	6	14	68	8.5	0.99	.213
	22	Reading (EL)	AA	1	4	4.91	11	11	0	59	55	10	19	64	9.8	1.26	.241
2019	23	Phillies West (GCL)	R	0	0	0.00	2	2	0	5	1	0	0	10	18.0	0.20	.063
	23	Phillies East (GCL)	R	0	1	11.57	1	1	0	2	6	0	0	2	7.7	2.57	.462
	23	Clearwater (FSL)	HiA	1	0	1.00	2	1	0	9	4	1	1	10	10.0	0.56	.133
	23	Reading (EL)	AA	3	1	2.25	7	7	0	40	35	2	10	36	8.1	1.13	.240
Minor League Totals				11	10	3.52	40	34	0	196	163	19	46	203	9.3	1.06	.222

Pittsburgh Pirates

BY TIM WILLIAMS

Just five years ago, the Pirates were Baseball America's Organization of the Year. It feels like a lifetime ago.

The Pirates won 98 games in 2015, made their third straight playoff appearance and had five Top 100 Prospects in Tyler Glasnow, Jameson Taillon, Austin Meadows, Josh Bell and Reese McGuire. Four seasons later, everything has changed.

President Frank Coonelly, general manager Neal Huntington and manager Clint Hurdle, who oversaw the Pirates' rebirth as a competitive franchise, were all fired following a last-place finish in the National League Central. Former Pittsburgh Penguins executive Travis Williams was named team president, Ben Cherington came on as GM and ex-Twins bench coach Derek Shelton was brought in as manager. Those were only the most prominent moves, with many more changes under the surface such as the firing of assistant GM Kyle Stark and the hiring of former Blue Jays scouting director Steve Sanders to take his place. Farm director Larry Broadway and scouting director Joe DelliCarri survived the initial wave of change.

To see how the organization changed so much in less than five years, all you need to do is look at those aforementioned Top 100 Prospects. The Pirates have a long history of failing to get the most out of their talented prospects. This issue became especially glaring when they traded Gerrit Cole to the Astros prior to the 2018 season and saw Cole emerge as the ace the Pirates expected when they drafted him first overall in 2011.

Things got worse at the trade deadline in 2018. The Pirates made a big splash by acquiring Chris Archer from the Rays for Glasnow, Meadows and 2017 first-round pick Shane Baz. Neither Meadows nor Glasnow had accomplished much with the Pirates, but in their first seasons after the trade Meadows hit 33 home runs in an all-star campaign and Glasnow posted a 1.78 ERA as a starter in an injury-abbreviated season.

That was the upside the Pirates expected from both players, yet it didn't happen until after they left the organization. The players who stayed have delivered mixed performances. Taillon has shown flashes of being an ace but hasn't been able to sustain that status and will miss all of 2020 after his second Tommy John surgery. Bell broke out with an all-star campaign in 2019, but McGuire was one of three players traded to the Blue Jays in 2016 for Drew Hutchsion—another deal that has not turned out favorably for the Pirates.

Prospects don't always work out. That's a reality that can't be ignored. It also can't be ignored that the Pirates have seen too many of their top prospects struggle in Pittsburgh, only to approach and reach their potential ceilings with their new organizations.

The Pirates fell behind the last few years on modern hitting and pitching philosophies, which hurt the development of their prospects. Cherington will have to figure out what went wrong while updating some of these philosophies to fit the modern game.

With Top 100 Prospects Mitch Keller, Ke'Bryan Hayes and Oneil Cruz in the system, the Pirates have promising talent once again. In order to return to contention, they'll need those players to flourish in Pittsburgh rather than someplace else.

JUSTIN BERL/GETTY IMAGES

Bryan Reynolds showed feel to hit, power and versatility in a remarkable rookie season.

PROJECTED 2023 LINEUP

Position	Player	Age
Catcher	Jacob Stallings	33
First Base	Josh Bell	30
Second Base	Kevin Newman	29
Third Base	Ke'Bryan Hayes (2)	26
Shortstop	Cole Tucker	26
Left Field	Bryan Reynolds	28
Center Field	Travis Swaggerty (9)	25
Right Field	Oneil Cruz (3)	24
No. 1 Starter	Jameson Taillon	31
No. 2 Starter	Mitch Keller (1)	27
No. 3 Starter	Joe Musgrove	30
No. 4 Starter	Cody Bolton (4)	25
No. 5 Starter	Quinn Priester (6)	22
Closer	Tahnaj Thomas (5)	24

DEPTH CHART

PITTSBURGH PIRATES

TOP 2020 ROOKIE: Mitch Keller, RHP. A rotation spot is Keller's for the taking after making his debut last year.

BREAKOUT PROSPECT: Santiago Florez, RHP. He already features a mid-90s fastball with a big frame that portends even more velocity to come.

SLEEPER: Deion Walker, OF. Drafted in the 35th round in 2019, Walker impressed in his pro debut as a toolsy center fielder with power to all fields.

SOURCE OF TOP 30 TALENT

Homegrown	27	Acquired	3
College	9	Trade	3
Junior college	0	Rule 5 draft	0
High school	13	Independent league	0
Nondrafted free agent	1	Free agent/waivers	0
International	4		

LF
Calvin Mitchell (12)
Juan Pie
Matt Fraizer
Fabricio Macias

CF
Sammy Siani (8)
Travis Swaggerty (9)
Jared Oliva (18)
Lolo Sanchez (26)
Jasiah Dixon (28)
Jase Bowen
Deion Walker

RF
Jack Herman (27)
Matt Gorski (30)
Jason Martin

3B
Ke'Bryan Hayes (2)
Alexander Mojica (14)

SS
Oneil Cruz (3)
Ji-Hwan Bae (7)
Stephen Alemais

2B
Kevin Kramer (19)
Rodolfo Castro

1B
Mason Martin (13)
Will Craig (22)

C
Christian Kelley
Arden Pabst
Jason Delay
Deon Stafford

LHP

LHSP	LHRP
Cam Vieaux	Blake Weiman
Domingo Robles	Braeden Ogle
	Sam Howard
	Brandon Waddell

RHP

RHSP	RHRP
Mitch Keller (1)	Nick Mears (17)
Cody Bolton (4)	Nick Burdi (23)
Tahnaj Thomas (5)	Blake Cederlind (25)
Quinn Priester (6)	J.C. Flowers (29)
Braxton Ashcraft (10)	Cody Ponce
Michael Burrows (11)	Geoff Hartlieb
Travis MacGregor (15)	Luis Escobar
JT Brubaker (16)	James Marvel
Santiago Florez (20)	Shea Murray
Max Kranick (21)	Noe Toribio
Osvaldo Bido (24)	Yerry De Los Santos
Aaron Shortridge (30)	
Colin Selby	
Luis Ortiz	
Gage Hinsz	
Ryan Harbin	

DRAFT ANALYSIS

2019

BEST PURE HITTER: OF Sammy Siani (1s) has plenty of hitting traits, with a handsy lefthanded swing that is simple and consistent, a quiet load and loose movements throughout. The Pirates also like the hitting traits that 3B Jared Triolo (2s) possesses, with an ability to use the opposite field and a strong track record of hitting at Houston.

BEST POWER HITTER: OF Matt Gorski (2) has plus raw power, though it didn't fully translate to games during his pro debut in the short-season New York-Penn League. OF Will Matthiesen (6) was a two-way player at Stanford, but the Pirates like his power potential as a hitter. A 6-foot-7, 220-pound righthanded hitter, Matthiessen has plus raw power as well and might better tap into that juice with an exclusive focus on hitting.

FASTEST RUNNER: Orange (Calif.) Lutheran High product OF Jasiah Dixon (23) has plus-plus speed and is likely the quickest runner in the class.

BEST DEFENSIVE PLAYER: Siani doesn't have game-changing speed, but he's a polished center fielder thanks to standout instincts. Gorski is athletic—he was also a standout soccer player—and quick enough for the position, while Triolo has impressive enough body control and instincts that he played some shortstop in his pro debut.

BEST ATHLETE: RHP J.C. Flowers (4) has athleticism that would stand out on a field with football players or in a basketball gym. He has elite body control and an impressive vertical leap, giving him significant upside now that he's beginning to focus exclusively on pitching.

BEST FASTBALL: RHP Austin Roberts (8) touches 97 mph and sits in the 92-96 mph range. RHP Quinn Priester (1) has been up to 96 mph, though he pitches in the low 90s with solid life.

BEST SECONDARY PITCH: Priester pairs his fastball and changeup with a curveball that has good shape and flashed plus potential as an amateur. The pitch could take big steps forward with some of the first real pitching instruction of his life.

BEST PRO DEBUT: Dixon could wind up being a steal in the 25th round after hitting .329/.417/.425 in his debut in the Rookie-level Gulf Coast League. His tools were enough to make him a talent worthy of the top 10 rounds, but scouts wondered about his contact rate. So far, so good.

MOST INTRIGUING BACKGROUND: The Pirates drafted a number of players with athletic bloodlines and family ties, including OF Blake Sabol (7), who is cousins with former Steelers safety Troy Polamalu and C Eli Wilson (16), who is the son of 14-year big leaguer Dan Wilson. 2B Josh Bissonette's (31) father Matt is a bass player who has performed with David Lee Roth and Ringo Starr and currently plays with Elton John.

CLOSEST TO THE MAJORS: Priester and Triolo are two of the most advanced players in the class, though Roberts or Flowers could move quickly if they were pushed to a reliever role.

BEST LATE-ROUND PICK: Dixon has a solid case for this selection thanks to his previously mentioned accolades, as does OF Deion Walker (35), whom the Pirates signed for $200,000 late on Day 3. Walker is 6-foot-4, 180 pounds and impacts the ball with long levers and some feel for the barrel.

THE ONE WHO GOT AWAY: 1B Will Simpson (18) had hitting qualities that the Pirates appreciated, but he'll make it to campus at Washington, where he flipped his commitment after originally being a Washington State commit. RHP Dawson McCarville (30) is a strong strike-thrower who will go from junior college to Grand Canyon for his junior season.

— CARLOS COLLAZO

TOP DRAFT PICKS OF THE DECADE

Year	Player, Pos	2019 Org
2010	Jameson Taillon, RHP	Pirates
2011	Gerrit Cole, RHP	Astros
2012	*Mark Appel, RHP	Did not play
2013	Austin Meadows, OF	Rays
2014	Cole Tucker, SS	Pirates
2015	Kevin Newman, SS	Pirates
2016	Will Craig, 3B	Pirates
2017	Shane Baz, RHP	Rays
2018	Travis Swaggerty, OF	Pirates
2019	Quinn Priester, RHP	Pirates

* Did not sign

2018

The class didn't set the minors alight in 2019. OF Travis Swaggerty (1) was solid at high Class A, while prep RHPs Braxton Ashcraft (2) and Michael Burrows (11) showed their potential.

GRADE: C

2017

RHP Shane Baz (1) was a key part of the Chris Archer trade and turned in a strong season in his first year with the Rays. RHP Cody Bolton (6) and 1B Mason Martin (17) are impressive finds later in the draft.

GRADE: B

2016

It was a tough year for this class. 1B Will Craig (1) scuffled at Triple-A and RHP Travis MacGregor (2) missed the year due to injury. RHP Geoff Hartlieb (29) made his MLB debut in the bullpen, however.

GRADE: C

1 MITCH KELLER, RHP

Born: April 4, 1996. **B-T:** R-R. **HT:** 6-2. **WT:** 210.
Drafted: HS—Cedar Rapids, Iowa, 2014 (2nd round).
Signed by: Matt Bimeal.

TRACK RECORD: Keller is the latest pitcher to top the Pirates' system, joining the likes of Gerrit Cole, Jameson Taillon and Tyler Glasnow. Keller has flashed the pure stuff to be a top-of-the-rotation starter, though the Pirates haven't gotten those results consistently from the previous group. Keller's chances might be better. He will work with a new big league pitching coach and likely a more updated organizational pitching philosophy, which has held Pirates pitching prospects back in recent years. Keller made his big league debut in 2019 and has already started to abandon the Pirates' penchant for heavy fastball usage. He ran up a 7.13 ERA over 48 innings in his debut, but he put a late emphasis on his slider and curveball and saw an uptick in strikeouts.

SCOUTING REPORT: Velocity has been Keller's calling card since hitting 94 mph in the Rookie-level Gulf Coast League out of high school. He has since increased that velocity to sit 94-96 with sink down in the zone and has touched 99. He improved the control and command of his fastball after a mechanical adjustment in 2015 but has seen his control regress the last two seasons. His curveball has long looked like a plus pitch, with sharp 12-to-6 movement that leads to strikeouts and grounders. He added a slider last year, which is quickly looking like a plus offering with a 26.8 percent swinging strike rate. It was his second most-used pitch in the majors and was used more than his curveball in all but three starts at the end of the season. The slider was developed because of issues with Keller's changeup, which flashes average with fade but has largely been inconsistent and ineffective. He has big stuff and throws strikes, but he often gets too much of the plate and struggles with sequencing.

THE FUTURE: The Pirates plan for Keller to be a critical part of their rotation, whether their plan is to win now or rebuild. If his slider is as good as it appeared in 2019, then a high strikeout rate should remain. If he can maintain the strikeout and walk rates and fine-tune his command, he should provide the Pirates with a mid- or front-of-the-rotation starter. He will open 2020 in the majors.

MIKE JANES/FOUR SEAM

BA GRADE

55 **Risk: Medium**

SCOUTING GRADES

Fastball: 70. **CB:** 60. **SL:** 60. **CHG:** 45. **Control:** 55.

Projected future grades on 20-80 scouting scale.

TOP PROSPECTS OF THE DECADE

Year	Player, Pos	2019 Org
2010	Pedro Alvarez, 3B	Did not play
2011	Jameson Taillon, RHP	Pirates
2012	Gerrit Cole, RHP	Astros
2013	Gerrit Cole, RHP	Astros
2014	Gregory Polanco, OF	Pirates
2015	Tyler Glasnow, RHP	Rays
2016	Tyler Glasnow, RHP	Rays
2017	Austin Meadows, OF	Rays
2018	Mitch Keller, RHP	Pirates
2019	Mitch Keller, RHP	Pirates

BEST TOOLS

Best Hitter for Average	Ji-Hwan Bae
Best Power Hitter	Oneil Cruz
Best Strike-Zone Discipline	Ke'Bryan Hayes
Fastest Baserunner	Jasiah Dixon
Best Athlete	Oneil Cruz
Best Fastball	Tahnaj Thomas
Best Curveball	Mitch Keller
Best Slider	Mitch Keller
Best Changeup	James Marvel
Best Control	Brad Case
Best Defensive Catcher	Christian Kelley
Best Defensive Infielder	Ke'Bryan Hayes
Best Infield Arm	Oneil Cruz
Best Defensive Outfielder	Jared Oliva
Best Outfield Arm	Travis Swaggerty

Year	Age	Club (League)	Class	W	L	ERA	G	GS	SV	IP	H	HR	BB	SO	K/9	WHIP	AVG
2017	21	West Virginia (NYP)	SS	0	0	0.00	2	2	0	4	2	0	1	7	15.8	0.75	.143
	21	Bradenton (FSL)	HiA	6	3	3.14	15	15	0	77	57	5	20	64	7.4	1.00	.207
	21	Altoona (EL)	AA	2	2	3.12	6	6	0	35	25	2	11	45	11.7	1.04	.197
2018	22	Altoona (EL)	AA	9	2	2.72	14	14	0	86	64	7	32	76	8.0	1.12	.208
	22	Bradenton (FSL)	HiA	0	0	2.25	1	1	0	4	7	0	1	2	4.5	2.00	.389
	22	Indianapolis (IL)	AAA	3	2	4.82	10	10	0	52	59	3	22	57	9.8	1.55	.280
2019	23	Indianapolis (IL)	AAA	7	5	3.56	19	19	0	104	94	9	35	123	10.7	1.24	.243
	23	Pittsburgh (NL)	MAJ	1	5	7.13	11	11	0	48	72	6	16	65	12.2	1.83	.348
Major League Totals				1	5	7.13	11	11	0	48	72	6	16	65	12.2	1.83	.348
Minor League Totals				36	22	3.12	106	105	0	539	453	31	170	566	9.4	1.16	.228

2 KE'BRYAN HAYES, 3B

BA GRADE
55 Risk: Medium

Born: Jan. 28, 1997. **B-T:** R-R. **HT:** 6-1. **WT:** 210. **Drafted:** HS—Tomball, Texas, 2015 (1st round). **Signed by:** Tyler Stohr.

TRACK RECORD: Ke'Bryan's father Charlie Hayes spent 14 years in the majors at third base, including one with the Pirates. Ke'Bryan has been one of the best defenders at the position in the minors since the Pirates drafted him 32nd overall in 2015. His offense has caught up in recent years, capped by a .265 average and a career-high 10 home runs at Triple-A Indianapolis in 2019.

SCOUTING REPORT: Hayes' plus-plus defense is his obvious carrying tool. He has multi-Gold Glove potential at third base thanks to smooth hands, quick reaction times, good routes to the ball and a plus arm. He is athletic enough to play shortstop in a pinch as well. Hayes shows plus hitting ability with a smooth, quick swing, natural lift and a patient approach. He has improved his power the last two years after recovering from a cracked rib at the end of 2016, which led to significant weight loss in 2017. Hayes regained the weight and muscle and added more in the process. He lost some speed, but he's still an above-average runner who is smart on the bases and capable of stealing double-digit bags each year.

THE FUTURE: Hayes has the foundation of an everyday third baseman with his hitting ability, defense and baserunning tools. His ceiling will depend on how much his power improves.

SCOUTING GRADES: **Hitting:** 55 **Power:** 50 **Running:** 55 **Fielding:** 70 **Arm:** 60

Year	Age	Club (League)	Class	AVG	G	AB	R	H	2B	3B	HR	RBI	BB	SO	SB	OBP	SLG
2017	20	Bradenton (FSL)	HiA	.278	108	421	66	117	16	7	2	43	41	76	27	.345	.363
2018	21	Altoona (EL)	AA	.293	117	437	64	128	31	7	7	47	57	84	12	.375	.444
2019	22	West Virginia (NYP)	SS	.111	3	9	1	1	1	0	0	2	2	2	1	.250	.222
	22	Indianapolis (IL)	AAA	.265	110	427	64	113	30	2	10	53	43	90	12	.336	.415
Minor League Totals				.279	461	1731	254	483	96	18	25	202	188	335	66	.354	.399

3 ONEIL CRUZ, SS

BA GRADE
60 Risk: High

Born: Oct. 4, 1998. **B-T:** L-R. **HT:** 6-7. **WT:** 202. **Signed:** Dominican Republic, 2015. **Signed by:** Patrick Guerrero/Franklin Taveras/Bob Engle (Dodgers).

TRACK RECORD: The Dodgers originally signed Cruz for $950,000 in 2015. The Pirates were interested in Cruz at the time and ended up getting him two years later for Tony Watson at the trade deadline. He broke out with mesmerizing power displays at low Class A West Virginia in 2018 and overcame a right foot fracture to reach Double-A in 2019.

SCOUTING REPORT: Cruz has a lot of solid tools to work with and the highest ceiling of anyone in the Pirates' system, though he also is the hardest to project. At 6-foot-7, Cruz is unusually tall for shortstop, though he is a plus runner with surprising dexterity to play the position. Scouts are mixed on whether he will stick at shortstop, with the safer projection being right field with his plus arm strength. Cruz's bat has fueled his rise and will be what determines his future. His hand strength and long levers give him massive raw power that some scouts grade as an 80, though with his long limbs come natural holes in his swing that lead to strikeouts. His approach is inconsistent as well.

THE FUTURE: Cruz will likely return to Double-A to start the 2020 season. With the right strides as a hitter, he should be batting in the middle of the Pirates' lineup by 2021.

SCOUTING GRADES: **Hitting:** 50 **Power:** 70 **Running:** 60 **Fielding:** 50 **Arm:** 60

Year	Age	Club (League)	Class	AVG	G	AB	R	H	2B	3B	HR	RBI	BB	SO	SB	OBP	SLG
2017	18	Great Lakes (MWL)	LoA	.240	89	342	51	82	9	1	8	36	28	110	8	.293	.342
	18	West Virginia (SAL)	LoA	.218	16	55	9	12	2	1	2	8	8	22	0	.317	.400
2018	19	West Virginia (SAL)	LoA	.286	103	402	66	115	25	7	14	59	34	100	11	.343	.488
2019	20	Pirates (GCL)	R	.600	3	10	0	6	1	0	0	1	1	1	1	.636	.700
	20	Bradenton (FSL)	HiA	.301	35	136	21	41	6	1	7	16	8	38	7	.345	.515
	20	Altoona (EL)	AA	.269	35	119	14	32	8	3	1	17	15	35	3	.346	.412
Minor League Totals				.274	336	1251	189	343	69	18	32	160	116	350	41	.335	.435

4 CODY BOLTON, RHP

Born: June 19, 1998. **B-T:** R-R. **HT:** 6-3. **WT:** 185. **Drafted:** HS—Tracy, Calif., 2017 (6th round). **Signed by:** Mike Sansoe.

TRACK RECORD: The Pirates signed Bolton for $300,000 in the sixth round in 2017 and he has since emerged as one of their top pitching prospects thanks to rapid improvements with his velocity and control. He was shut down with forearm soreness at the end of 2018 and received a platelet-rich plasma injection. He stayed healthy in 2019 and reached Double-A Altoona while pitching with an innings limit.

SCOUTING REPORT: Bolton sits 93-96 mph and touches 97 with sink on his four-seam fastball. He has worked with his two-seam fastball more in the last year and keeps it down in the zone in the low 90s. Bolton added an above-average, hard cutter in 2019 to pair with his two-seamer and has worked on his average changeup to make it an effective complement to his four-seam fastball. Both secondary pitches need improvement to ensure he can remain in the rotation. He could also benefit from a slower pitch in the low 80s, because everything now is thrown hard. Bolton has had issues keeping the ball in the park, but his command should improve along with his secondary pitches.

THE FUTURE: Bolton could move quickly through the system as a power reliever, but his starter upside will keep him in the rotation for now. He should return to Altoona to start 2020.

BA GRADE
50 Risk: High

SCOUTING GRADES: **Fastball:** 60 **Cutter:** 55 **Changeup:** 50 **Control:** 55

Year	Age	Club (League)	Class	W	L	ERA	G	GS	SV	IP	H	HR	BB	SO	K/9	WHIP	AVG
2017	19	Pirates (GCL)	R	0	2	3.16	9	9	0	26	23	1	8	22	7.7	1.21	.240
2018	20	West Virginia (SAL)	LoA	3	3	3.65	9	9	0	44	43	6	7	45	9.1	1.13	.253
2019	21	Bradenton (FSL)	HiA	6	3	1.61	12	12	0	62	39	1	14	69	10.1	0.86	.174
	21	Altoona (EL)	AA	2	3	5.85	9	9	0	40	37	6	16	33	7.4	1.33	.248
Minor League Totals				11	11	3.36	39	39	0	171	142	14	45	169	8.9	1.09	.222

5 TAHNAJ THOMAS, RHP

Born: June 16, 1999. **B-T:** R-R. **HT:** 6-4. **WT:** 190. **Signed:** Bahamas, 2016. **Signed by:** Koby Perez (Indians).

TRACK RECORD: Thomas trained as a shortstop in the Bahamas before moving to the mound when he turned pro with the Indians. The Pirates traded Jordan Luplow and Max Moroff to Cleveland after the 2018 season in a deal centered around shortstop Erik Gonzalez, but Thomas looks like the biggest talent in the trade. He had minor shoulder injury in spring training, but made slight mechanical changes to clean up his delivery and began throwing harder with better control. He finished eighth in the Rookie-level Appalachian League with 59 strikeouts.

ZACHARY LUCY

BA GRADE
55 Risk: Extreme

SCOUTING REPORT: Thomas saw his fastball go from sitting 92-95 mph at the time of the trade to 95-99 by the end of the 2019. He reached as high as 101 mph. Thomas also worked to improve his control, throwing more strikes with the improved velocity and showing average strike-throwing potential overall. His slider started to look like a potentially above-average, swing-and-miss pitch, though there is room for improvement. His fringe-average changeup will need to improve.

THE FUTURE: Thomas' velocity and slider upside give him a path to be a dominant reliever in the majors, but the 20-year-old has plenty of upside in the rotation and should remain in that role going forward. He will head to low Class A Greensboro in 2020 to make his full-season debut.

SCOUTING GRADES: **Fastball:** 70 **Slider:** 55 **Changeup:** 45 **Control:** 50

Year	Age	Club (League)	Class	W	L	ERA	G	GS	SV	IP	H	HR	BB	SO	K/9	WHIP	AVG
2017	18	Indians (DSL)	R	0	2	3.38	3	3	0	5	3	0	8	5	8.4	2.06	.167
	18	Indians (AZL)	R	0	3	6.00	13	10	0	33	35	4	25	29	7.9	1.82	.282
2018	19	Indians 1 (AZL)	R	0	0	4.58	8	6	0	20	13	2	10	27	12.4	1.17	.188
2019	20	Bristol (APP)	R	2	3	3.17	12	12	0	48	40	5	14	59	11.0	1.12	.217
Minor League Totals				2	8	4.32	36	31	0	106	91	11	57	120	10.2	1.39	.230

6 QUINN PRIESTER, RHP

Born: Sept. 15, 2000. **B-T:** R-R. **HT:** 6-3. **WT:** 195. **Drafted:** HS—Cary, Ill., 2019 (1st round). **Signed by:** Anthony Wycklendt.

MIKE JANES/FOUR SEAM IMAGES

BA GRADE
55 **Risk: Extreme**

TRACK RECORD: Priester was one of the top prep pitchers in the 2019 draft and passed up a commitment to Texas Christian after the Pirates drafted him 18th overall and signed him for $3.4 million. He didn't have a pitching coach as an amateur, with a lot of his development self-taught from watching other pitchers on YouTube. He took it upon himself to add strength to his lower half prior to 2019, resulting in added velocity.

SCOUTING REPORT: In addition to his high aptitude for the game, Priester has the stuff to be a high-end starter. His four-seam fastball can get up to 97 mph with a smooth delivery from a three-quarters arm slot. He has more command of his four-seamer but more movement on his low-90s two-seamer. Priester's curveball is his best offering at the moment and a future plus pitch. He can both land it for strikes and generate swings and misses thanks to good shape and deception. His changeup is a work in progress, but he has a grip he likes and is gradually getting a better feel for it. His smooth delivery portends future above-average control.

THE FUTURE: Priester is advanced enough that he could move up to low Class A Greensboro in 2020. His physicality, stuff and aptitude give him a chance to move quicker than a typical high school pitcher.

SCOUTING GRADES: **Fastball:** 60 **Curveball:** 60 **Changeup:** 50 **Control:** 55

Year	Age	Club (League)	Class	W	L	ERA	G	GS	SV	IP	H	HR	BB	SO	K/9	WHIP	AVG
2019	18	Pirates (GCL)	R	1	1	3.03	8	7	0	33	29	1	10	37	10.2	1.19	.238
	18	West Virginia (NYP)	SS	0	0	4.50	1	1	0	4	3	0	4	4	9.0	1.75	.214
Minor League Totals				1	1	3.19	9	8	0	36	32	1	14	41	10.1	1.25	.235

7 JI-HWAN BAE, SS

Born: July 26, 1999. **B-T:** L-R. **HT:** 6-1. **WT:** 170. **Signed:** South Korea, 2018. **Signed by:** Fu-chun Chiang/Tony Harris.

JAK KERLEY

BA GRADE
50 **Risk: High**

TRACK RECORD: The Braves originally agreed to sign Bae for $300,000 late in 2017, but Major League Baseball rejected the deal as part of the punishment handed out for Atlanta's international signing scandal. The Pirates signed him four months later for $1.25 million. Bae was convicted of assaulting his girlfriend in South Korea and served a 30-game suspension during the 2019 season. He returned to low Class A Greensboro in May and won the South Atlantic League batting title with a .323 average.

SCOUTING REPORT: Bae is a speedy contact hitter who projects to hit at either the top or bottom of a lineup. He is a slap hitter with power to the gaps, and his 80-grade speed helps him take plenty of extra bases. Bae has yet to homer in 121 career games and doesn't project to ever have much home run power, but he hits enough doubles and triples to post respectable slugging percentages. Bae has the athleticism and range to be an above-average defender at shortstop, though a fringe-average, inaccurate arm raises questions about his ability to stick there. There are obvious makeup concerns after his assault conviction.

THE FUTURE: Bae profiles as a future top-of-the-order hitter with speed and on-base ability. His development as a shortstop will be key to watch in 2020.

SCOUTING GRADES: **Hitting:** 60 **Power:** 30 **Running:** 80 **Fielding:** 55 **Arm:** 45

Year	Age	Club (League)	Class	AVG	G	AB	R	H	2B	3B	HR	RBI	BB	SO	SB	OBP	SLG
2018	18	Pirates (GCL)	R	.271	35	129	24	35	6	2	0	13	15	16	10	.362	.349
2019	19	Greensboro (SAL)	LoA	.323	86	328	69	106	25	5	0	38	43	77	31	.403	.430
Minor League Totals				.309	121	457	93	141	31	7	0	51	58	93	41	.391	.407

8 SAMMY SIANI, OF

TOM DIPACE

BA GRADE
55 **Risk: Extreme**

Born: Dec. 14, 2000. **B-T:** L-L. **HT:** 6-0. **WT:** 195. **Drafted:** HS—Philadelphia, 2019 (1st round supplemental). **Signed by:** Dan Radcliff.

TRACK RECORD: Siani followed his older brother Mike as a top draft prospect out of Philadelphia's Penn Charter School. The Reds drafted Mike Siani in the fourth round in 2018, and the Pirates made Sammy the 37th overall pick one year later. He signed for $2.15 million to forgo a Duke commitment.

SCOUTING REPORT: Siani is a solid all-around player who does nearly everything well. He has an easy swing from the left side with extra-base power that could improve to average home run power. He manages the strike zone and has a knack for getting on base. Siani has some swing-and-miss to his game right now, but he has the tools to hit .270 or better down the road. Siani has plus speed and could stick in center field, but his below-average arm is an issue. The Pirates moved him around to all three outfield spots in his debut to see where he fits best.

THE FUTURE: Siani's career could go a number of ways depending on his power and defensive development. Whether he becomes a top-of-the-order center fielder or a power-hitting left fielder, the Pirates believe there is enough of a foundation for him to become an everyday regular.

SCOUTING GRADES: **Hitting:** 55 **Power:** 50 **Running:** 60 **Fielding:** 55 **Arm:** 40

Year	Age	Club (League)	Class	AVG	G	AB	R	H	2B	3B	HR	RBI	BB	SO	SB	OBP	SLG
2019	18	Pirates (GCL)	R	.241	39	133	21	32	3	3	0	9	26	41	5	.372	.308
Minor League Totals				.241	39	133	21	32	3	3	0	9	26	41	5	.372	.308

9 TRAVIS SWAGGERTY, OF

BA GRADE
50 **Risk: High**

Born: Aug. 19, 1997. **B-T:** L-L. **HT:** 5-11. **WT:** 180. **Drafted:** South Alabama, 2018 (1st round). **Signed by:** Darren Mazeroski.

TRACK RECORD: Swaggerty emerged as a top draft prospect in 2018 after showing promising a power-speed combo at South Alabama, but some scouts had concerns after he hit just .296 playing against mid-major competition. The Pirates drafted Swaggerty 10th overall and signed him for $4.4 million. He showed bits of power and speed at high Class A Bradenton in his first full season, but he underwhelmed with his contact skills.

SCOUTING REPORT: Swaggerty flashes average or better tools across the board, but he too often falls into the trap of selling out for power and swings and misses too often. Swaggerty's power is only average, and he is at his best when he tones it down and focuses on making contact. Swaggerty hit just .219 with a 25-percent strikeout rate through June, but he recovered to bat .328 with an 18-percent strikeout rate the rest of the season, showing the bat-to-ball skills the Pirates believe is present when he takes the right approach. Swaggerty is an above-average defensive center fielder with an above-average arm and should stick at the position. He also is a plus runner capable of stealing 20-plus bases a year.

THE FUTURE: Swaggerty hasn't lived up to his draft slot, with his contact issues holding him back. He will try to carry his second-half improvement into 2020 with Double-A Altoona.

SCOUTING GRADES: **Hitting:** 50 **Power:** 50 **Running:** 60 **Fielding:** 55 **Arm:** 55

Year	Age	Club (League)	Class	AVG	G	AB	R	H	2B	3B	HR	RBI	BB	SO	SB	OBP	SLG
2018	20	West Virginia (NYP)	SS	.288	36	139	22	40	9	1	4	15	15	40	9	.365	.453
	20	West Virginia (SAL)	LoA	.129	16	62	6	8	1	1	1	5	7	18	0	.225	.226
2019	21	Bradenton (FSL)	HiA	.265	121	457	79	121	20	3	9	40	57	116	23	.347	.381
Minor League Totals				.257	173	658	107	169	30	5	14	60	79	174	32	.339	.381

10 BRAXTON ASHCRAFT, RHP

BA GRADE
50 Risk: Very High

Born: Oct. 5, 1999. **B-T:** L-R. **HT:** 6-5. **WT:** 195. **Drafted:** HS—Robinson, Texas, 2018 (2nd round). **Signed by:** Phil Huttmann.

TRACK RECORD: The Pirates signed Ashcraft for $1.825 million in 2018 to break his commitment to Baylor. It was the third-highest bonus in franchise history for a player drafted after the first round. The young righty struggled to a 5.77 ERA with short-season West Virginia in 2019, but he handled himself well in a college-heavy league.

SCOUTING REPORT: Ashcraft is a tall, projectable righthander with loads of athleticism. He was a star wide receiver in high school and touched 95 mph on the mound his senior year. His velocity dipped into the upper 80s after he signed, but he jumped back into the low-to-mid-90s at West Virginia. He has the loose, projectable frame to project to grow into even more velocity. Ashcraft's upper-70s slider is a slurvy offering that has a long way to go, but he shows feel to spin and could make it an average offering as he adds power and shape. He has feel for an average, low-80s changeup. Like many tall pitchers, the 6-foot-5 Ashcraft has struggled with his control at times. His athleticism provides optimism he will grow into average control.

THE FUTURE: Ashcraft offers a lot to dream on, but his growth will take time. Low Class A Greensboro is next in 2020.

SCOUTING GRADES: Fastball: 60 | Slider: 50 | Changeup: 50 | Control: 50

Year	Age	Club (League)	Class	W	L	ERA	G	GS	SV	IP	H	HR	BB	SO	K/9	WHIP	AVG
2018	18	Pirates (GCL)	R	0	1	4.58	5	5	0	18	16	2	5	12	6.1	1.19	.242
2019	19	West Virginia (NYP)	SS	1	9	5.77	11	11	0	53	49	4	22	39	6.6	1.34	.239
Minor League Totals				1	10	5.48	16	16	0	70	65	6	27	51	6.5	1.30	.240

11 MICHAEL BURROWS, RHP

BA GRADE
50 Risk: Very High

Born: Nov. 8, 1999. **B-T:** R-R. **HT:** 6-2. **WT:** 185. **Drafted:** HS—Waterford, Conn., 2018 (11th round). **Signed by:** Eddie Charles.

TRACK RECORD: The Pirates made Burrows their 11th-round pick in 2018 and signed him away from Connecticut for an above-slot $500,000 signing bonus. Burrows quickly established he was more advanced than the typical Northeast prep arm. The Pirates typically send their drafted high school pitchers to the Rookie-level Appalachian League for their first season, but Burrows impressed enough in extended spring training to make the jump to the college-heavy New York-Penn League.

SCOUTING REPORT: Burrows saw an increase in his fastball velocity, hitting 93-95 mph more consistently, after being in the low 90s in 2018. His fastball has good sink and he pairs it with a slider that features sharp, late break. Burrows lacked control at times, but his fastball/slider combination was good enough to get him 43 strikeouts in 43.2 innings with short-season West Virginia. He spent the year working on his changeup and developed more of a feel for the pitch throughout the season. There's not a lot of projection left for Burrows' frame, but he might not need it with his current velocity and how well his fastball and slider play off each other.

THE FUTURE: Burrows has the makings of a potential back-end starter. He can move closer to that goal in 2020 with improvements to his control and changeup.

Year	Age	Club (League)	Class	W	L	ERA	G	GS	SV	IP	H	HR	BB	SO	K/9	WHIP	AVG
2018	18	Pirates (GCL)	R	0	0	0.00	4	3	0	14	6	0	4	9	5.8	0.71	.133
2019	19	West Virginia (NYP)	SS	2	3	4.33	11	11	0	44	44	2	20	43	8.9	1.47	.262
Minor League Totals				2	3	3.28	15	14	0	57	50	2	24	52	8.1	1.28	.235

12 CALVIN MITCHELL, OF

BA GRADE
50 Risk: Very High

Born: March 8, 1999. **B-T:** L-L. **HT:** 6-0. **WT:** 206. **Drafted:** HS—San Diego, 2017 (2nd round). **Signed by:** Brian Tracy.

TRACK RECORD: There was a time during Mitchell's senior year in high school when he looked like a potential first-round pick. He struggled offensively his senior year, trying to pull the ball too often while adding too much swing-and-miss to his game. So far, that's been the story of his career.

SCOUTING REPORT: Mitchell has plus power potential and has shown it at times, including hitting 15 homers in the pitcher-friendly Florida State League in 2019. The power came with a spike in his strikeout rate to nearly 30 percent, while his walk rate dropped to 6.5 percent. Mitchell has the ability to hit to all fields and shows flashes of an advanced, patient approach, but he loses both of them when he tries to hit for power. Mitchell's bat is going to have to be his carrying tool. He's a below-average runner with an average arm, making left field the most likely position.

THE FUTURE: Mitchell has drawn comparisons to all-star hitters like Michael Brantley and Garret Anderson but only when he tamps down his approach and focuses on hard contact rather than power. He should go to Double-A in 2020 with the hope he can get the most from his bat away from the FSL.

Year	Age	Club (League)	Class	AVG	G	AB	R	H	2B	3B	HR	RBI	BB	SO	SB	OBP	SLG
2017	18	Pirates (GCL)	R	.245	43	159	17	39	11	0	2	20	24	35	2	.351	.352
2018	19	West Virginia (SAL)	LoA	.280	119	443	55	124	29	3	10	65	41	109	4	.344	.427
2019	20	Bradenton (FSL)	HiA	.251	118	451	54	113	21	2	15	64	32	142	1	.304	.406
Minor League Totals				.262	280	1053	126	276	61	5	27	149	97	286	7	.328	.406

13 MASON MARTIN, 1B

BA GRADE
50 **Risk: Very High**

Born: June 2, 1999. **B-T:** L-R. **HT:** 5-9. **WT:** 188. **Drafted:** HS—Kennewick, Wash., 2017 (17th round). **Signed by:** Max Kwan.

TRACK RECORD: An unheralded 17th-round pick in 2017, Martin was a big surprise in his pro debut when he set a GCL Pirates home run record with 11 in 127 at-bats. He struggled in his full-season debut the following year, but rediscovered his power stroke in 2019 and finished tied for fourth in the minors with 35 home runs while seeing time at both Class A levels. That total includes a day when he hit walk-off home runs in both ends of a doubleheader.

SCOUTING REPORT: Martin is a stout lefthanded masher with plus raw power and a patient approach, but he also strikes out at alarming rates. He can be too selective at times and passes on good pitches early in the count while waiting for a pitch he can crush. This frequently leads to long at-bats and a lot of pitches seen, but also unfavorable counts when he's at the mercy of the pitcher. Martin has worked on being more aggressive earlier in the count but hasn't completely solved the problem. He immediately moved to first base upon being drafted and will be solely reliant on his bat to carry him up the ladder. He's a below-average defender without much speed or athleticism

THE FUTURE: It's easy to dream of Martin hitting 30-plus home runs per year, but he needs time and a lot of work to get there. His approach will be key to watch in 2020.

Year	Age	Club (League)	Class	AVG	G	AB	R	H	2B	3B	HR	RBI	BB	SO	SB	OBP	SLG
2017	18	Pirates (GCL)	R	.307	39	127	37	39	8	0	11	22	32	41	2	.457	.630
2018	19	West Virginia (SAL)	LoA	.200	45	150	16	30	8	0	4	18	18	62	1	.302	.333
	19	Bristol (APP)	R	.233	59	223	42	52	10	1	10	40	42	87	2	.357	.422
2019	20	Greensboro (SAL)	LoA	.262	82	301	58	79	19	3	23	83	46	103	8	.361	.575
	20	Bradenton (FSL)	HiA	.239	49	176	32	42	13	1	12	46	22	65	0	.333	.528
Minor League Totals				.248	274	977	185	242	58	5	60	209	160	358	13	.360	.502

14 ALEXANDER MOJICA, 3B

BA GRADE
50 **Risk: Extreme**

Born: Aug. 2, 2002. **B-T:** R-R. **HT:** 6-1. **WT:** 195. **Signed:** Dominican Republic, 2018. **Signed by:** Victor Santana.

TRACK RECORD: Mojica celebrated his 16th birthday in 2018 by signing with the Pirates for $390,000. One of the youngest players in his class, Mojica spent most of his first season in the Dominican Summer League as a 16-year-old but was also one of the league's best hitters. Mojica ranked second in the DSL in OPS, ranked fifth in on-base percentage and third in slugging.

SCOUTING REPORT: Mojica has the upside to hit in the middle of a lineup. He has a sound swing with a good path through the hitting zone. He shows good plate discipline for his age, walking more than he struck out in his first season. That helped him get on base at a high clip and helped his plus power translate to games. Mojica has a big frame, but as long as he maintains his conditioning and mobility, he has the attributes to stay at third base, where he has good hands and a plus arm.

THE FUTURE: Mojica has emerged as the Pirates' prized signing from their 2018 international class with a chance to be an impact bat, albeit with significant risk because of how far he is from the majors. He will make his U.S. debut in 2020, likely in the Rookie-level Gulf Coast League.

Year	Age	Club (League)	Class	AVG	G	AB	R	H	2B	3B	HR	RBI	BB	SO	SB	OBP	SLG
2019	16	Pirates2 (DSL)	R	.351	55	174	37	61	14	1	8	46	37	34	2	.468	.580
Minor League Totals				.351	55	174	37	61	14	1	8	46	37	34	2	.468	.580

15 TRAVIS MACGREGOR, RHP

BA GRADE
50 Risk: Extreme

Born: Oct. 15, 1997. **B-T:** R-R. **HT:** 6-3. **WT:** 180. **Drafted:** HS—Tarpon Springs, Fla., 2016 (2nd round). **Signed by:** Nick Presto.

TRACK RECORD: After three years in rookie ball, MacGregor finally appeared to make progress with a solid season at low Class A West Virginia in 2018 before having Tommy John surgery late in the year. He missed the entire 2019 season rehabbing from the procedure.

SCOUTING REPORT: MacGregor has a tall, skinny frame which provided a lot of moving parts for his delivery when he entered pro ball. He quieted the delivery down after working on an adjustment with pitching coach Joel Hanrahan in 2018. That fix led to better control, along with a velocity increase that saw MacGregor throwing in the low-to-mid-90s prior to surgery. He also added a slider to give himself a sharper breaking ball instead of his loopy curveball. MacGregor saw an increase in strikeouts in 2018, but most of that came from the fastball and wasn't a sign of early success from the new slider. He has a feel for a changeup, giving him the makings of a three-pitch mix needed to project as a starter.

THE FUTURE: MacGregor is set to return with high Class A Bradenton in 2020. He'll need to maintain the developments that led to better control and velocity from the fastball, while trying to turn his slider into an out pitch.

Year	Age	Club (League)	Class	W	L	ERA	G	GS	SV	IP	H	HR	BB	SO	K/9	WHIP	AVG
2017	19	Bristol (APP)	R	1	4	7.84	12	12	0	41	61	3	20	32	7.0	1.96	.339
2018	20	Pirates (GCL)	R	0	0	2.57	2	2	0	7	6	1	1	6	7.7	1.00	.222
	20	West Virginia (SAL)	LoA	1	4	3.25	15	15	0	64	58	7	21	74	10.5	1.24	.239
2019	21	Did not play—Injured															
Minor League Totals				3	9	4.51	38	38	0	143	154	12	52	131	8.2	1.43	.272

16 JT BRUBAKER, RHP

BA GRADE
45 Risk: High

Born: Nov. 17, 1993. **B-T:** R-R. **HT:** 6-3. **WT:** 185. **Drafted:** Akron, 2015 (6th round). **Signed by:** Trevor Haley.

TRACK RECORD: Brubaker entered the 2019 season expecting to be one of the Pirates' first callups to the rotation, but injuries got in the way. After opening the year strong at Triple-A Indianapolis, he missed two months with a forearm strain and then was shut down for the year with right elbow irritation after two rehab starts.

SCOUTING REPORT: Brubaker has a big, sturdy frame that allows him to eat innings as a starter. He progressively ramped up his fastball velocity to the point it now touches 99 mph. He also added a hard cutter in 2018 that increased his strikeout rate and made him very tough against righthanded hitters. Brubaker has struggled against lefties at times and will need a better changeup to stick as a starter. It currently is a fringe-average pitch that is often too firm.

THE FUTURE: Brubaker projects to be healthy for the start of the 2020 season and should enter the season once again as a top depth option. His fastball and cutter could work wonders out of the bullpen and give him a chance to eventually pitch in late relief if needed.

Year	Age	Club (League)	Class	W	L	ERA	G	GS	SV	IP	H	HR	BB	SO	K/9	WHIP	AVG
2017	23	Altoona (EL)	AA	7	6	4.44	26	24	0	130	150	9	45	109	7.6	1.50	.291
2018	24	Altoona (EL)	AA	2	2	1.80	6	6	0	35	29	1	8	35	9.0	1.06	.218
	24	Indianapolis (IL)	AAA	8	4	3.10	22	22	0	119	121	7	36	96	7.3	1.32	.268
2019	25	Indianapolis (IL)	AAA	2	1	2.57	4	4	0	21	19	2	4	20	8.6	1.10	.241
	25	West Virginia (NYP)	SS	0	0	1.35	2	2	0	7	5	0	4	4	5.4	1.35	.217
Minor League Totals				31	28	3.60	101	99	0	514	514	37	155	433	7.6	1.30	.262

17 NICK MEARS, RHP

BA GRADE
45 Risk: High

Born: Oct. 7, 1996. **B-T:** R-R. **HT:** 6-3. **WT:** 215. **Signed:** Sacramento JC, 2018 (NDFA). **Signed by:** Mike Sansoe.

TRACK RECORD: Mears went from an undrafted pitcher signed as an injury replacement to a legitimate relief prospect in the span of a year. The 6-foot-3 righthander added 30 pounds to his frame following the 2018 season and saw his velocity spike. The Pirates moved him all the way up to Double-A in his first full season, then sent him to the Arizona Fall League, where he finished the season with 8.2 shutout innings.

SCOUTING REPORT: Mears' added weight led to an increase in velocity. His fastball now sits 96-98 mph most nights and touches as high as 101. Mears likes to throw his fastball high in the zone, and it was the primary pitch that helped him notch 50 strikeouts in 35 innings. His control also improved as the year went on. In the past, Mears has paired his fastball with a slider, which wasn't an effective pitch. He's since been working on a 1-to-7 curveball, aimed at playing off his high fastball with a north-south approach.

THE FUTURE: The velocity and control improvements have Mears looking like a potential late-inning reliever. A better breaking pitch could cement his future status in a big league bullpen.

Year	Age	Club (League)	Class	W	L	ERA	G	GS	SV	IP	H	HR	BB	SO	K/9	WHIP	AVG
2018	21	West Virginia (NYP)	SS	0	0	0.00	3	0	0	4	1	0	1	8	18.0	0.50	.077
2019	22	Greensboro (SAL)	LoA	1	1	3.09	7	0	0	12	5	2	7	19	14.7	1.03	.128
	22	Bradenton (FSL)	HiA	4	2	3.60	23	0	5	30	22	3	9	43	12.9	1.03	.202
	22	Altoona (EL)	AA	0	0	1.80	4	0	0	5	4	0	2	7	12.6	1.20	.211
Minor League Totals				5	3	3.02	37	0	5	50	32	5	19	77	13.7	1.01	.178

18 JARED OLIVA, OF

BA GRADE
45 Risk: High

Born: Nov. 27, 1995. **B-T:** R-R. **HT:** 6-2. **WT:** 203. **Drafted:** Arizona, 2017 (7th round). **Signed by:** Derrick Van Dusen.

TRACK RECORD: A walk-on turned starter at Arizona, Oliva became the Pirates' seventh-round pick in 2017 following a junior year that saw his offense rapidly improve. He has continued that upward trajectory in pro ball. After emerging as a prospect to watch in his first full season, Oliva moved to Double-A Altoona in 2019 and finished fourth in the Eastern League in hits (124) and second in stolen bases (36).

SCOUTING REPORT: Oliva does all the little things well to be a successful hitter. He commands the strike zone, controls the barrel, shortens his swing and puts the ball in play to take advantage of his plus speed. He takes efficient routes in center field with that plus speed and should have no problem sticking there, although his above-average arm will allow him to move around the outfield as needed. Oliva is a contact hitter with below-average game power, but he knows who he is and gets the most from his skill set.

THE FUTURE: Oliva profiles as an extra outfielder for most evaluators, but he has made a living out of exceeding expectations. he will head to Triple-A Indianapolis in 2020 with a big league callup in his sights.

Year	Age	Club (League)	Class	AVG	G	AB	R	H	2B	3B	HR	RBI	BB	SO	SB	OBP	SLG
2017	21	West Virginia (NYP)	SS	.266	56	222	30	59	10	7	0	17	17	57	15	.327	.374
2018	22	Bradenton (FSL)	HiA	.275	108	396	75	109	24	4	9	47	40	91	33	.354	.424
2019	23	Altoona (EL)	AA	.277	123	447	70	124	24	6	6	42	42	104	36	.352	.398
Minor League Totals				.274	287	1065	175	292	58	17	15	106	99	252	84	.348	.403

19 KEVIN KRAMER, 2B

BA GRADE
40 Risk: Medium

Born: Oct. 3, 1993. **B-T:** L-R. **HT:** 6-0. **WT:** 200. **Drafted:** UCLA, 2015 (2nd round). **Signed by:** Rick Allen.

TRACK RECORD: Kramer showed advanced hitting ability from the time the Pirates drafted him in the second round out of UCLA, and he generated extra excitement as he began to tap into his raw power in the upper minors. Kramer made his major league debut in 2018 and looked like a part of the club's plans for 2019, but instead he took a step back and spent most of the season at Triple-A Indianapolis.

SCOUTING REPORT: At his best, Kramer controls the strike zone and hits for average with a line-drive stroke that drives balls to the gaps. In 2019, however, his power went down and his strikeout numbers went up. He got 42 at-bats in the majors and struck out in 17 of them. Kramer offers some defensive versatility. He profiles best at second base with his smooth glove and above-average range, and he has enough ability that he can fill in at shortstop in a pinch. He also began seeing time at both corner outfield spots.

THE FUTURE: Kramer is now 26 and coming off a down year. He should serve as bench depth in 2020 and could work his way back into the second base mix with a rebound season at the plate.

Year	Age	Club (League)	Class	AVG	G	AB	R	H	2B	3B	HR	RBI	BB	SO	SB	OBP	SLG
2017	23	Altoona (EL)	AA	.297	53	202	31	60	17	3	6	27	17	50	7	.380	.500
	23	Pirates (GCL)	R	.000	1	2	0	0	0	0	0	1	0	1	0	.000	.000
	23	West Virginia (NYP)	SS	.231	3	13	1	3	0	0	0	2	0	2	1	.286	.231
2018	24	Indianapolis (IL)	AAA	.311	129	476	73	148	35	3	15	59	38	127	13	.365	.492
	24	Pittsburgh (NL)	MAJ	.135	21	37	5	5	0	0	0	4	2	20	0	.175	.135
2019	25	Indianapolis (IL)	AAA	.260	113	393	49	102	30	1	10	54	43	116	4	.335	.417
	25	Pittsburgh (NL)	MAJ	.167	22	42	5	7	1	0	0	5	6	17	0	.260	.190
Major League Totals				.152	43	79	10	12	1	0	0	9	8	37	0	.222	.165
Minor League Totals				.286	475	1757	253	502	120	13	35	220	176	395	40	.357	.429

20 SANTIAGO FLOREZ, RHP

BA GRADE
50 Risk: Extreme

Born: May 9, 2000. **B-T:** R-R. **HT:** 6-5. **WT:** 222. **Signed:** Colombia, 2016. **Signed by:** Rene Gayo, Orlando Covo & Jose Mosquera.

TRACK RECORD: The Pirates signed Florez for $150,000 out of Colombia as the top pitcher in their 2016 international signing class. They moved him step-by-step to each Rookie-ball affiliate after signing, and he

turned in a 3.46 ERA in 10 starts at Rookie-level Bristol in the Appalachian League in 2019.
SCOUTING REPORT: Florez already has a huge 6-foot-5, 222-pound frame, which has led to premium velocity early in his career. He already reaches the mid-90s with his fastball and even sat 95-97 mph during part of the 2019 season. Florez throws hard but needs to improve his control. He struck out just 36 and walked 21 in 43.2 innings at Bristol, largely because he couldn't control his fastball. Florez has made strides in other areas of his game. His changeup has developed into a usable pitch with average or better potential. He switched from a loopy curveball to a hard slider this year, but it's still a work in progress.
THE FUTURE: Florez's focus going forward will be improving his control and adding an out pitch. He may see low Class A Greensboro in 2020.

Year	Age	Club (League)	Class	W	L	ERA	G	GS	SV	IP	H	HR	BB	SO	K/9	WHIP	AVG
2017	17	Pirates (DSL)	R	2	5	4.56	14	14	0	53	43	2	38	30	5.1	1.52	.222
2018	18	Pirates (GCL)	R	5	2	4.15	10	10	0	43	37	0	23	35	7.3	1.38	.230
2019	19	Bristol (APP)	R	2	2	3.46	10	10	0	42	35	4	21	36	7.8	1.34	.226
Minor League Totals				9	9	4.10	34	34	0	138	115	6	82	101	6.6	1.42	.225

21 MAX KRANICK, RHP

BA GRADE
45 Risk: High

Born: July 21, 1997. **B-T:** R-R. **HT:** 6-3. **WT:** 200. **Drafted:** HS—Archbald, Pa., 2016 (11th round). **Signed by:** Dan Radcliff.

TRACK RECORD: Kranick fell to the Pirates in the 11th round in 2016 due to signability concerns, but signed for $300,000 to break his commitment to Virginia. After a stop-and-go start to his pro career, he reached high Class A Bradenton in 2019 and turned in a 3.79 ERA over 20 starts.
SCOUTING REPORT: Kranick has shown above-average control since turning pro and made improvements and adjustments to his pitch selection last season. After sitting in the low-90s with his fastball in 2018, he began sitting 94-96 mph and touching 97 in 2019. Kranick's fastball stands out, but his other pitches need work. He switched from a 12-to-6 curveball to a hard slider he typically throws in the mid-80s, though he will throw it harder at times with more cutter action. He also has a changeup he has flashed feel for since high school. Kranick used all three of his pitches by the end of the year and finished strong with a 2.95 ERA in his final 10 starts before reaching his innings limit.
THE FUTURE: Kranick shows the makings of a potential back-of-the-rotation starter with his improving fastball and sharp control. He'll need to improve his secondaries.

Year	Age	Club (League)	Class	W	L	ERA	G	GS	SV	IP	H	HR	BB	SO	K/9	WHIP	AVG
2017	19	Pirates (GCL)	R	0	0	0.00	3	3	0	13	12	0	4	9	6.4	1.26	.255
	19	Bristol (APP)	R	1	0	2.31	2	2	0	12	10	1	2	9	6.9	1.03	.233
2018	20	West Virginia (SAL)	LoA	4	5	3.81	17	16	1	78	72	7	18	77	8.9	1.15	.242
2019	21	Bradenton (FSL)	HiA	6	7	3.79	20	20	0	109	100	11	30	78	6.4	1.19	.246
Minor League Totals				12	14	3.34	51	47	1	245	225	20	58	194	7.1	1.16	.244

22 WILL CRAIG, 1B

Born: Nov. 6, 1994. **B-T:** R-R. **HT:** 6-3. **WT:** 235. **Drafted:** Wake Forest, 2016 (1st round). **Signed by:** Jerry Jordan.

TRACK RECORD: The Pirates drafted Craig with the 22nd overall pick in 2016 after he finished third in the nation in slugging percentage at Wake Forest, but things quickly went south in pro ball. He moved from third base to first base due to shoulder soreness and has yet to hit for average and power together. He hit a career-high 23 home runs at Triple-A Indianapolis in 2019, but also had a career-high 146 strikeouts.
SCOUTING REPORT: Craig alternately shows flashes of plus power or the ability to hit for average and get on base with a line-drive approach, but can't sync it up. When he hits for average, he shows little power. When he hits for power, his average and on-base percentage drop precipitously. He's emphasized power each of the last two years and shown average power and below-average hitting ability, which is not enough to project as an everyday regular at first base. Craig is a below-average runner and defender limited to first base, where he is solid-average.
THE FUTURE: Craig won't get a shot in Pittsburgh unless Josh Bell gets injured, and even then it would be a short-term fix. He'll return to Triple-A in 2020.

Year	Age	Club (League)	Class	AVG	G	AB	R	H	2B	3B	HR	RBI	BB	SO	SB	OBP	SLG
2017	22	Bradenton (FSL)	HiA	.271	123	458	59	124	26	1	6	61	62	106	1	.373	.371
2018	23	Altoona (EL)	AA	.248	132	480	73	119	30	3	20	102	42	128	6	.321	.448
2019	24	Indianapolis (IL)	AAA	.249	131	494	69	123	23	0	23	78	44	146	2	.326	.435
Minor League Totals				.259	449	1650	229	427	91	4	51	264	189	417	11	.350	.412

23 NICK BURDI, RHP

BA GRADE **50** Risk: Extreme

Born: Jan. 19, 1993. **B-T:** R-R. **HT:** 6-3. **WT:** 225. **Drafted:** Louisville, 2014 (2nd round). **Signed by:** Alan Sandberg (Twins).

TRACK RECORD: The Pirates acquired Burdi from the Phillies after the 2017 Rule 5 draft knowing he would miss most of 2018 recovering from Tommy John surgery. Burdi returned at the end of the season and opened 2019 in the Pirates bullpen, but in April he went down clutching his right biceps after a pitch. Burdi had thoracic outlet surgery and missed the rest of the year.

SCOUTING REPORT: Burdi brings a power arsenal in relief befitting a closer. His fastball sits 96-97 mph and has reached triple-digits, and he backs it up with a devastating hard slider in the 87-90 mph range. Burdi's command is imprecise and he occasionally leaves pitches over the plate, but his stuff is good enough to miss bats even when he makes mistakes. He struck out 42.5 percent of the batters he faced in his brief time in the majors last season, and that was with him still rounding into form.

THE FUTURE: Burdi will be under Rule 5 roster restrictions for the third straight year in 2020. Few pitchers successfully return from thoracic outlet surgery, but Burdi will try to beat the odds.

Year	Age	Club (League)	Class	W	L	ERA	G	GS	SV	IP	H	HR	BB	SO	K/9	WHIP	AVG
2017	24	Chattanooga (SL)	AA	2	0	0.53	14	0	1	17	9	1	4	20	10.6	0.76	.161
2018	25	Bradenton (FSL)	HiA	0	0	4.50	2	2	0	2	1	1	0	6	27.0	0.50	.143
	25	Altoona (EL)	AA	0	0	6.75	3	0	0	4	6	0	2	3	6.8	2.00	.375
	25	Indianapolis (IL)	AAA	0	2	5.40	5	0	0	5	9	0	4	5	9.0	2.60	.375
	25	Pittsburgh (NL)	MAJ	0	0	20.25	2	0	0	1	3	1	2	2	13.5	3.75	.375
2019	26	Pittsburgh (NL)	MAJ	2	1	9.35	11	0	0	9	11	1	3	17	17.7	1.62	.297
Major League Totals				2	1	10.80	13	0	0	10	14	2	5	19	17.1	1.90	.311
Minor League Totals				10	8	3.44	90	2	10	115	94	6	56	156	12.2	1.30	.225

24 OSVALDO BIDO, RHP

BA GRADE **45** Risk: High

Born: Oct. 18, 1995. **B-T:** R-R. **HT:** 6-3. **WT:** 175. **Signed:** Dominican Republic, 2017. **Signed by:** Juan Mercado.

TRACK RECORD: Bido got a late start to his pro career after signing with the Pirates for $20,000 as a 21-year-old in 2017. He made the jump to full-season ball in 2019 and finished fourth in the organization with a 3.32 ERA while advancing to high Class A Bradenton.

SCOUTING REPORT: Bido has plenty of stuff to compensate for his advanced age. He sits 92-95 mph on his fastball and touches 97. Despite turning 24 after the season, he still has a lanky frame with more room to add velocity as he fills out. Bido's control has improved a great deal year over year. He's still wild at times, but the throws enough strikes with quality stuff to overcome it. Bido pairs his fastball with an upper-80s cutter and also throws a slider and a changeup. None of his secondaries are bat-missing pitches, but his cutter in particular has shown flashes of being an effective offering.

THE FUTURE: Bido projects best as a reliever in the majors who works off of his fastball and cutter. He'll see Double-A Altoona in 2020 and will continue starting for now.

Year	Age	Club (League)	Class	W	L	ERA	G	GS	SV	IP	H	HR	BB	SO	K/9	WHIP	AVG
2017	21	Pirates (DSL)	R	1	8	5.33	15	13	0	51	53	1	36	41	7.3	1.76	.270
2018	22	West Virginia (NYP)	SS	4	6	4.18	14	14	0	75	74	2	19	58	6.9	1.23	.263
2019	23	Greensboro (SAL)	LoA	11	5	3.55	20	20	0	112	94	9	29	90	7.3	1.10	.228
	23	Bradenton (FSL)	HiA	1	3	2.25	5	5	0	24	18	1	9	17	6.4	1.13	.205
Minor League Totals				17	22	3.96	54	52	0	261	239	13	93	206	7.1	1.27	.244

25 BLAKE CEDERLIND, RHP

BA GRADE **40** Risk: Medium

Born: Jan. 4, 1996. **B-T:** R-R. **HT:** 6-3. **WT:** 190. **Drafted:** Merced (Calif.) JC, 2016 (5th round). **Signed by:** Mike Sansoe.

TRACK RECORD: Cederlind's fastball sat in the mid-90s when the Pirates drafted him in the fifth round in 2016, but he has boosted both his velocity and his prospect stock the last two years after moving to the bullpen. He jumped three levels from high Class A Bradenton to Triple-A Indianapolis in 2019 and logged a combined 2.43 ERA as a late-inning reliever.

SCOUTING REPORT: Cederlind's fastball jumped into the 97-101 mph range with his move to the bullpen and has touched as high as 102. It's a power offering befitting a late-inning reliever, but Cederlind still has a few things to work out. Cederlind's below-average control has improved but still rears its ugly head during bouts of extreme wildness and he doesn't have a secondary pitch that will play in the majors. His slider is currently fringy and his changeup below-average, although there is hope his slider can tick up to average if he stops overthrowing it.

THE FUTURE: The Pirates placed Cederlind on their 40-man roster after the season, putting him in position to make his major league debut in 2020. His control and secondaries will have to improve for him to stick in Pittsburgh's bullpen.

Year	Age	Club (League)	Class	W	L	ERA	G	GS	SV	IP	H	HR	BB	SO	K/9	WHIP	AVG
2017	21	West Virginia (SAL)	LoA	2	3	7.76	25	7	0	58	67	9	34	55	8.5	1.74	.289
2018	22	West Virginia (SAL)	LoA	3	2	2.86	19	1	1	28	21	1	9	36	11.4	1.06	.208
	22	Bradenton (FSL)	HiA	1	2	7.59	17	0	3	21	26	2	19	18	7.6	2.11	.302
2019	23	Bradenton (FSL)	HiA	0	0	1.17	7	0	2	8	4	0	6	8	9.4	1.30	.143
	23	Altoona (EL)	AA	5	1	1.77	31	0	2	46	31	1	16	42	8.3	1.03	.191
	23	Indianapolis (IL)	AAA	0	1	7.50	3	0	0	6	11	1	2	5	7.5	2.17	.393
Minor League Totals				11	10	4.93	108	14	8	184	178	16	93	178	8.7	1.47	.254

26 LOLO SANCHEZ, OF

Born: April 23, 1999. **B-T:** R-R. **HT:** 5-11. **WT:** 167. **Signed:** Dominican Republic, 2015. **Signed by:** Rene Gayo/Juan Mercado/Victor Santana.

TRACK RECORD: The Pirates signed Sanchez for $450,000 as the headline player of their 2015 international class. Sanchez was lauded for his five-tool talent at the time of his signing, but after five pro seasons, the most important tool—his bat—has yet to come around.

SCOUTING REPORT: Sanchez's one consistent tool is his speed. He's an above-average to plus runner who has stolen at least 30 bases each of the last two seasons, and that speed gives him plenty of range in center field. Sanchez's problem is at the plate. Though he doesn't strike out an overwhelming amount, he's an extreme free swinger who, in the words of one scout, "hasn't met a fastball he won't swing at." Sanchez often undermines his game by trying to hit for power when he should focus on driving the ball, and his over-swinging often leads to empty at-bats. Sanchez has flashed average power, but most feel he'd be better off focusing on line-drive contact and letting his speed work.

THE FUTURE: Sanchez's entire approach needs an overhaul. Without it, his upside is limited to a fifth outfielder who only provide values with his defense and speed, a rarity in today's game.

Year	Age	Club (League)	Class	AVG	G	AB	R	H	2B	3B	HR	RBI	BB	SO	SB	OBP	SLG
2017	18	Pirates (GCL)	R	.284	51	204	42	58	11	2	4	20	21	19	14	.359	.417
2018	19	West Virginia (SAL)	LoA	.243	114	378	57	92	18	1	4	34	41	72	30	.322	.328
2019	20	Greensboro (SAL)	LoA	.301	61	226	43	68	10	6	4	26	17	28	20	.377	.451
	20	Bradenton (FSL)	HiA	.196	52	163	21	32	3	3	1	9	18	31	13	.300	.270
Minor League Totals				.254	323	1124	182	286	46	13	13	99	121	168	81	.342	.353

27 JACK HERMAN, OF

BA GRADE
40
Risk: High

Born: Sept. 30, 1999. **B-T:** R-R. **HT:** 5-10. **WT:** 179. **Drafted:** HS—Voorhees Township, N.J., 2018 (30th round). **Signed by:** Dan Radcliff.

TRACK RECORD: The Pirates drafted Herman out of high school in the 30th round in 2018, a spot where high school picks normally end up going to college. Herman, however, signed with the Pirates for $50,000 instead of heading to Maryland and already looks like a good value. He hit .340 after signing in his pro debut and moved to low Class A Greensboro in 2019, where he posted an .804 OPS in 75 games.

SCOUTING REPORT: Previously regarded as a contact hitter, Herman added muscle in the offseason to improve his power production and saw results. He hit 13 home runs in just 75 games at Greensboro and finished fourth on the team with a .464 slugging percentage. That increased power came with a drop in his contact skills, however, and a strikeout rate that nearly doubled from 2018. Herman has quick hands and sound swing mechanics and now needs to find the balance between hitting for average and hitting for power. He profiles as a right fielder, with plus arm strength and enough range that he could play center field in a pinch.

THE FUTURE: Herman will likely see high Class A Bradenton in 2020, where he'll be challenged to find out who he is as a hitter.

Year	Age	Club (League)	Class	AVG	G	AB	R	H	2B	3B	HR	RBI	BB	SO	SB	OBP	SLG
2018	18	Pirates (GCL)	R	.340	37	141	28	48	9	3	2	22	23	24	2	.435	.489
2019	19	Greensboro (SAL)	LoA	.257	75	265	47	68	12	2	13	34	28	88	6	.340	.464
Minor League Totals				.286	112	406	75	116	21	5	15	56	51	112	8	.374	.473

28 JASIAH DIXON, OF

BA GRADE **45** Risk: Extreme

Born: Aug. 31, 2001. **B-T:** R-R. **HT:** 6-0. **WT:** 180. **Drafted:** HS—Orange, Calif., 2019 (23rd round). **Signed by:** Brian Tracy.

TRACK RECORD: Dixon was one of the most-seen high school players in the country as a four-year starter at national power Orange (Calif.) Lutheran. Questions about his bat and the strength of his commitment to Southern California caused him to fall to the 23rd of the draft, where the Pirates grabbed him and signed him for an above-slot $225,000. Dixon promptly went out and hit .329 in his pro debut while showing some of the best speed in the Pirates' system.

SCOUTING REPORT: Dixon has the tools to be a dynamic player. He's a plus-plus runner, has pure arm strength and the ingredients to be an above-average to plus defender in center field. Dixon has plus bat speed and makes contact, but his lack of natural timing or feel for the barrel led to a lot of mis-hit balls and poor quality contact in high school. He answered questions about his bat by showing excellent plate discipline and better quality contact in his pro debut, with flashes of average raw power.

THE FUTURE: Dixon has the look of a speedy, leadoff-hitting center fielder. He will try to show his hitting strides weren't a fluke at low Class A Greensboro in 2020.

Year	Age	Club (League)	Class	AVG	G	AB	R	H	2B	3B	HR	RBI	BB	SO	SB	OBP	SLG
2019	17	Pirates (GCL)	R	.329	22	73	12	24	5	1	0	7	10	11	8	.417	.425
Minor League Totals				.329	22	73	12	24	5	1	0	7	10	11	8	.417	.425

29 J.C. FLOWERS, RHP

BA GRADE **45** Risk: Extreme

Born: May 19, 1998. **B-T:** R-R. **HT:** 6-3. **WT:** 190. **Drafted:** Florida State, 2019 (4th round). **Signed by:** Darren Mazeroski

TRACK RECORD: Flowers was a two-way player at Florida State who played center field and pitched in relief. The Pirates drafted him in the fourth round exclusively as a pitcher, the position Flowers prefers. He signed for $497,500 and made his pro debut as a starter at short-season West Virginia.

SCOUTING REPORT: Flowers' best attribute is his athleticism. He was a standout wide receiver in high school as well as an above-average center fielder with plenty of range. As a pitcher, Flowers' fastball currently sits in the low 90s and can reach the mid-90s. He complements his heater with an upper-80s cutter that flashes above-average but is inconsistent. He also has a solid, third-pitch changeup. Flowers is raw as a pitcher after not pitching prior to his junior year and had command issues in his pro debut, which followed an up-and-down spring on the mound with the Seminoles.

THE FUTURE: Many two-way college players see their velocity tick up once they focus solely on pitching in pro ball, and the Pirates hope the same will happens with Flowers. His athleticism and three-pitch mix give him a the foundation to start, although his development will take time.

Year	Age	Club (League)	Class	W	L	ERA	G	GS	SV	IP	H	HR	BB	SO	K/9	WHIP	AVG
2019	21	West Virginia (NYP)	SS	0	2	4.30	9	8	0	29	33	5	11	24	7.4	1.50	.282
Minor League Totals				0	2	4.30	9	8	0	29	33	5	11	24	7.4	1.50	.282

30 MATT GORSKI, OF

BA GRADE **45** Risk: Extreme

Born: Dec. 22, 1997. **B-T:** R-R. **HT:** 6-4. **WT:** 198. **Drafted:** Indiana, 2019 (2nd round). **Signed by:** Anthony Wycklendt

TRACK RECORD: Gorski established a reputation for big home runs and big strikeout totals at Indiana and was viewed as one of the riskiest players in the 2019 draft. The Pirates drafted him in the second round, well above industry consensus, and signed him for $1 million.

SCOUTING REPORT: Gorski has plenty of tools as a plus runner with plus raw power and an above-average arm, but no one is sure how much he'll hit. He has a big leg kick and long swing he will need to tamp down to reduce his swing-and-miss shortcomings and become even a below-average hitter. He worked to adjust his point of contact after signing to get out in front of the plate to drive the ball more often, but that has adjustment has yet to hold. Gorski has the skills to remain in center field. He makes good reads, gets good jumps and has the arm strength for both center or a corner.

THE FUTURE: Gorski remains very raw with a swing that needs a lot of work if he's to reach even the upper levels of the minors. He should start 2020 in low Class A Greensboro.

Year	Age	Club (League)	Class	AVG	G	AB	R	H	2B	3B	HR	RBI	BB	SO	SB	OBP	SLG
2019	21	West Virginia (NYP)	SS	.223	49	179	32	40	9	2	3	22	19	48	11	.297	.346
Minor League Totals				.223	49	179	32	40	9	2	3	22	19	48	11	.297	.346

St. Louis Cardinals

BY KYLE GLASER

After three years without October baseball, the Cardinals returned to their usual status as postseason participants in 2019.

The acquisition of Paul Goldschmidt and signing of Andrew Miller in the offseason signaled the Cardinals were serious about ending their playoff hiatus, and while neither all-star delivered his usual performance, they provided enough of a boost to lift the Cardinals to a 91-71 record and the National League Central division title.

The short-term payoff of a division title was important, because the Cardinals gave up lots young talent in recent years to achieve it. Within the past two years the Cardinals traded Carson Kelly, Luke Weaver, Sandy Alcantara, Zac Gallen, Tommy Pham, Marco Gonzales and Luke Voit, all of whom are now flourishing elsewhere.

The Cardinals have overcome that talent exodus in part because of the strength of their farm system. Dakota Hudson followed Jack Flaherty to give the Cardinals a standout rookie starter for the second straight year, while Tommy Edman debuted as the Cardinals' latest unassuming college infielder-turned-everyday player. Ryan Helsley, Giovanny Gallegos, Daniel Ponce de Leon and Genesis Cabrera all rose from the minors to help fortify the Cardinals' pitching staff. Even with top prospects Alex Reyes and Tyler O'Neill missing most of the season with injuries, the system still provided enough of a boost to push the club over the top.

Maintaining that moving forward will be tricky. The combination of graduations and the aforementioned trades has significantly thinned the Cardinals' young talent base, and recent misses at the top of the draft have prevented the club from fully backfilling the system, although quality players have still been found in later rounds.

The Cardinals still have potential impact players coming up the pipeline. Outfielder Dylan Carlson became one of baseball's best prospects in 2019, putting together a 20-20 season and winning MVP of the Double-A Texas League at age 20. Talented teens Nolan Gorman and Ivan Herrera reached high Class A as 19-year-olds, while catcher Andrew Knizner and outfielder Lane Thomas made their big league debuts.

Where the Cardinals need help is on the pitching side. Flaherty is a burgeoning ace and Hudson provides another solid young arm, but the trades of Weaver, Alcantara and Gallen have thinned the available options for the Cardinals long-term rotation. A return to health from Reyes—who had season-ending surgery for the third straight year—and a quick rise from first-round pick Zack Thompson would help address that shortage.

NORM HALL/GETTY IMAGES

Rookie Tommy Edman started games at three positions and provided a second-half boost.

PROJECTED 2023 LINEUP

Position	Player	Age
Catcher	Ivan Herrera (5)	23
First Base	Paul Goldschmidt	35
Second Base	Tommy Edman	28
Third Base	Nolan Gorman (2)	23
Shortstop	Paul DeJong	29
Left Field	Dylan Carlson (1)	24
Center Field	Harrison Bader	29
Right Field	Tyler O'Neill	28
No. 1 Starter	Jack Flaherty	27
No. 2 Starter	Dakota Hudson	28
No. 3 Starter	Miles Mikolas	34
No. 4 Starter	Genesis Cabrera (3)	26
No. 5 Starter	Ryan Helsley (4)	28
Closer	Jordan Hicks	26

The up-and-coming young Cardinals will be tasked with replacing franchise icons in the coming years. Adam Wainright's contract expired after 2019, Yadier Molina will be in the final year of his contract in 2020 and Matt Carpenter will be a free agent after 2021. Combined with Marcell Ozuna and Michael Wacha hitting free agency after 2019 as well, the Cardinals have some brand-name players who will need to be replaced.

Whether the Cardinals' remaining young players are up to the task will go a long way toward determining if their 2019 division title is the start of another sustained playoff run, or if it becomes just a flash in the pan.

DEPTH CHART

ST. LOUIS CARDINALS

TOP 2020 ROOKIE: Dylan Carlson, OF. Carlson's considerable physical abilities and advanced, mature instincts have him ready to make an impact in the majors, even at 21.

BREAKOUT PROSPECT: Mateo Gil, SS. Gil has a potent mix of athleticism, instincts and the foundation to hit, and should only get better as he gets stronger.

SLEEPER: Leonardo Taveras, RHP. The 6-foot-5 righthander shows big stuff with a lively 93-97 mph fastball and above-average curveball and now must hone in his control.

SOURCE OF TOP 30 TALENT			
Homegrown	**24**	**Acquired**	**6**
College	9	Trade	5
Junior college	0	Rule 5 draft	0
High school	5	Independent league	0
Nondrafted free agent	0	Free agent/waivers	1
International	10		

LF
Dylan Carlson (1)
Diowill Burgos

CF
Lane Thomas (8)
Randy Arozarena (10)
Trejyn Fletcher (22)
Conner Capel
Adanson Cruz

RF
Jhon Torres (14)
Justin Williams (19)
Justin Toerner (29)
Johan Mieses

3B
Nolan Gorman (2)
Elehuris Montero (9)
Malcom Nunez (17)
Yariel Gonzalez

SS
Mateo Gil (20)
Edmundo Sosa (21)
Delvin Perez
Kramer Robertson

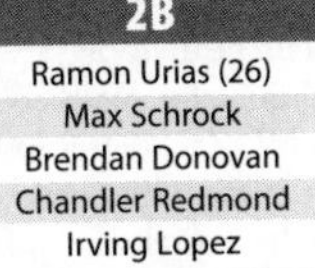

2B
Ramon Urias (26)
Max Schrock
Brendan Donovan
Chandler Redmond
Irving Lopez

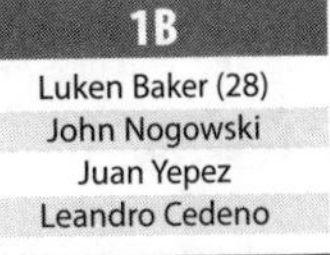

1B
Luken Baker (28)
John Nogowski
Juan Yepez
Leandro Cedeno

C
Ivan Herrera (5)
Andrew Knizner (7)
Julio Rodriguez (15)

LHP

LHSP	LHRP
Genesis Cabrera (3)	Evan Kruczynski
Zack Thompson (6)	Connor Thomas
Austin Warner	
Steven Gingery	

RHP

RHSP	RHRP
Ryan Helsley (4)	Junior Fernandez (12)
Johan Oviedo (11)	Kodi Whitley (18)
Jake Woodford (13)	Seth Elledge (24)
Angel Rondon (16)	Griffin Roberts (27)
Tony Locey (23)	Leonardo Taveras
Alvaro Seijas (25)	Connor Jones (30)
Tommy Parsons	Roel Ramirez
Edgar Gonzalez	Jesus Cruz
Luis Ortiz	Jack Ralston
Jeffry Abreu	Cole Aker
Alex Fagalde	
Kyle Leahy	

DRAFT ANALYSIS

2019

BEST PURE HITTER: The field is limited after the Cardinals drafted pitchers with eight of their first 11 picks, but C Pedro Pages (6) showed excellent plate discipline, a well-rounded approach and growing power both at Florida Atlantic and in his pro debut. His power has a chance to tick up as he gets more comfortable swinging a wood bat.

BEST POWER: OF Patrick Romeri (12) finished tied for third in the Rookie-level Gulf Coast League in home runs as an 18-year-old. His bat speed, natural strength and projectable 6-foot-3, 195-pound frame create optimism for potential above-average or better power.

FASTEST RUNNER: OF Trejyn Fletcher (2) is a consistently plus runner who has flashed 80-grade run times. He is an explosive runner who reaches top speed quickly on the bases and in the outfield.

BEST DEFENSIVE PLAYER: Fletcher's speed gives him tremendous range and closing speed in center field. He needs to refine his reads, but has the potential to develop into a plus center fielder.

BEST ATHLETE: Fletcher was seen doing backflips at the 2018 Area Code Games and was considered one of the top athletes in the draft with his speed and quick-twitch athleticism.

BEST FASTBALL: RHP Tony Locey (3) sits 93-96 mph and touches 98 mph. His fastball plays well up in the zone and is a consensus plus pitch.

BEST SECONDARY PITCH: LHP Zack Thompson (1) struggled to find consistency with his curveball in college at Kentucky, but he corralled it after signing and began breaking it off as a plus pitch. He can both land his 74-77 mph curveball in the strike zone and bury it to put hitters away.

BEST PRO DEBUT: Thompson jumped to the high Class A Florida State League and delivered a 3.77 ERA with 21 strikeouts and four walks in 14.1 innings. His quick jump and immediate success in the FSL put him in position to move aggressively.

TOP DRAFT PICKS OF THE DECADE

Year	Player, Pos	2019 Org
2010	Zack Cox, 3B	Did not play
2011	Kolten Wong, 2B	Cardinals
2012	Michael Wacha, RHP	Cardinals
2013	Marco Gonzales, LHP	Mariners
2014	Luke Weaver, RHP	D-backs
2015	Nick Plummer, OF	Cardinals
2016	Delvin Perez, SS	Cardinals
2017	Scott Hurst, OF (3rd round)	Cardinals
2018	Nolan Gorman, 3B	Cardinals
2019	Zack Thompson, LHP	Cardinals

MOST INTRIGUING BACKGROUND: Fletcher was originally supposed to be a member of the 2020 draft class, but he re-classified late and only became eligible for 2019 three months before the draft. He was Maine's highest-drafted high school player since Mark Rogers went fifth overall in 2004.

CLOSEST TO THE MAJORS: Thompson's polished four-pitch mix from the left side, combined with his confident, aggressive demeanor, has him poised to move through the system quickly.

BEST LATE-ROUND PICK: 2B Chandler Redmond (32) finished tied for third in the Rookie-level Appalachian League in home runs and was near the top of the Cardinals' scale in exit velocity. The $3,000 senior sign from Gardner-Webb has a strong, 6-foot-2, 230-pound frame and a track record of lefthanded power production.

THE ONE WHO GOT AWAY: RHP Alex McFarlane (25) possesses an intriguing frame, a quick arm and a feel for spin, but he stuck with his commitment to Miami. The Cardinals also took a late flyer on OF Chris Newell (37), who maintained his strong commitment to Virginia. His hitter traits and above-average raw power give him a chance to develop into a middle-of-the-order hitter in college.

—KYLE GLASER

2018

3B Nolan Gorman (1) has impressed from the get-go in pro ball and established himself as a top 50 prospect. He's largely carrying the banner for the class, but SS Mateo Gil (3) has solid upside as well.

GRADE: B

2017

The Cardinals worked from a disadvantage without a pick until No. 94 overall, but they've come up empty. RHP Kody Whitley (27) is the only player from the class to appear in the Handbook.

GRADE: F

2016

With three first-round picks, this class was a strong one. It has produced four big leaguers, including RHP Dakota Hudson (1) and 2B Tommy Edman (6). OF Dylan Carlson (1) is the system's top prospect.

GRADE: A

1 DYLAN CARLSON, OF

Born: Oct. 23, 1998. **B-T:** B-L. **HT:** 6-3. **WT:** 205.
Drafted: HS—Elk Grove, Calif., 2016. (1st round).
Signed by: Zach Mortimer.

TRACK RECORD: Carlson's father Jeff built a renowned program as the coach at Elk Grove (Calif.) High, where he won eight CIF section titles and produced a long list of future major leaguers. Carlson entered high school at 13 and made varsity as a freshman, the start of a decorated four-year career playing for his dad that culminated with the Cardinals drafting him 33rd overall in 2016. After steady production as one of the youngest players at each level, Carlson broke out in 2019 at Double-A Springfield. He opened the year as the second-youngest position player in the Texas League and finished second in OPS (.882), home runs (21), runs scored (81) and extra-base hits (51) en route to winning the league's MVP award. He made the Futures Game, earned a late-season promotion to Triple-A Memphis and finished the year as one of only 10 players in the minors with at least 20 home runs and 20 stolen bases.

SCOUTING REPORT: Carlson long showed advanced instincts, controlled the strike zone and flashed the ingredients to hit with above-average bat speed and hand-eye coordination. An added 10 pounds of muscle allowed him to impact the ball more, and as a result he jumped from 11 home runs in 2018 to 26 in 2019. A switch-hitter, Carlson ironed out his once-loopy lefthanded swing and is now at least an above-average hitter from both sides. He studies pitchers' tendencies, stays within the strike zone and doesn't miss his pitch. Carlson's pure power is average, but his growing strength and sound swing mechanics give him a chance to exceed that projection and hit 20 or more home runs per year. Carlson is an above-average runner who steals bases efficiently. Those same instincts allow him to capably man center field, though he's better as an above-average defender on the corners. His fringy to average arm fits best in left field. Long lauded for his plus-plus makeup, Carlson plays a mature game and knows how to handle adversity. His mother Caryn survived breast cancer and is confined to a wheelchair by an inflammatory disease that affected her spinal cord and left her partially paralyzed.

THE FUTURE: With a well-rounded game and few weaknesses, Carlson is a safe bet to be a solid everyday player and has a chance to be more. His major league debut should come in 2020.

JOHN WILLIAMSON

BA GRADE
60 **Risk: Medium**

SCOUTING GRADES
Hit: 55. **Power:** 60. **Run:** 55. **Field:** 55. **Arm:** 50.

Projected future grades on 20-80 scouting scale.

TOP PROSPECTS OF THE DECADE

Year	Player, Pos	2019 Org
2010	Shelby Miller, RHP	Brewers
2011	Shelby Miller, RHP	Brewers
2012	Shelby Miller, RHP	Brewers
2013	Oscar Taveras, OF	Deceased
2014	Oscar Taveras, OF	Deceased
2015	Marco Gonzales, LHP	Mariners
2016	Alex Reyes, RHP	Cardinals
2017	Alex Reyes, RHP	Cardinals
2018	Alex Reyes, RHP	Cardinals
2019	Alex Reyes, RHP	Cardinals

BEST TOOLS

Best Hitter for Average	Dylan Carlson
Best Power Hitter	Nolan Gorman
Best Strike-Zone Discipline	John Nogowski
Fastest Baserunner	Lane Thomas
Best Athlete	Trejyn Fletcher
Best Fastball	Ryan Helsley
Best Curveball	Zack Thompson
Best Slider	Johan Oviedo
Best Changeup	Junior Fernandez
Best Control	Tommy Parsons
Best Defensive Catcher	Julio Rodriguez
Best Defensive Infielder	Delvin Perez
Best Infield Arm	Elehuris Montero
Best Defensive Outfielder	Lane Thomas
Best Outfield Arm	Adolis Garcia

Year	Age	Club (League)	Class	AVG	G	AB	R	H	2B	3B	HR	RBI	BB	SO	SB	OBP	SLG
2017	18	Peoria (MWL)	LoA	.240	115	383	63	92	18	1	7	42	52	116	6	.342	.347
2018	19	Peoria (MWL)	LoA	.234	13	47	5	11	3	0	2	9	10	10	2	.368	.426
	19	Palm Beach (FSL)	HiA	.247	99	376	63	93	19	3	9	53	52	78	6	.345	.386
2019	20	Springfield (TL)	AA	.281	108	417	81	117	24	6	21	59	52	98	18	.364	.518
	20	Memphis (PCL)	AAA	.361	18	72	14	26	4	2	5	9	6	18	2	.418	.681
Minor League Totals				.260	403	1478	256	385	81	15	47	194	188	372	38	.350	.431

2 NOLAN GORMAN, 3B

Born: May 10, 2000. **B-T:** L-R. **HT:** 6-1. **WT:** 210. **Drafted:** HS—Phoenix, 2018 (1st round). **Signed by:** Mauricio Rubio.

TRACK RECORD: Gorman emerged early as the top power prospect in the 2018 draft, winning the high school home run derby at Marlins Park and the Under Armour All-America home run derby at Wrigley Field. Gorman got off to a scorching start with 24 home runs in his first 85 career games, but he cooled off and hit just eight home runs in his next 104 games. He still reached high Class A Palm Beach in his first full season as an 19-year-old.

SCOUTING REPORT: Muscular with a broad chest and strong hands, Gorman possesses the plus-plus raw power to makes balls disappear. He flashes the approach to get to his power, but he often gets too pull-oriented and uphill in his swing path, opening him up for strikeouts. He has the ingredients to be an average hitter as he improves his approach. Gorman makes the routine plays at third base with a quick exchange and an above-average arm, but he needs to improve his first-step quickness to become an average defender. He is somewhat stiff and a below-average runner.

THE FUTURE: Gorman has the power to hit in the middle of the lineup. He has time to improve his approach and show he can make adjustments.

SCOUTING GRADES: **Hitting:** 50 **Power:** 70 **Running:** 40 **Fielding:** 50 **Arm:** 55

Year	Age	Club (League)	Class	AVG	G	AB	R	H	2B	3B	HR	RBI	BB	SO	SB	OBP	SLG
2018	18	Johnson City (APP)	R	.350	38	143	41	50	10	1	11	28	24	37	1	.443	.664
	18	Peoria (MWL)	LoA	.202	25	94	8	19	3	0	6	16	10	39	0	.280	.426
2019	19	Peoria (MWL)	LoA	.241	67	241	41	58	14	3	10	41	32	79	2	.344	.448
	19	Palm Beach (FSL)	HiA	.256	58	215	24	55	16	3	5	21	13	73	0	.304	.428
Minor League Totals				.263	188	693	114	182	43	7	32	106	79	228	3	.345	.483

3 GENESIS CABRERA, LHP

BA GRADE
50 Risk: Medium

MARY DECICCO

Born: Oct. 10, 1996. **B-T:** L-L. **HT:** 6-2. **WT:** 190. **Signed:** Dominican Republic, 2013. **Signed by:** Carlos Batista/Danny Santana (Rays).

TRACK RECORD: Cabrera pitched for the Astros on a tryout basis in the Dominican Republic's informal Tricky League in the summer of 2013. Rays international director Carlos Rodriguez liked what he saw when Cabrera threw against the Rays and signed him for $34,000. Cabrera rose swiftly through Tampa's system, and the Cardinals acquired him as one of three prospects for Tommy Pham at the 2018 trade deadline. Cabrera made his major league debut with the Cardinals in May as a starter but later settled in the bullpen.

SCOUTING REPORT: Cabrera has long drawn comparisons with all-star closer Felipe Vazquez for his electric stuff, violent delivery and shoddy control. Cabrera's fastball sits 94-97 mph as a starter and ticks up to 99 as a reliever. He hides the ball well and it explodes out of his hand, inducing swings and misses even when he leaves it over the plate. Cabrera's power mid-80s breaking ball waffles between a curveball and slider, but it has the depth and snap to be an above-average, swing-and-miss pitch. His hard, upper-80s changeup plays up to average off his fastball. He is highly athletic, but his inconsistent delivery and violent arm action yield bouts of extreme wildness.

THE FUTURE: The Cardinals plan to bring Cabrera to spring training as a starter. If his control doesn't take a step forward, he has a solid fallback option as an impact reliever.

SCOUTING GRADES: **Fastball:** 70 **Slider:** 55 **Changeup:** 50 **Control:** 40

Year	Age	Club (League)	Class	W	L	ERA	G	GS	SV	IP	H	HR	BB	SO	K/9	WHIP	AVG
2017	20	Charlotte, FL (FSL)	HiA	4	5	2.84	13	12	0	70	45	3	25	60	7.8	1.00	.185
	20	Montgomery (SL)	AA	5	4	3.62	12	12	0	65	75	6	27	51	7.1	1.58	.292
2018	21	Montgomery (SL)	AA	7	6	4.12	21	20	0	114	90	11	57	124	9.8	1.29	.218
	21	Springfield (TL)	AA	1	3	4.74	5	5	0	25	24	3	13	21	7.7	1.50	.255
	21	Memphis (PCL)	AAA	0	0	0.00	1	0	0	2	0	0	1	3	13.5	0.50	.000
2019	22	Memphis (PCL)	AAA	5	6	5.91	20	18	0	99	107	20	39	106	9.6	1.47	.277
	22	St. Louis (NL)	MAJ	0	2	4.87	13	2	1	20	23	2	11	19	8.4	1.67	.274
Major League Totals				0	2	4.87	13	2	1	20	23	2	11	19	8.4	1.67	.274
Minor League Totals				35	30	4.06	114	92	0	536	487	52	217	506	8.5	1.31	.244

4 RYAN HELSLEY, RHP

Born: July 18,1994. **B-T:** R-R. **Ht.:** 6-1. **Wt.:** 195. **Drafted:** Northeastern State (Okla.), 2015 (5th round). **Signed by:** Aaron Looper

TRACK RECORD: Helsley grew up in rural Tahlequah, Okla., and received his only college scholarship offer from Division II Northeastern State. A star turn in the California Collegiate Summer League pulled scouts to Helsley's games, and the Cardinals drafted him in the fifth round in 2015. Helsley raced up the system until shoulder fatigue sidetracked him in 2018, but he rebounded to make his major league debut in 2019 and became a key part of the Cardinals' bullpen.

MARY DECICCO

BA GRADE
50 Risk: Medium

SCOUTING REPORT: With thick, sturdy legs and an explosive right arm, Helsley overpowers hitters with a fastball that sits 97-98 mph and touches 101 in relief. It features elite spin and is a potentially plus-plus pitch, though it presently plays down because he struggles to locate it. Helsley's plus upper-80s cutter is a strikeout pitch that slides off of barrels with short, late movement. He can land it for strikes or induce chases below the zone. Helsley uses his average power curveball and fringy changeup as a starter, but rarely throws them in relief.

THE FUTURE: Helsley will be stretched out as a starter in spring training. If his health and command aren't up for it, he has a future as an impact, late-inning reliever.

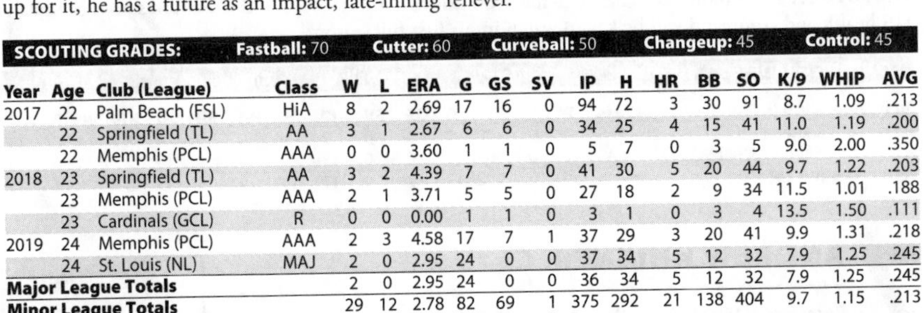

SCOUTING GRADES: Fastball: 70 Cutter: 60 Curveball: 50 Changeup: 45 Control: 45

Year	Age	Club (League)	Class	W	L	ERA	G	GS	SV	IP	H	HR	BB	SO	K/9	WHIP	AVG
2017	22	Palm Beach (FSL)	HiA	8	2	2.69	17	16	0	94	72	3	30	91	8.7	1.09	.213
	22	Springfield (TL)	AA	3	1	2.67	6	6	0	34	25	4	15	41	11.0	1.19	.200
	22	Memphis (PCL)	AAA	0	0	3.60	1	1	0	5	7	0	3	5	9.0	2.00	.350
2018	23	Springfield (TL)	AA	3	2	4.39	7	7	0	41	30	5	20	44	9.7	1.22	.203
	23	Memphis (PCL)	AAA	2	1	3.71	5	5	0	27	18	2	9	34	11.5	1.01	.188
	23	Cardinals (GCL)	R	0	0	0.00	1	1	0	3	1	0	3	4	13.5	1.50	.111
2019	24	Memphis (PCL)	AAA	2	3	4.58	17	7	1	37	29	3	20	41	9.9	1.31	.218
	24	St. Louis (NL)	MAJ	2	0	2.95	24	0	0	37	34	5	12	32	7.9	1.25	.245
Major League Totals				2	0	2.95	24	0	0	36	34	5	12	32	7.9	1.25	.245
Minor League Totals				29	12	2.78	82	69	1	375	292	21	138	404	9.7	1.15	.213

5 IVAN HERRERA, C

Born: June 1, 2000. **B-T:** R-R. **Ht.:** 6-0. **Wt.:** 180. **Signed:** Panama, 2016. **Signed by:** Damaso Espino.

TRACK RECORD: A veteran of Panama's junior national teams, Herrera signed with the Cardinals for $200,000 in 2016 and quickly established himself as one of the system's top hitters. He hit .335 in the Dominican Summer League and .348 in the Rookie-level Gulf Coast League to start his career, then jumped to full-season ball in 2019 and hit .286 with an .805 OPS as the third-youngest player in the low Class A Midwest League on Opening Day. He finished the year at high Class A Palm Beach.

BA GRADE
55 Risk: High

SCOUTING REPORT: Herrera is an offensive catcher who makes frequent contact with a compact, righthanded swing. He is short to the ball, rarely swings and misses in the strike zone and lines the ball to all fields. He continues to get stronger and has a chance to hit 12-15 home runs as he fills out. Herrera has the strong, athletic frame to catch and is willing to learn, but his blocking and receiving are inconsistent and his above-average arm strength plays down with a slow release. He threw out 31 percent of basestealers in 2019.

THE FUTURE: Herrera will be just 19 on Opening Day and has lots of time to polish his game. He has the upside of an everyday catcher who can provide impact on both sides of the ball.

SCOUTING GRADES: Hitting: 55 Power: 45 Running: 30 Fielding: 55 Arm: 50

Year	Age	Club (League)	Class	AVG	G	AB	R	H	2B	3B	HR	RBI	BB	SO	SB	OBP	SLG
2017	17	Cardinals (DSL)	R	.335	49	170	21	57	15	0	1	27	18	36	2	.425	.441
2018	18	Cardinals (GCL)	R	.348	28	112	23	39	6	4	1	25	11	20	1	.423	.500
	18	Springfield (TL)	AA	.000	2	4	0	0	0	0	0	0	0	2	0	.200	.000
2019	19	Peoria (MWL)	LoA	.286	69	248	41	71	10	0	8	42	35	56	1	.381	.423
	19	Palm Beach (FSL)	HiA	.276	18	58	7	16	0	0	1	5	5	16	0	.338	.328
Minor League Totals				.309	166	592	92	183	31	4	11	99	69	130	4	.397	.431

6 ZACK THOMPSON, LHP

CHET WHITE

BA GRADE
55 **Risk: High**

Born: Oct. 28, 1997. **B-T:** L-L. **HT:** 6-2. **WT:** 225. **Drafted:** Kentucky, 2019 (1st round). **Signed by:** Jason Bryans.

TRACK RECORD: The Rays drafted Thompson in the 11th round out of high school and made him an over-slot bonus offer, but he attended Kentucky instead. Elbow soreness sidetracked Thompson's sophomore season, but he returned to pitch 8.2 scoreless innings for USA Baseball's Collegiate National Team in the summer and rebounded with a strong junior season. He struck out 130 batters for the Wildcats, breaking James Paxton's school record for a lefthander, and was a Golden Spikes Award semifinalist. The Cardinals drafted him 19th overall and signed him for $3 million.

SCOUTING REPORT: Thompson's fastball sits 91-94 mph as a starter and touched 97 in relief at high Class A Palm Beach after he signed. His slider was better than his curveball in college, but his curveball showed better in pro ball as a plus 74-77 mph offering he could land in the strike zone or get batters to chase. His above-average mid-80s slider plays like a cutter at times, and his 83-85 mph changeup gives him an average fourth offering. Thompson mixes all his pitches and has a confident, aggressive demeanor. His control is average, but his command and consistency waver.

THE FUTURE: Thompson has a chance to move quickly as a mid-to-back of the rotation starter candidate. His health and command will be key to watch in his first full season.

SCOUTING GRADES: **Fastball:** 55 **Slider:** 55 **Curveball:** 60 **Changeup:** 50 **Control:** 50

Year	Age	Club (League)	Class	W	L	ERA	G	GS	SV	IP	H	HR	BB	SO	K/9	WHIP	AVG
2019	21	Cardinals (GCL)	R	0	0	0.00	2	2	0	2	3	0	0	4	18.0	1.50	.300
	21	Palm Beach (FSL)	HiA	0	0	4.05	11	0	0	13	16	0	4	19	12.8	1.50	.302
Minor League Totals				0	0	3.52	13	2	0	15	19	0	4	23	13.5	1.50	.302

7 ANDREW KNIZNER, C

BA GRADE
45 **Risk: Medium**

Born: Feb. 3, 1995. **B-T:** R-R. **Ht.:** 6-1. **Wt.:** 200. **Drafted:** North Carolina State, 2016 (7th round). **Signed by:** Charles Peterson.

TRACK RECORD: Knizner converted from third base to catcher in college and regressed offensively as he focused on learning his new position. The Cardinals drafted him in the seventh round in 2016 and quickly realized they had a steal. With his bat rejuvenated in pro ball, Knizner hit his way to Double-A in his first full season, advanced to Triple-A in his second and made his big league debut in 2019.

SCOUTING REPORT: Knizner's bat separates him from other catchers. He keeps his barrel in the zone, uses the whole field and has the hand-eye coordination to make frequent contact and limit his strikeouts despite an aggressive approach. Knizner's line-drive stroke and average power limit his home run output, but he has the strength to elevate to his pull side and reach double-digit homers. Knizner is an adequate but fringe-average defensive catcher still working to improve. He moves well laterally, has an average arm and calls a good game, but his rough hands make him a well below-average receiver and pitch-framer. He is still working on controlling his blocks, as well.

THE FUTURE: Knizner's bat will earn him at least a part-time role in the majors. Whether he eventually replaces Yadier Molina as the Cardinals' everyday catcher will depend on how well he continues his defensive growth.

SCOUTING GRADES: **Hitting:** 55 **Power:** 45 **Running:** 30 **Fielding:** 45 **Arm:** 50

Year	Age	Club (League)	Class	AVG	G	AB	R	H	2B	3B	HR	RBI	BB	SO	SB	OBP	SLG
2017	22	Peoria (MWL)	LoA	.279	44	179	18	50	10	1	8	29	9	22	1	.325	.480
	22	Springfield (TL)	AA	.324	51	182	27	59	13	0	4	22	14	27	0	.371	.462
2018	23	Springfield (TL)	AA	.313	77	281	39	88	13	0	7	41	23	40	0	.365	.434
	23	Memphis (PCL)	AAA	.315	17	54	3	17	5	0	0	4	4	8	0	.383	.407
2019	24	Memphis (PCL)	AAA	.276	66	246	41	68	10	0	12	34	24	37	2	.357	.463
	24	St. Louis (NL)	MAJ	.226	18	53	7	12	2	0	2	7	4	14	2	.293	.377
Major League Totals				.226	18	53	7	12	2	0	2	7	4	14	2	.293	.377
Minor League Totals				.303	308	1127	163	341	63	2	37	172	95	155	3	.369	.461

8 LANE THOMAS, OF

Born: Aug. 23, 1995. **B-T:** R-R. **HT:** 6-1. **WT:** 210. **Drafted:** HS—Knoxville, 2014 (5th round). **Signed by:** Nate Murrie (Blue Jays).

BA GRADE 45 **Risk:** Medium

TRACK RECORD: Thomas failed to advance past high Class A in four seasons with the Blue Jays after they made him a fifth-round pick in 2014. The Cardinals acquired him for $500,000 in international bonus pool money in July 2017, and he promptly broke out with his new organization. Thomas led the Cardinals' system with 27 home runs in 2018 and made his major league debut in 2019, homering in his first career at-bat. He spent most of August in the majors before suffering a season-ending right wrist fracture.

SCOUTING REPORT: Thomas has an intriguing blend of strength, speed and instincts. He takes a simple approach at the plate and stays within the strike zone. When he connects he makes consistent, hard contact, and he has learned to elevate to make the most of his average, line-drive power. He is prone to swinging and missing in the zone. Thomas is a plus runner who makes better use of his speed in center field than on the bases. He positions himself well, gets good jumps and runs down balls in every direction to be a borderline plus defender with an above-average arm. Staying healthy has been an issue for Thomas. He has played a full season just once in five years.

THE FUTURE: Thomas is a major league-ready fourth outfielder. If stays healthy, he could be more.

SCOUTING GRADES: **Hitting:** 45 **Power:** 50 **Running:** 60 **Fielding:** 60 **Arm:** 55

Year	Age	Club (League)	Class	AVG	G	AB	R	H	2B	3B	HR	RBI	BB	SO	SB	OBP	SLG
2017	21	Dunedin (FSL)	HiA	.252	73	274	34	69	12	6	4	38	27	84	8	.319	.383
	21	Palm Beach (FSL)	HiA	.257	9	35	5	9	0	1	0	3	3	10	2	.308	.314
2018	22	Springfield (TL)	AA	.260	100	384	63	100	16	4	21	67	43	101	13	.337	.487
	22	Memphis (PCL)	AAA	.275	32	131	21	36	7	2	6	21	7	33	4	.321	.496
2019	23	Memphis (PCL)	AAA	.268	75	265	42	71	17	2	10	44	32	80	11	.352	.460
	23	St. Louis (NL)	MAJ	.316	34	38	6	12	0	1	4	12	4	8	1	.409	.684
Major League Totals				.316	34	38	6	12	0	1	4	12	4	8	1	.409	.684
Minor League Totals				.252	480	1792	275	452	98	20	55	258	197	514	72	.329	.421

9 ELEHURIS MONTERO, 3B

Born: Aug. 17, 1998. **B-T:** R-R. **HT:** 6-3. **WT:** 215. **Signed:** Dominican Republic, 2014. **Signed by:** Angel Ovalles.

BA GRADE 55 **Risk:** Extreme

TRACK RECORD: Montero raced up the Cardinals' system after signing for $300,000. He won MVP of the low Class A Midwest League in 2018 and was pushed aggressively to Double-A in 2019, when he hit his first speed bump. Montero missed three weeks with a wrist injury and another two months with a broken hamate. The combination of injuries, interrupted playing time and older competition contributed to a .188 average in 59 Double-A games.

SCOUTING REPORT: Montero's youth and tools hold promise despite his down year. He is a physical, strong hitter with excellent hand-eye coordination, bat speed and plus raw power. He does damage when he connects and uses the whole field. Montero got by on his natural gifts at lower levels and is still learning to develop a plan against upper-level pitchers. He has the physical skills to be an above-average hitter, though his pitch recognition and swing path regressed in 2019. Montero has the plus arm for third base, but his thick body limits his range and makes him a fringe-average defender likely to move to first base.

THE FUTURE: Evaluators remain bullish on Montero's bat and consider 2019 a lost year. His health and improvements to his approach will be key to watch in 2020.

SCOUTING GRADES: **Hitting:** 55 **Power:** 55 **Running:** 40 **Fielding:** 45 **Arm:** 60

Year	Age	Club (League)	Class	AVG	G	AB	R	H	2B	3B	HR	RBI	BB	SO	SB	OBP	SLG
2017	18	Cardinals (GCL)	R	.277	52	173	30	48	16	1	5	36	22	33	0	.370	.468
2018	19	Peoria (MWL)	LoA	.322	103	382	68	123	28	3	15	69	33	81	2	.381	.529
	19	Palm Beach (FSL)	HiA	.286	24	98	13	28	9	0	1	13	5	22	1	.330	.408
2019	20	Cardinals (GCL)	R	.308	4	13	1	4	0	0	0	0	1	2	0	.400	.308
	20	Springfield (TL)	AA	.188	59	224	23	42	8	0	7	18	14	74	0	.235	.317
Minor League Totals				.269	360	1347	207	362	84	7	32	192	129	319	5	.339	.413

10 RANDY AROZARENA, OF

MARY DECICCO

BA GRADE
45 **Risk: Medium**

Born: Feb. 28, 1995. **B-T:** R-R. **Ht.:** 5-11. **Wt.:** 170. **Signed:** Cuba, 2016. **Signed by:** Ramon Garcia.

TRACK RECORD: Arozarena starred in Cuba's junior national leagues growing up and signed with the Cardinals for $1.25 million in 2016 after a brief stint in the Mexican League. After a steady three-year climb through the system, Arozarena made his major league debut in 2019 and earned a spot on the Cardinals' postseason roster.

SCOUTING REPORT: Arozarena is an energetic spark plug with tools, but he is still learning to take consistent at-bats. He separates balls from strikes and drives the ball gap-to-gap when he connects. He is extremely aggressive and prone to over-swinging, which results in lots of whiffs against breaking stuff and inconsistent quality of contact. His pure bat speed and feel for the zone make him a potentially average hitter, and he showed flashes by batting .344 in the minors in 2019. He has sneaky pop and hit a career-high 16 home runs as well. Arozarena's best tool is plus speed, though he can be reckless on the bases and is prone to running into outs. He adequately plays all three outfield positions with his plus athleticism and average arm.

THE FUTURE: Arozarena's speed and defensive versatility give him a chance to stick as a fourth outfielder.

SCOUTING GRADES: **Hitting:** 50 **Power:** 45 **Running:** 60 **Fielding:** 55 **Arm:** 50

Year	Age	Club (League)	Class	AVG	G	AB	R	H	2B	3B	HR	RBI	BB	SO	SB	OBP	SLG
2017	22	Palm Beach (FSL)	HiA	.275	70	265	38	73	22	3	8	40	13	53	10	.333	.472
	22	Springfield (TL)	AA	.252	51	163	34	41	10	1	3	9	27	34	8	.366	.380
2018	23	Springfield (TL)	AA	.396	24	91	22	36	5	0	7	21	6	25	9	.455	.681
	23	Memphis (PCL)	AAA	.232	89	267	42	62	16	0	5	28	28	59	17	.328	.348
2019	24	Springfield (TL)	AA	.309	28	97	14	30	7	2	3	15	13	23	8	.422	.515
	24	Memphis (PCL)	AAA	.358	64	246	51	88	18	2	12	38	24	48	9	.435	.593
	24	St. Louis (NL)	MAJ	.300	19	20	4	6	1	0	1	2	2	4	2	.391	.500
Major League Totals				.300	19	20	4	6	1	0	1	2	2	4	2	.391	.500
Minor League Totals				.289	331	1149	204	332	79	8	38	151	113	245	61	.373	.471

11 JOHAN OVIEDO, RHP

BA GRADE
50 **Risk: High**

Born: March 2, 1998. **B-T:** R-R. **Ht.:** 6-6. **Wt.:** 210. **Signed:** Cuba, 2016. **Signed by:** Angel Ovalles.

TRACK RECORD: The towering Oviedo has been a frustrating blend of big stuff and poor control since he signed with the Cardinals for $1.9 million out of Cuba in 2016. He reached Double-A Springfield as a 21-year-old in 2019 and led the system with 163 strikeouts, but he also led it with 76 walks.

SCOUTING REPORT: Oviedo stands an imposing 6-foot-6 with long limbs that are both a blessing and a curse. He generates easy velocity on a 94-98 mph fastball that plays up with extension out of his large frame, making it a potential plus pitch. He can get his average curveball over for a strike and put hitters away with a tilting, snapping slider that earns above-average to plus grades. He also teases an above-average changeup. Oviedo flashes a good delivery and shows feel to pitch, but his command and control vary wildly from start to start. His preparation and maturity are improving but still need work.

THE FUTURE: Oviedo's size, stuff and delivery are that of a starter, and evaluators are optimistic he will grow into his body and improve his control and consistency. He should see Triple-A Memphis in 2020.

Year	Age	Club (League)	Class	W	L	ERA	G	GS	SV	IP	H	HR	BB	SO	K/9	WHIP	AVG
2017	19	Johnson City (APP)	R	2	1	4.88	6	6	0	28	22	0	18	31	10.1	1.45	.220
	19	State College (NYP)	SS	2	2	4.56	8	8	0	47	53	3	18	39	7.4	1.50	.285
2018	20	Peoria (MWL)	LoA	10	10	4.22	25	23	1	122	108	6	79	118	8.7	1.54	.238
2019	21	Palm Beach (FSL)	HiA	5	0	1.60	6	5	0	34	29	1	12	35	9.4	1.22	.230
	21	Springfield (TL)	AA	7	8	5.65	23	23	0	113	120	9	64	128	10.2	1.63	.273
Minor League Totals				26	22	4.36	75	72	1	365	351	19	197	380	9.4	1.50	.253

12 JUNIOR FERNANDEZ, RHP

BA GRADE
45 **Risk: Medium**

Born: March 2, 1997. **B-T:** R-R. **HT:** 6-1. **WT:** 180. **Signed:** Dominican Republic, 2014. **Signed by:** Rodney Jimenez/Angel Ovalles.

TRACK RECORD: Fernandez grew up in Miami but moved to the Dominican Republic in high school so he could sign as an international free agent. The Cardinals signed him for for $400,000. Fernandez's career got off to a fast start, but shoddy control and repeated arm injuries halted his rise and forced him to move to the bullpen. He logged a 1.52 ERA over 45 appearance across three levels in 2019 and made his major league debut in August.

SCOUTING REPORT: Fernandez is a high-octane righthander with a 95-97 mph fastball with heavy sink. He was previously over-reliant on his fastball and got hit, so the Cardinals implored him to use his secondaries more last season. Fernandez's plus mid-80s changeup with armside fade is a swing-and-miss offering, and his hard, upper 80s slider improved to begin flashing plus. Fernandez's control is below-average, but he was far more effective with a better pitch mix.

THE FUTURE: Fernandez has the stuff to pitch in late relief. He'll be in the Cardinals bullpen in 2020.

Year	Age	Club (League)	Class	W	L	ERA	G	GS	SV	IP	H	HR	BB	SO	K/9	WHIP	AVG
2017	20	Palm Beach (FSL)	HiA	5	3	3.69	16	16	0	90	82	5	39	58	5.8	1.34	.249
2018	21	Palm Beach (FSL)	HiA	1	0	0.00	8	0	3	10	9	0	2	7	6.5	1.14	.265
	21	Springfield (TL)	AA	0	0	5.14	16	0	0	21	19	1	16	17	7.3	1.67	.253
2019	22	Palm Beach (FSL)	HiA	0	0	1.54	9	0	4	12	8	0	8	11	8.5	1.37	.191
	22	Springfield (TL)	AA	1	1	1.55	18	0	5	29	18	0	11	42	13.0	1.00	.177
	22	Memphis (PCL)	AAA	2	1	1.48	18	0	2	24	17	0	11	27	10.0	1.15	.191
	22	St. Louis (NL)	MAJ	0	1	5.40	13	0	0	12	9	2	6	16	12.3	1.29	.205
Major League Totals				0	1	5.40	13	0	0	11	9	2	6	16	12.3	1.29	.205
Minor League Totals				20	19	3.57	129	52	14	393	363	14	170	326	7.5	1.35	.247

13 JAKE WOODFORD, RHP

BA GRADE 45 **Risk:** Medium

Born: Oct. 28, 1996. **B-T:** R-R. **Ht.:** 6-4. **Wt.:** 220. **Drafted:** HS—Tampa, 2015 (1st round supplemental). **Signed by:** Mike Dibiase.

TRACK RECORD: The Cardinals drafted Woodford 39th overall in 2015 and signed him for $1.8 million. He spent all of 2019 at Triple-A Memphis and finished third in the Pacific Coast League in ERA (4.15) and strikeouts (131), but he also issued a league-high 75 walks.

SCOUTING REPORT: Woodford is a burly 6-foot-4, 220-pound righthander who flashes big stuff. His fastball sits 94-96 mph and his cutter works 87-89 mph in short bursts, but both lose steam as his outings progress and settle in as average offerings. His mid-80s changeup and upper 70s curveball flash average as well. Woodford struggles to maintain his aggressiveness or throw the right pitches in the right situations, often taking his foot off the gas against weaker hitters and getting tentative in the strike zone. The result is long innings and elevated walk totals.

THE FUTURE: Woodford may break in as a starter, but most see his future as a short-burst reliever. His ML debut should come in 2020.

Year	Age	Club (League)	Class	W	L	ERA	G	GS	SV	IP	H	HR	BB	SO	K/9	WHIP	AVG
2017	20	Palm Beach (FSL)	HiA	7	6	3.10	23	21	0	119	128	7	39	72	5.4	1.40	.280
2018	21	Springfield (TL)	AA	3	8	5.22	16	16	0	81	94	13	35	56	6.2	1.59	.290
	21	Memphis (PCL)	AAA	5	5	4.50	12	12	0	64	64	5	27	45	6.3	1.42	.261
2019	22	Memphis (PCL)	AAA	9	8	4.15	26	26	0	152	124	22	75	131	7.8	1.31	.223
Minor League Totals				30	32	3.87	106	101	1	550	540	55	220	407	6.7	1.38	.258

14 JHON TORRES, OF

BA GRADE 55 **Risk:** Extreme

Born: March 29, 2000. **B-T:** R-R. **HT:** 6-4. **WT:** 199. **Signed:** Colombia, 2016. **Signed by:** Domingo Toribio/Felix Nivar/Koby Perez (Indians).

TRACK RECORD: Torres signed with the Indians for $150,000 in 2016 and emerged as a rising prospect in their system, leading the Cardinals to acquire him with outfielder Conner Capel at the 2018 trade deadline for Oscar Mercado. Torres struggled after the Cardinals pushed him to low Class A Peoria to open the 2019 season, but he flourished after dropping down to Rookie-level Johnson City.

SCOUTING REPORT: Torres stands an imposing 6-foot-4 with long levers and flashes quality at-bats. He makes loud contact when he connects and has the bat speed, strength and leverage to grow into above-average power. Torres has the physical tools to hit for a solid average, but he is prone to chasing out of the strike zone and is still learning to pick out which pitches he can drive. He is a deceptively good right fielder who gets anticipates well, gets good jumps and takes proper angles to the ball. He has a plus arm.

THE FUTURE: Torres has the tools of a prototypical right fielder. He will return to Peoria in 2020.

Year	Age	Club (League)	Class	AVG	G	AB	R	H	2B	3B	HR	RBI	BB	SO	SB	OBP	SLG
2017	17	Indians (DSL)	R	.255	54	184	25	47	7	3	5	35	28	41	4	.363	.408
2018	18	Indians 2 (AZL)	R	.273	27	99	16	27	3	0	4	16	11	24	3	.351	.424
	18	Cardinals (GCL)	R	.397	17	63	11	25	6	0	4	14	8	13	1	.493	.683
2019	19	Peoria (MWL)	LoA	.167	21	66	4	11	3	0	0	8	7	29	0	.240	.212
	19	Johnson City (APP)	R	.286	33	112	24	32	9	0	6	17	19	36	0	.391	.527
Minor League Totals				.271	152	524	80	142	28	3	19	90	73	143	8	.368	.445

15 JULIO RODRIGUEZ, C

BA GRADE 50 Risk: High

Born: June 11, 1997. **B-T:** R-R. **HT:** 6-0. **WT:** 197. **Signed:** Dominican Republic, 2016. **Signed by:** Braly Guzman/Angel Ovalles.

TRACK RECORD: The Cardinals invite 60-70 unsigned international players to their Dominican academy each winter for a tournament to try and find players who were overlooked. Rodriguez was one of those unsigned invitees in 2016 and quickly impressed the Cardinals with his catch-and-throw skills. They signed him for $25,000. Rodriguez led high Class A Palm Beach in batting average and OPS through the first half of 2019 to earn Florida State League all-star honors, then was promoted to Double-A.

SCOUTING REPORT: Rodriguez stands out for his solid all-around game more than any individual tool. He makes frequent contact with a short, compact stroke, drives the ball with gap power and flashes occasional home-run power to his pull side. He controls the strike zone and limits his strikeouts. Though thick, Rodriguez is an above-average receiver and blocker who keeps wild pitches and passed balls to a minimum. His arm strength is average and plays up with his above-average footwork, transfer and accuracy, resulting in consistent sub-2.00 second pop times.

THE FUTURE: Rodriguez has a quiet personality and is still working to improve his leadership and game-calling. If he does, he has a chance to be a steady everyday catcher.

Year	Age	Club (League)	Class	AVG	G	AB	R	H	2B	3B	HR	RBI	BB	SO	SB	OBP	SLG
2017	20	Johnson City (APP)	R	.280	47	182	28	51	14	1	5	36	17	31	0	.343	.451
	20	Palm Beach (FSL)	HiA	.000	1	3	0	0	0	0	0	0	0	0	0	.000	.000
2018	21	Peoria (MWL)	LoA	.258	76	291	26	75	15	2	8	47	13	60	0	.288	.405
2019	22	Palm Beach (FSL)	HiA	.276	71	268	28	74	14	0	7	31	16	53	0	.321	.407
	22	Springfield (TL)	AA	.222	14	45	2	10	1	0	1	7	2	15	0	.255	.311
Minor League Totals				.275	249	932	114	256	54	6	28	158	67	178	0	.324	.436

16 ANGEL RONDON, RHP

BA GRADE 50 Risk: High

Born: Dec. 1, 1997. **B-T:** R-R. **HT:** 6-2. **WT:** 185. **Signed:** Dominican Republic, 2016. **Signed by:** Raymi Dicent/Angel Ovalles.

TRACK RECORD: Rondon was already 18 when the Cardinals signed him for $25,000 out of the Dominican Republic in Jan. 2016. He made his age irrelevant with a quick ascent through the Cardinals system. After cruising through the low minors, Rondon earned All-Star honors in the high Class A Florida State League and jumped to Double-A Springfield in 2019. He finished second in the Cardinals system in ERA (2.93) and strikeouts (159) and was named their minor league pitcher of the year.

SCOUTING REPORT: Rondon has a potent mix of funk and power. He dials his fastball up and down anywhere from 90-97 mph, sitting 93, and keeps hitters further off balance with a long, pronounced delivery. He complements his fastball with an above-average hard slider that drops under barrels. Rondon's delivery leads to scattered command and fringe-average control, but he keeps everything around the strike zone and has advanced feel for throwing the right pitch in the right situation. He won the Texas League ERA title and finished second in the league with a 1.23 WHIP.

THE FUTURE: Rondon became a favorite of rival evaluators during the season, who mostly think he will end up a power reliever. He will move to Triple-A Memphis in 2020.

Year	Age	Club (League)	Class	W	L	ERA	G	GS	SV	IP	H	HR	BB	SO	K/9	WHIP	AVG
2017	19	Cardinals (DSL)	R	0	1	4.76	2	2	0	6	4	0	3	6	9.5	1.24	.211
	19	Johnson City (APP)	R	0	0	6.75	1	1	0	4	6	2	3	5	11.3	2.25	.353
	19	Cardinals (GCL)	R	3	3	2.64	11	8	0	48	46	2	17	41	7.7	1.32	.254
2018	20	State College (NYP)	SS	0	4	3.72	5	5	0	29	29	3	7	23	7.1	1.24	.264
	20	Peoria (MWL)	LoA	3	2	2.90	10	10	0	59	49	7	17	57	8.7	1.12	.220
2019	21	Palm Beach (FSL)	HiA	5	1	2.20	8	8	0	45	26	3	17	47	9.4	0.96	.165
	21	Springfield (TL)	AA	6	6	3.21	20	20	0	115	99	11	42	112	8.8	1.23	.230
Minor League Totals				19	19	3.01	71	61	1	347	298	28	119	341	8.8	1.20	.229

17 MALCOM NUNEZ, 3B

BA GRADE 55 Risk: Extreme

Born: March 9, 2001. **B-T:** R-R. **HT:** 5-11. **WT:** 205. **Signed:** Cuba, 2018. **Signed by:** Alix Martinez/Angel Ovalles.

TRACK RECORD: Nunez starred for Cuba's junior national teams as a teenager and signed with the Cardinals for $300,000 in 2018. He won the Dominican Summer League triple crown after signing, but fell flat in his U.S. debut in 2019. Nunez hit .183 in 21 games at low Class A Peoria before being demoted, then drew mixed reviews at Rookie-level Johnson City.

SCOUTING REPORT: Nunez is a thick-bodied masher defined by his bat. He flashes plus raw power and has the bat speed to turn around velocity. Nunez makes loud contact when he connects, but his approach

is very raw. He is still learning to stay back on breaking balls and struggles to get to his power in games. Nunez is listed at 205 pounds but is closer to 225. He flashes soft hands and a plus arm at third base, but his throwing is inconsistent and his size limits his range. He is a well below-average runner.
THE FUTURE: Nunez has a thunderous bat, but he is very raw as both a hitter and defender and will have to watch his weight. He'll get another crack at low Class A Peoria in 2020.

Year	Age	Club (League)	Class	AVG	G	AB	R	H	2B	3B	HR	RBI	BB	SO	SB	OBP	SLG
2018	17	Cardinals Blue (DSL)	R	.415	44	164	44	68	16	2	13	59	26	29	3	.497	.774
2019	18	Peoria (MWL)	LoA	.183	21	71	5	13	1	0	0	5	5	15	0	.247	.197
	18	Johnson City (APP)	R	.254	37	130	14	33	11	0	2	13	13	32	3	.336	.385
Minor League Totals				.312	102	365	63	114	28	2	15	77	44	76	6	.396	.523

18 KODI WHITLEY, RHP

BA GRADE
45 **Risk: Medium**

Born: Feb. 21, 1995. **B-T:** R-R. **HT:** 6-4. **WT:** 220. **Drafted:** Mount Olive (N.C.), 2017 (27th round). **Signed by:** T.C. Calhoun

TRACK RECORD: Whitley missed all of 2016 after having Tommy John surgery and pitched only three games the following season for Division II Mount Olive (N.C.). The Cardinals saw enough to draft him in the 27th round and sign him for $75,000. Whitley quickly rewarded their faith, reaching Triple-A Memphis in his second full season and logging a 2.01 ERA over 104 career appearances.
SCOUTING REPORT: Whitley is a big-armed, 6-foot-4 righthander who looks the part of a major league reliever. He powers his four-seam fastball downhill at 94-97 mph, getting swings and misses in all parts of the strike zone. Whitley complements his heater with a vertical 84-85 mph slider that dives under barrels and a fading 83-84 mph changeup that neutralizes lefties. Whitley's control occasionally escapes him, but he stays around the strike zone enough to be competitive. Despite being a fly-ball pitcher, he has allowed only five home runs in 156.2 career professional innings.
THE FUTURE: He has the stuff and steady demeanor to pitch in high-leverage relief. He should join the Cardinals bullpen in 2020.

Year	Age	Club (League)	Class	W	L	ERA	G	GS	SV	IP	H	HR	BB	SO	K/9	WHIP	AVG
2017	22	Cardinals (GCL)	R	0	0	1.84	12	0	2	15	15	0	3	19	11.7	1.23	.283
	22	Palm Beach (FSL)	HiA	0	0	0.00	1	0	0	3	1	0	1	3	9.0	0.67	.100
2018	23	Peoria (MWL)	LoA	4	2	2.51	41	2	9	72	67	2	26	68	8.5	1.30	.248
2019	24	Palm Beach (FSL)	HiA	0	0	0.00	3	0	0	4	1	0	2	5	10.4	0.69	.077
	24	Springfield (TL)	AA	1	4	1.83	31	0	7	39	31	3	13	46	10.5	1.12	.208
	24	Memphis (PCL)	AAA	2	0	1.52	16	0	2	24	21	0	4	27	10.3	1.06	.233
Minor League Totals				7	6	2.01	104	2	20	156	136	5	49	168	9.7	1.18	.232

19 JUSTIN WILLIAMS, OF

BA GRADE
45 **Risk: Medium**

Born: Aug. 20, 1995. **B-T:** L-R. **HT:** 6-2. **WT:** 215. **Drafted:** HS—Houma, La., 2013 (2nd round). **Signed by:** Rusty Pendergrass (D-backs).

TRACK RECORD: The D-backs drafted Williams 52nd overall in 2013 and traded him to the Rays one year later as part of the package for Jeremy Hellickson. The Rays sent him to the Cardinals as one of three prospects for Tommy Pham at the 2018 trade deadline. Williams' first full season in the Cardinals organization was limited to 53 games by injuries. He missed the start of the season after punching a television, then went on the injured list twice with hamstring injuries during the year. He still managed to finish strong with a 1.045 OPS in 36 games at Triple-A Memphis.
SCOUTING REPORT: Williams intrigues as a natural athlete with above-average raw power from the left side. He manages the strike zone and recognizes pitches, but his segmented swing results in too many ground balls. At his best he drives the ball to all fields and can elevate for home runs. Williams is a fringe-average runner whose reads and effort waver in the outfield. His best position is right field where he can utilize his plus, accurate arm.
THE FUTURE: Williams has a chance to see the majors in 2020. He'll break in as a reserve.

Year	Age	Club (League)	Class	AVG	G	AB	R	H	2B	3B	HR	RBI	BB	SO	SB	OBP	SLG
2017	21	Montgomery (SL)	AA	.301	96	366	53	110	21	3	14	72	37	69	6	.364	.489
2018	22	Tampa Bay (AL)	MAJ	.000	1	1	0	0	0	0	0	0	0	0	0	.000	.000
	22	Durham (IL)	AAA	.258	94	356	41	92	18	0	8	46	25	81	4	.313	.376
	22	Memphis (PCL)	AAA	.217	21	69	8	15	3	0	3	11	5	17	0	.276	.391
2019	23	Springfield (TL)	AA	.193	17	57	7	11	1	0	1	3	4	17	1	.246	.263
	23	Memphis (PCL)	AAA	.353	36	102	20	36	5	0	7	26	16	30	0	.437	.608
Major League Totals				.000	1	1	0	0	0	0	0	0	0	0	0	.000	.000
Minor League Totals				.296	601	2261	302	670	126	12	55	348	147	471	18	.342	.436

20 MATEO GIL, SS

BA GRADE
50 Risk: Extreme

Born: July 24, 2000. **B-T:** R-R. **HT:** 6-1. **WT:** 180. **Drafted:** HS—Keller, Texas, 2018 (3rd round). **Signed by:** Tom Lipari.

TRACK RECORD: Gil largely split teams as a prospect in the 2018 draft, but the Cardinals liked his athleticism and instincts and drafted him in the third round. Gil's skills and athleticism proved even better than expected when he reported to the Cardinals after signing, and he followed up with a solid season as an 18-year-old in the Rookie-level Appalachian League.

SCOUTING REPORT: Gil is the son of former Rangers and Angels infielder Benji Gil. He is a smooth, confident shortstop with soft hands and mature actions, and he can make throws from anywhere on the diamond with his above-average, accurate arm. Gil takes an advanced approach at the plate and makes hard contact when he connects. He has a fast, loose swing and the strong hands and wrists to project power as he matures physically. Gil doesn't have any plus tools, but he has no major weaknesses, either.

THE FUTURE: Gil will move to low Class A Peoria in 2020. He projects as a solid all-around infielder.

Year	Age	Club (League)	Class	AVG	G	AB	R	H	2B	3B	HR	RBI	BB	SO	SB	OBP	SLG
2018	17	Cardinals (GCL)	R	.251	45	171	27	43	6	1	1	20	20	51	2	.340	.316
2019	18	Palm Beach (FSL)	HiA	.000	2	6	0	0	0	0	0	0	0	2	0	.000	.000
	18	Johnson City (APP)	R	.270	51	204	42	55	8	2	7	30	17	56	1	.324	.431
Minor League Totals				.257	98	381	69	98	14	3	8	50	37	109	3	.327	.373

21 EDMUNDO SOSA, SS

BA GRADE
40 Risk: Medium

Born: March 6, 1996. **B-T:** R-R. **Ht.:** 5-11. **Wt.:** 170. **Signed:** Panama, 2012. **Signed by:** Arquimedes Nieto.

TRACK RECORD: Sosa signed with the Cardinals for $425,000 in 2012. After missing much of 2016 and 2017 with wrist and hand injuries, Sosa stayed healthy in 2018 and jumped three levels to the majors. He spent most of 2019 at Triple-A Memphis and returned to the majors twice as a callup.

SCOUTING REPORT: Previously known for his defense, Sosa made an adjustment to use his hands more in his swing and keeps adding power. He hit a career-high 17 home runs in 2019 and slugged .466. Sosa is a free swinger who is aggressive early in counts and rarely walks, but his growing power gives him a chance to make some offensive impact. Defensively, Sosa has the hands and above-average arm to be an above-average shortstop. His defense previously played down due to poor instincts, but he has started positioning himself better and playing with more effort.

THE FUTURE: Sosa began playing second and third base the last two years to prepare for a future utility role. He will try to win a spot on the Cardinals' bench in 2020.

Year	Age	Club (League)	Class	AVG	G	AB	R	H	2B	3B	HR	RBI	BB	SO	SB	OBP	SLG
2017	21	Springfield (TL)	AA	.000	1	4	0	0	0	0	0	0	1	0	0	.200	.000
	21	Cardinals (GCL)	R	.364	6	22	7	8	1	0	1	2	1	2	0	.391	.545
	21	Palm Beach (FSL)	HiA	.285	51	193	25	55	10	1	0	14	12	34	3	.329	.347
2018	22	Springfield (TL)	AA	.276	67	261	34	72	17	1	7	32	9	52	1	.308	.429
	22	Memphis (PCL)	AAA	.262	56	191	31	50	13	0	5	27	13	42	5	.321	.408
	22	St. Louis (NL)	MAJ	.000	3	2	1	0	0	0	0	0	1	1	0	.333	.000
2019	23	Memphis (PCL)	AAA	.291	118	453	70	132	18	5	17	62	17	96	2	.335	.466
	23	St. Louis (NL)	MAJ	.250	8	8	2	2	0	0	0	0	1	2	1	.400	.250
Major League Totals				.200	11	10	3	2	0	0	0	0	2	3	1	.385	.200
Minor League Totals				.283	547	2090	312	592	96	22	44	237	129	389	37	.334	.413

22 TREJYN FLETCHER, OF

BA GRADE
50 Risk: Extreme

Born: April 30, 2001. **B-T:** R-R. **HT:** 6-2. **WT:** 200. **Drafted:** HS—Portland, Maine, 2019 (2nd round). **Signed by:** Jim Negrych.

TRACK RECORD: Fletcher reclassified from the 2020 draft class to the 2019 class three months before the draft, sending scouts scurrying up to Maine to see him. The Cardinals drafted him in the second round, No. 58 overall, and signed him for $1.5 million to forgo a Vanderbilt commitment.

SCOUTING REPORT: Fletcher is a plus-plus runner and has explosive quick-twitch movements in both the outfield and the batter's box. He has plus raw power, but he's very raw as a hitter. Fletcher is extremely pull-oriented with a long swing and a big leg kick, and opponents found him an easy out if they just threw him breaking balls. He struck out 76 times in 175 plate appearances (43 percent) in his pro debut. Fletcher has excellent range and closing speed in center field and should be a plus defender as his reads and jumps improve with experience. He has a plus arm that notched nine assists in 38 games.

THE FUTURE: Fletcher has a long way to develop as a hitter. He'll spend most of 2020 at Rookie levels.

Year	Age	Club (League)	Class	AVG	G	AB	R	H	2B	3B	HR	RBI	BB	SO	SB	OBP	SLG
2019	18	Cardinals (GCL)	R	.297	9	37	6	11	3	0	2	8	4	17	0	.357	.541
	18	Johnson City (APP)	R	.228	34	123	9	28	4	1	2	18	7	59	7	.271	.325
Minor League Totals				.244	43	160	15	39	7	1	4	26	11	76	7	.291	.375

23 TONY LOCEY, RHP

BA GRADE
45 Risk: High

Born: July 29, 1998. **B-T:** R-R. **HT:** 6-3. **WT:** 239. **Drafted:** Georgia, 2019 (3rd round). **Signed by:** Charles Peterson.

TRACK RECORD: Locey teamed with Orioles prospect D.L. Hall and Georgia quarterback Jake Fromm to lead Warner Robins (Ga.) High to a state title in 2016. Locey went on to Georgia and spent two years in the Bulldogs rotation, taking over as their Friday starter midway through his junior year. The Cardinals drafted him in the third round, No. 96 overall, and signed him for $604,800.

SCOUTING REPORT: Locey's primary weapon is his plus fastball. It's an explosive pitch that sits 94-96 mph and touches 98, and it plays at the top of the strike zone despite the lack of an elite spin rate. Locey complements his heater with a sharp, short slider with late break that flashes plus at its best, although it plays down because he has trouble locating it in the strike zone. His fringy curveball serves as a usable early count pitch. Locey's control ranges from below-average to average.

THE FUTURE: Locey's control and lack of a reliable third pitch make him a future reliever for many evaluators. The Cardinals will keep him as a starter for now.

Year	Age	Club (League)	Class	W	L	ERA	G	GS	SV	IP	H	HR	BB	SO	K/9	WHIP	AVG
2019	20	Cardinals (GCL)	R	0	0	0.00	2	0	0	2	1	0	2	3	13.5	1.50	.143
	20	Peoria (MWL)	LoA	1	2	6.00	10	0	0	15	15	1	10	28	16.8	1.67	.259
Minor League Totals				1	2	5.29	12	0	0	17	16	1	12	31	16.4	1.65	.246

24 SETH ELLEDGE, RHP

BA GRADE
40 Risk: Medium

Born: May 20, 1996. **B-T:** R-R. **HT:** 6-3. **WT:** 230. **Drafted:** Dallas Baptist, 2017 (4th round). **Signed by:** Ty Bowman (Mariners).

TRACK RECORD: Elledge followed a long line of hard-throwing Dallas Baptist relievers and set the school record with 26 saves. The Mariners drafted him in the fourth round in 2017 and traded him to the Cardinals one year later for Sam Tuivailala.

SCOUTING REPORT: Elledge has an imposing frame at 6-foot-3, 240 pounds and uses it to his advantage. He has a slight cross-body delivery, helping him hide the ball and prevent hitters from picking it up. Elledge's high-spin fastball sits 91-93 mph and plays up with late life and carry through the zone. He backs it up with a hard, downer curveball in the low 80s that flashes average. Elledge's big body and high-effort delivery cause him to lose his balance and result in below-average control and spotty fastball command.

THE FUTURE: Elledge is in position to join the Cardinals bullpen in 2020. He'll open back at Triple-A.

Year	Age	Club (League)	Class	W	L	ERA	G	GS	SV	IP	H	HR	BB	SO	K/9	WHIP	AVG
2017	21	Everett (NWL)	SS	0	0	4.50	4	0	0	4	2	0	2	7	15.8	1.00	.154
	21	Clinton (MWL)	LoA	3	0	3.00	15	0	5	21	14	1	6	35	15.0	0.95	.182
2018	22	Modesto (CAL)	HiA	5	1	1.17	31	0	9	38	18	1	15	54	12.7	0.86	.140
	22	Springfield (TL)	AA	3	1	4.32	13	0	4	17	13	3	6	20	10.8	1.14	.220
2019	23	Springfield (TL)	AA	3	3	3.78	26	0	3	33	34	3	13	43	11.6	1.41	.276
	23	Memphis (PCL)	AAA	3	1	4.72	21	3	0	34	28	3	19	32	8.4	1.37	.233
Minor League Totals				17	6	3.29	110	3	21	147	109	11	61	191	11.6	1.15	.209

25 ALVARO SEIJAS, RHP

BA GRADE
45 Risk: High

Born: Oct. 10, 1998. **B-T:** R-R. **HT:** 6-1. **WT:** 175. **Signed:** Venezuela, 2015. **Signed by:** Jose Gonzalez Maestre.

TRACK RECORD: Seijas signed for $762,500 as the headliner of the Cardinals' 2015 international class and quickly conquered the Rookie levels before struggling with the jump to full-season ball. He returned to low Class A Peoria in 2019 and improved his control, earning a promotion to high Class A Palm Beach.

SCOUTING REPORT: Seijas is undersized at 6-foot-1 but has plenty of arm strength with a fastball that reaches the mid-90s. His breaking ball gets slurvy at times but flashes as an average curveball, and his changeup is a fringy but usable offering off his fastball. Seijas is still working on the mental part of the game. He often lacks a plan to set hitters up and is prone to losing his focus. He is a solid competitor who stays poised, but he needs to be more consistent with his focus and command.

THE FUTURE: Seijas has the stuff and pitch mix to project as a potential back-end starter or middle reliever. He'll see Double-A Springfield in 2020.

Year	Age	Club (League)	Class	W	L	ERA	G	GS	SV	IP	H	HR	BB	SO	K/9	WHIP	AVG
2017	18	Johnson City (APP)	R	4	3	4.97	12	12	0	63	79	2	20	63	9.0	1.56	.306
2018	19	Peoria (MWL)	LoA	5	8	4.52	25	22	1	129	149	14	61	84	5.8	1.62	.301
2019	20	Peoria (MWL)	LoA	4	5	2.93	14	14	0	80	73	6	28	71	8.0	1.26	.246
	20	Palm Beach (FSL)	HiA	4	1	2.65	10	10	0	54	54	2	26	43	7.1	1.47	.262
Minor League Totals				22	19	3.81	75	71	1	396	423	28	154	316	7.2	1.46	.277

26 RAMON URIAS, 2B

BA GRADE 40 Risk: Medium

Born: June 3, 1994. **B-T:** R-R. **HT:** 5-10. **WT:** 150. **Signed:** Mexico, 2010. **Signed by:** Bill McLaughlin (Rangers).

TRACK RECORD: The Rangers signed Urias as a 16-year-old in 2010 but relinquished his rights to the Mexican League before the 2013 season. Urias grew into one of the league's top hitters over the next five seasons, batting a combined .323, and signed with the Cardinals as a free agent in 2018.

SCOUTING REPORT: The older brother of Padres second baseman Luis Urias, Ramon resembles his little brother as an undersized middle infielder with natural hitting instincts. He recognizes pitches, works himself into favorable counts and has the hand-eye coordination to consistently put the barrel on the ball. He is an average hitter with enough power to keep pitchers honest, reaching double-digit home runs each of the last two seasons. Urias is an average defender at both second and third base and is playable at shortstop in short spurts. He is an average runner who covers the requisite ground in the infield.

THE FUTURE: Urias is on the 40-man roster and in position to make his big league debut as a utilityman.

Year	Age	Club (League)	Class	AVG	G	AB	R	H	2B	3B	HR	RBI	BB	SO	SB	OBP	SLG
2017	23	Mexico City (MEX)	AAA	.340	106	388	91	132	29	3	19	79	41	75	12	.433	.577
2018	24	Springfield (TL)	AA	.333	44	168	28	56	19	0	8	27	18	29	1	.406	.589
	24	Memphis (PCL)	AAA	.261	46	142	20	37	9	0	5	17	6	29	0	.291	.430
2019	25	Palm Beach (FSL)	HiA	.200	5	20	5	4	0	0	1	2	1	8	0	.238	.350
	25	Springfield (TL)	AA	.375	2	8	1	3	0	0	0	1	0	2	0	.375	.375
	25	Memphis (PCL)	AAA	.263	96	316	51	83	24	0	9	52	44	71	4	.369	.424
Minor League Totals				.299	650	2132	411	637	139	11	60	344	202	376	44	.382	.459

27 GRIFFIN ROBERTS, RHP

BA GRADE 50 Risk: Extreme

Born: June 13, 1996. **B-T:** R-R. **HT:** 6-3. **WT:** 205. **Drafted:** Wake Forest, 2018 (1st round supplemental). **Signed by:** T.C. Calhoun.

TRACK RECORD: Roberts led the Atlantic Coast Conference in strikeouts in 2018 and was drafted by the Cardinals 43rd overall. He got off to a bad start when he twice tested positive for marijuana and received a 50-game suspension to start the 2019 season. Roberts struggled when he returned, posting a 6.44 ERA with nearly as many walks (35) as strikeouts (36) at high Class A Palm Beach.

SCOUTING REPORT: Roberts' fastball sits in the low-to-mid 90s and reaches 97 mph with running life, while his slider is a plus pitch with exceptional movement and depth. Roberts also flashes an average changeup with fade. Roberts's high-effort delivery and low arm slot make him a likely reliever for many evaluators, but the Cardinals will continue to start him. He rebuilt his stock with an excellent showing in the Arizona Fall League, where he posted a 3.07 ERA over four starts with 18 strikeouts and two walks in 14.2 innings.

THE FUTURE: Roberts has early red flags, but the Cardinals believe an uninterrupted 2020 will allow his best to come out.

Year	Age	Club (League)	Class	W	L	ERA	G	GS	SV	IP	H	HR	BB	SO	K/9	WHIP	AVG
2018	22	Cardinals (GCL)	R	0	1	6.23	7	2	1	9	6	0	4	11	11.4	1.15	.194
	22	Palm Beach (FSL)	HiA	0	0	0.00	1	0	0	1	0	0	0	2	18.0	0.00	.000
2019	23	Palm Beach (FSL)	HiA	1	7	6.44	15	13	0	66	79	3	35	36	4.9	1.74	.305
Minor League Totals				1	8	6.33	23	15	1	75	85	3	39	49	5.9	1.65	.290

28 LUKEN BAKER, 1B

BA GRADE 45 Risk: High

Born: March 10, 1997. **B-T:** R-R. **HT:** 6-4. **WT:** 270. **Drafted:** Texas Christian, 2018 (2nd round supplemental). **Signed by:** Tom Lipari.

TRACK RECORD: Baker achieved folk hero status at Texas Christian as a hefty masher who became one of college baseball's top sluggers. The Cardinals drafted him 75th overall in 2018 and signed him for $800,000. Baker struggled his first full season as his towering flies fell short of the wall at cavernous high Class A Palm Beach, but he adjusted his pitch selection late in the year and slugged .654 in August.

SCOUTING REPORT: A burly 270 pounds with a physique likened to a lumberjack, Baker boasts plus

raw power and doesn't have to swing hard to get to it. He began chasing pitches out of the zone as his early-season power drought extended, but by the end he returned to recognizing pitches, taking a patient approach and showing the mix of discipline and bat control to project as an average hitter. Baker is limited to first base by his size and below-average range. He picks balls out of the dirt well enough to be playable.
THE FUTURE: Baker's late-season improvement and a move to hitter-friendly Double-A Springfield bode well for a bounceback season in 2020. He will go as far as his bat takes him.

Year	Age	Club (League)	Class	AVG	G	AB	R	H	2B	3B	HR	RBI	BB	SO	SB	OBP	SLG
2018	21	Cardinals (GCL)	R	.500	8	24	10	12	2	0	1	7	3	4	0	.536	.708
	21	Peoria (MWL)	LoA	.288	37	139	16	40	9	0	3	15	16	31	0	.359	.417
2019	22	Palm Beach (FSL)	HiA	.244	122	439	47	107	32	1	10	53	52	112	1	.327	.390
Minor League Totals				.264	167	602	73	159	43	1	14	75	71	147	1	.343	.409

29 JUSTIN TOERNER, OF

BA GRADE
40 Risk: High

Born: Aug. 11, 1996. **B-T:** L-L. **HT:** 5-10. **WT:** 165. **Drafted:** Cal State Northridge, 2018 (28th round). **Signed by:** Mike Garciaparra.
TRACK RECORD: Toerner started all four years at Cal State Northridge, where his late father Sean was an All-American infielder and a 1980 draft pick of the Giants. He signed with the Cardinals for $3,000 as a 28th-rounder in 2018 and quickly outplayed his draft spot, reaching high Class A two months after signing and finishing his first full season in Double-A.
SCOUTING REPORT: Toerner is 5-foot-10 but plays above his size with a high effort level and sneaky tools. He is a patient lefthanded hitter who makes frequent contact with a short, whippy swing. He controls the strike zone, makes pitchers work and rarely strikes out. Toerner's power is more suited for doubles, but he can drive the ball out to both gaps. Toerner is an above-average runner, has an average arm and has the range and instincts to play all three outfield positions.
THE FUTURE: Toerner does everything well enough to be a potential fourth outfielder. He'll open 2020 back at Double-A.

Year	Age	Club (League)	Class	AVG	G	AB	R	H	2B	3B	HR	RBI	BB	SO	SB	OBP	SLG
2018	21	State College (NYP)	SS	.292	50	171	26	50	5	1	1	10	24	34	11	.390	.351
	21	Palm Beach (FSL)	HiA	.300	10	40	8	12	5	0	0	3	5	9	0	.391	.425
	21	Peoria (MWL)	LoA	.500	7	20	4	10	0	1	0	4	5	2	0	.600	.600
2019	22	Palm Beach (FSL)	HiA	.290	54	193	39	56	5	1	4	29	33	50	4	.403	.389
	22	Springfield (TL)	AA	.211	49	166	30	35	5	0	7	18	28	55	10	.338	.367
Minor League Totals				.276	170	590	107	163	20	3	12	64	95	150	25	.387	.381

30 CONNOR JONES, RHP

BA GRADE
40 Risk: High

Born: Oct. 10, 1994. **B-T:** R-R. **HT:** 6-3. **WT:** 200. **Drafted:** Virginia, 2016 (2nd round). **Signed by:** Sean Moran
BACKGROUND: Jones anchored Virginia's national championship-winning staff as a sophomore and emerged as its Friday night starter as a junior. The Cardinals drafted him in the second round in 2016 and signed him for $1.1 million. Considered a "safe" pick out of the draft, Jones' control instead abandoned him as a pro, and the Cardinals moved him to the bullpen full-time in 2019.
SCOUTING REPORT: Jones' stuff ticked up with his move to the bullpen. A sinker that sat 92-93 mph as a starter is now a heavy, 95-98 mph bowling ball that breaks bats and induces ground ball rates north of 60 percent. Jones complements his sinker with an above-average, 84-87 mph power curveball with sharp downward bite, and he keeps an average mid-80s changeup with depth in his back pocket. Jones tends to overthink and nibble rather than attack, resulting in a troublesome walk rate even in relief.
THE FUTURE: Jones has the stuff to pitch in relief, but he needs to get out of his own head and throw strikes.

Year	Age	Club (League)	Class	W	L	ERA	G	GS	SV	IP	H	HR	BB	SO	K/9	WHIP	AVG
2017	22	Palm Beach (FSL)	HiA	8	5	3.97	24	21	1	113	120	3	49	76	6.0	1.49	.275
	22	Springfield, MO (TL)	AA	1	0	2.70	1	1	0	7	6	1	3	2	2.7	1.35	.261
2018	23	Memphis (PCL)	AAA	1	0	6.46	4	4	0	15	20	1	14	16	9.4	2.22	.317
	23	Springfield, MO (TL)	AA	5	5	3.80	22	17	0	95	96	4	51	66	6.3	1.55	.264
2019	24	Springfield, MO (TL)	AA	1	1	4.66	42	0	9	48	54	5	35	49	9.1	1.84	.284
	24	Memphis (PCL)	AAA	0	0	0.00	1	0	0	2	0	0	0	1	4.5	0.00	.000
Minor League Totals				16	11	4.09	105	43	11	295	314	14	155	221	6.7	1.59	.275

San Diego Padres

BY KYLE GLASER

No one has ever doubted A.J. Preller's ability to identify amateur talent. The Padres general manager's ability to construct a winning major league roster, however, remains an open question.

Propelled by the promise of baseball's No. 1 farm system and the debuts of Fernando Tatis Jr. and Chris Paddack, the Padres began 2019 as optimistic as they've been years. They got off to an 11-5 start and held a 45-45 record at the all-star break, leading Preller to declare he expected the team to contend for a wild card spot.

Instead, the club traded away popular outfielder Franmil Reyes at the deadline, Tatis suffered a season-ending back injury in August and the Padres cratered with a 2-15 finish to the season. Manager Andy Green was fired in the midst of that skid, and the Padres finished 72-90 and in last place in the National League West once again.

Preller has repeatedly pronounced the Padres about to improve, only to have them fall short each time. After the Padres picked seventh overall in the 2018 draft, he declared it the last time the Padres would pick in the top 10.

Instead, they picked in the top 10 again in 2019 and will do so again in 2020.

Preller's proclamation of wild card contention raised eyebrows, and he didn't help by trading Reyes and lefthander Logan Allen—two major leaguers—for Double-A prospect Taylor Trammell at the deadline.

With each proclamation of future that falls short, Preller's ability to accurately gauge what it takes to win in the major leagues comes under further scrutiny. That scrutiny became even greater when owner Ron Fowler told a fan gathering after the season "heads will roll" if the team does not improve in 2020.

Tatis and Paddack had brilliant, albeit abbreviated, rookie seasons in 2019, but it wasn't enough to overcome a subpar campaign from $300 million offseason signee Manny Machado, who followed in the footsteps of Eric Hosmer, Wil Myers and James Shields in disappointing after signing large contracts with the Padres.

Supposed young cornerstones Austin Hedges and Manny Margot continue to struggle at the plate, while Luis Urias fell into the all-too-familiar pattern of becoming a worse hitter once he reached San Diego and was traded to the Brewers after the season. Catcher Francisco Mejia and outfielder Josh Naylor showed the ability to hit, but their defensive shortcomings make them questionable fits in the National League.

For all the hype about their farm system, the Padres largely have a roster of underperformers and ill-fitting pieces in the major leagues.

The Padres' farm system is still among baseball's best, led by lefthander MacKenzie Gore and righthander Luis Patiño. There are more position players on the way too, headlined by 2019 first-round pick CJ Abrams and catcher Luis Campusano.

But the question is whether Preller and his staff can accurately mold that prospect talent into a winning major league team. Preller hired Jayce Tingler, whom he worked with in Texas, to replace Green as manager and help turn things around.

If that turnaround doesn't begin in 2020, with a winning record the bare minimum, Preller's head may be the first to roll.

BRIAN ROTHMULLER/ICON SPORTSWIRE VIA GETTY IMAGES

Shortstop Fernando Tatis Jr. showed power, speed and flair in his huge rookie season.

PROJECTED 2023 LINEUP

Position	Player	Age
Catcher	Francisco Mejia	27
First Base	Eric Hosmer	33
Second Base	CJ Abrams (3)	22
Third Base	Manny Machado	30
Shortstop	Fernando Tatis Jr.	24
Left Field	Trent Grisham	26
Center Field	Taylor Trammell (4)	25
Right Field	Josh Naylor	26
No. 1 Starter	MacKenzie Gore (1)	24
No. 2 Starter	Luis Patiño (2)	23
No. 3 Starter	Chris Paddack	27
No. 4 Starter	Dinelson Lamet	30
No. 5 Starter	Joey Lucchesi	30
Closer	Andres Muñoz (9)	24

DEPTH CHART

SAN DIEGO PADRES

TOP 2020 ROOKIE: Andres Muñoz, RHP. As long as he stays healthy, the flame-throwing righthander has a chance to be the Padres' closer.

BREAKOUT PROSPECT: Hudson Head, OF. Head became a favorite of Padres coaches during instructional league and has seen his skills improve rapidly in a short time.

SLEEPER: Yeison Santana, SS. Santana hit .346 in his pro debut and owns a promising mix of bat-to-ball skills, plate discipline and excellent athleticism.

SOURCE OF TOP 30 TALENT

Homegrown	**26**	**Acquired**	**4**
College	3	Trade	4
Junior college	0	Rule 5 draft	0
High school	10	Independent league	0
Nondrafted free agent	0	Free agent/waivers	0
International	13		

LF
Taylor Trammell (4)
Esteury Ruiz

CF
Hudson Head (20)
Jeisson Rosario (24)
Ismael Mena (28)
Michael Gettys

RF
Edward Olivares (17)
Joshua Mears (22)
Tirso Ornelas (25)
Jorge Ona (26)
Junior Perez

3B
Hudson Potts (16)
Tucupita Marcano (18)

SS
CJ Abrams (3)
Gabriel Arias (9)
Jake Cronenworth (15)
Reggie Preciado (21)
Yeison Santana
Justin Lopez

2B
Owen Miller (12)
Eguy Rosario (29)
Esteban Quiroz
Ivan Castillo

1B
Seth Mejias-Brean
Brad Zunica

C
Luis Campusano (5)
Blake Hunt (19)
Logan Driscoll (27)

LHP

LHSP
MacKenzie Gore (1)
Adrian Morejon (6)
Ryan Weathers (10)
Joey Cantillo (11)
Omar Cruz
Aaron Leasher
Osvaldo Hernandez
Jesus Gonzalez

LHRP
Hazahel Quijada
Dan Dallas

RHP

RHSP
Luis Patino (2)
Michel Baez (8)
Ronald Bolanos (13)
Reggie Lawson (14)
Lake Bachar (30)
Jacob Nix
Anderson Espinoza
Adrian Martinez
Matt Brash
Efrain Contreras
Luarbert Arias

RHRP
Andres Muñoz (7)
Javy Guerra (23)
David Bednar
Steven Wilson
Dauris Valdez
Gerardo Reyes
Jordan Guerrero
Evan Miller
Henry Henry
Chris Lincoln

DRAFT ANALYSIS

2019

BEST PURE HITTER: SS CJ Abrams (1) had some of the best hand-eye coordination and bat-to-ball skills in the draft class. He lived up to that by hitting .401 in the Rookie-level Arizona League. Abrams' simple approach, rhythmic swing, direct bat path and ability to make adjustments all portend a future plus or better hitter.

BEST POWER HITTER: OF Joshua Mears (2) teases future plus-plus raw power out of his strapping, 6-foot-3, 230-pound frame. He has a thick, strong body with easy power to all fields out of a short, compact swing for his size.

FASTEST RUNNER: Abrams is an 80-grade runner who often clocked 3.90 seconds from home to first base as an amateur. He reaches top speed in a few strides and projects to be a plus runner even as he bulks up.

BEST DEFENSIVE PLAYER: Abrams' speed and quick-twitch athleticism give him the ability to make spectacular plays at shortstop, although he gets caught flat-footed on routine plays at times. SS Chris Givin (19) committed only four errors his senior year at Xavier playing on a natural surface. He has steady actions, sure hands and average, accurate arm.

BEST ATHLETE: Abrams played high school football and basketball in addition to baseball and can do a windmill dunk. OF Hudson Head (3) was a high school quarterback who would throw with his right hand when he rolled right and with his left hand when he rolled left. He is a plus runner with a lean, twitchy body.

BEST FASTBALL: RHP Matt Brash (4) gets up to 96 mph on his fastball with arm-side run and sink, and he holds his velocity deep into games as a starter. RHP Chris Lincoln (5) reaches 97-98 mph in short bursts out of the bullpen.

BEST SECONDARY PITCH: Brash's power, 77-78 mph curveball and tilting, 85-86 mph slider both have plus potential in the Padres' eyes. His slider was more prominent in college at Niagara, but his curveball has a chance to end up being the better of the two offerings.

TOP DRAFT PICKS OF THE DECADE

Year	Player, Pos.	2019 Org
2010	*Karsten Whitson, RHP	Did not play
2011	Cory Spangenberg, 2B	Brewers
2012	Max Fried, LHP	Braves
2013	Hunter Renfroe, OF	Padres
2014	Trea Turner, SS	Nationals
2015	Austin Smith, RHP (2nd round)	Padres
2016	Cal Quantrill, RHP	Padres
2017	MacKenzie Gore, LHP	Padres
2018	Ryan Weathers, LHP	Padres
2019	CJ Abrams, SS	Padres

* Did not sign

BEST PRO DEBUT: Abrams won Arizona League MVP after batting .401/.442/.662 and was promoted to low Class A Fort Wayne less than two months after signing.

MOST INTRIGUING BACKGROUND: OF Jack Stronach (21) was a top-10 ranked tennis player in California at age 12 and is the nephew of former major league catcher Damon Berryhill. LHP Dylan Hoffman (39) is the son of Padres third base coach Glenn Hoffman and nephew of Hall of Fame closer Trevor Hoffman.

CLOSEST TO THE MAJORS: Abrams has the approach, athleticism and skills to move quickly even as a high school pick. Brash's pure stuff gives him a chance to rise quickly if the Padres put him in the bullpen.

BEST LATE-ROUND PICK: OF Taylor Lomack (24) and RHP Blake Baker (25) impressed after being taken out of Florida junior colleges. Lomack is a plus-plus runner who could grow into a plus defensive center fielder with more game experience. Baker flashed a plus, 95 mph fastball with sink and an above-average curveball in relief.

THE ONE WHO GOT AWAY: 3B Joshua Rivera (22) could be a high draft pick out of Florida in three years with his loose swing and plus power potential. The Padres took a flyer on OF Maurice Hampton (23), but the two-sport star stuck with his commitment to play both football and baseball at Louisiana State.

—KYLE GLASER

2018

LHP Ryan Weathers (1) and SS Xavier Edwards (1s) still headline the class after solid first full pro seasons, while 2B Owen Miller (3) sped to Double-A. Edwards was a part of the trade for Tommy Pham.

GRADE: B

2017

LHP MacKenzie Gore (1) has become one of the best pitching prospects in baseball, giving the class a star. LHP Nick Margevicius (7) has reached MLB and LHP Joey Cantillo (16) provides late-round value.

GRADE: A

2016

The class has produced four big leaguers, all pitchers drafted from the college ranks. RHP Cal Quantrill (1) still headlines, with LHPs Eric Lauer (1) and Joey Lucchesi (4) and RHP David Bednar (35) joining him.

GRADE: A

1 MacKENZIE GORE, LHP

Born: Feb. 24, 1999. **B-T:** L-L. **HT:** 6-3. **WT:** 195.
Drafted: HS—Whiteville, N.C., 2017 (1st round).
Signed by: Nick Brannon.

TRACK RECORD: Gore led Whiteville (N.C.) High to three state championships and went 11-0, 0.19 as a senior with 158 strikeouts and five walks in 74.1 innings to win BA's High School Player of the Year award. The Padres drafted him third overall and signed him for $6.7 million to forgo an East Carolina commitment. Gore's first full season was limited to 16 starts by blisters, but his full ability came out with full health in 2019. He posted a 1.02 ERA at high Class A Lake Elsinore, the lowest ERA by a starter with at least 70 innings in California League history, and earned an invitation to the Futures Game before a late-season promotion to Double-A Amarillo. Among pitchers who threw at least 100 innings in 2019, Gore led the minors in ERA (1.69) and WHIP (0.83).

SCOUTING REPORT: Gore's supreme athleticism sets him apart from other pitchers. He brings his knee nearly to his chin out of the windup during a sky-high leg kick, then explodes down and out over the mound to generate tremendous reach and extension. Gore's fastball ranges from 91-96 mph and gets on hitters quickly because of his nearly seven feet of extension. The result is late, confused swings from batters who think they have his fastball timed up, only to have the ball nearly in the catcher's mitt by the time they swing. Gore's slider and curveball are each swing-and-miss weapons at their best, but they are rarely good together and alternate as his better breaking ball depending on the day. His slider comes at hitters from 83-87 mph with tight spin and late break, and he locates it to both sides of the plate to make it a plus offering. His 76-79 mph curveball also flashes plus with tight 1-to-7 snap, though it is less consistent than his slider. Gore's changeup is his most consistent secondary at 79-83 mph with sink at the bottom of the zone, but he doesn't use it very often. It's still a plus pitch when he does. Gore is a superb athlete who repeats his complicated delivery and has plus control. He is a fearless competitor who works quickly, attacks hitters and has an unshakable inner confidence. Gore's only negative is he struggles holding runners. His pickoff move lacks deception, and at times he rushes through his delivery and loses command when opponents run on him.

THE FUTURE: Gore has the rare mix of stuff, athleticism, poise and control to be a true No. 1 starter. Few think he'll be worse than a No. 3.

JOHN E. MOORE III/GETTY IMAGES

BA GRADE
70 Risk: High

SCOUTING GRADES
Fastball: 60. **SL:** 60. **CHG:** 60. **Curveball:** 55. **Control:** 60

Projected future grades on 20-80 scouting scale.

TOP PROSPECTS OF THE DECADE

Year	Player, Pos.	2019 Org
2010	Donavan Tate, OF	Did not play
2011	Casey Kelly, RHP	Korea
2012	Anthony Rizzo, 1B	Cubs
2013	Casey Kelly, RHP	Korea
2014	Austin Hedges, C	Padres
2015	Matt Wisler, RHP	Mariners
2016	Javier Guerra, SS	Padres
2017	Anderson Espinoza, RHP	Padres
2018	Fernando Tatis Jr., SS	Padres
2019	Fernando Tatis Jr., SS	Padres

BEST TOOLS

Best Hitter for Average	CJ Abrams
Best Power Hitter	Luis Campusano
Best Strike-Zone Discipline	Luis Campusano
Fastest Baserunner	CJ Abrams
Best Athlete	CJ Abrams
Best Fastball	Andres Muñoz
Best Curveball	Adrian Morejon
Best Slider	Luis Patiño
Best Changeup	Joey Cantillo
Best Control	Ryan Weathers
Best Defensive Catcher	Blake Hunt
Best Defensive Infielder	Gabriel Arias
Best Infield Arm	Gabriel Arias
Best Defensive Outfielder	Michael Gettys
Best Outfield Arm	Michael Gettys

Year	Age	Club (League)	Class	W	L	ERA	G	GS	SV	IP	H	HR	BB	SO	K/9	WHIP	AVG
2017	18	Padres (AZL)	R	0	1	1.27	7	7	0	21	14	0	7	34	14.3	0.98	.184
2018	19	Fort Wayne (MWL)	LoA	2	5	4.45	16	16	0	61	61	5	18	74	11.0	1.30	.260
2019	20	Lake Elsinore (CAL)	HiA	7	1	1.02	15	15	0	79	36	4	20	110	12.5	0.71	.137
	20	Amarillo (TL)	AA	2	1	4.15	5	5	0	22	20	3	8	25	10.4	1.29	.250
Minor League Totals				11	8	2.56	43	43	0	183	131	12	53	243	12.0	1.01	.201

2 LUIS PATIÑO, RHP

Born: Oct. 26, 1999. **B-T:** R-R. **HT:** 6-0. **WT:** 192. **Signed:** Colombia, 2016.
Signed by: Andres Cabadias/Chris Kemp.

COURTESY OF LE STORM

BA GRADE
65 Risk: High

TRACK RECORD: Patiño weighed 150 pounds when he signed for $130,000 in 2016. He rapidly added weight and strength and gained 10-12 mph in two years, resulting in a swift ascent up the system. Patiño began 2019 as the youngest pitcher in the high Class A California League and posted a 2.69 ERA, earning a promotion to Double-A.

SCOUTING REPORT: The 6-foot Patiño pitches much bigger than his size. His quick arm, powerful legs and twitchy athleticism yield a vicious 94-95 mph fastball that touches 99 and explodes with late life through the zone. He can elevate it for swings and misses or dot it on the corners, leaving batters largely helpless against it. Patiño's 85-88 mph slider with late, biting tilt is another plus swing-and-miss offering, and he lands his average 82-84 mph curveball early in counts to give hitters a different look. Patiño's changeup is too firm at times, but it flashes plus with late drop when he dials it back to 85-87 mph. Patiño pitches with energy and exuberance, but he generally maintains his poise and above-average control in tight situations.

THE FUTURE: Patiño's stuff is that of a potential No. 2 starter. He'll head back to Double-A to start 2020.

SCOUTING GRADES: **Fastball:** 70 **Slider:** 60 **Curveball:** 55 **Changeup:** 50 **Control:** 55

Year	Age	Club (League)	Class	W	L	ERA	G	GS	SV	IP	H	HR	BB	SO	K/9	WHIP	AVG
2017	17	Padres (DSL)	R	2	1	1.69	4	4	0	16	11	0	2	15	8.4	0.81	.193
	17	Padres (AZL)	R	2	1	2.48	9	8	0	40	32	2	16	43	9.7	1.20	.213
2018	18	Fort Wayne (MWL)	LoA	6	3	2.16	17	17	0	83	65	1	24	98	10.6	1.07	.220
2019	19	Lake Elsinore (CAL)	HiA	6	8	2.69	18	17	0	87	61	4	34	113	11.7	1.09	.192
	19	Amarillo (TL)	AA	0	0	1.17	2	2	0	8	8	0	4	10	11.7	1.57	.258
Minor League Totals				16	13	2.35	50	48	0	234	177	7	80	279	10.7	1.10	.208

3 CJ ABRAMS, SS

Born: Oct. 3, 2000. **B-T:** L-R. **HT:** 6-2. **WT:** 185. **Drafted:** HS—Roswell, Ga., 2019 (1st round). **Signed by:** Tyler Stubblefield.

COURTESY OF LE STORM

BA GRADE
65 Risk: Very High

TRACK RECORD: Most teams considered Bobby Witt Jr. the top high school player in the 2019 draft class, but the Padres were one of a few clubs who preferred Abrams. They eagerly drafted him sixth overall when he fell to them and signed him for $5.2 million to forgo an Alabama commitment. Abrams promptly hit .401 in the Rookie-level Arizona League, winning league MVP honors, and earned a promotion to low Class A Fort Wayne before he suffered a season-ending bone bruise in his left shoulder sliding into a base.

SCOUTING REPORT: Abrams' lean, athletic frame jumps out, but it's his hand-eye coordination that makes him special. He once went 113 consecutive at-bats without swinging and missing as a teenager and possesses a preternatural ability to find the barrel. Abrams takes easy, rhythmic swings with a direct path to the ball. He has a simple approach and makes adjustments, altogether projecting as a potential .300 hitter. Abrams' frame has plenty of room to add strength and grow into 20-plus home run power. An elite athlete who can do a windmill dunk, Abrams possesses nearly 80-grade speed and went 14-for-15 on stolen bases in his debut. He has the footwork, hands and athleticism to be a plus shortstop, with many scouts surmising he could be a plus defender at second base or in center field, too.

THE FUTURE: Abrams has the skills and makeup to move quickly despite his youth. He will open 2020 back at Fort Wayne.

SCOUTING GRADES: **Batting:** 70 **Power:** 55 **Running:** 80 **Fielding:** 60 **Arm:** 55

Year	Age	Club (League)	Class	AVG	G	AB	R	H	2B	3B	HR	RBI	BB	SO	SB	OBP	SLG
2019	18	Padres 1 (AZL)	R	.401	32	142	40	57	12	8	3	22	10	14	14	.442	.662
	18	Fort Wayne (MWL)	LoA	.250	2	8	1	2	1	0	0	0	1	0	1	.333	.375
Minor League Totals				.393	34	150	41	59	13	8	3	22	11	14	15	.436	.647

4 TAYLOR TRAMMELL, OF

Born: Sept. 13, 1997. **B-T:** L-L. **HT:** 6-2. **WT:** 215. **Drafted:** HS—Kennesaw, Ga., 2016 (1st round supplemental). **Signed by:** Jon Poloni (Reds).

JOHN MOORE

BA GRADE
55 Risk: High

TRACK RECORD: The Padres eyed Trammell with their second-round pick in 2016, but the Reds beat them to it and grabbed him in the supplemental first round. After Trammell won MVP of the 2018 Futures Game and starred again at the 2019 edition, the Padres acquired him from Cincinnati in a three-team trade that sent Franmil Reyes and Logan Allen to the Indians. Trammell scuffled after joining Double-A Amarillo, but he ended on a high note when he hit the go-ahead grand slam in the Texas League finals.

SCOUTING REPORT: Trammell won Georgia high school football player of the year as a senior and brings that athleticism to the diamond. He is a plus runner who makes game-changing plays on the bases and plays with a high motor. Trammell is a patient hitter adept at working counts, but his swing is often not on time. The Padres made adjustments to his load and posture and saw results in the Texas League playoffs, when he hit three home runs and posted a .998 OPS. Trammell isn't a natural center fielder despite his speed, and his below-average arm makes him best suited for left field.

THE FUTURE: Trammell's athleticism and patience give him a strong foundation. How well he maintains his swing improvements will determine his future.

SCOUTING GRADES: **Batting:** 55 **Power:** 50 **Running:** 60 **Fielding:** 50 **Arm:** 40

Year	Age	Club (League)	Class	AVG	G	AB	R	H	2B	3B	HR	RBI	BB	SO	SB	OBP	SLG
2017	19	Dayton (MWL)	LoA	.281	129	491	80	138	24	10	13	77	71	123	41	.368	.450
2018	20	Daytona (FSL)	HiA	.277	110	397	71	110	19	4	8	41	58	105	25	.375	.406
2019	21	Chattanooga (SL)	AA	.236	94	318	47	75	8	3	6	33	54	86	17	.349	.336
	21	Amarillo (TL)	AA	.229	32	118	14	27	4	1	4	10	13	36	3	.316	.381
Minor League Totals				.270	426	1552	251	419	64	24	33	195	219	407	110	.363	.406

5 LUIS CAMPUSANO, C

Born: Sept. 29, 1998. **B-T:** R-R. **HT:** 6-0. **WT:** 213. **Drafted:** HS—Augusta, Ga., 2017 (2nd round). **Signed by:** Tyler Stubblefield.

BA GRADE
55 Risk: High

TRACK RECORD: Campusano failed to make USA Baseball's 18U national team in high school and used it as motivation to get in better shape. He slimmed down, added muscle and became the first catcher selected in the 2017 draft when the Padres took him 39th overall. Campusano's first two seasons were interrupted by concussions, but he stayed healthy in 2019 at high Class A Lake Elsinore and won the California League batting title (.325) and co-MVP award.

SCOUTING REPORT: Campusano is one of the strongest players in the Padres system. He sometimes swings a 40-ounce bat in games and still manages to get the barrel through the zone. Campusano swings hard and punishes pitches over the plate while rarely straying outside the strike zone. He mostly smokes hard line drives, but he is progressively learning to elevate and put the ball over the fence to project as an above-average hitter with above-average power. Campusano's strong, flexible lower half makes him an agile blocker, and he turned his framing from a negative into a positive in 2019. His effort level wavers depending on the caliber of pitcher he's catching and his plus arm strength is often negated by a tendency to unnecessarily throw from his knees.

THE FUTURE: Campusano has defensive work ahead, but his bat is special. He'll move to Double-A Amarillo in 2020.

SCOUTING GRADES: **Batting:** 55 **Power:** 55 **Running:** 30 **Fielding:** 50 **Arm:** 55

Year	Age	Club (League)	Class	AVG	G	AB	R	H	2B	3B	HR	RBI	BB	SO	SB	OBP	SLG
2017	18	Padres (AZL)	R	.278	24	90	3	25	4	0	1	13	6	14	0	.327	.356
	18	Padres (AZL)	R	.250	13	44	5	11	0	0	3	12	9	11	0	.377	.455
2018	19	Fort Wayne (MWL)	LoA	.288	70	260	26	75	11	0	3	40	19	43	0	.345	.365
2019	20	Lake Elsinore (CAL)	HiA	.325	110	422	63	137	31	1	15	81	52	57	0	.396	.509
Minor League Totals				.304	217	816	97	248	46	1	22	146	86	125	0	.372	.444

6 ADRIAN MOREJON, LHP

MATT THOMAS

BA GRADE 55 Risk: High

Born: Feb. 27, 1999. **B-T:** L-L. **HT:** 6-1. **WT:** 210. **Signed:** Cuba, 2016. **Signed by:** David Post/Trevor Schumm/Felix Feliz.

TRACK RECORD: Morejon pitched Cuba to the gold medal at the 2014 15U World Cup with a complete game victory over the U.S. The Padres signed him two years later for $11 million, a franchise record for an amateur player. Morejon struggled with injuries every year since signing, but he still jumped from Double-A to the majors last year as a 20-year-old. He got hit hard in five appearances before suffering a season-ending left should impingement.

SCOUTING REPORT: Morejon tantalizes with premium raw stuff. His fastball sits 94-96 and touches 98 mph with startlingly little effort, and when his arm slot is right he snaps off plus low-80s curveballs that draw swings and misses below the strike zone. His traditional changeup flashes plus with fade, and he has a knuckle-change that acts like a splitter. The issue is Morejon often spins out of his rotational delivery, leaving his fastball over the plate and pulling his secondaries out of the strike zone. His delivery also puts tremendous strain on his shoulder and upper arm and is the root of his injury problems. He has yet to pitch more than 65.1 innings in a season.

THE FUTURE: Morejon has plenty of stuff, but his below-average command and durability draw scrutiny.

SCOUTING GRADES: **Fastball:** 60 **Curveball:** 60 **Changeup:** 55 **Control:** 45

Year	Age	Club (League)	Class	W	L	ERA	G	GS	SV	IP	H	HR	BB	SO	K/9	WHIP	AVG
2017	18	Tri-City (NWL)	SS	2	2	3.57	7	7	0	35	37	2	3	35	8.9	1.13	.266
	18	Fort Wayne (MWL)	LoA	1	2	4.23	6	6	0	28	28	2	13	23	7.5	1.48	.264
2018	19	Padres 1 (AZL)	R	0	1	6.75	1	1	0	3	5	0	0	4	13.5	1.88	.385
	19	Lake Elsinore (CAL)	HiA	4	4	3.30	13	13	0	63	54	6	24	70	10.1	1.24	.233
2019	20	Amarillo (TL)	AA	0	4	4.25	16	16	0	36	29	3	15	44	11.0	1.22	.215
	20	San Diego (NL)	MAJ	0	0	10.13	5	2	0	8	15	1	3	9	10.1	2.25	.385
Major League Totals				0	0	10.13	5	2	0	8	15	1	3	9	10.1	2.25	.385
Minor League Totals				7	13	3.78	43	43	0	164	153	13	55	176	9.6	1.27	.245

7 ANDRES MUÑOZ, RHP

MATT THOMAS

BA GRADE 55 Risk: High

Born: Jan. 16, 1999. **B-T:** R-R. **HT:** 6-2. **WT:** 165. **Signed:** Mexico, 2015. **Signed by:** Trevor Schumm.

TRACK RECORD: The Padres purchased Muñoz's rights for $700,000 from the Mexican League's Mexico City franchise when he was 16. He rapidly added velocity as he filled out and touched 100 mph for the first time the following season, beginning an ascent to of the hardest-throwing prospects in the game. He reached 103 as a closer at Double-A in 2018 and made his major league debut at age 20 last year, where he struck out 30 of the 97 batters he faced.

SCOUTING REPORT: Munoz is the embodiment of a power reliever. His fastball sits 99-100 mph and touches 103, and it plays up with explosive late life. He can elevate his fastball for swings and misses or spot it on the corners, making it a true 80-grade pitch. Munoz is still working to find consistency with his average slider. At it's best it features short, late life at 86-87 mph and rolls off the barrel of righthanded hitters. Munoz's high-effort delivery makes it difficult for him to stay on line to the plate and results in below-average control. He's also pitched more than 30 innings only once in four seasons and has already had a platelet-rich plasma injection in his elbow.

THE FUTURE: Muñoz has closer stuff, but his health and control are question marks. He'll open 2020 where he ended 2019: in the Padres' bullpen.

SCOUTING GRADES: **Fastball:** 80 **Slider:** 50 **Control:** 45

Year	Age	Club (League)	Class	W	L	ERA	G	GS	SV	IP	H	HR	BB	SO	K/9	WHIP	AVG
2017	18	Tri-City (NWL)	SS	3	0	3.80	21	0	1	24	15	2	16	35	13.3	1.31	.177
	18	Fort Wayne (MWL)	LoA	0	0	3.86	3	0	0	2	2	0	2	3	11.6	1.71	.222
2018	19	Tri-City (NWL)	SS	0	0	0.00	5	0	0	6	0	0	2	9	14.3	0.35	.000
	19	San Antonio (TL)	AA	2	1	0.95	20	0	7	19	11	0	11	19	9.0	1.16	.175
2019	20	El Paso (PCL)	AAA	3	2	3.79	19	0	2	19	16	3	7	24	11.4	1.21	.235
	20	Amarillo (TL)	AA	0	2	2.16	16	0	4	17	9	1	11	34	18.4	1.20	.153
	20	San Diego (NL)	MAJ	1	1	3.91	22	0	1	23	16	2	11	30	11.7	1.17	.188
Major League Totals				1	1	3.91	22	0	1	23	16	2	11	30	11.7	1.17	.188
Minor League Totals				9	6	3.14	100	1	14	106	69	7	65	150	12.7	1.26	.184

8 MICHEL BAEZ, RHP

Born: Jan. 21, 1996. **B-T:** R-R. **HT:** 6-8. **WT:** 220. **Signed:** Cuba, 2016. **Signed by:** Trevor Schumm/Jake Koenig.

TRACK RECORD: Baez briefly pitched in Cuba's major league before leaving the island and singing with the Padres for $3 million in December 2016. After starting in the low minors, Baez made 15 relief appearances at Double-A Amarillo before receiving his first major league callup in July. He settled into the Padres bullpen and held opponents scoreless in 19 of his 24 appearances.

SCOUTING REPORT: The 6-foot-8 Baez is an imposing presence who repeats his delivery better than most pitchers his size. His plus fastball sits 94-96 mph and touches 99, though inconsistent mechanics cause his velocity to fluctuate. Baez's above-average mid-80s changeup plays well off his fastball and has become his primary swing-and-miss pitch, drawing whiffs nearly a third of the time he throws it. Baez's slider and curveball both stalled in their development as fringy to below-average pitches and make him a better fit in the bullpen, where his fringe-average control is less of an issue. Baez has also missed the start of every season with either a back or shoulder injury.

THE FUTURE: The Padres haven't given up on Baez as a starter, but his pitch mix, control and health all point to a future in relief.

SCOUTING GRADES: **Fastball:** 60 **Slider:** 45 **Curveball:** 40 **Changeup:** 55 **Control:** 40

Year	Age	Club (League)	Class	W	L	ERA	G	GS	SV	IP	H	HR	BB	SO	K/9	WHIP	AVG
2017	21	Padres (AZL)	R	1	0	3.60	1	1	0	5	2	1	2	7	12.6	0.80	.133
	21	Fort Wayne (MWL)	LoA	6	2	2.45	10	10	0	59	41	8	8	82	12.6	0.84	.192
2018	22	Lake Elsinore (CAL)	HiA	4	7	2.91	17	17	0	87	73	5	33	92	9.6	1.22	.229
	22	San Antonio (TL)	AA	0	3	7.36	4	4	0	18	22	4	12	21	10.3	1.85	.301
2019	23	Amarillo (TL)	AA	3	2	2.00	15	0	1	27	22	1	11	38	12.7	1.22	.216
	23	San Diego (NL)	MAJ	1	1	3.03	24	1	0	30	25	3	14	28	8.5	1.31	.223
Major League Totals				1	1	3.03	24	1	0	29	25	3	14	28	8.5	1.31	.223
Minor League Totals				14	14	3.08	47	32	1	195	160	19	66	240	11.0	1.16	.221

9 GABRIEL ARIAS, SS

Born: Feb. 27, 2000. **B-T:** R-R. **HT:** 6-1. **WT:** 201. **Signed:** Venezuela, 2016. **Signed by:** Luis Prieto/Yfrain Linares/Trevor Schumm.

TRACK RECORD: Arias ranked as one of the top prospects in the 2016 international class and signed with the Padres for $1.9 million out of Venezuela. He shined defensively but scuffled offensively his first two and half years as a pro, but he flashed his vast potential with a .344/.376/.533 slash line in the second half of 2019 at high Class A Lake Elsinore.

SCOUTING REPORT: Arias is a long, lean athlete with tremendous raw ability. He is a gifted defensive shortstop who plays under control, smoothly ranges in all directions, has reliable hands and owns plus-plus arm that allows him to make jaw dropping throws. Evaluators use words like "special", "elite" and "unbelievable" to describe his shortstop defense. Arias has a smooth swing that stays through the ball, and his long levers and wiry strength give him surprising plus raw power. Arias' problem is his breaking ball recognition is exceedingly poor and has resulted in a nearly 30 percent career strikeout rate. Arias hits breaking balls in the zone, but flails at ones below the zone. Once he minimized his movements at the plate, he recognized pitches better and took off in the second half.

THE FUTURE: How well Arias improves his plate discipline will determine if he hits enough to play everyday. He'll be just 20 years old at Double-A Amarillo next year.

SCOUTING GRADES: **Batting:** 50 **Power:** 55 **Running:** 40 **Fielding:** 70 **Arm:** 70

Year	Age	Club (League)	Class	AVG	G	AB	R	H	2B	3B	HR	RBI	BB	SO	SB	OBP	SLG
2017	17	Padres (AZL)	R	.275	37	153	18	42	6	3	0	13	10	51	4	.329	.353
	17	Fort Wayne (MWL)	LoA	.242	16	62	8	15	1	0	0	4	2	16	1	.266	.258
2018	18	Fort Wayne (MWL)	LoA	.240	124	455	54	109	27	3	6	55	41	149	3	.302	.352
2019	19	Lake Elsinore (CAL)	HiA	.302	120	477	62	144	21	4	17	75	25	128	8	.339	.470
Minor League Totals				.270	297	1147	142	310	55	10	23	147	78	344	16	.319	.396

10 RYAN WEATHERS, LHP

Born: Dec. 17, 1999. **B-T:** L-L. **HT:** 6-1. **WT:** 230. **Drafted:** HS—Loretto, Tenn., 2018 (1st round). **Signed by:** Tyler Stubblefield.

TRACK RECORD: Weathers is the son of longtime big league reliever David Weathers and led Loretto (Tenn.) High to the state championship game in both basketball and baseball as a senior. The Padres drafted him seventh overall in 2018 and signed him for $5.23 million. Weathers started his first full season strong at low Class A Fort Wayne, but he went on the injured list for arm fatigue in mid-May and didn't have the same stuff when he returned.

SCOUTING REPORT: At his best, Weathers demonstrates an advanced feel for pitching with a three-pitch mix. He pounds the lower third of the strike zone with a 90-93 mph fastball to both sides of the plate and keeps hitters off balance with a potential plus mid-80s changeup with heavy fade. His low-80s slider flashes average with good shape and break, and he ties it all together with plus control and an advanced feel for sequencing. Weathers' fastball often sat 87-89 mph after his injured list stint, however, and his conditioning became a concern after he gained 20 pounds.

THE FUTURE: The Padres freely acknowledge Weathers needs to get in better shape to reach his mid-rotation ceiling. They have challenged him to do so in 2020.

SCOUTING GRADES: **Fastball:** 55 **Slider:** 50 **Changeup:** 60 **Control:** 60

Year	Age	Club (League)	Class	W	L	ERA	G	GS	SV	IP	H	HR	BB	SO	K/9	WHIP	AVG
2018	18	Padres (AZL)	R	0	2	3.86	4	4	0	9	8	2	3	9	8.7	1.18	.211
	18	Fort Wayne (MWL)	LoA	0	1	3.00	3	3	0	9	11	0	1	9	9.0	1.33	.282
2019	19	Fort Wayne (MWL)	LoA	3	7	3.84	22	22	0	96	101	6	18	90	8.4	1.24	.275
Minor League Totals				3	10	3.78	29	29	0	114	120	8	22	108	8.5	1.24	.270

11 JOEY CANTILLO, LHP

Born: Dec. 18, 1999. **B-T:** L-L. **HT:** 6-4. **WT:** 220. **Drafted:** HS—Kailua, Hawaii, 2017 (16th round). **Signed by:** Justin Baughman.

TRACK RECORD: Cantillo drew limited interest after sitting 83-88 mph in high school, but he intrigued the Padres by touching 91 mph in a pre-draft workout. They drafted him in the 16th round and signed him for $302,500—fifth-round money—to keep him from a Kentucky commitment. Cantillo spent most of his first two seasons in Rookie ball before the Padres unleashed him in 2019. He led the low Class A Midwest League in ERA until an August promotion and led the organization with 144 strikeouts.

SCOUTING REPORT: Cantillo has a long, angular body at 6-foot-4, 220 pounds and keeps growing into more velocity. His fastball now sits 88-91 mph and touches 94. Cantillo's devastating upper-70s changeup at the bottom of the zone is a borderline plus-plus offering with the added separation from his fastball, while his low-70s, downer curveball shows good shape and spin and could become average. Cantillo is a smart worker who attacks the strike zone and understands how to mix his pitches.

THE FUTURE: Cantillo put himself on the map as a potential back-of-the-rotation starter. He will begin 2020 at high Class A Lake Elsinore.

Year	Age	Club (League)	Class	W	L	ERA	G	GS	SV	IP	H	HR	BB	SO	K/9	WHIP	AVG
2017	17	Padres (AZL)	R	1	0	4.50	7	0	0	8	5	0	6	14	15.8	1.38	.179
2018	18	Padres (AZL)	R	2	2	2.18	11	9	0	45	33	0	12	58	11.5	0.99	.198
	18	Fort Wayne (MWL)	LoA	0	1	9.82	1	1	0	4	4	0	3	5	12.3	1.91	.286
2019	19	Fort Wayne (MWL)	LoA	9	3	1.93	19	19	0	98	58	3	27	128	11.8	0.87	.173
	19	Lake Elsinore (CAL)	HiA	1	1	4.61	3	3	0	14	12	2	7	16	10.5	1.39	.222
Minor League Totals				13	7	2.51	41	32	0	168	112	5	55	221	11.8	0.99	.187

12 OWEN MILLER, SS/2B

BA GRADE
45 **Risk: Medium**

Born: Nov. 15, 1996. **B-T:** R-R. **HT:** 6-0. **WT:** 190. **Drafted:** Illinois State, 2018 (3rd round). **Signed by:** Troy Hoerner.

TRACK RECORD: Miller hit at least .325 every season at Illinois State and signed with the Padres for $500,000 as a third-round pick in 2018. After notching 100 hits in 75 games after signing, Miller spent his first full season at Double-A Amarillo in 2019 and led the Texas League with 147 hits.

SCOUTING REPORT: Miller is a pure hitter with a long track record of performance. He squares balls up with a balanced, controlled swing and drives pitches from line-to-line. He hits velocity, recognizes breaking pitches and has an innate feel for finding the barrel. Miller's flat stroke is more geared for line drives, but he has average pullside power and elevates enough to project 12-15 homers a year. Miller is a sneaky

athlete with above-average speed and reliable hands. He primarily played shortstop for Amarillo, but his lateral agility and fringe-average arm are better suited for second base.
THE FUTURE: Miller's pure hitting ability is among the best in the Padres organization. He'll begin 2020 at Triple-A El Paso and has a chance to make his major league debut during the year.

Year	Age	Club (League)	Class	AVG	G	AB	R	H	2B	3B	HR	RBI	BB	SO	SB	OBP	SLG
2018	21	Tri-City (NWL)	SS	.335	49	191	22	64	8	3	2	20	15	24	4	.395	.440
	21	Fort Wayne (MWL)	LoA	.336	26	107	18	36	11	0	2	13	4	17	0	.368	.495
2019	22	Amarillo (TL)	AA	.290	130	507	76	147	28	2	13	68	46	86	5	.355	.430
Minor League Totals				.307	205	805	116	247	47	5	17	101	65	127	9	.367	.441

13 RONALD BOLAÑOS, RHP

BA GRADE
45 **Risk: Medium**

Born: Aug. 23, 1996. **B-T:** R-R. **HT:** 6-3. **WT:** 220. **Signed:** Cuba, 2016.
Signed by: Chris Kemp/Trevor Schumm.

TRACK RECORD: Bolaños initially developed as an outfielder in Cuba's junior leagues but converted to pitching and took to it quickly. He earned a spot on Cuba's 18U national team in 2014 and led the team with 15 strikeouts over nine scoreless innings at the Pan American Championships. The Padres signed him for $2.25 million in Aug. 2016. Bolaños struggled with his control his first two years in the U.S., but he improved his strike-throwing in 2019 and jumped from high Class A all the way to the majors.
SCOUTING REPORT: Bolaños is a power-armed righthander with a heavy fastball that sits 94-96 mph, but he has tremendous feel to manipulate the baseball. He'll throttle his fastball anywhere from 89-98 mph and add cut, sink or rise to it, keeping hitters wildly off-balance and unsure what they'll see pitch-to-pitch. Bolaños fastball operates like multiple different pitches, but he also has an above-average, high-spin mid-70s curveball he lands for strikes and an average mid-80s slider with an above-average spin rate. Bolaños has a lot of moving parts to his delivery and has yet to fully harness his lively stuff, resulting in fringe-average control.
THE FUTURE: Bolaños needs to improve his control to remain a starter, but he has a solid fallback as a power-armed reliever.

Year	Age	Club (League)	Class	W	L	ERA	G	GS	SV	IP	H	HR	BB	SO	K/9	WHIP	AVG
2017	20	Fort Wayne (MWL)	LoA	5	2	4.41	16	11	0	69	65	3	34	51	6.6	1.43	.253
2018	21	Lake Elsinore (CAL)	HiA	6	9	5.11	25	23	0	125	138	13	50	118	8.5	1.50	.282
2019	22	Lake Elsinore (CAL)	HiA	5	2	2.85	10	10	0	54	37	4	23	54	9.1	1.12	.193
	22	Amarillo (TL)	AA	8	5	4.23	15	13	0	77	71	7	30	88	10.3	1.32	.249
	22	San Diego (NL)	MAJ	0	2	5.95	5	3	0	20	17	3	12	19	8.7	1.47	.230
Major League Totals				0	2	5.95	5	3	0	19	17	3	12	19	8.7	1.47	.230
Minor League Totals				24	18	4.38	66	57	0	324	311	27	137	311	8.6	1.38	.254

14 REGGIE LAWSON, RHP

BA GRADE
50 **Risk: High**

Born: Aug. 2, 1997. **B-T:** R-R. **HT:** 6-4. **WT:** 205. **Drafted:** HS—Victorville, Calif., 2016 (2nd round supplemental). **Signed by:** Jeff Stevens.

TRACK RECORD: Lawson projected to go in the first round of the 2016 draft before an oblique injury limited him to six starts his senior year. He fell to the supplemental second round, where the Padres grabbed him and signed him for an over-slot $1.9 million. After tantalizing with flashes of brilliance his first three seasons, an elbow strain limited Lawson to six starts at Double-A Amarillo in 2019. He received a platelet-rich plasma injection and returned to pitch in the Arizona Fall League, where he threw 11 dominant innings with three hits and one run allowed, two walks and 14 strikeouts.
SCOUTING REPORT: Lawson is built like a scout's dream at 6-foot-4, 205 pounds with a loose, athletic delivery and a strong, well-proportioned frame. His fastball sits 93-96 mph and maintains its velocity deep into outings, and his previously loopy curveball has added power to sit 76-80 mph and flash as an average pitch. His developing changeup continues to progress and flashes above-average in the mid-80s with sink at the bottom of the zone. A hard landing in his delivery has caused Lawson below-average control his whole career and led to wildly inconsistent performances from outing-to-outing. He is a fierce competitor who performs best when the stakes are highest.
THE FUTURE: Lawson needs to find health and consistency, but he has the ingredients of a promising starter. He will return to Double-A Amarillo in 2020.

Year	Age	Club (League)	Class	W	L	ERA	G	GS	SV	IP	H	HR	BB	SO	K/9	WHIP	AVG
2017	19	Fort Wayne (MWL)	LoA	4	6	5.30	17	17	0	73	65	8	35	89	11.0	1.37	.236
2018	20	Lake Elsinore (CAL)	HiA	8	5	4.69	24	22	0	117	130	11	51	117	9.0	1.55	.280
2019	21	Amarillo (TL)	AA	3	1	5.20	6	6	0	28	28	4	13	36	11.7	1.48	.262
Minor League Totals				15	12	5.09	52	48	0	226	235	23	102	249	9.9	1.49	.265

15 JAKE CRONENWORTH, SS/RHP

BA GRADE 45 Risk: Medium

Born: Jan. 21, 1994. **B-T:** L-R. **HT:** 6-1. **WT:** 185. **Drafted:** Michigan, 2015 (7th round). **Signed by:** James Bonnici (Rays).

TRACK RECORD: Cronenworth started, relieved and played first base and second base at Michigan. The Rays drafted him as a second baseman, but quickly discovered he could play shortstop as well. He hit his way to the International League batting crown in 2019 and also made six starts as an opener. The Padres acquired him with Tommy Pham for Hunter Renfroe and Xavier Edwards after the season.

SCOUTING REPORT: Cronenworth is a heady player who gets the most out of his average tools. He learned to be more aggressive in 2019, and added strength helped him turn from a singles hitter into one who drives doubles and the sporadic home run. He's an above-average runner who can swipe a bag. Cronenworth is an average shortstop with modest range, reliable hands and good anticipation. His arm is more above-average than plus in the field, but he reaches 96 mph on the mound and flashes an above-average slider and usable cutter. His high walk rate in 2019 can be blamed on rust.

THE FUTURE: Cronenworth has a chance to break camp with the Padres. He projects as a super-sub with two-way ability as a low-leverage reliever.

Year	Age	Club (League)	Class	W	L	ERA	G	GS	SV	IP	H	HR	BB	SO	K/9	WHIP	AVG
2019	25	Durham (IL)	AAA	0	0	0.00	7	6	0	7	4	0	8	9	11.0	1.64	.160
Minor League Totals				0	0	0.00	7	6	0	7	4	0	8	9	11.1	1.64	.160

Year	Age	Club (League)	Class	AVG	G	AB	R	H	2B	3B	HR	RBI	BB	SO	SB	OBP	SLG
2017	23	Charlotte, FL (FSL)	HiA	.268	87	328	58	88	16	5	2	29	47	69	12	.364	.366
	23	Montgomery (SL)	AA	.285	38	158	15	45	6	0	1	20	19	19	1	.363	.342
2018	24	Montgomery (SL)	AA	.254	108	418	75	106	18	4	4	50	43	69	21	.323	.344
	24	Durham (IL)	AAA	.240	7	25	4	6	3	0	0	2	1	5	1	.269	.360
2019	25	Rays (GCL)	R	.167	3	12	2	2	1	0	0	0	1	2	0	.231	.250
	25	Durham (IL)	AAA	.334	88	344	75	115	26	4	10	45	49	62	12	.429	.520
Minor League Totals				.283	498	1906	341	539	100	23	22	219	258	368	73	.375	.394

16 HUDSON POTTS, 3B

BA GRADE 50 Risk: High

Born: Oct. 28, 1998. **B-T:** R-R. **HT:** 6-3. **WT:** 205. **Drafted:** HS—Southlake, Texas, 2016 (1st round). **Signed by:** Matt Schaffner.

TRACK RECORD: The Padres went above industry consensus to draft Potts 24th overall in 2016. He cruised through the lower minors but hit a wall at Double-A Amarillo in 2019 with a .290 on-base percentage, fourth-lowest of any qualified hitter in the Texas League.

SCOUTING REPORT: Potts is a physical specimen with plus raw power. He hits towering home runs to left and can drive the ball to right with authority, but he is still immature in his approach. Potts swings without having a plan, and he vacillates between being short and long to the ball. He generally stays within the strike zone, but he swings and misses in the zone at an alarming rate. A high school shortstop, Potts has grown into a reliable defender at third base with sure hands and an above-average, accurate arm.

THE FUTURE: Potts' power still has teams interested in him as a trade candidate. Finding a consistent swing and approach are his top priorities for 2020.

Year	Age	Club (League)	Class	AVG	G	AB	R	H	2B	3B	HR	RBI	BB	SO	SB	OBP	SLG
2017	18	Fort Wayne (MWL)	LoA	.253	125	491	67	124	23	4	20	69	23	140	0	.293	.438
2018	19	Lake Elsinore (CAL)	HiA	.281	106	406	66	114	35	1	17	58	37	112	3	.350	.498
	19	San Antonio (TL)	AA	.154	22	78	5	12	0	0	2	5	10	33	1	.258	.231
2019	20	Padres 1 (AZL)	R	.667	4	12	3	8	1	0	1	6	0	3	0	.692	1.000
	20	Amarillo (TL)	AA	.227	107	409	56	93	23	1	16	59	32	128	3	.290	.406
Minor League Totals				.256	423	1639	239	419	94	9	57	224	120	463	17	.315	.428

17 EDWARD OLIVARES, OF

BA GRADE 45 Risk: Medium

Born: March 6, 1996. **B-T:** R-R. **HT:** 6-2. **WT:** 186. **Signed:** Venezuela, 2014. **Signed by:** Ismael Cruz/Luis Marquez/Jose Contreras (Blue Jays).

TRACK RECORD: Olivares signed with the Blue Jays for just $1,000 out of Venezuela in 2014. He began drawing attention playing alongside Bo Bichette and Vladimir Guerrero Jr. at low Class A Lansing in 2017, and the Padres acquired him after the season for Yangervis Solarte. After progressively improving throughout 2018, Olivares broke out in with Double-A Amarillo in 2019. He led Texas League in total bases (221) and runs scored (85), ranked second in RBIs (77) and finished third in stolen bases (35).

SCOUTING REPORT: An athletic righthanded hitter, Olivares has a compact swing and teases above-average power. His pitch selection has long been below-average, but it is improving and was the catalyst behind his big season. Olivares is an above-average runner with long strides in both center and right field,

but late jumps and bad routes previously made him a well below-average defender. He made great strides to improve both in 2019, although he's still a tick below average. He has an above-average arm.
THE FUTURE: Most scouts peg Olivares as a future reserve outfielder, but he's trending upward to possibly become more. He'll head to Triple-A El Paso in 2020.

Year	Age	Club (League)	Class	AVG	G	AB	R	H	2B	3B	HR	RBI	BB	SO	SB	OBP	SLG
2017	21	Lansing (MWL)	LoA	.277	101	426	82	118	26	9	17	65	22	82	18	.330	.500
	21	Dunedin (FSL)	HiA	.221	19	68	11	15	1	1	0	7	8	17	2	.312	.265
2018	22	Lake Elsinore (CAL)	HiA	.277	129	531	79	147	25	10	12	62	29	102	21	.321	.429
2019	23	Amarillo (TL)	AA	.283	127	488	85	138	25	2	18	77	43	98	35	.349	.453
Minor League Totals				.274	469	1824	317	500	93	27	52	249	138	361	103	.342	.440

18 TUCUPITA MARCANO, 3B/SS/2B

BA GRADE
50 Risk: Very High

Born: Sept. 16, 1999. **B-T:** L-R. **HT:** 6-0. **WT:** 170. **Signed:** Venezuela, 2016. **Signed by:** Antonio Alejos/Yfrain Linares.

TRACK RECORD: Marcano signed with the Padres for $320,000 during their 2016 international signing spree and quickly surpassed many players who signed for more. He held his own as one of the youngest players in the low Class A Midwest League in 2019 and earned a promotion to high Class A Lake Elsinore for the California League playoffs, where he hit .370.
SCOUTING REPORT: Marcano is the son of former Venezuelan baseball star Raul Marcano and plays beyond his years. He has an extraordinarily lean frame that lacks power, but he knows his game and doesn't try to do too much. He keeps his barrel in the zone with his smooth lefthanded swing, rarely chases with a disciplined approach and uses the whole field. He is a prolific bunter with a keen sense for the right time to lay one down. Marcano is a plus runner who plays with energy, although he makes poor decisions on the basepaths. He is an adequate defender at second base, third base and shortstop with an average, accurate arm.
THE FUTURE: The Padres envision Marcano growing into a multi-positional everyday player like Marwin Gonzalez. He needs to make significant strength gains, but is only 20 and has time to do so.

Year	Age	Club (League)	Class	AVG	G	AB	R	H	2B	3B	HR	RBI	BB	SO	SB	OBP	SLG
2017	17	Padres (DSL)	R	.206	49	170	17	35	4	2	0	15	34	15	10	.337	.253
2018	18	Padres (AZL)	R	.395	35	124	33	49	4	1	0	17	26	10	10	.497	.444
	18	Tri-City (NWL)	SS	.314	17	70	12	22	1	2	1	9	4	6	5	.355	.429
2019	19	Fort Wayne (MWL)	LoA	.270	111	460	55	124	19	3	2	45	35	45	15	.323	.337
Minor League Totals				.279	212	824	117	230	28	8	3	86	99	76	40	.357	.343

19 BLAKE HUNT, C

BA GRADE
50 Risk: Very High

Born: Nov. 10, 1998. **B-T:** R-R. **HT:** 6-3. **WT:** 215. **Drafted:** HS—Santa Ana, Calif., 2017 (2nd round supplemental). **Signed by:** Nick Long

TRACK RECORD: Hunt played at national prep power Mater Dei (Calif.) HS and vaulted into first-day draft consideration with a standout showing at the Boras Classic in 2017. The Padres drafted him 69th overall and signed him for $1.6 million to forgo a Pepperdine commitment. Hunt made his full-season debut with low Class A Fort Wayne in 2019 and impressed as one of the Midwest League's top defensive catchers. He finished third among league catchers with a .990 fielding percentage and threw out 33 percent of runners.
SCOUTING REPORT: Hunt is a physical, righthanded hitter with excellent natural timing in the batter's box. He stays within strike zone, rarely swings and misses and hits the ball to all fields. He has above-average pullside power and is learning to translate it into games. Hunt's swing gets long at times, but he puts together quality at-bats and hits the ball hard. Hunt's plus arm is his best defensive tool and he gets out of the crouch well for a big catcher. He's an advanced receiver with a knack for framing and moves well laterally in blocking, projecting as an above-average-to-plus defender overall.
THE FUTURE: Hunt is frequently requested by opposing teams in trade discussions. The Padres think he's a potential everyday backstop and are keen to hold onto him.

Year	Age	Club (League)	Class	AVG	G	AB	R	H	2B	3B	HR	RBI	BB	SO	SB	OBP	SLG
2017	18	Padres (AZL)	R	.214	8	28	7	6	2	0	1	4	3	13	0	.313	.393
	18	Padres (AZL)	R	.250	22	88	14	22	7	2	1	15	5	29	1	.316	.409
2018	19	Tri-City (NWL)	SS	.271	56	207	34	56	13	0	3	25	27	56	2	.371	.377
2019	20	Fort Wayne (MWL)	LoA	.255	89	333	40	85	21	3	5	39	35	67	4	.331	.381
Minor League Totals				.258	175	656	95	169	43	5	10	83	70	165	7	.341	.384

20 HUDSON HEAD, OF

Born: April 8, 2001. **B-T:** L-L. **HT:** 6-1. **WT:** 180. **Drafted:** HS—San Antonio, 2019 (3rd round). **Signed by:** Kevin Ham.

TRACK RECORD: Head entered 2019 virtually unknown as a draft prospect, in part because his dual role as a high school quarterback kept him off baseball's showcase circuit. He hit .615 with 13 home runs and 54 RBIs for San Antonio's Churchill High in the spring to become one of the draft's biggest risers, and the Padres drafted him in the third round and signed him for $3 million—a record bonus for the third round.

SCOUTING REPORT: Head has a tall, lean, wiry body with quick-twitch actions. His bat speed is already among the fastest in the Padres organization, and he's a plus runner with the athleticism and quickness to stay in center field. Head plays with an aggressive football mentality and sometimes swings too hard or takes too aggressive a route in the outfield. When he slows down, he shows a sound swing with surprising plus raw power for his frame. He is supremely confident and has an above-average, accurate arm.

THE FUTURE: Head needs experience to fine-tune his plate discipline and outfield routes, but he has the ability to be an impact player on both sides of the ball. He'll head to low Class A Fort Wayne in 2020.

Year	Age	Club (League)	Class	AVG	G	AB	R	H	2B	3B	HR	RBI	BB	SO	SB	OBP	SLG
2019	18	Padres 1 (AZL)	R	.283	32	120	19	34	7	3	1	12	15	29	3	.383	.417
Minor League Totals				.283	32	120	19	34	7	3	1	12	15	29	3	.383	.417

21 REGGIE PRECIADO, SS

Born: May 16, 2003. **B-T:** B-R. **HT:** 6-4. **WT:** 185. **Signed:** Panama, 2019. **Signed by:** Chris Kemp/Richard Montenegro.

TRACK RECORD: Preciado led Panama to a silver medal at the 2018 U15 World Cup and made the all-tournament team. He cemented himself as Panama's top prospect in the 2019 international class and signed with the Padres for $1.3 million on July 2.

SCOUTING REPORT: Preciado intrigues with a projectable 6-foot-4 frame and natural bat-to-ball skills. A switch-hitter, he is stronger from the right side but shows the ability to find the barrel from both sides with a rhythmic, controlled swing. Preciado's power is only starting to emerge, and his frame provides hope he can grow into 20-plus home run power as he matures physically. Signed as a shortstop, Preciado isn't much of a runner and may move to third base as he fills out, where his above-average, accurate arm will play. His father Victor spent two years in the Yankees system as a first baseman and corner outfielder, and Reggie shows outstanding game awareness and aptitude.

THE FUTURE: Preciado became a favorite of the Padres' player development staff during fall instructional league. He doesn't turn 17 until May, but the Padres believe he'll move quicker than most his age.

Year	Age	Club (League)	Class	AVG	G	AB	R	H	2B	3B	HR	RBI	BB	SO	SB	OBP	SLG
2019	16	Did not play — Signed 2020 contract															

22 JOSHUA MEARS, OF

BA GRADE
50 Risk: Extreme

Born: Feb. 21, 2001. **B-T:** R-R. **HT:** 6-3. **WT:** 230. **Drafted:** HS—Federal Way, Wash., 2019 (2nd round). **Signed by:** Justin Baughman.

TRACK RECORD: Mears long stood out for his physicality and put himself on draft radars with a strong performance at the 2018 Area Code Games. He carried that momentum through his senior season and was drafted by the Padres in the second round, No. 48 overall. He signed for $1 million to forgo a Purdue commitment and impressed in his pro debut in the Rookie-level Arizona League.

SCOUTING REPORT: Mears is already built like a major league slugger at 6-foot-3, 230 pounds. Big, strong, and physical, Mears possesses plus-plus raw power to all fields and gets to it easy with a fast, compact swing for his size. Mears rarely saw premium velocity growing up in the Pacific Northwest and struggled to catch up to it early in his pro debut, but he adjusted to gear up for fastballs and hit .313 with a .937 OPS over the final month of the season. He hit one ball 117 mph off the bat, the same maximum exit velocity as Nelson Cruz in 2019. Mears is a prototypical right fielder with below-average speed and a plus arm. He has sneaky athleticism but has work to do to become an average defender.

THE FUTURE: Mears is a bright individual who took college courses while still in high school. His physicality, strong work ethic and intelligence make for a promising foundation.

Year	Age	Club (League)	Class	AVG	G	AB	R	H	2B	3B	HR	RBI	BB	SO	SB	OBP	SLG
2019	18	Padres 1 (AZL)	R	.253	43	166	30	42	4	3	7	24	23	59	9	.354	.440
Minor League Totals				.253	43	166	30	42	4	3	7	24	23	59	9	.354	.440

23 JAVY GUERRA, RHP

BA GRADE **50** Risk: Extreme

Born: Sept. 25, 1995. **B-T:** R-R. **HT:** 6-0. **WT:** 184. **Signed:** Panama, 2012. **Signed by:** Cristobal Garibaldo (Red Sox).

TRACK RECORD: Guerra ranked among the top prospects in baseball when the Padres acquired him from the Red Sox as part of the Craig Kimbrel trade in Nov. 2015. Abysmal pitch recognition led to a 33 percent strikeout rate and spiraling confidence after the trade, and the Padres converted Guerra to a pitcher during 2019 spring training. Guerra sat 96-100 mph in his first bullpen session and maintained that velocity when he reported to high Class A Lake Elsinore in June. He bounded up to Double-A Amarillo in August and received a big league callup Sept. 1, less than six months after he started pitching.

SCOUTING REPORT: Guerra's wiry athleticism and plus-plus arm from shortstop translated seamlessly to the mound. His fastball sits 96-100 with late armside life through the strike zone, and he already shows feel for an above-average 87-89 mph slider. Guerra throws his fastball over the plate but doesn't have command yet and was punished for it in the majors. He is still learning to land his slider in the strike zone. Guerra struggled mentally during his struggles as a position player. Once he began pitching, club officials noted he started smiling again.

THE FUTURE: The Padres hope Guerra will develop average command and control in time. If he does, he has the stuff to be a closer.

Year	Age	Club (League)	Class	W	L	ERA	G	GS	SV	IP	H	HR	BB	SO	K/9	WHIP	AVG
2019	23	Lake Elsinore (CAL)	HiA	0	0	3.71	17	0	1	17	13	2	5	23	12.2	1.06	.213
	23	Amarillo (TL)	AA	0	0	2.08	4	0	0	4	2	1	5	7	14.5	1.62	.133
	23	San Diego (NL)	MAJ	0	0	5.19	8	0	0	9	7	3	3	6	6.2	1.15	.219
Major League Totals				0	0	5.19	8	0	0	8	7	3	3	6	6.2	1.15	.219
Minor League Totals				0	0	3.38	21	0	1	21	15	3	10	30	12.7	1.17	.197

24 JEISSON ROSARIO, OF

BA GRADE **45** Risk: High

Born: Oct. 22, 1999. **B-T:** L-L. **HT:** 6-1. **WT:** 191. **Signed:** Dominican Republic, 2016. **Signed by:** Felix Feliz/Ysrael Rojas/Alvin Duran.

TRACK RECORD: Rosario ranked as one of the top prospects in the 2016 international class and signed with the Padres for $1.85 million. He held his own at first after the Padres pushed him aggressively, but a hamstring injury hampered him in 2019 and led to an underwhelming year at high Class A Lake Elsinore.

SCOUTING REPORT: Rosario is a special athlete who can do a standing backflip and throw with both arms. He's a plus runner in the outfield with excellent closing speed and frequently makes highlight-reel catches. He is a consensus above-average defender in center field, with an average arm strong enough to keep baserunners honest. Rosario has a discerning eye and finished fifth in the California League with a .372 on-base percentage, but not much happens when he swings. He crouches low in his stance and gets his body contorted, resulting in poor contact on the ground and minimal impact off the bat. He flashes above-average power in batting practice, but never gets close to it in games. Though he's a plus runner in the outfield, Rosario shows average speed on the bases and runs less often than he should.

THE FUTURE: Fixing his swing will be Rosario's top priority in 2020. He is set to repeat Lake Elsinore.

Year	Age	Club (League)	Class	AVG	G	AB	R	H	2B	3B	HR	RBI	BB	SO	SB	OBP	SLG
2017	17	Padres (AZL)	R	.299	52	187	31	56	10	0	1	24	33	36	8	.404	.369
2018	18	Fort Wayne (MWL)	LoA	.271	117	436	79	118	17	5	3	34	66	108	18	.368	.353
2019	19	Lake Elsinore (CAL)	HiA	.242	120	430	67	104	14	4	3	35	87	114	11	.372	.314
Minor League Totals				.264	289	1053	177	278	41	9	7	93	186	258	37	.376	.340

25 TIRSO ORNELAS, OF

BA GRADE **45** Risk: High

Born: March 11, 2000. **B-T:** L-L. **HT:** 6-3. **WT:** 200. **Signed:** Mexico, 2016. **Signed by:** Chris Kemp/Bill McLaughlin.

TRACK RECORD: The Padres purchased Ornelas' rights from the Mexican League for $1.5 million during their 2016 international signing spree. They aggressively pushed him to high Class A Lake Elsinore in 2019, but Ornelas fell flat. His swing became so long and slow the Padres demoted him to the Rookie-level Arizona League for a complete swing construction midseason, and he finished the year batting .220 with one home run.

SCOUTING REPORT: Ornelas is a hulking lefthanded slugger with an advanced eye at the plate. He stays within the strike zone and swings at strikes, but his swing needs work. Ornelas is often too steep entering the zone and lacks twitch, so he's often late as well. When he levels out his swing and is on time he drives the ball gap-to-gap and teases plus raw power. Ornelas moves well for a big man and has a chance to become an average defensive right fielder, although his fringe-average arm needs to improve.

THE FUTURE: Ornelas' youth and strength provide reasons for optimism, but his bat speed and swing length keep trending the wrong direction. He is slated to repeat Lake Elsinore in 2020.

Year	Age	Club (League)	Class	AVG	G	AB	R	H	2B	3B	HR	RBI	BB	SO	SB	OBP	SLG
2017	17	Padres (AZL)	R	.276	53	196	46	54	11	3	3	26	40	61	0	.399	.408
2018	18	Fort Wayne (MWL)	LoA	.252	86	309	45	78	13	3	8	40	40	68	5	.341	.392
2019	19	Padres 1 (AZL)	R	.205	21	88	6	18	2	0	0	11	9	22	4	.278	.227
	19	Lake Elsinore (CAL)	HiA	.220	89	332	41	73	11	5	1	30	44	91	3	.309	.292
Minor League Totals				.241	249	925	138	223	37	11	12	107	133	242	12	.337	.344

26 JORGE OÑA, OF

BA GRADE
50 Risk: Extreme

Born: Dec. 31, 1996. **B-T:** R-R. **HT:** 6-0. **WT:** 220. **Signed:** Cuba, 2016. **Signed by:** Felix Feliz/Trevor Schumm/Chris Kemp.

TRACK RECORD: Oña hit .636 with four home runs in eight games for Cuba at the 2014 18U Pan American Championships. He left the island in 2015 and landed a $7 million signing bonus from the Padres in 2016. Oña struggled with the transition to the U.S and underwhelmed his first two seasons, but he found his stride at Double-A Amarillo in 2019 before suffering a season-ending torn labrum.

SCOUTING REPORT: Oña is a thick, muscular specimen with massive raw power. He punishes balls and hits towering drives that demoralize opposing pitchers. His plus raw power plays to all fields, and he is particularly adept at driving the ball the other way. Oña is an aggressive hitter who hunts fastballs and swings at the first one around the strike zone. That freewheeling approach limits him to a potential fringe-average hitter, and his bulky body results in stiff actions in his swing despite above-average bat speed. Oña's below-average running speed and limited range make him a liability in the outfield, although he has flashed above-average arm strength when healthy.

THE FUTURE: The Padres put Oña on the 40-man roster despite his abbreviated season. Whether he makes enough contact to access his power will determine his future.

Year	Age	Club (League)	Class	AVG	G	AB	R	H	2B	3B	HR	RBI	BB	SO	SB	OBP	SLG
2017	20	Fort Wayne (MWL)	LoA	.277	107	415	54	115	18	1	11	64	40	115	8	.351	.405
2018	21	Lake Elsinore (CAL)	HiA	.239	100	368	44	88	24	2	8	44	33	110	0	.312	.380
2019	22	Amarillo (TL)	AA	.348	25	89	11	31	2	0	5	18	11	26	2	.417	.539
Minor League Totals				.268	232	872	109	234	44	3	24	126	84	251	10	.342	.408

27 LOGAN DRISCOLL, C

Born: Nov. 3, 1997. **B-T:** L-R. **HT:** 6-1. **WT:** 195. **Drafted:** George Mason, 2019 (2nd round supplemental). **Signed by:** Danny Sader.

TRACK RECORD: Driscoll started all three years at George Mason and became the school's highest-drafted player when the Padres selected him 73rd overall, nine picks higher than fellow catcher Chris Widger in 1992. Driscoll signed for $600,000 and delivered 19 extra-base hits in 39 games at short-season Tri-City to earn a late invitation to the Arizona Fall League, where he homered twice in his first game.

SCOUTING REPORT: Driscoll is a built like a hunk of granite with a muscular, protruding chest, bulging biceps and thick forearms. He takes a patient, contact-first approach from the left side and lets his natural strength provide his average power. He is a disciplined hitter who recorded more nearly as many walks (74) as strikeouts (75) in college. Driscoll called his own games at George Mason and runs a staff well, but his bulky build generates split opinions whether he can stay behind the plate. His setup needs work and his receiving is adequate at best. His above-average arm and blocking ability are two strengths in his favor.

THE FUTURE: The Padres believe Driscoll can be a serviceable catcher and provide thump with his bat. He'll move to full-season ball in 2020.

Year	Age	Club (League)	Class	AVG	G	AB	R	H	2B	3B	HR	RBI	BB	SO	SB	OBP	SLG
2019	21	Tri-City (NWL)	SS	.268	39	142	20	38	14	2	3	20	15	23	0	.340	.458
Minor League Totals				.268	39	142	20	38	14	2	3	20	15	23	0	.340	.458

28 ISMAEL MENA, OF

BA GRADE
50 Risk: Extreme

Born: Nov. 30, 2002. **B-T:** L-L. **HT:** 6-3. **WT:** 185. **Signed:** Dominican Republic, 2019. **Signed by:** Chris Kemp/Alvin Duran/Felix Feliz.

TRACK RECORD: Mena established himself early as one of the best athletes and fastest runners in the 2019 international class. He signed with the Padres for $2.2 million on July 2, the largest signing bonus the club awarded in the period.

SCOUTING REPORT: A wiry 6-foot-3 center fielder, Mena defends his position well with plus-plus speed and excellent range. He picks balls up off the bat, gets excellent jumps and takes advanced, efficient routes for a 16-year-old. His above-average arm rounds out his potential to a plus or better defensive center fielder. At the plate, Mena stays behind the ball from the left side and consistently puts it in play to take advantage of his speed. His power is mostly to the gaps now, but he has the projectable frame and leverage in his swing to dream on 15-20 home run power as he gets stronger.

THE FUTURE: Mena has a lot of room to grow into his body. His athleticism, defense and contact skills are a promising starter's kit for a potential everyday center fielder.

Year	Age	Club (League)	Class	AVG	G	AB	R	H	2B	3B	HR	RBI	BB	SO	SB	OBP	SLG
2019	16	Did not play — Signed 2020 contract															

29 EGUY ROSARIO, 2B/3B

BA GRADE
40 Risk: High

Born: Aug. 25, 1999. **B-T:** R-R. **HT:** 5-9. **WT:** 150. **Signed:** Dominican Republic, 2015. **Signed by:** Felix Feliz/Trevor Schumm/Chris Kemp.

TRACK RECORD: The Padres signed Rosario for $300,000 on his 16th birthday and pushed him quickly, sending him to high Class A Lake Elsinore as an 18-year-old in 2018. He repeated the California League in 2019 and was still the league's sixth-youngest player on Opening Day. He finished sixth in the league in hits (129), tied for ninth in doubles (25) and sixth in triples (8).

SCOUTING REPORT: Rosario is nicknamed "Eggy" because of his egg-shaped build. He's round, stout and thick, but he's sneaky-quick and packs a punch. Rosario uses his thick forearms to generate surprising impact with his short, quick swing. He catches up to velocity and has matured in his approach to use the whole field. Rosario flashes above-average raw power, but he's at his best when he focuses on hitting line drives up the middle. Rosario is an above-average runner on the bases, but his agility is limited in the field. He's naturally a second baseman and his plus arm fits at third base. His hands, footwork and short-area quickness have room to grow. Rosario a feisty, fiery presence who energizes his team and irritates opponents.

THE FUTURE: Both the Padres and opposing clubs view Rosario as a potential utilityman. He'll head to Double-A Amarillo in 2020.

Year	Age	Club (League)	Class	AVG	G	AB	R	H	2B	3B	HR	RBI	BB	SO	SB	OBP	SLG
2017	17	Fort Wayne (MWL)	LoA	.206	50	180	15	37	9	2	0	13	20	51	17	.296	.278
	17	Padres (AZL)	R	.282	50	206	36	58	12	7	1	33	24	43	16	.363	.422
2018	18	San Antonio (TL)	AA	.182	3	11	2	2	0	0	0	2	2	5	1	.357	.182
	18	Lake Elsinore (CAL)	HiA	.239	121	457	60	109	28	1	9	45	38	119	9	.307	.363
2019	19	Lake Elsinore (CAL)	HiA	.278	122	464	60	129	25	8	7	72	37	103	21	.331	.412
Minor League Totals				.267	406	1532	218	409	96	19	18	190	146	359	86	.338	.390

30 LAKE BACHAR, RHP

BA GRADE
40 Risk: High

Born: June 3, 1995. **B-T:** R-R. **HT:** 6-3. **WT:** 215. **Drafted:** Wisconsin-Whitewater, 2016 (5th round). **Signed by:** Troy Hoerner.

TRACK RECORD: Bachar played football exclusively his first two years at Division III Wisconsin-Whitewater and was an all-conference kicker/punter. He went out for baseball as a junior in 2015 and played both sports before focusing solely on baseball as a senior. Bachar touched 95 mph that season, and his fresh, live arm led the Padres to draft him in the fifth round and sign him for $350,000.

SCOUTING REPORT: Bachar bounced between starting and relieving his first three seasons, but he found his role as a starter with Double-A Amarillo in 2019. He finished fifth in the Texas League in strikeouts (126) and sixth in ERA (3.98). Bachar's fastball averages 92-93 mph on his fastball, but his real weapons are his breaking pitches. He generates above-average spin rates on both his slider and curveball, with his slider flashing above-average and his downer curveball flashing average. He's a good athlete and fierce competitor whose control is getting better the more he pitches and has a chance to become average.

THE FUTURE: Evaluators are intrigued by the possibility of Bachar's stuff ticking up with a move to the bullpen. He'll open the season at Triple-A El Paso with his big league debut in reach.

Year	Age	Club (League)	Class	W	L	ERA	G	GS	SV	IP	H	HR	BB	SO	K/9	WHIP	AVG
2017	22	Padres (AZL)	R	1	0	1.00	5	0	0	9	5	1	6	15	15.0	1.22	.156
	22	Padres (AZL)	R	0	0	2.25	1	1	0	4	2	0	2	4	9.0	1.00	.154
	22	Fort Wayne (MWL)	LoA	4	1	4.06	7	6	0	38	33	6	6	28	6.7	1.04	.239
2018	23	Lake Elsinore (CAL)	HiA	2	2	1.91	7	4	1	28	16	3	9	18	5.7	0.88	.167
	23	San Antonio (TL)	AA	3	7	5.59	20	14	1	87	99	15	38	62	6.4	1.57	.292
2019	24	Lake Elsinore (CAL)	HiA	0	0	3.00	1	1	0	6	6	0	2	7	10.5	1.33	.273
	24	Amarillo (TL)	AA	8	4	3.98	24	19	0	127	121	18	58	126	9.0	1.41	.259
Minor League Totals				20	16	4.03	80	50	3	335	311	44	128	301	8.1	1.31	.251

San Francisco Giants

BY JOSH NORRIS

With Farhan Zaidi imported from the Dodgers to oversee baseball operations, the Giants began the process of trying to creep back into relevancy.

They improved their win total by four games, from 73 to 77, but were two games back of the second National League wild card on July 31, so they only made minor moves. They dealt relievers Sam Dyson (Twins), Mark Melancon (Braves) and Drew Pomeranz (Brewers), while hanging on to their biggest prize, looming free agent lefty Madison Bumgarner. The hope faded quickly, however, and the team finished August and September with a record of 22-32.

Even a long-shot postseason berth was unexpected for the Giants, who were counting on their next waves of prospects to lead them back to October. Instead, they got production from unexpected sources. Most notably, journeyman outfielder Mike Yastrzemski led the team's position players in wins above replacement and slugged 21 home runs to tie outfielder Kevin Pillar for the team lead. Yastrzemski also authored the season's arguable high point when on Sept. 18 he homered to dead center field at Fenway Park, where his grandfather Carl Yastrzemski became a Hall of Famer over the course of a 23-year big league career.

Franchise turnarounds aren't usually built on the backs of 29-year-old rookies, however, so the bulk of San Francisco's hope is pinned on the top tier of their rejuvenated farm system. The group is led by a trio of Top 100 Prospects—shortstop Marco Luciano, catcher Joey Bart and outfielder Heliot Ramos. Ramos and Bart were the team's first-round selections in 2017 and 2018, while Luciano was the jewel of the team's excellent 2018 international signing class. In his pro debut, Luciano blew away all reasonable expectations by skipping over the Dominican Summer League and obliterating the Rookie-level Arizona League as a 17-year-old. Bart and Ramos each dealt with injuries but showed their talents when healthy. All three have the potential to make their marks on future Giants playoff teams.

Those three can't do it all, though, and toward season's end the Giants got a look at a few of the players who might play complementary roles over the next few years. Beyond Yastrzemski, the Giants welcomed middle infielder Mauricio Dubon (who arrived from Milwaukee in the Pomeranz trade), outfielder Jaylin Davis (from Minnesota in the Dyson deal) and lefthander Conner Menez to the big leagues. Menez, in particular, came from relative anonymity to reach the big leagues. He had struck out more than 150 hitters in each of the previous two seasons but hadn't made much noise on the national radar. Now, he looks like a potential back-of-the-rotation starter.

There's a wave bubbling at the lower levels, too, that includes top 10 prospects Hunter Bishop, the Giants' 2019 first-rounder, as well as international additions Alexander Canario, Luis Toribio and Luis Matos. All are years away but could play a big role in the team's attempts to re-ascend to the peak of the NL West.

After the season, the Giants hired Scott Harris away from the Cubs to work under Zaidi as the team's new general manager. They have the pieces in place to get the Giants back to contention. Now all they have to do is put them together.

THEARON W. HENDERSON/GETTY IMAGES

Mike Yastrzemski had a big rookie year, but at 29 he probably isn't part of the Giants' future.

PROJECTED 2023 LINEUP

Catcher	Joey Bart (2)	26
First Base	Buster Posey	36
Second Base	Mauricio Dubon (10)	28
Third Base	Luis Toribio (6)	22
Shortstop	Marco Luciano (1)	21
Left Field	Hunter Bishop (4)	24
Center Field	Heliot Ramos (3)	23
Right Field	Alexander Canario (5)	22
No. 1 Starter	Seth Corry (7)	24
No. 2 Starter	Shaun Anderson	28
No. 3 Starter	Tyler Beede	29
No. 4 Starter	Sean Hjelle (9)	25
No. 5 Starter	Logan Webb	26
Closer	Reyes Moronta	30

DEPTH CHART

SAN FRANCISCO GIANTS

TOP 2020 ROOKIE: Mauricio Dubon, SS/2B. The new Giant should get plenty of chances to play up the middle.
BREAKOUT PROSPECT: Tristan Beck, RHP. The imported arm could thrive thanks to the Giants' pitching philosophy.
SLEEPER: Matt Frisbee, RHP. Frisbee tied with Conner Menez for the system's strikeout lead and could prove himself big time in 2020.

SOURCE OF TOP 30 TALENT

Homegrown	**23**	**Acquired**	**7**
College	7	Trade	6
Junior college	1	Rule 5 draft	1
High school	4	Independent league	0
Nondrafted free agent	0	Free agent/waivers	0
International	11		

LF
- Hunter Bishop (4)
- Jairo Pomares (15)
- Victor Bericoto (24)
- Jacob Heyward

CF
- Heliot Ramos (3)
- Luis Matos (8)

RF
- Alexander Canario (5)
- Jaylin Davis (16)
- Sandro Fabian (29)
- Diego Rincones

3B
- Luis Toribio (6)
- Jacob Gonzalez
- Sean Roby
- Elian Rayo

SS
- Marco Luciano (1)
- Will Wilson (12)
- Aeverson Arteaga (26)
- Tyler Fitzgerald (28)
- Anthony Rodriguez
- Abiatal Avelino

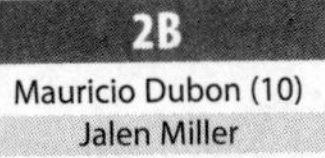

2B
- Mauricio Dubon (10)
- Jalen Miller

1B
- Logan Wyatt (13)
- Garrett Frechette
- Connor Cannon
- Gio Brusa

C
- Joey Bart (2)
- Rayner Santana (23)
- Ronaldo Flores
- Onil Perez
- Victor Coronil
- Adrian Sugastey
- Aramis Garcia
- Ricardo Genoves

LHP

LHSP
- Seth Corry (7)
- Conner Menez (17)
- Esmerlin Vinicio (27)

LHRP
- Garrett Williams
- Mac Marshall
- John Gavin

RHP

RHSP
- Sean Hjelle (9)
- Logan Webb (11)
- Tristan Beck (14)
- Kai Wei-Teng (19)
- Jake Wong (20)
- Gregory Santos (21)
- Jose Marte (22)
- Trevor McDonald (25)
- Matt Frisbee
- Kervin Castro

RHRP
- Blake Rivera (18)
- Dany Jimenez (30)
- Camilo Doval
- Melvin Adon
- Raffi Vizcaino
- Prelander Berroa

DRAFT ANALYSIS

2019

BEST PURE HITTER: OF Hunter Bishop (1) eased concerns about his hitting ability by batting .342/.479/.748 with 22 home runs as a junior at Arizona State. The lefthanded-hitting outfielder has worked to quiet his swing mechanics, which helped him significantly cut his strikeout rate while still allowing him to tap into his plus raw power.

BEST POWER: 1B Connor Cannon (17) set school records for most home runs in a single season (18) and career home runs (36) while at UC Riverside, and he continued showing off his power with 13 home runs in his first 35 games in the Rookie-level Arizona League this summer. He generates impressive, natural loft with his swing, and he routinely hits towering home runs.

FASTEST RUNNER: OF Grant McCray (3) ran track and played football in addition to baseball for Lakewood Ranch High in Bradenton, Fla., and he's described as a toolsy center fielder with plus speed. After signing with the Giants for $697,500 as the 87th overall pick, McCray stole 17 bases in 48 games in the Arizona League.

BEST DEFENSIVE PLAYER: SS Simon Whiteman (9) is a 5-foot-10, 165-pound infielder capable of playing all over the diamond. The Yale product split his time between shortstop and second base during his pro debut, and the Giants believe he can stick at shortstop.

BEST ATHLETE: Bishop is a potential five-tool player. Despite his 6-foot-5, 210-pound frame, the Giants believe Bishop has the requisite athleticism and speed to stick in center field, but he also has the arm strength and power potential to profile well in right field.

BEST FASTBALL: RHP Caleb Kilian (8) and RHP Cole Waites (18) both feature low-to-mid-90s fastballs that are capable of touching 97 mph. A Texas Tech product who started 16 games as a junior, Kilian is more polished than Waites, who appeared in 42 games for West Alabama.

BEST SECONDARY PITCH: A 6-foot-2, 180-pound righthander out of George County High in Mississippi, RHP Trevor McDonald (11) has the makings of a future plus curveball. Many evaluators believe his curveball, which features solid depth and impressive top-to-bottom break, has the makings of a future swing-and-miss pitch.

BEST PRO DEBUT: Kilian struck out 17 batters, walked only two and surrendered just seven hits in his first 16 professional innings. Opponents hit just .135 off Kilian, who attacks hitters with a low- to mid-90s fastball, an above-average curveball and effective, third-pitch changeup.

MOST INTRIGUING BACKGROUND: 2B Carter Aldrete (15) is the son of Rich Aldrete, a first baseman/corner outfielder who played six seasons in the minors for the Giants and Cardinals organizations from 1987-92, reaching as high as Triple-A. Carter is also the nephew of former big leaguer Mike Aldrete, who played 10 years in the majors.

CLOSEST TO THE MAJORS: Bishop has the established college track record of a hitter who could move through the minors at an accelerated pace.

BEST LATE-ROUND PICK: Regardless of his draft spot, the Giants believe McDonald has the chance to be one of the true gems of their 2019 draft class.

THE ONE WHO GOT AWAY: One of the top amateur players coming out of Southern California in 2019, SS Brooks Lee (35) was considered a tough sign and dropped in the draft in large part because his father, Larry, is the head coach at Cal Poly, where Lee now attends college.

—KEGAN LOWE

TOP DRAFT PICKS OF THE DECADE

Year	Player, Pos.	2019 Org
2010	Gary Brown, OF	Did not play
2011	Joe Panik, SS	Mets
2012	Chris Stratton, RHP	Pirates
2013	Christian Arroyo, SS	Indians
2014	Tyler Beede, RHP	Giants
2015	Phil Bickford, RHP	Brewers
2016	Bryan Reynolds, OF (2nd round)	Pirates
2017	Heliot Ramos, OF	Giants
2018	Joey Bart, C	Giants
2019	Hunter Bishop, OF	Giants

2018

C Joey Bart (1) has lived up to his status as the No. 2 overall pick, though he was limited by injury in 2019. RHPs Sean Hjelle (2), Jake Wong (3) and Blake Rivera (4) all started their careers strong.

GRADE: B

2017

OF Heliot Ramos (1) took off in 2019 by advancing to Double-A, and LHP Seth Corry (3) now ranks as the system's top pitcher. Aside from those two, however, the class has come up a bit empty.

GRADE: C

2016

The Giants have traded five players from this class already. That includes OF Bryan Reynolds (2), who finished fourth in the 2019 NL Rookie of the Year voting, and is one of two big leaguers from the class.

GRADE: B

1 MARCO LUCIANO, SS

Born: Sept. 10, 2001. **B-T:** R-R. **HT:** 6-2. **WT:** 178.
Signed: Dominican Republic, 2018.
Signed by: Jonathan Bautista.

TRACK RECORD: The Giants spent $6 million to sign Lucius Fox in 2015, thus putting themselves in the international penalty box for the next two signing periods. Once they were free of those restrictions, they quickly signed three of the top available talents: Venezuelan outfielder Luis Matos, Cuban outfielder Jairo Pomares and Luciano, the second-ranked player on the market behind only Victor Victor Mesa. The Giants paid $2.6 million to acquire Luciano, who dabbled in the outfield as an amateur but moved back to shortstop before signing. In 2019, the 17-year-old skipped over the Dominican Summer League and headed straight to the Rookie-level Arizona League, where he ranked as the league's No. 2 prospect. In 35 games in the AZL, Luciano slammed nine doubles and 10 home runs and produced a 1.055 OPS, which ranked fourth in the league. He was promoted to short-season Salem-Keizer for its playoff run but had his year end because of a hamstring injury.

SCOUTING REPORT: Luciano has already proven himself as a prodigious offensive talent. His raw power—which, according to one evaluator, sounds like "a cannon going off"—ranks as double-plus. He produces that power through picturesque swing mechanics which feature a quiet hand load, huge bat speed and big-time strength that allows him to snap the barrel through the zone with controlled violence. Even before he had begun to add muscle to his wiry frame, Luciano's strength was apparent in his hands, wrists and forearms. Beyond his physical gifts, Luciano has tremendous aptitude for the game. He quickly recognizes sequences and patterns and rarely allows pitchers to beat him the same way twice. Whereas his offensive game is advanced for a player his age, Luciano still needs plenty of work in the field. His instincts are strong and his arm projects as plus, but he still needs to clean up his footwork in order to stay at shortstop. If he has to move off shortstop his arm strength will make him a good fit for third base, and he has the athleticism to possibly move to the outfield. The AZL coaching staff worked with Luciano on the smaller details of shortstop, including pre-pitch positioning and learning how to slow the game down.

THE FUTURE: Luciano is just the latest in a growing line of players from the Dominican Republic whose talent puts them on an accelerated development track. His skills are so scintillating that he could start 2020 at low Class A Augusta.

BILL MITCHELL

BA GRADE
65 **Risk:** **V. High**

SCOUTING GRADES
Hit: 60. **Power:** 70. **Run:** 40.
Field: 50. **Arm:** 60.

Projected future grades on 20-80 scouting scale.

TOP PROSPECTS OF THE DECADE

Year	Player, Pos.	2019 Org
2010	Buster Posey, C	Giants
2011	Brandon Belt, 1B	Giants
2012	Gary Brown, OF	Did not play
2013	Kyle Crick, RHP	Pirates
2014	Kyle Crick, RHP	Pirates
2015	Andrew Susac, C	Royals
2016	Christian Arroyo, SS	Indians
2017	Tyler Beede, RHP	Giants
2018	Heliot Ramos, OF	Giants
2019	Joey Bart, C	Giants

BEST TOOLS

Best Hitter for Average	Marco Luciano
Best Power Hitter	Marco Luciano
Best Strike-Zone Discipline	Logan Wyatt
Fastest Baserunner	Simon Whiteman
Best Athlete	Hunter Bishop
Best Fastball	Melvin Adon
Best Curveball	Seth Corry
Best Slider	Blake Rivera
Best Changeup	Logan Webb
Best Control	Sean Hjelle
Best Defensive Catcher	Joey Bart
Best Defensive Infielder	Ghordy Santos
Best Infield Arm	Dilan Rosario
Best Defensive Outfielder	Hunter Bishop
Best Outfield Arm	Diego Rincones

Year	Age	Club (League)	Class	AVG	G	AB	R	H	2B	3B	HR	RBI	BB	SO	SB	OBP	SLG
2019	17	Giants Orange (AZL)	R	.322	38	146	46	47	9	2	10	38	27	39	8	.438	.616
	17	Salem-Keizer (NWL)	SS	.212	9	33	6	7	4	0	0	4	5	6	1	.316	.333
Minor League Totals				.302	47	179	52	54	13	2	10	42	32	45	9	.417	.564

2 JOEY BART, C

Born: Dec. 15, 1996. **B-T:** R-R. **HT:** 6-3. **WT:** 235. **Drafted:** Georgia Tech, 2018 (1st round). **Signed by:** Luke Murton.

BA GRADE 60 Risk: High

TRACK RECORD: After three stellar seasons at Georgia Tech, Bart found himself in contention for the No. 1 overall pick in the 2018 draft. The Tigers snapped up Auburn righthander Casey Mize in that spot, and the Giants were happy to select Bart a few minutes later. Since moving to pro ball, Bart has steadily proved himself an excellent prospect on both sides of the ball. He dealt with a pair of hand injuries in 2019 that cost him significant chunks of the season.

SCOUTING REPORT: When healthy, Bart shows few flaws. He puts the bat on the ball often and has the strength and bat speed to produce potentially plus power, especially to the pull side. He has a hole on the inner half that he'll need to close if he's to be an average big league hitter. If he does that, he could be an all-star. Behind the plate, Bart has a quick exchange and release and plus arm strength that should help him erase would-be basestealers. He also shows strong abilities to block and receive and call games.

THE FUTURE: The injuries limited Bart to 89 games between the regular season and the AFL, which delays his big league debut a little. When he does get there, potentially in the middle of 2020, he has all the makings of a player poised to receive the torch from Buster Posey.

SCOUTING GRADES: **Hitting:** 45 **Power:** 60 **Running:** 40 **Fielding:** 50 **Arm:** 60

Year	Age	Club (League)	Class	AVG	G	AB	R	H	2B	3B	HR	RBI	BB	SO	SB	OBP	SLG
2018	21	Giants Orange (AZL)	R	.261	6	23	3	6	1	1	0	1	1	7	0	.320	.391
	21	Salem-Keizer (NWL)	SS	.298	45	181	35	54	14	2	13	39	12	40	2	.369	.613
2019	22	San Jose (CAL)	HiA	.265	57	234	37	62	10	2	12	37	14	50	5	.315	.479
	22	Richmond (EL)	AA	.316	22	79	9	25	4	1	4	11	7	21	0	.368	.544
Minor League Totals				.284	130	517	84	147	29	6	29	88	34	118	7	.343	.532

3 HELIOT RAMOS, OF

Born: Sept. 7, 1999. **B-T:** R-R. **HT:** 6-0. **WT:** 188. **Drafted:** HS—Guaynabo, P.R., 2017 (1st round). **Signed by:** Junior Roman.

BA GRADE 60 Risk: High

TRACK RECORD: Ramos' athletic bloodlines and baseball skills showed up often in his amateur days, which led the Giants to spend $3.1 million on him in the first round of the 2017 draft. The organization was so impressed by his talent and makeup that they jumped him to the South Atlantic League on Opening Day 2018 and he struggled to perform against more advanced competition. The Giants made the move knowing failure was a possibility and believed his strong makeup would allow him to rebound.

SCOUTING REPORT: The first key to Ramos' rebound was improved pitch-recognition. The Giants noticed the improvement immediately in the high Class A California League. The improved approach combined with a much better body composition also led to an increase in power. Despite missing time with a knee injury, Ramos socked a career-best 16 homers. There's still a chance Ramos sticks in center field, but he could move to a corner depending on how his body develops as he matures.

THE FUTURE: In the Arizona Fall League and Double-A Eastern League, Ramos showed a need to continue refining his approach. If he can do that, he has a future as an above-average everyday outfielder with hitting ability and power.

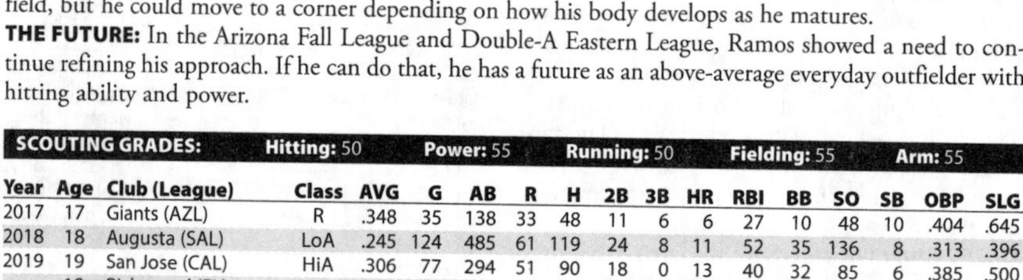

SCOUTING GRADES: **Hitting:** 50 **Power:** 55 **Running:** 50 **Fielding:** 55 **Arm:** 55

Year	Age	Club (League)	Class	AVG	G	AB	R	H	2B	3B	HR	RBI	BB	SO	SB	OBP	SLG
2017	17	Giants (AZL)	R	.348	35	138	33	48	11	6	6	27	10	48	10	.404	.645
2018	18	Augusta (SAL)	LoA	.245	124	485	61	119	24	8	11	52	35	136	8	.313	.396
2019	19	San Jose (CAL)	HiA	.306	77	294	51	90	18	0	13	40	32	85	6	.385	.500
	19	Richmond (EL)	AA	.242	25	95	13	23	6	1	3	15	10	33	2	.321	.421
Minor League Totals				.277	261	1012	158	280	59	15	33	134	87	302	26	.347	.462

4 HUNTER BISHOP, OF

Born: June 25, 1998. **B-T:** L-R. **HT:** 6-5. **WT:** 210. **Drafted:** Arizona State, 2019 (1st round). **Signed by:** Chuck Hensley.

BILL MITCHELL

BA GRADE
55 Risk: High

TRACK RECORD: Bishop was drafted by the Padres out of high school but chose to attend Arizona State. He spent the three seasons in Tempe sharpening his hit tool, and a breakout junior season led to the Giants selecting him in the first round and paying him $4,097,500 to sign. He spent most of his first pro season at short-season Salem-Keizer, where he struggled before being shut down late in the year with a case of turf toe.

SCOUTING REPORT: The improvements Bishop made to his hit tool in college were good enough to get him drafted, but his first exposure to pro ball proved more work is needed. In particular, the Giants would like to see Bishop improve his bat path. Opposing scouts noted that Bishop needed to refine his approach to allow him to cover more of the plate. His athletic frame is capable of generating plenty of power, and his excellent knowledge of the strike zone will help him pick the best pitches to drive. The Giants believe that Bishop has a chance to stay in center field because of his above-average speed, range and route-running abilities, but a player of his size usually ends up in a corner.

THE FUTURE: Bishop will likely begin the year at low Class A Augusta and has the ceiling of a powerful corner outfielder.

SCOUTING GRADES: **Hitting:** 40 **Power:** 60 **Running:** 55 **Fielding:** 50 **Arm:** 55

Year	Age	Club (League)	Class	AVG	G	AB	R	H	2B	3B	HR	RBI	BB	SO	SB	OBP	SLG
2019	21	Giants Orange (AZL)	R	.250	7	20	4	5	3	0	1	3	9	11	2	.483	.550
	21	Salem-Keizer (NWL)	SS	.224	25	85	21	19	1	1	4	9	29	28	6	.427	.400
Minor League Totals				.229	32	105	25	24	4	1	5	12	38	39	8	.438	.429

5 ALEXANDER CANARIO, OF

Born: May 7, 2000. **B-T:** R-R. **HT:** 6-1. **WT:** 200. **Signed:** Dominican Republic, 2016. **Signed by:** Ruddy Moreta.

ZACHARY LUCY/FOUR SEAM IMAGES

TRACK RECORD: Canario signed with the Giants for $60,000 and quickly proved his worth with an intriguing blend of speed, power and athleticism.

SCOUTING REPORT: Much like Hunter Bishop, with whom he was teammates in Salem-Keizer, Canario has serious swing-and-miss issues. He's extremely prone to chasing pitches when he gets to two strikes and posted a strikeout rate of 32.4 percent in the short-season Northwest League. If he learns to be more selective, however, the sky is the limit. His bat speed is the best in the organization and his stroke is flat through the zone. Those two qualities lead to plenty of extra-base impact when he makes contact, and a little more lift in his swing would turn doubles off the wall into majestic home runs. Canario plays center field now but nobody expects him to stay there because his route-running and poor reads on flyballs haven't improved over three pro seasons. He has a plus arm to profile in right field and above-average speed as well. Scouts also praise the fun-loving attitude Canario takes with him to the plate and in the field as well.

THE FUTURE: After showing off his tools and his flaws for a half-season in the Northwest League, Canario will take his talents to full-season ball in 2020. He has the ceiling of a corner outfielder with a coveted blend of power and speed.

SCOUTING GRADES: **Hitting:** 40 **Power:** 60 **Running:** 55 **Fielding:** 50 **Arm:** 60

Year	Age	Club (League)	Class	AVG	G	AB	R	H	2B	3B	HR	RBI	BB	SO	SB	OBP	SLG
2017	17	Giants (DSL)	R	.294	66	235	42	69	17	4	5	45	33	40	18	.391	.464
2018	18	Giants Black (AZL)	R	.250	45	176	36	44	5	2	6	19	27	51	8	.357	.403
2019	19	Giants Orange (AZL)	R	.395	10	43	13	17	3	1	7	14	2	9	1	.435	1.000
	19	Salem-Keizer (NWL)	SS	.301	49	193	38	58	17	1	9	40	18	71	3	.365	.539
Minor League Totals				.291	170	647	129	188	42	8	27	118	80	171	30	.377	.505

6 LUIS TORIBIO, 3B

Born: Sept. 28, 2000. **B-T:** L-R. **HT:** 6-1. **WT:** 165. **Drafted:** Dominican Republic, 2017. **Signed by:** Ruddy Moreta.

BILL MITCHELL

BA GRADE 55 **Risk:** Very High

TRACK RECORD: Toribio was a bit too young for the 2016 signing class, so he had to wait until 2017 to ink with the Giants for $300,000. His .902 OPS in the DSL in 2018 ranked just outside the top 10. For an encore, he moved to the Rookie-level Arizona League and continued to show an impressive blend of hittability and on-base skills.

SCOUTING REPORT: Despite playing all season at 18 years old, Toribio already boasts the best approach in the system. He knows where he can do damage and is disciplined enough to lay off pitches outside that hot zone, and also shows the aptitude to shorten his swing with two strikes. Though he's not a particularly big-time power threat yet, the Giants believe Toribio's solid plate discipline and emerging strength will combine with an on-plane bat path to produce more thump as he matures. He's a third baseman now, but Toribio needs to improve his hands and footwork to stay at the position. He has enough arm to make the necessary throws, but serious refinement is necessary to keep him from moving to first base. Opposing scouts were impressed enough by Toribio that he was made a target in potential trade talks.

THE FUTURE: Low Class A Augusta is the next step for Toribio, who has the ceiling of a corner infielder who can hit for both average and power in equal measure.

SCOUTING GRADES: **Hitting:** 55 **Power:** 50 **Running:** 40 **Fielding:** 40 **Arm:** 55

Year	Age	Club (League)	Class	AVG	G	AB	R	H	2B	3B	HR	RBI	BB	SO	SB	OBP	SLG
2018	17	Giants (DSL)	R	.270	64	215	44	58	13	1	10	39	51	62	4	.423	.479
2019	18	Giants Orange (AZL)	R	.297	51	185	45	55	15	3	3	33	45	54	4	.436	.459
	18	Salem-Keizer (NWL)	SS	.273	3	11	2	3	1	0	0	0	2	5	0	.385	.364
Minor League Totals				.282	118	411	91	116	29	4	13	72	98	121	8	.428	.467

7 SETH CORRY, LHP

Born: Nov. 3, 1998. **B-T:** L-L. **HT:** 6-2. **WT:** 195. **Drafted:** HS—Highland, Utah, 2017 (3rd round). **Signed by:** Chuck Hensley.

BA GRADE 55 **Risk:** Very High

TRACK RECORD: Command and control issues caused Corry to slip to the third round in 2017 despite having one of the best fastball/curveball combinations in the class. Those problems persisted early in his career and appeared to put a cap on his ceiling. Adjustments in the second half of 2019 helped him finish with 172 strikeouts, which tied Corry with Braves righthander Ian Anderson for fourth in the minor leagues.

SCOUTING REPORT: In the first half of 2019, Corry's control was nearly nonexistent. The Giants ironed out his delivery in the second half and asked him to increase his focus from pitch to pitch. Corry walked just 21 hitters over 73.1 second-half innings and dropped his WHIP to 0.80. His fastball sits in the low-to-mid-90s and touches up to 96 mph. Corry works his fastball toward the top of the zone and then pairs it with a hard, downer curveball. Corry's curveball is a tick away from a true 12-to-6 hammer and projects as an above-average pitch. He also improved his ability to work inside with his changeup, and the result was a pitch that increased its ceiling to above-average.

THE FUTURE: Even with plenty of improvement in 2019, the Giants still want to see Corry refine his command and control. He'll aim to do that at high Class A San Jose in 2020, when he'll work toward his ceiling as a No. 3 starter.

SCOUTING GRADES: **Fastball:** 60 **Slider:** 50 **Changeup:** 50 **Control:** 40

Year	Age	Club (League)	Class	W	L	ERA	G	GS	SV	IP	H	HR	BB	SO	K/9	WHIP	AVG
2017	18	Giants (AZL)	R	0	2	5.55	13	10	0	24	14	1	22	21	7.8	1.48	.163
2018	19	Giants Orange (AZL)	R	3	1	2.61	9	9	0	38	38	1	17	42	9.9	1.45	.260
	19	Salem-Keizer (NWL)	SS	1	2	5.49	5	5	0	20	14	1	15	17	7.8	1.47	.200
2019	20	Augusta (SAL)	LoA	9	3	1.76	27	26	0	123	73	4	58	172	12.6	1.07	.171
Minor League Totals				13	8	2.73	54	50	0	204	139	7	112	252	11.1	1.23	.191

8 LUIS MATOS, OF

BILL MITCHELL

Born: Jan. 28, 2002. **B-T:** R-R. **HT:** 5-11. **WT:** 175. **Signed:** Venezuela, 2018. **Signed by:** Edgar Matos.

TRACK RECORD: When the Giants emerged from the international penalty box in 2018, they made three big-name signings: Shortstop Marco Luciano, outfielder Jairo Pomares and Matos. As an amateur, Matos was known for an advanced approach which produced plenty of line drives. That scouting report has rung true as a pro, but he's begun showing more power than was expected.

SCOUTING REPORT: Refining his strike-zone discipline was one of the first orders of business for Matos once he turned pro. He worked toward that goal and showed immediate results in his first season by sticking to the organization's mantra of "drive the ball or walk." His 1.000 OPS placed third in the DSL. The Giants project Matos to have average or better tools across the board, and are optimistic his clean swing will make him a plus hitter and additional strength will give him above-average power. He's an above-average runner as well and has the range and aptitude to stick in center field.

THE FUTURE: After a cameo in the Rookie-level Arizona League, Matos is likely to return to the level in 2020 with a chance at short-season Salem-Keizer in the second half. He has the upside of a center fielder with a blend of gifts on both sides of the ball.

SCOUTING GRADES: **Hitting:** 50 **Power:** 50 **Running:** 55 **Fielding:** 50 **Arm:** 50

Year	Age	Club (League)	Class	AVG	G	AB	R	H	2B	3B	HR	RBI	BB	SO	SB	OBP	SLG
2019	17	Giants (DSL)	R	.362	55	235	60	85	24	2	7	47	19	30	20	.430	.570
	17	Giants Orange (AZL)	R	.438	5	16	5	7	1	0	0	1	1	1	1	.550	.500
Minor League Totals				.367	60	251	65	92	25	2	7	48	20	31	21	.438	.566

9 SEAN HJELLE, RHP

Born: May 7, 1997. **B-T:** R-R. **HT:** 6-11. **WT:** 230. **Drafted:** Kentucky, 2018 (2nd round). **Signed by:** Kevin Christman.

TRACK RECORD: At Kentucky, Hjelle transitioned from the closer's role as a freshman into the team's Friday starter for his sophomore and junior seasons. There's always a level of uneasiness with extraordinarily tall pitchers, but the Giants believed enough in Hjelle's athleticism to draft him in the second round and sign him for $1.5 million. He moved three levels in his first full season as a pro, from low Class A Augusta all the way to Double-A Richmond.

SCOUTING REPORT: Hjelle's 6-foot-11 frame isn't the only reason he stands out among Giants pitchers. That height helps him create extreme downhill angle with his fastball, which is why he's one of the only pitchers in the system encouraged to go against the trend of high fastballs tunneled with diving curveballs. The fastball itself sits in the low 90s and can scrape up to 95 mph. He pairs it with an average, 12-to-6 curveball in the low 80s and a potentially average changeup that took great strides in 2019 when he changed the grip from four-seam to two-seam. The alteration helped him create more velocity separation between his fastball and changeup.

THE FUTURE: Hjelle will likely return to Double-A Richmond in 2020 and has the potential to be a No. 4 starter.

SCOUTING GRADES: **Fastball:** 55 **Curveball:** 50 **Changeup:** 50 **Control:** 50

Year	Age	Club (League)	Class	W	L	ERA	G	GS	SV	IP	H	HR	BB	SO	K/9	WHIP	AVG
2018	21	Salem-Keizer (NWL)	SS	0	0	5.06	12	12	0	21	24	4	4	22	9.3	1.31	.273
2019	22	Augusta (SAL)	LoA	1	2	2.66	9	9	0	41	41	3	9	44	9.7	1.23	.256
	22	San Jose (CAL)	HiA	5	5	2.78	14	14	0	78	73	2	19	74	8.6	1.18	.251
	22	Richmond (EL)	AA	1	2	6.04	5	5	0	25	38	1	9	21	7.5	1.86	.355
Minor League Totals				7	9	3.55	40	40	0	165	176	10	41	161	8.8	1.32	.272

10 MAURICIO DUBON, 2B/SS

SUZANNA MITCHELL

BA GRADE
45 **Risk: Medium**

Born: July 19, 1994. **B-T:** R-R. **HT:** 6-0. **WT:** 175. **Drafted:** HS—Sacramento, 2013 (26th round). **Signed by:** Demond Smith (Red Sox).

TRACK RECORD: Drafted in 2013, Dubon was dealt to the Brewers in 2016. He appeared on the cusp of the big leagues in 2018 before a torn ACL ended his season. He came back strong in 2019 and made his big league debut on July 7. Three weeks later, the Brewers dealt Dubon to the Giants for lefty reliever Drew Pomeranz. He appeared in 28 games for the Giants.

SCOUTING REPORT: Dubon's blend of skills and incredible makeup give him a chance to be a versatile middle infielder. He still needs to alter his approach and focus on swinging on pitches he can impact. If he makes that adjustment, he has the potential to be an average hitter with enough pop to produce 8-12 homers per season. He has the range and instincts to play either shortstop or second base and will likely alternate between those two in the big leagues. He's an above-average runner as well with the aggression on the basepaths to steal double-digit bags per season.

THE FUTURE: Nearly a finished product, Dubon will come to spring training with the Giants and compete for what appears to be a wide-open path to the everyday second baseman's job in San Francisco.

SCOUTING GRADES: **Hitting:** 50 **Power:** 40 **Running:** 55 **Fielding:** 55 **Arm:** 55

Year	Age	Club (League)	Class	AVG	G	AB	R	H	2B	3B	HR	RBI	BB	SO	SB	OBP	SLG
2017	22	Biloxi (SL)	AA	.272	71	268	34	73	14	0	2	24	25	42	31	.334	.347
	22	Colorado Springs (PCL)	AAA	.272	58	224	40	61	15	0	6	33	14	34	7	.320	.420
2018	23	Colorado Springs (PCL)	AAA	.343	27	108	18	37	9	2	4	18	2	19	6	.348	.574
2019	24	Milwaukee (NL)	MAJ	.000	2	2	0	0	0	0	0	0	0	1	0	.000	.000
	24	San Antonio (PCL)	AAA	.297	98	404	59	120	22	1	16	47	18	59	9	.333	.475
	24	Sacramento (PCL)	AAA	.323	25	99	23	32	4	0	4	9	10	9	1	.391	.485
	24	San Francisco (NL)	MAJ	.279	28	104	12	29	5	0	4	9	5	19	3	.312	.442
Major League Totals				.274	30	106	12	29	5	0	4	9	5	20	3	.306	.434
Minor League Totals				.300	609	2371	393	712	127	16	46	285	164	334	127	.348	.426

11 LOGAN WEBB, RHP

BA GRADE
45 **Risk: Medium**

Born: Nov. 18, 1996. **B-T:** R-R. **HT:** 6-2. **WT:** 219. **Drafted:** HS—Rocklin, Calif., 2014 (4th round). **Signed by:** Keith Snider.

TRACK RECORD: Webb caught late helium in the 2014 draft cycle. The Giants were convinced enough by what they saw to draft Webb in the fourth round and keep him from a commitment to Cal Poly. He moved methodically through the system and didn't make his upper-level debut until 2018. His 2019 season was stopped on May 1 when he was suspended 80 games for testing positive for a performance-enhancing substance, but he returned in time to make his major league debut on Aug. 17.

SCOUTING REPORT: The Giants still have tremendous faith in Webb, whom they believe is one of the best athletes in the system. The righthander starts his arsenal with a low-to-mid-90s fastball that has touched as high as 98 mph, but Webb must refine the command of his fastball. The pitch gets tremendous lateral movement, which Webb hasn't learned how to consistently harness. He backs the fastball with a low-80s slider and mid-80s changeup that he uses in near-equal measure. He also worked in 2019 to make his arm slot consistent on all of his pitches. Once he'd done that, he quickly moved through the system.

THE FUTURE: Webb will have a chance to earn a spot in the back of San Francisco's rotation in spring training. He has a a ceiling of a No. 4 starter.

Year	Age	Club (League)	Class	W	L	ERA	G	GS	SV	IP	H	HR	BB	SO	K/9	WHIP	AVG
2017	20	Salem-Keizer (NWL)	SS	2	0	2.89	15	0	0	28	26	1	7	31	10.0	1.18	.241
2018	21	San Jose (CAL)	HiA	1	3	1.82	21	20	0	74	54	2	36	74	9.0	1.22	.207
	21	Richmond (EL)	AA	1	2	3.82	6	6	0	31	30	4	11	26	7.6	1.34	.254
2019	22	Giants Orange (AZL)	R	0	0	1.80	1	1	0	5	6	0	0	6	10.8	1.20	.333
	22	Augusta (SAL)	LoA	1	0	0.90	2	1	0	10	4	0	3	9	8.1	0.70	.125
	22	Richmond (EL)	AA	1	4	2.18	8	7	0	41	41	2	12	47	10.2	1.28	.246
	22	Sacramento (PCL)	AAA	0	0	1.29	1	1	0	7	7	0	0	7	9.0	1.00	.269
	22	San Francisco (NL)	MAJ	2	3	5.22	8	8	0	40	44	5	14	37	8.4	1.46	.279
Major League Totals				2	3	5.22	8	8	0	39	44	5	14	37	8.4	1.46	.278
Minor League Totals				11	18	3.36	80	60	0	302	301	18	100	275	8.2	1.33	.259

12 WILL WILSON, SS/2B

Born: July 21, 1998. **B-T:** R-R. **Ht.:** 6-0 **Wt.:** 184. **Drafted:** North Carolina State, 2019 (1st round). **Signed by:** Chris McAlpin (Angels).

TRACK RECORD: Wilson started for three years in North Carolina State's middle infield and capped his college career by hitting .339 with 16 home runs and winning the Atlantic Coast Conference defensive player of the year as a junior. The Angels drafted him 15th overall and sent him to Rookie-level Orem. He showed solid foundational tools at the level, but scouts were skeptical of his ultimate impact. The Angels traded him—and Zack Cozart's contract—to the Giants in December for lefthander Garrett Williams.

SCOUTING REPORT: Wilson has quick hands and deceptive strength at the plate and makes frequent contact with excellent bat-to-ball skills. He has a contact-oriented swing that mostly sends line drives up the middle, but he flashes gap power that could grow into more as he adds weight and strength. Wilson shows great vision, reliable hands and good feel at shortstop and quickly picked up the nuances and double-play pivot at second base in his pro debut. He is a below-average runner.

THE FUTURE: Wilson could move quickly if he hits, but some fear he profiles more as a utility player than a starter in the major leagues. He will make his full-season debut in 2020.

Year	Age	Club (League)	Class	AVG	G	AB	R	H	2B	3B	HR	RBI	BB	SO	SB	OBP	SLG
2019	20	Orem (PIO)	R	.275	46	189	23	52	10	3	5	18	14	47	0	.328	.439
Minor League Totals				.275	46	189	23	52	10	3	5	18	14	47	0	.328	.439

13 LOGAN WYATT, 1B

BA GRADE
50 Risk: High

Born: Nov. 15, 1997. **Age:** 22. **B-T:** L-R. **HT:** 6-4. **WT:** 230. **Drafted:** Louisville, 2019 (2nd round). Signed by: Todd Coryell.

TRACK RECORD: In college, Wyatt became known for his extraordinarily selective approach at the plate. That approach, plus hints of burgeoning power, was good enough to convince the Giants to select him in the second round and sign him for $997,500. After a quick tune-up in the Rookie-level Arizona League, Wyatt split most of his first pro season between short-season Salem-Keizer and low Class A Augusta.

SCOUTING REPORT: Wyatt's already the kind of player who seems to know the strike zone better than minor league umpires. His strength and swing plane makes the Giants believe he'll have plus power once he becomes a little more aggressive with pitches he can impact. They point to Brandon Belt as a player who faced similar challenges to start his pro career. Wyatt is a fringe-average defender at first base.

THE FUTURE: Wyatt will likely return to low Class A Augusta in 2020 to continue working to unleash the power that he'll need in order to profile at his position.

Year	Age	Club (League)	Class	AVG	G	AB	R	H	2B	3B	HR	RBI	BB	SO	SB	OBP	SLG
2019	21	Giants Black (AZL)	R	.375	7	24	7	9	1	0	0	9	4	6	0	.448	.417
	21	Salem-Keizer (NWL)	SS	.284	18	67	10	19	2	0	2	12	10	9	0	.385	.403
	21	Augusta (SAL)	LoA	.233	19	60	9	14	3	0	1	9	12	14	0	.368	.333
Minor League Totals				.278	44	151	26	42	6	0	3	30	26	29	0	.388	.377

14 TRISTAN BECK, RHP

BA GRADE
50 Risk: High

Born: June 24, 1996. **Age:** 23. **B-T:** R-R. **HT:** 6-4. **WT:** 199. **Drafted:** Stanford, 2018 (4th round). **Signed by:** Jim Blueberg (Braves).

TRACK RECORD: After suffering a stress fracture in his back that caused Beck to miss his sophomore year, he pitched all season for the Cardinal as a junior, but injury concerns meant he landed in the fourth round. The Braves snapped him up there and signed him for $900,000, but traded Beck to San Francisco in 2019 to acquire reliever Mark Melancon.

SCOUTING REPORT: Beck's scouting report is a little different now that he's with the Giants. His pitch mix is still the same, but he's utilizing it differently. Now he's taking his mid-90s fastball and using it more often at the top of the strike zone, where it tunnels well with his solid-average 12-6 curveball. He also throws a solid-average slider and a below-average changeup that he'll continue to develop in 2020.

THE FUTURE: After spending time at high Class A with both the Braves and Giants in 2019, Beck should move to Double-A Richmond in 2020. He has the stuff to pitch as a No. 4 starter in the big leagues.

Year	Age	Club (League)	Class	W	L	ERA	G	GS	SV	IP	H	HR	BB	SO	K/9	WHIP	AVG
2018	22	Braves (GCL)	R	0	0	0.00	3	1	0	5	4	0	2	7	13.5	1.29	.235
2019	23	Braves (GCL)	R	0	0	4.00	2	2	0	9	9	0	4	14	14.0	1.44	.257
	23	Florida (FSL)	HiA	2	2	5.65	8	8	0	37	45	2	14	39	9.6	1.61	.313
	23	San Jose (CAL)	HiA	3	2	2.27	6	6	0	36	33	1	13	37	9.3	1.29	.250
Minor League Totals				5	4	3.77	19	17	0	86	91	3	33	97	10.2	1.44	.277

15 JAIRO POMARES, OF

BA GRADE 50 Risk: Very High

Born: Aug. 4, 2000. **Age:** 19. **B-T:** L-R. **HT:** 6-0. **WT:** 196. **Signed:** Cuba, 2018. **Signed by:** Jonathan Bautista/Gabriel Elias.

TRACK RECORD: Freed from the international penalty box in 2018, the Giants spent big to acquire shortstop Marco Luciano, outfielder Luis Matos and Pomares. Pomares made his pro debut in 2019 and ranked as the No. 19 prospect in the Rookie-level Arizona League, where he spent most of the season before a promotion to short-season for the team's playoff run.

SCOUTING REPORT: Pomares blends a simple swing from the left side with a feel for the strike zone and an ability to manipulate the barrel to pitches in many different locations. Pomares showed potentially average power, especially to the pull side, in the AZL as well as an excellent approach to his batting practice and at-bats in games. Pomares is not likely to stick in center field unless he improves his first-step quickness and ability to read swings and position himself accordingly. His plus arm will play in right field, and his average speed will give him the range necessary for the position as well.

THE FUTURE: After reaching the Northwest League in 2019, the Giants could decide to be aggressive and move Pomares to low Class A Augusta. No matter where he lands, he'll need to develop the impact power required of a player who will likely wind up in a corner-outfield spot.

Year	Age	Club (League)	Class	AVG	G	AB	R	H	2B	3B	HR	RBI	BB	SO	SB	OBP	SLG
2019	18	Giants Black (AZL)	R	.368	37	155	17	57	10	4	3	33	10	26	5	.401	.542
	18	Salem-Keizer (NWL)	SS	.207	14	58	7	12	3	0	0	4	1	17	0	.258	.259
Minor League Totals				.324	51	213	24	69	13	4	3	37	11	43	5	.362	.465

16 JAYLIN DAVIS, OF

BA GRADE 40 Risk: Medium

Born: July 1, 1994. **B-T:** R-R. **HT:** 6-1. **WT:** 190. **Drafted:** Appalachian State, 2015 (24th round). **Signed by:** Ricky Daniel (Twins).

TRACK RECORD: The Twins took a flier on Davis in the 24th round of 2015 on the strength of what projected to be a bargain combination of power and speed. He was traded to the Giants in July as part of a three-player package for reliever Sam Dyson.

SCOUTING REPORT: Simply looking at the stat line, it's easy to see Davis' breakout year in 2019. He entered the year with 42 home runs in three seasons, then slugged 35 between Double-A and Triple-A, plus one more in the big leagues. To get there, he worked with Twins hitting coordinator Peter Fatse to redesign his swing. Specifically, he focused on using his legs more often and keeping a steadier head during his swing. The changes helped him see the ball better and utilize more of his raw strength. Beyond the power, he's also deceptively fast for a player who has 11 stolen bases in 435 MiLB games. His sprint speed, as measured by StatCast, puts him with elite big leaguers like Ronald Acuña Jr. Scouts peg Davis as a potentially average defender in right field, where his strong arm will play well.

THE FUTURE: Davis will have a chance to return to the big leagues out of spring training. If he doesn't, he'll head back to Triple-A for a bit more seasoning.

Year	Age	Club (League)	Class	AVG	G	AB	R	H	2B	3B	HR	RBI	BB	SO	SB	OBP	SLG
2017	22	Cedar Rapids (MWL)	LoA	.267	66	251	36	67	13	3	12	41	16	77	9	.316	.486
	22	Fort Myers (FSL)	HiA	.237	59	215	26	51	8	2	3	25	12	70	1	.288	.335
2018	23	Fort Myers (FSL)	HiA	.271	57	199	23	54	10	0	5	19	23	57	3	.354	.397
	23	Chattanooga (SL)	AA	.275	63	240	30	66	14	2	6	34	21	69	5	.341	.425
2019	24	Pensacola (SL)	AA	.274	58	212	34	58	9	0	10	25	36	64	7	.382	.458
	24	Rochester (IL)	AAA	.331	41	154	39	51	11	1	15	42	15	46	2	.405	.708
	24	Sacramento (PCL)	AAA	.333	27	102	21	34	6	0	10	27	14	28	1	.419	.686
	24	San Francisco (NL)	MAJ	.167	17	42	2	7	0	0	1	3	3	11	1	.255	.238
Major League Totals				.167	17	42	2	7	0	0	1	3	3	11	1	.255	.238
Minor League Totals				.274	435	1612	253	442	85	9	77	254	162	498	33	.349	.481

17 CONNER MENEZ, LHP

BA GRADE 40 Risk: Medium

Born: May 29, 1995. **B-T:** L-L. **HT:** 6-2. **WT:** 197. **Drafted:** The Master's (Calif.), 2016 (14th round). **Signed by:** Chuck Fick.

TRACK RECORD: Menez has moved slowly through the system after being drafted in 2016. He bounced among high Class A, Double-A and Triple-A over the past two seasons before making his big league debut on July 21. The callup was a reward for a strikeout renaissance from Menez at Double-A and Triple-A.

SCOUTING REPORT: Menez fits perfectly into the mold of a sneaky lefthander; his stuff won't overwhelm hitters, but it will get them out. Menez brings his fastball in the low 90s, but it plays much harder. Menez generates exceptional extension in his delivery, so an average heater in terms of pure velocity gets more swings and misses than would be expected. He backs up the fastball with a low-80s curveball that projects as solid-average and an improved changeup. If he can bring the changeup along even further, his odds of sticking in the rotation will improve.

THE FUTURE: Menez will battle for a rotation spot in spring training but could return to Triple-A for more seasoning.

Year	Age	Club (League)	Class	W	L	ERA	G	GS	SV	IP	H	HR	BB	SO	K/9	WHIP	AVG
2017	22	San Jose (CAL)	HiA	7	7	4.41	23	22	0	114	127	5	50	99	7.8	1.55	.282
2018	23	Sacramento (PCL)	AAA	1	1	3.27	2	2	0	11	6	0	5	9	7.4	1.00	.162
	23	San Jose (CAL)	HiA	2	5	4.83	11	11	0	50	48	2	21	70	12.5	1.37	.250
	23	Richmond (EL)	AA	6	4	4.38	15	15	0	74	73	1	34	92	11.2	1.45	.261
2019	24	Richmond (EL)	AA	3	3	2.72	11	11	0	60	37	5	20	70	10.6	0.96	.179
	24	Sacramento (PCL)	AAA	3	1	4.84	12	11	0	61	60	12	30	84	12.3	1.47	.256
	24	San Francisco (NL)	MAJ	0	1	5.29	8	3	0	17	13	4	12	22	11.6	1.47	.220
Major League Totals				0	1	5.29	8	3	0	17	13	4	12	22	11.7	1.47	.220
Minor League Totals				26	22	4.22	89	80	0	424	400	29	176	474	10.1	1.36	.249

18 BLAKE RIVERA, RHP

BA GRADE
45 Risk: High

Born: Jan. 9, 1998. **B-T:** R-R. **HT:** 6-4. **WT:** 221. **Drafted:** Wallace State (Ala.) JC, 2018 (4th round). **Signed by:** Jeff Wood.

TRACK RECORD: The Giants drafted Rivera in the 32nd round in 2017 after his freshman season at Wallace State (Ala.) JC but Rivera chose to return to school. That move paid off in 2018 when the Giants drafted him again, this time in the fourth round. He signed for an $800,000 bonus and split his first pro season between the Rookie-level Arizona League and the short-season Northwest League.

SCOUTING REPORT: The Giants believe Rivera has some of the best pure stuff in the organization. Now, the challenge is getting it to its top level more frequently. He starts his arsenal with a heavy, cutting fastball that averages 94 mph and touched as high as 98 in 2019. With refinement, outside evaluators believe Rivera's fastball could play as high as a 70 on the 20-to-80 scouting scale. He couples the fastball with a 12-to-6 curveball that some scouts project as above-average. His third-pitch changeup could get there, too, but the pitch's quality varies wildly. Scouts have also noticed that Rivera doesn't always hold his top-end velocity deep into starts.

THE FUTURE: Rivera will move to high Class A San Jose in 2020, where he will work to remain in the rotation. If he has to move to the pen, his stuff has the potential to be dominant in the later innings.

Year	Age	Club (League)	Class	W	L	ERA	G	GS	SV	IP	H	HR	BB	SO	K/9	WHIP	AVG
2018	20	Salem-Keizer (NWL)	SS	0	0	6.16	9	8	0	19	20	2	11	14	6.6	1.63	.263
2019	21	Giants Orange (AZL)	R	0	1	18.00	2	2	0	2	4	0	2	0	0.0	3.00	.500
	21	Augusta (SAL)	LoA	4	6	3.95	16	15	0	73	59	3	39	87	10.7	1.34	.215
Minor League Totals				4	7	4.69	27	25	0	94	83	5	52	101	9.7	1.44	.232

19 KAI-WEI TENG, RHP

BA GRADE
45 Risk: High

Born: Dec. 1, 1998. **B-T:** R-R. **HT:** 6-4. **WT:** 260. **Signed:** Taiwan, 2017. **Signed by:** Cary Broder (Twins).

TRACK RECORD: The Twins signed Teng for $500,000 as a part of their 2017 international class on the strength of an advanced pitch mix and excellent command for a pitcher his age. Teng was sent to San Francisco at the trade deadline as part of a deal for reliever Sam Dyson. Teng split his 2019 between each organization's low Class A affiliate and showed excellent feel to pitch at both stops.

SCOUTING REPORT: Giants evaluators were pleasantly surprised by what they saw once Teng got into their system. He showed a three-pitch mix fronted by a low-90s fastball which peaked at 93 mph. He threw the fastball less than 50 percent of the time, however, and relied more often on his slider and changeup. The Giants are working with Teng to increase the spin efficiency on his fastball. Both of Teng's offspeed pitches project to be above-average, and their effectiveness is amplified by his ability to consistently throw them for strikes. He did an excellent job pounding the strike zone overall and threw 66 percent of his pitches for strikes.

THE FUTURE: Teng will advance to high Class A San Jose in 2020 and has the ceiling of an innings-eater at the back of a rotation.

Year	Age	Club (League)	Class	W	L	ERA	G	GS	SV	IP	H	HR	BB	SO	K/9	WHIP	AVG
2018	19	Twins (GCL)	R	3	3	3.59	10	9	0	43	36	0	15	47	9.9	1.20	.226
2019	20	Cedar Rapids (MWL)	LoA	4	0	1.60	9	8	0	51	40	1	14	49	8.7	1.07	.212
	20	Augusta (SAL)	LoA	3	0	1.55	5	5	0	29	16	0	7	39	12.1	0.79	.160
Minor League Totals				10	3	2.28	24	22	0	122	92	1	36	135	9.9	1.05	.205

20 JAKE WONG, RHP

Born: Sept. 3, 1996. **B-T:** R-R. **HT:** 6-2. **WT:** 219. **Drafted:** Grand Canyon, 2018 (3rd round). **Signed by:** Chuck Hensley.

TRACK RECORD: Strong sophomore and junior seasons at Grand Canyon, coupled with an excellent showing in the Cape Cod League, boosted Wong's stock high enough for the Giants to take him in the third round. He signed for $850,000 then impressed in the short-season Northwest League, where he ranked as the No. 11 prospect at season's end. He dominated at low Class A Augusta in 2019 before running into trouble in the hitter-friendly California League.

SCOUTING REPORT: Now that he's fully immersed in their system, the Giants want to begin overhauling Wong's pitch package. The 92-95 mph fastball, they'll keep, but his offspeeds are going to get a bit of a makeover. Wong's goal entering the offseason was to develop a slider, which the Giants eventually want to see become his go-to offspeed pitch. High speed revealed that his curveball came out of his hand like a slider, which was limiting its effectiveness, so the Giants decided to turn the pitch into a full-fledged slider. His changeup is below-average now but projects as average. Scouts also note that Wong repeats his delivery well, which will be key if he is to remain a starter.

THE FUTURE: Wong will likely head back to San Jose in 2020 and has a ceiling in the back of a rotation.

Year	Age	Club (League)	Class	W	L	ERA	G	GS	SV	IP	H	HR	BB	SO	K/9	WHIP	AVG
2018	21	Salem-Keizer (NWL)	SS	0	2	2.30	11	11	0	27	28	1	6	27	8.9	1.24	.259
2019	22	Augusta (SAL)	LoA	2	1	1.99	8	8	0	41	26	2	11	34	7.5	0.91	.186
	22	San Jose (CAL)	HiA	3	2	4.98	15	15	0	72	76	6	24	67	8.3	1.38	.275
Minor League Totals				5	5	3.59	34	34	0	140	130	9	41	128	8.2	1.22	.248

21 GREGORY SANTOS, RHP

BA GRADE 50 Risk: Very High

Born: Aug. 28, 1999. **Age:** 20. **B-T:** R-R. **HT:** 6-4. **WT:** 238. **Signed:** Dominican Republic, 2015. **Signed by:** Eddie Romero/Manny Nanita (Red Sox).

TRACK RECORD: Santos signed with the Red Sox on Aug. 28, 2015—the exact date is important because it means he is not eligible for the Rule 5 draft until after 2020—and spent two seasons in their system. He was dealt to the Giants in 2017 along with righthander Shaun Anderson in the deal that brought shortstop Eduardo Nunez to Boston. Since then, his promising right arm has been shelved multiple times due to injuries. He missed time in 2018 after being hit in the head with a line drive, and then was limited to just eight starts in 2019 because of injuries to muscles in his shoulder and lat.

SCOUTING REPORT: Santos uses an imposing frame to pump naturally cutting fastballs in the mid-to-upper 90s and couples the pitch with a potentially plus slider. He has a changeup as a third pitch, but it's behind the fastball and slider. Coming into 2020, the Giants wanted to accomplish two goals with Santos: Figure out why hitters see his fastball so well despite its velocity and movement, and keep him healthy for a full season. In order to achieve the latter goal, he'll need to focus on improving his conditioning.

THE FUTURE: Though 2019 was a lost season for Santos, there's still plenty of hope. He'll return to low Class A Augusta to work toward his ceiling at the back of a rotation.

Year	Age	Club (League)	Class	W	L	ERA	G	GS	SV	IP	H	HR	BB	SO	K/9	WHIP	AVG
2017	17	Red Sox (DSL)	R	2	0	0.89	8	8	0	30	22	0	15	24	7.1	1.22	.206
	17	Giants (DSL)	R	1	0	1.93	4	4	0	19	21	2	5	17	8.2	1.39	.273
2018	18	Salem-Keizer (NWL)	SS	2	5	4.53	12	12	0	50	64	3	15	46	8.3	1.59	.311
2019	19	Augusta (SAL)	LoA	1	5	2.86	8	8	0	35	34	4	9	26	6.8	1.24	.256
Minor League Totals				9	13	3.20	48	42	1	174	181	10	70	138	7.1	1.44	.267

22 JOSE MARTE, RHP

BA GRADE 45 Risk: High

Born: June 14, 1996. **B-T:** R-R. **HT:** 6-5. **WT:** 236. **Signed:** Dominican Republic, 2015. **Signed by:** Ruddy Moreta.

TRACK RECORD: The Giants signed Marte in 2015 and then watched as he plodded through the system, teasing them with some of the best stuff in the organization. He made it to high Class A San Jose in 2019 and showed increased strikeout numbers but dramatically worse walks totals.

SCOUTING REPORT: Despite the command and control issues, the Giants still have tremendous belief in Marte's stuff. His fastball consistently sits between 95-97 mph and has touched as high as 99 mph. He backs it up with a hard slider in the low 90s and an improved changeup. One symptom for Marte's poor control, the Giants believe, is a lack of trust in his own stuff. He'll get to favorable counts before trying to make the perfect pitch and missing badly. That happens for several pitches in a row, leading to a frustrating number of walks. The Giants' analytical and biomechanical departments also peg Marte as one of their highest-ceiling pitching prospects.

THE FUTURE: Marte's likely to return to high Class A San Jose for a season that could determine whether he stays as a starter or moves to the pen.

Year	Age	Club (League)	Class	W	L	ERA	G	GS	SV	IP	H	HR	BB	SO	K/9	WHIP	AVG
2017	21	Salem-Keizer (NWL)	SS	2	5	5.33	14	14	0	54	61	2	34	42	7.0	1.76	.281
	21	Giants (AZL)	R	0	0	0.00	1	0	0	1	0	0	0	2	18.0	0.00	.000
2018	22	Augusta (SAL)	LoA	7	7	4.70	25	25	0	119	127	10	50	112	8.5	1.49	.275
2019	23	San Jose (CAL)	HiA	3	9	5.59	18	17	0	74	70	7	44	80	9.7	1.54	.255
Minor League Totals				13	22	4.86	63	61	0	266	270	19	138	254	8.6	1.53	.264

23 RAYNER SANTANA, C

BA GRADE 50 Risk: Extreme

Born: Aug. 15, 2002. **Age:** 17. **B-T:** R-R. **HT:** 6-3. **WT:** 232. **Signed:** Venezuela, 2018. **Signed by:** Daniel Mavarez.

TRACK RECORD: Santana was signed out of Venezuela as part of a strong 2018 class. His appeal stemmed from his raw power and strong throwing arm behind the plate. He made his pro debut in the Dominican Summer League and finished the season with a .992 OPS. The figure ranked fifth overall in the league but second behind Luis Matos among Giants prospects.

SCOUTING REPORT: When the Giants saw Santana during the team's Dominican instructional league, their evaluators were concerned that his swing appeared stiff and rigid. Santana showed off a much more fluid swing in his official pro debut, and the results were loud. He boasts plus or better raw power, which shows up to all fields in batting practice and to the pull side and center field in games. Three of his 10 homers went to dead-center field. Santana's power was also boosted by a weight loss of 22 pounds and the addition of roughly 3 percent more muscle mass. There's still more work to be done in that department, but his first steps were strong. The changes to his body composition will also help behind the plate, where he has a strong, accurate arm but could improve his blocking and receiving through increased mobility.

THE FUTURE: Santana will make his stateside debut in 2020, likely in the Rookie-level Arizona League.

Year	Age	Club (League)	Class	AVG	G	AB	R	H	2B	3B	HR	RBI	BB	SO	SB	OBP	SLG
2019	16	Giants (DSL)	R	.294	48	170	31	50	14	0	10	36	37	58	2	.439	.553
Minor League Totals				.294	48	170	31	50	14	0	10	36	37	58	2	.439	.553

24 VICTOR BERICOTO, OF

BA GRADE 50 Risk: Extreme

Born: Dec. 3, 2001. **B-T:** R-R. **HT:** 6-1. **WT:** 174. **Signed:** Venezuela, 2018. **Signed by:** Neriel Morillo.

TRACK RECORD: Bericoto was another piece of the Giants' massive 2018 international recruiting class. Somewhat of a low-profile signing, Bericoto was attractive because of his combination of an easy swing and loft power that should help him profile in a corner-outfield spot. He was excellent in the Dominican Summer League in his pro debut, posting a .472 on-base percentage that ranked just three spots behind White Sox prospect Benyamin Bailey.

SCOUTING REPORT: The Giants were extremely pleased with what they got from Bericoto in 2019. They saw a player with a strong, advanced approach for someone his age and a swing that produces power with the help of big-time strength. His swing is quick and short to the ball with a bit of loft while staying firmly on plane throughout most of the strike zone. Bericoto needs to improve his outfield play in order to stay there—he'd likely wind up in left field—but could move to first base if he doesn't make the necessary adjustments.

THE FUTURE: Bericoto will likely return to the AZL in 2020, when he'll look to build on the progress he's already made and reach his ceiling of an everyday corner outfielder.

Year	Age	Club (League)	Class	AVG	G	AB	R	H	2B	3B	HR	RBI	BB	SO	SB	OBP	SLG
2019	17	Giants (DSL)	R	.344	60	227	58	78	15	1	5	41	53	56	10	.472	.485
	17	Giants Orange (AZL)	R	.273	5	22	3	6	1	0	0	4	0	6	3	.273	.318
Minor League Totals				.337	65	249	61	84	16	1	5	45	53	62	13	.458	.470

25 TREVOR MCDONALD, RHP

BA GRADE 50 Risk: Extreme

Born: Feb. 26, 2001. **B-T:** R-R. **HT:** 6-0. **WT:** 180. **Drafted:** HS—Lucedale, Miss., 2019 (11th round). **Signed by:** Jeff Wood.

TRACK RECORD: McDonald's jump began after his junior season at George County (Miss.) HS. He worked diligently and added 20 pounds of muscle, which helped turn a high-80s fastball into a pitch that now sits in the low 90s. Improved arsenal in tow, McDonald dominated in his draft year. The gem of his year might have been a 12-punchout performance that included two whiffs of Jerrion Ealy, a two-sport prospect who signed with Ole Miss and starred on the football field. The Giants signed him for a bonus of $797,500 that stands as the highest amount given to an 11th-rounder over the last three drafts.

SCOUTING REPORT: The first thing that makes McDonald stand out is his improved fastball. The pitch now ticks as high as 95 mph thanks his recomposed body and an already fast arm. He pairs the pitch with a hard-diving curveball that the Giants, who believe strongly in the art of pitch tunneling, believe fits nicely into their system. The curve could get to plus with further refinement. Like many high school arms, McDonald has a changeup but it is in the very early stages of its development because of infrequent use. McDonald also draws praise for his strong work ethic and smart approach to pitching.

THE FUTURE: McDonald pitched just four innings in the Rookie-level Arizona League, so a return there in 2020 seems likely. He has the upside of a big league rotation piece.

Year	Age	Club (League)	Class	W	L	ERA	G	GS	SV	IP	H	HR	BB	SO	K/9	WHIP	AVG
2019	18	Giants Black (AZL)	R	0	0	2.25	3	3	0	4	2	0	2	8	18.0	1.00	.143
Minor League Totals				0	0	2.25	3	3	0	4	2	0	2	8	18.0	1.00	.143

26 AEVERSON ARTEAGA, SS

BA GRADE
50 Risk: Extreme

Born: March 16, 2003. **B-T:** R-R. **HT:** 6-0. **WT:** 174. **Signed:** Venezuela, 2019. **Signed by:** Edgar Fernandez.

TRACK RECORD: After hauling in Marco Luciano in 2018, the Giants bolstered their system with even more shortstops from the international market in 2019. The class was headlined by Arteaga, who trained in Venezuela with Luis Biasini. Arteaga has athletic bloodlines thanks to a father who played professional basketball. Those genes are apparent from the smooth actions Aretaga displays on defense.

SCOUTING REPORT: Arteaga made a name for himself as an amateur thanks to solid bat-to-ball skills. He shows present gap power but has enough projectability remaining in his frame to think 15 or more home runs are possible in a season when he's done maturing. His plus speed shows up on the basepaths and on defense, where he shows quick hands, strong body control and solid instincts, all of which are required to play shortstop in the long-term. He also has an above-average arm that will help him make all the throws required.

THE FUTURE: To start his career, Arteaga will likely begin in the Dominican Summer League.

Year	Age	Club (League)	Class	AVG	G	AB	R	H	2B	3B	HR	RBI	BB	SO	SB	OBP	SLG
2019	16	Did not play—Signed 2020 contract															

27 ESMERLIN VINICIO, LHP

Born: Jan. 31, 2003. **B-T:** L-L. **HT:** 6-2. **WT:** 140. **Signed:** Dominican Republic, 2019. **Signed by:** Abner Abreu.

TRACK RECORD: Vinicio was one of the top lefthanders available in the 2019 international class, and he earned a $750,000 signing bonus from San Francisco. He trained in the Dominican Republic with Alfredo Arias and did not face hitters—even in the Tricky League—after inking his contract.

SCOUTING REPORT: Getting stronger will be one of Vinicio's key goals before he makes his professional debut. He's slight at 140 pounds, which means there's likely plenty of projectability remaining. That's encouraging, because his fastball already has been clocked up to 92 mph. With strength gains, the pitch could jump into the mid-90s. Vinicio generates that velocity from a smooth delivery that belies a whip-quick arm and he repeats his delivery fairly consistently. He backs up his fastball with a curveball and a changeup that have each shown signs of promise.

THE FUTURE: Vinicio will likely make his professional debut in the Dominican Summer League, which will give him time to add strength to his frame so he can achieve his ceiling of a big league starter.

Year	Age	Club (League)	Class	W	L	ERA	G	GS	SV	IP	H	HR	BB	SO	K/9	WHIP	AVG
2019	16	Did not play—Signed 2020 contract															

28 TYLER FITZGERALD, SS

Born: Sept. 15, 1997. **B-T:** R-R. **HT:** 6-2. **WT:** 200. **Drafted:** Louisville, 2019 (4th round). **Signed by:** Todd Coryell.

TRACK RECORD: Fitzgerald fits the mold of the well-rounded college shortstop with a well-rounded game. He was selected by the Red Sox in the 30th round of the 2016 draft but chose to attend Louisville instead. Fitzgerald posted a solid season in the Cape Cod League in 2018, then hit .324/.397/.490 in his junior season in college. He signed for $495,000 and showed an advanced enough game to make it to low Class A Augusta, where he was reunited with Louisville teammate Logan Wyatt.

SCOUTING REPORT: Fitzgerald is the classic college player without a particularly standout tool but also without many weak points to his game. He's a solid hitter with a little bit of pop now—he hit 10 home runs in three years in college—that he plans to improve in the offseason. Specifically, he wants to do a better job of incorporating his lower half and adding rhythm to his swing, which should lead to more consistent power. Though Fitzgerald is an average defender at shortstop with enough arm to play the position, the expectation is that he'll move all over the infield as he ascends through the system. Fitzgerald is a solid-average runner.

THE FUTURE: Fitzgerald has the chops to move up to high Class A San Jose in 2020 and projects as a utility infielder in the big leagues.

Year	Age	Club (League)	Class	AVG	G	AB	R	H	2B	3B	HR	RBI	BB	SO	SB	OBP	SLG
2019	21	Giants Black (AZL)	R	.273	3	11	2	3	1	0	1	5	1	0	0	.308	.636
	21	Salem-Keizer (NWL)	SS	.284	26	102	20	29	11	2	0	16	15	24	2	.381	.431
	21	Augusta (SAL)	LoA	.264	19	72	11	19	3	0	0	9	8	17	4	.333	.306
Minor League Totals				.276	48	185	33	51	15	2	1	30	24	41	6	.358	.395

29 SANDRO FABIAN, OF

BA GRADE
45 Risk: High

Born: March 6, 1998. **B-T:** R-R. **HT:** 6-2. **WT:** 225. **Signed:** Dominican Republic, 2014. **Signed by:** Pablo Peguero/Felix Pegeuro/Jonathan Bautista.

TRACK RECORD: The Giants signed Fabian for $500,000 in 2014 and then watched as he reached high Class A by 20 years old. He was the sixth-youngest player in the league to open 2018 but struggled mightily and was looking for a rebound in 2019. That didn't quite happen as planned. Instead, the Giants discovered a thyroid issue that had been attacking Fabian's immune system and shut him down to get treatment. Once that was treated, Fabian regained some strength and began to look like the player the Giants envisioned when they signed him.

SCOUTING REPORT: When healthy, Fabian shows the potential to be a gap-to-gap hitter with the ability to drive the ball over the wall at a major league-average rate. The biggest hurdle to reaching that ceiling is plate discipline, an area in which he seemed to make progress during his brief return to the Cal League. He struck out just 33 times in 187 plate appearances, which works out to a 17.6-percent rate. That's a huge improvement from 2018, when he struck out 32 percent of the time at the same level. Fabian is an average runner and has the strong throwing arm required to play a potentially above-average right field.

THE FUTURE: After a brief taste of success in high Class A, Fabian could see his first time at Double-A in 2020.

Year	Age	Club (League)	Class	AVG	G	AB	R	H	2B	3B	HR	RBI	BB	SO	SB	OBP	SLG
2017	19	Augusta (SAL)	LoA	.277	122	480	51	133	30	0	11	61	10	88	5	.297	.408
2018	20	San Jose (CAL)	HiA	.200	112	406	47	81	19	1	10	35	26	107	1	.260	.325
2019	21	Giants Black (AZL)	R	.219	10	32	4	7	3	0	2	8	5	13	0	.366	.500
	21	San Jose (CAL)	HiA	.287	44	167	20	48	4	1	5	33	14	33	3	.353	.413
Minor League Totals				.261	395	1486	199	388	79	9	33	209	77	316	14	.311	.393

30 DANY JIMENEZ, RHP

BA GRADE
40 Risk: Medium

Born: Dec. 23, 1993. **B-T:** R-R. **HT:** 6-3. **WT:** 190. **Signed:** Dominican Republic, 2015. **Signed by:** Ismael Cruz/Sandy Rosario (Blue Jays).

TRACK RECORD: Jimenez signed with the Blue Jays in 2015 and he slowly wound his way through the system. He's pitched mostly in relief, and has racked up a career mark of 11.7 strikeouts per nine innings against 3.2 walks per nine. The Giants selected him in the major league phase of the 2019 Rule 5 draft.

SCOUTING REPORT: Jimenez was impressive in 2019 between high Class A Dunedin and Double-A New Hampshire. As would be expected from a reliever with those kinds of strikeout numbers, Jimenez can bring the heat. His fastball sits in the high-90s and shows armside run. He backs it up with a potentially plus slider and a low-80s changeup that has come on as well. Even with just a half-season of upper-level minor league experience, Jimenez has the kind of power arsenal that fits in a big league bullpen.

THE FUTURE: As a Rule 5 pick, Jimenez has to stay on the Giants' big league roster all year. So he'll get every chance to stick in their bullpen.

Year	Age	Club (League)	Class	W	L	ERA	G	GS	SV	IP	H	HR	BB	SO	K/9	WHIP	AVG
2017	23	Blue Jays (GCL)	R	0	0	9.00	1	0	0	1	1	0	0	1	9.0	1.00	.200
	23	Vancouver (NWL)	SS	2	3	5.30	6	3	0	19	13	3	4	23	11.1	0.91	.183
2018	24	Lansing (MWL)	LoA	6	2	3.84	38	0	13	63	58	10	24	80	11.4	1.29	.237
2019	25	Dunedin (FSL)	HiA	5	1	3.55	20	0	4	25	23	2	9	47	16.7	1.26	.240
	25	New Hampshire (EL)	AA	2	2	1.87	25	0	6	34	22	4	12	46	12.3	1.01	.183
Minor League Totals				19	10	3.43	104	11	24	197	151	22	71	257	11.7	1.13	.207

Seattle Mariners

BY BILL MITCHELL

General manager Jerry Dipoto made a sharp shift in the direction of the Mariners' franchise in the 2018 offseason by trading veterans for prospects, turning what was by far the worst farm system in baseball into a top-flight one.

Dipoto's biggest blockbuster deal involved trading second baseman Robinson Cano and closer Edwin Diaz to the Mets for a package centered on outfielder Jarred Kelenic and righthander Justin Dunn. Then he traded ace starter James Paxton to the Yankees for a package headlined by lefthander Justus Sheffield. Shortstop J.P. Crawford was acquired from the Phillies for all-star Jean Segura.

While veteran outfielder Mallex Smith was the more notable return from the Rays for catcher Mike Zunino, the long-term key to the deal may be outfielder Jake Fraley, who hit well at both Double-A and Triple-A before getting into 12 late-season games for Seattle.

After the rebuilding effort was underway, the Mariners then teased their fans with a strong start before playing more to the lower expectations for the season. They raced to a 13-2 start, with the first two wins coming on the mid-March excursion to Japan to play the Athletics, giving fans the hope that they could field a competitive team even after trading away key veterans.

The euphoria of the blazing start came crashing down on April 12 when the Mariners lost the first of six straight games. But what really sank the season for Seattle was the 7-21 record during the month of May, with the team posting losing records in each subsequent month and finishing in last place in the American League West at 68-94.

For the second straight year, Double-A Arkansas was the only one of six Mariners affiliates to post a record above .500, finishing at 81-57 and qualifying for the Texas League playoffs by winning the first half of the Northern Division before losing to Tulsa in a five-game semifinal series.

The most positive note for the Mariners' system was the development of outfielders Kelenic and Julio Rodriguez, both now ranked among the best players in the minor leagues. The duo started together at low Class A West Virginia, with Kelenic being promoted twice during a season in which he finished at Double-A. Rodriguez was slowed by an early-season injury but eventually made the jump to high Class A Modesto.

Righthander Logan Gilbert, a 2018 first-round pick, made his pro debut by pitching well across three levels, going a combined 10-5 with a 2.13 ERA at low Class A, high Class A and Double-A. He struck out 165 and walked just 33 in 26 starts.

Diving even lower, shortstop Noelvi Marte trounced the competition in the Dominican Summer League by hitting .309/.371/.511 as a 17-year-old while making his pro debut.

ROB LEITER/MLB PHOTOS VIA GETTY IMAGES

Kyle Lewis recovered from a gruesome knee injury to make his major league debut in 2019.

PROJECTED 2023 LINEUP

Position	Player	Age
Catcher	Tom Murphy	32
First Base	Evan White (3)	27
Second Base	Shed Long	27
Third Base	Noelvi Marte (6)	21
Shortstop	J.P. Crawford	28
Left Field	Mitch Haniger	32
Center Field	Jarred Kelenic (2)	23
Right Field	Julio Rodriguez (1)	22
Designated Hitter	Kyle Lewis (10)	27
No. 1 Starter	Logan Gilbert (4)	26
No. 2 Starter	George Kirby (5)	25
No. 3 Starter	Marco Gonzales	31
No. 4 Starter	Yusei Kikuchi	32
No. 5 Starter	Justus Sheffield (7)	27
Closer	Justin Dunn (8)	27

The Mariners continued to add more advanced college pitchers to the organization in the 2019 draft, selecting Elon righthander George Kirby with their first-round pick, followed closely by Texas Christian southpaw Brandon Williamson and Arkansas righty Isaiah Campbell. Kirby's debut was noteworthy in that he did not walk a batter in his 23 innings with short-season Everett.

The Mariners are dependent on their farm system for future success. The development shown by Rodriguez, Kelenic, White, Gilbert and Kirby in 2019 indicates that the front office's faith is not misplaced.

DEPTH CHART

SEATTLE MARINERS

TOP 2020 ROOKIE: Justus Sheffield, LHP. Sheffield rebounded after a rough start in 2019 and will get another shot at the Mariners' rotation.

BREAKOUT PROSPECT: Jonatan Clase, OF. He combines tools with a strong work ethic, and he'll get the opportunity to further develop those extraordinary tools.

SOURCE OF TOP 30 TALENT			
Homegrown	**22**	**Acquired**	**8**
College	14	Trade	8
Junior college	0	Rule 5 draft	0
High school	1	Independent league	0
Nondrafted free agent	0	Free agent/waivers	0
International	7		

SLEEPER: Tim Elliott, RHP. Elliott was coming off a long college season at Georgia when he reported to short-season Everett, but an offseason of rest should allow his stuff to tick up in 2020.

LF

Kyle Lewis (10)
Keegan McGovern

CF

Jarred Kelenic (2)
Jake Fraley (11)
Dom Thompson-Williams (17)
Braden Bishop (19)
Jonatan Clase (25)
George Feliz
Luis Liberato

RF

Julio Rodriguez (1)
Trent Tingelstad
Jack Larsen

3B

Austin Shenton (15)
Milkar Perez (16)
Joe Rizzo
Jose Caballero
Jake Scheiner

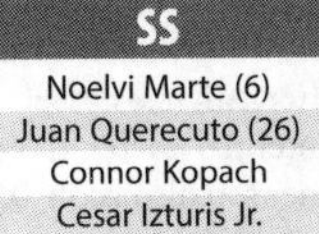

SS

Noelvi Marte (6)
Juan Querecuto (26)
Connor Kopach
Cesar Izturis Jr.

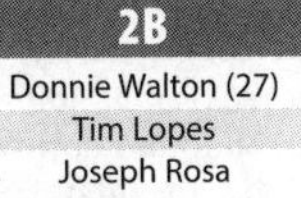

2B

Donnie Walton (27)
Tim Lopes
Joseph Rosa

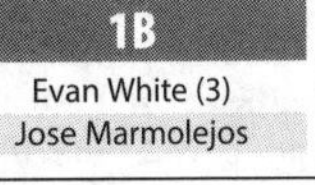

1B

Evan White (3)
Jose Marmolejos

C

Cal Raleigh (12)
Carter Bins
Jake Anchia

LHP

LHSP	LHRP
Justus Sheffield (7)	Aaron Fletcher (22)
Brandon Williamson (9)	Taylor Guilbeau
Anthony Misiewicz (28)	Raymond Kerr
Brayan Perez	
Adam Macko	
Ricardo Sanchez	
Holden Laws	
Ian McKinney	

RHP

RHSP	RHRP
Logan Gilbert (4)	Sam Delaplane (18)
George Kirby (5)	Joey Gerber (23)
Justin Dunn (8)	Wyatt Mills (24)
Isaiah Campbell (13)	Matt Festa
Juan Then (14)	Art Warren
Jose Corniel (20)	Elvis Alvarado
Sam Carlson (21)	Gerson Bautista
Penn Murfee (29)	
Yeury Tatiz (30)	
Tim Elliott	
Damon Casetta-Stubbs	
Ljay Newsome	
Levi Stoudt	
Michael Limoncelli	
Dutch Landis	
Anthony Tomczak	
Darren McCaughan	
Reggie McClain	

DRAFT ANALYSIS

2019

BEST PURE HITTER: 3B Austin Shenton (5), a native of Bellingham, Wash., had a standout summer in the Cape Cod League last year and was named MVP of the championship series. His hittability is his best asset as he consistently barrels balls and does a good job controlling the strike zone.

BEST POWER HITTER: In a draft class that was heavy on pitching—nine of the Mariners' first 11 picks were pitchers—C Carter Bins (11) is the chief power threat. He produces big exit velocity and after signing hit seven home runs in 49 games with short-season Everett.

FASTEST RUNNER: OF Antoine Mistico (12) is a well above-average runner that has registered some elite run times. He profiles as a potential top-of-the-order hitter.

BEST DEFENSIVE PLAYER: While Bins has raw power, he's more known for his catch-and-throw skills. He has soft hands, a plus arm and handles a pitching staff well. SS Patrick Frick (14) is a dependable defender who figures to be able to stay up the middle on the infield.

BEST ATHLETE: RHP Ty Adcock (8) was Kirby's teammate at Elon and pulled double duty as an outfielder and pitcher. He hit .251/.335/.480 this spring, and while the Mariners shut him down for the summer after his busy spring, they did entertain the possibility of using him as a DH.

BEST FASTBALL: RHP George Kirby (1) has a big arm and touched 99 mph while working in short stints this summer. Even as a starter, he consistently ran his fastball up to 94-95 mph this spring. LHP Brandon Williamson (2) came on strong this spring and was up to 97 mph late.

BEST SECONDARY PITCH: Kirby throws two breaking balls, and both have plus potential, but it's his slider that gets the edge right now. RHP Tim Elliott (4) has a plus changeup that helped him have a strong year.

BEST PRO DEBUT: Shenton started his pro career with Everett and hit .367/.446/.595 in 21 games and was in the mix for the Northwest League batting title when he was promoted to low Class A West Virginia. He had some initial struggles in the South Atlantic League but was back on track before his season ended a couple of weeks early when he was hit in the face by a pitch.

MOST INTRIGUING BACKGROUND: LHP Adam Macko (7) was born in Slovakia and is trying to become just the third native-born Slovakian to make the big leagues. He began playing baseball in Slovakia before moving to Ireland, where he played little league baseball, and eventually Canada.

CLOSEST TO THE MAJORS: Kirby, Williamson and RHP Isaiah Campbell (2s)—who didn't pitch after Arkansas' deep postseason run—all have the potential to hit the ground running next season. Shenton also is on an accelerated track after reaching West Virginia this summer.

BEST LATE-ROUND PICK: Bins has the biggest upside and could have been an early Day 2 pick. RHP Logan Rinehart (16) has a big arm, and his fastball has reached 96-97 mph. RHP Dutch Landis (17) presents plenty of upside and can also throw his fastball in the mid-90s.

THE ONE WHO GOT AWAY: The Mariners signed their first 31 picks before drafting RHP Jacob Meador (31). He upheld his commitment to Texas Christian, where he figures to take on a big role. C Dominic Tamez (35), who went on to Arkansas, is an advanced hitter and good athlete.

—TEDDY CAHILL

TOP DRAFT PICKS OF THE DECADE

Year	Player, Pos.	2019 Org
2010	Taijuan Walker, RHP (1st round supp)	D-backs
2011	Danny Hultzen, LHP	Cubs
2012	Mike Zunino, C	Rays
2013	D.J. Peterson, 3B	Atlantic League
2014	Alex Jackson, OF	Braves
2015	Nick Neidert, RHP (2nd round)	Marlins
2016	Kyle Lewis, OF	Mariners
2017	Evan White, 1B	Mariners
2018	Logan Gilbert, RHP	Mariners
2019	George Kirby, RHP	Mariners

2018

RHP Logan Gilbert (1) hit the ground running and reached Double-A in a strong pro debut. Seattle used five players from this class in trades, including OF Josh Stowers (2) and LHP Michael Plassmeyer (4).

GRADE: B

2017

1B Evan White (1) is set to make his MLB debut in 2020 after inking a long-term deal in the fall. RHP Sam Carlson (2) offers strong upside, and they found value in RHP Sam Delaplane (23).

GRADE: B

2016

OF Kyle Lewis (1) rebounded from his terrible knee injury to reach Seattle in 2019, giving the class five big leaguers so far. How much impact comes from that group is an open question, however.

GRADE: C

1 JULIO RODRIGUEZ, OF

Born: Dec. 29, 2000. **B-T:** R-R. **HT:** 6-4. **WT:** 225.
Signed: Dominican Republic, 2017.
Signed by: Eddy Toledo/Tim Kissner.

TRACK RECORD: Rodriguez was one of the premier hitters in the 2017 international class and signed with the Mariners for $1.75 million. He won MVP of the Dominican Summer League in his pro debut in 2018 and jumped to low Class A West Virginia to start 2019, where he teamed with fellow top prospect Jarred Kelenic in the outfield.The only speed bump Rodriguez encountered was a broken hand in mid-April that kept him out of action for two months. When on the field, Rodriguez was the talk of scouts, managers and opposing players. The Mariners promoted Rodriguez to high Class A Modesto in August, and he further embellished his lofty reputation by annihilating California League pitchers with a .462/.514/.738 slash line in 17 games. He finished his year in the Arizona Fall League and held his own as one of the youngest players there.

SCOUTING REPORT: Often described as a man-child, Rodriguez packs an impressive set of tools into a large, muscular frame. He has unbelievable feel to hit, especially for his age, and shows a good approach with the ability to retain information and make adjustments at the plate. With plus bat speed and quick hands, Rodriguez shows a swing with a solid bat path through the zone. He controls the zone well and struck out just a shade over 20 percent of the time in 2019. Rodriguez's most exhilarating tool is his plus-plus raw power to all fields. He makes loud contact and projects to hit for both average and power when he's fully developed. Rodriguez is no more than an average runner now and will slow with age, especially since he's already getting thicker in his lower half. He split time between center and right field, but a plus-plus arm profiles him perfectly for right field. Rodriguez gets good reads and jumps in the outfield, projecting to be an average defender. Rodriguez has outstanding makeup and character and is frequently described as a joy to be around. He has learned English rapidly and takes pride in being able to do interviews in his second language.

THE FUTURE: Rodriguez will continue to be pushed quickly through the Mariners' system, with some observers saying it wouldn't be a surprise to see him in the major leagues as a teenager. He has a chance to break camp with Double-A Arkansas to start 2020 and gives the Mariners a potential franchise, middle-of-the-order hitter to build around.

TRACY PROFFITT/FOUR SEAM IMAGES

BA GRADE
70 **Risk: High**

SCOUTING GRADES
Hit: 70. **Power:** 70. **Run:** 45. **Field:** 50. **Arm:** 70.

Projected future grades on 20-80 scouting scale.

TOP PROSPECTS OF THE DECADE

Year	Player, Pos	2019 Org
2010	Dustin Ackley, OF	Did not play
2011	Dustin Ackley, 2B	Did not play
2012	Taijuan Walker, RHP	D-backs
2013	Mike Zunino, C	Rays
2014	Taijuan Walker, RHP	D-backs
2015	Alex Jackson, OF	Braves
2016	Alex Jackson, OF	Braves
2017	Kyle Lewis, OF	Mariners
2018	Kyle Lewis, OF	Mariners
2019	Justus Sheffield, LHP	Mariners

BEST TOOLS

Best Hitter for Average	Jarred Kelenic
Best Power Hitter	Julio Rodriguez
Best Strike-Zone Discipline	Austin Shenton
Fastest Baserunner	Jonatan Clase
Best Athlete	Jarred Kelenic
Best Fastball	Logan Gilbert
Best Curveball	Brandon Williamson
Best Slider	Sam Delaplane
Best Changeup	Devin Sweet
Best Control	George Kirby
Best Defensive Catcher	Cal Raleigh
Best Defensive Infielder	Evan White
Best Infield Arm	Milkar Perez
Best Defensive Outfielder	Luis Liberato
Best Outfield Arm	Julio Rodriguez

Year	Age	Club (League)	Class	AVG	G	AB	R	H	2B	3B	HR	RBI	BB	SO	SB	OBP	SLG
2018	17	Mariners (DSL)	R	.315	59	219	50	69	13	9	5	36	30	40	10	.404	.525
2019	18	West Virginia (SAL)	LoA	.293	67	263	50	77	20	1	10	50	20	66	1	.359	.490
	18	Modesto (CAL)	HiA	.462	17	65	13	30	6	3	2	19	5	10	0	.514	.738
Minor League Totals				.322	143	547	113	176	39	13	17	105	55	116	11	.395	.534

2 JARRED KELENIC, OF

BA GRADE
65 Risk: High

Born: July 16, 1999. **B-T:** L-L. **HT:** 6-1. **WT:** 196. **Drafted:** HS—Waukesha, Wis., 2018 (1st round). **Signed by:** Chris Hervey (Mets).

TRACK RECORD: Kelenic was the consensus top high school hitter available in the 2018 draft and became the first prep taken when the Mets picked him sixth overall. Six months later, the Mariners acquired him in the deal that sent Robinson Cano and Edwin Diaz to New York. Kelenic shot through Seattle's system in 2019, jumping three levels to Double-A and posting a 20-20 season. He reported late to the Arizona Fall League due to dental work, then was shut down early with a sore back.

SCOUTING REPORT: Kelenic is a precocious hitter who hits to his strengths and lays off his weaknesses. He has an advanced feel for his swing and makes quick adjustments. Kelenic uses a short, compact swing with powerful hip rotation that allows him to drive balls with above-average power, and he has good enough strike-zone awareness to hit for power without striking out much. A plus runner now, Kelenic may slow down as his body matures but should be a basestealing threat because of his advanced instincts. He has the foundation to be an average defender in center field with a plus arm, but his focus and effort on defense need to improve.

THE FUTURE: Kelenic is a potential all-star in the mold of Jim Edmonds or Grady Sizemore. He'll see Triple-A in 2020.

SCOUTING GRADES: **Hitting:** 70 **Power:** 60 **Running:** 55 **Fielding:** 50 **Arm:** 60

Year	Age	Club (League)	Class	AVG	G	AB	R	H	2B	3B	HR	RBI	BB	SO	SB	OBP	SLG
2018	18	Mets (GCL)	R	.413	12	46	9	19	2	2	1	9	4	11	4	.451	.609
	18	Kingsport (APP)	R	.253	44	174	33	44	8	4	5	33	22	39	11	.350	.431
2019	19	West Virginia (SAL)	LoA	.309	50	191	33	59	14	3	11	29	25	45	7	.394	.586
	19	Modesto (CAL)	HiA	.290	46	169	36	49	13	1	6	22	17	49	10	.353	.485
	19	Arkansas (TL)	AA	.253	21	83	11	21	4	1	6	17	8	17	3	.315	.542
Minor League Totals				.290	173	663	122	192	41	11	29	110	76	161	35	.366	.516

3 EVAN WHITE, 1B

BA GRADE
55 Risk: Medium

Born: April 26, 1996. **B-T:** R-L. **HT:** 6-3. **WT:** 205. **Drafted:** Kentucky, 2017 (1st round). **Signed by:** Jackson Laumann.

TRACK RECORD: White's plus athleticism and premium defense date back to his college days at Kentucky, but the 2017 first-rounder long faced questions about whether he had enough power to profile at first base. White answered the doubters in 2019 with 18 home runs in 92 games at Double-A Arkansas while maintaining a high average. After the season, the Mariners signed him to a six-year, $24 million major league deal and added him to the 40-man roster.

SCOUTING REPORT: White's defining tool will always be his defense. He's a plus-plus defender with a plus arm, with scouts praising his glove work as the best since J.T. Snow. His footwork, soft hands and instincts are all top notch and should result in multiple Gold Glove awards. A plus runner, White could also handle an outfield position and possibly even be a plus defender there with his natural athleticism. At the plate, White has very good feel for the barrel, excellent hand-eye coordination and keen strike-zone awareness. He lowered his hands to increase the loft in his swing and now shows 20-home run power to go with above-average or better hitting ability.

THE FUTURE: White is on the fast track to Seattle after signing his big league deal. If he spends any time at all at Triple-A Tacoma in 2020, it won't be for very long.

SCOUTING GRADES: **Hitting:** 55 **Power:** 50 **Running:** 60 **Fielding:** 70 **Arm:** 55

Year	Age	Club (League)	Class	AVG	G	AB	R	H	2B	3B	HR	RBI	BB	SO	SB	OBP	SLG
2017	21	Everett (NWL)	SS	.277	14	47	6	13	1	1	3	12	6	6	1	.345	.532
2018	22	Tacoma (PCL)	AAA	.222	4	18	0	4	2	0	0	0	0	5	0	.222	.333
	22	Modesto (CAL)	HiA	.303	120	476	72	144	27	7	11	66	52	103	4	.375	.458
2019	23	Arkansas (TL)	AA	.293	92	365	61	107	13	2	18	55	29	92	2	.350	.488
Minor League Totals				.296	230	906	139	268	43	10	32	133	87	206	7	.361	.471

4 LOGAN GILBERT, RHP

Born: May 5, 1997. **B-T:** R-R. **HT:** 6-6. **WT:** 225. **Drafted:** Stetson, 2018 (1st round). **Signed by:** Rob Mummau.

TRACK RECORD: Gilbert didn't pitch in 2018 after the Mariners made him their first-round pick but made up for lost time by jumping three levels to Double-A Arkansas in 2019. The former all-American showed his college success was no fluke with a combined 2.13 ERA and 165 strikeouts, tied for 10th in the minors. The Mariners named him their minor league pitcher of the year.

SCOUTING REPORT: The velocity Gilbert lost near the end of his college career returned in 2019, with his plus fastball generally sitting 92-93 mph and touching 96. Gilbert's fastball is a separator with extra life, carry and ride due to the plus extension he generates with his long limbs. He is still inconsistent in commanding his breaking balls, but they both play up because of his pitchability. Gilbert's 72-77 mph curveball is an 11-to-5 pitch with consistent shape and high spin rates. His 78-84 mph slider comes in with a 10-to-4 shape with more horizontal movement. Both breaking balls are below-average but project average to above-average in time. He has feel for an average changeup in the low 80s, though he needs to throw it more frequently. Despite a long arm action, Gilbert is a good athlete who pounds the strike zone with above-average control.

THE FUTURE: Gilbert projects as a solid mid-rotation starter and could make his debut in 2020.

SCOUTING GRADES: **Fastball:** 60 **Slider:** 55 **Curveball:** 50 **Changeup:** 50 **Control:** 50

Year	Age	Club (League)	Class	W	L	ERA	G	GS	SV	IP	H	HR	BB	SO	K/9	WHIP	AVG
2018	21	Did not play—Injured															
2019	22	West Virginia (SAL)	LoA	1	0	1.59	5	5	0	23	9	2	6	36	14.3	0.66	.118
	22	Modesto (CAL)	HiA	5	3	1.73	12	12	0	62	52	3	12	73	10.5	1.03	.228
	22	Arkansas (TL)	AA	4	2	2.88	9	9	0	50	34	2	15	56	10.1	0.98	.194
Minor League Totals				10	5	2.13	26	26	0	135	95	7	33	165	11.0	0.95	.198

5 GEORGE KIRBY, RHP

SHARI SOMMERFELD

Born: Feb. 4, 1998. **B-T:** R-R. **HT:** 6-4. **WT:** 201. **Drafted:** Elon, 2019 (1st round). **Signed by:** Ty Holub.

TRACK RECORD: Kirby walked just six batters in 88 innings in his final season at Elon and became the highest drafted player in school history when the Mariners selected him 20th overall. He signed for $3,242,900. Kirby reported to short-season Everett after signing and didn't walk a batter in 23 innings while striking out 25.

SCOUTING REPORT: Kirby is more than just a strike-thrower and possesses an impressive arsenal of pitches. His fastball sat 93-95 mph and touched 98 in his pro debut, though those velocities were higher than usual because he was limited to shorter outings. He generally sits in the low 90s and touches 95. His best secondary pitch is a potentially above-average to plus slider at 83-88 mph with depth and a crisp break. His 79-83 mph curveball with 11-to-5 break projects to be an average pitch, while his 85-87 changeup flashes above-average, though he didn't use it much after signing. Where Kirby stands out most is his plus-plus control. He has a clean arm action and plus command, allowing him to put the ball wherever he wants in the strike zone.

THE FUTURE: Kirby has a chance to jump straight to high Class A Modesto and rejoin his college pitching coach, Sean McGrath, whom the Mariners hired in the offseason. He's a likely No. 3 or 4 starter.

SCOUTING GRADES: **Fastball:** 60 **Slider:** 55 **Curveball:** 50 **Changeup:** 55 **Control:** 70

Year	Age	Club (League)	Class	W	L	ERA	G	GS	SV	IP	H	HR	BB	SO	K/9	WHIP	AVG
2019	21	Everett (NWL)	SS	0	0	2.35	9	8	0	23	24	1	0	25	9.8	1.04	.270
Minor League Totals				0	0	2.35	9	8	0	23	24	1	0	25	9.8	1.04	.270

6 NOELVI MARTE, SS

Born: Oct. 16, 2001 **B-T:** R-R. **HT:** 6-0. **WT:** 187. **Signed:** Dominican Republic, 2018. **Signed by:** Eddy Toledo/Tim Kissner.

BILL MITCHELL

BA GRADE

60 Risk: Extreme

TRACK RECORD: Marte signed with the Mariners for $1.55 million during the 2018 international signing period and made his pro debut in 2019 with an outstanding season in the Dominican Summer League. He batted .309/.371/.511, led the league with 54 RBIs and 134 total bases, finished second with 31 extra-base hits and, significantly, stayed strong late with a 1.041 OPS in August.

SCOUTING REPORT: Marte is a five-tool athlete with plenty of upside. He has an advanced approach at the plate and uses a compact stroke with whippy bat speed and makes good swing decisions. An intriguing power-speed threat, Marte stole 19 bases in addition to hitting seven home runs in his pro debut. A plus-plus runner when he signed, Marte is now more of a plus runner and closer to 200 pounds after filling out. After having some throwing issues early in the season, Marte's shortstop defense improved thanks to a throwing program that boosted both his arm strength and accuracy. Concerns he would eventually move to the outfield have been lessened, but whether he remains at shortstop or slides to third base will be determined as his body continues to grow.

THE FUTURE: Marte is following in the footsteps of Julio Rodriguez as another potential impact Dominican signee. He will make his U.S. debut in 2020.

SCOUTING GRADES: **Hitting:** 60 **Power:** 55 **Running:** 60 **Fielding:** 50 **Arm:** 60

Year	Age	Club (League)	Class	AVG	G	AB	R	H	2B	3B	HR	RBI	BB	SO	SB	OBP	SLG
2019	17	Mariners (DSL)	R	.309	65	262	56	81	18	4	9	54	29	55	17	.371	.511
Minor League Totals				.309	65	262	56	81	18	4	9	54	29	55	17	.371	.511

7 JUSTUS SHEFFIELD, LHP

Born: May 13, 1996. **B-T:** L-L. **HT:** 6-0. **WT:** 200. **Drafted:** HS—Tullahoma, Tenn., 2014 (1st round). **Signed by:** Chuck Bartlett (Indians).

ALEX TRAUTWIG

BA GRADE

50 Risk: Medium

TRACK RECORD: Originally drafted by the Indians and traded to the Yankees in the 2016 Andrew Miller deal, Sheffield had an up-and-down first season in the Mariners' system after coming over in the James Paxton trade. He began the year at Triple-A and got bombed for a 6.87 ERA, then dropped down to Double-A and rediscovered his form. He then jumped to the majors, finishing the year with eight appearances, including seven starts, in Seattle.

SCOUTING REPORT: When he's on, Sheffield delivers a plus power fastball from the left side that sits at 93 mph and touches 97. The key to his improvement during his time in Double-A was commanding his fastball better after working with pitching coach Pete Woodworth, who will be the Mariners' big league pitching coach in 2020. Sheffield can vary the shape of his above-average mid-80s slider and gained confidence throwing his 84-88 mph average changeup with fade late in the year. Sheffield's effortful delivery has long resulted in below-average command, but he improved as the season progressed and stayed better on line to the plate.

THE FUTURE: Sheffield's command shortcomings have most rival evaluators projecting him to the bullpen, but he will enter 2020 with a chance to make the Mariners' rotation.

SCOUTING GRADES: **Fastball:** 60 **Slider:** 55 **Changeup:** 50 **Control:** 45

Year	Age	Club (League)	Class	W	L	ERA	G	GS	SV	IP	H	HR	BB	SO	K/9	WHIP	AVG
2017	21	Yankees2 (GCL)	R	0	1	1.93	2	2	0	5	4	0	1	6	11.6	1.07	.235
	21	Trenton (EL)	AA	7	6	3.18	17	17	0	93	94	14	33	82	7.9	1.36	.258
2018	22	Trenton (EL)	AA	1	2	2.25	5	5	0	28	16	1	14	39	12.5	1.07	.163
	22	Scranton/W-B (IL)	AAA	6	4	2.56	20	15	0	88	66	3	36	84	8.6	1.16	.204
	22	New York (AL)	MAJ	0	0	10.13	3	0	0	3	4	1	3	0	0.0	2.63	.364
2019	23	Tacoma (PCL)	AAA	2	6	6.87	13	12	0	55	59	12	41	48	7.9	1.82	.268
	23	Arkansas (TL)	AA	5	3	2.19	12	12	0	78	62	4	18	85	9.8	1.03	.218
	23	Seattle (AL)	MAJ	0	1	5.50	8	7	0	36	44	5	18	37	9.3	1.72	.303
Major League Totals				0	1	5.82	11	7	0	38	48	6	21	37	8.6	1.78	.308
Minor League Totals				43	33	3.31	128	118	0	620	567	48	243	640	9.3	1.31	.239

8 JUSTIN DUNN, RHP

ALEX TRAUTWIG

BA GRADE
50 **Risk: Medium**

Born: Sept. 22, 1995. **B-T:** R-R. **HT:** 6-2. **WT:** 185. **Drafted:** Boston College, 2016 (1st round). **Signed by:** Michael Pesce (Mets).

TRACK RECORD: Dunn mostly pitched in relief at Boston College but turned himself into a first-round pick with a successful move to the rotation as a junior. The Mets drafted him 19th overall in 2016, and the Mariners acquired him in the Dec. 2018 trade that sent Robinson Cano and Edwin Diaz to New York. Dunn's first year in the Mariners' system went splendidly at Double-A Arkansas. He led the Texas League in strikeouts, made the Futures Game and earned his first major league callup in September.

SCOUTING REPORT: Dunn's fastball sits 90-94 mph and averages 92, but it gets on hitters quick from his easy, effortless delivery. His separator is a plus low-80s slider he can land in the strike zone or bury for chases. It drew swings and misses nearly 40 percent of the time he threw it in the majors and gives him an out pitch. Dunn has the makings of an average changeup, though it is presently too firm in the upper 80s, and he also has a get-me-over curveball he'll occasionally throw. Dunn noticeably gained bad weight in 2019 and struggled to throw strikes in the majors, so he spent the fall improving his conditioning.

THE FUTURE: Dunn will get another shot in Seattle in 2020. Most see his future as a two-pitch late reliever.

SCOUTING GRADES: **Fastball:** 55 **Slider:** 60 **Curveball:** 45 **Changeup:** 40 **Control:** 50

Year	Age	Club (League)	Class	W	L	ERA	G	GS	SV	IP	H	HR	BB	SO	K/9	WHIP	AVG
2017	21	St. Lucie (FSL)	HiA	5	6	5.00	20	16	0	95	101	5	48	75	7.1	1.56	.273
2018	22	St. Lucie (FSL)	HiA	2	3	2.36	9	9	0	46	43	2	15	51	10.1	1.27	.243
	22	Binghamton (EL)	AA	6	5	4.22	15	15	0	90	85	7	37	105	10.5	1.36	.258
2019	23	Arkansas (TL)	AA	9	5	3.55	25	25	0	132	118	13	39	158	10.8	1.19	.236
	23	Seattle (AL)	MAJ	0	0	2.70	4	4	0	7	2	0	9	5	6.8	1.65	.105
Major League Totals				0	0	2.70	4	4	0	6	2	0	9	5	6.8	1.65	.105
Minor League Totals				23	20	3.76	80	73	0	392	372	28	149	424	9.7	1.33	.250

9 BRANDON WILLIAMSON, LHP

COURTESY OF TCU ATHLETICS

BA GRADE
55 **Risk: High**

Born: April 2, 1998. **B-T:** L-L. **HT:** 6-6. **WT:** 210. **Drafted:** Texas Christian, 2019 (2nd round). **Signed by:** Jordan Bley.

TRACK RECORD: Williamson transferred from Northern Iowa Area JC to Texas Christian before the 2019 season and missed the fall after having surgery on both hips. He recovered to settle in as the Horned Frogs' No. 2 starter behind fellow lefthander Nick Lodolo and showed enough for the Mariners to draft him in the second round and sign him for $925,000. Williamson reported to short-season Everett after signing and showed an uptick in stuff.

SCOUTING REPORT: After living in the low 90s in college, Williamson's heater came out sitting 91-96 mph with electric life at Everett. The result was an overall swinging-strike rate of 20 percent, one of the best in the minors, and plus grades on a pitch that was seen as average in college. Williamson generates high spin and good shape on his mid-70s curveball, another above-average pitch batters typically swing through, and he also has a low-80s slider that flashes average. He has feel for an above-average changeup but didn't use it much at Everett. Williamson uses a three-quarters delivery that is high on the front side and provides deception, and he maintains average control.

THE FUTURE: The Mariners may have a second-round steal in Williamson. He will make his full-season debut in 2020 and projects as a possible No. 3 or 4 starter.

SCOUTING GRADES: **Fastball:** 60 **Slider:** 50 **Curveball:** 55 **Changeup:** 50 **Control:** 50

Year	Age	Club (League)	Class	W	L	ERA	G	GS	SV	IP	H	HR	BB	SO	K/9	WHIP	AVG
2019	21	Everett (NWL)	SS	0	0	2.35	10	9	0	15	9	0	5	25	14.7	0.91	.167
Minor League Totals				0	0	2.35	10	9	0	15	9	0	5	25	14.7	0.91	.167

10 KYLE LEWIS, OF

ALEX TRAUTWIG

Born: July 13, 1995. **B-T:** R-R. **HT:** 6-4. **WT:** 210. **Drafted:** Mercer, 2016 (1st round). **Signed by:** John Wiedenbauer.

TRACK RECORD: It's been an arduous climb through the system for Lewis since the Mariners drafted him 11th overall in 2016, when he was the BA College Player of the Year. He tore the anterior cruciate ligament in his right knee in a grisly home plate collision in his pro debut and struggled with setbacks throughout 2017 and 2018. But he finally made it to the majors in 2019 after a solid, healthy season at Double-A Arkansas and made a splash by homering in each of his first three major league games.

SCOUTING REPORT: Lewis is a power-over-hit type with high strikeout totals part of the package. There are a lot of moving parts to his swing, with a hand trigger and a leg kick, but he sees the ball well and generates the bat speed through the zone to produce high exit velocities. Now a tick below-average runner, Lewis' time in center field is likely coming to an end. The Mariners plan to station him in left field in 2020, where he'll be an above-average defender with solid instincts and an above-average arm.

THE FUTURE: Lewis may skip over Triple-A Tacoma and win the wide-open left field job in Seattle. It will likely be his job to lose in spring training.

SCOUTING GRADES: **Hitting:** 50 **Power:** 55 **Running:** 45 **Fielding:** 55 **Arm:** 55

Year	Age	Club (League)	Class	AVG	G	AB	R	H	2B	3B	HR	RBI	BB	SO	SB	OBP	SLG
2017	21	Mariners (AZL)	R	.263	11	38	9	10	2	1	1	7	4	14	1	.348	.447
	21	Modesto (CAL)	HiA	.255	38	149	20	38	4	0	6	24	15	38	2	.323	.403
2018	22	Modesto (CAL)	HiA	.260	49	196	21	51	18	0	5	32	11	55	0	.303	.429
	22	Arkansas (TL)	AA	.220	37	132	18	29	8	0	4	20	17	32	1	.309	.371
2019	23	Arkansas (TL)	AA	.263	122	457	61	120	25	2	11	62	56	152	3	.342	.398
	23	Seattle (AL)	MAJ	.268	18	71	10	19	5	0	6	13	3	29	0	.293	.592
Major League Totals				.268	18	71	10	19	5	0	6	13	3	29	0	.293	.592
Minor League Totals				.260	287	1089	155	283	65	8	30	171	119	313	10	.334	.417

11 JAKE FRALEY, OF

BA GRADE
45 **Risk: Medium**

Born: May 25, 1995. **B-T:** L-L. **HT:** 6-0. **WT:** 195. **Drafted:** Louisiana State, 2016 (2nd round supplemental). **Signed by:** Rickey Drexler (Rays).

TRACK RECORD: The key for Fraley in his first season with the Mariners' organization was to get healthy and stay healthy after injury-plagued seasons in 2017 and 2018. The Louisiana State product accomplished that mission by getting into 99 minor league games before making his big league debut for Seattle on August 21. He was shut down early with a sore thumb, but overall it was a valuable growth season for the former Rays' farmhand.

SCOUTING REPORT: Being able to play every day helped Fraley turn himself into an impact hitter with solid tools. He has a solid approach at the plate with strong hands that help him drive balls to all fields, but needs to improve against lefthanders. While the swing is not particularly fluid, Fraley has the hand-eye coordination to compensate. It's more gap power, but he still hit a career-high 19 home runs in his 99 games split between two levels. A plus runner, Fraley's speed plays up even further because of his aggressiveness. Defensively, he can handle all three outfield positions with the chance to be a plus defender with an above-average arm.

THE FUTURE: Fraley projects to be a starting major league outfielder who plays above his tools because of his intensity on the field and very good instincts. He should see a significant amount of time in Seattle in 2020.

Year	Age	Club (League)	Class	AVG	G	AB	R	H	2B	3B	HR	RBI	BB	SO	SB	OBP	SLG
2017	22	Charlotte, FL (FSL)	HiA	.170	26	94	6	16	3	1	1	12	7	24	1	.238	.255
	22	Rays (GCL)	R	.467	4	15	6	7	3	0	1	2	2	3	3	.529	.867
2018	23	Charlotte, FL (FSL)	HiA	.347	66	225	39	78	19	7	4	41	26	44	11	.415	.547
2019	24	Arkansas (TL)	AA	.313	61	230	40	72	15	2	11	47	23	55	16	.386	.539
	24	Tacoma (PCL)	AAA	.276	38	152	28	42	12	3	8	33	11	34	6	.333	.553
	24	Seattle (AL)	MAJ	.150	12	40	3	6	2	0	0	1	0	14	0	.171	.200
Major League Totals				.150	12	40	3	6	2	0	0	1	0	14	0	.171	.200
Minor League Totals				.286	250	922	153	264	61	20	26	153	95	194	70	.362	.480

12 CAL RALEIGH, C

BA GRADE 50 Risk: High

Born: Nov. 26, 1996. **B-T:** B-R. **HT:** 6-3. **WT:** 215. **Drafted:** Florida State, 2018 (3rd round). **Signed by:** Rob Mummau.

TRACK RECORD: After a three-year career at Florida State and 38 games at short-season Everett in his pro debut in 2018, Raleigh jumped a level to high Class A Modesto and then to Double-A Arkansas for his first full season. The big switch-hitting catcher finished third in the Cal League in home runs (22).

SCOUTING REPORT: A rare switch-hitting catcher with big power, Raleigh gets to his raw power thanks to good direction in his bat, which makes up for below-average bat speed and a lack of lower-half mobility in the box. Scouts have seen Raleigh having to cheat to hit good velocity and he'll need to improve the quality of his at-bats as he advances. Behind the plate, Raleigh communicates well with his pitchers and frames and receives well. Because of his size he has to go to one knee to catch, but he transfers the ball well and his throws are accurate, with grades on his arm varying from below-average to just above.

THE FUTURE: Raleigh will provide value if he continues developing his approach and improving as a defender. He'll return to Double-A in 2020 with a probable move to Triple-A later in the summer.

Year	Age	Club (League)	Class	AVG	G	AB	R	H	2B	3B	HR	RBI	BB	SO	SB	OBP	SLG
2018	21	Everett (NWL)	SS	.288	38	146	25	42	10	1	8	29	18	29	1	.367	.534
2019	22	Modesto (CAL)	HiA	.261	82	310	48	81	19	0	22	66	33	69	4	.336	.535
	22	Arkansas (TL)	AA	.228	39	145	16	33	6	0	7	16	14	47	0	.296	.414
Minor League Totals				.260	159	601	89	156	35	1	37	111	65	145	5	.334	.506

13 ISAIAH CAMPBELL, RHP

BA GRADE 50 Risk: High

Born: Aug. 15, 1997. **B-T:** R-R. **HT:** 6-4. **WT:** 225. **Drafted:** Arkansas, 2019 (2nd round supplemental). **Signed by:** Ben Collman.

TRACK RECORD: Drafted in the second compensation round after a strong season as the Arkansas' Friday night starter, Campbell sat out his first pro summer after a long college season. He posted an outstanding 12-1 record and 2.26 ERA in his final year at Arkansas.

SCOUTING REPORT: Campbell validated his decision to return to campus by improving the power, shape and command of his slider. His above-average fastball sat 92-95 mph in college, with the 84-87 mph slider being the pitch that allows the heater to play up. Rounding out his four-pitch mix is a split-changeup that flashes above-average with deception and tumble, as well as a 75-80 mph curveball. He locates his pitches well, keeping them at the bottom of the zone but also elevating the fastball as needed.

THE FUTURE: Campbell's pure physicality convinces observers that he can remain in the rotation, projecting to be a No. 3 or No. 4 starter. He'll likely launch his pro career at low Class A West Virginia.

Year	Age	Club (League)	Class	W	L	ERA	G	GS	SV	IP	H	HR	BB	SO	K/9	WHIP	AVG
2019	21	Did not play															

14 JUAN THEN, RHP

BA GRADE 50 Risk: High

Born: Feb. 7, 2000. **B-T:** R-R. **HT:** 6-0. **WT:** 178. **Signed:** Dominican Republic, 2016. **Signed by:** Eddy Toledo.

TRACK RECORD: The Mariners would have been wise to purchase a round-trip ticket for Then when they traded the lanky Dominican to the Yankees in late 2017, as he headed back to the organization last year in the trade involving big leaguer Edwin Encarnacion.

SCOUTING REPORT: Then shows confidence on the mound, attacking hitters with his electric stuff. His fastball sits 92-93 mph, touching 96, and there's room on his frame to add strength. His heater comes out effortlessly and with late action. Still a work-in-progress that projects as an average pitch, Then's 80-84 mph slider has late break and 10-to-4 movement. The 83-88 mph changeup is a hard pitch that flashes plus, but he doesn't use it much. He throws his fastball for strikes but needs to get more swings and misses over the plate from his secondary pitches. He repeats a high-three-quarters delivery.

THE FUTURE: We'll have a better idea about Then's future projection after more time in full-season ball, but for now mark him down as an intriguing starting pitching prospect.

Year	Age	Club (League)	Class	W	L	ERA	G	GS	SV	IP	H	HR	BB	SO	K/9	WHIP	AVG
2017	17	Mariners (DSL)	R	2	2	2.64	13	13	0	61	50	3	15	56	8.2	1.06	.220
2018	18	Yankees1 (GCL)	R	0	3	2.70	11	11	0	50	38	2	11	42	7.6	0.98	.210
2019	19	Mariners (AZL)	R	0	0	0.00	1	0	0	2	2	0	0	2	9.0	1.00	.286
	19	Everett (NWL)	SS	0	3	3.56	7	6	0	30	24	1	9	32	9.5	1.09	.222
	19	West Virginia (SAL)	LoA	1	2	2.25	3	3	0	16	7	1	4	14	7.9	0.69	.127
Minor League Totals				3	10	2.76	35	33	0	159	121	7	39	146	8.2	1.00	.209

15 AUSTIN SHENTON, 3B

BA GRADE
50 Risk: Very High

Born: Jan. 22, 1998. **B-T:** L-R. **HT:** 6-0. **WT:** 195. **Drafted:** Florida International, 2019 (5th round). **Signed by:** Dan Rovetto.

TRACK RECORD: After taking five pitchers to begin the 2019 draft, the Mariners went for a proven pure hitter in Shenton, who spent the last two years of his college career at Florida International after a freshman season at Bellevue (Wash.) CC. He split his first pro season between short-season Everett, ranking as the Northwest League's 16th best prospect, and low Class A West Virginia.

SCOUTING REPORT: Shenton has real feel for hitting, consistently barreling balls and controlling the strike zone with advanced pitch recognition. He uses the whole field, showing average power mostly to the gaps but also with some pull-side home run pop. There are plenty of questions about where Shenton winds up defensively, as he's not particulary athletic but is a hard worker with a chance to stay at third base. He's a below-average defender with an average arm, but he could provide defensive versatility by also spending time at both left field and first base. Shenton is a below-average runner, but it's all about the bat for him.

THE FUTURE: With a quarter of a season in low Class A already under his belt, Shenton could head to high Class A Modesto to start the 2020 season.

Year	Age	Club (League)	Class	AVG	G	AB	R	H	2B	3B	HR	RBI	BB	SO	SB	OBP	SLG
2019	21	Everett (NWL)	SS	.367	21	79	16	29	10	1	2	16	8	15	0	.446	.595
	21	West Virginia (SAL)	LoA	.252	32	119	13	30	7	1	5	20	11	29	0	.328	.454
Minor League Totals				.298	53	198	29	59	17	2	7	36	19	44	0	.376	.510

16 MILKAR PEREZ, 3B

BA GRADE
50 Risk: Extreme

Born: Oct. 16, 2001. **B-T:** B-R. **HT:** 5-11. **WT:** 175. **Signed:** Nicaragua, 2018. **Signed by:** Tom Shafer.

TRACK RECORD: Perez's $175,000 bonus was tops for a player from Nicaragua in the 2018 international class, and based on his pro debut he could turn into a bargain for Seattle. Shortly after signing with the Mariners, Perez played for his native country at the COPABE 18U Pan American Championships in Panama, where he made the all-tournament team. Launching his professional career one year later in the Dominican Summer League, Perez was one of the top performers for the Mariners' squad, hitting .274/.381/.388 and walking in just over 13 percent of his plate appearances.

SCOUTING REPORT: Perez has an advanced approach from both sides of the plate, with a more compact swing from the left side, projecting as a potential hit/power combo. His best tool is a plus-plus arm, already graded as the best infield arm in the organization. He has below-average range but above-average hands, with the likelihood of being at least an above-average defender at the hot corner. He's a below-average runner.

THE FUTURE: Perez will make his stateside debut after extended spring training, most likely in the Rookie-level Arizona League.

Year	Age	Club (League)	Class	AVG	G	AB	R	H	2B	3B	HR	RBI	BB	SO	SB	OBP	SLG
2019	17	Mariners (DSL)	R	.274	64	237	38	65	11	2	4	44	37	55	8	.381	.388
Minor League Totals				.274	64	237	38	65	11	2	4	44	37	55	8	.381	.388

17 DOM THOMPSON-WILLIAMS, OF

Born: April 21, 1995. **B-T:** L-L. **HT:** 6-0. **WT:** 190. **Drafted:** South Carolina, 2016 (5th round). **Signed by:** Billy Godwin (Yankees).

TRACK RECORD: A 2016 fifth-round pick from South Carolina, Thompson-Williams joined the Mariners after three years in the Yankees' organization as part of the James Paxton trade and spent the entire 2019 season with Double-A Arkansas. At first glance, the numbers from his initial season with his new organization aren't impressive, but he hit much better (.277/.332/.509) away from the pitcher-friendly ballpark in Arkansas.

SCOUTING REPORT: It's not the tools, athleticism or makeup that would hold Thompson-Williams back. He's got quick-twitch athleticism and is an average runner out of the box but is plus on the bases, as shown by the 35 bases he's stolen in his two years of full-season ball. Thompson-Williams has plenty of raw power and knows the strike zone, but his swing gets uphill at times and he struggles against better velocity. An average defender, he gets good jumps and reads in the outfield, and his tick below-average arm will be enough for any outfield position in a backup role.

THE FUTURE: With a strong work ethic and willingness to hold himself accountable, Thompson-Williams could still bloom into a starting outfielder with more consistency in his swing.

Year	Age	Club (League)	Class	AVG	G	AB	R	H	2B	3B	HR	RBI	BB	SO	SB	OBP	SLG
2017	22	Staten Island (NYP)	SS	.277	41	141	17	39	7	0	3	22	18	30	7	.366	.390
	22	Charleston, SC (SAL)	LoA	.188	23	80	6	15	2	0	0	6	9	15	2	.270	.213
2018	23	Charleston, SC (SAL)	LoA	.378	10	37	7	14	1	0	5	9	2	7	3	.425	.811
	23	Tampa (FSL)	HiA	.290	90	331	56	96	16	4	17	65	31	95	17	.356	.517
2019	24	Arkansas (TL)	AA	.234	115	432	46	101	24	4	12	41	35	152	15	.298	.391
Minor League Totals				.257	335	1216	162	313	58	9	40	159	123	342	59	.332	.419

18 SAM DELAPLANE, RHP

BA GRADE **45** Risk: High

Born: March 27, 1995. **B-T:** R-R. **HT:** 5-11. **WT:** 175. **Drafted:** Eastern Michigan, 2017 (23rd round). **Signed by:** Ross Vecchio.

TRACK RECORD: Despite pitching well at every level since being drafted in the 23rd round in 2017, Delaplane wasn't a highly regarded prospect because he's a righthanded pitcher who stands under 6 feet tall. After striking out nearly 50 percent of batters he faced at high Class A Modesto, followed by a strong turn in the Arizona Fall League, Delaplane is getting more recognition.

SCOUTING REPORT: Coming into pro ball, Delaplane had so-so stuff and thrived more with deception. He now attacks hitters with a plus fastball that sits in the mid 90s and touches 98 mph. The pitch shows good riding from Delaplane's deceptive, high-three-quarters delivery. His other pitch is a mid-80s hard slider that generates high spin rates and is thrown with a curveball grip. The breaking ball has strong tilt and gets swings and misses from lefties and righties. Delaplane has an undersized frame but with a sturdy build is often compared physically to major league reliever Greg Holland.

THE FUTURE: Delaplane has averaged an astonishing 15 strikeouts per 9 innings in his career. He'll have to keep proving himself at higher levels, but his dominance in the Fall League shows that he's capable of thriving against better hitters. He profiles as a high-leverage reliever. He will likely head to Triple-A Tacoma in 2020 but with his eyes on Seattle.

Year	Age	Club (League)	Class	W	L	ERA	G	GS	SV	IP	H	HR	BB	SO	K/9	WHIP	AVG
2017	22	Mariners (AZL)	R	2	1	2.90	14	0	0	31	27	2	8	47	13.6	1.13	.223
	22	Tacoma (PCL)	AAA	0	0	4.50	1	0	0	2	3	0	1	3	13.5	2.00	.333
2018	23	Clinton (MWL)	LoA	4	2	1.96	39	0	10	60	54	5	22	100	15.1	1.27	.234
2019	24	Modesto (CAL)	HiA	3	2	4.26	21	0	2	32	22	2	14	62	17.6	1.14	.200
	24	Arkansas (TL)	AA	3	1	0.49	25	0	5	37	13	2	9	58	14.1	0.59	.107
Minor League Totals				12	6	2.29	100	0	17	161	119	11	54	270	15.1	1.07	.201

19 BRADEN BISHOP, OF

BA GRADE **40** Risk: Medium

Born: Aug. 22, 1993. **B-T:** R-R. **HT:** 6-1. **WT:** 190. **Drafted:** Washington, 2015 (3rd round). **Signed by:** Jeff Sakamoto.

TRACK RECORD: Bishop couldn't avoid the injury bug for the second year in a row, this time missing a significant amount of time due to surgery to repair a lacerated spleen in a season in which the Washington product made his major league debut.

SCOUTING REPORT: Bishop fits the profile of a fourth outfielder, but he's going to have to show more with the bat than he did during his big league trial in 2019. He hit with more power during his abbreviated season in Triple-A, but whether that translates to MLB performance is still in question. The strength he's added over the past two years hasn't resulted in significantly more impact at the plate, and a hitch in his swing requires him to get his bat started early. Bishop can do it all on the field, where he's a plus-plus defender with an above-average arm and has plus makeup and aptitude. Despite having plus speed, he's never been a big threat to steal bases.

THE FUTURE: Bishop should break camp as an extra outfielder in Seattle, but that's likely his ceiling. Injury issues have kept him from putting more oomph into his swing, so staying healthy all year will give a more accurate picture of Bishop's offensive ceiling.

Year	Age	Club (League)	Class	AVG	G	AB	R	H	2B	3B	HR	RBI	BB	SO	SB	OBP	SLG
2017	23	Modesto (CAL)	HiA	.296	88	355	71	105	25	3	2	32	45	65	16	.385	.400
	23	Arkansas (TL)	AA	.336	31	125	18	42	9	1	1	11	15	15	6	.417	.448
2018	24	Arkansas (TL)	AA	.284	84	345	70	98	20	0	8	33	37	68	5	.361	.412
2019	25	Modesto (CAL)	HiA	.240	7	25	7	6	1	1	0	3	2	9	0	.345	.360
	25	Tacoma (PCL)	AAA	.276	43	185	29	51	15	0	8	31	23	44	2	.360	.486
	25	Seattle (AL)	MAJ	.107	27	56	3	6	0	0	0	4	3	21	0	.153	.107
Major League Totals				.107	27	56	3	6	0	0	0	4	3	21	0	.153	.107
Minor League Totals				.291	413	1668	286	485	89	7	24	175	163	321	50	.365	.396

20 JOSE CORNIEL, RHP

BA GRADE 50 Risk: Extreme

Born: June 22, 2003. **B-T:** R-R. **HT:** 6-3. **WT:** 185. **Signed:** Dominican Republic, 2019. **Signed by:** Francisco Rosario.

TRACK RECORD: Corniel, a product of the Marmolejos Baseball Academy in his native Dominican Republic, was one of the better pitchers in the 2019 class and signed with the Mariners for a $630,000 bonus on July 2.

SCOUTING REPORT: Corniel has a very physical, projectable build with long levers and uses an effortless, balanced delivery with control rather than one that's explosive and effortful. A strike-thrower, he shows the ability to move the ball around the zone. His fastball ticked up to the low 90s during early workouts at the Mariners' academy in the Dominican Republic. Corniel can spin his above-average curveball and should have a solid changeup in time, giving him a three-pitch mix with above-average feel to pitch.

THE FUTURE: Corniel won't turn 17 until June, so he likely won't get to the states for another year or two. He'll start his pro career in the Dominican Summer League in 2020.

Year	Age	Club (League)	Class	W	L	ERA	G	GS	SV	IP	H	HR	BB	SO	K/9	WHIP	AVG
2019	16	Did not play—Signed 2020 contract															

21 SAM CARLSON, RHP

BA GRADE 50 Risk: Extreme

Born: Dec. 3, 1998. **B-T:** R-R. **HT:** 6-3. **WT:** 200. **Drafted:** HS—Burnsville, Minn., 2017 (2nd round). **Signed by:** Ben Collman.

TRACK RECORD: It would be easy to have forgotten about Carlson by now, considering that the Mariners' 2017 second-round pick has pitched in just two games since being drafted. Arm troubles kept him out of action for a full year before he had Tommy John surgery last July.

SCOUTING REPORT: Carlson is worth keeping on the radar because of his high school résumé, which shows that the Minnesota high school product was one of the better pitchers in the 2017 draft class. Prior to the injuries that wiped out much of the early part of his career, Carlson sported a heavy fastball up to 96 mph with late action and sink. He complemented that with an above-average slider with late action and tilt and a changeup that flashed plus.

THE FUTURE: Carlson was expected to start long tossing in the fall with bullpen sessions to follow prior to spring training.

Year	Age	Club (League)	Class	W	L	ERA	G	GS	SV	IP	H	HR	BB	SO	K/9	WHIP	AVG
2017	18	Mariners (AZL)	R	0	0	3.00	2	2	0	3	4	0	0	3	9.0	1.33	.364
2018	19	Did not play—Injured															
2019	20	Did not play—Injured															
Minor League Totals				0	0	3.00	2	2	0	3	4	0	0	3	9.0	1.33	.364

22 AARON FLETCHER, LHP

Born: Feb. 25, 1996. **B-T:** L-L. **HT:** 6-0. **WT:** 220. **Drafted:** Houston, 2018 (14th round). **Signed by:** Tyler Witt (Nationals).

TRACK RECORD: Fletcher pitched four years at the University of Houston, mostly in a bullpen role. He signed with the Nationals after being drafted in the 14th round in 2018 and jumped three levels in the first part of the 2019 season before being included in a trade to Seattle as one of three prospects acquired for Roenis Elias and Hunter Strickland. He finished 2019 with an assignment to the Arizona Fall League.

SCOUTING REPORT: Fletcher is a reliever all the way, with the potential to be a good one because of the velocity from the left side. He gets sink and run on his 91-96 mph fastball, delivered from a funky, deceptive delivery with a high front side. His fringy slider plays up because its sweep makes it tough for lefthanded batters and he gets it to the back foot of righthanded hitters. He rounds out his repertoire with an average changeup.

THE FUTURE: While he doesn't have a high ceiling, Fletcher will likely get big league time as an extra bullpen arm. He's likely to start 2020 back at Double-A Arkansas with a promotion to Tacoma to follow.

Year	Age	Club (League)	Class	W	L	ERA	G	GS	SV	IP	H	HR	BB	SO	K/9	WHIP	AVG
2018	22	Nationals (GCL)	R	0	0	9.00	1	0	0	2	4	0	1	2	9.0	2.50	.500
	22	Auburn (NYP)	SS	2	1	2.48	12	7	0	29	30	0	3	32	9.9	1.14	.265
2019	23	Hagerstown (SAL)	LoA	2	3	1.61	15	0	1	28	14	0	5	28	9.0	0.68	.149
	23	Potomac (CAR)	HiA	3	1	1.38	12	0	0	26	15	1	8	32	11.1	0.88	.165
	23	Harrisburg (EL)	AA	0	0	4.26	5	0	0	6	7	0	2	9	12.8	1.42	.280
	23	Arkansas (TL)	AA	0	0	3.46	9	0	0	13	14	0	3	15	10.4	1.31	.275
Minor League Totals				7	5	2.33	54	7	1	104	84	1	22	118	10.2	1.02	.220

23 JOEY GERBER, RHP

BA GRADE 45 Risk: High

Born: May 3, 1997. **B-T:** R-R. **HT:** 6-4. **WT:** 215. **Drafted:** Illinois, 2018 (8th round). **Signed by:** Ben Collman.

TRACK RECORD: Drafted in the eighth round in 2018, Gerber is a hard-throwing reliever. After striking out just over 12 batters per nine innings in college, Gerber has surpassed that number as a pro, fanning 13.6 batters per nine in his two pro seasons.

SCOUTING REPORT: Gerber delivers an electric fastball that regularly touches 97-98 mph with a funky, crossfire delivery that gives batters uncomfortable at-bats, especially since he rushes his pitches from a quick set and quick action to the plate. Hitters get a short arm view from Gerber's low-three-quarters delivery. His 83-85 mph slider often flashes plus and pairs well with the heater. That's all he should need in his role as a potential high-leverage reliever, especially if he improves his below-average command.

THE FUTURE: After splitting the 2019 season between high Class A Modesto and Double-A Arkansas, Gerber should break camp with Triple-A Tacoma to start the 2020 season. Don't be surprised if he gets big league time later in the year.

Year	Age	Club (League)	Class	W	L	ERA	G	GS	SV	IP	H	HR	BB	SO	K/9	WHIP	AVG
2018	21	Everett (NWL)	SS	1	0	1.93	13	0	6	14	9	0	6	21	13.5	1.07	.188
	21	Clinton (MWL)	LoA	0	0	2.31	9	0	2	12	9	0	5	22	17.0	1.20	.220
2019	22	Modesto (CAL)	HiA	0	2	3.46	25	0	8	26	17	0	12	39	13.5	1.12	.185
	22	Arkansas (TL)	AA	1	2	1.59	19	0	0	23	21	2	7	30	11.9	1.24	.247
Minor League Totals				2	4	2.42	66	0	16	74	56	2	30	112	13.6	1.16	.211

24 WYATT MILLS, RHP

BA GRADE 40 Risk: Medium

Born: Jan. 25, 1995**. B-T:** R-R. **HT:** 6-4. **WT:** 190. **Drafted:** Gonzaga, 2017 (3rd round). **Signed by:** Alex Ross/Jeff Sakamoto.

TRACK RECORD: Mills was slated to move quickly through the system after the Mariners drafted him in the third round in 2017 from Gonzaga, but the sidearm reliever spent all of 2019 at Double-A Arkansas followed by time in the fall with USA Baseball's Premier 12 team.

SCOUTING REPORT: Using a funky, deceptive delivery with the ball looking like it's coming out of his hip, Mills primarily relies on his sinker/slider combo to dominate righthanded hitters. He consistently throws both pitches for strikes. The plus fastball sits 92-94 mph, touching 95-96, with tail and sink, and he's gotten more aggressive with it to the inner half of the plate against lefthanded batters. His average, sweepy slider with tilt sits 80-84 mph and also flashes plus as he uses it to get ahead in the count. Mills uses his 82-85 mph changeup more to lefthanded hitters but needs to be more consistent with the pitch.

THE FUTURE: Mills profiles as a situational reliever most effective against righthanders. With improvement of the changeup, he could pitch in higher leverage situations. He'll head to Triple-A to start 2020 but will likely join the Tacoma-Seattle shuttle as bullpen reinforcements are needed by the Mariners.

Year	Age	Club (League)	Class	W	L	ERA	G	GS	SV	IP	H	HR	BB	SO	K/9	WHIP	AVG
2017	22	Everett (NWL)	SS	0	1	2.57	7	0	2	7	3	0	3	11	14.1	0.86	.120
	22	Clinton (MWL)	LoA	0	1	1.35	11	0	4	13	5	0	6	18	12.2	0.83	.111
2018	23	Modesto (CAL)	HiA	6	0	1.91	35	0	11	42	29	1	9	49	10.4	0.90	.193
	23	Arkansas (TL)	AA	0	2	10.13	9	0	0	11	18	0	4	10	8.4	2.06	.367
2019	24	Arkansas (TL)	AA	4	2	4.27	41	0	8	53	43	2	17	66	11.3	1.14	.222
Minor League Totals				10	6	3.57	103	0	25	126	98	3	39	154	11.0	1.09	.212

25 JONATAN CLASE, OF

BA GRADE 50 Risk: Extreme

Born: May 23, 2002. **B-T:** L-R. **HT:** 5-9. **WT:** 180. **Signed:** Dominican Republic, 2018. **Signed by:** Audo Vicente.

TRACK RECORD: Signed for just $35,000 in 2018, Clase surprised with a strong first pro season in the Dominican Republic when he posted a batting line of .300/.434/.444 with 31 stolen bases. He was extremely raw when he first came to the Mariners' academy in the DR but has made big strides through hard work. Clase has already added 30 pounds to his athletic frame by spending significant time in the weight room.

SCOUTING REPORT: Clase's defining tool is his plus-plus speed, graded as a 70 runner on the 20-80 scouting scale. He uses a short, compact swing, making contact with sneaky power for his size. Clase's 18 percent walk rate is impressive for a player so unrefined. Currently he shows more range than feel in the outfield, with some of the routes he takes being called "adventurous," but he has the closing speed to get to balls and will improve his routes with more experience.

THE FUTURE: Clase will make his stateside debut in 2020 with an assignment to the Rookie-level Arizona League after time in extended spring training. He's an intriguing talent.

Year	Age	Club (League)	Class	AVG	G	AB	R	H	2B	3B	HR	RBI	BB	SO	SB	OBP	SLG
2019	17	Mariners (DSL)	R	.300	63	223	64	67	12	7	2	22	51	56	31	.434	.444
Minor League Totals				.300	63	223	64	67	12	7	2	22	51	56	31	.434	.444

26 JUAN QUERECUTO, SS

BA GRADE 50 **Risk:** Extreme

Born: Sept. 21, 2000. **B-T:** R-R. **HT:** 6-2. **WT:** 175. **Signed:** Venezuela, 2017. **Signed by:** Emilio Carrasquel/Tim Kissner.

TRACK RECORD: Querecuto has been on the Mariners' prospect radar since signing in 2017 for a $1.225 million bonus. He comes from a family of ballplayers, with father Juan playing in the Blue Jays' system and older brother Juniel a veteran minor league infielder who got into four games with the Rays in 2016. Querecuto made it to the states in 2019 but was limited by a knee injury that kept him out for most of extended spring training and limited his time in the Rookie-level Arizona League season to 23 games.

SCOUTING REPORT: Querecuto is the type of player whose instincts allow him to play above his tools. More of a defense-first shortstop, he still has work to do to improve his glovework, especially on making decisions whether to charge balls or hold back. His athleticism allows him to make the tougher plays, with his plus-plus arm being one of the best in the organization. There's still plenty of development ahead as a hitter, but he made good strides during the Mariners' fall hitters camp in working on the movement patterns with his body in the box and being more selective.

THE FUTURE: Querecuto may need more time in the AZL before he's ready to head to the next level.

Year	Age	Club (League)	Class	AVG	G	AB	R	H	2B	3B	HR	RBI	BB	SO	SB	OBP	SLG
2018	17	Mariners (DSL)	R	.243	64	243	37	59	8	2	3	29	25	54	3	.331	.329
2019	18	Mariners (AZL)	R	.203	23	79	10	16	3	0	0	8	12	35	2	.315	.241
Minor League Totals				.233	87	322	47	75	11	2	3	37	37	89	5	.327	.307

27 DONNIE WALTON, 2B/SS

BA GRADE 40 **Risk:** Medium

Born: May 25, 1994. **B-T:** L-R. **HT:** 5-10. **WT:** 184. **Drafted:** Oklahoma State, 2016 (5th round). **Signed by:** Ty Bowman.

TRACK RECORD: A prototypical grinder and baseball rat, Walton made it to the major leagues in his fourth pro season after a four-year career at Oklahoma State. His callup followed a strong performance at Double-A Arkansas, where he was a sparkplug who batted leadoff in the Travelers' order and saw time at both middle infield positions.

SCOUTING REPORT: The son of Oklahoma State's pitching coach, Walton has the ceiling of a utility infielder at the big league level with a good chance of having a nice career in that role. He's gritty and plays hard and consistently performs above his tools. While he doesn't have the strength or bat speed to drive the baseball, he has a good approach at the plate, understands the strike zone and consistently puts balls in play. Despite having only average speed, Walton has good instincts on the bases. He's an average or slightly better defender at both middle infield positions, although a below-average arm is an impediment to regular play on the left side.

THE FUTURE: Walton will head to spring training looking to earn a spot on the Mariners' 25-man roster as an extra infielder. He knows his role and thrives in being that extra guy.

Year	Age	Club (League)	Class	AVG	G	AB	R	H	2B	3B	HR	RBI	BB	SO	SB	OBP	SLG
2017	23	Mariners (AZL)	R	.313	5	16	2	5	0	0	2	5	1	0	2	.353	.688
	23	Modesto (CAL)	HiA	.269	67	242	37	65	16	1	2	24	27	49	6	.349	.368
2018	24	Modesto (CAL)	HiA	.309	57	217	35	67	12	3	3	19	30	37	8	.402	.433
	24	Arkansas (TL)	AA	.236	62	208	22	49	14	1	1	22	21	34	3	.325	.327
2019	25	Arkansas (TL)	AA	.300	124	480	72	144	22	3	11	50	63	72	10	.390	.427
	25	Seattle (AL)	MAJ	.188	7	16	2	3	0	0	0	2	3	5	0	.316	.188
Major League Totals				.188	7	16	2	3	0	0	0	2	3	5	0	.316	.188
Minor League Totals				.283	358	1341	211	380	72	9	24	143	164	216	35	.371	.404

28 ANTHONY MISIEWICZ, LHP

BA GRADE 40 **Risk:** Medium

Born: Nov. 1, 1994. **B-T:** R-L. **HT:** 6-1. **WT:** 200. **Drafted:** Michigan State, 2015 (18th round). **Signed by:** Jay Catalano.

TRACK RECORD: Misiewicz spent most of the 2019 season as a starting pitcher, but the value he can bring to a big league team is a bit more diverse. Spot starter? Long reliever? Lefty specialist? The answer is all of the above. After spending most of the season in Triple-A, Misiewicz easily fits the label of "major league ready."

SCOUTING REPORT: Often described in the past as being more of a finesse pitcher with good pitchability,

Misiewicz improved his command and became more aggressive with his low-90s fastball, touching 94 mph with natural movement and good extension. He uses the heater to set up a curveball that flashes plus, and also mixed in a cutter/slider in the high 80s and an average changeup. Consistently scattering his pitches around the zone to keep batters from getting too comfortable, Misiewicz has been described as being effectively wild, using a delivery that has him falling off a bit toward third base.

THE FUTURE: There's a really good chance that Misiewicz makes his big league debut at some point in the 2020 season, especially since he could be that staff's Swiss army knife by filling multiple roles.

Year	Age	Club (League)	Class	W	L	ERA	G	GS	SV	IP	H	HR	BB	SO	K/9	WHIP	AVG
2017	22	Modesto (CAL)	HiA	5	2	4.96	16	16	0	78	82	6	27	85	9.8	1.40	.265
	22	Arkansas (TL)	AA	3	3	4.35	7	7	0	41	40	4	11	32	7.0	1.23	.270
	22	Montgomery (SL)	AA	3	1	3.49	5	5	0	28	26	3	5	24	7.6	1.09	.239
2018	23	Mariners (AZL)	R	0	0	0.00	2	2	0	5	2	0	0	4	7.2	0.40	.118
	23	Arkansas (TL)	AA	3	12	5.51	21	21	0	98	133	14	29	91	8.4	1.65	.319
2019	24	Arkansas (TL)	AA	1	2	2.52	7	7	0	36	36	0	7	36	9.1	1.21	.269
	24	Tacoma (PCL)	AAA	8	6	5.36	19	17	0	96	95	17	28	89	8.4	1.29	.256
Minor League Totals				33	38	4.55	120	111	0	586	610	66	164	516	7.9	1.32	.268

29 PENN MURFEE, RHP

BA GRADE 40 **Risk: Medium**

Born: May 2, 1994. **B-T:** R-R. **HT:** 6-2. **WT:** 195. **Drafted:** Santa Clara, 2018 (33rd round). **Signed by:** Jordan Bley.

TRACK RECORD: Murfee spent most of three seasons at Vanderbilt as a reserve infielder before transferring to Santa Clara for his redshirt senior year. He pitched well enough to interest the Mariners in picking him in the 33rd round in 2018. After a rocky pro debut, Murfee pitched effectively as a starter at high Class A Modesto, with a 3.07 ERA and 10.7 strikeouts per 9 innings. He was then one of the better starters in the Arizona Fall League before finishing his long season with USA Baseball's Premier 12 team.

SCOUTING REPORT: A smart, well-prepared pitcher who throws strikes to both sides of the plate, Murfee is light on stuff but commands his three pitches, competes well and gets the most out of his arsenal of pitches from a nearly sidearm slot. He's not a high-velocity guy, with a fastball from 88-92 mph with tailing action and sink. He gets swings and misses from an average or better 78-83 mph slider that he commands. His third pitch is a future average changeup, with both secondaries coming from the same arm slot as the fastball.

THE FUTURE: Murfee doesn't have a high ceiling but could get some big league time if he continues to make the most of his repertoire, probably in a swingman's role.

Year	Age	Club (League)	Class	W	L	ERA	G	GS	SV	IP	H	HR	BB	SO	K/9	WHIP	AVG
2018	24	Everett (NWL)	SS	3	2	6.55	19	0	0	33	35	6	12	23	6.3	1.42	.278
2019	25	Tacoma (PCL)	AAA	0	0	10.38	5	0	0	9	13	3	7	12	12.5	2.31	.342
	25	Arkansas (TL)	AA	1	0	0.00	1	0	0	2	0	0	1	2	9.0	0.50	.000
	25	Modesto (CAL)	HiA	5	5	3.07	26	20	0	103	95	3	23	122	10.7	1.15	.245
Minor League Totals				9	7	4.24	51	20	0	146	143	12	43	159	9.8	1.27	.256

30 YEURY TATIZ, RHP

BA GRADE 45 **Risk: Extreme**

Born: Nov. 22, 2000. **B-T:** R-R. **HT:** 6-3. **WT:** 205. **Signed:** Dominican Republic, 2017. **Signed by:** Francisco Rosario.

TRACK RECORD: It's been a bittersweet start to Tatiz's career since signing with the Mariners in 2017 for $425,000. He lost both of his parents, one year apart, but has added 35 pounds to his 6-foot-3 frame and about five to six mph to his fastball to turn himself into an intriguing yet lesser-known pitching prospect.

SCOUTING REPORT: Tatiz started strong in his second season back in the DSL before struggling with consistency after being promoted to the Rookie-level Arizona League, but threw higher-quality strikes in his later outings. He doesn't get a lot of movement on a fastball up to 95-96 mph, but it has plus life and ride up in the zone. His 80-83 mph slider projects to be an above-average pitch, showing late break at times. He rarely uses his changeup.

THE FUTURE: With a strong, physical build, Tatiz has the makings of a power arm. Improving his command and developing that third pitch will be the key factors in determining whether he's a starter or a reliever. He may return to the Arizona League after extended spring training but could get to short-season Everett later in the summer.

Year	Age	Club (League)	Class	W	L	ERA	G	GS	SV	IP	H	HR	BB	SO	K/9	WHIP	AVG
2018	17	Mariners (DSL)	R	0	3	5.92	12	9	0	38	38	4	20	26	6.2	1.53	.268
2019	18	Mariners (DSL)	R	1	1	2.14	5	5	0	21	15	0	6	25	10.7	1.00	.195
	18	Mariners (AZL)	R	1	2	5.70	8	2	0	24	29	1	13	19	7.2	1.77	.302
Minor League Totals				2	6	4.90	25	16	0	82	82	5	39	70	7.6	1.46	.260

Tampa Bay Rays

BY J.J. COOPER

Branch Rickey famously said that he would rather trade a player a year too early than a year too late.

Nearly 100 years later, the Rays embody Rickey's wisdom. In move after move, the Rays never-ceasing drive to balance value and production remains consistent.

So Tommy Pham, one of the best players on the Rays' 96-win team in 2019, was traded away. The newly acquired Hunter Renfroe is not expected to match Pham's production, but the Rays view Renfroe, plus players acquired with the money freed by dealing Pham, will match his output, and the addition of prospect Xavier Edwards could help the big league club in 2022 and beyond.

It was a move that seemingly could make the Rays slightly worse in 2020 but could make them better in 2022 and beyond. That's also the Rays' way. The team did not embrace a full-blown tank job after David Price, Evan Longoria and Carl Crawford departed. Moves for the long-term were made, but the team averaged 76 wins a year during its downswing.

And midway through Tampa Bay's 90-win season in 2018, the Rays traded away righthander Chris Archer, one of their best starters. That trade ended up setting the stage for success

That's the Rays' way. With one of the smallest payrolls in baseball year after year, Tampa Bay figured out how to return to the playoffs. And the Rays should be able to build on back-to-back 90-win seasons in 2020 and beyond.

Adding Austin Meadows and Tyler Glasnow in the Chris Archer trade gave Tampa Bay two young cornerstones. And it added Shane Baz, a live arm in one of the baseball's best farm systems, led by the No. 1 prospect in baseball, Wander Franco.

Not everything is bright for the Rays. While the state of the talent in the system and on the major league roster is on the upswing, the stadium situation continues to have no signs of any resolution. The Rays have floated several stadium proposals over the past few years, but none have gained any significant traction.

The Rays closed off their top deck of Tropicana Field for the regular season, limiting the stadium's capacity to roughly 25,000 fans. The club averaged fewer than 15,000 fans per game, second worst in the major leagues.

The Rays floated a proposal to split the season between St. Petersburg and Montreal. But negotiations with the city of St. Petersburg failed to come to an agreement on such a split schedule and the club's stadium lease is clear that the team must play its games at Tropicana Field through 2027.

ADAM HUNGER/GETTY IMAGES

Versatile Brandon Lowe hit 17 homers to finish third in AL Rookie of the Year balloting.

PROJECTED 2023 LINEUP

Position	Player	Age
Catcher	Ronaldo Hernandez (9)	25
First Base	Nate Lowe	27
Second Base	Xavier Edwards (8)	27
Third Base	Wander Franco (1)	22
Shortstop	Willy Adames	27
Left Field	Brandon Lowe	28
Center Field	Vidal Brujan (4)	25
Right Field	Austin Meadows	28
Designated Hitter	Yandy Diaz	31
No. 1 Starter	Blake Snell	30
No. 2 Starter	Tyler Glasnow	29
No. 3 Starter	Brendan McKay (2)	27
No. 4 Starter	Matthew Liberatore (3)	23
No. 5 Starter	Brent Honeywell (6)	28
Closer	Shane Baz (5)	24

With no signs of a new ballpark in the offing, the Rays likely will remain one of the smallest payroll teams in baseball. And that is where the challenge for the Rays front office remains quite difficult. The big league club is young and talented. The farm system is deep. But as the best players of the current team get more expensive, the Rays will likely continue their never-ending roster shuffle.

The Rays' front office is similarly subjected to brain drain. Andrew Friedman and Chaim Bloom have left in recent years to head up baseball operations for the large-revenue Dodgers and Red Sox.

That leaves Tampa Bay with very little margin for error. Which is why the club also continues to trade some of its best players. It's the Rays' way.

DEPTH CHART

TAMPA BAY RAYS

TOP 2020 ROOKIE: Brendan McKay, LHP. He made spot starts in 2019 but should be a fixture in 2020. He needs to improve his pitch efficiency to finish batters.

BREAKOUT PROSPECT: Greg Jones, SS. He has impressive athleticism to go with offensive impact.

SLEEPER: Graeme Stinson, LHP. Stinson was a likely first-round pick coming into 2019. His stuff disappeared during an awful junior season. He has to prove he can return to form, but if he does, he has the fastball/slider combo to be a high-leverage reliever.

SOURCE OF TOP 30 TALENT

Homegrown	**21**	**Acquired**	**9**
College	11	Trade	9
High School	5	Rule 5 draft	0
Junior College	0	Independent leagues	0
Nondrafted free agent	0	Free agents/waivers	0
International	4		

LF
Moises Gomez (14)
Zach Huffins
Patrick Merino
Garrett Whitley

CF
Josh Lowe (11)
Nick Schnell (16)
Lucius Fox (23)
Jhon Diaz (26)
Shane Sasaki

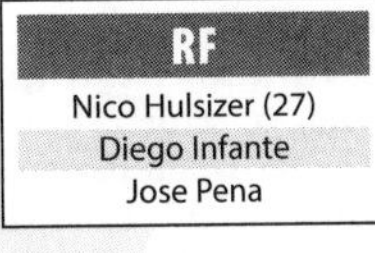

RF
Nico Hulsizer (27)
Diego Infante
Jose Pena

3B
Kevin Padlo (17)
Jim Haley

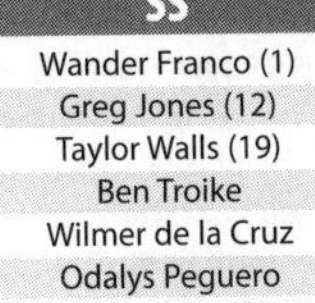

SS
Wander Franco (1)
Greg Jones (12)
Taylor Walls (19)
Ben Troike
Wilmer de la Cruz
Odalys Peguero

2B
Vidal Brujan (4)
Xavier Edwards (8)
Nick Sogard
Tristan Gray

1B
Dalton Kelly
Jake Guenther

C
Ronaldo Hernandez (9)
Chris Betts
Cristian Cerda

LHP

LHSP
Brendan McKay (2)
Matthew Liberatore (3)
Shane McClanahan (7)
Riley O'Brien (20)
John Doxakis (21)
Michael Plassmeyer (28)
Josh Fleming (29)
Anthony Banda (30)

LHRP
Sam McWilliams
Graeme Stinson
Matt Krook

RHP

RHSP
Shane Baz (5)
Brent Honeywell (6)
Joe Ryan (10)
JJ Goss (13)
Taj Bradley (15)
Caleb Sampen (24)
Drew Strotman (25)
Ben Peoples
Tommy Romero
Yoniel Curet

RHRP
Seth Johnson (18)
Peter Fairbanks (22)
Neraldo Catalina
Tanner Dodson
Hector Figueroa
Colby White
Jayden Murray

DRAFT ANALYSIS

2019

BEST PURE HITTER: SS Greg Jones (1) is a switch-hitter who generates above-average bat speed thanks to strong, whippy hands that bring the bat through the zone without a big load or weight transfer. He uses the whole field, hitting plenty of line drives. His plus-plus speed also helps him beat out infield hits.

BEST POWER: The Rays didn't land an abundance of power. 1B Jake Guenther (7) has strength to add power potential down the road, but his approach and level swing plane are not really geared for home runs.

FASTEST RUNNER: Jones is a plus-plus runner out of the box, and he really gets going when going home to second, first to third or first to home. The Rays landed a number of other plus runners including OF Shane Sasaki (3), OFs Zach Huffins (13), Logan Allen (14) and Garret Hiott (25).

BEST DEFENSIVE PLAYER: SS Ben Troike (11) and SS Nick Sogard (12) are a pair of middle infielders with reliable hands, solid actions and the steadiness to stay up the middle. Troike's stronger arm makes him more likely to stay at shortstop long term, although it's worth noting that the Rays like to move most of their infielders around to various positions.

BEST ATHLETE: Jones was one of the best athletes in the 2017 draft coming out of high school and was considered the best athlete in the 2019 college draft class.

BEST FASTBALL: RHP Seth Johnson (3) is relatively new to pitching, but he has a plus, 93-95 mph fastball with life. In one of his last outings of the season in a short two-inning stint, he was consistently getting to 96-98 mph. RHP JJ Goss (1s) sat 90-96 mph this spring. His fastball shows promising life and has projection remaining.

BEST SECONDARY PITCH: Goss' slider and changeup both could end up as plus pitches. Not surprisingly, neither is consistent, but he flashes plenty of promise with both offerings. LHP John Doxakis (2) will show a plus slider which can sit 84-85 mph with sharp, late break.

BEST PRO DEBUT: Jones hit .335/.413/.461 for short-season Hudson Valley, finishing third in the New York-Penn League in batting average and OPS and seventh in slugging percentage. RHP Jayden Murray (23) went 1-2, 2.45 with 47 strikeouts, eight walks and 31 hits allowed in 40.1 innings.

BEST LATE-ROUND PICK: Area scout David Hamlett liked RHP Jayden Murray's (23) 93-94 mph fastball, promising slider as well as his understanding of how to set up hitters.

MOST INTRIGUING BACKGROUND: Johnson was a shortstop in junior college, but after struggling at the plate for two years, he moved to the mound. After just one year at Campbell, he was a supplemental first round pick.

CLOSEST TO THE MAJORS: The Rays are not an organization that speeds players to the majors—they like to make sure that players are fully ready to contribute before they call them up to the majors—but Doxakis could be a fast-mover by Rays' standards as a polished, strike-throwing lefty.

THE ONE WHO GOT AWAY: RHP Andrew Peters (23) was considered one of the top junior college pitchers in the draft class before blowing out his elbow. The Rays would have liked to have signed him, but he opted to head to South Carolina to improve his draft stock.

—J.J. COOPER

TOP DRAFT PICKS OF THE DECADE

Year	Player, Pos.	2019 Org
2010	Justin O'Conner, C	White Sox
2011	Taylor Guerrieri, RHP	Rangers
2012	Richie Shaffer, 3B	Atlantic League
2013	Nick Ciuffo, C	Reds
2014	Casey Gillaspie, 1B	American Association
2015	Garrett Whitley, OF	Rays
2016	Josh Lowe, 3B	Rays
2017	Brendan McKay, LHP/1B	Rays
2018	Matthew Liberatore, LHP	Rays
2019	Greg Jones, SS	Rays

2018

First-round LHPs Matthew Liberatore and Shane McClanahan are living up to the hype early in their career and offer significant upside. RHP Joe Ryan (7) broke out in 2019 and looks to be a strong find.

GRADE: A

2017

LHP/1B Brendan McKay (1) is carrying the banner for this class and made his major league debut in 2019. He's still one of the game's best prospects. SS Taylor Walls (3) and RHP Riley O'Brien (8) are also promising.

GRADE: A

2016

The Lowe brothers—OF Josh (1) and 1B Nate (13)—are this class' standouts. Nate graduated to the big leagues in 2019 and Josh broke out at Double-A. The rest of the class hasn't returned much value.

GRADE: C

1 WANDER FRANCO, SS

Born: March 1, 2001. **B-T:** B-R. **HT:** 5-10. **WT:** 170.
Signed: Dominican Republic, 2017.
Signed by: Danny Santana.

TRACK RECORD: Franco has always been able to hit. He hit .325 in 2019 and managed to lower his career batting average. His .339 average was the best among all Florida State Leaguers with 200 or more plate appearances. He did that while being four years younger than the average FSL hitter and a year younger than anyone else in the league. Franco has always had a knack for being his team's vocal leader. It's partly because of his talent, but it's also because of his high-energy personality. He is exceptionally competitive in whatever he does, and he's comfortable in the spotlight that has followed him ever since he signed as the No. 1 prospect in the 2017 international amateur class. It helps that he's part of a baseball family—his older brothers are also minor leaguers, and his uncle is longtime major league shortstop Erick Aybar and his friend and neighbor is Indians infielder Jose Ramirez.

SCOUTING REPORT: There are hitters with exceptional awareness of the strike zone. There are others who do an excellent job of identifying pitches. There are those who have a knack of controlling the barrel and covering the entire plate. Franco has all of those attributes, plus the ability to drive the ball with power. He has some of the best bat-to-ball skills in the minors and an excellent feel for the strike zone. He's comfortable hitting down in the count because he can spoil pitches. He shows plus-plus raw power from both sides of the plate in batting practice, but in games he hits a large number of stinging ground balls. He'd get to more home runs if he lifted the ball more, but it's hard to argue with the results. Franco has soft, agile hands, but his thicker body gives him little margin for error to remain at shortstop. His above-average arm is enough to allow him to make the play in the hole in part because of a quick release and average range, but if he slows as he matures he'll have a hard time staying at the position. He projects as an above-average defender at second or third base.

THE FUTURE: The Rays generally move minor leaguers slowly to ensure they are ready to contribute the day they reach the majors, but Franco's talent has made it hard to keep him on the organization's typical timetable. He's ready to head to Double-A as a 19-year-old. He's only played shortstop so far, but it makes sense for the Rays to begin letting Franco play other infield positions because by the end of 2020 he may be a big league option if the Rays are making another postseason push.

MIKE JANES/FOUR SEAM

BA GRADE
75 **Risk:** High

SCOUTING GRADES
Hit: 80. **Power:** 60. **Run:** 50. **Field:** 55. **Arm:** 55.

Projected future grades on 20-80 scouting scale.

TOP PROSPECTS OF THE DECADE

Year	Player, Pos.	2019 Org
2010	Desmond Jennings, OF	Did not play
2011	Jeremy Hellickson, RHP	Nationals
2012	Matt Moore, LHP	Tigers
2013	Wil Myers, OF	Padres
2014	Jake Odorizzi, RHP	Twins
2015	Willy Adames, SS	Rays
2016	Blake Snell, LHP	Rays
2017	Willy Adames, SS	Rays
2018	Brent Honeywell, RHP	Rays
2019	Wander Franco, SS	Rays

BEST TOOLS

Best Hitter For Average	Wander Franco
Best Power Hitter	Moises Gomez
Best Strike-Zone Discipline	Wander Franco
Fastest Baserunner	Vidal Brujan
Best Athlete	Greg Jones
Best Fastball	Shane Baz
Best Curveball	Matthew Liberatore
Best Slider	Shane Baz
Best Changeup	Brent Honeywell
Best Control	Brendan McKay
Best Defensive Catcher	Roberto Alvarez
Best Defensive Infielder	Taylor Walls
Best Infield Arm	Jermaine Palacios
Best Defensive Outfielder	Josh Lowe
Best Outfield Arm	Tanner Dodson

Year	Age	Club (League)	Class	AVG	G	AB	R	H	2B	3B	HR	RBI	BB	SO	SB	OBP	SLG
2018	17	Princeton (APP)	R	.351	61	242	46	85	10	7	11	57	27	19	4	.418	.587
2019	18	Bowling Green (MWL)	LoA	.318	62	233	42	74	16	5	6	29	30	20	14	.390	.506
	18	Charlotte (FSL)	HiA	.339	52	192	40	65	11	2	3	24	26	15	4	.408	.464
Minor League Totals				.336	175	667	128	224	37	14	20	110	83	54	22	.405	.523

2 BRENDAN MCKAY, LHP/DH

Born: Dec. 18, 1995. **B-T:** L-L. **HT:** 6-2. **WT:** 212. **Drafted:** Louisville, 2017 (1st round). **Signed by:** James Bonnici.

WILL VRAGOVIC

BA GRADE
60 **Risk: Medium**

BACKGROUND: McKay finished his time at Louisville as one of the best two-way players in NCAA history. He toyed with Double-A hitters in the first half of 2019, then blitzed through Triple-A Durham and made his major league debut on June 29. McKay was sent back to Triple-A for a couple of resets but was one of just two 2017 draftees to make a postseason roster.

SCOUTING REPORT: McKay's success is based around having plus command of solid stuff. None of his pitches are dominant, but his ability to precisely spot all four allows everything to play up, even if only his fastball and cutter are plus. In the majors, McKay struggled at times to finish off hitters—his fastball is relatively true and his cutter is more of a weak-contact pitch than one to generate whiffs. The changeup is an effective, average pitch against righthanders while his 80-82 mph curve has average depth. The Rays have let McKay continue to work at DH but stopped playing him at first base in 2019. While it is unlikely that McKay will ever be a true two-way player like Shohei Ohtani, his hitting ability helps deepen the Rays bench. He pinch-hit three times in September and homered, going 2-for-3 with two runs and a home run.

THE FUTURE: McKay should be in the big league rotation in 2020. He profiles as a solid mid-rotation starter who can provide value as a bench bat.

SCOUTING GRADES: **Fastball:** 60 **Cutter:** 60 **Curveball:** 50 **Changeup:** 50 **Control:** 60

Year	Age	Club (League)	Class	W	L	ERA	G	GS	SV	IP	H	HR	BB	SO	K/9	WHIP	AVG
2017	21	Hudson Valley (NYP)	SS	1	0	1.80	6	6	0	20	10	3	5	21	9.5	0.75	.149
2018	22	Bowling Green (MWL)	LoA	2	0	1.09	6	6	0	25	8	1	2	40	14.6	0.41	.096
	22	Rays (GCL)	R	0	0	1.50	2	2	0	6	2	0	1	9	13.5	0.50	.095
	22	Charlotte (FSL)	HiA	3	2	3.21	11	9	0	48	45	2	11	54	10.2	1.17	.256
2019	23	Montgomery (SL)	AA	3	0	1.30	8	7	0	42	25	2	9	62	13.4	0.82	.172
	23	Durham (IL)	AAA	3	0	0.84	7	6	0	32	17	1	9	40	11.3	0.81	.156
	23	Tampa Bay (AL)	MAJ	2	4	5.14	13	11	0	49	53	8	16	56	10.3	1.41	.268
Major League Totals				2	4	5.14	13	11	0	49	53	8	16	56	10.3	1.41	.268
Minor League Totals				12	2	1.78	40	36	0	172	107	9	37	226	11.8	0.84	.178

3 MATTHEW LIBERATORE, LHP

Born: Nov. 6, 1999. **B-T:** L-L. **HT:** 6-5. **WT:** 200. **Drafted:** HS—Glendale, Ariz., 2018, (1st round). **Signed by:** David Hamlett.

COURTESY OF BC HOT RODS

BACKGROUND: Liberatore was the ace of USA Baseball's World Cup gold medal-winning 18U team in 2017, but he had to settle for a runner-up finish to friend Nolan Gorman's team in the Arizona 6A state championship. He was expected to be one of the first prep players off the board, but slid to the Rays at pick 16. He's lived up to expectations so far, though his 2019 was briefly interrupted in August by back spasms.

SCOUTING REPORT: Liberatore is notably polished for a young, 6-foot-6 lefthander. He spots his 91-95 mph fastball well (he can touch 97) and he shuffles between a slider, changeup and curveball that all are at least average now with above-average or plus potential. Liberatore's best curveballs are plus-plus, high-70s downers with power and depth. His 82-84 mph slider is usually a little slurvy, but he can induce chases when he gets more tilt. He shows feel for his average changeup but uses it less than his breaking stuff.

THE FUTURE: Like Brendan McKay, Liberatore projects as a polished middle-of-the-rotation lefty. He thrives thanks to a wide assortment of pitches combined with excellent command. He's about as safe a bet as a teen pitching prospect can be, and his size and smooth delivery give him a high upside as well. The excellent pitching environment of the Florida State League is the next test.

SCOUTING GRADES: **Fastball:** 60 **Slider:** 45 **Curveball:** 60 **Changeup:** 55 **Control:** 55

Year	Age	Club (League)	Class	W	L	ERA	G	GS	SV	IP	H	HR	BB	SO	K/9	WHIP	AVG
2018	18	Rays (GCL)	R	1	2	0.98	8	8	0	28	16	0	11	32	10.4	0.98	.170
	18	Princeton (APP)	R	1	0	3.60	1	1	0	5	5	0	2	5	9.0	1.40	.294
2019	19	Bowling Green (MWL)	LoA	6	2	3.10	16	15	0	78	70	2	31	76	8.7	1.29	.237
Minor League Totals				8	4	2.59	25	24	0	111	91	2	44	113	9.2	1.22	.224

4 VIDAL BRUJAN, 2B/SS

Born: Feb. 9, 1998. **B-T:** B-R. **HT:** 5-9. **WT:** 155. **Signed:** Dominican Republic, 2014. **Signed by:** Danny Santana.

BA GRADE
55 Risk: Medium

BACKGROUND: Brujan's $15,000 signing bonus was par for the course for a short middle infielder on the international market, but he's earned plenty of attention with his speed and his high energy.

SCOUTING REPORT: Brujan is twitchy and deceptively strong, but it gets hidden at the plate because he hits so many grounders. He's much better against righthanders. He has a simple, short swing with little load from both sides. He understands the strike zone and rarely swings and misses. The Rays gave him his first extended exposure to shortstop in 2019, and he showed enough to make himself at least a viable backup option. Brujan has one of the quickest first steps in the organization and his hands work well, but what he doesn't have is a refined internal clock. His all-out, high-energy style sometimes leads to him rushing on plays where he should slow everything down. His footwork is only adequate.

THE FUTURE: Brujan's speed, athleticism and versatility fits the Rays' love of multi-position regulars. Though he hasn't yet played center field, Brujan's athleticism and speed make him a potential fit there, and it wouldn't be surprising to see the Rays work him there in 2019. His ceiling is as a high-average, on-base-oriented table-setter who runs into 8-10 home runs a year while providing defensive value at multiple spots.

SCOUTING GRADES: **Hitting:** 60 **Power:** 40 **Running:** 80 **Fielding:** 55 **Arm:** 50

Year	Age	Club (League)	Class	AVG	G	AB	R	H	2B	3B	HR	RBI	BB	SO	SB	OBP	SLG
2017	19	Hudson Valley (NYP)	SS	.285	67	260	51	74	15	5	3	20	34	36	16	.378	.415
2018	20	Bowling Green (MWL)	LoA	.313	95	377	86	118	18	5	5	41	48	53	43	.395	.427
	20	Charlotte (FSL)	HiA	.347	27	98	26	34	7	2	4	12	15	15	12	.434	.582
2019	21	Charlotte (FSL)	HiA	.290	44	176	28	51	8	3	1	15	17	26	24	.357	.386
	21	Montgomery (SL)	AA	.266	55	207	28	55	9	4	3	25	20	35	24	.336	.391
Minor League Totals				.294	399	1554	309	457	78	28	19	141	187	197	151	.377	.417

5 SHANE BAZ, RHP

Born: June 17, 1999. **B-T:** R-R. **HT:** 6-3. **WT:** 190. **Drafted:** HS—Tomball, Texas, 2017 (1st round). **Signed by:** Wayne Mathis (Pirates).

BACKGROUND: Baz battled Hunter Greene for the title of best pure arm in the 2017 high school class, and the Rays pushed hard to make him the third piece in the trade that also imported Austin Meadows and Tyler Glasnow while sending Chris Archer to the Pirates. Baz was the player to be named in a deal that quickly became a massive win for the Rays.

SCOUTING REPORT: When the Rays acquired Baz, they helped the righthander shift from a predominantly two-seam fastball/curveball pitcher to a four-seam/slider pitcher, which proved to fit his strengths. Baz's arm is exceptionally fast—his fastball sits 92-98 mph and can touch 100. That arm speed means he sometimes struggles to keep his arm timed with his lower body and sometimes means he lands jarringly into a stiff front side, but his arm path is clear and he is direct to the plate. With an easier-to-command fastball, Baz went from throwing strikes on 59.5 percent of pitches in 2018 to 61.5 percent in 2019. Baz's 84-87 mph slider is a plus pitch with a short, tight two-plane break. His changeup ranges between below-average to average. His curveball, a weapon in high school, is now more of a fringy early-count pitch but flashes 12-to-6 depth at its best. Baz is now regularly around the strike zone, but he sporadically spikes a pitch badly.

THE FUTURE: Baz should at least be an effective fastball/slider reliever, but his strong frame and improvement portends hope that he can remain a starter. He is ready for high Class A Charlotte.

SCOUTING GRADES: **Fastball:** 70 **Slider:** 70 **Curveball:** 50 **Changeup:** 50 **Control:** 40

Year	Age	Club (League)	Class	W	L	ERA	G	GS	SV	IP	H	HR	BB	SO	K/9	WHIP	AVG
2017	18	Pirates (GCL)	R	0	3	3.80	10	10	0	24	26	2	14	19	7.2	1.69	.289
2018	19	Bristol (APP)	R	4	3	3.97	10	10	0	45	45	2	23	54	10.7	1.50	.250
	19	Princeton (APP)	R	0	2	7.71	2	2	0	7	11	1	6	5	6.4	2.43	.367
2019	20	Bowling Green (MWL)	LoA	3	2	2.99	17	17	0	81	63	5	37	87	9.6	1.23	.213
Minor League Totals				7	10	3.60	39	39	0	157	145	10	80	165	9.4	1.43	.243

6 BRENT HONEYWELL, RHP

BA GRADE
60 Risk: Very High

Born: March 31, 1995. **B-T:** R-R. **HT:** 6-2. **WT:** 180. **Drafted:** Walters State (Tenn.) JC, 2014 (2nd round supplemental). **Signed by:** Brian Hickman.

BACKGROUND: Honeywell's father Brent was a pitcher in the Pirates farm system in the 1980s. While he didn't get to the majors, he did pass on his love of pitching and his screwball to his namesake. The younger Honeywell dominated at every level of the minors and headed into spring training in 2018 battling for a big league job, but he tore his ulnar collateral ligament in a side session. He returned to the mound in spring 2019 after Tommy John surgery but fractured his elbow. His repaired ligament was intact, but the injury forced him out for another season.

SCOUTING REPORT: Before his two full years of elbow problems, Honeywell was a big league-ready starter with five pitches and was comfortable with using all five. Honeywell was again throwing in the low 90s before his elbow fracture. When healthy he sat 93-95 mph and has touched 99. Honeywell's plus changeup has enough tumble to get swings and misses. His above-average mid-80s slider has some power and generates swings and misses. His screwball is a plus-plus pitch, in part because it's something hitters are not used to seeing, but also because of its quality. His curveball is his weakest pitch, but it still flashed average.

THE FUTURE: Honeywell will likely need time to shake off the rust, but if healthy he should pitch in Tampa Bay in 2020. He isn't likely to be ready in spring training, but should be back on the mound soon afterward.

SCOUTING GRADES: **Fastball:** 60 **Screwball:** 70 **Change:** 60 **Curve:** 55 **Slider:** 55 **Control:** 45

Year	Age	Club (League)	Class	W	L	ERA	G	GS	SV	IP	H	HR	BB	SO	K/9	WHIP	AVG
2017	22	Montgomery (SL)	AA	1	1	2.08	2	2	0	13	4	1	4	20	13.8	0.62	.100
	22	Durham (IL)	AAA	12	8	3.64	24	24	0	124	130	11	31	152	11.1	1.30	.268
2018	23	Did not play—Injured															
2019	24	Did not play—Injured															
Minor League Totals				31	19	2.88	79	78	0	416	357	27	93	458	9.9	1.08	.230

7 SHANE MCCLANAHAN, LHP

COURTESY OF CLT STONE CRABS

BA GRADE
60 Risk: Very High

Born: April 28, 1997. **B-T:** L-L. **HT:** 6-1. **WT:** 190. **Drafted:** South Florida (1st round), 2018. **Signed by:** Brett Foley.

BACKGROUND: A Tommy John survivor, McClanahan entered his junior year at South Florida as a candidate to go first overall in the 2018 draft. An erratic spring ruined those hopes, but he was still seen as one of the best arms in that class, albeit one with reliever risk. He made big strides in body control during 2019. After walking 30 batters in his first 48 innings, he walked 15 over his final 73 innings.

SCOUTING REPORT: In addition to finding his control, McClanahan refined his changeup while working with high Class A Charlotte pitching coach Doc Watson. His fastball remains a plus-plus marvel. He can sit 93-98 mph and has touched 100. McClanahan explodes off the rubber to get to his velocity, though early in the season his arm struggled to catch up to his lower half. He doesn't need to rely on only one pitch because he shows excellent feel for spin. His power downer curveball gives him a second plus pitch, though it sometimes morphs into a hard, tilting slider. He started to figure out his changeup in the second half, though he needs to make more strides with the pitch.

THE FUTURE: The easiest assumption is to expect to see McClanahan turn into an impact reliever. His fastball and breaking balls need little projection for that role. But the improvement he's made in his control and with his changeup gives the Rays a reason to keep trying him as a starter. He'll be part of a potent roster at Double-A Montgomery.

SCOUTING GRADES: **Fastball:** 70 **Slider:** 50 **Curveball:** 60 **Changeup:** 50 **Control:** 45

Year	Age	Club (League)	Class	W	L	ERA	G	GS	SV	IP	H	HR	BB	SO	K/9	WHIP	AVG
2018	21	Rays (GCL)	R	0	0	0.00	2	2	0	3	1	0	0	6	18.0	0.33	.100
	21	Princeton (APP)	R	0	0	0.00	2	2	0	4	2	0	1	7	15.8	0.75	.154
2019	22	Bowling Green (MWL)	LoA	4	4	3.40	11	10	0	53	38	3	31	74	12.6	1.30	.199
	22	Charlotte (FSL)	HiA	6	1	1.46	9	8	0	49	33	1	8	59	10.8	0.83	.183
	22	Montgomery (SL)	AA	1	1	8.35	4	4	0	18	30	3	6	21	10.3	1.96	.366
Minor League Totals				11	6	3.17	28	26	0	127	104	7	46	167	11.8	1.17	.218

8 XAVIER EDWARDS, 2B/SS

BA GRADE
55 Risk: High

Born: Aug. 9, 1999. **B-T:** B-R. **HT:** 5-10. **WT:** 175. **Drafted:** HS—Coconut Creek, Fla., 2018 (1st round supplemental). **Signed by:** Brian Cruz (Padres).

TRACK RECORD: Edwards had the skills of a first-round pick in 2018 but fell due to concerns about his size. The Padres snatched him 38th overall and signed him for $1.3 million to forgo a Vanderbilt commitment. Listed at 5-foot-10 but really closer to 5-foot-7, Edwards rendered his size moot by hitting .322 and finishing tied for third in the minors in hits (162) in his first full season. He was selected for Team USA's Olympic qualifying roster after the year. The Rays acquired him with Hunter Renfroe in the trade that sent Tommy Pham to the Padres.

SCOUTING REPORT: Edwards is quiet in the box, shows a feel for the strike zone and consistently puts good swings on pitches. His diminutive size and flat swing path aren't conducive to hitting home runs, but he has enough strength and barrel awareness to hit the ball hard in play. He is a true switch-hitter equally capable from both sides of the plate. Edwards' plus-plus speed is his top asset. He is a prolific basestealer with advanced instincts, and is altogether 56 for 78 (72 percent) on stolen bases in his career. Edwards is a reliable defender with a quick first step and sure hands at both middle infield positions, but his fringe-average arm is best suited for second base.

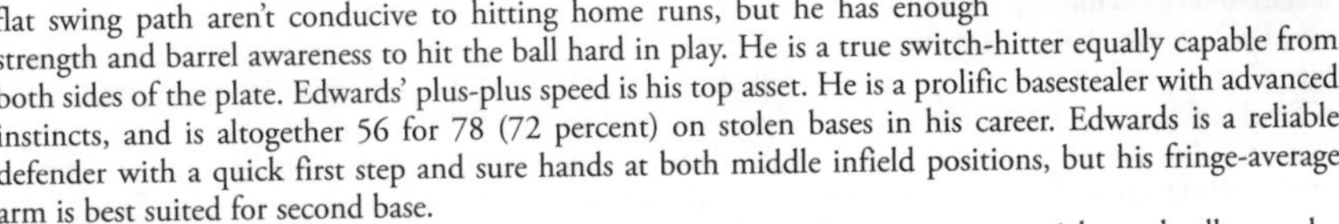

THE FUTURE: Edwards draws frequent comparisons to Chone Figgins as a potential speedy all-star who hits atop the lineup. He'll see Double-A Montgomery in 2020.

SCOUTING GRADES: Hitting: 60 | Power: 30 | Running: 70 | Fielding: 55 | Arm: 45

Year	Age	Club (League)	Class	AVG	G	AB	R	H	2B	3B	HR	RBI	BB	SO	SB	OBP	SLG
2018	18	Padres 1 (AZL)	R	.384	21	73	19	28	4	1	0	11	13	10	12	.471	.466
	18	Tri-City (NWL)	SS	.314	24	86	21	27	4	0	0	5	18	15	10	.438	.360
2019	19	Fort Wayne (MWL)	LoA	.336	77	307	44	103	13	4	1	30	30	35	20	.392	.414
	19	Lake Elsinore (CAL)	HiA	.301	46	196	32	59	5	4	0	13	14	19	14	.349	.367
Minor League Totals				.328	168	662	116	217	26	9	1	59	75	79	56	.395	.399

9 RONALDO HERNANDEZ, C

COURTESY OF CLT STONE CRABS

BA GRADE
55 Risk: High

Born: Nov. 11, 1997. **B-T:** R-R. **HT:** 6-1. **WT:** 190. **Signed:** Colombia, 2014. **Signed by:** Angel Contreras.

BACKGROUND: Catcher is one of the few thin positions in the Rays' farm system, which makes Hernandez even more important. An infielder as an amateur, Hernandez quickly took to catching as a pro. He had a breakout season with low Class A Bowling Green in 2018, but offensively he took a step back in 2019, largely because the Florida State League seemed to sap his power.

SCOUTING REPORT: Hernandez has already filled out and has a relatively mature, physical body. He has plus raw power. His bat speed is average at best and he too often hits pitchers' pitches, but he has solid bat-to-ball skills to go with his plus power. He will have to work to stay flexible enough to catch. He has tried a variety of setups to better present low pitches and has made improvement in his receiving, game-calling and English. He projects as an average defender with a plus-plus arm—he threw out 39 percent of basestealers in 2019.

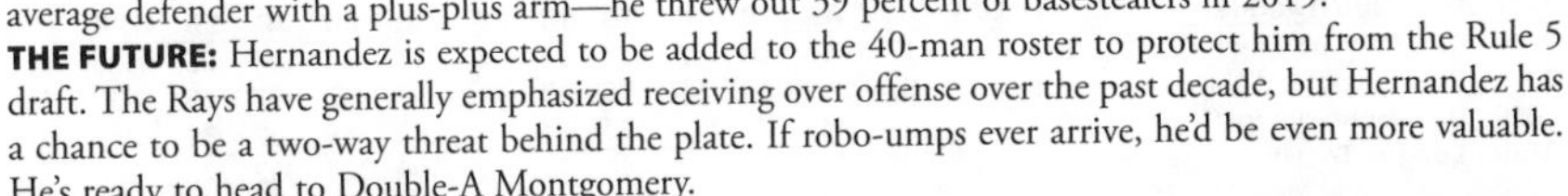

THE FUTURE: Hernandez is expected to be added to the 40-man roster to protect him from the Rule 5 draft. The Rays have generally emphasized receiving over offense over the past decade, but Hernandez has a chance to be a two-way threat behind the plate. If robo-umps ever arrive, he'd be even more valuable. He's ready to head to Double-A Montgomery.

SCOUTING GRADES: Hitting: 45 | Power: 60 | Running: 30 | Fielding: 45 | Arm: 70

Year	Age	Club (League)	Class	AVG	G	AB	R	H	2B	3B	HR	RBI	BB	SO	SB	OBP	SLG
2017	19	Princeton (APP)	R	.332	54	223	42	74	22	1	5	40	16	39	2	.382	.507
2018	20	Bowling Green (MWL)	LoA	.284	109	405	68	115	20	1	21	79	31	69	10	.339	.494
2019	21	Charlotte (FSL)	HiA	.265	103	393	43	104	19	3	9	60	17	65	7	.299	.397
Minor League Totals				.293	333	1271	190	373	73	6	41	218	87	191	22	.345	.457

10 JOE RYAN, RHP

Born: June 5, 1996. **B-T:** R-R. **HT:** 6-1. **WT:** 185. **Drafted:** Cal State-Stanislaus, 2018 (7th round). **Signed by:** Alan Hull.

BA GRADE
55 Risk: High

BACKGROUND: Ryan went undrafted after an injury-plagued junior year at Cal State Northridge. After a strong summer in the Cape Cod League, he transferred to Division II Cal State Stanislaus for his senior year and impressed enough to become a seventh-round pick.

SCOUTING REPORT: While many pitchers have simplified their deliveries and even junked pitching from a windup, Ryan begins with an old-school windup, bringing his arms high above and behind his head, then usually deals an elevated 92-96 mph fastball. He commands the pitch so well that hitters can't seem to touch it. Ryan's 2,250-rpm spin rate is merely average, but he hides the ball well and gets good extension. He credits his time skipping the ball in water polo for helping him get so much backspin on his fastball. He has toyed with a curveball, cutter and slider but has yet to find a breaking ball that he can spin consistently. His 83-85 mph changeup, which tunnels well off his fastball, gives him a potentially above-average second pitch. Double-A will be a useful test after dominating Class A with 75 percent fastballs.

THE FUTURE: The effectiveness of Ryan's fastball can't be ignored, but he is going to have to keep improving his changeup or figure out how to spin a breaking ball to keep more experienced hitters from keying on his fastball in his return to Montgomery.

SCOUTING GRADES: Fastball: 60 | Slider: 40 | Curveball: 30 | Changeup: 55 | Control: 55

Year	Age	Club (League)	Class	W	L	ERA	G	GS	SV	IP	H	HR	BB	SO	K/9	WHIP	AVG
2018	22	Hudson Valley (NYP)	SS	2	1	3.72	12	7	0	36	26	3	14	51	12.6	1.10	.202
2019	23	Bowling Green (MWL)	LoA	2	2	2.93	6	6	0	28	19	2	11	47	15.3	1.08	.185
	23	Charlotte (FSL)	HiA	7	2	1.42	15	13	0	83	47	3	12	112	12.2	0.71	.161
	23	Montgomery (SL)	AA	0	0	3.38	3	3	0	13	11	2	4	24	16.2	1.13	.220
Minor League Totals				11	5	2.36	36	29	0	160	103	10	41	234	13.2	0.90	.179

11 JOSH LOWE, OF

Born: Feb. 2, 1998. **B-T:** L-R. **HT:** 6-4. **WT:** 205. **Drafted:** HS—Marietta, Ga., 2016 (1st round). **Signed by:** Milt Hill.

BA GRADE
50 Risk: High

BACKGROUND: Lowe was an athletic third baseman and pitcher in high school, but the Rays moved him to center field as a pro, wanting to better use his plus speed and range. The brother of Rays first baseman Nate Lowe, Josh is much more athletic but not as bat savvy. The younger Lowe had his best season as a pro, ranking among the top 10 in the Double-A Southern League in a multitude of categories.

SCOUTING REPORT: Lowe can run, throw, field and drive the ball. The only question has always been how much he will hit. Lowe's swing is a bit grooved, and he struggles to stay inside the ball. He aims to drive balls pitches low and on the outer half where he can extend his arms, but if a pitcher comes inside with velocity, he can get tied up. Lowe is a little passive at times at the plate and doesn't use his legs particularly well. His 27 percent strikeout rate is adequate considering his power potential.

THE FUTURE: As a plus runner who can play all three outfield positions, Lowe can be a productive big leaguer even if he doesn't hit for much average. But his lofty ceiling depends on him continuing to make significant strides at the plate. He should have a solid floor as a useful part-time outfielder.

Year	Age	Club (League)	Class	AVG	G	AB	R	H	2B	3B	HR	RBI	BB	SO	SB	OBP	SLG
2017	19	Bowling Green (MWL)	LoA	.268	118	456	60	122	26	2	8	55	42	144	22	.326	.386
2018	20	Charlotte (FSL)	HiA	.238	105	399	62	95	25	3	6	47	47	117	18	.322	.361
2019	21	Montgomery (SL)	AA	.252	121	448	70	113	23	4	18	62	59	132	30	.341	.442
Minor League Totals				.253	398	1476	217	373	80	12	37	190	185	452	72	.336	.398

12 GREG JONES, SS

Born: March 7, 1988. **B-T:** B-R. **HT:** 6-2. **WT:** 175. **Drafted:** UNC Wilmington, 2019 (1st round). **Signed by:** Joe Hastings.

TRACK RECORD: After a modest freshman season and a summer in the Cape Cod League where he struggled with strikeouts, Jones blossomed as a draft-eligible sophomore at UNC-Wilmington and finished in the top 10 in Division I in triples and stolen bases. A sore shoulder limited his time at shortstop in college and early in his pro debut, but he played shortstop almost everyday in July and August.

SCOUTING REPORT: Jones is the most athletic player in the Rays' system. He will turn in 70 times on the 20-to-80 scouting scale from home to first and better than that when he's going first-to-third. He has

above-average bat speed and average power potential long-term thanks to strong hands, and an ability to whip the bat through the strike zone. He finished among the New York-Penn League's leaders in most offensive categories in his pro debut, helped in part by a likely unsustainable .467 batting average on balls in play. There remains plenty of debate over whether he's best at shortstop or center fielder. Jones can make the highlight play and has above-average arm strength, but his hands are fringy so far and his throwing accuracy needs to improve. His speed and athleticism would make him a plus defender in center.
THE FUTURE: Jones has explosive athleticism, but it's his ability to be a switch hitter who hits stinging line-drives that makes him a fascinating prospect. The Rays love multi-position players, so it wouldn't be surprising if they moved Jones around eventually, but for now he needs to try to master shortstop.

Year	Age	Club (League)	Class	AVG	G	AB	R	H	2B	3B	HR	RBI	BB	SO	SB	OBP	SLG
2019	21	Hudson Valley (NYP)	SS	.335	48	191	39	64	13	4	1	24	22	56	19	.413	.461
Minor League Totals				.335	48	191	39	64	13	4	1	24	22	56	19	.413	.461

13 JJ GOSS, RHP

BA GRADE
55 **Risk: Extreme**

Born: Dec. 25, 2000. **B-T:** R-R. **HT:** 6-3. **WT:** 185. **Drafted:** HS—Houston, 2019 (1st round supplemental). **Signed by:** Pat Murphy.

TRACK RECORD: Goss began his senior season as the second-best pitcher on his high school team, but his team was anything but normal. Paired with righthander Matthew Thompson, the duo had a chance to become the second pair of first-round pitchers to be drafted from Houston's Cypress Ranch High. Goss and Thompson had to settle for both being drafted in the top 50 picks.
SCOUTING REPORT: Until 2019, Goss was known for his feel for pitching, his projectability and a fast arm. His fastball took a big step forward his senior season as he went from pitching at 88-92 to sitting at 90-95 mph. His above-average fastball has carry up in the zone. He's a true three-pitch pitcher with a slider that projects as plus and a changeup that is advanced for his age and experience with solid deception and good fade. It flashes plus but is inconsistent. Goss is a strike-thrower who has smoothed out a head whack he once had as he got stronger.
THE FUTURE: The Rays have drafted seven prep pitchers in the top 100 picks in the 2010s. Six of them spent their second pro season in short-season or rookie ball. So it's realistic to think that Goss will be held back in extended spring training before heading to short-season ball. Goss has the athleticism, delivery and control to be a future No. 3 starter, although there's a lot of steps ahead for him to reach that upside.

Year	Age	Club (League)	Class	W	L	ERA	G	GS	SV	IP	H	HR	BB	SO	K/9	WHIP	AVG
2019	18	Rays (GCL)	R	1	3	5.82	9	8	0	17	19	1	2	16	8.5	1.24	.279
Minor League Totals				1	3	5.82	9	8	0	17	19	1	2	16	8.5	1.24	.279

14 MOISES GOMEZ, OF

BA GRADE
55 **Risk: Extreme**

Born: Aug. 27, 1988. **B-T:** R-R. **HT:** 5-11. **WT:** 200. **Signed:** Venezuela, 2015. **Signed by:** Juan Castillo/Ronnie Blanco.

TRACK RECORD: Gomez was the best player the Rays signed internationally in 2015. He was one of the best hitters in the Venezuelan Summer League in his pro debut and repeated that feat in the Midwest League in 2018, but 2019 was a significant step back. He had the fifth-worst strikeout rate among Florida State League batting qualifiers.
SCOUTING REPORT: Gomez has many of the attributes to be an above-average MLB corner outfielder with an average arm. He hits the ball as hard or harder than any other Rays minor leaguer thanks to well above-average bat speed. He's an above-average runner who can be an above-average corner outfielder as well. But none of that will matter if he doesn't improve his plate discipline and stop chasing pitches out of the strike zone. His bat control is fringy right now and he needs to get better at getting to advantageous counts where he can fully deploy his plus power.
THE FUTURE: It's fair to say 2020 is the pivot point in Gomez's career. The Rays were comfortable leaving him unprotected for the Rule 5 draft because of his struggles in high Class A. He has a chance to make adjustments and learn from his struggles, but a repeat of his contact issues in 2020 may be a sign that he's yet another slugger tripped up by overaggressiveness.

Year	Age	Club (League)	Class	AVG	G	AB	R	H	2B	3B	HR	RBI	BB	SO	SB	OBP	SLG
2017	18	Princeton (APP)	R	.275	53	211	37	58	11	0	5	28	13	52	10	.328	.398
2018	19	Bowling Green (MWL)	LoA	.280	122	471	67	132	34	7	19	82	34	137	4	.328	.503
2019	20	Charlotte (FSL)	HiA	.220	119	428	55	94	26	2	16	66	48	164	3	.297	.402
Minor League Totals				.259	388	1458	217	378	90	14	47	220	130	418	30	.320	.437

15 TAJ BRADLEY, RHP

BA GRADE
50 Risk: High

Born: March 20, 2001. **B-T:** R-R. **HT:** 6-2. **WT:** 190. **Drafted:** HS—Stone Mountain, Ga., 2018 (5th round). **Signed by:** Milt Hill.

TRACK RECORD: Taken in the 2018 draft, Bradley is younger than nine of the first 10 prep pitchers drafted in 2019. The Rays took a chance on his upside and have understandably moved him along slowly.

SCOUTING REPORT: A two-way player in high school who was primarily an outfielder until late in his prep career, Bradley's athleticism and upside is obvious to scouts. He has a clean arm action. His 91-94 mph fastball has excellent running life and he's sharpened his once loopy curveball into a tighter, more promising pitch that could be plus eventually. There's a lot of development still ahead for Bradley as he's still relatively new to pitching, but he's extremely intelligent and has demonstrated that he's a sponge at soaking up instruction.

THE FUTURE: Bradley will jump to Bowling Green next year as one of the younger pitchers in the Midwest League. He has the athleticism, projectability and stuff to develop into a No. 3 or No. 4 starter.

Year	Age	Club (League)	Class	W	L	ERA	G	GS	SV	IP	H	HR	BB	SO	K/9	WHIP	AVG
2018	17	Rays (GCL)	R	1	4	5.09	10	9	0	23	26	1	12	24	9.4	1.65	.277
2019	18	Princeton (APP)	R	2	5	3.18	12	11	0	51	42	4	19	57	10.1	1.20	.219
Minor League Totals				3	9	3.77	22	20	0	74	68	5	31	81	9.9	1.34	.238

16 NICK SCHNELL, OF

BA GRADE
50 Risk: High

Born: March 27, 2000. **B-T:** L-R. **HT:** 6-3. **HT:** 180. **Drafted:** HS—Indianapolis, 2018 (1st round). **Signed:** James Bonnici.

TRACK RECORD: Since signing, Schnell's biggest hurdle has been staying healthy. A wrist injury hampered his pro debut and a knee injury slowed him in 2019. Once he did get to full strength he hit for power at Rookie-level Princeton and received a late promotion to low Class A Bowling Green, but he was also the only 2018 first-round hitter who didn't spend the majority of the season at low Class A or higher.

SCOUTING REPORT: He's not as athletic, but Schnell has a profile similar to that of Rays center field prospect Josh Lowe as a center fielder with significant power potential and concerns about his ability to generate consistent contact. He's proven to be a better center fielder than he was projected out of high school. An above-average runner, Schnell has improved his routes as a pro and now covers plenty of ground in center. He projects as someone who should be able to remain at the position with above-average range. Schnell has plus power potential, but scouts worry about his ability to hit for average. His swing involves a deep load and a minor arm bar, which makes him vulnerable to fastballs in on his hands. He swung through a lot of strikes in 2019.

THE FUTURE: Schnell will return to low Class A Bowling Green. He could rank among the best power hitters in the Midwest League, but he has some cleaning up to do with his swing to make better contact.

Year	Age	Club (League)	Class	AVG	G	AB	R	H	2B	3B	HR	RBI	BB	SO	SB	OBP	SLG
2018	18	Rays (GCL)	R	.239	19	67	8	16	4	1	1	4	14	23	2	.378	.373
2019	19	Rays (GCL)	R	.190	4	21	4	4	0	2	0	1	0	9	0	.190	.381
	19	Princeton (APP)	R	.286	37	147	28	42	11	3	5	27	18	51	5	.361	.503
	19	Bowling Green (MWL)	LoA	.236	14	55	7	13	3	1	0	3	2	24	0	.271	.327
Minor League Totals				.259	74	290	47	75	18	7	6	35	34	107	7	.338	.431

17 KEVIN PADLO, 3B

BA GRADE
45 Risk: Medium

Born: July 15, 1996. **B-T:** R-R. **HT:** 6-2. **WT:** 200. **Drafted:** HS—Murietta, Calif., 2014 (5th round). **Signed by:** Jon Lukens (Rockies).

TRACK RECORD: The Rays acquired Padlo from the Rockies in Jan. 2016 along with Corey Dickerson in a trade that sent German Marquez and Jake McGee to Colorado. After being unprotected and unpicked in the 2018 Rule 5 draft, Padlo hit his way to Triple-A Durham and earned a spot on the 40-man roster.

SCOUTING REPORT: Padlo was an excellent basketball player in high school and retains some of that athleticism. He's average defensively at third base and first base but his above-average arm and fringe-average speed may allow him to pick up corner outfield spots as well in 2020. Padlo has always had plus-plus raw power. He draws walks and hits home runs. His big step forward in 2019 revolved around making more consistent contact. He's still quite pitchable thanks to a pull-heavy approach that leaves him in trouble covering the outer third of the plate, but he has improved his recognition of breaking balls and he'll take his walks if pitchers try to get him to chase. With his plus productive power, he can be a productive player as a .230-.240 hitter, but he'll have to keep improving to get there.

THE FUTURE: The Rays lack righthanded power, so Padlo could find a role at some point in 2020 as a slugger who can man both infield corners. His power gives him second-division regular potential.

Year	Age	Club (League)	Class	AVG	G	AB	R	H	2B	3B	HR	RBI	BB	SO	SB	OBP	SLG
2017	20	Rays (GCL)	R	.118	5	17	3	2	0	1	0	1	3	1	1	.286	.235
	20	Charlotte (FSL)	HiA	.223	64	220	28	49	13	3	6	34	35	60	4	.324	.391
2018	21	Charlotte (FSL)	HiA	.223	115	385	54	86	26	0	8	54	47	119	5	.318	.353
2019	22	Montgomery (SL)	AA	.250	70	220	39	55	20	0	12	35	47	70	11	.383	.505
	22	Durham (IL)	AAA	.290	40	131	25	38	11	1	9	27	21	46	1	.400	.595
Minor League Totals				.244	554	1885	307	460	134	14	70	314	322	556	77	.359	.441

18 SETH JOHNSON, RHP

BA GRADE
50 Risk: High

Born: Sept. 19, 1998. **B-T:** R-R. **HT:** 6-1. **WT:** 200. **Drafted:** Campbell, 2019 (1st round supplemental). **Signed by:** Joe Hastings.

TRACK RECORD: After two years at Louisburg (N.C.) JC as a light-hitting shortstop, Johnson discovered his path to Division I baseball was on the mound. In just one year at Campbell, he pitched his way into a top-40 spot in the 2019 draft. After signing, he was held on a strict two inning per outing limit.

SCOUTING REPORT: Johnson generally sat at 93-95 mph on his plus fastball, but in his best stints, he sat 96-97 to go with a plus 84-86 mph late breaking slider and average changeup. Johnson's velocity has steadily ticked up since he started pitching just a year ago and his changeup is something he picked up very quickly. It has some late fade at its best. Johnson's delivery is clean and athletic and he's surprisingly adept at the mental side of pitching for someone who is relatively new to the mound. Johnson's still figuring out how to command his fastball, but he has the athleticism and delivery to have average control.

THE FUTURE: Johnson is set to head to low Class A Bowling Green in 2020. He has a starter's clean delivery and a fresh arm.

Year	Age	Club (League)	Class	W	L	ERA	G	GS	SV	IP	H	HR	BB	SO	K/9	WHIP	AVG
2019	20	Rays (GCL)	R	0	0	0.00	5	5	0	10	7	0	2	7	6.3	0.90	.189
	20	Princeton (APP)	R	0	1	5.14	4	4	0	7	10	0	1	9	11.6	1.57	.345
Minor League Totals				0	1	2.12	9	9	0	17	17	0	3	16	8.5	1.18	.258

19 TAYLOR WALLS, SS

BA GRADE
45 Risk: Medium

Born: July 10, 1996. **B-T:** B-R. **HT:** 5-10. **WT:** 180. **Drafted:** Florida State, 2017 (3rd round). **Signed by:** Brett Foley.

TRACK RECORD: After playing for a state title as a high school senior at Cordele, Ga.'s Crisp County High, Walls' three Florida State teams all made the NCAA tournament. He was the starting shortstop on back-to-back league champions in 2017 (Hudson Valley) and 2018 (Bowling Green). In 2019, both high Class A Charlotte and Double-A Montgomery made the playoffs.

SCOUTING REPORT: Walls' best attribute is his steady glove. He has plus hands and average range with an arm that will flash above-average when needed. Thanks to a solid internal clock, he doesn't always let it rip with his throws. He can play second and third base as well and should be able to slide to the outfield if needed thanks to above-average speed and solid instincts. Offensively, Walls is likely a bottom-of-the-order hitter, but he can string together good at-bats and he can spray line drives in the gaps. He projects as an average hitter with belove-average power, but his barrel control makes it hard to strike him out.

THE FUTURE: Walls' solid all-around game makes him a versatile future utilityman who could be a second-division regular on a less-talented roster.

Year	Age	Club (League)	Class	AVG	G	AB	R	H	2B	3B	HR	RBI	BB	SO	SB	OBP	SLG
2017	20	Hudson Valley (NYP)	SS	.213	46	164	22	35	9	0	1	21	29	53	5	.330	.287
2018	21	Bowling Green (MWL)	LoA	.304	120	467	87	142	28	6	6	57	66	80	31	.393	.428
2019	22	Charlotte (FSL)	HiA	.269	41	156	22	42	7	2	4	26	19	28	13	.339	.417
	22	Montgomery (SL)	AA	.270	55	211	42	57	16	5	6	20	26	51	15	.346	.479
Minor League Totals				.277	262	998	173	276	60	13	17	124	140	212	64	.364	.414

20 RILEY O'BRIEN, RHP

BA GRADE
50 Risk: High

Born: Feb. 6, 1995. **B-T:** R-R. **HT:** 6-4. **WT:** 170. **Drafted:** College of Idaho, 2017 (8th round). **Signed:** Paul Kirsch.

TRACK RECORD: O'Brien pitched two years in junior college before becoming the highest-drafted player ever picked out of NAIA College of Idaho. He quickly pitched his way out of high Class A Charlotte and was putting together a successful season with Double-A Montgomery when he was shut down in late July with a sore elbow.

SCOUTING REPORT: O'Brien is the epitome of a lanky, long-armed pitcher. He has a loose arm as well, which means his 91-95 mph plus fastball (he brushes 97) and his big-breaking plus slider gives him two swing-and-miss pitches. What he doesn't have yet is the control to fully take advantage of them. O'Brien's slider can be dastardly, but he has a tendency to snap off 58-footers that land in the batter's box for lefty's.

His catchers have to be nimble and stay alert. O'Brien has shown some feel for a below-average changeup. His stuff is good enough to retire MLB hitters, but his below-average control needs to improve and that's where his long arms, and long takeaway in the back of his delivery makes it more difficult.
THE FUTURE: O'Brien's fringy control and fastball/slider combination may eventually lead to the bullpen, but there's no reason to do so just yet. In each of the past two seasons, O'Brien has earned quick promotions. He'll likely return to Montgomery with a chance to move up to Triple-A Durham before long.

Year	Age	Club (League)	Class	W	L	ERA	G	GS	SV	IP	H	HR	BB	SO	K/9	WHIP	AVG
2017	22	Princeton (APP)	R	1	0	2.20	11	10	0	41	28	1	17	40	8.8	1.10	.211
2018	23	Bowling Green (MWL)	LoA	4	1	2.05	15	5	0	48	23	3	21	66	12.3	0.91	.143
	23	Charlotte (FSL)	HiA	4	3	3.60	10	8	0	40	36	1	21	37	8.3	1.43	.240
2019	24	Charlotte (FSL)	HiA	2	0	1.59	6	6	0	34	20	2	15	35	9.3	1.03	.172
	24	Montgomery (SL)	AA	5	6	3.93	14	11	0	69	56	4	29	72	9.4	1.24	.215
Minor League Totals				16	10	2.83	56	40	0	232	163	11	103	250	9.7	1.15	.199

21 JOHN DOXAKIS, LHP

BA GRADE 50 Risk: High

Born: Aug. 20, 1998. **B-T:** B-L. **HT:** 6-4. **WT:** 215. **Drafted:** Texas A&M, 2019 (2nd round). **Signed by:** Pat Murphy.
TRACK RECORD: Doxakis pitched his way into the second round with a strong 2019, showing excellent control and improved fastball velocity.
SCOUTING REPORT: Doxakis' improved arm speed helped both his now average fastball (he now sits 89-92 mph and touches 94, an increase of 2-3 mph) and his slider. Doxakis' slider has morphed from a slow, below-average pitch in 2018 to a harder, 84-85 mph two-planer he can back foot to righthanded hitters and can induce chases from lefties. His changeup is a fringe-average pitch as well. All of them are more effective because of his ability to dot the corners with plus control and above-average command.
THE FUTURE: Doxakis throws harder, but he doesn't throw hard. His ability to locate his fastball and get his slider in on righthanded hitters gives him a solid chance to be a durable, productive starter. Whether he starts there or in Bowling Green, he should spend a good bit of 2020 at high Class A Charlotte.

Year	Age	Club (League)	Class	W	L	ERA	G	GS	SV	IP	H	HR	BB	SO	K/9	WHIP	AVG
2019	20	Hudson Valley (NYP)	SS	0	0	1.93	12	10	0	33	20	0	11	31	8.5	0.95	.174
Minor League Totals				0	0	1.93	12	10	0	32	20	0	11	31	8.5	0.95	.174

22 PETER FAIRBANKS, RHP

BA GRADE 45 Risk: Medium

Born: Dec. 16, 1993. **B-T:** R-R. **HT:** 6-6. **WT:** 219. **Drafted:** Missouri, 2015 (9th round). **Signed by:** Dustin Smith (Rangers).
TRACK RECORD: Fairbanks first endured Tommy John rehab when he blew out his ulnar collateral ligament as a high school junior. That ligament only lasted six seasons, as he blew out his elbow again in 2017 and had a second Tommy John surgery. Fairbanks has reworked his delivery with an extremely short arm action where he never fully unwinds his elbow in his takeaway—instead he uses a bow-and-arrow like delivery. It has paid off as Fairbanks has found improved velocity and sharpened his slider.
SCOUTING REPORT: Fairbanks missed all of 2018 because of his elbow surgery, but he leapt from high Class A to the majors in just two and a half months. He was soon afterward traded to the Rays in a swap for second baseman Nick Solak. He has the fastball-slider combination to pitch in the late innings. His fastball sits 96-99 mph and can blow away some hitters, but it is relatively true. His slider is his best pitch. It's easily plus with downward dive and sporadic two-plane action. It sometimes runs in on righthanders like a screwball when he's focused on throwing it in the zone for strikes. Like many power relievers, his goal is to improve his fringe-average control to average.
THE FUTURE: Fairbanks has already shown impressive aptitude and he has the run-through-a-wall intensity teams like to see in a late-inning reliever. He should be a part of the Rays bullpen in 2020. With options remaining, he may go up and down as the MLB team's needs warrant.

Year	Age	Club (League)	Class	W	L	ERA	G	GS	SV	IP	H	HR	BB	SO	K/9	WHIP	AVG
2017	23	Down East (CAR)	HiA	2	1	5.79	9	1	0	19	22	1	13	10	4.8	1.88	.301
2018	24	Did not play—Injured															
2019	25	Down East (CAR)	HiA	1	0	2.92	11	0	2	12	10	0	4	15	10.9	1.14	.213
	25	Frisco (TL)	AA	1	0	0.00	6	0	0	7	2	0	0	14	17.2	0.27	.083
	25	Texas (AL)	MAJ	0	2	9.35	8	0	0	9	8	4	7	15	15.6	1.73	.235
	25	Nashville (PCL)	AAA	0	0	11.37	7	0	0	6	10	1	2	11	15.6	1.89	.370
	25	Durham (IL)	AAA	1	2	5.09	16	1	0	18	15	3	6	30	15.3	1.19	.221
	25	Tampa Bay (AL)	MAJ	2	1	5.11	13	0	2	12	17	1	3	13	9.5	1.62	.309
Major League Totals				2	3	6.86	21	0	2	21	25	5	10	28	12.0	1.67	.281
Minor League Totals				10	10	4.44	86	29	4	221	223	17	78	207	8.4	1.36	.263

23 LUCIUS FOX, SS

BA GRADE
45 Risk: High

Born: July 2, 1997. **B-T:** B-R. **HT:** 6-1. **WT:** 180. **Signed:** Bahamas, 2015. **Signed by:** Jose Alou/Joe Salermo (Giants).

TRACK RECORD: The Rays acquired Fox with Matt Duffy in the 2016 Matt Moore trade. While remaining primarily a shortstop, Fox began playing second and third base in 2019 to add to his versatility.

SCOUTING REPORT: Fox is one of the most athletic players in the Rays system. He is an above-average defender at shortstop with excellent range. He has the potential to be a plus defender at second and third base and his above-average arm works at either spot. His plus-plus speed would also work well if the Rays try him in center field. Fox has gotten more selective and he has improved his barrel control at the plate, but he just doesn't impact the ball. The hope remains that he will add size and strength to his frame to add to his bottom-of-the-scale power, but it hasn't happened in his first four pro seasons. He does know how to draw a walk, so if he can raise his .220-.230 average to just .260-.270 his secondary skills would make him playable, but he needs to hit the ball over outfielders' heads more to make that happen.

THE FUTURE: Fox's defense, speed and athleticism are useful, but he has to get to being at least an average hitter to have a future as a utilityman. The Rays added Fox to the 40-man roster and will likely play him at multiple positions with Triple-A Durham in 2020.

Year	Age	Club (League)	Class	AVG	G	AB	R	H	2B	3B	HR	RBI	BB	SO	SB	OBP	SLG
2017	19	Bowling Green (MWL)	LoA	.275	77	302	45	83	13	3	2	27	33	80	27	.359	.358
	19	Charlotte (FSL)	HiA	.235	30	115	19	27	3	0	1	12	12	33	3	.321	.287
2018	20	Charlotte (FSL)	HiA	.282	89	351	54	99	17	1	2	30	42	79	23	.371	.353
	20	Montgomery (SL)	AA	.221	27	104	14	23	3	1	1	9	8	20	6	.284	.298
2019	21	Durham (IL)	AAA	.143	15	42	6	6	0	1	0	1	6	15	2	.250	.190
	21	Montgomery (SL)	AA	.230	104	365	60	84	16	8	3	33	53	89	37	.340	.342
Minor League Totals				.244	417	1564	244	382	58	18	11	128	191	392	123	.337	.325

24 CALEB SAMPEN, RHP

BA GRADE
45 Risk: High

Born: July 23, 1996. **B-T:** R-R. **HT:** 6-2. **WT:** 185. **Drafted:** Wright State, 2018 (20th round). **Signed by:** Marty Lamb (Dodgers).

TRACK RECORD: Sampen was the 2016 Horizon League Freshman of the Year and beat Ohio State in the NCAA tournament that season. After missing the 2017 season because of ulnar nerve transposition surgery, Sampen was impressive again as a redshirt sophomore. Drafted by the Dodgers, the skinny Sampen was traded to the Rays in Jan. 2019 for Jamie Schultz.

SCOUTING REPORT: Sampen dominates hitters with a plus cutter that is hard (88-89 mph) with near slider-like tilt. He discovered the pitch in a side-session in the final month of his college career. His newfound cutter quickly helped keep lefthanded hitters off his two-seam fastball. It has made his 91-93 mph average fastball more effective. Sampen's cutter is his lone plus pitch, but he has four fringe-average or better offerings. He's athletic with above-average control and future above-average command. He touches 95 mph now, and there is some belief in the organization that he may eventually get to those upper reaches more regularly. His curveball is average, but he throws it for strikes. His fringe-average changeup has improved.

THE FUTURE: Sampen is athletic and can keep hitters off balance with a varied arsenal and above-average control, giving him a path to being a back-end starter. He's ready for high Class A Charlotte.

Year	Age	Club (League)	Class	W	L	ERA	G	GS	SV	IP	H	HR	BB	SO	K/9	WHIP	AVG
2018	21	Ogden (PIO)	R	0	2	5.04	13	11	0	30	31	2	9	43	12.8	1.32	.250
2019	22	Bowling Green (MWL)	LoA	9	4	2.68	22	21	0	121	91	3	32	104	7.7	1.02	.206
Minor League Totals				9	6	3.15	35	32	0	151	122	5	41	147	8.7	1.08	.216

25 DREW STROTMAN, RHP

BA GRADE
50 Risk: Extreme

Born: Sept. 3, 1996. **B-T:** R-R. **HT:** 6-3. **WT:** 195. **Drafted:** St. Mary's, 2017 (4th round). **Signed by:** Alan Hull.

TRACK RECORD: A reliever for most of his St. Mary's career, the Rays liked Strotman's athleticism and believed he could start. After a solid start to his pro career he blew out his elbow in May 2018. He returned from Tommy John surgery in July 2019 and pitched 21 innings in the Arizona Fall League.

SCOUTING REPORT: By the end of Srotman's AFL stint he was sitting 92-94 mph, touching 96 and he had regained the feel for his potentially above-average slider, although it had a little less power in his return. As a starter, Strotman doesn't have a true plus pitch, but he has an average fastball and an average changeup to go with his slider. He also throws an early count get-over curveball. Pre-injury he had average control, but he dealt with bouts of wildness in his return.

THE FUTURE: Strotman will look to return to his pre-TJ form in 2020. He's lauded for his competitiveness and intensity. He will likely begin back at high Class A Charlotte, but the hope is he will pitch his way to Double-A Mongtomery. His upside is as a No. 4 starter/setup man.

Year	Age	Club (League)	Class	W	L	ERA	G	GS	SV	IP	H	HR	BB	SO	K/9	WHIP	AVG
2017	20	Hudson Valley (NYP)	SS	2	3	1.78	11	7	0	51	29	0	9	42	7.5	0.75	.168
2018	21	Bowling Green (MWL)	LoA	3	0	3.52	9	9	0	46	40	0	18	43	8.4	1.26	.241
2019	22	Rays (GCL)	R	0	1	3.38	4	4	0	8	9	0	3	11	12.4	1.50	.265
	22	Charlotte (FSL)	HiA	0	2	5.06	5	5	0	16	20	3	9	13	7.3	1.81	.318
Minor League Totals				5	6	2.98	29	25	0	120	98	3	39	109	8.1	1.14	.225

26 JHON DIAZ, OF

BA GRADE **50** Risk: Extreme

Born: Oct. 1, 2002. **B-T:** L-L. **HT:** 5-8. **WT:** 160. **Signed:** Dominican Republic, 2019. **Signed by:** Danny Santana.

TRACK RECORD: One of the top international prospects in the 2019 class, Diaz was initially expected to sign with the Yankees. But when the Yankees weren't able to come up with more bonus pool money to sign Diaz, he ended up signing with the Rays instead for $1.5 million.

SCOUTING REPORT: Diaz is diminutive but has an exciting combination of tools and refined baseball skills for his age. He has the potential to be a plus hitter at the top of a lineup, showing good bat control and strike-zone judgment and the ability to consistently barrel balls all over the field in games, squaring up all types of pitches with good plate coverage. Diaz puts a surprising charge into the ball for his size, driving the ball out of the park already in BP with signs of average power and a strong chance to tap into it during games because of his pure hitting ability. Diaz has the tools to play center field, with his speed and arm strength both grading above-average. He has an extremely high baseball IQ for his age, with instincts that stand out in the field, at the plate and running the bases.

THE FUTURE: Diaz is advanced enough that he could skip the Dominican Summer League and go straight to the Rookie-level Gulf Coast League in 2020.

Year	Age	Club (League)	Class	AVG	G	AB	R	H	2B	3B	HR	RBI	BB	SO	SB	OBP	SLG
2019	16	Did not play–Signed 2020 contract															

27 NIKO HULSIZER, OF

BA GRADE **50** Risk: Extreme

Born: Feb. 1, 1997. **B-T:** R-R. **HT:** 6-2. **WT:** 225. **Drafted:** Morehead State, 2018 (18th round). **Signed by:** Marty Lamb (Dodgers).

TRACK RECORD: At Morehead State, Hulsizer finished second in Division I with 27 home runs in 2017 and won the college home run derby in Omaha that season. In 2018 a hamate injury cost him time and led to a dip to 12 home runs, but he once again showed the plus-plus raw power that entices scouts. He had already hit 20 home runs in 2019 before he was traded to the Rays on July 31 for Adam Kolarek.

SCOUTING REPORT: Hulsizer has a powerful, muscular build. He hits the ball as hard as pretty much anyone in the Rays organization with a pull-heavy approach that uses his legs well. Hulsizer has yet to find a fastball he can't catch up to, but he's yet to show nearly the same confidence when facing breaking balls. He's starting to show the ability to work to more advantageous counts, but for now he still projects as the .230-.240 hitter that could limit his power potential. Defensively, he's fringe-average in the corners thanks to average speed and an average arm.

THE FUTURE: Hulsizer is a high-risk, high-reward player who could hit 30-plus big league home runs, or could end up stuck in Double-A because of too many strikeouts.

Year	Age	Club (League)	Class	AVG	G	AB	R	H	2B	3B	HR	RBI	BB	SO	SB	OBP	SLG
2018	21	Ogden (PIO)	R	.281	48	160	47	45	13	0	9	32	30	52	12	.426	.531
2019	22	Great Lakes (MWL)	LoA	.268	58	209	46	56	17	1	15	49	37	75	4	.395	.574
	22	R. Cucamonga (CAL)	HiA	.259	25	85	15	22	6	0	5	18	9	33	3	.327	.506
	22	Rays (GCL)	R	.111	4	9	0	1	0	0	0	1	2	4	0	.273	.111
	22	Charlotte (FSL)	HiA	.235	9	34	4	8	2	0	1	4	4	11	0	.308	.382
Minor League Totals				.266	144	497	112	132	38	1	30	104	82	175	19	.386	.527

28 MICHAEL PLASSMEYER, LHP

BA GRADE **40** Risk: Medium

Born: Nov. 5, 1996. **B-T:** L-L. **HT:** 6-2. **WT:** 195. **Drafted:** Missouri, 2018 (4th round). **Signed by:** Ben Collman (Mariners).

TRACK RECORD: Plassmeyer impressed scouts with a strong junior year at Missouri as he went from being a swingman as a sophomore to a consistent Saturday starter for the Tigers. He ranked in the top 30 in Division I in strikeout-to-walk ratio in 2018. The Rays acquired him along with Mike Zunino and Guillermo Heredia in the Nov. 2018 deal that sent Mallex Smith and Jake Fraley to Seattle.

SCOUTING REPORT: The only really plus tool Plassmeyer has is his control and command—his control

is a 70 on the 20-to-80 scale. That control has allowed him to dominate so far. His 90-92 mph fastball and slider are both average, but his ability to work in and out and dot the corners with his fastball and his ability to throw his slider for strikes or get it to dive out of the bottom of the zone allow the two pitches to work well together. He's improved his changeup to give him a third average pitch with some late drop.
THE FUTURE: Plassmeyer's durability and consistency make him a solid No. 5 starter candidate or he could fill the bulk-reliever role that Ryan Yarborough has thrived in.

Year	Age	Club (League)	Class	W	L	ERA	G	GS	SV	IP	H	HR	BB	SO	K/9	WHIP	AVG
2018	21	Everett (NWL)	SS	0	1	2.25	13	12	0	24	16	1	4	44	16.5	0.83	.182
2019	22	Bowling Green (MWL)	LoA	2	1	1.23	5	5	0	29	21	3	7	32	9.8	0.95	.208
	22	Charlotte (FSL)	HiA	7	2	2.12	19	18	0	102	89	5	16	76	6.7	1.03	.235
	22	Durham (IL)	AAA	0	0	0.00	1	0	0	1	0	0	0	1	9.0	0.00	.000
Minor League Totals				9	4	1.96	38	35	0	156	126	9	27	153	8.8	0.98	.221

29 JOSH FLEMING, LHP

BA GRADE
40 Risk: Medium

Born: May 18, 1996. **B-T:** L-L. **HT:** 6-2. **WT:** 190. **Drafted:** Webster (Mo.), 2017 (5th round). **Signed by:** Matt Allison.

TRACK RECORD: Fleming is trying to follow in Ryan Yarborough's footsteps as a crafty lefthander with plus control. Fleming was the first player ever drafted out of Division III Webster (Mo.).
SCOUTING REPORT: Fleming doesn't have a plus pitch, but he does have plus-plus control. He tries to avoid the heart of the plate and the barrel of the bat with a 90-92 mph fastball, a low-80s slider and a mid-70s changeup that relies on deception more than movement. Without increased velocity, none of the three likely ever will be plus. But he stays out of predictable patterns and uses three quadrants of the strike zone (outside, inside and the bottom of the zone) well. He relies on getting plenty of ground ball outs.
THE FUTURE: Fleming's upside is relatively limited, but his control and craftiness should help him carve out a major league role. For most teams, he'd be looking to be a back-of-the-rotation starter, but he could also handle a long-relief, bulk-innings role for the Rays.

Year	Age	Club (League)	Class	W	L	ERA	G	GS	SV	IP	H	HR	BB	SO	K/9	WHIP	AVG
2017	21	Princeton (APP)	R	1	2	5.40	12	9	0	35	42	5	7	26	6.7	1.40	.300
2018	22	Bowling Green (MWL)	LoA	6	1	1.20	10	10	0	60	41	1	10	42	6.3	0.85	.193
	22	Charlotte (FSL)	HiA	3	3	4.11	9	7	0	50	51	4	9	38	6.8	1.19	.258
2019	23	Montgomery (SL)	AA	11	4	3.31	21	17	0	128	127	9	19	92	6.5	1.14	.259
	23	Durham (IL)	AAA	1	3	5.14	4	3	0	21	24	6	8	16	6.9	1.52	.286
Minor League Totals				22	13	3.40	56	46	0	294	285	25	53	214	6.6	1.15	.254

30 ANTHONY BANDA, LHP

BA GRADE
45 Risk: High

Born: Aug. 10, 1993. **B-T:** L-L. **HT:** 6-2. **WT:** 225. **Drafted:** San Jacinto (Texas) JC, 2012 (10th round). **Signed by:** Brian Sankey (Brewers).

TRACK RECORD: To put into perspective how many years Banda has spent trying to graduate from prospect status, he was traded from the Brewers to the D-backs in 2014 for Gerardo Parra. Parra has played for five different MLB teams since that trade. Banda has been traded again (in a three-team 2018 swap that brought him to the Rays), had Tommy John surgery and made it back to the mound. He struggled at Triple-A Durham and didn't make it back to the majors until the September roster expansion.
SCOUTING REPORT: His 90-94 mph average fastball was 2-3 mph less than it was pre-surgery and his reduced arm speed also took something away from his slurvy slider—an average pitch pre-injury, it was fringe-average in 2019. Banda generally works in and out to hitters, but he does like to elevate his fastball to finish off batters. He found that 92-93 up in the zone isn't as effective as 95-97. In the majors, he relied more heavily on a mid-80s fringe-average changeup that lacked the late fade he's had in the past. He often missed badly to his glove-side and showed below-average control and command.
THE FUTURE: Banda and the Rays have to hope he regains the velocity, bite on his slider and command he had pre-surgery. If he does, he can be a bulk-innings reliever/lefty setup man.

Year	Age	Club (League)	Class	W	L	ERA	G	GS	SV	IP	H	HR	BB	SO	K/9	WHIP	AVG
2017	23	Reno (PCL)	AAA	8	7	5.39	22	22	0	122	125	15	51	116	8.6	1.44	.266
	23	Arizona (NL)	MAJ	2	3	5.96	8	4	0	26	26	1	10	25	8.8	1.40	.255
2018	24	Tampa Bay (AL)	MAJ	1	0	3.68	3	1	0	15	12	1	3	10	6.1	1.02	.235
	24	Durham (IL)	AAA	4	3	3.64	8	8	0	42	43	3	18	49	10.5	1.45	.272
2019	25	Charlotte (FSL)	HiA	0	0	0.00	2	2	0	3	1	0	0	2	6.8	0.38	.111
	25	Rays (GCL)	R	0	1	7.71	2	2	0	2	6	0	3	4	15.4	3.86	.462
	25	Durham (IL)	AAA	2	3	6.04	9	4	0	28	28	7	11	27	8.6	1.38	.262
	25	Tampa Bay (AL)	MAJ	0	0	6.75	3	0	0	4	6	0	0	2	4.5	1.50	.333
Major League Totals				3	3	5.28	14	5	0	44	44	2	13	37	7.5	1.29	.257
Minor League Totals				46	41	3.90	151	129	2	720	730	59	271	707	8.8	1.39	.263

Texas Rangers

BY BEN BADLER

For the third straight season, the Rangers finished below .500. However, instead of having a revamped minor league pipeline built up during those losing years, the Rangers have a deep farm system, but not an elite one.

That prospect depth has been bolstered by a slew of promising international signings in the lower levels. They added to that wave by signing two of the premier prospects in the 2019 international class, Venezuelan shortstop Maximo Acosta and Dominican outfielder Bayron Lora, both of whom join Venezuelan shortstop Luisangel Acuña in their Top 10 Prospects.

The Rangers lack elite talent—they don't have a top 50 prospect in baseball—particularly in the upper levels. Nick Solak should help in 2020, but among the organization's top 30 prospects, the only hitter besides Solak to have reached Double-A is center fielder Leody Taveras, a talented defender who faces questions about his future offensive impact.

Catcher Sam Huff and third baseman Sherten Apostel both should reach Double-A in 2020 and boosted their stock last year. Huff has some free-swinging tendencies, but he has elite power and arm strength and made significant defensive progress to show he can stay behind the plate. Drafting third baseman Josh Jung with the No. 8 overall pick in the 2019 draft gives the Rangers their new top prospect and an advanced college hitter with the potential to join them in the upper levels soon.

On the pitching side, righthanders Ronny Henriquez and Ricky Vanasco took steps forward in 2019. But injuries chewed up many of the Rangers' most promising arms. Two of their top 2018 draft picks—righthanders Owen White (second round) and Mason Englert (fourth)—both had Tommy John surgery. Lefthander Cole Ragans had a second TJ and will miss another year.

Lefties Taylor Hearn and Brock Burke and righthanders Yerry Rodriguez and A.J. Alexy all missed significant time with arm issues. Even on on the position player side, three of their toolsiest prospects—outfielder Bubba Thompson and shortstops Anderson Tejeda and Chris Seise—spent significant time on the injured list.

The Rangers' best pitching prospect, righthander Hans Crouse, dealt with injuries as well, pitching through bone spurs that he had surgery on after the season but that took a toll on his stuff and performance during the season. Crouse and righthander Cole Winn, their 2018 first-round pick who struggled in his first full season, will try to get back on track in 2020.

After three straight losing seasons and with a new ballpark opening in 2020, the Rangers are trying to contend this year. The lineup needs more help, but they bolstered their rotation by trading for Corey Kluber and signing Kyle Gibson and Jordan Lyles as free agents. They join Mike Minor and Lance Lynn in the rotation.

There's a path for the Rangers to reach the playoffs in 2020, but there are still obstacles on that road. Without one of the best teams in the major leagues or one of the best farm systems in the minors, it's an uncomfortable middle ground for the Rangers to navigate their way back to being the perennial contenders they were in the first half of the 2010s.

RICHARD RODRIGUEZ/GETTY IMAGES

Nick Solak hit well as a 2019 callup but is the only big league-ready bat on the horizon.

PROJECTED 2023 LINEUP

Position	Player	Age
Catcher	Sam Huff (2)	25
First Base	Ronald Guzman	28
Second Base	Rougned Odor	29
Third Base	Josh Jung (1)	25
Shortstop	Elvis Andrus	34
Left Field	Nick Solak (4)	28
Center Field	Leody Taveras (3)	25
Right Field	Joey Gallo	29
Designated Hitter	Willie Calhoun	28
No. 1 Starter	Mike Minor	35
No. 2 Starter	Hans Crouse (6)	24
No. 3 Starter	Joe Palumbo (7)	28
No. 4 Starter	Ronny Henriquez (10)	23
No. 5 Starter	Kolby Allard	25
Closer	Demarcus Evans	26

DEPTH CHART

TEXAS RANGERS

TOP 2020 ROOKIE: Nick Solak, 2B/3B/OF. His ultimate defensive home remains to be determined, but he has hit well at every level.

BREAKOUT PROSPECT: Heriberto Hernandez, OF. The $10,000 signing from the Dominican Republic has done nothing but mash in his first two seasons of Rookie ball, with an easy swing and big power, albeit with defensive questions.

SLEEPER: Justin Slaten, RHP. A third-round pick out of New Mexico in 2019, he has a promising fastball/slider combination that should help him miss bats.

SOURCE OF TOP 30 TALENT

Homegrown	25	Acquired	5
College	3	Trade	5
Junior college	0	Rule 5 draft	0
High school	8	Independent league	0
Nondrafted free agent	0	Free agent/waivers	0
International	14		

LF
Scott Heineman
Alexander Ovalles

CF
Leody Taveras (3)
Steele Walker (22)
Bubba Thompson (23)
Julio Pablo Martinez (27)
Zion Bannister (29)

RF
Bayron Lora (9)
Heriberto Hernandez (20)
Pedro Gonzalez

3B
Josh Jung (1)
Sherten Apostel (11)
Davis Wendzel (15)

SS
Maximo Acosta (5)
Luisangei Acuña (8)
Osleivis Basabe (13)
Anderson Tejeda (18)
Chris Seise
Eli White
Yonny Hernandez

2B
Nick Solak (4)
Keithron Moss (25)
Jonathan Ornelas
Cody Freeman
Keyber Rodriguez
Charles Leblanc

1B
Curtis Terry
Tyreque Reed

C
Sam Huff (2)
David Garcia (24)
Randy Florentino (26)
Jose Trevino
Efrenyer Narvaez

LHP

LHSP
Joe Palumbo (7)
Brock Burke (21)
Taylor Hearn (28)
John King
Jake Latz
Cole Ragans

LHRP
Cody Bradford

RHP

RHSP
Hans Crouse (6)
Ronny Henriquez (10)
Ricky Vanasco (12)
Cole Winn (14)
Jonathan Hernandez (17)
Ryan Garcia (19)
Tyler Phillips (30)
Mason Englert
Owen White
Yerry Rodriguez
Justin Slaten
Kyle Cody
A.J. Alexy
Jason Bahr
Orceli Gomez

RHRP
DeMarcus Evans (16)
Scott Engler
Joe Barlow
Nick Snyder
Kelvin Gonzalez
Michael Matuella

DRAFT ANALYSIS

2019

BEST PURE HITTER: The Rangers used the No. 8 overall pick to select 3B Josh Jung (1), one of the top offensive performers in college baseball over the last three seasons. He's a potential plus hitter with a solid grasp of the strike zone. He recognizes pitches well and has an approach geared to use all fields.

BEST POWER: The Rangers didn't draft a hitter who jumped out for power as a carrying tool. Jung has a hit-first profile with questions on how much power he will develop, and while it hasn't shown up yet, the Rangers drafted him as high as they did in part because they believe his future power grade will tick up due to his contact frequency and the potential adjustments he can make to develop more impact.

FASTEST RUNNER: The Rangers took a late-round flier on Hillsdale (Mich.) SS Jake Hoover (28), an elite runner who ran the 60-yard dash in the 6.2 seconds—which is an 80-grade run time.

BEST DEFENSIVE PLAYER: 3B Davis Wendzel (1s) projected as an above-average defensive third baseman coming out of Baylor. He played a little bit of shortstop for the Bears, and the Rangers plan to experiment with Wendzel all over the field next year, with shortstop, third and second base all in the mix. He's an instinctual defender with secure hands and a strong arm.

BEST ATHLETE: When the Rangers hosted Hoover at a pre-draft workout, he posted dazzling marks on their athletic testing markers, from vertical jump to grip strength, in addition to his blazing speed.

BEST FASTBALL: RHP Justin Slaten (3) can reach the mid-90s, though RHP Ryan Garcia (2) gets the edge here despite having a little less pure velocity. Garcia sits in the low 90s and has topped out at 94-95 mph, but he draws a lot of swings and misses due to the pitch's carrying life through the zone and overall deception.

BEST SECONDARY PITCH: Scouts from other clubs had Slaten's slider as an average to a tick better pitch, but the Rangers saw him a lot before the draft and graded it out even higher as a wipeout offering.

TOP DRAFT PICKS OF THE DECADE

Year	Player, Pos.	2019 Org
2010	Kellin Deglan, C	Yankees
2011	Kevin Matthews, LHP	American Association
2012	Lewis Brinson, OF	Marlins
2013	Chi Chi Gonzalez, RHP	Rockies
2014	Luis Ortiz, RHP	Orioles
2015	Dillon Tate, RHP	Orioles
2016	Cole Ragans, LHP	Rangers
2017	Bubba Thompson, OF	Rangers
2018	Cole Winn, RHP	Rangers
2019	Josh Jung, 3B	Rangers

BEST PRO DEBUT: Jung jumped to low Class A Hickory, where he hit .287/.363/.389 in 40 games. 1B Blaine Crim (19) didn't face the same level of competition, but he posted big numbers for short-season Spokane, batting .335/.398/.528 to win Northwest League MVP.

MOST INTRIGUING BACKGROUND: Garcia went to UCLA as a walk-on, then developed into UCLA's ace, the 2019 Pac-12 pitcher of the year and No. 50 overall pick in the draft with a $1,469,900 signing bonus.

CLOSEST TO THE MAJORS: As a college hitter drafted with a top-10 overall pick, Jung should be able to move relatively quickly.

BEST LATE-ROUND PICK: As a 22-year-old first baseman drafted in the 19th round, Crim will have to keep mashing and proving himself at higher levels, but winning the Northwest League MVP award is a good start.

THE ONE WHO GOT AWAY: RHP Brandon Sproat (8) opted to become a Florida Gator instead of signing. He has a lot of space to fill out his lanky, projectable frame and add to a fastball that has already been up to 94 mph. Sproat was one of just two players drafted among the top 10 rounds who did not sign—the other was catcher Wyatt Hendrie, who was drafted by the Cubs in the 10th round.

—BEN BADLER

2018

It was an injury-plagued first full pro season for this class. RHP Cole Winn (1) is the only player to make the Handbook and the rest of the group will look to bounce back with better health in 2020.

GRADE: D

2017

RHP Hans Crouse (2) has been one of the better prep pitchers the Rangers have drafted in recent years. RHP Ricky Vanesco (15) was a nice find and OF Bubba Thompson (1) still has a shot.

GRADE: C

2016

C Sam Huff (7) is the only player from this class to make the Handbook, but he also offers plenty of upside as the system's No. 2 prospect. OF Jonah McReynolds (13) was traded for Welington Castillo.

GRADE: C

1 JOSH JUNG, 3B

Born: Feb. 12, 1998. **B-T:** R-R. **HT:** 6-2. **WT:** 215.
Drafted: Texas Tech, 2019 (1st round).
Signed by: Josh Simpson.

TRACK RECORD: Jung was one of the best hitters in college baseball during his three seasons at Texas Tech. He was a first-team Freshman All-American in 2017, then a second-team All-American in both 2018 and 2019. The Rangers drafted Jung with the No. 8 overall pick in 2019 and signed him for $4.4 million. After a quick tune-up in the Rookie-level Arizona League, Jung went to the low Class A South Atlantic League in mid-July and helped Hickory capture the second-half crown in the Northern Division.

SCOUTING REPORT: Jung's bat is his calling card. He's calm and under control at the plate and stays inside the ball well with a short stroke and a straightaway hitting approach. He drives the ball well to the middle of the field and right-center field. He's a patient, disciplined hitter who walked more than he struck out in each of his final two college seasons. He recognizes pitches well and puts himself into favorable counts, though his bat-to-ball skills make him comfortable hitting in pitcher's counts. Jung has a chance to develop into a plus hitter, though the question is how much power he will have. Some scouts think he could have average power, but it's a hit-first profile, with Jung's approach geared for line drives and spreading the ball around the park rather than trying to turn on the ball for extra-base damage, and he hit only one home run in 40 games with Hickory, a team that plays its home games at power-friendly park. While a lot of teams had Jung stacked up as a middle of the first-round pick on their draft boards, the Rangers took him as high as they did in part because of their belief in his ability to develop more power. Defensively, Jung draws a split camp among scouts, but he should be able to provide average defense at third base. He moved from third base to shortstop his junior year at Texas Tech, but he went back to third base in pro ball. A below-average runner, Jung needs to improve his agility in the field, but his hands work well. He's good on the slow roller and he has a plus arm with the ability to make accurate throws on the run.

THE FUTURE: Jung should open the season at one of the Class A levels and could finish the year at Double-A Frisco. He has a chance to develop into a solid-average regular at third base with the upside for more if he can make the adjustments to unlock more game power. If not he should be a solid hit-over-power regular.

TRACY PROFFITT/FOUR SEAM IMAGES

BA GRADE
55 Risk: High

SCOUTING GRADES
Hit: 60. **Power:** 50. **Run:** 40. **Field:** 50. **Arm:** 60.

Projected future grades on 20-80 scouting scale.

TOP PROSPECTS OF THE DECADE

Year	Player, Pos.	2019 Org
2010	Neftali Feliz, RHP	Did not play
2011	Martin Perez, LHP	Twins
2012	Jurickson Profar, SS	Athletics
2013	Jurickson Profar, SS/2B	Athletics
2014	Rougned Odor, 2B	Rangers
2015	Joey Gallo, 3B	Rangers
2016	Joey Gallo, 3B	Rangers
2017	Leody Taveras ,OF	Rangers
2018	Willie Calhoun, OF	Rangers
2019	Hans Crouse, RHP	Rangers

BEST TOOLS

Best Hitter for Average	Josh Jung
Best Power Hitter	Sam Huff
Best Strike-Zone Discipline	Yonny Hernandez
Fastest Baserunner	Jake Hoover
Best Athlete	Bubba Thompson
Best Fastball	DeMarcus Evans
Best Curveball	Joe Palumbo
Best Slider	Jonathan Hernandez
Best Changeup	Tyler Phillips
Best Control	Tyler Phillips
Best Defensive Catcher	Sam Huff
Best Defensive Infielder	Anderson Tejeda
Best Infield Arm	Anderson Tejeda
Best Defensive Outfielder	Leody Taveras
Best Outfield Arm	Leody Taveras

Year	Age	Club (League)	Class	AVG	G	AB	R	H	2B	3B	HR	RBI	BB	SO	SB	OBP	SLG
2019	21	Rangers (AZL)	R	.588	4	17	5	10	1	1	1	5	2	3	0	.632	.941
	21	Hickory (SAL)	LoA	.287	40	157	18	45	13	0	1	23	16	29	4	.363	.389
Minor League Totals				.316	44	174	23	55	14	1	2	28	18	32	4	.389	.443

2 SAM HUFF, C

BA GRADE
55 **Risk: High**

Born: Jan. 14, 1998. **B-T:** R-R. **HT:** 6-4. **WT:** 230. **Drafted:** HS—Phoenix, 2016 (7th round). **Signed by:** Josh Simpson.

TRACK RECORD: Huff raised his profile in 2019, stamped with an MVP trophy from the Futures Game. The Rangers had him return low Class A Hickory to open the year, but he hit 15 home runs in his first 30 games to earn a bump to high Class A Down East, where he continued to show a power stroke.

SCOUTING REPORT: Huff is a tall, physical catcher with two loud tools between his power and arm strength. It's 70 raw power on the 20-80 scale, with Huff having the strength, bat speed and leverage in his swing to drive the ball out to any part of the park. He has the raw power to hit 30-plus homers if everything clicks, but he's susceptible to chasing off the plate and has trouble covering the inner third. As a result, he doesn't walk much and his strikeout rate is high. Where Huff made significant strides in 2019 was behind the plate. At 6-foot-4, 230 pounds, he's a big man for a catcher, but he frames pitches well and improved his footwork and blocking. He did an outstanding job of shutting down the running game with his plus arm, throwing out 48 percent of basestealers.

THE FUTURE: Now that Huff looks like a true catcher, there's less demand on his bat, though he will still need to improve his plate discipline. He heads to Double-A Frisco in 2020.

SCOUTING GRADES: **Hitting:** 40 **Power:** 70 **Running:** 40 **Fielding:** 45 **Arm:** 60

Year	Age	Club (League)	Class	AVG	G	AB	R	H	2B	3B	HR	RBI	BB	SO	SB	OBP	SLG
2017	19	Rangers (AZL)	R	.249	49	197	34	49	9	2	9	31	24	66	3	.329	.452
2018	20	Hickory (SAL)	LoA	.241	118	415	53	100	22	3	18	55	23	140	9	.292	.439
2019	21	Hickory (SAL)	LoA	.333	30	108	22	36	5	0	15	29	6	37	4	.368	.796
	21	Down East (CAR)	HiA	.262	97	367	49	96	17	2	13	43	27	117	2	.326	.425
Minor League Totals				.264	322	1184	177	313	63	8	56	175	96	389	18	.328	.473

3 LEODY TAVERAS, OF

BRIAN WESTERHOLT FOUR SEAM IMAGES

BA GRADE
55 **Risk: Very High**

Born: Sept. 8, 1998. **B-T:** B-R. **HT:** 6-1. **WT:** 190. **Signed:** Dominican Republic, 2015. **Signed by:** Willy Espinal/Gil Kim/Thad Levine.

TRACK RECORD: Taveras was one of the elite international prospects in 2015, when he signed with the Rangers for $2.1 million. A cousin of former major league center fielder Willy Taveras, Leody has moved quickly through the Rangers' system to reach Double-A as a 20-year-old.

SCOUTING REPORT: Taveras plays plus defense at a premium position. He's a plus runner with a quick first step who reads the ball well off the bat with good range, both to the gaps and running down balls hit over his head. His strong arm is another plus tool. While Taveras' defense grades out well, there are more questions about his bat. He has always been one of the youngest players at his level and has solid bat-to-ball skills, though his strikeout rate jumped from 17 percent in 2018 to 21 percent in 2019. Taveras has strong hands and the frame that suggests more power could come, but for now his contact is mostly soft. He's still entering his age-21 season, so there's time for Taveras to grow into more juice, but it's the biggest risk factor in his profile right now.

THE FUTURE: Scouts continue to want to see more offensive impact from Taveras to feel comfortable with him realizing his upside. He could return to Double-A Frisco to open 2019, but should be in Triple-A by the end of the year.

SCOUTING GRADES: **Hitting:** 50 **Power:** 40 **Running:** 60 **Fielding:** 60 **Arm:** 60

Year	Age	Club (League)	Class	AVG	G	AB	R	H	2B	3B	HR	RBI	BB	SO	SB	OBP	SLG
2017	18	Hickory (SAL)	LoA	.249	134	522	73	130	20	7	8	50	47	92	20	.312	.360
2018	19	Down East (CAR)	HiA	.246	132	521	65	128	16	7	5	48	51	96	19	.312	.332
2019	20	Down East (CAR)	HiA	.294	66	255	44	75	7	4	2	25	31	62	21	.368	.376
	20	Frisco (TL)	AA	.265	65	264	32	70	12	4	3	31	23	60	11	.320	.375
Minor League Totals				.260	470	1868	256	486	69	28	19	187	177	365	89	.323	.358

4 NICK SOLAK, 2B/OF

Born: Jan. 11, 1995. **B-T:** R-R. **HT:** 5-10. **WT:** 180. **Drafted:** Louisville, 2016 (2nd round). **Signed by:** Mike Gibbons (Yankees).

TRACK RECORD: Solak has been traded twice in his career, first from the Yankees to Rays, then in July 2019 to the Rangers for reliever Peter Fairbanks. He made his big league debut with the Rangers on Aug. 20 and performed well the rest of the season.

SCOUTING REPORT: Solak has major defensive questions, but his track record of hitting is impressive. He has a short swing with a level path that stays on plane with the pitch for a long time, with solid bat-to-ball skills. He has a good eye for the strike zone and makes good swing decisions with consistent quality at-bats. He has solid-average raw power but hit a combined 32 home runs last year, with his contact frequency and the baseball in Triple-A enhancing his power numbers. Solak is a plus runner, but his infield defense is rough. He's a well below-average defender at second base, where he has an average arm but stiff actions and footwork. He played fringe-average defense in left field with the Rays, though the Rangers mostly used him at second and third base.

THE FUTURE: Even if Solak goes to left field, his ability to create runs might be enough to carry him as a league-average player there.

SCOUTING GRADES: **Hitting:** 55 **Power:** 50 **Running:** 60 **Fielding:** 40 **Arm:** 50

Year	Age	Club (League)	Class	AVG	G	AB	R	H	2B	3B	HR	RBI	BB	SO	SB	OBP	SLG
2017	22	Tampa (FSL)	HiA	.301	100	346	56	104	17	4	10	44	53	76	13	.397	.460
	22	Trenton (EL)	AA	.286	30	119	16	34	9	1	2	9	10	24	1	.344	.429
2018	23	Montgomery (SL)	AA	.282	126	478	91	135	17	3	19	76	68	112	21	.384	.450
2019	24	Durham (IL)	AAA	.266	85	301	56	80	13	1	17	47	39	80	3	.353	.485
	24	Nashville (PCL)	AAA	.347	30	118	23	41	6	0	10	27	6	25	2	.386	.653
	24	Texas (AL)	MAJ	.293	33	116	19	34	6	1	5	17	15	29	2	.393	.491
Major League Totals				.293	33	116	19	34	6	1	5	17	15	29	2	.393	.491
Minor League Totals				.294	435	1602	290	471	75	10	61	228	206	356	48	.383	.468

5 MAXIMO ACOSTA, SS

BILL MITCHELL

Born: Oct. 29, 2002. **B-T:** R-R. **HT:** 6-1. **WT:** 170. **Signed:** Venezuela, 2019. **Signed by:** Carlos Gonzalez/Jhonny Gomez/Rafic Saab.

TRACK RECORD: The Rangers gave Dominican outfielder Bayron Lora more money in 2019, but Acosta has trended up so much that he has surpassed Lora as the team's best international signing in the 2019 class.

SCOUTING REPORT: Acosta combines plus tools in a well-rounded skill set. He plays with a calm, controlled style and easy actions on both sides of the ball, drawing comparisons to Gleyber Torres both physically and in his all-around game. He has a short, fluid swing with good rhythm, balance and timing. He recognizes spin, controls the strike zone and is a high-contact hitter who barrels pitches in all areas of the strike zone with an all-fields approach. Acosta has a chance to be a plus hitter and has at least average power now that should be above-average soon. His feel for the barrel should allow that power to translate in games. Acosta has a thicker lower half than some other shortstops his age, but he should stay at the position. A plus runner with a plus arm, Acosta has a good internal clock at shortstop with good footwork, range and athleticism.

THE FUTURE: Acosta is advanced enough that he should make his pro debut in 2020 in the U.S., most likely in the Rookie-level Arizona League. His upside makes him one of the most exciting players in the organization.

SCOUTING GRADES: **Hitting:** 60 **Power:** 55 **Running:** 60 **Fielding:** 50 **Arm:** 60

Year	Age	Club (League)	Class	AVG	G	AB	R	H	2B	3B	HR	RBI	BB	SO	SB	OBP	SLG
2019	16	Did not play—Signed 2020 contract															

6 HANS CROUSE, RHP

BA GRADE
55 Risk: Very High

Born: Sept. 15, 1998. **B-T:** R-R. **HT:** 6-4. **WT:** 185. **Signed:** HS—Dana Point, Calif., 2017 (2nd round). **Signed by:** Steve Flores.

TRACK RECORD: The No. 1 prospect in the organization a year ago, Crouse pitched through a bone spur in his pitching elbow in 2019 that hampered his stuff. He missed a month in the middle of the season, then had surgery after the season.

SCOUTING REPORT: Crouse didn't have the same electricity to his stuff in 2019 that he showed in 2018 as he pitched through the bone spur. Even with it, though, he still threw 92-96 mph with his fastball. At his best, Crouse has shown a plus slider that looks like a fastball out of his hand before diving late. In 2019, the nagging elbow issues took a toll on his slider, leading to a drop in his strikeout rate. He still got swings and misses with his slider, but he had trouble landing it in the zone, and it often was softer without the same finish it showed in 2018. He throws a fringe-average changeup that he shows enough feel for to tick up with more development. There's some violence to Crouse's energetic, herky-jerky delivery, so some scouts think he might end up in the bullpen, but he has the stuff to start and control to develop as a starter.

THE FUTURE: Crouse is headed to high Class A Down East in 2020. If he returns healthy and showing the stuff he did in 2018, he has a chance to be a No. 2 or 3 starter, but the stuff he showed in 2019 adds more risk to him reaching that upside.

SCOUTING GRADES: **Fastball:** 60 **Slider:** 60 **Changeup:** 50 **Control:** 55

Year	Age	Club (League)	Class	W	L	ERA	G	GS	SV	IP	H	HR	BB	SO	K/9	WHIP	AVG
2017	18	Rangers (AZL)	R	0	0	0.45	10	6	0	20	7	1	7	30	13.5	0.70	.109
2018	19	Spokane (NWL)	SS	5	1	2.37	8	8	0	38	25	2	11	47	11.1	0.95	.179
	19	Hickory (SAL)	LoA	0	2	2.70	5	5	0	17	18	1	8	15	8.1	1.56	.273
2019	20	Hickory (SAL)	LoA	6	1	4.41	19	19	0	88	86	12	19	76	7.8	1.20	.256
Minor League Totals				11	4	3.27	42	38	0	162	136	16	45	168	9.3	1.11	.224

7 JOE PALUMBO, LHP

BA GRADE
45 Risk: Medium

Born: Oct. 26, 1994. **B-T:** L-L. **HT:** 6-1. **WT:** 190. **Drafted:** HS—West Islip, N.Y., 2013 (30th round). **Signed by:** Takeshi Sakurayama.

TRACK RECORD: Palumbo didn't generate much attention during his first few seasons in the minors after signing for $32,000 as a 30th-round pick. He broke out as a prospect in 2016, but missed most of the 2017 season with Tommy John surgery. He returned in 2018 and got his first taste of the major leagues in 2019.

SCOUTING REPORT: Palumbo operates off a plus fastball from the left side, sitting 91-94 mph with the ability to reach 96. He has a short arm stroke and conceals the ball well in his delivery, which helps his fastball sneak up on hitters. When Palumbo gets ahead in the count he can put hitters away with his 77-80 mph curveball, a plus pitch that dives underneath barrels. He gained more confidence in his changeup in 2019 and it flashes as an average pitch. Palumbo has been a solid strike-thrower for most of his minor league career and projects to have average control. Entering his age-25 season, Palumbo has never topped 100 innings in a season, and given his medical history, there's durability risk with him handling a starter's full season workload.

THE FUTURE: If Palumbo proves durable, he has the stuff and control to be a solid No. 4 starter. He will get a chance to hold down a spot in the back of the Rangers' rotation in 2020.

SCOUTING GRADES: **Fastball:** 55 **Curveball:** 60 **Changeup:** 50 **Control:** 50

Year	Age	Club (League)	Class	W	L	ERA	G	GS	SV	IP	H	HR	BB	SO	K/9	WHIP	AVG
2017	22	Down East (CAR)	HiA	1	0	0.66	3	3	0	14	4	0	4	22	14.5	0.59	.087
2018	23	Rangers (AZL)	R	0	0	4.00	3	3	0	9	5	1	1	15	15.0	0.67	.161
	23	Down East (CAR)	HiA	1	4	2.67	6	6	0	27	24	3	6	34	11.3	1.11	.226
	23	Frisco (TL)	AA	1	0	1.93	2	2	0	9	6	0	3	10	9.6	0.96	.182
2019	24	Frisco (TL)	AA	0	0	3.19	11	10	0	54	43	5	25	69	11.6	1.27	.221
	24	Nashville (PCL)	AAA	3	0	2.67	6	6	0	27	13	4	10	39	13.0	0.85	.143
	24	Texas (AL)	MAJ	0	3	9.18	7	4	0	17	21	7	8	21	11.3	1.74	.300
Major League Totals				0	3	9.18	7	4	0	16	21	7	8	21	11.3	1.74	.300
Minor League Totals				21	17	2.72	104	53	8	357	271	21	139	425	10.7	1.15	.207

8 LUISANGEL ACUÑA, SS

BA GRADE
55 Risk: Extreme

BILL MITCHELL

Born: March 12, 2002. **B-T:** R-R. **HT:** 5-8. **WT:** 160. **Signed:** Venezuela, 2018. **Signed by:** Carlos Plaza/Rafic Saab.

TRACK RECORD: A younger brother of Braves outfielder Ronald Acuña Jr., Luisangel signed with the Rangers out of Venezuela in 2018. He made the Dominican Summer League all-star team in his pro debut and has separated himself as the team's best signing from that international class.

SCOUTING REPORT: Acuña is small but packed with explosiveness and aggression. With swing mechanics patterned after his brother, Acuña goes up to the plate looking to do damage with a quick, whippy stroke. He swings so hard that at times he will drop to one knee, but he sees the ball well and makes a lot of contact. He's a disciplined hitter with good barrel awareness who walked more than he struck out in the DSL. His power is mostly to the gaps but he has enough juice to pull one out of the park occasionally. He's an athletic player with plus speed. When Acuña was an amateur, a lot of scouts figured he would move over to second base or possibly center field. That's still a possibility, but he increased his chances to stay at shortstop in 2019 with his defensive improvements. He has a plus arm.

THE FUTURE: Acuña has a chance to develop into an on-base threat who could hit at the top of a lineup and play somewhere in the middle of the diamond.

SCOUTING GRADES: **Hitting:** 60 **Power:** 45 **Running:** 60 **Fielding:** 50 **Arm:** 60

Year	Age	Club (League)	Class	AVG	G	AB	R	H	2B	3B	HR	RBI	BB	SO	SB	OBP	SLG
2019	17	Rangers1 (DSL)	R	.342	51	202	61	69	11	3	2	29	34	26	17	.438	.455
Minor League Totals				.342	51	202	61	69	11	3	2	29	34	26	17	.438	.455

9 BAYRON LORA, OF

BILL MITCHELL

Born: Sept. 29, 2002. **B-T:** R-R. **HT:** 6-5. **WT:** 230. **Signed:** Dominican Republic, 2019. **Signed by:** Willy Espinal.

TRACK RECORD: Lora stood out as an amateur in the Dominican Republic for having the biggest raw power in the 2019 international signing class. He signed with the Rangers for $3.9 million, the third biggest international bonus of the class.

SCOUTING REPORT: Lora is a massive, hulking slugger with the upside to be a 40-homer threat. He has 70-grade raw power, producing exit velocities up to 112 mph already, and there's potential for his power to tick up to the top of the scale. Lora has plenty of strength and bat speed, but his power comes with high swing-and-miss risk. As an amateur, Lora would get pull-heavy and swing for the fences, causing him to fly open early. He has shown better at-bats since then in an attempt to shorten his swing and stay through the middle of the field. Lora is going to develop as a right fielder, where he's still learning to improve his reads and routes. He's so big already that there's risk he might end up at first base.

THE FUTURE: If Lora can draw walks and keep his strikeout rate in check, he has the potential to be a power-hitting force in the middle of a lineup, but it's a profile with considerable risk. He's expected to make his pro debut in the Dominican Summer League.

SCOUTING GRADES: **Hitting:** 50 **Power:** 70 **Running:** 40 **Fielding:** 40 **Arm:** 45

Year	Age	Club (League)	Class	AVG	G	AB	R	H	2B	3B	HR	RBI	BB	SO	SB	OBP	SLG
2019	16	Did not play—Signed 2020 contract															

10 RONNY HENRIQUEZ, RHP

Born: June 20, 2000. **B-T:** R-R. **HT:** 5-10. **WT:** 165. **Signed:** Dominican Republic, 2017. **Signed by:** Willy Espinal.

TRACK RECORD: The Rangers saw Henriquez pitch as an amateur at a tryout in the Tricky League. He threw 91 mph and they ended up signing him for $10,000, which quickly proved a bargain when his velocity spiked and he dominated the Dominican Summer League. The Rangers pushed him in 2019 to low Class A Hickory, where he had a solid year.

SCOUTING REPORT: Henriquez is a power arm who pitches off a fastball that's mostly 93-96 mph and can crank up to 98. He started to get more swinging strikes off it in the second half when he elevated the pitch more often. He fills the zone and has the ability to generate swing-and-miss with both his slider and changeup. His slider has above-average potential and his changeup can miss bats, too, though it would benefit from more separation off his fastball

THE FUTURE: Henriquez has a chance to develop into a mid-rotation starter. He's headed to high Class A Down East in 2020.

SCOUTING GRADES: **Fastball:** 60 **Slider** 55 **Changeup:** 50 **Control:** 50

Year	Age	Club (League)	Class	W	L	ERA	G	GS	SV	IP	H	HR	BB	SO	K/9	WHIP	AVG
2018	18	Rangers2 (DSL)	R	5	0	1.55	11	11	0	58	37	2	8	79	12.3	0.78	.177
2019	19	Hickory (SAL)	LoA	6	6	4.50	21	19	0	82	91	6	27	99	10.9	1.44	.284
Minor League Totals				11	6	3.28	32	30	0	140	128	8	35	178	11.4	1.16	.242

11 SHERTEN APOSTEL, 3B

Born: March 11, 1999. **B-T:** R-R. **HT:** 6-4. **WT:** 200. **Signed:** Curacao, 2015. **Signed by:** Rene Gayo/Juan Mercado/Mark VanZanten (Pirates).

TRACK RECORD: The Pirates signed Apostel for $200,000 when the 2015 international signing period opened that year on July 2. Three years later, the Pirates acquired reliever Keone Kela from the Rangers in exchange for lefthander Taylor Hearn and a player to be named later, which ended up being Apostel. His stock has climbed since then, with Apostel making his full-season debut in 2019 and finishing the year in high Class A Down East as a 20-year-old.

SCOUTING REPORT: Apostel has a large frame for a third baseman with above-average raw power, something he tapped into with more lift in his swing in 2019. He has a patient approach as well, but the Rangers challenged him to be more aggressive and hunt extra-base hits. At his best, he has a promising combination of plate discipline and power, with the ability to leave the park from right-center over to his pull side without excessive swing-and-miss. A below-average runner, Apostel moves well for a big man, but he has good hands and a plus arm at third base. Even so, he has a thick lower half and there's risk he could get so big that he outgrows the position and flips over to first base.

THE FUTURE: Apostel has the upside to be a regular at third base if he can replicate what he showed there at the upper levels. He should get his first taste of it at Double-A Frisco at some point in 2020.

Year	Age	Club (League)	Class	AVG	G	AB	R	H	2B	3B	HR	RBI	BB	SO	SB	OBP	SLG
2017	18	Pirates (DSL)	R	.258	61	198	43	51	12	4	9	48	56	49	4	.422	.495
2018	19	Bristol (APP)	R	.259	41	139	28	36	7	0	7	26	32	42	3	.406	.460
	19	Spokane (NWL)	SS	.351	12	37	7	13	1	0	1	10	9	8	0	.469	.459
2019	20	Hickory (SAL)	LoA	.258	80	283	38	73	13	1	15	43	28	71	2	.332	.470
	20	Down East (CAR)	HiA	.237	41	135	18	32	5	1	4	16	23	49	0	.352	.378
Minor League Totals				.249	283	963	158	240	45	7	37	152	172	280	10	.368	.426

12 RICKY VANASCO, RHP

BA GRADE
50 Risk: Very High

Born: Oct. 13, 1998. **B-T:** R-R. **HT:** 6-3. **WT:** 205. **Drafted:** HS—Williston, Fla., 2017 (15th round). **Signed by:** Brett Campbell.

TRACK RECORD: The Rangers signed Vanasco for $200,000 as a 15th-round pick in 2017, when he was a lanky and projectable but raw pitcher with a fastball that hit 93 mph. With more strength has come more velocity, as Vanasco generated buzz around the short-season Northwest League for his power arm while he was there before a late August bump to low Class A Hickory.

SCOUTING REPORT: Vanasco has an explosive fastball, sitting in the mid-90s with the ability to reach 99 mph. It's outstanding velocity, especially for a starter, and he mostly just rode that fastball to blow away hitters when he was in the Northwest League. He shows feel to spin a curveball with good depth that serves as his most reliable secondary pitch, flashing above-average at times. The Rangers required Vanasco

to throw a certain number of changeups in his starts to focus on that pitch, which is still below-average and needs more separation off his fastball but showed strides with improved sink. Vanasco can get away with mistakes at this level, but he has scatted control and needs to throw more strikes with his fastball.
THE FUTURE: After emerging as a prospect in 2019, Vanasco will head to low Class A Hickory next.

Year	Age	Club (League)	Class	W	L	ERA	G	GS	SV	IP	H	HR	BB	SO	K/9	WHIP	AVG
2017	18	Rangers (AZL)	R	0	1	0.00	10	0	0	9	8	0	5	16	16.0	1.44	.229
2018	19	Rangers (AZL)	R	3	3	4.38	7	3	0	25	25	1	13	25	9.1	1.54	.287
2019	20	Spokane (NWL)	SS	3	1	1.85	9	9	0	39	23	2	22	59	13.6	1.15	.173
	20	Hickory (SAL)	LoA	0	0	1.69	2	2	0	11	5	0	3	16	13.5	0.75	.143
Minor League Totals				6	5	2.38	28	14	0	83	61	3	43	116	12.5	1.25	.210

13 OSLEIVIS BASABE, SS

BA GRADE 50 Risk: Very High

Born: Sept. 13, 2001. **B-T:** R-R. **HT:** 6-1. **WT:** 165. **Signed:** Venezuela, 2017. **Signed by:** Carlos Plaza/Rafic Saab.

TRACK RECORD: Basabe, who was signed for $500,000 as part of the 2017 international signing class, stood out as an amateur because of his quick-twitch athleticism, but he has also posted impressive offensive numbers in his first two years of pro ball.
SCOUTING REPORT: Basabe's swing isn't pure and his bat path isn't ideal, but he has quick hands, generates fast bat speed and has the hand-eye coordination to make a lot of contact. He's susceptible to chasing, but when he swings at a pitch in the zone, he doesn't miss much. He mostly has gap power with a line-drive approach, but he could grow into 10-15 home run juice once he gets stronger. Basabe is a plus runner with a plus arm. He has the tools to stick at shortstop and could be an average fielder there, though he's still cleaning up his defensive actions to get to that point.
THE FUTURE: There's still rawness to Basabe's game despite his numbers, but the combination of barrel awareness and athleticism up the middle is promising. Low Class A Hickory is his next step.

Year	Age	Club (League)	Class	AVG	G	AB	R	H	2B	3B	HR	RBI	BB	SO	SB	OBP	SLG
2018	17	Rangers1 (DSL)	R	.344	52	192	37	66	16	3	1	34	23	25	12	.414	.474
2019	18	Rangers (AZL)	R	.325	35	151	29	49	2	5	0	31	8	20	7	.355	.404
	18	Spokane (NWL)	SS	.300	2	10	0	3	0	0	0	1	0	1	0	.300	.300
Minor League Totals				.334	89	353	66	118	18	8	1	66	31	46	19	.386	.439

14 COLE WINN, RHP

BA GRADE 50 Risk: Very High

Born: Nov. 25, 1999. **B-T:** R-R. **HT:** 6-2. **WT:** 190. **Drafted:** HS—Orange, Calif., 2018 (1st round). **Signed by:** Steve Flores.

TRACK RECORD: Winn was the BA High School Player of the Year in 2018, the year he went 10th overall in the draft, but it was a rocky debut in 2019. Winn finished June with a 7.59 ERA as he struggled to find the strike zone, but in the second half he rebounded with a 2.81 ERA after the all-star break.
SCOUTING REPORT: Winn has a solid four-pitch mix, working off a low-90s fastball that reaches 95 mph. His curveball was his money pitch in high school, and it flashed a tick above-average in 2019, but it also got slurvy and would blend into his slider. Winn shows good tilt on his slider at times with average potential, but at others it gets loopy, so getting better separation in shape and speed differential will be important for him. The pitch that made the most progress in 2019 was Winn's changeup, a pitch that flashed above-average at best and that some scouts think might end up being his best pitch. Winn has an athletic, explosive delivery and did a better job of staying calm and in sync with his delivery in the second half, which helped him throw more strikes, but he still needs to improve his control and command.
THE FUTURE: With a mix of average to a tick better pitches in his arsenal, Winn has enough upside to develop into a No. 3 or 4 starter. High Class A Down East is up next.

Year	Age	Club (League)	Class	W	L	ERA	G	GS	SV	IP	H	HR	BB	SO	K/9	WHIP	AVG
2018	18	Did not play—Injured															
2019	19	Hickory (SAL)	LoA	4	4	4.46	18	18	0	69	59	5	39	65	8.5	1.43	.233
Minor League Totals				4	4	4.46	18	18	0	68	59	5	39	65	8.5	1.43	.233

15 DAVIS WENDZEL, 3B

BA GRADE 50 Risk: Very High

Born: May 23, 1997. **B-T:** R-R. **HT:** 6-0. **WT:** 205. **Drafted:** Baylor, 2019 (1st round supplemental). **Signed by:** Josh Simpson.

TRACK RECORD: The Rangers used the No. 41 selection in the 2019 draft to take Wendzel, who at 22 was old for his class but consistently performed at a high level for Baylor.

SCOUTING REPORT: Wendzel's swing has some length to it, and he drops his hands to begin his load but is usually on time to make contact, with his ability to recognize pitches and control the strike zone helping to make it work. His power is below-average, with gap shots and occasional over-the-fence pop, but he will probably need to develop at least average power to project as an everyday player. A fringe-average runner, He has the potential to become an above-average fielder at third base. He's a reliable defender with secure hands, good instincts and an above-average arm. He played some shortstop at Baylor, and while he doesn't project to play there long term, the Rangers plan to give him time at third, shortstop and second base.
THE FUTURE: Wendzel's defensive ability should help him get playing time, with an assignment still to be determined for 2020. Developing more power will be key for Wendzel as he faces better competition.

Year	Age	Club (League)	Class	AVG	G	AB	R	H	2B	3B	HR	RBI	BB	SO	SB	OBP	SLG
2019	22	Rangers (AZL)	R	.444	4	9	4	4	1	0	1	2	2	3	0	.545	.889
	22	Spokane (NWL)	SS	.200	3	10	4	2	0	0	0	0	3	3	2	.385	.200
Minor League Totals				.316	7	19	8	6	1	0	1	2	5	6	2	.458	.526

16 DEMARCUS EVANS, RHP

BA GRADE
45 Risk: Medium

Born: Oct. 22, 1996. **B-T:** R-R. **HT:** 6-4. **WT:** 270. **Drafted:** HS—Petal, Miss., 2015 (25th round). **Signed by:** Brian Morrison.

TRACK RECORD: As a reliever between two levels in 2019, Evans struck out 43 percent of the batters he faced. After the season, he went on the 40-man roster to be protected from the Rule 5 draft.
SCOUTING REPORT: Evans is a huge, physical reliever who throws a power invisiball up in the zone, a high-spin fastball at 92-96 mph that hops over bats at an elite rate when he rides it up above the belt. Evans generates a tremendous amount of swing-and-miss off his fastball, to the point where he can carve up minor league hitters with just that pitch. His curveball also flashes above-average, and in the second half he started mixing that pitch in with more frequency, which will be important for him against better hitters. Below-average control is a weakness for Evans, who walked 5.9 batters per nine innings in 2019.
THE FUTURE: Evans is a potential late-inning reliever who could end up a closer if he can throw strikes. He is probably headed for Triple-A to begin 2020 but should be up in Texas at some point during the year.

Year	Age	Club (League)	Class	W	L	ERA	G	GS	SV	IP	H	HR	BB	SO	K/9	WHIP	AVG
2017	20	Rangers (AZL)	R	0	1	11.12	3	3	0	6	6	0	6	10	15.9	2.12	.273
	20	Hickory (SAL)	LoA	2	5	4.85	12	6	0	30	22	1	25	46	14.0	1.58	.198
	20	Spokane (NWL)	SS	0	2	2.59	5	5	0	24	15	0	9	25	9.2	0.99	.171
2018	21	Hickory (SAL)	LoA	4	1	1.77	35	0	9	56	28	1	27	103	16.6	0.98	.149
2019	22	Down East (CAR)	HiA	4	0	0.81	17	0	6	22	9	0	17	40	16.1	1.16	.127
	22	Frisco (TL)	AA	2	0	0.96	30	0	6	38	14	2	22	60	14.3	0.96	.114
Minor League Totals				13	11	2.53	125	26	21	242	147	7	149	369	13.7	1.22	.173

17 JONATHAN HERNANDEZ, RHP

BA GRADE
45 Risk: Medium

Born: July 6, 1996. **B-T:** R-R. **HT:** 6-2. **WT:** 185. **Signed:** Dominican Republic, 2013. **Signed by:** Willy Espinal/Mike Daly.

TRACK RECORD: Hernandez has flashed exciting stuff but, aside from brief spurts, has yet to connect it all consistently in games. With a 5.78 ERA in Triple-A in late July, Hernandez moved to the bullpen and made his major league debut in that role a month later.
SCOUTING REPORT: As a starter, Hernandez sits at 93-96 mph. When he moved to the bullpen, his fastball jumped to the upper 90s with a max of 99 mph. During the first half, his fastball got flat and hitters squared him up for hard contact, so later in the season he went to a heavy two-seam approach to create more sink. He throws a plus slider and he gets a surprising amount of swing-and-miss on a changeup that flashes average. Hernandez has the arsenal of a starter, but his command continues to plague him. He falls behind in the count too often and doesn't locate his fastball well, leading to his struggles.
THE FUTURE: There's a chance Hernandez could still end up as a starter, but he might just stay in the bullpen. He has the weapons be a multi-inning relief threat if he can improve his command.

Year	Age	Club (League)	Class	W	L	ERA	G	GS	SV	IP	H	HR	BB	SO	K/9	WHIP	AVG
2017	20	Hickory (SAL)	LoA	2	5	4.86	9	9	0	46	55	5	13	46	8.9	1.47	.306
	20	Down East (CAR)	HiA	3	6	3.44	14	13	0	65	66	2	31	64	8.8	1.48	.271
2018	21	Down East (CAR)	HiA	4	2	2.20	10	10	0	57	37	6	17	77	12.1	0.94	.184
	21	Frisco (TL)	AA	4	4	4.92	12	12	0	64	58	6	36	57	8.0	1.47	.247
2019	22	Frisco (TL)	AA	5	9	5.16	22	16	0	96	100	11	38	95	8.9	1.44	.267
	22	Texas (AL)	MAJ	2	1	4.32	9	2	0	17	14	3	13	19	10.3	1.62	.219
Major League Totals				2	1	4.32	9	2	0	16	14	3	13	19	10.3	1.62	.219
Minor League Totals				37	39	3.80	129	113	0	610	571	52	235	552	8.1	1.32	.248

18 ANDERSON TEJEDA, SS

BA GRADE
50 Risk: Very High

Born: May 1, 1998. **B-T:** B-R. **HT:** 5-11. **WT:** 185. **Signed:** Dominican Republic, 2014. **Signed by:** Rodolfo Rosario/Roberto Aquino.

TRACK RECORD: Tejeda has shown big tools since signing out of the Dominican Republic for $100,000 in 2014, but with up-and-down performance. His 2019 season lasted just 43 games before a subluxation of his left shoulder while sliding into a base ended his season.

SCOUTING REPORT: Tejeda began switch-hitting in games in 2019. He has little experience from the right side and is understandably raw, so it's not certain he will continue with it long term, though the Rangers plan to have him continue with it in 2020. From the left side, Tejeda has whippy bat speed and plus raw power, a potential 25-plus homer threat who can go deep to all fields. He also has a high swing-and-miss rate in the strike zone and chases too many pitches. Tejeda once faced questions about his ability to stick at shortstop, but improved first-step quickness and footwork have quieted those concerns. There's no question about his arm, a 70 tool that's among the best in the game.

THE FUTURE: Added to the 40-man roster after the season, Tejeda has a chance to be a power-hitting shortstop, but he needs to make more contact as he faces better pitching that can exploit his weaknesses.

Year	Age	Club (League)	Class	AVG	G	AB	R	H	2B	3B	HR	RBI	BB	SO	SB	OBP	SLG
2017	19	Hickory (SAL)	LoA	.247	115	401	68	99	24	9	8	53	36	132	10	.309	.411
2018	20	Down East (CAR)	HiA	.259	121	467	76	121	17	5	19	74	49	142	11	.331	.439
2019	21	Down East (CAR)	HiA	.234	43	158	22	37	10	1	4	24	17	58	9	.315	.386
Minor League Totals				.265	400	1500	248	397	84	31	45	238	145	454	46	.332	.452

19 RYAN GARCIA, RHP

BA GRADE
50 Risk: Very High

Born: Jan. 24, 1998. **B-T:** R-R. **HT:** 6-0. **WT:** 180. **Drafted:** UCLA, 2019 (2nd round). **Signed by:** Todd Guggiana.

TRACK RECORD: After his sophomore year in 2018, Garcia went to the Cape Cod League and struck out 49 batters in 39 innings with a 0.92 ERA. He missed the first three weeks of his junior year at UCLA in 2019 with flexor inflammation, but after returning he earned Pac-12 pitcher of the year honors. The Rangers drafted him in the second round and signed him for $1,469,900 with the No. 50 overall pick.

SCOUTING REPORT: Garcia pitches off a fastball that sits in the low-90s and reaches 95. The pitch plays up because of its late riding life, which helps him miss bats up in the zone. Garcia doesn't have one pitch that grades out plus, but his slider and changeup both flash as 55s on the 20-80 scale and he sprinkles in a fringy curveball at times. It's a solid arsenal that Garcia makes the most out of because of his command and feel for pitching, with deception and ability to mix his stuff to disrupt hitters' timing.

THE FUTURE: Garcia should start 2020 at low Class A Hickory and has the type of pitchability that could help him get to Double-A by the end of the year. He profiles as a back-of-the-rotation starter.

Year	Age	Club (League)	Class	W	L	ERA	G	GS	SV	IP	H	HR	BB	SO	K/9	WHIP	AVG
2019	21	Rangers (AZL)	R	0	0	9.00	1	1	0	1	1	0	1	2	18.0	2.00	.250
	21	Spokane (NWL)	SS	0	0	2.25	2	2	0	4	2	0	1	6	13.5	0.75	.154
Minor League Totals				0	0	3.60	3	3	0	5	3	0	2	8	14.4	1.00	.176

20 HERIBERTO HERNANDEZ, OF/1B/C

BA GRADE
50 Risk: Very High

Born: Dec. 16, 1999. **B-T:** R-R. **HT:** 6-1. **WT:** 180. **Signed:** Dominican Republic, 2017. **Signed by:** Willy Espinal.

TRACK RECORD: Since being signed from the Dominican Republic as a catcher for $10,000 in December 2017, Hernandez has raked, finishing second in the Dominican Summer League in OPS in his debut in 2018, then ranking third in that category in his jump to the Rookie-level Arizona League in 2019.

SCOUTING REPORT: Hernandez gets in a balanced hitting position, generates good leverage and hammers baseballs with raw power that grades out at least plus and translates in games. The best position for Hernandez is in the batter's box. He did catch last year, but he spent most of his time in right field and first base. The Rangers plan to keep giving some exposure to catching in 2020, but if he doesn't play there regularly, it's unlikely he stays there long term. A below-average runner, Hernandez has enough athleticism that he could be able to stay in right field with a slightly above-average arm.

THE FUTURE: A likely right fielder/first baseman coming off his age-19 season in a complex league carries a lot of risk, but Hernandez may have enough offensive impact to deliver. He will have an opportunity to convert more believers if he keeps mashing at low Class A Hickory in 2020.

Year	Age	Club (League)	Class	AVG	G	AB	R	H	2B	3B	HR	RBI	BB	SO	SB	OBP	SLG
2018	18	Rangers2 (DSL)	R	.292	60	178	56	52	15	5	12	49	53	41	5	.464	.635
2019	19	Rangers (AZL)	R	.344	50	192	42	66	17	4	11	48	27	57	3	.433	.646
	19	Spokane (NWL)	SS	.375	3	8	4	3	0	0	0	1	2	3	3	.500	.375
Minor League Totals				.320	113	378	102	121	32	9	23	98	82	101	11	.450	.635

21 BROCK BURKE, LHP

BA GRADE
40 **Risk: Medium**

Born: Aug. 4, 1996. **B-T:** L-L. **HT:** 6-4. **WT:** 200. **Drafted:** HS—Evergreen, Colo., 2014 (3rd round). **Signed by:** Ryan Henderson (Rays).

TRACK RECORD: The Rays traded Burke to the Rangers in the December 2018 deal that sent Jurickson Profar to the Athletics. Early in 2019, Burke dealt with a blister issue and a shoulder impingement that kept him out for two months. He pitched well in Double-A Frisco and reached the major leagues in August, though he got hit around with Texas and his shoulder issues resurfaced at the end of the season.

SCOUTING REPORT: Burke sits at 90-93 mph, with the ability to reach back for 96. He has a four-seamer and a two-seamer, but his fastball didn't have the same zip that it showed in 2018, and Burke ended up relying more heavily on his sinker in 2019. His low-80s slider was an effective pitch for him against Double-A hitters, but it was inconsistent when he reached the major leagues and ran into a lot of barrels. His mid-80s changeup comes in relatively firm off his fastball, and while it doesn't have any standout action or movement, it's a surprisingly effective pitch for him because of his ability to sell it with good arm speed and deception to keep hitters off balance.

THE FUTURE: Burke doesn't have one knockout pitch, but his stuff across the board is good enough to give him a chance as a back-end starter. He should get another shot to fill that role in Texas in 2020.

Year	Age	Club (League)	Class	W	L	ERA	G	GS	SV	IP	H	HR	BB	SO	K/9	WHIP	AVG
2017	20	Bowling Green (MWL)	LoA	6	0	1.10	10	10	0	57	37	0	20	59	9.3	0.99	.181
	20	Charlotte, FL (FSL)	HiA	5	6	4.64	13	13	0	66	75	6	16	49	6.7	1.38	.291
2018	21	Charlotte, FL (FSL)	HiA	3	5	3.84	16	13	0	82	85	4	30	87	9.5	1.40	.263
	21	Montgomery (SL)	AA	6	1	1.95	9	9	0	55	39	2	14	71	11.5	0.96	.193
2019	22	Rangers (AZL)	R	0	0	0.00	1	1	0	4	2	0	0	3	6.8	0.50	.154
	22	Hickory (SAL)	LoA	0	0	7.20	1	1	0	5	9	0	0	1	1.8	1.80	.429
	22	Frisco (TL)	AA	3	5	3.18	9	9	0	45	34	2	12	49	9.7	1.01	.205
	22	Nashville (PCL)	AAA	0	0	7.88	2	2	0	8	12	1	6	11	12.4	2.25	.343
	22	Texas (AL)	MAJ	0	2	7.43	6	6	0	27	30	6	11	14	4.7	1.54	.286
Major League Totals				0	2	7.43	6	6	0	26	30	6	11	14	4.7	1.54	.286
Minor League Totals				30	25	3.48	93	87	0	450	416	20	150	438	8.8	1.26	.244

22 STEELE WALKER, OF

BA GRADE
45 **Risk: High**

Age: 23. **B-T:** L-L. **HT:** 5-11. **WT:** 190. **Drafted:** Oklahoma, 2018 (2nd round). **Signed by:** Rob Cummings (White Sox).

TRACK RECORD: Walker earned a rep as an amateur—both at Oklahoma and in summer college leagues—as a talented hitter and the White Sox selected him in 2018 and signed him for $2 million. A lingering oblique injury put a damper on his production in his first pro season, then in December the White Sox traded him to the Rangers for outfielder Nomar Mazara.

SCOUTING REPORT: Walker turned 23 during the 2019 season, putting him on the older side for a Class A prospect, with a mix of average or near-average tools across the board. He's a high-contact hitter who tracks pitches well, striking out in just 15 percent of his plate appearances. He has lift in his swing with average power that shows up mostly to the pull side. With average speed and arm strength, Walker is athletic enough to play center field in the minors, but a lot of scouts expect him to slide over to a corner, creating some tweener risk in his profile unless his power jumps.

THE FUTURE: Walker will get his first taste of the upper levels when he heads to Double-A Frisco in 2020. He might be a reserve outfielder, though there's a chance his hitting is good enough to carry him in an everyday role.

Year	Age	Club (League)	Class	AVG	G	AB	R	H	2B	3B	HR	RBI	BB	SO	SB	OBP	SLG
2018	21	White Sox (AZL)	R	.455	4	11	0	5	0	0	0	0	1	1	0	.538	.455
	21	Great Falls (PIO)	R	.206	9	34	4	7	1	0	2	4	1	7	1	.263	.412
	21	Kannapolis (SAL)	LoA	.186	31	113	13	21	5	0	3	17	8	29	5	.246	.310
2019	22	Kannapolis (SAL)	LoA	.365	20	74	6	27	10	3	0	11	8	15	4	.437	.581
	22	Winston-Salem (CAR)	HiA	.269	100	383	59	103	26	2	10	51	42	63	9	.346	.426
Minor League Totals				.265	164	615	82	163	42	5	15	83	60	115	19	.338	.423

23 BUBBA THOMPSON, OF

BA GRADE
50 **Risk: Extreme**

Born: June 9, 1998. **B-T:** R-R. **HT:** 6-2. **WT:** 185. **Drafted:** HS—Mobile, Ala., 2017 (1st round). **Signed by:** Brian Morrison.

TRACK RECORD: An all-state quarterback who could have played Division 1 football, Thompson took his athleticism to the Rangers instead, signing for $2.1 million out of high school. Still an elite athlete, Thompson is also raw and missed significant development time in 2019 having surgery to repair a broken hamate bone in his left hand, then after returning missed a month after running into an outfield wall.

SCOUTING REPORT: Thompson is an athletic center fielder and a plus-plus runner underway. His reads and routes still need work, but he has good range and closing speed to go with an average arm. Thompson has fast hands and slightly above-average pop that has a chance to be plus. However, Thompson's swing and approach will need significant adjustments. He will have to shorten up his stroke to close holes and cut down on his chase rate, all of which contributes to too many empty swings.

THE FUTURE: Thompson's athleticism and raw tools stack up among the best in the system, with a shot as a dynamic power/speed threat, but he will need to iron out a lot at the plate to reach that upside.

Year	Age	Club (League)	Class	AVG	G	AB	R	H	2B	3B	HR	RBI	BB	SO	SB	OBP	SLG
2017	19	Rangers (AZL)	R	.257	30	113	23	29	7	2	3	12	6	28	5	.317	.434
2018	20	Hickory (SAL)	LoA	.289	84	332	52	96	18	5	8	42	23	104	32	.344	.446
2019	21	Down East (CAR)	HiA	.178	57	202	24	36	8	2	5	21	21	72	12	.261	.312
Minor League Totals				.249	171	647	99	161	33	9	16	75	50	204	49	.313	.402

24 DAVID GARCIA, C

BA GRADE
50 **Risk: Extreme**

Born: Feb. 6, 2000. **B-T:** B-R. **HT:** 5-11. **WT:** 170. **Signed:** Venezuela, 2016. **Signed by:** Johnny Gomez.

TRACK RECORD: Garcia was one of the top catchers in the 2016 international class when the Rangers signed him out of Venezuela for $800,000. He struggled in his pro debut in the Dominican Summer League and didn't deliver much offensive impact his first two seasons, but added strength helped his performance tick up in 2019 as a top prospect in the short-season Northwest League.

SCOUTING REPORT: Garcia has the attributes to be an average to above-average defensive catcher. He receives and blocks well for his age and he has a plus arm. His feet work well behind the plate, he gets rid of the ball quickly and makes on-target throws. Garcia has a simple, fluid swing from both sides of the plate, showing good bat-to-ball skills and a solid eye for the strike zone. Getting stronger led to a jump in his extra-base hit numbers, though he's more of a line-drive hitter with enough strength projection to grow into a 10-15 home run hitter.

THE FUTURE: Going to full-season ball in the low Class A South Atlantic League in 2020 will be a big test for Garcia to show he has enough offensive ability to be a starting catcher.

Year	Age	Club (League)	Class	AVG	G	AB	R	H	2B	3B	HR	RBI	BB	SO	SB	OBP	SLG
2017	17	Rangers2 (DSL)	R	.215	58	186	27	40	7	1	1	26	25	49	1	.321	.280
2018	18	Rangers (AZL)	R	.269	34	119	10	32	8	0	1	20	9	26	0	.320	.361
2019	19	Spokane (NWL)	SS	.277	48	184	33	51	14	0	5	29	21	42	1	.351	.435
Minor League Totals				.252	140	489	70	123	29	1	7	75	55	117	2	.332	.358

25 KEITHRON MOSS, 2B/3B

BA GRADE
50 **Risk: Extreme**

Born: Aug. 20, 2001. **B-T:** B-R. **HT:** 5-11. **WT:** 165. **Signed:** Bahamas, 2017. **Signed by:** Cliff Terracuso/Ross Fenstermaker.

TRACK RECORD: Moss signed for $800,000 out of the Bahamas as part of the 2017 international class. After struggling in his pro debut in the Dominican Summer League as an athletic 16-year-old, Moss moved up to the Rookie-level in 2019 and showed vast improvement, drawing buzz around the Arizona League as one of the league's top prospects.

SCOUTING REPORT: Getting stronger in 2019 was important for Moss, who was physically underdeveloped when he arrived in pro ball, and didn't have much experience against good competition coming out of the Bahamas. As Moss got more repetitions facing better velocity, his results improved. He's a good athlete with fast hands and a line-drive stroke, with some swing-and-miss to his game but a patient, all-fields approach and puts a surprising charge into the ball to his pull side, though his power is mostly to the gaps. A solid-average runner, Moss is still trying to find a defensive position, splitting time between second and third base, with a fringe-average arm that probably makes second base his best fit.

THE FUTURE: Moss is raw, but he was one of the most improved players in the system in 2019. Short-season Spokane could be up next, but he might be ready for low Class A Hickory at some point in 2020.

Year	Age	Club (League)	Class	AVG	G	AB	R	H	2B	3B	HR	RBI	BB	SO	SB	OBP	SLG
2018	16	Rangers1 (DSL)	R	.196	51	163	29	32	11	1	0	23	35	62	8	.350	.276
2019	17	Rangers (AZL)	R	.308	34	120	27	37	4	3	2	14	21	40	8	.425	.442
Minor League Totals				.244	85	283	56	69	15	4	2	37	56	102	16	.381	.346

26 RANDY FLORENTINO, C

Born: July 5, 2000. **B-T:** L-R. **HT:** 5-11. **WT:** 175. **Signed:** Dominican Republic, 2017. **Signed by:** Danilo Troncoso.

TRACK RECORD: Florentino didn't generate a lot of attention when he signed with the Rangers out of the Dominican Republic for $25,000 in 2017, but he did the next year after ranking third in the Dominican Summer League in OPS. In 2019, Florentino hit well in the beginning of the Rookie-level Arizona League season but looked worn down by the end and his performance regressed.

SCOUTING REPORT: Florentino makes frequent hard, quality contact with a smooth lefthanded swing that's short and stays through the hitting zone a long time. He takes a good path to the ball and does a good job of knowing which pitches to turn on for extra-base damage, with the power potential to eventually be a 20-25 home run guy. An offensive-minded catcher when he signed, Florentino made progress defensively the last two years and looks like he should stick behind the plate. He has a slightly above-average arm and did significant work cleaning up his blocking and receiving in 2019, with the athleticism and flexibility to get into good positions and move around well behind the dish.

THE FUTURE: Florentino needs to get stronger to handle a full season's workload. There's a long way to go for him to be an everyday guy, but there's upside for him to be a power-hitting catcher. With David Garcia ahead of him at low Class A Hickory, Florentino might go to short-season Spokane in 2020.

Year	Age	Club (League)	Class	AVG	G	AB	R	H	2B	3B	HR	RBI	BB	SO	SB	OBP	SLG
2018	17	Rangers2 (DSL)	R	.309	60	191	48	59	18	5	6	35	53	51	8	.454	.550
2019	18	Rangers (AZL)	R	.243	39	140	18	34	4	1	2	19	25	39	0	.353	.329
	18	Spokane (NWL)	SS	.250	1	4	0	1	0	0	0	2	0	2	0	.250	.250
Minor League Totals				.281	100	335	66	94	22	6	8	56	78	92	8	.411	.454

27 JULIO PABLO MARTINEZ, OF

BA GRADE **45** Risk: High

Born: March 21, 1996. **B-T:** L-L. **HT:** 5-9. **WT:** 175. **Drafted:** Cuba, 2018. **Signed by:** Willy Espinal/Jose Fernndez.

TRACK RECORD: Martinez was one of the best players his age in Cuba before he left the country and signed with the Rangers for $2.8 million in March 2018. After making his debut that year in short-season Spokane, Martinez jumped to high Class A Down East in 2019 and struggled there at first, batting .191/.263/.365 in the first half, but he rebounded to hit .293/.362/.467 in the second half.

SCOUTING REPORT: Martinez has a smaller frame but good tools, with strong wrists that help him whip the barrel through the zone and produce slightly above-average raw power. His swing can get long and he struggled to track breaking pitches in the first half, leading to a 32 percent strikeout rate in Down East, but he did a better job recognizing pitches in the second half. Martinez has plus speed to handle center field with average defense and an average arm.

THE FUTURE: Martinez has a promising power/speed combo, but now that he's had a full season in pro ball he has to to shorten his swing and make more contact. Double-A Frisco is up next.

Year	Age	Club (League)	Class	AVG	G	AB	R	H	2B	3B	HR	RBI	BB	SO	SB	OBP	SLG
2017	21	Trois-Rivieres (C-A)	IND	.297	57	236	48	70	11	2	7	21	17	56	20	.345	.449
2018	22	Rangers1 (DSL)	R	.409	7	22	10	9	1	1	1	3	9	7	2	.606	.682
	22	Spokane (NWL)	SS	.252	60	234	49	59	9	5	8	21	34	69	11	.351	.436
2019	23	Hickory (SAL)	LoA	.250	10	40	7	10	1	1	1	5	3	12	4	.295	.400
	23	Down East (CAR)	HiA	.248	113	407	59	101	21	4	14	58	39	144	28	.319	.423
Minor League Totals				.255	190	703	125	179	32	11	24	87	85	232	45	.340	.434

28 TAYLOR HEARN, LHP

BA GRADE **40** Risk: Medium

Born: Aug. 30, 1994. **B-T:** L-L. **HT:** 6-5. **WT:** 210. **Drafted:** Oklahoma Baptist, 2015 (5th round). **Signed by:** Ed Gustafson (Nationals).

TRACK RECORD: The Nationals drafted Hearn, traded him and Felipe Vasquez to the Pirates one year later for Mark Melancon. Two seasons later, the Pirates flipped him to the Rangers for Keone Kela. In 2019, Hearn made four Triple-A starts and made his major league debut in April, but he injured his elbow during that outing and didn't pitch the rest of the season.

SCOUTING REPORT: Hearn has a big fastball, sitting in the mid-90s with the ability to reach 98 mph.

He gives hitters a difficult angle on his fastball and he creates good extension out front, which helps his fastball play up, especially when he elevates. Everything beyond Hearn's fastball lagged behind last year. He showed progress with his slider the previous year, but it wasn't effective for him, while his changeup is a fringe-average offering. Hearn needs to sharpen his secondary pitches to be able to miss more bats, but he also needs to improve his fastball command.

THE FUTURE: Hearn, who will turn 26 before the end of the season, is healthy and ready to go for spring training. The Rangers plan to keep him as a starter, but there's a good chance he ends up in a relief role.

Year	Age	Club (League)	Class	W	L	ERA	G	GS	SV	IP	H	HR	BB	SO	K/9	WHIP	AVG
2017	22	Bradenton (FSL)	HiA	4	6	4.12	18	17	0	87	65	8	37	106	10.9	1.17	.207
	22	Pirates (GCL)	R	0	0	0.00	1	1	0	2	0	0	0	3	13.5	0.00	.000
2018	23	Altoona (EL)	AA	3	6	3.12	19	19	0	104	75	6	38	107	9.3	1.09	.198
	23	Frisco (TL)	AA	1	2	5.04	5	5	0	25	29	5	9	33	11.9	1.52	.284
2019	24	Nashville (PCL)	AAA	1	3	4.05	4	4	0	20	14	3	10	26	11.7	1.20	.200
	24	Texas (AL)	MAJ	0	1	108.00	1	1	0	0	3	0	4	0	0.0	21.00	.750
Major League Totals				0	1	108.00	1	1	0	0	3	0	4	0	0.0	21.00	.750
Minor League Totals				12	23	3.51	77	64	0	338	278	30	132	395	10.5	1.21	.222

29 ZION BANNISTER, OF

BA GRADE 50 Risk: Extreme

Born: Sept. 9, 2001. **B-T:** R-R. **HT:** 6-3. **WT:** 191. **Signed:** Bahamas, 2019. **Signed by:** Cliff Terracuso/Ross Fenstermaker.

TRACK RECORD: Born in the Bahamas, Bannister moved to Maryland from 2015-17 and played high school baseball there. In 2017, he moved to the Dominican Republic to train, then moved back to the Bahamas before signing with the Rangers for $836,000 as a 17-year-old on July 2, 2019.

SCOUTING REPORT: Bannister is an impressive, physical athlete with power/speed potential at a premium position. He played shortstop as an amateur but has spent most of his time in center field since signing and fits best there. He's a plus runner who moves around well in the outfield with fluid actions and the potential for good range, though he's still learning to take better reads and routes. Before signing, Bannister hit from both sides of the plate, but he's now batting righthanded only. It's a power-over-hit profile, with the bat speed, strength projection and leverage in his swing to develop plus raw power in the future. He has an efficient swing and stays through the ball well, but his power will probably come with strikeouts, as he needs to improve his timing to make more frequent contact.

THE FUTURE: Bannister's upside is exciting, but he's still a project. He's not advanced enough for a full-season assignment yet, so he's likely staying back in extended spring training to start 2020.

Year	Age	Club (League)	Class	AVG	G	AB	R	H	2B	3B	HR	RBI	BB	SO	SB	OBP	SLG
2019	17	Rangers2 (DSL)	R	.300	2	10	2	3	0	0	0	0	0	1	0	.300	.300
	17	Rangers (AZL)	R	.250	4	12	1	3	1	0	0	1	2	8	0	.357	.333
Minor League Totals				.273	6	22	3	6	1	0	0	1	2	9	0	.333	.318

30 TYLER PHILLIPS, RHP

BA GRADE 45 Risk: High

Born: Oct. 27, 1997. **B-T:** R-R. **HT:** 6-5. **WT:** 200. **Drafted:** HS—Pennsauken, N.J., 2015 (16th round). **Signed by:** Takeshi Sakurayama.

TRACK RECORD: Phillips put himself on the prospect map in 2018 and started strong in 2019, breezing through six starts in the high Class A Carolina League before a promotion to Double-A Frisco, where he struggled and got hit harder against better hitters.

SCOUTING REPORT: Phillips has plus control of a low-90s fastball. It's not overpowering, but he locates it well to all quadrants of the strike zone. His best pitch is his plus changeup, which he sells well to disguise as a fastball coming out of his hand before it drops with late sink and fade to get swings and misses or weak contact. Phillips' lack of a reliable breaking ball has been a red flag with him. His curveball is below-average, so the Rangers introduced a slider into his repertoire later in the 2019 season that he's still working on.

THE FUTURE: If the slider turns into a reliable pitch for Phillips he could develop into a back-end starter.

Year	Age	Club (League)	Class	W	L	ERA	G	GS	SV	IP	H	HR	BB	SO	K/9	WHIP	AVG
2017	19	Hickory (SAL)	LoA	1	2	6.39	7	4	0	25	28	2	9	15	5.3	1.46	.280
	19	Spokane (NWL)	SS	4	2	3.45	13	13	0	73	78	6	11	78	9.6	1.22	.265
2018	20	Hickory (SAL)	LoA	11	5	2.67	22	22	0	128	117	4	14	124	8.7	1.02	.239
	20	Down East (CAR)	HiA	1	0	1.80	1	1	0	5	2	0	2	3	5.4	0.80	.125
2019	21	Down East (CAR)	HiA	2	2	1.19	6	6	0	38	28	1	6	28	6.7	0.90	.212
	21	Frisco (TL)	AA	7	9	4.73	18	16	0	93	95	15	20	74	7.1	1.23	.263
Minor League Totals				30	28	3.86	93	75	1	436	439	32	83	389	8.0	1.20	.257

Toronto Blue Jays

BY BEN BADLER

After three straight losing seasons in Toronto, the Blue Jays look likely to miss the playoffs again in 2020.

Yes, there are promising signs for the future, starting with the Vlad and Bo show that arrived in Toronto in 2019. Third baseman Vladimir Guerrero Jr. debuted in the big leagues at 20, and while he didn't immediately provide Juan Soto-level production, he showed the combination of hitting ability and elite power that could one day put him in MVP conversations. Bo Bichette took over at shortstop right before the trade deadline and raked, looking like a future perennial all-star candidate.

Guerrero and Bichette could form one of the best left sides of the infield in baseball for the next half decade in Toronto, and the emergence of Lourdes Gurriel Jr. and Cavan Biggio give the Blue Jays two more young players who could be regulars in the lineup of their next playoff team.

To get back to the playoffs for the first time since 2016, however, they're going to need a lot of help, especially on the pitching side. The Blue Jays rotation is full of back-end, up-and-down starter types who don't project to be league-average pitchers. That should change as soon as their top prospect, righthander Nate Pearson, arrives in 2020. Pearson should be the Blue Jays' best starter right away, armed with one of the best fastballs in the game, an out pitch slider and the stuff to develop into a true No. 1 starter who can anchor their rotation.

Whether it's through trades, free agency or both, the Blue Jays will need to find more pitching to help Pearson. They started that process in 2019 at the trade deadline when they moved Marcus Stroman to the Mets in exchange for righthander Simeon Woods Richardson and lefthander Anthony Kay. Woods Richardson has more upside, with a chance to develop into a mid-rotation or better arm, but he has yet to pitch above high Class A. Kay projects as a back-end starter who should be ready to contribute in 2020.

And even after graduating two of the top 10 prospects in baseball in 2019, the Blue Jays still have a strong farm system. Pearson is one of the game's best pitching prospects. Shortstop Jordan Groshans spent most of the year on the injured list and is still at least a couple years away from the big leagues, but when healthy, he showed the potential to be an impact player. Catchers Alejandro Kirk and Gabriel Moreno both performed well at the Class A levels, while shortstops Orelvis Martinez and Miguel Hiraldo and righthander

MITCHELL LAYTON/GETTY IMAGES

Vladimir Guerrero Jr. ranked as the No. 1 prospect in baseball when he made his debut.

PROJECTED 2023 LINEUP

Position	Player	Age
Catcher	Danny Jansen	28
First Base	Vladimir Guerrero Jr.	24
Second Base	Cavan Biggio	28
Third Base	Jordan Groshans (2)	23
Shortstop	Bo Bichette	25
Left Field	Lourdes Gurriel Jr.	29
Center Field	Teoscar Hernandez	30
Right Field	Griffin Conine	26
Designated Hitter	Alejandro Kirk (4)	24
No. 1 Starter	Nate Pearson (1)	26
No. 2 Starter	Simeon Woods Richardson (3)	22
No. 3 Starter	Alek Manoah (5)	25
No. 4 Starter	Anthony Kay (9)	28
No. 5 Starter	Trent Thornton	29
Closer	Sean Reid-Foley	27

Adam Kloffenstein all ranked as top five prospects in their short-season and Rookie-level leagues. The system is filled with promising Latin American prospects at the lower levels, bolstered by another deep group of international signings the Blue Jays added in 2019.

With more development from their young core of hitters who reached Toronto the last two seasons, the Blue Jays should be better in 2020 than they were last year.

But even with a strong farm system, they will need to supplement their major league roster through smart free agent signings and trades if they want to compete for a playoff spot in 2021 and beyond.

DEPTH CHART

TORONTO BLUE JAYS

TOP 2020 ROOKIE: Nate Pearson, RHP. He should be Toronto's best starter as soon as he gets to the big leagues, with an electric arsenal led be one of the best fastballs in the game.

BREAKOUT PROSPECT: Estiven Machado, SS. A 2019 international signing from Venezuela, Machado is a quick-twitch athlete with a compact swing from both sides of the plate.

SLEEPER: Dahian Santos, rhp. Santos was a July 2 signing out of Venezuela in 2019 and his stuff has already jumped, reaching 94 mph with his fastball as a 16-year-old.

SOURCE OF TOP 30 TALENT

Homegrown	**26**	**Acquired**	**4**
College	6	Trade	4
Junior college	1	Rule 5 draft	0
High school	6	Independent league	0
Nondrafted free agent	0	Free agent/waivers	0
International	13		

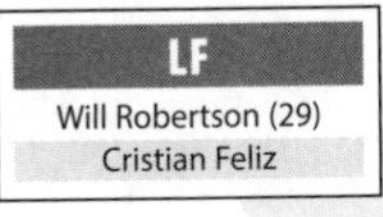

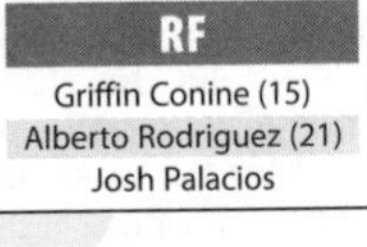

SS

Jordan Groshans (2)
Orelvis Martinez (6)
Miguel Hiraldo (8)
Estiven Machado (13)
Leonardo Jimenez (16)
Rikelvin de Castro (17)
Santiago Espinal (20)
Kevin Smith (25)
Kevin Vicuna
Addison Barger

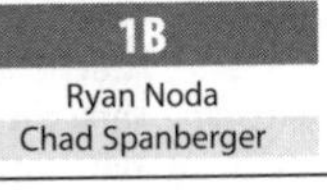

C

Alejandro Kirk (4)
Gabriel Moreno (7)
Victor Mesia (19)
Reese McGuire (23)
Riley Adams
Javier D'Orazio
Philip Clarke

LHP

LHSP	LHRP
Anthony Kay (9)	Rafael Monsion

RHP

RHSP	RHRP
Nate Pearson (1)	Hector Perez
Simeon Woods Richardson (3)	
Alek Manoah (5)	
Adam Kloffenstein (10)	
Eric Pardinho (11)	
Kendall Williams (14)	
Patrick Murphy (18)	
Joey Murray (26)	
Yennsy Diaz (27)	
Sem Robberse (30)	
Dahian Santos	
Yosver Zulueta	
T.J. Zeuch	
Maximo Castillo	
Josh Winckowski	

DRAFT ANALYSIS

2019

BEST PURE HITTER: SS Tanner Morris (5) put together three seasons of high offensive performance at Virginia. Between his pure hitting ability and plate discipline, he has a chance to be a high on-base percentage player, with an approach geared toward hitting the ball toward the middle or opposite field. OF Will Robertson (4) and C Philip Clarke (9) are two other college bats who stood out from Toronto's draft class.

BEST POWER: Robertson has above-average power from the left side. He hit 15 home runs at Creighton, then tacked on six more with short-season Vancouver. OF Nick Neal (11), a two-sport athlete who also played football in high school, also stood out for his power.

FASTEST RUNNER: OF Dasan Brown (3) immediately becomes one of the fastest players in baseball, an 80-grade runner on the 20-to-80 scouting scale.

BEST DEFENSIVE PLAYER: Brown's top-of-the-scale speed gives him a chance to be an elite defender. SS Glenn Santiago (10) has shown promising athleticism and defensive potential at shortstop, while the Blue Jays value SS Cameron Eden's (6) versatility to play either shortstop or center field.

BEST ATHLETE: Brown has some crudeness to his baseball skills, but he is an outstanding athlete.

BEST FASTBALL: RHP Alek Manoah (1) was the prize of the Toronto's draft class. He can overpower hitters with a fastball in the mid- to upper 90s.

BEST SECONDARY PITCH: Manoah's slider is a plus pitch at times. As a high school draft pick, RHP Kendall Williams (2) is younger than Manoah and doesn't have as much present stuff, but his curveball, slider and changeup all flash promising projection indicators for the future, especially his breaking pitches.

BEST PRO DEBUT: Manoah didn't get to pitch much, but he dominated in his 17 innings, posting a 27-to-5 strikeout-to-walk ratio with a 2.65 ERA. Williams also made the most of his limited work in the Rookie-level Gulf Coast League, while former Penn State C Dalton Sloninger (38) hit .304/.379/.551 between Rookie-level Bluefield and short-season Vancouver.

MOST INTRIGUING BACKGROUND: The Blue Jays drafted RHP Braden Halladay (32), son of Roy Halladay, knowing he would go to Penn State rather than sign out of high school.

CLOSEST TO THE MAJORS: Manoah shouldn't need much time at the Class A levels, so he could end 2020 in the upper levels with a chance to make his major league debut in 2021.

BEST LATE-ROUND PICK: With a smaller, compact frame at 5-foot-10, 180 pounds, RHP Michael Dominguez (15) doesn't jump out physically, but he had immediate success in the Rookie-level Gulf Coast League. He's a strike-thrower who pitches at 89-93 mph with good deception, reaches 95 mph and throws a solid breaking ball.

THE ONE WHO GOT AWAY: The Blue Jays knew there was a slim chance of signing RHP/C Nathaniel LaRue (25) that late in the draft based on his asking price and their pool limits. He has a chance to boost his stock at Auburn, armed with a low-90s fastball and a breaking ball flashing plus.

—**BEN BADLER**

TOP DRAFT PICKS OF THE DECADE

Year	Player, Pos.	2019 Org
2010	Deck McGuire, RHP	Korea
2011	*Tyler Beede, RHP	Giants
2012	D.J. Davis, OF	Did not play
2013	*Phil Bickford, RHP	Brewers
2014	Jeff Hoffman, RHP	Rockies
2015	Jon Harris, RHP	Blue Jays
2016	T.J. Zeuch, RHP	Blue Jays
2017	Logan Warmoth, SS	Blue Jays
2018	Jordan Groshans, SS	Blue Jays
2019	Alek Manoah, RHP	Blue Jays

* Did not sign

2018

SS Jordan Groshans (1) continues to be the class' headliner, despite a foot injury that cost him most of his first full pro season. OF Griffin Conine (2) and RHP Adam Kloffenstein (3) also offer strong upside.

GRADE: B

2017

RHP Nate Pearson (1) has become one of baseball's best pitching prospects and should soon reach Toronto. The class' grade takes a hit because fellow first-round pick SS Logan Warmoth (1) has struggled.

GRADE: B

2016

The Blue Jays have gotten three big leaguers from this class, led by SS Bo Bichette (2) and 2B Cavan Biggio (5), who could form their double-play combination for years to come. Bichette has all-star upside.

GRADE: A

1 NATE PEARSON, RHP

Born: Aug. 20, 1996. **B-T:** R-R. **HT:** 6-6. **WT:** 245.
Drafted: JC of Central Florida, 2017 (1st round).
Signed by: Matt Bishoff.

TRACK RECORD: Pearson pitched mostly out of the bullpen for Florida International as a freshman before transferring to the JC of Central Florida in 2017. While there, his stock climbed. The Blue Jays drafted him 28th overall that year and signed him for $2,452,900. In 2018, a back injury prevented Pearson from pitching until May 7. He returned, threw 1.2 innings, then didn't pitch again during the regular season when a line drive fractured his forearm, though he came back for the Arizona Fall League. In 2019, Pearson made a case as the best pitching prospect in the minors as he rose three levels to finish the year in Triple-A.

SCOUTING REPORT: Pearson has an extra-large frame and an elite fastball. He sits in the upper 90s, regularly touches triple digits and has climbed as high as 104 mph in the AFL in 2018. His fastball rides up and explodes with late life in the zone. One of the biggest leaps forward for Pearson came with his slider. It was a slurvy, low-80s pitch in college that he sharpened after his first year. Now it's a legitimate out pitch, earning plus or better grades and flashing plus-plus potential with power and late tilt. Pearson hasn't needed to use his changeup much, but it gives him a third legitimate weapon as a solid-average pitch, while his curveball is more of a fringy pitch he mixes in every once in a while. Pearson fills the strike zone and has an athletic, efficient delivery that he repeats well. That all points to a durable starter, but questions remain. His 101.2 innings were a career high, though he hasn't missed time due to operations or issues with his throwing arm. However, the Blue Jays kept Pearson on a restrictive workload. He alternated between starts of five and two innings by design for most of his Double-A time, though he threw 90-plus pitches in five of his final seven starts, including 100-plus pitches in two of them. The fact that Pearson throws with so much velocity on every fastball also gives some scouts concerns about whether that's a durability risk.

THE FUTURE: If Pearson shows he can handle a starter's workload, he can be a frontline arm with potential to be a No. 1 or 2 starter. He's probably headed back to Triple-A to begin 2020, but he's one of the Blue Jays' five best starting pitchers right now and should be in Toronto by midseason.

MIKE JANES/FOUR SEAM

BA GRADE
70 **Risk:** Medium

SCOUTING GRADES
FB: 80. **SL:** 60. **CHG:** 55. **CB:** 45. **CTL:** 55.

Projected future grades on 20-80 scouting scale.

TOP PROSPECTS OF THE DECADE

Year	Player, Pos.	2019 Org
2010	Zach Stewart, RHP	Atlantic League
2011	Kyle Drabek, RHP	Did not play
2012	Travis d'Arnaud, C	Rays
2013	Travis d'Arnaud, C	Rays
2014	Aaron Sanchez, RHP	Astros
2015	Daniel Norris, LHP	Tigers
2016	Anthony Alford, OF	Blue Jays
2017	Vladimir Guerrero Jr., 3B	Blue Jays
2018	Vladimir Guerrero Jr., 3B	Blue Jays
2019	Vladimir Guerrero Jr., 3B	Blue Jays

BEST TOOLS

Best Hitter for Average	Jordan Groshans
Best Power Hitter	Griffin Conine
Best Strike-Zone Discipline	Alejandro Kirk
Fastest Baserunner	Dasan Brown
Best Athlete	Dasan Brown
Best Fastball	Nate Pearson
Best Curveball	Eric Pardinho
Best Slider	Nate Pearson
Best Changeup	Nate Pearson
Best Control	Simeon Woods Richardson
Best Defensive Catcher	Reese McGuire
Best Defensive Infielder	Rikelbin de Castro
Best Infield Arm	Jordan Groshans
Best Defensive Outfielder	Dasan Brown
Best Outfield Arm	Chavez Young

Year	Age	Club (League)	Class	W	L	ERA	G	GS	SV	IP	H	HR	BB	SO	K/9	WHIP	AVG
2017	20	Blue Jays (GCL)	R	0	0	0.00	1	1	0	1	1	0	0	2	18.0	1.00	.250
	20	Vancouver (NWL)	SS	0	0	0.95	7	7	0	19	6	0	5	24	11.4	0.58	.097
2018	21	Dunedin (FSL)	HiA	0	1	10.80	1	1	0	2	5	1	0	1	5.4	3.00	.500
2019	22	Dunedin (FSL)	HiA	3	0	0.86	6	6	0	21	10	2	3	35	15.0	0.62	.139
	22	New Hampshire (EL)	AA	1	4	2.59	16	16	0	63	41	4	21	69	9.9	0.99	.186
	22	Buffalo (IL)	AAA	1	0	3.00	3	3	0	18	12	2	3	15	7.5	0.83	.185
Minor League Totals				5	5	2.19	34	34	0	123	75	9	32	146	10.7	0.87	.173

2 JORDAN GROSHANS, SS

Born: July 20, 1998. **B-T:** R-R. **HT:** 6-3. **WT:** 205. **Drafted:** HS—Magnolia, Texas, 2018 (1st round). **Signed by:** Brian Johnston.

BA GRADE
65 Risk: Very High

TRACK RECORD: Groshans generated positive buzz the summer after he signed for $3.4 million as the 12th overall pick in the 2018 draft. The arrows continued pointing up in 2019 after a hot start at low Class A, but a left foot injury limited him to just 23 games the entire season and he didn't play after May 13.

SCOUTING REPORT: When healthy, Groshans looked like one of the top offensive forces in the lower levels. He has a long frame and generates fast bat speed, with a knack for being on time. He has athletic hitting actions and an advanced approach for his age, with the ability to hammer premium velocity while also recognizing offspeed pitches and has the malleability in his body and swing to barrel soft stuff. He has good plate coverage, particularly for a taller hitter, and he has plus power to drive the ball out of the park from right-center over to his pull side. At shortstop, Groshans has an above-average arm and gets good reads off the bat, though his first-step quickness and range lead a lot of scouts to project a move to third base. He has the attributes to develop into an above-average defender if he moves to third base.

THE FUTURE: Health is the only thing that has held back Groshans, who has a chance to develop into a plus regular who could hit toward the top or middle of a big league lineup.

SCOUTING GRADES: **Hitting:** 60 **Power:** 60 **Running:** 50 **Fielding:** 50 **Arm:** 60

Year	Age	Club (League)	Class	AVG	G	AB	R	H	2B	3B	HR	RBI	BB	SO	SB	OBP	SLG
2018	18	Blue Jays (GCL)	R	.331	37	142	17	47	12	0	4	39	13	29	0	.390	.500
	18	Bluefield (APP)	R	.182	11	44	4	8	1	0	1	4	2	8	0	.229	.273
2019	19	Lansing (MWL)	LoA	.337	23	83	12	28	6	0	2	13	13	21	1	.427	.482
Minor League Totals				.309	71	269	33	83	19	0	7	56	28	58	1	.376	.457

3 SIMEON WOODS RICHARDSON, RHP

Born: Sept. 27, 2000. **B-T:** R-R. **HT:** 6-3. **WT:** 215. **Drafted:** HS—Sugar Land, Texas, 2018 (2nd round). **Signed by:** Ray Corbett (Mets).

TRACK RECORD: Woods Richardson was one of the youngest players in the 2018 draft when he signed with the Mets as the 48th overall pick. One year later, he was the key prospect the Mets sent to Toronto in the Marcus Stroman deal and finished the year with a strong showing at high Class A.

SCOUTING REPORT: Woods Richardson posted a sparkling K/BB ratio in his first full season, especially for a pitcher who is the same age as many 2019 high school draft picks. Little about him resembled an 18-year-old, from his strong, athletic frame to his advanced pitchability and poise on the mound. His fastball sits at 91-95 mph and he fills up the strike zone, projecting to have plus control. His fastball plays up because of its riding life, high spin rate and ability to generate extension out front, allowing him to get swings and misses up in the zone. He throws a slider and a curveball, with his slider the go-to when he's ahead in the count, grading out as an above-average pitch with a chance to tick up. His changeup has a chance to be average or better. He spent time working on his changeup in 2019 and it has a chance to be an average or better pitch.

THE FUTURE: Between his stuff, control and strong, durable frame, Woods Richardson has a chance to develop into a No. 2 or 3 starter. He should be in Double-A at some point in 2020 as a 19-year-old, putting himself in position to make his major league debut by age 20 or 21.

SCOUTING GRADES: **Fastball:** 60 **Slider:** 55 **Curveball:** 50 **Changeup:** 50 **Control:** 70

Year	Age	Club (League)	Class	W	L	ERA	G	GS	SV	IP	H	HR	BB	SO	K/9	WHIP	AVG
2018	17	Mets (GCL)	R	1	0	0.00	5	2	1	11	9	0	4	15	11.9	1.15	.209
	17	Kingsport (APP)	R	0	0	4.50	2	2	0	6	6	1	0	11	16.5	1.00	.250
2019	18	Columbia (SAL)	LoA	3	8	4.25	20	20	0	78	78	5	17	97	11.1	1.21	.256
	18	Dunedin (FSL)	HiA	3	2	2.54	6	6	0	28	18	1	7	29	9.2	0.88	.182
Minor League Totals				7	10	3.48	33	30	1	124	111	7	28	152	11.0	1.12	.236

4 ALEJANDRO KIRK, C

Born: Nov. 6, 1998. **B-T:** R-R. **HT:** 5-9. **WT:** 220. **Signed:** Mexico, 2016. **Signed by:** Dean Decillis/Sandy Rosario.

BA GRADE
55 Risk: High

TRACK RECORD: The Blue Jays signed Kirk out of Mexico in 2016, but he only played one game the next year due to a hand injury. Since then, Kirk has raked, even after a promotion to high Class A in May.

SCOUTING REPORT: The first thing that jumps out is Kirk's body, like a shorter version of Pablo Sandoval, which is an immediate turnoff for many scouts. But Kirk is also one of the best pure hitters in the minors. He has short arms, a compact swing and outstanding bat control. His tight stroke, bat speed and ability to track pitches helps him let the ball travel deep before deciding to swing. Kirk shows a sharp eye for the strike zone and has drawn more walks than strikeouts at every level. He struck out just 10 percent of the time in 2019, barreling good fastballs and offspeed pitches in all quadrants of the zone. Kirk has a hit-over-power profile, though there's more impact potential to unlock if he takes a more aggressive approach ahead in the count. Kirk's skeptics think his body will force him off the plate and question what they believe are below-average defensive skills. Others see a solid blocker who excels at framing, is prepared and works well with pitchers. He has an average, accurate arm, and threw out 38 percent of runners in 2019.

THE FUTURE: Kirk will get a chance to stick behind the plate and will head to Double-A New Hampshire in 2020.

SCOUTING GRADES: **Hitting:** 70 **Power:** 45 **Running:** 20 **Fielding:** 45 **Arm:** 50

Year	Age	Club (League)	Class	AVG	G	AB	R	H	2B	3B	HR	RBI	BB	SO	SB	OBP	SLG
2017	18	Blue Jays (GCL)	R	.000	1	2	0	0	0	0	0	0	0	0	0	.333	.000
2018	19	Bluefield (APP)	R	.354	58	206	31	73	10	1	10	57	33	21	2	.443	.558
2019	20	Lansing (MWL)	LoA	.299	21	77	15	23	6	1	3	8	18	8	1	.427	.519
	20	Dunedin (FSL)	HiA	.288	71	233	26	67	25	0	4	36	38	31	2	.395	.446
Minor League Totals				.315	151	518	72	163	41	2	17	101	89	60	5	.418	.500

5 ALEK MANOAH, RHP

Born: Jan. 9, 1998. **B-T:** R-R. **HT:** 6-6. **WT:** 270. **Drafted:** West Virginia, 2019 (1st round). **Signed by:** Coulson Barbiche.

BA GRADE
55 Risk: High

TRACK RECORD: During his first two seasons at West Virginia, Manoah moved between the starting rotation and the bullpen. After his sophomore year, he had an electric summer in the Cape Cod League, then continued to dominate in his junior year. He was the No. 11 overall pick in 2019, with the Blue Jays signing him for $4,547,500, and he had immediate success in the short-season Northwest League.

SCOUTING REPORT: Manoah is enormous. He's built like Aaron Harang, and will have to keep his conditioning in check. He uses that massive frame to produce a huge fastball. It's a lively, running pitch that sits around 93-96 mph and touches 98 mph. When Manoah needs a putaway pitch, he goes to his slider, which flashes plus and gets him swings and misses. Manoah was primarily a two-pitch guy in college, though his changeup has shown average potential. Manoah is more athletic than he looks, with a repertoire and delivery that should allow him to remain a starter. He has improved his strike-throwing over the past year and didn't walk many hitters in college or pro ball in 2019, though he needs to sharpen his fastball command.

THE FUTURE: Manoah is trending in the right direction, with the ability to develop into a No. 2 or 3 starter. He should open 2020 at a Class A affiliate with a chance to reach Toronto by 2021.

SCOUTING GRADES: **Fastball:** 60 **Slider:** 55 **Changeup:** 50 **Control:** 50

Year	Age	Club (League)	Class	W	L	ERA	G	GS	SV	IP	H	HR	BB	SO	K/9	WHIP	AVG
2019	21	Vancouver (NWL)	SS	0	1	2.65	6	6	0	17	13	1	5	27	14.3	1.06	.213
Minor League Totals				0	1	2.65	6	6	0	17	13	1	5	27	14.3	1.06	.213

6 ORELVIS MARTINEZ, SS/3B

Born: Nov. 19, 2001. **B-T:** R-R. **HT:** 6-1. **WT:** 190. **Signed:** Dominican Republic, 2018. **Signed by:** Alexis de la Cruz/Sandy Rosario.

MIKE JANES/FOUR SEAM IMAGES

BA GRADE
60 **Risk: Very High**

TRACK RECORD: The Blue Jays signed Martinez in 2018 for $3.51 million, the largest bonus for a 16-year-old in the 2018-19 international signing period. He immediately showed why the Blue Jays were so high on him, ranking as the top prospect in the Rookie-level Gulf Coast League as a 17-year-old in his pro debut.

SCOUTING REPORT: Martinez uses his body well in his swing. There are a lot of moving parts, but he's usually able to keep his swing in sync, which enables him to generate quick bat speed and easy plus power. He taps into that power in games (his seven home runs tied for second in the GCL), taking advantage of good hitters' hands to make frequent contact. Martinez can get too jumpy early in the count, but he mostly has a calm, advanced approach for his age and condenses his leg kick when he gets to two strikes. Martinez's hands play well at the plate and in the field. He has a strong arm, but his range and footwork are stretched thin at shortstop, and given how much bigger he's likely to get, third base is where he probably lands.

THE FUTURE: With Miguel Hiraldo and Leonardo Jimenez one level ahead of Martinez, the Blue Jays have to sort out where they're going to send all their infielders in 2019. Martinez could be ready for low Class A Lansing if the Blue Jays want to push him aggressively.

SCOUTING GRADES: **Hitting:** 60 **Power:** 60 **Running:** 45 **Fielding:** 40 **Arm:** 60

Year	Age	Club (League)	Class	AVG	G	AB	R	H	2B	3B	HR	RBI	BB	SO	SB	OBP	SLG
2019	17	Blue Jays (GCL)	R	.275	40	142	20	39	8	5	7	32	14	29	2	.352	.549
Minor League Totals				.275	40	142	20	39	8	5	7	32	14	29	2	.352	.549

7 GABRIEL MORENO, C

Born: Feb. 14, 2000. **B-T:** R-R. **HT:** 5-11. **WT:** 170. **Signed:** Venezuela, 2016. **Signed by:** Francisco Plasencia.

TRACK RECORD: Moreno had a low profile in Venezuela when the Blue Jays signed him for $25,000 in 2016. He has raised his status considerably over the last two seasons, emerging as one of the better catching prospects in the lower levels of the minors.

SCOUTING REPORT: Moreno's hand-eye coordination is elite. He rarely swings and misses, with a strikeout rate of just 11 percent in 2019. His swing has evolved since signing—he has added bigger, more athletic movements in an effort to drive the ball with more impact—and his athleticism and body awareness help him make adjustments quickly. Moreno isn't that big, but those changes have helped him display more power, with a chance to be a 15-20 home run hitter. Moreno isn't a free-swinger, but he walked in just 6 percent of his plate appearances. He will get himself into trouble when he expands the zone and makes soft contact on pitches he should lay off, though he did a better job in those areas last season. Moreno is athletic and gets rid of the ball quickly to get to an average arm, throwing out 33 percent of runners in 2019, but his blocking and receiving need to improve.

THE FUTURE: Moreno will head to high Class A Dunedin in 2020. He has the upside to develop into an average or possibly better regular behind the plate.

SCOUTING GRADES: **Hitting:** 55 **Power:** 45 **Running:** 30 **Fielding:** 45 **Arm:** 50

Year	Age	Club (League)	Class	AVG	G	AB	R	H	2B	3B	HR	RBI	BB	SO	SB	OBP	SLG
2017	17	Blue Jays (DSL)	R	.248	32	125	9	31	4	1	0	17	6	5	5	.274	.296
2018	18	Blue Jays (GCL)	R	.413	23	92	14	38	12	2	2	22	4	7	1	.455	.652
	18	Bluefield (APP)	R	.279	17	61	10	17	5	0	2	14	3	13	1	.303	.459
2019	19	Lansing (MWL)	LoA	.280	82	307	47	86	17	5	12	52	22	38	7	.337	.485
Minor League Totals				.294	154	585	80	172	38	8	16	105	35	63	14	.339	.468

8 MIGUEL HIRALDO, SS/2B

BA GRADE
55 Risk: Very High

Born: Sept. 5, 2000. **B-T:** R-R. **HT:** 5-11. **WT:** 175. **Signed:** Dominican Republic, 2017. **Signed by:** Luciano del Rosario.

TRACK RECORD: Hiraldo signed for $750,000 in 2017, when several clubs considered him one of the best hitters in his international class. Hiraldo performed well his first two seasons and stood out as one of the top prospects in 2019 in the Rookie-level Appalachian League.

SCOUTING REPORT: Hiraldo has a lot of qualities of a good hitter, with a knack for barreling baseballs. He doesn't load his hands back much to start his swing, but hand speed helps his bat explode through the zone. It's a direct, compact swing, and Hirado uses his legs and hips well to usually be on time and produce average power that should increase. Hiraldo clobbers fastballs and he generally has a good approach for his age. However, he needs to improve his breaking ball recognition and he has a pull-heavy approach, so he will need to make adjustments to better handle pitches on the outer third. His hands and arm are fine at shortstop, but his range is stretched thin there already. His stocky body suggests he's going to slow down as he gets bigger. He has the defensive skill set and offensive profile for third base.

THE FUTURE: Hiraldo should be ready in 2020 for low Class A Lansing, where he'll continue refining his hitting approach.

SCOUTING GRADES: Hitting: 55 Power: 60 Running: 45 Fielding: 45 Arm: 55

Year	Age	Club (League)	Class	AVG	G	AB	R	H	2B	3B	HR	RBI	BB	SO	SB	OBP	SLG
2018	17	Blue Jays (DSL)	R	.313	54	214	41	67	18	3	2	33	23	30	15	.381	.453
	17	Blue Jays (GCL)	R	.231	10	39	3	9	4	0	0	3	1	12	3	.250	.333
2019	18	Bluefield (APP)	R	.300	56	237	43	71	20	1	7	37	14	36	11	.348	.481
	18	Lansing (MWL)	LoA	.250	1	4	0	1	0	1	0	0	0	0	0	.250	.750
Minor League Totals				.300	121	494	87	148	42	5	9	73	38	78	29	.354	.460

9 ANTHONY KAY, LHP

TONY FIRRIOLO/MLB PHOTOS VIA GETTY IMAGES

BA GRADE
45 Risk: Medium

Born: March 21, 1995. **B-T:** L-L. **HT:** 6-0. **WT:** 218. **Drafted:** Connecticut, 2016 (1st round). **Signed by:** Michael Pesce (Mets).

TRACK RECORD: The Mets drafted Kay with the 31st overall pick in 2016, but he missed the entire 2017 season due to Tommy John surgery. He returned in 2018, and in July 2019 the Mets traded him and righthander Simeon Woods Richardson to the Blue Jays for Marcus Stroman. He made his major league debut as a September callup.

SCOUTING REPORT: Kay has a strong fastball from the left side, sitting at 92-94 mph with the ability to reach 96. Early in the year at Double-A, Kay commanded his fastball well to both sides of the plate, though when he moved up he got himself into trouble when his command escaped him and he fell behind in the count too often. Kay mixes in a curveball and changeup, with scouts split on which pitch they prefer depending on when they see him. When Kay got to Toronto, his curveball was more effective, an average pitch in the upper 70s. His mid-80s changeup is a fringe-average pitch that can flash a tick better.

THE FUTURE: If Kay tightens his fastball command, he projects as a back-end starer. He should be in Toronto's rotation immediately. His future could improve with a better third pitch.

SCOUTING GRADES: Fastball: 55 Slider: 50 Curveball: 50 Changeup: 50 Control: 50

Year	Age	Club (League)	Class	W	L	ERA	G	GS	SV	IP	H	HR	BB	SO	K/9	WHIP	AVG
2017	22	Did not play—Injured															
2018	23	Columbia (SAL)	LoA	4	4	4.54	13	13	0	69	73	6	22	78	10.1	1.37	.275
	23	St. Lucie (FSL)	HiA	3	7	3.88	10	10	0	53	51	1	27	45	7.6	1.46	.262
2019	24	Binghamton (EL)	AA	7	3	1.49	12	12	0	66	38	2	23	70	9.5	0.92	.165
	24	Syracuse (IL)	AAA	1	3	6.61	7	7	0	31	40	7	11	26	7.5	1.63	.325
	24	Buffalo (IL)	AAA	2	2	2.50	7	7	0	36	33	3	22	39	9.8	1.53	.244
	24	Toronto (AL)	MAJ	1	0	5.79	3	2	0	14	15	0	5	13	8.4	1.43	.263
Major League Totals				1	0	5.79	3	2	0	14	15	0	5	13	8.4	1.43	.263
Minor League Totals				17	19	3.58	49	49	0	256	235	19	105	258	9.1	1.33	.248

10 ADAM KLOFFENSTEIN, RHP

Born: Aug. 25, 2000. **B-T:** R-R. **HT:** 6-5. **WT:** 245. **Drafted:** HS—Magnolia, Texas, 2018 (3rd round). **Signed By:** Brian Johnston.

TRACK RECORD: In the first round of the 2018 draft, the Blue Jays picked shortstop Jordan Groshans, then in the third round they took Kloffenstein, his Magnolia (Texas) High teammate. Kloffenstein was one the youngest players in his draft class and didn't turn 19 until the end of the 2019 season, which he spent carving up hitters in the college-heavy, short-season Northwest League. He ranked No. 5 in the league's loaded Top 20 prospects list.

SCOUTING REPORT: Kloffenstein is built like a power pitcher with a solid fastball, but also has impressive feel for his age, both with his control and ability to manipulate his breaking stuff. His fastball sits at 90-93 mph, with a peak of 95. Kloffenstein has an innate feel for spinning his mid-70s curveball and low-80s slider. Both are at least average with a chance to be plus. He shows feel for a potentially average or better changeup as well that fades away from lefties.

THE FUTURE: Kloffenstein has a starter profile and, given his youth, there might be another gear coming for his stuff. If it does, he could be a mid-rotation starter, with low Class A Lansing as his next step.

SCOUTING GRADES: **Fastball:** 55 **Slider:** 55 **Curveball:** 55 **Changeup:** 50 **Control:** 50

Year	Age	Club (League)	Class	W	L	ERA	G	GS	SV	IP	H	HR	BB	SO	K/9	WHIP	AVG
2018	17	Blue Jays (GCL)	R	0	0	0.00	2	2	0	2	1	0	2	4	18.0	1.50	.143
2019	18	Vancouver (NWL)	SS	4	4	2.24	13	13	0	64	47	4	23	64	9.0	1.09	.205
Minor League Totals				4	4	2.17	15	15	0	66	48	4	25	68	9.2	1.10	.203

11 ERIC PARDINHO, RHP

BA GRADE
55 Risk: Extreme

Born: Jan. 5, 2001. **B-T:** R-R. **HT:** 5-9. **WT:** 200. **Signed:** Brazil, 2017. **Signed by:** Andrew Tinnish/Sandy Rosario.

TRACK RECORD: Pardinho was the best pitching prospect in the 2017 international class when he signed with the Blue Jays out of Brazil for $1.4 million. He showed why international scouts raved about his polish, skipping two levels to the Rookie-level Appalachian League in his pro debut and dominating there in 2018. His 2019 season was a disappointment, however, as a sore right elbow prevented him from pitching until June 26. When he returned, his stuff wasn't as explosive as it was the previous year.

SCOUTING REPORT: With a small, compact frame, Pardinho has a free-and-easy delivery with smooth arm action, but he mostly worked at 88-92 mph in 2019, down from the previous year when he sat in the low-90s and reached 96. When Pardinho is at his best, his curveball flashes plus and he can elicit empty swings with a slider that could develop into another above-average pitch. His changeup isn't there yet, but there's potential for it to develop into an average pitch

THE FUTURE: It's possible that Pardinho just wasn't at 100 percent when he returned, so if he pitches in 2020 with the stuff he showed in 2018, his stuff will bounce back. But the step back in his stuff in 2019 combined with the missed time due to elbow issues adds more risk to his profile.

Year	Age	Club (League)	Class	W	L	ERA	G	GS	SV	IP	H	HR	BB	SO	K/9	WHIP	AVG
2018	17	Bluefield (APP)	R	4	3	2.88	11	11	0	50	37	5	16	64	11.5	1.06	.199
2019	18	Blue Jays (GCL)	R	1	0	0.00	1	0	0	4	1	0	3	5	11.3	1.00	.091
	18	Lansing (MWL)	LoA	1	1	2.41	7	7	0	34	29	1	13	30	8.0	1.25	.240
Minor League Totals				6	4	2.57	19	18	0	87	67	6	32	99	10.2	1.13	.211

12 OTTO LOPEZ, SS/2B

Born: Oct. 1, 1998. **B-T:** R-R. **HT:** 5-10. **WT:** 160. **Signed:** Dominican Republic, 2016. **Signed by:** Sandy Rosario/Lorenzo Perez/Alexis De La Cruz.

TRACK RECORD: The Blue Jays signed Lopez out of the Dominican Republic for $60,000 in 2016. He had a low profile until 2019, when he won the batting title in the low Class A Midwest League in his full-season debut.

SCOUTING REPORT: Lopez doesn't have flashy tools, so he doesn't jump out immediately, but he's a baseball rat and a gamer with a knack for barreling baseballs. Lopez has good bat control with a line-drive, all-fields approach. While it doesn't show in his numbers, Lopez is strong and has at least average raw power. There's more untapped power potential if Lopez can make an adjustment to his approach. He generally shows a sound feel for the strike zone, though there are times he could be more selective. Lopez spent most of his time at shortstop, though he played some second base and corner outfield as well.

THE FUTURE: Moving around the diamond may be his role going forward, as his defense might be stretched thin as an everyday shortstop, with average speed and arm strength. High Class A Dunedin should be his next step.

Year	Age	Club (League)	Class	AVG	G	AB	R	H	2B	3B	HR	RBI	BB	SO	SB	OBP	SLG
2017	18	Blue Jays (GCL)	R	.275	51	178	30	49	6	3	1	15	19	23	7	.361	.360
2018	19	Bluefield (APP)	R	.364	7	33	8	12	5	2	0	6	0	5	1	.382	.636
	19	Vancouver (NWL)	SS	.297	51	175	31	52	7	4	3	22	26	21	13	.390	.434
2019	20	Lansing (MWL)	LoA	.324	108	447	61	145	20	5	5	50	34	63	20	.371	.425
Minor League Totals				.310	217	833	130	258	38	14	9	93	79	112	41	.374	.421

13 ESTIVEN MACHADO, SS

BA GRADE
55 **Risk: Extreme**

Born: Oct. 4, 2002. **B-T:** B-R. **HT:** 5-10. **WT:** 165. **Drafted:** Venezuela, 2019. **Signed by:** Sandy Rosario/Francisco Plasencia.

TRACK RECORD: Machado was one of the most promising players the Blue Jays signed from a deep 2019 international signing class.

SCOUTING REPORT: He has an exciting blend of explosive athleticism, tools and advanced game skills for his age with the ability to play a premium position. Machado has a direct, compact swing from both sides of the plate and a good approach, leading to a high contact rate. It's an efficient stroke with fast bat speed, showing gap power now with the bat speed and strength projection to potentially develop average pop. He's around an average runner now, and while speed is a tricky tool to project up, that could end up happening with Machado given his explosiveness and running gait. Machado is a notch behind Rikelvin de Castro as a defender, but he also projects to stick at shortstop. He has a quick first step and moves his feet well, with the range for the position and secure hands as well. His arm is a slightly above-average tool that's tickling plus and should be there consistently in the near future.

THE FUTURE: The Dominican Summer League is likely where he will make his pro debut in 2020.

Year	Age	Club (League)	Class	AVG	G	AB	R	H	2B	3B	HR	RBI	BB	SO	SB	OBP	SLG
2019	16	Did not play—Signed 2020 contract															

14 KENDALL WILLIAMS, RHP

BA GRADE
55 **Risk: Extreme**

Born: Aug. 24, 2000. **B-T:** R-R. **HT:** 6-6. **WT:** 205. **Drafted:** HS—Bradenton, Fla., 2019 (2nd round). **Signed by:** Brandon Bishoff.

TRACK RECORD: The Blue Jays have made a habit in recent years of drafting extra-large framed pitchers with their top picks. They added two more in 2019, taking Alek Manoah in the first round and another 6-foot-6 righthander in Williams with their second-round pick, signing Williams for $1,547,500.

SCOUTING REPORT: Williams has some similarities to righthander Adam Kloffenstein, Toronto's third-round pick the previous year, as a big-bodied righthander with good but not overpowering stuff that has a chance to tick up in the next few years. Williams throws strikes with downhill plane on a fastball that sits in the low-90s and can reach 95. He doesn't have a plus pitch, but he has feel for three secondary pitches—particularly his breaking stuff—that could all be average or better. That includes a mid-70s curveball that can miss bats at times, though he does tend to get around it sometimes, along with a slider and changeup both in the low 80s.

THE FUTURE: Williams has the stuff of a back-end starter, but he has the physical projection for his stuff to improve and potentially slot in higher up in a rotation. He could follow Kloffenstein's path by going to short-season Vancouver in 2020.

Year	Age	Club (League)	Class	W	L	ERA	G	GS	SV	IP	H	HR	BB	SO	K/9	WHIP	AVG
2019	18	Blue Jays (GCL)	R	0	0	1.13	6	5	0	16	6	0	7	19	10.7	0.81	.111
Minor League Totals				0	0	1.13	6	5	0	16	6	0	7	19	10.7	0.81	.111

15 GRIFFIN CONINE, OF

BA GRADE
50 **Risk: Very High**

Born: July 11, 1997. **B-T:** L-R. **HT:** 6-1. **WT:** 200. **Drafted:** Duke, 2018 (2nd round). **Signed by:** Jason Beverlin.

TRACK RECORD: The son of former Marlins outfielder Jeff Conine, Griffin looked like a potential first-round pick as he entered his junior year at Duke. He didn't live up to those expectations, dropping him to the second round in 2018, and after the season he tested positive for the stimulant ritalinic acid, prompting a suspension for the first 50 games of the 2019 season. Conine played just 80 games but still led the low Class A Midwest League with 22 home runs, with a .576 slugging average that was 97 points above the next qualified hitter.

SCOUTING REPORT: Conine has a straightforward profile: gigantic power with a lot of strikeouts. Conine is strong, has fast bat speed and plus-plus raw power. Conine clobbers the ball when he connects, especially when he gets a pitch in the middle to lower part of the strike zone. But Conine's swing also has holes and he swings and misses too often on pitches in the strike zone, especially when pitchers attack him up, leading to a 36-percent strikeout rate, a significant red flag for a college hitter in low Class A.
THE FUTURE: He showed more plate patience than he did the previous year, so if Conine can cut his swing-and-miss rate, he could have success as a three true outcomes player. He's a below-average runner with a plus arm in right field. He will head to high Class A Dunedin to begin 2020.

Year	Age	Club (League)	Class	AVG	G	AB	R	H	2B	3B	HR	RBI	BB	SO	SB	OBP	SLG
2018	20	Blue Jays (GCL)	R	.375	2	8	1	3	1	0	0	3	1	2	0	.444	.500
	20	Vancouver (NWL)	SS	.238	55	206	24	49	14	2	7	30	19	63	5	.309	.427
2019	21	Lansing (MWL)	LoA	.283	80	304	59	86	19	2	22	64	38	125	2	.371	.576
Minor League Totals				.266	137	518	84	138	34	4	29	97	58	190	7	.348	.515

16 LEONARDO JIMENEZ, SS

BA GRADE
50 **Risk: Very High**

Born: May 17, 2001. **B-T:** R-R. **HT:** 5-11. **WT:** 165. **Signed:** Panama, 2017. **Signed by:** Alex Zapata/Sandy Rosario.

TRACK RECORD: Jimenez played for Panama in multiple international tournaments growing up, and his instincts for the game were part of what drew the Blue Jays to sign him for $825,000 in 2017. While Jimenez doesn't have much physical strength yet, his swing and high baseball IQ have helped him perform well so far through Rookie ball.
SCOUTING REPORT: Jimenez is a savvy, fundamentally sound player who doesn't have the same quick-twitch explosion as some other young shortstops, but he does a better job than many of his peers of being able to slow the game down and play under control. He manages his at-bats well, usually staying within the strike zone with good bat path, plate coverage and solid bat-to-ball skills for his age. Jimenez got a little stronger in 2019 and his average exit velocity jumped a few miles per hour, but he has yet to hit a home run in pro ball and probably will never have more than below-average power, so his offensive game will rely more on his on-base skills. Jimenez doesn't have the quick-twitch athleticism some clubs prefer at shortstop, so some scouts see him as a second baseman, but he has a chance to stay at shortstop. He's a fringe-average runner with soft hands, an average arm and good body control at shortstop, where he reads the ball well off the bat.
THE FUTURE: Jimenez has the upside to be a top 10 prospect in the system a year from now, but how much stronger he gets will have a major impact on his future.

Year	Age	Club (League)	Class	AVG	G	AB	R	H	2B	3B	HR	RBI	BB	SO	SB	OBP	SLG
2018	17	Blue Jays (GCL)	R	.250	37	132	13	33	8	2	0	19	16	17	0	.333	.341
2019	18	Bluefield (APP)	R	.298	56	215	34	64	13	2	0	22	21	42	2	.377	.377
	18	Lansing (MWL)	LoA	.167	2	6	0	1	0	0	0	0	0	2	0	.167	.167
Minor League Totals				278	95	353	47	98	21	4	0	41	37	61	2	.358	.360

17 RIKELVIN DE CASTRO, SS

BA GRADE
50 **Risk: Extreme**

Born: Jan. 23, 2003. **B-T:** R-R. **HT:** 6-0. **WT:** 150. **Signed:** Dominican Republic, 2019. **Signed by:** Sandy Rosario/Lorenzo Perez/Luis Natera.

TRACK RECORD: The top international signing bonus from the Blue Jays in 2019 went to de Castro, who got $1.2 million at 16 years old out of the Dominican Republic.
SCOUTING REPORT: A loose, wiry athlete, de Castro quickly draws attention for the way he moves at shortstop. He's a fast-twitch, high-energy defender with clean actions, showing smooth hands, quick footwork and a nose for the ball. He's a potential plus glove at shortstop, with average speed and arm strength that could tick up as he gets stronger. That's especially for his arm given his arm speed. De Castro has a simple, compact stroke from the right side and makes consistent contact, showing good rhythm and timing in the box. It's an approach geared to hit line drives to all fields with occasional gap shots. He should grow into more extra-base thump once he gets stronger, though power doesn't project to be a big part of his game.
THE FUTURE: The Dominican Summer League should be his first step in pro ball.

Year	Age	Club (League)	Class	AVG	G	AB	R	H	2B	3B	HR	RBI	BB	SO	SB	OBP	SLG
2019	16	Did not play—Signed 2020 contract															

18 PATRICK MURPHY, RHP

BA GRADE 45 Risk: High

Born: June 10, 1995. **B-T:** R-R. **HT:** 6-4. **WT:** 220. **Drafted:** HS—Chandler, Ariz., 2013 (3rd round). **Signed by:** Blake Crosby.

TRACK RECORD: Murphy was in the midst of a strong stretch with Double-A New Hampshire heading into early June when umpires informed him that they determined the toe tap with his left foot in his delivery was illegal. Murphy stayed in the rotation, but he got knocked around in his next two starts, and even with time off to re-work his mechanics, he never got in sync trying to adjust to a new delivery.

SCOUTING REPORT: It was another setback for Murphy, who has had Tommy John surgery, an operation for thoracic outlet syndrome and another operation to reposition nerves in his pitching elbow. The delivery setback adds a lot of uncertainty to Murphy's projection, but he has a power arm, sitting in the low-to-mid-90s with his fastball with the ability to dial it up to the upper 90s. He pairs it with a power curveball that has good shape, sharp bite and that he does a good job landing for strikes, flashing as a plus pitch. He throws a fringe-average change, but he's primarily a fastball/breaking ball pitcher.

THE FUTURE: Murphy will try to regroup in 2020 and has a chance to be a back-end starter, though he could fit as a multi-inning reliever as well.

Year	Age	Club (League)	Class	W	L	ERA	G	GS	SV	IP	H	HR	BB	SO	K/9	WHIP	AVG
2017	22	Blue Jays (GCL)	R	1	0	0.00	3	2	0	9	7	0	1	15	15.0	0.89	.212
	22	Lansing (MWL)	LoA	4	3	2.94	15	15	0	89	87	5	33	57	5.8	1.35	.263
	22	Dunedin (FSL)	HiA	0	1	7.00	2	2	0	9	14	0	3	5	5.0	1.89	.368
2018	23	New Hampshire (EL)	AA	0	0	3.00	1	1	0	6	4	0	3	6	9.0	1.17	.200
	23	Dunedin (FSL)	HiA	10	5	2.64	26	26	0	147	126	5	50	135	8.3	1.20	.233
2019	24	New Hampshire (EL)	AA	4	7	4.71	18	18	0	84	75	7	27	86	9.2	1.21	.227
Minor League Totals				23	23	3.33	89	81	2	438	416	20	156	376	7.7	1.31	.250

19 VICTOR MESIA, C

BA GRADE 50 Risk: Extreme

Born: Jan. 18, 2003. **B-T:** R-R. **HT:** 5-10. **WT:** 175. **Signed:** Venezuela, 2019. **Signed by:** Sandy Rosario/Jose Contreras/Miguel Leal.

TRACK RECORD: The Blue Jays spread their international bonus pool money around in the 2019-20 signing period, coming away with a deep collection of talent. Part of that depth includes Mesia, who signed out of Venezuela at 16 and has emerged as one of the club's best 2019 signings.

SCOUTING REPORT: Mesia has power and explosiveness to his actions. He performed well in Tricky League and Dominican instructional league games since signing, with a compact swing from the right side of the plate. He has fast bat speed, a knack for the barrel and makes hard contact with an all-fields approach. He shows flashes of above-average raw power right now, giving him a chance to hit and hit for power at a high clip for a catcher. Mesia has strong legs, is athletic for a catcher and projects to stay behind the plate, with a strong arm that tickles plus now and projects to be there consistently soon.

THE FUTURE: Mesia will likely debut in the Dominican Summer League.

Year	Age	Club (League)	Class	AVG	G	AB	R	H	2B	3B	HR	RBI	BB	SO	SB	OBP	SLG
2019	16	Did not play—Signed 2020 contract															

20 SANTIAGO ESPINAL, SS/2B

BA GRADE 40 Risk: Medium

Born: Nov. 13, 1994. **B-T:** R-R. **HT:** 5-10. **WT:** 175. **Drafted:** Miami-Dade JC, 2016 (10th round). **Signed by:** Willie Romay (Red Sox).

TRACK RECORD: Born in the Dominican Republic, Espinal grew up in Florida and was a $50,000 signing as a 10th-round pick of the Red Sox in 2016. Two years later, the Red Sox traded him to the Blue Jays for outfielder/first baseman Steve Pearce. In 2019, Espinal performed well enough at the upper levels for the Blue Jays to add him to the 40-man roster after the season to protect him from the Rule 5 draft.

SCOUTING REPORT: Espinal doesn't have a big ceiling, but he should carve out a major league career with his ability to make contact and fill in at different positions. Espinal has good bat control and a mature two-strike approach, striking out in just 14 percent of his plate appearances in 2019. He has well below-average power, enough for perhaps 8-12 home runs in a full season, but his bat-to-ball skills and feel for the strike zone help him get on base at a solid clip for someone who can play up the middle. An average runner with a slightly above-average arm, Espinal is an athletic player who bounces around between shortstop, second base and center field, with average or better defense at each spot.

THE FUTURE: Unless his power jumps, he is probably stretched thin as an everyday regular, but he has the contact skills and defensive flexibility to be a utilityman, with a good chance to make his major league debut at some point in 2020.

Year	Age	Club (League)	Class	AVG	G	AB	R	H	2B	3B	HR	RBI	BB	SO	SB	OBP	SLG
2017	22	Greenville (SAL)	LoA	.280	123	492	64	138	18	4	4	46	39	67	20	.334	.358
2018	23	Salem (CAR)	HiA	.313	65	256	53	80	15	3	7	32	18	35	9	.363	.477
	23	Dunedin (FSL)	HiA	.262	17	65	9	17	3	1	2	8	6	10	0	.333	.431
	23	New Hampshire (EL)	AA	.286	42	147	17	42	9	2	1	20	14	22	2	.354	.395
2019	24	New Hampshire (EL)	AA	.278	94	367	46	102	21	1	5	57	35	50	10	.343	.381
	24	Buffalo (IL)	AAA	.317	28	104	11	33	6	0	2	14	7	23	2	.360	.433
Minor League Totals				.285	395	1517	208	433	74	11	21	187	129	218	44	.345	.390

21 ALBERTO RODRIGUEZ, OF

BA GRADE 45 Risk: Very High

Born: Oct. 6, 2000. **B-T:** L-L. **HT:** 5-11. **WT:** 180. **Signed:** Dominican Republic, 2017. **Signed by:** Sandy Rosario/Lorenzo Perez/Luciano del Rosario.

TRACK RECORD: Rodriguez was a famous name early on in the scouting process of the 2017 signing class and ended up signing for $500,000 that year. After debuting in the Dominican Summer League in 2018, he took a step forward in 2019 in his first season in the United States.

SCOUTING REPORT: Rodriguez is a high-contact hitter from the left side with a swing geared for low line drives. There are some unconventional parts to his swing, but he uses his hands well and puts the ball in play with a loose, quick stroke. Rodriguez has a solid eye for the strike zone for his age and he makes hard contact when he connects, but his swing doesn't have much loft and he doesn't project to be a big power threat, creating more risk for his profile as a right fielder. He improved his defense in right field, with his speed and arm strength both grading out around average.

THE FUTURE: Developing more home run power will be the key for Rodriguez to develop into an everyday player on a corner.

Year	Age	Club (League)	Class	AVG	G	AB	R	H	2B	3B	HR	RBI	BB	SO	SB	OBP	SLG
2018	17	Blue Jays (DSL)	R	.254	61	228	44	58	9	1	5	34	32	55	21	.350	.368
2019	18	Blue Jays (GCL)	R	.301	47	173	19	52	13	1	2	29	19	32	13	.364	.422
Minor League Totals				.274	108	401	63	110	22	2	7	63	51	87	34	.356	.392

22 DASAN BROWN, OF

BA GRADE 50 Risk: Extreme

Born: Sept. 25, 2001. **B-T:** R-R. **HT:** 6-0. **WT:** 185. **Drafted:** HS—Oakville, Ont., 2019 (3rd round). **Signed by:** Kory Lafreniere.

TRACK RECORD: Brown was the first Canadian player selected in the 2019 draft, with the Blue Jays picking him at No. 88 overall and signing him for $797,500. Brown was one of the youngest players in the class, only turning 18 after his first season in the Rookie-level Gulf Coast League ended.

SCOUTING REPORT: Brown is bursting with quick-twitch, explosive athleticism, with a large gap between his physical potential and the rawness of his baseball skills. He's an 80 runner on the 20-80 scouting scale, with the instincts and average arm strength that give him the tools to develop into a plus or better defender in center field with plenty of range and closing speed. Those wheels should also make him a high stolen base threat once he improves his technique and ability to read pitchers. As a hitter, Brown has excellent bat speed, enabling him to catch up to good velocity even when it's in on his body, and he puts himself into good hitting positions, but his feel for hitting and timing are still raw, especially when it comes to adjusting to offspeed pitches. Brown doesn't have much in-game power right now, but for a long, slender player, he shows surprising ability to drive the ball with impact in BP because of his bat speed.

THE FUTURE: Given his youth and present hitting ability, Brown will likely head to either Rookie-level Bluefield or short-season Vancouver in 2020.

Year	Age	Club (League)	Class	AVG	G	AB	R	H	2B	3B	HR	RBI	BB	SO	SB	OBP	SLG
2019	17	Blue Jays (GCL)	R	.222	14	45	8	10	2	2	0	5	9	17	6	.444	.356
Minor League Totals				.222	14	45	8	10	2	2	0	5	9	17	6	.444	.356

23 REESE MCGUIRE, C

BA GRADE 40 Risk: Medium

Born: March 2, 1995. **B-T:** L-R. **HT:** 5-11. **WT:** 215. **Drafted:** HS—Covington, Wash., 2013 (1st round). **Signed by:** Greg Hopkins (Pirates).

TRACK RECORD: It's the seventh year in the Prospect Handbook for McGuire, a first-round pick of the Pirates out of high school who they traded to the Blue Jays in 2016. McGuire spent most of 2019 in Triple-A Buffalo until the Blue Jays brought him up to Toronto at the end of July, his second stint in the big leagues after he was a September callup in 2018.

SCOUTING REPORT: McGuire's defense is what carries him. He's a smart player who is well prepared and earns high marks for his ability to handle a pitching staff and call games. He receives pitches well with soft hands, and while his arm strength is average, his quick footwork helps him get his throws off swiftly and on target. Offensively, McGuire has a short swing and makes a lot of contact, but his power is well below-average, so there isn't much impact when he does connect.

THE FUTURE: Unless he can develop more power, McGuire's offensive upside at this point may be limited, but he could have enough ability at the plate to stick around as a backup catcher, a role he should fill in Toronto in 2020.

Year	Age	Club (League)	Class	AVG	G	AB	R	H	2B	3B	HR	RBI	BB	SO	SB	OBP	SLG
2017	22	Blue Jays (GCL)	R	.409	8	22	4	9	2	0	0	7	3	1	0	.462	.500
	22	Dunedin (FSL)	HiA	.250	3	12	1	3	1	0	0	1	1	2	0	.308	.333
	22	New Hampshire (EL)	AA	.278	34	115	19	32	5	1	6	20	16	19	2	.366	.496
2018	23	Buffalo (IL)	AAA	.233	96	322	31	75	9	2	7	37	33	77	3	.312	.339
	23	Toronto (AL)	MAJ	.290	14	31	5	9	3	0	2	4	2	9	1	.333	.581
2019	24	Buffalo (IL)	AAA	.247	72	243	30	60	12	1	5	29	25	44	4	.316	.366
	24	Toronto (AL)	MAJ	.299	30	97	14	29	7	0	5	11	7	18	0	.346	.526
Major League Totals				.297	44	128	19	38	10	0	7	15	9	27	1	.343	.539
Minor League Totals				.261	551	1988	230	519	84	10	22	236	180	279	42	.325	.347

24 ANTHONY ALFORD, OF

BA GRADE 45 Risk: High

Born: July 20, 1994. **B-T:** R-R. **HT:** 6-1. **WT:** 215. **Drafted:** HS—Petal, Miss., 2012 (3rd round). **Signed by:** Brian Johnston.

TRACK RECORD: Alford was a top three prospect in Toronto's farm system for three straight years after the 2015-17 seasons. But the last two years, Alford has struggled at the upper levels because of a mixture of complications with his swing and nagging injuries. Alford, who spent most of 2012-14 focused on football as the quarterback at Southern Miss and later a defensive back for Ole Miss, has flashed tantalizing athleticism and hit well in Double-A New Hampshire in 2017, but he has yet to take the next leap.

SCOUTING REPORT: Alford has above-average bat speed but he gets into an awkward launch position with a high back elbow and doesn't keep his barrel through the hitting zone very long. That leads to timing issues, with Alford often late or caught in between on his swings. Alford has worked to make adjustments, but he missed a month in the middle of the 2019 season with an oblique injury, and being on the cusp of the big leagues and in Toronto as a September callup, those changes were difficult to make when the results are what matter. He's strong, but his game power is below-average. Alford is a plus runner who can play solid-average defense in center field with a 40 arm.

THE FUTURE: Now 25, Alford has to show he can produce quickly, whether that comes with Toronto or another organization

Year	Age	Club (League)	Class	AVG	G	AB	R	H	2B	3B	HR	RBI	BB	SO	SB	OBP	SLG
2017	22	Toronto (AL)	MAJ	.125	4	8	0	1	1	0	0	0	0	3	0	.125	.250
	22	Dunedin (FSL)	HiA	.143	6	21	1	3	0	0	0	2	0	8	1	.182	.143
	22	New Hampshire (EL)	AA	.310	68	245	41	76	14	0	5	24	35	45	18	.406	.429
	22	Buffalo (IL)	AAA	.333	3	12	1	4	1	0	0	0	1	2	0	.385	.417
2018	23	Dunedin (FSL)	HiA	.200	7	20	2	4	1	0	0	2	3	8	0	.360	.250
	23	Buffalo (IL)	AAA	.240	105	375	52	90	22	1	5	34	30	112	17	.312	.344
	23	Toronto (AL)	MAJ	.105	13	19	3	2	0	0	0	1	2	9	1	.190	.105
2019	24	Blue Jays (GCL)	R	.385	4	13	3	5	2	1	1	1	2	1	0	.467	.923
	24	Buffalo (IL)	AAA	.259	76	282	46	73	16	3	7	37	31	94	22	.343	.411
	24	Toronto (AL)	MAJ	.179	16	28	3	5	0	0	1	1	1	11	2	.233	.286
Major League Totals				.145	33	55	6	8	1	0	1	2	3	23	3	.203	.218
Minor League Totals				.265	493	1814	303	480	101	15	34	187	235	527	114	.358	.393

25 KEVIN SMITH, SS

BA GRADE 45 Risk: Very High

Born: July 4, 1996. **B-T:** R-R. **HT:** 6-1. **WT:** 190. **Drafted:** Maryland, 2017 (4th round). **Signed by:** Doug Witt.

TRACK RECORD: After the 2018 season, Smith was trending up. He spent his first full season raking through two Class A levels, with a swing adjustment that clicked to go with impressive power from a shortstop. However, in 2019, everything seemed to go wrong.

SCOUTING REPORT: Smith got off to a slow start in Double-A New Hampshire, and he tried to self-correct and tinker with his swing, but those adjustments never led to better results. After the season, Smith went to the Arizona Fall League, where he led the league with 38 strikeouts in just 67 plate appearances. Smith isn't that far removed from a successful 2018 campaign, and he still shows quick bat speed and above-average raw power. Smith is a student of the game and made different tweaks to his swing last year, but he has to find a way to get his swing back to where it was in 2018, and to stay more disciplined in the strike zone.

THE FUTURE: There's a split camp among scouts on his fielding, with some thinking he's a position change candidate, while others like his defense at shortstop, where he has good hands and an above-average arm with a quick release.

Year	Age	Club (League)	Class	AVG	G	AB	R	H	2B	3B	HR	RBI	BB	SO	SB	OBP	SLG
2017	20	Bluefield (APP)	R	.271	61	262	43	71	25	1	8	43	16	70	9	.312	.466
2018	21	Lansing (MWL)	LoA	.355	46	183	36	65	23	4	7	44	17	33	12	.407	.639
	21	Dunedin (FSL)	HiA	.274	83	340	57	93	8	2	18	49	23	88	17	.332	.468
2019	22	New Hampshire (EL)	AA	.209	116	430	49	90	22	2	19	61	29	151	11	.263	.402
Minor League Totals				.263	306	1215	185	319	78	9	52	197	85	342	49	.315	.470

26 JOEY MURRAY, RHP

BA GRADE 40 Risk: High

Born: Sept. 23, 1996. **B-T:** R-R. **HT:** 6-2. **WT:** 195. **Drafted:** Kent State, 2018 (8th round). **Signed by:** Coulson Barbiche.

TRACK RECORD: Murray has cruised through the Blue Jays farm system quickly, with performances that jump out more than his raw stuff. In his first full season, Murray led Toronto's farm system with 169 strikeouts, 50 more than the No. 2 player in the organization.

SCOUTING REPORT: He does it without overpowering anyone—his fastball mostly ranges from 87-92 mph—but with a tremendous amount of deception. It's a high-spin fastball relative to his velocity, and because of how difficult it is for hitters to track the ball out of his hand, Murray is able to generate surprising swing-and-miss when he throws his fastball. He throws a slow curveball that gets mixed reviews from scouts, with the ability to miss bats and keep hitters off-balance at times, but it's often a fringe-average pitch and still inconsistent. Developing a better changeup would be big for Murray to play off his fastball, but it's still a below-average pitch for him. Murray is a solid-strike thrower who is smart and well prepared, studying the strengths and weaknesses of opposing lineups. It's an unconventional profile, and while a lot of pitchers who rely on deception get filtered out once they reach the upper levels, Murray has already had some success at Double-A.

THE FUTURE: He could end up breaking through along the lines of Josh Collmenter to develop into a back-end starter.

Year	Age	Club (League)	Class	W	L	ERA	G	GS	SV	IP	H	HR	BB	SO	K/9	WHIP	AVG
2018	21	Vancouver (NWL)	SS	1	1	1.75	13	6	0	26	19	1	10	39	13.7	1.13	.204
2019	22	Lansing (MWL)	LoA	3	1	3.82	6	6	0	31	28	3	12	40	11.7	1.30	.239
	22	Dunedin (FSL)	HiA	5	2	1.71	12	11	1	63	40	3	19	77	11.0	0.94	.179
	22	New Hampshire (EL)	AA	2	4	3.50	9	8	0	44	37	4	18	52	10.7	1.26	.231
Minor League Totals				11	8	2.60	40	31	1	163	124	11	59	208	11.5	1.12	.209

27 YENNSY DIAZ, RHP

BA GRADE 40 Risk: High

Born: Nov. 15, 1996. **B-T:** R-R. **HT:** 6-1. **WT:** 210. **Signed:** Dominican Republic, 2014. **Signed by:** Ismael Cruz/Sandy Rosario/Luciano Del Rosario.

TRACK RECORD: The Blue Jays signed Diaz out of the Dominican Republic for $70,000 when he was 17 in 2014. He reached the upper levels of the system in 2019, eventually making his major league debut on Aug. 4 before getting sent back down to the Eastern League.

SCOUTING REPORT: Diaz has a plus fastball, sitting at 92-96 mph, with the ability to reach back for 98 mph. He's able to get swing-and-miss with his fastball, thanks to the velocity and the life on that pitch. Despite that, Diaz's overall strikeout rate is modest, as he doesn't have a true out pitch among his secondary offerings. His changeup is a 45 to 50 on the 20-80 scouting scale, while his breaking ball has its moments but is a fringe-average pitch. Diaz has made strides with his control, but he throws across his body and needs to still throw more strikes, especially without a bat-missing secondary weapon to fall back on.

THE FUTURE: Diaz should head to Triple-A Buffalo to open 2020 and, while there's some chance he can develop enough to pitch as a back-end starter, it's more likely he ends up in the bullpen—possibly a multi-inning relief role—where his fastball could play up in shorter stints and he wouldn't have to work over a lineup multiple times.

Year	Age	Club (League)	Class	W	L	ERA	G	GS	SV	IP	H	HR	BB	SO	K/9	WHIP	AVG
2017	20	Lansing (MWL)	LoA	5	2	4.79	16	16	0	77	71	10	41	82	9.6	1.45	.249
2018	21	Lansing (MWL)	LoA	5	1	2.08	9	9	0	48	22	4	25	42	7.9	0.99	.135
	21	Dunedin (FSL)	HiA	5	4	3.52	18	16	0	100	91	5	28	83	7.5	1.19	.242
2019	22	Toronto (AL)	MAJ	0	0	27.00	1	0	0	1	1	0	4	0	0.0	7.50	.333
	22	New Hampshire (EL)	AA	11	9	3.74	26	24	0	144	125	12	53	116	7.2	1.23	.234
Major League Totals				0	0	27.00	1	0	0	0	1	0	4	0	0.0	7.50	.333
Minor League Totals				34	26	3.84	96	84	1	481	422	40	197	429	8.0	1.29	.235

28 TANNER MORRIS, SS

BA GRADE
40 Risk: High

Born: Sept. 13, 1998. **B-T:** L-R. **HT:** 6-2. **WT:** 190. **Drafted:** Virginia, 2019 (5th round). **Signed by:** Coulson Barbiche.

TRACK RECORD: Morris performed at a high-level as a draft-eligible sophomore at Virginia in 2019, then signed with the Blue Jays for $397,500 as a fifth-round pick. Morris had a good track record of getting on base as an amateur and he continued to do that when he got to the short-season Northwest League.

SCOUTING REPORT: Morris is a disciplined hitter who does an excellent job controlling the strike zone. He doesn't chase much, working himself into favorable counts and has good bat control with a simple lefty stroke, so the components are there for him to be a high on-base threat. His swing and approach are geared toward hitting line drives and sending the ball the opposite way, which limits his power. There could be more untapped power in there for Morris if he adjusts his approach and learns how to pull pitches with authority, but he probably will always have a hit-over-power profile. Morris was a shortstop in college but is likely to end up at second or third base eventually, with some scouts thinking he might head to the outfield. He has a strong arm for the left side of the infield, but he's a below-average runner who lacks the first-step quickness or range for shortstop.

THE FUTURE: He should be in low Class A Lansing to start 2020.

Year	Age	Club (League)	Class	AVG	G	AB	R	H	2B	3B	HR	RBI	BB	SO	SB	OBP	SLG
2019	20	Vancouver (NWL)	SS	.246	64	240	37	59	16	1	2	28	49	56	4	.384	.346
Minor League Totals				.246	64	240	37	59	16	1	2	28	49	56	4	.384	.346

29 WILL ROBERTSON, OF

BA GRADE
40 Risk: High

Born: Dec. 26, 1997. **B-T:** L-L. **HT:** 6-2. **WT:** 215. **Drafted:** Creighton, 2019 (4th round). **Signed by:** Wes Penick.

TRACK RECORD: Robertson had two big years at Creighton and helped his stock with a strong summer in the Cape Cod League in 2018. The Blue Jays drafted him in the fourth round in 2019 and signed him for $422,500 before making his pro debut in the short-season Northwest League.

SCOUTING REPORT: Roberton has plenty of bat speed and strength to produce above-average raw power. He doesn't need to sell out to generate that power, with a short, level stroke that leads to a good amount of contact for a power hitter. There is some stiffness to his stroke, however, and he has an aggressive approach, so there are concerns about how that will affect him once he starts facing more advanced pitching. Robertson will have to mash as a corner outfielder with limited defensive value. He's a below-average runner with an average arm and needs to improve his reads and routes, projecting as a below-average defender.

THE FUTURE: He should be ticketed for low Class A Lansing to begin 2020.

Year	Age	Club (League)	Class	AVG	G	AB	R	H	2B	3B	HR	RBI	BB	SO	SB	OBP	SLG
2019	21	Vancouver (NWL)	SS	.268	61	228	33	61	11	1	6	33	31	49	1	.365	.404
Minor League Totals				.268	61	228	33	61	11	1	6	33	31	49	1	.365	.404

30 SEM ROBBERSE, RHP

BA GRADE
45 Risk: Extreme

Born: Oct. 12, 2001. **B-T:** R-R. **HT:** 6-1. **WT:** 180. **Signed:** Netherlands, 2019. **Signed by:** Andrew Tinnish.

TRACK RECORD: The Blue Jays also ventured into Europe to land Robberse, a promising, under-the-radar righthander from the Netherlands who signed for $125,000 in June 2019. Robberse's stock has been rising over the past year, with a plethora of projection indicators pointing up.

SCOUTING REPORT: In the summer of 2018, Robberse was a skinny 16-year-old throwing in the mid-80s. This spring before signing with the Blue Jays, Robberse pitched in Honkbal Hoofdklasse and reached 88 mph. After signing, Robberse came to the United States and hit 90 mph, then during the Rookie-level Gulf Coast League season he was sitting at 89-92 mph and touched 93. His lively fastball has come on as he's gotten stronger, adding 20 pounds since signing. There's probably more velocity coming, with Robberse having more physical upside and clean mechanics with a free-and-easy delivery. Robberse is athletic, which helps him repeat his delivery and command his fastball, a mix of two- and four-seamers. He shows feel for a breaking ball that flashes as a 55 pitch on the 20-80 scale, with a changeup that he's just learning

THE FUTURE: Rookie-level Bluefield or short-season Vancouver is likely up next for him.

Year	Age	Club (League)	Class	W	L	ERA	G	GS	SV	IP	H	HR	BB	SO	K/9	WHIP	AVG
2019	17	Blue Jays (GCL)	R	2	0	0.87	5	3	0	10	11	0	0	9	7.8	1.06	.275
Minor League Totals				2	0	0.87	5	3	0	10	11	0	0	9	7.8	1.06	.275

Washington Nationals

BY LACY LUSK

A pair of young outfielders helped the Nationals transition out of the Bryce Harper era and win a World Series for the first time in franchise history.

Left fielder Juan Soto, who turned 21 during the World Series against the 107-win Astros, was runner-up for National League Rookie of the Year in 2018 and had a comparable 2019. Then he delivered some of the biggest hits in the team's run toward D.C.'s first World Series title since the 1924 Senators.

In the NL Wild Card Game, Soto's eighth-inning single off Brewers closer Josh Hader drove in two runs—and a third scored on an error to give Washington the lead. Soto's eighth-inning home run off Clayton Kershaw tied the decisive NL Division Series Game 5 against the 106-win Dodgers before Howie Kendrick won it with a 10th-inning grand slam. After the Nationals swept the Cardinals in the Championship Series, Soto became the youngest player to hit three home runs in a World Series.

Also in 2019, center fielder Victor Robles, who entered the year ranked as the organization's No. 1 prospect, made the Opening Day roster as a 21-year-old. He was a Gold Glove finalist while hitting 17 home runs and stealing 28 bases.

New No. 1 prospect Carter Kieboom was one of four Nationals to make his major league debut in 2019, joining Jake Noll, James Bourque and Tres Barrera. Six other original Nationals signees, including Athletics prospect Jesus Luzardo, also made their debuts.

At the big league level, Washington rallied from a 19-31 start to finish with 93 wins and claim the top wild card. The franchise has four division titles and one wild card berth since 2012, and homegrown talent has played a large role in that either directly or through trades.

The current farm system likely doesn't have anyone as dominant as World Series MVP Stephen Strasburg and now-Phillies $330 million man Harper, the first overall picks in 2009 and 2010, but it has two high-level hitters leading the Top 10. Kieboom could have a role in Washington's infield in 2020, and Luis Garcia held his own as a 19-year-old in the Double-A Eastern League.

After those two, the organization features a mix of intriguing arms. Jackson Rutledge, a 2019 first-round pick, leads the way after a stellar showing at low Class A Hagerstown. Team officials also were encouraged by what they saw at instructional league in October, particularly from international signees Andry Lara and Eddy Yean

MITCHELL LAYTON/GETTY IMAGES

Rookie center fielder Victor Robles swiped 28 bases and was a Gold Glove finalist.

PROJECTED 2023 LINEUP

Position	Player	Age
Catcher	Tres Barrera	29
First Base	Drew Mendoza (6)	25
Second Base	Luis Garcia (2)	23
Third Base	Carter Kieboom (1)	25
Shortstop	Trea Turner	30
Left Field	Juan Soto	24
Center Field	Victor Robles	26
Right Field	Adam Eaton	34
No. 1 Starter	Stephen Strasburg	34
No. 2 Starter	Patrick Corbin	33
No. 3 Starter	Max Scherzer	38
No. 4 Starter	Jackson Rutledge (3)	24
No. 5 Starter	Wil Crowe (4)	28
Closer	Tanner Rainey	30

along with lefthander Seth Romero, who was returning from Tommy John surgery.

Washington player development weathered a season with its top affiliate stationed in Fresno. The Nationals frequently stashed players at Double-A Harrisburg instead because of proximity. The Nationals were unable to land a closer Triple-A affiliate after having to leave Syracuse when the Mets bought that franchise. They can search for a new Player Development Contract at Triple-A after the 2020 season.

Trades and promotions have hurt the depth of the Nationals' system, but the team believes several prospects, particularly on the pitching side, are set up to have breakout years in 2020.

DEPTH CHART

WASHINGTON NATIONALS

TOP 2020 ROOKIE: Carter Kieboom, SS/2B. The club's top prospect likely will get a longer look at a major league infield spot this season. He's the most seasoned and has the most opportunity of the organization's prospects.

BREAKOUT PROSPECT: Eddy Yean, RHP. He reached short-season Auburn as an 18-year-old and has the "it" factor according to officials.

SLEEPER: Jhonathan German, RHP. The 6-foot-4 reliever rose to Double-A on the strength of a high-90s fastball and a power slider. Throwing more strikes will be the key to him taking another step forward.

SOURCE OF TOP 30 TALENT

Homegrown	**30**	**Acquired**	**0**
College	16	Trade	0
Junior college	2	Rule 5 draft	0
High school	3	Independent league	0
Nondrafted free agent	0	Free agent/waivers	0
International	9		

LF
Jeremy De La Rosa (13)
Nick Banks (26)
Telmito Agustin
Yadiel Hernandez
Ricardo Mendez

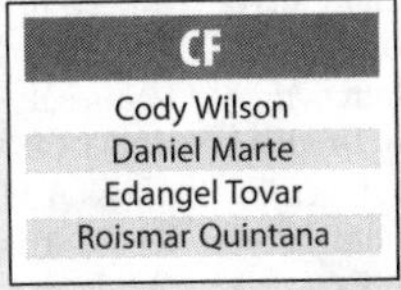

CF
Cody Wilson
Daniel Marte
Edangel Tovar
Roismar Quintana

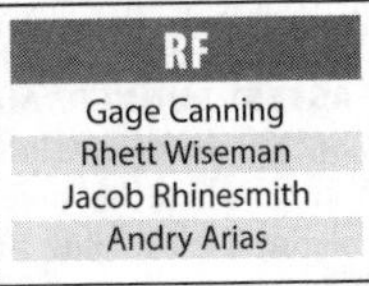

RF
Gage Canning
Rhett Wiseman
Jacob Rhinesmith
Andry Arias

3B
Jake Noll
Gilbert Lara
Ian Sagdal

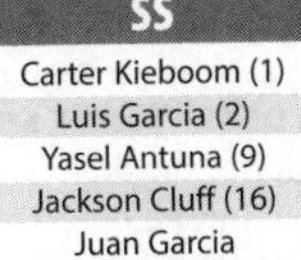

SS
Carter Kieboom (1)
Luis Garcia (2)
Yasel Antuna (9)
Jackson Cluff (16)
Juan Garcia

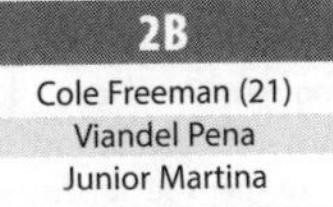

2B
Cole Freeman (21)
Viandel Pena
Junior Martina

1B
Drew Mendoza (6)
Drew Ward
Aldrem Corredor
K.J. Harrison
Leandro Emiliani

C
Tres Barrera (11)
Israel Pineda (19)
Jakson Reetz (28)
Raudy Read

LHP

LHSP
Tim Cate (5)
Seth Romero (10)
Nick Raquet (29)

LHRP
Matt Cronin (14)
Ben Braymer (20)
Bryan Pena

RHP

RHSP
Jackson Rutledge (3)
Wil Crowe (4)
Andry Lara (7)
Mason Denaburg (8)
Eddy Yean (12)
Jake Irvin (15)
Tyler Dyson (17)
Reid Schaller (18)
Joan Adon (23)
Jackson Tetreault (24)
Malvin Pena (25)
Tomas Alastre
Niomar Gomez

RHRP
James Bourque (22)
Steven Fuentes (27)
Jhonatan German (30)
Trey Turner
Francys Peguero
Kyle McGowin
Andrew Lee
Joan Baez
Jacob Condra-Bogan

DRAFT ANALYSIS

2019

BEST PURE HITTER: 3B Drew Mendoza hit .304/.447/.549 over a three-year career at Florida State. Mendoza will need to cut down his strikeout rate (23.8 percent at low Class A Hagerstown) and get a bit more aggressive in hitter's counts, but he has a solid understanding of the strike zone and good feel to hit.

BEST POWER HITTER: Mendoza currently has a power-over-hit profile, with at least 60-grade power that some scouts would describe as double-plus. He never had an issue tapping into that juice in college with a metal bat, but he might need some refinement to get the most out of his power.

FASTEST RUNNER: After a two-year church mission, SS Jackson Cluff (6) returned to Brigham Young, where he stole 12 bases without getting caught. He's a plus runner, which should allow him to be a distraction on the bases and cover a good amount of ground defensively.

BEST DEFENSIVE PLAYER: The Nationals got aggressive with Cluff's initial pro assignment because of his age—he will turn 23 in December—and his current defensive polish. He has solid hands and good footwork and can play both middle infield positions, though almost all of his professional innings were spent at shortstop, where he managed a .971 fielding percentage.

BEST ATHLETE: Cluff is a solid athlete, as is OF Jeremy Ydens (8), who missed time during the spring at UCLA thanks to a broken finger. Ydens has advanced feel to hit due to a loose, athletic swing that's consistently on time.

BEST FASTBALL: The Nationals made RHP Jackson Rutledge (1) the highest-drafted junior college pitcher this century when they took him with the 17th overall pick. Rutledge had the best pure stuff of any pitcher in the 2019 class, including a fastball that has touched as high as 102 mph and sits in the upper 90s deep into starts. It's an 80-grade offering.

BEST SECONDARY PITCH: LHP Matt Cronin (4) improved his curveball significantly during his junior season with Arkansas, to the point where his 12-to-6 curve is an easy plus offering. Rutledge will show a plus slider at times and also has a plus curveball.

BEST PRO DEBUT: In 17 games and 22 innings in Class A Hagerstown, Cronin struck out 41 batters (16.8 strikeouts per nine innings) to just 11 walks while posting a 0.82 ERA and holding opposing hitters to a .153 batting average.

MOST INTRIGUING BACKGROUND: Cluff didn't skip a beat once he returned to BYU. His added strength allowed him to hit for significantly more extra-base hits. OF Jake Randa (13) is the son of 12-year major leaguer Joe Randa.

CLOSEST TO THE MAJORS: Cronin was identified prior to the draft as the sort of power reliever who could move quickly through the minors thanks to a fast arm, above-average fastball and plus curveball. In Washington's system, he should be able to move quickly to help a major league bullpen.

BEST LATE-ROUND PICK: Washington signed SS Junior Martina (16) for $100,000 early on Day 3, and he went to the Rookie-level Gulf Coast League, where he finished 10th in batting with a .338/.461/.515 slash line before earning a late-season promotion to the New York-Penn League.

THE ONE WHO GOT AWAY: Washington signed each of its first picks through 25 rounds, but really liked RHP Bryce Osmond (35) and C Tyler LaRue (38). Osmond has legitimate two-way talent but most scouts prefer his upside on the mound.

—CARLOS COLLAZO

TOP DRAFT PICKS OF THE DECADE

Year	Player, Pos	2019 Org
2010	Bryce Harper, OF	Phillies
2011	Anthony Rendon, 3B	Nationals
2012	Lucas Giolito, RHP	White Sox
2013	Jake Johansen, RHP (2nd round)	Did not play
2014	Erick Fedde, RHP	Nationals
2015	Andrew Stevenson, OF (2nd round)	Nationals
2016	Carter Kieboom, SS	Nationals
2017	Seth Romero, LHP	Nationals
2018	Mason Denaburg, RHP	Nationals
2019	Jackson Rutledge, RHP	Nationals

2018

RHP Mason Denaburg (1) has promise but has dealt with injury problems throughout his young pro career. LHP Tim Cate (2) was solid in 2019, while RHPs Reid Schaller (3) and Jake Irvin (4) show promise.

GRADE: C

2017

LHP Seth Romero (1) remains an enigma after missing time due to Tommy John surgery and suspension. But he and RHP Wil Crowe (2) have real upside going forward as they continue their development.

GRADE: D

2016

This class is star-studded and has already gotten five players to the big leagues, including SS Carter Kieboom (1). LHP Jesus Luzardo (3), part of the deal for Sean Doolittle, has the most upside of the group.

GRADE: A

1 CARTER KIEBOOM, SS/2B

Born: Sept. 3, 1997. **B-T:** R-R. **HT:** 6-2. **WT:** 190.
Drafted: HS—Marietta, Ga., 2016 (1st round).
Signed by: Eric Robinson.

TRACK RECORD: Carter became the second Kieboom to play for the Nationals when he made his debut on April 26 and homered in his first major league game. His older brother Spencer is a catcher who played for the Nationals in 2016 and 2018. The younger Kieboom spent two weeks in the majors when Trea Turner was injured before returning to Triple-A Fresno for the rest of the season, where he ranked in the top 10 in the Pacific Coast League in on-base percentage (.405) despite being one of the circuit's youngest players. He was a Futures Game selection for the second straight year.

SCOUTING REPORT: Nationals manager Davey Martinez noted that all the skills are there for Kieboom to succeed and that it's just a matter of time until the game slows down enough for him to succeed in the majors. Kieboom is a patient hitter who habitually gets into good counts and punishes fastballs over the plate. He has a steady, consistent approach and never seems overwhelmed. He hits to all fields and recognizes breaking pitches well, grading as a future plus hitter with blossoming power that will be average or better. He has a steady heartbeat and flourishes in big situations. Kieboom is a fringe-average runner, but he has the hands and range to be an average defensive shortstop. He pushes the ball on his throws due to an irregular arm action, affecting his accuracy just enough for most evaluators to prefer him at second base. He played a career-high 41 games at second base with Fresno and is still learning the angles and shifts for the position. He plays under control at second base and could have above-average arm strength for the position, with the reflexes, hands and arm to handle third base as well.

THE FUTURE: Where Kieboom plays in Washington depends largely on need, but his ability to play all over the infield has put him in a good position. He projects as a No. 2 hitter with the potential to grow into enough power to hit in the middle of a lineup one day. He should get his first extended exposure to the big leagues in 2020, where the Nationals could have openings at second base and possibly third base now that Anthony Rendon has departed as a free agent.

PATRICK SMITH/GETTY IMAGES

BA GRADE
60 **Risk: Medium**

SCOUTING GRADES
Hit: 60. **Power:** 50. **Run:** 45. **Field:** 50. **Arm:** 55.

Projected future grades on 20-80 scouting scale.

TOP PROSPECTS OF THE DECADE

Year	Player, Pos.	2019 Org
2010	Stephen Strasburg, RHP	Nationals
2011	Bryce Harper, OF	Phillies
2012	Bryce Harper, OF	Phillies
2013	Anthony Rendon, 3B	Nationals
2014	Lucas Giolito, RHP	White Sox
2015	Lucas Giolito, RHP	White Sox
2016	Lucas Giolito, RHP	White Sox
2017	Victor Robles, OF	Nationals
2018	Victor Robles, OF	Nationals
2019	Victor Robles, OF	Nationals

BEST TOOLS

Best Hitter for Average	Luis Garcia
Best Power Hitter	Yadiel Hernandez
Best Strike-Zone Discipline	Drew Mendoza
Fastest Baserunner	Cole Freeman
Best Athlete	Sterling Sharp
Best Fastball	Jackson Rutledge
Best Curveball	James Bourque
Best Slider	Seth Romero
Best Changeup	Wil Crowe
Best Control	Tim Cate
Best Defensive Catcher	Tres Barrera
Best Defensive Infielder	Luis Garcia
Best Infield Arm	Luis Garcia
Best Defensive Outfielder	Cody Wilson
Best Outfield Arm	Rhett Wiseman.

Year	Age	Club (League)	Class	AVG	G	AB	R	H	2B	3B	HR	RBI	BB	SO	SB	OBP	SLG
2017	19	Nationals (GCL)	R	.417	6	12	1	5	3	0	0	5	3	0	0	.563	.667
	19	Auburn (NYP)	SS	.250	7	28	4	7	1	0	1	4	1	2	1	.276	.393
	19	Hagerstown (SAL)	LoA	.296	48	179	36	53	12	0	8	26	28	40	2	.400	.497
2018	20	Potomac (CAR)	HiA	.298	61	245	48	73	15	0	11	46	36	50	6	.386	.494
	20	Harrisburg (EL)	AA	.262	62	248	36	65	16	1	5	23	22	59	3	.326	.395
2019	21	Washington (NL)	MAJ	.128	11	39	4	5	0	0	2	2	4	16	0	.209	.282
	21	Fresno (PCL)	AAA	.303	109	412	79	125	24	3	16	79	68	100	5	.409	.493
Major League Totals				.128	11	39	4	5	0	0	2	2	4	16	0	.209	.282
Minor League Totals				.287	329	1259	226	361	79	8	45	208	170	294	18	.378	.469

2 LUIS GARCIA, SS/2B

Born: May 16, 2000. **B-T:** L-R. **HT:** 6-2. **WT:** 190. **Signed:** Dominican Republic, 2016. **Signed by:** Carlos Ulloa.

TRACK RECORD: Garcia, whose father Luis played in the majors, was born in New York and moved to the Dominican Republic when he was 3. He grew into one of the top international prospects for his age and signed for $1.3 million in 2016. After hitting nearly .300 at both Class A levels in 2018, Garcia struggled to handle a tough assignment at Double-A. He did hit .278 in August and he also hit .276/.345/.382 in an impressive stint in the Arizona Fall League.

SCOUTING REPORT: Garcia was a teenager in a man's league in 2019, but he never wavered. He has solid bat-to-ball skills but needs to improve his strike-zone knowledge and connect his upper and lower half in his swing. He shows hints of fringe-average power but the lefthanded batter primarily is a contact hitter. Garcia makes all the plays at shortstop laterally with a precise internal clock. His plus, accurate arm gives him the chance to be a plus shortstop. Garcia is an above-average runner now but will likely slow down to average as he becomes older and more physical.

THE FUTURE: Even if Garcia returns to the Eastern League in 2020, he would be one of the youngest players on the field each night. He'll get another crack at Double-A in 2020.

SCOUTING GRADES: **Hitting:** 55 **Power:** 45 **Running:** 50 **Fielding:** 60 **Arm:** 60

Year	Age	Club (League)	Class	AVG	G	AB	R	H	2B	3B	HR	RBI	BB	SO	SB	OBP	SLG
2017	17	Nationals (GCL)	R	.302	49	199	25	60	8	3	1	22	9	32	11	.330	.387
2018	18	Hagerstown (SAL)	LoA	.297	78	296	48	88	14	4	3	31	19	49	8	.335	.402
	18	Potomac (CAR)	HiA	.299	49	204	34	61	7	2	4	23	12	33	4	.338	.412
2019	19	Harrisburg (EL)	AA	.257	129	525	66	135	22	4	4	30	17	86	11	.280	.337
Minor League Totals				.281	305	1224	173	344	51	13	12	106	57	200	34	.312	.373

3 JACKSON RUTLEDGE, RHP

MIKE JANES/FOUR SEAM IMAGES

Born: April 1, 1999. **B-T:** R-R. **HT:** 6-8. **WT:** 250. **Drafted:** San Jacinto (Texas) JC, 2019 (1st round). **Signed by:** Brandon Larson.

TRACK RECORD: Rutledge began his college career at Arkansas, but he barely pitched and suffered a season-ending hip injury before transferring to San Jacinto JC. He experienced a velocity bump after rehabbing, touching 101 mph, and became one of the top pitching prospects in the 2019 draft class. The Nationals drafted him No. 17 overall and signed for $3.45 million.

SCOUTING REPORT: Though Rutledge is 6-foot-8, he has a short arm action and a shorter stride than expected. His arm action, reminiscent of former Nationals prospect Lucas Giolito, helps Rutledge maintain command of his 94-98 mph fastball. Rutledge also has good present secondary stuff, especially his plus slider. He's athletic for his size and is capable of throwing four above-average pitches, with his curveball and changeup showing above-average to plus. Rutledge is still honing in on his control and shows average strike-throwing potential, though he will occasionally get wild. He has shown an interest in analytics and takes a studious approach to his starts.

THE FUTURE: Rutledge was dominant in his six low Class A starts, and his next test could be at high Class A Fredericksburg. His biggest task will be adapting to a five-day schedule.

SCOUTING GRADES: **Fastball:** 80 **Slider:** 60 **Curveball:** 55 **Changeup:** 55 **Control:** 45

Year	Age	Club (League)	Class	W	L	ERA	G	GS	SV	IP	H	HR	BB	SO	K/9	WHIP	AVG
2019	20	Nationals (GCL)	R	0	0	27.00	1	1	0	1	4	0	1	2	18.0	5.00	.571
	20	Auburn (NYP)	SS	0	0	3.00	3	3	0	9	4	2	3	6	6.0	0.78	.133
	20	Hagerstown (SAL)	LoA	2	0	2.30	6	6	0	27	14	0	11	31	10.2	0.91	.151
Minor League Totals				2	0	3.13	10	10	0	37	22	2	15	39	9.4	0.99	.169

SAMUEL GETTY

BA GRADE

50 **Risk: Medium**

4 WIL CROWE, RHP

Born: Sept. 9, 1994. **B-T:** R-R. **HT:** 6-2. **WT:** 240. **Drafted:** South Carolina, 2017 (2nd round). **Signed by:** Paul Faulk.

TRACK RECORD: Crowe had Tommy John surgery in 2015 and missed all of 2016 at South Carolina, but rebounded in 2017 to become the Nationals' second-round pick. He won high Class A Carolina League Pitcher of the Year honors in his first full season but struggled after being bumped to Double-A. He fared much better in his second Eastern League try in 2019, posting a 3.87 ERA, and finished the year at Triple-A Fresno.

SCOUTING REPORT: Crowe is continuing to learn which of his four pitches works best at which times. His fastball velocity has increased each year and he now sits 92-93 mph with the ability to reach 95. His four-seam fastball plays up more than its raw velocity would suggest due to an elite spin rate that makes it an above-average pitch, and he can mix in a sinker to change hitters' eye levels. His changeup is a swing-and-miss pitch that draws above-average grades, and he shows feel to spin both an average curveball and slider. Crowe has the actions and durability to remain a starter, but his stuff would play up in the bullpen, too.

THE FUTURE: Crowe will continue to see what his stuff can do against more advanced hitters. He's seen as a future major leaguer, but the question could be what role he'll play.

SCOUTING GRADES: **Fastball:** 55 **Slider:** 50 **Curveball:** 50 **Changeup:** 55 **Control:** 50

Year	Age	Club (League)	Class	W	L	ERA	G	GS	SV	IP	H	HR	BB	SO	K/9	WHIP	AVG
2017	22	Nationals (GCL)	R	0	0	4.91	2	2	0	4	3	0	1	2	4.9	1.09	.250
	22	Auburn (NYP)	SS	0	0	2.61	7	7	0	21	18	3	3	15	6.5	1.02	.234
2018	23	Auburn (NYP)	SS	0	0	0.00	1	1	0	3	2	0	2	1	3.0	1.33	.222
	23	Potomac (CAR)	HiA	11	0	2.69	16	15	0	87	71	6	30	78	8.1	1.16	.220
	23	Harrisburg (EL)	AA	0	5	6.15	5	5	0	26	31	4	16	15	5.1	1.78	.307
2019	24	Harrisburg (EL)	AA	7	6	3.87	16	16	0	95	85	8	22	89	8.4	1.12	.242
	24	Fresno (PCL)	AAA	0	4	6.17	10	10	0	54	66	7	26	41	6.8	1.70	.303
Minor League Totals				18	15	4.03	57	56	0	290	276	28	100	241	7.5	1.30	.253

5 TIM CATE, LHP

BA GRADE

50 **Risk: High**

Born: Sept. 30, 1997. **B-T:** L-L. **HT:** 6-0. **WT:** 185. **Drafted:** Connecticut, 2018 (2nd round). **Signed by:** John Malzone.

TRACK RECORD: When he was at Connecticut, Cate was famous for having one of the best curveballs in the nation, although his small stature raised some durability concerns. Cate is ambidextrous. He had Tommy John surgery on his left elbow in high school, but while he recovered, he just batted, pitched and played the outfield as a righthander.

SCOUTING REPORT: When the Nationals drafted Cate, the hope was his 90-92 mph velocity would steadily tick up. Instead, he's struggled to maintain that, often dipping to 89-90 in starts. Even with only a fringe-average fastball at best, Cate transitioned smoothly to high Class A in 2019 after thriving at low A Hagerstown thanks to plus control. Cate's curveball has teeth and depth to it. A previously below-average changeup has improved, and he still had life on a fastball that he can cut, sink or run. At instructional league, he worked on his changeup and a small tweak to his delivery. He didn't pitch in any games but focused on preparing himself for 2020. He's a student of the game who has adjusted well to a five-day schedule in pro ball.

THE FUTURE: Some scouts believe Cate needs to build more stamina, but he has the workings of a potential back-of-the-rotation starter if the improvement he's made with his changeup sticks. If not, his fastball and curveball should play up in shorter bullpen stints.

SCOUTING GRADES: **Fastball:** 45 **Curveball:** 70 **Changeup:** 50 **Control:** 55

Year	Age	Club (League)	Class	W	L	ERA	G	GS	SV	IP	H	HR	BB	SO	K/9	WHIP	AVG
2018	20	Auburn (NYP)	SS	2	3	4.65	9	8	0	31	34	1	10	26	7.5	1.42	.272
	20	Hagerstown (SAL)	LoA	0	3	5.57	4	4	0	21	23	4	6	19	8.1	1.38	.271
2019	21	Hagerstown (SAL)	LoA	4	5	2.82	13	13	0	70	61	2	13	73	9.3	1.05	.232
	21	Potomac (CAR)	HiA	7	4	3.31	13	13	0	73	71	4	19	66	8.1	1.23	.255
Minor League Totals				13	15	3.59	39	38	0	195	189	11	48	184	8.5	1.21	.252

6 DREW MENDOZA, 1B

Born: Oct. 10, 1997. **B-T:** L-R. **HT:** 6-5. **WT:** 230. **Drafted:** Florida State, 2019 (3rd round). **Signed by:** Alan Marr.

BA GRADE
50 Risk: High

TRACK RECORD: Mendoza ranked as one of the top high school prospects in the 2016 draft but was strongly committed to Florida State, where both of his parents attended. After leading the Seminoles to two College World Series appearances in three years, he signed with the Nationals for $800,000 as their third-round pick in 2019. A college third baseman and shortstop, Mendoza moved to first base in his first summer as a professional with low Class A Hagerstown.

SCOUTING REPORT: Mendoza has the tools to hit and is extremely knowledgeable of the strike zone, but at times he is overly passive. The Nationals are looking for more of a ready-to-hit mentality, which should get him into fewer two-strike counts. Mendoza hits drives to center field and the opposite field and is athletic for such a big man. He can be an average hitter with above-average power as he hones his approach. Mendoza's athleticism was on display defensively when he quickly took to playing first base, looking like a natural around the bag as he worked out with infield coordinator Jeff Garber. He has soft hands and an above-average arm for a first baseman.

THE FUTURE: Mendoza is expected to take his calm hitting approach to high Class A in 2020. He has room to fill out and hit for more power.

SCOUTING GRADES: Hitting: 50 | Power: 55 | Running: 40 | Fielding: 55 | Arm: 55

Year	Age	Club (League)	Class	AVG	G	AB	R	H	2B	3B	HR	RBI	BB	SO	SB	OBP	SLG
2019	21	Hagerstown (SAL)	LoA	.264	55	201	23	53	12	0	4	25	34	57	3	.377	.383
Minor League Totals				.264	55	201	23	53	12	0	4	25	34	57	3	.377	.383

7 ANDRY LARA, RHP

Born: Jan. 6, 2003. **B-T:** R-R. **HT:** 6-4. **WT:** 217. **Signed:** Venezuela, 2019. **Signed by:** Ronald Morillo.

TRACK RECORD: Scouts German Robles and Juan Indriago quickly identified Lara as a priority target for the Nationals in the 2019 international signing class, and international director Johnny DiPuglia liked what he saw in the loose-limbed power pitcher as well. The Nationals signed him for $1.25 million on July 2. Lara focused on a throwing program and drills before starting a mound progression in mid-August. He pitched in instructional league and then for seven weeks at Dominican instructs.

SCOUTING REPORT: The 16-year-old Lara quickly won over club officials who saw him for the first time in Florida. His fastball was clocked at 92-95 mph. He has an advanced feel for pitching and repeats his delivery well for someone his age. He has a power curveball and can manipulate its depth and velocity. He has the makings of a changeup, and he throws all his pitches with a downhill angle. Lara has a strong and durable pitcher's frame. He's a confident young pitcher with a fluid delivery.

THE FUTURE: It's easy to dream on Lara, who is slated to start his first pro season in extended spring training. He has a chance to pitch in the Rookie-level Gulf Coast League before the end of the season and has the ingredients to emerge as a breakout prospect.

SCOUTING GRADES: Fastball: 60 | Curveball: 55 | Changeup: 50 | Control: 50

Year	Age	Club (League)	Class	W	L	ERA	G	GS	SV	IP	H	HR	BB	SO	K/9	WHIP	AVG
2019	16	Did not play—Signed 2020 contract															

8 MASON DENABURG, RHP

MIKE JANES/FOUR SEAM IMAGES

BA GRADE
55 **Risk: Extreme**

Born: Aug. 8, 1999. **B-T:** R-R. **HT:** 6-4. **WT:** 195. **Drafted:** HS—Merritt Island, Fla., 2018 (1st round). **Signed by:** Alan Marr.

TRACK RECORD: Denaburg was the 27th overall pick in 2018 despite missing time in high school with biceps tendinitis. He signed for $3 million, some of which he used for a Christmas gift for his parents by paying off their loans. The video of his appreciative moment has more than 2,600 likes on Twitter. Denaburg pitched in instructional league during his draft year, but he didn't make his minor league debut until 2019, when he again wasn't healthy. He had minor shoulder surgery after the season and is expected to be back for the start of spring training.

SCOUTING REPORT: When healthy, Denaburg has a mid-90s fastball and an above-average curveball and changeup. The secondary stuff needs more consistency. The Nationals are hoping he can be a righthanded version of Robbie Ray, a 2010 Nationals draft pick who needed time to overcome injuries and reach the majors. Though Denaburg's velocity was down in the Gulf Coast League, he has a strong repertoire when healthy. He's also a good athlete capable of repeating his delivery.

THE FUTURE: Denaburg will continue to learn the pro game. In 2019, he pitched through adversity, but he's still a young pitcher with a high upside.

SCOUTING GRADES: **Fastball:** 60 **Curveball:** 55 **Changeup:** 55 **Control:** 50

Year	Age	Club (League)	Class	W	L	ERA	G	GS	SV	IP	H	HR	BB	SO	K/9	WHIP	AVG
2019	19	Nationals (GCL)	R	1	1	7.52	7	4	0	20	23	1	14	19	8.4	1.82	.288
Minor League Totals				1	1	7.52	7	4	0	20	23	1	14	19	8.4	1.82	.288

9 YASEL ANTUNA, SS

BA GRADE
55 **Risk: Extreme**

Born: Oct. 26, 1999. **B-T:** B-R. **HT:** 6-0. **WT:** 170. **Signed:** Dominican Republic, 2016. **Signed by:** Pablo Arias.

TRACK RECORD: Antuna signed for $3.85 million on July 2 as the Nationals' top signee in the 2016 international class. While fellow 2016 signee Luis Garcia has played a full season in Double-A, Antuna has yet to reach high Class A. He was limited to just three games in 2019 due to Tommy John surgery and leg injuries. He has just 502 at-bats in three years.

SCOUTING REPORT: When healthy, the switch-hitting Antuna has a smooth swing from both sides of the plate and the strength to impact the ball. He has shown plus raw power potential and an easy looseness to his swing. He flashed his potential at low Class A Hagerstown in the middle of 2018 before going down with an elbow injury that required surgery. Before Tommy John, Antuna had a plus arm from shortstop and the soft hands and body control to remain at the position. Antuna posted a .220/.293/.331 line before his surgery at low Class A Hagerstown of the South Atlantic League.

THE FUTURE: Antuna got bigger and stronger during his rehab, so the organization expects to see a more physical player with line-drive power when he returns in 2020. He'll be just 20 years old all of next season and has time to get back on track.

SCOUTING GRADES: **Hitting:** 50 **Power:** 55 **Running:** 50 **Fielding:** 50 **Arm:** 60

Year	Age	Club (League)	Class	AVG	G	AB	R	H	2B	3B	HR	RBI	BB	SO	SB	OBP	SLG
2017	17	Nationals (GCL)	R	.301	48	173	25	52	8	3	1	17	23	29	5	.382	.399
2018	18	Hagerstown (SAL)	LoA	.220	87	323	44	71	14	2	6	27	32	79	8	.293	.331
2019	19	Nationals (GCL)	R	.167	3	6	1	1	0	0	0	0	2	1	0	.375	.167
Minor League Totals				.247	138	502	70	124	22	5	7	44	57	109	13	.325	.353

10 SETH ROMERO, LHP

Born: April 19, 1996. **B-T:** L-L. **HT:** 6-3. **WT:** 240. **Drafted:** Houston, 2017 (1st round). **Signed by:** Tyler Wilt.

GLEN GASTON

BA GRADE
55 **Risk: Extreme**

TRACK RECORD: Romero had 290 strikeouts in 226.1 innings in his college career at Houston, but he was suspended his sophomore year and kicked off the team his junior year. The Nationals still took him 25th overall and signed him for $2.8 million. The next spring, he was sent home for violating team rules. Romero returned to strike out 34 in 25.1 innings at low Class A Hagerstown but then needed Tommy John surgery and missed the 2019 season. He was able to pitch one inning in instructional league, a dazzling outing in which he pumped strikes with all of his pitches.

SCOUTING REPORT: On stuff alone, Romero is among the best pitchers in the Nationals' system. The ball comes out clean in his delivery, and he's a strike-thrower. Prior to surgery, Romero had feel for locating his 93-95 mph fastball, and his plus low-80s slider drew swings and misses from batters on both sides of the plate. He throws the best slider in the Nationals' system. His changeup flashed above-average as well, giving him the raw stuff of a mid-rotation starter.

THE FUTURE: At 23, Romero can still set a positive course. His main goals will be building back up and staying out of trouble, two things he has yet to show he can do.

SCOUTING GRADES: **Fastball:** 60 **Slider:** 60 **Changeup:** 55 **Control:** 50

Year	Age	Club (League)	Class	W	L	ERA	G	GS	SV	IP	H	HR	BB	SO	K/9	WHIP	AVG
2017	21	Nationals (GCL)	R	0	0	0.00	1	1	0	2	0	0	2	3	13.5	1.00	.000
	21	Auburn (NYP)	SS	0	1	5.40	6	6	0	20	19	0	6	32	14.4	1.25	.244
2018	22	Hagerstown (SAL)	LoA	0	1	3.91	7	7	0	25	20	3	8	34	12.1	1.11	.206
2019	23	Did not play—Injured															
Minor League Totals				0	2	4.37	14	14	0	47	39	3	16	69	13.1	1.16	.215

11 TRES BARRERA, C

BA GRADE
45 **Risk: High**

Born: Sept. 15, 1994. **B-T:** R-R. **HT:** 6-0. **WT:** 215. **Drafted:** Texas, 2016 (6th round). **Signed by:** Tyler Wilt.

TRACK RECORD: Barrera, who signed for $210,000, has risen through the system one rung at a time, starting at short-season Auburn in his draft year. In 2019 at Double-A Harrisburg, he set a career high in home runs. He thought his season was over but was summoned to the major leagues when Nationals catcher Kurt Suzuki needed time to rest his elbow in September.

SCOUTING REPORT: The Nationals see Barrera as someone who will eventually stick in the major leagues, and his bat will determine whether he's a regular or a backup. He found a consistent hitting position at Harrisburg and used the whole field. He kept his hands inside the ball and had a repeatable swing. Barrera has decent strike-zone knowledge as a hitter. He's slow on the bases, but scouts say he's athletic behind the plate. His receiving, blocking and throwing are all good, and his leadership skills are even better. One team official noted that "all he cares about is winning."

THE FUTURE: Triple-A Fresno is the next progression for Barrera, who now has his spot on the 40-man roster.

Year	Age	Club (League)	Class	AVG	G	AB	R	H	2B	3B	HR	RBI	BB	SO	SB	OBP	SLG
2017	22	Hagerstown (SAL)	LoA	.278	67	237	28	66	18	1	8	27	23	58	1	.354	.464
2018	23	Potomac (CAR)	HiA	.263	68	259	36	68	14	0	6	24	22	53	3	.334	.386
2019	24	Harrisburg (EL)	AA	.249	101	357	42	89	23	0	8	46	36	69	1	.323	.381
	24	Washington (NL)	MAJ	.000	2	2	0	0	0	0	0	0	0	0	0	.000	.000
Major League Totals				.000	2	2	0	0	0	0	0	0	0	0	0	.000	.000
Minor League Totals				.259	284	1017	125	263	64	2	25	114	96	202	5	.336	.399

12 EDDY YEAN, RHP

Born: June 25, 2001. **B-T:** R-R. **HT:** 6-1. **WT:** 180. **Signed:** Dominican Republic, 2017 **Signed by:** Pablo Arias.

TRACK RECORD: Yean signed for $100,000 in 2017 and has since upped his fastball velocity to the 92-97 mph range. He earned a promotion to short-season Auburn for his final two starts of 2019. In his last outing, he threw just 73 pitches in a six-inning complete-game loss at Williamsport in the first game of a doubleheader on Aug. 28. He allowed two runs in that outing and two (one earned) in five innings in his other start with the Doubledays.

SCOUTING REPORT: Yean's a physical athlete with a power pitcher's body. He has a clean delivery, and the ball jumps out of his hand. He has electric stuff and one of the highest ceilings among pitchers in the system. He has increased the depth on his slider, which is a swing-and-miss pitch for him. Yean is also improving the feel of his changeup.

THE FUTURE: After closing the year with a strong showing in the instructional league, Yean has momentum going into 2020. He has only 90 career minor league innings, but he has quickly improved his stock.

Year	Age	Club (League)	Class	W	L	ERA	G	GS	SV	IP	H	HR	BB	SO	K/9	WHIP	AVG
2018	17	Nationals (DSL)	R	1	2	5.98	11	10	0	44	57	1	23	32	6.6	1.83	.322
2019	18	Nationals (GCL)	R	1	2	3.82	8	8	0	35	30	3	12	36	9.2	1.19	.233
	18	Auburn (NYP)	SS	1	1	2.45	2	2	0	11	7	0	5	7	5.7	1.09	.180
Minor League Totals				3	5	4.70	21	20	0	90	94	4	40	75	7.5	1.49	.272

13 JEREMY DE LA ROSA, OF

BA GRADE 50 Risk: Extreme

Born: Jan. 16, 2002. **B-T:** L-L. **HT:** 5-11. **WT:** 160. **Signed:** Dominican Republic, 2018 **Signed by:** Modesto Ulloa.

TRACK RECORD: De La Rosa signed for $300,000 and participated stateside in instructional league three months later. In 2019, he was back in Florida as a 17-year-old in the Gulf Coast League. He has the potential to have five above-average tools, especially in hitting, power and speed.

SCOUTING REPORT: Leg issues limited De La Rosa in his debut professional season, but he still flashed his array of skills. He has an advanced feel for the strike zone and swings a quick bat. The compact, strong De La Rosa is capable of playing all three outfield spots. In the GCL, he improved the use of his bottom half in his swing. He gets into a good hitting position and has good power for a player his age. His bat-to-ball skills project to be among the best in the organization. De La Rosa may not be a burner, but he has good speed.

THE FUTURE: De La Rosa is raw at this point, but he has a high ceiling and could be pushed quickly, perhaps to low Class A Hagerstown early in 2020.

Year	Age	Club (League)	Class	AVG	G	AB	R	H	2B	3B	HR	RBI	BB	SO	SB	OBP	SLG
2019	17	Nationals (GCL)	R	.232	26	82	14	19	1	2	2	10	12	29	3	.343	.366
Minor League Totals				.232	26	82	14	19	1	2	2	10	12	29	3	.343	.366

14 MATT CRONIN, LHP

BA GRADE 45 Risk: High

Born: Sept. 20, 1997. **B-T:** L-L. **HT:** 6-2. **WT:** 195. **Drafted:** Arkansas, 2019 (4th round). **Signed by:** Jerad Head.

TRACK RECORD: One of the top relievers in the Southeastern Conference, Cronin had 26 saves in his final two seasons at Arkansas, helping the Razorbacks reach the College World Series both years. He had a mild case of mononucleosis as a sophomore but still broke a single-season school record with 14 saves. He sharpened his curveball in his junior year, showing a 12-to-6 hammer that helped persuade the Nationals to sign him for $464,500.

SCOUTING REPORT: Cronin has a plus fastball and curveball, and at times his slider is plus as well. He's working on dialing back his full-effort delivery. Even with the major leagues scheduled to go to a three-batter minimum in 2020, Cronin fills a dire need in a system short on lefthanded relievers. He has a chance to move quickly through the organization.

THE FUTURE: Cronin held South Atlantic League hitters to a .153 average and probably could've thrived at a higher level. He should go to at least high Class A Fredericksburg to start his first full pro season.

Year	Age	Club (League)	Class	W	L	ERA	G	GS	SV	IP	H	HR	BB	SO	K/9	WHIP	AVG
2019	21	Hagerstown (SAL)	LoA	0	0	0.82	17	0	1	22	11	1	11	41	16.8	1.00	.153
Minor League Totals				0	0	0.82	17	0	1	22	11	1	11	41	16.8	1.00	.153

15 JAKE IRVIN, RHP

BA GRADE 45 Risk: High

Born: Feb 18, 1997. **B-T:** R-R. **HT:** 6-6. **WT:** 225. **Drafted:** Oklahoma, 2018 (4th round). **Signed by:** Ed Gustafson.

TRACK RECORD: A Minnesota native, Irvin was a three-year starter at Oklahoma, including the last two as a Friday night ace. He won six games in each of his three seasons with the Sooners. In his draft year, he led the Big 12 with 115 strikeouts in 95 innings and was the conference's Scholar Athlete of the Year with a 3.83 GPA as a human resources major. He signed for $550,000.

SCOUTING REPORT: Irvin was able to grind through a season that didn't come easy at Hagerstown. In April, he had an 8.24 ERA in five starts. But he shot up at the end of the year, showing a 94-96 mph fastball in instructional league with a plus curveball and at least an average changeup. After throwing a slider in college, he has developed a hard-breaking curve as a professional. Irvin is durable and athletic on the mound.

THE FUTURE: Irvin had a 1.67 ERA with 29 strikeouts in 27 innings over his five August starts for the Suns. That finish has him on track to go to the high Class A Carolina League in 2020.

Year	Age	Club (League)	Class	W	L	ERA	G	GS	SV	IP	H	HR	BB	SO	K/9	WHIP	AVG
2018	21	Nationals (GCL)	R	1	0	1.42	7	3	0	13	10	0	3	9	6.4	1.03	.213
	21	Auburn (NYP)	SS	0	0	2.25	4	4	0	8	6	0	4	6	6.8	1.25	.207
2019	22	Hagerstown (SAL)	LoA	8	8	3.79	25	25	0	128	122	14	38	113	7.9	1.25	.250
Minor League Totals				9	8	3.50	36	32	0	149	138	14	45	128	7.7	1.23	.244

16 JACKSON CLUFF, SS

BA GRADE
45 Risk: High

Born: Dec. 3, 1996. **B-T:** L-R. **HT:** 6-0. **WT:** 185. **Drafted:** Brigham Young, 2019 (6th round). **Signed by:** Mitch Sokol.

TRACK RECORD: Nationals player development officials believe the scouting department found a gem in Cluff, who served a two-year mission in Atlanta before returning to BYU in 2019. He hit in cages and off a tee once a week for those two years. In his first season with the Cougars since 2016, he hit .327/.458/.518 with 20 doubles in 199 at-bats while walking almost as many times (37) as he struck out (39).

SCOUTING REPORT: Cluff has above-average running ability, an above-average arm and a short, line-drive stroke. He does have a tendency to chase fastballs, so he'll have to be more selective. He has sneaky pop but still needs to learn more about repeating his swing. Cluff held his own defensively and has a good internal clock. The Idaho native is a quick-twitch athlete who plays the game as hard as anyone in the organization. Over the course of the summer, he improved at driving balls to center field and left-center field for doubles and triples.

THE FUTURE: Cluff will likely head to high Class A Fredericksburg. If he continues to adapt quickly, as he has since returning from his mission, he could be a fast riser through the system.

Year	Age	Club (League)	Class	AVG	G	AB	R	H	2B	3B	HR	RBI	BB	SO	SB	OBP	SLG
2019	22	Hagerstown (SAL)	LoA	.229	62	240	33	55	8	5	5	19	26	63	11	.320	.367
Minor League Totals				.229	62	240	33	55	8	5	5	19	26	63	11	.320	.367

17 TYLER DYSON, RHP

Born: Dec. 24, 1997. **B-T:** R-R. **HT:** 6-3. **WT:** 210. **Drafted:** Florida, 2019 (5th round). **Signed by:** Alan Marr.

TRACK RECORD: Dyson played mostly infield in high school in Bradenton, Fla., before dominating on the mound as a senior. He adjusted well to pitching in the SEC, managing a 3.23 ERA in 39 innings as a freshman on Florida's 2017 national championship team. In 2019, he was projected as a possible first-round pick, but he had a 4.95 ERA and a 1.50 WHIP. Two of his college appearances as a junior were out of the bullpen, but the Nationals would like to use him as a starter as long as possible. Dyson signed for $500,000.

SCOUTING REPORT: Scouts clocked Dyson's fastball as high as 99 mph in the SEC tournament. He was hitting 96 this summer with short-season Auburn. His slider needs work, but he has a pitcher's frame and a strong, quick arm. He has the ability to repeat his clean, easy delivery but struggles at times with his control.

THE FUTURE: Dyson appears ready to make his full-season debut, likely at low Class A Hagerstown. He'll focus on gaining movement on his fastball and improving his secondary pitches while increasing his workload.

Year	Age	Club (League)	Class	W	L	ERA	G	GS	SV	IP	H	HR	BB	SO	K/9	WHIP	AVG
2019	21	Nationals (GCL)	R	0	0	0.00	1	1	0	2	0	0	0	3	13.5	0.00	.000
	21	Auburn (NYP)	SS	2	1	1.14	8	8	0	32	20	1	8	14	4.0	0.88	.192
Minor League Totals				2	1	1.07	9	9	0	33	20	1	8	17	4.5	0.83	.182

18 REID SCHALLER, RHP

BA GRADE
45 Risk: High

Born: April 2, 1997. **B-T:** R-R. **HT:** 6-3. **WT:** 210. **Drafted:** Vanderbilt, 2018 (3rd round). **Signed by:** Brian Cleary.

TRACK RECORD: Schaller lettered for four years in baseball and one in football at Lebanon (Ind.) Senior High before heading to Vanderbilt. He missed the 2017 season after having Tommy John surgery but was still picked 101st overall. Schaller recorded a 3.77 ERA with 39 strikeouts and nine walks in 28.2 innings as a draft-eligible redshirt freshman for the Commodores. He made 21 appearances in college that year, including two starts, before taking a starting role in pro ball. Schaller signed for $551,100.

SCOUTING REPORT: Schaller's season at low Class A Hagerstown didn't begin until June 24 because of an injured oblique. He got off to a slow start but was extended to five innings in six of his final nine starts. Schaller has good carry on his mid-90s fastball, pitches to the top of the zone and has a short and quick pitching motion. In instructional league, he altered his motion a bit and focused on his slider. He has improved his changeup and will be asked to throw it more frequently.

THE FUTURE: If he stays healthy, Schaller has a chance to move quickly, whether it's in a starting or relief role.

year	Age	Club (League)	Class	W	L	ERA	G	GS	SV	IP	H	HR	BB	SO	K/9	WHIP	AVG
2018	21	Nationals (GCL)	R	0	1	1.54	5	5	0	12	9	1	3	16	12.3	1.03	.209
	21	Auburn (NYP)	SS	2	2	5.90	7	7	0	29	30	0	9	16	5.0	1.34	.268
2019	22	Hagerstown (SAL)	LoA	4	3	3.29	12	12	0	52	38	5	25	47	8.1	1.21	.205
Minor League Totals				6	6	3.88	24	24	0	92	77	6	37	79	7.7	1.23	.226

19 ISRAEL PINEDA, C

BA GRADE **50** Risk: High

Born: April 3, 2000. **B-T:** R-R. **HT:** 5-11. **WT:** 190. **Signed:** Venezuela, 2016. **Signed by:** Eduardo Rosario.

TRACK RECORD: Pineda, who signed for $450,000, hit .288/.323/.441 as a 17-year-old in the Rookie-level Gulf Coast League and .273/.341/.388 at age 18 in the short-season New York-Penn League, but he struggled offensively this past year in low A ball. His bat-to-ball skills dipped in full-season action, but he was one of the youngest players in the league.

SCOUTING REPORT: Despite the drop-off at Hagerstown, Pineda has above-average future hit and power tools. He has a quick bat and hits fastballs in the strike zone. In the second half of the season, he improved at hitting the ball to the opposite field. The Nationals wanted to test Pineda by putting him in the middle of the order, and 358 of his at-bats were from the third, fourth or fifth spot. He tends to get overly aggressive and needs to better recognize off-speed pitches. Pineda is an average fielder with an above-average arm and little speed.

THE FUTURE: After a good learning year in the South Atlantic League, Pineda may well return there in 2020.

Year	Age	Club (League)	Class	AVG	G	AB	R	H	2B	3B	HR	RBI	BB	SO	SB	OBP	SLG
2017	17	Nationals (GCL)	R	.288	17	59	10	17	5	2	0	12	4	13	0	.323	.441
2018	18	Auburn (NYP)	SS	.273	46	165	25	45	7	0	4	24	12	35	0	.341	.388
2019	19	Hagerstown (SAL)	LoA	.217	101	374	48	81	12	0	7	35	30	102	1	.278	.305
Minor League Totals				.239	164	598	83	143	24	2	11	71	46	150	1	.300	.341

20 BEN BRAYMER, LHP

BA GRADE **40** Risk: Medium

Born: April 28, 1994. **B-T:** L-L **HT:** 6-2. **WT:** 215. **Drafted:** Auburn, 2016 (18th round). **Signed by:** Eric Robinson.

TRACK RECORD: A late-round find who pitched for one year out of Auburn's bullpen after transferring from junior college national champion Louisiana State-Eunice, Braymer was the organization's co-pitcher of the year in 2018 along with Wil Crowe. He made only 11 starts in 28 appearances in his breakout season and then was exclusively a starter this past year.

SCOUTING REPORT: Braymer has a deceptive, low-90s fastball and an above-average power curveball. He also has improved the feel and action on his changeup, which gives him a chance to become a back-end starter in the major leagues. Braymer throws his change consistently out of the same slot and has improved the tunneling of the pitch. He hides the ball well and is able to pitch up in the zone. The Nationals believe his sparkling Double-A numbers are more representative of his stuff than the subpar statistics he put up in Triple-A.

THE FUTURE: Scouts like Braymer's pitchability. His stuff isn't overwhelming, but he could serve as a long man or be a good emergency option for a big league start. His curveball, especially dangerous against lefthanded hitters, could serve him well if he's moved back to the bullpen.

Year	Age	Club (League)	Class	W	L	ERA	G	GS	SV	IP	H	HR	BB	SO	K/9	WHIP	AVG
2017	23	Auburn (NYP)	SS	2	0	2.28	6	6	0	28	24	1	13	39	12.7	1.34	.226
	23	Hagerstown (SAL)	LoA	3	2	5.26	7	7	0	38	46	3	8	37	8.8	1.43	.295
2018	24	Hagerstown (SAL)	LoA	3	0	1.75	7	0	0	26	18	2	5	25	8.8	0.90	.205
	24	Potomac (CAR)	HiA	6	3	2.43	21	11	2	89	73	4	29	93	9.4	1.15	.223
2019	25	Harrisburg (EL)	AA	4	4	2.51	13	13	0	79	56	7	21	69	7.9	0.97	.194
	25	Fresno (PCL)	AAA	0	6	7.20	13	13	0	60	81	18	35	47	7.1	1.93	.328
Minor League Totals				18	17	3.64	75	52	2	338	311	35	124	334	8.9	1.28	.243

21 COLE FREEMAN, 2B/OF

BA GRADE 45 **Risk: High**

Born: Sept. 27, 1994. **B-T:** R-R. **HT:** 5-9. **WT:** 175. **Drafted:** Louisiana State, 2017 (4th round). **Signed by:** Ed Gustafson.

TRACK RECORD: Freeman helped lead LSU to the 2017 College World Series finals, but a right wrist injury limited him in Omaha and delayed his professional debut until the next season. He's a grinder who doesn't have much power but draws walks and steals bases.

SCOUTING REPORT: Though Freeman was named the Carolina League's postseason all-star second baseman, he struggled with his throwing so much in the infield that he played mostly center field in the second half at Potomac. He's still working on his routes in the outfield, but he has plus running speed and the all-out drive needed to play in center with more time and reps. Freeman has impressive contact ability and bat-to-ball skills, which scouts like and believe could allow him to become a top-of-the-order, cataylst type hitter, but he has well below-average raw power and is unlikely to ever turn into a real home run threat. The extra-base hits he does get will come from line drives in the gap and his speed more than real power.

THE FUTURE: The more versatility Freeman can show, the better. He'll have a shot at the major leagues, especially in a utility role. His fine season in the Carolina League has him on track to play at Double-A Harrisburg. He'll likely split time between second base and center field again but his throwing accuracy has to improve for him to stick in the infield.

Year	Age	Club (League)	Class	AVG	G	AB	R	H	2B	3B	HR	RBI	BB	SO	SB	OBP	SLG
2017	22	Did not play—Injured															
2018	23	Hagerstown (SAL)	LoA	.266	122	447	78	119	32	3	3	43	47	59	26	.354	.371
2019	24	Potomac (CAR)	HiA	.311	123	453	82	141	27	3	3	49	53	60	31	.394	.404
Minor League Totals				.289	245	900	160	260	59	6	6	92	100	119	57	.374	.388

22 JAMES BOURQUE, RHP

BA GRADE 40 **Risk: High**

Born: July 9, 1993. **B-T:** R-R HT: 6-4. **WT:** 215. **Drafted:** Michigan, 2014 (14th round). **Signed by:** Steve Arnieri.

TRACK RECORD: Mostly a reliever in college, Bourque began his professional career as a starter. He moved back to the bullpen in 2018 and has risen quickly since then. His two plus pitches helped him earn a promotion from Double-A Harrisburg to Washington on May 26 for his major league debut. But he allowed four runs in two-thirds of an inning in the Nationals' 9-6 win over Miami and then spent the rest of the season at Triple-A Fresno.

SCOUTING REPORT: Bourque, who missed the 2015 season after having Tommy John surgery, throws at 96-98 mph with high-effort mechanics. He also has a hard, downer curveball thrown at 84-85 mph from an overhand delivery. Those two pitches can both wipe out hitters, but his control is lagging. He occasionally throws a below-average changeup.

THE FUTURE: As a bet on pure stuff, Bourque has a chance to slide into the Nationals' bullpen as a seventh-inning option. His command, though, will have to get better for that to happen.

Year	Age	Club (League)	Class	W	L	ERA	G	GS	SV	IP	H	HR	BB	SO	K/9	WHIP	AVG
2017	23	Hagerstown (SAL)	LoA	5	7	5.05	23	20	0	114	123	8	35	90	7.1	1.39	.273
2018	24	Potomac (CAR)	HiA	3	2	2.16	26	0	5	33	19	3	12	52	14.0	0.93	.170
	24	Harrisburg (EL)	AA	1	0	0.92	15	0	1	20	11	0	14	24	11.0	1.27	.167
2019	25	Harrisburg (EL)	AA	3	0	1.33	14	0	6	20	17	1	6	33	14.6	1.13	.224
	25	Washington (NL)	MAJ	0	0	54.00	1	0	0	1	3	0	2	0	0.0	7.50	.750
	25	Fresno (PCL)	AAA	4	1	5.56	33	0	3	44	41	6	30	53	10.9	1.63	.247
Major League Totals				0	0	54.00	1	0	0	0	3	0	2	0	0.0	7.50	.750
Minor League Totals				24	21	4.24	140	44	15	343	345	29	137	340	8.9	1.40	.259

23 JOAN ADON, RHP

BA GRADE 40 **Risk: High**

Born: Aug. 12, 1998. **B-T:** R-R. **HT:** 6-2. **WT:** 185. **Signed:** Dominican Republic, 2016. **Signed by:** Pablo Arias.

TRACK RECORD: Adon has risen faster than organization officials expected. He moved into a starting role for the first time in 2019, exceeding 100 innings in his age 20 season against mostly older players in the South Atlantic League. This fall and last, he impressed at instructional league with his eagerness to learn.

SCOUTING REPORT: Hagerstown's top winner in 2019, Adon held his 95-96 mph fastball velocity for several innings in most of his starts. He also has a power slider and an improving changeup. Toward the end of the year, he used the changeup with more confidence. His mechanics could use refinement, but he does a good job of repeating his delivery and staying on line. One South Atlantic League reliever said Adon reminds him of big league reliever Pedro Strop, although Adon is a little bit better at this stage.

THE FUTURE: The maximized innings will give Adon a chance to show what he can do as a starter, and then he could become a medium-leverage reliever if needed in the future.

Year	Age	Club (League)	Class	W	L	ERA	G	GS	SV	IP	H	HR	BB	SO	K/9	WHIP	AVG
2017	18	Nationals (DSL)	R	2	1	3.54	13	0	1	28	24	1	9	31	10.0	1.18	.240
2018	19	Nationals (GCL)	R	2	0	2.29	13	0	2	20	20	0	13	29	13.3	1.68	.250
	19	Auburn (NYP)	SS	1	1	7.36	7	0	0	11	13	2	9	11	9.0	2.00	.310
2019	20	Hagerstown (SAL)	LoA	11	3	3.86	22	21	0	105	93	8	44	90	7.7	1.30	.237
Minor League Totals				16	5	3.85	55	21	3	163	150	11	75	161	8.9	1.37	.244

24 JACKSON TETREAULT, RHP

BA GRADE 40 Risk: High

Born: June 3, 1996. **B-T:** R-R. **HT:** 6-5. **WT:** 189. **Drafted:** State JC of Florida, 2017 (7th round). **Signed by:** Buddy Hernandez.

TRACK RECORD: Tetreault signed for $300,000, the fourth-most of anyone in the Nationals' 2017 draft class. In his one year of junior college ball, he struck out 105 in 80.1 innings and had a 2.58 ERA. Tetreault has a plus fastball and reached Double-A Harrisburg in 2019, but he closed out the season where he started it—at high Class A Potomac.

SCOUTING REPORT: Scouts like Tetreault's fastball, which touches the mid-90s thanks to a fast and whippy arm. It was a plus pitch in Harrisburg, but what continues to hold Tetreault back is the development of his secondaries. He made progress with a changeup last year but scouts who saw Tetreault thought all of his secondaries were below-average offerings this year. He has shown the ability to spin his curveball, but doesn't land the pitch for strike consistently, and without improvement of either his change or curve, more advanced hitters will be able to sit on his fastball. Tetreault walked 4.2 batters per nine innings in Double-A after walking just 2.8 per nine innings in both low Class A and high Class A in 2018.

THE FUTURE: Tetreault's stuff is good enough to work at higher levels, perhaps in the bullpen. After allowing one run over 11 innings in his final two starts in the Carolina League, he appears ready for another go at the Eastern League. The Nationals hope to see more confidence out of Tetreault in the season ahead.

Year	Age	Club (League)	Class	W	L	ERA	G	GS	SV	IP	H	HR	BB	SO	K/9	WHIP	AVG
2017	21	Nationals (GCL)	R	0	0	4.50	1	0	0	2	1	1	1	2	9.0	1.00	.143
	21	Auburn (NYP)	SS	2	2	2.58	11	6	0	38	32	1	16	36	8.5	1.25	.216
2018	22	Hagerstown (SAL)	LoA	3	8	4.01	20	20	0	110	108	10	34	118	9.7	1.29	.255
	22	Potomac (CAR)	HiA	1	1	4.37	4	4	0	23	21	2	7	20	7.9	1.24	.241
2019	23	Harrisburg (EL)	AA	4	5	4.73	18	18	0	86	98	8	40	63	6.6	1.61	.292
	23	Potomac (CAR)	HiA	4	2	1.91	7	7	0	38	29	0	13	29	6.9	1.12	.213
Minor League Totals				14	18	3.80	61	55	0	296	289	22	111	268	8.1	1.35	.254

25 MALVIN PENA, RHP

BA GRADE 40 Risk: High

Born: June 24, 1997. **B-T:** R-R. **HT:** 6-2. **WT:** 180. **Signed:** Dominican Republic, 2014. **Signed by:** Modesto Ulloa.

TRACK RECORD: Pena had a breakout year in 2018 at short-season Auburn and low Class A Hagerstown. His numbers didn't show it at high Class A Potomac, but he has enough stuff to keep rising through the system. He had Tommy John surgery and missed the entire 2015 season before making just two appearances in 2016. Pena's high point of this past season came in early June when he was named Carolina League pitcher of the week after allowing two hits over seven scoreless innings in a win over Lynchburg.

SCOUTING REPORT: The biggest key for Pena will be the development of his secondary pitches. He throws a firm, 92-93 mph fastball that touches 95 at its best and also has good riding life. This season, Pena worked on improving a hard, power slider and increasing the consistency of his changeup, but both of those pitches need to get better to become even average. Pena has a deceptive delivery that he's able to repeat well. His walk rate spiked compared to the 2018 season, and while he does a decent job putting the ball in and around the zone, he's safely a control over command pitcher at this point and will need to make strides in that area to remain competitive as he climbs the minor league ladder barring improvement with his secondary offerings.

THE FUTURE: Pena more than doubled his career high for innings in 2019, and he proved to be a tough competitor. The uptick in innings should help him, whether he continues to start or moves to a relief role.

Year	Age	Club (League)	Class	W	L	ERA	G	GS	SV	IP	H	HR	BB	SO	K/9	WHIP	AVG
2017	20	Auburn (NYP)	SS	0	0	3.86	2	0	1	7	10	0	4	5	6.4	2.00	.357
	20	Nationals (GCL)	R	1	3	5.44	10	7	0	41	45	7	18	39	8.5	1.52	.274
2018	21	Auburn (NYP)	SS	3	0	1.80	4	4	0	20	20	0	3	20	9.0	1.15	.253
	21	Hagerstown (SAL)	LoA	3	1	3.60	6	6	0	30	37	1	4	27	8.1	1.37	.289
2019	22	Potomac (CAR)	HiA	5	9	6.20	23	23	0	107	112	20	38	87	7.3	1.40	.265
Minor League Totals				13	16	5.36	60	45	1	241	267	30	85	204	7.6	1.46	.276

26 NICK BANKS, OF

Born: Nov. 18, 1994. **B-T:** L-L. **HT:** 6-0. **WT:** 215. **Drafted:** Texas A&M, 2016 (4th round). **Signed by:** Tyler Wilt.

TRACK RECORD: After winning MVP of the 2016 Southeastern Conference tournament and helping Texas A&M reach super regionals that year, the athletic Banks joined the Nationals system with a $500,000 bonus. In 2019, he was MVP of the high Class A Carolina League All-Star Game, going 3-for-4 with a three-run homer to lead the Northern Division to a win in Frederick.

SCOUTING REPORT: Banks has a calm stance at the plate and puts together quality at-bats. He's well-rounded enough to play all three outfield positions. He's an above-average runner who hasn't shown big power in games but is capable of improving his home run totals. The Nationals believe his future floor is as a good extra player in the major leagues, and that he could develop into something more than that. He played in the Arizona Fall League, hitting .250/.295/.464 with three home runs in 56 at-bats for the Surprise Saguaros.

THE FUTURE: In the AFL, Banks struck out 20 times and drew three walks. He could use improvement in his strike-zone judgment, but he has an intriguing power/speed combination and at age 25 will be close to the big leagues.

Year	Age	Club (League)	Class	AVG	G	AB	R	H	2B	3B	HR	RBI	BB	SO	SB	OBP	SLG
2017	22	Hagerstown (SAL)	LoA	.252	122	440	52	111	24	4	7	58	31	90	14	.303	.373
2018	23	Hagerstown (SAL)	LoA	.260	56	200	25	52	9	0	6	27	13	45	10	.307	.395
	23	Potomac (CAR)	HiA	.263	64	232	27	61	11	2	4	30	14	52	1	.310	.379
2019	24	Potomac (CAR)	HiA	.271	69	280	41	76	21	0	9	35	19	54	2	.327	.443
	24	Harrisburg (EL)	AA	.288	45	156	19	45	12	2	1	21	15	41	6	.358	.410
Minor League Totals				.266	416	1539	182	409	85	9	27	190	103	319	40	.316	.385

27 STEVEN FUENTES, RHP

BA GRADE
40 Risk: Very High

Born: May 4, 1997. **B-T:** R-R. **HT:** 6-2. **WT:** 175. **Signed:** Panama, 2013. **Signed by:** Miguel Ruiz.

TRACK RECORD: For the first time since Fuentes was an 18-year-old in the Rookie-level Gulf Coast League, he was used primarily as a starter. He was having a breakout season at Double-A Harrisburg before he was suspended 50 games for testing positive for a stimulant.

SCOUTING REPORT: Fuentes is a throwback. He's bigger than Anibal Sanchez but tries to get batters out in much the same way. He has a good changeup, commands his 90-95 mph fastball and has a tight slider that is at least average. Fuentes' fastball and slider both have good life. His sink on the ball led to a 55 percent groundball rate in Double-A, and he allowed only one home run in more than 80 innings between Harrisburg and high Class A Potomac. For his career, he has allowed 16 homers in 358 minor league innings. He has made 29 starts in 126 professional games.

THE FUTURE: Fuentes will continue to work as a starter and has a chance to become a major leaguer in the back end of a rotation. His versatility also could help him find a spot in the bullpen.

Year	Age	Club (League)	Class	W	L	ERA	G	GS	SV	IP	H	HR	BB	SO	K/9	WHIP	AVG
2017	20	Hagerstown (SAL)	LoA	4	3	4.41	25	1	2	63	80	9	13	53	7.5	1.47	.308
	20	Potomac (CAR)	HiA	0	1	7.71	2	1	0	2	2	0	4	0	0.0	2.57	.250
2018	21	Hagerstown (SAL)	LoA	2	1	2.35	9	0	3	23	17	0	2	27	10.6	0.83	.198
	21	Potomac (CAR)	HiA	3	3	3.00	24	0	3	45	33	1	16	43	8.6	1.09	.201
2019	22	Potomac (CAR)	HiA	1	1	0.53	8	0	1	17	8	0	7	26	13.8	0.88	.136
	22	Harrisburg (EL)	AA	5	4	2.69	15	11	0	64	63	1	15	63	8.9	1.23	.252
Minor League Totals				22	21	3.29	126	29	12	358	352	16	99	354	8.9	1.26	.252

28 JAKSON REETZ, C

BA GRADE
40 Risk: Very High

Born: Jan. 3, 1996. **B-T:** R-R. **HT:** 6-0. **WT:** 195. **Drafted:** HS—Firth, Neb., 2014 (3rd round). **Signed by:** Ed Gustafson

TRACK RECORD: Reetz signed out of high school for $800,000 instead of playing baseball at Nebraska, where his father played linebacker in the football program. He's a hard worker who won the organization's Bob Boone Award in 2019 for playing the "Nationals Way."

SCOUTING REPORT: The question with Reetz has been his bat, and something clicked for him in the second half of the season at high Class A Potomac. He hit .282/.378/.563 in 174 at-bats after the Carolina League all-star break. He went 1-for-2 in the all-star game, but up to that point he was known more for his makeup and leadership skills than for his offense. Reetz has learned to relax more and let his ability take over. He threw out 41 percent of opposing base stealers last season and has soft hands and good blocking skills. He's also a decent runner.

THE FUTURE: Reetz even hit well in his 27 at-bats for Surprise in the Arizona Fall League, putting up .333/.455/.519 numbers. After 2 1/2 seasons of high-A ball, there's a good chance he'll start 2020 at Double-A Harrisburg.

Year	Age	Club (League)	Class	AVG	G	AB	R	H	2B	3B	HR	RBI	BB	SO	SB	OBP	SLG
2017	21	Hagerstown (SAL)	LoA	.238	37	122	16	29	7	0	2	11	15	41	1	.345	.344
	21	Potomac (CAR)	HiA	.236	26	89	8	21	6	0	2	11	9	32	2	.327	.371
2018	22	Potomac (CAR)	HiA	.224	69	232	25	52	8	0	5	27	35	46	1	.342	.323
2019	23	Potomac (CAR)	HiA	.253	96	324	54	82	18	2	13	55	46	95	3	.370	.441
Minor League Totals				**.238**	**395**	**1280**	**182**	**305**	**73**	**3**	**27**	**162**	**182**	**360**	**20**	**.357**	**.363**

29 NICK RAQUET, LHP

BA GRADE
40 Risk: Very High

Born: Dec. 12, 1995. **B-T:** R-L. **HT:** 6-0. **WT:** 215. **Drafted:** William & Mary, 2017 (3rd round). **Signed by:** Bobby Myrick.

TRACK RECORD: Raquet started his college career at North Carolina before transferring to William & Mary, where he was able to play alongside his brother Brandon. He struck out 95 in 77 innings for the Tribe, impressing the Nationals enough for them to take him 103rd overall and give him a $475,000 bonus. He breezed up to high Class A within a year of being drafted, but he found the going tougher in the Carolina League.

SCOUTING REPORT: After struggling to a 4.91 ERA and allowing 72 hits in 55 innings at Potomac in 2018, Raquet was more consistent last season. He held lefthanded batters to .209/.260/.338 numbers while starting each of the 25 games he appeared in before pitching in relief during the Arizona Fall League. Raquet throws a low- to mid-90s fastball that has heavy armside run and also features a slider, curveball and changeup. The slider has been the better of his two breaking balls, and he might be better off scrapping one and focusing on a simplified, three-pitch arsenal—especially if his future is in the bullpen. Raquet pitches with an up-tempo delivery that includes some funk that adds deception, particularly against same-sided hitters.

THE FUTURE: Raquet has been a starter to get as many repetitions as possible, but his long-term role could be in the bullpen. He recorded an 8.49 ERA in 11.2 relief innings in the Arizona Fall League, so he'll have adjustments to make when he likely heads to Double-A Harrisburg for the first time in 2020.

Year	Age	Club (League)	Class	W	L	ERA	G	GS	SV	IP	H	HR	BB	SO	K/9	WHIP	AVG
2017	21	Nationals (GCL)	R	0	0	0.00	1	1	0	2	2	0	0	2	9.0	1.00	.250
	21	Auburn (NYP)	SS	3	2	2.45	11	11	0	51	56	2	7	22	3.9	1.23	.283
2018	22	Hagerstown (SAL)	LoA	4	6	2.79	12	12	0	68	68	1	18	56	7.4	1.27	.262
	22	Potomac (CAR)	HiA	5	3	4.91	12	12	0	55	72	3	21	36	5.9	1.69	.319
2019	23	Potomac (CAR)	HiA	11	9	4.07	25	25	0	130	129	12	43	122	8.4	1.32	.257
Minor League Totals				23	20	3.64	61	61	0	306	327	18	89	238	7.0	1.36	.274

30 JHONATAN GERMAN, RHP

BA GRADE
40 Risk: Extreme

Born: Jan. 24, 1995. **B-T:** R-R. **HT:** 6-4. **WT:** 215. **Signed:** Dominican Republic, 2015. **Signed by:** Pablo Arias.

TRACK RECORD: When German began his professional career, he had little ability to throw strikes. He walked eight in 4.1 innings in the Rookie-level Dominican Summer League in 2015, but Nationals pitching coaches have helped him move in the right direction with his big arm. It has been a sudden rise for German, who didn't sign until he was 20 and spent half of his age-23 season at short-season Auburn before finally reaching low Class A Hagerstown.

SCOUTING REPORT: German throws a 95 mph fastball and a plus slider. He's working on mixing in changeups against lefthanded hitters. German's control has improved to the point where he averaged 1.93 walks per nine innings in 2019 and walked only one batter in 13 innings in Double-A, but he still needs to show more command.

THE FUTURE: German saved 12 games over three levels last season. He'll be given late-inning opportunities again and has a chance to eventually work his way into a major league bullpen.

Year	Age	Club (League)	Class	W	L	ERA	G	GS	SV	IP	H	HR	BB	SO	K/9	WHIP	AVG
2017	21	Nationals (GCL)	R	0	0	0.00	1	1	0	2	2	0	0	2	9.0	1.00	.250
	21	Auburn (NYP)	SS	3	2	2.45	11	11	0	51	56	2	7	22	3.9	1.23	.283
2018	22	Hagerstown (SAL)	LoA	4	6	2.79	12	12	0	68	68	1	18	56	7.4	1.27	.262
	22	Potomac (CAR)	HiA	5	3	4.91	12	12	0	55	72	3	21	36	5.9	1.69	.319
2019	23	Potomac (CAR)	HiA	11	9	4.07	25	25	0	130	129	12	43	122	8.4	1.32	.257
Minor League Totals				23	20	3.64	61	61	0	306	327	18	89	238	7.0	1.36	.274

APPENDIX

Baseball America's J.J. Cooper, Justin Coleman, Kyle Glaser, Josh Norris and freelancer Jason Coskrey report on international players who were eligible to sign with major league organizations for 2020 or were available free agents as the Prospect Handbook went to press.

YOSHITOMO TSUTSUGO, OF

YUKI TAGUCHI/WBCI/MLB VIA GETTY IMAGES

BA GRADE
50 **Risk: Medium**

Born: Nov. 26, 1991. **Age:** 28. **B-T:** L-R. **Ht.:** 6-0. **Wt.:** 209.

TRACK RECORD: Tsutsugo has spent most of his life in Yokohama, playing at Yokohama High before being drafted by the Yokohama BayStars in 2009. He has been extremely productive, hitting 205 home runs and posting a .910 OPS over 10 seasons in Nippon Professional Baseball. He hit 44 home runs in 2016 and also hit three home runs at the 2017 World Baseball Classic.
SCOUTING REPORT: Tsutsugo has some feel to hit and the ability to draw walks to go with plus power. He posts excellent exit velocities and showed in Japan that he could catch up to mid-90s fastballs while staying inside the ball. His power should translate well to the U.S. game, though he projects as more of a fringe-average hitter whose ability to draw walks makes up for his proclivity to strike out. He's a fringe-average runner at best. Tsutsugo has played third base and first base as well as left field, but he's below-average at all three spots and has mainly focused on left field in recent years. He likely will play a good bit of DH if he signs with an American League team.
THE FUTURE: Tsutsugo has the power to help a major league team, especially if he is kept away from the toughest lefthanders. His makeup and temperament impress evaluators and he should be able to make the transition to a new culture and a longer season. He went to the Dominican Republic to play winter ball a few years ago, showing both his love of the game and his willingness to adapt to other cultures.

Year	Age	Club (League)	Class	AVG	G	AB	R	H	2B	3B	HR	RBI	BB	SO	SB	OBP	SLG
2017	25	Yokohama (CL)	JPN	.284	139	503	85	143	31	0	28	94	93	115	1	.396	.513
2018	26	Yokohama (CL)	JPN	.295	139	495	77	146	33	1	38	89	80	107	0	.393	.596
2019	27	Yokohama (CL)	JPN	.272	131	464	74	126	24	0	29	79	88	141	0	.388	.511

SHUN YAMAGUCHI, RHP

GENE WANG/GETTY IMAGES

BA GRADE
45 **Risk: Medium**

Born: July 11, 1987. **Age:** 32. **B-T:** R-R. **Ht.:** 6-1. **Wt.:** 216.

TRACK RECORD: Yamaguchi is the son of sumo wrestler Taniarashi. Yamaguchi has played in Nippon Professional Baseball for 14 seasons, long enough that he has earned international free agent rights, meaning a team signing him does not need to pay a posting fee. He began his career as a closer before moving to the rotation in 2014. Yamaguchi was suspended in 2017 for an incident when he was accused of shoving a security guard and doing damage at a hospital.
SCOUTING REPORT: Yamaguchi does not blow hitters away. His below-average fastball sits at 87-93 mph. It actually gained a tick in 2019 to average 90 mph after sitting at 89 for several previous years. But Yamaguchi uses a forkball, slider, curveball and changeup as well. His forkball has become a bigger and bigger part of his approach in recent years, and is a pitch that induces chases out of the zone. Yamaguchi's delivery adds deception as well. He can be difficult for opposing batters to time because he hangs over his balance point on the rubber. He has average command and control.
THE FUTURE: Yamaguchi provides value to a major league team because of his durability and his ability to slide between starting and relieving roles. He carries some risk because of his lack of velocity, but North American hitters aren't used to seeing many forkballs, which may help Yamaguchi.

Year	Age	Club (League)	Class	W	L	ERA	G	GS	SV	IP	H	HR	BB	SO	K/9	BB/9	WHIP
2017	29	Yomiuri (CL)	JPN	1	1	6.43	4	4	0	21	24	5	16	22	9.4	6.9	1.91
2018	30	Yomiuri (CL)	JPN	9	9	3.68	30	21	1	154	127	18	60	144	8.4	3.5	1.21
2019	31	Yomiuri (CL)	JPN	15	4	2.91	26	26	0	170	137	8	60	188	10.0	3.2	1.16

KWANG-HYUN KIM, LHP

Born: July 22, 1988. **Age:** 31. **B-T:** L-L. **Ht.:** 6-2. **Wt.:** 185.

TRACK RECORD: Scouts first got to see Kim on a major international stage when he beat Japan in the 2008 Olympic semifinals, setting up South Korea's gold medal win over Cuba in the championship game. That gold medal helped him and Hyun-Jin Ryu be exempted from the mandatory two years of military service that all South Korean males normally have to serve. He also pitched in the 2009 World Baseball Classic. Kim, who lost the 2017 season to Tommy John surgery, has been one of the most reliable starters in the Korean Baseball Organization over the past decade.

SCOUTING REPORT: Kim throws a high-spin 89-94 mph fastball that grades as average. He elevates a four-seamer but relies more on his 90-92 mph two-seamer which he can locate to both his arm and glove side. He also throws an average low-80s slider, an average high-70s curveball, an average changeup and an occasional cutter. He has steadily improved his control and command as he has matured, and he is pitching some of his best baseball in his early 30s.

THE FUTURE: While Kim worked as a starter in Korea, he may be a better fit as a high-leverage reliever in the U.S. However, a team wanting to start him would get to take advantage of his ability to mix and match five fringe-average to average pitches.

Year	Age	Club (League)	Class	W	L	ERA	G	GS	SV	IP	H	HR	BB	SO	K/9	BB/9	WHIP
2017	28	SK Wyverns (KBO)	KOR	Did not play—Injured													
2018	29	SK Wyverns (KBO)	KOR	11	8	2.98	25	25	0	136	125	16	30	130	8.6	2.0	1.14
2019	30	SK Wyverns (KBO)	KOR	17	6	2.51	31	30	0	190	198	13	38	180	8.5	1.8	1.24

2019 INTERNATIONAL SIGNING CLASS: BEST TOOLS

BY BEN BADLER

The international signing period opened on July 2, 2019. Among players who signed in the 2019-20 period, these players stood out as having the best tools, with a focus on the most prominent players in the 2019 class.

BILL MITCHELL

Bayron Lora generates incredible raw power from his 6-foot-5 frame.

BEST HITTER: Not only is Yankees OF Jasson Dominguez one of the best athletes in the class, he's also an elite hitter for his age, with a sweet swing from both sides and a mature approach for his age. Dodgers OF Luis Rodriguez, Royals OF Erick Peña, Rangers SS Maximo Acosta, Rockies SS Adael Amador, Brewers OF Hedbert Perez and Rays OF Jhon Diaz all have impressive swings and hitting track records.

BEST POWER: Rangers OF Bayron Lora has 70-grade raw power with exit velocities up to 112 mph from his massive 6-foot-5 frame. There are plenty of other players in the class who project to have at least plus power, including Dominguez, Brewers OF Luis Medina, Tigers OF Roberto Campos, Twins OF Malfrin Sosa, Rockies OF Yanquiel Fernandez, Blue Jays OF Cristian Feliz and Pirates OF Ewry Espinal.

BEST SPEED: The 60-yard dash times players show can change quickly—both up and down—as they get stronger and heavier. Dominguez ran 6.4 seconds consistently as an amateur with an explosive first step. Padres OF Ismael Mena, Indians OF Luis Durango Jr., Rockies SS Adrian Pinto and Nationals SSs Juan Garcia and Dawry Martinez can also fly.

BEST DEFENSIVE INFIELDER: It only takes a few ground balls to see what stands out about Blue Jays SS Rikelvin de Castro, a high-energy defender with slick actions, clean hands and swift feet. Orioles SS Leonel Sanchez, Giants SS Aeverson Arteaga, Brewers SS Jose Caballero and D-backs SS Juan Corniel all stood out for their glovework as well.

BEST DEFENSIVE OUTFIELDER: Padres OF Ismael Mena has a chance to be a plus or better defender in center field, with elite athleticism, speed and range. Dominguez and Brewers OF Hedbert Perez are both quick-burst athletes with high-end speed, arm strength and defensive instincts in center.

BEST DEFENSIVE CATCHER: Brewers C Jeferson Quero has the tools to be a plus defender. He's advanced in his blocking and receiving, with a plus arm and pop times down to the low 1.9 seconds on throws to second base. Giants C Adrian Sugastey, Padres C Carlos Rodriguez and Blue Jays C Victor Mesia are also advanced catch-and-throw guys.

BEST INFIELD ARM: Angels 3B/SS Jose Bonilla probably fits best at third base, where his arm grades out at least plus with signs of becoming a 70 tool. Mariners SS Andres Mesa, Red Sox SS Johnfrank Salazar and Cubs SS Kevin Made all have huge arms with plus-plus potential.

BEST OUTFIELD ARM: Dominguez earns plus to plus-plus grades for his arm. So does Astros OF Richi Gonzalez and Reds OF Yerlin Confidan.

BEST FASTBALL: Mets RHP Robert Dominguez, who was eligible to sign in 2018 but signed in 2019, saw his fastball jump to 97 mph as an amateur. He then touched 99 shortly before his 18th birthday. Red Sox RHP Chih-Jung Liu, a 20-year-old from Taiwan, has hit 98 mph. Padres RHP Bryan Medina, Nationals RHP Andry Lara, Giants RHP Manuel Mercedes, Red Sox RHP Luis Perales, Rays RHP Yoniel Curet and Pirates RHP Roelmy Garcia have all touched the mid-90s.

BEST OFFSPEED PITCH: At this age, some pitchers show the components in place to eventually throw a plus breaking ball or changeup, but it's rare to see a true present 60. Padres RHP Bryan Medina shows the attributes to get there with his slider, which has hard, sharp bite when it's on. Orioles LHP Luis Ortiz, Astros RHP Elvis Garcia and Perales and all show feel to spin tight curveballs that can miss bats.

2019 RULE 5 DRAFT

The major league Rule 5 draft occurred on Dec. 12, 2019. A few of these players rank in their new organizations' Top 30 Prospects, but since all 11 will be in big league spring training camp in 2020, we provide thumbnail scouting reports for all of them in this space.

Pick	2020 Org	Player	Pos	2019 Org	BA Grade/Risk

1. Tigers — Rony Garcia — RHP — Yankees — 45/High

Garcia gained a couple of ticks on his fastball at Double-A in 2019, which helped turn him from an organization arm into something more interesting. He can now touch 97 mph and sits 92-94. He has a bat-missing, above-average low-80s slider. His hard high-80s changeup is designed to be a chase pitch. He also mixes in a cutter. He is effective against righthanded batters but has had trouble retiring lefthanders. A move to the bullpen could allow everything to play up.

2. Orioles — Brandon Bailey — RHP — Astros — 45/High

He's a 5-foot-10 righthander with a 92-94 mph fastball and a plus changeup. Bailey throws a pair of breaking balls that are both fringy at best, but Bailey competes very well and is coming off of a solid season at Double-A Corpus Christi. He has the craftiness and feel to potentially succeed as a swingman.

3. Marlins — Sterling Sharp — RHP — Nationals — 40/High

Sharp is one of the more athletic pitchers in the minors. Nothing about his arsenal is spectacular, but he's a sinkerballer who keeps the ball in the park and allowed only one home run at Double-A last year. His fastball and changeup are hard to hit in the air. He used his fringe-average slider more often in 2019. Sharp missed some time with an oblique injury in 2019, but he's an upside play, albeit one with modest 89-92 mph velocity.

4. Royals — Stephen Woods — RHP — Rays — 40/High

Woods has long been known as a pitcher with a big arm and bigger walk totals. He walked seven batters per nine innings for his college career and more than five batters per nine in his first three pro stops. After missing all of 2018 with a labrum injury, Woods showed better control at high Class A in 2019. He got better as the season progressed and pitches with a plus fastball/curveball combination.

5. Mariners — Yohan Ramirez — RHP — Astros — 45/Extreme

Ramirez is one of the seeming multitude of Astros pitchers who sits 94-97 and touches 99 mph. He spent half the season at high Class A Fayetteville and the other half at Double-A Corpus Christi. He ate up righthanded hitters, who hit .138 and slugged .199 in 251 plate appearances in 2019. Ramirez also throws a hard low-80s curveball that flashes above-average. His control at Double-A was frightening—nearly eight walks per nine innings—but his strikeout rate was also impressive—13.5 per nine between the two levels.

6. Reds — Mark Payton — OF — Athletics — 40/Medium

Payton impressed at the Premier12 international tournament in November. He also found the new Triple-A ball and a move to the Pacific Coast League to his liking. After hitting six home runs at Triple-A Scranton/Wilkes-Barre in 2018, he hit 30 with Las Vegas in 2019. That was 20 more than he had ever hit in any previous season. If Payton's power surge is sustainable, the 28-year-old could stick as a disciplined, lefthanded-hitting corner outfielder.

7. Giants — Dany Jimenez — RHP — Blue Jays — 45/Very High

Jimenez was outstanding in 2019. He struck out 14 batters per nine innings between high Class A and Double-A while allowing a 1.12 WHIP. He has a high-90s fastball with armside run, a plus slider and a low-80s changeup that shows promise. Most power arms with his kind of stuff who are available in the Rule 5 draft either have zero upper-level minor league experience or well-below-average control. Jimenez spent half of the year at Double-A and has average control.

8. Athletics — Vimael Machin — SS/2B — Cubs — 40/High

Machin doesn't really do anything particularly well. He's limited at shortstop, and as a fringe-average runner he doesn't have much value as a pinch-runner. But he is a lefthanded-hitting utility infielder who can play all four infield spots to varying degrees of ability. He hit .295/.390/.412 for Triple-A Iowa in 2019. Machin's chances to contribute in Oakland revolve around showing enough defensive versatility to prove he can be a backup infielder.

9. Cubs — Trevor Megill — RHP — Padres — 40/High

Megill is more major league-ready than most available Rule 5 prospects. He has nearly 75 innings at Double-A and Triple-A, he throws strikes (2.7 walks per nine innings) and he has three average or better pitches with a 93-96 mph fastball as well as a slider and changeup.

10. Red Sox — Jonathan Arauz — SS/3B — Astros — 40/High

Arauz has been a name for quite a while. He was signed by the Phillies, then shipped to the Astros in the Ken Giles trade. The Red Sox will see if he can fit as a switch-hitting utility infielder. Arauz has primarily been a shortstop, but the Astros have moved him to second base and third base throughout his career. His bat may be stretched against major league pitchers. He hit .249/.319/.388 in a season spent primarily at high Class A.

11. Orioles — Michael Rucker — RHP — Cubs — 40/High

Rucker's stuff drew varying opinions in 2019. Some scouts saw a pitcher with vanilla stuff, but scouts who saw him in other outings saw arm speed and a quality fastball. He's a 6-foot-1 righthander who spent most of the year at Double-A. Rucker's 92-96 mph fastball earns above-average grades from some scouts. He has a pair of breaking balls and a changeup that are all fringe-average to average, so he has to succeed with location and staying a step ahead of hitters.

SIGNING BONUSES

2019 DRAFT

TOP 100 PICKS

FIRST ROUND

No.	Team: Player, Pos.	Bonus
1.	Orioles: Adley Rutschman, C	$8,100,000
2.	Royals: Bobby Witt Jr., SS	$7,787,400
3.	White Sox: Andrew Vaughn, 1B	$7,221,200
4.	Marlins: JJ Bleday, OF	$6,670,000
5.	Tigers: Riley Greene, OF	$6,180,700
6.	Padres: CJ Abrams, SS	$5,200,000
7.	Reds: Nick Lodolo, LHP	$5,432,400
8.	Rangers: Josh Jung, 3B	$4,400,000
9.	Braves: Shea Langeliers, C	$3,997,500
10.	Giants: Hunter Bishop, OF	$4,097,500
11.	Blue Jays: Alek Manoah, RHP	$4,547,500
12.	Mets: Brett Baty, 3B	$3,900,000
13.	Twins: Keoni Cavaco, SS	$4,050,000
14.	Phillies: Bryson Stott, SS	$3,900,000
15.	Angels: Will Wilson, SS	$3,397,500
16.	D-backs: Corbin Carroll, OF	$3,745,500
17.	Nationals: Jackson Rutledge, RHP	$3,450,000
18.	Pirates: Quinn Priester, RHP	$3,400,000
19.	Cardinals: Zack Thompson, LHP	$3,000,000
20.	Mariners: George Kirby, RHP	$3,242,900
21.	Braves: Braden Shewmake, SS	$3,129,800
22.	Rays: Greg Jones, SS	$3,024,500
23.	Rockies: Michael Toglia, 1B	$2,725,000
24.	Indians: Daniel Espino, RHP	$2,500,000
25.	Dodgers: Kody Hoese, 3B	$2,740,300
26.	D-backs: Blake Walston, LHP	$2,450,000
27.	Cubs: Ryan Jensen, RHP	$2,000,000
28.	Brewers: Ethan Small, LHP	$1,800,000
29.	Athletics: Logan Davidson, SS	$2,424,600
30.	Yankees: Anthony Volpe, SS	$2,740,300
31.	Dodgers: Michael Busch, 2B	$2,312,000
32.	Astros: Korey Lee, C	$1,750,000
33.	D-backs: Brennan Malone, RHP	$2,202,200
34.	D-backs: Drey Jameson, RHP	$1,400,000

SUPPLEMENTAL FIRST ROUND

No.	Team: Player, Pos.	Bonus
35.	Marlins: Kameron Misner, OF	$2,115,000
36.	Rays: JJ Goss, RHP	$2,042,900
37.	Pirates: Sammy Siani, OF	$2,150,000
38.	Yankees: TJ Sikkema, LHP	$1,949,800
39.	Twins: Matt Wallner, OF	$1,800,000
40.	Rays: Seth Johnson, RHP	$1,722,500
41.	Rangers: Davis Wendzel, 3B	$1,600,000

SECOND ROUND

No.	Team: Player, Pos.	Bonus
42.	Orioles: Gunnar Henderson, SS	$2,300,000
43.	Red Sox: Cameron Cannon, SS	$1,300,000
44.	Royals: Brady McConnell, SS	$2,222,500
45.	White Sox: Matthew Thompson, RHP	$2,100,000
46.	Marlins: Nasim Nuñez, SS	$2,200,000
47.	Tigers: Nick Quintana, 3B	$1,580,200
48.	Padres: Joshua Mears, OF	$1,000,000
49.	Reds: Rece Hinds, SS	$1,797,500
50.	Rangers: Ryan Garcia, RHP	$1,469,900
51.	Giants: Logan Wyatt, 1B	$997,500
52.	Blue Jays: Kendall Williams, RHP	$1,547,500
53.	Mets: Josh Wolf, RHP	$2,150,000
54.	Twins: Matt Canterino, RHP	$1,100,000
55.	Angels: Kyren Paris, SS	$1,400,000
56.	D-backs: Ryne Nelson, RHP	$1,100,000
57.	Pirates: Matt Gorski, OF	$1,000,000
58.	Cardinals: Trejyn Fletcher, OF	$1,500,000
59.	Mariners: Brandon Williamson, LHP	$925,000
60.	Braves: Beau Philip, SS	$697,500
61.	Rays: John Doxakis, LHP	$1,127,200
62.	Rockies: Aaron Schunk, 3B	$1,102,700
63.	Indians: Yordys Valdes, SS	$1,001,000
64.	Cubs: Chase Strumpf, 2B	$1,050,300
65.	Brewers: Antoine Kelly, LHP	$1,025,100
66.	Athletics: Tyler Baum, RHP	$900,000
67.	Yankees: Josh Smith, 2B	$976,700
68.	Astros: Grae Kessinger, SS	$750,000
69.	Red Sox: Matthew Lugo, SS	$1,100,000

SUPPLEMENTAL SECOND ROUND

No.	Team: Player, Pos.	Bonus
70.	Royals: Alec Marsh, RHP	$904,300
71.	Orioles: Kyle Stowers, OF	$884,200
72.	Pirates: Jared Triolo, 3B	$868,200
73.	Padres: Logan Driscoll, C	$600,000
74.	D-backs: Tommy Henry, LHP	$750,000
75.	D-backs: Dominic Fletcher, OF	$700,000
76.	Mariners: Isaiah Campbell, RHP	$850,000
77.	Rockies: Karl Kauffmann, RHP	$805,600
78.	Dodgers: Jimmy Lewis, RHP	$1,097,500

SECOND ROUND

No.	Team: Player, Pos.	Bonus
79.	Orioles: Zach Watson, OF	$780,400
80.	Royals: Grant Gambrell, RHP	$647,500
81.	White Sox: Andrew Dalquist, RHP	$2,000,000
82.	Marlins: Peyton Burdick, OF	$397,500
83.	Tigers: Andre Lipcius, 3B	$733,100
84.	Padres: Hudson Head, OF	$3,000,000
85.	Reds: Tyler Callihan, 2B	$1,497,500
86.	Rangers: Justin Slaten, RHP	$575,000
87.	Giants: Grant McCray, OF	$697,500
88.	Blue Jays: Dasan Brown, OF	$797,500
89.	Mets: Matt Allan, RHP	$2,500,000
90.	Twins: Spencer Steer, SS	$575,000
91.	Phillies: Jamari Baylor, SS	$675,000
92.	Angels: Jack Kochanowicz, RHP	$1,247,500
93.	D-backs: Tristin English, 1B	$500,000
94.	Nationals: Drew Mendoza, 3B	$800,000
95.	Pirates: Matt Fraizer, OF	$525,000
96.	Cardinals: Tony Locey, RHP	$604,800
97.	Mariners: Levi Stoudt, RHP	$339,000
98.	Braves: Michael Harris, OF	$547,500
99.	Rays: Shane Sasaki, OF	$472,500
100.	Rockies: Jacob Wallace, RHP	$581,600

2018 DRAFT

TOP 100 PICKS

FIRST ROUND

No.	Team: Player, Pos.	Bonus
1.	Tigers: Casey Mize, RHP	$7,500,000
2.	Giants: Joey Bart, C	$7,025,000
3.	Phillies: Alec Bohm, 3B	$5,850,000
4.	White Sox: Nick Madrigal, SS	$6,411,400
5.	Reds: Jonathan India, 3B	$5,297,500
6.	Mets: Jarred Kelenic, OF	$4,500,000
7.	Padres: Ryan Weathers, LHP	$5,226,500
8.	Braves: Carter Stewart, RHP	Did not sign
9.	Athletics: Kyler Murray, OF	$4,660,000
10.	Pirates: Travis Swaggerty, OF	$4,400,000
11.	Orioles: Grayson Rodriguez, RHP	$4,300,000
12.	Blue Jays: Jordan Groshans, SS	$3,400,000
13.	Marlins: Connor Scott, OF	$4,038,200
14.	Mariners: Logan Gilbert, RHP	$3,883,800
15.	Rangers: Cole Winn, RHP	$3,150,000
16.	Rays: Matthew Liberatore, LHP	$3,497,500
17.	Angels: Jordyn Adams, OF	$4,100,000
18.	Royals: Brady Singer, RHP	$4,247,500
19.	Cardinals: Nolan Gorman, 3B	$3,231,700
20.	Twins: Trevor Larnach, OF	$2,550,000
21.	Brewers: Brice Turang, SS	$3,411,100
22.	Rockies: Ryan Rolison, LHP	$2,912,300
23.	Yankees: Anthony Seigler, C	$2,815,900
24.	Cubs: Nico Hoerner, SS	$2,724,000
25.	D-backs: Matt McLain, SS	Did not sign
26.	Red Sox: Triston Casas, 3B	$2,552,800
27.	Nationals: Mason Denaburg, RHP	$3,000,000
28.	Astros: Seth Beer, OF	$2,250,000
29.	Indians: Bo Naylor, C	$2,578,137
30.	Dodgers: J.T. Ginn, RHP	Did not sign
31.	Rays: Shane McClanahan, LHP	$2,230,100
32.	Rays: Nick Schnell, OF	$2,297,500
33.	Royals: Jackson Kowar, RHP	$2,147,500
34.	Royals: Daniel Lynch, LHP	$1,697,500
35.	Indians: Ethan Hankins, RHP	$2,246,022

SUPPLEMENTAL FIRST ROUND

No.	Team: Player, Pos.	Bonus
36.	Pirates: Gunnar Hoglund, RHP	Did not sign
37.	Orioles: Cadyn Grenier, SS	$1,800,000
38.	Padres: Xavier Edwards, SS	$2,600,000
39.	D-backs: Jake McCarthy, OF	$1,650,000
40.	Royals: Kris Bubic, LHP	$1,597,500
41.	Indians: Lenny Torres, RHP	$1,350,000
42.	Rockies: Grant Lavigne, 1B	$2,000,000
43.	Cardinals: Griffin Roberts, RHP	$1,664,200

SECOND ROUND

No.	Team: Player, Pos.	Bonus
44.	Tigers: Parker Meadows, OF	$2,500,000
45.	Giants: Sean Hjelle, RHP	$1,500,000
46.	White Sox: Steele Walker, OF	$2,000,000
47.	Reds: Lyon Richardson, RHP	$1,997,500
48.	Mets: Simeon Woods Richardson, RHP	$1,850,000
49.	Braves: Greyson Jenista, OF	$1,200,000
50.	Athletics: Jameson Hannah, OF	$1,800,000
51.	Pirates: Braxton Ashcraft, RHP	$1,825,000
52.	Blue Jays: Griffin Conine, OF	$1,350,000
53.	Marlins: Osiris Johnson, SS	$1,350,000
54.	Mariners: Josh Stowers, OF	$1,100,000
55.	Rangers: Owen White, RHP	$1,500,000
56.	Rays: Tyler Frank, SS	$997,500
57.	Angels: Jeremiah Jackson, SS	$1,194,000
58.	Royals: Jonathan Bowlan, RHP	$697,500
59.	Twins: Ryan Jeffers, C	$800,000
60.	Brewers: Joe Gray, OF	$1,113,500
61.	Yankees: Josh Breaux, C	$1,497,500
62.	Cubs: Brennen Davis, OF	$1,100,000
63.	D-backs: Alek Thomas, OF	$1,200,000
64.	Red Sox: Nick Decker, OF	$1,250,000
65.	Nationals: Tim Cate, LHP	$986,200
66.	Astros: Jayson Schroeder, RHP	$1,200,000
67.	Indians: Nick Sandlin, RHP	$750,000
68.	Dodgers: Michael Grove, RHP	$1,229,500

SUPPLEMENTAL SECOND ROUND

No.	Team: Player, Pos.	Bonus
69.	Marlins: Will Banfield, C	$1,800,000
70.	Athletics: Jeremy Eierman, SS	$1,232,000
71.	Rays: Tanner Dodson, RHP	$772,500
72.	Reds: Josiah Gray, RHP	$772,500
73.	Brewers: Micah Bello, OF	$550,000
74.	Padres: Grant Little, OF	$800,000
75.	Cardinals: Luken Baker, 1B	$800,000
76.	Rockies: Mitchell Kilkenny, RHP	$550,000
77.	Cubs: Cole Roederer, OF	$1,200,000
78.	Cubs: Paul Richan, RHP	$450,000

SECOND ROUND

No.	Team: Player, Pos.	Bonus
79.	Tigers: Kody Clemens, 2B	$600,000
80.	Giants: Jake Wong, RHP	$850,000
81.	White Sox: Konnor Pilkington, LHP	$650,000
82.	Reds: Bren Spillane, OF	$597,500
83.	Mets: Carlos Cortes, 2B	$1,000,038
84.	Padres: Owen Miller, SS	$500,000
85.	Athletics: Hogan Harris, LHP	$660,000
86.	Pirates: Connor Kaiser, SS	$625,000
87.	Orioles: Blaine Knight, RHP	$1,100,000
88.	Blue Jays: Adam Kloffenstein, RHP	$2,450,000
89.	Marlins: Tristan Pompey, OF	$645,000
90.	Mariners: Cal Raleigh, C	$854,000
91.	Rangers: Jonathan Ornelas, SS	$622,800
92.	Rays: Ford Proctor, SS	$572,500
93.	Angels: Aaron Hernandez, RHP	$547,500
94.	Royals: Kyle Isbel, 2B	$592,300
95.	Cardinals: Mateo Gil, SS	$900,000
96.	Rockies: Terrin Vavra, SS	$550,000
97.	Yankees: Ryder Green, OF	$997,500
98.	Cubs: Jimmy Herron, OF	$520,000
99.	D-backs: Jackson Goddard, RHP	$550,000
100.	Red Sox: Durbin Feltman, RHP	$559,600

SIGNING BONUSES

2017 DRAFT

TOP 100 PICKS

FIRST ROUND

No.	Team: Player, Pos.	Bonus
1.	Twins: Royce Lewis, SS	$6,725,000
2.	Reds: Hunter Greene, RHP	$7,230,000
3.	Padres: MacKenzie Gore, LHP	$6,700,000
4.	Rays: Brendan McKay, 1B	$7,005,000
5.	Braves: Kyle Wright, RHP	$7,000,000
6.	Athletics: Austin Beck, OF	$5,303,000
7.	D-backs: Pavin Smith, 1B	$5,016,300
8.	Phillies: Adam Haseley, OF	$5,100,000
9.	Brewers: Keston Hiura, 2B	$4,000,000
10.	Angels: Jo Adell, OF	$4,376,800
11.	White Sox: Jake Burger, 3B	$3,700,000
12.	Pirates: Shane Baz, RHP	$4,100,000
13.	Marlins: Trevor Rogers, LHP	$3,400,000
14.	Royals: Nick Pratto, 1B	$3,450,000
15.	Astros: J.B. Bukauskas, RHP	$3,600,000
16.	Yankees: Clarke Schmidt, RHP	$2,184,300
17.	Mariners: Evan White, 1B	$3,125,000
18.	Tigers: Alex Faedo, RHP	$3,500,000
19.	Giants: Heliot Ramos, OF	$3,101,700
20.	Mets: David Peterson, LHP	$2,994,500
21.	Orioles: D.L. Hall, LHP	$3,000,000
22.	Blue Jays: Logan Warmoth, SS	$2,820,200
23.	Dodgers: Jeren Kendall, OF	$2,897,500
24.	Red Sox: Tanner Houck, RHP	$2,614,500
25.	Nationals: Seth Romero, LHP	$2,800,000
26.	Rangers: Bubba Thompson, OF	$2,100,000
27.	Cubs: Brendon Little, LHP	$2,200,000
28.	Blue Jays: Nate Pearson, RHP	$2,452,900
29.	Rangers: Chris Seise, SS	$2,000,000
30.	Cubs: Alex Lange, RHP	$1,925,000

SUPPLEMENTAL FIRST ROUND

No.	Team: Player, Pos.	Bonus
31.	Rays: Drew Rasmussen, RHP	Did not sign
32.	Reds: Jeter Downs, SS	$1,822,500
33.	Athletics: Kevin Merrell, SS	$1,800,000
34.	Brewers: Tristen Lutz, OF	$2,352,000
35.	Twins: Brent Rooker, OF	$1,935,300
36.	Marlins: Brian Miller, OF	$1,888,800

SECOND ROUND

No.	Team: Player, Pos.	Bonus
37.	Twins: Landon Leach, RHP	$1,400,000
38.	Reds: Stuart Fairchild, OF	$1,800,300
39.	Padres: Luis Campusano, C	$1,300,000
40.	Rays: Michael Mercado, RHP	$2,132,400
41.	Braves: Drew Waters, OF	$1,500,000
42.	Pirates: Steven Jennings, RHP	$1,900,000
43.	Athletics: Greg Deichmann, OF	$1,700,000
44.	D-backs: Drew Ellis, 3B	$1,560,100
45.	Phillies: Spencer Howard, RHP	$1,150,000
46.	Brewers: Caden Lemons, RHP	$1,450,000
47.	Angels: Griffin Canning, RHP	$1,459,200
48.	Rockies: Ryan Vilade, 3B	$1,425,400
49.	White Sox: Gavin Sheets, 1B	$2,000,000
50.	Pirates: Calvin Mitchell, OF	$1,357,300
51.	Marlins: Joe Dunand, 3B	$1,200,000
52.	Royals: M.J. Melendez, C	$2,097,500
53.	Astros: Joe Perez, 3B	$1,600,000
54.	Yankees: Matt Sauer, RHP	$2,497,500
55.	Mariners: Sam Carlson, RHP	$2,000,000
56.	Astros: Corbin Martin, RHP	$1,000,000
57.	Tigers: Rey Rivera, OF	$850,000
58.	Giants: Jacob Gonzalez, 3B	$950,000
59.	Mets: Mark Vientos, 3B	$1,500,000
60.	Orioles: Adam Hall, SS	$1,300,000
61.	Blue Jays: Hagen Danner, C	$1,500,000
62.	Dodgers: Morgan Cooper	$867,500
63.	Red Sox: Cole Brannen, OF	$1,300,000
64.	Indians: Quentin Holmes	$988,970
65.	Nationals: Wil Crowe, RHP	$946,500
66.	Rangers: Hans Crouse, RHP	$1,450,000
67.	Cubs: Cory Abbott, RHP	$901,900

SUPPLEMENTAL SECOND ROUND

No.	Team: Player, Pos.	Bonus
68.	D-backs: Daulton Varsho, C	$881,100
69.	Padres: Blake Hunt, C	$1,600,000
70.	Rockies: Tommy Doyle, RHP	$837,300
71.	Indians: Tyler Freeman, SS	$816,500
72.	Pirates: Conner Uselton, OF	$900,000
73.	Royals: Evan Steele, LHP	$826,500
74.	Orioles: Zac Lowther, LHP	$779,500
75.	Astros: J.J. Matijevic, 2B	$700,000

THIRD ROUND

No.	Team: Player, Pos.	Bonus
76.	Twins: Blayne Enlow, RHP	$2,000,000
77.	Reds: Jacob Heatherly, LHP	$1,047,500
78.	Padres: Mason House, OF	$732,200
79.	Rays: Taylor Walls, SS	$612,500
80.	Braves: Freddy Tarnok, RHP	$1,445,000
81.	Athletics: Nick Allen, SS	$2,000,000
82.	D-backs: Matt Tabor, RHP	$1,000,000
83.	Phillies: Connor Seabold, RHP	$525,000
84.	Brewers: K.J. Harrison, C	$667,000
85.	Angels: Jacob Pearson, OF	$1,000,000
86.	Rockies: Will Gaddis, RHP	$600,000
87.	White Sox: Luis Gonzalez, OF	$517,000
88.	Pirates: Dylan Busby, 3B	$575,000
89.	Marlins: Riley Mahan, 2B	$525,000
90.	Royals: Daniel Tillo, LHP	$557,500
91.	Astros: Tyler Ivey, RHP	$450,000
92.	Yankees: Trevor Stephan, RHP	$797,500
93.	Mariners: Wyatt Mills, RHP	$125,000
94.	Cardinals: Scott Hurst, OF	$450,000
95.	Tigers: Joey Morgan, C	$564,000
96.	Giants: Seth Corry, LHP	$1,000,000
97.	Mets: Quinn Brodey, OF	$500,000
98.	Orioles: Mike Baumann, RHP	$500,000
99.	Blue Jays: Riley Adams, C	$542,400
100.	Dodgers: Connor Wong, C	$547,500

TOP 20 PROSPECTS

FROM EVERY MINOR LEAGUE

TRIPLE-A

International League

1. Luis Robert, OF, Charlotte (White Sox)
2. Bo Bichette, SS, Buffalo (Blue Jays)
3. Brendan McKay, LHP/DH, Durham (Rays)
4. Austin Riley, 3B/OF, Gwinnett (Braves)
5. Oscar Mercado, OF, Columbus (Indians)
6. Mitch Keller, RHP, Indianapolis (Pirates)
7. Ryan Mountcastle, 1B/OF, Norfolk (Orioles)
8. Ke'Bryan Hayes, 3B, Indianapolis (Pirates)
9. Kyle Wright, RHP, Gwinnett (Braves)
10. Aristides Aquino, OF, Louisville (Reds)
11. Bryse Wilson, RHP, Gwinnett (Braves)
12. Dylan Cease, RHP, Charlotte (White Sox)
13. Bobby Bradley, 1B, Columbus (Indians)
14. Nate Lowe, 1B, Durham (Rays)
15. Kolby Allard, LHP, Gwinnett (Braves)
16. Nick Solak, 2B/OF, Durham (Rays)
17. Jaylin Davis, OF, Rochester (Twins)
18. Cole Tucker, SS, Indianapolis (Pirates)
19. Jake Cronenworth, SS, Durham (Rays)
20. Keegan Akin, LHP, Norfolk (Orioles)

Pacific Coast League

1. Yordan Alvarez, OF, Fresno (Astros)
2. Keston Hiura, 2B, San Antonio (Brewers)
3. Gavin Lux, SS/2B, Oklahoma City (Dodgers)
4. Carter Kieboom, SS/2B, Fresno (Nationals)
5. Kyle Tucker, OF, Round Rock (Astros)
6. Sean Murphy, C, Las Vegas (Athletics)
7. Zac Gallen, RHP, New Orleans (Marlins)
8. Will Smith, C, Oklahoma City (Dodgers)
9. Brendan Rodgers, 2B/SS, Albuquerque (Rockies)
10. Luis Urias, SS/2B, El Paso (Padres)
11. Tommy Edman, 2B/SS, Memphis (Cardinals)
12. Tyler O'Neill, OF, Memphis (Cardinals)
13. Josh Naylor, OF, El Paso (Padres)
14. Peter Lambert, RHP, Albuquerque (Rockies)
15. Mauricio Dubon, SS, San Antonio (MIL)/Sacramento (SF)
16. Trent Grisham, OF, San Antonio (Brewers)
17. Lane Thomas, OF, Memphis (Cardinals)
18. Patrick Sandoval, LHP, Salt Lake (Angels)
19. Isan Diaz, 2B, New Orleans (Marlins)
20. Justus Sheffield, LHP, Tacoma (Mariners)

DOUBLE-A

Eastern League

1. Nate Pearson, RHP, New Hampshire (Blue Jays)
2. Casey Mize, RHP, Erie (Tigers)
3. Matt Manning, RHP, Erie (Tigers)
4. Alec Bohm, 3B, Reading (Phillies)
5. Deivi Garcia, RHP, Trenton (Yankees)
6. Nolan Jones, 3B, Akron (Indians)
7. Bryan Mata, RHP, Portland (Red Sox)
8. Bobby Dalbec, 3B, Portland (Red Sox)
9. Andres Gimenez, SS, Binghamton (Mets)
10. Isaac Paredes, 3B/SS, Erie (Tigers)
11. Anthony Kay, LHP, Binghamton (Mets)
12. Alex Faedo, RHP, Erie (Tigers)
13. Jarren Duran, OF, Portland (Red Sox)
14. Yusniel Diaz, OF, Bowie (Orioles)
15. Mike Baumann, RHP, Bowie (Orioles)
16. Luis Garcia, SS, Harrisburg (Nationals)
17. Albert Abreu, RHP, Trenton (Yankees)
18. Adonis Medina, RHP, Reading (Phillies)
19. Adam Haseley, OF, Reading (Phillies)
20. Patrick Murphy, RHP, New Hampshire (Blue Jays)

Southern League

1. Jo Adell, OF, Mobile (Angels)
2. Luis Robert, OF, Birmingham (White Sox)
3. Cristian Pache, OF, Mississippi (Braves)
4. Sixto Sanchez, RHP, Jacksonville (Marlins)
5. Drew Waters, OF, Mississippi (Braves)
6. Brendan McKay, LHP/DH, Montgomery (Rays)
7. Jazz Chisholm, SS, Jackson (ARI)/Jacksonville (MIA)
8. Ian Anderson, RHP, Mississippi (Braves)
9. Brusdar Graterol, RHP, Pensacola (Twins)
10. Brandon Marsh, OF, Mobile (Angels)
11. Trevor Larnach, OF, Pensacola (Twins)
12. Alex Kirilloff, OF/1B, Pensacola (Twins)
13. Lewin Diaz, 1B, Pensacola (MIN)/Jacksonville (MIA)
14. Daulton Varsho, C/OF, Jackson (D-backs)
15. Nico Hoerner, SS/2B, Tennessee (Cubs)
16. Taylor Trammell, OF, Chattanooga (Reds)
17. Nick Madrigal, 2B, Birmingham (White Sox)
18. Royce Lewis, SS, Pensacola (Twins)
19. Jesus Sanchez, OF, Montgomery (Rays)
20. Josh Lowe, OF, Montgomery (Rays)

Texas League

1. Gavin Lux, SS, Tulsa (Dodgers)
2. Dylan Carlson, OF, Springfield (Cardinals)
3. Dustin May, RHP, Tulsa (Dodgers)
4. Logan Gilbert, RHP, Arkansas (Mariners)
5. Justus Sheffield, LHP, Arkansas (Mariners)
6. Evan White, 1B, Arkansas (Mariners)
7. Keibert Ruiz, C, Tulsa (Dodgers)
8. Justin Dunn, RHP, Arkansas (Mariners)
9. Brady Singer, RHP, Northwest Arkansas (Royals)
10. Jackson Kowar, RHP, Northwest Arkansas (Royals)
11. Seth Beer, 1B, Corpus Christi (Astros)
12. Elehuris Montero, 3B, Springfield (Cardinals)
13. Abraham Toro, 3B, Corpus Christi (Astros)
14. Leody Taveras, OF, Frisco (Rangers)
15. Daulton Jefferies, RHP, Midland (Athletics)
16. Khalil Lee, OF, Northwest Arkansas (Royals)
17. Jake Fraley, OF, Arkansas (Mariners)
18. Edward Olivares, OF, Amarillo (Padres)
19. Owen Miller, 2B, Amarillo (Padres)
20. Ronald Bolaños, RHP, Amarillo (Padres)

HIGH CLASS A

California League

1. MacKenzie Gore, LHP, Lake Elsinore (Padres)
2. Joey Bart, C, San Jose (Giants)
3. Jarred Kelenic, OF, Modesto (Mariners)
4. Luis Patiño, RHP, Lake Elsinore (Padres)

5. Heliot Ramos, OF, San Jose (Giants)
6. Josiah Gray, RHP, Rancho Cucamonga (Dodgers)
7. Logan Gilbert, RHP, Modesto (Mariners)
8. Luis Campusano, C, Lake Elsinore (Padres)
9. Jeter Downs, SS, Rancho Cucamonga (Dodgers)
10. Xavier Edwards, 2B, Lake Elsinore (Padres)
11. Sean Hjelle, RHP, San Jose (Giants)
12. Gabriel Arias, SS, Lake Elsinore (Padres)
13. Ryan Rolison, LHP, Lancaster (Rockies)
14. Cal Raleigh, C, Modesto (Mariners)
15. Josh Green, RHP, Visalia (D-backs)
16. Ronald Bolaños, RHP, Lake Elsinore (Padres)
17. Nick Allen, SS, Stockton (Athletics)
18. Devin Mann, 2B/3B, Rancho Cucamonga (Dodgers)
19. Oliver Ortega, RHP, Inland Empire (Angels)
20. Ryan Vilade, SS/3B, Lancaster (Rockies)

Carolina League

1. DL Hall, LHP, Frederick (Orioles)
2. Nolan Jones, 3B, Lynchburg (Indians)
3. Jackson Kowar, RHP, Wilmington (Royals)
4. Nick Madrigal, 2B, Winston-Salem (White Sox)
5. Sam Huff, C/1B, Down East (Rangers)
6. Daniel Lynch, LHP, Wilmington (Royals)
7. Jarren Duran, OF, Salem (Red Sox)
8. Bryan Mata, RHP, Salem (Red Sox)
9. Brady Singer, RHP, Wilmington (Royals)
10. Tyler Freeman, SS, Lynchburg (Indians)
11. Miguel Amaya, C, Myrtle Beach (Cubs)
12. Kris Bubic, LHP, Wilmington (Royals)
13. Leody Taveras, OF, Down East (Rangers)
14. Mario Feliciano, C, Carolina (Brewers)
15. Tim Cate, LHP, Potomac (Nationals)
16. Brice Turang, SS, Carolina (Brewers)
17. Kyle Isbel, OF, Wilmington (Royals)
18. Payton Henry, C, Carolina (Brewers)
19. Shawn Dubin, RHP, Fayetteville (Astros)
20. Steele Walker, OF, Winston-Salem (White Sox)

Florida State League

1. Wander Franco, SS, Charlotte (Rays)
2. Alec Bohm, 3B, Clearwater (Phillies)
3. Trevor Larnach, OF, Fort Myers (Twins)
4. Tarik Skubal, LHP, Lakeland (Tigers)
5. JJ Bleday, OF, Jupiter (Marlins)
6. Edward Cabrera, RHP, Jupiter (Marlins)
7. Oneil Cruz, SS, Bradenton (Pirates)
8. Nolan Gorman, 3B, Palm Beach (Cardinals)
9. Jordan Balazovic, RHP, Fort Myers (Twins)
10. Joe Ryan, RHP, Charlotte (Rays)
11. Shane McClanahan, LHP, Charlotte (Rays)
12. Clarke Schmidt, RHP, Tampa (Yankees)
13. Royce Lewis, SS, Fort Myers (Twins)
14. Jhoan Duran, RHP, Fort Myers (Twins)
15. Vidal Brujan, 2B, Charlotte (Rays)
16. Jose Garcia, SS, Daytona (Reds)
17. Lewin Diaz, 1B, Fort Myers (Twins)
18. Jonathan India, 3B, Daytona (Reds)
19. Ryan Jeffers, C, Fort Myers (Twins)
20. Ronaldo Hernandez, C, Charlotte (Rays)

LOW CLASS A

Midwest League

1. Wander Franco, SS, Bowling Green (Rays)
2. Matthew Liberatore, LHP, Bowling Green (Rays)
3. Brailyn Marquez, LHP, South Bend (Cubs)
4. Shane Baz, RHP, Bowling Green (Rays)
5. Shane McClanahan, LHP, Bowling Green (Rays)
6. Xavier Edwards, SS, Fort Wayne (Padres)
7. Tyler Freeman, SS, Lake County (Indians)
8. Nolan Gorman, 3B, Peoria (Cardinals)
9. Alek Thomas, OF, Kane County (D-backs)
10. Brennan Davis, OF, South Bend (Cubs)
11. Joey Cantillo, LHP, Fort Wayne (Padres)
12. Gabriel Moreno, C, Lansing (Blue Jays)
13. Geraldo Perdomo, SS, Kane County (D-backs)
14. Miguel Vargas, 3B, Great Lakes (Dodgers)
15. Levi Kelly, RHP, Kane County (D-backs)
16. Ryan Weathers, LHP, Fort Wayne (Padres)
17. Brice Turang, SS, Wisconsin (Brewers)
18. Otto Lopez, 2B, Lansing (Blue Jays)
19. Riley Thompson, RHP, South Bend (Cubs)
20. Will Benson, OF, Lake County (Indians)

South Atlantic League

1. Jarred Kelenic, OF, West Virginia (Mariners)
2. Julio Rodriguez, OF, West Virginia (Mariners)
3. Grayson Rodriguez, RHP, Delmarva (Orioles)
4. Triston Casas, 1B, Greenville (Red Sox)
5. Ronny Mauricio, SS, Columbia (Mets)
6. Seth Corry, LHP, Augusta (Giants)
7. Simeon Woods-Richardson, RHP, Columbia (Mets)
8. Kris Bubic, LHP, Lexington (Royals)
9. Braden Shewmake, SS, Rome (Braves)
10. Josh Jung, 3B, Hickory (Rangers)
11. Cole Winn, RHP, Hickory (Rangers)
12. Roansy Contreras, RHP, Charleston (Yankees)
13. Alexander Vizcaino, RHP, Charleston (Yankees)
14. Luis Gil, RHP, Charleston (Yankees)
15. Luis Medina, RHP, Charleston (Yankees)
16. Sherten Apostel, 3B, Hickory (Rangers)
17. Hans Crouse, RHP, Hickory (Rangers)
18. Ji-Hwan Bae, 2B/SS, Greensboro (Pirates)
19. Trey Harris, OF, Rome (Braves)
20. Canaan Smith, OF, Charleston (Yankees)

SHORT-SEASON

Northwest League

1. Kristian Robinson, OF, Hillsboro (D-Backs)
2. Luis Frias, RHP, Hillsboro (D-backs)
3. Hunter Bishop, OF, Salem-Keizer (Giants)
4. Aaron Schunk, 3B, Boise (Rockies)
5. Adam Kloffenstein, RHP, Vancouver (Blue Jays)
6. Chase Strumpf, 2B, Eugene (Cubs)
7. Ezequiel Tovar, SS, Boise (Rockies)
8. Liover Peguero, SS, Hillsboro (D-backs)
9. Alexander Canario, OF, Salem-Keizer (Giants)
10. Ricky Vanasco, RHP, Spokane (Rangers)
11. Michael Toglia, 1B, Boise (Rockies)
12. David Garcia, C, Spokane (Rangers)
13. Kohl Franklin, RHP, Eugene (Cubs)

14. Logan Wyatt, 1B, Salem-Keizer (Giants)
15. Edmond Americaan, OF, Eugene (Cubs)
16. Austin Shenton, 3B, Everett (Mariners)
17. Armani Smith, OF, Salem-Keizer (Giants)
18. Franklin Labour, OF, Salem-Keizer (Giants)
19. Pedro Martinez, SS, Eugene (Cubs)
20. Bladimir Restituyo, 2B/OF, Boise (Rockies)

New York-Penn League

1. Adley Rutschman, C, Aberdeen (Orioles)
2. Riley Greene, OF, Connecticut (Tigers)
3. Greg Jones, SS, Hudson Valley (Rays)
4. Gilberto Jimenez, OF, Lowell (Red Sox)
5. Brayan Rocchio, SS/2B, Mahoning Valley (Indians)
6. George Valera, OF, Mahoning Valley (Indians)
7. Ezequiel Duran, 2B, Staten Island (Yankees)
8. Jordan Diaz, 3B, Vermont (Athletics)
9. Ethan Hankins, RHP, Mahoning Valley (Indians)
10. Leonardo Rodriguez, RHP, Aberdeen (Orioles)
11. Bryson Stott, SS, Williamsport (Phillies)
12. Tyler Baum, RHP, Vermont (Athletics)
13. John Doxakis, LHP, Hudson Valley (Rays)
14. Oswald Peraza, SS, Staten Island (Yankees)
15. Kendall Simmons, 2B, Williamsport (Phillies)
16. Josh Smith, 2B, Staten Island (Yankees)
17. Korey Lee, C, Tri-City (Astros)
18. Aldo Ramirez, RHP, Lowell (Red Sox)
19. Dalvy Rosario, SS, Batavia (Marlins)
20. Eliezer Alfonzo, C, Connecticut (Tigers)

ROOKIE-ADVANCED

Appalachian League

1. Francisco Alvarez, C, Kingsport (Mets)
2. Brett Baty, 3B, Kingsport (Mets)
3. Miguel Hiraldo, SS/2B, Bluefield (Blue Jays)
4. Jhon Torres, OF, Johnson City (Cardinals)
5. Antonio Cabello, OF, Pulaski (Yankees)
6. Matt Wallner, OF, Elizabethton (Twins)
7. Anthony Volpe, SS, Pulaski (Yankees)
8. Nick Schnell, OF, Princeton (Rays)
9. Yoendrys Gomez, RHP, Pulaski (Yankees)
10. Jaylen Palmer, SS/3B, Kingsport (Mets)
11. Tyler Callihan, 3B/2B, Greeneville (Reds)
12. Junior Santos, RHP, Kingsport (Mets)
13. Ivan Johnson, SS/2B, Greeneville (Reds)
14. Leonardo Jimenez, SS/2B, Bluefield (Blue Jays)
15. Bryce Ball, 1B, Danville (Braves)
16. Spencer Steer, SS/2B, Elizabethton (Twins)
17. Ryder Green, OF, Pulaski (Yankees)
18. Adrian Alcantara, RHP, Burlington (Royals)
19. Tahnaj Thomas, RHP, Bristol (Pirates)
20. Jose Salvador, LHP, Greeneville (Reds)

Pioneer League

1. Liover Peguero, SS, Missoula (D-Backs)
2. Andy Pages, OF, Ogden (Dodgers)
3. Jeremiah Jackson, SS/2B, Orem (Angels)
4. Helcris Olivarez, LHP, Grand Junction (Rockies)
5. Will Wilson, SS/2B, Orem (Angels)
6. Brenton Doyle, OF, Grand Junction (Rockies)
7. Alec Marsh, RHP, Idaho Falls (Royals)
8. Noah Davis, RHP, Billings (Reds)
9. Carlos Rodriguez, OF, Rocky Mountain (Brewers)
10. Miguel Medrano, RHP, Billings (Reds)
11. Brady McConnell, SS, Idaho Falls (Royals)
12. Julio Carreras, 3B/SS, Grand Junction (Rockies)
13. Eddy Davis, SS/2B, Grand Junction (Rockies)
14. Mitchell Kilkenny, RHP, Grand Junction (Rockies)
15. Brandon Lewis, 3B/1B, Ogden (Dodgers)
16. Christian Koss, INF, Grand Junction (Rockies)
17. Ezequiel Tovar, SS, Grand Junction (Rockies)
18. Nick Kahle, C, Rocky Mountain (Brewers)
19. Eric Yang, C, Billings (Reds)
20. Grant Gambrell, RHP, Idaho Falls (Royals)

ROOKIE-LEVEL

Arizona League

1. CJ Abrams, SS, Padres
2. Marco Luciano, SS, Giants
3. Bobby Witt Jr., SS, Royals
4. Corbin Carroll, OF, D-backs
5. Diego Cartaya, C, Dodgers
6. Kody Hoese, 3B, Dodgers
7. Antoine Kelly, LHP, Brewers
8. Aaron Bracho, 2B, Indians
9. Wilderd Patiño, OF, D-backs
10. Hudson Head, OF, Padres
11. Alex De Jesus, SS, Dodgers
12. Keithron Moss, 2B/3B, Rangers
13. Hyun-il Choi, RHP, Dodgers
14. H. Hernandez, OF/C/1B, Rangers
15. Jose Tena, SS, Indians
16. Luis Toribio, 3B, Giants
17. Jairo Pomares, OF, Giants
18. Pedro Martinez, SS/2B, Cubs
19. Brayan Buelvas, OF, Athletics
20. Joshua Mears, OF, Padres

Gulf Coast League

1. Orelvis Martinez, SS/3B, Blue Jays
2. Quinn Priester, RHP, Pirates
3. Gunnar Henderson, SS, Orioles
4. Sammy Siani, OF, Pirates
5. Antonio Gomez, C, Yankees
6. Andrick Nava, C, Phillies
7. Victor Mesa Jr., OF, Marlins
8. Kevin Alcantara, OF, Yankees
9. Alexander Vargas, SS, Yankees
10. Nasim Nuñez, SS, Marlins
11. Raimfer Salinas, OF, Yankees
12. Jairo Lopez, RHP, Astros
13. Keoni Cavaco, SS, Twins
14. Matthew Lugo, SS, Red Sox
15. Michael Harris, OF, Braves
16. Evan Fitterer, RHP, Marlins
17. Alberto Rodriguez, Blue Jays
18. Jeremy de la Rosa, OF, Nationals
19. Dasan Brown, OF, Blue Jays
20. Viandel Pena, INF, Nationals

INDEX

A

Abbott, Cory (Cubs) 90
Abrams, CJ (Padres) 390
Abreu, Albert (Yankees) 314
Abreu, Bryan (Astros) 183
Acosta, Daison (Mets) 303
Acosta, Maximo (Rangers) 455
Acuña, Luisangel (Rangers) 457
Adams, Jordyn (Angels) 214
Adell, Jo (Angels) 213
Ademan, Aramis (Cubs) 96
Adolfo, Micker (White Sox) 106
Adon, Joan (Nationals) 494
Akin, Keegan (Orioles) 57
Alcala, Jorge (Twins) 285
Alcantara, Kevin (Yankees) 318
Alcantara, Sergio (Tigers) 174
Alexander, Blaze (D-backs) 29
Alford, Anthony (Blue Jays) 479
Allan, Matt (Mets) 295
Allen, Austin (Athletics) 330
Allen, Logan (Indians) 138
Allen, Nick (Athletics) 330
Altuve, Brayan (Cubs) 95
Alvarez, Francisco (Mets) 294
Alzolay, Adbert (Cubs) 90
Amador, Adael (Rockies) 154
Amaya, Jacob (Dodgers) 238
Amaya, Miguel (Cubs) 87
Americaan, Edmond (Cubs) 92
Anderson, Ian (Braves) 38
Andrews, Clayton (Brewers) 272
Antone, Tejay (Reds) 126
Antuna, Yasel (Nationals) 489
Apostel, Sherten (Rangers) 458
Aquino, Stiward (Angels) 219
Arias, Gabriel (Padres) 393
Armenteros, Lazaro (Athletics) 330
Armenteros, Rogelio (Astros) 192
Arozarena, Randy (Cardinals) 378
Arteaga, Aeverson (Giants) 416
Ashby, Aaron (Brewers) 263
Ashcraft, Braxton (Pirates) 362
Aybar, Yoan (Red Sox) 78
Azocar, Jose (Tigers) 176

B

Bachar, Lake (Padres) 401
Baddoo, Akil (Twins) 286
Bae, Ji-Hwan (Pirates) 360
Baez, Michel (Padres) 393
Bailey, Benyamin (White Sox) 110
Baker, Luken (Cardinals) 384
Balazovic, Jordan (Twins) 279
Ball, Bryce (Braves) 45
Ball, Matt (Angels) 225
Banda, Anthony (Rays) 449
Banfield, Will (Marlins) 253
Banks, Nick (Nationals) 496
Bannister, Zion (Rangers) 465
Bannon, Rylan (Orioles) 65
Barber, Colin (Astros) 188
Barrera, Luis (Athletics) 334
Barrera, Tres (Nationals) 490
Bart, Joey (Giants) 406
Basabe, Luis Alexander (White Sox) 108
Basabe, Osleivis (Rangers) 459
Baty, Brett (Mets) 294
Baum, Tyler (Athletics) 331
Baumann, Mike (Orioles) 58
Bautista, Mariel (Reds) 127
Baylor, Jamari (Phillies) 349
Baz, Shane (Rays) 439
Beard, James (White Sox) 109
Beasley, Jeremy (Angels) 224
Beck, Austin (Athletics) 327
Beck, Tristan (Giants) 411
Beer, Seth (D-backs) 27
Bello, Brayan (Red Sox) 75
Bello, Micah (Brewers) 273
Benson, Will (Indians) 143
Bericoto, Victor (Giants) 415
Bettinger, Alec (Brewers) 270
Bido, Osvaldo (Pirates) 367
Bielak, Brandon (Astros) 187
Bishop, Braden (Mariners) 429
Bishop, Hunter (Giants) 407
Blankenhorn, Travis (Twins) 287
Bleday, JJ (Marlins) 246
Bohm, Alec (Phillies) 342
Bolanos, Ronald (Padres) 395
Bolt, Skye (Athletics) 331
Bolton, Cody (Pirates) 359
Bonaci, Brainer (Red Sox) 76
Bonilla, Jose (Angels) 223
Bourque, James (Nationals) 494
Bowden, Ben (Rockies) 154
Bowlan, Jonathan (Royals) 202
Bracho, Aaron (Indians) 137
Bradley, Bobby (Indians) 138
Bradley, Taj (Rays) 444
Braymer, Ben (Nationals) 493
Brewer, Jordan (Astros) 186
Brodey, Quinn (Mets) 305
Brodgon, Connor (Phillies) 351
Brown, Dasan (Blue Jays) 478
Brown, Hunter (Astros) 185
Brown, Logan (Braves) 47
Brown, Seth (Athletics) 335
Brown, Zack (Brewers) 266
Brubaker, JT (Pirates) 364
Brujan, Vidal (Rays) 439
Bubic, Kris (Royals) 201
Buelvas, Brayan (Athletics) 333
Bukauskas, J.B. (D-backs) 26
Burdi, Nick (Pirates) 367
Burdick, Peyton (Marlins) 253
Burke, Brock (Rangers) 462
Burrows, Beau (Tigers) 172
Burrows, Michael (Pirates) 362
Busch, Michael (Dodgers) 233
Bush, Bryce (White Sox) 107
Butto, Jose (Mets) 301

C

Cabello, Antonio (Yankees) 317
Cabrera, Edward (Marlins) 247
Cabrera, Gensis (Cardinals) 374
Callihan, Tyler (Reds) 123
Cameron, Daz (Tigers) 168
Campbell, Isaiah (Mariners) 427
Campos, Roberto (Tigers) 171
Campusano, Luis (Padres) 391
Canario, Alexander (Giants) 407
Cannon, Cameron (Red Sox) 77
Canterino, Matt (Twins) 281
Cantillo, Joey (Padres) 394
Carillo, Gerardo (Dodgers) 240
Carlson, Dylan (Cardinals) 373
Carlson, Sam (Mariners) 430
Carreras, Julio (Rockies) 158
Carroll, Corbin (D-backs) 23
Cartaya, Diego (Dodgers) 232
Casas, Triston (Red Sox) 69
Castellani, Ryan (Rockies) 152
Castro, Anthony (Tigers) 173
Castro, Willi (Tigers) 169
Cate, Tim (Nationals) 487
Cavaco, Keoni (Twins) 282
Cederlind, Blake (Pirates) 367
Celestino, Gilberto (Twins) 283
Chang, Yu (Indians) 142
Chatham, C.J. (Red Sox) 74
Chisholm, Jazz (Marlins) 247
Clarke, Chris (Cubs) 91
Clase, Emmanuel (Indians) 140
Clase, Jonatan (Mariners) 431
Clemens, Kody (Tigers) 172
Clement, Ernie (Indians) 142
Clementina, Hendrick (Reds) 127
Cluff, Jackson (Nationals) 492
Colina, Edwar (Twins) 288
Collins, Zack (White Sox) 108
Comas, Alexander (White Sox) 111
Conine, Brett (Astros) 190
Conine, Griffin (Blue Jays) 475
Contreras, Roansy (Yankees) 313
Contreras, William (Braves) 41
Contreras, Yan (Reds) 125
Corniel, Jose (Mariners) 430
Corry, Seth (Giants) 408
Cortes, Carlos (Mets) 304
Cox, Austin (Royals) 201
Craig, Will (Pirates) 366
Cronenworth, Jake (Padres) 396
Cronin, Matt (Nationals) 491
Crouse, Hans (Rangers) 456
Crowe, Wil (Nationals) 487
Cruz, Oneil (Pirates) 358

D

Dalbec, Bobby (Red Sox) 70
Dalquist, Andrew (White Sox) 104
Davidson, Logan (Athletics) 329
Davidson, Tucker (Braves) 42
Davis, Brennen (Cubs) 86
Davis, Jaylin (Giants) 412
Davis, Noah (Reds) 123
Daza, Yonathan (Rockies) 159
De Castro, Rikelvin (Blue Jays) 476
De Jesus, Alex (Dodgers) 240
De la Cruz, Jassel (Braves) 42
De la Cruz, Jose (Tigers) 175
De la Rosa, Jeremy (Nationals) 491
De los Santos, Enyel (Phillies) 345
Dean, Justin (Braves) 48
Decker, Nick (Red Sox) 77
Deichmann, Greg (Athletics) 332
Del Rosario, Yefri (Royals) 205
Delaplane, Sam (Mariners) 429
Denaburg, Mason (Nationals) 489
Devers, Jose (Marlins) 251
Diaz, Eddy (Rockies) 157

Diaz, Eduardo (D-backs) 31
Diaz, Jhon (Rays) 448
Diaz, Jordan (Athletics) 332
Diaz, Lewin (Marlins) 248
Diaz, Yennsy (Blue Jays) 480
Diaz, Yusniel (Orioles) 56
Dibrell, Tony (Mets) 303
Dillard, Thomas (Brewers) 271
Dixon, Jasiah (Pirates) 369
Dobnak, Randy (Twins) 283
Dominguez, Jasson (Yankees) 309
Dominguez, Robert (Mets) 300
Downs, Jeter (Dodgers) 232
Doxakis, John (Rays) 446
Doyle, Brenton (Rockies) 156
Doyle, Tommy (Rockies) 157
Driscoll, Logan (Padres) 400
Dubin, Shawn (Astros) 189
Dubon, Mauricio (Giants) 410
Dugger, Robert (Marlins) 256
Dunn, Justin (Mariners) 425
Dunning, Dane (White Sox) 105
Dunshee, Parker (Athletics) 334
Duplantier, Jon (D-backs) 27
Duran, Ezequiel (Yankees) 319
Duran, Jarren (Red Sox) 71
Duran, Jhoan (Twins) 280
Dyson, Tyler (Nationals) 492

E

Edwards, Xavier (Rays) 441
Eierman, Jeremy (Athletics) 335
Elledge, Seth (Cardinals) 383
Encarnacion, Jean Carlos (Orioles) 65
Encarnacion, Jerar (Marlins) 252
English, Tristin (D-backs) 32
Enlow, Blayne (Twins) 281
Escotto, Maikol (Yankees) 320
Espinal, Santiago (Blue Jays) 477
Espino, Daniel (Indians) 136
Esplin, Tyler (Red Sox) 80
Estevez, Omar (Dodgers) 236
Ethridge, Will (Rockies) 161
Evans, DeMarcus (Rangers) 460

F

Fabian, Sandro (Giants) 417
Faedo, Alex (Tigers) 168
Fairbanks, Peter (Rays) 446
Fairchild, Stuart (Reds) 121
Feliciano, Mario (Brewers) 264
Feltman, Durbin (Red Sox) 81
Fenter, Gray (Orioles) 62
Fernandez, Eduarqui (Brewers) 273
Fernandez, Junior (Cardinals) 378
Fernandez, Yanquiel (Rockies) 158
File, Dylan (Brewers) 270
Fitterer, Evan (Marlins) 255
Fitzgerald, Tyler (Giants) 416
Fleming, Josh (Rays) 449
Fletcher, Aaron (Mariners) 430
Fletcher, Dominic (D-backs) 30
Fletcher, Trejyn (Cardinals) 382
Florentino, Randy (Rangers) 464
Flores, Antoni (Red Sox) 81
Florez, Santiago (Pirates) 365
Florial, Estevan (Yankees) 315
Flowers, J.C. (Pirates) 369
Fox, Lucius (Rays) 447
Fraley, Jake (Mariners) 426
Franco, Sadrac (Angels) 220
Franco, Wander (Rays) 437
Franklin, Kohl (Cubs) 91
Freeman, Cole (Nationals) 494
Freeman, Tyler (Indians) 134
Frias, Luis (D-backs) 26
Friedl, TJ (Reds) 125
Fuentes, Josh (Rockies) 160
Fuentes, Steven (Nationals) 496
Funkhouser, Kyle (Tigers) 176

G

Gallardo, Richard (Cubs) 93
Garcia, Bryan (Tigers) 172
Garcia, David (Rangers) 463
Garcia, Deivi (Yankees) 310
Garcia, Eduardo (Brewers) 265
Garcia, Jose (Reds) 120
Garcia, Luis (Astros) 187
Garcia, Luis (Nationals) 486
Garcia, Luis (Phillies) 344
Garcia, Ryan (Rangers) 461
Garrett, Braxton (Marlins) 249
Gerber, Joey (Mariners) 431
German, Jhonatan (Nationals) 497
Gigliotti, Michael (Royals) 208
Gil, Luis (Yankees) 311
Gil, Mateo (Cardinals) 382
Gilbert, Logan (Mariners) 423
Gilliam, Ryley (Mets) 304
Gimenez, Andres (Mets) 295
Ginkel, Kevin (D-backs) 31
Gladney, Damon (White Sox) 111
Gomez, Antonio (Yankees) 318
Gomez, Moises (Rays) 443
Gomez, Yoendrys (Yankees) 315
Gonsolin, Tony (Dodgers) 231
Gonzalez, Luis (White Sox) 106
Gonzalez, Oscar (Indians) 144
Gonzalez, Victor (Dodgers) 241
Gordon, Nick (Twins) 284
Gore, Mackenzie (Padres) 389
Gorman, Nolan (Cardinals) 374
Gorski, Matt (Pirates) 369
Goss, JJ (Rays) 443
Goudeau, Ashton (Rockies) 159
Graffanino, AJ (Braves) 48
Grammes, Conor (D-backs) 33
Graterol, Brusdar (Twins) 279
Gray, Joe (Brewers) 271
Gray, Josiah (Dodgers) 231
Green, Josh (D-backs) 28
Green, Ryder (Yankees) 321
Greene, Hunter (Reds) 117
Greene, Riley (Tigers) 167
Grenier, Cadyn (Orioles) 63
Griffin, Foster (Royals) 209
Groome, Jay (Red Sox) 72
Groshans, Jordan (Blue Jays) 470
Gruillon, Deivi (Phillies) 348
Guerra, Javy (Padres) 399
Gutierrez, Abrahan (Phillies) 352
Gutierrez, Kelvin (Royals) 205
Gutierrez, Vladimir (Reds) 122
Guzman, Jeison (Royals) 203
Guzman, Jonathan (Phillies) 353
Guzman, Jorge (Marlins) 251

H

Haake, Zach (Royals) 204
Haggerty, Sam (Mets) 303
Hall, Adam (Orioles) 59
Hall, DL (Orioles) 54
Hamilton, Ian (White Sox) 113
Hanifee, Brenan (Orioles) 63
Hankins, Ethan (Indians) 137
Hannah, Jameson (Reds) 122
Hansen, Austin (Astros) 192
Harris, Hogan (Athletics) 336
Harris, Michael (Braves) 43
Harris, Trey (Braves) 46
Harrison, Monte (Marlins) 248
Hart, Kyle (Red Sox) 80
Harvey, Hunter (Orioles) 57
Hayes, Ke'Bryan (Pirates) 358
Hays, Austin (Orioles) 55
Head, Hudson (Padres) 398
Hearn, Ethan (Cubs) 89
Hearn, Taylor (Rangers) 464
Heasley, Jon (Royals) 206
Heath, Nick (Royals) 208
Heatherly, Jacob (Reds) 129
Heim, Jonah (Athletics) 335
Helsley, Ryan (Cardinals) 375
Henderson, Gunnar (Orioles) 56
Hendrix, Ryan (Reds) 129
Henley, Blair (Astros) 190
Henriquez, Ronny (Rangers) 458
Henry, Payton (Brewers) 268
Henry, Tommy (D-backs) 31
Hentges, Sam (Indians) 140
Herman, Jack (Pirates) 368
Hernaiz, Darell (Orioles) 63
Hernandez, Aaron (Angels) 225
Hernandez, Carlos (Royals) 203
Hernandez, Darwinzon (Red Sox) 71
Hernandez, Daysbel (Braves) 47
Hernandez, Heriberto (Rangers) 461
Hernandez, Jonathan (Rangers) 460
Hernandez, Ronaldo (Rays) 441
Hernandez, Wilkel (Tigers) 177
Herrera, Ivan (Cardinals) 375
Heuer, Codi (White Sox) 112
Hicklen, Brewer (Royals) 205
Hill, Derek (Tigers) 174
Hilliard, Sam (Rockies) 152
Hinds, Rece (Reds) 122
Hiraldo, Miguel (Blue Jays) 473
Hjelle, Sean (Giants) 409
Hoerner, Nico (Cubs) 86
Hoese, Kody (Dodgers) 233
Holloway, Jordan (Marlins) 254
Holmes, Grant (Athletics) 332
Holmes, William (Angels) 221
Holt, Gabe (Brewers) 273
Honeywell, Brent (Rays) 440
Houck, Tanner (Red Sox) 74
Howard, Spencer (Phillies) 341
Howlett, Brandon (Red Sox) 77
Huff, Sam (Rangers) 454
Hulsizer, Nico (Rays) 448
Humphreys, Jordan (Mets) 298
Hunt, Blake (Padres) 397

I

India, Jonathan (Reds) 118
Irvin, Cole (Phillies) 352
Irvin, Jake (Nationals) 491
Isabel, Ibandel (Reds) 128
Isbel, Kyle (Royals) 199
Ivey, Tyler (Astros) 186

J

Jackson, Alex (Braves) 44
Jackson, Andre (Dodgers) 239
Jackson, Jeremiah (Angels) 215

Jameson, Drey (D-backs) 28
Javier, Cristian (Astros) 185
Javier, Wander (Twins) 289
Jefferies, Daulton (Athletics) 327
Jeffers, Ryan (Twins) 280
Jenista, Greyson (Braves) 45
Jensen, Ryan (Cubs) 88
Jimenez, Dany (Giants) 417
Jimenez, Gilberto (Red Sox) 73
Jimenez, Leonardo (Blue Jays) 476
Johnson, Daniel (Indians) 143
Johnson, Ivan (Reds) 126
Johnson, Osiris (Marlins) 255
Johnson, Seth (Rays) 445
Jones, Connor (Cardinals) 385
Jones, Damon (Phillies) 349
Jones, Greg (Rays) 442
Jones, Jahmai (Angels) 218
Jones, Nolan (Indians) 133
Jung, Josh (Rangers) 453

K

Kahle, Nick (Brewers) 268
Kalich, Kasey (Braves) 46
Kaprielian, James (Athletics) 331
Karinchak, James (Indians) 140
Kauffman, Karl (Rockies) 155
Kay, Anthony (Blue Jays) 473
Kelenic, Jarred (Mariners) 422
Keller, Mitch (Pirates) 357
Kelly, Antoine (Brewers) 264
Kelly, Levi (D-backs) 26
Kessinger, Grae (Astros) 186
Kieboom, Carter (Nationals) 485
Kilome, Franklyn (Mets) 299
King, Michael (Yankees) 315
Kirby, George (Mariners) 423
Kirilloff, Alex (Twins) 278
Kirk, Alejandro (Blue Jays) 471
Kloffenstein, Adam (Blue Jays) 474
Knight, Blaine (Orioles) 62
Knizner, Andrew (Cardinals) 376
Knowles, D'Shawn (Angels) 219
Kochanowicz, Jack (Angels) 218
Kopech, Michael (White Sox) 102
Koss, Christian (Rockies) 160
Kowar, Jackson (Royals) 198
Kramer, Kevin (Pirates) 365
Kranick, Max (Pirates) 366
Kremer, Dean (Orioles) 58
Kuhnel, Joel (Reds) 125

L

Lambert, Jimmy (White Sox) 106
Lange, Alex (Tigers) 177
Langeliers, Shea (Braves) 40
Lara, Andry (Nationals) 488
Larnach, Trevor (Twins) 278
Lavigne, Grant (Rockies) 151
Lawson, Reggie (Padres) 395
Lazar, Max (Brewers) 271
Lee, Khalil (Royals) 200
Lee, Korey (Astros) 184
Lewis, Jimmy (Dodgers) 239
Lewis, Kyle (Mariners) 426
Lewis, Royce (Twins) 277
Liberatore, Matthew (Rays) 438
Lindow, Ethan (Phillies) 351
Liu, Chih-Jung (Red Sox) 79
Llovera, Mauricio (Phillies) 351
Locey, Tony (Cardinals) 383
Lockett, Walker (Mets) 302
Lodolo, Nick (Reds) 118
Lopez, Jairo (Astros) 189
Lopez, Otto (Blue Jays) 474
Lora, Bayron (Rangers) 457
Lorenzo, Dauri (Astros) 193
Lovelady, Richard (Royals) 207
Lowe, Josh (Rays) 442
Lowther, Zac (Orioles) 59
Luciano, Marco (Giants) 405
Lugo, Matthew (Red Sox) 74
Lutz, Tristen (Brewers) 262
Lux, Gavin (Dodgers) 229
Luzardo, Jesus (Athletics) 325
Lynch, Daniel (Royals) 198

M

MacGregor, Travis (Pirates) 364
Machado, Estiven (Blue Jays) 475
Made, Kevin (Cubs) 93
Madrigal, Nick (White Sox) 103
Malone, Brennan (D-backs) 25
Mann, Devin (Dodgers) 237
Manning, Matt (Tigers) 166
Manoah, Alek (Blue Jays) 471
Marcano, Tucupita (Padres) 397
Marchan, Rafael (Phillies) 344
Marinan, James (Reds) 127
Marquez, Brailyn (Cubs) 85
Marsh, Alec (Royals) 206
Marsh, Brandon (Angels) 214
Marte, Jose (Giants) 414
Marte, Noelvi (Mariners) 424
Martin, Corbin (D-backs) 25
Martin, Mason (Pirates) 363
Martinez, Angel (Indians) 141
Martinez, Julio Pablo (Rangers) 464
Martinez, Justin (D-backs) 33
Martinez, Orelvis (Blue Jays) 472
Martinez, Orlando (Angels) 221
Martinez, Pedro (Cubs) 92
Mata, Bryan (Red Sox) 70
Mateo, Jorge (Athletics) 329
Matias, Seuly (Royals) 204
Maton, Nick (Phillies) 346
Matos, Luis (Giants) 409
Mauricio, Ronny (Mets) 293
May, Dustin (Dodgers) 230
McAvene, Michael (Cubs) 92
McCann, Kyle (Athletics) 337
McClanahan, Shane (Rays) 440
McConnell, Brady (Royals) 204
McCoy, Mason (Orioles) 64
McDonald, Trevor (Giants) 415
McGuire, Reese (Blue Jays) 478
McKay, Brendan (Rays) 438
McKenna, Ryan (Orioles) 60
McKenzie, Triston (Indians) 136
McKinstry, Zach (Dodgers) 238
Meadows, Parker (Tigers) 170
Mears, Joshua (Padres) 398
Mears, Nick (Pirates) 364
Medina, Adonis (Phillies) 343
Medina, Luis (Brewers) 267
Medina, Luis (Yankees) 312
Mejia, Humberto (Marlins) 256
Mejia, Jean Carlos (Indians) 145
Melendez, MJ (Royals) 202
Mena, Ismael (Padres) 400
Mendick, Danny (White Sox) 112
Mendoza, Drew (Nationals) 488
Mendoza, Jefferson (White Sox) 113
Menez, Conor (Giants) 412
Mesa Jr., Victor (Marlins) 254
Mesa, Victor Victor (Marlins) 252
Mesia, Victor (Blue Jays) 477
Mieses, Luis (White Sox) 110
Miller, Brian (Marlins) 256
Miller, Erik (Phillies) 347
Miller, Owen (Padres) 394
Miller, Tyson (Cubs) 90
Mills, Wyatt (Mariners) 431
Misiewicz, Anthony (Mariners) 432
Misner, Kameron (Marlins) 250
Mitchell, Calvin (Pirates) 362
Mize, Casey (Tigers) 165
Mojica, Alexander (Pirates) 363
Mokma, Chris (Marlins) 257
Moniak, Mickey (Phillies) 345
Montero, Elehuris (Cardinals) 377
Morales, Francisco (Phillies) 343
Morejon, Adrian (Padres) 392
Morel, Christopher (Cubs) 96
Morel, Rafael (Cubs) 94
Morel, Yohanse (Royals) 209
Moreno, Gabriel (Blue Jays) 472
Morris, Tanner (Blue Jays) 481
Moss, Keithron (Rangers) 463
Moss, Scott (Indians) 139
Mountcastle, Ryan (Orioles) 55
Muller, Kyle (Braves) 39
Munoz, Andres (Padres) 392
Murfee, Penn (Mariners) 433
Murphy, Chris (Red Sox) 75
Murphy, Patrick (Blue Jays) 477
Murphy, Sean (Athletics) 326
Murray, Joey (Blue Jays) 480
Muzziotti, Simon (Phillies) 346

N

Naughton, Packy (Reds) 124
Nava, Andrick (Phillies) 347
Naylor, Bo (Indians) 134
Neidert, Nick (Marlins) 250
Nelson, Nick (Yankees) 320
Nelson, Ryne (D-backs) 32
Neuse, Sheldon (Athletics) 328
Nevin, Tyler (Rockies) 154
Newton, Shervyen (Mets) 300
Nova, Freudis (Astros) 183
Nunez, Dedniel (Mets) 302
Nunez, Malcom (Cardinals) 380
Nunez, Nasim (Marlins) 253

O

O'Brien, Riley (Rays) 445
O'Hoppe, Logan (Phillies) 350
Oliva, Jared (Pirates) 365
Olivares, Edward (Padres) 396
Olivarez, Helcris (Rockies) 156
Ona, Jorge (Padres) 400
Ornelas, Tirso (Padres) 399
Ortega, Oliver (Angels) 220
Ortiz, Jhailyn (Phillies) 352
Ortiz, Robinson (Dodgers) 241
Ota, Scott (Mets) 305
Otañez, Michel (Mets) 299
Oviedo, Johan (Cardinals) 378
Oviedo, Luis (Indians) 141

P

Pache, Cristian (Braves) 37
Padlo, Kevin (Rays) 444
Pages, Andy (Dodgers) 239
Palmer, Jaylen (Mets) 301

Palumbo, Joe (Rangers) 456
Paolini, Stephen (Braves) 49
Pardinho, Eric (Blue Jays) 474
Paredes, Enoli (Astros) 192
Paredes, Isaac (Tigers) 167
Paris, Kyren (Angels) 218
Parra, Jesus (Brewers) 269
Pastrano, Jose (Indians) 144
Patino, Luis (Padres) 390
Patino, Wilderd (D-backs) 28
Patterson, Jack (Cubs) 97
Pearson, Nate (Blue Jays) 469
Peguero, Liover (D-backs) 24
Pena, Erick (Royals) 200
Pena, Jeremy (Astros) 182
Pena, Malvin (Nationals) 495
Pepiot, Ryan (Dodgers) 240
Peraza, Oswald (Yankees) 311
Perdomo, Geraldo (D-backs) 22
Pereira, Everson (Yankees) 317
Perez, Franklin (Tigers) 169
Perez, Hedbert (Brewers) 266
Perez, Milkar (Mariners) 428
Perez, Wenceel (Tigers) 171
Pertuz, Fabian (Cubs) 95
Peters, DJ (Dodgers) 235
Peterson, David (Mets) 298
Phillip, Beau (Braves) 47
Phillips, Tyler (Rangers) 465
Pilkington, Konnor (White Sox) 109
Pina, Robinson (Angels) 221
Pinango, Yohendrick (Cubs) 94
Pineda, Israel (Nationals) 493
Pint, Riley (Rockies) 161
Pinto, Wladimir (Tigers) 176
Placencia, Adrian (Angels) 223
Plassmeyer, Michael (Rays) 448
Politi, Andrew (Red Sox) 78
Pomares, Jairo (Giants) 412
Pop, Zach (Orioles) 64
Potts, Hudson (Padres) 396
Poulin, PJ (Rockies) 161
Pratto, Nick (Royals) 202
Preciado, Reggie (Padres) 398
Priester, Quinn (Pirates) 360
Puason, Robert (Athletics) 328
Puk, A.J. (Athletics) 326

Q

Querecuto, Juan (Mariners) 432
Quero, Jeferson (Brewers) 269
Quintana, Nick (Tigers) 173
Quintero, Ronnier (Cubs) 94

R

Rafaela, Ceddanne (Red Sox) 78
Raleigh, Cal (Mariners) 427
Raley, Luke (Twins) 287
Ramirez, Aldo (Red Sox) 79
Ramirez, Alexander (Angels) 219
Ramirez, Alexander (Mets) 300
Ramos, Bryan (White Sox) 110
Ramos, Heliot (Giants) 406
Ramos, Jefrey (Braves) 49
Raquet, Nick (Nationals) 497
Rasmussen, Drew (Brewers) 265
Ray, Corey (Brewers) 262
Reetz, Jakson (Nationals) 496
Restituyo, Bladimir (Rockies) 160
Reyes, Adinso (Tigers) 175
Richan, Paul (Tigers) 175
Richardson, Lyon (Reds) 120
Riley, Trey (Braves) 49
Rios, Edwin (Dodgers) 235
Rivas, Alfonso (Athletics) 333
Rivera, Blake (Giants) 413
Rivera, Erik (Angels) 224
Rivera, Jose Alberto (Astros) 189
Robberse, Sem (Blue Jays) 481
Robert, Luis (White Sox) 101
Roberts, Griffin (Cardinals) 384
Robertson, Will (Blue Jays) 481
Robinson, Kristian (D-backs) 22
Rocchio, Brayan (Indians) 135
Rodgers, Brendan (Rockies) 149
Rodriguez, Alberto (Blue Jays) 478
Rodriguez, Carlos (Brewers) 266
Rodriguez, Chris (Angels) 215
Rodriguez, Elvin (Tigers) 173
Rodriguez, Emmanuel (Twins) 288
Rodriguez, Gabriel (Indians) 138
Rodriguez, Grayson (Orioles) 54
Rodriguez, Jose (White Sox) 113
Rodriguez, Jose D. (Angels) 222
Rodriguez, Julio (Cardinals) 380
Rodriguez, Julio (Mariners) 421
Rodriguez, Luis (Dodgers) 234
Rodriguez, Manuel (Cubs) 97
Rodriguez, Nivaldo (Astros) 190
Roederer, Cole (Cubs) 88
Rogers, Jake (Tigers) 170
Rogers, Trevor (Marlins) 249
Rojas, Johan (Phillies) 346
Rolison, Ryan (Rockies) 150
Rom, Drew (Orioles) 60
Romero, JoJo (Phillies) 348
Romero, Miguel (Athletics) 336
Romero, Seth (Nationals) 490
Rondon, Angel (Cardinals) 380
Rooker, Brent (Twins) 283
Rortvedt, Ben (Twins) 287
Rosario, Eguy (Padres) 401
Rosario, Jeisson (Padres) 399
Ruiz, Keibert (Dodgers) 230
Russ, Addison (Phillies) 350
Rutherford, Blake (White Sox) 105
Rutledge, Jackon (Nationals) 486
Rutschman, Adley (Orioles) 53
Ryan, Joe (Rays) 442

S

Salas, Jose (Marlins) 255
Salinas, Raimfer (Yankees) 320
Sampen, Caleb (Rays) 447
Sanchez, Ali (Mets) 304
Sanchez, Christopher (Phillies) 348
Sanchez, Jesus (Marlins) 246
Sanchez, Lolo (Pirates) 368
Sanchez, Sixto (Marlins) 245
Sanchez, Yolbert (White Sox) 109
Sandlin, Nick (Indians) 145
Sandoval, Patrick (Angels) 216
Sands, Cole (Twins) 286
Santana, Cristian (Dodgers) 236
Santana, Debby (Reds) 128
Santana, Dennis (Dodgers) 234
Santana, Rayner (Giants) 415
Santillan, Tony (Reds) 119
Santos, Gregory (Giants) 414
Santos, Junior (Mets) 298
Sauer, Matt (Yankees) 317
Schaller, Reid (Nationals) 492
Schmidt, Clarke (Yankees) 310
Schnell, Nick (Rays) 444
Schunk, Aaron (Rockies) 153
Scott, Connor (Marlins) 250
Seabold, Connor (Phillies) 353
Sedlock, Cody (Orioles) 61
Seigler, Anthony (Yankees) 319
Seijas, Alvaro (Cardinals) 383
Sharp, Sterling (Marlins) 254
Sheets, Gavin (White Sox) 107
Sheffield, Justus (Mariners) 424
Shenton, Austin (Mariners) 428
Shewmake, Braden (Braves) 41
Short, Zack (Cubs) 96
Shugart, Chase (Red Sox) 80
Siani, Mike (Reds) 121
Siani, Sammy (Pirates) 361
Sikkema, T.J. (Yankees) 316
Simmons, Kendall (Phillies) 350
Singer, Brady (Royals) 199
Siri, Jose (Reds) 124
Skubal, Tarik (Tigers) 166
Small, Ethan (Brewers) 263
Smeltzer, Devin (Twins) 282
Smith, Canaan (Yankees) 316
Smith, Josh (Yankees) 319
Smith, Kevin (Blue Jays) 479
Smith, Kevin (Mets) 297
Smith, Marcus (Athletics) 333
Smith, Pavin (D-backs) 29
Solak, Nick (Rangers) 455
Solis, Jairo (Astros) 187
Soloman, Jared (Reds) 126
Solomon, Peter (Astros) 191
Song, Noah (Red Sox) 73
Soriano, Jose (Angels) 216
Sosa, Edmundo (Cardinals) 382
Soto, Livan (Angels) 223
Stallings, Garrett (Angels) 224
Stashak, Cody (Twins) 289
Staumont, Josh (Royals) 207
Steele, Evan (Royals) 208
Steele, Justin (Cubs) 95
Stephenson, Tyler (Reds) 119
Stewart, Will (Marlins) 257
Stiever, Jonathan (White Sox) 104
Stott, Bryson (Phillies) 342
Stowers, Josh (Yankees) 321
Stowers, Kyle (Orioles) 61
Strotman, Drew (Rays) 447
Strumpf, Chase (Cubs) 87
Stubbs, Garrett (Astros) 191
Supak, Trey (Brewers) 267
Swaggerty, Travis (Pirates) 361
Szapucki, Thomas (Mets) 296

T

Tabor, Matt (D-backs) 30
Tarnok, Freddy (Braves) 43
Tate, Dillon (Orioles) 64
Tatis, Yeury (Mariners) 433
Taveras, Leody (Rangers) 454
Taylor, Chandler (Astros) 193
Taylor, Tyrone (Brewers) 270
Tejeda, Anderson (Rangers) 461
Tena, Jose (Indians) 144
Teng, Kai-Wei (Giants) 413
Tetreault, Jackson (Nationals) 495
Then, Juan (Mariners) 427
Thomas, Alek (D-backs) 23
Thomas, Lane (Cardinals) 377
Thomas, Tahnaj (Pirates) 359
Thompson-Williams, Dom (Mariners) 428
Thompson, Bubba (Rangers) 463
Thompson, Matthew (White Sox) 103
Thompson, Riley (Cubs) 89

Thompson, Zack (Cardinals) 376
Thorpe, Lewis (Twins) 284
Tillo, Daniel (Royals) 206
Toerner, Justin (Cardinals) 385
Toglia, Michael (Rockies) 150
Toribio, Luis (Giants) 408
Toro, Abraham (Astros) 184
Torres, Jhon (Cardinals) 379
Torres, Jojanse (Astros) 188
Torres, Lenny (Indians) 143
Torres, Victor (White Sox) 112
Tovar, Ezeuqiel (Rockies) 158
Trammell, Taylor (Padres) 391
Triana, Michel (Reds) 123
Turang, Brice (Brewers) 261

U

Uceta, Edwin (Dodgers) 237
Urbina, Misael (Twins) 282
Urias, Ramon (Cardinals) 384
Urquidy, Jose (Astros) 182

V

Valdes, Yordys (Indians) 141
Valdez, Freddy (Mets) 301
Valera, George (Indians) 135
Vanasco, Ricky (Rangers) 458
Vargas, Alexander (Yankees) 318
Vargas, Carlos (Indians) 139
Vargas, Jheremy (Brewers) 272
Vargas, Miguel (Dodgers) 238
Varland, Gus (Athletics) 337
Varsho, Daulton (D-backs) 21
Vaughn, Andrew (White Sox) 102
Vavra, Terrin (Rockies) 155
Vera, Arol (Angels) 217
Vientos, Mark (Mets) 296
Vilade, Ryan (Rockies) 153
Vinicio, Esmerlin (Giants) 416
Vizcaino, Alexander (Yankees) 313
Vodnik, Victor (Braves) 43
Volpe, Anthony (Yankees) 312

W

Wade, Lamonte (Twins) 285
Walker, Jeremy (Braves) 46
Walker, Steele (Rangers) 462
Wallace, Jacob (Rockies) 156
Wallner, Matt (Twins) 286
Walls, Taylor (Rays) 445
Walsh, Jared (Angels) 222
Walston, Blake (D-backs) 24
Walton, Donnie (Mariners) 432
Ward, Thad (Red Sox) 72
Waters, Drew (Braves) 38
Watson, Zach (Orioles) 61
Weathers, Ryan (Padres) 394
Webb, Logan (Giants) 410
Weigel, Patrick (Braves) 42
Welker, Colton (Rockies) 151
Wells, Alex (Orioles) 59
Wendzel, Davis (Rangers) 459
Wentz, Joey (Tigers) 170
White, Evan (Mariners) 422
White, Mitchell (Dodgers) 234
Whitley, Forrest (Astros) 181
Whitley, Kodi (Cardinals) 381
Widener, Taylor (D-backs) 32
Williams, Devin (Brewers) 268
Williams, Justin (Cardinals) 381
Williams, Kendall (Blue Jays) 475
Williamson, Brandon (Mariners) 425
Wilson, Bryse (Braves) 40
Wilson, Marcus (Red Sox) 76
Wilson, Will (Giants) 411
Winder, Josh (Twins) 288
Winn, Cole (Rangers) 459
Witt Jr., Bobby (Royals) 197
Wolf, Josh (Mets) 297
Wong, Connor (Dodgers) 236
Wong, Jake (Giants) 414
Woodford, Jake (Cardinals) 379
Woods Richardson, Simeon (Blue Jays) 470
Wright, Kyle (Braves) 39
Wyatt, Logan (Giants) 411

Y

Yajure, Miguel (Yankees) 314
Yan, Hector (Angels) 217
Yean, Eddy (Nationals) 490
Ynoa, Huascar (Braves) 44
Young, Andy (D-backs) 30

Z

Zeferjahn, Ryan (Red Sox) 76
Zimmerman, Bruce (Orioles) 60